Collins

Collins
German
Dictionary

D0774806

Glasgow
G64 2QT
Great Britain

Second Edition 2009

Reprint 10 9 8 7 6 5 4 3

© HarperCollins Publishers 2006, 2009

ISBN 978-0-00-729883-9

Collins® is a registered trademark of
HarperCollins Publishers Limited

www.collinslanguage.com

A catalogue record for this book is
available from the British Library

Typeset by RefineCatch Ltd,
Bungay, Suffolk

Printed and bound in Great Britain by
Clays Ltd, St Ives, plc

Acknowledgements

We would like to thank those
authors and publishers who kindly
gave permission for copyright
material to be used in the Collins
Word Web. We would also like to
thank Times Newspapers Ltd for
providing valuable data.

MANAGING EDITOR
Gaëlle Amiot-Cadey

CONTRIBUTORS
Howard Atkinson
Stuart Fortey
Helen Galloway
Silke Probst
Robin Sawers
Veronika Schnorr
Yvonne Stein
Karin Weindl

EDITORIAL COORDINATION
Susie Beattie

SERIES EDITOR
Rob Scriven

INHALT

Einleitung	vi
Abkürzungen	vii
Lautschrift	x
Regelmäßige deutsche Substantivendungen	xii
Unregelmäßige englische Verben	xiii
Unregelmäßige deutsche Verben	xvi
DEUTSCH-ENGLISCH	1
ENGLISCH-DEUTSCH	201

CONTENTS

Introduction	vi
Abbreviations	vii
Phonetic symbols	x
Regular German noun endings	xii
Irregular English verbs	xiii
Irregular German verbs	xvi
GERMAN-ENGLISH	1
ENGLISH-GERMAN	201

WARENZEICHEN

Warenzeichen, die unseres Wissens eingetragene Warenzeichen darstellen, sind als solche gekennzeichnet. Es ist jedoch zu beachten, dass weder das Vorhandensein noch das Fehlen derartiger Kennzeichnungen die Rechtslage hinsichtlich eingetragener Warenzeichen berührt.

NOTE ON TRADEMARKS

Words which we have reason to believe constitute trademarks have been designated as such. However, neither the presence nor the absence of such designation should be regarded as affecting the legal status of any trademark.

William Collins' dream of knowledge for all began with the publication of his first book in 1819. A self-educated mill worker, he not only enriched millions of lives, but also founded a flourishing publishing house. Today, staying true to this spirit, Collins books are packed with inspiration, innovation, and practical expertise. They place you at the centre of a world of possibility and give you exactly what you need to explore it.

Language is the key to this exploration, and at the heart of Collins Dictionaries is language as it is really used. New words, phrases, and meanings spring up every day, and all of them are captured and analysed by the Collins Word Web. Constantly updated, and with over 2.5 billion entries, this living language resource is unique to our dictionaries.

Words are tools for life. And a Collins Dictionary makes them work for you.

Collins. Do more

EINFÜHRUNG

Wir freuen uns sehr, dass Sie sich zum Kauf eines Collins Wörterbuchs Deutsch entschlossen haben. Wir wünschen Ihnen viel Spaß beim Gebrauch in der Schule, zu Hause, im Urlaub und im Beruf.

INTRODUCTION

We are delighted you have decided to buy the Collins German Dictionary and hope you will enjoy and benefit from using it at school, at home, on holiday or at work.

ABKÜRZUNGEN

ABBREVIATIONS

auch	*a.*	also
Abkürzung	*abk, abbr*	abbreviation
Akronym	*acr*	acronym
Adjektiv	*adj*	adjective
Adverb	*adv*	adverb
Landwirtschaft	*Agr*	agriculture
Akkusativ	*akk*	accusative
Akronym	*akr*	acronym
Anatomie	*Anat*	anatomy
Artikel	*art*	article
Bildende Künste	*Art*	fine arts
Astronomie, Astrologie	*Astr*	astronomy, astrology
Auto, Verkehr	*Auto*	automobiles, traffic
Luftfahrt	*Aviat*	aviation
Biologie	*Bio*	biology
Botanik	*Bot*	botany
britisch	*BRIT*	British
schweizerisch	*CH*	Swiss
Chemie	*Chem*	chemistry
Film	*Cine*	cinema
Wirtschaft	*Comm*	commerce
Konjunktion	*conj*	conjunction
Dativ	*dat*	dative
Eisenbahn	*Eisenb*	railways
Elektrizität	*Elek, Elec*	electricity
besonders	*esp*	especially
und so weiter	*etc*	et cetera
etwas	*etw*	
Femininum	*f*	feminine
umgangssprachlich	*fam*	familiar, informal
übertragen	*fig*	figurative
Finanzen, Börse	*Fin*	finance
Fotografie	*Foto*	photography
Gastronomie	*Gastr*	cooking, gastronomy
Genitiv	*gen*	genitive
Geographie, Geologie	*Geo*	geography, geology
Geschichte	*Hist*	history
Imperativ	*imper*	imperative
Imperfekt	*imperf*	past tense
Informatik und Computer	*Inform*	computing
Interjektion, Ausruf	*interj*	interjection
unveränderlich	*inv*	invariable
unregelmäßig	*irr*	irregular
jemand	*jd*	
jemandem	*jdm*	
jemanden	*jdn*	

jemandes	*jds*	
Rechtsprechung	*Jur*	law
Konjunktion	*konj*	conjunction
Bildende Künste	*Kunst*	fine arts
Sprachwissenschaft, Grammatik	*Ling*	linguistics, grammar
Maskulinum	*m*	masculine
Mathematik	*Math*	mathematics
Medizin	*Med*	medicine
Meteorologie	*Meteo*	meteorology
Maskulinum und Femininum	*mf*	masculine and feminine
Militär	*Mil*	military
Musik	*Mus*	music
Substantiv	*n*	noun
Seefahrt	*Naut*	nautical, naval
Neutrum	*nt*	neuter
Zahlwort	*num*	numeral
oder	*o*	or
pejorativ, abwertend	*pej*	pejorative
Physik	*Phys*	physics
Plural	*pl*	plural
Politik	*Pol*	politics
Partizip Perfekt	*pp*	past participle
Präfix	*pref*	prefix
Präposition	*prep*	preposition
Pronomen	*pron*	pronoun
1. Vergangenheit	*pt*	past tense
Warenzeichen	®	registered trademark
Radio	*Radio*	radio
Eisenbahn	*Rail*	railways
Religion	*Rel*	religion
siehe	*s.*	see
	sb	someone, somebody
schottisch	*SCOT*	Scottish
Singular	*sing*	singular
Skisport	*Ski*	skiing
Sport	*Sport*	sports
	sth	something
Technik	*Tech*	technology
Nachrichtentechnik	*Tel*	telecommunications
Theater	*Theat*	theatre
Fernsehen	*TV*	television
Typographie, Buchdruck	*Typo*	printing
unpersönlich	*unpers*	impersonal
(nord)amerikanisch	*US*	(North) American
Verb	*vb*	verb
Hilfsverb	*vb aux*	auxiliary verb
intransitives Verb	*vi*	intransitive verb
reflexives Verb	*vr*	reflexive verb

transitives Verb	*vt*	transitive verb
vulgär	*vulg*	vulgar
Zoologie	*Zool*	zoology
zwischen zwei Sprechern	-	change of speaker
ungefähre Entsprechung	≈	cultural equivalent
abtrennbares Präfix	|	separable prefix

LAUTSCHRIFT   PHONETIC SYMBOLS

[:] Längezeichen, length mark
['] Betonung, stress mark
[*] Bindungs-R, 'r' pronounced before a vowel

alle Vokallaute sind nur ungefähre Entsprechungen
all vowel sounds are approximate only

VOKALE UND DIPHTHONGE

plant, arm, father	[ɑ:]	Bahn
fiancé	[ɑ̃:]	Ensemble
life	[aɪ]	weit
house	[au]	Haut
man, sad	[æ]	
but, son	[ʌ]	Butler
get, bed	[e]	Metall
name, lame	[eɪ]	
ago, better	[ə]	bitte
bird, her	[ɜ:]	
there, care	[ɛə]	mehr
it, wish	[ɪ]	Bischof
bee, me, beat, belief	[i:]	viel
here	[ɪə]	Bier
no, low	[əʊ]	
not, long	[ɒ]	Post
law, all	[ɔ:]	Mond
boy, oil	[ɔɪ]	Heu
push, look	[ʊ]	Pult
you, do	[u:]	Hut
poor, sure	[ʊə]	

KONSONANTEN

been, blind	[b]	Ball
do, had	[d]	dann
jam, object	[dʒ]	
father, wolf	[f]	Fass
go, beg	[g]	Gast
house	[h]	Herr
youth, Indian	[j]	ja
keep, milk	[k]	kalt
lamp, oil, ill	[l]	Last
man, am	[m]	Mast
no, manner	[n]	Nuss
long, sing	[ŋ]	lang

El Niño	[ɲ]	El Niño
paper, happy	[p]	Pakt
red, dry	[r]	rot
stand, sand, yes	[s]	Rasse
ship, station	[ʃ]	Schal
tell, fat	[t]	Tal
thank, death	[θ]	
this, father	[ð]	
church, catch	[tʃ]	Rutsch
voice, live	[v]	was
water, we, which	[w]	
loch	[x]	Bach
zeal, these, gaze	[z]	Hase
pleasure	[ʒ]	Genie

REGULAR GERMAN NOUN ENDINGS

nominative		genitive	plural	nominative		genitive	plural
-ade	f	-ade	-aden	-ist	m	-isten	-isten
-ant	m	-anten	-anten	-ium	nt	-iums	-ien
-anz	f	-anz	-anzen	-ius	m	-ius	-iusse
-ar	m	-ars	-are	-ive	f	-ive	-iven
-är	m	-ärs	-äre	-keit	f	-keit	-keiten
-at	nt	-at(e)s	-ate	-lein	nt	-leins	-lein
-atte	f	-atte	-atten	-ling	m	-lings	-linge
-chen	nt	-chens	-chen	-ment	nt	-ments	-mente
-ei	f	-ei	-eien	-mus	m	-mus	-men
-elle	f	-elle	-ellen	-nis	f	-nis	-nisse
-ent	m	-enten	-enten	-nis	nt	-nisses	-nisse
-enz	f	-enz	-enzen	-nom	m	-nomen	-nomen
-ette	f	-ette	-etten	-rich	m	-richs	-riche
-eur	m	-eurs	-eure	-schaft	f	-schaft	-schaften
-euse	f	-euse	-eusen	-sel	nt	-sels	-sel
-heit	f	-heit	-heiten	-tät	f	-tät	-täten
-ie	f	-ie	-ien	-tiv	nt, m	-tivs	-tive
-ik	f	-ik	-iken	-tor	m	-tors	-toren
-in	f	-in	-innen	-tum	m, nt	-tums	-tümer
-ine	f	-ine	-inen	-ung	f	-ung	-ungen
-ion	f	-ion	-ionen	-ur	f	-ur	-uren

Substantive, die mit einem geklammerten 'r' oder 's' enden (z.B. **Angestellte(r)** mf, **Beamte(r)** m, **Gute(s)** nt) werden wie Adjektive dekliniert:

Nouns listed with an 'r' or an 's' in brackets (eg **Angestellte(r)** mf, **Beamte(r)** m, **Gute(s)** nt) take the same endings as adjectives:

der Angestellte m	**die Angestellte** f	**die Angestellten** pl
ein Angestellter m	**eine Angestellte** f	**Angestellte** pl
der Beamte m		**die Beamten** pl
ein Beamter m		**Beamte** pl
das Gute nt		
ein Gutes nt		

UNREGELMÄßIGE ENGLISCHE VERBEN

present	past tense	past participle	present	past tense	past participle
arise (arising)	arose	arisen	drink	drank	drunk
awake (awaking)	awoke	awaked	drive (driving)	drove	driven
be (am, is, are; being)	was, were	been	eat	ate	eaten
			fall	fell	fallen
bear	bore	born(e)	feed	fed	fed
beat	beat	beaten	feel	felt	felt
become (becoming)	became	become	fight	fought	fought
			find	found	found
begin (beginning)	began	begun	flee	fled	fled
			fling	flung	flung
bend	bent	bent	fly (flies)	flew	flown
bet (betting)	bet	bet	forbid (forbidding)	forbade	forbidden
bid (bidding)	bid	bid			
bind	bound	bound	foresee	foresaw	foreseen
bite (biting)	bit	bitten	forget (forgetting)	forgot	forgotten
bleed	bled	bled			
blow	blew	blown	forgive (forgiving)	forgave	forgiven
break	broke	broken			
breed	bred	bred	freeze (freezing)	froze	frozen
bring	brought	brought			
build	built	built	get (getting)	got	got, (US) gotten
burn	burnt (o burned)	burnt (o burned)	give (giving)	gave	given
burst	burst	burst	go (goes)	went	gone
buy	bought	bought	grind	ground	ground
can	could	(been able)	grow	grew	grown
cast	cast	cast	hang	hung (o hanged)	hung (o hanged)
catch	caught	caught			
choose (choosing)	chose	chosen	have (has; having)	had	had
cling	clung	clung	hear	heard	heard
come (coming)	came	come	hide (hiding)	hid	hidden
cost	cost	cost	hit (hitting)	hit	hit
creep	crept	crept	hold	held	held
cut (cutting)	cut	cut	hurt	hurt	hurt
deal	dealt	dealt	keep	kept	kept
dig (digging)	dug	dug	kneel	knelt (o kneeled)	knelt (o kneeled)
do (does)	did	done			
draw	drew	drawn	know	knew	known
dream	dreamed (o dreamt)	dreamed (o dreamt)	lay	laid	laid
			lead	led	led

present	past tense	past participle	present	past tense	past participle
lean	leant	leant	**shoot**	shot	shot
	(o leaned)	(o leaned)	**show**	showed	shown
leap	leapt	leapt	**shrink**	shrank	shrunk
	(o leaped)	(o leaped)	**shut**	shut	shut
learn	learnt (o	learnt (o	**(shutting)**		
	learned)	learned)	**sing**	sang	sung
leave	left	left	**sink**	sank	sunk
(leaving)			**sit (sitting)**	sat	sat
lend	lent	lent	**sleep**	slept	slept
let (letting)	let	let	**slide**	slid	slid
lie (lying)	lay	lain	**(sliding)**		
light	lit (o	lit (o	**sling**	slung	slung
	lighted)	lighted)	**slit (slitting)**	slit	slit
lose (losing)	lost	lost	**smell**	smelt (o	smelt (o
make	made	made		smelled)	smelled)
(making)			**sow**	sowed	sown
may	might	–			(o sowed)
mean	meant	meant	**speak**	spoke	spoken
meet	met	met	**speed**	sped (o	sped (o
mow	mowed	mown		speeded)	speeded)
		(o mowed)	**spell**	spelt (o	spelt (o
must	(had to)	(had to)		spelled)	spelled)
pay	paid	paid	**spend**	spent	spent
put	put	put	**spin**	spun	spun
(putting)			**(spinning)**		
quit	quit (o	quit (o	**spit**	spat	spat
(quitting)	quitted)	quitted)	**(spitting)**		
read	read	read	**split**	split	split
rid (ridding)	rid	rid	**(splitting)**		
ride (riding)	rode	ridden	**spoil**	spoiled	spoiled
ring	rang	rung		(o spoilt)	(o spoilt)
rise (rising)	rose	risen	**spread**	spread	spread
run	ran	run	**spring**	sprang	sprung
(running)			**stand**	stood	stood
saw	sawed	sawn	**steal**	stole	stolen
say	said	said	**stick**	stuck	stuck
see	saw	seen	**sting**	stung	stung
seek	sought	sought	**stink**	stank	stunk
sell	sold	sold	**strike**	struck	struck
send	sent	sent	**(striking)**		
set (setting)	set	set	**strive**	strove	striven
shake	shook	shaken	**(striving)**		
(shaking)			**swear**	swore	sworn
shall	should	–	**sweep**	swept	swept
shine	shone	shone	**swell**	swelled	swollen (o
(shining)					swelled)

present	past tense	past participle	present	past tense	past participle
swim (**swimming**)	swam	swum	**wake** (**waking**)	woke (*o* waked)	woken (*o* waked)
swing	swung	swung	**wear**	wore	worn
take (**taking**)	took	taken	**weave** (**weaving**)	wove (*o* weaved)	woven (*o* weaved)
teach	taught	taught	**weep**	wept	wept
tear	tore	torn	**win** (**winning**)	won	won
tell	told	told			
think	thought	thought	**wind**	wound	wound
throw	threw	thrown	**write** (**writing**)	wrote	written
thrust	thrust	thrust			
tread	trod	trodden			

GERMAN IRREGULAR VERBS

Infinitiv	Präsens 2., 3. Singular	Imperfekt	Partizip Perfekt
backen	bäckst, bäckt	backte o buk	gebacken
befehlen	befiehlst, befiehlt	befahl	befohlen
beginnen	beginnst, beginnt	begann	begonnen
beißen	beißt, beißt	biss	gebissen
bergen	birgst, birgt	barg	geborgen
betrügen	betrügst, betrügt	betrog	betrogen
biegen	biegst, biegt	bog	gebogen
bieten	bietest, bietet	bot	geboten
binden	bindest, bindet	band	gebunden
bitten	bittest, bittet	bat	gebeten
blasen	bläst, bläst	blies	geblasen
bleiben	bleibst, bleibt	blieb	geblieben
braten	brätst, brät	briet	gebraten
brechen	brichst, bricht	brach	gebrochen
brennen	brennst, brennt	brannte	gebrannt
bringen	bringst, bringt	brachte	gebracht
denken	denkst, denkt	dachte	gedacht
dringen	dringst, dringt	drang	gedrungen
dürfen	darfst, darf	durfte	gedurft
empfangen	empfängst, empfängt	empfing	empfangen
empfehlen	empfiehlst, empfiehlt	empfahl	empfohlen
empfinden	empfindest, empfindet	empfand	empfunden
erschrecken	erschrickst, erschrickt	erschrak	erschrocken
essen	isst, isst	aß	gegessen
fahren	fährst, fährt	fuhr	gefahren
fallen	fällst, fällt	fiel	gefallen
fangen	fängst, fängt	fing	gefangen
finden	findest, findet	fand	gefunden
flechten	flichtst, flicht	flocht	geflochten
fliegen	fliegst, fliegt	flog	geflogen
fließen	fließt, fließt	floss	geflossen
fressen	frisst, frisst	fraß	gefressen
frieren	frierst, friert	fror	gefroren
geben	gibst, gibt	gab	gegeben
gehen	gehst, geht	ging	gegangen
gelingen	–, gelingt	gelang	gelungen
gelten	giltst, gilt	galt	gegolten
genießen	genießt, genießt	genoss	genossen
geraten	gerätst, gerät	geriet	geraten
geschehen	–, geschieht	geschah	geschehen
gewinnen	gewinnst, gewinnt	gewann	gewonnen
gießen	gießt, gießt	goss	gegossen
gleichen	gleichst, gleicht	glich	geglichen
gleiten	gleitest, gleitet	glitt	geglitten

Infinitiv	Präsens 2., 3. Singular	Imperfekt	Partizip Perfekt
graben	gräbst, gräbt	grub	gegraben
greifen	greifst, greift	griff	gegriffen
haben	hast, hat	hatte	gehabt
halten	hältst, hält	hielt	gehalten
hängen	hängst, hängt	hing	gehangen
hauen	haust, haut	haute	gehauen
heben	hebst, hebt	hob	gehoben
heißen	heißt, heißt	hieß	geheißen
helfen	hilfst, hilft	half	geholfen
kennen	kennst, kennt	kannte	gekannt
klingen	klingst, klingt	klang	geklungen
kneifen	kneifst, kneift	kniff	gekniffen
kommen	kommst, kommt	kam	gekommen
können	kannst, kann	konnte	gekonnt
kriechen	kriechst, kriecht	kroch	gekrochen
laden	lädst, lädt	lud	geladen
lassen	lässt, lässt	ließ	gelassen
laufen	läufst, läuft	lief	gelaufen
leiden	leidest, leidet	litt	gelitten
leihen	leihst, leiht	lieh	geliehen
lesen	liest, liest	las	gelesen
liegen	liegst, liegt	lag	gelegen
lügen	lügst, lügt	log	gelogen
mahlen	mahlst, mahlt	mahlte	gemahlen
meiden	meidest, meidet	mied	gemieden
messen	misst, misst	maß	gemessen
misslingen	–, misslingt	misslang	misslungen
mögen	magst, mag	mochte	gemocht
müssen	musst, muss	musste	gemusst
nehmen	nimmst, nimmt	nahm	genommen
nennen	nennst, nennt	nannte	genannt
pfeifen	pfeifst, pfeift	pfiff	gepfiffen
quellen	quillst, quillt	quoll	gequollen
raten	rätst, rät	riet	geraten
reiben	reibst, reibt	rieb	gerieben
reißen	reißt, reißt	riss	gerissen
reiten	reitest, reitet	ritt	geritten
rennen	rennst, rennt	rannte	gerannt
riechen	riechst, riecht	roch	gerochen
ringen	ringst, ringt	rang	gerungen
rufen	rufst, ruft	rief	gerufen
salzen	salzt, salzt	salzte	gesalzen
saufen	säufst, säuft	soff	gesoffen
saugen	saugst, saugt	sog o saugte	gesogen o gesaugt
schaffen	schaffst, schafft	schuf	geschaffen
scheiden	scheidest, scheidet	schied	geschieden

Infinitiv	Präsens 2., 3. Singular	Imperfekt	Partizip Perfekt
scheinen	scheinst, scheint	schien	geschienen
scheißen	scheißt, scheißt	schiss	geschissen
schieben	schiebst, schiebt	schob	geschoben
schießen	schießt, schießt	schoss	geschossen
schlafen	schläfst, schläft	schlief	geschlafen
schlagen	schlägst, schlägt	schlug	geschlagen
schleichen	schleichst, schleicht	schlich	geschlichen
schleifen	schleifst, schleift	schliff	geschliffen
schließen	schließt, schließt	schloss	geschlossen
schmeißen	schmeißt, schmeißt	schmiss	geschmissen
schmelzen	schmilzt, schmilzt	schmolz	geschmolzen
schneiden	schneidest, schneidet	schnitt	geschnitten
schreiben	schreibst, schreibt	schrieb	geschrieben
schreien	schreist, schreit	schrie	geschrie(e)n
schweigen	schweigst, schweigt	schwieg	geschwiegen
schwellen	schwillst, schwillt	schwoll	geschwollen
schwimmen	schwimmst, schwimmt	schwamm	geschwommen
schwören	schwörst, schwört	schwor	geschworen
sehen	siehst, sieht	sah	gesehen
sein	bist, ist	war	gewesen
senden	sendest, sendet	sandte	gesandt
singen	singst, singt	sang	gesungen
sinken	sinkst, sinkt	sank	gesunken
sitzen	sitzt, sitzt	saß	gesessen
sollen	sollst, soll	sollte	gesollt
spinnen	spinnst, spinnt	spann	gesponnen
sprechen	sprichst, spricht	sprach	gesprochen
springen	springst, springt	sprang	gesprungen
stechen	stichst, sticht	stach	gestochen
stehen	stehst, steht	stand	gestanden
stehlen	stiehlst, stiehlt	stahl	gestohlen
steigen	steigst, steigt	stieg	gestiegen
sterben	stirbst, stirbt	starb	gestorben
stinken	stinkst, stinkt	stank	gestunken
stoßen	stößt, stößt	stieß	gestoßen
streichen	streichst, streicht	strich	gestrichen
streiten	streitest, streitet	stritt	gestritten
tragen	trägst, trägt	trug	getragen
treffen	triffst, trifft	traf	getroffen
treiben	treibst, treibt	trieb	getrieben
treten	trittst, tritt	trat	getreten
trinken	trinkst, trinkt	trank	getrunken
tun	tust, tut	tat	getan
verderben	verdirbst, verdirbt	verdarb	verdorben
vergessen	vergisst, vergisst	vergaß	vergessen
verlieren	verlierst, verliert	verlor	verloren

Infinitiv	Präsens 2., 3. Singular	Imperfekt	Partizip Perfekt
verschwinden	verschwindest, verschwindet	verschwand	verschwunden
verzeihen	verzeihst, verzeiht	verzieh	verziehen
wachsen	wächst, wächst	wuchs	gewachsen
waschen	wäschst, wäscht	wusch	gewaschen
weisen	weist, weist	wies	gewiesen
wenden	wendest, wendet	wandte	gewandt
werben	wirbst, wirbt	warb	geworben
werden	wirst, wird	wurde	geworden
werfen	wirfst, wirft	warf	geworfen
wiegen	wiegst, wiegt	wog	gewogen
wissen	weißt, weiß	wusste	gewusst
wollen	willst, will	wollte	gewollt
ziehen	ziehst, zieht	zog	gezogen
zwingen	zwingst, zwingt	zwang	gezwungen

à *prep* +akk at … each; **4 Tickets ~ 8 Euro** 4 tickets at 8 euros each
A *abk* = **Autobahn** ≈ M (*Brit*), ≈ I (*US*)
Aal (-(e)s, -e) *m* eel

 SCHLÜSSELWORT

ab *präp* +dat from; **Kinder ab 12 Jahren** children from the age of 12; **ab morgen** from tomorrow; **ab sofort** as of now ▷ *adv* **1** off; **links ab** to the left; **der Knopf ist ab** the button has come off; **ab nach Hause!** off you go home
2 (*zeitlich*): **von da ab** from then on; **von heute ab** from today, as of today
3 (*auf Fahrplänen*): **München ab 12.20** leaving Munich 12.20
4: **ab und zu** *od* **an** now and then *od* again

ab|bauen *vt* (*Zelt*) to take down; (*verringern*) to reduce
ab|beißen *irr vt* to bite off
ab|bestellen *vt* to cancel
ab|biegen *irr vi* to turn off; (*Straße*) to bend; **nach links/rechts ~** to turn left/right; **Abbiegespur** *f* filter lane

Abbildung *f* illustration
ab|blasen *irr vt* (*fig*) to call off
ab|blenden *vt, vi* (*Auto*) (**die Scheinwerfer**) **~** to dip (*Brit*) (*o* to dim (*US*)) one's headlights; **Abblendlicht** *nt* dipped (*Brit*) (*o* dimmed (*US*)) headlights *pl*
ab|brechen *irr vt* to break off; (*Gebäude*) to pull down; (*aufhören*) to stop; (*Computerprogramm*) to abort
ab|bremsen *vi* to brake, to slow down
ab|bringen *irr vt* **jdn von einer Idee ~** to talk sb out of an idea; **jdn vom Thema ~** to get sb away from the subject; **davon lasse ich mich nicht ~** nothing will make me change my mind about it
ab|buchen *vt* to debit (*von* to)
ab|danken *vi* to resign
ab|drehen *vt* (*Gas, Wasser*) to turn off; (*Licht*) to switch off ▷ *vi* (*Schiff, Flugzeug*) to change course
Abend (-s, -e) *m* evening; **am ~** in the evening; **zu ~ essen** to have dinner; **heute/morgen/gestern ~** this/tomorrow/yesterday evening; **guten ~!** good evening; **Abendbrot** *nt* supper; **Abendessen** *nt* dinner; **Abendgarderobe** *f* evening dress (*o* gown); **Abendkasse** *f* box office; **Abendkleid** *nt* evening dress (*o* gown); **Abendkurs** *m* evening class; **Abendmahl** *nt* **das ~** (*Holy*) Communion; **abends** *adv* in the evening; **montags ~** on Monday evenings
Abenteuer (-s, -) *nt* adventure; **Abenteuerurlaub** *m* adventure holiday
aber *conj* but; (*jedoch*) however; **oder ~** alternatively; **~ ja!** (*but*) of course; **das ist ~ nett von Ihnen** that's really nice of you
abergläubisch *adj* superstitious
ab|fahren *irr vi* to leave (*o* to depart) (*nach* for); (*Ski*) to ski down; **Abfahrt** *f* departure; (*von Autobahn*) exit; (*Ski*) descent; (*Piste*) run; **Abfahrtslauf** *m* (*Ski*) downhill; **Abfahrtszeit** *f* departure time
Abfall *m* waste; (*Müll*) rubbish (*Brit*), garbage (*US*); **Abfalleimer** *m* rubbish bin (*Brit*), garbage can (*US*)
abfällig *adj* disparaging; **~ von jdm sprechen** to make disparaging remarks about sb
ab|färben *vi* (*Wäsche*) to run; (*fig*) to rub off

ab|fertigen vt (Pakete) to prepare for dispatch; (an der Grenze) to clear; **Abfertigungsschalter** m (am Flughafen) check-in desk

ab|finden irr vt to pay off ▷ vr **sich mit etw ~** to come to terms with sth; **Abfindung** f (Entschädigung) compensation; (von Angestellten) redundancy payment

ab|fliegen irr vi (Flugzeug) to take off; (Passagier a.) to fly off; **Abflug** m departure; (Start) takeoff; **Abflughalle** f departure lounge; **Abflugzeit** f departure time

Abfluss m drain; (am Waschbecken) plughole (Brit); **Abflussrohr** nt waste pipe; (außen) drainpipe

ab|fragen vt to test; (Inform) to call up

ab|führen vi (Med) to have a laxative effect ▷ vt (Steuern, Gebühren) to pay; **jdn ~ lassen** to take sb into custody; **Abführmittel** nt laxative

Abgabe f handing in; (von Ball) pass; (Steuer) tax; (einer Erklärung) making; **abgabenfrei** adj tax-free; **abgabenpflichtig** adj liable to tax

Abgase pl (Auto) exhaust fumes pl; **Abgas(sonder)untersuchung** f exhaust emission test

ab|geben irr vt (Gepäck, Schlüssel) to leave (bei with); (Schularbeit etc) to hand in; (Wärme) to give off; (Erklärung, Urteil) to make ▷ vr **sich mit jdm ~** to associate with sb; **sich mit etw ~** to bother with sth

abgebildet adj **wie oben ~** as shown above

ab|gehen irr vi (Post) to go; (Knopf etc) to come off; (abgezogen werden) to be taken off; (Straße) to branch off; **von der Schule ~** to leave school; **sie geht mir ab** I really miss her; **was geht denn hier ab?** (fam) what's going on here?

abgehetzt adj exhausted, shattered

abgelaufen adj (Pass) expired; (Zeit, Frist) up; **die Milch ist ~** the milk is past its sell-by date

abgelegen adj remote

abgemacht interj OK, it's a deal, that's settled, then

abgeneigt adj **einer Sache** (dat) **~ sein** to be averse to sth; **ich wäre nicht ~, das zu tun** I wouldn't mind doing that

Abgeordnete(r) mf Member of Parliament

abgepackt adj prepacked

abgerissen adj **der Knopf ist ~** the button has come off

abgesehen adj **es auf jdn/etw ~ haben** to be after sb/sth; **~ von** apart from

abgespannt adj (Person) exhausted, worn out

abgestanden adj stale; (Bier) flat

abgestorben adj (Pflanze) dead; (Finger) numb

abgestumpft adj (Person) insensitive

abgetragen adj (Kleidung) worn

ab|gewöhnen vt **jdm etw ~** to cure sb of sth; **sich etw ~** to give sth up

ab|haken vt to tick off; **das (Thema) ist schon abgehakt** that's been dealt with

ab|halten irr vt (Versammlung) to hold; **jdn von etw ~** (fernhalten) to keep sb away from sth; (hindern) to keep sb from sth

abhanden adj **~ kommen** to get lost

Abhang m slope

ab|hängen vt (Bild) to take down; (Anhänger) to uncouple; (Verfolger) to shake off ▷ irr vi **von jdm/etw ~** to depend on sb/sth; **das hängt davon ab, ob ...** it depends (on) whether ...; **abhängig** adj dependent (von on)

ab|hauen irr vt (abschlagen) to cut off ▷ vi (fam: verschwinden) to clear off; **hau ab!** get lost!, beat it!

ab|heben irr vt (Geld) to withdraw; (Telefonhörer, Spielkarte) to pick up ▷ vi (Flugzeug) to take off; (Rakete) to lift off; (Karten) to cut

ab|holen vt to collect; (am Bahnhof etc) to meet; (mit dem Auto) to pick up; **Abholmarkt** m cash and carry

ab|horchen vt (Med) to listen to

ab|hören vt (Vokabeln) to test; (Telefongespräch) to tap; (Tonband etc) to listen to

Abitur (-s, -e) nt German school-leaving examination, ≈ A-levels (Brit), ≈ High School Diploma (US)

● **Abitur**
●
● The **Abitur** is the German
● school-leaving examination which is
● taken at the age of 18 or 19 by pupils
● at a **Gymnasium**. It is taken in four
● subjects and is necessary for entry to
● university.

ab|kaufen vt **jdm etw ~** to buy sth from sb; **das kauf ich dir nicht ab!** (fam: glauben) I don't believe you

ab|klingen irr vi (Schmerz) to ease; (Wirkung) to wear off

ab|kommen irr vi to get away; **von der Straße ~** to leave the road; **von einem Plan ~** to give up a plan; **vom Thema ~** to stray from the point

Abkommen (-s, -) nt agreement

ab|koppeln vt (Anhänger) to unhitch

ab|kratzen vt to scrape off ▷ vi (fam: sterben) to kick the bucket, to croak

ab|kühlen vi, vt to cool down ▷ vr **sich ~** to cool down

ab|kürzen vt (Wort) to abbreviate; **den Weg ~** to take a short cut; **Abkürzung** f (Wort) abbreviation; (Weg) short cut

ab|laden irr vt to unload

Ablage f (für Akten) tray; (Aktenordnung) filing system

Ablauf m (Abfluss) drain; (von Ereignissen) course; (einer Frist, Zeit) expiry; **ab|laufen** irr vi (abfließen) to drain away; (Ereignisse) to happen; (Frist, Zeit, Pass) to expire

ab|legen vt to put down; (Kleider) to take off; (Gewohnheit) to get out of; (Prüfung) to take, to sit; (Akten) to file away ▷ vi (Schiff) to cast off

ab|lehnen vt to reject; (Einladung) to decline; (missbilligen) to disapprove of; (Bewerber) to turn down ▷ vi to decline

ab|lenken vt to distract; **jdn von der Arbeit ~** to distract sb from their work; **vom Thema ~** to change the subject; **Ablenkung** f distraction

ab|lesen vt (Text, Rede) to read; **das Gas/den Strom ~** to read the gas/electricity meter

ab|liefern vt to deliver

ab|machen vt (entfernen) to take off; (vereinbaren) to agree; **Abmachung** f agreement

ab|melden vt (Zeitung) to cancel; (Auto) to take off the road ▷ vr **sich ~** to give notice of one's departure; (im Hotel) to check out; (vom Verein) to cancel one's membership

ab|messen irr vt to measure

ab|nehmen irr vt to take off, to remove; (Hörer) to pick up; (Führerschein) to take away; (Geld) to get (jdm out of sb); (kaufen, umg: glauben) to buy (jdm from sb) ▷ vi to decrease; (schlanker werden) to lose weight; (Tel) to pick up the phone; **fünf Kilo ~** to lose five kilos

Abneigung f dislike (gegen of); (stärker) aversion (gegen to)

ab|nutzen vt to wear out ▷ vr **sich ~** to wear out

Abonnement (-s, -s) nt subscription; **Abonnent(in)** m(f) subscriber; **abonnieren** vt to subscribe to

ab|raten irr vi **jdm von etw ~** to advise sb against sth

ab|räumen vt **den Tisch ~** to clear the table; **das Geschirr ~** to clear away the dishes; (Preis etc) to walk off with

Abrechnung f settlement; (Rechnung) bill

ab|regen vr **sich ~** (fam) to calm (o to cool) down; **reg dich ab!** take it easy

Abreise f departure; **ab|reisen** vi to leave (nach for)

ab|reißen irr vt (Haus) to pull down; (Blatt) to tear off; **den Kontakt nicht ~ lassen** to stay in touch ▷ vi (Knopf etc) to come off

ab|runden vt **eine Zahl nach oben/unten ~** to round a number up/down

abrupt adj abrupt

ABS nt abk = **Antiblockiersystem** (Auto) ABS

Abs. abk = **Absender** from

ab|sagen vt to cancel, to call off; (Einladung) to turn down ▷ vi (ablehnen) to decline; **ich muss leider ~** I'm afraid I can't come

Absatz m (Comm) sales pl; (neuer Abschnitt) paragraph; (Schuh) heel

ab|schaffen vt to abolish, to do away with

ab|schalten vt, vi (a. fig) to switch off

ab|schätzen vt to estimate; (Lage) to assess; **jdn ~** to size sb up

abscheulich adj disgusting

ab|schicken vt to send off

ab|schieben irr vt (ausweisen) to deport

Abschied (-(e)s, -e) m parting; **~ nehmen** to say good-bye (von jdm to sb); **Abschiedsfeier** f farewell party

Abschlagszahlung f interim payment

Abschleppdienst m (Auto) breakdown service; **ab|schleppen** vt to tow; **Abschleppseil** nt towrope;

Abschleppwagen m breakdown truck (Brit), tow truck (US)

ab|schließen irr vt (Tür) to lock; (beenden) to conclude, to finish; (Vertrag, Handel) to conclude; **Abschluss** m (Beendigung) close, conclusion; (von Vertrag, Handel) conclusion

ab|schmecken vt (kosten) to taste; (würzen) to season

ab|schminken vr **sich ~** to take one's make-up off ▷ vt (fam) **sich** (dat) **etw ~** to get sth out of one's mind

ab|schnallen vr **sich ~** to undo one's seatbelt

ab|schneiden irr vt to cut off ▷ vi **gut/schlecht ~** to do well/badly

Abschnitt m (von Buch, Text) section; (Kontrollabschnitt) stub

ab|schrauben vt to unscrew

ab|schrecken vt to deter, to put off

ab|schreiben irr vt to copy (bei, von from, off); (verloren geben) to write off; (Comm: absetzen) to deduct

abschüssig adj steep

ab|schwächen vt to lessen; (Behauptung, Kritik) to tone down

ab|schwellen irr vi (Entzündung) to go down; (Lärm) to die down

absehbar adj foreseeable; **in ~er Zeit** in the foreseeable future; **ab|sehen** irr vt (Ende, Folgen) to foresee ▷ vi **von etw ~** to refrain from sth

abseits adv out of the way; (Sport) offside ▷ prep +gen away from; **Abseits** nt (Sport) offside; **Abseitsfalle** f (Sport) offside trap

ab|senden irr vt to send off; (Post) to post; **Absender(in)** (-s, -) m(f) sender

ab|setzen vt (Glas, Brille etc) to put down; (aussteigen lassen) to drop (off); (Comm) to sell; (Fin) to deduct; (streichen) to drop ▷ vr **sich ~** (sich entfernen) to clear off; (sich ablagern) to be deposited

Absicht f intention; **mit ~** on purpose; **absichtlich** adj intentional, deliberate

absolut adj absolute

ab|specken vi (fam) to lose weight

ab|speichern vt (Inform) to save

ab|sperren vt to block (o to close) off; (Tür) to lock; **Absperrung** f (Vorgang) blocking (o closing) off; (Sperre) barricade

ab|spielen vt (CD etc) to play ▷ vr **sich ~** to happen

ab|springen irr vi to jump down/off; (von etw Geplantem) to drop out (von of)

ab|spülen vt to rinse; (Geschirr) to wash (up)

Abstand m distance; (zeitlich) interval; **~ halten** to keep one's distance

ab|stauben vt, vi to dust; (fam: stehlen) to pinch

Abstecher (-s, -) m detour

ab|steigen irr vi (vom Rad etc) to get off, to dismount; (in Gasthof) to stay (in +dat at)

ab|stellen vt (niederstellen) to put down; (Auto) to park; (ausschalten) to turn (o to switch) off; (Missstand, Unsitte) to stop; **Abstellraum** m store room

Abstieg (-(e)s, -e) m (vom Berg) descent; (Sport) relegation

ab|stimmen vi to vote ▷ vt (Termine, Ziele) to fit in (auf +akk with); **Dinge aufeinander ~** to coordinate things ▷ vr **sich ~** to come to an agreement (o arrangement)

abstoßend adj repulsive

abstrakt adj abstract

ab|streiten irr vt to deny

Abstrich m (Med) smear; **~e machen** to cut back (an +dat on); (weniger erwarten) to lower one's sights

Absturz m fall; (Aviat, Inform) crash; **ab|stürzen** vi to fall; (Aviat, Inform) to crash

absurd adj absurd

Abszess (-es, -e) m abscess

ab|tauen vt, vi to thaw; (Kühlschrank) to defrost

Abtei (-, -en) f abbey

Abteil (-(e)s, -e) nt compartment

Abteilung f (in Firma, Kaufhaus) department; (in Krankenhaus) section

ab|treiben irr vt (Kind) to abort ▷ vi to be driven off course; (Med: Abtreibung vornehmen) to carry out an abortion; (Abtreibung vornehmen lassen) to have an abortion; **Abtreibung** f abortion

ab|trocknen vt to dry

ab|warten vt to wait for; **das bleibt abzuwarten** that remains to be seen ▷ vi to wait

abwärts adv down

Abwasch (-(e)s) m washing-up; **ab|waschen** irr vt (Schmutz) to wash off; (Geschirr) to wash (up)

Abwasser (-s, Abwässer) nt sewage

ab|wechseln vr **sich ~** to alternate; **sich mit jdm ~** to take turns with sb; **abwechselnd** adv alternately; **Abwechslung** f change; **zur ~** for a change

ab|weisen irr vt to turn away; (Antrag) to turn down; **abweisend** adj unfriendly

abwesend adj absent; **Abwesenheit** f absence

ab|wiegen irr vt to weigh (out)

ab|wischen vt (Gesicht, Tisch etc) to wipe; (Schmutz) to wipe off

ab|zählen vt to count; (Geld) to count out

Abzeichen nt badge

ab|zeichnen vt to draw, to copy; (Dokument) to initial ▷ vr **sich ~** to stand out; (fig: bevorstehen) to loom

ab|ziehen irr vt to take off; (Bett) to strip; (Schlüssel) to take out; (subtrahieren) to take away, to subtract ▷ vi to go away

Abzug m (Foto) print; (Öffnung) vent; (Truppen) withdrawal; (Betrag) deduction; **nach ~ der Kosten** charges deducted; **abzüglich** prep +gen minus; **~ 20% Rabatt** less 20% discount

ab|zweigen vi to branch off ▷ vt to set aside; **Abzweigung** f junction

Accessoires pl accessories pl

ach interj oh; **~ so!** oh, I see; **~ was!** (Überraschung) really?; (Ärger) don't talk nonsense

Achse (-, -n) f axis; (Auto) axle

Achsel (-, -n) f shoulder; (Achselhöhle) armpit

acht num eight; **heute in ~ Tagen** in a week('s time), a week from today

Acht (-) f **sich in ~ nehmen** to be careful (vor +dat of), to watch out (vor +dat for); **~ geben** to take care (auf +akk of); **etw außer ~ lassen** to disregard sth

achte(r, s) adj eighth; siehe auch **dritte**; **Achtel** (-s, -) nt (Bruchteil) eighth; (Wein etc) eighth of a litre; (Glas Wein) ≈ small glass

achten vt to respect ▷ vi to pay attention (auf +akk to)

Achterbahn f big dipper, roller coaster

achthundert num eight hundred; **achtmal** adv eight times

Achtung f attention; (Ehrfurcht) respect ▷ interj look out

achtzehn num eighteen; **achtzehnte(r, s)** adj eighteenth; siehe auch **dritte**; **achtzig** num eighty; **in den ~er Jahren** in the eighties; **achtzigste(r, s)** adj eightieth

Acker (-s, Äcker) m field

Action (-, -s) f (fam) action; **Actionfilm** m action film

Adapter (-s, -) m adapter

addieren vt to add (up)

Adel (-s) m nobility; **adelig** adj noble

Ader (-, -n) f vein

Adjektiv nt adjective

Adler (-s, -) m eagle

adoptieren vt to adopt; **Adoption** f adoption; **Adoptiveltern** pl adoptive parents pl; **Adoptivkind** nt adopted child

Adrenalin (-s) nt adrenalin

Adressbuch nt directory; (persönliches) address book; **Adresse** (-, -n) f address; **adressieren** vt to address (an +akk to)

Advent (-s, -) m Advent; **Adventskranz** m Advent wreath

Adverb nt adverb

Aerobic (-s) nt aerobics sing

Affäre (-, -n) f affair

Affe (-n, -n) m monkey

Afghanistan (-s) nt Afghanistan

Afrika (-s) nt Africa; **Afrikaner(in)** (-s, -) m(f) African; **afrikanisch** adj African

After (-s, -) m anus

Aftershave (-(s), -s) nt aftershave

AG (-, -s) f abk = **Aktiengesellschaft** plc (Brit), corp. (US)

Agent(in) m(f) agent; **Agentur** f agency

aggressiv adj aggressive

Ägypten (-s) nt Egypt

ah interj ah, ooh

äh interj (Sprechpause) er, um; (angeekelt) ugh

aha interj I see, aha

ähneln vi +dat to be like, to resemble ▷ vr **sich ~** to be alike (o similar)

ahnen vt to suspect; **du ahnst es nicht!** would you believe it?

ähnlich adj similar (dat to); **jdm ~ sehen** to look like sb; **Ähnlichkeit** f similarity

Ahnung f idea; (Vermutung) suspicion; **keine ~!** no idea; **ahnungslos** adj unsuspecting

Ahorn (-s, -e) m maple

Aids (-) nt Aids; **aidskrank** adj suffering

from Aids; **aidspositiv** adj tested positive for Aids; **Aidstest** m Aids test

Airbag (-s, -s) m (Auto) airbag; **Airbus** m airbus

Akademie (-, -n) f academy; **Akademiker(in)** (-s, -) m(f) (university) graduate

akklimatisieren vr **sich ~** to acclimatize oneself

Akkordeon (-s, -s) nt accordion

Akku (-s, -s) m (storage) battery

Akkusativ m accusative (case)

Akne (-, -) f acne

Akrobat(in) (-s, -en) m(f) acrobat

Akt (-(e)s, -e) m act; (Kunst) nude

Akte (-, -n) f file; **etw zu den ~n legen** (a. fig) to file sth away; **Aktenkoffer** m briefcase

Aktie (-, -n) f share; **Aktiengesellschaft** f public limited company (Brit), corporation (US)

Aktion f (Kampagne) campaign; (Einsatz) operation

Aktionär(in) (-s, -e) m(f) shareholder

aktiv adj active

aktualisieren vt to update; **aktuell** adj (Thema) topical; (modern) up-to-date; (Problem) current; **nicht mehr ~** no longer relevant

Akupunktur f acupuncture

akustisch adj acoustic; **Akustik** f acoustics sing

akut adj acute

AKW (-s, -s) nt abk = **Atomkraftwerk** nuclear power station

Akzent (-(e)s, -e) m accent; (Betonung) stress; **mit starkem schottischen ~** with a strong Scottish accent

akzeptieren vt to accept

Alarm (-(e)s, -e) m alarm; **Alarmanlage** f alarm system; **alarmieren** vt to alarm; **die Polizei ~** to call the police

Albanien (-s) nt Albania

Albatros (-ses, -se) m albatross

albern adj silly

Albtraum m nightmare

Album (-s, Alben) nt album

Algen pl algae pl; (Meeresalgen) seaweed sing

Algerien (-s) nt Algeria

Alibi (-s, -s) nt alibi

Alimente pl maintenance sing

Alkohol (-s, -e) m alcohol; **alkoholfrei** adj non-alcoholic; **~es Getränk** soft drink; **Alkoholiker(in)** (-s, -) m(f) alcoholic; **alkoholisch** adj alcoholic

All (-s) nt universe

🔵 **SCHLÜSSELWORT**

alle(r, s) adj **1** (sämtliche) all; **wir alle** all of us; **alle Kinder waren da** all the children were there; **alle Kinder mögen ...** all children like ...; **alle beide** both of us/them; **sie kamen alle** they all came; **alles Gute** all the best; **alles in allem** all in all

2 (mit Zeit- oder Maßangaben) every; **alle vier Jahre** every four years; **alle fünf Meter** every five metres

▷ pron everything; **alles was er sagt** everything he says, all that he says

▷ adv (zu Ende, aufgebraucht) finished; **die Milch ist alle** the milk's all gone, there's no milk left; **etw alle machen** to finish sth up

Allee (-, -n) f avenue

allein adj, adv alone; (ohne Hilfe) on one's own, by oneself; **nicht ~** (nicht nur) not only; **~ erziehende Mutter** single mother; **~ stehend** single, unmarried; **Alleinerziehende(r)** mf single mother/father/parent

allerbeste(r, s) adj very best

allerdings adv (zwar) admittedly; (gewiss) certainly, sure (US)

allererste(r, s) adj very first; **zu allererst** first of all

Allergie f allergy; **Allergiker(in)** (-s, -) m(f) allergy sufferer; **allergisch** adj allergic (gegen to)

allerhand adj inv (fam) all sorts of; **das ist doch ~!** (Vorwurf) that's the limit; **~!** (lobend) that's pretty good

Allerheiligen (-) nt All Saints' Day

allerhöchste(r, s) adj very highest; **allerhöchstens** adv at the very most; **allerlei** adj inv all sorts of; **allerletzte(r, s)** adj very last; **allerwenigste(r, s)** adj very least

alles pron everything; **~ in allem** all in all; siehe auch **alle**

Alleskleber (-s, -) m all-purpose glue

allgemein *adj* general; **im Allgemeinen** in general
Alligator (*-s*, *-en*) *m* alligator
alljährlich *adj* annual
allmählich *adj* gradual ▷ *adv* gradually
Allradantrieb *m* all-wheel drive
Alltag *m* everyday life; **alltäglich** *adj* everyday; (*gewöhnlich*) ordinary; (*tagtäglich*) daily
allzu *adv* all too
Allzweckreiniger (*-s*, *-*) *m* multi-purpose cleaner
Alpen *pl* **die ~** the Alps *pl*
Alphabet (*-(e)s*, *-e*) *nt* alphabet; **alphabetisch** *adj* alphabetical
Alptraum *m siehe* Albtraum

⊙ SCHLÜSSELWORT

als *konj* **1** (*zeitlich*) when; (*gleichzeitig*) as; **damals, als ...** (in the days) when ...; **gerade, als ...** just as ...
2 (*in der Eigenschaft*) than; **als Antwort** as an answer; **als Kind** as a child
3 (*bei Vergleichen*) than; **ich kam später als er** I came later than he (did) *od* later than him; **lieber ... als ...** rather ... than ...; **nichts als Ärger** nothing but trouble
4: **als ob/wenn** as if

also *conj* (*folglich*) so, therefore ▷ *adv, interj* so; **~ gut** (*o* **schön**)! okay then
alt *adj* old; **wie ~ sind Sie?** how old are you?; **28 Jahre ~** 28 years old; **vier Jahre älter** four years older
Altar (*-(e)s*, *Altäre*) *m* altar
Alter (*-s*, *-*) *nt* age; (*hohes*) old age; **im ~ von** at the age of; **er ist in meinem ~** he's my age
alternativ *adj* alternative; (*umweltbewusst*) ecologically minded; (*Landwirtschaft*) organic; **Alternative** *f* alternative
Altersheim *nt* old people's home
Altglas *nt* used glass; **Altglascontainer** *m* bottle bank; **altmodisch** *adj* old-fashioned; **Altöl** *nt* used (*o* waste) oil; **Altpapier** *nt* waste paper; **Altstadt** *f* old town
Alt-Taste *f* Alt key
Alufolie *f* tin (*o* kitchen) foil
Aluminium (*-s*) *nt* aluminium (*Brit*), aluminum (*US*)

Alzheimerkrankheit *f* Alzheimer's (disease)
am *kontr von* **an dem**; **~ 2. Januar** on January 2(nd); **~ Morgen** in the morning; **~ Strand** on the beach; **~ Bahnhof** at the station; **was gefällt Ihnen ~ besten?** what do you like best?; **~ besten bleiben wir hier** it would be best if we stayed here
Amateur(in) *m(f)* amateur
ambulant *adj* outpatient; **kann ich ~ behandelt werden?** can I have it done as an outpatient?; **Ambulanz** *f* (*Krankenwagen*) ambulance; (*in der Klinik*) outpatients' department
Ameise (*-*, *-n*) *f* ant
amen *interj* amen
Amerika (*-s*) *nt* America; **Amerikaner(in)** (*-s*, *-*) *m(f)* American; **amerikanisch** *adj* American
Ampel (*-*, *-n*) *f* traffic lights *pl*
Amphitheater *nt* amphitheatre
Amsel (*-*, *-n*) *f* blackbird
Amt (*-(e)s*, *Ämter*) *nt* (*Dienststelle*) office, department; (*Posten*) post; **amtlich** *adj* official; **Amtszeichen** *nt* (*Tel*) dialling tone (*Brit*), dial tone (*US*)
amüsant *adj* amusing; **amüsieren** *vt* to amuse ▷ *vr* **sich ~** to enjoy oneself, to have a good time

⊙ SCHLÜSSELWORT

an *präp* +*dat* **1** (*räumlich: wo?*) at; (*auf, bei*) on; (*nahe bei*) near; **an diesem Ort** at this place; **an der Wand** on the wall; **zu nahe an etw** too near to sth; **unten am Fluss** down by the river; **Köln liegt am Rhein** Cologne is on the Rhine
2 (*zeitlich: wann?*) on; **an diesem Tag** on this day; **an Ostern** at Easter
3: **arm an Fett** low in fat; **an etw sterben** to die of sth; **an (und für) sich** actually
▷ *präp* +*akk* **1** (*räumlich: wohin?*) to; **er ging ans Fenster** he went (over) to the window; **etw an die Wand hängen/ schreiben** to hang/write sth on the wall
2 (*zeitlich: woran?*) **an etw denken** to think of sth
3 (*gerichtet an*) to; **ein Gruß/eine Frage an dich** greetings/a question to you

▷ *adv* **1** (*ungefähr*) about; **an die hundert** about a hundred

2 (*auf Fahrplänen*): **Frankfurt an 18.30** arriving Frankfurt 18.30

3 (*ab*): **von dort/heute an** from there/today onwards

4 (*angeschaltet, angezogen*) on; **das Licht ist an** the light is on; **ohne etwas an** with nothing on; *siehe auch* **am**

anal *adj* anal

analog *adj* analogous; (*Inform*) analog

Analyse (-, -n) *f* analysis; **analysieren** *vt* to analyse

Ananas (-, - *o* -se) *f* pineapple

an|baggern *vt* (*fam*) to chat up (*Brit*), to come on to (*US*)

Anbau *m* (*Agr*) cultivation; (*Gebäude*) extension; **an|bauen** *vt* (*Agr*) to cultivate; (*Gebäudeteil*) to build on

an|behalten *irr vt* to keep on

anbei *adv* enclosed; **~ sende ich ...** please find enclosed ...

an|beten *vt* to worship

an|bieten *irr vt* to offer ▷ *vr* **sich ~** to volunteer

an|binden *irr vt* to tie up

Anblick *m* sight

an|braten *irr vt* to brown

an|brechen *irr vt* to start; (*Vorräte, Ersparnisse*) to break into; (*Flasche, Packung*) to open ▷ *vi* to start; (*Tag*) to break; (*Nacht*) to fall

an|brennen *irr vt, vi* to burn; **das Fleisch schmeckt angebrannt** the meat tastes burnt

an|bringen *irr vt* (*herbeibringen*) to bring; (*befestigen*) to fix, to attach

Andacht (-, -en) *f* devotion; (*Gottesdienst*) prayers *pl*

an|dauern *vi* to continue, to go on; **andauernd** *adj* continual

Andenken (-s, -) *nt* memory; (*Gegenstand*) souvenir

andere(r, s) *adj* (*weitere*) other; (*verschieden*) different; (*folgend*) next; **am ~n Tag** the next day; **von etw/jmd ~m sprechen** to talk about sth/sb else; **unter ~m** among other things; **andererseits** *adv* on the other hand

ändern *vt* to alter, to change ▷ *vr* **sich ~** to change

andernfalls *adv* otherwise

anders *adv* differently (*als* from); **jemand/irgendwo ~** someone/somewhere else; **sie ist ~ als ihre Schwester** she's not like her sister; **es geht nicht ~** there's no other way; **anders(he)rum** *adv* the other way round; **anderswo** *adv* somewhere else

anderthalb *num* one and a half

Änderung *f* change, alteration

an|deuten *vt* to indicate; (*Wink geben*) to hint at

Andorra (-s) *nt* Andorra

Andrang *m* **es herrschte großer ~** there was a huge crowd

an|drohen *vt* **jdm etw ~** to threaten sb with sth

aneinander *adv* at/on/to one another (*o* each other); **~ denken** think of each other; **~ geraten** to clash; **sich ~ gewöhnen** to get used to each other; **~ legen** to put together

Anemone (-, -n) *f* anemone

an|erkennen *irr vt* (*Staat, Zeugnis etc*) to recognize; (*würdigen*) to appreciate; **Anerkennung** *f* recognition; (*Würdigung*) appreciation

an|fahren *irr vt* (*fahren gegen*) to run into; (*Ort, Hafen*) to stop (*o* call) at; (*liefern*) to deliver; (*fig: schimpfen*) to jump on sb ▷ *vi* to start; (*losfahren*) to drive off

Anfall *m* (*Med*) attack; **anfällig** *adj* delicate; (*Maschine*) temperamental; **~ für** prone to

Anfang (-(e)s, Anfänge) *m* beginning, start; **zu/am ~** to start with; **~ Mai** at the beginning of May; **sie ist ~ 20** she's in her early twenties; **an|fangen** *irr vt, vi* to begin, to start; **damit kann ich nichts ~** that's no use to me; **Anfänger(in)** (-s, -) *m(f)* beginner; **anfangs** *adv* at first; **Anfangsbuchstabe** *m* first (*o* initial) letter

an|fassen *vt* (*berühren*) to touch ▷ *vi* **kannst du mal mit ~?** can you give me a hand? ▷ *vr* **sich weich ~** to feel soft

Anflug *m* (*Aviat*) approach; (*Hauch*) trace

an|fordern *vt* to demand; **Anforderung** *f* request (*von* for); (*Anspruch*) demand

Anfrage *f* inquiry

an|freunden *vr* **sich mit jdm ~** to make (*o* to become) friends with sb

an|fühlen *vr* **sich ~** to feel; **es fühlt sich gut an** it feels good

Anführungszeichen *pl* quotation marks *pl*

Angabe *f* (*Tech*) specification; (*fam: Prahlerei*) showing off; (*Tennis*) serve; **~n** *pl* (*Auskunft*) particulars *pl*; **die ~n waren falsch** (*Info*) the information was wrong; **an|geben** *irr vt* (*Name, Grund*) to give; (*zeigen*) to indicate; (*bestimmen*) to set ▷ *vi* (*fam: prahlen*) to boast; (*Sport*) to serve; **Angeber(in)** (-s, -) *m(f)* (*fam*) show-off; **angeblich** *adj* alleged

angeboren *adj* inborn

Angebot *nt* offer; (*Comm*) supply (*an +dat* of); **~ und Nachfrage** supply and demand

angebracht *adj* appropriate

angebunden *adj* **kurz ~** curt

angeheitert *adj* tipsy

an|gehen *irr vt* to concern; **das geht dich nichts an** that's none of your business; **ein Problem ~** to tackle a problem; **was ihn angeht** as far as he's concerned, as for him ▷ *vi* (*Feuer*) to catch; (*fam: beginnen*) to begin; **angehend** *adj* prospective

Angehörige(r) *mf* relative

Angeklagte(r) *mf* accused, defendant

Angel (-, -n) *f* fishing rod; (*an der Tür*) hinge

Angelegenheit *f* affair, matter

Angelhaken *m* fish hook; **angeln** *vt* to catch ▷ *vi* to fish; **Angeln** (-s) *nt* angling, fishing; **Angelrute** (-, -n) *f* fishing rod

angemessen *adj* appropriate, suitable

angenehm *adj* pleasant; **~!** (*bei Vorstellung*) pleased to meet you; **das ist mir gar nicht ~** I don't like the idea of that

angenommen *adj* assumed ▷ *conj* **~, es regnet, was machen wir dann?** suppose it rains, what do we do then?

angesehen *adj* respected

angesichts *prep +gen* in view of, considering

Angestellte(r) *mf* employee

angetan *adj* **von jdm/etw ~ sein** to be impressed by (*o* taken with) sb/sth

angewiesen *adj* **auf jdn/etw ~ sein** to be dependent on sb/sth

an|gewöhnen *vt* **sich etw ~** to get used to doing sth; **Angewohnheit** *f* habit

Angina (-, *Anginen*) *f* tonsillitis; **Angina Pectoris** (-) *f* angina

Angler(in) (-s, -) *m(f)* angler

Angora (-s) *nt* angora

an|greifen *irr vt* to attack; (*anfassen*) to

touch; (*beschädigen*) to damage; **Angriff** *m* attack; **etw in ~ nehmen** to get started on sth

Angst (-, *Ängste*) *f* fear; **~ haben** to be afraid (*o* scared) (*vor +dat* of); **jdm ~ machen** to scare sb; **ängstigen** *vt* to frighten ▷ *vr* **sich ~** to worry (*um, wegen +dat* about); **ängstlich** *adj* nervous; (*besorgt*) worried

an|haben *irr vt* (*Kleidung*) to have on, to wear; (*Licht*) to have on

an|halten *irr vi* to stop; (*andauern*) to continue; **anhaltend** *adj* continuous; **Anhalter(in)** (-s, -) *m(f)* hitch-hiker; **per ~ fahren** to hitch-hike

anhand *prep +gen* with; **~ von** by means of

an|hängen *vt* to hang up; (*Eisenb: Wagen*) to couple; (*Zusatz*) to add (on); **jdm etw ~** (*fam: unterschieben*) to pin sth on sb; **Anhänger** (-s, -) *m* (*Auto*) trailer; (*am Koffer*) tag; (*Schmuck*) pendant; **Anhänger(in)** (-s, -) *m(f)* supporter; **Anhängerkupplung** *f* towbar; **anhänglich** *adj* affectionate; (*pej*) clinging

Anhieb *m* **auf ~** straight away; **das kann ich nicht auf ~ sagen** I can't say offhand

an|himmeln *vt* to worship, to idolize

an|hören *vt* to listen to ▷ *vr* **sich ~** to sound; **das hört sich gut an** that sounds good

Animateur(in) *m(f)* host/hostess

Anis (-es, -e) *m* aniseed

Anker (-s, -) *m* anchor; **ankern** *vt*, *vi* to anchor; **Ankerplatz** *m* anchorage

Ankleidekabine *f* changing cubicle

an|klicken *vt* (*Inform*) to click on

an|klopfen *vi* to knock (*an +akk* on)

an|kommen *irr vi* to arrive; **bei jdm gut ~** to go down well with sb; **es kommt darauf an** it depends (*ob* on whether); **darauf kommt es nicht an** that doesn't matter

an|kotzen *vt* (*vulg*) **es kotzt mich an** it makes me sick

an|kreuzen *vt* to mark with a cross

an|kündigen *vt* to announce

Ankunft (-, *Ankünfte*) *f* arrival; **Ankunftszeit** *f* arrival time

Anlage *f* (*Veranlagung*) disposition; (*Begabung*) talent; (*Park*) gardens *pl*, grounds *pl*; (*zu Brief etc*) enclosure; (*Stereoanlage*) stereo (system); (*Tech*) plant; (*Fin*) investment

Anlass (-es, Anlässe) m cause (zu for); (Ereignis) occasion; **aus diesem ~** for this reason; **an|lassen** irr vt (Motor) to start; (Licht, Kleidung) to leave on; **Anlasser** (-s, -) m (Auto) starter; **anlässlich** prep +gen on the occasion of

Anlauf m run-up; **an|laufen** irr vi to begin; (Film) to open; (Fenster) to mist up; (Metall) to tarnish

an|legen vt to put (an +akk against/on); (Schmuck) to put on; (Garten) to lay out; (Geld) to invest; (Gewehr) to aim (auf +akk at); **es auf etw** (akk) **~** to be out for sth ⊳ vi (Schiff) to berth, to dock ⊳ vr **sich mit jdm ~** (fam) to pick a quarrel with sb; **Anlegestelle** f moorings pl

an|lehnen vt to lean (an +akk against); (Tür) to leave ajar ⊳ vr **sich ~** to lean (an +akk against)

an|leiern vt etw **~** (fam) to get sth going

Anleitung f instructions pl

Anliegen (-s, -) nt matter; (Wunsch) request

Anlieger(in) (-s, -) m(f) resident; **~ frei** residents only

an|lügen irr vt to lie to

an|machen vt (befestigen) to attach; (einschalten) to switch on; (Salat) to dress; (fam: aufreizen) to turn on; (fam: ansprechen) to chat up (Brit), to come on to (US); (fam: beschimpfen) to have a go at

Anmeldeformular nt application form; (bei Amt) registration form; **an|melden** vt (Besuch etc) to announce ⊳ vr **sich ~** (beim Arzt etc) to make an appointment; (bei Amt, für Kurs etc) to register; **Anmeldeschluss** m deadline for applications, registration deadline; **Anmeldung** f registration, (Antrag) application

an|nähen vt **einen Knopf** (**an den Mantel**) **~** to sew a button on (one's coat)

annähernd adv roughly; **nicht ~** nowhere near

Annahme (-, -n) f acceptance; (Vermutung) assumption; **annehmbar** adj acceptable; **an|nehmen** irr vt to accept; (Namen) to take; (Kind) to adopt; (vermuten) to suppose, to assume

Annonce (-, -n) f advertisement

an|öden vt (fam) to bore stiff (o silly)

annullieren vt to cancel

anonym adj anonymous

Anorak (-s, -s) m anorak

an|packen vt (Problem, Aufgabe) to tackle; **mit ~** to lend a hand

an|passen vt (fig) to adapt (dat to) ⊳ vr **sich ~** to adapt (an +akk to)

an|pfeifen irr vt (Fußballspiel) **das Spiel ~** to start the game; **Anpfiff** m (Sport) (starting) whistle; (Beginn) kick-off; (fam: Tadel) roasting

an|probieren vt to try on

Anrede f form of address; **an|reden** vt to address

an|regen vt to stimulate; **Anregung** f stimulation; (Vorschlag) suggestion

Anreise f journey; **der Tag der ~** the day of arrival; **an|reisen** vi to arrive

Anreiz m incentive

an|richten vt (Speisen) to prepare; (Schaden) to cause

Anruf m call; **Anrufbeantworter** (-s, -) m answering machine, answerphone; **an|rufen** irr vt (Tel) to call, to phone, to ring (Brit)

ans kontr von **an das**

Ansage f announcement; (auf Anrufbeantworter) recorded message; **an|sagen** vt to announce; **angesagt sein** to be recommended; (modisch sein) to be the in thing; **Spannung ist angesagt** we are in for some excitement ⊳ vr **er sagte sich an** he said he would come

an|schaffen vt to buy

an|schauen vt to look at

Anschein m appearance; **dem** (o allem) **~ nach ...** it looks as if ...; **den ~ erwecken, hart zu arbeiten** to give the impression of working hard; **anscheinend** adj apparent ⊳ adv apparently

an|schieben irr vt **könnten Sie mich mal ~?** (Auto) could you give me a push?

Anschlag m notice; (Attentat) attack; **an|schlagen** irr vt (Plakat) to put up; (beschädigen) to chip ⊳ vi (wirken) to take effect; **mit etw an etw** (akk) **~** to bang sth against sth

an|schließen irr vt (Elek, Tech) to connect (an +akk to); (mit Stecker) to plug in ⊳ vi, vr (**sich**) **an etw** (akk) **~** (Gebäude etc) to adjoin sth; (zeitlich) to follow sth ⊳ vr **sich ~** to join (jdm/einer Gruppe sb/a group); **anschließend** adj adjacent; (zeitlich) subsequent ⊳ adv afterwards; **~ an** (+akk) following; **Anschluss** m (Elek, Eisenb) connection; (*von Wasser, Gas etc*) supply; **im ~ an** (+*akk*) following; **kein ~ unter dieser Nummer** (*Tel*) the number you have dialled has not been recognized; **Anschlussflug** *m* connecting flight

an|schnallen *vt* (*Skier*) to put on ▷ *vr* **sich ~** to fasten one's seat belt

Anschrift *f* address

an|schwellen *irr vi* to swell (up)

an|sehen *irr vt* to look at; (*bei etw zuschauen*) to watch; **jdn/etw als etw ~** to look on sb/sth as sth; **das sieht man ihm an** he looks it

an sein *irr vi* siehe **an**

an|setzen *vt* (*Termin*) to fix; (*zubereiten*) to prepare ▷ *vi* (*anfangen*) to start, to begin; **zu etw ~** to prepare to do sth

Ansicht *f* (*Meinung*) view, opinion; (*Anblick*) sight; **meiner ~ nach** in my opinion; **zur ~** on approval; **Ansichtskarte** *f* postcard

ansonsten *adv* otherwise

Anspiel *nt* (*Sport*) start of play; **anspielen** *vi* **auf etw** (*akk*) **~** to allude to sth; **Anspielung** *f* allusion (*auf* +*akk* to)

an|sprechen *irr vt* to speak to; (*gefallen*) to appeal to ▷ *vi* **auf etw** (*akk*) **~** (*Patient*) to respond ▷ sth; **ansprechend** *adj* attractive; **Ansprechpartner(in)** *m(f)* contact

an|springen *irr vi* (*Auto*) to start

Anspruch *m* claim; (*Recht*) right (*auf* +*akk* to); **etw in ~ nehmen** to take advantage of sth; **~ auf etw haben** to be entitled to sth; **anspruchslos** *adj* undemanding; (*bescheiden*) modest; **anspruchsvoll** *adj* demanding

Anstalt (-, -en) *f* institution

Anstand *m* decency; **anständig** *adj* decent; (*fig, fam*) proper; (*groß*) considerable

an|starren *vt* to stare at

anstatt *prep* +*gen* instead of

an|stecken *vt* to pin on; (*Med*) to infect; **jdn mit einer Erkältung ~** to pass one's cold on to sb ▷ *vr* **ich habe mich bei ihm angesteckt** I caught it from him ▷ *vi* (*fig*) to be infectious; **ansteckend** *adj* infectious; **Ansteckungsgefahr** *f* danger of infection

an|stehen *irr vi* (*in Warteschlange*) to queue (*Brit*), to stand in line (*US*); (*erledigt werden müssen*) to be on the agenda

anstelle *prep* +*gen* instead of

an|stellen *vt* (*einschalten*) to turn on; (*Arbeit geben*) to employ; (*machen*) to do; **was hast du wieder angestellt?** what have you been up to now? ▷ *vr* **sich ~ to** queue (*Brit*), to stand in line (*US*); (*fam*) **stell dich nicht so an!** stop making such a fuss

Anstoß *m* impetus; (*Sport*) kick-off; **an|stoßen** *irr vt* to push; (*mit Fuß*) to kick ▷ *vi* to knock, to bump; (*mit Gläsern*) to drink (a toast) (*auf* +*akk* to); **anstößig** *adj* offensive; (*Kleidung etc*) indecent

an|strengen *vt* to strain ▷ *vr* **sich ~ to** make an effort; **anstrengend** *adj* tiring

Antarktis *f* Antarctic

Anteil *m* share (*an* +*dat* in); **~ nehmen an** (+*dat*) (*mitleidig*) to sympathize with; (*sich interessieren*) to take an interest in

Antenne (-, -*n*) *f* aerial

Antibabypille *f* **die ~** the pill; **Antibiotikum** (-*s*, *Antibiotika*) *nt* (*Med*) antibiotic

antik *adj* antique

Antilope (-, -*n*) *f* antelope

Antiquariat *nt* (*für Bücher*) second-hand bookshop

Antiquitäten *pl* antiques *pl*; **Antiquitätenhändler(in)** *m(f)* antique dealer

an|törnen *vt* (*fam*) to turn on

Antrag (-(*e*)*s*, *Anträge*) *m* proposal; (*Pol*) motion; (*Formular*) application form; **einen ~ stellen auf** (+*akk*) to make an application for

an|treffen *irr vt* to find

an|treiben *irr vt* (*Tech*) to drive; (*anschwemmen*) to wash up; **jdn zur Arbeit ~** to make sb work

an|treten *irr vt* **eine Reise ~** to set off on a journey

Antrieb *m* (*Tech*) drive; (*Motivation*) impetus

an|tun *irr vt* **jdm etwas ~** to do sth to sb; **sich** (*dat*) **etwas ~** (*Selbstmord begehen*) to kill oneself

Antwort (-, -*en*) *f* answer, reply; **um ~ wird gebeten** RSVP (*répondez s'il vous plaît*); **antworten** *vi* to answer, to reply; **jdm ~** to answer sb; **auf etw** (*akk*) **~** to answer sth

an|vertrauen *vt* **jdm etw ~** to entrust sb with sth

Anwalt (-s, Anwälte) m, **Anwältin** f
lawyer

an|weisen irr vt (anleiten) to instruct;
(zuteilen) to allocate (jdm etw sth to sb);
Anweisung f instruction; (von Geld)
money order

an|wenden irr vt to use; (Gesetz, Regel)
to apply; **Anwender(in)** (-s, -) m(f)
user; **Anwendung** f use; (Inform)
application

anwesend adj present; **Anwesenheit** f
presence

an|widern vt to disgust

Anwohner(in) (-s, -) m(f) resident

Anzahl f number (an +dat of); **an|zahlen**
vt to pay a deposit on; **100 Euro ~** to pay
100 euros as a deposit; **Anzahlung** f
deposit

Anzeichen nt sign; (Med) symptom

Anzeige (-, -n) f (Werbung) advertisement;
(elektronisch) display; (bei Polizei) report;
an|zeigen vt (Temperatur, Zeit) to indicate,
to show; (elektronisch) to display; (bekannt
geben) to announce; **jdn/einen
Autodiebstahl bei der Polizei ~** to report
sb/a stolen car to the police

an|ziehen irr vt to attract; (Kleidung) to
put on; (Schraube, Seil) to tighten ▷ vr **sich
~** to get dressed; **anziehend** adj
attractive

Anzug m suit

anzüglich adj suggestive

an|zünden vt to light; (Haus etc) to set
fire to

an|zweifeln vt to doubt

Aperitif (-s, -s (o -e)) m aperitif

Apfel (-s, Äpfel) m apple; **Apfelbaum** m
apple tree; **Apfelkuchen** m apple cake;
Apfelmus nt apple purée; **Apfelsaft** m
apple juice; **Apfelsine** f orange;
Apfelwein m cider

Apostroph (-s, -e) m apostrophe

Apotheke (-, -n) f chemist's (shop) (Brit),
pharmacy (US); **apothekenpflichtig** adj
only available at the chemist's (o
pharmacy); **Apotheker(in)** (-s, -) m(f)
chemist (Brit), pharmacist (US)

Apparat (-(e)s, -e) m (piece of) apparatus;
(Tel) telephone; (Radio, Tv) set; **am ~!** (Tel)
speaking; **am ~ bleiben** (Tel) to hold the
line

Appartement (-s, -s) nt studio flat (Brit)
(o apartment (US))

Appetit (-(e)s, -e) m appetite; **guten ~!**
bon appétit; **appetitlich** adj appetizing

Applaus (-es, -e) m applause

Aprikose (-, -n) f apricot

April (-(s), -e) m April; siehe auch **Juni ~, ~!**
April fool!; **Aprilscherz** (-es, -e) m April
fool's joke

apropos adv by the way; **~ Urlaub ...**
while we're on the subject of holidays ...

Aquaplaning (-(s)) nt aquaplaning

Aquarell (-s, -e) nt watercolour

Aquarium nt aquarium

Äquator m equator

Araber(in) (-s, -) m(f) Arab; **arabisch** adj
Arab; (Ziffer, Sprache) Arabic; (Meer, Wüste)
Arabian

Arbeit (-, -en) f work; (Stelle) job;
(Erzeugnis) piece of work; **arbeiten** vi to
work; **Arbeiter(in)** (-s, -) m(f) worker;
(ungelernt) labourer; **Arbeitgeber(in)**
(-s, -) m(f) employer; **Arbeitnehmer(in)**
(-s, -) m(f) employee; **Arbeitsamt** nt job
centre (Brit), employment office (US);
Arbeitserlaubnis f work permit;
arbeitslos adj unemployed;
Arbeitslose(r) mf unemployed person;
die ~n pl the unemployed pl;
Arbeitslosengeld nt (income-related)
unemployment benefit, job-seeker's
allowance (Brit); **Arbeitslosenhilfe** f
(non-income related) unemployment
benefit; **Arbeitslosigkeit** f
unemployment; **Arbeitsplatz** m job;
(Ort) workplace; **Arbeitsspeicher** m
(Inform) main memory; **Arbeitszeit** f
working hours pl; **gleitende ~** flexible
working hours pl, flexitime;
Arbeitszimmer nt study

Archäologe (-n, -n) m, **Archäologin** f
archaeologist

Architekt(in) (-en, -en) m(f) architect;
Architektur f architecture

Archiv (-s, -e) nt archives pl

arg adj bad; (schrecklich) awful ▷ adv (sehr)
terribly

Argentinien (-s) nt Argentina

Ärger (-s) m annoyance; (stärker) anger;
(Unannehmlichkeiten) trouble; **ärgerlich**
adj (zornig) angry; (lästig) annoying;
ärgern vt to annoy ▷ vr **sich ~** to get
annoyed

Argument (-s, -e) nt argument

Arktis (-) f Arctic

arm adj poor

Arm (-(e)s, -e) m arm; (Fluss) branch

Armaturenbrett nt instrument panel; (Auto) dashboard

Armband nt bracelet; **Armbanduhr** f (wrist)watch

Armee (-, -n) f army

Ärmel (-s, -) m sleeve; **Ärmelkanal** m (English) Channel

Armut (-) f poverty

Aroma (-s, Aromen) nt aroma; **Aromatherapie** f aromatherapy

arrogant adj arrogant

Art (-, -en) f (Weise) way; (Sorte) kind, sort; (bei Tieren) species; **nach ~ des Hauses** à la maison; **auf diese ~ (und Weise)** in this way; **das ist nicht seine ~** that's not like him

Arterie (-, -n) f artery

artig adj good, well-behaved

Artikel (-s, -) m (Ware) article, item; (Zeitung) article

Artischocke (-, -n) f artichoke

Artist(in) (-en, -en) m(f) (circus) performer

Arznei f medicine; **Arzt** (-es, Ärzte) m doctor; **Arzthelfer(in)** m(f) doctor's assistant; **Ärztin** f (female) doctor; **ärztlich** adj medical; **sich ~ behandeln lassen** to undergo medical treatment

Asche (-, -n) f ashes pl; (von Zigarette) ash; **Aschenbecher** m ashtray; **Aschermittwoch** m Ash Wednesday

Asiat(in) (-en, -en) m(f) Asian; **asiatisch** adj Asian; **Asien** (-s) nt Asia

Aspekt (-(e)s, -e) m aspect

Asphalt (-(e)s, -e) m asphalt

Aspirin® (-s, -e) nt aspirin

aß imperf von **essen**

Ass (-es, -e) nt (Karten, Tennis) ace

Assistent(in) m(f) assistant

Ast (-(e)s, Äste) m branch

Asthma (-s) nt asthma

Astrologie f astrology; **Astronaut(in)** (-en, -en) m(f) astronaut; **Astronomie** f astronomy

ASU (-, -s) f abk = **Abgassonderuntersuchung** exhaust emission test

Asyl (-s, -e) nt asylum; (Heim) home; (für Obdachlose) shelter; **Asylant(in)** m(f), **Asylbewerber(in)** m(f) asylum seeker

Atelier (-s, -s) nt studio

Atem (-s) m breath; **atemberaubend** adj breathtaking; **Atembeschwerden** pl breathing difficulties pl; **atemlos** adj breathless; **Atempause** f breather

Athen nt Athens

Äthiopien (-s) nt Ethiopia

Athlet(in) (-en, -en) m(f) athlete

Atlantik (-s) m Atlantic (Ocean)

Atlas (- o Atlasses, Atlanten) m atlas

atmen vt, vi to breathe; **Atmung** f breathing

Atom (-s, -e) nt atom; **Atombombe** f atom bomb; **Atomkraftwerk** nt nuclear power station; **Atommüll** m nuclear waste; **Atomwaffen** pl nuclear weapons pl

Attentat (-(e)s, -e) nt assassination (auf +akk of); (Versuch) assassination attempt

Attest (-(e)s, -e) nt certificate

attraktiv adj attractive

Attrappe (-, -n) f dummy

ätzend adj (fam) revolting; (schlecht) lousy

au interj ouch; **~ ja!** yeah

Aubergine (-, -n) f aubergine, eggplant (US)

🔵 **SCHLÜSSELWORT**

auch adv 1 (ebenfalls) also, too, as well; **das ist auch schön** that's nice too od as well; **er kommt — ich auch** he's coming — so am I me too; **auch nicht** not ... either; **ich auch nicht** nor I, me neither; **oder auch** or; **auch das noch!** not that as well!

2 (selbst, sogar) even; **auch wenn das Wetter schlecht ist** even if the weather is bad; **ohne auch nur zu fragen** without even asking

3 (wirklich) really; **du siehst müde aus — bin ich auch** you look tired — (so) I am; **so sieht es auch aus** it looks like it too

4 (auch immer); **wer auch** whoever; **was auch** whatever; **wie dem auch sei** be that as it may; **wie sehr er sich auch bemühte** however much he tried

audiovisuell adj audiovisual

○ SCHLÜSSELWORT

auf *präp* +dat (*wo?*) on; **auf dem Tisch** on the table; **auf der Reise** on the way; **auf der Post/dem Fest** at the post office/party; **auf der Straße** on the road; **auf dem Land/der ganzen Welt** in the country/the whole world

▷ *präp* +akk **1** (*wohin?*) on(to); **auf den Tisch** on(to) the table; **auf die Post gehen** go to the post office; **auf das Land** into the country; **etw auf einen Zettel schreiben** to write sth on a piece of paper

2: **auf Deutsch** in German; **auf Lebenszeit** for my/his lifetime; **bis auf ihn** except for him; **auf einmal** at once; **auf seinen Vorschlag (hin)** at his suggestion

▷ *adv* **1** (*offen*) open; **auf sein** (*umg*) (*Tür, Geschäft*) to be open; **das Fenster ist auf** the window is open

2 (*hinauf*) up; **auf und ab** up and down; **auf und davon** up and away; **auf!** (*los!*) come on!

3 (*aufgestanden*) up; **auf sein** to be up; **ist er schon auf?** is he up yet?

▷ *konj*: **auf dass** (so) that

auf|atmen *vi* to breathe a sigh of relief

auf|bauen *vt* (*errichten*) to put up; (*schaffen*) to build up; (*gestalten*) to construct; (*gründen*) to found, to base (*auf* +akk on); **sich eine Existenz ~** to make a life for oneself

auf|bewahren *vt* to keep, to store

auf|bleiben *irr vi* (*Tür, Laden etc*) to stay open; (*Mensch*) to stay up

auf|blenden *vi, vt* (**die Scheinwerfer**) **~** to put one's headlights on full beam

auf|brechen *irr vt* to break open ▷ *vi* to burst open; (*gehen*) to leave; (*abreisen*) to set off; **Aufbruch** *m* departure

auf|drängen *vt* **jdm etw ~** to force sth on sb ▷ *vr* **sich ~** to intrude (*jdm* on sb); **aufdringlich** *adj* pushy

aufeinander *adv* (*übereinander*) on top of each other; **~ achten** to look after each other; **~ schießen** to shoot at each other; **~ vertrauen** to trust each other; **~ folgen** to follow one another; **~ prallen** to crash into one another

Aufenthalt *m* stay; (*Zug*) stop; **Aufenthaltsgenehmigung** *f* residence permit; **Aufenthaltsraum** *m* lounge

auf|essen *irr vt* to eat up

auf|fahren *irr vi* (*Auto*) to run (*o* to crash) (*auf* +akk into); (*herankommen*) to drive up; **Auffahrt** *f* (*am Haus*) drive; (*Autobahn*) slip road (*Brit*), ramp (*US*); **Auffahrunfall** *m* rear-end collision; (*mehrere Fahrzeuge*) pile-up

auf|fallen *irr vi* to stand out; **jdm ~** to strike sb; **das fällt gar nicht auf** nobody will notice; **auffallend** *adj* striking; **auffällig** *adj* conspicuous; (*Kleidung, Farbe*) striking

auf|fangen *irr vt* (*Ball*) to catch; (*Stoß*) to cushion

auf|fassen *vt* to understand; **Auffassung** *f* view; (*Meinung*) opinion; (*Auslegung*) concept; (*Auffassungsgabe*) grasp

auf|fordern *vt* (*befehlen*) to call upon; (*bitten*) to ask

auf|frischen *vt* (*Kenntnisse*) to brush up

auf|führen *vt* (*Theat*) to perform; (*in einem Verzeichnis*) to list; (*Beispiel*) to give ▷ *vr* **sich ~** (*sich benehmen*) to behave; **Aufführung** *f* (*Theat*) performance

Aufgabe *f* job, task; (*Schule*) exercise; (*Hausaufgabe*) homework

Aufgang *m* (*Treppe*) staircase

auf|geben *irr vt* (*verzichten auf*) to give up; (*Paket*) to post; (*Gepäck*) to check in; (*Bestellung*) to place; (*Inserat*) to insert; (*Rätsel, Problem*) to set ▷ *vi* to give up

auf|gehen *irr vi* (*Sonne, Teig*) to rise; (*sich öffnen*) to open; (*klar werden*) to dawn (*jdm* on sb)

aufgelegt *adj*: **gut/schlecht ~** in a good/bad mood

aufgeregt *adj* excited

aufgeschlossen *adj* open(minded)

aufgeschmissen *adj* (*fam*) in a fix

aufgrund, auf Grund *prep* +gen on the basis of; (*wegen*) because of

auf|haben *irr vt* (*Hut etc*) to have on; **viel ~** (*Schule*) to have a lot of homework to do ▷ *vi* (*Geschäft*) to be open

auf|halten *irr vt* (*jdn*) to detain; (*Entwicklung*) to stop; (*Tür, Hand*) to hold open; (*Augen*) to keep open ▷ *vr* **sich ~** (*wohnen*) to live; (*vorübergehend*) to stay

auf|hängen irr vt to hang up

auf|heben irr vt (vom Boden etc) to pick up; (aufbewahren) to keep

auf|holen vt (Zeit) to make up ▷ vi to catch up

auf|hören vi to stop; **~, etw zu tun** to stop doing sth

auf|klären vt (Geheimnis etc) to clear up; **jdn ~** to enlighten sb; (sexuell) to tell sb the facts of life

Aufkleber (-s, -) m sticker

auf|kommen irr vi (Wind) to come up; (Zweifel, Gefühl) to arise; (Mode etc) to appear on the scene; **für den Schaden ~** to pay for the damage

auf|laden irr vt to load; (Handy etc) to charge; **Aufladegerät** nt charger

Auflage f edition; (von Zeitung) circulation; (Bedingung) condition

auf|lassen vt (Hut, Brille) to keep on; (Tür) to leave open

Auflauf m (Menschen) crowd; (Speise) bake

auf|legen vt (CD, Schminke etc) to put on; (Hörer) to put down ▷ vi (Tel) to hang up

auf|leuchten vi to light up

auf|lösen vt (in Flüssigkeit) to dissolve ▷ vr **sich ~** (in Flüssigkeit) to dissolve; **der Stau hat sich aufgelöst** traffic is back to normal; **Auflösung** f (von Rätsel) solution; (von Bildschirm) resolution

auf|machen vt to open; (Kleidung) to undo ▷ vr **sich ~** to set out (nach for)

aufmerksam adj attentive; **jdn auf etw (akk) ~ machen** to draw sb's attention to sth; **Aufmerksamkeit** f attention; (Konzentration) attentiveness; (Geschenk) small token

auf|muntern vt (ermutigen) to encourage; (aufheitern) to cheer up

Aufnahme (-, -n) f (Foto) photo(graph); (einzelne) shot; (in Verein, Krankenhaus etc) admission; (Beginn) beginning; (auf Tonband etc) recording; **Aufnahmeprüfung** f entrance exam; **auf|nehmen** irr vt (in Verein, Krankenhaus etc) to admit; (Musik) to record; (beginnen) to take up; (in Liste) to include; (begreifen) to take in; **mit jdm Kontakt ~** to get in touch with sb

auf|passen vi (aufmerksam sein) to pay attention; (vorsichtig sein) to take care; **auf jdn/etw ~** to keep an eye on sb/sth

Aufprall (-s, -e) m impact; **auf|prallen** vi **auf etw (akk) ~** to hit sth, to crash into sth

Aufpreis m extra charge

auf|pumpen vt to pump up

Aufputschmittel nt stimulant

auf|räumen vt, vi (Dinge) to clear away; (Zimmer) to tidy up

aufrecht adj upright

auf|regen vt to excite; (ärgern) to annoy ▷ vr **sich ~** to get worked up; **aufregend** adj exciting; **Aufregung** f excitement

auf|reißen irr vt (Tüte) to tear open; (Tür) to fling open; (fam: Person) to pick up

Aufruf m (Aviat, Inform) call; (öffentlicher) appeal; **auf|rufen** irr vt (auffordern) to call upon (zu for); (Namen) to call out; (Aviat) to call; (Inform) to call up

auf|runden vt (Summe) to round up

aufs kontr von **auf das**

Aufsatz m essay

auf|schieben irr vt (verschieben) to postpone; (verzögern) to put off; (Tür) to slide open

Aufschlag m (auf Preis) extra charge; (Tennis) service; **auf|schlagen** irr vt (öffnen) to open; (verletzen) to cut open; (Zelt) to pitch, to put up; (Lager) to set up ▷ vi (Tennis) to serve; **auf etw (+akk) ~** (aufprallen) to hit sth

auf|schließen irr vt to unlock, to open up ▷ vi (aufrücken) to close up

auf|schneiden irr vt to cut open; (in Scheiben) to slice ▷ vi (angeben) to boast, to show off

Aufschnitt m (slices pl of) cold meat; (bei Käse) (assorted) sliced cheeses pl

auf|schreiben irr vt to write down

Aufschrift f inscription; (Etikett) label

Aufschub m (Verzögerung) delay; (Vertagung) postponement

Aufsehen (-s) nt stir; **großes ~ erregen** to cause a sensation; **Aufseher(in)** (-s, -) m(f) guard; (im Betrieb) supervisor; (im Museum) attendant; (im Park) keeper

auf sein irr vi siehe **auf**

auf|setzen vt to put on; (Dokument) to draw up ▷ vi (Flugzeug) to touch down

Aufsicht f supervision; (bei Prüfung) invigilation; **die ~ haben** to be in charge

auf|spannen vt (Schirm) to put up

auf|sperren vt (Mund) to open wide; (aufschließen) to unlock

auf|springen irr vi to jump (auf +akk

onto); (*hochspringen*) to jump up; (*sich öffnen*) to spring open

auf|stehen *irr vi* to get up; (*Tür*) to be open

auf|stellen *vt* (*aufrecht stellen*) to put up; (*aufreihen*) to line up; (*nominieren*) to put up; (*Liste, Programm*) to draw up; (*Rekord*) to set up

Aufstieg (-(e)s, -e) *m* (*auf Berg*) ascent; (*Fortschritt*) rise; (*beruflich, im Sport*) promotion

Aufstrich *m* spread

auf|tanken *vt, vi* (*Auto*) to tank up; (*Flugzeug*) to refuel

auf|tauchen *vi* to turn up; (*aus Wasser etc*) to surface; (*Frage, Problem*) to come up

auf|tauen *vt* (*Speisen*) to defrost ▷ *vi* to thaw; (*fig: Person*) to unbend

Auftrag (-(e)s, *Aufträge*) *m* (*Comm*) order; (*Arbeit*) job; (*Anweisung*) instructions *pl*; (*Aufgabe*) task; **im ~ von** on behalf of;

auf|tragen *irr vt* (*Salbe etc*) to apply; (*Essen*) to serve

auf|treten *irr vi* to appear; (*Problem*) to come up; (*sich verhalten*) to behave;

Auftritt *m* (*des Schauspielers*) entrance; (*fig: Szene*) scene

auf|wachen *vi* to wake up

auf|wachsen *irr vi* to grow up

Aufwand (-(e)s) *m* expenditure; (*Kosten a.*) expense; (*Anstrengung*) effort; **aufwändig** *adj* costly; **das ist zu ~** that's too much trouble

auf|wärmen *vt* to warm up ▷ *vr* **sich ~** to warm up

aufwärts *adv* upwards; **mit etw geht es ~** things are looking up for sth

auf|wecken *vt* to wake up

aufwendig *adj siehe* **aufwändig**

auf|wischen *vt* to wipe up; (*Fußboden*) to wipe

auf|zählen *vt* to list; **Aufzählungszeichen** *nt* bullet

auf|zeichnen *vt* to sketch; (*schriftlich*) to jot down; (*auf Band etc*) to record; **Aufzeichnung** *f* (*schriftlich*) note; (*Tonband etc*) recording; (*Film*) record

auf|ziehen *irr vt* (*öffnen*) to pull open; (*Uhr*) to wind (up); (*fam: necken*) to tease; (*Kinder*) to bring up; (*Tiere*) to rear ▷ *vi* (*Gewitter*) to come up

Aufzug *m* (*Fahrstuhl*) lift (*Brit*), elevator (*US*); (*Kleidung*) get-up; (*Theat*) act

Auge (-s, -n) *nt* eye; **jdm etw aufs ~ drücken** (*fam*) to force sth on sb; **ins ~ gehen** (*fam*) to go wrong; **unter vier ~n** in private; **etw im ~ behalten** to keep sth in mind; **Augenarzt** *m*, **Augenärztin** *f* eye specialist, eye doctor (*US*); **Augenblick** *m* moment; **im ~** at the moment; **Augenbraue** (-, -n) *f* eyebrow; **Augenbrauenstift** *m* eyebrow pencil; **Augenfarbe** *f* eye colour; **seine ~** the colour of his eyes; **Augenlid** *nt* eyelid; **Augenoptiker(in)** (-s, -) *m(f)* optician; **Augentropfen** *pl* eyedrops *pl*; **Augenzeuge** *m*, **Augenzeugin** *f* eyewitness

August (-(e)s *o* -, -e) *m* August; *siehe auch* **Juni**

Auktion *f* auction

⭕ **SCHLÜSSELWORT**

aus *präp* +dat **1** (*räumlich*) out of (*von ... her*) from; **er ist aus Berlin** he's from Berlin; **aus dem Fenster** out of the window

2 (*gemacht/hergestellt aus*) made of; **ein Herz aus Stein** a heart of stone

3 (*auf Ursache deutend*) out of; **aus Mitleid** out of sympathy; **aus Erfahrung** from experience; **aus Spaß** for fun

4: **aus ihr wird nie etwas** she'll never get anywhere

▷ *adv* **1** (*zu Ende*) finished, over; **aus sein** to be over; **aus und vorbei** over and done with

2 (*ausgeschaltet, ausgezogen*) out (*Aufschrift an Geräten*) off; **aus sein** (*nicht brennen*) to be out, (*abgeschaltet sein: Radio, Herd*) to be off; **Licht aus!** lights out!

3 (*nicht zu Hause*): **aus sein** to be out

4 (*in Verbindung mit von*): **von Rom aus** from Rome; **vom Fenster aus** out of the window; **von sich aus** (*selbstständig*) of one's own accord; **von ihm aus** as far as he's concerned

---

aus|atmen *vi* to breathe out

aus|bauen *vt* (*Haus, Straße*) to extend; (*Motor etc*) to remove

aus|bessern *vt* to repair; (*Kleidung*) to mend

aus|bilden *vt* to educate; (*Lehrling etc*) to train; (*Fähigkeiten*) to develop; **Ausbildung**

f education; (*von Lehrling etc*) training; (*von Fähigkeiten*) development

Ausblick *m* view; (*fig*) outlook

aus|brechen *irr vi* to break out; **in Tränen ~** to burst into tears; **in Gelächter ~** to burst out laughing

aus|breiten *vt* to spread (out); (*Arme*) to stretch out ▷ *vr* **sich ~** to spread

Ausbruch *m* (*Krieg, Seuche etc*) outbreak; (*Vulkan*) eruption; (*Gefühle*) outburst; (*von Gefangenen*) escape

aus|buhen *vt* to boo

Ausdauer *f* perseverance; (*Sport*) stamina

aus|dehnen *vt* to stretch; (*fig: Macht*) to extend

aus|denken *irr vt* **sich** (*dat*) **etw ~** to come up with sth

Ausdruck *m* (*Ausdrücke*) expression ▷ *m* (*Ausdrucke*) (*Computerausdruck*) print-out; **aus|drucken** *vt* (*Inform*) to print (out)

aus|drücken *vt* (*formulieren*) to express; (*Zigarette*) to put out; (*Zitrone etc*) to squeeze ▷ *vr* **sich ~** to express oneself; **ausdrücklich** *adj* express ▷ *adv* expressly

auseinander *adv* (*getrennt*) apart; **~ gehen** (*Menschen*) to separate; (*Meinungen*) to differ; (*Gegenstand*) to fall apart; **~ halten** to tell apart; **~ schreiben** to write as separate words; **~ setzen** (*erklären*) to explain; **sich ~ setzen** (*sich beschäftigen*) to look (*mit* at); (*sich streiten*) to argue (*mit* with); **Auseinandersetzung** *f* (*Streit*) argument; (*Diskussion*) debate

Ausfahrt *f* (*des Zuges etc*) departure; (*Autobahn, Garage etc*) exit

aus|fallen *irr vi* (*Haare*) to fall out; (*nicht stattfinden*) to be cancelled; (*nicht funktionieren*) to break down; (*Strom*) to be cut off; (*Resultat haben*) to turn out; **groß/klein ~** (*Kleidung, Schuhe*) to be too big/too small

ausfindig machen *vt* to discover

aus|flippen *vi* (*fam*) to freak out

Ausflug *m* excursion, outing; **Ausflugsziel** *nt* destination

Ausfluss *m* (*Med*) discharge

aus|fragen *vt* to question

Ausfuhr (-, -*en*) *f* export

aus|führen *vt* (*verwirklichen*) to carry

out; (*Person*) to take out; (*Comm*) to export; (*darlegen*) to explain

ausführlich *adj* detailed ▷ *adv* in detail

aus|füllen *vt* to fill up; (*Fragebogen etc*) to fill in (*o* out)

Ausgabe *f* (*Geld*) expenditure; (*Inform*) output; (*Buch*) edition; (*Nummer*) issue

Ausgang *m* way out, exit; (*Flugsteig*) gate; (*Ende*) end; (*Ergebnis*) result; „**kein ~**" 'no exit'

aus|geben *irr vt* (*Geld*) to spend; (*austeilen*) to distribute; **jdm etw ~** (*spendieren*) to buy sb sth ▷ *vr* **sich für etw/jdn ~** to pass oneself off as sth/sb

ausgebucht *adj* fully booked

ausgefallen *adj* (*ungewöhnlich*) unusual

aus|gehen *irr vi* (*abends etc*) to go out; (*Benzin, Kaffee etc*) to run out; (*Haare*) to fall out; (*Feuer, Licht etc*) to go out; (*Resultat haben*) to turn out; **davon ~, dass** to assume that; **ihm ging das Geld aus** he ran out of money

ausgelassen *adj* exuberant

ausgeleiert *adj* worn out

ausgenommen *conj, prep +gen o dat* except

ausgerechnet *adv* **~ du** you of all people; **~ heute** today of all days

ausgeschildert *adj* signposted

ausgeschlafen *adj* **bist du ~?** have you had enough sleep?

ausgeschlossen *adj* (*unmöglich*) impossible, out of the question

ausgesprochen *adj* (*absolut*) out-and-out; (*unverkennbar*) marked ▷ *adv* extremely; **~ gut** really good

ausgezeichnet *adj* excellent

ausgiebig *adj* (*Gebrauch*) thorough; (*Essen*) substantial

aus|gießen *irr vt* (*Getränk*) to pour out; (*Gefäß*) to empty

aus|gleichen *irr vt* to even out ▷ *vi* (*Sport*) to equalize

Ausguss *m* (*Spüle*) sink; (*Abfluss*) outlet

aus|halten *irr vt* to bear, to stand; **auszuhalten sein** to be unbearable ▷ *vi* to hold out

aus|händigen *vt* **jdm etw ~** to hand sth over to sb

Aushang *m* notice

Aushilfe *f* temporary help; (*im Büro*) temp

aus|kennen *irr vr* **sich ~** to know a lot

(*bei, mit* about); (*an einem Ort*) to know one's way around

aus|kommen *irr vi* **gut/schlecht mit jdm ~** to get on well/badly with sb; **mit etw ~** to get by with sth

Auskunft (-, *Auskünfte*) *f* information; (*nähere*) details *pl*; (*Schalter*) information desk; (*Tel*) (directory) enquiries *sing* (*kein Artikel*, *Brit*), information (*US*)

aus|lachen *vt* to laugh at

aus|laden *irr vt* (*Gepäck etc*) to unload; **jdn ~** (*Gast*) to tell sb not to come

Auslage *f* window display; **~n** *pl* (*Kosten*) expenses

Ausland *nt* foreign countries *pl*; **im/ins ~** abroad; **Ausländer(in)** (-*s*, -) *m(f)* foreigner; **ausländerfeindlich** *adj* hostile to foreigners, xenophobic; **ausländisch** *adj* foreign; **Auslandsgespräch** *nt* international call; **Auslandskrankenschein** *m* health insurance certificate for foreign countries, ≈ E111 (*Brit*); **Auslandsschutzbrief** *m* international (*motor*) insurance cover (*documents pl*)

aus|lassen *irr vt* to leave out; (*Wort etc a.*) to omit; (*überspringen*) to skip; (*Wut, Ärger*) to vent (*an +dat* on) ▷ *vr* **sich über etw** (*akk*) **~** to speak one's mind about sth

aus|laufen *irr vi* (*Flüssigkeit*) to run out; (*Tank etc*) to leak; (*Schiff*) to leave port; (*Vertrag*) to expire

aus|legen *vt* (*Waren*) to display; (*Geld*) to lend; (*Text etc*) to interpret; (*technisch ausstatten*) to design (*für, auf +akk* for)

aus|leihen *irr vt* (*verleihen*) to lend; **sich** (*dat*) **etw ~** to borrow sth

aus|loggen *vi* (*Inform*) to log out (*o* off)

aus|lösen *vt* (*Explosion, Alarm*) to set off; (*hervorrufen*) to cause; **Auslöser** (-*s*, -) *m* (*Foto*) shutter release

aus|machen *vt* (*Licht, Radio*) to turn off; (*Feuer*) to put out; (*Termin, Preis*) to fix; (*vereinbaren*) to agree; (*Anteil darstellen, betragen*) to represent; (*bedeuten*) to matter; **macht es Ihnen etwas aus, wenn ...?** would you mind if ...?; **das macht mir nichts aus** I don't mind

Ausmaß *nt* extent

Ausnahme (-, -*n*) *f* exception; **ausnahmsweise** *adv* as an exception, just this once

aus|nutzen *vt* (*Zeit, Gelegenheit, Einfluss*) to use; (*jdn, Gutmütigkeit*) to take advantage of

aus|packen *vt* to unpack

aus|probieren *vt* to try (out)

Auspuff (-(*e*)*s*, -*e*) *m* (*Tech*) exhaust; **Auspuffrohr** *nt* exhaust (pipe); **Auspufftopf** *m* (*Auto*) silencer (*Brit*), muffler (*US*)

aus|rauben *vt* to rob

aus|räumen *vt* (*Dinge*) to clear away; (*Schrank, Zimmer*) to empty; (*Bedenken*) to put aside

aus|rechnen *vt* to calculate, to work out

Ausrede *f* excuse

aus|reden *vi* to finish speaking ▷ *vt* **jdm etw ~** to talk sb out of sth

ausreichend *adj* sufficient, satisfactory; (*Schulnote*) ≈ D

Ausreise *f* departure; **bei der ~** on leaving the country; **Ausreiseerlaubnis** *f* exit visa; **aus|reisen** *vi* to leave the country

aus|reißen *irr vt* to tear out ▷ *vi* to come off; (*fam: davonlaufen*) to run away

aus|renken *vt* **sich** (*dat*) **den Arm ~** to dislocate one's arm

aus|richten *vt* (*Botschaft*) to deliver; (*Gruß*) to pass on; (*erreichen*) **ich konnte bei ihr nichts ~** I couldn't get anywhere with her; **jdm etw ~** to tell sb sth

aus|rufen *irr vt* (*über Lautsprecher*) to announce; **jdn ~ lassen** to page sb; **Ausrufezeichen** *nt* exclamation mark

aus|ruhen *vi* to rest ▷ *vr* **sich ~** to rest

Ausrüstung *f* equipment

aus|rutschen *vi* to slip

aus|schalten *vt* to switch off; (*fig*) to eliminate

Ausschau *f* **~ halten** to look out (*nach* for)

aus|scheiden *irr vt* (*Med*) to give off, to secrete ▷ *vi* to leave (*aus etw* sth); (*Sport*) to be eliminated

aus|schlafen *irr vi* to have a lie-in ▷ *vr* **sich ~** to have a lie-in ▷ *vt* to sleep off

Ausschlag *m* (*Med*) rash; **den ~ geben** (*fig*) to tip the balance; **aus|schlagen** *irr vt* (*Zahn*) to knock out; (*Einladung*) to turn down ▷ *vi* (*Pferd*) to kick out; **ausschlaggebend** *adj* decisive

aus|schließen *irr vt* to lock out; (*fig*) to exclude; **ausschließlich** *adv* exclusively ▷ *prep* +*gen* excluding

Ausschnitt m (*Teil*) section; (*von Kleid*) neckline; (*aus Zeitung*) cutting

Ausschreitungen pl riots pl

aus|schütten vt (*Flüssigkeit*) to pour out; (*Gefäß*) to empty

aus|sehen irr vi to look; **krank ~** to look ill; **gut ~** (*Person*) to be good-looking; (*Sache*) to be looking good; **es sieht nach Regen aus** it looks like rain; **es sieht schlecht aus** things look bad

aus sein irr vi siehe **aus**

außen adv outside; **nach ~** outwards; **von ~** from (the) outside; **Außenbordmotor** m outboard motor; **Außenminister(in)** m(f) foreign minister, Foreign Secretary (*Brit*); **Außenseite** f outside; **Außenseiter(in)** m(f) outsider; **Außenspiegel** m wing mirror (*Brit*), side mirror (*US*)

außer prep +dat (*abgesehen von*) except (for); **nichts ~** nothing but; **~ Betrieb** out of order; **~ sich sein** to be beside oneself (*vor* with); **~ Atem** out of breath ▷ conj (*ausgenommen*) except; **~ wenn** unless; **~ dass** except; **außerdem** conj besides

äußere(r, s) adj outer, external

außergewöhnlich adj unusual ▷ adv exceptionally; **~ kalt** exceptionally cold; **außerhalb** prep +gen outside

äußerlich adj external

äußern vt to express; (*zeigen*) to show ▷ vr **sich ~** to give one's opinion; (*sich zeigen*) to show itself

außerordentlich adj extraordinary; **außerplanmäßig** adj unscheduled

äußerst adv extremely; **äußerste(r, s)** adj utmost; (*räumlich*) farthest; (*Termin*) last possible

Äußerung f remark

aus|setzen vt (*Kind, Tier*) to abandon; (*Belohnung*) to offer; **ich habe nichts daran auszusetzen** I have no objection to it ▷ vi (*aufhören*) to stop; (*Pause machen*) to drop out; (*beim Spiel*) to miss a turn

Aussicht f (*Blick*) view; (*Chance*) prospect; **aussichtslos** adj hopeless; **Aussichtsplattform** f observation platform; **Aussichtsturm** m observation tower

Aussiedler(in) (-s, -) m(f) émigré (*person of German descent from Eastern Europe*)

aus|spannen vi (*erholen*) to relax ▷ vt **er hat ihm die Freundin ausgespannt** (*fam*) he's nicked his girlfriend

aus|sperren vt to lock out ▷ vr **sich ~** to lock oneself out

Aussprache f (*von Wörtern*) pronunciation; (*Gespräch*) (frank) discussion; **aus|sprechen** irr vt to pronounce; (*äußern*) to express ▷ vr **sich ~** to talk (*über +akk* about) ▷ vi (*zu Ende sprechen*) to finish speaking

aus|spülen vt to rinse (out)

Ausstattung f (*Ausrüstung*) equipment; (*Einrichtung*) furnishings pl; (*von Auto*) fittings pl

aus|stehen irr vt to endure; **ich kann ihn nicht ~** I can't stand him ▷ vi (*noch nicht da sein*) to be outstanding

aus|steigen irr vi to get out (*aus* of); **aus dem Bus/Zug ~** to get off the bus/train; **Aussteiger(in)** m(f) dropout

aus|stellen vt to display; (*auf Messe, in Museum etc*) to exhibit; (*fam: ausschalten*) to switch off; (*Scheck etc*) to make out; (*Pass etc*) to issue; **Ausstellung** f exhibition

aus|sterben irr vi to die out

aus|strahlen vt to radiate; (*Programm*) to broadcast; **Ausstrahlung** f (*Radio, Tv*) broadcast; (*fig: von Person*) charisma

aus|strecken vr **sich ~** to stretch out ▷ vt (*Hand*) to reach out (*nach* for)

aus|suchen vt to choose

Austausch m exchange; **aus|tauschen** vt to exchange (*gegen* for)

aus|teilen vt to distribute; (*aushändigen*) to hand out

Auster (-, -n) f oyster; **Austernpilz** m oyster mushroom

aus|tragen irr vt (*Post*) to deliver; (*Wettkampf*) to hold

Australien (-s) nt Australia; **Australier(in)** (-s, -) m(f) Australian; **australisch** adj Australian

aus|trinken irr vt (*Glas*) to drain; (*Getränk*) to drink up ▷ vi to finish one's drink

aus|trocknen vi to dry out; (*Fluss*) to dry up

aus|üben vt (*Beruf, Sport*) to practise; (*Einfluss*) to exert

Ausverkauf m sale; **ausverkauft** adj (*Karten, Artikel*) sold out

Auswahl f selection, choice (*an +dat* of); **aus|wählen** vt to select, to choose

aus|wandern vi to emigrate

auswärtig adj (*nicht am/vom Ort*) not

local; (*ausländisch*) foreign; **auswärts** *adv*
(*außerhalb der Stadt*) out of town; (*Sport*)
~ spielen to play away; **Auswärtsspiel** *nt*
away match
aus|wechseln *vt* to replace; (*Sport*) to
substitute
Ausweg *m* way out
aus|weichen *irr vi* to get out of the way;
jdm/einer Sache ~ to move aside for
sb/sth; (*fig*) to avoid sb/sth
Ausweis (*-es, -e*) *m* (*Personalausweis*)
identity card, ID; (*für Bibliothek etc*) card;
aus|weisen *irr vt* to expel ▷ *vr* **sich ~** to
prove one's identity; **Ausweiskontrolle** *f*
ID check; **Ausweispapiere** *pl*
identification documents *pl*
auswendig *adv* by heart
aus|wuchten *vt* (*Auto: Räder*) to balance
aus|zahlen *vt* (*Summe*) to pay (out);
(*Person*) to pay off ▷ *vr* **sich ~** to be worth
it
aus|zeichnen *vt* (*ehren*) to honour;
(*Comm*) to price ▷ *vr* **sich ~** to distinguish
oneself
aus|ziehen *irr vt* (*Kleidung*) to take off ▷ *vr*
sich ~ to undress ▷ *vi* (*aus Wohnung*) to
move out
Auszubildende(r) *mf* trainee
Auto (*-s, -s*) *nt* car; **~ fahren** to drive;
Autoatlas *m* road atlas; **Autobahn** *f*
motorway (*Brit*), freeway (*US*);
Autobahnauffahrt *f* motorway access
road (*Brit*), on-ramp (*US*);
Autobahnausfahrt *f* motorway exit (*Brit*),
off-ramp (*US*); **Autobahngebühr** *f* toll;
Autobahnkreuz *nt* motorway
interchange; **Autobahnring** *m* motorway
ring (*Brit*), beltway (*US*); **Autobombe** *f* car
bomb; **Autofähre** *f* car ferry;
Autofahrer(in) *m(f)* driver, motorist;
Autofahrt *f* drive
Autogramm (*-s, -e*) *nt* autograph
Automarke *f* make of car
Automat (*-en, -en*) *m* vending machine
Automatik (*-, -en*) *f* (*Auto*) automatic
transmission; **Automatikschaltung** *f*
automatic gear change (*Brit*) (*o shift* (*US*));
Automatikwagen *m* automatic
automatisch *adj* automatic ▷ *adv*
automatically
Automechaniker(in) *m(f)* car
mechanic; **Autonummer** *f* registration
(*Brit*) (*o license* (*US*)) number; **Autoradio**

nt car radio; **Autoreifen** *m* car tyre;
Autoreisezug *m* Motorail train® (*Brit*),
auto train (*US*); **Autorennen** *nt* motor
racing; (*einzelnes Rennen*) motor race;
Autoschlüssel *m* car key; **Autotelefon**
nt car phone; **Autounfall** *m* car accident;
Autoverleih *m*, **Autovermietung** *f* car
hire (*Brit*) (*o rental* (*US*)); (*Firma*) car hire
(*Brit*) (*o rental* (*US*)) company;
Autowaschanlage *f* car wash;
Autowerkstatt *f* car repair shop, garage;
Autozubehör *nt* car accessories *pl*
Avocado (*-, -s*) *f* avocado
Axt (*-, Äxte*) *f* axe
Azubi (*-s, -s*) *m* (*-, -s*) *f akr* =
Auszubildende trainee

B *abk* = **Bundesstraße**

Baby (-s, -s) *nt* baby; **Babybett** *nt* cot (*Brit*), crib (*US*); **Babyfläschchen** *nt* baby's bottle; **Babynahrung** *f* baby food; **Babysitter(in)** *m(f)* babysitter; **Babysitz** *m* child seat; **Babywickelraum** *m* baby-changing room

Bach (-(e)s, Bäche) *m* stream

Backblech *nt* baking tray (*Brit*), cookie sheet (*US*)

Backbord *nt* port (side)

Backe (-, -n) *f* cheek

backen (backte, gebacken) *vt, vi* to bake

Backenzahn *m* molar

Bäcker(in) (-s, -) *m(f)* baker; **Bäckerei** *f* bakery; (Laden) baker's (shop)

Backofen *m* oven; **Backpulver** *nt* baking powder

Backspace-Taste *f* (Inform) backspace key

Backstein *m* brick

Backwaren *pl* bread, cakes and pastries *pl*

Bad (-(e)s, Bäder) *nt* bath; (Schwimmen) swim; (Ort) spa; **ein ~ nehmen** to have (o take) a bath; **Badeanzug** *m* swimsuit, swimming costume (*Brit*); **Badehose** *f* swimming trunks *pl*; **Badekappe** *f* swimming cap; **Bademantel** *m* bathrobe; **Bademeister(in)** *m(f)* pool attendant; **Bademütze** *f* swimming cap

baden *vi* to have a bath; (schwimmen) to swim, to bathe (*Brit*) ▷ *vt* to bath (*Brit*), to bathe (*US*)

Baden-Württemberg (-s) *nt* Baden-Württemberg

Badeort *m* spa; **Badesachen** *pl* swimming things *pl*; **Badetuch** *nt* bath towel; **Badewanne** *f* bath (tub); **Badezimmer** *nt* bathroom

Badminton *nt* badminton

baff *adj* **~ sein** (fam) to be flabbergasted (o gobsmacked)

Bagger (-s, -) *m* excavator; **Baggersee** *m* artificial lake in quarry etc, used for bathing

Bahamas *pl* **die ~** the Bahamas *pl*

Bahn (-, -en) *f* (Eisenbahn) railway (*Brit*), railroad (*US*); (Rennbahn) track; (für Läufer) lane; (Astr) orbit; **bahnbrechend** *adj* groundbreaking; **BahnCard®** (-, -s) *f* rail card (allowing 50% or 25% reduction on tickets); **Bahnfahrt** *f* railway (*Brit*) (o railroad (*US*)) journey; **Bahnhof** *m* station; **am** (o **auf dem**) **~** at the station; **Bahnlinie** *f* railway (*Brit*) (o railroad (*US*)) line; **Bahnpolizei** *f* railway (*Brit*) (o railroad (*US*)) police; **Bahnsteig** (-(e)s, -e) *m* platform; **Bahnstrecke** *f* railway (*Brit*) (o railroad (*US*)) line; **Bahnübergang** *m* level crossing (*Brit*), grade crossing (*US*)

Bakterien *pl* bacteria *pl*, germs *pl*

bald *adv* (zeitlich) soon; (beinahe) almost; **bis ~!** see you soon (o later); **baldig** *adj* quick, speedy

Balkan (-s) *m* **der ~** the Balkans *pl*

Balken (-s, -) *m* beam

Balkon (-s, -s o -e) *m* balcony

Ball (-(e)s, Bälle) *m* ball; (Tanz) dance, ball

Ballett (-s, -) *nt* ballet

Ballon (-s, -s) *m* balloon

Ballspiel *nt* ball game

Ballungsgebiet *nt* conurbation

Baltikum (-s) *nt* **das ~** the Baltic States *pl*

Bambus (-ses, -se) *m* bamboo; **Bambussprossen** *pl* bamboo shoots *pl*

banal *adj* banal; (Frage, Bemerkung) trite

Banane (-, -n) *f* banana

band *imperf von* **binden**

Band (-(e)s, Bände) *m* (Buch) volume ▷ (-(e)s, Bänder) *nt* (aus Stoff) ribbon, tape;

(*Fließband*) production line; (*Tonband*) tape; (*Anat*) ligament; **etw auf ~ aufnehmen** to tape sth ▷ (-, -s) f (*Musikgruppe*) band
Bandage (-, -n) f bandage; **bandagieren** vt to bandage
Bande (-, -n) f (*Gruppe*) gang
Bänderriss m (*Med*) torn ligament
Bandscheibe f (*Anat*) disc; **Bandwurm** m tapeworm
Bank (-, *Bänke*) f (*Sitzbank*) bench ▷ (-, -en) f (*Fin*) bank
Bankautomat m cash dispenser; **Bankkarte** f bank card; **Bankkonto** nt bank account; **Bankleitzahl** f bank sort code; **Banknote** f banknote; **Bankverbindung** f (*Kontonummer etc*) banking (o account) details pl
bar adj **~es Geld** cash; **etw (in) ~ bezahlen** to pay sth (in) cash
Bar (-, -s) f bar
Bär (-en, -en) m bear
barfuß adj barefoot
barg imperf von **bergen**
Bargeld nt cash; **bargeldlos** adj non-cash
Barkeeper (-s, -) m, **Barmann** m barman, bartender (*US*)
barock adj baroque
Barometer (-s, -) m barometer
barsch adj brusque
Barsch (-(e)s, -e) m perch
Barscheck m open (o uncrossed) cheque
Bart (-(e)s, *Bärte*) m beard; **bärtig** adj bearded
Barzahlung f cash payment
Basar (-s, -e) m bazaar
Baseballmütze f baseball cap
Basel (-s) nt Basle
Basilikum (-s) nt basil
Basis (-, *Basen*) f basis
Baskenland nt Basque region
Basketball m basketball
Bass (-es, *Bässe*) m bass
basta interj **und damit ~!** and that's that
basteln vt to make ▷ vi to make things, to do handicrafts
bat imperf von **bitten**
Batterie f battery; **batteriebetrieben** adj battery-powered
Bau (-(e)s) m (*Bauen*) building, construction; (*Aufbau*) structure; (*Baustelle*) building site ▷ m (*Baue*) (*Tier*) burrow ▷ m (*Bauten*) (*Gebäude*) building;

Bauarbeiten pl construction work sing; (*Straßenbau*) roadworks pl (*Brit*), roadwork (*US*); **Bauarbeiter(in)** m(f) construction worker
Bauch (-(e)s, *Bäuche*) m stomach; **Bauchnabel** m navel; **Bauchredner(in)** m(f) ventriloquist; **Bauchschmerzen** pl stomach-ache sing; **Bauchspeicheldrüse** f pancreas; **Bauchtanz** m belly dance; (*das Tanzen*) belly dancing; **Bauchweh** (-s) nt stomach-ache
Baudenkmal nt monument
bauen vt, vi to build; (*Tech*) to construct
Bauer (-n o -s, -n) m farmer; (*Schach*) pawn; **Bäuerin** f farmer; (*Frau des Bauern*) farmer's wife; **Bauernhof** m farm
baufällig adj dilapidated; **Baujahr** nt year of construction; **der Wagen ist ~ 2002** the car is a 2002 model, the car was made in 2002
Baum (-(e)s, *Bäume*) m tree
Baumarkt m DIY centre
Baumwolle f cotton
Bauplatz m building site; **Baustein** m (*für Haus*) stone; (*Spielzeug*) brick; (*fig*) element; **elektronischer ~** chip; **Baustelle** f building site; (*bei Straßenbau*) roadworks pl (*Brit*), roadwork (*US*); **Bauteil** nt prefabricated part; **Bauunternehmer(in)** m(f) building contractor; **Bauwerk** nt building
Bayern (-s) nt Bavaria
beabsichtigen vt to intend
beachten vt (*Aufmerksamkeit schenken*) to pay attention to; (*Vorschrift etc*) to observe; **nicht ~** to ignore; **beachtlich** adj considerable
Beachvolleyball nt beach volleyball
Beamte(r) (-n, -n) m, **Beamtin** f official; (*Staatsbeamter*) civil servant
beanspruchen vt to claim; (*Zeit, Platz*) to take up; **jdn ~** to keep sb busy
beanstanden vt to complain about
beantragen vt to apply for
beantworten vt to answer
bearbeiten vt to work; (*Material, Daten*) to process; (*Chem*) to treat; (*Fall etc*) to deal with; (*Buch etc*) to revise; (*fam: beeinflussen wollen*) to work on; **Bearbeitungsgebühr** f handling (o service) charge
beatmen vt **jdn ~** to give sb artificial respiration

beaufsichtigen vt to supervise; (bei Prüfung) to invigilate

beauftragen vt to instruct; **jdn mit etw ~** to give sb the job of doing sth

Becher (-s, -) m mug; (ohne Henkel) tumbler; (für Jogurt) pot; (aus Pappe) tub

Becken (-s, -) nt basin; (Spüle) sink; (zum Schwimmen) pool; (Mus) cymbal; (Anat) pelvis

bedanken vr sich **~** to say thank you; **sich bei jdm für etw ~** to thank sb for sth

Bedarf (-(e)s) m need (an +dat for); (Comm) demand (an +dat for); **je nach ~** according to demand; **bei ~** if necessary; **Bedarfshaltestelle** f request stop, flag stop (US)

bedauerlich adj regrettable; **bedauern** vt to regret; (bemitleiden) to feel sorry for; **bedauernswert** adj (Zustände) regrettable; (Mensch) unfortunate

bedeckt adj covered; (Himmel) overcast

bedenken irr vt to consider; **Bedenken** (-s, -) nt (Überlegen) consideration; (Zweifel) doubt; (Skrupel) scruples pl; **bedenklich** adj dubious; (Zustand) serious

bedeuten vt to mean; **jdm nichts/viel ~** to mean nothing/a lot to sb; **bedeutend** adj important; (beträchtlich) considerable; **Bedeutung** f meaning; (Wichtigkeit) importance

bedienen vt to serve; (Maschine) to operate ▷ vr sich **~** (beim Essen) to help oneself; **Bedienung** f service; (Kellner/Kellnerin) waiter/waitress; (Verkäufer(in)) shop assistant; (Zuschlag) service (charge); **Bedienungsanleitung** f operating instructions pl; **Bedienungshandbuch** nt instruction manual; **Bedingung** f condition; **unter der ~, dass** on condition that; **unter diesen ~en** under these circumstances

bedrohen vt to threaten

Bedürfnis nt need

beeilen vr sich **~** to hurry

beeindrucken vt to impress

beeinflussen vt to influence

beeinträchtigen vt to affect

beenden vt to end; (fertigstellen) to finish

beerdigen vt to bury; **Beerdigung** f burial; (Feier) funeral

Beere (-, -n) f berry; (Traubenbeere) grape

Beet (-(e)s, -e) nt bed

befahl imperf von **befehlen**

befahrbar adj passable; (Naut) navigable; **befahren** irr vt (Straße) to use; (Pass) to drive over; (Fluss etc) to navigate ▷ adj **stark/wenig ~** busy/quiet

Befehl (-(e)s, -e) m order; (Inform) command; **befehlen** (befahl, befohlen) vt to order; **jdm ~, etw zu tun** to order sb to do sth ▷ vi to give orders

befestigen vt to fix; (mit Schnur, Seil) to attach; (mit Klebestoff) to stick

befeuchten vt to moisten

befinden irr vr sich **~** to be

befohlen pp von **befehlen**

befolgen vt (Rat etc) to follow

befördern vt (transportieren) to transport; (beruflich) to promote; **Beförderung** f transport; (beruflich) promotion; **Beförderungsbedingungen** pl conditions pl of carriage

Befragung f questioning; (Umfrage) opinion poll

befreundet adj friendly; **~ sein** to be friends (mit jdm with sb)

befriedigen vt to satisfy; **befriedigend** adj satisfactory; (Schulnote) ≈ C; **Befriedigung** f satisfaction

befristet adj limited (auf +akk to)

befruchten vt to fertilize; (fig) to stimulate

Befund (-(e)s, -e) m findings pl; (Med) diagnosis

befürchten vt to fear

befürworten vt to support

begabt adj gifted, talented; **Begabung** f talent, gift

begann imperf von **beginnen**

begegnen vi to meet (jdm sb), to meet with (einer Sache dat sth)

begehen irr vt (Straftat) to commit; (Jubiläum etc) to celebrate

begehrt adj sought-after; (Junggeselle) eligible

begeistern vt to fill with enthusiasm; (inspirieren) to inspire ▷ vr sich für etw **~** to be/get enthusiastic about sth; **begeistert** adj enthusiastic

Beginn (-(e)s) m beginning; **zu ~** at the beginning; **beginnen** (begann, begonnen) vt, vi to start, to begin

beglaubigen vt to certify; **Beglaubigung** f certification

begleiten vt to accompany;

Begleiter(in) *m(f)* companion; **Begleitung** *f* company; (*Mus*) accompaniment

beglückwünschen *vt* to congratulate (*zu* on)

begonnen *pp von* **beginnen**

begraben *irr vt* to bury; **Begräbnis** *nt* burial; (*Feier*) funeral

begreifen *irr vt* to understand

Begrenzung *f* boundary; (*fig*) restriction

Begriff (-(e)s, -e) *m* concept; (*Vorstellung*) idea; **im ~ sein, etw zu tun** to be on the point of doing sth; **schwer von ~ sein** to be slow on the uptake

begründen *vt* (*rechtfertigen*) to justify; **Begründung** *f* explanation; (*Rechtfertigung*) justification

begrüßen *vt* to greet; (*willkommen heißen*) to welcome; **Begrüßung** *f* greeting; (*Empfang*) welcome

behaart *adj* hairy

behalten *irr vt* to keep; (*im Gedächtnis*) to remember; **etw für sich ~** to keep sth to oneself

Behälter (-s, -) *m* container

behandeln *vt* to treat; **Behandlung** *f* treatment

behaupten *vt* to claim, to maintain ▷ *vr* **sich ~** to assert oneself; **Behauptung** *f* claim

beheizen *vt* to heat

behelfen *irr vr* **sich mit/ohne etw ~** to make do with/without sth

beherbergen *vt* to accommodate

beherrschen *vt* (*Situation, Gefühle*) to control; (*Instrument*) to master ▷ *vr* **sich ~** to control oneself; **Beherrschung** *f* control; (*über +akk* of); **die ~ verlieren** to lose one's self-control

behilflich *adj* helpful; **jdm ~ sein** to help sb (*bei* with)

behindern *vt* to hinder; (*Verkehr, Sicht*) to obstruct; **Behinderte(r)** *mf* disabled person; **behindertengerecht** *adj* suitable for disabled people

Behörde (-, -n) *f* authority; **die ~n** *pl* the authorities *pl*

🔘 SCHLÜSSELWORT

bei *präp* +*dat* **1** (*nahe bei*) near; (*zum Aufenthalt*) at, with; (*unter, zwischen*) among; **bei München** near Munich; **bei uns** at our place; **beim Friseur** at the hairdresser's; **bei seinen Eltern wohnen** to live with one's parents; **bei einer Firma arbeiten** to work for a firm; **etw bei sich haben** to have sth on one; **jdn bei sich haben** to have sb with one; **bei Goethe** in Goethe; **beim Militär** in the army

2 (*zeitlich*) at, on; (*während*) during (*Zustand, Umstand*) in; **bei Nacht** at night; **bei Nebel** in fog; **bei Regen** if it rains; **bei solcher Hitze** in such heat; **bei meiner Ankuft** on my arrival; **bei der Arbeit** when I'm *etc* working; **beim Fahren** while driving

bei|behalten *irr vt* to keep

Beiboot *nt* dinghy

bei|bringen *irr vt* **jdm etw ~** (*mitteilen*) to break sth to sb; (*lehren*) to teach sb sth

beide(s) *pron* both; **meine ~n Brüder** my two brothers, both my brothers; **wir ~** both (*o* the two) of us; **keiner von ~n** neither of them; **alle ~** both (of them); **~s ist sehr schön** both are very nice; **30 ~** (*beim Tennis*) 30 all

beieinander *adv* together

Beifahrer(in) *m(f)* passenger; **Beifahrerairbag** *m* passenger airbag; **Beifahrersitz** *m* passenger seat

Beifall (-(e)s) *m* applause

beige *adj inv* beige

Beigeschmack *m* aftertaste

Beil (-(e)s, -e) *nt* axe

Beilage *f* (*Gastr*) side dish; (*Gemüse*) vegetables *pl*; (*zu Buch etc*) supplement

beiläufig *adj* casual ▷ *adv* casually

Beileid *nt* condolences *pl*; (*mein*) **herzliches ~** please accept my sincere condolences

beiliegend *adj* enclosed

beim *kontr von* **bei dem**

Bein (-(e)s, -e) *nt* leg

beinah(e) *adv* almost, nearly

beinhalten *vt* to contain

Beipackzettel *m* instruction leaflet

beisammen *adv* together; **Beisammensein** (-s) *nt* get-together

Beischlaf *m* sexual intercourse

beiseite *adv* aside; **etw ~ legen** (*sparen*) to put sth by

Beispiel (-(e)s, -e) *nt* example; **sich** (*dat*) **an jdm/etw ein ~ nehmen** to take sb/sth as an example; **zum ~** for example

beißen (biss, gebissen) vt to bite ▷ vi to bite; (stechen: Rauch, Säure) to sting ▷ vr **sich ~** (Farben) to clash

Beitrag (-(e)s, Beiträge) m contribution; (für Mitgliedschaft) subscription; (Versicherung) premium; **bei|tragen** irr vt, vi to contribute (zu to)

bekannt adj well-known; (nicht fremd) familiar; **mit jdm ~ sein** to know sb; **~ geben** to announce; **jdn mit jdm ~ machen** to introduce sb to sb; **Bekannte(r)** mf friend; (entfernter) acquaintance; **bekanntlich** adv as everyone knows; **Bekanntschaft** f acquaintance

bekiffen vr **sich ~** (fam) to get stoned

beklagen vr **sich ~** to complain

Bekleidung f clothing

bekommen irr vt to get; (erhalten) to receive; (Kind) to have; (Zug, Grippe) to catch, to get; **wie viel ~ Sie dafür?** how much is that? ▷ vi **jdm ~** (Essen) to agree with sb; **wir ~ schon** (bedient werden) we're being served

beladen irr vt to load

Belag (-(e)s, Beläge) m coating; (auf Zähnen) plaque; (auf Zunge) fur

belasten vt to load; (Körper) to strain; (Umwelt) to pollute; (fig: mit Sorgen etc) to burden; (Comm: Konto) to debit; (Jur) to incriminate

belästigen vt to bother; (stärker) to pester; (sexuell) to harass; **Belästigung** f annoyance; **sexuelle ~** sexual harassment

belebt adj (Straße etc) busy

Beleg (-(e)s, -e) m (Comm) receipt; (Beweis) proof; **belegen** vt (Brot) to spread; (Platz) to reserve; (Kurs, Vorlesung) to register for; (beweisen) to prove

belegt adj (Tel) engaged (Brit), busy (US); (Hotel) full; (Zunge) coated; **~es Brötchen** sandwich; **der Platz ist ~** this seat is taken; **Belegtzeichen** nt (Tel) engaged tone (Brit), busy tone (US)

beleidigen vt to insult; (kränken) to offend; **Beleidigung** f insult; (Jur) slander; (schriftliche) libel

beleuchten vt to light; (bestrahlen) to illuminate; (fig) to examine; **Beleuchtung** f lighting; (Bestrahlung) illumination

Belgien (-s) nt Belgium; **Belgier(in)** (-s, -) m(f) Belgian; **belgisch** adj Belgian

belichten vt to expose; **Belichtung** f exposure; **Belichtungsmesser** (-s, -) m light meter

Belieben nt **(ganz) nach ~** (just) as you wish

beliebig adj **jedes ~e Muster** any pattern; **jeder ~e** anyone ▷ adv **~ lange** as long as you like; **~ viel** as many (o much) as you like

beliebt adj popular; **sich bei jdm ~ machen** to make oneself popular with sb

beliefern vt to supply

bellen vi to bark

Belohnung f reward

Belüftung f ventilation

belügen irr vt to lie to

bemerkbar adj noticeable; **sich ~ machen** (Mensch) to attract attention; (Zustand) to become noticeable; **bemerken** vt (wahrnehmen) to notice; (sagen) to remark; **bemerkenswert** adj remarkable; **Bemerkung** f remark

bemitleiden vt to pity

bemühen vr **sich ~** to try (hard), to make an effort; **Bemühung** f effort

bemuttern vt to mother

benachbart adj neighbouring

benachrichtigen vt to inform; **Benachrichtigung** f notification

benachteiligen vt to (put at a) disadvantage; (wegen Rasse etc) to discriminate against

benehmen irr vr **sich ~** to behave; **Benehmen** (-s) nt behaviour

beneiden vt to envy; **jdn um etw ~** to envy sb sth

Beneluxländer pl Benelux countries pl

benommen adj dazed

benötigen vt to need

benutzen vt to use; **Benutzer(in)** (-s, -) m(f) user; **benutzerfreundlich** adj user-friendly; **Benutzerhandbuch** nt user's guide; **Benutzerkennung** f user ID; **Benutzeroberfläche** f (Inform) user/system interface

Benzin (-s, -e) nt (Auto) petrol (Brit), gas (US); **Benzingutschein** m petrol (Brit) (o gas (US)) coupon; **Benzinkanister** m petrol (Brit) (o gas (US)) can; **Benzinpumpe** f petrol (Brit) (o gas (US)) pump; **Benzintank** m petrol (Brit) (o gas (US)) tank; **Benzinuhr** f fuel gauge

beobachten vt to observe;
Beobachtung f observation

bequem adj comfortable; (Ausrede)
convenient; (faul) lazy; **machen Sie es
sich ~** make yourself at home;
Bequemlichkeit f comfort; (Faulheit)
laziness

beraten irr vt to advise; (besprechen) to
discuss ▷ vr **sich ~** to consult; **Beratung** f
advice; (bei Arzt etc) consultation

berauben vt to rob

berechnen vt to calculate; (Comm) to
charge; **berechnend** adj (Mensch)
calculating

berechtigen vt to entitle (zu to); (fig) to
justify; **berechtigt** adj justified; **zu etw
~ sein** to be entitled to sth

bereden vt (besprechen) to discuss

Bereich (-(e)s, -e) m area; (Ressort, Gebiet)
field

bereisen vt to travel through

bereit adj ready; **zu etw ~ sein** to be
ready for sth; **sich ~ erklären, etw zu tun**
to agree to do sth

bereiten vt to prepare; (Kummer) to
cause; (Freude) to give

bereit|legen vt to lay out

bereit|machen vr **sich ~** to get ready

bereits adv already

Bereitschaft f readiness; **~ haben** (Arzt)
to be on call

bereit|stehen vi to be ready

bereuen vt to regret

Berg (-(e)s, -e) m mountain; (kleiner) hill; **in
die ~e fahren** to go to the mountains;
bergab adv downhill; **bergauf** adv uphill;
Bergbahn f mountain railway (Brit) (o
railroad (US))

bergen (barg, geborgen) vt (retten) to
rescue; (enthalten) to contain

Bergführer(in) m(f) mountain guide;
Berghütte f mountain hut; **bergig** adj
mountainous; **Bergkette** f mountain
range; **Bergschuh** m climbing boot;
Bergsteigen (-s) nt mountaineering;
Bergsteiger(in) (-s, -) m(f) mountaineer;
Bergtour f mountain hike

Bergung f (Rettung) rescue; (von Toten,
Fahrzeugen) recovery

Bergwacht (-, -en) f mountain rescue
service; **Bergwerk** nt mine

Bericht (-(e)s, -e) m report; **berichten** vt,
vi to report

berichtigen vt to correct

Bermudadreieck nt Bermuda triangle;
Bermudainseln pl Bermuda sing;
Bermudashorts pl Bermuda shorts pl

Bernstein m amber

berüchtigt adj notorious, infamous

berücksichtigen vt to take into
account; (Antrag, Bewerber) to consider

Beruf (-(e)s, -e) m occupation;
(akademischer) profession; (Gewerbe)
trade; **was sind Sie von ~?** what do you
do (for a living)?; **beruflich** adj
professional

Berufsausbildung f vocational training;
Berufsschule f vocational college;
berufstätig adj employed;
Berufsverkehr m commuter traffic

beruhigen vt to calm ▷ vr **sich ~** (Mensch,
Situation) to calm down; **beruhigend** adj
reassuring; **Beruhigungsmittel** nt
sedative

berühmt adj famous

berühren vt to touch; (gefühlsmäßig
bewegen) to move; (betreffen) to affect;
(flüchtig erwähnen) to mention, to touch on
▷ vr **sich ~** to touch

besaufen irr vr **sich ~** (fam) to get
plastered

beschädigen vt to damage

beschäftigen vt to occupy; (beruflich) to
employ ▷ vr **sich mit etw ~** to occupy
oneself with sth; (sich befassen) to deal
with sth; **beschäftigt** adj busy, occupied;
Beschäftigung f (Beruf) employment;
(Tätigkeit) occupation; (geistige)
preoccupation (mit with)

Bescheid (-(e)s, -e) m information;
~ wissen to be informed (o know) (über
+akk about); **ich weiß ~** I know; **jdm
~ geben** (o sagen) to let sb know

bescheiden adj modest

bescheinigen vt to certify; (bestätigen) to
acknowledge; **Bescheinigung** f
certificate; (Quittung) receipt

bescheißen irr vt (vulg) to cheat (um out
of)

beschimpfen vt (mit Kraftausdrücken) to
swear at

Beschiss (-es) m **das ist ~** (vulg) that's
a rip-off; **beschissen** adj (vulg)
shitty

beschlagnahmen vt to confiscate

Beschleunigung f acceleration;

Beschleunigungsspur f acceleration lane

beschließen irr vt to decide on; (beenden) to end; **Beschluss** m decision

beschränken vt to limit, to restrict (auf +akk to) ▷ vr **sich ~** to restrict oneself (auf +akk to); **Beschränkung** f limitation, restriction

beschreiben irr vt to describe; (Papier) to write on; **Beschreibung** f description

beschuldigen vt to accuse (gen of); **Beschuldigung** f accusation

beschummeln vt, vi (fam) to cheat (um out of)

beschützen vt to protect (vor +dat from)

Beschwerde (-, -n) f complaint; **~n** pl (Leiden) trouble sing; **beschweren** vt to weight down; (fig) to burden ▷ vr **sich ~** to complain

beschwipst adj tipsy

beseitigen vt to remove; (Problem) to get rid of; (Müll) to dispose of; **Beseitigung** f removal; (von Müll) disposal

Besen (-s, -) m broom

besetzen vt (Haus, Land) to occupy; (Platz) to take; (Posten) to fill; (Rolle) to cast; **besetzt** adj full; (Tel) engaged (Brit), busy (US); (Platz) taken; (WC) engaged; **Besetztzeichen** nt engaged tone (Brit), busy tone (US)

besichtigen vt (Museum) to visit; (Sehenswürdigkeit) to have a look at; (Stadt) to tour

besiegen vt to defeat

Besitz (-es) m possession; (Eigentum) property; **besitzen** irr vt to own; (Eigenschaft) to have; **Besitzer(in)** (-s, -) m(f) owner

besoffen adj (fam) plastered

besondere(r, s) adj special; (bestimmt) particular; (eigentümlich) peculiar; **nichts ~s** nothing special; **Besonderheit** f special feature; (besondere Eigenschaft) peculiarity; **besonders** adv especially, particularly; (getrennt) separately

besorgen vt (beschaffen) to get (jdm for sb); (kaufen a.) to purchase; (erledigen: Geschäfte) to deal with

besprechen irr vt to discuss; **Besprechung** f discussion; (Konferenz) meeting

besser adj better; **es geht ihm ~** he feels better; **~ gesagt** or rather; **~ werden** to improve; **bessern** vt to improve ▷ vr **sich ~** to improve; (Mensch) to mend one's ways; **Besserung** f improvement; **gute ~!** get well soon

beständig adj constant; (Wetter) settled

Bestandteil m component

bestätigen vt to confirm; (Empfang, Brief) to acknowledge; **Bestätigung** f confirmation; (von Brief) acknowledgement

beste(r, s) adj best; **das ~ wäre, wir ...** it would be best if we ... ▷ adv **sie singt am ~n** she sings best; **so ist es am ~n** it's best that way; **am ~n gehst du gleich** you'd better go at once

bestechen irr vt to bribe; **Bestechung** f bribery

Besteck (-(e)s, -e) nt cutlery

bestehen irr vi to be, to exist; (andauern) to last; **~ auf** (+dat) to insist on; **~ aus** to consist of ▷ vt (Probe, Prüfung) to pass; (Kampf) to win

bestehlen irr vt to rob

bestellen vt to order; (reservieren) to book; (Grüße, Auftrag) to pass on (jdm sb); (kommen lassen) to send for; **Bestellnummer** f order number; **Bestellung** f (Comm) order; (das Bestellen) ordering

bestens adv very well

bestimmen vt to determine; (Regeln) to lay down; (Tag, Ort) to fix; (ernennen) to appoint; (vorsehen) to mean (für for); **bestimmt** adj definite; (gewiss) certain; (entschlossen) firm ▷ adv definitely; (wissen) for sure; **Bestimmung** f (Verordnung) regulation; (Zweck) purpose

Best.-Nr. abk = **Bestellnummer** order number

bestrafen vt to punish

bestrahlen vt to illuminate; (Med) to treat with radiotherapy

bestreiten irr vt (leugnen) to deny

Bestseller (-s, -) m bestseller

bestürzt adj dismayed

Besuch (-(e)s, -e) m visit; (Mensch) visitor; **~ haben** to have visitors/a visitor; **besuchen** vt to visit; (Schule, Kino etc) to go to; **Besucher(in)** (-s, -) m(f) visitor; **Besuchszeit** f visiting hours pl

betäuben vt (Med) to anaesthetize; **Betäubungsmittel** nt anaesthetic

Bete (-, -n) f **Rote ~** beetroot

beteiligen vr **sich an etw** (dat) **~** to take part in sth, to participate in sth ▷ vt **jdn an etw** (dat) **~** to involve sb in sth; **Beteiligung** f participation; (Anteil) share; (Besucherzahl) attendance

beten vi to pray

Beton (-s, -s) m concrete

betonen vt to stress; (hervorheben) to emphasize; **Betonung** f stress; (fig) emphasis

Betr. abk = **Betreff** re

Betracht m **in ~ ziehen** to take into consideration; **in ~ kommen** to be a possibility; **nicht in ~ kommen** to be out of the question; **betrachten** vt to look at; **~ als** to regard as; **beträchtlich** adj considerable

Betrag (-(e)s, Beträge) m amount, sum; **betragen** irr vt to amount to (o come) to ▷ vr **sich ~** to behave

betreffen irr vt to concern; (Regelung etc) to affect; **was mich betrifft** as for me; **betreffend** adj relevant, in question

betreten irr vt to enter; (Bühne etc) to step onto; **„Betreten verboten"** 'keep off/out'

betreuen vt to look after; (Reisegruppe, Abteilung) to be in charge of; **Betreuer(in)** (-s, -) m(f) (Pfleger) carer; (von Kind) child minder; (von Reisegruppe) groupleader

Betrieb (-(e)s, -e) m (Firma) firm; (Anlage) plant; (Tätigkeit) operation; (Treiben) bustle; **außer ~ sein** to be out of order; **in ~ sein** to be in operation; **betriebsbereit** adj operational; **Betriebsrat** m (Gremium) works council; **Betriebssystem** nt (Inform) operating system

betrinken irr vr **sich ~** to get drunk

betroffen adj (bestürzt) shaken; **von etw ~ werden/sein** to be affected by sth

betrog imperf von **betrügen**; **betrogen** pp von **betrügen**

Betrug (-(e)s) m deception; (Jur) fraud; **betrügen** (betrog, betrogen) vt to deceive; (Jur) to defraud; (Partner) to cheat on; **Betrüger(in)** (-s, -) m(f) cheat

betrunken adj drunk

Bett (-(e)s, -en) nt bed; **ins** (o zu) **~ gehen** to go to bed; **das ~ machen** to make the bed; **Bettbezug** m duvet cover; **Bettdecke** f blanket

betteln vi to beg

Bettlaken nt sheet

Bettler(in) (-s, -) m(f) beggar

Bettsofa nt sofa bed; **Betttuch** nt sheet; **Bettwäsche** f bed linen; **Bettzeug** m bedding

beugen vt to bend ▷ vr **sich ~** to bend; (sich fügen) to submit (dat to)

Beule (-, -n) f (Schwellung) bump; (Delle) dent

beunruhigen vt to worry ▷ vr **sich ~** to worry

beurteilen vt to judge

Beute (-) f (von Dieb) booty, loot; (von Tier) prey

Beutel (-s, -) m bag

Bevölkerung f population

bevollmächtigt adj authorized (zu etw to do sth)

bevor conj before; **bevor|stehen** irr vi (Schwierigkeiten) to lie ahead; (Gefahr) to be imminent; **jdm ~** (Überraschung etc) to be in store for sb; **bevorstehend** adj forthcoming; **bevorzugen** vt to prefer

bewachen vt to guard; **bewacht** adj **~er Parkplatz** supervised car park (Brit), guarded parking lot (US)

bewegen vt to move; **jdn dazu ~, etw zu tun** to get sb to do sth ▷ vr **sich ~** to move; **es bewegt sich etwas** (fig) things are beginning to happen; **Bewegung** f movement; (Phys) motion; (innere) emotion; (körperlich) exercise; **Bewegungsmelder** (-s, -) m sensor (which reacts to movement)

Beweis (-es, -e) m proof; (Zeugnis) evidence; **beweisen** irr vt to prove; (zeigen) to show

bewerben irr vr **sich ~** to apply (um for); **Bewerbung** f application; **Bewerbungsunterlagen** pl application documents pl

bewilligen vt to allow; (Geld) to grant

bewirken vt to cause, to bring about

bewohnen vt to live in; **Bewohner(in)** (-s, -) m(f) inhabitant; (von Haus) resident

bewölkt adj cloudy, overcast; **Bewölkung** f clouds pl

bewundern vt to admire; **bewundernswert** adj admirable

bewusst adj conscious; (absichtlich) deliberate; **sich** (dat) **einer Sache** (gen) **~ sein** to be aware of sth ▷ adv consciously; (absichtlich) deliberately; **bewusstlos** adj unconscious; **Bewusstlosigkeit** f unconsciousness;

Bewusstsein (-s) nt consciousness; **bei ~** conscious

bezahlen vt to pay; (Ware, Leistung) to pay for; **kann ich bar/mit Kreditkarte ~?** can I pay cash/by credit card?; **sich bezahlt machen** to be worth it; **Bezahlung** f payment

bezeichnen vt (kennzeichnen) to mark; (nennen) to call; (beschreiben) to describe; **Bezeichnung** f (Name) name; (Begriff) term

beziehen irr vt (Bett) to change; (Haus, Position) to move into; (erhalten) to receive; (Zeitung) to take; **einen Standpunkt ~** (fig) to take up a position ▷ vr **sich ~** to refer (auf +akk to); **Beziehung** f (Verbindung) connection; (Verhältnis) relationship; **~en haben** (vorteilhaft) to have connections (o contacts); **in dieser ~** in this respect; **beziehungsweise** adv or; (genauer gesagt) or rather

Bezirk (-(e)s, -e) m district

Bezug (-(e)s, Bezüge) m (Überzug) cover; (von Kopfkissen) pillowcase; **in ~ auf** (+akk) with regard to; **bezüglich** prep +gen concerning

bezweifeln vt to doubt

BH (-s, -s) m bra

Bhf. abk = **Bahnhof** station

Biathlon (-s, -s) nt biathlon

Bibel (-, -n) f Bible

Biber (-s, -) m beaver

Bibliothek (-, -en) f library

biegen (bog, gebogen) vt to bend ▷ vr **sich ~** to bend ▷ vi to turn (in +akk into); **Biegung** f bend

Biene (-, -n) f bee

Bier (-(e)s, -e) nt beer; **helles ~** ≈ lager (Brit), beer (US); **dunkles ~** ≈ brown ale (Brit), dark beer (US); **zwei ~, bitte!** two beers, please; **Biergarten** m beer garden; **Bierzelt** nt beer tent

bieten (bot, geboten) vt to offer; (bei Versteigerung) bid; **sich** (dat) **etw ~ lassen** to put up with sth ▷ vr **sich ~** (Gelegenheit) to present itself (dat to)

Bikini (-s, -s) m bikini

Bild (-(e)s, -er) nt picture; (gedankliches) image; (Foto) photo

bilden vt to form; (geistig) to educate; (ausmachen) to constitute ▷ vr **sich ~** (entstehen) to form; (lernen) to educate oneself

Bilderbuch nt picture book

Bildhauer(in) (-s, -) m(f) sculptor

Bildschirm m screen; **Bildschirmschoner** (-s, -) m screen saver; **Bildschirmtext** m viewdata, videotext

Bildung f formation; (Wissen, Benehmen) education; **Bildungsurlaub** m educational holiday; (von Firma) study leave

Billard nt billiards sing

billig adj cheap; (gerecht) fair

Binde (-, -n) f bandage; (Armbinde) band; (Damenbinde) sanitary towel (Brit), sanitary napkin (US)

Bindehautentzündung f conjunctivitis

binden (band, gebunden) vt to tie; (Buch) to bind; (Soße) to thicken

Bindestrich m hyphen

Bindfaden m string

Bindung f bond, tie; (Skibindung) binding

Bio- in zW bio-; **Biokost** f health food

● **Bioladen**
●
● A **Bioladen** is a shop which specializes
● in selling environmentally friendly
● products such as phosphate-free
● washing powders, recycled paper
● and organically grown vegetables.

Biologie f biology; **biologisch** adj biological; (Anbau) organic

Birke (-, -n) f birch

Birne (-, -n) f (Obst) pear; (Elek) (light) bulb

 SCHLÜSSELWORT

bis präp +akk, adv **1** (zeitlich) till, until; (bis spätestens) by; **Sie haben bis Dienstag Zeit** you have until od till Tuesday; **bis Dienstag muss es fertig sein** it must be ready by Tuesday; **bis auf weiteres** until further notice; **bis in die Nacht** into the night; **bis bald/gleich** see you later/ soon

2 (räumlich) (up) to; **ich fahre bis Köln** I'm going od I'm going as far as Cologne; **bis an unser Grundstück** (right od up) to our plot; **bis hierher** this far

3 (bei Zahlen) up to; **bis zu** up to

4 : **bis auf etw** akk (außer) except sth (einschließlich) including sth

▷ *konj* **1** (*mit Zahlen*) to; **10 bis 20** 10 to 20

2 (*zeitlich*) till, until; **bis es dunkel wird** till *od* until it gets dark; **von ... bis ...** from ... to ...

Bischof (*-s, Bischöfe*) *m* bishop
bisher *adv* up to now, so far
Biskuit (*-(e)s, -s o -e*) *nt* sponge
biss *imperf von* **beißen**
Biss (*-es, -e*) *m* bite
bisschen *adj* **ein ~** a bit of; **ein ~ Salz/Liebe** a bit of salt/love; **ich habe kein ~ Hunger** I'm not a bit hungry ▷ *adv* **ein ~** a bit; **kein ~** not at all
bissig *adj* (*Hund*) vicious; (*Bemerkung*) cutting
Bit (*-s, -s*) *nt* (*Inform*) bit
bitte *interj* please; (*wie*) **~?** (I beg your) pardon?; **~** (**schön**)! (*als Antwort auf Dank*) you're welcome; that's allright; **hier, ~** here you are; **Bitte** (*-, -n*) *f* request; **bitten** (*bat, gebeten*) *vt, vi* to ask (*um for*)
bitter *adj* bitter
Blähungen *pl* (*Med*) wind *sing*
blamieren *vr* **sich ~** to make a fool of oneself ▷ *vt* **jdn ~** to make sb look a fool
Blankoscheck *m* blank cheque
Blase (*-, -n*) *f* bubble; (*Med*) blister; (*Anat*) bladder
blasen (*blies, geblasen*) *vi* to blow; **jdm einen ~** (*vulg*) to give sb a blow job
Blasenentzündung *f* cystitis
blass *adj* pale
Blatt (*-(e)s, Blätter*) *nt* leaf; (*von Papier*) sheet; **blättern** *vi* (*Inform*) to scroll; **in etw** (*dat*) **~** to leaf through sth; **Blätterteig** *m* puff pastry; **Blattsalat** *m* green salad; **Blattspinat** *m* spinach
blau *adj* blue; (*fam: betrunken*) plastered; (*Gastr*) boiled; **~es Auge** black eye; **~er Fleck** bruise; **Blaubeere** *f* bilberry, blueberry; **Blaulicht** *nt* flashing blue light; **blau|machen** *vi* to skip work; (*in Schule*) to skip school; **Blauschimmelkäse** *m* blue cheese
Blazer (*-s, -*) *m* blazer
Blech (*-(e)s, -e*) *nt* sheet metal; (*Backblech*) baking tray (*Brit*), cookie sheet (*US*); **Blechschaden** *m* (*Auto*) damage to the bodywork
Blei (*-(e)s, -e*) *nt* lead
bleiben (*blieb, geblieben*) *vi* to stay; **lass**

das ~! stop it; **das bleibt unter uns** that's (just) between ourselves; **mir bleibt keine andere Wahl** I have no other choice
bleich *adj* pale; **bleichen** *vt* to bleach
bleifrei *adj* (*Benzin*) unleaded; **bleihaltig** *adj* (*Benzin*) leaded
Bleistift *m* pencil
Blende (*-, -n*) *f* (*Foto*) aperture
Blick (*-(e)s, -e*) *m* look; (*kurz*) glance; (*Aussicht*) view; **auf den ersten ~** at first sight; **einen ~ auf etw** (*akk*) **werfen** to have a look at sth; **blicken** *vi* to look; **sich ~ lassen** to show up
blieb *imperf von* **bleiben**
blies *imperf von* **blasen**
blind *adj* blind; (*Glas etc*) dull; **Blinddarm** *m* appendix; **Blinddarmentzündung** *f* appendicitis; **Blinde(r)** *mf* blind person/man/woman; **die ~n** *pl* the blind *pl*; **Blindenhund** *m* guide dog; **Blindenschrift** *f* braille
blinken *vi* (*Stern, Lichter*) to twinkle; (*aufleuchten*) to flash; (*Auto*) to indicate; **Blinker** (*-s, -*) *m* (*Auto*) indicator (*Brit*), turn signal (*US*)
blinzeln *vi* (*mit beiden Augen*) to blink; (*mit einem Auge*) to wink
Blitz (*-es, -e*) *m* (flash of) lightning; (*Foto*) flash; **blitzen** *vi* (*Foto*) to use a/the flash; **es blitzte und donnerte** there was thunder and lightning; **Blitzlicht** *nt* flash
Block (*-(e)s, Blöcke*) *m* (*a. fig*) block; (*von Papier*) pad; **Blockflöte** *f* recorder; **Blockhaus** *nt* log cabin; **blockieren** *vt* to block ▷ *vi* to jam; (*Räder*) to lock; **Blockschrift** *f* block letters *pl*
blöd *adj* stupid; **blödeln** *vi* (*fam*) to fool around
blond *adj* blond; (*Frau*) blonde

⭕ **SCHLÜSSELWORT**

bloß *adj* **1** (*unbedeckt*) bare (*nackt*) naked; **mit der bloßen Hand** with one's bare hand; **mit bloßem Auge** with the naked eye

2 (*alleinig, nur*) mere; **der bloße Gedanke** the very thought; **bloßer Neid** sheer envy

▷ *adv* only, merely; **lass das bloß!** just don't do that!; **wie ist das bloß passiert?** how on earth did that happen?

blühen vi to bloom; (fig) to flourish

Blume (-, -n) f flower; (von Wein) bouquet; **Blumenkohl** m cauliflower; **Blumenladen** m flower shop; **Blumenstrauß** m bunch of flowers; **Blumentopf** m flowerpot; **Blumenvase** f vase

Bluse (-, -n) f blouse

Blut (-(e)s) nt blood; **Blutbild** nt blood count; **Blutdruck** m blood pressure

Blüte (-, -n) f (Pflanzenteil) flower, bloom; (Baumblüte) blossom; (fig) prime

bluten vi to bleed

Blütenstaub m pollen

Bluter (-s, -) m (Med) haemophiliac; **Bluterguss** m haematoma; (blauer Fleck) bruise; **Blutgruppe** f blood group; **blutig** adj bloody; **Blutkonserve** f unit of stored blood; **Blutprobe** f blood sample; **Blutspende** f blood donation; **Bluttransfusion** f blood transfusion; **Blutung** f bleeding; **Blutvergiftung** f blood poisoning; **Blutwurst** f black pudding (Brit), blood sausage (US)

BLZ abk = **Bankleitzahl**

Bob (-s, -s) m bob(sleigh)

Bock (-(e)s, Böcke) m (Reh) buck; (Schaf) ram; (Gestell) trestle; (Sport) vaulting horse; **ich hab keinen ~ (drauf)** (fam) I don't feel like it

Boden (-s, Böden) m ground; (Fußboden) floor; (von Meer, Fass) bottom; (Speicher) attic; **Bodennebel** m ground mist; **Bodenpersonal** nt ground staff; **Bodenschätze** pl mineral resources pl

Bodensee m **der ~** Lake Constance

Body (-s, -s) m body; **Bodybuilding** (-s) nt bodybuilding

bog imperf von **biegen**

Bogen (-s, -) m (Biegung) curve; (in der Architektur) arch; (Waffe, Instrument) bow; (Papier) sheet

Bohne (-, -n) f bean; **grüne ~n** pl green (o French (Brit)) beans pl; **weiße ~n** pl haricot beans pl; **Bohnenkaffee** m real coffee; **Bohnensprosse** f bean sprout

bohren vt to drill; **Bohrer** (-s, -) m drill

Boiler (-s, -) m water heater

Boje (-, -n) f buoy

Bolivien (-s) nt Bolivia

Bombe (-, -n) f bomb

Bon (-s, -s) m (Kassenzettel) receipt; (Gutschein) voucher, coupon

Bonbon (-s, -s) nt sweet (Brit), candy (US)

Bonus (- o -ses, -se o Boni) m bonus; (Punktvorteil) bonus points pl; (Schadenfreiheitsrabatt) no-claims bonus

Boot (-(e)s, -e) nt boat; **Bootsverleih** m boat hire (Brit) (o rental (US))

Bord (-(e)s, -e) m **an ~** (eines Schiffes) on board (a ship); **an ~ gehen** (Schiff) to go on board; (Flugzeug) to board; **von ~ gehen** to disembark; **Bordcomputer** m dashboard computer

Bordell (-s, -e) nt brothel

Bordkarte f boarding card

Bordstein m kerb (Brit), curb (US)

borgen vt to borrow; **jdm etw ~** to lend sb sth; **sich** (dat) **etw ~** to borrow sth

Börse (-, -n) f stock exchange; (Geldbörse) purse

bös adj siehe **böse**; **bösartig** adj malicious; (Med) malignant

Böschung f slope; (Uferböschung) embankment

böse adj bad; (stärker) evil; (Wunde) nasty; (zornig) angry; **bist du mir ~?** are you angry with me?

boshaft adj malicious

Bosnien (-s) nt Bosnia; **Bosnien-Herzegowina** (-s) nt Bosnia-Herzegovina

böswillig adj malicious

bot imperf von **bieten**

botanisch adj **~er Garten** botanical gardens pl

Botschaft f message; (Pol) embassy; **Botschafter(in)** m(f) ambassador

Botsuana (-s) nt Botswana

Bouillon (-, -s) f stock

Boutique (-, -n) f boutique

Bowle (-, -n) f punch

Box (-, -en) f (Behälter, Pferdebox) box; (Lautsprecher) speaker; (bei Autorennen) pit

boxen vi to box; **Boxer** (-s, -) m (Hund, Sportler) boxer; **Boxershorts** pl boxer shorts pl; **Boxkampf** m boxing match

Boykott (-s, -e) m boycott

brach imperf von **brechen**

brachte imperf von **bringen**

Brainstorming (-s) nt brainstorming

Branchenverzeichnis nt yellow pages® pl

Brand (-(e)s, Brände) m fire; **einen ~ haben** (fam) to be parched

Brandenburg (-s) nt Brandenburg

Brandsalbe f ointment for burns
Brandung f surf
Brandwunde f burn
brannte imperf von **brennen**
Brasilien (-s) nt Brazil
braten (briet, gebraten) vt to roast; (auf dem Rost) to grill; (in der Pfanne) to fry; **Braten** (-s, -) m roast; (roher) joint; **Bratensoße** f gravy; **Brathähnchen** nt roast chicken; **Bratkartoffeln** pl fried potatoes pl; **Bratpfanne** f frying pan; **Bratspieß** m spit; **Bratwurst** f fried sausage; (gegrillte) grilled sausage
Brauch (-s, Bräuche) m custom
brauchen vt (nötig haben) to need (für, zu for); (erfordern) to require; (Zeit) to take; (gebrauchen) to use; **wie lange wird er ~?** how long will it take him?; **du brauchst es nur zu sagen** you only need to say; **das braucht (seine) Zeit** it takes time; **ihr braucht es nicht zu tun** you don't have (o need) to do it; **sie hätte nicht zu kommen ~** she needn't have come
brauen vt to brew; **Brauerei** f brewery
braun adj brown; (von Sonne) tanned; **Bräune** (-, -n) f brownness; (von Sonne) tan; **Bräunungsstudio** nt tanning studio
Brause (-, -n) f (Dusche) shower; (Getränk) fizzy drink (Brit), soda (US)
Braut (-, Bräute) f bride; **Bräutigam** (-s, -e) m bridegroom
brav adj (artig) good, well-behaved
bravo interj well done
BRD (-) f abk = **Bundesrepublik Deutschland** FRG

● **BRD**
●
● The **BRD** is the official name for the
● Federal Republic of Germany. It
● comprises 16 **Länder** (see **Land**). It was
● the name given to the former West
● Germany as opposed to East
● Germany (the **DDR**). The two
● Germanies were reunited on 3rd
● October 1990.

brechen (brach, gebrochen) vt to break; (erbrechen) to bring up; **sich** (dat) **den Arm ~** to break one's arm ▷ vi to break; (erbrechen) to vomit, to be sick; **Brechreiz** m nausea

Brei (-(e)s, -e) m (Breimasse) mush, pulp; (Haferbrei) porridge; (für Kinder) pap
breit adj wide; (Schultern) broad; **zwei Meter ~** two metres wide; **Breite** (-, -n) f breadth; (bei Maßangaben) width; (Geo) latitude; **der ~ nach** widthways; **Breitengrad** m (degree of) latitude
Bremen (-s) nt Bremen
Bremsbelag m brake lining; **Bremse** (-, -n) f brake; (Zool) horsefly; **bremsen** vi to brake ▷ vt (Auto) to brake; (fig) to slow down; **Bremsflüssigkeit** f brake fluid; **Bremslicht** nt brake light; **Bremspedal** nt brake pedal; **Bremsspur** f tyre marks pl; **Bremsweg** m braking distance
brennen (brannte, gebrannt) vi to burn; (in Flammen stehen) to be on fire; **es brennt!** fire!; **mir ~ die Augen** my eyes are smarting; **das Licht ~ lassen** to leave the light on; **Brennholz** nt firewood; **Brennnessel** f stinging nettle; **Brennspiritus** m methylated spirits pl; **Brennstab** m fuel rod; **Brennstoff** m fuel
Brett (-(e)s, -er) nt board; (länger) plank; (Regal) shelf; (Spielbrett) board; **schwarzes ~** notice board, bulletin board (US); **-er** pl (ski) skis pl; **Brettspiel** nt board game
Brezel (-, -n) f pretzel
Brief (-(e)s, -e) m letter; **Briefbombe** f letter bomb; **Brieffreund(in)** m(f) penfriend, pen pal; **Briefkasten** m letterbox (Brit), mailbox (US); **elektronischer ~** electronic mailbox; **Briefmarke** f stamp; **Briefpapier** nt writing paper; **Brieftasche** f wallet; **Briefträger(in)** m(f) postman/-woman; **Briefumschlag** m envelope; **Briefwaage** f letter scales pl
briet imperf von **braten**
Brille (-, -n) f glasses pl; (Schutzbrille) goggles pl; **Brillenetui** nt glasses case
bringen (brachte, gebracht) vt (herbringen) to bring; (mitnehmen, vom Sprecher weg) to take; (holen, herbringen) to get, to fetch; (Theat, Cine) to show; (Radio, TV) to broadcast; **~ Sie mir bitte noch ein Bier** could you bring me another beer, please?; **jdn nach Hause ~** to take sb home; **jdn dazu ~, etw zu tun** to make sb do sth; **jdn auf eine Idee ~** to give sb an idea
Brise (-, -n) f breeze
Brite (-n, -n) m, **Britin** f British person,

Briton; **er ist ~** he is British; **die ~n** the British; **britisch** adj British

Brocken (-s, -) m bit; (*größer*) lump, chunk

Brokkoli m broccoli

Brombeere f blackberry

Bronchitis (-) f bronchitis

Bronze (-, -n) f bronze

Brosche (-, -n) f brooch

Brot (-(e)s, -e) nt bread; (*Laib*) loaf; **Brotaufstrich** m spread; **Brötchen** nt roll; **Brotzeit** f (*Pause*) break; (*Essen*) snack; **~ machen** to have a snack

Browser (-s, -) m (*Inform*) browser

Bruch (-(e)s, Brüche) m (*Brechen*) breaking; (*Bruchstelle; mit Partei, Tradition etc*) break; (*Med: Eingeweidebruch*) rupture, hernia; (*Knochenbruch*) fracture; (*Math*) fraction; **brüchig** adj brittle

Brücke (-, -n) f bridge

Bruder (-s, Brüder) m brother

Brühe (-, -n) f (*Suppe*) (clear) soup; (*Grundlage*) stock; (*pej: Getränk*) muck; **Brühwürfel** m stock cube

brüllen vi to roar; (*Stier*) to bellow; (*vor Schmerzen*) to scream (with pain)

brummen vi (*Bär, Mensch*) to growl; (*brummeln*) to mutter; (*Insekt*) to buzz; (*Motor, Radio*) to drone ▷ vt to growl

brünett adj brunette

Brunnen (-s, -) m fountain; (*tief*) well; (*natürlich*) spring

Brust (-, Brüste) f breast; (*beim Mann*) chest; **Brustschwimmen** (-s) nt breaststroke; **Brustwarze** f nipple

brutal adj brutal

brutto adv gross

BSE (-) nt abk = **bovine spongiforme Enzephalopathie** BSE

Bube (-n, -n) m boy, lad; (*Karten*) jack

Buch (-(e)s, Bücher) nt book

Buche (-, -n) f beech (tree)

buchen vt to book; (*Betrag*) to enter

Bücherei f library

Buchfink m chaffinch

Buchhalter(in) m(f) accountant

Buchhandlung f bookshop

Büchse (-, -n) f tin (*Brit*), can; **Büchsenfleisch** nt tinned meat (*Brit*), canned meat; **Büchsenmilch** f tinned milk (*Brit*), canned milk; **Büchsenöffner** m tin opener (*Brit*), can opener

Buchstabe (-ns, -n) m letter; **buchstabieren** vt to spell

Bucht (-, -en) f bay

Buchung f booking; (*Comm*) entry

Buckel (-s, -) m hump

bücken vr **sich ~** to bend down

Buddhismus (-) m Buddhism

Bude (-, -en) f (*auf Markt*) stall; (*fam: Wohnung*) pad, place

Büfett (-s, -s) nt sideboard; **kaltes ~** cold buffet

Büffel (-s, -) m buffalo

Bügel (-s, -) m (*Kleidung*) hanger; (*Steigbügel*) stirrup; (*Brille*) sidepiece; (*von Skilift*) T-bar; **Bügelbrett** nt ironing board; **Bügeleisen** nt iron; **Bügelfalte** f crease; **bügelfrei** adj non-iron; **bügeln** vt, vi to iron

buh interj boo

Bühne (-, -n) f stage; **Bühnenbild** nt set

Bulgare (-n, -n) m, **Bulgarin** f Bulgarian; **Bulgarien** (-s) nt Bulgaria; **bulgarisch** adj Bulgarian; **Bulgarisch** nt Bulgarian

Bulimie f bulimia

Bulle (-n, -n) m bull; (*fam: Polizist*) cop

Bummel (-s, -) m stroll; **bummeln** vi to stroll; (*trödeln*) to dawdle; (*faulenzen*) to loaf around; **Bummelzug** m slow train

bums interj bang

bumsen vi (*vulg*) to screw

Bund (-(e)s, Bünde) m (*von Hose, Rock*) waistband; (*Freundschaftsbund*) bond; (*Organisation*) association; (*Pol*) confederation; **der ~** (*fam: Bundeswehr*) the army ▷ (-(e)s, -e) nt bunch; (*von Stroh etc*) bundle

Bundes- in zW Federal; (*auf Deutschland bezogen a.*) German; **Bundesbahn** f German railway company; **Bundeskanzler(in)** m(f) Chancellor; **Bundesland** nt state, Land; **Bundesliga** f **erste/zweite ~** First/Second Division; **Bundespräsident(in)** m(f) President; **Bundesrat** m (*in Deutschland*) Upper House (of the German Parliament); (*in der Schweiz*) Council of Ministers; **Bundesregierung** f Federal Government; **Bundesrepublik** f Federal Republic; **~ Deutschland** Federal Republic of Germany; **Bundesstraße** f ≈ A road (*Brit*), ≈ state highway (*US*); **Bundestag** m Lower House (of the German Parliament); **Bundeswehr** f (German) armed forces pl

● **Bundeswehr**
●
● The **Bundeswehr** is the name for the
● German armed forces. It was
● established in 1955, first of all for
● volunteers, but since 1956 there has
● been compulsory military service for
● all able-bodied young men of 18. In
● peacetime the Defence Minister is
● the head of the 'Bundeswehr', but in
● wartime the **Bundeskanzler** takes over.
● The 'Bundeswehr' comes under the
● jurisdiction of NATO.

Bündnis nt alliance
Bungalow (-s, -s) m bungalow
Bungeejumping (-s) nt bungee jumping
bunt adj colourful; (von Programm etc)
   varied; **~e Farben** bright colours ▷ adv
   (anstreichen) in bright colours; **Buntstift** m
   crayon, coloured pencil
Burg (-, -en) f castle
Bürger(in) (-s, -) m(f) citizen; **bürgerlich**
   adj (Rechte, Ehe etc) civil; (vom Mittelstand)
   middle-class; (pej) bourgeois; **Bürger-
   meister(in)** m(f) mayor; **Bürgersteig**
   (-(e)s, -e) m pavement (Brit), sidewalk (US)
Büro (-s, -s) nt office; **Büroklammer** f
   paper clip
Bürokratie f bureaucracy
Bursche (-n, -n) m lad; (Typ) guy
Bürste (-, -n) f brush; **bürsten** vt to brush
Bus (-ses, -se) m bus; (Reisebus) coach (Brit),
   bus; **Busbahnhof** m bus station
Busch (-(e)s, Büsche) m bush; (Strauch) shrub
Busen (-s, -) m breasts pl, bosom
Busfahrer(in) m(f) bus driver;
   Bushaltestelle f bus stop
Businessclass (-) f business class
Busreise f coach tour (Brit), bus tour
Bußgeld nt fine
Büstenhalter (-s, -) m bra
Busverbindung f bus connection
Butter (-) f butter; **Butterbrot** nt slice of
   bread and butter; **Butterkäse** m type of
   mild, full-fat cheese; **Buttermilch** f butter-
   milk; **Butterschmalz** nt clarified butter
Button (-s, -s) m badge (Brit), button (US)
b. w. abk = **bitte wenden** pto
Byte (-s, -s) nt byte
bzw. adv abk = **beziehungsweise**

C

ca. adv abk = **circa** approx

Cabrio (-s, -s) nt convertible

Café (-s, -s) nt café

Cafeteria (-, -s) f cafeteria

Call-Center (-s, -) nt call centre

campen vi to camp; **Camping** (-s) nt camping; **Campingbus** m camper; **Campingplatz** m campsite, camping ground (US)

Cappuccino (-s, -) m cappuccino

Carving (-s) nt (Ski) carving; **Carvingski** m carving ski

CD (-, -s) f abk = **Compact Disc** CD; **CD-Brenner** (-s, -) m CD burner, CD writer; **CD-Player** (-s, -) m CD player; **CD-ROM** (-, -s) f abk = **Compact Disc Read Only Memory** CD-ROM; **CD-ROM-Laufwerk** nt CD-ROM drive, **CD-Spieler** m CD player

Cello (-s, -s o Celli) nt cello

Celsius nt celsius; **20 Grad ~** 20 degrees Celsius, 68 degrees Fahrenheit

Cent (-s, -s) m (von Dollar und Euro) cent

Chamäleon (-s, -s) nt chameleon

Champagner (-s, -) m champagne

Champignon (-s, -s) m mushroom

Champions League (-, -s) f Champions League

Chance (-, -n) f chance; **die ~n stehen gut** the prospects are good

Chaos (-) nt chaos; **Chaot(in)** (-en, -en) m(f) (fam) disorganized person, scatterbrain; **chaotisch** adj chaotic

Charakter (-s, -e) m character; **charakteristisch** adj characteristic (für of)

Charisma (-s, Charismen o Charismata) nt charisma

charmant adj charming

Charterflug m charter flight; **chartern** vt to charter

checken vt (überprüfen) to check; (fam: verstehen) to get

Check-in (-s, -s) m check-in; **Check-in-Schalter** m check-in desk

Chef(in) (-s, -s) m(f) boss; **Chefarzt** m, **Chefärztin** f senior consultant (Brit), medical director (US)

Chemie (-) f chemistry; **chemisch** adj chemical; **~e Reinigung** dry cleaning

Chemotherapie f chemotherapy

Chicoree (-s) m chicory

Chiffre (-, -n) f (Geheimzeichen) cipher; (in Zeitung) box number

Chile (-s) nt Chile

Chili (-s, -s) m chilli

China (-s) nt China; **Chinakohl** m Chinese leaves pl (Brit), bok choy (US); **Chinarestaurant** nt Chinese restaurant; **Chinese** (-n, -n) m Chinese; **Chinesin** (-, -nen) f Chinese (woman); **sie ist ~** she's Chinese; **chinesisch** adj Chinese; **Chinesisch** nt Chinese

Chip (-s, -s) m (Inform) chip; **Chipkarte** f smart card

Chips pl (Kartoffelchips) crisps pl (Brit), chips pl (US)

Chirurg(in) (-en, -en) m(f) surgeon

Chlor (-s) nt chlorine

Choke (-s, -s) m choke

Cholera (-) f cholera

Cholesterin (-s) nt cholesterol

Chor (-(e), Chöre) m choir; (Theat) chorus

Choreografie f choreography

Christ(in) (-en, -en) m(f) Christian; **Christbaum** m Christmas tree; **Christi Himmelfahrt** f the Ascension (of Christ); **Christkind** nt baby Jesus; (das Geschenke

bringt) = Father Christmas, Santa Claus;
christlich *adj* Christian
Chrom (*-s*) *nt* chrome; (*Chem*) chromium
chronisch *adj* chronic
chronologisch *adj* chronological ▷ *adv*
in chronological order
Chrysantheme (*-, -n*) *f* chrysanthemum
circa *adv* about, approximately
City (*-*) *f* city centre, downtown (*US*)
Clementine (*-, -n*) *f* clementine
clever *adj* clever, smart
Clique (*-, -n*) *f* group; (*pej*) clique;
David und seine ~ David and his lot *o*
crowd
Clown (*-s, -s*) *m* clown
Club (*-s, -s*) *m* club; **Cluburlaub** *m* club
holiday (*Brit*), club vacation (*US*)
Cocktail (*-s, -s*) *m* cocktail;
Cocktailtomate *f* cherry tomato
Cognac (*-s*) *m* cognac
Cola (*-, -s*) *f* Coke®, cola
Comic (*-s, -s*) *m* comic strip; (*Heft*) comic
Compact Disc (*-, -s*) *f* compact disc
Computer (*-s, -*) *m* computer;
Computerfreak *m* computer nerd;
computergesteuert *adj*
computer-controlled; **Computergrafik** *f*
computer graphics *pl*; **computerlesbar**
adj machine-readable; **Computerspiel** *nt*
computer game; **Computertomografie** *f*
computer tomography, scan;
Computervirus *m* computer virus
Container (*-s, -*) *m* (*zum Transport*)
container; (*für Bauschutt etc*) skip
Control-Taste *f* control key
Cookie (*-s, -s*) *nt* (*Inform*) cookie
cool *adj* (*fam*) cool
Cornflakes *pl* cornflakes *pl*
Couch (*-, -en*) *f* couch; **Couchtisch** *m*
coffee table
Coupé (*-s, -s*) *nt* coupé
Coupon (*-s, -s*) *m* coupon
Cousin (*-s, -s*) *m* cousin; **Cousine** *f*
cousin
Crack (*-s*) *nt* (*Droge*) crack
Creme (*-, -s*) *f* cream; (*Gastr*) mousse
Creutzfeld-Jakob-Krankheit *f*
Creutzfeld-Jakob disease, CJD
Croissant (*-s, -s*) *nt* croissant
Curry (*-s*) *m* curry powder ▷ (*-s*) *nt*
(*indisches Gericht*) curry; **Currywurst** *f* fried
sausage with ketchup and curry powder
Cursor (*-s, -*) *m* (*Inform*) cursor

Cybercafé *nt* cybercafé; **Cyberspace** (*-*)
m cyberspace

d

ich bleibe dabei I'm not changing my mind

dabei|haben *irr vt* **er hat seine Schwester dabei** he's brought his sister; **ich habe kein Geld dabei** I haven't got any money on me

Dach (-(e)s, *Dächer*) *nt* roof; **Dachboden** *m* attic, loft; **Dachgepäckträger** *m* roofrack; **Dachrinne** *f* gutter

Dachs (-es, -e) *m* badger

dachte *imperf von* **denken**

Dackel (-s, -) *m* dachshund

dadurch *adv* (*räumlich*) through it; (*durch diesen Umstand*) in that way; (*deshalb*) because of that, for that reason ▷ *conj* **~, dass** because; **~, dass er hart arbeitete** (*indem*) by working hard

dafür *adv* for it; (*anstatt*) instead; **~ habe ich 50 Euro bezahlt** I paid 50 euros for it; **ich bin ~ zu bleiben** I'm for (*o* in favour of) staying; **~ ist er ja da** that's what he's there for; **er kann nichts ~** he can't help it

dagegen *adv* against it; (*im Vergleich damit*) in comparison; (*bei Tausch*) for it; **ich habe nichts ~** I don't mind

daheim *adv* at home

daher *adv* (*räumlich*) from there; (*Ursache*) that's why ▷ *conj* (*deshalb*) that's why

dahin *adv* (*räumlich*) there; (*zeitlich*) then; (*vergangen*) gone; **bis ~** (*zeitlich*) till then; (*örtlich*) up to there; **bis ~ muss die Arbeit fertig sein** the work must be finished by then

dahinter *adv* behind it; **~ kommen** to find out

dahinterkommen *vi* to find out

Dahlie *f* dahlia

Dalmatiner (-s, -) *m* dalmatian

damals *adv* at that time, then

Dame (-, -n) *f* lady; (*Karten*) queen; (*Spiel*) draughts *sing* (Brit), checkers *sing* (US); **Damenbinde** *f* sanitary towel (Brit), sanitary napkin (US); **Damenfriseur** *m* ladies' hairdresser; **Damenkleidung** *f* ladies' wear; **Damentoilette** *f* ladies' toilet (*o* restroom (US))

damit *adv* with it; (*begründend*) by that; **was meint er ~?** what does he mean by that?; **genug ~!** that's enough ▷ *conj* so that

Damm (-(e)s, *Dämme*) *m* dyke; (*Staudamm*) dam; (*am Hafen*) mole; (*Bahn-, Straßendamm*) embankment

SCHLÜSSELWORT

da *adv* 1 (*örtlich*) there (*hier*) here; **da draußen** out there; **da sein** to be there; **da bin ich** here I am; **da, wo** where; **ist noch Milch da?** is there any milk left?
2 (*zeitlich*) then; (*folglich*) so
3: **da haben wir Glück gehabt** we were lucky there; **da kann man nichts machen** nothing can be done about it
▷ *konj* (*weil*) as since

dabei *adv* (*räumlich*) close to it; (*zeitlich*) at the same time; (*obwohl, doch*) though; **sie hörte Radio und rauchte ~** she was listening to the radio and smoking (at the same time); **~ fällt mir ein ...** that reminds me ...; **~ kam es zu einem Unfall** this led to an accident; **... und ~ hat er gar keine Ahnung ...** even though he has no idea; **ich finde nichts ~** I don't see anything wrong with it; **es bleibt ~** that's settled; **~ sein** (*anwesend*) to be present; (*beteiligt*) to be involved; **ich bin ~!** count me in; **er war gerade ~ zu gehen** he was just (*o* on the point of) leaving

dabei|bleiben *irr vi* to stick with it;

Dämmerung f twilight; (am Morgen) dawn; (am Abend) dusk

Dampf (-(e)s, Dämpfe) m steam; (Dunst) vapour; **Dampfbad** nt Turkish bath; **Dampfbügeleisen** nt steam iron; **dampfen** vi to steam

dämpfen vt (Gastr) to steam; (Geräusch) to deaden; (Begeisterung) to dampen

Dampfer (-s, -) m steamer

Dampfkochtopf m pressure cooker

danach adv after that; (zeitlich a.) afterwards; (demgemäß) accordingly; **mir ist nicht ~** I don't feel like it; **~ sieht es aus** that's what it looks like

Däne (-n, -n) m Dane

daneben adv beside it; (im Vergleich) in comparison

Dänemark (-s) nt Denmark; **Dänin** f Dane, Danish woman/girl; **dänisch** adj Danish; **Dänisch** nt Danish

dank prep +dat o gen thanks to; **Dank** (-(e)s) m thanks pl; **vielen ~!** thank you very much; **jdm ~ sagen** to thank sb; **dankbar** adj grateful; (Aufgabe) rewarding; **danke** interj thank you, thanks; **nein ~!** no, thank you; **~, gerne!** yes, please; **~, gleichfalls!** thanks, and the same to you; **danken** vi jdm für etw ~ to thank sb for sth; **nichts zu ~!** you're welcome

dann adv then; **bis ~!** see you (later); **~ eben nicht** okay, forget it, suit yourself

daran adv (räumlich) on it; (befestigen) to it; (stoßen) against it; **es liegt ~, dass ...** it's because ...

darauf adv (räumlich) on it; (zielgerichtet) towards it; (danach) afterwards; **es kommt ganz ~ an, ob ...** it all depends whether ...; **ich freue mich ~** I'm looking forward to it; **am Tag ~** the next day; **~ folgend** (Tag, Jahr) next, following

darauffolgend adj (Tag, Jahr) next, following

daraus adv from it; **was ist ~ geworden?** what became of it?

darin adv in it; **das Problem liegt ~, dass ...** the basic problem is that ...

Darlehen (-s, -) nt loan

Darm (-(e)s, Därme) m intestine; (Wurstdarm) skin; **Darmgrippe** f gastroenteritis

dar|stellen vt to represent; (Theat) to play; (beschreiben) to describe;

Darsteller(in) m(f) actor/actress; **Darstellung** f representation; (Beschreibung) description

darüber adv (räumlich) above it, over it; (fahren) over it; (mehr) more; (währenddessen) meanwhile; (sprechen, streiten, sich freuen) about it

darum adv (deshalb) that's why; **es geht ~, dass ...** the point (o thing) is that ...

darunter adv (räumlich) under it; (dazwischen) among them; (weniger) less; **was verstehen Sie ~?** what do you understand by that?; **~ fallen** to be included

darunterfallen vi to be included

das art the; **~ Auto da** that car; **er hat sich ~ Bein gebrochen** he's broken his leg; **vier Euro ~ Kilo** four euros a kilo ▷ pron that (one), this (one); (relativ, Sache) that, which; (relativ, Person) who, that; (demonstrativ) this/that one; **~ Auto da** that car; **ich nehme ~ da** I'll take that one; **~ Auto, ~ er kaufte** the car (that (o which)) he bought; **~ Mädchen, ~ nebenan wohnt** the girl who (o that) lives next door; **~ heißt** that is; **~ sind Amerikaner** they're American

da sein irr vi siehe da

dass conj that; **so ~** so that; **es sei denn, ~** unless; **ohne ~ er grüßte** without saying hello

dasselbe pron the same

Datei f (Inform) file; **Dateimanager** m file manager

Daten pl data pl; **Datenbank** f database; **Datenmissbrauch** m misuse of data; **Datenschutz** m data protection; **Datenträger** m data carrier; **Datenverarbeitung** f data processing

datieren vt to date

Dativ m dative (case)

Dattel (-, -n) f date

Datum (-s, Daten) nt date

Dauer (-, -n) f duration; (Länge) length; **auf die ~** in the long run; **für die ~ von zwei Jahren** for (a period of) two years; **Dauerauftrag** m (Fin) standing order; **dauerhaft** adj lasting; (Material) durable; **Dauerkarte** f season ticket; **dauern** vi to last; (Zeit benötigen) to take; **es hat sehr lange gedauert, bis er ...** it took him a long time to ...; **wie lange dauert es denn noch?** how much longer will it be?; **das**

dauert mir zu lange I can't wait that long; **dauernd** adj lasting; (ständig) constant ▷ adv always, constantly; **er lachte ~** he kept laughing; **unterbrich mich nicht ~** stop interrupting me; **Dauerwelle** f perm (Brit), permanent (US)

Daumen (-s, -) m thumb

Daunendecke f eiderdown

davon adv of it; (räumlich) away; (weg von) from it; (Grund) because of it; **ich hätte gerne ein Kilo ~** I'd like one kilo of that; **~ habe ich gehört** I've heard of it; (Geschehen) I've heard about it; **das kommt ~, wenn ...** that's what happens when ...; **was habe ich ~?** what's the point?; **auf und ~** up and away; **davon|laufen** irr vi to run away

davor adv (räumlich) in front of it; (zeitlich) before; **ich habe Angst ~** I'm afraid of it

dazu adv (zusätzlich) on top of that, as well; (zu diesem Zweck) for it, for that purpose; **ich möchte Reis ~** I'd like rice with it; **und ~ noch** and in addition; **~ fähig sein, etw zu tun** to be capable of doing sth; **wie kam es ~?** how did it happen?; **dazu|gehören** vi to belong to it; **dazu|kommen** irr vi (zu jdm ~) to join sb; **kommt noch etwas dazu?** anything else?

dazwischen adv in between; (Unterschied etc) between them; (in einer Gruppe) among them

dazwischen|kommen irr vi **wenn nichts dazwischenkommt** if all goes well; **mir ist etwas dazwischengekommen** something has cropped up

DDR (-) f abk = **Deutsche Demokratische Republik** (Hist) GDR

dealen vi (fam: mit Drogen) to deal in drugs; **Dealer(in)** (-s, -) m(f) (fam) dealer, pusher

Deck (-(e)s, -s o -e) nt deck; **an ~ on** deck

Decke (-, -n) f cover; (für Bett) blanket; (für Tisch) tablecloth; (von Zimmer) ceiling

Deckel (-s, -) m lid

decken vt to cover; (Tisch) to lay, to set ▷ vr **sich ~** (Interessen) to coincide; (Aussagen) to correspond ▷ vi (den Tisch decken) to lay (o set) the table

Decoder (-s, -) m decoder

defekt adj faulty; **Defekt** (-(e)s, -e) m fault, defect

definieren vt to define; **Definition** (-, -en) f definition

deftig adj (Preise) steep; **ein ~es Essen** a good solid meal

dehnbar adj flexible, elastic; **dehnen** vt to stretch ▷ vr **sich ~** to stretch

Deich (-(e)s, -e) m dyke

dein pron (adjektivisch) your; **deine(r, s)** pron (substantivisch) yours, of you; **deiner** pron gen von **du**; of you; **deinetwegen** adv (wegen dir) because of you; (dir zuliebe) for your sake; (um dich) about you

deinstallieren vt (Programm) to uninstall

Dekolleté (-s, -s) nt low neckline

Dekoration f decoration; (in Laden) window dressing; **dekorativ** adj decorative; **dekorieren** vt to decorate; (Schaufenster) to dress

Delfin (-s, -e) m dolphin

delikat adj (lecker) delicious; (heikel) delicate

Delikatesse (-, -n) f delicacy

Delle (-, -en) f (fam) dent

Delphin (-s, -e) m dolphin

dem dat sing von **der/das**; **wie ~ auch sein mag** be that as it may

demnächst adv shortly, soon

Demo (-, -s) f (fam) demo

Demokratie (-, -n) f democracy; **demokratisch** adj democratic

demolieren vt to demolish

Demonstration f demonstration; **demonstrieren** vt, vi to demonstrate

den art akk sing, dat pl von **der**; **sie hat sich ~ Arm gebrochen** she's broken her arm ▷ pron him; (Sache) that one; (relativ: Person) who, that, whom; (relativ: Sache) which, that; **~ hab ich schon ewig nicht mehr gesehen** I haven't seen him in ages ▷ pron (Person) who, that, whom; (Sache) which, that; **der Typ, auf ~ sie steht** the guy (who) she fancies; **der Berg, auf ~ wir geklettert sind** the mountain (that) we climbed

denkbar adj **das ist ~** that's possible ▷ adv **~ einfach** extremely simple; **denken** (dachte, gedacht) vt, vi to think (über +akk about); **an jdn/etw ~** to think of sb/sth; (sich erinnern, berücksichtigen) to remember sb/sth; **woran denkst Du?** what are you thinking about?; **denk an den Kaffee!** don't forget the coffee ▷ vr

sich ~ (*sich vorstellen*) to imagine; **das kann ich mir ~** I can (well) imagine

Denkmal (*-s, Denkmäler*) *nt* monument; **Denkmalschutz** *m* monument preservation; **unter ~ stehen** to be listed

denn *conj* for, because ▷ *adv* then; (*nach Komparativ*) than; **was ist ~?** what's wrong?; **ist das ~ so schwierig?** is it really that difficult?

dennoch *conj* still, nevertheless

Deo (*-s, -s*) *nt*, **Deodorant** (*-s, -s*) *nt* deodorant; **Deoroller** *m* roll-on deodorant; **Deospray** *m o nt* deodorant spray

Deponie (*-, -n*) *f* waste disposal site, tip

Depressionen *pl* **an ~ leiden** to suffer from depression *sing*; **deprimieren** *vt* to depress

SCHLÜSSELWORT

der (*f* **die**, *nt* **das**, *gen* **des, der, des**, *dat* **dem, der, dem**, *akk* **den, die, das**, *pl* **die**) *def art* the; **der Rhein** the Rhine; **der Klaus** (*umg*) Klaus; **die Frau** (*im Allgemeinen*) women; **der Tod/das Leben** death/life; **der Fuß des Berges** the foot of the hill; **gib es der Frau** give it to the woman; **er hat sich die Hand verletzt** he has hurt his hand ▷ *relativ pron* (*bei Menschen*) who, that (*bei Tieren, Sachen*) which, that; **der Mann, den ich gesehen habe** the man who *od* whom *od* that I saw ▷ *demonstrativ pron* he/she/it (*jener, dieser*) that, (*pl*) those; **der/die war es** it was him/her; **der mit der Brille** the one with glasses; **ich will den (da)** I want that one

derart *adv* so; (*solcher Art*) such; **derartig** *adj* **ein ~er Fehler** such a mistake, a mistake like that

deren *gen von* **die** ▷ *pron* (*Person*) her; (*Sache*) its; (*Plural*) their ▷ *pron* (*Person*) whose; (*Sache*) of which; **meine Freundin und ~ Mutter** my friend and her mother; **das sind ~ Sachen** that's their stuff; **die Frau, ~ Tochter ...** the woman whose daughter ...; **ich bin mir ~ bewusst** I'm aware of that

dergleichen *pron* **und ~ mehr** and the like, and so on; **nichts ~** no such thing

derjenige *pron* the one; **~, der** (*relativ*) the one who (*o that*)

dermaßen *adv* so much; (*mit Adj*) so

derselbe *pron* the same (person/thing)

deshalb *adv* therefore; **~ frage ich ja** that's why I'm asking

Design (*-s, -s*) *nt* design; **Designer(in)** (*-s, -*) *m(f)* designer

Desinfektionsmittel *nt* disinfectant; **desinfizieren** *vt* to disinfect

dessen *gen von* **der, das** ▷ *pron* (*Person*) his; (*Sache*) its; **ich bin mir ~ bewusst** I'm aware of that ▷ *pron* (*Person*) whose; (*Sache*) of which; **mein Freund und ~ Mutter** my friend and his mother; **der Mann, ~ Tochter ...** the man whose daughter ...; **ich bin mir ~ bewusst** I'm aware of that

Dessert (*-s, -s*) *nt* dessert; **zum** (*o* **als**) **~** for dessert

destilliert *adj* distilled

desto *adv* **je eher, ~ besser** the sooner, the better

deswegen *conj* therefore

Detail (*-s, -s*) *nt* detail; **ins ~ gehen** to go into detail

Detektiv(in) (*-s, -e*) *m(f)* detective

deutlich *adj* clear; (*Unterschied*) distinct

deutsch *adj* German; **Deutsch** *nt* German; **auf ~** in German; **ins ~e übersetzen** to translate into German; **Deutsche(r)** *mf* German; **Deutschland** *nt* Germany

Devise (*-, -n*) *f* motto; **~n** *pl* (*Fin*) foreign currency *sing*; **Devisenkurs** *m* exchange rate

Dezember (*-(s), -*) *m* December; *siehe auch* **Juni**

dezent *adj* discreet

d.h. *abk von* **das heißt** i.e. (*gesprochen: i.e. oder that is*)

Dia (*-s, -s*) *nt* slide

Diabetes (*-, -*) *m* (*Med*) diabetes; **Diabetiker(in)** (*-s, -*) *m(f)* diabetic

Diagnose (*-, -n*) *f* diagnosis

diagonal *adj* diagonal

Dialekt (*-(e)s, -e*) *m* dialect

Dialog (*-(e)s, -e*) *m* dialogue; (*Inform*) dialog

Dialyse (*-, -n*) *f* (*Med*) dialysis

Diamant *m* diamond

Diaprojektor *m* slide projector

Diät (*-, -en*) *f* diet; **eine ~ machen** to be on a diet; (*anfangen*) to go on a diet

dich *pron akk von* **du** you; **~ (selbst)**

(*reflexiv*) yourself; **pass auf ~ auf** look after yourself; **reg ~ nicht auf** don't get upset

dicht *adj* dense; (*Nebel*) thick; (*Gewebe*) close; (*wasserdicht*) watertight; (*Verkehr*) heavy ▷ *adv* **~ an/bei** close to; **~ bevölkert** densely populated

Dichter(in) (*-s, -*) *m(f)* poet; (*Autor*) writer

Dichtung *f* (*Auto*) gasket; (*Dichtungsring*) washer; (*Gedichte*) poetry

Dichtungsring *m* (*Tech*) washer

dick *adj* thick; (*Person*) fat; **jdn ~ haben** to be sick of sb; **Dickdarm** *m* colon; **Dickkopf** *m* stubborn (*o* pig-headed) person; **Dickmilch** *f* sour milk

die *art* the; **~ arme Sarah** poor Sarah ▷ *pron* (*sing, Person, als Subjekt*) she; (*Person, als Subjekt, Plural*) they; (*Person, als Objekt*) her; (*Person, als Objekt, Plural*) them; (*Sache*) that (one), this (one); (*Plural*) those (ones); (*Sache, Plural*) those (ones); (*relativ, auf Person*) who, that; (*relativ, auf Sache*) which, that; **~ mit den langen Haaren** the one (*o* her) with the long hair; **sie war ~ erste, ~ es erfuhr** she was the first to know; **ich nehme ~ da** I'll take that one/those ▷ *pl* *von* **der, die, das**

Dieb(in) (*-(e)s, -e*) *m(f)* thief; **Diebstahl** (*-(e)s, Diebstähle*) *m* theft; **Diebstahlsicherung** *f* burglar alarm

diejenige *pron* the one; **~, die** (*relativ*) the one who (*o* that); **~n** *pl* those *pl*, the ones

Diele (*-, -n*) *f* hall

Dienst (*-(e)s, -e*) *m* service; **außer ~** retired; **~ haben** to be on duty; **der ~ habende Arzt** the doctor on duty

Dienstag *m* Tuesday; *siehe auch* **Mittwoch; dienstags** *adv* on Tuesdays; *siehe auch* **mittwochs**

Dienstbereitschaft *f* **~ haben** (*Arzt*) to be on call; **Dienstleistung** *f* service; **dienstlich** *adj* official; **er ist ~ unterwegs** he's away on business; **Dienstreise** *f* business trip; **Dienststelle** *f* department; **Dienstwagen** *m* company car; **Dienstzeit** *f* office hours *pl*; (*Mil*) period of service

diesbezüglich *adj* (*formell*) on this matter

diese(r, s) *pron* this (one); *pl* these; **~ Frau** this woman; **~r Mann** this man; **~s Mädchen** this girl; **~ Leute** these people; **ich nehme ~/~n/~s** (*hier*) I'll take this one; (*dort*) I'll take that one; **ich nehme ~** *pl*

(*hier*) I'll take these (ones); (*dort*) I'll take those (ones)

Diesel (*-s, -*) *m* (*Auto*) diesel

dieselbe *pron* the same; **es sind immer ~n** it's always the same people

Dieselmotor *m* diesel engine; **Dieselöl** *nt* diesel (oil)

diesig *adj* hazy, misty

diesmal *adv* this time

Dietrich (*-s, -e*) *m* skeleton key

Differenz (*-, -en*) *f* difference

digital *adj* digital; **Digital-** *in zW* (*Kamera, Anzeige etc*) digital

Diktat (*-(e)s, -e*) *nt* dictation

Diktatur *f* dictatorship

Dill (*-s*) *m* dill

DIN *abk* = **Deutsche Industrienorm** DIN; **~ A4** A4

Ding (*-(e)s, -e*) *nt* thing; **vor allen ~en** above all; **der Stand der ~e** the state of affairs; **das ist nicht mein ~** (*fam*) it's not my sort of thing (*o* cup of tea); **Dingsbums** (*-*) *nt* (*fam*) thingy, thingummybob

Dinosaurier *m* dinosaur

Diphtherie *f* diphtheria

Diplom (*-(e)s, -e*) *nt* diploma

Diplomat(in) (*-en, -en*) *m(f)* diplomat

dir *pron* *dat von* **du** (to) you; **hat er ~ geholfen?** did he help you?; **ich werde es ~ erklären** I'll explain it to you; (*reflexiv*) **wasch ~ die Hände** go and wash your hands; **ein Freund von ~** a friend of yours

direkt *adj* direct; (*Frage*) straight; **~e Verbindung** through service ▷ *adv* directly; (*sofort*) immediately; **~ am Bahnhof** right next to the station; **Direktflug** *m* direct flight

Direktor(in) *m(f)* director; (*Schule*) headmaster/-mistress (*Brit*), principal (*US*)

Direktübertragung *f* live broadcast

Dirigent(in) *m(f)* conductor; **dirigieren** *vt* to direct; (*Mus*) to conduct

Discman® (*-s, -s*) *m* Discman®

Diskette *f* disk, diskette; **Diskettenlaufwerk** *nt* disk drive

Diskjockey (*-s, -s*) *m* disc jockey; **Disko** (*-, -s*) *f* (*fam*) disco, club; **Diskothek** (*-, -en*) *f* discotheque, club

diskret *adj* discreet

diskriminieren *vt* to discriminate against

Diskussion f discussion; **diskutieren** vt, vi to discuss

Display (-s, -s) nt display

disqualifizieren vt to disqualify

Distanz f distance

Distel (-, -n) f thistle

Disziplin (-, -en) f discipline

divers adj various

dividieren vt to divide (durch by); **8 dividiert durch 2 ist 4** 8 divided by 2 is 4

DJ (-s, -s) m abk = **Diskjockey** DJ

🔘 SCHLÜSSELWORT

doch adv **1** (dennoch) after all (sowieso) anyway; **er kam doch noch** he came after all; **du weißt es ja doch besser** you know better than I do anyway; **und doch ...** and yet ...

2 (als bejahende Antwort) yes I do/it does etc; **das ist nicht wahr — doch!** that's not true — yes it is!

3 (auffordernd): **komm doch** do come; **lass ihn doch** just leave him; **nicht doch!** oh no!

4: **sie ist doch noch so jung** but she's still so young; **Sie wissen doch, wie das ist** you know how it is(, don't you?); **wenn doch** if only

▷ konj (aber) but (trotzdem) all the same; **und doch hat er es getan** but still he did it

Doktor(in) m(f) doctor

Dokument nt document; **Dokumentarfilm** m documentary (film); **dokumentieren** vt to document; **Dokumentvorlage** f (Inform) document template

Dolch (-(e)s, -e) m dagger

Dollar (-(s), -s) m dollar

dolmetschen vt, vi to interpret; **Dolmetscher(in)** (-s, -) m(f) interpreter

Dolomiten pl Dolomites pl

Dom (-(e)s, -e) m cathedral

Domäne (-, -n) f domain, province; (Inform: Domain) domain

Dominikanische Republik f Dominican Republic

Domino (-s, -s) nt dominoes sing

Donau (-) f Danube

Döner (-s, -) m, **Döner Kebab** (-(s), -s) m doner kebab

Donner (-s, -) m thunder; **donnern** vi **es donnert** it's thundering

Donnerstag m Thursday; siehe auch **Mittwoch**; **donnerstags** adv on Thursdays; siehe auch **mittwochs**

doof adj (fam) stupid

dopen vt to dope; **Doping** (-s) nt doping; **Dopingkontrolle** f drugs test

Doppel (-s, -) nt duplicate; (Sport) doubles sing; **Doppelbett** nt double bed; **Doppeldecker** m double-decker; **Doppelhaushälfte** f semi-detached house (Brit), duplex (US); **doppelklicken** vi to double-click; **Doppelname** m double-barrelled name; **Doppelpunkt** m colon; **Doppelstecker** m two-way adaptor; **doppelt** adj double; **in ~er Ausführung** in duplicate; **Doppelzimmer** nt double room

Dorf (-(e)s, Dörfer) nt village

Dorn (-(e)s, -en) m (Bot) thorn

Dörrobst nt dried fruit

Dorsch (-(e)s, -e) m cod

dort adv there; **~ drüben** over there; **dorther** adv from there

Dose (-, -n) f box; (Blechdose) tin (Brit), can; (Bierdose) can

dösen vi to doze

Dosenbier nt canned beer; **Dosenmilch** f canned milk, tinned milk (Brit); **Dosenöffner** m tin opener (Brit), can opener

Dotter (-s, -) m (egg) yolk

downloaden vt to download

Downsyndrom (-(e)s, -e) nt (Med) Down's syndrome

Dozent(in) m(f) lecturer

Dr. abk = **Doktor**

Drache (-n, -n) m dragon; **Drachen** (-s, -) m (Spielzeug) kite; (Sport) hang-glider; **Drachenfliegen** (-s) nt hang-gliding; **Drachenflieger(in)** (-s, -) m(f) hang-glider

Draht (-(e)s, Drähte) m wire; **Drahtseilbahn** f cable railway

Drama (-s, Dramen) nt drama; **dramatisch** adj dramatic

dran adv (fam) kontr von **daran**; **gut ~ sein** (reich) to be well-off; (glücklich) to be fortunate; (gesundheitlich) to be well; **schlecht ~ sein** to be in a bad way; **wer ist ~?** whose turn is it?; **ich bin ~** it's my turn; **bleib ~!** (Tel) hang on

drang imperf von **dringen**

Drang (-(e)s, Dränge) m (Trieb) urge (nach for); (Druck) pressure

drängeln vt, vi to push

drängen vt (schieben) to push; (antreiben) to urge ▷ vi (eilig sein) to be urgent; (Zeit) to press; **auf etw** (akk) **~ to** press for sth

dran|kommen irr vi **wer kommt dran?** who's turn is it?, who's next?

drauf (fam) kontr von **darauf**; **gut/schlecht ~ sein** to be in a good/bad mood

Draufgänger(in) (-s, -) m(f) daredevil

drauf|kommen irr vi to remember; **ich komme nicht drauf** I can't think of it

drauf|machen vi (fam) **einen ~ to** go on a binge

draußen adv outside

Dreck (-(e)s) m dirt, filth; **dreckig** adj dirty, filthy

drehen vt, vi to turn; (Zigaretten) to roll; (Film) to shoot ▷ vr **sich ~ to** turn; (um Achse) to rotate; **sich ~ um** (handeln von) to be about

Drehstrom m three-phase current; **Drehtür** f revolving door; **Drehzahlmesser** m rev counter

drei num three; **~ viertel voll** three-quarters full; **es ist ~ viertel neun** it's a quarter to nine; **Drei** (-, -en) f three; (Schulnote) ≈ C; **Dreieck** nt triangle; **dreieckig** adj triangular; **dreifach** adj triple ▷ adv three times; **dreihundert** num three hundred; **Dreikönigstag** m Epiphany; **dreimal** adv three times; **Dreirad** nt tricycle; **dreispurig** adj three-lane

dreißig num thirty; **dreißigste(r, s)** adj thirtieth; siehe auch **dritte**

Dreiviertelstunde f eine **~** three quarters of an hour

dreizehn num thirteen; **dreizehnte(r, s)** adj thirteenth; siehe auch **dritte**

dressieren vt to train

Dressing (-s, -s) nt (salad) dressing

Dressman (-s, Dressmen) m (male) model

Dressur (-, -en) f training

drin (fam) kontr von **darin** in it; **mehr war nicht ~ that** was the best I could do

dringen (drang, gedrungen) vi (Wasser, Licht, Kälte) to penetrate (durch through, in +akk into); **auf etw** (akk) **~ to** insist on sth; **dringend, dringlich** adj urgent

drinnen adv inside

dritt adv **wir sind zu ~ there** are three of us; **dritte(r, s)** adj third; **die Dritte Welt** the Third World; **7. Juni** 7(th) June (gesprochen: the seventh of June); **am 7. Juni** on 7(th) June, on June 7(th) (gesprochen: on the seventh of June); **München, den 7. Juni** Munich, June 7(th); **Drittel** (-s, -) nt (Bruchteil) third; **drittens** adv thirdly

Droge (-, -n) f drug; **drogenabhängig, drogensüchtig** adj addicted to drugs

Drogerie f chemist's (Brit), drugstore (US); **Drogeriemarkt** m discount chemist's (Brit) (o drugstore (US))

● **Drogerie**
●
● The **Drogerie** as opposed to the
● **Apotheke** sells medicines not
● requiring a prescription. It tends to
● be cheaper and also sells cosmetics,
● perfume and toiletries.

drohen vi to threaten (jdm sb); **mit etw ~ to** threaten to do sth

dröhnen vi (Motor) to roar; (Stimme, Musik) to boom; (Raum) to resound

Drohung f threat

Drossel (-, -n) f thrush

drüben adv over there; (auf der anderen Seite) on the other side

drüber (fam) kontr von **darüber**

Druck (-(e)s, Drücke) m (Phys) pressure; (fig: Belastung) stress; **jdn unter ~ setzen** to put sb under pressure ▷ (-(e)s, -e) m (Typo: Vorgang) printing; (Produkt, Schriftart) print; **Druckbuchstabe** m block letter; **in ~n schreiben** to print; **drucken** vt, vi to print

drücken vt, vi (Knopf, Hand) to press; (zu eng sein) to pinch; (fig: Preise) to keep down; **jdm etw in die Hand ~ to** press sth into sb's hand ▷ vr **sich vor etw** (dat) **~ to** get out of sth; **drückend** adj oppressive

Drucker (-s, -) m (Inform) printer; **Druckertreiber** m printer driver

Druckknopf m press stud (Brit), snap fastener (US); **Drucksache** f printed matter; **Druckschrift** f block letters pl

drunten adv down there

drunter (fam) kontr von **darunter**

Drüse (-, -n) f gland

Dschungel (-s, -) m jungle

du pron you; **bist ~ es?** is it you?; **wir sind per ~** we're on first-name terms

Dübel (-s, -) m Rawlplug®

ducken vt to duck ▷ vr **sich ~** to duck

Dudelsack m bagpipes pl

Duett (-s, -e) nt duet

Duft (-(e)s, Düfte) m scent; **duften** vi to smell nice; **es duftet nach ...** it smells of ...

dulden vt to tolerate

dumm adj stupid; **Dummheit** f stupidity; (Tat) stupid thing; **Dummkopf** m idiot

dumpf adj (Ton) muffled; (Erinnerung) vague; (Schmerz) dull

Düne (-, -n) f dune

Dünger (-s, -) m fertilizer

dunkel adj dark; (Stimme) deep; (Ahnung) vague; (rätselhaft) obscure; (verdächtig) dubious; **im Dunkeln tappen** (fig) to be in the dark; **dunkelblau** adj dark blue; **dunkelblond** adj light brown; **dunkelhaarig** adj dark-haired; **Dunkelheit** f darkness

dünn adj thin; (Kaffee) weak

Dunst (-es, Dünste) m haze; (leichter Nebel) mist; (Chem) vapour

dünsten vt (Gastr) to steam

Duo (-s, -s) nt duo

Dur (-) nt (Mus) major (key); **in G-~** in G major

O SCHLÜSSELWORT

durch präp +akk **1** (hindurch) through; **durch den Urwald** through the jungle; **durch die ganze Welt reisen** to travel all over the world
2 (mittels) through, by (means of) (aufgrund) due to, owing to; **Tod durch Herzschlag/den Strang** death from a heart attack/by hanging; **durch die Post** by post; **durch seine Bemühungen** through his efforts
▷ adv **1** (hindurch) through; **die ganze Nacht durch** all through the night; **den Sommer durch** during the summer; **8 Uhr durch** past 8 o'clock; **durch und durch** completely
2 (durchgebraten etc): **(gut) durch** well-done

durchaus adv absolutely; **~ nicht** not at all

Durchblick m view; **den ~ haben** (fig) to know what's going on; **durch|blicken** vi to look through; (fam: verstehen) to understand (bei etw sth); **etw ~ lassen** (fig) to hint at sth

Durchblutung f circulation

durch|brennen irr vi (Sicherung) to blow; (Draht) to burn through; (fam: davonlaufen) to run away

durchdacht adv **gut ~** well thought-out

durch|drehen vt (Fleisch) to mince ▷ vi (Räder) to spin; (fam: nervlich) to crack up

durcheinander adv in a mess; (fam: verwirrt) confused; **~ bringen** to mess up; (verwirren) to confuse; **~ reden** to talk all at the same time; **~ trinken** to mix one's drinks; **Durcheinander** (-s) nt (Verwirrung) confusion; (Unordnung) mess

Durchfahrt f way through; **„~ verboten!"** 'no thoroughfare'

Durchfall m (Med) diarrhoea

durch|fallen irr vi to fall through; (in Prüfung) to fail

durch|fragen vr **sich ~** to ask one's way

durch|führen vt to carry out

Durchgang m passage; (Sport) round; (bei Wahl) ballot; **Durchgangsverkehr** m through traffic

durchgebraten adj well done

durchgefroren adj frozen to the bone

durch|gehen irr vi to go through (durch etw sth); (ausreißen: Pferd) to break loose; (Mensch) to run away; **durchgehend** adj (Zug) through; **~ geöffnet** open all day

durch|halten irr vi to hold out ▷ vt (Tempo) to keep up; **etw ~** (bis zum Schluss) to see sth through

durch|kommen irr vi to get through; (Patient) to pull through

durch|lassen irr vt (jdn) to let through; (Wasser) to let in

Durchlauf(wasser)erhitzer (-s, -) m instantaneous water heater

durch|lesen irr vt to read through

durchleuchten vt to X-ray

durch|machen vt to go through; (Entwicklung) to undergo; **die Nacht ~** to make a night of it, to have an all-nighter

Durchmesser (-s, -) m diameter

Durchreise f journey through; **auf der ~** passing through; (Güter) in

transit; **Durchreisevisum** nt transit
visa
durch|reißen irr vt, vi to tear (in two)
durchs kontr von **durch das**
Durchsage (-, -n) f announcement
durchschauen vt (jdn, Lüge) to see
through
durch|schlagen irr vr **sich ~** to struggle
through
durch|schneiden irr vt to cut (in two)
Durchschnitt m (Mittelwert) average; **im
~** on average; **durchschnittlich** adj
average ▷ adv (im Durchschnitt) on
average; **Durchschnittsgeschwindigkeit**
f average speed
durch|setzen vt to get through ▷ vr **sich
~** (Erfolg haben) to succeed; (sich behaupten)
to get one's way
durchsichtig adj transparent,
see-through
durch|stellen vt (Tel) to put through
durch|streichen irr vt to cross out
durchsuchen vt to search (nach for);
Durchsuchung f search
durchwachsen adj (Speck) streaky; (fig:
mittelmäßig) so-so
Durchwahl f direct dialling; (Nummer)
extension
durch|ziehen irr vt (Plan) to carry
through
Durchzug m draught

○ **SCHLÜSSELWORT**

dürfen unreg vi **1** (Erlaubnis haben) to be
allowed to; **ich darf das** I'm allowed to
(do that); **darf ich?** may I?; **darf ich ins
Kino?** can od may I go to the cinema?;
es darf geraucht werden you may
smoke
2 (in Verneinungen): **er darf das nicht** he's
not allowed to (do that); **das darf nicht
geschehen** that must not happen; **da
darf sie sich nicht wundern** that
shouldn't surprise her
3 (in Höflichkeitsformeln): **darf ich Sie
bitten, das zu tun?** may od could I ask you
to do that?; **was darf es sein?** what can I
do for you?
4 (können): **das dürfen Sie mir glauben**
you can believe me
5 (Möglichkeit): **das dürfte genug sein**
that should be enough; **es dürfte Ihnen**

bekannt sein, dass ... as you will
probably know ...

dürftig adj (ärmlich) poor; (unzulänglich)
inadequate
dürr adj dried-up; (Land) arid; (mager)
skinny
Durst (-(e)s) m thirst; **~ haben** to be
thirsty; **durstig** adj thirsty
Dusche (-, -n) f shower; **duschen** vi to
have a shower ▷ vr **sich ~** to have a
shower; **Duschgel** nt shower gel;
Duschvorhang m shower curtain
Düse (-, -n) f nozzle; (Tech) jet;
Düsenflugzeug nt jet (aircraft)
Dussel (-s, -) m (fam) dope; **duss(e)lig** adj
(fam) stupid
düster adj dark; (Gedanken, Zukunft)
gloomy
Dutyfreeshop (-s, -s) m duty-free shop
Dutzend (-s, -e) nt dozen
duzen vt to address as 'du' ▷ vr **sich ~** (mit
jdm) to address each other as 'du', to be on
first-name terms
DVD (-, -s) f abk = **Digital Versatile Disk**
DVD
dynamisch adj dynamic
Dynamo (-s, -s) m dynamo
D-Zug m fast train

Ebbe (-, -n) f low tide
eben adj level; (glatt) smooth ▷ adv just; (bestätigend) exactly
Ebene (-, -n) f plain; (fig) level
ebenfalls adv also, as well; (Antwort: gleichfalls!) you too; **ebenso** adv just as; **~ gut** just as well; **~ viel** just as much
Eber (-s, -) m boar
EC (-, -s) m abk = **Eurocityzug**
Echo (-s, -s) nt echo
echt adj (Leder, Gold) real, genuine; **ein ~er Verlust** a real loss
EC-Karte f ≈ debit card
Ecke (-, -n) f corner; (Math) angle; **an der ~** at the corner; **gleich um die ~** just round the corner; **eckig** adj rectangular; **Eckzahn** m canine
Economyclass (-) f coach (class), economy class
Ecstasy (-) f (Droge) ecstasy
edel adj noble; **Edelstein** m precious stone
EDV (-) f abk = **elektronische Datenverarbeitung** EDP
Efeu (-s) m ivy
Effekt (-s, -e) m effect
egal adj **das ist ~** it doesn't matter; **das ist**
mir **~** I don't care, it's all the same to me; **~ wie teuer** no matter how expensive
egoistisch adj selfish
ehe conj before
Ehe (-, -n) f marriage; **Ehefrau** f wife; (verheiratete Frau) married woman; **Eheleute** pl married couple sing
ehemalig adj former; **ehemals** adv formerly
Ehemann m husband; (verheirateter Mann) married man; **Ehepaar** nt married couple
eher adv (früher) sooner; (lieber) rather, sooner; (mehr) more; **je ~, desto besser** the sooner the better
Ehering m wedding ring
eheste(r, s) adj (früheste) first ▷ adv **am ~n** (am wahrscheinlichsten) most likely
Ehre (-, -n) f honour; **ehren** vt to honour; **ehrenamtlich** adj voluntary; **Ehrengast** m guest of honour; **Ehrenwort** nt word of honour; **~!** I promise; **ich gebe dir mein ~** I give you my word
ehrgeizig adj ambitious
ehrlich adj honest
Ei (-(e)s, -er) nt egg; **hart gekochtes/weiches ~** hard-boiled/soft-boiled egg
Eiche (-, -n) f oak (tree); **Eichel** (-, -n) f acorn
Eichhörnchen nt squirrel
Eid (-(e)s, -e) m oath
Eidechse (-, -n) f lizard
Eierbecher m eggcup; **Eierstock** m ovary; **Eieruhr** f egg timer
Eifersucht f jealousy; **eifersüchtig** adj jealous (auf +akk of sb)
Eigelb (-(e)s, -) nt egg yolk
eigen adj own; (typisch) characteristic (jdm of sb); (eigenartig) peculiar; **eigenartig** adj peculiar; **Eigenschaft** f quality; (Chem, Phys) property; (Merkmal) characteristic
eigentlich adj actual, real ▷ adv actually, really; **was denken Sie sich ~ dabei?** what on earth do you think you're doing?
Eigentum nt property; **Eigentümer(in)** m(f) owner; **Eigentumswohnung** f owner-occupied flat (Brit), condominium (US)
eignen vr **sich ~ für** to be suited for; **er würde sich als Lehrer ~** he'd make a good teacher
Eilbrief m express letter, special-delivery

letter; **Eile** (-) f hurry; **eilen** vi (dringend sein) to be urgent; **es eilt nicht** there's no hurry; **eilig** adj hurried; (dringlich) urgent; **es ~ haben** to be in a hurry

Eimer (-s, -) m bucket

ein adv **nicht ~ noch aus wissen** not to know what to do; **~ - aus** (Schalter) on - off

ein(e) art a; (vor gesprochenem Vokal) an; **~ Mann** a man; **~ Apfel** an apple; **~e Stunde** an hour; **~ Haus** a house; **~ (gewisser) Herr Miller** a (certain) Mr Miller; **~es Tages** one day

einander pron one another, each other

ein|arbeiten vt to train ▷ vr **sich ~** to get used to the work

ein|atmen vt, vi to breathe in

Einbahnstraße f one-way street

ein|bauen vt to build in; (Motor etc) to install, to fit; **Einbauküche** f fitted kitchen

ein|biegen irr vi to turn (in +akk into)

ein|bilden vt **sich** (dat) **etw ~** to imagine sth

ein|brechen irr vi (in Haus) to break in; (Dach etc) to fall in, to collapse; **Einbrecher(in)** (-s, -) m(f) burglar

ein|bringen irr vt (Ernte) to bring in; (Gewinn) to yield; **jdm etw ~** to bring (o earn) sb sth ▷ vr **sich in** (akk) **etw ~** to make a contribution to sth

Einbruch m (Haus) break-in, burglary; **bei ~ der Nacht** at nightfall

Einbürgerung f naturalization

ein|checken vt to check in

ein|cremen vt to put some cream on ▷ vr **sich ~** to put some cream on

eindeutig adj clear, obvious ▷ adv clearly; **~ falsch** clearly wrong

ein|dringen irr vi (gewaltsam) to force one's way in (in +akk -to); (in Haus) to break in (in +akk -to); (Gas, Wasser) to get in (in +akk -to)

Eindruck m impression; **großen ~ auf jdn machen** to make a big impression on sb

eine(r, s) pron one; (jemand) someone; **~r meiner Freunde** one of my friends; **~r nach dem andern** one after the other

eineiig adj (Zwillinge) identical

eineinhalb num one and a half

einerseits adv on the one hand

einfach adj (nicht kompliziert) simple; (Mensch) ordinary; (Essen) plain; (nicht mehrfach) single; **~e Fahrkarte** single

ticket (Brit), one-way ticket (US) ▷ adv simply; (nicht mehrfach) once

Einfahrt f (Vorgang) driving in; (eines Zuges) arrival; (Ort) entrance

Einfall m (Idee) idea; **ein|fallen** irr vi (Licht etc) to fall in; (einstürzen) to collapse; **ihm fiel ein, dass ...** it occurred to him that ...; **ich werde mir etwas ~ lassen** I'll think of something; **was fällt Ihnen ein!** what do you think you're doing?

Einfamilienhaus nt detached house

einfarbig adj all one colour; (Stoff etc) self-coloured

Einfluss m influence

ein|frieren irr vt, vi to freeze

ein|fügen vt to fit in; (zusätzlich) to add; (Inform) to insert; **Einfügetaste** f (Inform) insert key

Einfuhr (-, -en) f import; **Einfuhrbestimmungen** pl import regulations pl

ein|führen vt to introduce; (Ware) to import; **Einführung** f introduction

Eingabe f (Dateneingabe) input; **Eingabetaste** f (Inform) return (o enter) key

Eingang m entrance; **Eingangshalle** f entrance hall, lobby (US)

ein|geben irr vt (Daten etc) to enter, to key in

eingebildet adj imaginary; (eitel) arrogant

Eingeborene(r) mf native

ein|gehen irr vi (Sendung, Geld) to come in, to arrive; (Tier, Pflanze) to die; (Stoff) to shrink; **auf etw** (akk) **~** to agree to sth; **auf jdn ~** to respond to sb ▷ vt (Vertrag) to enter into; (Wette) to make; (Risiko) to take

eingelegt adj (in Essig) pickled

eingeschaltet adj (switched) on

eingeschlossen adj locked in; (inklusive) included

ein|gewöhnen vr **sich ~** to settle in

ein|gießen irr vt to pour

ein|greifen irr vi to intervene; **Eingriff** m intervention; (Operation) operation

ein|halten irr vt (Versprechen etc) to keep

ein|hängen vt (Telefon) **(den Hörer) ~** to hang up

einheimisch adj (Produkt, Mannschaft) local; **Einheimische(r)** mf local

Einheit f (Geschlossenheit) unity; (Maß) unit; **einheitlich** adj uniform

ein|holen vt (Vorsprung aufholen) to catch

up with; (*Verspätung*) to make up for; (*Rat, Erlaubnis*) to ask for

Einhorn nt unicorn

einhundert num one (o a) hundred

einig adj (*vereint*) united; **sich** (*dat*) **~ sein** to agree

einige pron pl some; (*mehrere*) several ▷ adj some; **nach ~er Zeit** after some time; **~e hundert Euro** some hundred euros

einigen vr **sich ~** to agree (*auf* +akk on)

einigermaßen adv fairly, quite; (*leidlich*) reasonably

einiges pron something; (*ziemlich viel*) quite a bit; (*mehreres*) a few things; **es gibt noch ~ zu tun** there's still a fair bit to do

Einkauf m purchase; **Einkäufe (machen)** (to do one's) shopping; **ein|kaufen** vt to buy ▷ vi to go shopping; **Einkaufsbummel** m shopping trip; **Einkaufstasche** f, **Einkaufstüte** f shopping bag; **Einkaufswagen** m shopping trolley (*Brit*) (o cart (*US*)); **Einkaufszentrum** nt shopping centre (*Brit*) (o mall (*US*))

ein|klemmen vt to jam; **er hat sich** (*dat*) **den Finger eingeklemmt** he got his finger caught

Einkommen (-s, -) nt income

ein|laden irr vt (*jdn*) to invite; (*Gegenstände*) to load; **jdn zum Essen ~** to take sb out for a meal; **ich lade dich ein** (*bezahle*) it's my treat; **Einladung** f invitation

Einlass (-es, Einlässe) m admittance; **~ ab 18 Uhr** doors open at 6 pm; **ein|lassen** irr vr **sich mit jdm/auf etw** (*akk*) **~** to get involved with sb/sth

ein|leben vr **sich ~** to settle down

ein|legen vt (*Film etc*) to put in; (*marinieren*) to marinate; **eine Pause ~** to take a break

ein|leiten vt to start; (*Maßnahmen*) to introduce; (*Geburt*) to induce; **Einleitung** f introduction; (*von Geburt*) induction

ein|leuchten vi **jdm ~** to be (o become) clear to sb; **einleuchtend** adj clear

ein|loggen vi (*Inform*) to log on (o in)

ein|lösen vt (*Scheck*) to cash; (*Gutschein*) to redeem; (*Versprechen*) to keep

einmal adv once; (*früher*) before; (*in*

Zukunft) some day; (*erstens*) first; **~ im Jahr** once a year; **noch ~** once more, again; **ich war schon ~ hier** I've been here before; **warst du schon ~ in London?** have you ever been to London?; **nicht ~** not even; **auf ~** suddenly; (*gleichzeitig*) at once; **einmalig** adj unique; (*einmal geschehend*) single; (*prima*) fantastic

ein|mischen vr **sich ~** to interfere (*in* +akk with)

Einnahme (-, -n) f (*Geld*) takings pl; (*von Medizin*) taking; **ein|nehmen** irr vt (*Medizin*) to take; (*Geld*) to take in; (*Standpunkt, Raum*) to take up; **jdn für sich ~** to win sb over

ein|ordnen vt to put in order; (*klassifizieren*) to classify; (*Akten*) to file ▷ vr **sich ~** (*Auto*) to get in lane; **sich rechts/links ~** to get into the right/left lane

ein|packen vt to pack (up)

ein|parken vt, vi to park

ein|planen vt to allow for

ein|prägen vt **sich** (*dat*) **etw ~** to remember (o memorize) sth

ein|räumen vt (*Bücher, Geschirr*) to put away; (*Schrank*) to put things in

ein|reden vt **jdm/sich etw ~** to talk sb/oneself into (believing) sth

ein|reiben irr vt **sich mit etw ~** to rub sth into one's skin

ein|reichen vt to hand in; (*Antrag*) to submit

Einreise f entry; **Einreisebestimmungen** pl entry regulations pl; **Einreiseerlaubnis** f, **Einreisegenehmigung** f entry permit; **ein|reisen** vi to enter (*in ein Land* a country); **Einreisevisum** nt entry visa

ein|renken vt (*Arm, Bein*) to set

ein|richten vt (*Wohnung*) to furnish; (*gründen*) to establish, to set up; (*arrangieren*) to arrange ▷ vr **sich ~** (*in Haus*) to furnish one's home; (*sich vorbereiten*) to prepare oneself (*auf* +akk for); (*sich anpassen*) to adapt (*auf* +akk to); **Einrichtung** f (*Wohnung*) furnishings pl; (*öffentliche Anstalt*) institution; (*Schwimmbad etc*) facility

eins num one; **Eins** (-, -en) f one; (*Schulnote*) ≈ A

einsam adj lonely

ein|sammeln vt to collect

Einsatz m (*Teil*) insert; (*Verwendung*) use;

(*Spieleinsatz*) stake; (*Risiko*) risk; (*Mus*) entry

ein|schalten vt (*Elek*) to switch on

ein|schätzen vt to estimate, to assess

ein|schenken vt to pour

ein|schiffen vr **sich ~** to embark (*nach* for)

ein|schlafen irr vi to fall asleep, to drop off; **mir ist der Arm eingeschlafen** my arm's gone to sleep

ein|schlagen irr vt (*Fenster*) to smash; (*Zähne, Schädel*) to smash in; (*Weg, Richtung*) to take ▷ vi to hit (*in etw akk* sth, *auf jdn* sb); (*Blitz*) to strike; (*Anklang finden*) to be a success

ein|schließen irr vt (*jdn*) to lock in; (*Gegenstand*) to lock away; (*umgeben*) to surround; (*fig: beinhalten*) to include; **einschließlich** adv inclusive ▷ prep +gen including; **von Montag bis ~ Freitag** from Monday up to and including Friday, Monday through Friday (US)

ein|schränken vt to limit, to restrict; (*verringern*) to cut down on ▷ vr **sich ~** to cut down (on expenditure)

ein|schreiben irr vr **sich ~** to register; (*Schule*) to enrol; **Einschreiben** (*-s, -*) nt registered letter; **etw per ~ schicken** to send sth by special delivery

ein|schüchtern vt to intimidate

ein|sehen irr vt (*verstehen*) to see; (*Fehler*) to recognize; (*Akten*) to have a look at

einseitig adj one-sided

ein|senden irr vt to send in

ein|setzen vt to put in; (*in Amt*) to appoint; (*Geld*) to stake; (*verwenden*) to use ▷ vi (*beginnen*) to set in; (*Mus*) to enter, to come in ▷ vr **sich ~** to work hard; **sich für jdn/etw ~** to support sb/sth

Einsicht f insight; **zu der ~ kommen, dass ...** to come to realize that ...

ein|sperren vt to lock up

ein|spielen vt (*Geld*) to bring in

ein|springen irr vi (*aushelfen*) to step in (*für* for)

Einspruch m objection (*gegen* to)

einspurig adj single-lane

Einstand m (*Tennis*) deuce

ein|stecken vt to pocket; (*Elek: Stecker*) to plug in; (*Brief*) to post, to mail (US); (*mitnehmen*) to take; (*hinnehmen*) to swallow

ein|steigen irr vi (*in Auto*) to get in; (*in Bus, Zug, Flugzeug*) to get on; (*sich beteiligen*) to get involved

ein|stellen vt (*beenden*) to stop; (*Geräte*) to adjust; (*Kamera*) to focus; (*Sender, Radio*) to tune in; (*unterstellen*) to put; (*in Firma*) to employ, to take on ▷ vr **sich auf jdn/etw ~** to adapt to sb/prepare oneself for sth; **Einstellung** f (*von Gerät*) adjustment; (*von Kamera*) focusing; (*von Arbeiter*) taking on; (*Meinung*) attitude

ein|stürzen vi to collapse

eintägig adj one-day

ein|tauschen vt to exchange (*gegen* for)

eintausend num one (*o* a) thousand

ein|teilen vt (*in Teile*) to divide (up) (*in* +akk into); (*Zeit*) to organize

eintönig adj monotonous

Eintopf m stew

ein|tragen irr vt (*in eine Liste*) to put down, to enter ▷ vr **sich ~** to put one's name down, to register

ein|treffen irr vi to happen; (*ankommen*) to arrive

ein|treten irr vi (*hineingehen*) to enter (*in etw akk* sth); (*in Klub, Partei*) to join (*in etw akk* sth); (*sich ereignen*) to occur; **~ für** to support; **Eintritt** m admission; **„~ frei"** 'admission free'; **Eintrittskarte** f (entrance) ticket; **Eintrittspreis** m admission charge

einverstanden interj okay, all right ▷ adj **mit etwas ~ sein** to agree to sth, to accept sth

Einwanderer m, **Einwanderin** f immigrant; **ein|wandern** vi to immigrate

einwandfrei adj perfect, flawless

Einwegflasche f non-returnable bottle; **Einwegwaschlappen** m disposable flannel (*Brit*) (*o* washcloth (US))

ein|weichen vt to soak

ein|weihen vt (*Gebäude*) to inaugurate, to open; **jdn in etw** (akk) **~** to let sb in on sth; **Einweihungsparty** f housewarming party

ein|werfen irr vt (*Ball, Bemerkung etc*) to throw in; (*Brief*) to post, to mail (US); (*Geld*) to put in, to insert; (*Fenster*) to smash

ein|wickeln vt to wrap up; (*fig*) **jdn ~** to take sb in

Einwohner(in) (*-s, -*) m(f) inhabitant; **Einwohnermeldeamt** nt registration office for residents

Einwurf m (*Öffnung*) slot; (*Sport*) throw-in

Einzahl f singular
ein|zahlen vt to pay in (auf ein Konto -to an account)
Einzel (-s, -) nt (Tennis) singles sing; **Einzelbett** nt single bed; **Einzelfahrschein** m single ticket (Brit), one-way ticket (US); **Einzelgänger(in)** m(f) loner; **Einzelhandel** m retail trade; **Einzelkind** nt only child
einzeln adj individual; (getrennt) separate; (einzig) single; **~e ...** several ..., some ...; **der/die Einzelne** the individual; **im Einzelnen** in detail ▷ adv separately; (verpacken, aufführen) individually; **~ angeben** to specify; **~ eintreten** to enter one by one
Einzelzimmer nt single room; **Einzelzimmerzuschlag** m single-room supplement
ein|ziehen irr vt **den Kopf ~** to duck ▷ vi (in ein Haus) to move in
einzig adj only; (einzeln) single; (einzigartig) unique; **kein ~er Fehler** not a single mistake; **das Einzige** the only thing; **der/die Einzige** the only person ▷ adv only; **die ~ richtige Lösung** the only correct solution; **einzigartig** adj unique
Eis (-es, -) nt ice; (Speiseeis) ice-cream; **~ laufen** to skate; **Eisbahn** f ice(skating) rink; **Eisbär** m polar bear; **Eisbecher** m (ice-cream) sundae; **Eisberg** m iceberg; **Eiscafé** nt, **Eisdiele** f ice-cream parlour
Eisen (-s, -) nt iron; **Eisenbahn** f railway (Brit), railroad (US); **eisern** adj iron
eisgekühlt adj chilled; **Eishockey** nt ice hockey; **Eiskaffee** m iced coffee; **eiskalt** adj ice-cold; (Temperatur) freezing; **Eiskunstlauf** m figure skating; **Eissalat** m iceberg lettuce; **Eisschokolade** f iced chocolate; **Eisschrank** m fridge, ice-box (US); **Eistee** m iced tea; **Eiswürfel** m ice cube; **Eiszapfen** m icicle
eitel adj vain
Eiter (-s) m pus
Eiweiß (-es, -e) nt egg white; (Chem, Bio) protein
ekelhaft, ek(e)lig adj disgusting, revolting; **ekeln** vr **sich ~** to be disgusted (vor +dat at)
EKG (-s, -s) nt abk = **Elektrokardiogramm** ECG
Ekzem (-s, -e) nt (Med) eczema

Elastikbinde f elastic bandage; **elastisch** adj elastic
Elch (-(e)s, -e) m elk; (nordamerikanischer) moose
Elefant m elephant
elegant adj elegant
Elektriker(in) (-s, -) m(f) electrician; **elektrisch** adj electric; **Elektrizität** f electricity; **Elektroauto** nt electric car; **Elektrogerät** nt electrical appliance; **Elektrogeschäft** nt electrical shop; **Elektroherd** m electric cooker; **Elektromotor** m electric motor; **Elektronik** f electronics sing; **elektronisch** adj electronic; **Elektrorasierer** (-s, -) m electric razor
Element (-s, -e) nt element
elend adj miserable; **Elend** (-(e)s) nt misery
elf num eleven; **Elf** (-, -en) f (Sport) eleven
Elfenbein nt ivory
Elfmeter m (Sport) penalty (kick)
elfte(r, s) adj eleventh; siehe auch **dritte**
Ell(en)bogen m elbow
Elster (-, -n) f magpie
Eltern pl parents pl
EM f abk = **Europameisterschaft** European Championship(s)
Email (-s, -s) nt enamel
E-Mail (-, -s) f (Inform) e-mail; **jdm eine ~ schicken** to e-mail sb, to send sb an e-mail; **jdm etwas per ~ schicken** to e-mail sth to sb; **E-Mail-Adresse** f e-mail address; **e-mailen** vt to e-mail
Emoticon (-s, -s) nt emoticon
emotional adj emotional
empfahl imperf von **empfehlen**
empfand imperf von **empfinden**
Empfang (-(e)s, Empfänge) m (Rezeption; Veranstaltung) reception; (Erhalten) receipt; **in ~ nehmen** to receive; **empfangen** (empfing, empfangen) vt to receive; **Empfänger(in)** (-s, -) m(f) recipient; (Adressat) addressee ▷ m (Tech) receiver; **Empfängnisverhütung** f contraception; **Empfangshalle** f reception area
empfehlen (empfahl, empfohlen) vt to recommend; **Empfehlung** f recommendation
empfinden (empfand, empfunden) vt to feel; **empfindlich** adj (Mensch) sensitive; (Stelle) sore; (reizbar) touchy; (Material) delicate

empfing imperf von **empfangen**

empfohlen pp von **empfehlen**

empfunden pp von **empfinden**

empört adj indignant (über +akk at)

Ende (-s, -n) nt end; (Film, Roman) ending; **am ~** at the end; (schließlich) in the end; **~ Mai** at the end of May; **~ der Achtzigerjahre** in the late eighties; **sie ist ~ zwanzig** she's in her late twenties; **zu ~** over, finished; **enden** vi to end; **der Zug endet hier** this service (o train) terminates here; **endgültig** adj final; (Beweis) conclusive

Endivie f endive

endlich adv at last, finally; (am Ende) eventually; **Endspiel** nt final; (Endrunde) finals pl; **Endstation** f terminus; **Endung** f ending

Energie f energy; **~ sparend** energy-saving; **Energiebedarf** m energy requirement; **Energieverbrauch** m energy consumption

energisch adj (entschlossen) forceful

eng adj narrow; (Kleidung) tight; (fig: Freundschaft, Verhältnis) close; **das wird ~** (fam: zeitlich) we're running out of time, it's getting tight ▷ adv **~ befreundet sein** to be close friends

engagieren vt to engage ▷ vr **sich ~** to commit oneself, to be committed (für to)

Engel (-s, -) m angel

England nt England; **Engländer(in)** (-s, -) m(f) Englishman/ -woman; **die ~** pl the English pl; **englisch** adj English; (Gastr) rare; **Englisch** nt English; **ins ~e übersetzen** to translate into English

Enkel (-s, -) m grandson; **Enkelin** f granddaughter

enorm adj enormous; (fig) tremendous

Entbindung f (Med) delivery

entdecken vt to discover; **Entdeckung** f discovery

Ente (-, -n) f duck

Enter-Taste f (Inform) enter (o return) key

entfernen vt to remove; (Inform) to delete ▷ vr **sich ~** to go away; **entfernt** adj distant; **15 km von X ~** 15 km away from X; **20 km voneinander ~** 20 km apart; **Entfernung** f distance; **aus der ~** from a distance

entführen vt to kidnap; **Entführer(in)** m(f) kidnapper; **Entführung** f kidnapping

entgegen prep +dat contrary to ▷ adv towards; **dem Wind ~** against the wind; **entgegengesetzt** adj (Richtung) opposite; (Meinung) opposing; **entgegen|kommen** irr vi **jdm ~** to come to meet sb; (fig) to accommodate sb; **entgegenkommend** adj (Verkehr) oncoming; (fig) obliging

entgegnen vt to reply (auf +akk to)

entgehen irr vi **jdm ~** to escape sb's notice; **sich** (dat) **etw ~ lassen** to miss sth

entgleisen vi (Eisenb) to be derailed; (fig: Mensch) to misbehave

Enthaarungscreme f hair remover

enthalten irr vt (Behälter) to contain; (Preis) to include ▷ vr **sich ~** to abstain (gen from)

entkoffeiniert adj decaffeinated

entkommen irr vi to escape

entkorken vt to uncork

entlang prep +akk o dat **~ dem Fluss, den Fluss ~** along the river; **entlang|gehen** irr vi to walk along

entlassen irr vt (Patient) to discharge; (Arbeiter) to dismiss

entlasten vt **jdn ~** (Arbeit abnehmen) to relieve sb of some of his/her work

entmutigen vt to discourage

entnehmen vt to take (dat from)

entrahmt adj (Milch) skimmed

entschädigen vt to compensate; **Entschädigung** f compensation

entscheiden irr vt, vi to decide ▷ vr **sich ~** to decide; **sich für/gegen etw ~** to decide on/against sth; **wir haben uns entschieden, nicht zu gehen** we decided not to go; **das entscheidet sich morgen** that'll be decided tomorrow; **entscheidend** adj decisive; (Stimme) casting; (Frage, Problem) crucial; **Entscheidung** f decision

entschließen irr vr **sich ~** to decide (zu, für on), to make up one's mind; **Entschluss** m decision

entschuldigen vt to excuse ▷ vr **sich ~** to apologize; **sich bei jdm für etw ~** to apologize to sb for sth ▷ vi **entschuldige!, ~ Sie!** (vor einer Frage) excuse me; (Verzeihung!) (I'm) sorry, excuse me (US); **Entschuldigung** f apology; (Grund) excuse; **jdn um ~ bitten** to apologize to sb; **~!** (bei Zusammenstoß) (I'm) sorry, excuse me (US); (vor einer Frage) excuse me; (*wenn man etw nicht verstanden hat*) (I beg your) pardon?

entsetzlich *adj* dreadful, appalling

entsorgen *vt* to dispose of

entspannen *vt* (*Körper*) to relax; (*Pol: Lage*) to ease ▷ *vr* **sich ~** to relax; (*fam*) to chill out; **Entspannung** *f* relaxation

entsprechen *irr vi* +*dat* to correspond to; (*Anforderungen, Wünschen etc*) to comply with; **entsprechend** *adj* appropriate ▷ *adv* accordingly ▷ *prep* +*dat* according to, in accordance with

entstehen *vi* (*Schwierigkeiten*) to arise; (*gebaut werden*) to be built; (*hergestellt werden*) to be created

enttäuschen *vt* to disappoint; **Enttäuschung** *f* disappointment

entweder *conj* **~ ... oder ...** either ... or ...; **~ oder!** take it or leave it

entwerfen *irr vt* (*Möbel, Kleider*) to design; (*Plan, Vertrag*) to draft

entwerten *vt* to devalue; (*Fahrschein*) to cancel; **Entwerter** (*-s, -*) *m* ticket-cancelling machine

entwickeln *vt* (*a. Foto*) to develop; (*Mut, Energie*) to show, to display ▷ *vr* **sich ~** to develop; **Entwicklung** *f* development; (*Foto*) developing; **Entwicklungshelfer(in)** (*-s, -*) *m(f)* development worker; **Entwicklungsland** *nt* developing country

Entwurf *m* outline; (*Design*) design; (*Vertragsentwurf, Konzept*) draft

entzückend *adj* delightful, charming

Entzug *m* withdrawal; (*Behandlung*) detox; **Entzugserscheinung** *f* withdrawal symptom

entzünden *vr* **sich ~** to catch fire; (*Med*) to become inflamed; **Entzündung** *f* (*Med*) inflammation

Epidemie *f* epidemic

Epilepsie *f* epilepsy

er *pron* (*Person*) he; (*Sache*) it; **er ists** it's him; **wo ist mein Mantel? - ~ ist ...** where's my coat? - it's ...

Erbe (*-n, -n*) *m* heir ▷ (*-s*) *nt* inheritance; (*fig*) heritage; **erben** *vt* to inherit; **Erbin** *f* heiress; **erblich** *adj* hereditary

erbrechen *irr vt* to vomit ▷ *vr* **sich ~** to vomit; **Erbrechen** *nt* vomiting

Erbschaft *f* inheritance

Erbse (*-, -n*) *f* pea

Erdapfel *m* potato; **Erdbeben** *nt* earthquake; **Erdbeere** *f* strawberry; **Erde** (*-, -n*) *f* (*Planet*) earth; (*Boden*) ground; **Erdgas** *nt* natural gas; **Erdgeschoss** *nt* ground floor (*Brit*), first floor (*US*); **Erdkunde** *f* geography; **Erdnuss** *f* peanut; **Erdöl** *nt* (mineral) oil; **Erdrutsch** *m* landslide; **Erdteil** *m* continent

ereignen *vr* **sich ~** to happen, to take place; **Ereignis** *nt* event

erfahren *irr vt* to learn, to find out; (*erleben*) to experience ▷ *adj* experienced; **Erfahrung** *f* experience

erfinden *irr vt* to invent; **erfinderisch** *adj* inventive, creative; **Erfindung** *f* invention

Erfolg (*-(e)s, -e*) *m* success; (*Folge*) result; **~ versprechend** promising; **viel ~!** good luck; **erfolglos** *adj* unsuccessful; **erfolgreich** *adj* successful

erforderlich *adj* necessary

erforschen *vt* to explore; (*untersuchen*) investigate

erfreulich *adj* pleasing, pleasant; (*Nachricht*) good; **erfreulicherweise** *adv* fortunately

erfrieren *irr vi* to freeze to death; (*Pflanzen*) to be killed by frost

Erfrischung *f* refreshment

erfüllen *vt* (*Raum*) to fill; (*Bitte, Wunsch etc*) to fulfil ▷ *vr* **sich ~** to come true

ergänzen *vt* (*hinzufügen*) to add; (*vervollständigen*) to complete ▷ *vr* **sich ~** to complement one another; **Ergänzung** *f* completion; (*Zusatz*) supplement

ergeben *irr vt* (*Betrag*) to come to; (*zum Ergebnis haben*) to result in ▷ *irr vr* **sich ~** to surrender; (*folgen*) to result (*aus from*) ▷ *adj* devoted; (*demütig*) humble

Ergebnis *nt* result

ergreifen *irr vt* to seize; (*Beruf*) to take up; (*Maßnahme, Gelegenheit*) to take; (*rühren*) to move

erhalten *irr vt* (*bekommen*) to receive; (*bewahren*) to preserve; **gut ~ sein** to be in good condition; **erhältlich** *adj* available

erheblich *adj* considerable

erhitzen *vt* to heat (up)

erhöhen *vt* to raise; (*verstärken*) to increase ▷ *vr* **sich ~** to increase

erholen *vr* **sich ~** to recover; (*sich ausruhen*) to have a rest; **erholsam** *adj* restful; **Erholung** f recovery; (*Entspannung*) relaxation, rest

erinnern vt to remind (*an +akk* of) ▷ vr **sich ~** to remember (*an etw akk* sth); **Erinnerung** f memory; (*Andenken*) souvenir; (*Mahnung*) reminder

erkälten vr **sich ~** to catch a cold; **erkältet** adj (**stark**) **~ sein** to have a (bad) cold; **Erkältung** f cold

erkennen irr vt to recognize; (*sehen, verstehen*) to see; **~, dass ...** to realize that ...; **erkenntlich** adj **sich ~ zeigen** to show one's appreciation

Erker (*-s, -*) m bay

erklären vt to explain; (*kundtun*) to declare; **Erklärung** f explanation; (*Aussage*) declaration

erkundigen vr **sich ~** to enquire (*nach* about)

erlauben vt to allow, to permit; **jdm ~, etw zu tun** to allow (*o* permit) sb to do sth; **sich** (*dat*) **etw ~** to permit oneself sth; **~ Sie(, dass ich rauche)?** do you mind (if I smoke)?; **was ~ Sie sich?** what do you think you're doing?; **Erlaubnis** f permission

Erläuterung f explanation; (*zu Text*) comment

erleben vt to experience; (*schöne Tage etc*) to have; (*Schlimmes*) to go through; (*miterleben*) to witness; (*noch miterleben*) to live to see; **Erlebnis** nt experience

erledigen vt (*Angelegenheit, Aufgabe*) to deal with; (*fam: ruinieren*) to finish; **erledigt** adj (*beendet*) finished; (*gelöst*) dealt with; (*fam: erschöpft*) whacked, knackered (Brit)

erleichtert adj relieved

Erlös (*-es, -e*) m proceeds pl

ermahnen vt (*warnend*) to warn

ermäßigt adj reduced; **Ermäßigung** f reduction

ermitteln vt to find out; (*Täter*) to trace ▷ vi (*Jur*) to investigate

ermöglichen vt to make possible (*dat* for)

ermorden vt to murder

ermüdend adj tiring

ermutigen vt to encourage

ernähren vt to feed; (*Familie*) to support ▷ vr **sich ~** to support oneself; **sich ~ von** to live on; **Ernährung** f (*Essen*) food; **Ernährungsberater(in)** m(f) nutritional (*o* dietary) adviser

erneuern vt to renew; (*restaurieren*) to restore; (*renovieren*) to renovate; (*auswechseln*) to replace

ernst adj serious ▷ adv **jdn/etw ~ nehmen** take sb/sth seriously; **Ernst** (*-es*) m seriousness; **das ist mein ~** I'm quite serious; **im ~?** seriously?; **ernsthaft** adj serious ▷ adv seriously

Ernte (*-, -n*) f harvest; **Erntedankfest** nt harvest festival (Brit), Thanksgiving (Day) (US: 4. Donnerstag im November); **ernten** vt to harvest; (*Lob etc*) to earn

erobern vt to conquer

eröffnen vt to open; **Eröffnung** f opening

erogen adj erogenous

erotisch adj erotic

erpressen vt (*jdn*) to blackmail; (*Geld etc*) to extort; **Erpressung** f blackmail; (*von Geld*) extortion

erraten irr vt to guess

erregen vt to excite; (*sexuell*) to arouse; (*ärgern*) to annoy; (*hervorrufen*) to arouse ▷ vr **sich ~** to get worked up; **Erreger** (*-s, -*) m (Med) germ; (*Virus*) virus

erreichbar adj **~ sein** to be within reach; (*Person*) to be available; **das Stadtzentrum ist zu Fuß/mit dem Wagen leicht ~** the city centre is within easy walking/driving distance; **erreichen** vt to reach; (*Zug etc*) to catch

Ersatz (*-es*) m replacement; (*auf Zeit*) substitute; (*Ausgleich*) compensation; **Ersatzreifen** m (Auto) spare tyre; **Ersatzteil** nt spare (part)

erscheinen irr vi to appear; (*wirken*) to seem

erschöpft adj exhausted; **Erschöpfung** f exhaustion

erschrecken vt to frighten ▷ (*erschrak, erschrocken*) vi to get a fright; **erschreckend** adj alarming; **erschrocken** adj frightened

erschwinglich adj affordable

ersetzen vt to replace; (*Auslagen*) to reimburse

○ **SCHLÜSSELWORT**

erst adv **1** first; **mach erst mal die Arbeit fertig** finish your work first; **wenn du das erst mal hinter dir hast** once you've got that behind you

2 (*nicht früher als, nur*) only; (*nicht bis*) not

till; **erst gestern** only yesterday; **erst morgen** not until tomorrow; **erst als** only when not until; **wir fahren erst später** we're not going until later; **er ist (gerade) erst angekommen** he's only just arrived

3: **wäre er doch erst zurück!** if only he were back!

erstatten vt (Kosten) to refund; **Bericht ~** to report (über +akk on); **Anzeige gegen jdn ~** to report sb to the police

erstaunlich adj astonishing; **erstaunt** adj surprised

erstbeste(r, s) adj **das ~ Hotel** any old hotel; **der Erstbeste** just anyone

erste(r, s) adj first; siehe auch dritte **zum ~n Mal** for the first time; **er wurde Erster** he came first; **auf den ~n Blick** at first sight

erstens adv first(ly), in the first place

ersticken vi (Mensch) to suffocate; **in Arbeit ~** to be snowed under with work

erstklassig adj first-class; **erstmals** adv for the first time

erstrecken vr **sich ~** to extend, to stretch (auf +akk to; über +akk over)

ertappen vt to catch

erteilen vt (Rat, Erlaubnis) to give

Ertrag (-(e)s, Erträge) m yield; (Gewinn) proceeds pl; **ertragen** irr vt (Schmerzen) to bear, to stand; (dulden) to put up with; **erträglich** adj bearable; (nicht zu schlecht) tolerable

ertrinken irr vi to drown

erwachsen adj grown-up; **~ werden** to grow up; **Erwachsene(r)** mf adult, grown-up

erwähnen vt to mention

erwarten vt to expect; (warten auf) to wait for; **ich kann den Sommer kaum ~** I can hardly wait for the summer

erwerbstätig adj employed

erwidern vt to reply; (Gruß, Besuch) to return

erwischen vt (fam) to catch (bei etw doing sth)

erwünscht adj desired; (willkommen) welcome

Erz (-es, -e) nt ore

erzählen vt to tell (jdm etw sb sth); **Erzählung** f story, tale

erzeugen vt to produce; (Strom) to generate; **Erzeugnis** nt product

erziehen irr vt to bring up; (geistig) to educate; (Tier) to train; **Erzieher(in)** (-s, -) m(f) educator; (Kindergarten) (nursery school) teacher; **Erziehung** f upbringing; (Bildung) education

es pron (Sache, im Nom und Akk) it; (Baby, Tier) he/she; **ich bin ~** it's me; **~ ist kalt** it's cold; **~ gibt ...** there is .../there are ...; **ich hoffe ~** I hope so; **ich kann ~** I can do it

Escape-Taste f (Inform) escape key

Esel (-s, -) m donkey

Espresso (-s, -) m espresso

essbar adj edible; **essen** (aß, gegessen) vt, vi to eat; **zu Mittag/Abend ~** to have lunch/dinner; **was gibt's zu ~?** what's for lunch/dinner?; **~ gehen** to eat out; **gegessen sein** (fig, fam) to be history; **Essen** (-s, -) nt (Mahlzeit) meal; (Nahrung) food

Essig (-s, -e) m vinegar; **Essiggurke** f gherkin

Esslöffel m dessert spoon; **Esszimmer** nt dining room

Estland nt Estonia

Etage (-, -n) f floor, storey; **in** (o **auf**) **der ersten ~** on the first (Brit) (o second (US)) floor; **Etagenbett** nt bunk bed

Etappe (-, -n) f stage

ethnisch adj ethnic

Etikett (-(e)s, -e) nt label

etliche pron pl several, quite a few; **etliches** pron quite a lot

etwa adv (ungefähr) about; (vielleicht) perhaps; (beispielsweise) for instance

etwas pron something; (verneinend, fragend) anything; (ein wenig) a little; **~ Neues** something/anything new; **~ zu essen** something to eat; **~ Salz** some salt; **wenn ich noch ~ tun kann ...** if I can do anything else ... ▷ adv a bit, a little; **~ mehr** a little more

EU (-) f abk = **Europäische Union** EU

euch pron akk, dat von **ihr**; you, (to) you; **~ (selbst)** (reflexiv) yourselves; **wo kann ich ~ treffen?** where can I meet you?; **sie schickt es ~** she'll send it to you; **ein Freund von ~** a friend of yours; **setzt ~ bitte** please sit down; **habt ihr ~ amüsiert?** did you enjoy yourselves?

euer pron (adjektivisch) your; **~ David** (am

Briefende) Yours, David ▷ *pron gen von* **ihr**; of you; **euere(r, s)** *pron siehe* **eure**

Eule *(-, -n) f* owl

eure(r, s) *pron (substantivisch)* yours; **das ist ~** that's yours; **euretwegen** *adv (wegen euch)* because of you; *(euch zuliebe)* for your sake; *(um euch)* about you

Euro *(-, -) m (Währung)* euro; **Eurocent** *m* eurocent; **Eurocity** *(-(s), -s) m*, **Eurocityzug** *m* European Intercity train; **Europa** *(-s) nt* Europe; **Europäer(in)** *(-s, -) m(f)* European; **europäisch** *adj* European; **Europäische Union** European Union; **Europameister(in)** *m(f)* European champion; *(Mannschaft)* European champions *pl*; **Europaparlament** *nt* European Parliament

Euter *(-s, -) nt* udder

evangelisch *adj* Protestant

eventuell *adj* possible ▷ *adv* possibly, perhaps

ewig *adj* eternal; **er hat ~ gebraucht** it took him ages; **Ewigkeit** *f* eternity

Ex- *in zW* ex-, former; **~frau** ex-wife; **~minister** former minister

exakt *adj* precise

Examen *(-s, -) nt* exam

Exemplar *(-s, -e) nt* specimen; *(Buch)* copy

Exil *(-s, -e) nt* exile

Existenz *f* existence; *(Unterhalt)* livelihood, living; **existieren** *vi* to exist

exklusiv *adj* exclusive; **exklusive** *adv*, *prep +gen* excluding

exotisch *adj* exotic

Experte *(-n, -n) m*, **Expertin** *f* expert

explodieren *vi* to explode; **Explosion** *f* explosion

Export *(-(e)s, -e) m* export; **exportieren** *vt* to export

Express *(-es) m*, **Expresszug** *m* express (train)

extra *adj inv (fam: gesondert)* separate; *(zusätzlich)* extra ▷ *adv (gesondert)* separately; *(speziell)* specially; *(absichtlich)* on purpose; **Extra** *(-s, -s) nt* extra

extrem *adj* extreme ▷ *adv* extremely; **~ kalt** extremely cold

exzellent *adj* excellent

Eyeliner *(-s, -) m* eyeliner

e

f

fabelhaft *adj* fabulous, marvellous

Fabrik *f* factory

Fach (*-(e)s, Fächer*) *nt* compartment; (*Schulfach, Sachgebiet*) subject; **Facharzt** *m*, **Fachärztin** *f* specialist; **Fachausdruck** (*-s, Fachausdrücke*) *m* technical term

Fächer (*-s, -*) *m* fan

Fachfrau *f* specialist, expert; **Fachmann** (*-leute*) *m* specialist, expert; **Fachwerkhaus** *nt* half-timbered house

Fackel (*-, -n*) *f* torch

fad(e) *adj* (*Essen*) bland; (*langweilig*) dull

Faden (*-s, Fäden*) *m* thread

fähig *adj* capable (*zu, gen* of); **Fähigkeit** *f* ability

Fahndung *f* search

Fahne (*-, -n*) *f* flag

Fahrausweis *m* ticket; **Fahrausweisautomat** *m* ticket machine; **Fahrausweiskontrolle** *f* ticket inspection

Fahrbahn *f* road; (*Spur*) lane

Fähre (*-, -n*) *f* ferry

fahren (*fuhr, gefahren*) *vt* to drive; (*Rad*) to ride; (*befördern*) to drive, to take; **50 km/h ~** to drive at (*o* do) 50 kph ▷ *vi* (*sich bewegen*) to go; (*Autofahrer*) to drive; (*Schiff*) to sail; (*abfahren*) to leave; **mit dem Auto/Zug ~** to go by car/train; **rechts ~!** keep to the right; **Fahrer(in)** (*-s, -*) *m(f)* driver; **Fahrerairbag** *m* driver airbag; **Fahrerflucht** *f* **~ begehen** to fail to stop after an accident; **Fahrersitz** *m* driver's seat

Fahrgast *m* passenger; **Fahrgeld** *nt* fare; **Fahrgemeinschaft** *f* car pool; **Fahrkarte** *f* ticket; **Fahrkartenautomat** *m* ticket machine; **Fahrkartenschalter** *m* ticket office

fahrlässig *adj* negligent

Fahrlehrer(in) *m(f)* driving instructor; **Fahrplan** *m* timetable; **Fahrplanauszug** *m* individual timetable; **fahrplanmäßig** *adj* (*Eisenb*) scheduled; **Fahrpreis** *m* fare; **Fahrpreisermäßigung** *f* fare reduction; **Fahrrad** *nt* bicycle; **Fahrradschlauch** *m* bicycle tube; **Fahrradschloss** *nt* bicycle lock; **Fahrradverleih** *m* cycle hire (*Brit*) (*o* rental (*US*)); **Fahrradweg** *m* cycle path; **Fahrschein** *m* ticket; **Fahrscheinautomat** *m* ticket machine; **Fahrscheinentwerter** *m* ticket-cancelling machine; **Fahrschule** *f* driving school; **Fahrschüler(in)** *m(f)* learner (driver) (*Brit*), student driver (*US*); **Fahrspur** *f* lane; **Fahrstreifen** *m* lane; **Fahrstuhl** *m* lift (*Brit*), elevator (*US*)

Fahrt (*-, -en*) *f* journey; (*kurz*) trip; (*Auto*) drive; **auf der ~ nach London** on the way to London; **nach drei Stunden ~** after travelling for three hours; **gute ~!** have a good trip; **Fahrtkosten** *pl* travelling expenses *pl*; **Fahrtrichtung** *f* direction of travel

fahrtüchtig *f* (*Person*) fit to drive; (*Fahrzeug*) roadworthy

Fahrtunterbrechung *f* break in the journey, stop

Fahrverbot *nt* **~ erhalten/haben** to be banned from driving; **Fahrzeug** *nt* vehicle; **Fahrzeugbrief** *m* (vehicle) registration document; **Fahrzeughalter(in)** *m(f)* registered owner; **Fahrzeugpapiere** *pl* vehicle documents *pl*

fair *adj* fair

Fakultät *f* faculty

Falke (*-n, -n*) *m* falcon

Fall (*-(e)s, Fälle*) *m* (*Sturz*) fall; (*Sachverhalt, juristisch*) case; **auf jeden ~, auf alle Fälle**

in any case; (*bestimmt*) definitely; **auf keinen ~** on no account; **für den ~, dass ...** in case ...

Falle (-, -*n*) *f* trap

fallen (*fiel*, *gefallen*) *vi* to fall; **etw ~ lassen** to drop sth

fällig *adj* due

falls *adv* if; (*für den Fall, dass*) in case

Fallschirm *m* parachute; **Fallschirmspringen** *nt* parachuting, parachute jumping; **Fallschirmspringer(in)** *m(f)* parachutist

falsch *adj* (*unrichtig*) wrong; (*unehrlich, unecht*) false; (*Schmuck*) fake; **~ verbunden** sorry, wrong number; **fälschen** *vt* to forge; **Falschfahrer(in)** *m(f)* person driving the wrong way on the motorway; **Falschgeld** *nt* counterfeit money; **Fälschung** *f* forgery, fake

Faltblatt *nt* leaflet

Falte (-, -*n*) *f* (*Knick*) fold; (*Haut*) wrinkle; (*Rock*) pleat; (*Bügel*) crease; **falten** *vt* to fold; **faltig** *adj* (*zerknittert*) creased; (*Haut, Gesicht*) wrinkled

Familie *f* family; **Familienangehörige(r)** *mf* family member; **Familienname** *m* surname; **Familienstand** *m* marital status

Fan (-s, -s) *m* fan

fand *imperf von* **finden**

fangen (*fing, gefangen*) *vt* to catch ▷ *vr* **sich ~** (*nicht fallen*) to steady oneself; (*fig*) to compose oneself

Fantasie *f* imagination

fantastisch *adj* fantastic

Farbbild *nt* colour photograph; **Farbdrucker** *m* colour printer; **Farbe** (-, -*n*) *f* colour; (*zum Malen etc*) paint; (*für Stoff*) dye; **farbecht** *adj* colourfast; **färben** *vt* to colour; (*Stoff, Haar*) to dye; **Farbfernsehen** *nt* colour television; **Farbfilm** *m* colour film; **Farbfoto** *nt* colour photo; **farbig** *adj* coloured; **Farbkopierer** *m* colour copier; **farblos** *adj* colourless; **Farbstoff** *m* dye; (*für Lebensmittel*) colouring

Farn (-(*e*)s, -*e*) *m* fern

Fasan (-(*e*)s, -*e*(*n*)) *m* pheasant

Fasching (-s, -*e*) *m* carnival, Mardi Gras (US); **Faschingsdienstag** (-s, -*e*) *m* Shrove Tuesday, Mardi Gras (US)

Faschismus *m* fascism

Faser (-, -*n*) *f* fibre

Fass (-es, *Fässer*) *nt* barrel; (*Öl*) drum

fassen *vt* (*ergreifen*) to grasp; (*enthalten*) to hold; (*Entschluss*) to take; (*verstehen*) to understand; **nicht zu ~!** unbelievable ▷ *vr* **sich ~** to compose oneself; **Fassung** *f* (*Umrahmung*) mount; (*Brille*) frame; (*Lampe*) socket; (*Wortlaut*) version; (*Beherrschung*) composure; **jdn aus der ~ bringen** to throw sb; **die ~ verlieren** to lose one's cool

fast *adv* almost, nearly

fasten *vi* to fast; **Fastenzeit** *f* **die ~** (*christlich*) Lent; (*muslimisch*) Ramadan

Fast Food (-s) *nt* fast food

Fastnacht *f* (*Fasching*) carnival

fatal *adj* (*verhängnisvoll*) disastrous; (*peinlich*) embarrassing

faul *adj* (*Obst, Gemüse*) rotten; (*Mensch*) lazy; (*Ausreden*) lame; **faulen** *vi* to rot

faulenzen *vi* to do nothing, to hang around; **Faulheit** *f* laziness

faulig *adj* rotten; (*Geruch, Geschmack*) foul

Faust (-, *Fäuste*) *f* fist; **Fausthandschuh** *m* mitten

Fax (-, -(*e*)) *nt* fax; **faxen** *vi, vt* to fax; **Faxgerät** *nt* fax machine; **Faxnummer** *f* fax number

FCKW (-, -s) *nt abk =* **Fluorchlorkohlenwasserstoff** CFC

Februar (-(*s*), -*e*) *m* February; *siehe auch* **Juni**

Fechten *nt* fencing

Feder (-, -*n*) *f* feather; (*Schreibfeder*) (pen-)nib; (*Tech*) spring; **Federball** *m* (*Ball*) shuttlecock; (*Spiel*) badminton; **Federung** *f* suspension

Fee (-, -*n*) *f* fairy

fegen *vi, vt* to sweep

fehl *adj* **~ am Platz** (*o Ort*) out of place

fehlen *vi* (*abwesend sein*) to be absent; **etw fehlt jdm** sb lacks sth; **was fehlt ihm?** what's wrong with him?; **du fehlst mir** I miss you; **es fehlt an ...** there's no...

Fehler (-s, -) *m* mistake, error; (*Mangel, Schwäche*) fault; **Fehlermeldung** *f* (*Inform*) error message

Fehlzündung *f* (*Auto*) misfire

Feier (-, -*n*) *f* celebration; (*Party*) party; **Feierabend** *m* end of the working day; **~ haben** to finish work; **nach ~** after work; **feierlich** *adj* solemn; **feiern** *vt, vi* to celebrate, to have a party; **Feiertag** *m*

holiday; **gesetzlicher ~** public (*o* bank (*Brit*) *o* legal (*US*)) holiday

feig(e) *adj* cowardly

Feige (*-, -n*) *f* fig

Feigling *m* coward

Feile (*-, -n*) *f* file

fein *adj* fine; (*vornehm*) refined; **~!** great!; **das schmeckt ~** that tastes delicious

Feind(in) (*-(e)s, -e*) *m(f)* enemy; **feindlich** *adj* hostile

Feinkost (*-*) *f* delicacies *pl*; **Feinkostladen** *m* delicatessen; **Feinschmecker(in)** (*-s, -*) *m(f)* gourmet

Feinwaschmittel *nt* washing powder for delicate fabrics

Feld (*-(e)s, -er*) *nt* field; (*Schach*) square; (*Sport*) pitch; **Feldsalat** *m* lamb's lettuce; **Feldweg** *m* path across the fields

Felge (*-, -n*) *f* (wheel) rim

Fell (*-(e)s, -e*) *nt* fur; (*von Schaf*) fleece

Fels (*-en, -en*) *m*, **Felsen** (*-s, -*) *m* rock; (*Klippe*) cliff; **felsig** *adj* rocky

feminin *adj* feminine; **Femininum** (*-s, Feminina*) *nt* (*Ling*) feminine noun

feministisch *adj* feminist

Fenchel (*-s, -*) *m* fennel

Fenster (*-s, -*) *nt* window; **Fensterbrett** *nt* windowsill; **Fensterladen** *m* shutter; **Fensterplatz** *m* windowseat; **Fensterscheibe** *f* windowpane

Ferien *pl* holidays *pl* (*Brit*), vacation *sing* (*US*); **~ haben/machen** to be/go on holiday (*Brit*) (*o* vacation (*US*)); **Ferienhaus** *nt* holiday (*Brit*) (*o* vacation (*US*)) home; **Ferienkurs** *m* holiday (*Brit*) (*o* vacation (*US*)) course; **Ferienlager** *nt* holiday camp (*Brit*), vacation camp (*US*); (*für Kinder im Sommer*) summer camp; **Ferienort** *m* holiday (*Brit*) (*o* vacation (*US*)) resort; **Ferienwohnung** *f* holiday flat (*Brit*), vacation apartment (*US*)

Ferkel (*-s, -*) *nt* piglet

fern *adj* distant, far-off; **von ~** from a distance; **Fernabfrage** *f* remote-control access; **Fernbedienung** *f* remote control; **Ferne** *f* distance; **aus der ~** from a distance

ferner *adj, adv* further; (*außerdem*) besides

Fernflug *m* long-distance flight; **Ferngespräch** *nt* long-distance call; **ferngesteuert** *adj* remote-controlled; **Fernglas** *nt* binoculars *pl*; **Fernlicht** *nt* full beam (*Brit*), high beam (*US*)

Fernsehapparat *m* TV (set); **fern|sehen** *irr vi* to watch television; **Fernsehen** *nt* television; **im ~** on television; **Fernseher** *m* TV (set); **Fernsehkanal** *m* TV channel; **Fernsehprogramm** *nt* (*Sendung*) TV programme; (*Zeitschrift*) TV guide; **Fernsehserie** *f* TV series *sing*; **Fernsehturm** *m* TV tower; **Fernsehzeitschrift** *f* TV guide

Fernstraße *f* major road; **Ferntourismus** *m* long-haul tourism; **Fernverkehr** *m* long-distance traffic

Ferse (*-, -n*) *f* heel

fertig *adj* (*bereit*) ready; (*beendet*) finished; (*gebrauchsfertig*) ready-made; **~ machen** (*beenden*) to finish; **jdn ~ machen** (*kritisieren*) to give sb hell; (*zur Verzweiflung bringen*) to drive sb mad; (*deprimieren*) to get sb down; **sich ~ machen** to get ready; **mit etw ~ werden** to be able to cope with sth; **auf die Plätze, ~, los!** on your marks, get set, go!; **Fertiggericht** *nt* ready meal

fest *adj* firm; (*Nahrung*) solid; (*Gehalt*) regular; (*Schuhe*) sturdy; (*Schlaf*) sound

Fest (*-(e)s, -e*) *nt* party; (*Rel*) festival

Festbetrag *m* fixed amount

fest|binden *irr vt* to tie (*an +dat* to); **fest|halten** *irr vt* to hold onto ▷ *vr* **sich ~** to hold on (*an +dat* to)

Festiger (*-s, -*) *m* setting lotion

Festival (*-s, -s*) *nt* festival

Festland *nt* mainland; **das europäische ~** the (European) continent

fest|legen *vt* to fix ▷ *vr* **sich ~** to commit oneself

festlich *adj* festive

fest|machen *vt* to fasten; (*Termin etc*) to fix; **fest|nehmen** *irr vt* to arrest; **Festnetz** *nt* (*Tel*) fixed-line network; **Festplatte** *f* (*Inform*) hard disk

fest|setzen *vt* to fix

Festspiele *pl* festival *sing*

fest|stehen *irr vi* to be fixed

fest|stellen *vt* to establish; (*sagen*) to remark

Feststelltaste *f* shift lock

Festung *f* fortress

Festzelt *nt* marquee

Fete (*-, -n*) *f* party

fett *adj* (*dick*) fat; (*Essen etc*) greasy; (*Schrift*) bold; **Fett** (*-(e)s, -e*) *nt* fat; (*Tech*) grease; **fettarm** *adj* low-fat; **fettig** *adj* fatty; (*schmierig*) greasy

fetzig adj (fam: Musik) funky
feucht adj damp; (Luft) humid;
Feuchtigkeit f dampness;
(Luftfeuchtigkeit) humidity;
Feuchtigkeitscreme f moisturizing
cream
Feuer (-s, -) nt fire; **haben Sie ~?** have you
got a light?; **Feueralarm** m fire alarm;
feuerfest adj fireproof; **feuergefährlich**
adj inflammable; **Feuerlöscher** (-s, -) m
fire extinguisher; **Feuermelder** (-s, -) m
fire alarm; **Feuertreppe** f fire escape;
Feuerwehr (-, -en) f fire brigade;
Feuerwehrfrau f firewoman, fire
fighter; **Feuerwehrmann** m fireman,
fire fighter; **Feuerwerk** nt fireworks pl;
Feuerzeug nt (cigarette) lighter
Fichte (-, -n) f spruce
ficken vt, vi (vulg) to fuck
Fieber (-s, -) nt temperature, fever;
~ haben to have a high temperature;
Fieberthermometer nt thermometer
fiel imperf von **fallen**
fies adj (fam) nasty
Figur (-, -en) f figure; (im Schach) piece
Filet (-s, -s) nt fillet; **filetieren** vt to
fillet; **Filetsteak** nt fillet steak
Filiale (-, -n) f (Comm) branch
Film (-(e)s, -e) m film, movie; **filmen** vt, vi
to film
Filter (-s, -) m filter; **Filterkaffee** m filter
coffee; **filtern** vt to filter; **Filterpapier**
nt filter paper
Filz (-es, -e) m felt; **Filzschreiber** m,
Filzstift m felt(-tip) pen, felt-tip
Finale (-s, -) nt (Sport) final
Finanzamt nt tax office; **finanziell** adj
financial; **finanzieren** vt to finance
finden (fand, gefunden) vt to find; (meinen)
to think; **ich finde nichts dabei, wenn ...**
I don't see what's wrong if ...; **ich finde es
gut/schlecht** I like/don't like it ▷ vr **es
fanden sich nur wenige Helfer** there
were only a few helpers
fing imperf von **fangen**
Finger (-s, -) m finger; **Fingerabdruck** m
fingerprint; **Fingerhandschuh** m glove;
Fingernagel m fingernail
Fink (-en, -en) m finch
Finne (-n, -n) m, **Finnin** f Finn, Finnish
man/woman; **finnisch** adj Finnish;
Finnisch nt Finnish; **Finnland** nt Finland
finster adj dark; (verdächtig) dubious;

(verdrossen) grim; (Gedanke) dark;
Finsternis f darkness
Firewall (-, -s) f (Inform) firewall
Firma (-, Firmen) f firm
Fisch (-(e)s, -e) m fish; **~ pl** (Astr) Pisces
sing; **fischen** vt, vi to fish; **Fischer(in)**
(-s, -) m(f) fisherman/-woman;
Fischerboot nt fishing boat; **Fischgericht**
nt fish dish; **Fischhändler(in)** m(f)
fishmonger; **Fischstäbchen** nt fish
finger (Brit) (o stick (US))
Fisole (-, -n) f French bean
fit adj fit; **Fitness** (-) f fitness;
Fitnesscenter (-s, -) nt fitness centre
fix adj (schnell) quick; **~ und fertig**
exhausted
fixen vi (fam) to shoot up; **Fixer(in)** (-s, -)
m(f) (fam) junkie
FKK f abk = **Freikörperkultur** nudism;
FKK-Strand m nudist beach
flach adj flat; (Gewässer, Teller) shallow; **~er
Absatz** low heel; **Flachbildschirm** m flat
screen
Fläche (-, -n) f area; (Oberfläche) surface
Flagge (-, -n) f flag
flambiert adj flambé(ed)
Flamme (-, -n) f flame
Flanell (-s) m flannel
Flasche (-, -n) f bottle; **eine ~ sein** (fam)
to be useless; **Flaschenbier** nt bottled
beer; **Flaschenöffner** m bottle opener;
Flaschenpfand nt deposit;
Flaschentomate f plum tomato
flatterhaft adj fickle; **flattern** vi to
flutter
flauschig adj fluffy
Flausen pl (fam) daft ideas pl
Flaute (-, -n) f calm; (Comm) recession
Flechte (-, -n) f plait; (Med) scab; (Bot)
lichen; **flechten** (flocht, geflochten) vt to
plait; (Kranz) to bind
Fleck (-(e)s, -e) m, **Flecken** (-s, -) m spot;
(Schmutz) stain; (Stoff~) patch; (Makel)
blemish; **Fleckentferner** (-s, -) m stain
remover; **fleckig** adj spotted; (mit
Schmutzflecken) stained
Fledermaus f bat
Fleisch (-(e)s) nt flesh; (Essen) meat;
Fleischbrühe f meat stock; **Fleischer(in)**
(-s, -) m(f) butcher; **Fleischerei** f
butcher's (shop); **Fleischtomate** f beef
tomato
fleißig adj diligent, hard-working

flexibel adj flexible

flicken vt to mend; **Flickzeug** nt repair kit

Flieder (-s, -) m lilac

Fliege (-, -n) f fly; (Krawatte) bow tie

fliegen (flog, geflogen) vt, vi to fly

Fliese (-, -n) f tile

Fließband nt conveyor belt; (als Einrichtung) production (o assembly) line; **fließen** (floss, geflossen) vi to flow; **fließend** adj (Rede, Deutsch) fluent; (Übergänge) smooth; **~(es) Wasser** running water

Flipper (-s, -) m pinball machine; **flippern** vi to play pinball

flippig adj (fam) eccentric

flirten vi to flirt

Flitterwochen pl honeymoon sing

flocht imperf von **flechten**

Flocke (-, -n) f flake

flog imperf von **fliegen**

Floh (-(e)s, Flöhe) m flea; **Flohmarkt** m flea market

Flop (-s, -s) m flop

Floskel (-, -n) f empty phrase

floss imperf von **fließen**

Floß (-es, Flöße) nt raft

Flosse (-, -n) f fin; (Schwimmflosse) flipper

Flöte (-, -n) f flute; (Blockflöte) recorder

flott adj lively; (elegant) smart; (Naut) afloat

Fluch (-(e)s, Flüche) m curse; **fluchen** vi to swear, to curse

Flucht (-, -en) f flight; **flüchten** vi to flee (vor +dat from); **flüchtig** adj **ich kenne ihn nur ~** I don't know him very well at all; **Flüchtling** m refugee

Flug (-(e)s, Flüge) m flight; **Flugbegleiter(in)** (-s, -) m(f) flight attendant; **Flugblatt** nt leaflet

Flügel (-s, -) m wing; (Mus) grand piano

Fluggast m passenger (on a plane); **Fluggesellschaft** f airline; **Flughafen** m airport; **Fluglotse** m air-traffic controller; **Flugnummer** f flight number; **Flugplan** m flight schedule; **Flugplatz** m airport; (klein) airfield; **Flugschein** m plane ticket; **Flugschreiber** m flight recorder, black box; **Flugsteig** (-s, -e) m gate; **Flugstrecke** f air route; **Flugticket** nt plane ticket; **Flugverbindung** f flight connection; **Flugverkehr** m air traffic; **Flugzeit** f flying time; **Flugzeug** nt plane; **Flugzeugentführung** f hijacking

Flunder (-, -n) f flounder

Fluor (-s) nt fluorine

Flur (-(e)s, -e) m hall

Fluss (-es, Flüsse) m river; (Fließen) flow

flüssig adj liquid; **Flüssigkeit** f liquid

flüstern vt, vi to whisper

Flut (-, -en) f (a. fig) flood; (Gezeiten) high tide; **Flutlicht** nt floodlight

Fohlen (-s, -) nt foal

Föhn (-(e)s, -e) m hairdryer; (Wind) foehn; **föhnen** vt to dry; (beim Friseur) to blow-dry

Folge (-, -n) f (Reihe, Serie) series sing; (Aufeinanderfolge) sequence; (Fortsetzung eines Romans) instalment; (Fortsetzung einer Fernsehserie) episode; (Auswirkung) result; **etw zur ~ haben** to result in sth; **~n haben** to have consequences; **folgen** vi to follow (jdm sb); (gehorchen) to obey (jdm sb); **jdm ~ können** (fig) to be able to follow sb; **folgend** adj following; **folgendermaßen** adv as follows; **folglich** adv consequently

Folie f foil; (für Projektor) transparency

Fön® m siehe **Föhn**

Fondue (-s, -s) nt fondue

fönen vt siehe **föhnen**

fordern vt to demand

fördern vt to promote; (unterstützen) to help

Forderung f demand

Forelle f trout

Form (-, -en) f form; (Gestalt) shape; (Gussform) mould; (Backform) baking tin (Brit) (o pan (US)); **in ~ sein** to be in good form; **Formalität** f formality; **Format** nt format; **von internationalem ~** of international standing; **formatieren** vt (Diskette) to format; (Text) to edit

Formblatt nt form; **formen** vt to form, to shape; **förmlich** adj formal; (buchstäblich) real; **formlos** adj informal; **Formular** (-s, -e) nt form; **formulieren** vt to formulate

forschen vi to search (nach for); (wissenschaftlich) to (do) research; **Forscher(in)** m(f) researcher; **Forschung** f research

Förster(in) (-s, -) m(f) forester; (für Wild) gamekeeper

fort adv away; (verschwunden) gone; **fort|bewegen** vt to move away ▷ vr **sich ~** to move; **Fortbildung** f further education; (*im Beruf*) further training; **fort|fahren** *irr vi* to go away; (*weitermachen*) to continue; **fort|gehen** *irr vi* to go away; **fortgeschritten** *adj* advanced; **Fortpflanzung** *f* reproduction

Fortschritt *m* progress; **-e machen** to make progress; **fortschrittlich** *adj* progressive

fort|setzen *vt* to continue; **Fortsetzung** *f* continuation; (*folgender Teil*) instalment; **- folgt** to be continued

Foto (*-s, -s*) *nt* photo ▷ (*-s, -s*) *m* (*Fotoapparat*) camera; **Fotograf(in)** (*-en, -en*) *m(f)* photographer; **Fotografie** *f* photography; (*Bild*) photograph; **fotografieren** *vt* to photograph ▷ *vi* to take photographs; **Fotokopie** *f* photocopy; **fotokopieren** *vt* to photocopy

Foul (*-s, -s*) *nt* foul

Foyer (*-s, -s*) *nt* foyer

Fr. *f abk=***Frau** Mrs; (*unverheiratet, neutral*) Ms

Fracht (*-, -en*) *f* freight; (*Naut*) cargo; (*Preis*) carriage; **Frachter** (*-s, -*) *m* freighter

Frack (*-(e)s, Fräcke*) *m* tails *pl*

Frage (*-, -n*) *f* question; **das ist eine - der Zeit** that's a matter (*o* question) of time; **das kommt nicht in -** that's out of the question; **Fragebogen** *m* questionnaire; **fragen** *vt, vi* to ask; **Fragezeichen** *nt* question mark; **fragwürdig** *adj* dubious

Franken (*-s, -*) *m* (*Schweizer Währung*) Swiss franc ▷ (*-s*) *nt* (*Land*) Franconia

frankieren *vt* to stamp; (*maschinell*) to frank

Frankreich (*-s*) *nt* France; **Franzose** (*-n, -n*) *m*, **Französin** *f* Frenchman/-woman; **die ~n** *pl* the French *pl*; **französisch** *adj* French; **Französisch** *nt* French

fraß *imperf von* **fressen**

Frau (*-, -en*) *f* woman; (*Ehefrau*) wife; (*Anrede*) Mrs; (*unverheiratet, neutral*) Ms; **Frauenarzt** *m*, **Frauenärztin** *f* gynaecologist; **Frauenbewegung** *f* women's movement; **frauenfeindlich** *adj* misogynous; **Frauenhaus** *nt* refuge (for battered women)

Fräulein *nt* (*junge Dame*) young lady; (*veraltet als Anrede*) Miss

Freak (*-s, -s*) *m* (*fam*) freak

frech *adj* cheeky; **Frechheit** *f* cheek; **so eine ~!** what a cheek

Freeclimbing (*-s*) *nt* free climbing

frei *adj* free; (*Straße*) clear; (*Mitarbeiter*) freelance; **ein ~er Tag** a day off; **~e Arbeitsstelle** vacancy; **Zimmer ~** room(s) to let (*Brit*), room(s) for rent (*US*); **im Freien** in the open air; **Freibad** *nt* open-air (swimming) pool; **freiberuflich** *adj* freelance; **freig(i)ebig** *adj* generous; **Freiheit** *f* freedom; **Freikarte** *f* free ticket; **frei|lassen** *irr vt* to (set) free

freilich *adv* of course

Freilichtbühne *f* open-air theatre; **frei|machen** *vr* **sich ~** to undress; **frei|nehmen** *irr vt* **sich** (*dat*) **einen Tag ~** to take a day off; **Freisprechanlage** *f* hands-free phone; **Freistoß** *m* free kick

Freitag *m* Friday; *siehe auch* **Mittwoch**; **freitags** *adv* on Fridays; *siehe auch* **mittwochs**

freiwillig *adj* voluntary

Freizeichen *nt* (*Tel*) ringing tone

Freizeit *f* spare (*o* free) time; **Freizeithemd** *nt* sports shirt; **Freizeitkleidung** *f* leisure wear; **Freizeitpark** *m* leisure park

fremd *adj* (*nicht vertraut*) strange; (*ausländisch*) foreign; (*nicht eigen*) someone else's; **Fremde(r)** *mf* (*Unbekannter*) stranger; (*Ausländer*) foreigner; **fremdenfeindlich** *adj* anti-foreigner, xenophobic; **Fremdenführer(in)** *m(f)* (tourist) guide; **Fremdenverkehr** *m* tourism; **Fremdenverkehrsamt** *nt* tourist information office; **Fremdenzimmer** *nt* (guest) room; **Fremdsprache** *f* foreign language; **Fremdsprachenkenntnisse** *pl* knowledge *sing* of foreign languages; **Fremdwort** *nt* foreign word

Frequenz *f* (*Radio*) frequency

fressen (*fraß, gefressen*) *vt, vi* (*Tier*) to eat; (*Mensch*) to guzzle

Freude (*-, -n*) *f* joy, delight; **freuen** *vt* to please; **es freut mich, dass ...** I'm pleased that ... ▷ *vr* **sich ~** to be pleased (*über +akk* about); **sich auf etw** (*akk*) **~** to look forward to sth

Freund (*-(e)s, -e*) *m* friend; (*in Beziehung*) boyfriend; **Freundin** *f* friend; (*in Beziehung*) girlfriend; **freundlich** *adj* friendly; (*liebenswürdig*) kind; **freundlicherweise** *adv* kindly; **Freundlichkeit** *f* friendliness;

(*Liebenswürdigkeit*) kindness;
Freundschaft f friendship
Frieden (-s, -) m peace; **Friedhof** m
cemetery; **friedlich** adj peaceful
frieren (*fror*, *gefroren*) vt, vi to freeze; **ich
friere, es friert mich** I'm freezing
Frikadelle f rissole
Frisbeescheibe® f frisbee®
frisch adj fresh; (*lebhaft*) lively;
„**~ gestrichen**" 'wet paint'; **sich ~ machen**
to freshen up; **Frischhaltefolie** f
clingfilm® (*Brit*), plastic wrap (*US*);
Frischkäse m cream cheese
Friseur m, **Friseuse** f hairdresser;
frisieren vt **jdn ~** to do sb's hair ▷ vr **sich
~** to do one's hair; **Frisör** (-s, -e) m,
Frisöse (-, -n) f hairdresser
Frist (-, -en) f period; (*Zeitpunkt*) deadline;
**innerhalb einer ~ von zehn
Tagen** within a ten-day period; **eine
~ einhalten** to meet a deadline; **die ~ ist
abgelaufen** the deadline has expired;
fristgerecht adj, adv within the specified
time; **fristlos** adj **~e Entlassung**
dismissal without notice
Frisur f hairdo, hairstyle
frittieren vt to deep-fry
Frl. f abk = **Fräulein** Miss
froh adj happy; **~e Weihnachten!** Merry
Christmas
fröhlich adj happy, cheerful
Fronleichnam (-(e)s) m Corpus Christi
frontal adj frontal;
Frontalzusammenstoß m head-on
collision
fror imperf von **frieren**
Frosch (-(e)s, Frösche) m frog
Frost (-(e)s, Fröste) m frost; **bei ~** in frosty
weather; **Frostschutzmittel** nt
anti-freeze
Frottee nt terry(cloth); **frottieren** vt
to rub down; **Frottier(hand)tuch** nt
towel
Frucht (-, Früchte) f (*a. fig*) fruit; (*Getreide*)
corn; **Fruchteis** nt fruit-flavoured
ice-cream; **Früchtetee** m fruit tea;
fruchtig adj fruity; **Fruchtpresse** f
juicer; **Fruchtsaft** m fruit juice;
Fruchtsalat m fruit salad
früh adj, adv early; **heute ~** this morning;
um fünf Uhr ~ at five (o'clock) in the
morning; **~ genug** soon enough; **früher**
adj earlier; (*ehemalig*) former ▷ adv

formerly, in the past; **frühestens** adv at
the earliest
Frühjahr nt, **Frühling** m spring;
Frühlingsrolle f spring roll;
Frühlingszwiebel f spring onion (*Brit*),
scallion (*US*)
frühmorgens adv early in the morning
Frühschicht f **~ haben** to be on the early
shift
Frühstück nt breakfast; **frühstücken** vi
to have breakfast; **Frühstücksbüfett** nt
breakfast buffet; **Frühstücksfernsehen**
nt breakfast television; **Frühstücksspeck**
m bacon
frühzeitig adj early
Frust (-s) m (*fam*) frustration; **frustrieren**
vt to frustrate
Fuchs (-es, Füchse) m fox
fühlen vt, vi to feel ▷ vr **sich ~** to feel
fuhr imperf von **fahren**
führen vt to lead; (*Geschäft*) to run; (*Name*)
to bear; (*Buch*) to keep ▷ vi to lead, to be
in the lead ▷ vr **sich ~** to behave;
Führerschein m driving licence (*Brit*),
driver's license (*US*); **Führung** f
leadership; (*eines Unternehmens*)
management; (*Mil*) command; (*in Museum,
Stadt*) guided tour; **in ~ liegen** to be in the
lead
füllen vt to fill; (*Gastr*) to stuff ▷ vr **sich
~** to fill
Füller (-s, -) m, **Füllfederhalter** (-s, -) m
fountain pen
Füllung f filling
Fund (-(e)s, -e) m find; **Fundbüro** nt lost
property office (*Brit*), lost and found (*US*);
Fundsachen pl lost property sing
fünf num five; **Fünf** (-, -en) f five;
(*Schulnote*) ≈ E; **fünfhundert** num five
hundred; **fünfmal** adv five times;
fünfte(r, s) adj fifth; *siehe auch* **dritte**;
Fünftel (-s, -) nt (*Bruchteil*) fifth; **fünfzehn**
num fifteen; **fünfzehnte(r, s)** adj
fifteenth; *siehe auch* **dritte**; **fünfzig** num
fifty; **fünfzigste(r, s)** adj fiftieth
Funk (-s) m radio; **über ~** by radio
Funke (-ns, -n) m spark; **funkeln** vi to
sparkle
Funkgerät nt radio set; **Funktaxi** nt
radio taxi, radio cab
Funktion f function; **funktionieren** vi to
work, to function; **Funktionstaste** f
(*Inform*) function key

für prep +akk for; **was ~ (ein) ...?** what kind
(o sort) of ...?; **Tag ~ Tag** day after day
Furcht (-) f fear; **furchtbar** adj terrible;
fürchten vt to be afraid of, to fear ▷ vr
sich ~ to be afraid (vor +dat of);
fürchterlich adj awful
füreinander adv for each other
fürs kontr von **für das**
Fürst(in) (-en, -en) m(f) prince/princess;
Fürstentum nt principality; **fürstlich** adj
(fig) splendid
Furunkel (-s, -) nt boil
Furz (-es, -e) m (vulg) fart; **furzen** vi (vulg)
to fart
Fuß (-es, Füße) m foot; (von Glas, Säule etc)
base; (von Möbel) leg; **zu ~** on foot; **zu
~ gehen** to walk; **Fußball** m football (Brit),
soccer; **Fußballmannschaft** f football
(Brit) (o soccer) team; **Fußballplatz** m
football pitch (Brit), soccer field (US);
Fußballspiel nt football (Brit) (o soccer)
match; **Fußballspieler(in)** m(f)
footballer (Brit), soccer player; **Fußboden**
m floor; **Fußgänger(in)** (-s, -) m(f)
pedestrian; **Fußgängerüberweg** m
pedestrian crossing (Brit), crosswalk (US);
Fußgängerzone f pedestrian precinct
(Brit) (o zone (US)); **Fußgelenk** nt ankle;
Fußpilz m athlete's foot; **Fußtritt** m
kick; **jdm einen ~ geben** to give sb a kick,
to kick sb; **Fußweg** m footpath
Futon (-s, -s) m futon
futsch adj (fam: kaputt) broken;
(zerschlagen) smashed; (weg, verloren) gone
Futter (-s, -) nt feed; (Heu etc) fodder;
(Stoff) lining; **füttern** vt to feed; (Kleidung)
to line
Futur (-s, -e) nt (Ling) future (tense)
Fuzzi (-s, -s) m (fam) guy

g

gab imperf von **geben**

Gabe (-, -n) f gift

Gabel (-, -n) f fork; **Gabelung** f fork

gaffen vi to gape

Gage (-, -n) f fee

gähnen vi to yawn

Galerie f gallery

Galle (-, -n) f gall; (Organ) gall bladder; **Gallenstein** m gallstone

Galopp (-s) m gallop; **galoppieren** vi to gallop

galt imperf von **gelten**

Gameboy® (-s, -s) m Gameboy®

gammeln vi to loaf (o hang) around; **Gammler(in)** (-s, -) m(f) layabout

gang adj ~ **und gäbe sein** to be quite normal

Gang (-(e)s, Gänge) m walk; (im Flugzeug) aisle; (Essen, Ablauf) course; (Flur etc) corridor; (Durchgang) passage; (Auto) gear; **den zweiten ~ einlegen** to change into second (gear); **etw in ~ bringen** to get sth going; **Gangschaltung** f gears pl; **Gangway** (-, -s) f (Aviat) steps pl; (Naut) gangway

Gans (-, Gänse) f goose; **Gänseblümchen**
nt daisy; **Gänsehaut** f goose pimples pl (Brit), goose bumps pl (US)

ganz adj whole; (vollständig) complete; ~ **Europa** all of Europe; **sein ~es Geld** all his money; **den ~en Tag** all day; **die ~e Zeit** all the time ▷ adv quite; (völlig) completely; **es hat mir ~ gut gefallen** I quite liked it; ~ **schön viel** quite a lot; ~ **und gar nicht** not at all; **das ist etwas ~ anderes** that's a completely different matter; **ganztägig** adj all-day; (Arbeit, Stelle) full-time

gar adj done, cooked ▷ adv at all; ~ **nicht/nichts/keiner** not/nothing/nobody at all; ~ **nicht schlecht** not bad at all

Garage (-, -n) f garage

Garantie f guarantee; **garantieren** vt to guarantee

Garderobe (-, -n) f (Kleidung) wardrobe; (Abgabe) cloakroom

Gardine f curtain

Garn (-(e)s, -e) nt thread

Garnele (-, -n) f shrimp

garnieren vt to decorate; (Speisen) to garnish

Garten (-s, Gärten) m garden; **Gärtner(in)** (-s, -) m(f) gardener; **Gärtnerei** f nursery; (Gemüsegärtnerei) market garden (Brit), truck farm (US)

Garzeit f cooking time

Gas (-es, -e) nt gas; ~ **geben** (Auto) to accelerate; (fig) to get a move on; **Gasanzünder** m gas lighter; **Gasbrenner** m gas burner; **Gasflasche** f gas bottle; **Gasheizung** f gas heating; **Gasherd** m gas stove, gas cooker (Brit); **Gaskocher** m camping stove; **Gaspedal** nt accelerator, gas pedal (US)

Gasse (-, -n) f alley

Gast (-es, Gäste) m guest; **Gäste haben** to have guests; **Gastarbeiter(in)** m(f) foreign worker; **Gästebett** nt spare bed; **Gästebuch** nt visitors' book; **Gästehaus** nt guest house; **Gästezimmer** nt guest room; **gastfreundlich** adj hospitable; **Gastgeber(in)** (-s, -) m(f) host/hostess; **Gasthaus** nt, **Gasthof** m inn; **Gastland** nt host country

Gastritis (-) f gastritis

Gastronomie f (Gewerbe) catering trade

Gastspiel nt (Sport) away game; **Gaststätte** f restaurant; (Trinklokal) pub

(*Brit*), bar; **Gastwirt(in)** *m(f)* landlord/
-lady

GAU (*-s, -s*) *m akr* = **größter
anzunehmender Unfall** MCA

Gaumen (*-s, -*) *m* palate

Gaze (*-, -n*) *f* gauze

geb. *adj abk* = **geboren** b. ▷ *adj abk* =
geborene née; *siehe* **geboren**

Gebäck (*-(e)s, -e*) *nt* pastries *pl*; (*Kekse*)
biscuits *pl* (*Brit*), cookies *pl* (*US*)

gebacken *pp von* **backen**

Gebärdensprache *f* sign language

Gebärmutter *f* womb

Gebäude (*-s, -*) *nt* building

geben (*gab, gegeben*) *vt, vi* to give (*jdm etw*
sb sth, sth to sb); (*Karten*) to deal; **lass dir
eine Quittung** ~ ask for a receipt ▷ *vt
impers* **es gibt** there is/are; (*in Zukunft*)
there will be; **das gibt's nicht** I don't
believe it ▷ *vr* **sich** ~ (*sich verhalten*) to
behave, to act; **das gibt sich wieder** it'll
sort itself out

Gebet (*-(e)s, -e*) *nt* prayer

gebeten *pp von* **bitten**

Gebiet (*-(e)s, -e*) *nt* area; (*Hoheitsgebiet*)
territory; (*fig*) field

gebildet *adj* educated; (*belesen*) well-read

Gebirge (*-s, -*) *nt* mountains *pl*; **gebirgig**
adj mountainous

Gebiss (*-es, -e*) *nt* teeth *pl*; (*künstlich*)
dentures *pl*; **gebissen** *pp von* **beißen**;
Gebissreiniger *m* denture tablets *pl*

Gebläse (*-s, -*) *nt* fan, blower

geblasen *pp von* **blasen**

geblieben *pp von* **bleiben**

gebogen *pp von* **biegen**

geboren *pp von* **gebären** ▷ *adj* born;
Andrea Jordan, ~e Christian Andrea
Jordan, née Christian

geborgen *pp von* **bergen** ▷ *adj* secure,
safe

geboten *pp von* **bieten**

gebracht *pp von* **bringen**

gebrannt *pp von* **brennen**

gebraten *pp von* **braten**

gebrauchen *vt* to use;
Gebrauchsanweisung *f* directions *pl* for
use; **gebrauchsfertig** *adj* ready to use;
gebraucht *adj* used; **etw** ~ **kaufen** to buy
sth secondhand; **Gebrauchtwagen** *m*
secondhand (*o* used) car

gebräunt *adj* tanned

gebrochen *pp von* **brechen**

Gebühr (*-, -en*) *f* charge; (*Maut*) toll;
(*Honorar*) fee; **Gebühreneinheit** *f* (*Tel*)
unit; **gebührenfrei** *adj* free of charge;
(*Telefonnummer*) freefone® (*Brit*), toll-free
(*US*); **gebührenpflichtig** *adj* subject to
charges; **~e Straße** toll road

gebunden *pp von* **binden**

Geburt (*-, -en*) *f* birth; **gebürtig** *adj* **er ist
~er Schweizer** he is Swiss by birth;
Geburtsdatum *nt* date of birth;
Geburtsjahr *nt* year of birth;
Geburtsname *m* birth name; (*einer Frau*)
maiden name; **Geburtsort** *m* birthplace;
Geburtstag *m* birthday; **herzlichen
Glückwunsch zum ~!** Happy Birthday;
Geburtsurkunde *f* birth certificate

Gebüsch (*-(e)s, -e*) *nt* bushes *pl*

gedacht *pp von* **denken**

Gedächtnis *nt* memory; **im ~ behalten**
to remember

Gedanke (*-ns, -n*) *m* thought; **sich** (*dat*)
über etw (*akk*) **~n machen** to think about
sth; (*besorgt*) to be worried about sth;
Gedankenstrich *m* dash

Gedeck (*-(e)s, -e*) *nt* place setting;
(*Speisenfolge*) set meal

Gedenkstätte *f* memorial; **Gedenktafel**
f commemorative plaque

Gedicht (*-(e)s, -e*) *nt* poem

Gedränge (*-s*) *nt* crush, crowd

gedrungen *pp von* **dringen**

Geduld (*-*) *f* patience; **geduldig** *adj*
patient

gedurft *pp von* **dürfen**

geehrt *adj* **Sehr ~er Herr Young** Dear Mr
Young

geeignet *adj* suitable

Gefahr (*-, -en*) *f* danger; **auf eigene** ~ at
one's own risk; **außer** ~ out of danger;
gefährden *vt* to endanger

gefahren *pp von* **fahren**

gefährlich *adj* dangerous

Gefälle (*-s, -*) *nt* gradient, slope

gefallen *pp von* **fallen** ▷ *irr vi* **jdm** ~ to
please sb; **er/es gefällt mir** I like him/it;
sich (*dat*) **etw** ~ **lassen** to put up with
sth

Gefallen (*-s, -*) *m* favour; **jdm einen** ~ **tun**
to do sb a favour

gefälligst *adv* **...**, will you!; **sei** ~ **still!** be
quiet, will you!

gefangen *pp von* **fangen**

Gefängnis *nt* prison

Gefäß (-es, -e) nt (Behälter) container, receptacle; (Anat, Bot) vessel

gefasst adj composed, calm; **auf etw (akk) ~ sein** to be prepared (o ready) for sth

geflochten pp von **flechten**

geflogen pp von **fliegen**

geflossen pp von **fließen**

Geflügel (-s) nt poultry

gefragt adj in demand

gefressen pp von **fressen**

Gefrierbeutel m freezer bag; **gefrieren** irr vi to freeze; **Gefrierfach** nt freezer compartment; **Gefrierschrank** m (upright) freezer; **Gefriertruhe** f (chest) freezer

gefroren pp von **frieren**

Gefühl (-(e)s, -e) nt feeling

gefunden pp von **finden**

gegangen pp von **gehen**

gegeben pp von **geben**; **gegebenenfalls** adv if need be

O SCHLÜSSELWORT

gegen präp +akk **1** against; **nichts gegen jdn haben** to have nothing against sb; **X gegen Y** (Sport, Jur) X versus Y; **ein Mittel gegen Schnupfen** something for colds

2 (in Richtung auf) towards; **gegen Osten** to(wards) the east; **gegen Abend** towards evening; **gegen einen Baum fahren** to drive into a tree

3 (ungefähr) round about; **gegen 3 Uhr** around 3 o'clock

4 (gegenüber) towards (ungefähr) around; **gerecht gegen alle** fair to all

5 (im Austausch für) for; **gegen bar** for cash; **gegen Quittung** against a receipt

6 (verglichen mit) compared with

Gegend (-, -en) f area; **hier in der ~** around here

gegeneinander adv against one another

Gegenfahrbahn f opposite lane; **Gegenmittel** nt remedy (gegen for); **Gegenrichtung** f opposite direction; **Gegensatz** m contrast; **im ~ zu** in contrast to; **gegensätzlich** adj conflicting; **gegenseitig** adj mutual; **sich ~ helfen** to help each other

Gegenstand m object; (Thema) subject

Gegenteil nt opposite; **im ~** on the contrary; **gegenteilig** adj opposite, contrary

gegenüber prep +dat opposite; (zu jdm) to(wards); (angesichts) in the face of ▷ adv opposite; **gegenüber|stehen** vt to face; (Problemen) to be faced with; **gegenüber|stellen** vt to confront (dat with); (fig) compare (dat with)

Gegenverkehr m oncoming traffic; **Gegenwart** (-) f present (tense)

Gegenwind m headwind

gegessen pp von **essen**

geglichen pp von **gleichen**

geglitten pp von **gleiten**

Gegner(in) (-s, -) m(f) opponent

gegolten pp von **gelten**

gegossen pp von **gießen**

gegraben pp von **graben**

gegriffen pp von **greifen**

gehabt pp von **haben**

Gehackte(s) nt mince(d meat) (Brit), ground meat (US)

Gehalt (-(e)s, -e) m content ▷ (-(e)s, Gehälter) nt salary

gehalten pp von **halten**

gehangen pp von **hängen**

gehässig adj spiteful, nasty

gehauen pp von **hauen**

gehbehindert adj **sie ist ~** she can't walk properly

geheim adj secret; **etw ~ halten** to keep sth secret; **Geheimnis** nt secret; (rätselhaft) mystery; **geheimnisvoll** adj mysterious; **Geheimnummer** f, **Geheimzahl** f (von Kreditkarte) PIN number

geheißen pp von **heißen**

gehen (ging, gegangen) vt, vi to go; (zu Fuß) to walk; (funktionieren) to work; **über die Straße ~** to cross the street; **~ nach** (Fenster) to face
▷ vi impers **wie geht es (dir)?** how are you (o things)?; **mir/ihm geht es gut** I'm/he's (doing) fine; **geht das?** is that possible?; **geht's noch?** can you still manage?; **es geht** not too bad, OK; **das geht nicht** that's not on; **es geht um ...** it's about ...

Gehirn (-(e)s, -e) nt brain; **Gehirnerschütterung** f concussion

gehoben pp von **heben**

geholfen pp von **helfen**
Gehör (-(e)s) nt hearing
gehorchen vi to obey (jdm sb)
gehören vi to belong (jdm to sb); **wem gehört das Buch?** whose book is this?; **gehört es dir?** is it yours? ▷ vr impers **das gehört sich nicht** it's not done
gehörlos adj deaf
gehorsam adj obedient
Gehsteig m
Gehweg (-s, -e) m pavement (Brit), sidewalk (US)
Geier (-s, -) m vulture
Geige (-, -n) f violin
geil adj randy (Brit), horny (US); (fam: toll) fantastic
Geisel (-, -n) f hostage
Geist (-(e)s, -er) m spirit; (Gespenst) ghost; (Verstand) mind; **Geisterbahn** f ghost train, tunnel of horror (US); **Geisterfahrer(in)** m(f) person driving the wrong way on the motorway
geizig adj stingy
gekannt pp von **kennen**
geklungen pp von **klingen**
geknickt adj (fig) dejected
gekniffen pp von **kneifen**
gekommen pp von **kommen**
gekonnt pp von **können** ▷ adj skilful
gekrochen pp von **kriechen**
Gel (-s, -s) nt gel
Gelächter (-s, -) nt laughter
geladen pp von **laden** ▷ adj loaded; (Elek) live; (fig) furious
gelähmt adj paralysed
Gelände (-s, -) nt land, terrain; (Fabrik, Sportgelände) grounds pl; (Baugelände) site
Geländer (-s, -) nt railing; (Treppengeländer) banister
Geländewagen m off-road vehicle
gelang imperf von **gelingen**
gelassen pp von **lassen** ▷ adj calm, composed
Gelatine f gelatine
gelaufen pp von **laufen**
gelaunt adj **gut/schlecht ~** in a good/bad mood
gelb adj yellow; (Ampel) amber, yellow (US); **gelblich** adj yellowish; **Gelbsucht** f jaundice
Geld (-(e)s, -er) nt money; **Geldautomat** m cash machine (o dispenser (Brit)), ATM (US); **Geldbeutel** m, **Geldbörse** f purse;

Geldbuße f fine; **Geldschein** m (bank)note (Brit), bill (US); **Geldstrafe** f fine; **Geldstück** nt coin; **Geldwechsel** m exchange of money; (Ort) bureau de change; **Geldwechselautomat** m, **Geldwechsler** (-s, -) m change machine
Gelee (-s, -s) nt jelly
gelegen pp von **liegen** ▷ adj situated; (passend) convenient; **etw kommt jdm ~** sth is convenient for sb
Gelegenheit f opportunity; (Anlass) occasion
gelegentlich adj occasional ▷ adv occasionally; (bei Gelegenheit) some time (or other)
Gelenk (-(e)s, -e) nt joint
gelernt adj skilled
gelesen pp von **lesen**
geliehen pp von **leihen**
gelingen (gelang, gelungen) vi to succeed; **es ist mir gelungen, ihn zu erreichen** I managed to get hold of him
gelitten pp von **leiden**
gelockt adj curly
gelogen pp von **lügen**
gelten (galt, gegolten) vt (wert sein) to be worth; **jdm viel/wenig ~** to mean a lot/not to mean much to sb ▷ vi (gültig sein) to be valid; (erlaubt sein) to be allowed; **jdm ~** (gemünzt sein auf) to be meant for (o aimed at) sb; **etw ~ lassen** to accept sth; **als etw ~** to be considered to be sth; **Geltungsdauer** f **eine ~ von fünf Tagen haben** to be valid for five days
gelungen pp von **gelingen**
gemahlen pp von **mahlen**
Gemälde (-s, -) nt painting, picture
gemäß prep +dat in accordance with ▷ adj appropriate (dat to)
gemein adj (niederträchtig) mean, nasty; (gewöhnlich) common
Gemeinde (-, -n) f district, community; (Pfarrgemeinde) parish; (Kirchengemeinde) congregation
gemeinsam adj joint, common ▷ adv together, jointly; **das Haus gehört uns beiden ~** the house belongs to both of us
Gemeinschaft f community; **~ Unabhängiger Staaten** Commonwealth of Independent States
gemeint pp von **meinen**; **das war nicht so ~** I didn't mean it like that
gemessen pp von **messen**

gemieden pp von **meiden**
gemischt adj mixed
gemocht pp von **mögen**
Gemüse (-s, -) nt vegetables pl;
Gemüsehändler(in) m(f) greengrocer
gemusst pp von **müssen**
gemustert adj patterned
gemütlich adj comfortable, cosy;
(Mensch) good-natured, easy-going; **mach
es dir ~** make yourself at home
genannt pp von **nennen**
genau adj exact, precise ▷ adv exactly,
precisely; **~ in der Mitte** right in the
middle; **es mit etw ~ nehmen** to be
particular about sth; **~ genommen**
strictly speaking; **ich weiß es ~** I know for
certain (o for sure); **genauso** adv exactly
the same (way); **~ gut/viel/viele Leute**
just as well/much/many people (wie as)
genehmigen vt to approve; **sich** (dat)
etw ~ to indulge in sth; **Genehmigung** f
approval
Generalkonsulat nt consulate general
Generation f generation
Genf (-s) nt Geneva; **~er See** Lake
Geneva
genial adj brilliant
Genick (-(e)s, -e) nt (back of the) neck
Genie (-s, -s) nt genius
genieren vr **sich ~** to feel awkward; **ich
geniere mich vor ihm** he makes me feel
embarrassed
genießen (genoss, genossen) vt to enjoy
Genitiv m genitive (case)
genommen pp von **nehmen**
genoss imperf von **genießen**
genossen pp von **genießen**
genug adv enough
genügen vi to be enough (jdm for sb);
danke, das genügt thanks, that's enough
(o that will do)
Genuss (-es, Genüsse) m pleasure;
(Zusichnehmen) consumption
geöffnet adj (Geschäft etc) open
Geografie f geography
Geologie f geology
Georgien (-s) nt Georgia
Gepäck (-(e)s) nt luggage (Brit), baggage;
Gepäckabfertigung f luggage (Brit) (o
baggage) check-in; **Gepäckablage** f
luggage (Brit) (o baggage) rack;
Gepäckannahme f (zur Beförderung)
luggage (Brit) (o baggage) office; (zur

Aufbewahrung) left-luggage office (Brit),
baggage checkroom (US);
Gepäckaufbewahrung f left-luggage
office (Brit), baggage checkroom (US);
Gepäckausgabe f luggage (Brit) (o
baggage) office; (am Flughafen) baggage
reclaim; **Gepäckband** nt luggage (Brit) (o
baggage) conveyor; **Gepäckkontrolle** f
luggage (Brit) (o baggage) check;
Gepäckstück nt item of luggage (Brit) (o
baggage (US)); **Gepäckträger** m porter;
(an Fahrrad) carrier; **Gepäckversicherung**
f luggage (Brit) (o baggage) insurance;
Gepäckwagen m luggage van (Brit),
baggage car (US)
gepfiffen pp von **pfeifen**
gepflegt adj well-groomed; (Park) well
looked after
gequollen pp von **quellen**

○ **SCHLÜSSELWORT**

gerade adj straight (aufrecht) upright;
eine gerade Zahl an even number
▷ adv 1 (genau) just exactly; (speziell)
especially; **gerade deshalb** that's just od
exactly why; **das ist es ja gerade!** that's
just it!; **gerade du** you especially; **warum
gerade ich?** why me (of all people)?; **jetzt
gerade nicht!** not now!; **gerade neben**
right next to
2 (eben, soeben) just; **er wollte gerade
aufstehen** he was just about to get up;
gerade erst only just; **gerade noch** (only)
just

gerannt pp von **rennen**
geraspelt adj grated
Gerät (-(e)s, -e) nt device, gadget;
(Werkzeug) tool; (Radio, Fernseher) set;
(Zubehör) equipment
geraten pp von **raten** ▷ irr vi to turn out;
gut/schlecht ~ to turn out well/badly; **an
jdn ~** to come across sb; **in etw** (akk) **~** to
get into sth
geräuchert adj smoked
geräumig adj roomy
Geräusch (-(e)s, -e) nt sound;
(unangenehm) noise
gerecht adj fair; (Strafe, Belohnung) just;
jdm/einer Sache ~ werden to do justice
to sb/sth
gereizt adj irritable

Gericht (-(e)s, -e) nt (Jur) court; (Essen) dish
gerieben pp von **reiben**
gering adj small; (unbedeutend) slight; (niedrig) low; (Zeit) short; **geringfügig** adj slight, minor ▷ adv slightly
gerissen pp von **reißen**
geritten pp von **reiten**
gern(e) adv willingly, gladly; **~ haben, ~ mögen** to like; **etw ~ tun** to like doing sth; **~ geschehen** you're welcome
gerochen pp von **riechen**
Gerste (-, -n) f barley; **Gerstenkorn** nt (im Auge) stye
Geruch (-(e)s, Gerüche) m smell
Gerücht (-(e)s, -e) nt rumour
gerufen pp von **rufen**
Gerümpel (-s) nt junk
gerungen pp von **ringen**
Gerüst (-(e)s, -e) nt (auf Bau) scaffolding; (Gestell) trestle; (fig) framework (zu of)
gesalzen pp von **salzen**
gesamt adj whole, entire; (Kosten) total; (Werke) complete; **Gesamtschule** f ≈ comprehensive school
gesandt pp von **senden**
Gesäß (-es, -e) nt bottom
geschaffen pp von **schaffen**
Geschäft (-(e)s, -e) nt business; (Laden) shop; (Geschäftsabschluss) deal; **geschäftlich** adj commercial ▷ adv on business; **Geschäftsfrau** f businesswoman; **Geschäftsführer(in)** m(f) managing director; (von Laden) manager; **Geschäftsmann** m businessman; **Geschäftsreise** f business trip; **Geschäftsstraße** f shopping street; **Geschäftszeiten** pl business (o opening) hours pl
geschehen (geschah, geschehen) vi to happen
Geschenk (-(e)s, -e) nt present, gift; **Geschenkgutschein** m gift voucher; **Geschenkpapier** nt gift-wrapping paper, giftwrap
Geschichte (-, -n) f story; (Sache) affair; (Hist) history
geschickt adj skilful
geschieden pp von **scheiden** ▷ adj divorced
geschienen pp von **scheinen**
Geschirr (-(e)s, -e) nt crockery; (zum Kochen) pots and pans pl; (von Pferd)

harness; **~ spülen** to do (o wash) the dishes, to do the washing-up (Brit); **Geschirrspülmaschine** f dishwasher; **Geschirrspülmittel** nt washing-up liquid (Brit), dishwashing liquid (US); **Geschirrtuch** nt tea towel (Brit), dish towel (US)
geschissen pp von **scheißen**
geschlafen pp von **schlafen**
geschlagen pp von **schlagen**
Geschlecht (-(e)s, -er) nt sex; (Ling) gender; **Geschlechtskrankheit** f sexually transmitted disease, STD; **Geschlechtsorgan** nt sexual organ; **Geschlechtsverkehr** m sexual intercourse
geschlichen pp von **schleichen**
geschliffen pp von **schleifen**
geschlossen adj closed
Geschmack (-(e)s, Geschmäcke) m taste; **geschmacklos** adj tasteless; **Geschmack(s)sache** f das ist **~** that's a matter of taste; **geschmackvoll** adj tasteful
geschmissen pp von **schmeißen**
geschmolzen pp von **schmelzen**
geschnitten pp von **schneiden**
geschoben pp von **schieben**
Geschoss (-es, -e) nt (Stockwerk) floor
geschossen pp von **schießen**
Geschrei (-s) nt cries pl; (fig) fuss
geschrieben pp von **schreiben**
geschrie(e)n pp von **schreien**
geschützt adj protected
Geschwätz (-es) nt chatter; (Klatsch) gossip; **geschwätzig** adj talkative, gossipy
geschweige adv **~** (denn) let alone
geschwiegen pp von **schweigen**
Geschwindigkeit f speed; (Phys) velocity; **Geschwindigkeitsbegrenzung** f speed limit
Geschwister pl brothers and sisters pl
geschwollen adj (angeschwollen) swollen; (Rede) pompous
geschwommen pp von **schwimmen**
geschworen pp von **schwören**
Geschwulst (-, Geschwülste) f growth
Geschwür (-(e)s, -e) nt ulcer
gesehen pp von **sehen**
gesellig adj sociable; **Gesellschaft** f society; (Begleitung) company; (Abend~) party; **~ mit beschränkter Haftung**

g

limited company (Brit), limited corporation (US)

gesessen pp von **sitzen**

Gesetz (-es, -e) nt law; **gesetzlich** adj legal; **~er Feiertag** public (o bank (Brit) o legal (US)) holiday; **gesetzwidrig** adj illegal

Gesicht (-(e)s, -er) nt face; (Miene) expression; **mach doch nicht so ein ~!** stop pulling such a face; **Gesichtscreme** f face cream; **Gesichtswasser** nt toner

gesoffen pp von **saufen**

gesogen pp von **saugen**

gespannt adj tense; (begierig) eager; **ich bin ~, ob ...** I wonder if ...; **auf etw/jdn ~ sein** to look forward to sth/to seeing sb

Gespenst (-(e)s, -er) nt ghost

gesperrt adj closed

gesponnen pp von **spinnen**

Gespräch (-(e)s, -e) nt talk, conversation; (Diskussion) discussion; (Anruf) call

gesprochen pp von **sprechen**

gesprungen pp von **springen**

Gestalt (-, -en) f form, shape; (Mensch) figure

gestanden pp von **stehen, gestehen**

Gestank (-(e)s) m stench

gestatten vt to permit, to allow; **~ Sie?** may I?

Geste (-, -n) f gesture

gestehen irr vt to confess

gestern adv yesterday; **~ Abend/Morgen** yesterday evening/morning

gestiegen pp von **steigen**

gestochen pp von **stechen**

gestohlen pp von **stehlen**

gestorben pp von **sterben**

gestört adj disturbed; (Empfang) poor

gestoßen pp von **stoßen**

gestreift adj striped

gestrichen pp von **streichen**

gestritten pp von **streiten**

gestunken pp von **stinken**

gesund adj healthy; **wieder ~ werden** to get better; **Gesundheit** f health; **~!** bless you!; **gesundheitsschädlich** adj unhealthy

gesungen pp von **singen**

gesunken pp von **sinken**

getan pp von **tun**

getragen pp von **tragen**

Getränk (-(e)s, -e) nt drink;

Getränkeautomat m drinks machine; **Getränkekarte** f list of drinks

Getreide (-s, -) nt cereals pl, grain

getrennt adj separate; **~ leben** to live apart; **~ zahlen** to pay separately

getreten pp von **treten**

Getriebe (-s, -) nt (Auto) gearbox

getrieben pp von **treiben**

Getriebeschaden m gearbox damage

getroffen pp von **treffen**

getrunken pp von **trinken**

Getue nt fuss

geübt adj experienced

gewachsen pp von **wachsen** ▷ adj **jdm/einer Sache ~ sein** to be a match for sb/up to sth

Gewähr (-) f guarantee; **keine ~ übernehmen für** to accept no responsibility for

Gewalt (-, -en) f (Macht) power; (Kontrolle) control; (große Kraft) force; (~taten) violence; **mit aller ~** with all one's might; **gewaltig** adj tremendous; (Irrtum) huge

gewandt pp von **wenden** ▷ adj (flink) nimble; (geschickt) skilful

gewann imperf von **gewinnen**

gewaschen pp von **waschen**

Gewebe (-s, -) nt (Stoff) fabric; (Bio) tissue

Gewehr (-(e)s, -e) nt rifle, gun

Geweih (-(e)s, -e) nt antlers pl

gewellt adj (Haare) wavy

gewendet pp von **wenden**

Gewerbe (-s, -) nt trade; **Gewerbegebiet** nt industrial estate (Brit) (o park (US)); **gewerblich** adj commercial

Gewerkschaft f trade union

gewesen pp von **sein**

Gewicht (-(e)s, -e) nt weight; (fig) importance

gewiesen pp von **weisen**

Gewinn (-(e)s, -e) m profit; (bei Spiel) winnings pl; **gewinnen** (gewann, gewonnen) vt to win; (erwerben) to gain; (Kohle, Öl) to extract ▷ vi to win; (profitieren) to gain; **Gewinner(in)** (-s, -) m(f) winner

gewiss adj certain ▷ adv certainly

Gewissen (-s, -) nt conscience; **ein gutes/schlechtes ~ haben** to have a clear/bad conscience

Gewitter (-s, -) nt thunderstorm; **gewittern** vi impers **es gewittert** it's thundering

gewogen pp von **wiegen**

gewöhnen vt jdn an etw (akk) ~ to accustom sb to sth ▷ vr **sich an jdn/etw** ~ to get used (o accustomed) to sb/sth; **Gewohnheit** f habit; (Brauch) custom; **gewöhnlich** adj usual; (durchschnittlich) ordinary; (pej) common; **wie** ~ as usual; **gewohnt** adj usual; **etw** ~ **sein** to be used to sth

Gewölbe (-s, -) nt (Deckengewölbe) vault

gewonnen pp von **gewinnen**

geworben pp von **werben**

geworden pp von **werden**

geworfen pp von **werfen**

Gewürz (-es, -e) nt spice; **Gewürznelke** f clove; **gewürzt** adj seasoned

gewusst pp von **wissen**

Gezeiten pl tides pl

gezogen pp von **ziehen**

gezwungen pp von **zwingen**

Gibraltar (-s) nt Gibraltar

Gicht (-) f gout

Giebel (-s, -) m gable

gierig adj greedy

gießen (goss, gegossen) vt to pour; (Blumen) to water; (Metall) to cast; **Gießkanne** f watering can

Gift (-(e)s, -e) nt poison; **giftig** adj poisonous

Gigabyte nt gigabyte

Gin (-s, -s) m gin

ging imperf von **gehen**; **Gin Tonic** (-(s), -s) m gin and tonic

Gipfel (-s, -) m summit, peak; (Pol) summit; (fig: Höhepunkt) height

Gips (-es, -e) m (a. Med) plaster; **Gipsbein** nt **sie hat ein** ~ she's got her leg in plaster; **Gipsverband** m plaster cast

Giraffe (-, -n) f giraffe

Girokonto nt current account (Brit), checking account (US)

Gitarre (-, -n) f guitar

Gitter (-s, -) nt bars pl

glänzen vi (a. fig) to shine; **glänzend** adj shining; (fig) brilliant

Glas (-es, Gläser) nt glass; (Marmelade) jar; **zwei** ~ **Wein** two glasses of wine; **Glascontainer** m bottle bank; **Glaser(in)** m(f) glazier; **Glasscheibe** f pane (of glass); **Glassplitter** m splinter of glass

Glasur f glaze; (Gastr) icing

glatt adj smooth; (rutschig) slippery; (Lüge) downright; **Glatteis** nt (black) ice

Glatze (-, -n) f bald head; (fam: Skinhead) skinhead

glauben vt, vi to believe (an +akk in); (meinen) to think; **jdm** ~ to believe sb

gleich adj equal; (identisch) same, identical; **alle Menschen sind** ~ all people are the same; **es ist mir** ~ it's all the same to me ▷ adv equally; (sofort) straight away; (bald) in a minute; ~ **groß/alt** the same size/age; ~ **nach/an** right after/at; **Gleichberechtigung** f equal rights pl; **gleichen** (glich, geglichen) vi **jdm/einer Sache** ~ to be like sb/sth ▷ vr **sich** ~ to be alike; **gleichfalls** adv likewise; **danke** ~! thanks, and the same to you; **gleichgültig** adj indifferent; **gleichmäßig** adj regular; (Verteilung) even, equal; **gleichzeitig** adj simultaneous ▷ adv at the same time

Gleis (-es, -e) nt track, rails pl; (Bahnsteig) platform

gleiten (glitt, geglitten) vi to glide; (rutschen) to slide; **Gleitschirmfliegen** (-s) nt paragliding

Gletscher (-s, -) m glacier; **Gletscherskifahren** nt glacier skiing; **Gletscherspalte** f crevasse

glich imperf von **gleichen**

Glied (-(e)s, -er) nt (Arm, Bein) limb; (von Kette) link; (Penis) penis; **Gliedmaßen** pl limbs pl

glitschig adj slippery

glitt imperf von **gleiten**

glitzern vi to glitter; (Sterne) to twinkle

Glocke (-, -n) f bell; **Glockenspiel** nt chimes pl

Glotze (-, -n) f (fam: TV) box; **glotzen** vi (fam) to stare

Glück (-(e)s) nt luck; (Freude) happiness; ~ **haben** to be lucky; **viel** ~! good luck; **zum** ~ fortunately; **glücklich** adj lucky; (froh) happy; **glücklicherweise** adv fortunately; **Glückwunsch** m congratulations pl; **herzlichen** ~ **zur bestandenen Prüfung** congratulations on passing your exam; **herzlichen** ~ **zum Geburtstag!** Happy Birthday

Glühbirne f light bulb; **glühen** vi to glow; **Glühwein** m mulled wine

GmbH (-, -s) f abk = **Gesellschaft mit beschränkter Haftung** ≈ Ltd (Brit), ≈ Inc (US)

Gokart (-(s), -s) m go-kart

Gold (-(e)s) nt gold; **golden** adj gold; (fig)
golden; **Goldfisch** m goldfish;
Goldmedaille f gold medal;
Goldschmied(in) m(f) goldsmith

Golf (-(e)s, -e) m gulf; **der ~ von Biskaya**
the Bay of Biscay ▷ (-s) nt golf; **Golfplatz**
m golf course; **Golfschläger** m golf club

Gondel (-, -n) f gondola; (Seilbahn)
cable-car

gönnen vt **ich gönne es ihm** I'm really
pleased for him; **sich** (dat) **etw ~** to allow
oneself sth

goss imperf von **gießen**

gotisch adj Gothic

Gott (-es, Götter) m God; (Gottheit) god;
Gottesdienst m service; **Göttin** f
goddess

Grab (-(e)s, Gräber) nt grave

graben (grub, gegraben) vt to dig; **Graben**
(-s, Gräben) m ditch

Grabstein m gravestone

Grad (-(e)s, -e) m degree; **wir haben 30
~ Celsius** it's 30 degrees Celsius, it's 86
degrees Fahrenheit; **bis zu einem
gewissen ~** up to a certain extent

Graf (-en, -en) m count; (in Großbritannien)
earl

Graffiti pl graffiti sing

Grafik (-, -en) f graph; (Kunstwerk) graphic;
(Illustration) diagram; **Grafikkarte** f
(Inform) graphics card; **Grafikprogramm**
nt (Inform) graphics software

Gräfin (-, -nen) f countess

Gramm (-s) nt gram(me)

Grammatik f grammar

Grapefruit (-, -s) f grapefruit

Graphik f siehe **Grafik**

Gras (-es, Gräser) nt grass

grässlich adj horrible

Gräte (-, -n) f (fish)bone

gratis adj, adv free (of charge)

gratulieren vi **jdm** (**zu etw**) **~** to
congratulate sb (on sth); (**ich**) **gratuliere!**
congratulations!

grau adj grey, gray (US); **grauhaarig** adj
grey-haired

grausam adj cruel

gravierend adj (Fehler) serious

greifen (griff, gegriffen) vt to seize; **zu etw
~** (fig) to resort to sth ▷ vi (Regel etc) to
have an effect (bei on)

grell adj harsh

Grenze (-, -n) f boundary; (Staat) border;
(Schranke) limit; **grenzen** vi to border (an
+akk on); **Grenzkontrolle** f border control;
Grenzübergang m border crossing point;
Grenzverkehr m border traffic

Grieche (-n, -n) m Greek; **Griechenland** nt
Greece; **Griechin** f Greek; **griechisch** adj
Greek; **Griechisch** nt Greek

griesgrämig adj grumpy

Grieß (-es, -e) m (Gastr) semolina

griff imperf von **greifen**

Griff (-(e)s, -e) m grip; (Tür etc) handle;
griffbereit adj handy

Grill (-s, -s) m grill; (im Freien) barbecue

Grille (-, -n) f cricket

grillen vt to grill ▷ vi to have a barbecue;
Grillfest nt, **Grillfete** f barbecue;
Grillkohle f charcoal

grinsen vi to grin; (höhnisch) to sneer

Grippe (-, -n) f flu; **Grippeschutzimpfung**
f flu vaccination

grob adj coarse; (Fehler, Verstoß) gross;
(Einschätzung) rough

Grönland (-s) nt Greenland

groß adj big, large; (hoch) tall; (fig) great;
(Buchstabe) capital; (erwachsen) grown-up;
im Großen und Ganzen on the whole
▷ adv greatly; **großartig** adj wonderful

Großbritannien (-s) nt (Great) Britain

Großbuchstabe m capital letter

Größe (-, -n) f size; (Länge) height; (fig)
greatness; **welche ~ haben Sie?** what size
do you take?

Großeltern pl grandparents pl;
Großhandel m wholesale trade;
Großmarkt m hypermarket;
Großmutter f grandmother; **Großraum**
m **der ~ Manchester** Greater
Manchester; **groß|schreiben** irr vt to
write with a capital letter; **Großstadt** f
city; **Großvater** m grandfather;
großzügig adj generous; (Planung) on a
large scale

Grotte (-, -n) f grotto

grub imperf von **graben**

Grübchen nt dimple

Grube (-, -n) f pit

grüezi interj (schweizerisch) hello

Gruft -, -en f vault

grün adj green; **~er Salat** lettuce; **~e
Bohnen** French beans; **die Bananen sind
noch zu ~** the bananas aren't ripe yet; **der
~e Punkt** symbol for recyclable packaging; **im
~en Bereich** hunky-dory

● **grüner Punkt**
●
● The **grüner Punkt** is the green spot
● symbol which appears on packaging,
● indicating that the packaging should
● not be thrown into the normal
● household refuse but kept separate
● to be recycled through the **DSD**
● (Duales System Deutschland)
● system. The recycling is financed by
● licences bought by the manufacturer
● from the 'DSD' and the cost of this is
● often passed on to the consumer.

Grünanlage f park
Grund (-(e)s, Gründe) m (Ursache) reason;
(Erdboden) ground; (See, Gefäß) bottom;
(Grundbesitz) land, property; **aus
gesundheitlichen Gründen** for health
reasons; **im ~e** basically; **aus diesem ~** for
this reason
gründen vt to found; **Gründer(in)** m(f)
founder
Grundgebühr f basic charge;
Grundgesetz nt (German) Constitution
gründlich adj thorough
Gründonnerstag m Maundy Thursday
grundsätzlich adj fundamental, basic;
sie kommt ~ zu spät she's always late;
Grundschule f primary school;
Grundstück nt plot; (Anwesen) estate;
(Baugrundstück) site; **Grundwasser** nt
ground water
Grüne(r) mf (Pol) Green; **die ~n** the Green
Party
Gruppe (-, -n) f group;
Gruppenermäßigung f group discount;
Gruppenreise f group tour
Gruß (-es, Grüße) m greeting; **viele Grüße**
best wishes; **Grüße an** (+akk) regards to;
mit freundlichen Grüßen Yours sincerely
(Brit), Sincerely yours (US); **sag ihm einen
schönen ~ von mir** give him my regards;
grüßen vt to greet; **grüß deine Mutter
von mir** give your mother my regards;
Julia lässt (euch) ~ Julia sends (you) her
regards
gucken vi to look
Gulasch (-(e)s, -e) nt goulash
gültig adj valid
Gummi (-s, -s) m o nt rubber; **Gummiband**
nt rubber (o elastic (Brit)) band;
Gummibärchen pl gums pl (in the shape of

a bear) (Brit), gumdrops pl (in the shape of a
bear) (US); **Gummihandschuhe** pl rubber
gloves pl; **Gummistiefel** m wellington
(boot) (Brit), rubber boot (US)
günstig adj favourable; (Preis) good
gurgeln vi to gurgle; (im Mund) to gargle
Gurke (-, -n) f cucumber; **saure ~** gherkin
Gurt (-(e)s, -e) m belt
Gürtel (-s, -) m belt; (Geo) zone;
Gürtelrose f shingles sing
GUS (-) f akr = **Gemeinschaft
Unabhängiger Staaten** CIS

 SCHLÜSSELWORT

g

gut adj good; **alles Gute** all the best; **also
gut** all right then
▷ adv well; **gut gehen** to work, to come off;
es geht jdm gut sb's doing fine; **gut
gemeint** well meant; **gut schmecken** to
taste good; **jdm gut tun** to do sb good;
gut, aber ... OK, but ...; **(na) gut, ich
komme** all right, I'll come; **gut drei
Stunden** a good three hours; **das kann
gut sein** that may well be; **lass es gut
sein** that'll do

Gutachten (-s, -) nt report;
Gutachter(in) (-s, -) m(f) expert
gutartig adj (Med) benign
Güter pl goods pl; **Güterbahnhof** m
goods station; **Güterzug** m goods
train
gutgläubig adj trusting; **Guthaben** (-s)
nt (credit) balance
gutmütig adj good-natured
Gutschein m voucher; **Gutschrift** f
credit
Gymnasium nt = grammar school (Brit),
= high school (US)
Gymnastik f exercises pl, keep-fit
Gynäkologe m, **Gynäkologin** f
gynaecologist
Gyros (-, -) nt doner kebab

h

Haar (-(e)s, -e) nt hair; **um ein ~** nearly; **sich** (dat) **die ~e schneiden lassen** to have one's hair cut; **Haarbürste** f hairbrush; **Haarfestiger** m setting lotion; **Haargel** nt hair gel; **haarig** adj hairy; (fig) nasty; **Haarschnitt** m haircut; **Haarspange** f hair slide (Brit), barrette (US); **Haarspliss** m split ends pl; **Haarspray** nt hair spray; **Haartrockner** (-s, -) m hairdryer; **Haarwaschmittel** nt shampoo; **Haarwasser** nt hair tonic

haben (hatte, gehabt) vt, vaux to have; **Hunger/Angst ~** to be hungry/afraid; **Ferien ~** to be on holiday (Brit) (o vacation (US)); **welches Datum ~ wir heute?** what's the date today?; **ich hätte gerne ...** I'd like ...; **hätten Sie etwas dagegen, wenn ...?** would you mind if ...?; **was hast du denn?** what's the matter (with you)?

Haben nt (Comm) credit

Habicht (-(e)s, -e) m hawk

Hacke (-, -n) f (im Garten) hoe; (Ferse) heel; **hacken** vt to chop; (Loch) to hack; (Erde) to hoe; **Hacker(in)** (-s, -) m(f) (Inform) hacker; **Hackfleisch** nt mince(d meat) (Brit), ground meat (US)

Hafen (-s, Häfen) m harbour; (großer) port; **Hafenstadt** f port

Hafer (-s, -) m oats pl; **Haferflocken** pl rolled oats pl

Haft (-) f custody; **haftbar** adj liable, responsible; **haften** vi to stick; **~ für** to be liable (o responsible) for; **Haftnotiz** f Post-it®; **Haftpflichtversicherung** f third party insurance; **Haftung** f liability

Hagebutte (-, -n) f rose hip

Hagel (-s) m hail; **hageln** vi impers to hail

Hahn (-(e)s, Hähne) m cock; (Wasserhahn) tap (Brit), faucet (US); **Hähnchen** nt cockerel; (Gastr) chicken

Hai(fisch) (-(e)s, -e) m shark

häkeln vi, vt to crochet; **Häkelnadel** f crochet hook

Haken (-s, -) m hook; (Zeichen) tick

halb adj half; **~ eins** half past twelve; (fam) half twelve; **eine ~e Stunde** half an hour; **~ offen** half-open; **Halbfinale** nt semifinal; **halbieren** vt to halve; **Halbinsel** f peninsula; **Halbjahr** nt half-year; **halbjährlich** adj half-yearly; **Halbmond** m (Astr) half-moon; (Symbol) crescent; **Halbpension** f half board; **halbseitig** adj **~ gelähmt** paralyzed on one side; **halbtags** adv (arbeiten) part-time; **halbwegs** adv (leidlich) reasonably; **Halbzeit** f half; (Pause) half-time

half imperf von **helfen**; **Hälfte** (-, -n) f half

Halle (-, -n) f hall; **Hallenbad** nt indoor (swimming) pool

hallo interj hello, hi

Halogenlampe f halogen lamp; **Halogenscheinwerfer** m halogen headlight

Hals (-es, Hälse) m neck; (Kehle) throat; **Halsband** nt (für Tiere) collar; **Halsentzündung** f sore throat; **Halskette** f necklace; **Hals-Nasen-Ohren-Arzt** m, **Hals-Nasen-Ohren-Ärztin** f ear, nose and throat specialist; **Halsschmerzen** pl sore throat sing; **Halstuch** nt scarf

halt interj stop ▷ adv **das ist ~ so** that's just the way it is; **Halt** (-(e)s, -e) m stop; (fester) hold; (innerer) stability

haltbar adj durable; (Lebensmittel) non-perishable; **Haltbarkeitsdatum** nt best-before date

halten (*hielt, gehalten*) *vt* to keep; (*festhalten*) to hold; ~ **für** to regard as; ~ **von** to think of; **den Elfmeter** ~ to save the penalty; **eine Rede** ~ to give (*o* make) a speech ▷ *vi* to hold; (*frisch bleiben*) to keep; (*stoppen*) to stop; **zu jdm** ~ to stand by sb ▷ *vr* **sich** ~ (*frisch bleiben*) to keep; (*sich behaupten*) to hold out

Haltestelle *f* stop; **Halteverbot** *nt* **hier ist** ~ you can't stop here

Haltung *f* (*Körper*) posture; (*fig*) attitude; (*Selbstbeherrschung*) composure; ~ **bewahren** to keep one's composure

Hamburg (*-s*) *nt* Hamburg; **Hamburger** (*-s, -*) *m* (*Gastr*) hamburger

Hammelfleisch *nt* mutton

Hammer (*-s, Hämmer*) *m* hammer; (*fig, fam: Fehler*) howler; **das ist der** ~ (*unerhört*) that's a bit much

Hämorr(ho)iden *pl* haemorrhoids *pl*, piles *pl*

Hamster (*-s, -*) *m* hamster

Hand (*-, Hände*) *f* hand; **jdm die** ~ **geben** to shake hands with sb; **jdn bei der** ~ **nehmen** to take sb by the hand; **eine** ~ **voll Reis/Leute** a handful of rice/people; **zu Händen von** attention; **Handarbeit** *f* (*Schulfach*) handicraft; ~ **sein** to be handmade; **Handball** *m* handball; **Handbremse** *f* handbrake; **Handbuch** *nt* handbook, manual; **Handcreme** *f* hand cream; **Händedruck** *m* handshake

Handel (*-s*) *m* trade; (*Geschäft*) transaction; **handeln** *vi* to act; (*Comm*) to trade; ~ **von** to be about ▷ *vr impers* **sich** ~ **um** to be about; **es handelt sich um ...** it's about ...; **Handelskammer** *f* chamber of commerce; **Handelsschule** *f* business school

Handfeger (*-s, -*) *m* brush; **Handfläche** *f* palm; **Handgelenk** *nt* wrist; **handgemacht** *adj* handmade; **Handgepäck** *nt* hand luggage (*Brit*) (*o* baggage)

Händler(in) (*-s, -*) *m(f)* dealer

handlich *adj* handy

Handlung *f* act, action; (*von Roman, Film*) plot

Handschellen *pl* handcuffs *pl*; **Handschrift** *f* handwriting; **Handschuh** *m* glove; **Handschuhfach** *nt* glove compartment; **Handtasche** *f* handbag, purse (*US*); **Handtuch** *nt* towel;

Handwerk *nt* trade; (*Kunst~*) craft; **Handwerker** (*-s, -*) *m* workman

Handy (*-s, -s*) *nt* mobile (phone), cell phone (*US*)

Hanf (*-(e)s*) *m* hemp

Hang (*-(e)s, Hänge*) *m* (*Abhang*) slope; (*fig*) tendency

Hängebrücke *f* suspension bridge; **Hängematte** *f* hammock

hängen (*hing, gehangen*) *vi* to hang; **an der Wand/an der Decke** ~ to hang on the wall/from the ceiling; **an jdm** ~ (*fig*) to be attached to sb; ~ **bleiben** to get caught (*an +dat* on); (*fig*) to get stuck ▷ *vt* to hang (*an +akk* on)

Hantel (*-, -n*) *f* dumbbell

Hardware (*-, -s*) *f* (*Inform*) hardware

Harfe (*-, -n*) *f* harp

harmlos *adj* harmless

harmonisch *adj* harmonious

Harn (*-(e)s, -e*) *m* urine; **Harnblase** *f* bladder

Harpune (*-, -n*) *f* harpoon

hart *adj* hard; (*fig*) harsh; **zu jdm** ~ **sein** to be hard on sb; ~ **gekocht** (*Ei*) hard-boiled; **hartnäckig** *adj* stubborn

Haschee (*-s, -s*) *nt* hash

Haschisch (*-*) *nt* hashish

Hase (*-n, -n*) *m* hare

Haselnuss *f* hazelnut

Hasenscharte *f* (*Med*) harelip

Hass (*-es*) *m* hatred (*auf, gegen +akk* of), hate; **einen** ~ **kriegen** (*fam*) to see red; **hassen** *vt* to hate

hässlich *adj* ugly; (*gemein*) nasty

Hast (*-*) *f* haste, hurry; **hastig** *adj* hasty

hatte *imperf von* **haben**

Haube (*-, -n*) *f* hood; (*Mütze*) cap; (*Auto*) bonnet (*Brit*), hood (*US*)

Hauch (*-(e)s, -e*) *m* breath; (*Luft~*) breeze; (*fig*) trace; **hauchdünn** *adj* (*Schicht, Scheibe*) wafer-thin

hauen (*haute, gehauen*) *vt* to hit

Haufen (*-s, -*) *m* pile; **ein** ~ **Geld** (*viel Geld*) a lot of money

häufig *adj* frequent ▷ *adv* frequently, often

Haupt- *in zW* main; **Hauptbahnhof** *m* central (*o* main) station; **Hauptdarsteller(in)** *m(f)* leading actor/lady; **Haupteingang** *m* main entrance; **Hauptgericht** *nt* main course;

Hauptgeschäftszeiten pl peak shopping hours pl; **Hauptgewinn** m first prize

Häuptling m chief

Hauptquartier nt headquarters pl; **Hauptreisezeit** f peak tourist season; **Hauptrolle** f leading role; **Hauptsache** f main thing; **hauptsächlich** adv mainly, chiefly; **Hauptsaison** f high (o peak) season; **Hauptsatz** m main clause; **Hauptschule** f ≈ secondary school (Brit), ≈ junior high school (US); **Hauptspeicher** m (Inform) main storage (o memory); **Hauptstadt** f capital; **Hauptstraße** f main road; (im Stadtzentrum) main street; **Hauptverkehrszeit** f rush hour

Haus (-es, Häuser) nt house; **nach ~e** home; **zu ~e** at home; **jdn nach ~e bringen** to take sb home; **bei uns zu ~e** (Heimat) where we come from; (Familie) in my family; (Haus) at our place; **Hausarbeit** f housework; **Hausaufgabe** f (Schule) homework; **~n** pl homework sing; **Hausbesitzer(in)** (-s, -) m(f) house owner; (Vermieter) landlord/-lady; **Hausbesuch** m home visit; **Hausbewohner(in)** (-s, -) m(f) occupant; **Hausflur** m hall; **Hausfrau** f housewife; **hausgemacht** adj homemade; **Haushalt** m household; (Pol) budget; **Hausherr(in)** m(f) host/hostess; (Vermieter) landlord/-lady

häuslich adj domestic

Hausmann m house-husband; **Hausmannskost** f good plain cooking; **Hausmeister(in)** m(f) caretaker (Brit), janitor (US); **Hausnummer** f house number; **Hausordnung** f (house) rules pl; **Hausschlüssel** m front-door key; **Hausschuh** m slipper; **Haustier** nt pet; **Haustür** f front door

Haut (-, Häute) f skin; (Tier) hide; **Hautarzt** m, **Hautärztin** f dermatologist; **Hautausschlag** m skin rash; **Hautcreme** f skin cream; **Hautfarbe** f skin colour; **Hautkrankheit** f skin disease

Hawaii (-s) nt Hawaii

Hbf. abk = **Hauptbahnhof** central station

Hebamme (-, -n) f midwife

Hebel (-s, -) m lever

heben (hob, gehoben) vt to raise, to lift

Hebräisch (-) nt Hebrew

Hecht (-(e)s, -e) m pike

Heck (-(e)s, -e) nt (von Boot) stern; (von Auto) rear; **Heckantrieb** m rear-wheel drive

Hecke (-, -n) f hedge

Heckklappe f tailgate; **Hecklicht** nt tail-light; **Heckscheibe** f rear window; **Heckscheibenheizung** f rear-window defroster

Hefe (-, -n) f yeast

Heft (-(e)s, -e) nt notebook, exercise book; (Ausgabe) issue

heftig adj violent; (Kritik, Streit) fierce

Heftklammer f paper clip; **Heftpflaster** nt plaster (Brit), Band-Aid® (US)

Heide (-, -n) f heath, moor; **Heidekraut** nt heather

Heidelbeere f bilberry, blueberry

heidnisch adj (Brauch) pagan

heikel adj (Angelegenheit) awkward; (wählerisch) fussy

heil adj (Sache) in one piece, intact; (Person) unhurt; **heilbar** adj curable

Heilbutt (-(e)s, -e) m halibut

heilen vt to cure ▷ vi to heal

heilig adj holy; **Heiligabend** m Christmas Eve; **Heilige(r)** mf saint

Heilmittel n remedy, cure (gegen for); **Heilpraktiker(in)** (-s, -) m(f) non-medical practitioner

heim adv home; **Heim** (-(e), -e) nt home

Heimat (-, -en) f home (town/country); **Heimatland** nt home country

heim|fahren irr vi to drive home; **Heimfahrt** f journey home; **heimisch** adj (Bevölkerung, Brauchtum) local; (Tiere, Pflanzen) native; **heim|kommen** irr vi to come (o return) home

heimlich adj secret

Heimreise f journey home; **Heimspiel** nt (Sport) home game; **Heimvorteil** m (Sport) home advantage; **Heimweg** m way home; **Heimweh** (-s) nt homesickness; **~ haben** to be homesick; **Heimwerker(in)** m(f) DIY enthusiast

Heirat (-, -en) f marriage; **heiraten** vi to get married ▷ vt to marry; **Heiratsantrag** m proposal; **er hat ihr einen ~ gemacht** he proposed to her

heiser adj hoarse

heiß adj hot; (Diskussion) heated; **mir ist ~** I'm hot

heißen (hieß, geheißen) vi to be called; (bedeuten) to mean; **ich heiße Tom** my name is Tom; **wie ~ Sie?** what's your name?; **wie heißt sie mit Nachnamen?** what's her surname?; **wie heißt das auf**

Englisch? what's that in English? ▷ vi impers **es heißt** (man sagt) it is said; **es heißt in dem Brief ...** it says in the letter ...; **das heißt** that is
Heißluftherd m fan-assisted oven
heiter adj cheerful; (Wetter) bright
heizen vt to heat; **Heizkissen** m (Med) heated pad; **Heizkörper** m radiator; **Heizöl** nt fuel oil; **Heizung** f heating
Hektar (-s, -) nt hectare
Hektik (-, -en) f **nur keine ~!** take it easy; **hektisch** adj hectic
Held (-en, -en) m hero; **Heldin** f heroine
helfen (half, geholfen) vi to help (jdm bei etw sb with sth); (nützen) to be of use; **sie weiß sich** (dat) **zu ~** she can manage ▷ vi impers **es hilft nichts, du musst ...** it's no use, you have to ...; **Helfer(in)** m(f) helper; (Mitarbeiter) assistant
Helikopter-Skiing (-s) nt heliskiing, helicopter skiing
hell adj bright; (Farbe) light; (Hautfarbe) fair; **hellblau** adj light blue; **hellblond** adj ash-blond; **hellgelb** adj pale yellow; **hellgrün** adj light green; **Hellseher(in)** m(f) clairvoyant
Helm (-(e)s, -e) m helmet; **Helmpflicht** f compulsory wearing of helmets
Hemd (-(e)s, -en) nt shirt; (Unter~) vest
hemmen vt to check; (behindern) to hamper; **gehemmt sein** to be inhibited; **Hemmung** f (psychisch) inhibition; **sie hatte keine ~, ihn zu betrügen** she had no scruples about deceiving him; (moralisch) scruple
Henkel (-s, -) m handle
Henna (-s) nt henna
Henne (-, -n) f hen
Hepatitis (-, Hepatitiden) f hepatitis

🔵 **SCHLÜSSELWORT**

her adv **1** (Richtung): **komm her zu mir** come here (to me); **von England her** from England; **von weit her** from a long way away; **her damit!** hand it over!; **wo hat er das her?** where did he get that from?; **wo bist du her?** where do you come from?
2 (Blickpunkt): **von der Form her** as far as the form is concerned
3 (zeitlich): **das ist 5 Jahre her** that was 5

years ago; **ich kenne ihn von früher her** I know him from before

herab adv down; **herablassend** adj (Bemerkung) condescending; **herab|sehen** irr vt **auf jdn ~** to look down on sb; **herab|setzen** vt to reduce; (fig) to disparage
heran adv **näher ~!** come closer; **heran|kommen** irr vi to approach; **~ an** (+akk) to be able to get at; (fig) to be able to get hold of; **heran|wachsen** irr vi to grow up
herauf adv up; **herauf|beschwören** irr vt to evoke; (verursachen) to cause; **herauf|ziehen** irr vt to pull up ▷ vi to approach; (Sturm) to gather
heraus adv out; **heraus|bekommen** irr vt (Geheimnis) to find out; (Rätsel) to solve; **ich bekomme noch zwei Euro heraus** I've got two euros change to come; **heraus|bringen** irr vt to bring out; **heraus|finden** irr vt to find out; **heraus|fordern** vt to challenge; **Herausforderung** f challenge; **heraus|geben** irr vt (Buch) to edit; (veröffentlichen) to publish; **jdm zwei Euro ~** to give sb two euros change; **geben Sie mir bitte auf 20 Euro heraus** could you give me change for 20 euros, please?; **heraus|holen** vt to get out (aus of); **heraus|kommen** irr vi to come out; **dabei kommt nichts heraus** nothing will come of it; **heraus|stellen** vr **sich ~** to turn out (als to be); **heraus|ziehen** irr vt to pull out
Herbst (-(e)s, -e) m autumn, fall (US)
Herd (-(e)s, -e) m cooker, stove
Herde (-, -n) f herd; (Schafe) flock
herein adv in; **~!** come in; **herein|fallen** irr vi **wir sind auf einen Betrüger hereingefallen** we were taken in by a swindler; **herein|legen** vt **jdn ~** (fig) to take sb for a ride
Herfahrt f journey here; **auf der ~** on the way here
Hergang m course (of events); **schildern Sie mir den ~** tell me what happened
Hering (-s, -e) m herring
her|kommen irr vi to come; **wo kommt sie her?** where does she come from?
Heroin (-s) nt heroin
Herpes (-) m (Med) herpes

Herr (-(e)n, -en) m (vor Namen) Mr; (Mann) gentleman; (Adliger, Gott) Lord; **mein ~!** sir; **meine ~en!** gentlemen; **Sehr geehrte Damen und ~en** Dear Sir or Madam; **herrenlos** adj (Gepäckstück) abandoned; (Tier) stray; **Herrentoilette** f men's toilet, gents

her|richten vt to prepare

herrlich adj marvellous, splendid

Herrschaft f rule; (Macht) power; **meine ~en!** ladies and gentlemen!

herrschen vi to rule; (bestehen) to be

her|stellen vt to make; (industriell) to manufacture; **Hersteller(in)** m(f) manufacturer; **Herstellung** f production

herüber adv over

herum adv around; (im Kreis) round; **um etw ~** around sth; **du hast den Pulli falsch ~ an** you're wearing your sweater inside out; **anders ~** the other way round; **herum|fahren** irr vi to drive around; **herum|führen** vt **jdn in der Stadt ~** to show sb around the town ▷ vi **die Straße führt um das Zentrum herum** the road goes around the city centre; **herum|kommen** irr vi **sie ist viel in der Welt herumgekommen** she's been around the world; **um etw ~** (vermeiden) to get out of sth; **herum|kriegen** vt to talk round; **herum|treiben** irr vr **sich ~** to hang around

herunter adv down; **heruntergekommen** adj (Gebäude, Gegend) run-down; (Person) down-at-heel; **herunter|handeln** vt to get down; **herunter|holen** vt to bring down; **herunter|kommen** irr vi to come down; **herunter|laden** irr vt (Inform) to download

hervor adv out; **hervor|bringen** irr vt to produce; (Wort) to utter; **hervor|heben** irr vt to emphasize, to stress; **hervorragend** adj excellent; **hervor|rufen** irr vt to cause, to give rise to

Herz (-ens, -en) nt heart; (Karten) hearts pl; **von ganzem ~en** wholeheartedly; **sich** (dat) **etw zu ~en nehmen** to take sth to heart; **Herzanfall** m heart attack; **Herzbeschwerden** pl heart trouble sing; **Herzfehler** m heart defect; **herzhaft** adj (Essen) substantial; **~ lachen** to have a good laugh; **Herzinfarkt** m heart attack; **Herzklopfen** (-s) nt (Med) palpitations pl;

ich hatte ~ (vor Aufregung) my heart was pounding (with excitement); **herzkrank** adj **sie ist ~** she's got a heart condition; **herzlich** adj (Empfang, Mensch) warm; **~en Glückwunsch** congratulations

Herzog(in) (-s, Herzöge) m(f) duke/duchess

Herzschlag m heartbeat; (Herzversagen) heart failure; **Herzschrittmacher** m pacemaker; **Herzstillstand** m cardiac arrest

Hessen (-s) nt Hessen

heterosexuell adj heterosexual; **Heterosexuelle(r)** mf heterosexual

Hetze (-, -) f (Eile) rush; **hetzen** vt to rush ▷ vr **sich ~** to rush

Heu (-(e)s) nt hay

heuer adv this year

heulen vi to howl; (weinen) to cry

Heuschnupfen m hay fever; **Heuschrecke** (-, -n) f grasshopper; (größer) locust

heute adv today; **~ Abend/früh** this evening/morning; **~ Nacht** tonight; (letzte Nacht) last night; **~ in acht Tagen** a week (from) today; **sie hat bis ~ nicht bezahlt** she hasn't paid to this day; **heutig** adj **die ~e Zeitung/Generation** today's paper/generation; **heutzutage** adv nowadays

Hexe (-, -n) f witch; **Hexenschuss** m lumbago

hielt imperf von **halten**

hier adv here; **~ entlang** this way; **~ bleiben** to stay here; **~ lassen** to leave here; **ich bin auch nicht von ~** I'm a stranger here myself; **hierher** adv here; **das gehört nicht ~** that doesn't belong here; **hiermit** adv with this; **hierzulande**, **hier zu Lande** adv in this country

hiesig adj local

hieß imperf von **heißen**

Hi-Fi-Anlage f hi-fi (system)

high adj (fam) high; **Highlife** (-s) nt high life; **~ machen** to live it up; **Hightech** (-s) nt high tech

Hilfe (-, -n) f help; (für Notleidende, finanziell) aid; **~!** help!; **erste ~ leisten** to give first aid; **um ~ bitten** to ask for help; **hilflos** adj helpless; **hilfsbereit** adj helpful; **Hilfsmittel** nt aid

Himbeere f raspberry

Himmel (-s, -) m sky; (Rel) heaven;
  Himmelfahrt f Ascension;
  Himmelsrichtung f direction;
  himmlisch adj heavenly

🅞 SCHLÜSSELWORT

hin adv **1** Richtung): **hin und zurück** there
and back; **hin und her** to and fro; **bis zur
Mauer hin** up to the wall; **wo ist er hin?**
where has he gone?; **Geld hin, Geld her**
money or no money

2 (auf ... hin): **auf meine Bitte hin** at my
request; **auf seinen Rat hin** on the basis
of his advice

3: **mein Glück ist hin** my happiness has
gone

hinab adv down; **hinab|gehen** irr vi to go
down

hinauf adv up; **hinauf|gehen** irr vi, vt
to go up; **hinauf|steigen** irr vi to climb
(up)

hinaus adv out; **hinaus|gehen** irr vi to go
out; **das Zimmer geht auf den See
hinaus** the room looks out onto the lake;
~ über (+akk) to exceed; **hinaus|laufen** irr
vi to run out; **~ auf** (+akk) to come to, to
amount to; **hinaus|schieben** irr vt to put
off, to postpone; **hinaus|werfen** irr vt to
throw out; (aus Firma) to fire, to sack
(Brit); **hinaus|zögern** vr **sich ~** to take
longer than expected

Hinblick m in (o im) **~ auf** (+akk) with
regard to; (wegen) in view of

hin|bringen irr vt **ich bringe Sie hin** I'll
take you there

hindern vt to prevent; **jdn daran ~, etw
zu tun** to stop (o prevent) sb from doing
sth; **Hindernis** nt obstacle

Hinduismus m Hinduism

hindurch adv through; **das ganze Jahr
~** throughout the year, all year round; **die
ganze Nacht ~** all night (long)

hinein adv in; **hinein|gehen** irr vi to go
in; **~ in** (+akk) to go into, to enter;
hinein|passen vi to fit in; **~ in** (+akk) to
fit into

hin|fahren irr vi to go there ▷ vt to take
there; **Hinfahrt** f outward journey

hin|fallen irr vi to fall (down)

Hinflug m outward flight

hing imperf von **hängen**

hin|gehen irr vi to go there; (Zeit) to pass;
  hin|halten irr vt to hold out; (warten
  lassen) to put off

hinken vi to limp; **der Vergleich hinkt**
the comparison doesn't work

hin|knien vr **sich ~** to kneel down;
  hin|legen vt to put down ▷ vr **sich ~** to
  lie down; **hin|nehmen** irr vt (fig) to put
  up with, to take; **Hinreise** f outward
  journey; **hin|setzen** vr **sich ~** to sit down;
  hinsichtlich prep +gen with regard to;
  hin|stellen vt to put (down) ▷ vr **sich
  ~** to stand

hinten adv at the back; (im Auto) in the
back; (dahinter) behind

hinter prep +dat o akk behind; (nach) after;
  ~ jdm her sein to be after sb; **etw ~ sich**
  (akk) **bringen** to get sth over (and done)
  with; **Hinterachse** f rear axle;
  Hinterausgang m rear exit; **Hinterbein** nt
  hind leg; **Hinterbliebene(r)** mf
  dependant; **hintere(r, s)** adj rear, back;
  hintereinander adv (in einer Reihe) one
  behind the other; (hintereinander her) one
  after the other; **drei Tage ~** three days
  running (o in a row); **Hintereingang** m
  rear entrance; **Hintergedanke** m ulterior
  motive; **hintergehen** irr vt to deceive;
  Hintergrund m background; **hinterher**
  adv (zeitlich) afterwards; **los, ~!** come on,
  after him/her/them; **Hinterkopf** m back
  of the head; **hinterlassen** vt to leave;
  jdm eine Nachricht ~ to leave a
  message for sb; **hinterlegen** vt to leave
  (bei with)

Hintern (-, -) m (fam) backside, bum

Hinterradantrieb m (Auto) rear-wheel
drive; **Hinterteil** nt back (part); (Hintern)
behind; **Hintertür** f back door

hinüber adv over; **~ sein** (fam: kaputt) to
be ruined; (verdorben) to have gone bad;
hinüber|gehen irr vi to go over

hinunter adv down; **hinunter|gehen** irr
vi, vt to go down; **hinunter|schlucken** vt
(a. fig) to swallow

Hinweg m outward journey

hinweg|setzen vr **sich über etw** (akk)
~ to ignore sth

Hinweis (-es, -e) m (Andeutung) hint;
(Anweisung) instruction; (Verweis)
reference; **hin|weisen** irr vi **jdn auf etw**
(acc) **~** to point sth out to sb; **jdn nochmal
auf etw ~** to remind sb of sth

hinzu *adv* in addition; **hinzu|fügen** *vt* to add; **hinzu|kommen** *irr vi* **zu jdm ~** to join sb; **es war kalt, hinzu kam, dass es auch noch regnete** it was cold, and on top of that it was raining

Hirn (-(e)s, -e) *nt* brain; (*Verstand*) brains *pl*; **Hirnhautentzündung** *f* meningitis; **hirnverbrannt** *adj* crazy

Hirsch (-(e)s, -e) *m* deer; (*als Speise*) venison

Hirse (-, -n) *f* millet

Hirte (-n, -n) *m* shepherd

historisch *adj* historical

Hit (-s, -s) *m* (*fig, Mus, Inform*) hit; **Hitliste** *f*, **Hitparade** *f* charts *pl*

Hitze (-) *f* heat; **hitzebeständig** *adj* heat-resistant; **Hitzewelle** *f* heatwave; **hitzig** *adj* hot-tempered; (*Debatte*) heated; **Hitzschlag** *m* heatstroke

HIV (-(s), -(s)) *nt abk* = **Human Immunodeficiency Virus** HIV; **HIV-negativ** *adj* HIV-negative; **HIV-positiv** *adj* HIV-positive

H-Milch *f* long-life milk

hob *imperf von* **heben**

Hobby (-s, -s) *nt* hobby

Hobel (-s, -) *m* plane

hoch *adj* high; (*Baum, Haus*) tall; (*Schnee*) deep; **der Zaun ist drei Meter ~** the fence is three metres high; **~ auflösend** high-resolution; **~ begabt** extremely gifted; **das ist mir zu ~** that's above my head; **~ soll sie leben!, sie lebe ~!** three cheers for her; **4 ~ 2 ist 16** 4 squared is 16; **4 ~ 5** 4 to the power of 5

Hoch (-s, -s) *nt* (*Ruf*) cheer; (*Meteo*) high; **hochachtungsvoll** *adv* (*in Briefen*) Yours faithfully; **Hochbetrieb** *m* **es herrscht ~** they/we are extremely busy; **Hochdeutsch** *nt* High German; **Hochgebirge** *nt* high mountains *pl*; **Hochgeschwindigkeitszug** *m* high-speed train; **Hochhaus** *nt* high rise; **hoch|heben** *irr vt* to lift (up); **hochprozentig** *adj* (*Alkohol*) high-proof; **Hochsaison** *f* high season; **Hochschule** *f* college; (*Universität*) university; **hochschwanger** *adj* heavily pregnant; **Hochsommer** *m* midsummer; **Hochspannung** *f* great tension; (*Elek*) high voltage; **Hochsprung** *m* high jump

höchst *adv* highly, extremely; **höchste(r, s)** *adj* highest; (*äußerste*) extreme; **höchstens**

adv at the most; **Höchstgeschwindigkeit** *f* maximum speed; **Höchstparkdauer** *f* maximum stay

Hochstuhl *m* high chair

höchstwahrscheinlich *adv* very probably

Hochwasser *nt* high water; (*Überschwemmung*) floods *pl*; **hochwertig** *adj* high-quality

Hochzeit (-, -en) *f* wedding; **Hochzeitsnacht** *f* wedding night; **Hochzeitsreise** *f* honeymoon; **Hochzeitstag** *m* wedding day; (*Jahrestag*) wedding anniversary

hocken *vi* to squat, to crouch

Hocker (-s, -) *m* stool

Hockey (-s) *nt* hockey

Hoden (-s, -) *m* testicle

Hof (-(e)s, Höfe) *m* (*Hinterhof*) yard; (*Innenhof*) courtyard; (*Bauernhof*) farm; (*Königshof*) court

hoffen *vi* to hope (*auf* +*akk* for); **ich hoffe es** I hope so; **hoffentlich** *adv* hopefully; **~ nicht** I hope not; **Hoffnung** *f* hope; **hoffnungslos** *adj* hopeless; **höflich** *adj* polite; **Höflichkeit** *f* politeness

hohe(r, s) *adj siehe* **hoch**

Höhe (-, -n) *f* height; (*Anhöhe*) hill; (*einer Summe*) amount; **in einer ~ von 5000 Metern** at an altitude of 5,000 metres; (*Flughöhe*) altitude; **Höhenangst** *f* vertigo; **Höhensonne** *f* sun lamp

Höhepunkt *m* (*einer Reise*) high point; (*einer Veranstaltung*) highlight; (*eines Films, sexuell*) climax

höher *adj, adv* higher

hohl *adj* hollow

Höhle (-, -n) *f* cave

holen *vt* to get, to fetch; (*abholen*) to pick up; (*Atem*) to catch; **die Polizei ~** to call the police; **jdn/etw ~ lassen** to send for sb/sth

Holland *nt* Holland; **Holländer(in)** (-s, -) *m(f)* Dutchman/-woman; **holländisch** *adj* Dutch

Hölle (-, -n) *f* hell

Hologramm *nt* hologram

holperig *adj* bumpy

Holunder (-s, -) *m* elder

Holz (-es, Hölzer) *nt* wood; **Holzboden** *m* wooden floor; **hölzern** *adj* wooden; **holzig** *adj* (*Stängel*) woody; **Holzkohle** *f* charcoal

Homebanking (-s) nt home banking, online banking; **Homepage** (-, -s) f home page; **Hometrainer** m exercise machine

homöopathisch adj homeopathic

homosexuell adj homosexual; **Homosexuelle(r)** mf homosexual

Honig (-s, -e) m honey; **Honigmelone** f honeydew melon

Honorar (-s, -e) nt fee

Hopfen (-s, -) m (Bot) hop; (beim Brauen) hops pl

hoppla interj whoops, oops

horchen vi to listen (auf+akk to); (an der Tür) to eavesdrop

hören vt, vi (passiv, mitbekommen) to hear; (zufällig) to overhear; (aufmerksam zuhören, Radio, Musik) to listen to; **ich habe schon viel von Ihnen gehört** I've heard a lot about you; **Hörer** m (Tel) receiver; **Hörer(in)** m(f) listener; **Hörgerät** nt hearing aid

Horizont (-(e)s, -e) m horizon; **das geht über meinen ~** that's beyond me

Hormon (-s, -e) nt hormone

Hornhaut f hard skin; (des Auges) cornea

Hornisse (-, -n) f hornet

Horoskop (-s, -e) nt horoscope

Hörsaal m lecture hall; **Hörsturz** m acute hearing loss; **Hörweite** f **in/außer ~** within/out of earshot

Höschenwindel (-, -n) f nappy (Brit), diaper (US)

Hose (-, -n) f trousers pl (Brit), pants pl (US); (Unterhose) (under)pants pl; **eine ~** a pair of trousers/pants; **kurze ~** (pair of) shorts pl; **Hosenanzug** m trouser suit (Brit), pantsuit (US); **Hosenschlitz** m fly, flies (Brit); **Hosentasche** f trouser pocket (Brit), pant pocket (US); **Hosenträger** m braces pl (Brit), suspenders pl (US)

Hospital (-s, Hospitäler) nt hospital

Hotdog (-s, -s) nt o m hot dog

Hotel (-s, -s) nt hotel; **in welchem ~ seid ihr?** which hotel are you staying at?; **Hoteldirektor(in)** m(f) hotel manager; **Hotelkette** f hotel chain; **Hotelzimmer** nt hotel room

Hotline (-, -s) f hot line

Hubraum m cubic capacity

hübsch adj (Mädchen, Kind, Kleid) pretty; (gutaussehend; Mann, Frau) good-looking, cute

Hubschrauber (-s, -) m helicopter

Huf (-(e)s, -e) m hoof; **Hufeisen** nt horseshoe

Hüfte (-, -n) f hip

Hügel (-s, -) m hill; **hügelig** adj hilly

Huhn (-(e)s, Hühner) nt hen; (Gastr) chicken; **Hühnchen** nt chicken; **Hühnerauge** nt corn; **Hühnerbrühe** f chicken broth

Hülle (-, -n) f cover; (für Ausweis) case; (Zellophan) wrapping

Hummel (-, -n) f bumblebee

Hummer (-s, -) m lobster; **Hummerkrabbe** f king prawn

Humor (-s) m humour; **~ haben** to have a sense of humour; **humorvoll** adj humorous

humpeln vi hobble

Hund (-(e)s, -e) m dog; **Hundeleine** f dog lead (Brit), dog leash (US)

hundert num hundred; **Hundertjahrfeier** f centenary; **hundertprozentig** adj, adv one hundred per cent; **hundertste(r, s)** adj hundredth

Hündin f bitch

Hunger (-s) m hunger; **~ haben/bekommen** to be/get hungry; **hungern** vi to go hungry; (ernsthaft, dauernd) to starve

Hupe (-, -n) f horn; **hupen** vi to sound one's horn

Hüpfburg f bouncy castle®; **hüpfen** vi to hop; (springen) to jump

Hürde (-, -n) f hurdle

Hure (-, -n) f whore

hurra interj hooray

husten vi to cough; **Husten** (-s) m cough; **Hustenbonbon** nt cough sweet; **Hustensaft** m cough mixture

Hut (-(e)s, Hüte) m hat

hüten vt to look after ▷ vr **sich ~** to watch out; **sich ~, etw zu tun** to take care not to do sth; **sich ~ vor** (+dat) to beware of

Hütte (-, -n) f hut, cottage; **Hüttenkäse** m cottage cheese

Hyäne (-, -n) f hyena

Hydrant m hydrant

hygienisch adj hygienic

Hyperlink (-s, -s) m hyperlink

Hypnose (-, -n) f hypnosis; **Hypnotiseur(in)** m(f) hypnotist; **hypnotisieren** vt to hypnotize

Hypothek (-, -en) f mortgage

hysterisch adj hysterical

ihnen *pron dat pl von* **sie**; (to) them; **wie geht es ~?** how are they?; **ein Freund von ~** a friend of theirs

Ihnen *pron dat sing u pl von* **Sie**; (to) you; **wie geht es ~?** how are you?; **ein Freund von ~** a friend of yours

ihr *pron* **1** (*nom pl*) you; **ihr seid es** it's you
2 (*dat von sie*) to her; **gib es ihr** give it to her; **er steht neben ihr** he is standing beside her
▷ *possessiv pron* **1** (*sg*) her; (*bei Tieren, Dingen*) its; **ihr Mann** her husband
2 (*pl*) their; **die Bäume und ihre Blätter** the trees and their leaves

Ihr *pron von* **Sie**; (*adjektivisch*) your; **~(e) XY** (*am Briefende*) Yours, XY

ihre(r, s) *pron* (*substantivisch, sing*) hers; (*pl*) theirs; **das ist ~/~r/ihr(e)s** that's hers; (*pl*) that's theirs

Ihre(r, s) *pron* (*substantivisch*) yours; **das ist ~/~r/Ihr(e)s** that's yours

ihretwegen *adv* (*wegen ihr*) because of her; (*ihr zuliebe*) for her sake; (*um sie*) about her; (*von ihr aus*) as far as she is concerned ▷ *adv* (*wegen ihnen*) because of them; (*ihnen zuliebe*) for their sake; (*um sie*) about them; (*von ihnen aus*) as far as they are concerned; **Ihretwegen** *adv* (*wegen Ihnen*) because of you; (*Ihnen zuliebe*) for your sake; (*um Sie*) about you; (*von Ihnen aus*) as far as you are concerned

Ikone (*-, -n*) *f* icon

illegal *adj* illegal

Illusion *f* illusion; **sich** (*dat*) **~en machen** to delude oneself; **illusorisch** *adj* illusory

Illustration *f* illustration

Illustrierte (*-n, -n*) *f* (*glossy*) magazine

im *kontr von* **in dem**; **~ Bett** in bed; **~ Fernsehen** on TV; **~ Radio** on the radio; **~ Bus/Zug** on the bus/train; **~ Januar** in January; **~ Stehen** (*while*) standing up

Imbiss (*-es, -e*) *m* snack; **Imbissbude** *f*, **Imbissstube** *f* snack bar

Imbusschlüssel *m* hex key

immer *adv* always; **~ mehr** more and more; **~ wieder** again and again; **~ noch** still; **~ noch nicht** still not; **für ~** forever; **~ wenn ich ...** every time I ...;

---

i. A. *abk* = **im Auftrag** pp

IC (*-, -s*) *m abk* = **Intercityzug** Intercity (train)

ICE (*-, -s*) *m abk* = **Intercityexpresszug** German high-speed train

ich *pron* I; **~ bin's** it's me; **~ nicht** not me; **du und ~** you and me; **hier bin ~!** here I am; **~ Idiot!** stupid me

Icon (*-s, -s*) *nt* (*Inform*) icon

IC-Zuschlag *m* Intercity supplement

ideal *adj* ideal; **Ideal** (*-s, -e*) *nt* ideal

Idee (*-, -n*) *f* idea

identifizieren *vt* to identify ▷ *vr* **sich mit jdm/etw ~** to identify with sb/sth

identisch *adj* identical

Idiot(in) (*-en, -en*) *m(f)* idiot; **idiotisch** *adj* idiotic

Idol (*-s, -e*) *nt* idol

Idylle *f* idyll; **idyllisch** *adj* idyllic

Igel (*-s, -*) *m* hedgehog

ignorieren *vt* to ignore

ihm *pron dat sing von* **er/es**; (to) him, (to) it; **wie geht es ~?** how is he?; **ein Freund von ~** a friend of his ▷ *pron dat von* **es**; (to) it

ihn *pron akk sing von* **er**; (*Person*) him; (*Sache*) it

~ schöner/trauriger more and more beautiful/sadder and sadder; **was/wer/wo/wann (auch)** ~ whatever/whoever/wherever/whenever; **immerhin** adv after all; **immerzu** adv all the time

Immigrant(in) m(f) immigrant

Immobilien pl property sing, real estate sing; **Immobilienmakler(in)** m(f) estate agent (Brit), realtor (US)

immun adj immune (gegen to); **Immunschwäche** f immunodeficiency; **Immunschwächekrankheit** f immune deficiency syndrome; **Immunsystem** nt immune system

impfen vt to vaccinate; **ich muss mich gegen Pocken ~ lassen** I've got to get myself vaccinated against smallpox; **Impfpass** m vaccination card; **Impfstoff** m vaccine; **Impfung** f vaccination

imponieren vi to impress (jdm sb)

Import (-(e)s, -e) m import; **importieren** vt to import

impotent adj impotent

imstande adj ~ **sein** to be in a position; (fähig) to be able

○ SCHLÜSSELWORT

in präp +akk **1** (räumlich: wohin?) in, into; **in die Stadt** into town; **in die Schule gehen** to go to school
2 (zeitlich): **bis ins 20. Jahrhundert** into od up to the 20th century
▷ präp +dat **1** (räumlich: wo) in; **in der Stadt** in town; **in der Schule sein** to be at school
2 (zeitlich: wann); **in diesem Jahr** this year (in jenem Jahr) in that year; **heute in zwei Wochen** two weeks today

inbegriffen adj included

indem conj **sie gewann, ~ sie mogelte** she won by cheating

Inder(in) (-s, -) m(f) Indian

Indianer(in) (-s, -) m(f) American Indian, Native American; **indianisch** adj American Indian, Native American

Indien (-s) nt India

indirekt adj indirect

indisch adj Indian

indiskret adj indiscreet

individuell adj individual

Indonesien (-s) nt Indonesia

Industrie f industry; **Industrie-** in zW industrial; **Industriegebiet** nt industrial area; **industriell** adj industrial

ineinander adv in(to) one another (o each other)

Infarkt (-(e)s, -e) m (Herzinfarkt) heart attack

Infektion f infection; **Infektionskrankheit** f infectious disease; **infizieren** vt to infect ▷ vr **sich ~** to be infected

Info (-, -s) f (fam) info

infolge prep +gen as a result of, owing to; **infolgedessen** adv consequently

Informatik f computer science; **Informatiker(in)** (-s, -) m(f) computer scientist

Information f information; **Informationsschalter** m information desk; **informieren** vt to inform; **falsch ~** to misinform ▷ vr **sich ~** to find out (über +akk about)

infrage adv **das kommt nicht ~** that's out of the question; **etw ~ stellen** to question sth

Infrastruktur f infrastructure

Infusion f infusion

Ingenieur(in) m(f) engineer

Ingwer (-s) m ginger

Inhaber(in) (-s, -) m(f) owner; (Haus~) occupier; (von Lizenz) holder; (Fin) bearer

Inhalt (-(e)s, -e) m contents pl; (eines Buchs etc) content; (Math) volume; (Flächeninhalt) area; **Inhaltsangabe** f summary; **Inhaltsverzeichnis** nt table of contents

Initiative f initiative; **die ~ ergreifen** to take the initiative

Injektion f injection

inklusive adv, prep inclusive (gen of)

inkonsequent adj inconsistent

Inland nt (Pol, Comm) home; **im ~** at home; (Geo) inland; **inländisch** adj domestic; **Inlandsflug** m domestic flight; **Inlandsgespräch** nt national call

Inlineskates pl Rollerblades® pl, inline skates pl

innen adv inside; **Innenarchitekt(in)** m(f) interior designer; **Innenhof** m (inner) courtyard; **Innenminister(in)** m(f) minister of the interior, Home Secretary (Brit); **Innenseite** f inside; **Innenspiegel**

m rearview mirror; **Innenstadt** *f* town centre; (*von Großstadt*) city centre

innere(r, s) *adj* inner; (*im Körper, inländisch*) internal; **Innere(s)** *nt* inside; (*Mitte*) centre; (*fig*) heart

Innereien *pl* innards *pl*

innerhalb *adv, prep +gen* within; (*räumlich*) inside

innerlich *adj* internal; (*geistig*) inner

innerste(r, s) *adj* innermost

Innovation *f* innovation; **innovativ** *adj* innovative

inoffiziell *adj* unofficial; (*zwanglos*) informal

ins *kontr von* **in das**

Insasse (-n, -n) *m*, **Insassin** *f* (*Auto*) passenger; (*Anstalt*) inmate

insbesondere *adv* particularly, in particular

Inschrift *f* inscription

Insekt (-(e)s, -en) *nt* insect, bug (*US*); **Insektenschutzmittel** *nt* insect repellent; **Insektenstich** *m* insect bite

Insel (-, -n) *f* island

Inserat *nt* advertisement

insgesamt *adv* altogether, all in all

Insider(in) (-s, -) *m(f)* insider

insofern *adv* in that respect; (*deshalb*) (and) so ▷ *conj* if; **~ als** in so far as

Installateur(in) *m(f)* (*Klempner*) plumber; (*Elektroinstallateur*) electrician; **installieren** *vt* (*Inform*) to install

Instinkt (-(e)s, -e) *m* instinct

Institut (-(e)s, -e) *nt* institute

Institution *f* institution

Instrument *nt* instrument

Insulin (-s) *nt* insulin

Inszenierung *f* production

intakt *adj* intact

intellektuell *adj* intellectual

intelligent *adj* intelligent; **Intelligenz** *f* intelligence

intensiv *adj* (*gründlich*) intensive; (*Gefühl, Schmerz*) intense; **Intensivkurs** *m* crash course; **Intensivstation** *f* intensive care unit

interaktiv *adj* interactive

Intercityexpress(zug) *m* German high-speed train; **Intercityzug** *m* Intercity (train); **Intercityzuschlag** *m* Intercity supplement

interessant *adj* interesting; **Interesse** (-s, -n) *nt* interest; **~ haben an** (+*dat*) to be

interested in; **interessieren** *vt* to interest ▷ *vr* **sich ~** to be interested (*für* in)

Interface (-, -s) *nt* (*Inform*) interface

Internat *nt* boarding school

international *adj* international

Internet (-s) *nt* Internet, Net; **im ~** on the Internet; **im ~ surfen** to surf the Net; **Internetcafé** *nt* Internetcafé, cybercafé; **Internetfirma** *f* dotcom company; **Internethandel** *m* e-commerce; **Internetseite** *f* web page

interpretieren *vt* to interpret (*als* as)

Interpunktion *f* punctuation

Interregio (-s, -s) *m* regional train

Interview (-s, -s) *nt* interview; **interviewen** *vt* to interview

intim *adj* intimate

intolerant *adj* intolerant

investieren *vt* to invest

inwiefern *adv* in what way; (*in welchem Ausmaß*) to what extent; **inwieweit** *adv* to what extent

inzwischen *adv* meanwhile

Irak (-(s)) *m* (**der**) **~** Iraq

Iran (-(s)) *m* (**der**) **~** Iran

Ire (-n, -n) *m* Irishman

irgend *adv* **~ so ein Idiot** some idiot; **wenn ~ möglich** if at all possible; **irgendein** *pron*, **irgendeine(r, s)** *adj* some; (*fragend, im Bedingungssatz; beliebig*) any; **irgendetwas** *pron* something; (*fragend, im Bedingungssatz*) anything; **irgendjemand** *pron* somebody; (*fragend, im Bedingungssatz*) anybody; **irgendwann** *adv* sometime; (*zu beliebiger Zeit*) any time; **irgendwie** *adv* somehow; **irgendwo** *adv* somewhere; (*fragend, im Bedingungssatz*) anywhere

Irin *f* Irishwoman; **irisch** *adj* Irish; **Irland** *nt* Ireland

ironisch *adj* ironic

irre *adj* crazy, mad; (*toll*) terrific; **Irre(r)** *mf* lunatic; **irreführen** *irr vt* to mislead; **irremachen** *vt* to confuse; **irren** *vi* to be mistaken; (*umherirren*) to wander ▷ *vr* **sich ~** to be mistaken; **wenn ich mich nicht irre** if I'm not mistaken; **sich in der Nummer ~** (*Telefon*) to get the wrong number; **irrsinnig** *adj* mad, crazy; **Irrtum** (-s, -tümer) *m* mistake, error; **irrtümlich** *adj* mistaken ▷ *adv* by mistake

ISBN (-) *nt abk* = **industrial standard business network** ISBN ▷ (-) *f abk* =

Internationale Standard Buchnummer
ISBN
Ischias (-) *m* sciatica
ISDN (-) *nt* `abk =` **integrated services digital network** ISDN
Islam (-s) *m* Islam; **islamisch** *adj* Islamic
Island *nt* Iceland; **Isländer(in)** (-s, -) *m(f)* Icelander; **isländisch** *adj* Icelandic; **Isländisch** *nt* Icelandic
Isolierband *nt* insulating tape; **isolieren** *vt* to isolate; (*Elek*) to insulate
Isomatte *f* thermomat, karrymat®
Israel (-s) *nt* Israel; **Israeli** (-(s), -(s)) *m* (-, -(s)) *f* Israeli; **israelisch** *adj* Israeli
IT (-) *f* `abk =` **Informationstechnologie** IT
Italien (-s) *nt* Italy; **Italiener(in)** (-s, -) *m(f)* Italian; **italienisch** *adj* Italian; **Italienisch** *nt* Italian

j

ja adv **1** yes; **haben Sie das gesehen? — ja** did you see it? — yes(, I did); **ich glaube ja** (yes,) I think so

2 (fragend) really?; **ich habe gekündigt — ja?** I've quit — have you?; **du kommst, ja?** you're coming, aren't you?

3 : **sei ja vorsichtig** do be careful; **Sie wissen ja, dass ...** as you know, ...; **tu das ja nicht!** don't do that!; **ich habe es ja gewusst** I just knew it; **ja, also ...** well you see ...

Jacht (-, -en) f yacht; **Jachthafen** m marina

Jacke (-, -n) f jacket; (Wolljacke) cardigan

Jackett (-s, -s o -e) nt jacket

Jagd (-, -en) f hunt; (Jagen) hunting; **jagen** vi to hunt ▷ vt to hunt; (verfolgen) to chase; **Jäger(in)** m(f) hunter

Jaguar (-s, -e) m jaguar

Jahr (-(e)s, -e) nt year; **ein halbes ~** six months pl; **Anfang der neunziger ~e** in the early nineties; **mit sechzehn ~en** at (the age of) sixteen; **Jahrestag** m anniversary; **Jahreszahl** f date, year;

Jahreszeit f season; **Jahrgang** m (Wein) year, vintage; **der ~ 1989** (Personen) those born in 1989; **Jahrhundert** (-s, -e) nt century; **jährlich** adj yearly, annual; **Jahrmarkt** m fair; **Jahrtausend** nt millennium; **Jahrzehnt** nt decade

jähzornig adj hot-tempered

Jakobsmuschel f scallop

Jalousie f (venetian) blind

Jamaika (-s) nt Jamaica

jämmerlich adj pathetic

jammern vi to moan

Januar (-(s), -e) m January; siehe auch **Juni**

Japan (-s) nt Japan; **Japaner(in)** (-s, -) m(f) Japanese; **japanisch** adj Japanese; **Japanisch** nt Japanese

jaulen vi to howl

jawohl adv yes (of course)

Jazz (-) m jazz

je adv **1** (jemals) ever; **hast du so was je gesehen?** did you ever see anything like it?

2 (jeweils) every each; **sie zahlten je 3 Euro** they paid 3 euros each

▷ konj **1** : **je nach** depending on; **je nachdem** it depends; **je nachdem, ob ...** depending on whether ...

2 : **je eher, desto** od **umso besser** the sooner the better

Jeans (-, -) f jeans pl

jede(r, s) unbest Zahlwort (insgesamt gesehen) every; (einzeln gesehen) each; (jede(r, s) beliebige) any; **~s Mal** every time, each time; **~n zweiten Tag** every other day; **sie hat an ~m Finger einen Ring** she's got a ring on each finger; **~r Computer reicht aus** any computer will do; **bei ~m Wetter** in any weather ▷ pron everybody; (jeder Einzelne) each; **~r von euch/uns** each of you/us; **jedenfalls** adv in any case; **jederzeit** adv at any time; **jedesmal** adv every time

jedoch adv however

jemals adv ever

jemand pron somebody; (in Frage und Verneinung) anybody

Jemen (-(s)) m Yemen

jene(r, s) adj that, those pl ▷ pron that (one), those pl

jenseits adv on the other side ▷ prep +gen on the other side of; (fig) beyond

Jetlag (-s) m jet lag

jetzig adj present

jetzt adv now; **erst ~** only now; **~ gleich** right now; **bis ~** so far, up to now; **von ~ an** from now on

jeweils adv **~ zwei zusammen** two at a time; **zu ~ 5 Euro** at 5 euros each

Job (-s, -s) m job; **jobben** vi (fam) to work, to have a job

Jod (-(e)s) nt iodine

Joga (-s) nt yoga

joggen vi to jog; **Jogging** (-s) nt jogging; **Jogginganzug** m jogging suit, tracksuit; **Jogginghose** f jogging pants pl

Jog(h)urt (-s, -s) m o nt yoghurt

Johannisbeere f **Schwarze ~** blackcurrant; **Rote ~** redcurrant

Joint (-s, -s) m (fam) joint

jonglieren vi to juggle

Jordanien (-s) nt Jordan

Joule (-(s), -) nt joule

Journalist(in) m(f) journalist

Joystick (-s, -s) m (Inform) joystick

jubeln vi to cheer

Jubiläum (-s, Jubiläen) nt jubilee; (Jahrestag) anniversary

jucken vi to itch ▷ vt **es juckt mich am Arm** my arm is itching; **das juckt mich nicht** (fam) I couldn't care less; **Juckreiz** m itch

Jude (-n, -n) m, **Jüdin** f Jew; **sie ist Jüdin** she's Jewish; **jüdisch** adj Jewish

Judo (-(s)) nt judo

Jugend (-) f youth; **jugendfrei** adj **ein ~er Film** a U-rated film (Brit), a G-rated film (US); **ein nicht ~er Film** an X-rated film; **Jugendherberge** (-, -n) f youth hostel; **jugendlich** adj youthful; **Jugendliche(r)** mf young person; **Jugendstil** m art nouveau; **Jugendzentrum** nt youth centre

Jugoslawien (-s) nt (Hist) Yugoslavia; **das ehemalige ~** the former Yugoslavia

Juli (-(s), -s) m July; siehe auch **Juni**

jung adj young

Junge (-n, -n) m boy

Junge(s) (-n, -n) nt young animal; **die ~n** pl the young pl

Jungfrau f virgin; (Astr) Virgo

Junggeselle (-n, -n) m bachelor; **Junggesellin** f single woman

Juni (-(s), -s) m June; **im ~** in June; **am 4.**

~ on 4(th) June, on June 4(th) (gesprochen: on the fourth of June); **Anfang/Mitte/Ende ~** at the beginning/in the middle/at the end of June; **letzten/nächsten ~** last/next June

Jupiter (-s) m Jupiter

Jura ohne Artikel (Studienfach) law; **~ studieren** to study law; **Jurist(in)** m(f) lawyer; **juristisch** adj legal

Justiz (-) f justice; **Justizminister(in)** m(f) minister of justice

Juwel (-s, -en) nt jewel; **Juwelier(in)** (-s, -e) m(f) jeweller

Jux (-es, -e) m joke, lark

j

k

Kabel (-s, -) nt (Elek) wire; (stark) cable; **Kabelfernsehen** nt cable television

Kabeljau (-s, -e o -s) m cod

Kabine f cabin; (im Schwimmbad) cubicle

Kabrio (-s, -s) nt convertible

Kachel (-, -n) f tile; **Kachelofen** m tiled stove

Käfer (-s, -) m beetle, bug (US)

Kaff (-s, -s) nt dump, hole

Kaffee (-s, -s) m coffee; ~ **kochen** to make some coffee; **Kaffeefilter** m coffee filter; **Kaffeekanne** f coffeepot; **Kaffeeklatsch** (-(e)s, -e) m chat over coffee and cakes, coffee klatch (US); **Kaffeelöffel** m coffee spoon; **Kaffeemaschine** f coffee maker (o machine); **Kaffeetasse** f coffee cup

Käfig (-s, -e) m cage

kahl adj (Mensch, Kopf) bald; (Baum, Wand) bare

Kahn (-(e)s, Kähne) m boat; (Lastkahn) barge

Kai (-s, -e o -s) m quay

Kaiser (-s, -) m emperor; **Kaiserin** f empress; **Kaiserschnitt** m (Med) caesarean (section)

Kajak (-s, -s) nt kayak

Kajal (-s) m kohl

Kajüte (-, -n) f cabin

Kakao (-s, -s) m cocoa; (Getränk) (hot) chocolate

Kakerlake (-, -n) f cockroach

Kaki (-, -s) f kaki

Kaktee (-, -n) f, **Kaktus** (-, -se) m cactus

Kalb (-(e)s, Kälber) nt calf; **Kalbfleisch** nt veal; **Kalbsbraten** m roast veal; **Kalbsschnitzel** nt veal cutlet; (paniert) escalope of veal

Kalender (-s, -) m calendar; (Taschenkalender) diary

Kalk (-(e)s, -e) m lime; (in Knochen) calcium

Kalorie f calorie; **kalorienarm** adj low-calorie

kalt adj cold; **mir ist (es) ~** I'm cold; **kaltblütig** adj cold-blooded; **Kälte** (-) f cold; (fig) coldness

kam imperf von **kommen**

Kambodscha (-s) nt Cambodia

Kamel (-(e)s, -e) nt camel

Kamera (-, -s) f camera

Kamerad(in) (-en, -en) m(f) friend; (als Begleiter) companion

Kamerafrau f, **Kameramann** m camerawoman/-man

Kamille (-, -n) f camomile; **Kamillentee** m camomile tea

Kamin (-s, -e) m (außen) chimney; (innen) fireplace

Kamm (-(e)s, Kämme) m comb; (Berg) ridge; (Hahn) crest; **kämmen** vr **sich ~, sich** (dat) **die Haare ~** to comb one's hair; **Kammermusik** f chamber music

Kampf (-(e)s, Kämpfe) m fight; (Schlacht) battle; (Wettbewerb) contest; (fig: Anstrengung) struggle; **kämpfen** vi to fight (für, um for); **Kampfsport** m martial art

Kanada (-s) nt Canada; **Kanadier(in)** (-s, -) m(f) Canadian; **kanadisch** adj Canadian

Kanal (-s, Kanäle) m (Fluss) canal; (Rinne, TV) channel; (für Abfluss) drain; **der ~** (Ärmelkanal) the (English) Channel; **Kanalinseln** pl Channel Islands pl; **Kanalisation** f sewerage system; **Kanaltunnel** m Channel Tunnel

Kanarienvogel m canary

Kandidat(in) (-en, -en) m(f) candidate

Kandis(zucker) (-) m rock candy

Känguru (-s, -s) nt kangaroo

Kaninchen nt rabbit

Kanister (-s, -) m can

Kännchen nt pot; **ein ~ Kaffee/Tee** a pot

of coffee/tea; **Kanne** (-, -n) f (Krug) jug;
(Kaffeekanne) pot; (Milchkanne) churn;
(Gießkanne) can

kannte imperf von **kennen**

Kante (-, -n) f edge

Kantine f canteen

Kanton (-s, -e) m canton

Kanu (-s, -s) nt canoe

Kanzler(in) (-s, -) m(f) chancellor

Kap (-s, -s) nt cape

Kapazität f capacity; (Fachmann)
authority

Kapelle f (Gebäude) chapel; (Mus) band

Kaper (-, -n) f caper

kapieren vt, vi (fam) to understand;
kapiert? got it?

Kapital (-s, -e o -ien) nt capital

Kapitän (-s, -e) m captain

Kapitel (-s, -) nt chapter

Kappe (-, -n) f cap

Kapsel (-, -n) f capsule

kaputt adj (fam) broken; (Mensch)
exhausted; **kaputt|gehen** irr vi to break;
(Schuhe) to fall apart; (Firma) to go bust;
(Stoff) to wear out; **kaputt|machen** vt to
break; (jdn) to wear out

Kapuze (-, -n) f hood

Kap Verde (-s) nt Cape Verde

Karaffe (-, -n) f carafe; (mit Stöpsel)
decanter

Karambole (-, -n) f star fruit, carambola

Karamell (-s) m caramel, toffee

Karaoke (-(s)) nt karaoke

Karat (-s, -e) nt carat

Karate (-s) nt karate

Kardinal (-s, Kardinäle) m cardinal

Karfreitag m Good Friday

kariert adj checked; (Papier) squared

Karies (-) f (tooth) decay

Karikatur f caricature

Karneval (-s, -e o -s) m carnival

● **Karneval**
●
● **Karneval** is the name given to the days
● immediately before Lent when
● people gather to sing, dance, eat,
● drink and generally make merry
● before the fasting begins.
● **Rosenmontag**, the day before Shrove
● Tuesday, is the most important day
● of 'Karneval' on the Rhine. Most
● firms take a day's holiday on that day

● to enjoy the parades and revelry. In
● South Germany 'Karneval' is called
● **Fasching**.

Kärnten (-s) nt Carinthia

Karo (-s, -s) nt square; (Karten) diamonds
pl

Karosserie f (Auto) body(work)

Karotte (-, -n) f carrot

Karpfen (-s, -) m carp

Karriere (-, -n) f career

Karte (-, -n) f card; (Landkarte) map;
(Speisekarte) menu; (Eintrittskarte,
Fahrkarte) ticket; **mit ~ bezahlen** to pay by
credit card; **~n spielen** to play cards; **die
~n mischen/geben** to shuffle/deal the
cards

Kartei f card index; **Karteikarte** f index
card

Kartenspiel nt card game;
Kartentelefon nt cardphone;
Kartenvorverkauf m advance booking

Kartoffel (-, -n) f potato; **Kartoffelbrei** m
mashed potatoes pl; **Kartoffelchips** pl
crisps pl (Brit), chips pl (US);
Kartoffelpuffer m potato cake (made
from grated potatoes); **Kartoffelpüree** nt
mashed potatoes pl; **Kartoffelsalat** m
potato salad

Karton (-s, -s) m cardboard; (Schachtel)
(cardboard) box

Kartusche (-, -n) f cartridge

Karussell (-s, -s) nt roundabout (Brit),
merry-go-round

Kaschmir (-s, e) m (Stoff) cashmere

Käse (-s, -) m cheese; **Käsekuchen**
m cheesecake; **Käseplatte** f
cheeseboard

Kasino (-s, -s) nt (Spielkasino) casino

Kaskoversicherung f comprehensive
insurance

Kasper(l) (-s, -) m Punch; (fig) clown;
Kasperl(e)theater nt (Vorstellung) Punch
and Judy show; (Gebäude) Punch and Judy
theatre

Kasse (-, -n) f (in Geschäft) till, cash
register; (im Supermarkt) checkout;
(Geldkasten) cashbox; (Theater) box office;
(Kino) ticket office; (Krankenkasse) health
insurance; (Spar~) savings bank;
Kassenbon (-s, -s) m, **Kassenzettel** m
receipt; **Kassenzettel** m receipt

Kassette f (small) box; (Tonband)

k

cassette; **Kassettenrekorder** m cassette recorder

kassieren vt to take ▷ vi **darf ich ~?** would you like to pay now?; **Kassierer(in)** m(f) cashier

Kastanie f chestnut

Kasten (-s, Kästen) m (Behälter) box; (Getränkekasten) crate

Kat m abk = **Katalysator**

Katalog (-(e)s, -e) m catalogue

Katalysator m (Auto) catalytic converter; (Phys) catalyst

Katar (-s) nt Qatar

Katarr(h) (-s, -e) m catarrh

Katastrophe (-, -n) f catastrophe, disaster

Kategorie (-, -n) f category

Kater (-s, -) m tomcat; (fam: nach zu viel Alkohol) hangover

Kathedrale (-, -n) f cathedral

Katholik(in) m(f) Catholic; **katholisch** adj Catholic

Katze (-, -n) f cat

Kauderwelsch (-(s)) nt (unverständlich) gibberish; (Fachjargon) jargon

kauen vt, vi to chew

Kauf (-(e)s, Käufe) m purchase; (Kaufen) buying; **ein guter ~** a bargain; **etw in ~ nehmen** to put up with sth; **kaufen** vt to buy; **Käufer(in)** m(f) buyer; **Kauffrau** f businesswoman; **Kaufhaus** nt department store; **Kaufmann** m businessman; (im Einzelhandel) shopkeeper (Brit), storekeeper (US); **Kaufpreis** m purchase price; **Kaufvertrag** m purchase agreement

Kaugummi m chewing gum

Kaulquappe (-, -n) f tadpole

kaum adv hardly, scarcely

Kaution f deposit; (Jur) bail

Kaviar m caviar

KB (-, -) nt, **Kbyte** (-, -) nt abk = **Kilobyte** KB

Kebab (-(s), -s) m kebab

Kegel (-s, -) m skittle; (beim Bowling) pin; (Math) cone; **Kegelbahn** f bowling alley; **kegeln** vi to play skittles; (bowlen) to bowl

Kehle (-, -n) f throat; **Kehlkopf** m larynx

Kehre (-, -n) f sharp bend

kehren vt (fegen) to sweep

Keilriemen m (Auto) fan belt

kein pron no, not ... any; **ich habe ~ Geld** I have no money, I don't have money; **~ Mensch** no one; **du bist ~ Kind mehr**

you're not a child any more; **keine(r, s)** pron (Person) no one, nobody; (Sache) not ... any, none; **~r von ihnen** none of them; (bei zwei Personen/Sachen) neither of them; **ich will keins von beiden** I don't want either (of them); **keinesfalls** adv on no account, under no circumstances

Keks (-es, -e) m biscuit (Brit), cookie (US); **jdm auf den ~ gehen** (fam) to get on sb's nerves

Keller (-s, -) m cellar; (Geschoss) basement

Kellner (-s, -) m waiter; **Kellnerin** f waitress

Kenia (-s) nt Kenya

kennen (kannte, gekannt) vt to know; **wir ~ uns seit 1990** we've known each other since 1990; **wir ~ uns schon** we've already met; **kennst du mich noch?** do you remember me?; **~ lernen** to get to know; **sich ~ lernen** to get to know each other; (zum ersten Mal) to meet

Kenntnis f knowledge; **seine ~se** his knowledge

Kennwort nt (a. Inform) password; **Kennzeichen** nt mark, sign; (Auto) number plate (Brit), license plate (US); **besondere ~** distinguishing marks

Kerl (-s, -e) m guy, bloke (Brit)

Kern (-(e)s, -e) m (Obst) pip; (Pfirsich, Kirsche etc) stone; (Nuss) kernel; (Atomkern) nucleus; (fig) heart, core

Kernenergie f nuclear energy; **Kernkraft** f nuclear power; **Kernkraftwerk** nt nuclear power station

Kerze (-, -n) f candle; (Zündkerze) plug

Ket(s)chup (-(s), -s) m o nt ketchup

Kette (-, -n) f chain; (Halskette) necklace

keuchen vi to pant; **Keuchhusten** m whooping cough

Keule (-, -n) f club; (Gastr) leg; (von Hähnchen a.) drumstick

Keyboard (-s, -s) nt (Mus) keyboard

Kfz nt abk = **Kraftfahrzeug**

Kfz-Brief m ≈ logbook

Kfz-Steuer f ≈ road tax (Brit), vehicle tax (US)

KG (-, -s) f abk = **Kommanditgesellschaft** limited partnership

Kichererbse f chick pea

kichern vi to giggle

Kickboard® (-s, -s) nt micro scooter

Kicker (-s, -) m (Spiel) table football (Brit), foosball (US)

kidnappen vt to kidnap
Kidney-Bohne f kidney bean
Kiefer (-s, -) m jaw ▷ (-, -n) f pine
Kieme (-, -n) f gill
Kies (-es, -e) m gravel; **Kiesel** (-s, -) m,
  Kieselstein m pebble
kiffen vi (fam) to smoke pot
Kilo (-s, -(s)) nt kilo; **Kilobyte** nt kilobyte;
  Kilogramm nt kilogram; **Kilojoule** nt
  kilojoule; **Kilometer** m kilometre;
  Kilometerstand m ≈ mileage;
  Kilometerzähler m ≈ mileometer;
  Kilowatt nt kilowatt
Kind (-(e)s, -er) nt child; **sie bekommt ein
  ~** she's having a baby; **Kinderarzt** m,
  Kinderärztin f paediatrician;
  Kinderbetreuung f childcare;
  Kinderbett nt cot (Brit), crib (US);
  Kinderfahrkarte f child's ticket;
  Kindergarten m nursery school,
  kindergarten; **Kindergärtnerin** f
  nursery-school teacher; **Kindergeld** nt
  child benefit; **Kinderkrankheit** f
  children's illness; **Kinderkrippe** f crèche
  (Brit), daycare center (US);
  Kinderlähmung f polio;
  Kindermädchen nt nanny (Brit),
  nurse(maid); **kindersicher** adj childproof;
  Kindersicherung f childproof safety
  catch; (an Flasche) childproof cap;
  Kindersitz m child seat;
  Kindertagesstätte nt day nursery;
  Kinderteller m (im Restaurant) children's
  portion; **Kinderwagen** m pram (Brit),
  baby carriage (US); **Kinderzimmer** nt
  children's (bed)room; **Kindheit** f
  childhood; **kindisch** adj childish; **kindlich**
  adj childlike
Kinn (-(e)s, -e) nt chin
Kino (-s, -s) nt cinema (Brit), movie
  theater (US); **ins ~ gehen** to go to the
  cinema (Brit) (o to the movies (US))
Kiosk (-(e)s, -e) m kiosk
Kippe f (fam: Zigarettenstummel) cigarette
  end, fag end (Brit)
kippen vi to tip over ▷ vt to tilt;
  (Regierung, Minister) to topple
Kirche (-, -n) f church; **Kirchturm** m
  church tower; (mit Spitze) steeple
Kirmes (-, -sen) f fair
Kirsche (-, -n) f cherry; **Kirschtomate** f
  cherry tomato
Kissen (-s, -) nt cushion; (Kopfkissen)

pillow; **Kissenbezug** m cushion cover;
  (für Kopfkissen) pillowcase
Kiste (-, -n) f box; (Truhe) chest
kitschig adj kitschy, cheesy
kitzelig adj (a. fig) ticklish; **kitzeln** vt, vi
  to tickle
Kiwi (-, -s) f (Frucht) kiwi (fruit)
Klage (-, -n) f complaint; (Jur) lawsuit;
  klagen vi to complain (über +akk about,
  bei to); **kläglich** adj wretched
Klammer (-, -n) f (in Text) bracket;
  (Büroklammer) clip; (Wäscheklammer) peg
  (Brit), clothespin (US); (Zahnklammer)
  brace; **Klammeraffe** m (fam) at-sign, @;
  klammern vr **sich ~** to cling (an +akk to)
klang imperf von **klingen**
Klang (-(e)s, Klänge) m sound
Klappbett nt folding bed
klappen vi impers (gelingen) to work; **es
  hat gut geklappt** it went well
klappern vi to rattle; (Geschirr) to clatter;
  Klapperschlange f rattlesnake
Klappfahrrad nt folding bicycle;
  Klappstuhl m folding chair
klar adj clear; **sich** (dat) **im Klaren sein** to
  be clear (über +akk about); **alles ~?**
  everything okay?
klären vt (Flüssigkeit) to purify; (Probleme,
  Frage) to clarify ▷ vr **sich ~** to clear itself up
Klarinette (-, -n) f clarinet
klar|kommen irr vi **mit etw ~** to cope
  with something; **kommst du klar?** are
  you managing all right?; **mit jdm ~** to get
  along with sb; **klar|machen** vt **jdm etw
  ~** to make sth clear to sb; **Klarsichtfolie** f
  clingfilm (Brit), plastic wrap (US);
  klar|stellen vt to clarify
Klärung f (von Frage, Problem) clarification
klasse adj inv (fam) great, brilliant
Klasse (-, -n) f class; (Schuljahr) form (Brit),
  grade (US); **erster ~ reisen** to travel first
  class; **in welche ~ gehst du?** which form
  (Brit) (o grade (US)) are you in?;
  Klassenarbeit f test; **Klassenlehrer(in)**
  m(f) class teacher; **Klassenzimmer** nt
  classroom
Klassik f (Zeit) classical period; (Musik)
  classical music
Klatsch (-(e)s, -e) m (Gerede) gossip;
  klatschen vi (schlagen) to smack; (Beifall)
  to applaud, to clap; (reden) to gossip;
  Klatschmohn m (corn) poppy;
  klatschnass adj soaking (wet)

k

Klaue (-, -n) f claw; (fam: Schrift) scrawl; **klauen** vt (fam) to pinch

Klavier (-s, -e) nt piano

Klebeband nt adhesive tape; **kleben** vt to stick (an +akk to) ▷ vi (klebrig sein) to be sticky; **klebrig** adj sticky; **Klebstoff** m glue; **Klebstreifen** m adhesive tape

Klecks (-es, -e) m blob; (Tinte) blot

Klee (-s) m clover

Kleid (-(e)s, -er) nt (Frauen~) dress; **~er** pl (Kleidung) clothes pl; **Kleiderbügel** m coat hanger; **Kleiderschrank** m wardrobe (Brit), closet (US); **Kleidung** f clothing

klein adj small, little; (Finger) little; **mein ~er Bruder** my little (o younger) brother; **als ich noch ~ war** when I was a little boy/girl; **etw ~ schneiden** to chop sth up; **etw ~ schreiben** to write sth with a small letter; **Kleinanzeige** f classified ad; **Kleinbuchstabe** m small letter; **Kleinbus** m minibus; **Kleingeld** nt change; **Kleinigkeit** f trifle; (Zwischenmahlzeit) snack; **Kleinkind** nt toddler; **klein|schreiben** vt to write with a small letter; **Kleinstadt** f small town

Kleister (-s, -) m paste

Klempner(in) m(f) plumber

klettern vi to climb

Klettverschluss m Velcro® fastening

klicken vi (a. Inform) to click

Klient(in) (-en, -en) m(f) client

Klima (-s, -s) nt climate; **Klimaanlage** f air conditioning; **klimatisiert** adj air-conditioned

Klinge (-, -n) f blade

Klingel (-, -n) f bell; **klingeln** vi to ring

klingen (klang, geklungen) vi to sound

Klinik f clinic; (Krankenhaus) hospital

Klinke (-, -n) f handle

Klippe (-, -n) f cliff; (im Meer) reef; (fig) hurdle

Klischee (-s, -s) nt (fig) cliché

Klo (-s, -s) nt (fam) loo (Brit), john (US); **Klobrille** f toilet seat; **Klopapier** nt toilet paper

klopfen vt, vi to knock; (Herz) to thump

Kloß (-es, Klöße) m (im Hals) lump; (Gastr) dumpling

Kloster (-s, Klöster) nt (für Männer) monastery; (für Frauen) convent

Klub (-s, -s) m club

klug adj clever

knabbern vt, vi to nibble

Knäckebrot nt crispbread

knacken vt, vi to crack

Knall (-(e)s, -e) m bang; **Knallbonbon** nt cracker; **knallen** vi to bang

knapp adj (kaum ausreichend) scarce; (Sieg) narrow; **~ bei Kasse sein** to be short of money; **~ zwei Stunden** just under two hours

Knauf (-s, Knäufe) m knob

Knautschzone f (Auto) crumple zone

kneifen (kniff, gekniffen) vt, vi to pinch; (sich drücken) to back out (vor +dat of); **Kneifzange** f pincers pl

Kneipe (-, -n) f (fam) pub (Brit), bar

Knete (-) f (fam: Geld) dough; **kneten** vt to knead; (formen) to mould

knicken vt, vi (brechen) to break; (Papier) to fold; **geknickt sein** (fig) to be downcast

Knie (-s, -) nt knee; **in die ~ gehen** to bend one's knees; **Kniebeuge** f knee bend; **Kniegelenk** nt knee joint; **Kniekehle** f back of the knee; **knien** vi to kneel; **Kniescheibe** f kneecap; **Knieschoner** (-s, -) m, **Knieschützer** (-s, -) m knee pad; **Kniestrumpf** m knee-length sock

kniff imperf von **kneifen**

knipsen vt to punch; (Foto) to snap ▷ vi (Foto) to take snaps

knirschen vi to crunch; **mit den Zähnen ~** to grind one's teeth

knitterfrei adj non-crease; **knittern** vi to crease

Knoblauch m garlic; **Knoblauchbrot** nt garlic bread; **Knoblauchzehe** f clove of garlic

Knöchel (-s, -) m (Finger) knuckle; (Fuß) ankle

Knochen (-s, -) m bone; **Knochenbruch** m fracture; **Knochenmark** nt marrow

Knödel (-s, -) m dumpling

Knollensellerie m celeriac

Knopf (-(e)s, Knöpfe) m button; **Knopfdruck** m **auf ~** at the touch of a botton; **Knopfloch** nt buttonhole

Knospe (-, -n) f bud

knoten vt to knot; **Knoten** (-s, -) m knot; (Med) lump

Know-how (-(s)) nt know-how, expertise

knurren vi (Hund) to growl; (Magen) to rumble; (Mensch) to grumble

knusprig adj crisp; (Keks) crunchy

knutschen vi (fam) to smooch

k. o. adj inv (Sport) knocked out; (fig) knackered

Koalition f coalition

Koch (-(e)s, Köche) m cook; **Kochbuch** nt cookery book, cookbook; **kochen** vt, vi to cook; (Wasser) to boil; (Kaffee, Tee) to make; **Köchin** f cook; **Kochlöffel** m wooden spoon; **Kochnische** f kitchenette; **Kochplatte** f hotplate; **Kochrezept** nt recipe; **Kochtopf** m saucepan

Kode (-s, -s) m code

Köder (-s, -) m bait

Koffein (-s) nt caffeine; **koffeinfrei** adj decaffeinated

Koffer (-s, -) m (suit)case; **Kofferraum** m (Auto) boot (Brit), trunk (US)

Kognak (-s, -s) m brandy

Kohl (-(e)s, -e) m cabbage

Kohle (-, -n) f coal; (Holzkohle) charcoal; (Chem) carbon; (fam: Geld) cash, dough; **Kohlehydrat** nt carbohydrate; **Kohlendioxid** nt carbon dioxide; **Kohlensäure** f (in Getränken) fizz; **ohne ~** still, non-carbonated (US); **mit ~** sparkling, carbonated (US); **Kohletablette** f charcoal tablet

Kohlrabi (-(s), -(s)) m kohlrabi

Kohlrübe f swede (Brit), rutabaga (US)

Koje (-, -n) f cabin; (Bett) bunk

Kokain (-s) nt cocaine

Kokosnuss f coconut

Kolben (-s, -) m (Tech) piston; (Mais~) cob

Kolik (-, -en) f colic

Kollaps (-es, -e) m collapse

Kollege (-n, -n) m, **Kollegin** f colleague

Köln (-s) nt Cologne

Kolonne (-, -n) f convoy; **in ~ fahren** to drive in convoy

Kölsch (-, -) nt (Bier) (strong) lager (from the Cologne region)

Kolumbien (-s) nt Columbia

Koma (-s, -s) nt coma

Kombi (-(s), -s) m estate (car) (Brit), station wagon (US); **Kombination** f combination; (Folgerung) deduction; (Hemdhose) combinations pl; (Aviat) flying suit; **kombinieren** vt to combine ▷ vi to reason; (vermuten) to guess; **Kombizange** f (pair of) pliers pl

Komfort (-s) m conveniences pl; (Bequemlichkeit) comfort

Komiker(in) m(f) comedian, comic; **komisch** adj funny

Komma (-s, -s) nt comma

Kommanditgesellschaft f limited partnership

kommen (kam, gekommen) vi to come; (näher kommen) to approach; (passieren) to happen; (gelangen, geraten) to get; (erscheinen) to appear; (in die Schule, das Gefängnis etc) to go; **~ lassen** to send for; **zu sich ~** to come round (o to); **zu etw ~** (bekommen) to acquire sth; (Zeit dazu finden) to get round to sth; **wer kommt zuerst?** who's first?; **kommend** adj coming; **~e Woche** next week; **in den ~en Jahren** in the years to come

Kommentar m commentary; **kein ~** no comment

Kommilitone (-n, -n) m, **Kommilitonin** f fellow student

Kommissar(in) m(f) inspector

Kommode (-, -n) f chest of drawers

Kommunikation f communication

Kommunion f (Rel) communion

Kommunismus m communism

Komödie f comedy

kompakt adj compact

Kompass (-es, -e) m compass

kompatibel adj compatible

kompetent adj competent

komplett adj complete

Kompliment nt compliment; **jdm ein ~ machen** to pay sb a compliment; **~!** congratulations

Komplize (-n, -n) m accomplice

kompliziert adj complicated

Komponist(in) m(f) composer

Kompost (-(e)s, -e) m compost; **Komposthaufen** m compost heap; **kompostierbar** adj biodegradable

Kompott (-(e)s, -e) nt stewed fruit

Kompresse (-, -n) f compress

Kompromiss (-es, -e) m compromise

Kondensmilch f condensed milk, evaporated milk

Kondition f (Leistungsfähigkeit) condition; **sie hat eine gute ~** she's in good shape

Konditorei f cake shop; (mit Café) café

Kondom (-s, -e) nt condom

Konfektionsgröße f size

Konferenz f conference

Konfession f religion; (christlich) denomination

Konfetti (-(s)) nt confetti

Konfirmation f (Rel) confirmation
Konfitüre (-, -n) f jam
Konflikt (-(e)s, -e) m conflict
konfrontieren vt to confront
Kongo (-s) m Congo
Kongress (-es, -e) m conference; **der
~** (Parlament der USA) Congress
König (-(e)s, -e) m king; **Königin** f
queen; **Königinpastete** f vol-au-vent;
königlich adj royal; **Königreich** nt
kingdom
Konkurrenz f competition

⊙ **SCHLÜSSELWORT**

können (pt **konnte**, pp **gekonnt** od (als
Hilfsverb) **können**) vt, vi 1 to be able to;
ich kann es machen I can do it, I am able
to do it,; **ich kann es nicht machen** I can't
do it, I'm not able to do it; **ich kann nicht
...** I can't ..., I cannot ...; **ich kann nicht
mehr** I can't go on
2 (wissen, beherrschen) to know; **können
Sie Deutsch?** can you speak German?; **er
kann gut Englisch** he speaks English well;
sie kann keine Mathematik she can't do
mathematics
3 (dürfen) to be allowed to; **kann ich
gehen?** can I go?; **könnte ich ...?** could I
...?; **kann ich mit?** (umg) can I come with
you?
4 (möglich sein): **Sie könnten Recht
haben** you may be right; **das kann sein**
that's possible; **kann sein** maybe

konsequent adj consistent;
Konsequenz f consequence
konservativ adj conservative
Konserven pl tinned food sing (Brit),
canned food sing; **Konservendose** f tin
(Brit), can
konservieren vt to preserve;
Konservierungsmittel nt preservative
Konsonant m consonant
Konsul(in) (-s, -n) m(f) consul; **Konsulat**
nt consulate
Kontakt (-(e)s, -e) m contact;
kontaktarm adj **er ist ~** he lacks contact
with other people; **kontaktfreudig** adj
sociable; **Kontaktlinsen** pl contact
lenses pl
Kontinent m continent
Konto (-s, Konten) nt account;

Kontoauszug m (bank) statement;
Kontoauszugsdrucker m bank-statement
machine; **Kontoinhaber(in)** m(f) account
holder; **Kontonummer** f account
number; **Kontostand** m balance
Kontrabass m double bass
Kontrast (-(e)s, -e) m contrast
Kontrolle (-, -n) f control; (Aufsicht)
supervision; (Passkontrolle) passport
control; **kontrollieren** vt to control;
(nachprüfen) to check
Konzentration f concentration;
Konzentrationslager nt (Hist)
concentration camp; **konzentrieren** vt
to concentrate ▷ vr **sich ~** to concentrate
Konzept (-(e)s, -e) nt rough draft; **jdn aus
dem ~ bringen** to put sb off
Konzert (-(e)s, -e) nt concert; (Stück)
concerto; **Konzertsaal** m concert hall
koordinieren vt to coordinate
Kopf (-(e)s, Köpfe) m head; **pro ~** per
person; **sich den ~ zerbrechen** to rack
one's brains; **Kopfhörer** m headphones
pl; **Kopfkissen** nt pillow; **Kopfsalat** m
lettuce; **Kopfschmerzen** pl headache
sing; **Kopfstütze** f headrest; **Kopftuch** nt
headscarf; **kopfüber** adv headfirst
Kopie f copy; **kopieren** vt (a. Inform) to
copy; **Kopierer** (-s, -) m, **Kopiergerät** nt
copier
Kopilot(in) m(f) co-pilot
Koralle (-, -n) f coral
Koran (-s) m (Rel) Koran
Korb (-(e)s, Körbe) m basket; **jdm einen
~ geben** (fig) to turn sb down
Kord (-(e)s, -e) m corduroy
Kordel (-, -n) f cord
Korinthe (-e, -n) f currant
Kork (-(e)s, -e) m cork; **Korken** (-s, -) m
cork; **Korkenzieher** (-s, -) m corkscrew
Korn (-(e)s, Körner) nt grain; **Kornblume** f
cornflower
Körper (-s, -) m body; **Körperbau** m
build; **körperbehindert** adj disabled;
Körpergeruch m body odour;
Körpergröße f height; **körperlich** adj
physical; **Körperteil** m part of the body;
Körperverletzung f physical injury
korrekt adj correct
Korrespondent(in) m(f) correspondent;
Korrespondenz f correspondence
korrigieren vt to correct
Kosmetik f cosmetics pl;

Kosmetikkoffer m vanity case;
Kosmetiksalon m beauty parlour;
Kosmetiktuch nt paper tissue

Kost (-) f (Nahrung) food; (Verpflegung) board

kostbar adj precious; (teuer) costly, expensive

kosten vt to cost ▷ vt, vi (versuchen) to taste; **Kosten** pl costs pl, cost; (Ausgaben) expenses pl; **auf ~ von** at the expense of; **kostenlos** adj free (of charge); **Kostenvoranschlag** m estimate

köstlich adj (Essen) delicious; (Einfall) delightful; **sich ~ amüsieren** to have a marvellous time

Kostprobe f taster; (fig) sample; **kostspielig** adj expensive

Kostüm (-s, -e) nt costume; (Damenkostüm) suit

Kot (-(e)s) m excrement

Kotelett (-(e)s, -e o -s) nt chop, cutlet

Koteletten pl sideboards pl (Brit), sideburns pl (US)

Kotflügel m (Auto) wing

Krabbe (-, -n) f shrimp; (größer) prawn; (Krebs) crab

krabbeln vi to crawl

Krach (-(e)s, -s o -e) m crash; (andauernd) noise; (fam: Streit) row

Kraft (-, Kräfte) f strength; (Pol, Phys) force; (Fähigkeit) power; (Arbeits~) worker; **in ~ treten** to come into effect; **Kraftausdruck** m swearword; **Kraftfahrzeug** nt motor vehicle; **Kraftfahrzeugbrief** m ≈ logbook; **Kraftfahrzeugschein** m vehicle registration document; **Kraftfahrzeugsteuer** f ≈ road tax (Brit), vehicle tax (US); **Kraftfahrzeugversicherung** f car insurance; **kräftig** adj strong; (gesund) healthy; (Farben) intense, strong; **Kraftstoff** m fuel; **Kraftwerk** nt power station

Kragen (-s, -) m collar

Krähe (-, -n) f crow

Kralle (-, -n) f claw; (Parkkralle) wheel clamp

Kram (-(e)s) m stuff

Krampf (-(e)s, Krämpfe) m cramp; (zuckend) spasm; **Krampfader** f varicose vein

Kran (-(e)s, Kräne) m crane

Kranich (-s, -e) m (Zool) crane

krank adj ill, sick

kränken vt to hurt

Krankengymnastik f physiotherapy; **Krankenhaus** nt hospital; **Krankenkasse** f health insurance; **Krankenpfleger** (-s, -) m (male) nurse; **Krankenschein** m health insurance certificate; **Krankenschwester** f nurse; **Krankenversicherung** f health insurance; **Krankenwagen** m ambulance; **Krankheit** f illness; (durch Infektion hervorgerufen) disease

Kränkung f insult

Kranz (-es, Kränze) m wreath

krass adj crass; (fam: toll) wicked

kratzen vt, vi to scratch; **Kratzer** (-s, -) m scratch

kraulen vi (schwimmen) to do the crawl ▷ vt (streicheln) to pet

Kraut (-(e)s, Kräuter) nt plant; (Gewürz) herb; (Gemüse) cabbage; **Kräuter** pl herbs pl; **Kräuterbutter** f herb butter; **Kräutertee** m herbal tea; **Krautsalat** m coleslaw

Krawatte f tie

kreativ adj creative

Krebs (-es, -e) m (Zool) crab; (Med) cancer; (Astr) Cancer

Kredit (-(e)s, -e) m credit; **auf ~** on credit; **einen ~ aufnehmen** to take out a loan; **Kreditkarte** f credit card

Kreide (-, -n) f chalk

Kreis (-es, -e) m circle; (Bezirk) district

kreischen vi to shriek; (Bremsen, Säge) to screech

Kreisel (-s, -) m (Spielzeug) top; (Verkehrskreisel) roundabout (Brit), traffic circle (US)

Kreislauf m (Med) circulation; (fig: der Natur etc) cycle; **Kreislaufstörungen** pl (Med) **ich habe ~** I've got problems with my circulation; **Kreisverkehr** m roundabout (Brit), traffic circle (US), rotary (US)

Kren (-s) m horseradish

Kresse (-, -n) f cress

Kreuz (-es, -e) nt cross; (Anat) small of the back; (Karten) clubs pl; **mir tut das ~ weh** I've got backache; **Kreuzband** nt cruciate ligament; **kreuzen** vt to cross ▷ vr **sich ~** to cross ▷ vi (Naut) to cruise; **Kreuzfahrt** f cruise; **Kreuzgang** m

k

cloisters pl; **Kreuzotter** (-, -n) f adder;
Kreuzschlitzschraubenzieher m
Phillips® screwdriver; **Kreuzschlüssel** m
(Auto) wheel brace; **Kreuzschmerzen** pl
backache sing; **Kreuzung** f
(Verkehrskreuzung) crossroads sing,
intersection; (Züchtung) cross;
Kreuzworträtsel nt crossword (puzzle)
kriechen (kroch, gekrochen) vi to crawl;
(unauffällig) to creep; (fig, pej) (**vor jdm**) ~ to
crawl (to sb); **Kriechspur** f crawler lane
Krieg (-(e)s, -e) m war
kriegen vt (fam) to get; (erwischen) to
catch; **sie kriegt ein Kind** she's having a
baby; **ich kriege noch Geld von dir** you
still owe me some money
Krimi (-s, -s) m (fam) thriller; **Kriminalität**
f criminality; **Kriminalpolizei** f detective
force, ≈ CID (Brit), ≈ FBI (US);
Kriminalroman m detective novel;
kriminell adj criminal
Krippe (-, -n) f (Futterkrippe) manger;
(Weihnachtskrippe) crib (Brit), crèche (US);
(Kinderkrippe) crèche (Brit), daycare center
(US)
Krise (-, -n) f crisis
Kristall (-s, -e) m crystal ▷ (-s) nt (Glas)
crystal
Kritik f criticism; (Rezension) review;
Kritiker(in) m(f) critic; **kritisch** adj
critical
kritzeln vt, vi to scribble, to scrawl
Kroate (-n, -n) m Croat; **Kroatien** (-s) nt
Croatia; **Kroatin** f Croat; **kroatisch** adj
Croatian; **Kroatisch** nt Croatian
kroch imperf von **kriechen**
Krokodil (-s, -e) nt crocodile
Krokus (-, - o -se) m crocus
Krone (-, -n) f crown; **Kronleuchter** m
chandelier
Kropf (-(e)s, Kröpfe) m (Med) goitre; (von
Vogel) crop
Kröte (-, -n) f toad
Krücke (-, -n) f crutch
Krug (-(e)s, Krüge) m jug; (Bierkrug) mug
Krümel (-s, -) m crumb
krumm adj crooked
Krüppel (-s, -) m cripple
Kruste (-, -n) f crust
Kruzifix (-es, -e) nt crucifix
Kuba (-s) nt Cuba
Kübel (-s, -) m tub; (Eimer) bucket
Kubikmeter m cubic metre

Küche (-, -n) f kitchen; (Kochen) cooking
Kuchen (-s, -) m cake; (mit Teigdeckel) pie;
Kuchengabel f cake fork
Küchenmaschine f food processor;
Küchenpapier nt kitchen roll;
Küchenschrank m (kitchen) cupboard
Kuckuck (-s, -e) m cuckoo
Kugel (-, -n) f ball; (Math) sphere; (Mil)
bullet; (Weihnachtskugel) bauble;
Kugellager nt ball bearing;
Kugelschreiber m (ball-point) pen,
biro® (Brit); **Kugelstoßen** (-s) nt shot
put
Kuh (-, Kühe) f cow
kühl adj cool; **Kühlakku** (-s, -s) m ice
pack; **Kühlbox** f cool box; **kühlen** vt to
cool; **Kühler** (-s, -) m (Auto) radiator;
Kühlerhaube f (Auto) bonnet (Brit), hood
(US); **Kühlschrank** m fridge, refrigerator;
Kühltasche f cool bag; **Kühltruhe** f
freezer; **Kühlwasser** nt (Auto) radiator
water
Kuhstall m cowshed
Küken (-s, -) nt chick
Kuli (-s, -s) m (fam: Kugelschreiber) pen,
biro® (Brit)
Kulisse (-, -n) f scenery
Kult (-s, -e) m cult; **Kultfigur** f cult
figure
Kultur f culture; (Lebensform) civilization;
Kulturbeutel m toilet bag (Brit),
washbag; **kulturell** adj cultural
Kümmel (-s, -) m caraway seeds pl
Kummer (-s) m grief, sorrow
kümmern vr **sich um jdn** ~ to look after
sb; **sich um etw** ~ to see to sth ▷ vt to
concern; **das kümmert mich nicht** that
doesn't worry me
Kumpel (-s, -) m (fam) mate, pal
Kunde (-n, -n) m customer;
Kundendienst m after-sales (o customer)
service; **Kunden(kredit)karte** f
storecard, chargecard; **Kundennummer** f
customer number
kündigen vi to hand in one's notice; to
(Mieter) to give notice that one is moving
out; **jdm** ~ to give sb his/her notice;
(Vermieter) to give sb notice to quit ▷ vt to
cancel; (Vertrag) to terminate; **jdm die
Stellung** ~ to give sb his/her notice; **jdm
die Wohnung** ~ to give sb notice to quit;
Kündigung f (Arbeitsverhältnis) dismissal;
(Vertrag) termination; (Abonnement)

cancellation; (*Frist*) notice;
Kündigungsfrist f period of notice
Kundin f customer; **Kundschaft** f
customers pl
künftig adj future
Kunst (-, Künste) f art; (*Können*) skill;
Kunstausstellung f art exhibition;
Kunstgewerbe nt arts and crafts pl;
Künstler(in) (-s, -) m(f) artist;
künstlerisch adj artistic
künstlich adj artificial
Kunststoff m synthetic material;
Kunststück nt trick; **Kunstwerk** nt
work of art
Kupfer (-s, -) nt copper
Kuppel (-, -n) f dome
kuppeln vi (*Auto*) to operate the clutch;
Kupplung f coupling; (*Auto*) clutch
Kur (-, -en) f course of treatment; (*am
Kurort*) cure
Kür (-, -en) f (*Sport*) free programme
Kurbel (-, -n) f crank; (*von Rollo, Fenster*)
winder
Kürbis (-ses, -se) m pumpkin
Kurierdienst m courier service
kurieren vt to cure
Kurort m health resort
Kurs (-es, -e) m course; (*Fin*) rate;
(*Wechselkurs*) exchange rate
kursiv adj italic ▷ adv in italics
Kursleiter(in) m(f) course tutor;
Kursteilnehmer(in) m(f) (course)
participant; **Kurswagen** m (*Eisenb*)
through carriage
Kurve (-, -n) f curve; (*Straßenkurve*) bend;
kurvenreich adj (*Straße*) winding
kurz adj short; (*zeitlich a.*) brief;
~ **vorher/darauf** shortly before/after;
kannst du ~ kommen? could you come
here for a minute?; ~ **gesagt** in short;
kurzärmelig adj short-sleeved; **kürzen**
vt to cut short; (*in der Länge*) to shorten;
(*Gehalt*) to reduce; **kurzerhand** adv on the
spot; **kurzfristig** adj short-term; **das
Konzert wurde ~ abgesagt** the concert
was called off at short notice;
Kurzgeschichte f short story;
kurzhaarig adj short-haired; **kürzlich**
adv recently; **Kurznachrichten** pl news
summary sing; **Kurzparkzone** f
short-stay (*Brit*) (o short-term (*US*))
parking zone; **Kurzschluss** m (*Elek*) short
circuit; **kurzsichtig** adj short-sighted;

Kurzurlaub m short holiday (*Brit*), short
vacation (*US*); **Kurzwelle** f short wave
Kusine f cousin
Kuss (-es, Küsse) m kiss; **küssen** vt to kiss
▷ vr **sich ~** to kiss
Küste (-, -n) f coast; (*Ufer*) shore;
Küstenwache f coastguard
Kutsche (-, -n) f carriage; (*geschlossene*)
coach
Kuvert (-s, -s) nt envelope
Kuvertüre (-, -n) f coating
Kuwait (-s) nt Kuwait
KZ (-s, -s) nt abk = **Konzentrationslager**
(*Hist*) concentration camp

k

L

Labor (-s, -e o -s) nt lab
Labyrinth (-s, -e) nt maze
Lache (-, -n) f (Pfütze) puddle; (Blut~, Öl~) pool
lächeln vi to smile; **Lächeln** (-s) nt smile; **lachen** vi to laugh; **lächerlich** adj ridiculous
Lachs (-es, -e) m salmon
Lack (-(e)s, -e) m varnish; (Farblack) lacquer; (an Auto) paint; **lackieren** vt to varnish; (Auto) to spray; **Lackschaden** m scratch (on the paintwork)
Ladegerät nt (battery) charger; **laden** (lud, geladen) vt (a. Inform) to load; (einladen) to invite; (Handy etc) to charge
Laden (-s, Läden) m shop; (Fensterladen) shutter; **Ladendieb(in)** m(f) shoplifter; **Ladendiebstahl** m shoplifting; **Ladenschluss** m closing time
Ladung f load; (Naut, Aviat) cargo; (Jur) summons sing
lag imperf von **liegen**
Lage (-, -n) f position, situation; (Schicht) layer; **in der ~ sein zu** to be in a position to
Lager (-s, -) nt camp; (Comm) warehouse;

(Tech) bearing; **Lagerfeuer** nt campfire; **lagern** vi (Dinge) to be stored; (Menschen) to camp ▷ vt to store
Lagune f lagoon
lahm adj lame; (langweilig) dull; **lähmen** vt to paralyse; **Lähmung** f paralysis
Laib (-s, -e) m loaf
Laie (-n, -n) m layman
Laken (-s, -) nt sheet
Lakritze (-, -n) f liquorice
Lamm (-(e)s, Lämmer) nt (a. Lammfleisch) lamb
Lampe (-, -n) f lamp; (Glühbirne) bulb; **Lampenfieber** nt stage fright; **Lampenschirm** m lampshade
Lampion (-s, -s) m Chinese lantern
Land (-(e)s, Länder) nt (Gelände) land; (Nation) country; (Bundesland) state, Land; **auf dem ~(e)** in the country

- **Land**
-
- A **Land** (plural **Länder**) is a member
- state of the **BRD**. There are 16 **Länder**,
- namely Baden-Württemberg, Bayern,
- Berlin, Brandenburg, Bremen,
- Hamburg, Hessen,
- Mecklenburg-Vorpommern,
- Niedersachsen,
- Nordrhein-Westfalen,
- Rheinland-Pfalz, Saarland, Sachsen,
- Sachsen-Anhalt, Schleswig-Holstein
- and Thüringen. Each 'Land' has its
- own parliament and constitution.

Landebahn f runway; **landen** vt, vi to land; (Schiff) to dock
Länderspiel nt international (match)
Landesgrenze f national border, frontier; **Landesinnere** nt interior; **landesüblich** adj customary; **Landeswährung** f national currency; **landesweit** adj nationwide
Landhaus nt country house; **Landkarte** f map; **Landkreis** m administrative region, ≈ district
ländlich adj rural
Landschaft f countryside; (schöne) scenery; (Kunst) landscape; **Landstraße** f country road, B road (Brit)
Landung f landing; **Landungsbrücke** f, **Landungssteg** m gangway
Landwirt(in) m(f) farmer;

Landwirtschaft f agriculture, farming;
landwirtschaftlich adj agricultural
lang adj long; (Mensch) tall; **ein zwei
Meter ~er Tisch** a table two metres long;
den ganzen Tag ~ all day long; **die Straße
~** along the street; **langärmelig** adj
long-sleeved; **lange** adv (for) a long time;
ich musste ~ warten I had to wait (for) a
long time; **ich bleibe nicht ~** I won't stay
long; **es ist ~ her, dass wir uns gesehen
haben** it's a long time since we saw each
other; **Länge** (-, -n) f length; (Geo)
longitude
langen vi (fam: ausreichen) to be enough;
(fam: fassen) to reach (nach for); **mir
langt's** I've had enough
Langeweile f boredom
langfristig adj long-term ▷ adv in the
long term
Langlauf m cross-country skiing
längs prep +gen die Bäume ~ der Straße
the trees along(side) the road ▷ adv **die
Streifen laufen ~ über das Hemd** the
stripes run lengthways down the shirt
langsam adj slow ▷ adv slowly
Langschläfer(in) (-s, -) m(f) late riser
längst adv **das ist ~ fertig** that was
finished a long time ago; **sie sollte ~ da
sein** she should have been here long ago;
als sie kam, waren wir ~ weg when she
arrived we had long since left
Langstreckenflug m long-haul flight
Languste (-, -n) f crayfish, crawfish
(US)
langweilen vt to bore; **ich langweile
mich** I'm bored; **langweilig** adj boring;
Langwelle f long wave
Laos (-) nt Laos
Lappen (-s, -) m cloth, rag; (Staublappen)
duster
läppisch adj silly; (Summe) ridiculous
Laptop (-s, -s) m laptop
Lärche (-, -n) f larch
Lärm (-(e)s) m noise
las imperf von **lesen**
Lasche (-, -n) f flap
Laser (-s, -) m laser; **Laserdrucker** m
laser printer

SCHLÜSSELWORT

lassen (pt **ließ**, pp **gelassen** od (als
Hilfsverb) **lassen**) vt **1** (unterlassen) to stop

(momentan) to leave; **lass das (sein)!** don't
(do it)!; (hör auf!) stop it!; **lass mich!** leave
me alone; **lassen wir das!** let's leave it; **er
kann das Trinken nicht lassen** he can't
stop drinking
2 (zurücklassen) to leave; **etw lassen, wie
es ist** to leave sth (just) as it is
3 (überlassen): **jdn ins Haus lassen** to let
sb into the house
▷ vi; **lass mal, ich mache das schon**
leave it, I'll do it
▷ Hilfsverb **1** (veranlassen): **etw machen
lassen** to have od get sth done; **sich** dat
etw **schicken lassen** to have sth sent (to one)
2 (zulassen): **jdn etw wissen lassen** to let
sb know sth; **das Licht brennen lassen** to
leave the light on; **jdn warten lassen** to
keep sb waiting; **das lässt sich machen**
that can be done
3: lass uns gehen let's go

lässig adj casual
Last (-, -en) f load; (Bürde) burden; (Naut,
Aviat) cargo
Laster (-s, -) nt vice; (fam) truck, lorry
(Brit)
lästern vi **über jdn/etw ~** to make nasty
remarks about sb/sth
lästig adj annoying; (Person) tiresome
Last-Minute-Flug m last-minute flight;
Last-Minute-Ticket nt last-minute ticket
Lastwagen m truck, lorry (Brit)
Latein (-s) nt Latin
Laterne (-, -n) f lantern; (Straßenlaterne)
streetlight
Latte (-, -n) f slat; (Sport) bar
Latz (-es, Lätze) m bib; **Lätzchen** nt bib;
Latzhose f dungarees pl
lau adj (Wind, Luft) mild
Laub (-(e)s) nt foliage; **Laubfrosch** m tree
frog; **Laubsäge** f fretsaw
Lauch (-(e)s, -e) m leeks pl; **eine Stange
~** a leek; **Lauchzwiebel** f spring onions pl
(Brit), scallions pl (US)
Lauf (-(e)s, Läufe) m run; (Wettlauf) race;
(Entwicklung) course; (von Gewehr) barrel;
Laufbahn f career; **laufen** (lief, gelaufen) vi,
vt to run; (gehen) to walk; (funktionieren) to
work; **mir läuft die Nase** my nose is
running; **was läuft im Kino?** what's on at
the cinema?; **wie läuft's so?** how are
things?; **laufend** adj running; (Monat,
Ausgaben) current; **auf dem Laufenden**

sein/halten to be/to keep up-to-date;
Läufer (-s, -) m (Teppich) rug; (Schach)
bishop; **Läufer(in)** m(f) (Sport) runner;
Laufmasche f ladder (Brit), run (US);
Laufwerk nt (Inform) drive
Laune (-, -n) f mood; **gute/schlechte**
~ haben to be in a good/bad mood;
launisch adj moody
Laus (-, Läuse) f louse
lauschen vi to listen; (heimlich) to
eavesdrop
laut adj loud ▷ adv loudly; (lesen) aloud
▷ prep +gen o dat according to
läuten vt, vi to ring
lauter adv (fam: nichts als) nothing but
Lautsprecher m loudspeaker;
Lautstärke f loudness; (Radio, Tv) volume
lauwarm adj lukewarm
Lava (-, Laven) f lava
Lavendel (-s, -) m lavender
Lawine f avalanche
LCD-Anzeige f LCD-display
leasen vt to lease; **Leasing** (-s) nt leasing
leben vt, vi to live; (am Leben sein) to be
alive; **wie lange ~ Sie schon hier?** how
long have you been living here?; **von ...**
~ (Nahrungsmittel etc) to live on ...; (Beruf,
Beschäftigung) to make one's living from
...; **Leben** (-s, -) nt life; **lebend** adj living;
lebendig adj alive; (lebhaft) lively;
lebensgefährlich adj very dangerous;
(Verletzung) critical; **Lebensgefährte** m,
Lebensgefährtin f partner;
Lebenshaltungskosten pl cost sing of
living; **lebenslänglich** adj for life;
~ bekommen to get life; **Lebenslauf** m
curriculum vitae (Brit), CV (Brit), resumé
(US); **Lebensmittel** pl food sing;
Lebensmittelgeschäft nt grocer's (shop);
Lebensmittelvergiftung f food
poisoning; **lebensnotwendig** adj vital;
Lebensretter(in) m(f) rescuer;
Lebensstandard m standard of living;
Lebensunterhalt m livelihood;
Lebensversicherung f life insurance (o
assurance (Brit)); **Lebenszeichen** nt sign
of life
Leber (-, -n) f liver; **Leberfleck** m mole;
Leberpastete f liver pâté
Lebewesen nt living being
lebhaft adj lively; (Erinnerung, Eindruck)
vivid; **Lebkuchen** m gingerbread; **ein ~ a**
piece of gingerbread; **leblos** adj lifeless

Leck nt leak
lecken vi (Loch haben) to leak ▷ vt, vi
(schlecken) to lick
lecker adj delicious, tasty
Leder (-s, -) nt leather
ledig adj single
leer adj empty; (Seite) blank; (Batterie)
dead; **leeren** vt to empty ▷ vr **sich ~** to
empty; **Leerlauf** m (Gang) neutral;
Leertaste f space bar; **Leerung** f
emptying; (Briefkasten) collection;
Leerzeichen nt blank, space
legal adj legal, lawful
legen vt to put, to place; (Eier) to lay ▷ vr
sich ~ to lie down; (Sturm, Begeisterung) to
die down; (Schmerz, Gefühl) to wear off
Legende (-, -n) f legend
leger adj casual
Lehm (-(e)s, -e) m loam; (Ton) clay
Lehne (-, -n) f arm(rest); (Rückenlehne)
back(rest); **lehnen** vt to lean ▷ vr **sich**
~ to lean (an/gegen +akk against);
Lehnstuhl m armchair
Lehrbuch nt textbook; **Lehre** (-, -n) f
teaching; (beruflich) apprenticeship;
(moralisch) lesson; **lehren** vt to teach;
Lehrer(in) (-s, -) m(f) teacher; **Lehrgang**
m course; **Lehrling** m apprentice;
lehrreich adj instructive
Leib (-(e)s, -er) m body; **Leibgericht** nt,
Leibspeise f favourite dish;
Leibwächter(in) m(f) bodyguard
Leiche (-, -n) f corpse; **Leichenhalle** f
mortuary; **Leichenwagen** m hearse
leicht adj light; (einfach) easy, simple;
(Erkrankung) slight; **jdm ~ fallen** to be easy
for sb; **es sich** (dat) **~ machen** to take the
easy way out ▷ adv (mühelos, schnell)
easily; (geringfügig) slightly;
Leichtathletik f athletics sing;
leichtsinnig adj careless; (stärker)
reckless
leid adj **jdn/etw ~ sein** to be tired of
sb/sth; **Leid** (-(e)s) nt grief, sorrow; **es tut**
mir/ihm ~ I'm/he's sorry; **er tut mir ~** I'm
sorry for him; **~ tun**; siehe auch **leidtun**;
leiden (litt, gelitten) vi, vt to suffer (an,
unter +dat from); **ich kann ihn/es nicht ~** I
can't stand him/it; **Leiden** (-s, -) nt
suffering; (Krankheit) illness
Leidenschaft f passion;
leidenschaftlich adj passionate
leider adv unfortunately; **wir müssen**

jetzt ~ gehen I'm afraid we have to go now; **~ ja/nein** I'm afraid so/not
leidtun vi **es tut mir/ihm ~** I'm/he's sorry; **er tut mir ~** I'm sorry for him
Leihbücherei f lending library
leihen (lieh, geliehen) vt **jdm etw ~** to lend sb sth; **sich** (dat) **etw von jdm ~** to borrow sth from sb; **Leihfrist** f lending period; **Leihgebühr** f hire charge; (für Buch) lending charge; **Leihwagen** m hire car (Brit), rental car (US)
Leim (-(e)s, -e) m glue
Leine (-, -n) f cord; (für Wäsche) line; (Hundeleine) lead (Brit), leash (US)
Leinen (-s, -) nt linen; **Leintuch** nt (für Bett) sheet; **Leinwand** f (Kunst) canvas; (Cine) screen
leise adj quiet; (sanft) soft ▷ adv quietly
Leiste (-, -n) f ledge; (Zierleiste) strip; (Anat) groin
leisten vt (Arbeit) to do; (vollbringen) to achieve; **jdm Gesellschaft ~** to keep sb company; **sich** (dat) **etw ~** (gönnen) to treat oneself to sth; **ich kann es mir nicht ~** I can't afford it
Leistenbruch m hernia
Leistung f performance; (gute) achievement
Leitartikel m leading article (Brit), editorial (US)
leiten vt to lead; (Firma) to run; (in eine Richtung) to direct; (Elek) to conduct
Leiter (-, -n) f ladder
Leiter(in) (-s, -) m(f) (von Geschäft) manager
Leitplanke (-, -n) f crash barrier
Leitung f (Führung) direction; (Tel) line; (von Firma) management; (Wasserleitung) pipe; (Kabel) cable; **eine lange ~ haben** to be slow on the uptake; **Leitungswasser** nt tap water
Lektion f lesson
Lektüre (-, -n) f (Lesen) reading; (Lesestoff) reading matter
Lende (-, -n) f (Speise) loin; (vom Rind) sirloin; **die ~n** pl (Med) the lumbar region sing
lenken vt to steer; (Blick) to direct (auf +akk towards); **jds Aufmerksamkeit auf etw** (akk) **~** to draw sb's attention to sth; **Lenker** m (von Fahrrad, Motorrad) handlebars pl; **Lenkrad** nt steering

wheel; **Lenkradschloss** nt steering lock; **Lenkstange** f handlebars pl
Leopard (-en, -en) m leopard
Lepra (-) f leprosy
Lerche (-, -n) f lark
lernen vt, vi to learn; (für eine Prüfung) to study, to revise
lesbisch adj lesbian
Lesebuch nt reader; **lesen** (las, gelesen) vi, vt to read; (ernten) to pick; **Leser(in)** m(f) reader; **Leserbrief** m letter to the editor; **leserlich** adj legible; **Lesezeichen** nt bookmark
Lettland nt Latvia
letzte(r, s) adj last; (neueste) latest; (endgültig) final; **zum ~n Mal** for the last time; **am ~n Montag** last Monday; **in ~r Zeit** lately, recently; **letztens** adv (vor kurzem) recently; **letztere(r, s)** adj the latter
Leuchtanzeige f illuminated display; **Leuchte** (-, -n) f lamp, light; **leuchten** vi to shine; (Feuer, Zifferblatt) to glow; **Leuchter** (-s, -) m candlestick; **Leuchtfarbe** f fluorescent colour; (Anstrichfarbe) luminous paint; **Leuchtreklame** f neon sign; **Leuchtstift** m highlighter; **Leuchtstoffröhre** f strip light; **Leuchtturm** m lighthouse
leugnen vt to deny ▷ vi to deny everything
Leukämie f leukaemia (Brit), leukemia (US)
Leukoplast® (-(e)s, -e) nt Elastoplast® (Brit), Band-Aid® (US)
Leute pl people pl
Lexikon (-s, Lexika) nt encyclopaedia (Brit), encyclopedia (US); (Wörterbuch) dictionary
Libanon (-s) m **der ~** Lebanon
Libelle f dragonfly
liberal adj liberal
Libyen (-s) nt Libya
Licht (-(e)s, -er) nt light; **Lichtblick** m ray of hope; **lichtempfindlich** adj sensitive to light; **Lichempfindlichkeit** f (Foto) speed; **Lichthupe** f **die ~ betätigen** to flash one's lights; **Lichtjahr** nt light year; **Lichtmaschine** f dynamo; **Lichtschalter** m light switch; **Lichtschranke** f light barrier; **Lichtschutzfaktor** m sun protection factor, SPF
Lichtung f clearing

Lid (-(e)s, -er) nt eyelid; **Lidschatten** m eyeshadow

lieb adj (nett) nice; (teuer, geliebt) dear; (liebenswert) sweet; **das ist ~ von dir** that's nice of you; **Lieber Herr X** Dear Mr X; **Liebe** (-, -n) f love; **lieben** vt to love; (sexuell) to make love to; **liebenswürdig** adj kind; **lieber** adv rather; **ich möchte ~ nicht** I'd rather not; **welches ist dir ~?** which one do you prefer?; siehe auch **gern, lieb**; **Liebesbrief** m love letter; **Liebeskummer** m **~ haben** to be lovesick; **Liebespaar** nt lovers pl; **liebevoll** adj loving; **Liebhaber(in)** (-s, -) m(f) lover; **lieblich** adj lovely; (Wein) sweet; **Liebling** m darling; (Günstling) favourite; **Lieblings-** in zW favourite; **liebste(r, s)** adj favourite; **liebsten** adv **am ~ esse ich ...** my favourite food is ...; **am ~ würde ich bleiben** I'd really like to stay

Liechtenstein (-s) nt Liechtenstein

Lied (-(e)s, -er) nt song; (Rel) hymn

lief imperf von **laufen**

Lieferant(in) m(f) supplier

lieferbar adj available

liefern vt to deliver; (beschaffen) to supply

Lieferschein m delivery note; **Lieferung** f delivery; **Lieferwagen** m delivery van

Liege (-, -n) f (beim Arzt) couch; (Notbett) campbed; (Gartenliege) lounger; **liegen** (lag, gelegen) vi to lie; (sich befinden) to be; **mir liegt nichts/viel daran** it doesn't matter to me/it matters a lot to me; **woran liegt es nur, dass ...?** why is it that ...?; **~ bleiben** (Mensch) to stay lying down; (im Bett) to stay in bed; (Ding) to be left (behind); **~ lassen** (vergessen) to leave behind; **Liegestuhl** m deck chair; **Liegestütz** m press-up (Brit), push-up (US); **Liegewagen** m (Eisenb) couchette car

lieh imperf von **leihen**

ließ imperf von **lassen**

Lift (-(e)s, -e o -s) m lift, elevator (US)

Liga (-, Ligen) f league, division

light adj (Cola) diet; (fettarm) low-fat; (kalorienarm) low-calorie; (Zigaretten) mild

Likör (-s, -e) m liqueur

lila adj inv purple

Lilie f lily

Limette (-, -n) f lime

Limo (-, -s) f (fam) fizzy drink (Brit), soda

(US); **Limonade** f fizzy drink (Brit), soda (US); (mit Zitronengeschmack) lemonade

Limone (-, -n) f lime

Limousine (-, -n) f saloon (car) (Brit), sedan (US); (fam) limo

Linde (-, -n) f lime tree

lindern vt to relieve, to soothe

Lineal (-s, -e) nt ruler

Linie f line; **Linienflug** m scheduled flight; **Linienrichter** m linesman; **liniert** adj ruled, lined

Linke (-n, -n) f left-hand side; (Hand) left hand; (Pol) left (wing); **linke(r, s)** adj left; **auf der ~n Seite** on the left, on the left-hand side; **links** adv on the left; **~ abbiegen** to turn left; **~ von** to the left of; **~ oben** at the top left; **Linksaußen** m left winger; **Linkshänder(in)** (-s, -) m(f) left-hander; **linksherum** adv to the left, anticlockwise; **Linksverkehr** m driving on the left

Linse (-, -n) f lentil; (optisch) lens; **Linsensuppe** f lentil soup

Lippe (-, -n) f lip; **Lipgloss** nt lip gloss; **Lippenstift** m lipstick

lispeln vi to lisp

List (-, -en) f cunning; (Trick) trick

Liste (-, -n) f list

Litauen (-s) nt Lithuania

Liter (-s, -) m o nt litre

literarisch adj literary; **Literatur** f literature

Litschi (-, -s) f lychee, litchi

litt imperf von **leiden**

live adv (Radio, Tv) live

Lizenz f licence

Lkw (-(s), -(s)) m abk = **Lastkraftwagen** truck, lorry (Brit)

Lob (-(e)s) nt praise; **loben** vt to praise

Loch (-(e)s, Löcher) nt hole; **lochen** vt to punch; **Locher** (-s, -) m (hole) punch

Locke (-, -n) f curl; **locken** vt (anlocken) to lure; (Haare) to curl; **Lockenstab** m curling tongs pl (Brit), curling irons pl (US); **Lockenwickler** (-s, -) m curler

locker adj (Schraube, Zahn) loose; (Haltung) relaxed; (Person) easy-going; **das schaffe ich ~** (fam) I'll manage it, no problem; **lockern** vt to loosen ▷ vr **sich ~** to loosen

lockig adj curly

Löffel (-s, -) m spoon; **einen ~ Mehl zugeben** add a spoonful of flour; **Löffelbiskuit** (-s, -s) m sponge finger

log *imperf von* **lügen**
Loge (-, -n) *f* (*Theat*) box
logisch *adj* logical
Logo (-s, -s) *nt* logo
Lohn (-(e)s, Löhne) *m* reward; (*Arbeitslohn*) pay, wages *pl*
lohnen *vr* **sich ~** to be worth it; **es lohnt sich nicht zu warten** it's no use waiting
Lohnerhöhung *f* pay rise (*Brit*), pay raise (*US*); **Lohnsteuer** *f* income tax
Lokal (-(e)s, -e) *nt* (*Gaststätte*) restaurant; (*Kneipe*) pub (*Brit*), bar
Lokomotive *f* locomotive
London (-s) *nt* London
Lorbeer (-s, -en) *m* laurel; **Lorbeerblatt** *nt* (*Gastr*) bay leaf
los *adj* loose; **~!** go on!; **jdn/etw ~ sein** to be rid of sb/sth; **was ist ~?** what's the matter?, what's up?; **dort ist nichts/viel ~** there's nothing/a lot going on there
Los (-es, -e) *nt* (*Schicksal*) lot, fate; (*Lotterie etc*) ticket
los|binden *irr vt* to untie
löschen *vt* (*Feuer, Licht*) to put out, to extinguish; (*Durst*) to quench; (*Tonband*) to erase; (*Daten, Zeile*) to delete; **Löschtaste** *f* delete key
lose *adj* loose
Lösegeld *nt* ransom
losen *vi* to draw lots
lösen *vt* (*lockern*) to loosen; (*Rätsel*) to solve; (*Chem*) to dissolve; (*Fahrkarte*) to buy ▷ *vr* **sich ~** (*abgehen*) to come off; (*Zucker etc*) to dissolve; (*Problem, Schwierigkeit*) to (re)solve itself
los|fahren *irr vi* to leave; **los|gehen** *irr vi* to set out; (*anfangen*) to start; **los|lassen** *irr vt* to let go
löslich *adj* soluble
Lösung *f* (*eines Rätsels, Problems, Flüssigkeit*) solution
los|werden *irr vt* to get rid of
Lotterie *f* lottery; **Lotto** (-s) *nt* National Lottery; **~ spielen** to play the lottery
Löwe (-n, -n) *m* (*Zool*) lion; (*Astr*) Leo; **Löwenzahn** *m* dandelion
Luchs (-es, -e) *m* lynx
Lücke (-, -n) *f* gap; **Lückenbüßer(in)** (-s, -) *m(f)* stopgap
lud *imperf von* **laden**
Luft (-, Lüfte) *f* air; (*Atem*) breath; **Luftballon** *m* balloon; **Luftblase** *f* (air) bubble; **luftdicht** *adj* airtight; **Luftdruck**

m (*Meteo*) atmospheric pressure; (*in Reifen*) air pressure
lüften *vt* to air; (*Geheimnis*) to reveal
Luftfahrt *f* aviation; **Luftfeuchtigkeit** *f* humidity; **Luftfilter** *m* air filter; **Luftfracht** *f* air freight; **Luftkissenfahrzeug** *nt* hovercraft; **Luftlinie** *f* **10 km ~** 10 km as the crow flies; **Luftmatratze** *f* airbed; **Luftpirat(in)** *m(f)* hijacker; **Luftpost** *f* airmail; **Luftpumpe** *f* (bicycle) pump; **Luftröhre** *f* windpipe
Lüftung *f* ventilation
Luftveränderung *f* change of air; **Luftverschmutzung** *f* air pollution; **Luftwaffe** *f* air force; **Luftzug** *m* draught (*Brit*), draft (*US*)
Lüge (-, -n) *f* lie; **lügen** (log, gelogen) *vi* to lie; **Lügner(in)** (-s, -) *m(f)* liar
Luke (-, -n) *f* hatch
Lumpen (-s, -) *m* rag
Lunchpaket *nt* packed lunch
Lunge (-, -n) *f* lungs *pl*; **Lungenentzündung** *f* pneumonia
Lupe (-, -n) *f* magnifying glass; **etw unter die ~ nehmen** (*fig*) to have a close look at sth
Lust (-, Lüste) *f* joy, delight; (*Neigung*) desire; **~ auf etw** (*akk*) **haben** to feel like sth; **~ haben, etw zu tun** to feel like doing sth
lustig *adj* (*komisch*) amusing, funny; (*fröhlich*) cheerful
lutschen *vt* to suck ▷ *vi* **~ an** (+*dat*) to suck; **Lutscher** (-s, -) *m* lollipop
Luxemburg (-s) *nt* Luxembourg
luxuriös *adj* luxurious
Luxus (-) *m* luxury
Lymphdrüse *f* lymph gland; **Lymphknoten** *m* lymph node
Lyrik (-) *f* poetry

m

machbar *adj* feasible

machen *vt* **1** to do; (*herstellen, zubereiten*) to make; **was machst du da?** what are you doing (there)?; **das ist nicht zu machen** that can't be done; **das Radio leiser machen** to turn the radio down; **aus Holz gemacht** made of wood

2 (*verursachen, bewirken*) to make; **jdm Angst machen** to make sb afraid; **das macht die Kälte** it's the cold that does that

3 (*ausmachen*) to matter; **das macht nichts** that doesn't matter; **die Kälte macht mir nichts** I don't mind the cold

4 (*kosten, ergeben*) to be; **3 und 5 macht 8** 3 and 5 is o are 8; **was o wie viel macht das?** how much does that make?

5: **was macht die Arbeit?** how's the work going?; **was macht dein Bruder?** how is your brother doing?; **das Auto machen lassen** to have the car done; **machs gut!** take care!; (*viel Glück*) good luck!

▷ *vi*: **mach schnell!** hurry up!; **Schluss**

machen to finish (off); **mach schon!** come on!; **das macht müde** it makes you tired; **in etw** *dat* **machen** to be o deal in sth

▷ *vr* to come along (nicely); **sich an etw** *akk* **machen** to set about sth; **sich verständlich machen** to make o.s. understood; **sich** *dat* **viel aus jdm/etw machen** to like sb/sth

Macho (-s, -s) *m* (*fam*) macho (type)
Macht (-s, *Mächte*) *f* power; **mächtig** *adj* powerful; (*fam: ungeheuer*) enormous; **machtlos** *adj* powerless; **da ist man ~** there's nothing you can do (about it)
Mädchen *nt* girl; **Mädchenname** *m* maiden name
Made (-, -n) *f* maggot
Magazin (-s, -e) *nt* magazine
Magen (-s, - o *Mägen*) *m* stomach; **Magenbeschwerden** *pl* stomach trouble *sing*; **Magen-Darm-Infektion** *f* gastroenteritis; **Magengeschwür** *nt* stomach ulcer; **Magenschmerzen** *pl* stomachache *sing*
mager *adj* (*Fleisch, Wurst*) lean; (*Person*) thin; (*Käse, Joghurt*) low-fat; **Magermilch** *f* skimmed milk; **Magersucht** *f* anorexia; **magersüchtig** *adj* anorexic
magisch *adj* magical
Magnet (-s o -en, -en) *m* magnet
mähen *vt, vi* to mow
mahlen (*mahlte, gemahlen*) *vt* to grind
Mahlzeit *f* meal; (*für Baby*) feed ▷ *interj* (*guten Appetit*) enjoy your meal
Mähne (-, -n) *f* mane
mahnen *vt* to urge; **jdn schriftlich ~** to send sb a reminder; **Mahngebühr** *f* fine; **Mahnung** *f* warning; (*schriftlich*) reminder
Mai (-(s), -e) *m* May; *siehe auch* **Juni**; **Maifeiertag** *m* May Day; **Maiglöckchen** *nt* lily of the valley; **Maikäfer** *m* cockchafer
Mail (-, -s) *f* e-mail; **Mailbox** *f* (*Inform*) mailbox; **mailen** *vi, vt* to e-mail
Mais (-es, -e) *m* maize, corn (US); **Maiskolben** *m* corn cob; (*Gastr*) corn on the cob
Majestät (-, -en) *f* Majesty
Majonäse (-, -n) *f* mayonnaise
Majoran (-s, -e) *m* marjoram
makaber *adj* macabre
Make-up (-s, -s) *nt* make-up

Makler(in) (-s, -) m(f) broker;
(*Immobilienmakler*) estate agent (*Brit*),
realtor (*US*)

Makrele (-, -n) f mackerel

Makro (-s, -s) nt (*Inform*) macro

Makrone (-, -n) f macaroon

mal adv (*beim Rechnen*) times, multiplied
by; (*beim Messen*) by; (*fam: einmal = früher*)
once; (*einmal = zukünftig*) some day; **4 ~ 3
ist 12** 4 times 3 is (*o equals*) twelve; **da
habe ich ~ gewohnt** I used to live there;
irgendwann ~ werde ich dort hinfahren
I'll go there one day; **das ist nun ~ so** well,
that's just the way it is (*o goes*); **Mal** (-(e)s,
-e) nt (*Zeitpunkt*) time; (*Markierung*) mark;
jedes ~ every time; **ein paar ~** a few
times; **ein einziges ~** just once

Malaria (-) f malaria

Malaysia (-s) nt Malaysia

Malbuch nt colouring book

Malediven pl Maldives pl

malen vt, vi to paint; **Maler(in)** (-s, -) m(f)
painter; **Malerei** f painting; **malerisch**
adj picturesque

Mallorca (-s) nt Majorca, Mallorca

mal|nehmen irr vt to multiply (*mit* by)

Malta (-s) nt Malta

Malventee m mallow tea

Malz (-es) nt malt; **Malzbier** nt malt beer

Mama (-, -s) f mum(my) (*Brit*), mom(my)
(*US*)

man pron you; (*förmlich*) one; (*jemand*)
someone, somebody; (*die Leute*) they,
people pl; **wie schreibt ~ das?** how do you
spell that?; **~ hat ihr das Fahrrad
gestohlen** someone stole her bike;
~ sagt, dass ... they (*o people*) say that ...

managen vt (*fam*) to manage;
Manager(in) (-s, -) m(f) manager

manche(r, s) adj many a; (*mit pl*) a
number of, some ▷ pron (*einige*) some;
(*viele*) many; **~ Politiker** many politicians
pl, many a politician; **manchmal** adv
sometimes

Mandant(in) m(f) client

Mandarine f mandarin, tangerine

Mandel (-, -n) f almond; **~n** (*Anat*) tonsils
pl; **Mandelentzündung** f tonsillitis

Manege (-, -n) f ring

Mangel (-s, Mängel) m (*Fehlen*) lack;
(*Knappheit*) shortage (*an* +dat of); (*Fehler*)
defect, fault; **mangelhaft** adj (*Ware*)
faulty; (*Schulnote*) ≈ E

Mango (-, -s) f mango

Mangold (-s) m mangel(wurzel)

Manieren pl manners pl

Maniküre (-, -n) f manicure

manipulieren vt to manipulate

Manko (-s, -s) nt deficiency

Mann (-(e)s, Männer) m man; (*Ehemann*)
husband; **Männchen** nt **es ist ein ~** (*Tier*)
it's a he; **männlich** adj masculine; (*Bio*)
male

Mannschaft f (*Sport, fig*) team; (*Naut,
Aviat*) crew

Mansarde (-, -n) f attic

Manschettenknopf m cufflink

Mantel (-s, Mäntel) m coat; (*Tech*) casing,
jacket

Mappe (-, -n) f briefcase; (*Aktenmappe*)
folder

Maracuja (-, -s) f passion fruit

Marathon (-s, -s) m marathon

Märchen (-s, -) nt fairy tale

Marder (-s, -) m marten

Margarine f margarine

Marienkäfer m ladybird (*Brit*), ladybug
(*US*)

Marihuana (-s) nt marijuana

Marille (-, -n) f apricot

Marinade f marinade

Marine f navy

marinieren vt to marinate

Marionette f puppet

Mark (-(e)s) nt (*Knochenmark*) marrow;
(*Fruchtmark*) pulp

Marke (-, -n) f (*Warensorte*) brand;
(*Fabrikat*) make; (*Briefmarke*) stamp;
(*Essenmarke*) voucher, ticket; (*aus Metall
etc*) disc; (*Briefmarke*) mark;
Markenartikel m branded item, brand
name product; **Markenzeichen** nt
trademark

markieren vt to mark; **Markierung** f
marking; (*Zeichen*) mark

Markise (-, -n) f awning

Markt (-(e)s, Märkte) m market; **auf den
~ bringen** to launch; **Markthalle** f
covered market; **Marktlücke** f gap in
the market; **Marktplatz** m market
place; **Marktwirtschaft** f market
economy

Marmelade f jam; (*Orangenmarmelade*)
marmalade

Marmor (-s, -e) m marble;
Marmorkuchen m marble cake

Marokko (-s) nt Morocco
Marone (-, -n) f chestnut
Mars (-) m Mars
Marsch (-(e)s, Märsche) m march
Märtyrer(in) (-s, -) m(f) martyr
März (-(es), -e) m March; siehe auch **Juni**
Marzipan (-s, -e) nt marzipan
Maschine f machine; (Motor) engine;
  maschinell adj mechanical, machine-;
  Maschinenbau m mechanical
  engineering
Masern pl (Med) measles sing
Maske (-, -n) f mask; **Maskenball** m
  fancy-dress ball; **maskieren** vr **sich**
  ~ (Maske aufsetzen) to put on a mask;
  (verkleiden) to dress up
Maskottchen nt mascot
maß imperf von **messen**
Maß (-es, -e) nt measure; (Mäßigung)
  moderation; (Grad) degree, extent; **~e**
  (Person) measurements; (Raum)
  dimensions; **in gewissem/hohem ~e** to a
  certain/high degree; **in zunehmendem
  ~e** increasingly
Mass (-, -(en)) f (Bier) litre of beer
Massage (-, -n) f massage
Masse (-, -n) f mass; (von Menschen)
  crowd; (Großteil) majority; **massenhaft**
  adv masses (o loads) of; **am See sind
  ~ Mücken** there are masses of
  mosquitoes at the lake;
  Massenkarambolage f pile-up;
  Massenmedien pl mass media pl;
  Massenproduktion f mass production;
  Massentourismus m mass tourism
Masseur(in) m(f) masseur/masseuse
maßgeschneidert adj (Kleidung)
  made-to-measure
massieren vt to massage
mäßig adj moderate
massiv adj solid; (fig) massive
maßlos adj extreme
Maßnahme (-, -n) f measure, step
Maßstab m rule, measure; (fig) standard;
  im ~ von 1:5 on a scale of 1:5
Mast (-(e)s, -e(n)) m mast; (Elek) pylon
Material (-s, -ien) nt material;
  (Arbeitsmaterial) materials pl;
  materialistisch adj materialistic
Materie f matter; **materiell** adj material
Mathematik f mathematics sing;
  Mathematiker(in) m(f) mathematician
Matinee (-, -n) f ≈ matinee

Matratze (-, -n) f mattress
Matrose (-n, -n) m sailor
Matsch (-(e)s) m mud; (Schnee) slush;
  matschig adj (Boden) muddy; (Schnee)
  slushy; (Obst) mushy
matt adj weak; (glanzlos) dull; (Foto) matt;
  (Schach) mate
Matte (-, -n) f mat
Matura (-) f Austrian school-leaving
  examination; ≈ A-levels (Brit), ≈ High School
  Diploma (US)
Mauer (-, -n) f wall
Maul (-(e)s, Mäuler) nt mouth; (fam) gob;
  halt's ~! shut your face (o gob);
  Maulbeere f mulberry; **Maulesel** m
  mule; **Maulkorb** m muzzle; **Maul- und
  Klauenseuche** f foot-and-mouth
  disease; **Maulwurf** m mole
Maurer(in) (-s, -) m(f) bricklayer
Mauritius (-) nt Mauritius
Maus (-, Mäuse) f mouse; **Mausefalle** f
  mousetrap; **Mausklick** (-s, -s) m mouse
  click; **Mauspad** (-s, -s) nt mouse mat (o
  pad); **Maustaste** f mouse key (o button)
Maut (-, -en) f toll; **Mautgebühr** f toll;
  mautpflichtig adj **~e Straße** toll road,
  turnpike (US); **Mautstelle** f tollbooth,
  tollgate; **Mautstraße** f toll road,
  turnpike (US)
maximal adv **ihr habt ~ zwei Stunden
  Zeit** you've got two hours at (the) most;
  ~ vier Leute a maximum of four people
Mayonnaise f siehe **Majonäse**
Mazedonien (-s) nt Macedonia
MB (-, -) nt, **Mbyte** (-, -) nt abk =
  Megabyte MB
Mechanik f mechanics sing; (Getriebe)
  mechanics pl; **Mechaniker(in)** (-s, -) m(f)
  mechanic; **mechanisch** adj mechanical;
  Mechanismus m mechanism
meckern vi (Ziege) to bleat; (fam:
  schimpfen) to moan
Mecklenburg-Vorpommern (-s) nt
  Mecklenburg-Western Pomerania
Medaille (-, -n) f medal
Medien pl media pl
Medikament nt medicine
Meditation f meditation; **meditieren** vi
  to meditate
medium adj (Steak) medium
Medizin (-, -en) f medicine (gegen for);
  medizinisch adj medical
Meer (-(e)s, -e) nt sea; **am ~** by the sea;

Meerenge f straits pl; **Meeresfrüchte** pl seafood sing; **Meeresspiegel** m sea level; **Meerrettich** m horseradish; **Meerschweinchen** nt guinea pig; **Meerwasser** nt seawater

Megabyte nt megabyte; **Megahertz** nt megahertz

Mehl (-(e)s, -e) nt flour; **Mehlspeise** f sweet dish made from flour, eggs and milk

mehr pron, adv more; **~ will ich nicht ausgeben** I don't want to spend any more, that's as much as I want to spend; **was willst du ~?** what more do you want? ▷ adv **immer ~ (Leute)** more and more (people); **~ als fünf Minuten** more than five minutes; **je ~ ..., desto besser** the more ..., the better; **ich kann nicht ~ stehen** I can't stand any more (o longer); **es ist kein Brot ~ da** there's no bread left; **nie ~** never again; **mehrdeutig** adj ambiguous; **mehrere** pron several; **mehreres** pron several things; **mehrfach** adj multiple; (wiederholt) repeated; **Mehrfachstecker** m multiple plug; **Mehrheit** f majority; **mehrmals** adv repeatedly; **mehrsprachig** adj multilingual; **Mehrwegflasche** f returnable bottle, deposit bottle; **Mehrwertsteuer** f value added tax, VAT; **Mehrzahl** f majority; (Plural) plural

meiden (mied, gemieden) vt to avoid

Meile (-, -n) f mile

mein pron (adjektivisch) my; **meine(r, s)** pron (substantivisch) mine

meinen vt, vi (glauben, der Ansicht sein) to think; (sagen) to say; (sagen wollen, beabsichtigen) to mean; **das war nicht so gemeint** I didn't mean it like that

meinetwegen adv (wegen mir) because of me; (mir zuliebe) for my sake; (von mir aus) as far as I'm concerned

Meinung f opinion; **meiner ~ nach** in my opinion; **Meinungsumfrage** f opinion poll; **Meinungsverschiedenheit** f disagreement (über +akk about)

Meise (-, -n) f tit; **eine ~ haben** (fam) to be crazy

Meißel (-s, -) m chisel

meist adv mostly; **meiste(r, s)** pron (adjektivisch) most; **die ~n (Leute)** most people; **die ~ Zeit** most of the time; **das ~ (davon)** most of it; **die ~n von ihnen** most of them; (substantivisch) most of them; **am ~n** (the) most; **meistens** adv mostly; (zum größten Teil) for the most part

Meister(in) (-s, -) m(f) master; (Sport) champion; **Meisterschaft** f championship; **Meisterwerk** nt masterpiece

melden vt to report ▷ vr **sich ~** to report (bei to); (Schule) to put one's hand up; (freiwillig) to volunteer; (auf etw, am Telefon) to answer; **Meldung** f announcement; (Bericht) report; (Inform) message

Melodie f tune, melody

Melone (-, -n) f melon

Memoiren pl memoirs pl

Menge (-, -n) f quantity; (Menschen) crowd; **eine ~ (große Anzahl)** a lot (gen of); **Mengenrabatt** m bulk discount

Meniskus (-, Menisken) m meniscus

Mensa (-, Mensen) f canteen, cafeteria (US)

Mensch (-en, -en) m human being, man; (Person) person; **kein ~** nobody; **~!** (bewundernd) wow!; (verärgert) bloody hell!; **Menschenmenge** f crowd; **Menschenrechte** pl human rights pl; **Menschenverstand** m **gesunder ~** common sense; **Menschheit** f humanity, mankind; **menschlich** adj human; (human) humane

Menstruation f menstruation

Mentalität f mentality, mindset

Menthol (-s) nt menthol

Menü (-s, -s) nt set meal; (Inform) menu; **Menüleiste** f (Inform) menu bar

Merkblatt nt leaflet; **merken** vt (bemerken) to notice; **sich** (dat) **etw ~** to remember sth; **Merkmal** nt feature

Merkur (-s) m Mercury

merkwürdig adj odd

Messbecher m measuring jug

Messe (-, -n) f fair; (Rel) mass; **Messebesucher(in)** m(f) visitor to a/the fair; **Messegelände** nt exhibition site

messen (maß, gemessen) vt to measure; (Temperatur, Puls) to take ▷ vr **sich ~** to compete; **sie kann sich mit ihm nicht ~** she's no match for him

Messer (-s, -) nt knife

Messgerät nt measuring device, gauge

Messing (-s) nt brass

Metall (-s, -e) nt metal

Meteorologe m, **Meteorologin** f meteorologist

Meter (-s, -) m o nt metre; **Metermaß** nt
tape measure
Methode (-, -n) f method
Metzger(in) (-s, -) m(f) butcher;
Metzgerei f butcher's (shop)
Mexiko (-s) nt Mexico
MEZ f abk = **mitteleuropäische Zeit** CET
miau interj miaow
mich pron akk von **ich** me; ~ **(selbst)**
(reflexiv) myself; **stell dich hinter ~** stand
behind me; **ich fühle ~ wohl** I feel fine
mied imperf von **meiden**
Miene (-, -n) f look, expression
mies adj (fam) lousy
Miesmuschel f mussel
Mietauto nt siehe **Mietwagen**; **Miete**
(-, -n) f rent; **mieten** vt to rent; (Auto) to
hire (Brit), to rent (US); **Mieter(in)** (-s, -)
m(f) tenant; **Miethaus** nt block of flats
(Brit), apartment house (US); **Mietvertrag**
m rental agreement; **Mietwagen** m hire
car (Brit), rental car (US); **sich** (dat) **einen**
~ **nehmen** to hire (Brit) (o rent (US)) a car
Migräne (-, -n) f migraine
Mikrofon (-s, -e) nt microphone
Mikrowelle (-, -n) f, **Mikrowellenherd** m
microwave (oven)
Milch (-) f milk; **Milcheis** nt ice-cream
(made with milk); **Milchglas** nt (dickes,
trübes Glas) frosted glass; **Milchkaffee** m
milky coffee; **Milchprodukte** pl dairy
products pl; **Milchpulver** nt powdered
milk; **Milchreis** m rice pudding;
Milchshake m milk shake; **Milchstraße** f
Milky Way
mild adj mild; (Richter) lenient; (freundlich)
kind
Militär (-s) nt military, army
Milliarde (-, -n) f billion; **Milligramm** nt
milligram; **Milliliter** m millilitre;
Millimeter m millimetre; **Million** f million;
Millionär(in) m(f) millionaire
Milz (-, -en) f spleen
Mimik f facial expression(s)
Minderheit f minority
minderjährig adj underage
minderwertig adj inferior;
Minderwertigkeitskomplex m
inferiority complex
Mindest- in zW minimum; **mindeste(r, s)**
adj least; **mindestens** adv at least;
Mindesthaltbarkeitsdatum nt
best-before date, sell-by date (Brit)

Mine (-, -n) f mine; (Bleistift) lead;
(Kugelschreiber) refill
Mineralwasser nt mineral water
Minibar f minibar; **Minigolf** nt miniature
golf, crazy golf (Brit)
minimal adj minimal
Minimum (-s, Minima) nt minimum
Minirock m miniskirt
Minister(in) (-s, -) m(f) minister;
Ministerium nt ministry;
Ministerpräsident(in) m(f) (von
Bundesland) Minister President (Prime
Minister of a Bundesland)
minus adv minus; **Minus** (-, -) nt deficit;
im ~ sein to be in the red; (Konto) to be
overdrawn
Minute (-, -n) f minute
Minze (-, -n) f mint
Mio. nt abk von **Million(en)** m
mir pron dat von **ich** (to) me; **kannst du**
~ **helfen?** can you help me?; **kannst du**
es ~ erklären? can you explain it to me?;
ich habe ~ einen neuen Rechner
gekauft I bought (myself) a new
computer; **ein Freund von ~** a friend of
mine
Mirabelle (-, -n) f mirabelle (small yellow
plum)
mischen vt to mix; (Karten) to shuffle;
Mischmasch m (fam) hotchpotch;
Mischung f mixture (aus of)
missachten vt to ignore; **Missbrauch** m
abuse; (falscher Gebrauch) misuse;
missbrauchen vt to misuse (zu for);
(sexuell) to abuse; **Misserfolg** m failure;
Missgeschick nt (Panne) mishap;
misshandeln vt to ill-treat
Mission f mission
misslingen (misslang, misslungen) vi to
fail; **der Versuch ist mir misslungen** my
attempt failed; **misstrauen** vt +dat to
distrust; **Misstrauen** (-s) nt mistrust,
suspicion (gegenüber of); **misstrauisch**
adj distrustful; (argwöhnisch) suspicious;
Missverständnis nt misunderstanding;
missverstehen vt to misunderstand
Mist (-(e)s) m (fam) rubbish; (von Kühen)
dung; (als Dünger) manure
Mistel (-, -n) f mistletoe
mit prep +dat with; (mittels) by; ~ **der Bahn**
by train; ~ **der Kreditkarte bezahlen** to
pay by credit card; ~ **10 Jahren** at the age
of 10; **wie wärs ~ ...?** how about ...? ▷ adv

along, too; **wollen Sie ~?** do you want to come along?

Mitarbeiter(in) m(f) (Angestellter) employee; (an Projekt) collaborator; (freier) freelancer

mit|bekommen irr vt (fam: aufschnappen) to catch; (hören) to hear; (verstehen) to get

mit|benutzen vt to share

Mitbewohner(in) m(f) (in Wohnung) flatmate (Brit), roommate (US)

mit|bringen irr vt to bring along; **Mitbringsel** (-s, -) nt small present

miteinander adv with one another; (gemeinsam) together

mit|erleben vt to see (with one's own eyes)

Mitesser (-s, -) m blackhead

Mitfahrgelegenheit f ≈ lift, ride (US); **Mitfahrzentrale** f agency for arranging lifts

mit|geben irr vt jdm etw ~ to give sb sth (to take along)

Mitgefühl nt sympathy

mit|gehen irr vi to go/come along

mitgenommen adj worn out, exhausted

Mitglied nt member

mithilfe prep +gen ~ von with the help of

mit|kommen irr vi to come along; (verstehen) to follow

Mitleid nt pity; ~ **haben mit** to feel sorry for

mit|machen vt to take part in ▷ vi to take part

mit|nehmen irr vt to take along; (anstrengen) to wear out, to exhaust

mit|schreiben irr vi to take notes ▷ vt to take down

Mitschüler(in) m(f) schoolmate

mit|spielen vi (in Mannschaft) to play; (bei Spiel) to join in; **in einem Film/Stück ~** to act in a film/play

Mittag m midday; **gestern ~** at midday yesterday, yesterday lunchtime; **über ~ geschlossen** closed at lunchtime; **zu ~ essen** to have lunch; **Mittagessen** nt lunch; **mittags** adv at lunchtime, at midday; **Mittagspause** f lunch break

Mitte (-, -n) f middle; **~ Juni** in the middle of June; **sie ist ~ zwanzig** she's in her mid-twenties

mit|teilen vt jdm etw ~ to inform sb of sth; **Mitteilung** f notification

Mittel (-s -) nt means sing; (Maßnahme, Methode) method; (Med) remedy (gegen

for); **das ist ein gutes ~, (um) junge Leute zu erreichen** that's a good way of engaging with young people

Mittelalter nt Middle Ages pl; **mittelalterlich** adj medieval; **Mittelamerika** nt Central America; **Mitteleuropa** nt Central Europe; **Mittelfeld** nt midfield; **Mittelfinger** m middle finger; **mittelmäßig** adj mediocre; **Mittelmeer** nt Mediterranean (Sea); **Mittelohrentzündung** f inflammation of the middle ear; **Mittelpunkt** m centre; **im ~ stehen** to be the centre of attention

mittels prep +gen by means of

Mittelstreifen m central reservation (Brit), median (US); **Mittelstürmer(in)** m(f) striker, centre-forward; **Mittelwelle** f medium wave

mitten adv in the middle; **~ auf der Straße/in der Nacht** in the middle of the street/night

Mitternacht f midnight

mittlere(r, s) adj middle; (durchschnittlich) average

mittlerweile adv meanwhile

Mittwoch (-s, -e) m Wednesday; (am) **~** on Wednesday; (am) **~ Morgen/Nachmittag/Abend** (on) Wednesday morning/afternoon/evening; **diesen/letzten/nächsten ~** this/last/next Wednesday; **jeden ~** every Wednesday; **~ in einer Woche** a week on Wednesday, Wednesday week; **mittwochs** adv on Wednesdays; **~ abends** (jeden Mittwochabend) on Wednesday evenings

mixen vt to mix; **Mixer** (-s, -) m (Küchengerät) blender

MKS f abk = **Maul- und Klauenseuche** FMD

mobben vt to harass (o to bully) (at work)

Mobbing (-s) nt workplace bullying (o harassment)

Möbel (-s, -) nt piece of furniture; **die ~** pl the furniture sing; **Möbelwagen** m removal van

mobil adj mobile

Mobilfunknetz nt cellular network; **Mobiltelefon** nt mobile phone

möblieren vt to furnish

mochte imperf von **mögen**

Mode (-, -n) f fashion
Model (-s, -s) nt model
Modell (-s, -e) nt model
Modem (-s, -s) nt (Inform) modem
Mode(n)schau f fashion show
Moderator(in) m(f) presenter
modern adj modern; (modisch)
fashionable
Modeschmuck m costume jewellery;
modisch adj fashionable
Modus (-, Modi) m (Inform) mode; (fig) way
Mofa (-s, -s) nt moped
mogeln vi to cheat

 SCHLÜSSELWORT

mögen (pt mochte, pp gemocht od (als
Hilfsverb) mögen) vt, vi to like; **magst
du/mögen Sie ihn?** do you like him?; **ich
möchte ...** I would like ... I'd like ...; **er
möchte in die Stadt** he'd like to go into
town; **ich möchte nicht, dass du ...** I
wouldn't like you to ...; **ich mag nicht
mehr** I've had enough
▷ Hilfsverb to like to (wollen) to want;
möchtest du etwas essen? would you
like something to eat?; **sie mag nicht
bleiben** she doesn't want to stay; **das
mag wohl sein** that may well be; **was
mag das heißen?** what might that
mean?; **Sie möchten zu Hause anrufen**
could you please call home?

möglich adj possible; **so bald wie ~** as
soon as possible; **möglicherweise** adv
possibly; **Möglichkeit** f possibility;
möglichst adv as ... as possible
Mohn (-(e)s, -e) m (Blume) poppy; (Samen)
poppy seed
Möhre (-, -n) f, **Mohrrübe** f carrot
Mokka (-s, -s) m mocha
Moldawien (-s) nt Moldova
Molkerei (-, -en) f dairy
Moll (-) nt minor (key); **a-~** A minor
mollig adj cosy; (dicklich) plump
Moment (-(e)s, -e) m moment; **im ~** at the
moment; **einen ~ bitte!** just a minute;
momentan adj momentary ▷ adv at the
moment
Monaco (-s) nt Monaco
Monarchie f monarchy
Monat (-(e)s, -e) m month; **sie ist im
dritten ~** (schwanger) she's three months

pregnant; **monatlich** adj, adv monthly;
~ 100 Euro zahlen to pay 100 euros a
month (o every month); **Monatskarte** f
monthly season ticket
Mönch (-s, -e) m monk
Mond (-(e)s, -e) m moon; **Mondfinsternis**
f lunar eclipse
Mongolei (-) f **die ~** Mongolia
Monitor m (Inform) monitor
monoton adj monotonous
Monsun (-s, -e) m monsoon
Montag m Monday; siehe auch **Mittwoch**;
montags adv on Mondays; siehe auch
mittwochs
Montenegro (-s) nt Montenegro
Monteur(in) (-s, -e) m(f) fitter;
montieren vt to assemble, to set up
Monument nt monument
Moor (-(e)s, -e) nt moor
Moos (-es, -e) nt moss
Moped (-s, -s) nt moped
Moral (-) f (Werte) morals pl; (einer
Geschichte) moral; **moralisch** adj moral
Mord (-(e)s, -e) m murder; **Mörder(in)**
(-s, -) m(f) murderer/murderess
morgen adv tomorrow; **~ früh** tomorrow
morning
Morgen (-s, -) m morning; **am ~** in the
morning; **Morgenmantel** m,
Morgenrock m dressing gown;
Morgenmuffel m **er ist ein ~** he's not a
morning person; **morgens** adv in the
morning; **um 3 Uhr ~** at 3 (o'clock) in the
morning, at 3 am
Morphium (-s) nt morphine
morsch adj rotten
Mosaik (-s, -e(n)) nt mosaic
Mosambik (-s) nt Mozambique
Moschee (-, -n) f mosque
Moskau (-s) nt Moscow
Moskito (-s, -s) m mosquito;
Moskitonetz nt mosquito net
Moslem (-s, -s) m, **Moslime** (-, -n) f
Muslim
Most (-(e)s, -e) m (unfermented) fruit
juice; (Apfelwein) cider
Motel (-s, -s) nt motel
motivieren vt to motivate
Motor m engine; (Elek) motor;
Motorboot nt motorboat; **Motorenöl** nt
engine oil; **Motorhaube** f bonnet (Brit),
hood (US); **Motorrad** nt motorbike,
motorcycle; **Motorradfahrer(in)** m(f)

motorcyclist; **Motorroller** m (motor)
scooter; **Motorschaden** m engine
trouble
Motte (-, -n) f moth
Motto (-s, -s) nt motto
Mountainbike (-s, -s) nt mountain bike
Möwe (-, -n) f (sea)gull
Mrd. f abk = **Milliarde(n)**
MS (-) f abk = **multiple Sklerose** MS
Mücke (-, -n) f midge; (tropische)
mosquito; **Mückenstich** m mosquito bite
müde adj tired
muffig adj (Geruch) musty; (Gesicht,
Mensch) grumpy
Mühe (-, -n) f trouble, pains pl; **sich** (dat)
große ~ geben to go to a lot of trouble
muhen vi to moo
Mühle (-, -n) f mill; (Kaffeemühle) grinder
Mull (-(e)s, -e) m muslin; (Med) gauze
Müll (-(e)s) m rubbish (Brit), garbage (US);
Müllabfuhr f rubbish (Brit) (o garbage
(US)) disposal
Mullbinde f gauze bandage
Müllcontainer m waste container;
Mülldeponie f rubbish (Brit) (o garbage
(US)) dump; **Mülleimer** m rubbish bin
(Brit), garbage can (US); **Mülltonne** f
dustbin (Brit), garbage can (US);
Mülltrennung f sorting and collecting
household waste according to type of material;
Müllverbrennungsanlage f incineration
plant; **Müllwagen** m dustcart (Brit),
garbage truck (US)
multikulturell adj multicultural
Multimedia- in zW multimedia
Multiple-Choice-Verfahren nt
multiple choice
multiple Sklerose (-n, -n) f multiple
sclerosis
Multiplexkino nt multiplex (cinema)
multiplizieren vt to multiply (mit by)
Mumie f mummy
Mumps (-) m mumps sing
München (-s) nt Munich
Mund (-(e)s, Münder) m mouth; **halt den ~!**
shut up; **Mundart** f dialect;
Munddusche f dental water jet
münden vi to flow (in +akk into)
Mundgeruch m bad breath;
Mundharmonika (-, -s) f mouth organ
mündlich adj oral
Mundschutz m mask; **Mundwasser** nt
mouthwash

Munition f ammunition
Münster (-s, -) nt minster, cathedral
munter adj lively
Münzautomat m vending machine;
Münze (-, -n) f coin; **Münzeinwurf** m
slot; **Münzrückgabe** f coin return;
Münztelefon nt pay phone;
Münzwechsler m change machine
murmeln vt, vi to murmur, to mutter
Murmeltier nt marmot
mürrisch adj sullen, grumpy
Mus (-es, -e) nt puree
Muschel (-, -n) f mussel; (~schale) shell
Museum (-s, Museen) nt museum
Musical (-s, -s) nt musical
Musik f music; **musikalisch** adj musical;
Musiker(in) (-s, -) m(f) musician;
Musikinstrument nt musical
instrument; **musizieren** vi to play music
Muskat (-(e)s) m nutmeg
Muskel (-s, -n) m muscle; **Muskelkater** m
~ haben to be stiff; **Muskelriss** m torn
muscle; **Muskelzerrung** f pulled muscle;
muskulös adj muscular
Müsli (-s, -) nt muesli
Muslim(in) (-s, -s) m(f) Muslim
Muss (-) nt must

◯ SCHLÜSSELWORT

müssen (pt **musste**, pp **gemusst** od (als
Hilfsverb) **müssen**) vi **1** (Zwang) must; (nur
im Präsens) to have to; **ich muss es tun** I
must do it, I have to do it; **ich musste es
tun** I had to do it; **er muss es nicht tun** he
doesn't have to do it; **muss ich?** must I?,
do I have to?; **wann müsst ihr zur Schule?**
when do you have to go to school?; **er hat
gehen müssen** he (has) had to go; **muss
das sein?** is that really necessary?; **ich
muss mal** (umg) I need the toilet
2 (sollen): **das musst du nicht tun!** you
oughtn't to od shouldn't do that; **Sie
hätten ihn fragen müssen** you should
have asked him
3: **es muss geregnet haben** it must have
rained; **es muss nicht wahr sein** it
needn't be true

Muster (-s, -) nt (Dessin) pattern, design;
(Probe) sample; (Vorbild) model; **mustern**
vt to have a close look at; **jdn ~** to size sb
up and down

Mut (-(e)s) *m* courage; **jdm ~ machen** to encourage sb; **mutig** *adj* brave, courageous

Mutter (-, *Mütter*) *f* mother ▷ (-, *-n*) *f* (*Schraubenmutter*) nut; **Muttersprache** *f* mother tongue; **Muttertag** *m* Mother's Day; **Mutti** *f* mum(my) (*Brit*), mom(my) (*US*)

mutwillig *adj* deliberate

Mütze (-, *-n*) *f* cap

MwSt. *abk* = **Mehrwertsteuer** VAT

Myanmar (-s) *nt* Myanmar

n

N *abk* = **Nord** N

na *interj* ~ **also!**, ~ **bitte!** see?, what did I tell you?; ~ **ja** well; ~ **und?** so what?

Nabel (-s, -) *m* navel

 SCHLÜSSELWORT

nach *präp* +dat **1** (*örtlich*) to; **nach Berlin** to Berlin; **nach links/rechts** (to the) left/right; **nach oben/hinten** up/back

2 (*zeitlich*) after; **einer nach dem anderen** one after the other; **nach Ihnen!** after you!; **zehn (Minuten) nach drei** ten (minutes) past three

3 (*gemäß*) according to; **nach dem Gesetz** according to the law; **dem Namen nach** judging by his/her name; **nach allem, was ich weiß** as far as I know
▷ *adv*: **ihm nach!** after him!; **nach und nach** gradually little by little; **nach wie vor** still

Nachbar(in) (-n, -n) *m(f)* neighbour; **Nachbarschaft** *f* neighbourhood

nach|bestellen *vt* to order some more

nachdem *conj* after; (*weil*) since; **je ~ (ob/wie)** depending on (whether/how)

nach|denken *irr vi* to think (*über* +*akk* about); **nachdenklich** *adj* thoughtful

nacheinander *adv* one after another (o the other)

Nachfolger(in) (-s, -) *m(f)* successor

nach|forschen *vt* to investigate

Nachfrage *f* inquiry; (*Comm*) demand; **nach|fragen** *vi* to inquire

Nachfüllpack *m* refill pack

nach|geben *irr vi* to give in (*jdm* to sb)

Nachgebühr *f* surcharge; (*für Briefe etc*) excess postage

nach|gehen *irr vi* to follow (*jdm* sb); (*erforschen*) to inquire (*einer Sache dat* into sth); **die Uhr geht (zehn Minuten) nach** this watch is (ten minutes) slow

nachher *adv* afterwards; **bis ~!** see you later

Nachhilfe *f* extra tuition

nach|holen *vt* to catch up with; (*Versäumtes*) to make up for

nach|kommen *irr vi* to follow; **einer Verpflichtung** (*dat*) ~ to fulfil an obligation

nach|lassen *irr vt* (*Summe*) to take off ▷ *vi* to decrease, to ease off; (*schlechter werden*) to deteriorate; **nachlässig** *adj* negligent, careless

nach|laufen *irr vi* to run after, to chase (*jdm* sb)

nach|lösen *vt* **eine Fahrkarte ~** to buy a ticket on the bus/train

nach|machen *vt* to imitate, to copy (*jdm etw* sth from sb); (*fälschen*) to counterfeit

Nachmittag *m* afternoon; **heute ~** this afternoon; **am ~** in the afternoon; **nachmittags** *adv* in the afternoon; **um 3 Uhr ~** at 3 (o'clock) in the afternoon, at 3 pm

Nachnahme (-, -n) *f* cash on delivery; **per ~** COD

Nachname *m* surname

Nachporto *nt* excess postage

nach|prüfen *vt* to check

nach|rechnen *vt* to check

Nachricht (-, -en) *f* (piece of) news *sing*; (*Mitteilung*) message; **Nachrichten** *pl* news *sing*

Nachsaison *f* off-season

nach|schauen vi jdm ~ to gaze after sb
▷ vt (prüfen) to check
nach|schicken vt to forward
nach|schlagen irr vt to look up
nach|sehen irr vt (prüfen) to check
nach|senden irr vt to forward
Nachspeise f dessert
nächstbeste(r, s) adj der ~ Zug/Job the
first train/job that comes along;
nächste(r, s) adj next; (nächstgelegen)
nearest
Nacht (-, Nächte) f night; **in der ~** during
the night; (bei Nacht) at night; **Nachtclub**
m nightclub; **Nachtdienst** m night duty;
~ **haben** (Apotheke) to be open all night
Nachteil m disadvantage
Nachtflug m night flight; **Nachtfrost** m
overnight frost; **Nachthemd** nt (für
Damen) nightdress; (für Herren)
nightshirt
Nachtigall (-, -en) f nightingale
Nachtisch m dessert, sweet (Brit),
pudding (Brit); **Nachtleben** nt nightlife
nach|tragen irr vt jdm etw ~ (übel
nehmen) to hold sth against sb
nachträglich adv ~ alles Gute zum
Geburtstag! Happy belated birthday
nachts adv at night; **um 11 Uhr ~** at 11
(o'clock) at night, at 11 pm; **um 2 Uhr ~** at 2
(o'clock) in the morning, at 2 am;
Nachtschicht f night shift; **Nachttarif** m
off-peak rate; **Nachttisch** m bedside
table; **Nachtzug** m night train
Nachweis (-es, -e) m proof
Nachwirkung f after-effect
nach|zahlen vi to pay extra ▷ vt **20 Euro**
~ to pay 20 euros extra
nach|zählen vt to check
Nacken (-s, -) m (nape of the) neck
nackt adj naked; (Tatsachen) plain, bare;
Nacktbadestrand m nudist beach
Nadel (-, -n) f needle; (Stecknadel) pin;
Nadelstreifen pl pinstripes pl
Nagel (-s, Nägel) m nail; **Nagelfeile** f
nail-file; **Nagellack** m nail varnish (o
polish); **Nagellackentferner** (-s, -) m
nail-varnish (o nail-polish) remover;
Nagelschere f nail scissors pl
nah(e) adj, adv (räumlich) near(by);
(zeitlich) near; (Verwandte, Freunde) close;
jdm ~e **gehen** to upset sb; **jdm etw ~e**
legen to suggest sth to sb; **~e liegen** to be
obvious ▷ prep +dat near (to), close to;

Nähe (-) f (Umgebung) vicinity; **in der**
~ nearby; **in der ~ von** near to
nähen vt, vi to sew
nähere(r, s) adj (Erklärung, Erkundigung)
more detailed; **die ~ Umgebung** the
immediate area; **Nähere(s)** nt details pl;
nähern vr **sich ~** to approach
nahezu adv virtually, almost
nahm imperf von **nehmen**
Nähmaschine f sewing machine;
Nähnadel f (sewing) needle
nahrhaft adj nourishing, nutritious;
Nahrung f food; **Nahrungsmittel** nt
food
Naht (-, Nähte) f seam; (Med) stitches pl,
suture; (Tech) join
Nahverkehr m local traffic;
Nahverkehrszug m local train
Nähzeug nt sewing kit
naiv adj naive
Name (-ns, -n) m name
nämlich adv that is to say, namely; (denn)
since
nannte imperf von **nennen**
Napf (-(e)s, Näpfe) m bowl, dish
Narbe (-, -n) f scar
Narkose (-, -n) f anaesthetic
Narzisse (-, -n) f narcissus
naschen vt, vi to nibble; **Naschkatze** f
(fam) nibbler; **eine ~ sein** to have a sweet
tooth
Nase (-, -n) f nose; **Nasenbluten** (-s) nt
nosebleed; ~ **haben** to have a nosebleed;
Nasenloch nt nostril; **Nasentropfen** pl
nose drops pl
Nashorn nt rhinoceros
nass adj wet; **Nässe** (-) f wetness;
nässen vi (Wunde) to weep
Nation (-, -en) f nation; **national** adj
national; **Nationalfeiertag** m national
holiday; **Nationalhymne** (-, -n) f national
anthem; **Nationalität** f nationality;
Nationalmannschaft f national team;
Nationalspieler(in) m(f) international
(player)
NATO (-) f abk = North Atlantic Treaty
Organization NATO, Nato
Natur f nature; **Naturkost** f health food;
natürlich adj natural ▷ adv naturally;
(selbstverständlich) of course; **Naturpark** m
nature reserve; **naturrein** adj natural,
pure; **Naturschutz** m conservation;
Naturschutzgebiet nt nature reserve;

Naturwissenschaft f (natural) science; **Naturwissenschaftler(in)** m(f) scientist

Navigationssystem nt (Auto) navigation system

n. Chr. abk = **nach Christus** AD

Nebel (-s, -) m fog, mist; **nebelig** adj foggy, misty; **Nebelscheinwerfer** m foglamp; **Nebelschlussleuchte** f (Auto) rear foglight

neben prep +akk o dat next to; (außer) apart from, besides; **nebenan** adv next door; **Nebenausgang** m side exit; **nebenbei** adv at the same time; (außerdem) additionally; (beiläufig) incidentally; **nebeneinander** adv side by side; **Nebeneingang** m side entrance; **Nebenfach** nt subsidiary subject

nebenher adv (zusätzlich) besides; (gleichzeitig) at the same time; (daneben) alongside

Nebenkosten pl extra charges pl, extras pl; **Nebensache** f minor matter; **nebensächlich** adj minor; **Nebensaison** f low season; **Nebenstelle** f (Geschäft) branch; (Telefon) extension; **Nebenstraße** f side street; **Nebenwirkung** f side effect

neblig adj foggy, misty

necken vt to tease

Neffe (-n, -n) m nephew

negativ adj negative; **Negativ** nt (Foto) negative

nehmen (nahm, genommen) vt to take; **jdm etw ~** to take sth (away) from sb; **wie man's nimmt** it depends on how you look at it; **den Bus/Zug ~** to take the bus/train; **jdn/etw ernst ~** to take sb/sth seriously; **etw zu sich ~** to eat sth; **jdn zu sich ~** to have sb come and live with one; **jdn an die Hand ~** to take sb by the hand

neidisch adj envious

neigen vi **zu etw ~** to tend towards sth; **Neigung** f (des Geländes) slope; (Tendenz) inclination; (Vorliebe) liking

nein adv no

Nektarine f nectarine

Nelke (-, -n) f carnation; (Gewürz) clove

nennen (nannte, genannt) vt to name; (mit Namen) to call

Neonazi (-s, -s) m neo-Nazi

Neonlicht nt neon light; **Neonröhre** f neon tube

Nepal (-s) nt Nepal

Neptun (-s) m Neptune

Nerv (-s, -en) m nerve; **jdm auf die ~en gehen** to get on sb's nerves; **nerven** vt **jdn ~** (fam) to get on sb's nerves; **Nervenzusammenbruch** m nervous breakdown; **nervös** adj nervous

Nest (-(e)s, -er) nt nest; (pej: Ort) dump

nett adj nice; (freundlich) kind; **sei so ~ und ...** do me a favour and ...

netto adv net

Netz (-es, -e) nt net; (für Einkauf) string bag; (System) network; (Stromnetz) mains, power (US); **Netzanschluss** m mains connection; **Netzbetreiber(in)** m(f) network operator; (Inform) Internet (o Net) operator; **Netzgerät** nt power pack; **Netzkarte** f season ticket; **Netzwerk** nt (Inform) network; **Netzwerkkarte** f network card

neu adj new; (Sprache, Geschichte) modern; **die ~esten Nachrichten** the latest news; **Neubau** m new building; **neuerdings** adv recently; **Neueröffnung** f (Geschäft) new business; **Neuerung** f innovation; (Reform) reform

Neugier f curiosity; **neugierig** adj curious (auf +akk about); **ich bin ~, ob ...** I wonder whether (o if) ...; **ich bin ~, was du dazu sagst** I'll be interested to hear what you have to say about it

Neuheit f novelty; **Neuigkeit** f news sing; **eine ~** a piece of news; **Neujahr** nt New Year; **prosit ~!** Happy New Year;

neulich adv recently, the other day; **Neumond** m new moon

neun num nine; **neunhundert** num nine hundred; **neunmal** adv nine times; **neunte(r, s)** adj ninth; siehe auch **dritte**; **Neuntel** (-s, -) nt ninth; **neunzehn** num nineteen; **neunzehnte(r, s)** adj nineteenth; siehe auch **dritte**; **neunzig** num ninety; **in den ~er Jahren** in the nineties; **Neunzigerjahre** pl nineties pl; **neunzigste(r, s)** adj ninetieth

neureich adj nouveau riche

Neurologe m, **Neurologin** f neurologist; **Neurose** (-, -n) f neurosis; **neurotisch** adj neurotic

Neuseeland nt New Zealand

Neustart m (Inform) restart, reboot

neutral adj neutral

neuwertig adj nearly new

Nicaragua (-s) nt Nicaragua

n

○ SCHLÜSSELWORT

nicht adv 1 (Verneinung) not; **er ist es nicht** it's not him it isn't him; **er raucht nicht** (gerade) he isn't smoking (gewöhnlich) he doesn't smoke; **ich kann das nicht — ich auch nicht** I can't do it — neither od nor can I; **es regnet nicht mehr** it's not raining any more; **nicht rostend** stainless

2 (Bitte, Verbot): **nicht!** don't!, no!; **nicht berühren!** do not touch!; **nicht doch!** don't!

3 (rhetorisch): **du bist müde, nicht (wahr)?** you're tired, aren't you?; **das ist schön, nicht (wahr)?** it's nice, isn't it?

4: **was du nicht sagst!** the things you say!

Nichte (-, -n) f niece
Nichtraucher(in) m(f) non-smoker; **Nichtraucherabteil** nt non-smoking compartment; **Nichtraucherzone** f non-smoking area
nichts pron nothing; **für ~ und wieder ~** for nothing at all; **ich habe ~ gesagt** I didn't say anything; **~ sagend** meaningless; **macht ~** never mind
Nichtschwimmer(in) m(f) non-swimmer
nicken vi to nod
Nickerchen nt nap
nie adv never; **~ wieder** (o **mehr**) never again; **fast ~** hardly ever
nieder adj (niedrig) low; (gering) inferior ▷ adv down; **niedergeschlagen** adj depressed; **Niederlage** f defeat
Niederlande pl Netherlands pl; **Niederländer(in)** m(f) Dutchman/Dutchwoman; **niederländisch** adj Dutch; **Niederländisch** nt Dutch
Niederlassung f branch
Niederösterreich nt Lower Austria; **Niedersachsen** nt Lower Saxony
Niederschlag m (Meteo) precipitation; (Regen) rainfall
niedlich adj sweet, cute
niedrig adj low; (Qualität) inferior
niemals adv never
niemand pron nobody, no one; **ich habe**

~en gesehen I haven't seen anyone; **~ von ihnen** none of them
Niere (-, -n) f kidney; **Nierenentzündung** f kidney infection; **Nierensteine** pl kidney stones pl
nieseln vi impers to drizzle; **Nieselregen** m drizzle
niesen vi to sneeze
Niete (-, -n) f (Los) blank; (Reinfall) flop; (pej: Mensch) failure; (Tech) rivet
Nigeria (-s) nt Nigeria
Nikotin (-s) nt nicotine; **nikotinarm** adj low in nicotine
Nilpferd nt hippopotamus
nippen vi to sip; **an etw** (dat) **~** to sip sth
nirgends adv nowhere
Nische (-, -n) f niche
Nitrat nt nitrate
Niveau (-s, -s) nt level; **sie hat ~** she's got class
nobel adj (großzügig) generous; (fam: luxuriös) classy, posh; **Nobelpreis** m Nobel Prize

○ SCHLÜSSELWORT

noch adv 1 (weiterhin) still; **noch nicht** not yet; **noch nie** never (yet); **noch immer** od **immer noch** still; **bleiben Sie doch noch** stay a bit longer

2 (in Zukunft) still, yet; **das kann noch passieren** that might still happen; **er wird noch kommen** he'll come (yet)

3 (nicht später als): **noch vor einer Woche** only a week ago; **noch am selben Tag** the very same day; **noch im 19. Jahrhundert** as late as the 19th century; **noch heute** today

4 (zusätzlich): **wer war noch da?** who else was there?; **noch einmal** once more again; **noch dreimal** three more times; **noch einer** another one

5 (bei Vergleichen): **noch größer** even bigger; **das ist noch besser** that's better still; **und wenn es noch so schwer ist** however hard it is

6: **Geld noch und noch** heaps (and heaps) of money; **sie hat noch und noch versucht, ...** she tried again and again to ...
▷ konj: **weder A noch B** neither A nor B

Nominativ *m* nominative (case)
Nonne (-, -n) *f* nun
Non-Stop-Flug *m* nonstop flight
Nord north; **Nordamerika** *nt* North
America; **Norddeutschland** *nt* Northern
Germany; **Norden** (-s) *m* north; **im
~ Deutschlands** in the north of Germany;
Nordeuropa *nt* Northern Europe;
Nordirland *nt* Northern Ireland;
nordisch *adj* (Völker, Sprache) Nordic;
Nordkorea (-s) *nt* North Korea; **nördlich**
adj northern; (Kurs, Richtung) northerly;
Nordost(en) *m* northeast; **Nordpol** *m*
North Pole; **Nordrhein-Westfalen** (-s) *nt*
North Rhine-Westphalia; **Nordsee** *f*
North Sea; **nordwärts** *adv* north,
northwards; **Nordwest(en)** *m*
northwest; **Nordwind** *m* north wind
nörgeln *vi* to grumble
Norm (-, -en) *f* norm; (Größenvorschrift)
standard
normal *adj* normal; **Normalbenzin** *nt*
regular (petrol (Brit) *o* gas (US));
normalerweise *adv* normally
normen *vt* to standardize
Norwegen (-s) *nt* Norway; **Norweger(in)**
m(f) Norwegian; **norwegisch** *adj*
Norwegian; **Norwegisch** *nt* Norwegian
Not (-, Nöte) *f* need; (Armut) poverty;
(Elend) hardship; (Bedrängnis) trouble;
(Mangel) want; (Mühe) trouble; (Zwang)
necessity; **zur ~** if necessary; (gerade noch)
just about
Notar(in) *m(f)* public notary; **notariell**
adj **~ beglaubigt** attested by a notary
Notarzt *m*, **Notärztin** *f* emergency
doctor; **Notarztwagen** *m* emergency
ambulance; **Notausgang** *m* emergency
exit; **Notbremse** *f* emergency brake;
Notdienst *m* emergency service,
after-hours service; **notdürftig** *adj*
scanty; (behelfsmäßig) makeshift
Note (-, -n) *f* note; (in Schule) mark, grade
(US); (Mus) note
Notebook (-(s), -s) *nt* (Inform) notebook
Notfall *m* emergency; **notfalls** *adv* if
necessary
notieren *vt* to note down
nötig *adj* necessary; **etw ~ haben** to need
sth
Notiz (-, -en) *f* note; (Zeitungs~) item;
Notizblock *m* notepad; **Notizbuch** *nt*
notebook

Notlage *f* crisis; (Elend) plight;
notlanden *vi* to make a forced
(*o* emergency) landing; **Notruf**
m emergency call; **Notrufnummer**
f emergency number;
Notrufsäule *f* emergency telephone
notwendig *adj* necessary
Nougat (-s, -s) *m* od *nt* nougat
November (-(s), -) *m* November; siehe
auch **Juni**
Nr. *abk* = **Nummer** No., no.
Nu *m* **im ~** in no time
nüchtern *adj* sober; (Magen) empty
Nudel (-, -n) *f* noodle; **~n** *pl* (italienische)
pasta *sing*; **Nudelsuppe** *f* noodle
soup
null *num* zero; (Tel) O (Brit), zero (US);
~ Fehler no mistakes; **~ Uhr** midnight;
Null (-, -en) *f* nought, zero; (pej: Mensch)
dead loss; **Nulltarif** *m* **zum ~** free of
charge
Numerus clausus (-) *m* restriction on the
number of students allowed to study a
particular subject
Nummer (-, -n) *f* number; **nummerieren**
vt to number; **Nummernschild** *nt* (Auto)
number plate (Brit), license plate (US)
nun *adv* now; **von ~ an** from now on
▷ *interj* well; **~ gut!** all right, then; **es ist
~ mal so** that's the way it is
nur *adv* only; **nicht ~ ..., sondern auch ...**
not only ..., but also ...; **~ Anna nicht**
except Anna
Nürnberg (-s) *nt* Nuremberg
Nuss (-, Nüsse) *f* nut; **Nussknacker** (-s, -)
m nutcracker; **Nuss-Nougat-Creme** *f*
chocolate nut cream
Nutte (-, -n) *f* (fam) tart
nutz, nütze *adj* **zu nichts ~ sein** to be
useless; **nutzen, nützen** *vt* to use (zu etw
for sth); **was nützt es?** what use is it? ▷ *vi*
to be of use; **das nützt nicht viel** that
doesn't help much; **es nützt nichts(, es
zu tun)** it's no use (doing it); **Nutzen** (-s, -)
m usefulness; (Gewinn) profit; **nützlich**
adj useful
Nylon (-s) *nt* nylon

O

o *interj* oh

O *abk* = **Ost** E

Oase (-, -n) *f* oasis

ob *conj* if, whether; **so als ~** as if; **er tut so, als ~ er krank wäre** he's pretending to be sick; **und ~!** you bet

obdachlos *adj* homeless

oben *adv* (*am oberen Ende*) at the top; (*obenauf*) on (the) top; (*im Haus*) upstairs; (*in einem Text*) above; **~ erwähnt** (*o genannt*) above-mentioned; **mit dem Gesicht nach ~** face up; **da ~** up there; **von ~ bis unten** from top to bottom; **siehe ~** see above

Ober (-s, -) *m* waiter

obere(r, s) *adj* upper, top

Oberfläche *f* surface; **oberflächlich** *adj* superficial; **Obergeschoss** *nt* upper floor

oberhalb *adv*, *prep* +*gen* above

Oberhemd *nt* shirt; **Oberkörper** *m* upper body; **Oberlippe** *f* upper lip; **Oberösterreich** *nt* Upper Austria; **Oberschenkel** *m* thigh

oberste(r, s) *adj* very top, topmost

Oberteil *nt* top; **Oberweite** *f* bust/chest measurement

obig *adj* above(-mentioned)

Objekt (-(e)s, -e) *nt* object

objektiv *adj* objective; **Objektiv** *nt* lens

obligatorisch *adj* compulsory, obligatory

Oboe (-, -n) *f* oboe

Observatorium *nt* observatory

Obst (-(e)s) *nt* fruit; **Obstkuchen** *m* fruit tart; **Obstsalat** *m* fruit salad

obszön *adj* obscene

obwohl *conj* although

Ochse (-n, -n) *m* ox; **Ochsenschwanzsuppe** *f* oxtail soup

ocker *adj* ochre

öd(e) *adj* waste; (*unbebaut*) barren; (*fig*) dull

oder *conj* or; **~ aber** or else; **er kommt doch, ~?** he's coming, isn't he?

Ofen (-s, Öfen) *m* oven; (*Heizofen*) heater; (*Kohleofen*) stove; (*Herd*) cooker, stove; **Ofenkartoffel** *f* baked (*o* jacket) potato

offen *adj* open; (*aufrichtig*) frank; (*Stelle*) vacant ▷ *adv* frankly; **~ gesagt** to be honest

offenbar *adj* obvious; **offensichtlich** *adj* evident, obvious

öffentlich *adj* public; **Öffentlichkeit** *f* (*Leute*) public; (*einer Versammlung etc*) public nature

offiziell *adj* official

offline *adv* (*Inform*) offline

öffnen *vt* to open ▷ *vr* **sich ~** to open; **Öffner** (-s, -) *m* opener; **Öffnung** *f* opening; **Öffnungszeiten** *pl* opening times *pl*

oft *adv* often; **schon ~** many times; **öfter** *adv* more often (*o* frequently); **öfters** *adv* often, frequently

ohne *conj*, *prep* +*akk* without; **~ weiteres** without a second thought; (*sofort*) immediately; **~ ein Wort zu sagen** without saying a word; **~ mich** count me out

Ohnmacht (-machten) *f* unconsciousness; (*Hilflosigkeit*) helplessness; **in ~ fallen** to faint; **ohnmächtig** *adj* unconscious; **sie ist ~** she has fainted

Ohr (-(e)s, -en) *nt* ear; (*Gehör*) hearing

Öhr (-(e)s, -e) *nt* eye

Ohrenarzt *m*, **Ohrenärztin** *f* ear specialist; **Ohrenschmerzen** *pl* earache; **Ohrentropfen** *pl* ear drops *pl*; **Ohrfeige** *f*

slap (in the face); **Ohrläppchen** nt earlobe; **Ohrringe** pl earrings pl

oje interj oh dear

okay interj OK, okay

Ökoladen m health food store; **ökologisch** adj ecological; **~e Landwirtschaft** organic farming

ökonomisch adj economic; (sparsam) economical

Ökosystem nt ecosystem

Oktanzahl f (bei Benzin) octane rating

Oktober (-(s), -) m October; siehe auch **Juni**

● **Oktoberfest**
●
● The annual October beer festival, the
● **Oktoberfest**, takes place in Munich on
● a huge field where beer tents, roller
● coasters and many other
● amusements are set up. People sit at
● long wooden tables, drink beer from
● enormous litre beer mugs, eat
● pretzels and listen to brass bands. It
● is a great attraction for tourists and
● locals alike.

Öl (-(e)s, -e) nt oil; **Ölbaum** m olive tree; **ölen** vt to oil; (Tech) to lubricate; **Ölfarbe** f oil paint; **Ölfilter** m oil filter; **Ölgemälde** nt oil painting; **Ölheizung** f oil-fired central heating; **ölig** adj oily

oliv adj inv olive-green; **Olive** (-, -n) f olive; **Olivenöl** nt olive oil

Ölmessstab m dipstick; **Ölofen** m oil stove; **Ölpest** f oil pollution; **Ölsardine** f sardine in oil; **Ölstandanzeiger** m (Auto) oil gauge; **Ölteppich** m oil slick; **Ölwechsel** m oil change

Olympiade f Olympic Games pl; **olympisch** adj Olympic

Oma f, **Omi** (-s, -s) f grandma, gran(ny)

Omelett (-(e)s, -s) nt, **Omelette** f omelette

Omnibus m bus

onanieren vi to masturbate

Onkel (-s, -) m uncle

online adv (Inform) online; **Onlinedienst** m (Inform) online service

OP (-s, -s) m abk = **Operationssaal** operating theatre (Brit) (o room (US))

Opa m, **Opi** (-s, -s) m grandpa, grandad

Openairkonzert nt open-air concert

Oper (-, -n) f opera; (Gebäude) opera house

Operation f operation

Operette f operetta

operieren vi to operate ▷ vt to operate on

Opernsänger(in) m(f) opera singer

Opfer (-s, -) nt sacrifice; (Mensch) victim; **ein ~ bringen** to make a sacrifice

Opium (-s) nt opium

Opposition f opposition

Optiker(in) (-s, -) m(f) optician

optimal adj optimal, optimum

optimistisch adj optimistic

oral adj oral; **Oralverkehr** m oral sex

orange adj inv orange; **Orange** (-, -n) f orange; **Orangenmarmelade** f marmalade; **Orangensaft** m orange juice

Orchester (-s, -) nt orchestra

Orchidee (-, -n) f orchid

Orden (-s, -) m (Rel) order; (Mil) decoration

ordentlich adj (anständig) respectable; (geordnet) tidy, neat; (fam: annehmbar) not bad; (fam: tüchtig) proper ▷ adv properly

ordinär adj common, vulgar; (Witz) dirty

ordnen vt to sort out; **Ordner** (-s, -) m (bei Veranstaltung) steward; (Aktenordner) file; **Ordnung** f order; (Geordnetsein) tidiness; **(geht) in ~!** (that's) all right; **mit dem Drucker ist etwas nicht in ~** there's something wrong with the printer

Oregano (-s) m oregano

Organ (-s, -e) nt organ; (Stimme) voice

Organisation f organization; **organisieren** vt to organize; (fam: beschaffen) to get hold of ▷ vr **sich ~** to organize

Organismus m organism

Orgasmus m orgasm

Orgel (-, -n) f organ

Orgie f orgy

orientalisch adj oriental

orientieren vr **sich ~** to get one's bearings; **Orientierung** f orientation; **Orientierungssinn** m sense of direction

original adj original; (echt) genuine; **Original** (-s, -e) nt original; **Originalfassung** f original version

originell adj original; (komisch) witty

Orkan (-(e)s, -e) m hurricane

Ort (-(e)s, -e) m place; (Dorf) village; **an ~ und Stelle, vor ~** on the spot

Orthopäde (-n, -n) m, **Orthopädin** f orthopaedist

örtlich adj local; **Ortschaft** f village,

small town; **Ortsgespräch** nt local call;
Ortstarif m local rate; **Ortszeit** f local
time

● **Ossi**
●
● **Ossi** is a colloquial and rather
● derogatory word used to describe a
● German from the former **DDR**.

Ost east; **Ostdeutschland** nt (als
Landesteil) Eastern Germany; (Hist) East
Germany; **Osten** (-s) m east
Osterei nt Easter egg; **Osterglocke** f
daffodil; **Osterhase** m Easter bunny;
Ostermontag m Easter Monday; **Ostern**
(-, -) nt Easter; **an** (o **zu**) ~ at Easter; **frohe**
~ Happy Easter
Österreich (-s) nt Austria;
Österreicher(in) (-s, -) m(f) Austrian;
österreichisch adj Austrian
Ostersonntag m Easter Sunday
Osteuropa nt Eastern Europe; **Ostküste**
f east coast; **östlich** adj eastern; (Kurs,
Richtung) easterly; **Ostsee** f **die** ~ the
Baltic (Sea); **Ostwind** m east(erly) wind
OSZE (-) f abk = **Organisation für
Sicherheit und Zusammenarbeit in
Europa** OSCE
Otter (-s, -) m otter
out adj (fam) out; **outen** vt to out
oval adj oval
Overheadprojektor m overhead
projector
Ozean (-s, -e) m ocean; **der Stille** ~ the
Pacific (Ocean)
Ozon (-s) nt ozone; **Ozonbelastung** f
ozone level; **Ozonloch** nt hole in the
ozone layer; **Ozonschicht** f ozone layer;
Ozonwerte pl ozone levels pl

paar adj inv **ein ~** a few; **ein ~ Mal** a few times; **ein ~ Äpfel** some apples

Paar (-(e)s, -e) nt pair; (Ehepaar) couple; **ein ~ Socken** a pair of socks

pachten vt to lease

Päckchen nt package; (Zigaretten) packet; (zum Verschicken) small parcel; **packen** vt to pack; (fassen) to grasp, to seize; (fam: schaffen) to manage; (fig: fesseln) to grip; **Packpapier** nt brown paper; **Packung** f packet, pack (US); **Packungsbeilage** f package insert, patient information leaflet

Pädagoge (-n, -n) m, **Pädagogin** f teacher; **pädagogisch** adj educational; **~e Hochschule** college of education

Paddel (-s, -) nt paddle; **Paddelboot** nt canoe; **paddeln** vi to paddle

Paket (-(e)s, -e) nt packet; (Postpaket) parcel; (Inform) package; **Paketbombe** f parcel bomb; **Paketkarte** f dispatch form (to be filled in with details of the sender and the addressee when handing in a parcel at the post office)

Pakistan (-s) nt Pakistan

Palast (-es, Paläste) m palace

Palästina (-s) nt Palestine; **Palästinenser(in)** (-s, -) m(f) Palestinian

Palatschinken pl filled pancakes pl

Palette f (von Maler) palette; (Ladepalette) pallet; (Vielfalt) range

Palme (-, -n) f palm (tree); **Palmsonntag** m Palm Sunday

Pampelmuse (-, -n) f grapefruit

pampig adj (fam: frech) cheeky; (breiig) gooey

Panda(bär) (-s, -s) m panda

panieren vt (Gastr) to coat with breadcrumbs; **paniert** adj breaded

Panik f panic

Panne (-, -n) f (Auto) breakdown; (Missgeschick) slip; **Pannendienst** m, **Pannenhilfe** f breakdown (o rescue) service

Pant(h)er (-s, -) m panther

Pantoffel (-s, -n) m slipper

Pantomime (-, -n) f mime

Panzer (-s, -) m (Panzerung) armour (plating); (Mil) tank

Papa (-s, -s) m dad(dy), pa (US)

Papagei (-s, -en) m parrot

Papaya (-, -s) f papaya

Papier (-s, -e) nt paper; **~e** pl (Ausweispapiere) papers pl; (Dokumente, Urkunden) papers pl, documents pl; **Papiercontainer** m paper bank; **Papierformat** nt paper size; **Papiergeld** nt paper money; **Papierkorb** m wastepaper basket; (Inform) recycle bin; **Papiertaschentuch** nt (paper) tissue; **Papiertonne** f paper bank

Pappbecher m paper cup; **Pappe** (-, -n) f cardboard; **Pappkarton** m cardboard box; **Pappteller** m paper plate

Paprika (-s, -s) m (Gewürz) paprika; (Schote) pepper

Papst (-(e)s, Päpste) m pope

Paradeiser (-s, -) m tomato

Paradies (-es, -e) nt paradise

Paragliding (-s) nt paragliding

Paragraph (-en, -en) m paragraph; (Jur) section

parallel adj parallel

Paranuss f Brazil nut

Parasit (-en, -en) m parasite

parat adj ready; **etw ~ haben** to have sth ready

Pärchen nt couple

Parfüm (-s, -s o -e) nt perfume; **Parfümerie** f perfumery; **parfümieren** vt to scent, to perfume

P

Pariser (-s, -) m (fam: Kondom) rubber
Park (-s, -s) m park
Park-and-ride-System nt
park-and-ride system; **Parkanlage** f
park; (um Gebäude) grounds pl; **Parkbank** f
park bench; **Parkdeck** nt parking level;
parken vt, vi to park
Parkett (-s, -e) nt parquet flooring; (Theat)
stalls pl (Brit), parquet (US)
Parkhaus nt multi-storey car park (Brit),
parking garage (US)
parkinsonsche Krankheit f
Parkinson's disease
Parkkralle f (Auto) wheel clamp;
Parklicht nt parking light; **Parklücke** f
parking space; **Parkplatz** m (für ein Auto)
parking space; (für mehrere Autos) car park
(Brit), parking lot (US); **Parkscheibe** f
parking disc; **Parkscheinautomat** m pay
point; (Parkscheinausgabegerät) ticket
machine; **Parkuhr** f parking meter;
Parkverbot nt (Stelle) no-parking zone;
hier ist ~ you can't park here
Parlament (-s) nt parliament
Parmesan (-s) m Parmesan (cheese)
Partei f party
Parterre (-s, -s) nt ground floor (Brit), first
floor (US)
Partie f part; (Spiel) game; (Mann, Frau)
catch; **mit von der ~ sein** to be in on it
Partitur f (Mus) score
Partizip (-s, -ien) nt participle
Partner(in) (-s, -) m(f) partner;
Partnerschaft f partnership;
eingetragene ~ civil partnership;
Partnerstadt f twin town
Party (-, -s) f party; **Partymuffel** (-s, -) m
party pooper; **Partyservice** m catering
service
Pass (-es, Pässe) m pass; (Ausweis) passport
passabel adj reasonable
Passagier (-s, -e) m passenger
Passamt nt passport office
Passant(in) m(f) passer-by; **Passbild** nt
passport photo
passen vi (Größe) to fit; (Farbe, Stil) to go
(zu with); (auf Frage) to pass; **passt (es) dir
morgen?** does tomorrow suit you?; **das
passt mir gut** that suits me fine;
passend adj suitable; (zusammenpassend)
matching; (angebracht) fitting; (Zeit)
convenient; **haben Sie es nicht ~?**
(Kleingeld) have you got the right change?

passieren vi to happen
passiv adj passive
Passkontrolle f passport control
Passwort nt password
Paste (-, -n) f paste
Pastellfarbe f pastel colour
Pastete (-, -n) f (warmes Gericht) pie;
(Pastetchen) vol-au-vent; (ohne Teig) pâté
Pastor(in) (-s, -en) m(f) minister, vicar
Pate (-n, -n) m godfather; **Patenkind** nt
godchild
Patient(in) m(f) patient
Patin f godmother
Patrone (-, -n) f cartridge
patsch interj splat; **Patsche** (-, -n) f
(Fliegen~) swat; (Bedrängnis) mess;
patschnass adj soaking wet
pauschal adj (Kosten) inclusive; (Urteil)
sweeping; **Pauschale** (-, -n) f,
Pauschalgebühr f flat rate (charge);
Pauschalpreis m flat rate; (für Hotel,
Reise) all-inclusive price; **Pauschalreise** f
package tour
Pause (-, -n) f break; (Theat) interval; (Kino
etc) intermission; (Innehalten) pause
Pavian (-s, -e) m baboon
Pavillon (-s, -s) m pavilion
Pay-TV (-s) nt pay-per-view television,
pay TV
Pazifik (-s) m Pacific (Ocean)
PC (-s, -s) m abk = **Personalcomputer** PC
Pech (-s, -e) nt (fig) bad luck; **~ haben** to
be unlucky; **~ gehabt!** tough (luck)
Pedal (-s, -e) nt pedal
Pediküre (-, -en) f pedicure
Peeling (-s, -s) nt (facial/body) scrub
peinlich adj (unangenehm) embarrassing,
awkward; (genau) painstaking; **es war mir
sehr ~** I was totally embarrassed
Peitsche (-, -n) f whip
Pelikan (-s, -e) m pelican
Pellkartoffeln pl potatoes pl boiled in
their skins
Pelz (-es, -e) m fur; **pelzig** adj (Zunge)
furred
pendeln vi (Zug, Bus) to shuttle; (Mensch)
to commute; **Pendelverkehr** m shuttle
traffic; (für Pendler) commuter traffic;
Pendler(in) (-s, -) m(f) commuter
penetrant adj sharp; (Mensch) pushy
Penis (-, -se) m penis
Pension f (Geld) pension; (Ruhestand)
retirement; (für Gäste) guesthouse, B&B;

pensioniert adj retired; **Pensionsgast** m guest (in a guesthouse)
Peperoni (-, -) f chilli
per prep +akk by, per; (pro) per; (bis) by
perfekt adj perfect
Pergamentpapier nt greaseproof paper
Periode (-, -n) f period
Perle (-, -n) f (a. fig) pearl
perplex adj dumbfounded
Person (-, -en) f person; **ein Tisch für drei ~en** a table for three; **Personal** (-s) nt staff, personnel; (Bedienung) servants pl; **Personalausweis** m identity card; **Personalien** pl particulars pl; **Personenschaden** m injury to persons; **Personenwaage** f (bathroom) scales pl; **Personenzug** m passenger train; **persönlich** adj personal; (auf Briefen) private ▷ adv personally; (selbst) in person; **Persönlichkeit** f personality
Peru (-s) nt Peru
Perücke (-, -n) f wig
pervers adj perverted
pessimistisch adj pessimistic
Pest (-) f plague
Petersilie f parsley
Petroleum (-s) nt paraffin (Brit), kerosene (US)
Pfad (-(e)s, -e) m path; **Pfadfinder** (-s, -) m boy scout; **Pfadfinderin** f girl guide
Pfahl (-(e)s, Pfähle) m post, stake
Pfand (-(e)s, Pfänder) nt security; (Flaschenpfand) deposit; (im Spiel) forfeit; **Pfandflasche** f returnable bottle
Pfanne (-, -n) f (frying) pan
Pfannkuchen m pancake
Pfarrei f parish; **Pfarrer(in)** (-s, -) m(f) priest
Pfau (-(e)s, -en) m peacock
Pfeffer (-s, -) m pepper; **Pfefferkuchen** m gingerbread; **Pfefferminze** (-e) f peppermint; **Pfefferminztee** m peppermint tea; **Pfeffermühle** f pepper mill; **pfeffern** vt to put pepper on/in; **Pfefferstreuer** (-s, -) m pepper pot
Pfeife (-, -n) f whistle; (für Tabak, von Orgel) pipe; **pfeifen** (pfiff, gepfiffen) vt, vi to whistle
Pfeil (-(e)s, -e) m arrow
Pfeiltaste f (Inform) arrow key
Pferd (-(e)s, -e) nt horse; **Pferdeschwanz** m (Frisur) ponytail; **Pferdestall** m stable; **Pferdestärke** f horsepower

pfiff imperf von **pfeifen**
Pfifferling m chanterelle
Pfingsten (-, -) nt Whitsun, Pentecost (US); **Pfingstmontag** m Whit Monday; **Pfingstsonntag** m Whit Sunday, Pentecost (US); **Pfingstrose** f peony
Pfirsich (-s, -e) m peach
Pflanze (-, -n) f plant; **pflanzen** vt to plant; **Pflanzenfett** nt vegetable fat
Pflaster (-s, -) nt (für Wunde) plaster, Band Aid® (US); (Straßenpflaster) road surface, pavement (US)
Pflaume (-, -n) f plum
Pflege (-, -n) f care; (Krankenpflege) nursing; (von Autos, Maschinen) maintenance; **pflegebedürftig** adj in need of care; **pflegeleicht** adj easy-care; (fig) easy to handle; **pflegen** vt to look after; (Kranke) to nurse; (Beziehungen) to foster; (Fingernägel, Gesicht) to take care of; (Daten) to maintain; **Pflegepersonal** nt nursing staff; **Pflegeversicherung** f long-term care insurance
Pflicht (-, -en) f duty; (Sport) compulsory section; **pflichtbewusst** adj conscientious; **Pflichtfach** nt (Schule) compulsory subject; **Pflichtversicherung** f compulsory insurance
pflücken vt to pick
Pforte (-, -n) f gate; **Pförtner(in)** (-s, -) m(f) porter
Pfosten (-s, -) m post
Pfote (-, -n) f paw
pfui interj ugh
Pfund (-(e)s, -e) nt pound
pfuschen vi (fam) to be sloppy
Pfütze (-, -n) f puddle
Phantasie f siehe Fantasie; **phantastisch** adj siehe fantastisch
Phase (-, -n) f phase
Philippinen pl Philippines pl
Philosophie f philosophy
Photo nt siehe Foto
pH-neutral adj pH-balanced; **pH-Wert** m pH-value
Physalis (-, Physalen) f physalis
Physik f physics sing
physisch adj physical
Pianist(in) (-en, -en) m(f) pianist
Pickel (-s, -) m pimple; (Werkzeug) pickaxe; (Berg~) ice-axe
Picknick (-s, -e o -s) nt picnic; **ein ~ machen** to have a picnic

P

piepsen vi to chirp

piercen vt **sich die Nase ~ lassen** to have one's nose pierced; **Piercing** (-s) nt (body) piercing

pieseln vi (fam) to pee

Pik (-, -) nt (Karten) spades pl

pikant adj spicy

Pilger(in) m(f) pilgrim; **Pilgerfahrt** f pilgrimage

Pille (-, -n) f pill; **sie nimmt die ~** she's on the pill

Pilot(in) (-en, -en) m(f) pilot

Pilz (-es, -e) m (essbar) mushroom; (giftig) toadstool; (Med) fungus

PIN (-, -s) f PIN (number)

pingelig adj (fam) fussy

Pinguin (-s, -e) m penguin

Pinie f pine; **Pinienkern** m pine nut

pink adj shocking pink

pinkeln vi (fam) to pee

Pinsel (-s, -) m (paint)brush

Pinzette f tweezers pl

Pistazie f pistachio

Piste (-, -n) f (Ski) piste; (Aviat) runway

Pistole (-, -n) f pistol

Pixel (-s) nt (Inform) pixel

Pizza (-, -s) f pizza; **Pizzaservice** m pizza delivery service; **Pizzeria** (-, Pizzerien) f pizzeria

Pkw (-(s), -(s)) m abk = **Personenkraftwagen** car

Plakat nt poster

Plakette f (Schildchen) badge; (Aufkleber) sticker

Plan (-(e)s, Pläne) m plan; (Karte) map; **planen** vt to plan

Planet (-en, -en) m planet; **Planetarium** nt planetarium

planmäßig adj scheduled

Plan(t)schbecken nt paddling pool; **plan(t)schen** vi to splash around

Planung f planning

Plastik f sculpture ▷ (-s) nt (Kunststoff) plastic; **Plastikfolie** f plastic film; **Plastiktüte** f plastic bag

Platin (-s) nt platinum

platsch interj splash

platt adj flat; (fam: überrascht) flabbergasted; (fig: geistlos) flat, boring

Platte (-, -n) f (Foto, Tech, Gastr) plate; (Steinplatte) flag; (Schallplatte) record; **Plattenspieler** m record player

Plattform f platform; **Plattfuß** m flat foot; (Reifen) flat (tyre)

Platz (-es, Plätze) m place; (Sitzplatz) seat; (freier Raum) space, room; (in Stadt) square; (Sportplatz) playing field; **nehmen Sie ~** please sit down, take a seat; **ist dieser ~ frei?** is this seat taken?; **Platzanweiser(in)** m(f) usher/usherette

Plätzchen nt spot; (Gebäck) biscuit

platzen vi to burst; (Bombe) to explode

Platzkarte f seat reservation; **Platzreservierung** f seat reservation; **Platzverweis** m **er erhielt einen ~** he was sent off; **Platzwunde** f laceration, cut

plaudern vi to chat, to talk

pleite adj (fam) broke; **Pleite** (-, -n) f (Bankrott) bankruptcy; (fam: Reinfall) flop

Plombe (-, -n) f lead seal; (Zahnplombe) filling; **plombieren** vt (Zahn) to fill

plötzlich adj sudden ▷ adv suddenly, all at once

plump adj clumsy; (Hände) ungainly; (Körper) shapeless

plumps interj thud; (in Flüssigkeit) plop

Plural (-s, -e) m plural

plus adv plus; **fünf ~ sieben ist zwölf** five plus seven is (o are) twelve; **zehn Grad ~** ten degrees above zero; **Plus** (-, -) nt plus; (Fin) profit; (Vorteil) advantage

Plüsch (-(e)s, -e) m plush

Pluto (-) m Pluto

PLZ abk = **Postleitzahl** postcode (Brit), zip code (US)

Po (-s, -s) m (fam) bottom, bum

Pocken pl smallpox sing

poetisch adj poetic

Pointe (-, -n) f punch line

Pokal (-s, -e) m goblet; (Sport) cup

pökeln vt to pickle

Pol (-s, -e) m pole

Pole (-n, -n) m Pole; **Polen** (-s) nt Poland

Police (-, -n) f (insurance) policy

polieren vt to polish

Polin f Pole, Polish woman

Politik f politics sing; (eine bestimmte) policy; **Politiker(in)** m(f) politician; **politisch** adj political

Politur f polish

Polizei f police pl; **Polizeibeamte(r)** m, **Polizeibeamtin** f police officer; **polizeilich** adj police; **sie wird ~ gesucht** the police are looking for her;

Polizeirevier nt, **Polizeiwache** f police station; **Polizeistunde** f closing time; **Polizeiwache** f police station; **Polizist(in)** m(f) policeman/-woman

Pollen (-s, -) m pollen; **Pollenflug** (-s) m pollen count

polnisch adj Polish; **Polnisch** nt Polish

Polo (-s) nt polo; **Polohemd** nt polo shirt

Polster (-s, -) nt cushion; (Polsterung) upholstery; (in Kleidung) padding; (fig: Geld) reserves pl; **Polstergarnitur** f living-room suite; **Polstermöbel** pl upholstered furniture sing; **polstern** vt to upholster; (Kleidung) to pad

Polterabend m party prior to a wedding, at which old crockery is smashed to bring good luck

poltern vi (Krach machen) to crash; (schimpfen) to rant

Polyester (-s, -) m polyester

Polypen pl (Med) adenoids pl

Pommes frites pl chips pl (Brit), French fries pl (US)

Pony (-s, -s) m (Frisur) fringe (Brit), bangs pl (US) ▷ (-s, -s) nt (Pferd) pony

Popcorn (-s) nt popcorn

Popmusik f pop (music)

populär adj popular

Pore (-, -n) f pore

Pornografie f pornography

Porree (-s, -s) m leeks pl; **eine Stange ~** a leek

Portemonnaie, Portmonee (-s, -s) nt purse

Portier (-s, -s) m porter; siehe auch **Pförtner**

Portion f portion, helping

Porto (-s, -s) nt postage

Portrait, Porträt (-s, -s) nt portrait

Portugal (-s) nt Portugal; **Portugiese** (-n, -n) m Portuguese; **Portugiesin** (-, -nen) f Portuguese; **portugiesisch** adj Portuguese; **Portugiesisch** nt Portuguese

Portwein (-s, -e) m port

Porzellan (-s, -e) nt china

Posaune (-, -n) f trombone

Position f position

positiv adj positive

Post® (-, -en) f post office; (Briefe) post (Brit), mail; **Postamt** nt post office; **Postanweisung** f postal order (Brit), money order (US); **Postbank** f German

post office bank; **Postbote** m, **-botin** f postman/-woman

Posten (-s, -) m post, position; (Comm) item; (auf Liste) entry

Poster (-s, -) nt poster

Postfach nt post-office box, PO box; **Postkarte** f postcard; **postlagernd** adv poste restante; **Postleitzahl** f postcode (Brit), zip code (US)

postmodern adj postmodern

Postsparkasse f post office savings bank; **Poststempel** m postmark; **Postweg** m **auf dem ~** by mail

Potenz f (Math) power; (eines Mannes) potency

PR (-, -s) f abk = **Public Relations** PR

prächtig adj splendid

prahlen vi to boast, to brag

Praktikant(in) m(f) trainee; **Praktikum** (-s, Praktika) nt practical training; **praktisch** adj practical; **~er Arzt** general practitioner

Praline f chocolate

Prämie f (bei Versicherung) premium; (Belohnung) reward; (von Arbeitgeber) bonus

Präparat nt (Med) medicine; (Bio) preparation

Präservativ nt condom

Präsident(in) m(f) president

Praxis (-, Praxen) f practice; (Behandlungsraum) surgery; (von Anwalt) office

präzise adj precise, exact

predigen vt, vi to preach; **Predigt** (-, -en) f sermon

Preis (-es, -e) m (zu zahlen) price; (bei Sieg) prize; **den ersten ~ gewinnen** to win first prize; **Preisausschreiben** nt competition

Preiselbeere f cranberry

preisgünstig adj inexpensive; **Preislage** f price range; **Preisliste** f price list; **Preisschild** nt price tag; **Preisträger(in)** m(f) prizewinner; **preiswert** adj inexpensive

Prellung f bruise

Premiere (-, -n) f premiere, first night

Premierminister(in) m(f) prime minister, premier

Presse (-, -n) f press

pressen vt to press

prickeln vi to tingle

Priester(in) (-s, -) m(f) priest/(woman) priest

P

Primel (-, -n) f primrose
primitiv adj primitive
Prinz (-en, -en) m prince; **Prinzessin** f princess
Prinzip (-s, -ien) nt principle; **im ~** basically; **aus ~** on principle
Priorität f priority
privat adj private; **Privatfernsehen** nt commercial television; **Privatgrundstück** nt private property; **privatisieren** vt to privatize; **Privatquartier** nt private accommodation
pro prep +akk per; **5 Euro ~ Stück/Person** 5 euros each/per person; **Pro** (-s) nt pro
Probe (-, -n) f test; (Teststück) sample; (Theat) rehearsal; **Probefahrt** f test drive; **eine ~ machen** to go for a test drive; **Probezeit** f trial period; **probieren** vt, vi to try; (Wein, Speise) to taste, to sample
Problem (-s, -e) nt problem
Produkt (-(e)s, -e) nt product; **Produktion** f production; (produzierte Menge) output; **produzieren** vt to produce
Professor(in) (-s, -en) m(f) professor
Profi (-s, -s) m pro
Profil (-s, -e) nt profile; (von Reifen, Schuhsohle) tread
Profit (-(e)s, -e) m profit; **profitieren** vi to profit (von from)
Prognose (-, -n) f prediction; (Wetter) forecast
Programm (-s, -e) nt programme; (Inform) program; (TV) channel; **Programmheft** nt programme; **programmieren** vt to program; **Programmierer(in)** (-s, -) m(f) programmer; **Programmkino** nt arts (o repertory (US)) cinema
Projekt (-(e)s, -e) nt project
Projektor m projector
Promenade (-, -n) f promenade
Promille (-(s), -) nt (blood) alcohol level; **0,8 ~** 0,08 per cent; **Promillegrenze** f legal alcohol limit
prominent adj prominent; **Prominenz** f VIPs pl, prominent figures pl; (fam: Stars) the glitterati pl
Propeller (-s, -) m propeller
prosit interj cheers
Prospekt (-(e)s, -e) m leaflet, brochure
prost interj cheers
Prostituierte(r) mf prostitute
Protest (-(e)s, -e) m protest

Protestant(in) m(f) Protestant; **protestantisch** adj Protestant
protestieren vi to protest (gegen against)
Prothese (-, -n) f artificial arm/leg; (Gebiss) dentures pl
Protokoll (-s, -e) nt (bei Sitzung) minutes pl; (diplomatisch) (Inform) protocol; (bei Polizei) statement
protzen vi to show off; **protzig** adj flashy
Proviant (-s, -e) m provisions pl
Provider (-s, -) m (Inform) (service) provider
Provinz (-, -en) f province
Provision f (Comm) commission
provisorisch adj provisional
provozieren vt to provoke
Prozent (-(e)s, -e) nt per cent
Prozess (-es, -e) m (Vorgang) process; (Jur) trial; (Rechtsfall) (court) case; **prozessieren** vi to go to law (mit against)
Prozession f procession
Prozessor (-s, -en) m (Inform) processor
prüde adj prudish
prüfen vt to test; (nachprüfen) to check; **Prüfung** f (Schule) exam; (Überprüfung) check; **eine ~ machen** (Schule) to take an exam
Prügelei f fight; **prügeln** vt to beat ▷ vr **sich ~** to fight
PS abk = **Pferdestärke** hp ▷ abk = **Postskript(um)** PS
pseudo- präf pseudo; **Pseudokrupp** (-s) m (Med) pseudocroup; **Pseudonym** (-s, -e) nt pseudonym
pst interj ssh
Psychiater(in) (-s, -) m(f) psychiatrist; **psychisch** adj psychological; (Krankheit) mental; **Psychoanalyse** f psychoanalysis; **Psychologe** (-n, -n) m, **Psychologin** f psychologist; **Psychologie** f psychology
Psychopharmaka pl mind-affecting drugs pl, psychotropic drugs pl; **psychosomatisch** adj psychosomatic; **Psychoterror** m psychological intimidation; **Psychotherapie** f psychotherapy
Pubertät f puberty
Publikum (-s) nt audience; (Sport) crowd
Pudding (-s, -e o -s) m blancmange
Pudel (-s, -) m poodle

Puder (-s, -) m powder; **Puderzucker** m icing sugar

Puerto Rico (-s) nt Puerto Rico

Pulli (-s, -s) m, **Pullover** (-s, -) m sweater, pullover, jumper (Brit)

Puls (-es, -e) m pulse

Pulver (-s, -) nt powder; **Pulverkaffee** m instant coffee; **Pulverschnee** m powder snow

pummelig adj chubby

Pumpe (-, -n) f pump; **pumpen** vt to pump; (fam: verleihen) to lend; (fam: sich ausleihen) to borrow

Pumps pl court shoes pl (Brit), pumps pl (US)

Punk (-s, -s) m (Musik, Mensch) punk

Punkt (-(e)s, -e) m point; (bei Muster) dot; (Satzzeichen) full stop (Brit), period (US); **~ zwei Uhr** at two o'clock sharp

pünktlich adj punctual, on time; **Pünktlichkeit** f punctuality

Punsch (-(e)s, -e) m punch

Pupille (-, -n) f pupil

Puppe (-, -n) f doll

pur adj pure; (völlig) sheer; (Whisky) neat

Püree (-s, -s) nt puree; (Kartoffelpüree) mashed potatoes pl

Puste (-) f (fam) puff; **außer ~ sein** to be puffed

Pustel (-, -n) f pustule; (Pickel) pimple; **pusten** vi to blow; (keuchen) to puff

Pute (-, -n) f turkey; **Putenschnitzel** nt turkey escalope

Putsch (-es, -e) m putsch

Putz (-es) m (Mörtel) plaster

putzen vt to clean; **sich** (dat) **die Nase ~** to blow one's nose; **sich** (dat) **die Zähne ~** to brush one's teeth; **Putzfrau** f cleaner; **Putzlappen** m cloth, **Putzmann** m cleaner; **Putzmittel** nt cleaning agent, cleaner

Puzzle (-s, -s) nt jigsaw (puzzle)

Pyjama (-s, -s) m pyjamas pl

Pyramide (-, -n) f pyramid

Python (-s, -s) m python

q

Quadrat *nt* square; **quadratisch** *adj* square; **Quadratmeter** *m* square metre

quaken *vi* (*Frosch*) to croak; (*Ente*) to quack

Qual (-, -en) *f* pain, agony; (*seelisch*) anguish; **quälen** *vt* to torment ▷ *vr* sich ~ to struggle; (*geistig*) to torment oneself; **Quälerei** *f* torture, torment

qualifizieren *vt* to qualify; (*einstufen*) to label ▷ *vr* **sich ~** to qualify

Qualität *f* quality

Qualle (-, -n) *f* jellyfish

Qualm (-(e)s) *m* thick smoke; **qualmen** *vt*, *vi* to smoke

Quantität *f* quantity

Quarantäne (-, -n) *f* quarantine

Quark (-s) *m* quark; (*fam: Unsinn*) rubbish

Quartett (-s, -e) *nt* quartet; (*Kartenspiel*) happy families *sing*

Quartier (-s, -e) *nt* accommodation

quasi *adv* more or less

Quatsch (-es) *m* (*fam*) rubbish; **quatschen** *vi* (*fam*) to chat

Quecksilber *nt* mercury

Quelle (-, -n) *f* spring; (*eines Flusses*) source

quellen *vi* to pour

quer *adv* crossways, diagonally; (*rechtwinklig*) at right angles; ~ **über die Straße** straight across the street; **querfeldein** *adv* across country; **Querflöte** *f* flute; **Querschnitt** *m* cross section; **querschnittsgelähmt** *adj* paraplegic; **Querstraße** *f* side street

quetschen *vt* to squash, to crush; (*Med*) to bruise; **Quetschung** *f* bruise

Queue (-s, -s) *m* (billiard) cue

quietschen *vi* to squeal; (*Tür, Bett*) to squeak; (*Bremsen*) to screech

Quirl (-s, -e) *m* whisk

quitt *adj* quits, even

Quitte (-, -n) *f* quince

Quittung *f* receipt

Quiz (-, -) *nt* quiz

Quote (-, -n) *f* rate; (*Comm*) quota

r

Rabatt (-(e)s, -e) m discount
Rabbi (-(s), -s) m rabbi; **Rabbiner** (-s, -) m rabbi
Rabe (-n, -n) m raven
Rache (-) f revenge, vengeance
Rachen (-s, -) m throat
rächen vt to avenge ▷ vr **sich ~** to take (one's) revenge (an +dat on)
Rad (-(e)s, Räder) nt wheel; (Fahrrad) bike; **~ fahren** to cycle; **mit dem ~ fahren** to go by bike
Radar (-s) m o nt radar; **Radarfalle** f speed trap; **Radarkontrolle** f radar speed check
radeln vi (fam) to cycle; **Radfahrer(in)** m(f) cyclist; **Radfahrweg** m cycle track (o path)
Radicchio (-s) m (Salatsorte) radicchio
radieren vt to rub out, to erase; **Radiergummi** m rubber (Brit), eraser; **Radierung** f (Kunst) etching
Radieschen nt radish
radikal adj radical
Radio (-s, -s) nt radio; **im ~** on the radio
radioaktiv adj radioactive
Radiologe (-n, -n) m, **Radiologin** f radiologist

Radiorekorder m radio cassette recorder; **Radiosender** m radio station; **Radiowecker** m radio alarm (clock)
Radkappe f (Auto) hub cap
Radler(in) (-s, -) m(f) cyclist
Radler (-s, -) nt ≈ shandy
Radlerhose f cycling shorts pl; **Radrennen** nt cycle racing; (einzelnes Rennen) cycle race; **Radtour** f cycling tour; **Radweg** m cycle track (o path)
raffiniert adj crafty, cunning; (Zucker) refined
Rafting (-s) nt white water rafting
Ragout (-s, -s) nt ragout
Rahm (-s) m cream
rahmen vt to frame; **Rahmen** (-s, -) m frame
Rakete (-, -n) f rocket
rammen vt to ram
Rampe (-, -n) f ramp
ramponieren vt (fam) to damage, to batter
Ramsch (-(e)s, -e) m junk
ran (fam) kontr von **heran**
Rand (-(e)s, Ränder) m edge; (von Brille, Tasse etc) rim; (auf Papier) margin; (Schmutzrand, unter Augen) ring; (fig) verge, brink
randalieren vi to (go on the) rampage; **Randalierer(in)** (-s, -) m(f) hooligan
Randstein m kerb (Brit), curb (US); **Randstreifen** m shoulder
rang imperf von **ringen**
Rang (-(e)s, Ränge) m rank; (in Wettbewerb) place; (Theat) circle
rannte imperf von **rennen**
ranzig adj rancid
Rap (-(s), -s) m (Mus) rap; **rappen** vi (Mus) to rap; **Rapper(in)** (-s, -) m(f) (Mus) rapper
rar adj rare, scarce
rasant adj quick, rapid
rasch adj quick
rascheln vi to rustle
rasen vi (sich schnell bewegen) to race; (toben) to rave; **gegen einen Baum ~** to crash into a tree
Rasen (-s, -) m lawn
rasend adj (vor Wut) furious
Rasenmäher (-s, -) m lawnmower
Rasierapparat m razor; (elektrischer) shaver; **Rasiercreme** f shaving cream;

rasieren vt to shave ▷ vr **sich ~** to shave;
Rasierer m shaver; **Rasiergel** nt shaving
gel; **Rasierklinge** f razor blade;
Rasiermesser nt (cutthroat) razor;
Rasierpinsel m shaving brush;
Rasierschaum m shaving foam
Rasse (-, -n) f race; (Tiere) breed
Rassismus m racism; **Rassist(in)** m(f)
racist; **rassistisch** adj racist
Rast (-, -en) f rest, break; **~ machen** to
have a rest (o break); **rasten** vi to rest;
Rastplatz m (Auto) rest area; **Raststätte**
f (Auto) service area; (Gaststätte)
motorway (Brit) (o highway (US))
restaurant
Rasur f shave
Rat (-(e)s, Ratschläge) m (piece of) advice;
sie hat mir einen ~ gegeben she gave me
some advice; **um ~ fragen** to ask for
advice
Rate (-, -n) f instalment; **etw auf ~n
kaufen** to buy sth in instalments (Brit), to
buy sth on the instalment plan (US)
raten (riet, geraten) vt, vi to guess;
(empfehlen) to advise (jdm sb)
Rathaus nt town hall
Ration f ration
ratlos adj at a loss, helpless; **ratsam** adj
advisable
Rätsel (-s, -) nt puzzle; (Worträtsel) riddle;
das ist mir ein ~ it's a mystery to me;
rätselhaft adj mysterious
Ratte (-, -n) f rat
rau adj rough, coarse; (Wetter) harsh
Raub (-(e)s) m robbery; (Beute) loot, booty;
rauben vt to steal; **jdm etw ~** to rob sb of
sth; **Räuber(in)** (-s, -) m(f) robber;
Raubfisch m predatory fish; **Raubkopie**
f pirate copy; **Raubmord** m robbery with
murder; **Raubtier** nt predator;
Raubüberfall m mugging; **Raubvogel** m
bird of prey
Rauch (-(e)s) m smoke; (Abgase) fumes pl;
rauchen vt, vi to smoke; **Raucher(in)**
(-s, -) m(f) smoker; **Raucherabteil** nt
smoking compartment
Räucherlachs m smoked salmon;
räuchern vt to smoke
rauchig adj smoky; **Rauchmelder** m
smoke detector; **Rauchverbot** nt
smoking ban; **hier ist ~** there's no
smoking here
rauf (fam) kontr von **herauf**

rauh adj siehe **rau**; **Rauhreif** m siehe
Raureif
Raum (-(e)s, Räume) m space; (Zimmer,
Platz) room; (Gebiet) area
räumen vt to clear; (Wohnung, Platz) to
vacate; (wegbringen) to shift, to move; (in
Schrank etc) to put away
Raumfähre f space shuttle; **Raumfahrt**
f space travel; **Raumschiff** nt spacecraft,
spaceship; **Raumsonde** f space probe;
Raumstation f space station
Raumtemperatur f room temperature
Räumungsverkauf m clearance sale,
closing-down sale
Raupe (-, -n) f caterpillar
Raureif m hoarfrost
raus (fam) kontr von **heraus, hinaus**; **~!**
(get) out!
Rausch (-(e)s, Räusche) m intoxication;
einen ~ haben/kriegen to be/get drunk
rauschen vi (Wasser) to rush; (Baum) to
rustle; (Radio etc) to hiss; **Rauschgift** nt
drug; **Rauschgiftsüchtige(r)** mf drug
addict
raus|fliegen irr vi (fam) to be kicked out
raus|halten irr vr (fam) **halt du dich da
raus!** you (just) keep out of it
räuspern vr **sich ~** to clear one's throat
raus|schmeißen irr vt (fam) to throw out
Razzia (-, Razzien) f raid
reagieren vi to react (auf +akk to);
Reaktion f reaction
real adj real; **realisieren** vt (merken) to
realize; (verwirklichen) to implement;
realistisch adj realistic; **Realität** (-, -en) f
reality; **Reality-TV** (-s) nt reality TV
Realschule f ≈ secondary school, junior
high (school) (US)
Rebe (-, -n) f vine
rebellieren vi to rebel
Rebhuhn nt partridge
rechnen vt, vi to calculate; **~ mit** to
expect; (bauen auf) to count on ▷ vr **sich
~** to pay off, to turn out to be profitable;
Rechner (-s, -) m calculator; (Computer)
computer; **Rechnung** f calculation(s);
(Comm) bill (Brit), check (US); **die ~, bitte!**
can I have the bill, please?; **das geht auf
meine ~** this is on me
recht adj (richtig, passend) right; **mir soll's
~ sein** it's alright by me; **mir ist es ~** I
don't mind ▷ adv really, quite; (richtig)
right(ly); **ich weiß nicht ~** I don't really

know; **es geschieht ihm ~** it serves him right

Recht (-(e)s, -e) nt right; (Jur) law; **~ haben** to be right; **jdm ~ geben** to agree with sb

Rechte (-n, -n) f right-hand side; (Hand) right hand; (Pol) right (wing); **rechte(r, s)** adj right; **auf der ~n Seite** on the right, on the right-hand side; **Rechte(s)** nt right thing; **etwas/nichts ~s** something/nothing proper

Rechteck (-s, -e) nt rectangle; **rechteckig** adj rectangular

rechtfertigen vt to justify ▷ vr **sich ~** to justify oneself

rechtlich adj legal; **rechtmäßig** adj legal, lawful

rechts adv on the right; **~ abbiegen** to turn right; **~ von** to the right of; **~ oben** at the top right

Rechtsanwalt m, **-anwältin** f lawyer

Rechtschreibung f spelling

Rechtshänder(in) (-s, -) m(f) right-hander; **rechtsherum** adv to the right, clockwise; **rechtsradikal** adj (Pol) extreme right-wing

Rechtsschutzversicherung f legal costs insurance

Rechtsverkehr m driving on the right

rechtswidrig adj illegal

rechtwinklig adj right-angled; **rechtzeitig** adj timely ▷ adv in time

recycelbar adj recyclable; **recyceln** vt to recycle; **Recycling** (-s) nt recycling; **Recyclingpapier** nt recycled paper

Redakteur(in) m(f) editor; **Redaktion** f editing; (Leute) editorial staff; (Büro) editorial office(s)

Rede (-, -n) f speech; (Gespräch) talk; **eine ~ halten** to make a speech; **reden** vi to talk, to speak ▷ vt to say; (Unsinn etc) to talk; **Redewendung** f idiom; **Redner(in)** m(f) speaker

reduzieren vt to reduce

Referat (-s, -e) nt paper; **ein ~ halten** to give a paper (über +akk on)

reflektieren vt to reflect

Reform (-, -en) f reform; **Reformhaus** nt health food shop; **reformieren** vt to reform

Regal (-s, -e) nt shelf; (Möbelstück) shelves pl

Regel (-, -n) f rule; (Med) period;

regelmäßig adj regular; **regeln** vt to regulate, to control; (Angelegenheit) to settle ▷ vr **sich von selbst ~** to sort itself out; **Regelung** f regulation

Regen (-s, -) m rain; **Regenbogen** m rainbow; **Regenmantel** m raincoat; **Regenrinne** f gutter; **Regenschauer** m shower; **Regenschirm** m umbrella; **Regenwald** m rainforest; **Regenwurm** m earthworm

Regie f direction

regieren vt, vi to govern, to rule; **Regierung** f government; (von Monarch) reign

Region f region; **regional** adj regional

Regisseur(in) m(f) director

registrieren vt to register; (bemerken) to notice

regnen vi impers to rain; **regnerisch** adj rainy

regulär adj regular; **regulieren** vt to regulate, to adjust

Reh (-(e)s, -e) nt deer; (Fleisch) venison

Rehabilitationszentrum nt (Med) rehabilitation centre

Reibe (-, -n) f, **Reibeisen** nt grater; **reiben** (rieb, gerieben) vt to rub; (Gastr) to grate; **reibungslos** adj smooth

reich adj rich

Reich (-(e)s, -e) nt empire; (eines Königs) kingdom

reichen vi to reach; (genügen) to be enough, to be sufficient (jdm for sb) ▷ vt to hold out; (geben) to pass, to hand; (anbieten) to offer

reichhaltig adj ample, rich; **reichlich** adj (Trinkgeld) generous; (Essen) ample; **~ Zeit** plenty of time; **Reichtum** (-s, -tümer) m wealth

reif adj ripe; (Mensch, Urteil) mature

Reif (-(e)s) m (Raureif) hoarfrost ▷ (-(e)s, -e) m (Ring) ring, hoop

reifen vi to mature; (Obst) to ripen

Reifen (-s, -) m ring, hoop; (von Auto) tyre; **Reifendruck** m tyre pressure; **Reifenpanne** f puncture; **Reifenwechsel** m tyre change

Reihe (-, -n) f row; (von Tagen etc, fam: Anzahl) series sing; **der ~ nach** one after the other; **er ist an der ~** it's his turn; **Reihenfolge** f order, sequence; **Reihenhaus** nt terraced house (Brit), row house (US)

r

Reiher (-s, -) m heron
rein (fam) kontr von **herein, hinein** ▷ adj
pure; (sauber) clean
Reinfall m (fam) letdown; **rein|fallen** irr vi
(fam) **auf etw** (akk) **~** to fall for sth
reinigen vt to clean; **Reinigung** f
cleaning; (Geschäft) (dry) cleaner's;
Reinigungsmittel nt cleaning agent,
cleaner
rein|legen vt jdn **~** to take sb for a ride
Reis (-es, -e) m rice
Reise (-, -n) f journey; (auf Schiff) voyage;
Reiseapotheke f first-aid kit; **Reisebüro**
nt travel agent's; **Reisebus** m coach;
Reiseführer(in) m(f) (Mensch) courier;
(Buch) guide(book); **Reisegepäck** nt
luggage (Brit), baggage;
Reisegesellschaft f (Veranstalter) tour
operator; **Reiseleiter(in)** m(f) courier;
reisen vi to travel; **~ nach** to go to;
Reisende(r) mf traveller; **Reisepass** m
passport; **Reiseroute** f route, itinerary;
Reiserücktrittversicherung f holiday
cancellation insurance; **Reisescheck** m
traveller's cheque; **Reisetasche** f holdall
(Brit), carryall (US); **Reiseveranstalter** m
tour operator; **Reiseverkehr** m holiday
traffic; **Reiseversicherung** f travel
insurance; **Reiseziel** nt destination
reißen (riss, gerissen) vt, vi to tear; (ziehen)
to pull, to drag; (Witz) to crack
Reißnagel m drawing pin (Brit),
thumbtack (US); **Reißverschluss** m zip
(Brit), zipper (US); **Reißzwecke** f drawing
pin (Brit), thumbtack (US)
reiten (ritt, geritten) vt, vi to ride;
Reiter(in) m(f) rider; **Reithose** f riding
breeches pl; **Reitsport** m riding;
Reitstiefel m riding boot
Reiz (-es, -e) m stimulus; (angenehm)
charm; (Verlockung) attraction; **reizen** vt
to stimulate; (unangenehm) to annoy;
(verlocken) to appeal to, to attract; **reizend**
adj charming; **Reizgas** nt irritant gas;
Reizung f irritation
Reklamation f complaint
Reklame (-, -n) f advertising;
(Einzelwerbung) advertisement; (im
Fernsehen) commercial
reklamieren vi to complain (wegen
about)
Rekord (-(e)s, -e) m record
relativ adj relative ▷ adv relatively

relaxen vi to relax, to chill out
Religion f religion; **religiös** adj religious
Remoulade (-, -n) f tartar sauce
Renaissance f renaissance, revival;
(Hist) Renaissance
Rennbahn f racecourse; (Auto) racetrack;
rennen (rannte, gerannt) vt, vi to run;
Rennen (-s, -) nt running; (Wettbewerb)
race; **Rennfahrer(in)** m(f) racing driver;
Rennrad nt racing bike; **Rennwagen** m
racing car
renommiert adj famous, noted (wegen,
für for)
renovieren vt to renovate; **Renovierung**
f renovation
rentabel adj profitable
Rente (-, -n) f pension;
Rentenversicherung f pension scheme
Rentier nt reindeer
rentieren vr sich **~** to pay, to be
profitable
Rentner(in) (-s, -) m(f) pensioner, senior
citizen
Reparatur f repair; **Reparaturwerkstatt**
f repair shop; (Auto) garage; **reparieren**
vt to repair
Reportage f report; **Reporter(in)** (-s, -)
m(f) reporter
Reptil (-s, -ien) nt reptile
Republik f republic
Reservat (-s, -e) nt nature reserve; (für
Ureinwohner) reservation; **Reserve** (-, -n) f
reserve; **Reservekanister** m spare can;
Reserverad nt (Auto) spare wheel;
Reservespieler(in) m(f) reserve;
reservieren vt to reserve; **Reservierung**
f reservation
resignieren vi to give up; **resigniert** adj
resigned
Respekt (-(e)s) m respect; **respektieren**
vt to respect
Rest (-(e)s, -e) m rest, remainder;
(Überreste) remains pl; **der ~ ist für Sie** (zur
Bedienung) keep the change
Restaurant (-s, -s) nt restaurant
restaurieren vt to restore
Restbetrag m balance; **restlich** adj
remaining; **restlos** adj complete
Resultat nt result
retten vt to save, to rescue
Rettich (-s, -e) m radish (large white or red
variety)
Rettung f rescue; (Hilfe) help;

(*Rettungsdienst*) ambulance service;
Rettungsboot *nt* lifeboat;
Rettungshubschrauber *m* rescue
helicopter; **Rettungsring** *m* lifebelt, life
preserver (*US*); **Rettungswagen** *m*
ambulance

Reue (-) *f* remorse; (*Bedauern*) regret;
reuen *vt* **es reut ihn** he regrets it

revanchieren *vr* **sich ~** (*sich rächen*)
to get one's own back, to get one's
revenge; (*für Hilfe etc*) to return the
favour

Revolution *f* revolution

Rezept (-(*e*)*s*, -*e*) *nt* (*Gastr*) recipe; (*Med*)
prescription; **rezeptfrei** *adj*
over-the-counter, non-prescription

Rezeption *f* (*im Hotel*) reception

rezeptpflichtig *adj* available only on
prescription

R-Gespräch *nt* reverse-charge (*Brit*)
(*o* collect (*US*)) call

Rhabarber (-*s*) *m* rhubarb

Rhein (-*s*) *m* Rhine; **Rheinland-Pfalz** (-)
nt Rhineland-Palatinate

Rheuma (-*s*) *nt* rheumatism

Rhythmus *m* rhythm

richten *vt* (*lenken*) to direct (*auf +akk* to);
(*Waffe, Kamera*) to point (*auf +akk* at); (*Brief,
Anfrage*) to address (*an +akk* to); (*einstellen*)
to adjust; (*instand setzen*) to repair;
(*zurechtmachen*) to prepare ▷ *vr* **sich
~ nach** (*Regel etc*) to keep to; (*Mode,
Beispiel*) to follow; (*abhängen von*) to
depend on

Richter(in) (-*s*, -) *m(f)* judge

Richtgeschwindigkeit *f* recommended
speed

richtig *adj* right, correct; (*echt*) proper;
etw ~ stellen to correct sth ▷ *adv* (*fam:
sehr*) really

Richtlinie *f* guideline

Richtung *f* direction; (*Tendenz*) tendency

rieb *imperf von* **reiben**

riechen (*roch, gerochen*) *vt, vi* to smell;
nach etw ~ to smell of sth; **an etw** (*dat*)
~ to smell sth

rief *imperf von* **rufen**

Riegel (-*s*, -) *m* bolt; (*Gastr*) bar

Riemen (-*s*, -) *m* strap; (*Gürtel*) belt

Riese (-*n*, -*n*) *m* giant; **Riesengarnele** *f*
king prawn; **riesengroß** *adj* gigantic,
huge; **Riesenrad** *nt* big wheel; **riesig** *adj*
enormous, huge

riet *imperf von* **raten**

Riff (-(*e*)*s*, -*e*) *nt* reef

Rind (-(*e*)*s*, -*er*) *nt* cow; (*Bulle*) bull; (*Gastr*)
beef; **~er** *pl* cattle *pl*

Rinde (-, -*n*) *f* (*Baum*) bark; (*Käse*) rind;
(*Brot*) crust

Rinderbraten *m* roast beef;
Rinderwahn(sinn) *m* mad cow disease;
Rindfleisch *nt* beef

Ring (-(*e*)*s*, -*e*) *m* ring; (*Straße*) ring road;
Ringbuch *nt* ring binder

ringen (*rang, gerungen*) *vi* to wrestle;
Ringer(in) *m(f)* wrestler; **Ringfinger** *m*
ring finger; **Ringkampf** *m* wrestling
match; **ringsherum** *adv* round about

Rippe (-, -*n*) *f* rib; **Rippenfellentzündung**
f pleurisy

Risiko (-*s*, -*s o* Risiken) *nt* risk; **auf eigenes
~** at one's own risk; **riskant** *adj* risky;
riskieren *vt* to risk

riss *imperf von* **reißen**

Riss (-*es*, -*e*) *m* tear; (*in Mauer, Tasse
etc*) crack; **rissig** *adj* cracked; (*Haut*)
chapped

ritt *imperf von* **reiten**

Ritter (-*s*, -) *m* knight

Rivale (-*n*, -*n*) *m*, **Rivalin** *f* rival

Rizinusöl *nt* castor oil

Robbe (-, -*n*) *f* seal

Roboter (-*s*, -) *m* robot

robust *adj* robust

roch *imperf von* **riechen**

Rock (-(*e*)*s*, Röcke) *m* skirt

Rockband *f* (*Musikgruppe*) rock band;
Rockmusik *f* rock (music)

Rodelbahn *f* toboggan run; **rodeln** *vi* to
toboggan

Roggen (-*s*, -) *m* rye; **Roggenbrot** *nt* rye
bread

roh *adj* raw; (*Mensch*) coarse, crude;
Rohkost *f* raw vegetables and fruit *pl*

Rohr (-(*e*)*s*, -*e*) *nt* pipe; (*Bot*) cane; (*Schilf*)
reed; **Röhre** (-, -*n*) *f* tube; (*Leitung*) pipe;
(*Elek*) valve; (*Backröhre*) oven; **Rohrzucker**
m cane sugar

Rohstoff *m* raw material

Rokoko (-*s*) *nt* rococo

Rolle (-, -*n*) *f* (*etw Zusammengerolltes*) roll;
(*Theat*) role

rollen *vt, vi* to roll

Roller (-*s*, -) *m* scooter

Rollerblades® *pl* Rollerblades® *pl*;
Rollerskates *pl* roller skates *pl*

Rollkragenpullover m polo-neck (*Brit*) (*o* turtleneck (*US*)) sweater; **Rollladen** m, **Rollo** (*-s, -s*) m (roller) shutters *pl*; **Rollschuh** m roller skate; **Rollstuhl** m wheelchair; **rollstuhlgerecht** *adj* suitable for wheelchairs; **Rolltreppe** f escalator

Roman (*-s, -e*) m novel

Romantik f romance; **romantisch** *adj* romantic

römisch-katholisch *adj* Roman Catholic

röntgen *vt* to X-ray; **Röntgenaufnahme** f, **Röntgenbild** *nt* X-ray; **Röntgenstrahlen** *pl* X-rays *pl*

rosa *adj inv* pink

Rose (*-, -n*) f rose

Rosenkohl m (Brussels) sprouts *pl*

Rosé(wein) m rosé (wine)

rosig *adj* rosy

Rosine f raisin

Rosmarin (*-s*) m rosemary

Rosskastanie f horse chestnut

Rost (*-(e)s, -e*) m rust; (*zum Braten*) grill, gridiron; **Rostbratwurst** f grilled sausage; **rosten** *vi* to rust; **rösten** *vt* to roast, to grill; (*Brot*) to toast; **rostfrei** *adj* rustproof; (*Stahl*) stainless; **rostig** *adj* rusty; **Rostschutz** m rustproofing

rot *adj* red; **~ werden** to blush; **~e Karte** red card; **~e Be(e)te** beetroot; **bei Rot über die Ampel fahren** to jump the lights; **das Rote Kreuz** the Red Cross

Röteln *pl* German measles *sing*

röten *vt* to redden ▷ *vr* **sich ~** to redden

rothaarig *adj* red-haired

rotieren *vi* to rotate; **am Rotieren sein** (*fam*) to be rushing around like a mad thing

Rotkehlchen *nt* robin; **Rotkohl** m, **Rotkraut** *nt* red cabbage; **Rotlichtviertel** *nt* red-light district; **Rotwein** m red wine

Rouge (*-s, -s*) *nt* rouge

Route (*-, -n*) f route

Routine f experience; (*Trott*) routine

Rubbellos *nt* scratchcard; **rubbeln** *vt* to rub

Rübe (*-, -n*) f turnip; **Gelbe ~** carrot; **Rote ~** beetroot

rüber (*fam*) *kontr von* **herüber, hinüber**

Rubin (*-s, -e*) m ruby

rücken *vt, vi* to move; **könntest du ein bisschen ~?** could you move over a bit?

Rücken (*-s, -*) m back; **Rückenlehne** f back(rest); **Rückenmark** *nt* spinal cord; **Rückenschmerzen** *pl* backache *sing*; **Rückenschwimmen** (*-s*) *nt* backstroke; **Rückenwind** m tailwind

Rückerstattung f refund; **Rückfahrkarte** f return ticket (*Brit*), round-trip ticket (*US*); **Rückfahrt** f return journey; **Rückfall** m relapse; **Rückflug** m return flight; **Rückgabe** f return; **rückgängig** *adj* **etw ~ machen** to cancel sth; **Rückgrat** (*-(e)s, -e*) *nt* spine, backbone; **Rückkehr** (*-, -en*) f return; **Rücklicht** *nt* rear light; **Rückreise** f return journey; **auf der ~** on the way back

Rucksack m rucksack, backpack; **Rucksacktourist(in)** m(f) backpacker

Rückschritt m step back; **Rückseite** f back; (*hinterer Teil*) rear; **siehe ~** see overleaf; **Rücksicht** f consideration; **~ nehmen auf** (*+akk*) to show consideration for; **rücksichtslos** *adj* inconsiderate; (*Fahren*) reckless; (*unbarmherzig*) ruthless; **rücksichtsvoll** *adj* considerate; **Rücksitz** m back seat; **Rückspiegel** m (*Auto*) rear-view mirror; **Rückstand** m **sie sind zwei Tore im ~** they're two goals down; **im ~ sein mit** (*Arbeit, Miete*) to be behind with; **Rücktaste** f backspace key; **Rückvergütung** f refund; **rückwärts** *adv* backwards, back; **Rückwärtsgang** m (*Auto*) reverse (gear); **Rückweg** m return journey, way back; **Rückzahlung** f repayment; **Rückzieher** m **einen ~ machen** to back out

Ruder (*-s, -*) *nt* oar; (*Steuer*) rudder; **Ruderboot** *nt* rowing boat (*Brit*), rowboat (*US*); **rudern** *vt, vi* to row

Ruf (*-(e)s, -e*) m call, cry; (*Ansehen*) reputation; **rufen** (*rief, gerufen*) *vt, vi* to call; (*schreien*) to cry; **Rufnummer** f telephone number

Ruhe (*-*) f rest; (*Ungestörtheit*) peace, quiet; (*Gelassenheit, Stille*) calm; (*Schweigen*) silence; **lass mich in ~!** leave me alone; **ruhen** *vi* to rest; **Ruhestand** m retirement; **im ~ sein** to be retired; **Ruhestörung** f disturbance of the peace; **Ruhetag** m closing day; **montags ~ haben** to be closed on Mondays

ruhig *adj* quiet; (*bewegungslos*) still; (*Hand*) steady; (*gelassen*) calm

Ruhm *(-(e)s) m* fame, glory

Rührei *nt* scrambled egg(s); **rühren** *vt* to move; *(umrühren)* to stir ▷ *vr* **sich ~** to move; *(sich bemerkbar machen)* to say something; **rührend** *adj* touching, moving; **Rührung** *f* emotion

Ruine *(-, -n) f* ruin; **ruinieren** *vt* to ruin

rülpsen *vi* to burp, to belch

rum *(fam) kontr von* **herum**

Rum *(-s, -s) m* rum

Rumänien *(-s) nt* Romania

Rummel *(-s) m (Trubel)* hustle and bustle; *(Jahrmarkt)* fair; *(Medienrummel)* hype; **Rummelplatz** *m* fairground

rumoren *vi* **es rumort in meinem Bauch/Kopf** my stomach is rumbling/my head is spinning

Rumpf *(-(e)s, Rümpfe) m (Anat)* trunk; *(Aviat)* fuselage; *(Naut)* hull

rümpfen *vt* **die Nase ~** to turn one's nose up *(über at)*

Rumpsteak *nt* rump steak

rund *adj* round ▷ *adv (etwa)* around; **~ um etw** (a)round sth; **Runde** *(-, -n) f* round; *(in Rennen)* lap; **Rundfahrt** *f* tour *(durch* of); **Rundfunk** *m* broadcasting; *(Rundfunkanstalt)* broadcasting service; **im ~** on the radio; **Rundgang** *m* tour *(durch* of); *(von Wächter)* round

rundlich *adj* plump; **Rundreise** *f* tour *(durch* of)

runter *(fam) kontr von* **herunter, hinunter**; **runterscrollen** *vt (Inform)* to scroll down

runzeln *vt* **die Stirn ~** to frown; **runzelig** *adj* wrinkled

ruppig *adj* gruff

Rüsche *(-, -n) f* frill

Ruß *(-es) m* soot

Russe *(-n, -n) m* Russian

Rüssel *(-s, -) m (Elefant)* trunk; *(Schwein)* snout

Russin *f* Russian; **russisch** *adj* Russian; **Russisch** *nt* Russian; **Russland** *nt* Russia

Rüstung *f (mit Waffen)* arming; *(Ritterrüstung)* armour; *(Waffen)* armaments *pl*

Rutsch *(-(e)s, -e) m* **guten ~ (ins neue Jahr)!** Happy New Year; **Rutschbahn** *f*, **Rutsche** *f* slide; **rutschen** *vi* to slide; *(ausrutschen)* to slip; **rutschig** *adj* slippery

rütteln *vt, vi* to shake

S

S _abk_ = **Süd** S

s. _abk_ = **siehe** see; **S.** _abk_ = **Seite** p.

Saal (-(e)s, Säle) m hall; (für Sitzungen) room

Saarland nt Saarland

sabotieren vt to sabotage

Sache (-, -n) f thing; (Angelegenheit) affair, business; (Frage) matter; **bei der ~ bleiben** to keep to the point; **sachkundig** adj competent; **Sachlage** f situation; **sachlich** adj (objektiv) objective; (nüchtern) matter-of-fact; (inhaltlich) factual; **sächlich** adj (Ling) neuter; **Sachschaden** m material damage

Sachsen (-s) nt Saxony; **Sachsen-Anhalt** (-s) nt Saxony-Anhalt

sacht(e) adv softly, gently

Sachverständige(r) mf expert

Sack (-(e)s, Säcke) m sack; (pej: Mensch) bastard, bugger; **Sackgasse** f dead end, cul-de-sac

Safe (-s, -s) m safe

Safer Sex m safe sex

Safran (-s, -e) m saffron

Saft (-(e)s, Säfte) m juice; **saftig** adj juicy

Sage (-, -n) f legend

Säge (-, -n) f saw; **Sägemehl** nt sawdust

sagen vt, vi to say (jdm to sb), to tell (jdm sb); **wie sagt man ... auf Englisch?** what's ... in English?; **ich will dir mal was ~** let me tell you something

sägen vt, vi to saw

sagenhaft adj legendary; (fam: großartig) fantastic

sah imperf von **sehen**

Sahne (-) f cream; **Sahnetorte** f gateau

Saison (-, -s) f season; **außerhalb der ~** out of season

Saite (-, -n) f string

Sakko (-s, -s) nt jacket

Salami (-, -s) f salami

Salat (-(e)s, -e) m salad; (Kopfsalat) lettuce; **Salatbar** f salad bar; **Salatschüssel** f salad bowl; **Salatsoße** f salad dressing

Salbe (-, -n) f ointment

Salbei (-s) m sage

Salmonellenvergiftung f salmonella (poisoning)

salopp adj (Kleidung) casual; (Sprache) slangy

Salsamusik f salsa (music)

Salto (-s, -s) m somersault

Salz (-es, -e) nt salt; **salzarm** adj low-salt; **salzen** (salzte, gesalzen) vt to salt; **Salzgurke** f pickled gherkin; **Salzhering** m pickled herring; **salzig** adj salty; **Salzkartoffeln** pl boiled potatoes pl; **Salzstange** f pretzel stick; **Salzstreuer** m salt cellar (Brit) (o shaker (US)); **Salzwasser** nt salt water

Samba (-, -s) f samba

Samen (-s, -) m seed; (Sperma) sperm

sammeln vt to collect; **Sammler(in)** m(f) collector; **Sammlung** f collection; (Ansammlung, Konzentration) concentration

Samstag m Saturday; siehe auch **Mittwoch**; **samstags** adv on Saturdays; siehe auch **mittwochs**

samt prep +dat (along) with, together with

Samt (-(e)s, -e) m velvet

sämtliche(r, s) adj all (the)

Sanatorium (-s, Sanatorien) nt sanatorium (Brit), sanitarium (US)

Sand (-(e)s, -e) m sand

Sandale (-, -n) f sandal

sandig adj sandy; **Sandkasten** m sandpit (Brit), sandbox (US); **Sandpapier** nt sandpaper; **Sandstrand** m sandy beach

sandte imperf von **senden**

sanft adj soft, gentle

sang imperf von **singen**; **Sänger(in)** (-s, -) m(f) singer

Sangria (-, -s) f sangria

sanieren vt to redevelop; (Gebäude) to renovate; (Betrieb) to restore to profitability

sanitär adj sanitary; **~e Anlagen** pl sanitation

Sanitäter(in) (-s, -) m(f) ambulance man/woman, paramedic

sank imperf von **sinken**

Sankt Gallen (-s) nt St Gallen

Saphir (-s, -e) m sapphire

Sardelle f anchovy

Sardine f sardine

Sarg (-(e)s, Särge) m coffin

saß imperf von **sitzen**

Satellit (-en, -en) m satellite; **Satellitenfernsehen** nt satellite TV; **Satellitenschüssel** f (fam) satellite dish

Satire (-, -n) f satire (auf +akk on)

satt adj full; (Farbe) rich, deep; **~ sein** (gesättigt) to be full; **~ machen** to be filling; **jdn/etw ~ sein** (o haben) to be fed up with sb/sth

Sattel (-s, Sättel) m saddle

Saturn (-s) m Saturn

Satz (-es, Sätze) m (Ling) sentence; (Mus) movement; (Tennis) set; (Kaffee) grounds pl; (Comm) rate; (Sprung) jump; (Comm) rate

Satzzeichen nt punctuation mark

Sau (-, Säue) f sow; (pej: Mensch) dirty bugger

sauber adj clean; (ironisch) fine; **~ machen** to clean; **Sauberkeit** f cleanness; (von Person) cleanliness; **säubern** vt to clean

saublöd adj (fam) really stupid, dumb

Sauce (-, -n) f sauce; (zu Braten) gravy

Saudi-Arabien (-s) nt Saudi Arabia

sauer adj sour; (Chem) acid; (fam: verärgert) cross; **saurer Regen** acid rain; **Sauerkirsche** f sour cherry; **Sauerkraut** nt sauerkraut; **säuerlich** adj slightly sour; **Sauermilch** f sour milk; **Sauerrahm** m sour cream; **Sauerstoff** m oxygen

saufen (soff, gesoffen) vt to drink; (fam: Mensch) to knock back ▷ vi to drink; (fam: Mensch) to booze

saugen (sog o saugte, gesogen o gesaugt) vt, vi to suck; (mit Staubsauger) to vacuum, to hoover (Brit); **Sauger** (-s, -) m (auf Flasche)

teat; **Säugetier** nt mammal; **Säugling** m infant, baby

Säule (-, -n) f column, pillar

Saum (-s, Säume) m hem; (Naht) seam

Sauna (-, -s) f sauna

Säure (-, -n) f acid

sausen vi (Ohren) to buzz; (Wind) to howl; (Mensch) to rush

Saustall m pigsty; **Sauwetter** nt **was für ein ~** (fam) what lousy weather

Saxophon (-s, -e) nt saxophone

S-Bahn f suburban railway; **S-Bahn-Haltestelle** f, **S-Bahnhof** m suburban (train) station

scannen vt to scan; **Scanner** (-s, -) m scanner

schäbig adj shabby

Schach (-s, -s) nt chess; (Stellung) check; **Schachbrett** nt chessboard; **Schachfigur** f chess piece; **schachmatt** adj checkmate

Schacht (-(e)s, Schächte) m shaft

Schachtel (-, -n) f box

schade interj what a pity

Schädel (-s, -) m skull; **Schädelbruch** m fractured skull

schaden vi to damage, to harm (jdm sb); **das schadet nichts** it won't do any harm; **Schaden** (-s, Schäden) m damage; (Verletzung) injury; (Nachteil) disadvantage; **einen ~ verursachen** to cause damage; **Schadenersatz** m compensation, damages pl; **schadhaft** adj faulty; (beschädigt) damaged; **schädigen** vt to damage; (jdn) to do harm to, to harm; **schädlich** adj harmful (für to); **Schadstoff** m harmful substance; **schadstoffarm** adj low-emission

Schaf (-(e)s, -e) nt sheep; **Schafbock** m ram; **Schäfer** (-s, -) m shepherd; **Schäferhund** m Alsatian (Brit), German shepherd; **Schäferin** f shepherdess

schaffen (schuf, geschaffen) vt to create; (Platz) to make ▷ vt (erreichen) to manage, to do; (erledigen) to finish; (Prüfung) to pass; (transportieren) to take; **jdm zu ~ machen** to cause sb trouble

Schaffner(in) (-s, -) m(f) (in Bus) conductor/conductress; (Eisenb) guard

Schafskäse m sheep's (milk) cheese

schal adj (Getränk) flat

Schal (-s, -e o -s) m scarf

s

Schälchen nt (small) bowl

Schale (-, -n) f skin; (abgeschält) peel; (Nuss, Muschel, Ei) shell; (Geschirr) bowl, dish

schälen vt to peel; (Tomate, Mandel) to skin; (Erbsen, Eier, Nüsse) to shell; (Getreide) to husk ▷ vr **sich ~** to peel

Schall (-(e)s, -e) m sound; **Schalldämpfer** (-s, -) m (Auto) silencer (Brit), muffler (US); **Schallplatte** f record

Schalotte (-, -n) f shallot

schalten vt to switch ▷ vi (Auto) to change gear; (fam: begreifen) to catch on; **Schalter** (-s, -) m (auf Post, Bank) counter; (an Gerät) switch; **Schalterhalle** f main hall; **Schalteröffnungszeiten** pl business hours pl

Schaltfläche f (Inform) button; **Schalthebel** m gear lever (Brit) (o shift (US)); **Schaltjahr** nt leap year; **Schaltknüppel** m gear lever (Brit) (o shift (US)); **Schaltung** f gear change (Brit), gearshift (US)

Scham (-) f shame; (Schamgefühl) modesty; **schämen** vr **sich ~** to be ashamed

Schande (-) f disgrace

Schanze (-, -n) f ski jump

Schar (-, -en) f (von Vögeln) flock; (Menge) crowd; **in ~en** in droves

scharf adj (Messer, Kritik) sharp; (Essen) hot; **auf etw** (akk) **~ sein** (fam) to be keen on sth

Schärfe (-, -n) f sharpness; (Strenge) rigour; (Foto) focus

Scharlach (-s) m (Med) scarlet fever

Scharnier (-s, -e) nt hinge

Schaschlik (-s, -s) m o nt (shish) kebab

Schatten (-s, -) m shadow; **30 Grad im ~** 30 degrees in the shade; **schattig** adj shady

Schatz (-es, Schätze) m treasure; (Mensch) love

schätzen vt (abschätzen) to estimate; (Gegenstand) to value; (würdigen) to value, to esteem; (vermuten) to reckon; **Schätzung** f estimate; (das Schätzen) estimation; (von Wertgegenstand) valuation; **schätzungsweise** adv roughly, approximately

Schau (-, -en) f show; (Ausstellung) exhibition

schauen vi to look; **ich schau mal, ob ...**

I'll go and have a look whether ...; **schau, dass ...** see (to it) that ...

Schauer (-s, -) m (Regen) shower; (Schreck) shudder

Schaufel (-, -n) f shovel; **~ und Besen** dustpan and brush; **schaufeln** vt to shovel; **Schnee ~** to clear the snow away

Schaufenster nt shop window; **Schaufensterbummel** m window-shopping expedition

Schaukel (-, -n) f swing; **schaukeln** vi to rock; (mit Schaukel) to swing; **Schaukelstuhl** m rocking chair

Schaulustige(r) mf gawper (Brit), rubbernecker (US)

Schaum (-(e)s, Schäume) m foam; (Seifenschaum) lather; (Bierschaum) froth; **Schaumbad** nt bubble bath; **schäumen** vi to foam; **Schaumfestiger** (-s, -) m styling mousse; **Schaumgummi** m foam (rubber); **Schaumwein** m sparkling wine

Schauplatz m scene; **Schauspiel** nt spectacle; (Theat) play; **Schauspieler(in)** m(f) actor/actress

Scheck (-s, -s) m cheque; **Scheckheft** nt chequebook; **Scheckkarte** f cheque card

Scheibe (-, -n) f disc; (von Brot, Käse etc) slice; (Glasscheibe) pane; **Scheibenbremse** f (Auto) disc brake; **Scheibenwaschanlage** f (Auto) windscreen (Brit (o windshield (US)) washer unit; **Scheibenwischer** (-s, -) m (Auto) windscreen (Brit (o windshield (US)) wiper

Scheich (-s, -s) m sheik(h)

Scheide (-, -n) f (Anat) vagina

scheiden (schied, geschieden) vt (trennen) to separate; (Ehe) to dissolve; **sich ~ lassen** to get a divorce; **sie hat sich von ihm ~ lassen** she divorced him; **Scheidung** f divorce

Schein (-(e)s, -e) m light; (Anschein) appearance; (Geld) (bank)note; **scheinbar** adj apparent; **scheinen** (schien, geschienen) vi (Sonne) to shine; (den Anschein haben) to seem; **Scheinwerfer** (-s, -) m floodlight; (Theat) spotlight; (Auto) headlight

Scheiß- in zW (vulg) damned, bloody (Brit); **Scheiße** (-) f (vulg) shit, crap; **scheißegal** adj (vulg) **das ist mir ~** I don't give a damn (o toss); **scheißen** (schiss, geschissen) vi (vulg) to shit

Scheitel (-s, -) m parting (Brit), part (US)

scheitern vi to fail (an +dat because of)

Schellfisch m haddock

Schema (-s, -s o Schemata) nt scheme, plan; (Darstellung) diagram

Schenkel (-s, -) m thigh

schenken vt to give; **er hat es mir geschenkt** he gave it to me (as a present); **sich** (dat) **etw ~** (fam: weglassen) to skip sth

Scherbe (-, -n) f broken piece, fragment

Schere (-, -n) f scissors pl; (groß) shears pl; **eine ~** a pair of scissors/shears

Scherz (-es, -e) m joke

scheu adj shy

scheuen vr **sich ~ vor** (+dat) to be afraid of, to shrink from ▷ vt to shun ▷ vi (Pferd) to shy

scheuern vt to scrub; **jdm eine ~** (fam) to slap sb in the face

Scheune (-, -n) f barn

scheußlich adj dreadful

Schi (-s, -er) m siehe **Ski**

Schicht (-, -en) f layer; (in Gesellschaft) class; (in Fabrik etc) shift

schick adj stylish, chic

schicken vt to send ▷ vr **sich ~** (sich beeilen) to hurry up

Schickimicki (-(s), -s) m (fam) trendy

Schicksal (-s, -e) nt fate

Schiebedach nt (Auto) sunroof; **schieben** (schob, geschoben) vt, vi to push; **die Schuld auf jdn ~** to put the blame on sb; **Schiebetür** f sliding door

schied imperf von **scheiden**

Schiedsrichter(in) m(f) referee; (Tennis) umpire; (Schlichter) arbitrator

schief adj crooked; (Blick) funny ▷ adv crooked(ly); **~ gehen** (fam) to go wrong

schielen vi to squint

schien imperf von **scheinen**

Schienbein nt shin

Schiene (-, -n) f rail; (Med) splint

schier adj pure; (fig) sheer ▷ adv nearly, almost

schießen (schoss, geschossen) vt to shoot; (Ball) to kick; (Tor) to score; (Foto) to take ▷ vi to shoot (auf +akk at)

Schiff (-(e)s, -e) nt ship; (in Kirche) nave; **Schifffahrt** f shipping; **Schiffsreise** f voyage

schikanieren vt to harass; (Schule) to bully

Schild (-(e)s, -e) m (Schutz) shield ▷ (-(e)s, -er) nt sign; **was steht auf dem ~?** what does the sign say?

Schilddrüse f thyroid gland

schildern vt to describe

Schildkröte f tortoise; (Wasserschildkröte) turtle

Schimmel (-s, -) m mould; (Pferd) white horse; **schimmeln** vi to go mouldy

schimpfen vt to tell off ▷ vi (sich beklagen) to complain; **mit jdm ~** to tell sb off; **Schimpfwort** nt swearword

Schinken (-s, -) m ham

Schirm (-(e)s, -e) m (Regenschirm) umbrella; (Sonnenschirm) parasol, sunshade

schiss imperf von **scheißen**

Schlacht (-, -en) f battle; **schlachten** vt to slaughter; **Schlachter(in)** (-s, -) m(f) butcher; **Schlachtfeld** nt battlefield

Schlaf (-(e)s) m sleep; **Schlafanzug** m pyjamas pl; **Schlafcouch** f bed settee

Schläfe (-, -n) f temple

schlafen (schlief, geschlafen) vi to sleep; **schlaf gut!** sleep well; **hast du gut geschlafen?** did you sleep all right?; **er schläft noch** he's still asleep; **~ gehen** to go to bed

schlaff adj slack; (kraftlos) limp; (erschöpft) exhausted

Schlafgelegenheit f place to sleep; **Schlaflosigkeit** f sleeplessness; **Schlafmittel** nt sleeping pill; **schläfrig** adj sleepy

Schlafsaal m dormitory; **Schlafsack** m sleeping bag; **Schlaftablette** f sleeping pill; **er ist eine richtige ~** (fam: langweilig) he's such a bore; **Schlafwagen** m sleeping car, sleeper; **Schlafzimmer** nt bedroom

Schlag (-(e)s, Schläge) m blow; (Puls) beat; (Elek) shock; (fam: Portion) helping; (Art) kind, type; **Schlagader** f artery; **Schlaganfall** m (Med) stroke; **schlagartig** adj sudden; **Schlagbohrmaschine** f hammer drill

schlagen (schlug, geschlagen) vt to hit; (besiegen) to beat; (Sahne) to whip; **jdn zu Boden ~** to knock sb down ▷ vi (Herz) to beat; (Uhr) to strike; **mit dem Kopf gegen etw ~** to bang one's head against sth ▷ vr **sich ~** to fight

Schläger (-s, -) m (Sport) bat; (Tennis)

racket; (*Golf*) (golf) club; (*Hockey*) hockey stick; (*Mensch*) brawler; **Schlägerei** *f* fight, brawl

schlagfertig *adj* quick-witted; **Schlagloch** *nt* pothole; **Schlagsahne** *f* whipping cream; (*geschlagen*) whipped cream; **Schlagzeile** *f* headline; **Schlagzeug** *nt* drums *pl*; (*in Orchester*) percussion

Schlamm (*-(e)s, -e*) *m* mud

schlampig *adj* (*fam*) sloppy

schlang *imperf von* **schlingen**

Schlange (*-, -n*) *f* snake; (*von Menschen*) queue (*Brit*), line (*US*); **~ stehen** to queue (*Brit*), to stand in line (*US*); **Schlangenlinie** *f* wavy line; **in ~n fahren** to swerve about

schlank *adj* slim

schlapp *adj* limp; (*locker*) slack

Schlappe (*-, -n*) *f* (*fam*) setback

schlau *adj* clever, smart; (*raffiniert*) crafty, cunning

Schlauch (*-(e)s, Schläuche*) *m* hose; (*in Reifen*) inner tube; **Schlauchboot** *nt* rubber dinghy

schlecht *adj* bad; **mir ist ~** I feel sick; **jdn ~ machen** to run sb down; **die Milch ist ~** the milk has gone off ▷ *adv* badly; **es geht ihm ~** he's having a hard time; (*gesundheitlich*) he's not feeling well; (*finanziell*) he's pretty hard up

schleichen (*schlich, geschlichen*) *vi* to creep

Schleier (*-s, -*) *m* veil

Schleife (*-, -n*) *f* (*Inform, Aviat, Elek*) loop; (*Band*) bow

schleifen *vt* (*ziehen, schleppen*) to drag ▷ (*schliff, geschliffen*) *vt* (*schärfen*) to grind; (*Edelstein*) to cut

Schleim (*-(e)s, -e*) *m* slime; (*Med*) mucus; **Schleimer** (*-s, -*) *m* (*fam*) creep; **Schleimhaut** *f* mucous membrane

schlendern *vi* to stroll

schleppen *vt* to drag; (*Auto, Schiff*) to tow; (*tragen*) to lug; **Schlepplift** *m* ski tow

Schleswig-Holstein (*-s*) *nt* Schleswig-Holstein

Schleuder (*-, -n*) *f* catapult; (*für Wäsche*) spin-dryer; **schleudern** *vt* to hurl; (*Wäsche*) to spin-dry ▷ *vi* (*Auto*) to skid; **Schleudersitz** *m* ejector seat

schleunigst *adv* straight away

schlich *imperf von* **schleichen**

schlicht *adj* simple, plain

schlichten *vt* (*Streit*) to settle

schlief *imperf von* **schlafen**

schließen (*schloss, geschlossen*) *vt, vi* to close, to shut; (*beenden*) to close; (*Freundschaft, Ehe*) to enter into; (*folgern*) to infer (*aus* from) ▷ *vr* **sich ~** to close, to shut; **Schließfach** *nt* locker

schließlich *adv* finally; (*schließlich doch*) after all

schliff *imperf von* **schleifen**

schlimm *adj* bad; **schlimmer** *adj* worse; **schlimmste(r, s)** *adj* worst; **schlimmstenfalls** *adv* at (the) worst

Schlinge (*-, -n*) *f* loop; (*Med*) sling

Schlips (*-es, -e*) *m* tie

Schlitten (*-s, -*) *m* sledge, toboggan; (*mit Pferden*) sleigh; **Schlittenfahren** (*-s*) *nt* tobogganing

Schlittschuh *m* ice skate; **~ laufen** to ice-skate

Schlitz (*-es, -e*) *m* slit; (*für Münze*) slot; (*an Hose*) flies *pl*

schloss *imperf von* **schließen**

Schloss (*-es, Schlösser*) *nt* lock; (*Burg*) castle

Schlosser(in) *m(f)* mechanic

Schlucht (*-, -en*) *f* gorge, ravine

schluchzen *vi* to sob

Schluck (*-(e)s, -e*) *m* swallow; **Schluckauf** (*-s*) *m* hiccups *pl*; **schlucken** *vt, vi* to swallow

schludern *vi* (*fam*) to do sloppy work

schlug *imperf von* **schlagen**

Schlüpfer (*-s, -*) *m* panties *pl*

schlüpfrig *adj* slippery; (*fig*) lewd; (*Witz*) risqué

schlürfen *vt, vi* to slurp

Schluss (*-es, Schlüsse*) *m* end; (*Schlussfolgerung*) conclusion; **am ~** at the end; **mit jdm ~ machen** to finish (*o* split up) with sb

Schlüssel (*-s, -*) *m* (*a. fig*) key; **Schlüsselbein** *nt* collarbone; **Schlüsselblume** *f* cowslip; **Schlüsselbund** *m* bunch of keys; **Schlüsseldienst** *m* key-cutting service; **Schlüsselloch** *nt* keyhole

Schlussfolgerung *f* conclusion; **Schlusslicht** *nt* tail-light; (*fig*) tail-ender; **Schlusspfiff** *m* final whistle; **Schlussverkauf** *m* clearance sale

schmächtig *adj* frail

schmal *adj* narrow; (*Mensch, Buch etc*) slim; (*karg*) meagre

Schmalz (*-es, -e*) nt dripping, lard; (*fig:* *Sentimentalitäten*) schmaltz

schmatzen vi to eat noisily

schmecken vt, vi to taste (*nach* of); **es schmeckt ihm** he likes it; **lass es dir ~!** bon appétit

Schmeichelei f flattery; **schmeichelhaft** adj flattering; **schmeicheln** vi **jdm ~ to** flatter sb

schmeißen (*schmiss, geschmissen*) vt (*fam*) to chuck, to throw

schmelzen (*schmolz, geschmolzen*) vt, vi to melt; (*Metall, Erz*) to smelt; **Schmelzkäse** m cheese spread

Schmerz (*-es, -en*) m pain; (*Trauer*) grief; **~en haben** to be in pain; **~en im Rücken haben** to have a pain in one's back; **schmerzen** vt, vi to hurt; **Schmerzensgeld** nt compensation; **schmerzhaft, schmerzlich** adj painful; **schmerzlos** adj painless; **Schmerzmittel** nt painkiller; **schmerzstillend** adj painkilling; **Schmerztablette** f painkiller

Schmetterling m butterfly

Schmied(in) (*-(e)s, -e*) m(f) blacksmith; **schmieden** vt to forge; (*Pläne*) to make

schmieren vt to smear; (*ölen*) to lubricate, to grease; (*bestechen*) to bribe ▷ vt, vi (*unsauber schreiben*) to scrawl; **Schmiergeld** nt (*fam*) bribe; **schmierig** adj greasy; **Schmiermittel** nt lubricant; **Schmierpapier** nt scrap paper; **Schmierseife** f soft soap

Schminke (*-, -n*) f make-up; **schminken** vr **sich ~** to put one's make-up on

schmiss imperf von **schmeißen**

schmollen vi to sulk; **schmollend** adj sulky

schmolz imperf von **schmelzen**

Schmuck (*-(e)s, -e*) m jewellery (*Brit*), jewelry (*US*); (*Verzierung*) decoration; **schmücken** vt to decorate

schmuggeln vt, vi to smuggle

schmunzeln vi to smile

schmusen vi to (kiss and) cuddle

Schmutz (*-es*) m dirt, filth; **schmutzig** adj dirty

Schnabel (*-s, Schnäbel*) m beak, bill; (*Ausguss*) spout

Schnake (*-, -n*) f mosquito

Schnalle (*-, -n*) f buckle

Schnäppchen nt (*fam*) bargain; **schnappen** vt (*fangen*) to catch ▷ vi **nach** **Luft ~** to gasp for breath; **Schnappschuss** m (*Foto*) snap(shot)

Schnaps (*-es, Schnäpse*) m schnapps

schnarchen vi to snore

schnaufen vi to puff, to pant

Schnauzbart m moustache; **Schnauze** (*-, -n*) f snout, muzzle; (*Ausguss*) spout; (*fam: Mund*) trap; **die ~ voll haben** to have had enough

schnäuzen vr **sich ~** to blow one's nose

Schnecke (*-, -n*) f snail; **Schneckenhaus** nt snail's shell

Schnee (*-s*) m snow; **Schneeball** m snowball; **Schneebob** m snowmobile; **Schneebrille** f snow goggles pl; **Schneeflocke** f snowflake; **Schneegestöber** (*-s, -*) nt snow flurry; **Schneeglöckchen** nt snowdrop; **Schneegrenze** f snowline; **Schneekanone** f snow thrower; **Schneekette** f (*Auto*) snow chain; **Schneemann** m snowman; **Schneematsch** m slush; **Schneepflug** m snowplough; **Schneeregen** m sleet; **Schneeschmelze** f thaw; **Schneesturm** m snowstorm, blizzard; **Schneetreiben** nt light blizzards pl; **Schneewehe** f snowdrift

Schneide (*-, -n*) f edge; (*Klinge*) blade; **schneiden** (*schnitt, geschnitten*) vt to cut; **sich** (*dat*) **die Haare ~ lassen** to have one's hair cut ▷ vr **sich ~** to cut oneself; **Schneider(in)** (*-s, -*) m(f) tailor; (*für Damenmode*) dressmaker; **Schneiderin** f dressmaker; **Schneidezahn** m incisor

schneien vi impers to snow

schnell adj quick, fast ▷ adv quickly, fast; **mach ~!** hurry up; **Schnelldienst** m express service; **Schnellhefter** m loose-leaf binder; **Schnellimbiss** m snack bar; **Schnellkochtopf** m pressure cooker; **Schnellreinigung** f express dry cleaning; (*Geschäft*) express (dry) cleaner's; **Schnellstraße** f expressway; **Schnellzug** m fast train

schneuzen vr siehe **schnäuzen**

schnitt imperf von **schneiden**

Schnitt (*-(e)s, -e*) m cut; (*Schnittpunkt*) intersection; (*Querschnitt*) (cross) section; (*Durchschnitt*) average; (*eines Kleides*) style; **Schnittblume** f cut flower; **Schnitte**

(-, -n) f slice; (*belegt*) sandwich;
Schnittkäse m cheese slices pl;
Schnittlauch m chives pl; **Schnittmuster**
nt pattern; **Schnittstelle** f (*Inform, fig*)
interface; **Schnittwunde** f cut, gash
Schnitzel (-s, -) nt (*Papier*) scrap; (*Gastr*)
escalope
schnitzen vt to carve
Schnorchel (-s, -) m snorkel;
schnorcheln vi to go snorkelling, to
snorkel; **Schnorcheln** (-s) nt snorkelling
schnüffeln vi to sniff
Schnuller (-s, -) m dummy (*Brit*), pacifier
(*US*)
Schnulze (-, -n) f (*Film, Roman*) weepie
Schnupfen (-s, -) m cold
schnuppern vi to sniff
Schnur (-, Schnüre) f string, cord; (*Elek*)
lead; **schnurlos** adj (*Telefon*) cordless
Schnurrbart m moustache
schnurren vi to purr
Schnürschuh m lace-up (shoe);
Schnürsenkel (-s, -) m shoelace
schob imperf von **schieben**
Schock (-(e)s, -e) m shock; **unter ~ stehen**
to be in a state of shock; **schockieren** vt
to shock
Schokolade f chocolate; **Schokoriegel**
m chocolate bar
Scholle (-, -n) f (*Fisch*) plaice; (*Eis*) ice floe

⊙ SCHLÜSSELWORT

schon adv **1** (*bereits*) already; **er ist schon
da** he's there already, he's already there;
ist er schon da? is he there yet?; **warst du
schon einmal da?** have you ever been
there?; **ich war schon einmal da** I've been
there before; **das war schon immer so**
that has always been the case; **schon oft**
often; **hast du schon gehört?** have you
heard?
2 (*bestimmt*) all right; **du wirst schon
sehen** you'll see (all right); **das wird
schon noch gut** that'll be OK
3 (*bloß*) just; **allein schon das Gefühl ...**
just the very feeling ...; **schon der
Gedanke** the very thought; **wenn ich
das schon höre** I only have to hear
that
4 (*einschränkend*): **ja schon, aber ...** yes
(well), but ...
5: **schon möglich** possible; **schon gut!**

OK!; **du weißt schon** you know; **komm
schon!** come on!

schön adj beautiful; (*nett*) nice; (*Frau*)
beautiful, pretty; (*Mann*) beautiful,
handsome; (*Wetter*) fine; **~e Grüße** best
wishes; **~es Wochenende** have a nice
weekend
schonen vt (*pfleglich behandeln*) to look
after ▷ vr **sich ~** to take it easy
Schönheit f beauty
Schonkost f light diet
schöpfen vt to scoop; (*mit Kelle*) to ladle;
Schöpfkelle f, **Schöpflöffel** m ladle
Schöpfung f creation
Schoppen (-s, -) m glass (of wine)
Schorf (-(e)s, -e) m scab
Schorle (-, -n) f spritzer
Schornstein m chimney;
Schornsteinfeger(in) (-s, -) m(f) chimney
sweep
schoss imperf von **schießen**
Schoß (-es, Schöße) m lap
Schotte (-n, -n) m Scot, Scotsman;
Schottin f Scot, Scotswoman;
schottisch adj Scottish, Scots;
Schottland nt Scotland
schräg adj slanting; (*Dach*) sloping; (*Linie*)
diagonal; (*fam: unkonventionell*) wacky
Schrank (-(e)s, Schränke) m cupboard;
(*Kleiderschrank*) wardrobe (*Brit*), closet
(*US*)
Schranke (-, -n) f barrier
Schrankwand f wall unit
Schraube (-, -n) f screw; **schrauben** vt to
screw; **Schraubendreher** (-s, -) m
screwdriver; **Schraubenschlüssel** m
spanner; **Schraubenzieher** (-s, -) m
screwdriver; **Schraubverschluss** m
screw top, screw cap
Schreck (-(e)s, -e) m, **Schrecken** (-s, -) m
terror; (*Angst*) fright; **jdm einen
~ einjagen** to give sb a fright;
schreckhaft adj jumpy; **schrecklich** adj
terrible, dreadful
Schrei (-(e)s, -e) m scream; (*Ruf*) shout
Schreibblock m writing pad; **schreiben**
(*schrieb, geschrieben*) vt, vi to write;
(*buchstabieren*) to spell; **wie schreibt man
...?** how do you spell ...?; **Schreiben** (-s, -)
nt writing; (*Brief*) letter; **Schreibfehler** m
spelling mistake; **schreibgeschützt** adj
(*Diskette*) write-protected; **Schreibtisch**

m desk; **Schreibwaren** *pl* stationery *sing*; **Schreibwarenladen** *m* stationer's

schreien *(schrie, geschrie(e)n) vt, vi* to scream; *(rufen)* to shout

Schreiner(in) *m(f)* joiner; **Schreinerei** *f* joiner's workshop

schrie *imperf von* **schreien**

schrieb *imperf von* **schreiben**

Schrift *(-, -en) f* writing; *(Handschrift)* handwriting; *(Schriftart)* typeface; *(Schrifttyp)* font; **schriftlich** *adj* written ▷ *adv* in writing; **würden Sie uns das bitte ~ geben?** could we have that in writing, please?; **Schriftsteller(in)** *(-s, -) m(f)* writer

Schritt *(-(e)s, -e) m* step; **~ für ~** step by step; **~e gegen etw unternehmen** to take steps against sth; **Schrittgeschwindigkeit** *f* walking speed; **Schrittmacher** *m (Med)* pacemaker

Schrott *(-(e)s, -e) m* scrap metal; *(fig)* rubbish

schrubben *vi, vt* to scrub; **Schrubber** *(-s, -) m* scrubbing brush

schrumpfen *vi* to shrink

Schubkarren *(-s, -) m* wheelbarrow; **Schublade** *f* drawer

schubsen *vt* to shove, to push

schüchtern *adj* shy

schuf *imperf von* **schaffen**

Schuh *(-(e)s, -e) m* shoe; **Schuhcreme** *f* shoe polish; **Schuhgeschäft** *nt* shoe shop; **Schuhgröße** *f* shoe size; **Schuhlöffel** *m* shoehorn; **Schuhsohle** *f* sole

Schulabschluss *m* school-leaving qualification

schuld *adj* **wer ist ~ daran?** whose fault is it?; **er ist ~** it's his fault, he's to blame; **Schuld** *(-) f* guilt; *(Verschulden)* fault; **~ haben** to be to blame *(an +dat* for); **er hat ~** it's his fault; **sie gibt mir die ~ an dem Unfall** she blames me for the accident; **schulden** *vt* to owe *(jdm etw* sb sth); **Schulden** *pl* debts *pl*; **~ haben** to be in debt; **~ machen** to run up debts; **seine ~ bezahlen** to pay off one's debts; **schuldig** *adj* guilty *(an +dat* of); *(gebührend)* due; **jdm etw ~ sein** to owe sb sth

Schule *(-, -n) f* school; **in der ~** at school; **in die ~ gehen** to go to school;

Schüler(in) *(-s, -) m(f) (jüngerer)* pupil; *(älterer)* student; **Schüleraustausch** *m* school exchange; **Schulfach** *nt* subject; **Schulferien** *pl* school holidays *pl (Brit) (o* vacation *(US))*; **schulfrei** *adj* **morgen ist ~** there's no school tomorrow; **Schulfreund(in)** *m(f)* schoolmate; **Schuljahr** *nt* school year; **Schulkenntnisse** *pl* **~ in Französisch** school(-level) French; **Schulklasse** *f* class; **Schulleiter(in)** *m(f)* headmaster/headmistress *(Brit)*, principal *(US)*

Schulter *(-, -n) f* shoulder; **Schulterblatt** *nt* shoulder blade

Schulung *f* training; *(Veranstaltung)* training course

Schund *(-(e)s) m* trash

Schuppe *(-, -n) f (von Fisch)* scale; **schuppen** *vt* to scale ▷ *vr* **sich ~** to peel; **Schuppen** *pl (im Haar)* dandruff *sing*

Schürfwunde *f* graze

Schürze *(-, -n) f* apron

Schuss *(-es, Schüsse) m* shot; **mit einem ~ Wodka** with a dash of vodka

Schüssel *(-, -n) f* bowl

Schuster(in) *(-s, -) m(f)* shoemaker

Schutt *(-(e)s) m* rubble

Schüttelfrost *m* shivering fit; **schütteln** *vt* to shake ▷ *vr* **sich ~** to shake

schütten *vt* to pour; *(Zucker, Kies etc)* to tip ▷ *vi impers* to pour (down)

Schutz *(-es) m* protection *(gegen, vor* against, from); *(Unterschlupf)* shelter; **jdn in ~ nehmen** to stand up for sb; **Schutzblech** *nt* mudguard; **Schutzbrief** *m* travel insurance document for drivers; **Schutzbrille** *f* (safety) goggles *pl*

Schütze *(-n, -n) m (beim Fußball)* scorer; *(Astr)* Sagittarius

schützen *vt* **jdn gegen/vor etw ~** to protect sb against/from sth; **Schutzimpfung** *f* inoculation, vaccination

schwach *adj* weak; **~e Augen** poor eyesight *sing*; **Schwäche** *(-, -n) f* weakness; **Schwachstelle** *f* weak point; **Schwachstrom** *m* low-voltage current

Schwager *(-s, Schwäger) m* brother-in-law; **Schwägerin** *f* sister-in-law

Schwalbe *(-, -n) f* swallow; *(beim Fußball)* dive

schwamm imperf von **schwimmen**

Schwamm (-(e)s, Schwämme) m sponge;
~ **drüber!** (fam) let's forget it!

Schwan (-(e)s, Schwäne) m swan

schwanger adj pregnant; **im vierten
Monat ~ sein** to be four months
pregnant; **Schwangerschaft** f
pregnancy; **Schwangerschaftsabbruch**
m abortion; **Schwangerschaftstest** m
pregnancy test

schwanken vi to sway; (Preise, Zahlen) to
fluctuate; (zögern) to hesitate; (taumeln) to
stagger; **ich schwanke zwischen A und B**
I can't decide between A and B

Schwanz (-es, Schwänze) m tail; (vulg:
Penis) cock

Schwarm (-(e)s, Schwärme) m swarm;
(fam: angehimmelte Person) heartthrob;
schwärmen vi to swarm; ~ **für** to be mad
about

schwarz adj black; ~ **sehen** (fam) to be
pessimistic (für about); **mir wurde ~ vor
Augen** everything went black;
Schwarzarbeit f illicit work; **Schwarzbrot**
nt black bread; **schwarz|fahren** irr vi to
travel without a ticket; (ohne Führerschein)
to drive without a licence;
Schwarzfahrer(in) m(f) fare-dodger;
Schwarzmarkt m black market;
Schwarzwald m Black Forest;
schwarzweiß adj black and white;
Schwarzwurzel f black salsify

schwatzen vi to chatter; **Schwätzer(in)**
(-s, -) m(f) chatterbox; (Schwafler) gasbag;
(Klatschmaul) gossip

Schwebebahn f suspension railway;
schweben vi to float; (hoch) to soar

Schwede (-n, -n) m Swede; **Schweden**
(-s) nt Sweden; **Schwedin** f Swede;
schwedisch adj Swedish; **Schwedisch** nt
Swedish

Schwefel (-s) m sulphur

schweigen (schwieg, geschwiegen) vi to be
silent; (nicht mehr reden) to stop talking;
Schweigen (-s) nt silence;
Schweigepflicht f duty of
confidentiality; **die ärztliche ~** medical
confidentiality

Schwein (-(e)s, -e) nt pig; (fam: Glück) luck;
(fam: gemeiner Mensch) swine;
Schweinebraten m roast pork;
Schweinefleisch nt pork; **Schweinerei** f
mess; (Gemeinheit) dirty trick

Schweiß (-es) m sweat

schweißen vt, vi to weld

Schweißfüße pl sweaty feet pl

Schweiz (-) f **die ~** Switzerland;
Schweizer(in) (-s, -) m(f) Swiss;
Schweizerdeutsch nt Swiss German;
schweizerisch adj Swiss

Schwelle (-, -n) f doorstep; (a. fig)
threshold

schwellen vi to swell (up); **Schwellung** f
swelling

schwer adj heavy; (schwierig) difficult,
hard; (schlimm) serious, bad; **er ist ~ zu
verstehen** it's difficult to understand
what he's saying ▷ adv (sehr) really;
(verletzt etc) seriously, badly; **jdm ~ fallen**
to be difficult for sb; **etw ~ nehmen** to
take sth hard; **Schwerbehinderte(r)** mf
severely disabled person; **schwerhörig**
adj hard of hearing

Schwert (-(e)s, -er) nt sword; **Schwertlilie**
f iris

Schwester (-, -n) f sister; (Med) nurse

schwieg imperf von **schweigen**

Schwiegereltern pl parents-in-law pl;
Schwiegermutter f mother-in-law;
Schwiegersohn m son-in-law;
Schwiegertochter f daughter-in-law;
Schwiegervater m father-in-law

schwierig adj difficult, hard;
Schwierigkeit f difficulty; **in ~en
kommen** to get into trouble; **jdm ~en
machen** to make things difficult for sb

Schwimmbad nt swimming pool;
Schwimmbecken nt swimming pool;
schwimmen (schwamm, geschwommen) vi
to swim; (treiben) to float; (fig: unsicher
sein) to be all at sea; **Schwimmer(in)** m(f)
swimmer; **Schwimmflosse** f flipper;
Schwimmflügel m water wing;
Schwimmreifen m rubber ring;
Schwimmweste f life jacket

Schwindel (-s) m dizziness; (Anfall) dizzy
spell; (Betrug) swindle; **schwindelfrei** adj
nicht ~ sein to suffer from vertigo; ~ **sein**
to have a head for heights; **schwindlig** adj
dizzy; **mir ist ~** I feel dizzy

Schwips m **einen ~ haben** to be tipsy

schwitzen vi to sweat

schwoll imperf von **schwellen**

schwor imperf von **schwören**

schwören (schwor, geschworen) vt, vi to
swear; **einen Eid ~** to take an oath

schwul *adj* gay

schwül *adj* close

Schwung (-(e)s, Schwünge) *m* swing; (Triebkraft) momentum; (fig: Energie) energy; (fam: Menge) batch; **in ~ kommen** to get going

Schwur (-s, Schwüre) *m* oath

scrollen *vi* (Inform) to scroll

sechs *num* six; **Sechs** (-, -en) *f* six; (Schulnote) ≈ F; **Sechserpack** *m* sixpack; **sechshundert** *num* six hundred; **sechsmal** *adv* six times; **sechste(r, s)** *adj* sixth; *siehe auch* **dritte**; **Sechstel** (-s, -) *nt* sixth; **sechzehn** *num* sixteen; **sechzehnte(r, s)** *adj* sixteenth; *siehe auch* **dritte**; **sechzig** *num* sixty; **in den ~er Jahren** in the sixties; **sechzigste(r, s)** *adj* sixtieth

Secondhandladen *m* secondhand shop

See (-, -n) *f* sea; **an der ~** by the sea ▷ (-s, -n) *m* lake; **am ~** by the lake; **Seegang** *m* waves; **hoher/schwerer/leichter ~** rough/heavy/calm seas *pl*; **Seehund** *m* seal; **Seeigel** *m* sea urchin; **seekrank** *adj* seasick

Seele (-, -n) *f* soul

Seeleute *pl* seamen *pl*, sailors *pl*

seelisch *adj* mental, psychological

Seelöwe *m* sea lion; **Seemann** *m* sailor, seaman; **Seemeile** *f* nautical mile; **Seemöwe** *f* seagull; **Seenot** *f* distress (at sea); **Seepferdchen** *nt* sea horse; **Seerose** *f* water lily; **Seestern** *m* starfish; **Seezunge** *f* sole

Segel (-s, -) *nt* sail; **Segelboot** *nt* yacht; **Segelfliegen** (-s) *nt* gliding; **Segelflugzeug** *nt* glider; **segeln** *vt, vi* to sail; **Segelschiff** *nt* sailing ship

sehbehindert *adj* partially sighted

sehen (sah, gesehen) *vt, vi* to see; (in bestimmte Richtung) to look; **gut/schlecht ~** to have good/bad eyesight; **auf die Uhr ~** to look at one's watch; **kann ich das mal ~?** can I have a look at it?; **wir ~ uns morgen!** see you tomorrow; **ich kenne sie nur vom Sehen** I only know her by sight; **Sehenswürdigkeiten** *pl* sights *pl*

Sehne (-, -n) *f* tendon; (an Bogen) string

sehnen *vr* **sich ~** to long (nach for)

Sehnenscheidenentzündung *f* (Med) tendovaginitis; **Sehnenzerrung** *f* (Med) pulled tendon

Sehnsucht *f* longing; **sehnsüchtig** *adj* longing

sehr *adv* (vor Adjektiv, Adverb) very; (mit Verben) a lot, very much; **zu ~** too much

seicht *adj* shallow

Seide (-, -n) *f* silk

Seife (-, -n) *f* soap; **Seifenoper** *f* soap (opera); **Seifenschale** *f* soap dish

Seil (-(e)s, -e) *nt* rope; (Kabel) cable; **Seilbahn** *f* cable railway

---

⬤ **SCHLÜSSELWORT**

sein (pt **war**, pp **gewesen**) *vi* **1** to be; **ich bin** I am; **du bist** you are; **er/sie/es ist** he/she/it is; **wir sind/ihr seid/sie sind** we/you/they are; **wir waren** we were; **wir sind gewesen** we have been

2: **seien Sie nicht böse** don't be angry; **sei so gut und ...** be so kind as to ...; **das wäre gut** that would *od* that'd be a good thing; **wenn ich Sie wäre** if I were *od* was you; **das wärs** that's all, that's it; **morgen bin ich in Rom** tomorrow I'll *od* I will be in Rome; **waren Sie mal in Rom?** have you ever been to Rome?

3: **wie ist das zu verstehen?** how is that to be understood?; **er ist nicht zu ersetzen** he cannot be replaced; **mit ihr ist nicht zu reden** you can't talk to her

4: **mir ist kalt** I'm cold; **was ist?** what's the matter?, what is it?; **ist was?** is something the matter?; **es sei denn, dass ...** unless ...; **wie dem auch sei** be that as it may; **wie wäre es mit ...?** how *od* what about ...?; **lass das sein!** stop that!

---

seit *conj* (bei Zeitpunkt) since; (bei Zeitraum) for; **er ist ~ Montag hier** he's been here since Monday; **er ist ~ einer Woche hier** he's been here for a week; **~ langem** for a long time; **seitdem** *adv, conj* since

Seite (-, -n) *f* side; (in Buch) page; **zur ~ gehen** to step aside; **Seitenairbag** *m* side-impact airbag; **Seitenaufprallschutz** *m* (Auto) side-impact protection; **Seitensprung** *m* affair; **Seitenstechen** (-s) *nt* **~ haben/bekommen** to have/get a stitch; **Seitenstraße** *f* side street; **Seitenstreifen** *m* hard shoulder (Brit), shoulder (US); **seitenverkehrt** *adj* the

S

wrong way round; **Seitenwind** m crosswind

seither adv since (then)

seitlich adj side

Sekretär(in) m(f) secretary

Sekt (-(e)s, -e) m sparkling wine (similar to champagne)

Sekte (-, -n) f sect

Sekunde (-, -n) f second; **Sekundenkleber** (-s, -) m superglue; **Sekundenschnelle** f **es geschah alles in ~** it was all over in a matter of seconds

○ SCHLÜSSELWORT

selbst pron 1: **ich/er/wir selbst** I myself/he himself/we ourselves; **sie ist die Tugend selbst** she's virtue itself; **er braut sein Bier selbst** he brews his own beer; **wie gehts? — gut, und selbst?** how are things? — fine, and yourself?
2 (ohne Hilfe) alone on my/his/one's etc own; **von selbst** by itself; **er kam von selbst** he came of his own accord; **selbst gemacht** home-made
▷ adv even; **selbst wenn** even if; **selbst Gott** even God (himself)

selbständig adj siehe **selbstständig**

Selbstauslöser (-s, -) m (Foto) self-timer; **Selbstbedienung** f self-service; **Selbstbefriedigung** f masturbation; **Selbstbeherrschung** f self-control; **Selbstbeteiligung** f (einer Versicherung) excess; **selbstbewusst** adj (self-)confident; **Selbstbräuner** (-s, -) m self-tanning lotion; **selbstgemacht** adj self-made; **Selbstgespräch** nt **~e führen** to talk to oneself; **selbstklebend** adj self-adhesive; **Selbstkostenpreis** m cost price; **Selbstlaut** m vowel; **Selbstmord** m suicide; **selbstsicher** adj self-assured; **selbstständig** adj independent; (arbeitend) self-employed; **Selbstverpflegung** f self-catering; **selbstverständlich** adj obvious; **ich halte das für ~** I take that for granted ▷ adv naturally; **Selbstvertrauen** nt self-confidence

Sellerie (-s, -(s)) m (-, -n) f (Knollensellerie) celeriac; (Stangensellerie) celery

selten adj rare ▷ adv seldom, rarely

seltsam adj strange;

~ schmecken/riechen to taste/smell strange

Semester (-s, -) nt semester; **Semesterferien** pl vacation sing

Semikolon (-s, Semikola) nt semicolon

Seminar (-s, -e) nt seminar

Semmel (-, -n) f roll; **Semmelbrösel** pl breadcrumbs

Senat (-(e)s, -e) m senate

senden (sandte, gesandt) vt to send ▷ vt, vi (Radio, Tv) to broadcast; **Sender** (-s, -) m (TV) channel; (Radio) station; (Anlage) transmitter; **Sendung** f (Radio, Tv) broadcasting; (Programm) programme

Senf (-(e)s, -e) m mustard

Senior(in) m(f) senior citizen; **Seniorenpass** m senior citizen's travel pass

senken vt to lower ▷ vr **sich ~** to sink

senkrecht adj vertical

Sensation (-, -en) f sensation

sensibel adj sensitive

sentimental adj sentimental

separat adj separate

September (-(s), -) m September; siehe auch **Juni**

Serbien (-s) nt Serbia

Serie f series sing

seriös adj (ernsthaft) serious; (anständig) respectable

Serpentine f hairpin (bend)

Serum (-s, Seren) nt serum

Server (-s, -) m (Inform) server

Service (-(s), -) nt (Geschirr) service ▷ (-, -s) m service

servieren vt, vi to serve

Serviette f napkin, serviette

Servolenkung f (Auto) power steering

Sesam (-s, -s) m sesame seeds pl

Sessel (-s, -) m armchair; **Sessellift** m chairlift

Set (-s, -s) m o nt set; (Tischset) tablemat

setzen vt to put; (Baum etc) to plant; (Segel) to set ▷ vr **sich ~** to settle; (hinsetzen) to sit down; **~ Sie sich doch** please sit down

Seuche (-, -n) f epidemic

seufzen vt, vi to sigh

Sex (-(es)) m sex; **Sexismus** m sexism; **sexistisch** adj sexist; **Sextourismus** m sex tourism; **Sexualität** f sexuality; **sexuell** adj sexual

Seychellen pl Seychelles pl
sfr abk = **Schweizer Franken** Swiss franc(s)
Shampoo (-s, -s) nt shampoo
Shareware (-, -s) f (Inform) shareware
Shorts pl shorts pl
Shuttlebus m shuttle bus

O SCHLÜSSELWORT

sich pron 1 (akk); **er/sie/es ... sich**
he/she/it ... himself/herself/itself; **sie**
pl/**man ... sich** they/one ...
themselves/oneself; **Sie ... sich** you ...
yourself/yourselves pl; **sich wiederholen**
to repeat oneself/itself
2 (dat): **er/sie/es ... sich** he/she/it ... to
himself/herself/itself; **sie** pl/**man ... sich**
they/one ... to themselves/oneself; **Sie ...
sich** you ... to yourself/yourselves pl; **sie
hat sich einen Pullover gekauft** she
bought herself a jumper; **sich die Haare
waschen** to wash one's hair
3 (mit Präposition): **haben Sie Ihren
Ausweis bei sich?** do you have your
pass on you?; **er hat nichts bei sich** he's
got nothing on him; **sie bleiben gern
unter sich** they keep themselves to
themselves
4 (einander) each other one another; **sie
bekämpfen sich** they fight each other od
one another
5: **dieses Auto fährt sich gut** this car
drives well; **hier sitzt es sich gut** it's good
to sit here

sicher adj safe (vor +dat from); (gewiss)
certain (gen of); (zuverlässig) reliable;
(selbstsicher) confident; **aber ~!** of course,
sure; **Sicherheit** f safety; (Aufgabe von
Sicherheitsbeamten) (Fin) security;
(Gewissheit) certainty; (Selbstsicherheit)
confidence; **mit ~** definitely;
Sicherheitsabstand m safe distance;
Sicherheitsgurt m seat belt;
sicherheitshalber adv just to be on the
safe side; **Sicherheitsnadel** f safety pin;
Sicherheitsvorkehrung f safety
precaution; **sicherlich** adv certainly;
(wahrscheinlich) probably
sichern vt to secure (gegen against);
(schützen) to protect; (Daten) to back up;
Sicherung f (Sichern) securing;

(Vorrichtung) safety device; (an Waffen)
safety catch; (Elek) fuse; (Inform) backup;
die ~ ist durchgebrannt the fuse has
blown
Sicht (-) f sight; (Aussicht) view; **sichtbar**
adj visible; **sichtlich** adj evident, obvious;
Sichtverhältnisse pl visibility sing;
Sichtweite f in/außer ~ within/out of
sight
sie pron (3. Person sing) she; (3. Person pl)
they; (akk von sing) her; (akk von pl) them;
(für eine Sache) it; **da ist ~ ja** there she is; **da
sind ~ ja** there they are; **ich kenne ~** (Frau)
I know her; (mehrere Personen) I know
them; **~ lag gerade noch hier** (meine Jacke,
Uhr) it was here just a minute ago; **ich hab
~ gefunden** (meine Jacke, Uhr) I've found it;
**hast du meine Brille/Hose gesehen? -
ich kann ~ nirgends finden** have you
seen my glasses/trousers? - I can't find
them anywhere
Sie pron (Höflichkeitsform, Nom und Akk) you
Sieb (-(e)s, -e) nt sieve; (Teesieb) strainer
sieben num seven; **siebenhundert** num
seven hundred; **siebenmal** adv seven
times; **siebte(r, s)** adj seventh; siehe auch
dritte; **Siebtel** (-s, -) nt seventh; **siebzehn**
num seventeen; **siebzehnte(r, s)** adj
seventeenth; siehe auch **dritte**; **siebzig**
num seventy; **in den ~er Jahren** in the
seventies; **siebzigste(r, s)** adj seventieth
Siedlung (-, -en) f (Wohngebiet) housing
estate (Brit) (o development (US))
Sieg (-(e)s, -e) m victory; **siegen** vi to win;
Sieger(in) (-s, -) m(f) winner;
Siegerehrung f presentation ceremony
siehe imper see
siezen vt to address as 'Sie'
Signal (-s, -e) nt signal
Silbe (-, -n) f syllable
Silber (-s) nt silver; **Silberhochzeit** f
silver wedding; **Silbermedaille** f silver
medal
Silikon (-s, -e) nt silicone
Silvester (-s, -) nt, **Silvesterabend** m
New Year's Eve, Hogmanay (SCOT)

● **Silvester**
●
● **Silvester** is the German name for New
● Year's Eve. Although not an official
● holiday, most businesses close early
● and shops shut at midday. Most

S

Germans celebrate in the evening
and at midnight they let off
fireworks and rockets; the revelry
usually lasts until the early hours of
the morning.

Simbabwe (-s) nt Zimbabwe

simpel adj simple

simultan adj simultaneous

simsen vt, vi (fam) to text

Sinfonie (-, -n) f symphony; **Sinfonieorchester** nt symphony orchestra

Singapur (-s) nt Singapore

singen (sang, gesungen) vt, vi to sing; **richtig/falsch ~** to sing in tune/out of tune

Single (-, -s) f (CD) single ▷ (-s, -s) m (Mensch) single

Singular m singular

sinken (sank, gesunken) vi to sink; (Preise etc) to fall, to go down

Sinn (-(e)s, -e) m (Denken) mind; (Wahrnehmung) sense; (Bedeutung) sense, meaning; **~ machen** to make sense; **das hat keinen ~** it's no use; **sinnlich** adj sensuous; (erotisch) sensual; (Wahrnehmung) sensory; **sinnlos** adj (unsinnig) stupid; (Verhalten) senseless; (zwecklos) pointless; (bedeutungslos) meaningless; **sinnvoll** adj meaningful; (vernünftig) sensible

Sirup (-s, -e) m syrup

Sitte (-, -n) f custom

Situation f situation

Sitz (-es, -e) m seat; **sitzen** (saß, gesessen) vi to sit; (Bemerkung, Schlag) to strike home; (Gelerntes) to have sunk in; **der Rock sitzt gut** the skirt is a good fit; **Sitzgelegenheit** f place to sit down; **Sitzplatz** m seat; **Sitzung** f meeting

Sizilien (-s) nt Sicily

Skandal (-s, -e) m scandal

Skandinavien (-s) nt Scandinavia

Skateboard (-s, -s) nt skateboard; **Skateboardfahrer(in)** m(f) skateboarder

Skelett (-s, -e) nt skeleton

skeptisch adj sceptical

Ski (-s, -er) m ski; **~ laufen** (o **fahren**) to ski; **Skianzug** m ski suit; **Skibrille** f ski goggles pl; **Skifahren** (-s) nt skiing; **Skigebiet** (-s, -e) nt skiing area; **Skihose** f skiing trousers pl; **Skikurs** m skiing course;

Skilanglauf m cross-country skiing; **Skiläufer(in)** m(f) skier; **Skilehrer(in)** m(f) ski instructor; **Skilift** m ski-lift

Skinhead (-s, -s) m skinhead

Skipiste f ski run; **Skischanze** (-, -n) f ski jump; **Skischuh** m ski boot; **Skischule** f ski school; **Skispringen** (-s, -n) nt ski jumping; **Skistiefel** (-s, -) m ski boot; **Skistock** m ski pole; **Skiträger** m ski rack; **Skiurlaub** m skiing holiday (Brit) (o vacation (US))

Skizze (-, -n) f sketch

Skonto (-s, -s) m o nt discount

Skorpion (-s, -e) m (Zool) scorpion; (Astr) Scorpio

Skulptur (-, -en) f sculpture

S-Kurve f double bend

Slalom (-s, -s) m slalom

Slip (-s, -s) m (pair of) briefs pl; **Slipeinlage** f panty liner

Slowakei (-) f Slovakia; **slowakisch** adj Slovakian; **Slowakische Republik** Slovak Republic; **Slowakisch** nt Slovakian

Slowenien (-s) nt Slovenia; **slowenisch** adj Slovenian; **Slowenisch** nt Slovenian

Smiley (-s, -s) m smiley

Smog (-s) m smog; **Smogalarm** m smog alert

Smoking (-s, -s) m dinner jacket (Brit), tuxedo (US)

SMS nt abk = **Short Message Service** ▷ f (Nachricht) text message; **ich schicke dir eine ~** I'll text you, I'll send you a text (message)

Snowboard (-s, -s) nt snowboard; **Snowboardfahren** (-s) nt snowboarding; **Snowboardfahrer(in)** m(f) snowboarder

◯ **SCHLÜSSELWORT**

so adv **1** (so sehr) so; **so groß/schön** etc so big/nice etc; **so groß/schön wie ...** as big/nice as ...; **so viel (wie)** as much as; **rede nicht so viel** don't talk so much; **so weit sein** to be ready; **so weit wie** od **als möglich** as far as possible; **ich bin so weit zufrieden** by and large I'm quite satisfied; **so wenig (wie)** as little (as); **das hat ihn so geärgert, dass ...** that annoyed him so much that ...; **so einer wie ich** somebody like me; **na so was!** well, well!

2 (auf diese Weise) like this; **mach es nicht**

so don't do it like that; **so oder so** in one way or the other; **und so weiter** and so on; **... oder so was** ... or something like that; **das ist gut so** that's fine; **so gennant** so-called
3 (*umg: umsonst*); **ich habe es so bekommen** I got it for nothing
▷ *konj:* **so dass; sodass; so wie es jetzt ist** as things are at the moment
▷ *excl:* **so?** really?; **so, das wärs** so, that's it then

s. o. *abk* = **siehe oben** see above
sobald *conj* as soon as
Socke (-, -*n*) *f* sock
Sodbrennen (-*s*) *nt* heartburn
Sofa (-*s*, -*s*) *nt* sofa
sofern *conj* if, provided (that)
soff *imperf von* **saufen**
sofort *adv* immediately, at once;
  Sofortbildkamera *f* instant camera
Softeis *nt* soft ice-cream
Software (-, -*s*) *f* software
sog *imperf von* **saugen**
sogar *adv* even; **kalt, ~ sehr kalt** cold, in fact very cold
Sohle (-, -*n*) *f* sole
Sohn (-(*e*)*s*, *Söhne*) *m* son
Soja (-, *Sojen*) *f* soya; **Sojasprossen** *pl* bean sprouts *pl*
solang(e) *conj* as long as
Solarium *nt* solarium
Solarzelle *f* solar cell
solche(r, s) *pron* such; **eine ~ Frau, solch eine Frau** such a woman, a woman like that; **~ Sachen** things like that, such things; **ich habe ~ Kopfschmerzen** I've got such a headache; **ich habe ~n Hunger** I'm so hungry
Soldat(in) (-*en*, -*en*) *m*(*f*) soldier
solidarisch *adj* showing solidarity; **sich ~ erklären mit** to declare one's solidarity with
solid(e) *adj* solid; (*Leben, Mensch*) respectable
Soll (-(*s*), -(*s*)) *nt* (*Fin*) debit; (*Arbeitsmenge*) quota, target

SCHLÜSSELWORT

sollen (*pt* **sollte**, *pp* **gesollt** *od* (*als Hilfsverb*) **sollen**) *Hilfsverb* **1** (*Pflicht, Befehl*) to be

supposed to; **du hättest nicht gehen sollen** you shouldn't have gone, you oughtn't to have gone, **soll ich?** shall I?; **soll ich dir helfen?** shall I help you?; **sag ihm, er soll warten** tell him he's to wait; **was soll ich machen?** what should I do?
2 (*Vermutung*): **sie soll verheiratet sein** she's said to be married; **was soll das heißen?** what's that supposed to mean?; **man sollte glauben, dass ...** you would think that ...; **sollte das passieren, ...** if that should happen ...
▷ *vt, vi:* **was soll das?** what's all this?; **das sollst du nicht** you shouldn't do that; **was solls?** what the hell!

Solo (-*s*, -) *nt* solo
Sommer (-*s*, -) *m* summer;
  Sommerfahrplan *m* summer timetable;
  Sommerferien *pl* summer holidays *pl* (*Brit*) (*o* vacation *sing* (*US*)); **sommerlich** *adj* summery; (*Sommer-*) summer;
  Sommerreifen *m* normal tyre;
  Sommersprossen *pl* freckles *pl*;
  Sommerzeit *f* summertime; (*Uhrzeit*) daylight saving time
Sonderangebot *nt* special offer;
  sonderbar *adj* strange, odd;
  Sondermarke *f* special stamp;
  Sondermaschine *f* special plane;
  Sondermüll *m* hazardous waste
sondern *conj* but; **nicht nur ..., ~ auch** not only ..., but also
Sonderpreis *m* special price;
  Sonderschule *f* special school;
  Sonderzeichen *nt* (*Inform*) special character; **Sonderzug** *m* special train
Song (-*s*, -*s*) *m* song
Sonnabend *m* Saturday; *siehe auch* **Mittwoch**; **sonnabends** *adv* on Saturdays; **~ morgens** on Saturday mornings; *siehe auch* **mittwochs**
Sonne (-, -*n*) *f* sun; **sonnen** *vr* **sich ~** to sunbathe; **Sonnenallergie** *f* sun allergy; **Sonnenaufgang** *m* sunrise; **Sonnenblume** *f* sunflower; **Sonnenblumenkern** *m* sunflower seed; **Sonnenbrand** *m* sunburn; **Sonnenbrille** *f* sunglasses *pl*, shades *pl*; **Sonnencreme** *f* sun cream; **Sonnendach** *nt* (*an Haus*) awning; (*Auto*) sunroof; **Sonnendeck** *nt* sun deck; **Sonnenmilch** *f* suntan lotion;

Sonnenöl nt suntan oil; **Sonnenschein** m sunshine; **Sonnenschirm** m parasol, sunshade; **Sonnenschutzcreme** f sunscreen; **Sonnenstich** m sunstroke; **Sonnenstudio** nt solarium; **Sonnenuhr** f sundial; **Sonnenuntergang** m sunset; **sonnig** adj sunny

Sonntag m Sunday; siehe auch **Mittwoch**; **sonntags** adv on Sundays; siehe auch **mittwochs**

sonst adv, conj (außerdem) else; (andernfalls) otherwise, (or) else; (mit Pron, in Fragen) else; (normalerweise) normally, usually; **~ noch etwas?** anything else?; **~ nichts** nothing else

sooft conj whenever

Sopran (-s, -e) m soprano

Sorge (-, -n) f worry; (Fürsorge) care; **sich** (dat) **um jdn ~n machen** to be worried about sb; **sorgen** vi **für jdn ~** to look after sb; **für etw ~** to take care of sth, to see to sth ▷ vr **sich ~** to worry (um about); **sorgfältig** adj careful

sortieren vt to sort (out)

Sortiment nt assortment

sosehr conj however much

Soße (-, -n) f sauce; (zu Braten) gravy

Soundkarte f (Inform) sound card

Souvenir (-s, -s) nt souvenir

soviel conj as far as

soweit conj as far as

sowie conj (wie auch) as well as; (sobald) as soon as

sowohl conj **~ ... als** (o **wie**) **auch** both ... and

sozial adj social; **Sozialhilfe** f income support (Brit), welfare (aid) (US); **Sozialismus** m socialism; **Sozialversicherung** f social security; **Sozialwohnung** f council flat (Brit), state-subsidized apartment (US)

Soziologie f sociology

sozusagen adv so to speak

Spachtel (-s, -) m spatula

Spag(h)etti pl spaghetti sing

Spalte (-, -n) f crack; (Gletscher) crevasse; (in Text) column

spalten vt to split ▷ vr **sich ~** to split

Spange (-, -n) f clasp; (Haarspange) hair slide (Brit), barrette (US)

Spanien (-s) nt Spain; **Spanier(in)** (-s, -) m(f) Spaniard; **spanisch** adj Spanish; **Spanisch** nt Spanish

spann imperf von **spinnen**

spannen vt (straffen) to tighten; (befestigen) to brace ▷ vi to be tight

spannend adj exciting, gripping; **Spannung** f tension; (Elek) voltage; (fig) suspense

Sparbuch nt savings book; (Konto) savings account; **sparen** vt, vi to save

Spargel (-s, -) m asparagus; **Spargelsuppe** f asparagus soup

Sparkasse f savings bank; **Sparkonto** f savings account

spärlich adj meagre; (Bekleidung) scanty

sparsam adj economical; **Sparschwein** nt piggy bank

Spaß (-es, Späße) m joke; (Freude) fun; **es macht mir ~** I enjoy it, it's (great) fun; **viel ~!** have fun

spät adj, adv late; **zu ~ kommen** to be late

Spaten (-s, -) m spade

später adj, adv later; **spätestens** adv at the latest; **Spätlese** f late vintage (wine); **Spätvorstellung** f late-night performance

Spatz (-en, -en) m sparrow

spazieren vi to stroll, to walk; **~ gehen** to go for a walk; **Spaziergang** m walk

Specht (-(e)s, -e) m woodpecker

Speck (-(e)s, -e) m bacon fat; (durchwachsen) bacon

Spedition f (für Umzug) removal firm

Speiche (-, -n) f spoke

Speichel (-s) m saliva

Speicher (-s, -) m storehouse; (Dachboden) attic; (Inform) memory; **speichern** vt (Inform) to store; (sichern) to save

Speise (-, -n) f food; (Gericht) dish; **Speisekarte** f menu; **Speiseröhre** f gullet, oesophagus; **Speisesaal** m dining hall; **Speisewagen** m dining car

Spende (-, -n) f donation; **spenden** vt to donate, to give

spendieren vt **jdm etw ~** to treat sb to sth

Sperre (-, -n) f barrier; (Verbot) ban; **sperren** vt to block; (Sport) to suspend; (verbieten) to ban

Sperrgepäck m bulky luggage; **Sperrmüll** m bulky refuse; **Sperrstunde** f closing time; **Sperrung** f closing

Spesen pl expenses pl

spezialisieren vr **sich ~** to specialize (auf

Spiegel (-s, -) m mirror; **Spiegelei** nt fried egg (sunny-side up (US)); **spiegelglatt** adj very slippery; **Spiegelreflexkamera** f reflex camera

Spiel (-(e)s, -e) nt game; (Tätigkeit) play(ing); (Karten) pack, deck; (Tech) (free) play; **Spielautomat** m (ohne Geldgewinn) gaming machine; (mit Geldgewinn) slot machine; **spielen** vt, vi to play; (um Geld) to gamble; (Theat) to perform, to act; **Klavier ~** to play the piano; **spielend** adv easily; **Spieler(in)** (-s, -) m(f) player; (um Geld) gambler; **Spielfeld** nt (für Fußball, Hockey) field; (für Basketball) court; **Spielfilm** m feature film; **Spielkasino** nt casino; **Spielplatz** m playground; **Spielraum** m room to manoeuvre; **Spielregel** f rule; **sich an die ~n halten** to stick to the rules; **Spielsachen** pl toys pl; **Spielverderber(in)** (-s, -) m(f) spoilsport; **Spielzeug** nt toys pl; (einzelnes) toy

Spieß (-es, -e) m spear; (Bratspieß) spit; **Spießer(in)** (-s, -) m(f) square, stuffy type; **spießig** adj square, uncool

Spikes pl (Sport) spikes pl; (Auto) studs pl

Spinat (-(e)s, -e) m spinach

Spinne (-, -n) f spider; **spinnen** (spann, gesponnen) vt, vi to spin; (fam: Unsinn reden) to talk rubbish; (verrückt sein) to be crazy; **du spinnst!** you must be mad; **Spinnwebe** (-, -n) f cobweb

Spion(in) (-s, -e) m(f) spy; **spionieren** vi to spy; (fig) to snoop around

Spirale (-, -n) f spiral; (Med) coil

Spirituosen pl spirits pl, liquor sing (US)

Spiritus (-, -se) m spirit

spitz adj (Nase, Kinn) pointed; (Bleistift, Messer) sharp; (Winkel) acute; **Spitze** (-, -n) f point; (von Finger, Nase) tip; (Bemerkung) taunt, dig; (erster Platz) lead; (Gewebe) lace; **Spitzengeschwindigkeit** f top speed; **Spitzer** (-s, -) m pencil sharpener; **Spitzname** m nickname

Spliss (-) m split ends pl

sponsern vt to sponsor; **Sponsor(in)** (-s, -en) m(f) sponsor

spontan adj spontaneous

Sport (-(e)s, -e) m sport; **~ treiben** to do sport; **Sportanlage** f sports grounds pl; **Sportart** f sport; **Sportbekleidung** f sportswear; **Sportgeschäft** nt sports shop; **Sporthalle** f gymnasium, gym; **Sportlehrer(in)** (-s, -) m(f) sports instructor; (Schule) PE teacher; **Sportler(in)** (-s, -) m(f) sportsman/ -woman; **sportlich** adj sporting; (Mensch) sporty; **Sportplatz** m playing field; **Sporttauchen** nt (skin-)diving; (mit Gerät) scuba-diving; **Sportverein** m sports club; **Sportwagen** m sports car

sprach imperf von **sprechen**

Sprache (-, -n) f language; (Sprechen) speech; **Sprachenschule** f language school; **Sprachführer** m phrasebook; **Sprachkenntnisse** pl knowledge sing of languages; **gute englische ~ haben** to have a good knowledge of English; **Sprachkurs** m language course; **Sprachunterricht** m language teaching

sprang imperf von **springen**

Spray (-s, -s) m o nt spray

Sprechanlage f intercom; **sprechen** (sprach, gesprochen) vt, vi to speak (jdn, mit jdm to sb); (sich unterhalten) to talk (mit to, über, von about); **~ Sie Deutsch?** do you speak German?; **kann ich bitte mit David ~?** (am Telefon) can I speak to David, please?; **Sprecher(in)** m(f) speaker; (Ansager) announcer; **Sprechstunde** f consultation; (Arzt) surgery hours pl; (Anwalt etc) office hours pl; **Sprechzimmer** nt consulting room

Sprengstoff m explosive

Sprichwort nt proverb

Springbrunnen m fountain

springen (sprang, gesprungen) vi to jump; (Glas) to crack; (mit Kopfsprung) to dive

Sprit (-(e)s, -e) m (fam: Benzin) petrol (Brit), gas (US)

Spritze (-, -n) f (Gegenstand) syringe; (Injektion) injection; (an Schlauch) nozzle; **spritzen** vt to spray; (Med) to inject ▷ vi to splash; (Med) to give injections

Spruch (-(e)s, Sprüche) m saying

Sprudel (-s, -) m sparkling mineral water; (süßer) fizzy drink (Brit), soda (US); **sprudeln** vi to bubble

Sprühdose f aerosol (can); **sprühen** vt, vi to spray; (fig) to sparkle; **Sprühregen** m drizzle

Sprung (-(e)s, Sprünge) m jump; (Riss) crack; **Sprungbrett** nt springboard;

S

Sprungschanze f ski jump; **Sprungturm** m diving platforms pl

Spucke (-) f spit; **spucken** vt, vi to spit; (fam: sich erbrechen) to vomit; **Spucktüte** f sick bag

spuken vi (Geist) to walk; **hier spukt es** this place is haunted

Spülbecken nt sink

Spule (-, -n) f spool; (Elek) coil

Spüle (-, -n) f sink; **spülen** vt, vi to rinse; (Geschirr) to wash up; (Toilette) to flush; **Spülmaschine** f dishwasher; **Spülmittel** nt washing-up liquid (Brit), dishwashing liquid (US); **Spültuch** nt dishcloth; **Spülung** f (von WC) flush

Spur (-, -en) f trace; (Fußspur, Radspur) track; (Fährte) trail; (Fahrspur) lane; **die ~ wechseln** to change lanes pl

spüren vt to feel; (merken) to notice; **Spürhund** m sniffer dog

Squash (-) nt squash; **Squashschläger** m squash racket

Sri Lanka (-s) nt Sri Lanka

Staat (-(e)s, -en) m state; **staatlich** adj state(-); (vom Staat betrieben) state-run; **Staatsangehörigkeit** f nationality; **Staatsanwalt** m, **-anwältin** f prosecuting counsel (Brit), district attorney (US); **Staatsbürger(in)** m(f) citizen; **Staatsbürgerschaft** f nationality; **doppelte ~** dual nationality; **Staatsexamen** nt final exam taken by trainee teachers, medical and law students

Stab (-(e)s, Stäbe) m rod; (Gitter) bar; **Stäbchen** nt (Essstäbchen) chopstick; **Stabhochsprung** m pole vault

stabil adj stable; (Möbel) sturdy

stach imperf von stechen

Stachel (-s, -n) m spike; (von Tier) spine; (von Insekten) sting; **Stachelbeere** f gooseberry; **Stacheldraht** m barbed wire; **stachelig** adj prickly

Stadion (-s, Stadien) nt stadium

Stadt (-, Städte) f town; (groß) city; **in der ~** in town; **Stadtautobahn** f urban motorway (Brit) (o expressway (US)); **Stadtbummel** (-s, -) m **einen ~ machen** to go round town; **Städtepartnerschaft** f twinning; **Stadtführer** m (Heft) city guide; **Stadtführung** f city sightseeing tour; **Stadthalle** f municipal hall; **städtisch** adj municipal; **Stadtmauer** f city wall(s); **Stadtmitte** f town/city

centre, downtown (US); **Stadtplan** m (street) map; **Stadtrand** m outskirts pl; **Stadtrundfahrt** f city tour; **Stadtteil** m, **Stadtviertel** nt district, part of town; **Stadtzentrum** nt town/city centre, downtown (US)

stahl imperf von stehlen

Stahl (-(e)s, Stähle) m steel

Stall (-(e)s, Ställe) m stable; (Kaninchen) hutch; (Schweine) pigsty; (Hühner) henhouse

Stamm (-(e)s, Stämme) m (Baum) trunk; (von Menschen) tribe; **stammen** vi **~ aus** to come from; **Stammgast** m regular (guest); **Stammkunde** m, **Stammkundin** f regular (customer); **Stammtisch** m table reserved for regulars

stampfen vt, vi to stamp; (mit Werkzeug) to pound; (stapfen) to tramp

stand imperf von stehen

Stand (-(e)s, Stände) m (Wasser, Benzin) level; (Stehen) standing position; (Zustand) state; (Spielstand) score; (auf Messe etc) stand; (Klasse) class; **im ~e sein** to be in a position; (fähig) to be able

Standby-Betrieb m stand-by; **Standby-Ticket** nt stand-by ticket

Ständer (-s, -) m (Gestell) stand; (fam: Erektion) hard-on

Standesamt nt registry office

ständig adj permanent; (ununterbrochen) constant, continual

Standlicht nt sidelights pl (Brit), parking lights pl (US); **Standort** m position; **Standpunkt** m standpoint; **Standspur** f (Auto) hard shoulder (Brit), shoulder (US)

Stange (-, -n) f stick; (Stab) pole; (Metall) bar; (Zigaretten) carton; **Stangenbohne** f runner (Brit) (o string (US)) bean; **Stangenbrot** nt French stick; **Stangensellerie** m celery

stank imperf von stinken

Stapel (-s, -) m pile

Star (-(e)s, -e) m (Vogel) starling; (Med) cataract ▷ (-s, -s) m (in Film etc) star

starb imperf von sterben

stark adj strong; (heftig, groß) heavy; (Maßangabe) thick; **Stärke** (-, -n) f strength; (Dicke) thickness; (Wäschestärke, Speisestärke) starch; **stärken** vt to strengthen; (Wäsche) to starch; **Starkstrom** m high-voltage current;

Stärkung f strengthening; (Essen) refreshment

starr adj stiff; (unnachgiebig) rigid; (Blick) staring

starren vi to stare

Start (-(e)s, -e) m start; (Aviat) takeoff; **Startautomatik** f automatic choke; **Startbahn** f runway; **starten** vt, vi to start; (Aviat) to take off; **Starthilfekabel** nt jump leads pl (Brit), jumper cables pl (US); **Startmenü** nt (Inform) start menu

Station f (Haltestelle) stop; (Bahnhof) station; (im Krankenhaus) ward; **stationär** adj stationary; **~e Behandlung** in-patient treatment; **jdn ~ behandeln** to treat sb as an in-patient

Statistik f statistics pl

Stativ nt tripod

statt conj, prep +gen o dat instead of; **~ zu arbeiten** instead of working

statt|finden irr vi to take place

Statue (-, -n) f statue

Statusleiste f, **Statuszeile** f (Inform) status bar

Stau (-(e)s, -e) m (im Verkehr) (traffic) jam; **im ~ stehen** to be stuck in a traffic jam

Staub (-(e)s) m dust; **~ wischen** to dust; **staubig** adj dusty; **staubsaugen** vt, vi to vacuum, to hoover (Brit); **Staubsauger** m vacuum cleaner, hoover® (Brit); **Staubtuch** nt duster

Staudamm m dam

staunen vi to be astonished (über +akk at)

Stausee m reservoir; **Stauung** f (von Wasser) damming-up; (von Blut, Verkehr) congestion; **Stauwarnung** f traffic report

Std. abk = **Stunde** h

Steak (-s, -s) nt steak

stechen (-(e)s, -e) m (mit Nadel etc) to prick; (mit Messer) to stab; (mit Finger) to poke; (Biene) to sting; (Mücke) to bite; (Sonne) to burn; (Kartenspiel) to trump; **Stechen** (-s, -) nt sharp pain, stabbing pain; **Stechmücke** f mosquito

Steckdose f socket; **stecken** vt to put; (Nadel) to stick; (beim Nähen) to pin ▷ vi (festsitzen) to be stuck; (Nadeln) to be (sticking); **der Schlüssel steckt** the key is in the door; **Stecker** (-s, -) m plug; **Stecknadel** f pin; **Steckrübe** f swede (Brit), rutabaga (US)

Steg (-s, -e) m bridge

stehen (stand, gestanden) vi to stand (zu by); (sich befinden) to be; (stillstehen) to have stopped; **was steht im Brief?** what does it say in the letter?; **jdm (gut) ~** to suit sb; **~ bleiben** (Uhr) to stop; **~ lassen** to leave ▷ vi impers **wie steht's?** (Sport) what's the score?; **Stehlampe** f standard lamp (Brit), floor lamp (US)

stehlen (stahl, gestohlen) vt to steal

Stehplatz m (im Konzert etc) standing ticket

Steiermark (-) f Styria

steif adj stiff

steigen (stieg, gestiegen) vi (Preise, Temperatur) to rise; (klettern) to climb; **~ in/auf** (+akk) to get in/on

steigern vt to increase ▷ vr **sich ~** to increase

Steigung f incline, gradient

steil adj steep; **Steilhang** m steep slope; **Steilküste** f steep coast

Stein (-(e)s, -e) m stone; **Steinbock** m (Zool) ibex; (Astr) Capricorn; **Steinbutt** (-s, -e) m turbot; **steinig** adj stony; **Steinschlag** m falling rocks pl

Stelle (-, -n) f place, spot; (Arbeit) post, job; (Amt) office; **ich an deiner ~** if I were you; **auf der ~** straightaway; **stellen** vt to put; (Uhr etc) to set (auf +akk to); (zur Verfügung stellen) to provide ▷ vr **sich ~** (bei Polizei) to give oneself up; **sich schlafend ~** to pretend to be asleep; **Stellenangebot** nt job offer, vacancy; **stellenweise** adv in places; **Stellenwert** m (fig) status; **einen hohen ~ haben** to play an important role; **Stellplatz** m parking space; **Stellung** f position; **zu etw ~ nehmen** to comment on sth; **Stellvertreter(in)** m(f) representative; (amtlich) deputy; (von Arzt) locum (Brit), locum tenens (US)

Stempel (-s, -) m stamp; **stempeln** vt to stamp; (Briefmarke) to cancel

sterben (starb, gestorben) vi to die

Stereoanlage f stereo (system)

steril adj sterile; **sterilisieren** vt to sterilize

Stern (-(e)s, -e) m star; **ein Hotel mit vier ~en** a four-star hotel; **Sternbild** nt constellation; (Sternzeichen) star sign, sign of the zodiac; **Sternfrucht** f star fruit; **Sternschnuppe** (-, -n) f shooting star; **Sternwarte** (-e, -n) f observatory; **Sternzeichen** nt star sign, sign of the

S

zodiac; **welches ~ bist du?** what's your star sign?

stets adv always

Steuer (-s, -) nt (Auto) steering wheel ▷ (-, -en) f tax; **Steuerberater(in)** m(f) tax adviser; **Steuerbord** nt starboard; **Steuererklärung** f tax declaration; **steuerfrei** adj tax-free; (Waren) duty-free; **Steuerknüppel** m control column; (Aviat, Inform) joystick; **steuern** vt, vi to steer; (Flugzeug) to pilot; (Entwicklung, Tonstärke) (Inform) to control; **steuerpflichtig** adj taxable; **Steuerung** f (Auto) steering; (Vorrichtung) controls pl; (Aviat) piloting; (fig) control; **Steuerungstaste** f (Inform) control key

Stich (-(e)s, -e) m (von Insekt) sting; (von Mücke) bite; (durch Messer) stab; (beim Nähen) stitch; (Färbung) tinge; (Kartenspiel) trick; (Kunst) engraving; **Stichprobe** f spot check

sticken vt, vi to embroider

Sticker (-s, -) m sticker

Stickerei f embroidery

stickig adj stuffy, close

Stiefbruder m stepbrother

Stiefel (-s, -) m boot

Stiefmutter f stepmother

Stiefmütterchen nt pansy

Stiefschwester f stepsister; **Stiefsohn** m stepson; **Stieftochter** f stepdaughter; **Stiefvater** m stepfather

stieg imperf von **steigen**

Stiege (-, -n) f steps pl

Stiel (-(e)s, -e) m handle; (Bot) stalk; **ein Eis am ~** an ice lolly (Brit), a Popsicle® (US)

Stier (-(e)s, -e) m (Zool) bull; (Astr) Taurus; **Stierkampf** m bullfight; **Stierkämpfer(in)** m(f) bullfighter

stieß imperf von **stoßen**

Stift (-(e)s, -e) m (aus Holz) peg; (Nagel) tack; (zum Schreiben) pen; (Farbstift) crayon; (Bleistift) pencil

Stil (-s, -e) m style

still adj quiet; (unbewegt) still

stillen vt (Säugling) to breast-feed

still|halten irr vi to keep still; **Stillleben** nt still life; **still|stehen** irr vi to stand still

Stimme (-, -n) f voice; (bei Wahl) vote

stimmen vi to be right; **stimmt!** that's right; **hier stimmt was nicht** there's something wrong here; **stimmt so!** (beim Bezahlen) keep the change

Stimmung f mood; (Atmosphäre) atmosphere

Stinkefinger m (fam) **jdm den ~ zeigen** to give sb the finger (o bird (US))

stinken (stank, gestunken) vi to stink (nach of)

Stipendium nt scholarship; (als Unterstützung) grant

Stirn (-, -en) f forehead; **Stirnhöhle** f sinus

Stock (-(e)s, Stöcke) m stick; (Bot) stock ▷ m (Stockwerke) floor, storey; **Stockbett** nt bunk bed; **Stöckelschuhe** pl high-heels; **Stockwerk** nt floor; **im ersten ~** on the first floor (Brit), on the second floor (US)

Stoff (-(e)s, -e) m (Gewebe) material; (Materie) matter; (von Buch etc) subject (matter); (fam: Rauschgift) stuff

stöhnen vi to groan (vor with)

stolpern vi to stumble, to trip

stolz adj proud

stopp interj hold it; (Moment mal!) hang on a minute; **stoppen** vt, vi to stop; (mit Uhr) to time; **Stoppschild** nt stop sign; **Stoppuhr** f stopwatch

Stöpsel (-s, -) m plug; (für Flaschen) stopper

Storch (-(e)s, Störche) m stork

stören vt to disturb; (behindern) to interfere with; **darf ich dich kurz ~?** can I trouble you for a minute?; **stört es dich, wenn ...?** do you mind if ...?

stornieren vt to cancel; **Stornogebühr** f cancellation fee

Störung f disturbance; (in der Leitung) fault

Stoß (-es, Stöße) m (Schub) push; (Schlag) blow; (mit Fuß) kick; (Haufen) pile; **Stoßdämpfer** (-s, -) m shock absorber

stoßen (stieß, gestoßen) vt (mit Druck) to shove, to push; (mit Schlag) to knock; (mit Fuß) to kick; (anstoßen) to bump; (zerkleinern) to pulverize ▷ vr **sich ~** to bang oneself; **sich ~ an** (+dat) (fig) to take exception to

Stoßstange f (Auto) bumper

stottern vt, vi to stutter

Str. abk von **Straße** St, Rd

Strafe (-, -n) f punishment; (Sport) penalty; (Gefängnisstrafe) sentence; (Geldstrafe) fine; **strafen** vt to punish; **Strafraum** m penalty area; **Strafstoß** m penalty kick; **Straftat** f (criminal) offence; **Strafzettel** m ticket

Strahl (-s, -en) m ray, beam; (Wasser) jet; **strahlen** vi to radiate; (fig) to beam

Strähne (-, -n) f strand; (weiß, gefärbt) streak

Strand (-(e)s, Strände) m beach; **am ~** on the beach; **Strandcafé** nt beach café; **Strandkorb** m wicker beach chair with a hood; **Strandpromenade** f promenade

strapazieren vt (Material) to be hard on; (Mensch, Kräfte) to be a strain on

Straße (-, -n) f road; (in der Stadt) street; **Straßenarbeiten** pl roadworks pl (Brit), road repairs pl (US); **Straßenbahn** f tram (Brit), streetcar (US); **Straßencafé** nt pavement café (Brit), sidewalk café (US); **Straßenfest** nt street party; **Straßenglätte** f slippery roads pl; **Straßenkarte** f road map; **Straßenrand** m **am ~** at the roadside; **Straßenschild** nt street sign; **Straßensperre** f roadblock; **Straßenverhältnisse** pl road conditions pl

Strategie (-, -n) f strategy

Strauch (-(e)s, Sträucher) m bush, shrub; **Strauchtomate** f vine-ripened tomato

Strauß (-es, Sträuße) m bunch; (als Geschenk) bouquet ▷ m (Strauße) (Vogel) ostrich

Strecke (-, -n) f route; (Entfernung) distance; (Eisenb) line

strecken vt to stretch ▷ vr **sich ~** to stretch

streckenweise adv (teilweise) in parts; (zeitweise) at times

Streich (-(e)s, -e) m trick, prank

streicheln vt to stroke

streichen (strich, gestrichen) vt (anmalen) to paint; (berühren) to stroke; (auftragen) to spread; (durchstreichen) to delete; (nicht genehmigen) to cancel

Streichholz nt match; **Streichholzschachtel** f matchbox; **Streichkäse** m cheese spread

Streifen (-s, -) m (Linie) stripe; (Stück) strip; (Film) film

Streifenwagen m patrol car

Streik (-(e)s, -s) m strike; **streiken** vi to be on strike

Streit (-(e)s, -e) m argument (um, wegen about, over); **streiten** (stritt, gestritten) vi to argue (um, wegen about, over) ▷ vr **sich ~** to argue (um, wegen about, over)

streng adj (Blick) severe; (Lehrer) strict; (Geruch) sharp

Stress (-es) m stress; **stressen** vt to stress (out); **stressig** adj (fam) stressful

Stretching (-s) nt (Sport) stretching exercises pl

streuen vt to scatter; **die Straßen ~** to grit the roads; (mit Salz) to put salt down on the roads; **Streufahrzeug** nt gritter lorry (Brit), salt truck (US)

strich imperf von **streichen**

Strich (-(e)s, -e) m (Linie) line; **Stricher** (fam: Strichjunge) rent boy (Brit), boy prostitute; **Strichkode** (-s, -s) m bar code; **Stricherin** f (fam: Strichmädchen) hooker; **Strichpunkt** m semicolon

Strick (-(e)s, -e) m rope

stricken vt, vi to knit; **Strickjacke** f cardigan; **Stricknadel** f knitting needle

Stripper(in) m(f) stripper; **Striptease** (-) m striptease

stritt imperf von **streiten**

Stroh (-(e)s) nt straw; **Strohdach** nt thatched roof; **Strohhalm** m (drinking) straw; **Strohhut** m straw hat

Strom (-(e)s, Ströme) m river; (fig) stream; (Elek) current; **Stromanschluss** m connection; **Stromausfall** m power failure

strömen vi to stream, to pour; **Strömung** f current

Stromverbrauch m power consumption; **Stromzähler** m electricity meter

Strophe (-, -n) f verse

Strudel (-s, -) m (in Fluss) whirlpool; (Gebäck) strudel

Struktur f structure; (von Material) texture

Strumpf (-(e)s, Strümpfe) m (Damenstrumpf) stocking; (Socke) sock; **Strumpfhose** f (pair of) tights pl (Brit), pantyhose (US)

Stück (-(e)s, -e) nt piece; (von Zucker) lump; (etwas) bit; (Zucker) lump; (Theat) play; **ein ~ Käse** a piece of cheese

Student(in) m(f) student; **Studentenausweis** m student card; **Studentenwohnheim** nt hall of residence (Brit), dormitory (US); **Studienabschluss** m qualification (at the end of a course of higher education); **Studienfahrt** f study trip; **Studienplatz** m university/college place; **studieren** vt, *vi* to study; **Studium** *nt* studies *pl*; **während seines ~s** while he is/was studying

Stufe (-, -n) *f* step; (*Entwicklungsstufe*) stage

Stuhl (-(e)s, Stühle) *m* chair

stumm *adj* silent; (*Med*) dumb

stumpf *adj* blunt; (*teilnahmslos, glanzlos*) dull; **stumpfsinnig** *adj* dull

Stunde (-, -n) *f* hour; (*Unterricht*) lesson; **eine halbe ~** half an hour; **Stundenkilometer** *m* **80 ~** 80 kilometres an hour; **stundenlang** *adv* for hours; **Stundenlohn** *m* hourly wage; **Stundenplan** *m* timetable; **stündlich** *adj* hourly

Stuntman (-s, Stuntmen) *m* stuntman; **Stuntwoman** (-, Stuntwomen) *f* stuntwoman

stur *adj* stubborn; (*stärker*) pigheaded

Sturm (-(e)s, Stürme) *m* storm; **stürmen** *vi* (*Wind*) to blow hard; (*rennen*) to storm; **Stürmer(in)** *m(f)* striker, forward; **Sturmflut** *f* storm tide; **stürmisch** *adj* stormy; (*fig*) tempestuous; (*Zeit*) turbulent; (*Liebhaber*) passionate; (*Beifall, Begrüßung*) tumultuous; **Sturmwarnung** *f* gale warning

Sturz (-es, Stürze) *m* fall; (*Pol*) overthrow; **stürzen** *vt* (*werfen*) to hurl; (*Pol*) to overthrow; (*umkehren*) to overturn ▷ *vi* to fall; (*rennen*) to dash; **Sturzhelm** *m* crash helmet

Stute (-, -n) *f* mare

Stütze (-, -n) *f* support; (*Hilfe*) help; (*fam: Arbeitslosenunterstützung*) dole (*Brit*), welfare (*US*)

stützen *vt* to support; (*Ellbogen*) to prop

stutzig *adj* perplexed, puzzled; (*misstrauisch*) suspicious

Styropor® (-s) *nt* polystyrene (*Brit*), styrofoam (*US*)

subjektiv *adj* subjective

Substanz (-, -en) *f* substance

subtrahieren *vt* to subtract

Subvention *f* subsidy; **subventionieren** *vt* to subsidize

Suche *f* search (*nach* for); **auf der ~ nach etw sein** to be looking for sth; **suchen** *vt* to look for; (*Inform*) to search ▷ *vi* to look, to search (*nach* for); **Suchmaschine** *f* (*Inform*) search engine

Sucht (-, Süchte) *f* mania; (*Med*) addiction;

süchtig *adj* addicted; **Süchtige(r)** *mf* addict

Süd south; **Südafrika** *nt* South Africa; **Südamerika** *nt* South America; **Süddeutschland** *nt* Southern Germany; **Süden** (-s) *m* south; **im ~ Deutschlands** in the south of Germany; **Südeuropa** *nt* Southern Europe; **Südkorea** (-s) *nt* South Korea; **südlich** *adj* southern; (*Kurs, Richtung*) southerly; **Verkehr in ~er Richtung** southbound traffic; **Südost(en)** *m* southeast; **Südpol** *m* South Pole; **Südstaaten** *pl* (*der USA*) the Southern States *pl*, the South *sing*; **südwärts** *adv* south, southwards; **Südwest(en)** *m* southwest; **Südwind** *m* south wind

Sultanine *f* sultana

Sülze (-, -n) *f* jellied meat

Summe (-, -n) *f* sum; (*Gesamtsumme*) total

summen *vi*, *vt* to hum; (*Insekt*) to buzz

Sumpf (-(e)s, Sümpfe) *m* marsh; (*subtropischer*) swamp; **sumpfig** *adj* marshy

Sünde (-, -n) *f* sin

super *adj* (*fam*) super, great; **Super** (-s) *nt* (*Benzin*) four star (petrol) (*Brit*), premium (*US*); **Supermarkt** *m* supermarket

Suppe (-, -n) *f* soup; **Suppengrün** *nt* bunch of herbs and vegetables for flavouring soup; **Suppenlöffel** *m* soup spoon; **Suppenschüssel** *f* soup tureen; **Suppentasse** *f* soup cup; **Suppenteller** *m* soup plate; **Suppenwürfel** *m* stock cube

Surfbrett *nt* surfboard; **surfen** *vi* to surf; **im Internet ~** to surf the Internet; **Surfer(in)** (-s, -) *m(f)* surfer

Surrealismus *m* surrealism

süß *adj* sweet; **süßen** *vt* to sweeten; **Süßigkeit** *f* (*Bonbon etc*) sweet (*Brit*), candy (*US*); **Süßkartoffel** *f* sweet potato, yam (*US*); **süßsauer** *adj* sweet-and-sour; **Süßspeise** *f* dessert; **Süßstoff** *m* sweetener; **Süßwasser** *nt* fresh water

Sweatshirt (-s, -s) *nt* sweatshirt

Swimmingpool (-s, -s) *m* (swimming) pool

Sylvester *nt siehe* **Silvester**

Symbol (-s, -e) *nt* symbol; **Symbolleiste** *f* (*Inform*) toolbar

Symmetrie (-, -n) *f* symmetry; **symmetrisch** *adj* symmetrical

sympathisch *adj* nice; **jdn ~ finden** to
 like sb
Symphonie (-, -n) *f* symphony
Symptom (-s, -e) *nt* symptom (*für* of)
Synagoge (-, -n) *f* synagogue
synchronisiert *adj* (*Film*) dubbed;
 Synchronstimme *f* dubbing voice
Synthesizer (-s, -) *m* (*Mus*) synthesizer
Synthetik (-, -en) *f* synthetic (fibre);
 synthetisch *adj* synthetic
Syrien (-s) *nt* Syria
System (-s, -e) *nt* system; **systematisch**
 adj systematic; **Systemsteuerung** *f*
 (*Inform*) control panel
Szene (-, -n) *f* scene

S

t

Tabak (-s, -e) m tobacco; **Tabakladen** m tobacconist's
Tabelle f table
Tablett (-s, -s) nt tray
Tablette f tablet, pill
Tabulator m tabulator, tab
Tacho(meter) (-s, -) m (Auto) speedometer
Tafel (-, -n) f (a. Math) table; (Anschlagtafel) board; (Wandtafel) blackboard; (Schiefer~) slate; (Gedenktafel) plaque; **eine ~ Schokolade** a bar of chocolate; **Tafelwasser** nt table water; **Tafelwein** m table wine
Tag (-(e)s, -e) m day; (Tageslicht) daylight; **guten ~!** good morning/afternoon; **am ~** during the day; **sie hat ihre ~e** she's got her period; **eines ~es** one day; **~ der Arbeit** Labour Day; **Tagebuch** nt diary; **tagelang** adj for days (on end); **Tagesanbruch** m daybreak; **Tagesausflug** m day trip; **Tagescreme** f day cream; **Tagesdecke** f bedspread; **Tagesgericht** nt dish of the day; **Tageskarte** f (Fahrkarte) day ticket; **die ~** (Speisekarte) today's menu; **Tageslicht** nt daylight; **Tagesmutter** f child minder;

Tagesordnung f agenda; **Tagestour** f day trip; **Tageszeitung** f daily newspaper; **täglich** adj, adv daily; **tags(über)** adv during the day; **Tagung** f conference
Tai Chi (-) nt tai chi
Taille (-, -n) f waist; **tailliert** adj fitted
Taiwan (-s) nt Taiwan
Takt (-(e)s, -e) m (Taktgefühl) tact; (Mus) time
Taktik (-, -en) f tactics pl
taktlos adj tactless; **taktvoll** adj tactful
Tal (-(e)s, Täler) nt valley
Talent (-(e)s, -e) nt talent; **talentiert** adj talented
Talkmaster(in) (-s, -) m(f) talk-show host; **Talkshow** (-, -s) f talkshow
Tampon (-s, -s) m tampon
Tandem (-s, -s) nt tandem
Tang (-s, -e) m seaweed
Tank (-s, -s) m tank; **Tankanzeige** f fuel gauge; **Tankdeckel** m fuel cap; **tanken** vi to get some petrol (Brit) (o gas (US)); (Aviat) to refuel; **Tanker** (-s, -) m (oil) tanker; **Tankstelle** f petrol station (Brit), gas station (US); **Tankwart(in)** (-s, -e) m(f) petrol pump attendant (Brit), gas station attendant (US)
Tanne (-, -n) f fir; **Tannenzapfen** m fir cone
Tansania (-s) nt Tanzania
Tante (-, -n) f aunt; **Tante-Emma-Laden** m corner shop (Brit), grocery store (US)
Tanz (-es, Tänze) m dance; **tanzen** vt, vi to dance; **Tänzer(in)** m(f) dancer; **Tanzfläche** f dance floor; **Tanzkurs** m dancing course; **Tanzlehrer(in)** m(f) dancing instructor; **Tanzstunde** f dancing lesson
Tapete (-, -n) f wallpaper; **tapezieren** vt, vi to wallpaper
Tarantel (-, -n) f tarantula
Tarif (-s, -e) m tariff, (scale of) fares/charges pl
Tasche (-, -n) f bag; (Hosentasche) pocket; (Handtasche) bag (Brit), purse (US); **Taschen-** in zW pocket; **Taschenbuch** nt paperback; **Taschendieb(in)** m(f) pickpocket; **Taschengeld** nt pocket money; **Taschenlampe** f torch (Brit), flashlight (US); **Taschenmesser** nt penknife; **Taschenrechner** m pocket calculator; **Taschentuch** nt handkerchief

Tasse (-, -n) f cup; **eine ~ Kaffee** a cup of coffee

Tastatur f keyboard; **Taste** (-, -n) f button; (von Klavier, Computer) key; **Tastenkombination** f (Inform) shortcut; **Tastentelefon** nt push-button telephone

tat imperf von **tun**

Tat (-, -en) f action

Tatar (-s, -s) nt raw minced beef

Täter(in) (-s, -) m(f) culprit

tätig adj active; **in einer Firma ~ sein** to work for a firm; **Tätigkeit** f activity; (Beruf) occupation

tätowieren vt to tattoo; **Tätowierung** f tattoo (an +dat on)

Tatsache f fact; **tatsächlich** adj actual ▷ adv really

Tau (-(e)s, -e) nt (Seil) rope ▷ (-(e)s) m dew

taub adj deaf; (Füße etc) numb (vor Kälte with cold)

Taube (-, -n) f pigeon; (Turtel~, fig: Friedenssymbol) dove

taubstumm adj deaf-and-dumb; **Taubstumme(r)** mf deaf-mute

tauchen vt to dip ▷ vi to dive; (Naut) to submerge; **Tauchen** (-s) nt diving; **Taucher(in)** (-s, -) m(f) diver; **Taucheranzug** m diving (o wet) suit; **Taucherbrille** f diving goggles pl; **Tauchermaske** f diving mask; **Tauchkurs** m diving course; **Tauchsieder** (-s, -) m portable immersion coil for heating water

tauen vi impers to thaw

Taufe (-, -n) f baptism; **taufen** vt to baptize; (nennen) to christen

taugen vi to be suitable (für for); **nichts ~** to be no good

Tausch (-(e)s, -e) m exchange; **tauschen** vt to exchange, to swap

täuschen vt to deceive ▷ vi to be deceptive ▷ vr **sich ~** to be wrong; **täuschend** adj deceptive; **Täuschung** f deception; (optisch) illusion

tausend num a thousand; **vier~** four thousand; **~ Dank!** thanks a lot; **tausendmal** adv a thousand times; **tausendste(r, s)** adj thousandth; **Tausendstel** (-s, -) nt (Bruchteil) thousandth

Tauwetter nt thaw

Taxi nt taxi; **Taxifahrer(in)** m(f) taxi driver; **Taxistand** m taxi rank (Brit), taxi stand (US)

Team (-s, -s) nt team; **Teamarbeit** f team work; **teamfähig** adj able to work in a team

Technik f technology; (angewandte) engineering; (Methode) technique; **Techniker(in)** (-s, -) m(f) engineer; (Sport, Mus) technician; **technisch** adj technical

Techno (-s) m (Mus) techno

Teddybär m teddy bear

Tee (-s, -s) m tea; **Teebeutel** m teabag; **Teekanne** f teapot; **Teelöffel** m teaspoon

Teer (-(e)s, -e) m tar

Teesieb nt tea strainer; **Teetasse** f teacup

Teich (-(e)s, -e) m pond

Teig (-(e)s, -e) m dough; **Teigwaren** pl pasta sing

Teil (-(e)s, -e) m part; (Anteil) share; **zum ~** partly ▷ (-(e)s, -e) nt part; (Bestandteil) component; **teilen** vt to divide; (mit jdm) to share (mit with); **20 durch 4 ~** to divide 20 by 4 ▷ vr **sich ~** to divide

Teilkaskoversicherung f third party, fire and theft insurance

teilmöbliert adj partly furnished

Teilnahme (-, -n) f participation (an +dat in); **teil|nehmen** irr vi to take part (an +dat in); **Teilnehmer(in)** (-s, -) m(f) participant

teils adv partly; **teilweise** adv partially, in part; **Teilzeit** f **~ arbeiten** to work part-time

Teint (-s, -s) m complexion

Tel. abk von **Telefon** tel.

Telefon (-s, -e) nt telephone; **Telefonanruf** m, **Telefonat** nt (tele)phone call; **Telefonanschluss** m telephone connection; **Telefonauskunft** f directory enquiries pl (Brit), directory assistance (US); **Telefonbuch** nt telephone directory; **Telefongebühren** pl telephone charges pl; **Telefongespräch** nt telephone conversation; **telefonieren** vi **ich telefoniere gerade (mit ...)** I'm on the phone (to ...); **telefonisch** adj telephone; (Benachrichtigung) by telephone; **Telefonkarte** f phonecard; **Telefonnummer** f (tele)phone number; **Telefonrechnung** f phone bill; **Telefonverbindung** f telephone connection; **Telefonzelle** f phone box (Brit), phone booth; **Telefonzentrale** f

t

switchboard; **über die ~** through the
switchboard

Telegramm nt telegram; **Teleobjektiv**
nt telephoto lens; **Teleshopping** (-s) nt
teleshopping; **Teleskop** (-s, -e) nt
telescope

Teller (-s, -) m plate

Tempel (-s, -) m temple

Temperament nt temperament;
(Schwung) liveliness; **temperamentvoll**
adj lively

Temperatur f temperature; **bei ~en von
30 Grad** at temperatures of 30 degrees;
~ haben to have a temperature; **~ bei jdm
messen** to take sb's temperature

Tempo (-s, -s) nt (Geschwindigkeit) speed;
Tempolimit (-s, -s) nt speed limit

Tempotaschentuch® nt
(Papiertaschentuch) (paper) tissue, ≈
Kleenex®

Tendenz f tendency; (Absicht) intention

Tennis (-) nt tennis; **Tennisball** m tennis
ball; **Tennisplatz** m tennis court;
Tennisschläger m tennis racket;
Tennisspieler(in) m(f) tennis player;
Tennisturnier nt tennis tournament

Tenor (-s, Tenöre) m tenor

Teppich (-s, -e) m carpet; **Teppichboden**
m (wall-to-wall) carpet

Termin (-s, -e) m (Zeitpunkt) date; (Frist)
deadline; (Arzttermin etc) appointment

Terminal (-s, -s) nt (Inform, Aviat) terminal

Terminkalender m diary; **Terminplaner**
m (in Buchform) personal organizer,
Filofax®; (Taschencomputer) personal
digital assistant, PDA

Terpentin (-s, -e) nt turpentine, turps sing

Terrasse (-, -n) f terrace; (hinter einem
Haus) patio

Terror (-s) m terror; **Terroranschlag** m
terrorist attack; **terrorisieren** vt to
terrorize; **Terrorismus** m terrorism;
Terrorist(in) m(f) terrorist

Tesafilm® m ≈ sellotape® (Brit), ≈ Scotch
tape® (US)

Test (-s, -s) m test

Testament nt will; **das Alte/Neue ~** the
Old/New Testament

testen vt to test; **Testergebnis** nt test
results pl

Tetanus (-) m tetanus; **Tetanusimpfung**
f (anti-)tetanus injection

teuer adj expensive, dear (Brit)

Teufel (-s, -) m devil; **was/wo zum
~** what/where the devil; **Teufelskreis** m
vicious circle

Text (-(e)s, -e) m text; (Liedertext) words pl,
lyrics pl; **Textmarker** (-s, -) m highlighter;
Textverarbeitung f word processing;
Textverarbeitungsprogramm nt word
processing program

Thailand nt Thailand

Theater (-s, -) nt theatre; (fam) fuss; **ins
~ gehen** to go to the theatre;
Theaterkasse f box office;
Theaterstück nt (stage) play;
Theatervorstellung f (stage)
performance

Theke (-, -n) f (Schanktisch) bar;
(Ladentisch) counter

Thema (-s, Themen) nt subject, topic; **kein
~!** no problem

Themse (-) f Thames

Theologie f theology

theoretisch adj theoretical; **~ stimmt
das** that's right in theory; **Theorie** f
theory

Therapeut(in) m(f) therapist; **Therapie**
f therapy; **eine ~ machen** to undergo
therapy

Thermalbad nt thermal bath; (Ort)
thermal spa; **Thermometer** (-s, -) nt
thermometer

Thermosflasche® f, **Thermoskanne®** f
Thermos® (flask); **Thermostat** (-(e)s, -e) m
thermostat

These (-, -n) f theory

Thron (-(e)s, -e) m throne

Thunfisch m tuna

Thüringen (-s) nt Thuringia

Thymian (-s, -e) m thyme

Tick (-(e)s, -s) m tic; (Eigenart) quirk;
(Fimmel) craze; **ticken** vi to tick; **er
tickt nicht ganz richtig** he's off his
rocker

Ticket (-s, -s) nt (plane) ticket

Tiebreak (-s, -s) m (Sport: Tennis) tie
break(er)

tief adj deep; (Ausschnitt, Ton, Sonne) low; **2
Meter ~** 2 metres deep; **Tief** (-s, -s) nt
(Meteo) low; (seelisch) depression;
Tiefdruck m (Meteo) low pressure; **Tiefe**
(-, -n) f depth; **Tiefgarage** f underground
car park (Brit) (o garage (US)); **tiefgekühlt**
adj frozen; **Tiefkühlfach** nt freezer
compartment; **Tiefkühlkost** f frozen

food; **Tiefkühltruhe** f freezer; **Tiefpunkt** m low

Tier (-(e)s, -e) nt animal; **Tierarzt** m, **Tierärztin** f vet; **Tiergarten** m zoo; **Tierhandlung** f pet shop; **Tierheim** nt animal shelter; **tierisch** adj animal ▷ adv (fam) really; ~ **ernst** deadly serious; **ich hatte ~ Angst** I was dead scared; **Tierkreiszeichen** nt sign of the zodiac; **Tierpark** m zoo; **Tierquälerei** f cruelty to animals; **Tierschützer(in)** (-s, -) m(f) animal rights campaigner; **Tierversuch** m animal experiment

Tiger (-s, -) m tiger

timen vt to time; **Timing** (-s) nt timing

Tinte (-, -n) f ink; **Tintenfisch** m cuttlefish; (klein) squid; (achtarmig) octopus; **Tintenfischringe** pl calamari pl; **Tintenstrahldrucker** m ink-jet printer

Tipp (-s, -s) m tip; **tippen** vt, vi to tap; (fam: schreiben) to type; (fam: raten) to guess

Tirol (-s) nt Tyrol

Tisch (-(e)s, -e) m table; **Tischdecke** f tablecloth; **Tischlerei** f joiner's workshop; (Arbeit) joinery; **Tischtennis** nt table tennis; **Tischtennisschläger** m table-tennis bat

Titel (-s, -) m title; **Titelbild** nt cover picture; **Titelmusik** f theme music; **Titelverteidiger(in)** m(f) defending champion

Toast (-(e)s, -s) m toast; **toasten** vt to toast; **Toaster** (-s, -) m toaster

Tochter (-, Töchter) f daughter

Tod (-(e)s, -e) m death; **Todesopfer** nt casualty; **Todesstrafe** f death penalty; **todkrank** adj terminally ill; (sehr krank) seriously ill; **tödlich** adj deadly, fatal; **er ist ~ verunglückt** he was killed in an accident; **todmüde** adj (fam) dead tired; **todsicher** adj (fam) dead certain

Tofu (-(s)) m tofu, bean curd

Toilette f toilet, restroom (US); **Toilettenpapier** nt toilet paper

toi, toi, toi interj good luck

tolerant adj tolerant (gegen of)

toll adj mad; (Treiben) wild; (fam: großartig) great; **Tollkirsche** f deadly nightshade; **Tollwut** f rabies sing

Tomate (-, -n) f tomato; **Tomatenmark** nt tomato purée (Brit) (o paste (US)); **Tomatensaft** m tomato juice

Tombola (-, -s) f raffle, tombola (Brit)

Ton (-(e)s, -e) m (Erde) clay ▷ m (Töne) (Laut) sound; (Mus) note; (Redeweise) tone; (Farbton, Nuance) shade; **Tonband** nt tape; **Tonbandgerät** nt tape recorder

tönen vi to sound ▷ vt to shade; (Haare) to tint

Toner (-s, -) m toner; **Tonerkassette** f toner cartridge

Tonne (-, -n) f (Fass) barrel; (Gewicht) tonne, metric ton

Tontechniker(in) m(f) sound engineer

Tönung f hue; (für Haar) rinse

Top (-s, -s) nt top

Topf (-(e)s, Töpfe) m pot

Töpfer(in) (-s, -) m(f) potter; **Töpferei** f pottery; (Gegenstand) piece of pottery

Tor (-(e)s, -e) nt gate; (Sport) goal; **ein ~ schießen** to score a goal; **Torhüter(in)** m(f) goalkeeper

torkeln vi to stagger

Torlinie f goal line

Tornado (-s, -s) m tornado

Torpfosten m goalpost; **Torschütze** m, **Torschützin** f (goal)scorer

Torte (-, -n) f cake; (Obsttorte) flan; (Sahnetorte) gateau

Torwart(in) (-s, -e) m(f) goalkeeper

tot adj dead; ~**er Winkel** blind spot

total adj total, complete; **Totalschaden** m complete write-off

Tote(r) mf dead man/woman; (Leiche) corpse; **töten** vt, vi to kill; **Totenkopf** m skull

tot|lachen vr **sich ~** to kill oneself laughing

Toto (-s, -s) m o nt pools pl

tot|schlagen irr vt to beat to death; **die Zeit ~** to kill time

Touchscreen (-s, -s) m touch screen

Toupet (-s, -s) nt toupee

Tour (-, -en) f trip; (Rundfahrt) tour; **eine ~ nach York machen** to go on a trip to York; **Tourenski** m touring ski

Tourismus m tourism; **Tourist(in)** m(f) tourist; **Touristenklasse** f tourist class; **touristisch** adj tourist; (pej) touristy

traben vi to trot

Tournee (-, -n) f tour

Tracht (-, -en) f (Kleidung) traditional costume

Trackball (-s, -s) m (Inform) trackball
Tradition f tradition; **traditionell** adj
traditional
traf imperf von **treffen**
Trafik (-, -en) f tobacconist's
Tragbahre (-, -n) f stretcher
tragbar adj portable
träge adj sluggish, slow
tragen (trug, getragen) vt to carry;
(Kleidung, Brille, Haare) to wear; (Namen,
Früchte) to bear; **Träger** (-s, -) m (an
Kleidung) strap; (Hosen~) braces pl (Brit),
suspenders pl (US); (in der Architektur)
beam; (Stahl~, Eisen~) girder
Tragfläche f wing; **Tragflügelboot** nt
hydrofoil
tragisch adj tragic; **Tragödie** f tragedy
Trainer(in) (-s, -) m(f) trainer, coach;
trainieren vt, vi to train; (jdn a.) to
coach; (Übung) to practise; **Training**
(-s, -s) nt training; **Trainingsanzug** m
tracksuit
Traktor m tractor
Trambahn f tram (Brit), streetcar (US)
trampen vi to hitchhike; **Tramper(in)**
m(f) hitchhiker
Träne (-, -n) f tear; **tränen** vi to water;
Tränengas nt teargas
trank imperf von **trinken**
Transfusion f transfusion
Transitverkehr m transit traffic;
Transitvisum nt transit visa
Transplantation f transplant;
(Hauttransplantation) graft
Transport (-(e)s, -e) m transport;
transportieren vt to transport;
Transportmittel nt means sing of
transport; **Transportunternehmen** nt
haulage firm
Transvestit (-en, -en) m transvestite
trat imperf von **treten**
Traube (-, -n) f (einzelne Beere) grape;
(ganze Frucht) bunch of grapes;
Traubensaft m grape juice;
Traubenzucker m glucose
trauen vi jdm/einer Sache ~ to trust
sb/sth; **ich traute meinen Ohren nicht** I
couldn't believe my ears ▷ vr **sich ~** to
dare ▷ vt to marry; **sich ~ lassen** to get
married
Trauer (-) f sorrow; (für Verstorbenen)
mourning
Traum (-(e)s, Träume) m dream; **träumen**

vt, vi to dream (von of, about); **traumhaft**
adj dreamlike; (fig) wonderful
traurig adj sad (über +akk about)
Trauschein m marriage certificate;
Trauung f wedding ceremony;
Trauzeuge m, **Trauzeugin** f witness (at
wedding ceremony), ≈ best man/maid of
honour
Travellerscheck m traveller's cheque
treffen (traf, getroffen) vr **sich ~** to meet
▷ vt, vi to hit; (Bemerkung) to hurt;
(begegnen) to meet; (Entscheidung) to
make; (Maßnahmen) to take; **Treffen** (-s, -)
nt meeting; **Treffer** (-s, -) m (Tor) goal;
Treffpunkt m meeting place
treiben (trieb, getrieben) vt to drive; (Sport)
to do ▷ vi (im Wasser) to drift; (Pflanzen) to
sprout; (Tee, Kaffee) to be diuretic; **Treiber**
(-s, -) m (Inform) driver
Treibgas nt propellant; **Treibhaus** nt
greenhouse; **Treibstoff** m fuel
trennen vt to separate; (teilen) to divide
▷ vr **sich ~** to separate; **sich von jdm ~** to
leave sb; **sich von etw ~** to part with sth;
Trennung f separation
Treppe (-, -n) f stairs pl; (im Freien) steps pl;
Treppengeländer nt banister;
Treppenhaus nt staircase
Tresen (-s, -) m (in Kneipe) bar; (in Laden)
counter
Tresor (-s, -e) m safe
Tretboot nt pedal boat; **treten** (trat,
getreten) vi to step; **~ nach** to kick at; **mit
jdm in Verbindung ~** to get in contact
with sb ▷ vt to kick; (nieder~) to tread
treu adj (gegenüber Partner) faithful; (Kunde,
Fan) loyal; **Treue** (-) f (eheliche)
faithfulness; (von Kunde, Fan) loyalty
Triathlon (-s, -s) m triathlon
Tribüne (-, -n) f stand; (Rednertribüne)
platform
Trick (-s, -e o -s) m trick; **Trickfilm** m
cartoon
trieb imperf von **treiben**
Trieb (-(e)s, -e) m urge; (Instinkt) drive;
(Neigung) inclination; (an Baum etc) shoot;
Triebwerk nt engine
Trikot (-s, -s) nt shirt, jersey
Trimm-Dich-Pfad m fitness trail
trinkbar adj drinkable; **trinken** (trank,
getrunken) vt, vi to drink; **einen ~ gehen** to
go out for a drink; **Trinkgeld** nt tip;
Trinkhalm m (drinking) straw;

Trinkschokolade f drinking chocolate; **Trinkwasser** nt drinking water

Trio (-s, -s) nt trio

Tripper (-s, -) m gonorrhoea

Tritt (-(e)s, -e) m (Schritt) step; (Fußtritt) kick; **Trittbrett** nt running board

Triumph (-(e)s, -e) m triumph; **triumphieren** vi to triumph (über +akk over)

trivial adj trivial

trocken adj dry; **Trockenhaube** f hair-dryer; **Trockenheit** f dryness; **trocken|legen** vt (Baby) to change; **trocknen** vt, vi to dry; **Trockner** (-s, -) m dryer

Trödel (-s) m (fam) junk; **Trödelmarkt** m flea market

trödeln vi (fam) to dawdle

Trommel (-, -n) f drum; **Trommelfell** nt eardrum; **trommeln** vt, vi to drum

Trompete (-, -n) f trumpet

Tropen pl tropics pl

Tropf (-(e)s, -e) m (Med) drip; **am ~ hängen** to be on a drip; **tröpfeln** vi to drip; **es tröpfelt** it's drizzling; **tropfen** vt, vi to drip; **Tropfen** (-s, -) m drop; **tropfenweise** adv drop by drop; **tropfnass** adj dripping wet; **Tropfsteinhöhle** f stalactite cave

tropisch adj tropical

Trost (-es) m consolation, comfort; **trösten** vt to console, to comfort; **trostlos** adj bleak; (Verhältnisse) wretched; **Trostpreis** m consolation prize

Trottoir (-s, -s) nt pavement (Brit), sidewalk (US)

trotz prep +gen o dat in spite of; **Trotz** (-es) m defiance; **trotzdem** adv nevertheless ▷ conj although; **trotzig** adj defiant

trüb adj dull; (Flüssigkeit, Glas) cloudy; (fig) gloomy

Trüffel (-, -n) f truffle

trug imperf von **tragen**

trügerisch adj deceptive

Truhe (-, -n) f chest

Trümmer pl wreckage sing; (Bau~) ruins pl

Trumpf (-(e)s, Trümpfe) m trump

Trunkenheit f intoxication; **~ am Steuer** drink driving (Brit), drunk driving (US)

Truthahn m turkey

Tscheche (-n, -n) m, **Tschechin** f Czech; **Tschechien** (-s) nt Czech Republic; **tschechisch** adj Czech; **Tschechische**

Republik Czech Republic; **Tschechisch** nt Czech

Tschetschenien (-s) nt Chechnya

tschüs(s) interj bye

T-Shirt (-s, -s) nt T-shirt

Tube (-, -n) f tube

Tuberkulose (-, -n) f tuberculosis, TB

Tuch (-(e)s, Tücher) nt cloth; (Halstuch) scarf; (Kopftuch) headscarf

tüchtig adj competent; (fleißig) efficient; (fam: kräftig) good

Tugend (-, -en) f virtue; **tugendhaft** adj virtuous

Tulpe (-, -n) f tulip

Tumor (-s, -en) m tumour

Tümpel (-s, -) m pond

tun (tat, getan) vt (machen) to do; (legen) to put; **was tust du da?** what are you doing?; **das tut man nicht** you shouldn't do that; **jdm etw ~** (antun) to do sth to sb; **das tut es auch** that'll do ▷ vi to act; **so ~, als ob** to act as if ▷ vr impers **es tut sich etwas/viel** something/a lot is happening

Tuner (-s, -) m tuner

Tunesien (-s) nt Tunisia

Tunfisch m siehe **Thunfisch** tuna

Tunnel (-s, -s o -) m tunnel

Tunte (-, -n) f (pej, fam) fairy

tupfen vt, vi to dab; (mit Farbe) to dot; **Tupfen** (-s, -) m dot

Tür (-, -en) f door; **vor/an der ~** at the door; **an die ~ gehen** to answer the door

Türke (-n, -n) m Turk; **Türkei** (-) f **die ~** Turkey; **Türkin** f Turk

Türkis (-es, -e) m turquoise

türkisch adj Turkish; **Türkisch** nt Turkish

Turm (-(e)s, Türme) m tower; (spitzer Kirchturm) steeple; (Sprung~) diving platform; (Schach) rook, castle

turnen vi to do gymnastics; **Turnen** (-s) nt gymnastics sing; (Schule) physical education, PE; **Turner(in)** m(f) gymnast; **Turnhalle** f gym(nasium); **Turnhose** f gym shorts pl

Turnier (-s, -e) nt tournament

Turnschuh m gym shoe, sneaker (US)

Türschild nt doorplate; **Türschloss** nt lock

tuscheln vt, vi to whisper

Tussi (-, -s) f (pej, fam) chick

Tüte (-, -n) f bag

TÜV (-s, -s) m akr = **Technischer Überwachungsverein**

● **TÜV**
●
● The **TÜV** is the organization
● responsible for checking the safety of
● machinery, particularly vehicles. Cars
● over three years old have to be
● examined every two years for their
● safety and for their exhaust
● emissions. **TÜV** is also the name
● given to the test itself.

TÜV-Plakette f badge attached to a vehicle's numberplate, indicating that it has passed the 'TÜV'

Tweed (-s, -s) m tweed

Typ (-s, -en) m type; (Auto) model; (Mann) guy, bloke

Typhus (-) m typhoid

typisch adj typical (für of); **ein ~er Fehler** a common mistake; **~ Marcus!** that's just like Marcus; **~ amerikanisch!** that's so American

u. abk = **und**

u. a. abk = **und andere(s)** and others; = **unter anderem, unter anderen** among other things

u. A. w. g. abk = **um Antwort wird gebeten** RSVP

U-Bahn f underground (Brit), subway (US)

übel adj bad; (moralisch) wicked; **mir ist ~** I feel sick; **diese Bemerkung hat er mir ~ genommen** he took offence at my remark; **Übelkeit** f nausea

üben vt, vi to practise

 SCHLÜSSELWORT

über präp +dat **1** (räumlich) over above; **zwei Grad über null** two degrees above zero

2 (zeitlich) over; **über der Arbeit einschlafen** to fall asleep over one's work
▷ präp +akk
1 (räumlich) over; (hoch über auch) above; (quer über auch) across

2 (zeitlich) over; **über kurz oder lang** sooner or later

3 (mit Zahlen): **Kinder über 12 Jahren** children over od above 12 years of age; **ein Scheck über 200 Euro** a cheque for 200 euros

4 (auf dem Wege) via; **nach Köln über Aachen** to Cologne via Aachen; **ich habe es über die Auskunft erfahren** I found out from information

5 (betreffend) about; **ein Buch über ...** a book about od on ...; **über jdn/etw lachen** to laugh about od at sb/sth

6: **Macht über jdn haben** to have power over sb; **sie liebt ihn über alles** she loves him more than everything
▷ adv over; **über und über** over and over; **den ganzen Tag über** all day long; **jdm in etw** dat **über sein** to be superior to sb in sth

überall adv everywhere

überanstrengen vr **sich ~** to overexert oneself

überbacken adj (mit Käse) **~** au gratin; **überbelichten** vt (Foto) to overexpose; **überbieten** irr vt to outbid; (übertreffen) to surpass; (Rekord) to break

Überbleibsel (-s, -) nt remnant

Überblick m overview; (fig: in Darstellung) survey; (Fähigkeit zu verstehen) grasp (über +akk of)

überbuchen vt to overbook; **Überbuchung** f overbooking

überdurchschnittlich adj above average

übereinander adv on top of each other; (sprechen etc) about each other

überein|stimmen vi to agree (mit with)

überempfindlich adj hypersensitive

überfahren irr vt (Auto) to run over; **Überfahrt** f crossing

Überfall m (Banküberfall) robbery; (Mil) raid; (auf jdn) assault; **überfallen** irr vt to attack; (Bank) to raid

überfällig adj overdue

überfliegen irr vt to fly over; (Buch) to skim through

Überfluss m overabundance, excess (an +dat of); **überflüssig** adj superfluous

überfordern vt to demand too much of; (Kräfte) to overtax; **da bin ich überfordert** (bei Antwort) you've got me there

Überführung f (Brücke) flyover (Brit), overpass (US)

überfüllt adj overcrowded

u

Übergabe f handover

Übergang m crossing; (Wandel, Überleitung) transition; **Übergangslösung** f temporary solution, stopgap

übergeben irr vt to hand over ▷ vr **sich ~** to be sick, to vomit

Übergepäck nt excess baggage

Übergewicht nt excess weight; (**10 Kilo**) **~ haben** to be (10 kilos) overweight

überglücklich adj overjoyed; (fam) over the moon

Übergröße f outsize

überhaupt adv at all; (im Allgemeinen) in general; (besonders) especially; **was willst du ~?** what is it you want?

überheblich adj arrogant

überholen vt to overtake; (Tech) to overhaul; **Überholspur** f overtaking (Brit) (o passing (US)) lane; **überholt** adj outdated

Überholverbot nt **hier herrscht ~** you can't overtake here

überhören vt to miss, not to catch; (absichtlich) to ignore; **überladen** irr vt to overload ▷ adj (fig) cluttered; **überlassen** irr vt **jdm etw ~** to leave sth to sb; **über|laufen** irr vi (Flüssigkeit) to overflow

überleben vt, vi to survive; **Überlebende(r)** mf survivor

überlegen vt to think about; **sich** (dat) **etw ~** to think about sth; **er hat es sich** (dat) **anders überlegt** he's changed his mind ▷ adj superior (dat to); **Überlegung** f consideration

überm kontr von **über dem**

übermäßig adj excessive

übermorgen adv the day after tomorrow

übernächste(r, s) adj **~ Woche** the week after next

übernachten vi to spend the night (bei jdm at sb's place); **übernächtigt** adj bleary-eyed, very tired; **Übernachtung** f overnight stay; **~ mit Frühstück** bed and breakfast

übernehmen irr vt to take on; (Amt, Geschäft) to take over ▷ vr **sich ~** to take on too much

überprüfen vt to check; **Überprüfung** f check; (Überprüfen) checking

überqueren vt to cross

überraschen vt to surprise; **Überraschung** f surprise

überreden vt to persuade; **er hat mich überredet** he talked me into it

überreichen vt to hand over

übers kontr von **über das**

überschätzen vt to overestimate; **überschlagen** irr vt (berechnen) to estimate; (auslassen: Seite) to skip ▷ vr **sich ~** to somersault; (Auto) to overturn; (Stimme) to crack; **überschneiden** irr vr **sich ~** (Linien etc) to intersect; (Termine) to clash

Überschrift f heading

Überschwemmung f flood

Übersee f **nach/in ~** overseas

übersehen irr vt (Gelände) to look (out) over; (nicht beachten) to overlook

übersetzen vt to translate (aus from, in +akk into); **Übersetzer(in)** (-s, -) m(f) translator; **Übersetzung** f translation

Übersicht f overall view; (Darstellung) survey; **übersichtlich** adj clear

überstehen irr vt (durchstehen) to get over; (Winter etc) to get through

Überstunden pl overtime sing

überstürzt adj hasty

überteuert adj overpriced

übertragbar adj transferable; (Med) infectious; **übertragen** irr vt to transfer (auf +akk to); (Radio) to broadcast; (Krankheit) to transmit ▷ vr to spread (auf +akk to) ▷ adj figurative; **Übertragung** f (Radio) broadcast; (von Daten) transmission

übertreffen irr vt to surpass

übertreiben irr vt, vi to exaggerate, to overdo; **Übertreibung** f exaggeration; **übertrieben** adj exaggerated, overdone

überwachen vt to supervise; (Verdächtigen) to keep under surveillance

überwand imperf von **überwinden**

überweisen irr vt to transfer; (Patienten) to refer (an +akk to); **Überweisung** f transfer; (von Patienten) referral

überwiegend adv mainly

überwinden (überwand, überwunden) vt to overcome ▷ vr **sich ~** to make an effort, to force oneself; **überwunden** pp von **überwinden**

Überzelt nt flysheet

überzeugen vt to convince; **Überzeugung** f conviction

überziehen irr vt (bedecken) to cover; (Jacke etc) to put on; (Konto) to overdraw;

die Betten frisch ~ to change the sheets; **Überziehungskredit** m overdraft facility

üblich adj usual

übrig adj remaining; **ist noch Saft ~?** is there any juice left?; **für jdn etwas ~ haben** (fam) to have a soft spot for sb; **die Übrigen** pl the rest pl; **im Übrigen** besides; **~ bleiben** to be left (over); **mir blieb nichts anderes ~(, als zu gehen)** I had no other choice (but to go); **übrigens** adv besides; (nebenbei bemerkt) by the way

Übung f practice; (im Sport, Aufgabe etc) exercise

Ufer (-s, -) nt (Fluss) bank; (Meer, See) shore; **am ~** on the bank/shore

Ufo (-(s), -s) nt akr = **unbekanntes Flugobjekt** UFO

Uhr (-, -en) f clock; (am Arm) watch; **wie viel ~ ist es?** what time is it?; **1 ~** 1 o'clock; **20 ~** 8 o'clock, 8 pm; **Uhrzeigersinn** m **im ~** clockwise; **gegen den ~** anticlockwise (Brit), counterclockwise (US); **Uhrzeit** f time (of day)

Ukraine (-) f **die ~** the Ukraine

UKW abk = **Ultrakurzwelle** VHF

Ulme (-, -n) f elm

Ultrakurzwelle f very high frequency; **Ultraschallaufnahme** f (Med) scan

⬤ **SCHLÜSSELWORT**

um präp +akk **1** (um herum) (a)round; **um Weihnachten** around Christmas; **er schlug um sich** he hit about him
2 (mit Zeitangabe) at; **um acht (Uhr)** at eight (o'clock)
3 (mit Größenangabe) by; **etw um 4 cm kürzen** to shorten sth by 4 cm; **um 10% teurer** 10% more expensive; **um vieles besser** better by far; **um so besser** so much the better
4: **der Kampf um den Titel** the battle for the title; **um Geld spielen** to play for money; **Stunde um Stunde** hour after hour; **Auge um Auge** an eye for an eye
▷ präp +gen: **um ... willen** for the sake of ...; **um Gottes willen** for goodness' od (stärker) God's sake
▷ konj: **um ... zu** (in order) to ...; **zu klug, um zu ...** too clever to ...; siehe **umso**
▷ adv **1** (ungefähr) about; **um (die) 30**

Leute about od around 30 people
2 (vorbei): **die 2 Stunden sind um** the two hours are up

umarmen vt to embrace

Umbau m rebuilding; (zu etwas) conversion (zu into); **um|bauen** vt to rebuild; (zu etwas) to convert (zu into)

um|blättern vt, vi to turn over

um|bringen irr vt to kill

um|buchen vi to change one's reservation/flight

um|drehen vt to turn (round); (obere Seite nach unten) to turn over ▷ vr **sich ~** to turn (round); **Umdrehung** f turn; (Phys, Auto) revolution

um|fahren irr vt to knock down

um|fallen irr vi to fall over

Umfang m (Ausmaß) extent; (von Buch) size; (Reichweite) range; (Math) circumference; **umfangreich** adj extensive

Umfeld nt environment

Umfrage f survey

Umgang m company; (mit jdm) dealings pl; **umgänglich** adj sociable; **Umgangssprache** f colloquial language, slang

Umgebung f surroundings pl; (Milieu) environment; (Personen) people around one

umgehen irr vi (Gerücht) to go round; **~ (können) mit** (know how to) handle ▷ irr vt to avoid; (Schwierigkeit, Verbot) to get round

um|gehen irr vi **mit etw ~** to handle sth; **Umgehungsstraße** f bypass

umgekehrt adj reverse; (gegenteilig) opposite ▷ adv the other way round; **und ~** and vice versa

um|hören vr **sich ~** to ask around; **um|kehren** vi to turn back ▷ vt to reverse; (Kleidungsstück) to turn inside out; **um|kippen** vt to tip over ▷ vi to overturn; (fig) to change one's mind; (fam: ohnmächtig werden) to pass out

Umkleidekabine f changing cubicle (Brit), dressing room (US); **Umkleideraum** m changing room

Umkreis m neighbourhood; **im ~ von** within a radius of

um|leiten vt to divert; **Umleitung** f diversion

um|rechnen vt to convert (in +akk into);

u

Umrechnung f conversion;
Umrechnungskurs m rate of exchange
Umriss m outline
um|rühren vi, vt to stir
ums kontr von **um das**
Umsatz m turnover
um|schalten vi to turn over
Umschlag m cover; (Buch) jacket; (Med) compress; (Brief) envelope
Umschulung f retraining
um|sehen irr vr **sich ~** to look around; (suchen) to look out (nach for)
umso adv all the; **~ mehr** all the more; **~ besser** so much the better
umsonst adv (vergeblich) in vain; (gratis) for nothing
Umstand m circumstance; **Umstände** (pl) (fig) fuss; **in anderen Umständen sein** to be pregnant; **jdm Umstände machen** to cause sb a lot of trouble; **machen Sie bitte keine Umstände** please, don't put yourself out; **unter diesen/keinen Umständen** under these/no circumstances; **unter Umständen** possibly; **umständlich** adj (Methode) complicated; (Ausdrucksweise) long-winded; (Mensch) ponderous; **Umstandsmode** f maternity wear
um|steigen irr vi to change (trains/buses)
um|stellen vt (an anderen Ort) to change round; (Tech) to convert ▷ vr **sich ~** to adapt (auf +akk to); **Umstellung** f change; (Umgewöhnung) adjustment; (Tech) conversion
Umtausch m exchange; **um|tauschen** vt to exchange; (Währung) to change
Umweg m detour
Umwelt f environment;
Umweltbelastung f ecological damage; **umweltbewusst** adj environmentally aware; **umweltfreundlich** adj environment-friendly; **Umweltpapier** nt recycled paper; **umweltschädlich** adj harmful to the environment;
Umweltschutz m environmental protection; **Umweltschützer(in)** (-s, -) m(f) environmentalist;
Umweltverschmutzung f pollution;
umweltverträglich adj environment-friendly
um|werfen irr vt to knock over; (fig:

ändern) to upset; (fig, fam: jdn) to flabbergast
um|ziehen irr vt to change ▷ vr **sich ~** to change ▷ vi to move (house); **Umzug** m (Straßenumzug) procession; (Wohnungsumzug) move
unabhängig adj independent;
Unabhängigkeitstag m Independence Day, Fourth of July (US)
unabsichtlich adv unintentionally
unangenehm adj unpleasant;
Unannehmlichkeit f inconvenience; **~en** pl trouble sing
unanständig adj indecent;
unappetitlich adj (Essen) unappetizing; (abstoßend) off-putting; **unbeabsichtigt** adj unintentional; **unbedeutend** adj insignificant, unimportant; (Fehler) slight
unbedingt adj unconditional ▷ adv absolutely
unbefriedigend adj unsatisfactory;
unbegrenzt adj unlimited; **unbekannt** adj unknown; **unbeliebt** adj unpopular; **unbemerkt** adj unnoticed; **unbequem** adj (Stuhl, Mensch) uncomfortable; (Regelung) inconvenient; **unbeständig** adj (Wetter) unsettled; (Lage) unstable; (Mensch) unreliable; **unbestimmt** adj indefinite; **unbeteiligt** adj (nicht dazugehörig) uninvolved; (innerlich nicht berührt) indifferent, unconcerned;
unbewacht adj unguarded; **unbewusst** adj unconscious; **unbezahlt** adj unpaid; **unbrauchbar** adj useless
und conj and; **~ so weiter** and so on; **na ~?** so what?
undankbar adj (Person) ungrateful; (Aufgabe) thankless; **undenkbar** adj inconceivable; **undeutlich** adj indistinct; **undicht** adj leaky; **uneben** adj uneven; **unecht** adj (Schmuck etc) fake; **unehelich** adj (Kind) illegitimate; **unendlich** adj endless; (Math) infinite; **unentbehrlich** adj indispensable; **unentgeltlich** adj free (of charge)
unentschieden adj undecided; **~ enden** (Sport) to end in a draw
unerfreulich adj unpleasant
unerhört adj unheard-of; (Bitte) outrageous; **unerlässlich** adj indispensable; **unerträglich** adj unbearable; **unerwartet** adj unexpected

unerwünscht adj unwelcome; (Eigenschaften) undesirable; **unfähig** adj incompetent; **~ sein, etw zu tun** to be incapable of doing sth; **unfair** adj unfair

Unfall m accident; **Unfallbericht** m accident report; **Unfallflucht** f failure to stop after an accident; **Unfallhergang** m **den ~ schildern** to give details of the accident; **Unfallstation** f casualty ward; **Unfallstelle** f scene of the accident; **Unfallversicherung** f accident insurance

unfreundlich adj unfriendly

Ungarn (-s) nt Hungary

Ungeduld f impatience; **ungeduldig** adj impatient

ungeeignet adj unsuitable

ungefähr adj approximate ▷ adv approximately; **~ 10 Kilometer** about 10 kilometres; **wann ~?** about what time?; **wo ~?** whereabouts?

ungefährlich adj harmless; (sicher) safe

ungeheuer adj huge ▷ adv (fam) enormously; **Ungeheuer** (-s, -) nt monster

ungehorsam adj disobedient (gegenüber to)

ungelegen adj inconvenient; **ungemütlich** adj unpleasant; (Mensch) disagreeable; **ungenießbar** adj inedible; (Getränk) undrinkable; **ungenügend** adj unsatisfactory; (Schulnote) ≈ F; **ungepflegt** adj (Garten) untended; (Aussehen) unkempt; (Hände) neglected; **ungerade** adj odd

ungerecht adj unjust; **ungerechtfertigt** adj unjustified; **Ungerechtigkeit** f injustice, unfairness

ungern adv reluctantly; **ungeschickt** adj clumsy; **ungeschminkt** adj without make-up; **ungesund** adj unhealthy; **ungewiss** adj uncertain; **ungewöhnlich** adj unusual

Ungeziefer (-s) nt vermin pl

ungezogen adj ill-mannered

ungezwungen adj relaxed

ungiftig adj non-toxic

unglaublich adj incredible

Unglück (-(e)s, -e) nt (Unheil) misfortune; (Pech) bad luck; (Unglücksfall) disaster; (Verkehrs~) accident; **das bringt ~** that's unlucky; **unglücklich** adj unhappy; (erfolglos) unlucky; (unerfreulich) unfortunate; **unglücklicherweise** adv unfortunately

ungültig adj invalid

ungünstig adj inconvenient

unheilbar adj incurable; **~ krank sein** to be terminally ill

unheimlich adj eerie ▷ adv (fam) incredibly

unhöflich adj impolite

uni adj plain

Uni (-, -s) f uni

Uniform (-, -en) f uniform

Universität f university

Unkenntnis f ignorance

unklar adj unclear

Unkosten pl expenses pl; **Unkostenbeitrag** m contribution (towards expenses)

Unkraut nt weeds pl, ~art, weed

unlogisch adj illogical

unmissverständlich adj unambiguous

unmittelbar adj immediate; **~ darauf** immediately afterwards

unmöbliert adj unfurnished

unmöglich adj impossible

unnahbar adj unapproachable

unnötig adj unnecessary

UNO (-) f akr = **United Nations Organization** UN

unordentlich adj untidy; **Unordnung** f disorder

unpassend adj inappropriate; (Zeit) inconvenient; **unpersönlich** adj impersonal; **unpraktisch** adj impractical

Unrecht nt wrong; **zu ~** wrongly; **~ haben, im ~ sein** to be wrong

unregelmäßig adj irregular; **unreif** adj unripe; **unruhig** adj restless; **~ schlafen** to have a bad night

uns pron akk, dat von **wir**; us, (to) us; **~ (selbst)** (reflexiv) ourselves; **sehen Sie ~?** can you see us?; **er schickte es ~** he sent it to us; **lasst ~ in Ruhe** leave us alone; **ein Freund von ~** a friend of ours; **wir haben ~ hingesetzt** we sat down; **wir haben ~ amüsiert** we enjoyed ourselves; **wir mögen ~** we like each other

unscharf adj (Foto) blurred, out of focus

unscheinbar adj insignificant; (Aussehen) unprepossessing

unschlüssig adj undecided

unschuldig adj innocent

unser pron (adjektivisch) our ▷ pron gen von **wir**; of us; **unsere(r, s)** pron (substantivisch) ours; **unseretwegen** adv (wegen uns) because of us; (uns zuliebe) for our sake; (um uns) about us; (von uns aus) as far as we are concerned

unseriös adj dubious; **unsicher** adj (ungewiss) uncertain; (Person, Job) insecure

Unsinn m nonsense

unsterblich adj immortal; **~ verliebt** madly in love

unsympathisch adj unpleasant; **er ist mir ~** I don't like him

unten adv below; (im Haus) downstairs; (an der Treppe etc) at the bottom; **nach ~** down; **unter** prep +akk o dat under, below; (bei Menschen) among; (während) during

○ **SCHLÜSSELWORT**

unter präp +dat **1** (räumlich, mit Zahlen) under; (drunter) underneath, below; **unter 18 Jahren** under 18 years

2 (zwischen) among(st); **sie waren unter sich** they were by themselves; **einer unter ihnen** one of them; **unter anderem** among other things

▷ präp +akk under below

Unterarm m forearm

unterbelichtet adj (Foto) underexposed

Unterbewusstsein nt subconscious

unterbrechen irr vt to interrupt; **Unterbrechung** f interruption; **ohne ~** nonstop

unterdrücken vt to suppress; (Leute) to oppress

unterdurchschnittlich adj below average

untere(r, s) adj lower

untereinander adv (räumlich) one below the other; (gegenseitig) each other; (miteinander) among themselves/yourselves/ourselves

Unterführung f underpass

unter|gehen irr vi to go down; (Sonne) to set; (Volk) to perish; (Welt) to come to an end; (im Lärm) to be drowned out

Untergeschoss nt basement; **Untergewicht** nt (3 Kilo) **~ haben** to be (3 kilos) underweight; **Untergrund** m foundation; (Pol) underground;

Untergrundbahn f underground (Brit), subway (US)

unterhalb adv, prep +gen below; **~ von** below

Unterhalt m maintenance; **unterhalten** irr vt to maintain; (belustigen) to entertain ▷ vr **sich ~** to talk; (sich belustigen) to enjoy oneself; **Unterhaltung** f (Belustigung) entertainment; (Gespräch) talk, conversation

Unterhemd nt vest (Brit), undershirt (US); **Unterhose** f underpants pl; (für Damen) briefs pl

unterirdisch adj underground

Unterkiefer m lower jaw

Unterkunft (-, -künfte) f accommodation

Unterlage f (Beleg) document; (Schreibunterlage) pad

unterlassen irr vt **es ~, etw zu tun** (versäumen) to fail to do sth; (bleiben lassen) to refrain from doing sth

unterlegen adj inferior (dat to); (besiegt) defeated

Unterleib m abdomen

Unterlippe f lower lip

Untermiete f **zur ~ wohnen** to be a subtenant; **Untermieter(in)** m(f) subtenant

unternehmen irr vt (Reise) to go on; (Versuch) to make; **etwas ~** to do something (gegen about); **Unternehmen** (-s, -) nt undertaking; (Comm) company; **Unternehmensberater(in)** (-s, -) m(f) management consultant; **Unternehmer(in)** (-s, -) m(f) entrepreneur

Unterricht (-(e)s, -e) m lessons pl; **unterrichten** vt to teach

unterschätzen vt to underestimate

unterscheiden irr vt to distinguish (von from, zwischen +dat between) ▷ vr **sich ~** to differ (von from)

Unterschenkel m lower leg

Unterschied (-(e)s, -e) m difference; **im ~ zu dir** unlike you; **unterschiedlich** adj different

unterschreiben irr vt to sign; **Unterschrift** f signature

Untersetzer (-s, -) m tablemat; (für Gläser) coaster

unterste(r, s) adj lowest, bottom

unter|stellen vr **sich ~** to take shelter

unterstellen vt (rangmäßig) to

subordinate (*dat* to); (*fig*) to impute (*jdm etw* sth to sb)

unterstreichen *irr vt* (*a. fig*) to underline

Unterstrich *m* (*Inform*) underscore

unterstützen *vt* to support; **Unterstützung** *f* support

untersuchen *vt* (*Med*) to examine; (*Polizei*) to investigate; **Untersuchung** *f* examination; (*polizeiliche*) investigation

untertags *adv* during the day

Untertasse *f* saucer

Unterteil *nt* lower part, bottom

Untertitel *m* subtitle

untervermieten *vt* to sublet

Unterwäsche *f* underwear

unterwegs *adv* on the way

unterzeichnen *vt* to sign

untreu *adj* unfaithful

untröstlich *adj* inconsolable; **unüberlegt** *adj* ill-considered ▷ *adv* without thinking; **unüblich** *adj* unusual; **unverantwortlich** *adj* irresponsible; (*unentschuldbar*) inexcusable

unverbindlich *adj* not binding; (*Antwort*) noncommittal ▷ *adv* (*Comm*) without obligation

unverbleit *adj* unleaded; **unverheiratet** *adj* unmarried, single; **unvermeidlich** *adj* unavoidable; **unvernünftig** *adj* silly; **unverschämt** *adj* impudent; **unverständlich** *adj* incomprehensible; **unverträglich** *adj* (*Person*) quarrelsome; (*Essen*) indigestible

unverwüstlich *adj* indestructible; (*Mensch*) irrepressible

unverzeihlich *adj* unpardonable; **unverzüglich** *adj* immediate; **unvollständig** *adj* incomplete; **unvorsichtig** *adj* careless

unwahrscheinlich *adj* improbable, unlikely ▷ *adv* (*fam*) incredibly

Unwetter *nt* thunderstorm

unwichtig *adj* unimportant

unwiderstehlich *adj* irresistible

unwillkürlich *adj* involuntary ▷ *adv* instinctively; **ich musste ~ lachen** I couldn't help laughing

unwohl *adj* unwell, ill

unzählig *adj* innumerable, countless

unzerbrechlich *adj* unbreakable; **unzertrennlich** *adj* inseparable; **unzufrieden** *adj* dissatisfied; **unzugänglich** *adj* inaccessible;

unzumutbar *adj* unacceptable

unzusammenhängend *adj* disconnected; (*Äußerung*) incoherent; **unzutreffend** *adj* inapplicable; (*unwahr*) incorrect; **unzuverlässig** *adj* unreliable

Update (*-s, -s*) *nt* (*Inform*) update

üppig *adj* (*Essen*) lavish; (*Vegetation*) lush

uralt *adj* ancient, very old

Uran (*-s*) *nt* uranium

Uranus (*-*) *m* Uranus

Uraufführung *f* premiere

Urenkel *m* great-grandson; **Urenkelin** *f* great-granddaughter; **Urgroßeltern** *pl* great-grandparents *pl*; **Urgroßmutter** *f* great-grandmother; **Urgroßvater** *m* great-grandfather

Urheber(in) (*-s, -*) *m(f)* originator; (*Autor*) author

Urin (*-s, -e*) *m* urine; **Urinprobe** *f* urine specimen

Urkunde (*-, -n*) *f* document

Urlaub (*-(e)s, -e*) *m* holiday (*Brit*), vacation (*US*); **im ~** on holiday (*Brit*), on vacation (*US*); **in ~ fahren** to go on holiday (*Brit*) (*o* vacation (*US*)); **Urlauber(in)** (*-s, -*) *m(f)* holiday-maker (*Brit*), vacationer (*US*); **Urlaubsort** *m* holiday resort; **urlaubsreif** *adj* ready for a holiday (*Brit*) (*o* vacation (*US*)); **Urlaubszeit** *f* holiday season (*Brit*), vacation period (*US*)

Urne (*-, -n*) *f* urn

Urologe *m*, **Urologin** *f* urologist

Ursache *f* cause (*für* of); **keine ~!** not at all; (*bei Entschuldigung*) that's all right

Ursprung *m* origin; (*von Fluss*) source; **ursprünglich** *adj* original ▷ *adv* originally; **Ursprungsland** *adj* country of origin

Urteil (*-s, -e*) *nt* (*Meinung*) opinion; (*Jur*) verdict; (*Strafmaß*) sentence; **urteilen** *vi* to judge

Uruguay (*-s*) *nt* Uruguay

Urwald *m* jungle

USA *pl* USA *sing*

User(in) (*-s, -*) *m(f)* (*Inform*) user

usw. *abk* = **und so weiter** etc

Utensilien *pl* utensils *pl*

u

V

vage adj vague

Vagina (-, Vaginen) f vagina

vakuumverpackt adj vacuum-packed

Valentinstag m St Valentine's Day

Vandalismus m vandalism

Vanille (-) f vanilla

variieren vt, vi to vary

Vase (-, -n) f vase

Vaseline (-) f Vaseline®

Vater (-s, Väter) m father; **väterlich** adj
paternal; **Vaterschaft** f fatherhood; (Jur)
paternity; **Vatertag** m Father's Day;
Vaterunser nt **das ~** (**beten**) (to say) the
Lord's Prayer

V-Ausschnitt m V-neck

v. Chr. abk = **vor Christus** BC

Veganer(in) (-s, -) m(f) vegan;
Vegetarier(in) (-s, -) m(f) vegetarian;
vegetarisch adj vegetarian

Veilchen nt violet

Velo (-s, -s) nt (schweizerisch) bicycle

Vene (-, -n) f vein

Venedig (-s) nt Venice

Venezuela (-s) nt Venezuela

Ventil (-s, -e) nt valve

Ventilator m ventilator

Venus (-) f Venus

Venusmuschel f clam

verabreden vt to arrange ▷ vr **sich ~** to
arrange to meet (mit jdm sb); **ich bin
schon verabredet** I'm already meeting
someone; **Verabredung** f arrangement;
(Termin) appointment; (zum Ausgehen) date

verabschieden vt (Gäste) to say goodbye
to; (Gesetz) to pass ▷ vr **sich ~** to say
goodbye

verachten vt to despise; **verächtlich** adj
contemptuous; (verachtenswert)
contemptible; **Verachtung** f contempt

verallgemeinern vt to generalize

Veranda (-, Veranden) f veranda, porch
(US)

veränderlich adj changeable; **verändern**
vt to change ▷ vr **sich ~** to change;
Veränderung f change

veranlassen vt to cause

veranstalten vt to organize;
Veranstalter(in) (-s, -) m(f) organizer;
Veranstaltung f event;
Veranstaltungsort m venue

verantworten vt to take responsibility
for ▷ vr **sich für etw ~** to answer for sth;
verantwortlich adj responsible (für for);
Verantwortung f responsibility (für for)

verärgern vt to annoy

verarschen vt (fam) to take the piss out
of (Brit), to make a sucker out of (US)

Verb (-s, -en) nt verb

Verband m (Med) bandage; (Bund)
association; **Verband(s)kasten** m
first-aid box; **Verband(s)zeug** nt
dressing material

verbergen irr vt to hide (vor +dat from)
▷ vr **sich ~** to hide (vor +dat from)

verbessern vt to improve; (berichtigen) to
correct ▷ vr **sich ~** to improve;
(berichtigen) to correct oneself;
Verbesserung f improvement;
(Berichtigung) correction

verbiegen irr vi to bend ▷ vr **sich ~** to
bend

verbieten irr vt to forbid; **jdm ~, etw zu
tun** to forbid sb to do sth

verbilligt adj reduced

verbinden irr vt to connect; (kombinieren)
to combine; (Med) to bandage; **können
Sie mich mit ... ~?** (Tel) can you put me
through to ...?; **ich verbinde** (Tel) I'm
putting you through ▷ vr (Chem) **sich ~** to
combine

verbindlich adj binding; (freundlich) friendly; **Verbindung** f connection

verbleit adj leaded

verblüffen vt to amaze

verblühen vi to fade

verborgen adj hidden

Verbot (-(e)s, -e) nt ban (für, von on); **verboten** adj forbidden; **es ist ~** it's not allowed; **es ist ~, hier zu parken** you're not allowed to park here; **Rauchen ~** no smoking

verbrannt adj burnt

Verbrauch (-(e)s) m consumption; **verbrauchen** vt to use up; **Verbraucher(in)** (-s, -) m(f) consumer

Verbrechen (-s, -) nt crime; **Verbrecher(in)** (-s, -) m(f) criminal

verbreiten vt to spread ▷ vr **sich ~** to spread

verbrennen irr vt to burn; **Verbrennung** f burning; (in Motor) combustion

verbringen irr vt to spend

verbunden adj **falsch ~** sorry, wrong number

Verdacht (-(e)s) m suspicion; **verdächtig** adj suspicious; **verdächtigen** vt to suspect

verdammt interj (fam) damn

verdanken vt **jdm etw ~** to owe sth to sb

verdarb imperf von **verderben**

verdauen vt (a. fig) to digest; **verdaulich** adj digestible; **das ist schwer ~** that is hard to digest; **Verdauung** f digestion

Verdeck (-(e)s, -e) nt top

verderben (verdarb, verdorben) vt to spoil; (schädigen) to ruin; (moralisch) to corrupt; **es sich** (dat) **mit jdm ~** to get into sb's bad books; **ich habe mir den Magen verdorben** I've got an upset stomach ▷ vi (Lebensmittel) to go off

verdienen vt to earn; (moralisch) to deserve; **Verdienst** (-(e)s, -e) m earnings pl ▷ (-(e)s, -e) nt merit; (Leistung) service (um to)

verdoppeln vt to double

verdorben pp von **verderben** ▷ adj spoilt; (geschädigt) ruined; (moralisch) corrupt

verdrehen vt to twist; (Augen) to roll; **jdm den Kopf ~** (fig) to turn sb's head

verdünnen vt to dilute

verdunsten vi to evaporate

verdursten vi to die of thirst

verehren vt to admire; (Rel) to worship; **Verehrer(in)** (-s, -) m(f) admirer

Verein (-(e)s, -e) m association; (Klub) club

vereinbar adj compatible

vereinbaren vt to arrange; **Vereinbarung** f agreement, arrangement

vereinigen vt to unite ▷ vr **sich ~** to unite; **Vereinigtes Königreich** nt United Kingdom; **Vereinigte Staaten (von Amerika)** pl United States sing (of America); **Vereinigung** f union; (Verein) association; **Vereinte Nationen** pl United Nations pl

vereisen vi (Straße) to freeze over; (Fenster) to ice up ▷ vt (Med) to freeze

vererben vt **jdm etw ~** to leave sth to sb; (Bio) to pass sth on to sb ▷ vr **sich ~** to be hereditary; **vererblich** adj hereditary

verfahren irr vi to proceed ▷ vr **sich ~** to get lost; **Verfahren** (-s, -) nt procedure; (Tech) method; (Jur) proceedings pl

verfallen irr vi to decline; (Haus) to be falling apart; (Fin) to lapse; (Fahrkarte etc) to expire; **~ in** (+akk) to lapse into; **Verfallsdatum** nt expiry (Brit) (o expiration (US)) date; (von Lebensmitteln) best-before date

verfärben vr **sich ~** to change colour; (Wäsche) to discolour

Verfasser(in) (-s, -) m(f) author, writer; **Verfassung** f (gesundheitlich) condition; (Pol) constitution

verfaulen vi to rot

verfehlen vt to miss

verfeinern vt to refine

Verfilmung f film (o screen) version

verfluchen vt to curse

verfolgen vt to pursue; (Pol) to persecute

verfügbar adj available; **verfügen** vi **über etw** (akk) **~** to have sth at one's disposal; **Verfügung** f order; **jdm zur ~ stehen** to be at sb's disposal; **jdm etw zur ~ stellen** to put sth at sb's disposal

verführen vt to tempt; (sexuell) to seduce; **verführerisch** adj seductive

vergangen adj past; **~e Woche** last week; **Vergangenheit** f past

Vergaser (-s, -) m (Auto) carburettor

vergaß imperf von **vergessen**

vergeben irr vt to forgive (jdm etw sb for sth); (weggeben) to award, to allocate;

vergebens *adv* in vain; **vergeblich** *adv* in vain ▷ *adj* vain, futile

vergehen *irr vi* to pass ▷ *vr* **sich an jdm ~** to indecently assault sb; **Vergehen** (*-s, -*) *nt* offence

Vergeltung *f* retaliation

vergessen (*vergaß, vergessen*) *vt* to forget; **vergesslich** *adj* forgetful

vergeuden *vt* to squander, to waste

vergewaltigen *vt* to rape; **Vergewaltigung** *f* rape

vergewissern *vr* **sich ~** to make sure

vergiften *vt* to poison; **Vergiftung** *f* poisoning

Vergissmeinnicht (*-(e)s, -e*) *nt* forget-me-not

Vergleich (*-(e)s, -e*) *m* comparison; (*Jur*) settlement; **im ~ zu** compared to (*o* with); **vergleichen** *irr vt* to compare (*mit* to, with)

Vergnügen (*-s, -*) *nt* pleasure; **viel ~!** enjoy yourself; **vergnügt** *adj* cheerful; **Vergnügungspark** *m* amusement park

vergoldet *adj* gold-plated

vergriffen *adj* (*Buch*) out of print; (*Ware*) out of stock

vergrößern *vt* to enlarge; (*Menge*) to increase; (*mit Lupe*) to magnify; **Vergrößerung** *f* enlargement; (*Menge*) increase; (*mit Lupe*) magnification; **Vergrößerungsglas** *nt* magnifying glass

verh. *adj abk* = **verheiratet** married

verhaften *vt* to arrest

verhalten *irr vr* **sich ~** (*sich benehmen*) to behave; (*Sache*) to be; **Verhalten** (*-s*) *nt* behaviour

Verhältnis *nt* relationship (*zu* with); (*Math*) ratio; **~se** *pl* circumstances *pl*, conditions *pl*; **im ~ von 1 zu 2** in a ratio of 1 to 2; **verhältnismäßig** *adj* relative ▷ *adv* relatively

verhandeln *vi* to negotiate (*über etw akk* sth); **Verhandlung** *f* negotiation

verheimlichen *vt* to keep secret (*jdm* from sb)

verheiratet *adj* married

verhindern *vt* to prevent; **sie ist verhindert** she can't make it

Verhör (*-(e)s, -e*) *nt* interrogation; (*gerichtlich*) examination; **verhören** *vt* to interrogate; (*bei Gericht*) to examine ▷ *vr* **sich ~** to mishear

verhungern *vi* to starve to death

verhüten *vt* to prevent; **Verhütung** *f* prevention; (*mit Pille, Kondom etc*) contraception; **Verhütungsmittel** *nt* contraceptive

verirren *vr* **sich ~** to get lost

Verkauf *m* sale; **verkaufen** *vt* to sell; **zu ~** for sale; **Verkäufer(in)** *m(f)* seller; (*beruflich*) salesperson; (*in Laden*) shop assistant (*Brit*), salesperson (*US*); **verkäuflich** *adj* for sale

Verkehr (*-s, -e*) *m* traffic; (*Sex*) intercourse; (*Umlauf*) circulation; **verkehren** *vi* (*Bus etc*) to run; **~ in** to frequent; **~ mit** to associate (*o* mix) with; **Verkehrsampel** *f* traffic lights *pl*; **Verkehrsamt** *nt* tourist information office; **verkehrsfrei** *adj* traffic-free; **Verkehrsfunk** *m* travel news *sing*; **Verkehrsinsel** *f* traffic island; **Verkehrsmeldung** *f* traffic report; **Verkehrsmittel** *nt* means *sing* of transport; **öffentliche ~** *pl* public transport *sing*; **Verkehrsschild** *nt* traffic sign; **Verkehrstote(r)** *mf* road casualty; **die Zahl der ~n** the number of deaths on the road; **Verkehrsunfall** *m* road accident; **Verkehrszeichen** *nt* traffic sign

verkehrt *adj* wrong; (*verkehrt herum*) the wrong way round; (*Pullover etc*) inside out; **du machst es ~** you're doing it wrong

verklagen *vt* to take to court

verkleiden *vt* to dress up (*als* as) ▷ *vr* **sich ~** to dress up (*als* as); (*um unerkannt zu bleiben*) to disguise oneself; **Verkleidung** *f* (*Karneval*) fancy dress; (*um nicht erkannt zu werden*) disguise

verkleinern *vt* to reduce; (*Zimmer, Gebiet etc*) to make smaller

verkneifen *irr vt* **sich** (*dat*) **etw ~** (*Lachen*) to stifle sth; (*Schmerz*) to hide sth; (*sich versagen*) to do without sth; **verkommen** *irr vi* to deteriorate; (*Mensch*) to go downhill ▷ *adj* (*Haus*) dilapidated; (*moralisch*) depraved; **verkraften** *vt* to cope with

verkratzt *adj* scratched

verkühlen *vr* **sich ~** to get a chill

verkürzen *vt* to shorten

Verlag (*-(e)s, -e*) *m* publishing company

verlangen *vt* (*fordern*) to demand; (*wollen*) to want; (*Preis*) to ask; (*Qualifikation*) to require; (*erwarten*) to ask (*von* of); (*fragen*

nach) to ask for; (*Pass etc*) to ask to see;
~ Sie Herrn X ask for Mr X ▷ *vi* **~ nach** to
ask for
verlängern *vt* to extend; (*Pass,
Erlaubnis*) renew; **Verlängerung** *f*
extension; (*Sport*) extra time; (*von Pass,
Erlaubnis*) renewal; **Verlängerungsschnur**
f extension cable; **Verlängerungswoche**
f extra week
verlassen *irr vt* to leave ▷ *irr vr* **sich
~** to rely (*auf +akk* on) ▷ *adj* desolate;
(*Mensch*) abandoned; **verlässlich** *adj*
reliable
Verlauf *m* course; **verlaufen** *irr vi* (*Weg,
Grenze*) to run (*entlang* along); (*zeitlich*) to
pass; (*Farben*) to run ▷ *vr* **sich ~** to get
lost; (*Menschenmenge*) to disperse
verlegen *vt* to move; (*verlieren*) to mislay;
(*Buch*) to publish ▷ *adj* embarrassed;
Verlegenheit *f* embarrassment;
(*Situation*) difficulty
Verleih (*-(e)s, -e*) *m* (*Firma*) hire company
(*Brit*), rental company (*US*); **verleihen** *irr
vt* to lend; (*vermieten*) to hire (out) (*Brit*), to
rent (out) (*US*); (*Preis, Medaille*) to award
verleiten *vt* **jdn dazu ~, etw zu tun** to
induce sb to do sth
verlernen *vt* to forget
verletzen *vt* to injure; (*fig*) to hurt;
Verletzte(r) *mf* injured person;
Verletzung *f* injury; (*Verstoß*) violation
verlieben *vr* **sich ~** to fall in love (*in jdn*
with sb); **verliebt** *adj* in love
verlieren (*verlor, verloren*) *vt, vi* to lose
verloben *vr* **sich ~** to get engaged (*mit*
to); **Verlobte(r)** *mf* fiancé/fiancée;
Verlobung *f* engagement
verlor *imperf von* **verlieren**
verloren *pp von* **verlieren** ▷ *adj* lost; (*Eier*)
poached; **~ gehen** to go missing
verlosen *vt* to raffle; **Verlosung** *f* raffle
Verlust (*-(e)s, -e*) *m* loss
vermehren *vt* to multiply; (*Menge*) to
increase ▷ *vr* **sich ~** to multiply; (*Menge*)
to increase
vermeiden *irr vt* to avoid
vermeintlich *adj* supposed
vermieten *vt* to rent (out), to let (out)
(*Brit*); (*Auto*) to hire (out) (*Brit*), to rent
(out) (*US*); **Vermieter(in)** *m(f)* landlord/
-lady
vermischen *vt* to mix ▷ *vr* **sich ~** to mix
vermissen *vt* to miss; **vermisst** *adj*

missing; **jdn als ~ melden** to report sb
missing
Vermittlung *f* (*bei Streit*) mediation;
(*Herbeiführung*) arranging; (*Stelle*) agency
Vermögen (*-s, -*) *nt* fortune
vermuten *vt* to suppose; (*argwöhnen*) to
suspect; **vermutlich** *adj* probable ▷ *adv*
probably; **Vermutung** *f* supposition;
(*Verdacht*) suspicion
vernachlässigen *vt* to neglect
vernichten *vt* to destroy; **vernichtend**
adj (*fig*) crushing; (*Blick*) withering; (*Kritik*)
scathing
Vernunft (*-*) *f* reason; **ich kann ihn nicht
zur ~ bringen** I can't make him see
reason; **vernünftig** *adj* sensible; (*Preis*)
reasonable
veröffentlichen *vt* to publish
verordnen *vt* (*Med*) to prescribe;
Verordnung *f* order; (*Med*) prescription
verpachten *vt* to lease (out) (*an +akk*
to)
verpacken *vt* to pack; (*einwickeln*) to
wrap up
Verpackung *f* packaging;
Verpackungskosten *pl* packing charges
pl
verpassen *vt* to miss
verpflegen *vt* to feed; **Verpflegung** *f*
feeding; (*Kost*) food; (*in Hotel*) board
verpflichten *vt* to oblige; (*anstellen*) to
engage ▷ *vr* **sich ~** to commit oneself (*etw
zu tun* to doing sth)
verpfuschen *vt* (*fam*) to make a mess of;
(*vulg*) to fuck up
verprügeln *vt* to beat up
verraten *irr vt* to betray; (*Geheimnis*) to
divulge; **aber nicht ~!** but don't tell
anyone ▷ *vr* **sich ~** to give oneself away
verrechnen *vt* **~ mit** to set off against
▷ *vr* **sich ~** to miscalculate;
Verrechnungsscheck *m* crossed cheque
(*Brit*), check for deposit only (*US*)
verregnet *adj* rainy
verreisen *vi* to go away (*nach* to); **sie ist
(geschäftlich) verreist** she's away (on
business); **verrenken** *vt* to contort; (*Med*)
to dislocate; **sich** (*dat*) **den Knöchel ~** to
sprain (*o* twist) one's ankle; **verringern** *vt*
to reduce
verrostet *adj* rusty
verrückt *adj* mad, crazy; **es macht mich
~** it's driving me mad

V

versagen vi to fail; **Versagen** (-s) nt
failure; **Versager(in)** (-s, -) m(f) failure
versalzen irr vt to put too much salt in/on
versammeln vt to assemble, to gather
▷ vr **sich ~** to assemble, to gather;
Versammlung f meeting
Versand (-(e)s) m dispatch; (Abteilung)
dispatch department; **Versandhaus** nt
mail-order company
versäumen vt to miss; (unterlassen) to
neglect; **~, etw zu tun** to fail to do sth
verschätzen vr **sich ~** to miscalculate
verschenken vt to give away; (Chance) to
waste
verschicken vt to send off
verschieben vt irr (auf später) to postpone,
to put off; (an anderen Ort) to move
verschieden adj (unterschiedlich)
different; (mehrere) various; **sie sind
~ groß** they are of different sizes;
Verschiedene pl various people/things pl;
Verschiedenes various things pl
verschimmelt adj mouldy
verschlafen irr vt to sleep through; (fig)
to miss ▷ vi to oversleep
verschlechtern vr **sich ~** to deteriorate,
to get worse; **Verschlechterung** f
deterioration
Verschleiß (-es) m wear and tear
verschließbar adj lockable;
verschließen irr vt to close; (mit Schlüssel)
to lock
verschlimmern vt to make worse ▷ vr
sich ~ to get worse
verschlossen adj locked; (fig) reserved
verschlucken vt to swallow ▷ vr **sich
~** to choke (an +dat on)
Verschluss m lock; (von Kleid) fastener;
(Foto) shutter; (Stöpsel) stopper
verschmutzen vt to get dirty; (Umwelt)
to pollute
verschnaufen vi **ich muss mal ~** I need
to get my breath back
verschneit adj snow-covered
verschnupft adj **~ sein** to have a cold;
(fam: beleidigt) to be peeved
verschonen vt to spare (jdn mit etw sb sth)
verschreiben irr vt (Med) to prescribe;
verschreibungspflichtig adj available
only on prescription
verschwand imperf von **verschwinden**
verschweigen irr vt to keep secret; **jdm
etw ~** to keep sth from sb

verschwenden vt to waste;
Verschwendung f waste
verschwiegen adj discreet; (Ort)
secluded
verschwinden (verschwand, verschwunden)
vi to disappear, to vanish; **verschwinde!**
get lost!; **verschwunden** pp von
verschwinden
Versehen (-s, -) nt **aus ~** by mistake;
versehentlich adv by mistake
versenden irr vt to send off
versessen adj **~ auf** (+akk) mad about
versetzen vt to transfer; (verpfänden) to
pawn; (fam: bei Verabredung) to stand up
▷ vr **sich in jdn** (o **jds Lage**) **~** to put
oneself in sb's place
verseuchen vt to contaminate
versichern vt to insure; (bestätigen) to
assure; **versichert sein** to be insured;
Versichertenkarte f health-insurance
card; **Versicherung** f insurance;
Versicherungskarte f **grüne ~** green card
(Brit), insurance document for driving abroad;
Versicherungspolice f insurance policy
versilbert adj silver-plated
versinken irr vi to sink
Version f version
versöhnen vt to reconcile ▷ vr **sich ~** to
become reconciled
versorgen vt to provide, to supply (mit
with); (Familie) to look after ▷ vr **sich ~** to
look after oneself; **Versorgung** f
provision; (Unterhalt) maintenance; (für
Alter etc) benefit
verspäten vr **sich ~** to be late; **verspätet**
adj late; **Verspätung** f delay; (eine
Stunde) **~ haben** to be (an hour) late
versprechen irr vt to promise ▷ vr **ich
habe mich versprochen** I didn't mean to
say that
Verstand m mind; (Vernunft) (common)
sense; **den ~ verlieren** to lose one's mind;
verständigen vt to inform ▷ vr **sich ~** to
communicate; (sich einigen) to come to an
understanding; **Verständigung** f
communication; **verständlich** adj
understandable; **Verständnis** nt
understanding (für of); (Mitgefühl)
sympathy; **verständnisvoll** adj
understanding
Verstärker (-s, -) m amplifier
verstauchen vt to sprain
Versteck (-(e)s, -e) nt hiding place;

~ **spielen** to play hide-and-seek;
verstecken vt to hide (vor +dat from) ▷ vr
sich ~ to hide (vor +dat from)
verstehen irr vt to understand; **falsch**
~ to misunderstand ▷ vr sich ~ to get on
(mit with)
Versteigerung f auction
verstellbar adj adjustable; **verstellen** vt
to move; (Uhr) to adjust; (versperren) to
block; (Stimme, Handschrift) to disguise ▷ vr
sich ~ to pretend, to put on an act
verstopfen vt to block up; (Med) to
constipate; **Verstopfung** f obstruction;
(Med) constipation
Verstoß m infringement, violation (gegen
of)
Versuch (-(e)s, -e) m attempt;
(wissenschaftlich) experiment; **versuchen**
vt to try
vertauschen vt to exchange;
(versehentlich) to mix up
verteidigen vt to defend;
Verteidiger(in) (-s, -) m(f) (Sport)
defender; (Jur) defence counsel;
Verteidigung f defence
verteilen vt to distribute
Vertrag (-(e)s, Verträge) m contract; (Pol)
treaty
vertragen irr vt to stand, to bear ▷ vr
sich ~ to get along (with each other); (sich
aussöhnen) to make it up
verträglich adj (Mensch) good-natured;
(Speisen) digestible
vertrauen vi **jdm/einer Sache ~** to trust
sb/sth; **Vertrauen** (-s) nt trust (in +akk in,
zu in); **ich habe kein ~ zu ihm** I don't trust
him; **ich hab's ihm im ~ gesagt** I told him
in confidence; **vertraulich** adj (geheim)
confidential; **vertraut** adj **sich mit etw
~ machen** to familiarize oneself with
sth
vertreten irr vt to represent; (Ansicht) to
hold; **Vertreter(in)** (-s, -) m(f)
representative
Vertrieb (-(e)s, -e) m (Abteilung) sales
department
vertrocknen vi to dry up
vertun irr vr sich ~ to make a mistake
vertuschen vt to cover up
verunglücken vi to have an accident;
tödlich ~ to be killed in an accident
verunsichern vt to make uneasy
verursachen vt to cause

verurteilen vt to condemn
vervielfältigen vt to make copies of
verwackeln vt (Foto) to blur
verwählen vr sich ~ to dial the wrong
number
verwalten vt to manage; (behördlich) to
administer; **Verwalter(in)** (-s, -) m(f)
manager; (Vermögens~) trustee;
Verwaltung f management; (amtlich)
administration
verwandt adj related (mit to);
Verwandte(r) mf relative, relation;
Verwandtschaft f relationship;
(Menschen) relations pl
verwarnen vt to warn; (Sport) to
caution
verwechseln vt to confuse (mit with);
(halten für) to mistake (mit for)
verweigern vt to refuse
verwenden vt to use; (Zeit) to spend;
Mühe auf etw (akk) ~ to take trouble over
sth; **Verwendung** f use
verwirklichen vt to realize; **sich selbst
~** to fulfil oneself
verwirren vt to confuse; **Verwirrung** f
confusion
verwitwet adj widowed
verwöhnen vt to spoil
verwunderlich adj surprising;
Verwunderung f astonishment
verwüsten vt to devastate
verzählen vr sich ~ to miscount
verzehren vt to consume
Verzeichnis nt (Liste) list; (Katalog) catalogue; (in Buch) index; (Inform) directory
verzeihen (verzieh, verziehen) vt, vi to
forgive (jdm etw sb for sth); **~ Sie bitte, ...**
(vor Frage etc) excuse me, ...; **~ Sie die
Störung** sorry to disturb you; **Verzeihung**
f **~!** sorry; **~, ...** (vor Frage etc) excuse me,
...; (**jdn**) **um ~ bitten** to apologize (to sb)
verzichten vi **auf etw** (akk) ~ to do
without sth; (aufgeben) to give sth up
verzieh imperf von verzeihen
verziehen pp von verzeihen
verziehen irr vt (Kind) to spoil; **das
Gesicht ~** to pull a face ▷ vr sich ~ to go
out of shape; (Gesicht) to contort;
(verschwinden) to disappear
verzieren vt to decorate
verzögern vt to delay ▷ vr sich ~ to be
delayed; **Verzögerung** f delay
verzweifeln vi to despair (an +dat of);

V

verzweifelt *adj* desperate; **Verzweiflung** *f* despair

Veterinär(in) (*-s, -e*) *m(f)* veterinary surgeon (*Brit*), veterinarian (*US*)

Vetter (*-s, -n*) *m* cousin

vgl. *abk* = **vergleiche** cf

Viagra® (*-s*) *nt* Viagra®

Vibrator (*-s, -en*) *m* vibrator; **vibrieren** *vi* to vibrate

Video (*-s, -s*) *nt* video; **auf ~ aufnehmen** to video; **Videoclip** (*-s, -s*) *m* video clip; **Videofilm** *m* video; **Videogerät** *nt* video (recorder); **Videokamera** *f* video camera; **Videokassette** *f* video (cassette); **Videorekorder** *m* video recorder; **Videospiel** *nt* video game; **Videothek** (*-, -en*) *f* video library

Vieh (*-(e)s*) *nt* cattle

viel *pron* a lot (of), lots of; **~ Arbeit** a lot of work, lots of work; **~e Leute** a lot of people, lots of people, many people; **zu ~** too much; **zu ~e** too many; **sehr ~** a great deal of; **sehr ~e** a great many; **ziemlich ~/~e** quite a lot of; **nicht ~** not much, not a lot of; **nicht ~e** not many, not a lot of ▷ *pron* a lot; **sie sagt nicht ~** she doesn't say a lot; **nicht ~** not much, not a lot of; **nicht ~e** not many, not a lot of; **gibt es ~?** is there much?, is there a lot?; **gibt es ~e?** are there many?, are there a lot? ▷ *adv* a lot; **er geht ~ ins Kino** he goes a lot to the cinema; **sehr ~** a great deal; **ziemlich ~** quite a lot; **~ besser** much better; **~ teurer** much more expensive; **~ zu ~** far too much

vielleicht *adv* perhaps; **~ ist sie krank** perhaps she's ill, she might be ill; **weißt du ~, wo er ist?** do you know where he is (by any chance)?

vielmal(s) *adv* many times; **danke ~s** many thanks; **vielmehr** *adv* rather; **vielseitig** *adj* very varied; (*Mensch, Gerät*) versatile

vier *num* four; **auf allen ~en** on all fours; **unter ~ Augen** in private, privately; **Vier** (*-, -en*) *f* four; (*Schulnote*) ≈ D; **Vierbettzimmer** *nt* four-bed room; **Viereck** (*-(e)s, -e*) *nt* four-sided figure; (*Quadrat*) square; **viereckig** *adj* four-sided; (*quadratisch*) square; **vierfach** *adj* **die ~e Menge** four times the amount; **vierhundert** *num* four hundred; **viermal** *adv* four times; **vierspurig** *adj* four-lane

viert *adv* **wir sind zu ~** there are four of us; **vierte(r, s)** *adj* fourth; *siehe auch* **dritte**

Viertel (*-s, -*) *nt* (*Stadtviertel*) quarter, district; (*Bruchteil*) quarter; (*Viertelliter*) quarter-litre; (*Uhrzeit*) quarter; **~ vor/nach drei** a quarter to/past three; **viertel drei** a quarter past two; **drei viertel drei** a quarter to three; **Viertelfinale** *nt* quarter-final; **vierteljährlich** *adj* quarterly; **Viertelstunde** *f* quarter of an hour

vierzehn *num* fourteen; **in ~ Tagen** in two weeks, in a fortnight (*Brit*); **vierzehntägig** *adj* two-week, fortnightly (*Brit*); **vierzehnte(r, s)** *adj* fourteenth; *siehe auch* **dritte**; **vierzig** *num* forty; **vierzigste(r, s)** *adj* fortieth

Vietnam (*-s*) *nt* Vietnam

Vignette *f* (*Autobahn~*) motorway (*Brit*) (*o* freeway (*US*)) permit

Villa (*-, Villen*) *f* villa

violett *adj* purple

Violine *f* violin

Virus (*-, Viren*) *m o nt* virus

Visitenkarte *f* card

Visum (*-s, Visa o Visen*) *nt* visa

Vitamin (*-s, -e*) *nt* vitamin

Vitrine (*-, -n*) *f* (glass) cabinet; (*Schaukasten*) display case

Vogel (*-s, Vögel*) *m* bird; **vögeln** *vi, vt* (*vulg*) to screw

Voicemail (*-, -s*) *f* voice mail

Vokal (*-s, -e*) *m* vowel

Volk (*-(e)s, Völker*) *nt* people *pl*; (*Nation*) nation; **Volksfest** *nt* festival; (*Jahrmarkt*) funfair; **Volkshochschule** *f* adult education centre; **Volkslied** *nt* folksong; **Volksmusik** *f* folk music; **volkstümlich** *adj* (*einfach und beliebt*) popular; (*herkömmlich*) traditional; (*Kunst*) folk

voll *adj* full (*von* of); **~ machen** to fill (up); **~ tanken** to fill up

Vollbart *m* beard; **Vollbremsung** *f* **eine ~ machen** to slam on the brakes; **vollends** *adv* completely

Volleyball *m* volleyball

Vollgas *nt* **mit ~** at full throttle; **~ geben** to step on it

völlig *adj* complete ▷ *adv* completely

volljährig *adj* of age; **Vollkaskoversicherung** *f* fully comprehensive insurance;

vollklimatisiert adj fully air-conditioned;
vollkommen adj perfect; **~er Unsinn**
complete rubbish ▷ adv completely
Vollkornbrot nt wholemeal (Brit) (o
whole wheat (US)) bread
Vollmacht (-, -en) f authority; (Urkunde)
power of attorney
Vollmilch f full-fat milk (Brit), whole milk
(US); **Vollmilchschokolade** f milk
chocolate; **Vollmond** m full moon;
Vollnarkose f general anaesthetic;
Vollpension f full board
vollständig adj complete
Volltreffer m direct hit; **Vollwaschmittel**
nt all-purpose washing powder;
Vollwertkost f wholefood; **vollzählig**
adj complete
Volt (-, -) nt volt
Volumen (-s, -) nt volume
vom kontr von **von dem** (räumlich, zeitlich,
Ursache) from; **ich kenne sie nur ~ Sehen** I
only know her by sight

SCHLÜSSELWORT

von präp +dat **1** (Ausgangspunkt) from; **von
... bis** from ... to; **von morgens bis
abends** from morning till night; **von ...
nach ...** from ... to ...; **von ... an** from ...;
von ... aus from ...; **von dort aus** from
there; **etw von sich aus tun** to do sth of
one's own accord; **von mir aus** (umg) if
you like I don't mind; **von wo/wann ...?**
where/when ... from?
2 (Urheber, im Passiv) by; **ein Gedicht von
Schiller** a poem by Schiller; **von etw
müde** tired from sth
3 (als Genitiv) of; **ein Freund von mir** a
friend of mine; **nett von dir** nice of you;
jeweils zwei von zehn two out of every
ten
4 (über) about; **er erzählte vom Urlaub**
he talked about his holiday
5: von wegen! (umg) no way!

SCHLÜSSELWORT

vor präp +dat **1** (räumlich) in front of; **vor
der Kirche links abbiegen** turn left before
the church
2 (zeitlich) before; **ich war vor ihm da** I
was there before him; **vor 2 Tagen** 2 days

ago; **5 (Minuten) vor 4** 5 (minutes) to 4;
vor kurzem a little while ago
3 (Ursache) with; **vor Wut/Liebe** with
rage/love; **vor Hunger sterben** to die of
hunger; **vor lauter Arbeit** because of
work
4: vor allem, vor allen Dingen most of all
▷ präp +akk (räumlich) in front of
▷ adv: **vor und zurück** backwards and
forwards

voran|gehen irr vi to go ahead; **einer
Sache** (dat) **~** to precede sth;
voran|kommen irr vi to make
progress
Vorarlberg (-s) nt Vorarlberg
voraus adv **jdm ~ sein** to be ahead of sb;
im Voraus in advance; **voraus|fahren** irr
vi to drive on ahead; **vorausgesetzt** conj
provided (that); **Voraussage** f
prediction; (Wetter) forecast;
voraus|sagen vt to predict;
voraus|sehen irr vt to foresee;
voraus|setzen vt to assume;
Voraussetzung f requirement,
prerequisite; **voraussichtlich** adj
expected ▷ adv probably; **voraus|zahlen**
vt to pay in advance
Vorbehalt (-(e)s, -e) m reservation;
vor|behalten irr vt **sich/jdm etw ~** to
reserve sth (for oneself)/for sb
vorbei adv past, over, finished;
vorbei|bringen irr vt to drop by (o in);
vorbei|fahren irr vi to drive past;
vorbei|gehen irr vi to pass by, to go past;
(verstreichen, aufhören) to pass;
vorbei|kommen irr vi to drop by;
vorbei|lassen irr vt **kannst du die Leute
~?** would you let these people pass?; **lässt
du mich bitte mal vorbei?** can I get past,
please?; **vorbei|reden** vi **aneinander ~** to
talk at cross-purposes
vor|bereiten vt to prepare ▷ vr **sich ~** to
get ready (auf +akk, für for); **Vorbereitung**
f preparation
vor|bestellen vt to book in advance;
(Essen) to order in advance;
Vorbestellung f booking, reservation
vor|beugen vi to prevent (dat sth);
vorbeugend adj preventive;
Vorbeugung f prevention
Vorbild nt (role) model; **vorbildlich** adj
model, ideal

V

Vorderachse f front axle; **vordere(r, s)** adj front; **Vordergrund** m foreground; **Vorderradantrieb** m (Auto) front-wheel drive; **Vorderseite** f front; **Vordersitz** m front seat; **Vorderteil** m o nt front (part)

vor|drängen vr **sich ~** to push forward

Vordruck m form

voreilig adj hasty, rash; **~e Schlüsse ziehen** to jump to conclusions; **voreingenommen** adj biased

vor|enthalten irr vt **jdm etw ~** to withhold sth from sb

vorerst adv for the moment

vor|fahren irr vi (vorausfahren) to drive on ahead; **vor das Haus ~** to drive up to the house; **fahren Sie bis zur Ampel vor** drive as far as the traffic lights

Vorfahrt f (Auto) right of way; **~ achten** give way (Brit), yield (US); **Vorfahrtsschild** nt give way (Brit) (o yield (US)) sign; **Vorfahrtsstraße** f major road

Vorfall m incident

vor|führen vt to demonstrate; (Film) to show; (Theaterstück, Trick) to perform

Vorgänger(in) m(f) predecessor

vor|gehen irr vi (vorausgehen) to go on ahead; (nach vorn) to go forward; (handeln) to act, to proceed; (Uhr) to be fast; (Vorrang haben) to take precedence; (passieren) to go on; **Vorgehen** (-s) nt procedure

Vorgesetzte(r) mf superior

vorgestern adv the day before yesterday

vor|haben irr vt to plan; **hast du schon was vor?** have you got anything on?; **ich habe vor, nach Rom zu fahren** I'm planning to go to Rome

vor|halten irr vt **jdm etw ~** to accuse sb of sth

Vorhand f forehand

vorhanden adj existing; (erhältlich) available

Vorhang m curtain

Vorhängeschloss nt padlock

Vorhaut f foreskin

vorher adv before; **zwei Tage ~** two days before; **~ essen wir** we'll eat first; **Vorhersage** f forecast; **vorher|sehen** irr vt to foresee

vorhin adv just now, a moment ago

vorig adj previous; (Woche etc) last

Vorkenntnisse pl previous knowledge sing

vor|kommen irr vi (nach vorne kommen) to come forward; (geschehen) to happen; (sich finden) to occur; (scheinen) to seem (to be); **sich** (dat) **dumm ~** to feel stupid

Vorlage f model

vor|lassen irr vt **jdn ~** to let sb go first

vorläufig adj temporary

vor|lesen irr vt to read out

Vorlesung f lecture

vorletzte(r, s) adj last but one; **am ~n Samstag** (on) the Saturday before last

Vorliebe f preference

vor|machen vt **kannst du es mir ~?** can you show me how to do it?; **jdm etwas ~** (fig: täuschen) to fool sb

vor|merken vt to note down; (Plätze) to book

Vormittag m morning; **am ~** in the morning; **heute ~** this morning; **vormittags** adv in the morning; **um 9 Uhr ~** at 9 (o'clock) in the morning, at 9 am

vorn(e) adv in front; **von ~ anfangen** to start at the beginning; **nach ~** to the front; **weiter ~** further up; **von ~ bis hinten** from beginning to end

Vorname m first name; **wie heißt du mit ~** what's your first name?

vornehm adj (von Rang) distinguished; (Benehmen) refined; (fein, elegant) elegant

vor|nehmen irr vt **sich** (dat) **etw ~** to start on sth; **sich** (dat) **~, etw zu tun** (beschließen) to decide to do sth

vornherein adv **von ~** from the start

Vorort m suburb

vorrangig adj priority

Vorrat m stock, supply; **vorrätig** adj in stock; **Vorratskammer** f pantry

Vorrecht nt privilege

Vorruhestand m early retirement

Vorsaison f early season

Vorsatz m intention; (Jur) intent; **vorsätzlich** adj intentional; (Jur) premeditated

Vorschau f preview; (Film) trailer

Vorschlag m suggestion, proposal; **vorschlagen** irr vt to suggest, to propose; **ich schlage vor, dass wir gehen** I suggest we go

vor|schreiben irr vt (befehlen) to stipulate; **jdm etw ~** to dictate sth to sb

Vorschrift f regulation, rule; (*Anweisung*) instruction; **vorschriftsmäßig** adj correct

Vorschule f nursery school, pre-school (*US*)

Vorsicht f care; **~!** look out; (*Schild*) caution; **~ Stufe!** mind the step; **vorsichtig** adj careful; **vorsichtshalber** adv just in case

Vorsorge f precaution; (*Vorbeugung*) prevention; **Vorsorgeuntersuchung** f checkup; **vorsorglich** adv as a precaution

Vorspann (*-(e)s, -e*) m credits pl

Vorspeise f starter

Vorsprung m projection; (*Abstand*) lead

vor|stellen vt (*bekannt machen*) to introduce; (*Uhr*) to put forward; (*vor etw*) to put in front; **sich** (*dat*) **etw ~** to imagine sth; **Vorstellung** f (*Bekanntmachen*) introduction; (*Theat*) performance; (*Gedanke*) idea; **Vorstellungsgespräch** nt interview

vor|täuschen vt to feign

Vorteil m advantage (*gegenüber* over); **die Vor- und Nachteile** the pros and cons; **vorteilhaft** adj advantageous

Vortrag (*-(e)s, Vorträge*) m talk (*über +akk* on); (*akademisch*) lecture; **einen ~ halten** to give a talk

vorüber adv over; **vorüber|gehen** irr vi to pass; **vorübergehend** adj temporary ▷ adv temporarily, for the time being

Vorurteil nt prejudice

Vorverkauf m advance booking

vor|verlegen vt to bring forward

Vorwahl f (*Tel*) dialling code (*Brit*), area code (*US*)

Vorwand (*-(e)s, Vorwände*) m pretext, excuse; **unter dem ~, dass** with the excuse that

vorwärts adv forward; **~ gehen** (*fig*) to progress; **Vorwärtsgang** m (*Auto*) forward gear

vorweg adv in advance; **vorweg|nehmen** irr vt to anticipate

Vorweihnachtszeit f pre-Christmas period, run-up to Christmas (*Brit*)

vor|werfen irr vt **jdm etw ~** to accuse sb of sth

vorwiegend adv mainly

Vorwort nt preface

Vorwurf m reproach; **sich** (*dat*) **Vorwürfe machen** to reproach oneself; **jdm**

Vorwürfe machen to accuse sb; **vorwurfsvoll** adj reproachful

vor|zeigen vt to show

vorzeitig adj premature, early

vor|ziehen irr vt (*lieber haben*) to prefer

Vorzug m preference; (*gute Eigenschaft*) merit; (*Vorteil*) advantage

vorzüglich adj excellent

vulgär adj vulgar

Vulkan (*-s, -e*) m volcano; **Vulkanausbruch** m volcanic eruption

W

W *abk* = **West** W

Waage (-, -n) *f* scales *pl*; (*Astr*) Libra; **waagerecht** *adj* horizontal

wach *adj* awake; **~ werden** to wake up; **Wache** (-, -n) *f* guard

Wachs (-es, -e) *nt* wax

wachsen (*wuchs, gewachsen*) *vi* to grow

wachsen *vt* (*Skier*) to wax

Wachstum *nt* growth

Wachtel (-, -n) *f* quail

Wächter(in) (-s, -) *m(f)* guard; (*auf Parkplatz*) attendant

wackelig *adj* wobbly; (*fig*) shaky; **Wackelkontakt** *m* loose connection; **wackeln** *vi* (*Stuhl*) to be wobbly; (*Zahn, Schraube*) to be loose; **mit dem Kopf ~** to waggle one's head

Wade (-, -n) *f* (*Anat*) calf

Waffe (-, -n) *f* weapon

Waffel (-, -n) *f* waffle; (*Keks, Eiswaffel*) wafer

wagen *vt* to risk; **es ~, etw zu tun** to dare to do sth

Wagen (-s, -) *m* (*Auto*) car; (*Eisenb*) carriage; **Wagenheber** (-s, -) *m* jack; **Wagentyp** *m* model, make

Wahl (-, -en) *f* choice; (*Pol*) election

wählen *vt* to choose; (*Tel*) to dial; (*Pol*) to vote for; (*durch Wahl ermitteln*) to elect ▷ *vi* to choose; (*Tel*) to dial; (*Pol*) to vote; **Wähler(in)** (-s, -) *m(f)* voter; **wählerisch** *adj* choosy

Wahlkampf *m* election campaign; **wahllos** *adv* at random; **Wahlwiederholung** *f* redial

Wahnsinn *m* madness; **~!** amazing!; **wahnsinnig** *adj* insane, mad ▷ *adv* (*fam*) incredibly

wahr *adj* true; **das darf doch nicht ~ sein!** I don't believe it; **nicht ~?** that's right, isn't it?

während *prep* +*gen* during ▷ *conj* while; **währenddessen** *adv* meanwhile, in the meantime

Wahrheit *f* truth

wahrnehmbar *adj* noticeable, perceptible; **wahr|nehmen** *irr vt* to perceive

Wahrsager(in) (-s, -) *m(f)* fortune-teller

wahrscheinlich *adj* probable, likely ▷ *adv* probably; **ich komme ~ zu spät** I'll probably be late; **Wahrscheinlichkeit** *f* probability

Währung *f* currency

Wahrzeichen *nt* symbol

Waise (-, -n) *f* orphan

Wal (-(e)s, -e) *m* whale

Wald (-(e)s, *Wälder*) *m* wood; (*groß*) forest; **Waldbrand** *m* forest fire; **Waldlauf** *m* cross-country run; **Waldsterben** (-s) *nt* forest dieback

Wales (-) *nt* Wales; **Waliser(in)** *m(f)* Welshman/Welshwoman; **walisisch** *adj* Welsh; **Walisisch** *nt* Welsh

Walkie-Talkie (-(s), -s) *nt* walkie-talkie

Walkman® (-s, -s) *m* walkman®, personal stereo

Wall (-(e)s, *Wälle*) *m* embankment

Wallfahrt *f* pilgrimage; **Wallfahrtsort** *m* place of pilgrimage

Walnuss *f* walnut

Walross (-es, -e) *nt* walrus

wälzen *vt* to roll; (*Bücher*) to pore over; (*Probleme*) to deliberate on ▷ *vr* **sich ~** to wallow; (*vor Schmerzen*) to roll about; (*im Bett*) to toss and turn

Walzer (-s, -) *m* waltz

Wand (-, *Wände*) *f* wall; (*Trenn~*) partition; (*Berg~*) (rock) face

Wandel (-s) *m* change; **wandeln** *vt* to change ▷ *vr* **sich ~** to change

Wanderer (-s, -) m, **Wanderin** f hiker; **Wanderkarte** f hiking map; **wandern** vi to hike; (Blick) to wander; (Gedanken) to stray; **Wanderschuh** m walking shoe; **Wanderstiefel** m hiking boot; **Wanderung** f hike; **eine ~ machen** to go on a hike; **Wanderweg** m walking (o hiking) trail

Wandleuchte f wall lamp; **Wandmalerei** f mural; **Wandschrank** m built-in cupboard (Brit), closet (US)

wandte imperf von **wenden**

Wange (-, -n) f cheek

wann adv when; **seit ~ ist sie da?** how long has she been here?; **bis ~ bleibt ihr?** how long are you staying?

Wanne (-, -n) f (bath) tub

Wappen (-s, -) nt coat of arms

war imperf von **sein**

warb imperf von **werben**

Ware (-, -n) f product; **~n** goods pl; **Warenhaus** nt department store; **Warenprobe** f sample; **Warensendung** f consignment; **Warenzeichen** nt trademark

warf imperf von **werfen**

warm adj warm; (Essen) hot; **~ laufen** to warm up; **mir ist es zu ~** I'm too warm; **Wärme** (-, -n) f warmth; **wärmen** vt to warm; (Essen) to warm (o to heat) up ▷ vi (Kleidung, Sonne) to be warm ▷ vr **sich ~** to warm up; (gegenseitig) to keep each other warm; **Wärmflasche** f hot-water bottle; **Warmstart** m (Inform) warm start

Warnblinkanlage f (Auto) warning flasher; **Warndreieck** nt (Auto) warning triangle; **warnen** vt to warn (vor +dat about, of); **Warnung** f warning

Warteliste f waiting list; **warten** vi to wait (auf +akk for); **warte mal!** wait (o hang on) a minute ▷ vt (Tech) to service

Wärter(in) m(f) attendant

Wartesaal m, **Wartezimmer** nt waiting room

Wartung f service; (das Warten) servicing

warum adv why

Warze (-, -n) f wart

was pron what; (fam: etwas) something; **~ kostet das?** what does it cost? how much is it?; **~ für ein Auto ist das?** what kind of car is that?; **~ für eine Farbe/Größe?** what colour/size?; **~?** (fam: wie bitte?) what?; **~ ist/gibt's?** what is it?

what's up? **du weißt, ~ ich meine** you know what I mean; **~ (auch) immer** whatever; **soll ich dir ~ mitbringen?** do you want me to bring you anything?; **alles, ~ er hat** everything he's got

Waschanlage f (Auto) car wash; **waschbar** adj washable; **Waschbär** m raccoon; **Waschbecken** nt washbasin

Wäsche (-, -n) f washing; (schmutzig) laundry; (Bettwäsche) linen; (Unterwäsche) underwear; **in der ~** in the wash; **Wäscheklammer** f clothes peg (Brit) (o pin (US)); **Wäscheleine** f clothesline

waschen (wusch, gewaschen) vt, vi to wash; **Waschen und Legen** shampoo and set ▷ vr **sich ~** to (have a) wash; **sich** (dat) **die Haare ~** to wash one's hair

Wäscherei f laundry; **Wäscheschleuder** f spin-drier; **Wäscheständer** m clothes horse; **Wäschetrockner** m tumble-drier

Waschgelegenheit f washing facilities pl; **Waschlappen** m flannel (Brit), washcloth (US); (fam: Mensch) wet blanket; **Waschmaschine** f washing machine; **Waschmittel** nt, **Waschpulver** nt washing powder; **Waschraum** m washroom; **Waschsalon** (-s, -s) m launderette (Brit), laundromat (US); **Waschstraße** f car wash

Wasser (-s, -) nt water; **fließendes ~** running water; **Wasserball** m (Sport) water polo; **Wasserbob** m jet ski; **wasserdicht** adj watertight; (Uhr etc) waterproof; **Wasserfall** m waterfall; **Wasserfarbe** f watercolour; **wasserfest** adj watertight, waterproof; **Wasserhahn** m tap (Brit), faucet (US); **wässerig** adj watery; **Wasserkessel** m kettle; **Wasserkocher** m electric kettle; **Wasserleitung** f water pipe; **wasserlöslich** adj water-soluble; **Wassermann** m (Astr) Aquarius; **Wassermelone** f water melon; **Wasserrutschbahn** f water chute; **Wasserschaden** m water damage; **wasserscheu** adj scared of water; **Wasserski** nt water-skiing; **Wasserspiegel** m surface of the water; (Wasserstand) water level; **Wassersport** m water sports pl; **Wasserspülung** f flush; **wasserundurchlässig** adj watertight, waterproof; **Wasserverbrauch** m water consumption; **Wasserversorgung** f

w

water supply; **Wasserwaage** f spirit
level; **Wasserwerk** nt waterworks pl
waten vi to wade
Watt (-(e)s, -en) nt (Geo) mud flats pl
▷ (-s, -) nt (Elek) watt
Watte (-, -n) f cotton wool; **Wattepad**
(-s, -s) m cotton pad; **Wattestäbchen** nt
cotton bud, Q-tip® (US)
WC (-s, -s) nt toilet, restroom (US);
WC-Reiniger m toilet cleaner
Web (-s) nt (Inform) Web; **Webseite** f
(Inform) web page
Wechsel (-s, -) m change; (Spieler~) (Sport)
substitution; **Wechselgeld** nt change;
wechselhaft adj (Wetter) changeable;
Wechseljahre pl menopause sing;
Wechselkurs m exchange rate;
wechseln vt to change; (Blicke) to
exchange; **Geld ~** to change some money;
(in Kleingeld) to get some change; **Euro in
Pfund ~** to change euros into pounds ▷ vi
to change; **kannst du ~?** can you change
this?; **Wechselstrom** m alternating
current, AC; **Wechselstube** f bureau de
change
Weckdienst m wake-up call service;
wecken vt to wake (up); **Wecker** (-s, -) m
alarm clock; **Weckruf** m wake-up call
wedeln vi (Ski) to wedel; **mit etw ~** to
wave sth; **mit dem Schwanz ~** to wag its
tail; **der Hund wedelte mit dem
Schwanz** the dog wagged its tail
weder conj **~ ... noch ...** neither ... nor ...
weg adv (entfernt, verreist) away; (los, ab)
off; **er war schon ~** he had already left (o
gone); **Hände ~!** hands off; **weit ~** a long
way away (o off)
Weg (-(e)s, -e) m way; (Pfad) path; (Route)
route; **jdn nach dem ~ fragen** to ask sb
the way; **auf dem ~ sein** to be on the
way
weg|bleiben irr vi to stay away;
weg|bringen irr vt to take away
wegen prep +gen o dat because of
weg|fahren irr vi to drive away; (abfahren)
to leave; (in Urlaub) to go away;
Wegfahrsperre f (Auto) (engine)
immobilizer; **weg|gehen** irr vi to go
away; **weg|kommen** irr vi to get away;
(fig) **gut/schlecht ~** to come off
well/badly; **weg|lassen** irr vt to leave
out; **weg|laufen** irr vi to run away;
weg|legen vt to put aside; **weg|machen**

vt (fam) to get rid of; **weg|müssen** irr vi
ich muss weg I've got to go;
weg|nehmen irr vt to take away;
weg|räumen vt to clear away;
weg|rennen irr vi to run away;
weg|schicken vt to send away;
weg|schmeißen irr vt to throw away;
weg|sehen irr vi to look away; **weg|tun**
irr vt to put away
Wegweiser (-s, -) m signpost
weg|werfen irr vt to throw away;
Wegwerfflasche f non-returnable bottle;
weg|wischen vt to wipe off; **weg|ziehen**
irr vi to move (away)
weh adj sore; siehe auch **wehtun**
wehen vt, vi to blow; (Fahne) to flutter
Wehen pl labour pains pl
Wehrdienst m military service
wehren vr **sich ~** to defend oneself
weh|tun irr vi to hurt; **jdm/sich ~** to hurt
sb/oneself
Weibchen nt **es ist ein ~** (Tier) it's a she;
weiblich adj feminine; (Bio) female
weich adj soft; **~ gekocht** (Ei) soft-boiled
Weichkäse m soft cheese; (Streichkäse)
cheese spread; **weichlich** adj soft;
(körperlich) weak; **Weichspüler** (-s, -) m
(für Wäsche) (fabric) softener
Weide (-, -n) f (Baum) willow; (Grasfläche)
meadow
weigern vr **sich ~** to refuse; **Weigerung** f
refusal
Weiher (-s, -) m pond
Weihnachten (-, -) nt Christmas;
Weihnachtsabend m Christmas Eve;
Weihnachtsbaum m Christmas tree;
Weihnachtsfeier f Christmas party;
Weihnachtsferien pl Christmas holidays
pl (Brit), Christmas vacation sing (US);
Weihnachtsgeschenk nt Christmas
present; **Weihnachtslied** nt Christmas
carol; **Weihnachtsmann** m Father
Christmas, Santa (Claus)

● **Weihnachtsmarkt**
●
● The **Weihnachtsmarkt** is a market held
● in most large towns in Germany in
● the weeks prior to Christmas. People
● visit it to buy presents, toys and
● Christmas decorations, and to enjoy
● the festive atmosphere. Food and
● drink associated with the Christmas

● festivities can also be eaten and
● drunk there, for example,
● gingerbread and mulled wine.

Weihnachtsstern m (Bot) poinsettia;
Weihnachtstag m **erster ~** Christmas
Day; **zweiter ~** Boxing Day;
Weihnachtszeit f Christmas season
weil conj because
Weile (-) f while, short time; **es kann
noch eine ~ dauern** it could take some
time
Wein (-(e)s, -e) m wine; (Pflanze) vine;
Weinbeere f grape; **Weinberg** m
vineyard; **Weinbergschnecke** f snail;
Weinbrand m brandy
weinen vt, vi to cry
Weinglas nt wine glass; **Weinkarte** f
wine list; **Weinkeller** m wine cellar;
Weinlese (-, -n) f vintage; **Weinprobe** f
wine tasting; **Weintraube** f grape
weise adj wise
Weise (-, -n) f manner, way; **auf diese
(Art und) ~** this way
weisen (wies, gewiesen) vt to show
Weisheit f wisdom; **Weisheitszahn** m
wisdom tooth
weiß adj white; **Weißbier** nt ≈ wheat
beer; **Weißbrot** nt white bread;
weißhaarig adj white-haired; **Weißkohl**
m, **Weißkraut** nt (white) cabbage;
Weißwein m white wine
weit adj wide; (Begriff) broad; (Reise, Wurf)
long; (Kleid) loose; **wie ~ ist es ...?** how
far is it ...?; **so ~ sein** to be ready ▷ adv
far; **~ verbreitet** widespread; **~ gereist**
widely travelled; **~ offen** wide open; **das
geht zu ~** that's going too far, that's
pushing it
weiter adj wider; (~ weg) farther (away);
(zusätzlich) further; **~e Informationen**
further information sing ▷ adv further; **~!**
go on; (weitergehen!) keep moving;
~ nichts/niemand nothing/nobody else;
und so ~ and so on; **weiter|arbeiten** vi to
carry on working; **Weiterbildung** f
further training (o education);
weiter|empfehlen irr vt to recommend;
weiter|erzählen vt **nicht ~!** don't tell
anyone; **weiter|fahren** irr vi to go on
(nach to, bis as far as); **weiter|geben** irr vt
to pass on; **weiter|gehen** irr vi to go on;
weiter|helfen irr vi **jdm ~** to help sb;

weiterhin adv **etw ~ tun** to go on doing
sth; **weiter|machen** vt, vi to continue;
weiter|reisen vi to continue one's
journey
weitgehend adj considerable ▷ adv
largely; **weitsichtig** adj long-sighted; (fig)
far-sighted; **Weitspringer(in)** m(f) long
jumper; **Weitsprung** m long jump;
Weitwinkelobjektiv nt (Foto) wide-angle
lens
Weizen (-s, -) m wheat; **Weizenbier** nt ≈
wheat beer

○ **SCHLÜSSELWORT**

welche(r, s) interrogativ pron which;
welcher von beiden? which (one) of the
two?; **welchen hast du genommen?**
which (one) did you take?; **welche eine
...!** what a ...!; **welche Freude!** what joy!
▷ indef pron some; (in Fragen) any; **ich habe
welche** I have some, **haben Sie welche?**
do you have any?
▷ relativ pron (bei Menschen) who (bei Sachen)
which that; **welche(r, s) auch immer**
whoever/whichever/whatever

welk adj withered; **welken** vi to wither
Welle (-, -n) f wave; **Wellengang** m
waves pl; **starker ~** heavy seas pl;
Wellenlänge f (a. fig) wavelength;
Wellenreiten nt surfing; **Wellensittich**
(-s, -e) m budgerigar, budgie; **wellig** adj
wavy
Welpe (-n, -n) m puppy
Welt (-, -en) f world; **auf der ~** in the
world; **auf die ~ kommen** to be born;
Weltall nt universe; **weltbekannt**,
weltberühmt adj world-famous;
Weltkrieg m world war; **Weltmacht** f
world power; **Weltmeister(in)** m(f)
world champion; **Weltmeisterschaft** f
world championship; (im Fußball) World
Cup; **Weltraum** m space; **Weltreise** f
trip round the world; **Weltrekord** m
world record; **Weltstadt** f metropolis;
weltweit adj worldwide, global
wem pron dat von **wer** who ... to, (to)
whom; **~ hast du's gegeben?** who did you
give it to?; **~ gehört es?** who does it
belong to?, whose is it?; **~ auch immer es
gehört** whoever it belongs to
wen pron akk von **wer** who, whom; **~ hast**

du besucht? who did you visit?;
~ möchten Sie sprechen? who would you
like to speak to?; **~ auch immer du
gesprochen hast** whoever you talked
to

Wende (-, -n) f turning point;
(*Veränderung*) change; **die ~** (*Hist*) the fall
of the Berlin Wall; **Wendekreis** m (*Auto*)
turning circle

Wendeltreppe f spiral staircase

wenden (wendete o wandte, gewendet o
gewandt) vt, vi to turn (round); (*um 180°*)
to make a U-turn; **sich an jdn ~** to turn
to sb; **bitte ~!** please turn over, PTO
▷ vr **sich ~** to turn; **sich an jdn ~** to turn
to sb

wenig pron, adv little; **~(e)** pl few; (**nur**) **ein**
(**klein**) **~** (just) a little (bit); **ein ~ Zucker** a
little bit of sugar, a little sugar; **wir haben
~ Zeit** we haven't got much time; **zu ~** too
little; pl too few; **nur ~ wissen** only a few
know ▷ adv **er spricht ~** he doesn't talk
much; **~ bekannt** little known; **wenige**
pron pl few pl; **wenigste(r, s)** adj least;
wenigstens adv at least

○ SCHLÜSSELWORT

wenn konj **1** (*falls, bei Wünschen*) if; **wenn
auch ..., selbst wenn ...** even if ...; **wenn
ich doch ...** if only I ...
2 (*zeitlich*) when; **immer wenn** whenever

wer pron who; **~ war das?** who was that?;
~ von euch? which (one) of you? ▷ pron
anybody who, anyone who; **~ das glaubt,
ist dumm** anyone who believes that is
stupid; **~ auch immer** whoever ▷ pron
somebody, someone; (*in Fragen*)
anybody, anyone; **ist da ~?** is (there)
anybody there?

Werbefernsehen nt TV commercials pl;
Werbegeschenk nt promotional gift;
werben (warb, geworben) vt to win;
(*Mitglied*) to recruit ▷ vi to advertise;
Werbespot (-s, -s) m commercial;
Werbung f advertising

○ SCHLÜSSELWORT

werden (pt **wurde**, pp **geworden** od (*bei
Passiv*) **worden**) vi to become; **was ist aus
ihm/aus der Sache geworden?** what

became of him/it?; **es ist nichts/gut
geworden** it came to nothing/turned out
well; **es wird Nacht/Tag** it's getting
dark/light; **mir wird kalt** I'm getting cold;
mir wird schlecht I feel ill; **Erster werden**
to come od be first; **das muss anders
werden** that'll have to change; **rot/zu Eis
werden** to turn red/to ice; **was willst du
(mal) werden?** what do you want to be?;
die Fotos sind gut geworden the photos
have come out nicely

▷ als Hilfsverb **1** (*bei Futur*): **er wird es tun**
he will od he'll do it; **er wird das nicht tun**
he will not od he won't do it; **es wird
gleich regnen** it's going to rain
2 (*bei Konjunktiv*): **ich würde ...** I would ...;
er würde gern ... he would od he'd like to
...; **ich würde lieber ...** I would od I'd
rather ...
3 (*bei Vermutung*): **sie wird in der Küche
sein** she will be in the kitchen
4 (*bei Passiv*): **gebraucht werden** to be
used; **er ist erschossen worden** he has od
he's been shot; **mir wurde gesagt, dass
...** I was told that ...

werfen (warf, geworfen) vt to throw

Werft (-, -en) f shipyard, dockyard

Werk (-(e)s, -e) nt (*Kunstwerk, Buch etc*)
work; (*Fabrik*) factory; (*Mechanismus*)
works pl; **Werkstatt** (-, -stätten) f
workshop; (*Auto*) garage; **Werktag** m
working day; **werktags** adv on weekdays,
during the week; **Werkzeug** nt tool;
Werkzeugkasten m toolbox

wert adj worth; **es ist etwa 50 Euro ~** it's
worth about 50 euros; **das ist nichts ~** it's
worthless; **Wert** (-(e)s, -e) m worth;
(*Zahlen~*) (*Fin*) value; **~ legen auf** (+akk) to
attach importance to; **es hat doch
keinen ~** (*Sinn*) it's pointless; **Wertangabe**
f declaration of value; **Wertbrief** m
insured letter; **Wertgegenstand** m
valuable object; **wertlos** adj worthless;
Wertmarke f token; **Wertpapiere** pl
securities pl; **Wertsachen** pl valuables pl;
Wertstoff m recyclable waste; **wertvoll**
adj valuable

Wesen (-s, -) nt being; (*Natur, Charakter*)
nature

wesentlich adj significant; (*beträchtlich*)
considerable ▷ adv considerably

weshalb adv why

Wespe (-, -n) f wasp; **Wespenstich** m wasp sting

wessen pron gen von **wer**; whose

● **Wessi**
●
● A **Wessi** is a colloquial and often
● derogatory word used to describe a
● German from the former West
● Germany. The expression
● 'Besserwessi' is used by East
● Germans to describe a West German
● who is considered to be a know-all.

West west; **Westdeutschland** nt (als Landesteil) Western Germany; (Hist) West Germany

Weste (-, -n) f waistcoat (Brit), vest (US); (Wollweste) cardigan

Westen (-s) m west; **im ~ Englands** in the west of England; **der Wilde ~** the Wild West; **Westeuropa** nt Western Europe; **Westküste** f west coast; **westlich** adj western; (Kurs, Richtung) westerly; **Westwind** m west(erly) wind

weswegen adv why

Wettbewerb m competition; **Wettbüro** nt betting office; **Wette** (-, -n) f bet; **eine ~ abschließen** to make a bet; **die ~ gilt!** you're on; **wetten** vt, vi to bet (auf+akk on); **ich habe mit ihm gewettet, dass ...** I bet him that ...; **ich wette mit dir um 50 Euro** I'll bet you 50 euros; **~, dass?** wanna bet?

Wetter (-s, -) nt weather; **Wetterbericht** m, **Wettervorhersage** f weather forecast; **Wetterkarte** f weather map; **Wetterlage** f weather situation; **Wettervorhersage** f weather forecast

Wettkampf m contest; **Wettlauf** m race; **Wettrennen** nt race

WG (-, -s) f abk = **Wohngemeinschaft**

Whirlpool® (-s, -s) m jacuzzi®

Whisky (-s, -s) m (schottisch) whisky; (irisch, amerikanisch) whiskey

wichtig adj important

wickeln vt (Schnur) to wind (um round); (Schal, Decke) to wrap (um round); **ein Baby ~** to change a baby's nappy (Brit) (o diaper (US)); **Wickelraum** m baby-changing room; **Wickeltisch** m baby-changing table

Widder (-s, -) m (Zool) ram; (Astr) Aries sing

wider prep +akk against

widerlich adj disgusting

widerrufen irr vt to withdraw; (Auftrag, Befehl etc) to cancel

widersprechen irr vi to contradict (jdm sb); **Widerspruch** m contradiction

Widerstand m resistance; **widerstandsfähig** adj resistant (gegen to)

widerwärtig adj disgusting

widerwillig adj unwilling, reluctant

widmen vt to dedicate ▷ vr **sich jdm/etw ~** to devote oneself to sb/sth; **Widmung** f dedication

○ SCHLÜSSELWORT

wie adv how; **wie groß/schnell?** how big/fast?; **wie wärs?** how about it?; **wie ist er?** what's he like?; **wie gut du das kannst!** you're very good at it; **wie bitte?** pardon?; (entrüstet) I beg your pardon!; **und wie!** and how!; **wie viel** how much; **wie viel Menschen** how many people; **wie weit** to what extent

▷ konj **1** (bei Vergleichen): **so schön wie ...** as beautiful as ...; **wie ich schon sagte** as I said; **wie du** like you; **singen wie ein ...** to sing like a ...; **wie (zum Beispiel)** such as (for example)

2 (zeitlich): **wie er das hörte, ging er** when he heard that he left; **er hörte, wie der Regen fiel** he heard the rain falling

wieder adv again; **~ ein(e) ...** another ...; **~ erkennen** to recognize; **etw ~ gutmachen** to make up for sth; **~ verwerten** to recycle

wieder|bekommen irr vt to get back

wiederholen vt to repeat; **Wiederholung** f repetition

Wiederhören nt (Tel) **auf ~** goodbye

wieder|kommen irr vi to come back

wieder|sehen irr vt to see again; (wieder treffen) to meet again; **Wiedersehen** (-s) nt reunion; **auf ~!** goodbye

Wiedervereinigung f reunification

Wiege (-, -n) f cradle; **wiegen** (wog, gewogen) vt, vi (Gewicht) to weigh

Wien (-s) nt Vienna

wies imperf von **weisen**

Wiese (-, -n) f meadow

Wiesel (-s, -) nt weasel

wieso adv why

w

wievielmal adv how often; **wievielte(r, s)** adj **zum ~n Mal?** how many times?; **den Wievielten haben wir heute?** what's the date today?; **am Wievielten hast du Geburtstag?** which day is your birthday?

wieweit conj to what extent

wild adj wild

Wild (-(e)s) nt game

wildfremd adj (fam) **ein ~er Mensch** a complete (o total) stranger; **Wildleder** nt suede; **Wildpark** m game park; **Wildschwein** nt (wild) boar; **Wildwasserfahren** (-s) nt whitewater canoeing (o rafting)

Wille (-ns, -n) m will

willen prep +gen **um ... ~** for the sake of ...; **um Himmels ~!** (vorwurfsvoll) for heaven's sake; (betroffen) goodness me

willkommen adj welcome

Wimper (-, -n) f eyelash; **Wimperntusche** f mascara

Wind (-(e)s, -e) m wind

Windel (-, -n) f nappy (Brit), diaper (US)

windgeschützt adj sheltered from the wind; **windig** adj windy; (fig) dubious; **Windjacke** f windcheater; **Windmühle** f windmill; **Windpocken** pl chickenpox sing; **Windschutzscheibe** f (Auto) windscreen (Brit), windshield (US); **Windstärke** f wind force; **Windsurfen** (-s) nt windsurfing; **Windsurfer(in)** m(f) windsurfer

Winkel (-s, -) m (Math) angle; (Gerät) set square; (in Raum) corner; **im rechten ~ zu** at right angles to

winken vt, vi to wave

Winter (-s, -) m winter; **Winterausrüstung** f (Auto) winter equipment; **Winterfahrplan** m winter timetable; **winterlich** adj wintry; **Wintermantel** m winter coat; **Winterreifen** m winter tyre; **Winterschlussverkauf** m winter sales pl; **Wintersport** m winter sports pl

Winterzeit f (Uhrzeit) winter time (Brit), standard time (US)

winzig adj tiny

wir pron we; **~ selbst** we ourselves; **~ alle** all of us; **~ drei** the three of us; **~ sind's** it's us; **~ nicht** not us

Wirbel (-s, -) m whirl; (Trubel) hurly-burly; (Aufsehen) fuss; (Anat) vertebra; **Wirbelsäule** f spine

wirken vi to be effective; (erfolgreich sein) to work; (scheinen) to seem

wirklich adj real; **Wirklichkeit** f reality

wirksam adj effective; **Wirkung** f effect

wirr adj confused; **Wirrwarr** (-s) m confusion

Wirsing (-s) m savoy cabbage

Wirt (-(e)s, -e) m landlord; **Wirtin** f landlady

Wirtschaft f (Comm) economy; (Gaststätte) pub; **wirtschaftlich** adj (Pol, Comm) economic; (sparsam) economical

Wirtshaus nt pub

wischen vt, vi to wipe; **Wischer** (-s, -) m wiper; **Wischlappen** m cloth

wissen (wusste, gewusst) vt to know; **weißt du schon, ...?** did you know ...?; **woher weißt du das?** how do you know?; **das musst du selbst ~** that's up to you; **Wissen** (-s) nt knowledge

Wissenschaft f science; **Wissenschaftler(in)** (-s, -) m(f) scientist; (Geisteswissenschaftler) academic; **wissenschaftlich** adj scientific; (geisteswissenschaftlich) academic

Witwe (-, -n) f widow; **Witwer** (-s, -) m widower

Witz (-(e)s, -e) m joke; **mach keine ~e!** you're kidding!; **das soll wohl ein ~ sein** you've got to be joking; **witzig** adj funny

wo adv where; **zu einer Zeit, ~ ...** at a time when ...; überall, **~ ich hingehe** wherever I go ▷ conj **jetzt, ~ du da bist** now that you're here; **~ ich dich gerade spreche** while I'm talking to you; **woanders** adv somewhere else

wobei adv **~ mir einfällt ...** which reminds me ...

Woche (-, -n) f week; **während** (o unter) **der ~** during the week; **einmal die ~** once a week; **Wochenende** nt weekend; **am ~** at (Brit) (o on (US)) the weekend; **wir fahren übers ~ weg** we're going away for the weekend; **Wochenendhaus** nt weekend cottage; **Wochenkarte** f weekly (season) ticket; **wochenlang** adv for weeks (on end); **Wochenmarkt** m weekly market; **Wochentag** m weekday; **wöchentlich** adj, adv weekly

Wodka (-s, -s) m vodka

wodurch adv **~ unterscheiden sie sich?** what's the difference between them?;

~ hast du es gemerkt? how did you notice?; **wofür** adv (relativ) for which; (Frage) what ... for; **~ brauchst du das?** what do you need that for?

wog imperf von **wiegen**

woher adv where ... from; **wohin** adv where ... to

○ SCHLÜSSELWORT

wohl adv 1: **sich wohl fühlen** (zufrieden) to feel happy; (gesundheitlich) to feel well; **jdm wohl tun** to do sb good; **wohl oder übel** whether one likes it or not

2 (wahrscheinlich) probably; (gewiss) certainly; (vielleicht) perhaps; **sie ist wohl zu Hause** she's probably at home; **das ist doch wohl nicht dein Ernst!** surely you're not serious!; **das mag wohl sein** that may well be; **ob das wohl stimmt?** I wonder if that's true; **er weiß das sehr wohl** he knows that perfectly well

Wohlwollen (-s) nt goodwill

Wohnblock m block of flats (Brit), apartment house (US); **wohnen** vi to live; **Wohngemeinschaft** f shared flat (Brit) (o apartment (US)); **ich wohne in einer ~** I share a flat (o apartment); **wohnhaft** adj resident; **Wohnküche** f kitchen-cum-living-room; **Wohnmobil** (-s, -e) nt camper, RV (US); **Wohnort** m place of residence; **Wohnsitz** m place of residence; **Wohnung** f flat (Brit), apartment (US); **Wohnungstür** f front door; **Wohnwagen** m caravan; **Wohnzimmer** nt living room

Wolf (-(e)s, **Wölfe**) m wolf

Wolke (-, -n) f cloud; **Wolkenkratzer** m skyscraper; **wolkenlos** adj cloudless; **wolkig** adj cloudy

Wolldecke f (woollen) blanket; **Wolle** (-, -n) f wool

○ SCHLÜSSELWORT

wollen (pt **wollte**, pp **gewollt** od (als Hilfsverb) **wollen**) vt, vi to want; **ich will nach Hause** I want to go home; **er will nicht** he doesn't want to; **er wollte das nicht** he didn't want it; **wenn du willst** if you like; **ich will, dass du mir zuhörst** I want you to listen to me

▷ Hilfsverb: **er will ein Haus kaufen** he wants to buy a house; **ich wollte, ich wäre ...** I wish I were ...; **etw gerade tun wollen** to be going to do sth

Wolljacke f cardigan

womit adv what ... with; **~ habe ich das verdient?** what have I done to deserve that?

womöglich adv possibly

woran adv **~ denkst du?** what are you thinking of?; **~ ist er gestorben?** what did he die of?; **~ sieht man das?** how can you tell?

worauf adv **~ wartest du?** what are you waiting for?

woraus adv **~ ist das gemacht?** what is it made of?

Workshop (-s, -s) m workshop

World Wide Web nt World Wide Web

Wort (-(e)s, **Wörter**) nt (Vokabel) word ▷ (-(e)s, -e) nt (Äußerung) word; **mit anderen ~en** in other words; **jdn beim ~ nehmen** to take sb at his/her word; **Wörterbuch** nt dictionary; **wörtlich** adj literal

worüber adv **~ redet sie?** what is she talking about?

worum adv **~ gehts?** what is it about?

worunter adv **~ leidet er?** what is he suffering from?

wovon adv (relativ) from which; **~ redest du?** what are you talking about?; **wozu** adv (relativ) to/for which; (interrogativ) what ... for/to; (warum) why; **~?** what for?; **~ brauchst du das?** what do you need that for?; **~ soll das gut sein?** what's it for?; **~ hast du Lust?** what do you feel like doing?

Wrack (-(e)s, -s) nt wreck

Wucher (-s) m profiteering; **das ist ~!** that's daylight robbery!

wuchs imperf von **wachsen**

wühlen vi to rummage; (Tier) to root; (Maulwurf) to burrow

Wühltisch m bargain counter

wund adj sore; **Wunde** (-, -n) f wound

Wunder (-s, -) nt miracle; **es ist kein ~** it's no wonder; **wunderbar** adj wonderful, marvellous; **Wunderkerze** f sparkler; **Wundermittel** nt wonder cure; **wundern** vr **sich ~** to be surprised (über +akk at) ▷ vt

W

to surprise; **wunderschön** *adj* beautiful;
wundervoll *adj* wonderful

Wundsalbe *f* antiseptic ointment;
Wundstarrkrampf *m* tetanus

Wunsch (-(e)s, Wünsche) *m* wish (*nach* for);
wünschen *vt* to wish; **sich** (*dat*) **etw ~** to
want sth; **ich wünsche dir alles Gute** I
wish you all the best; **wünschenswert**
adj desirable

wurde *imperf von* **werden**

Wurf (-s, Würfe) *m* throw; (*Zool*) litter

Würfel (-s, -) *m* dice; (*Math*) cube;
würfeln *vi* to throw (the dice); (*Würfel
spielen*) to play dice ▷ *vt* (*Zahl*) to throw;
(*Gastr*) to dice; **Würfelzucker** *m* lump
sugar

Wurm (-(e)s, Würmer) *m* worm

Wurst (-, Würste) *f* sausage; **das ist mir
~** (*fam*) I couldn't care less

Würstchen *nt* frankfurter

Würze (-, -n) *f* seasoning, spice

Wurzel (-, -n) *f* root

würzen *vt* to season, to spice; **würzig** *adj*
spicy

wusch *imperf von* **waschen**

wusste *imperf von* **wissen**

wüst *adj* (*unordentlich*) chaotic;
(*ausschweifend*) wild; (*öde*) desolate; (*fam:
heftig*) terrible

Wüste (-, -n) *f* desert

Wut (-) *f* rage, fury; **ich habe eine ~ auf
ihn** I'm really mad at him; **wütend** *adj*
furious

WWW (-) *nt abk* = **World Wide Web**
WWW

X-Beine *pl* knock-knees *pl*; **x-beinig** *adj* knock-kneed
x-beliebig *adj* **ein ~es Buch** any book (you like)
x-mal *adv* umpteen times
Xylophon (*-s, -e*) *nt* xylophone

Yacht (-, -*en*) *f* yacht
Yoga (-(*s*)) *m o nt* yoga
Yuppie (-*s*, -*s*) *m* (-, -*s*) *f* yuppie

Zacke (-, -n) f point; (*Säge, Kamm*) tooth; (*Gabel*) prong; **zackig** adj (*Linie etc*) jagged; (*fam: Tempo*) brisk

zaghaft adj timid

zäh adj tough; (*Flüssigkeit*) thick

Zahl (-, -en) f number; **zahlbar** adj payable; **zahlen** vt, vi to pay; **~ bitte!** could I have the bill (*Brit*) (*o* check (*US*)) please?; **bar ~** to pay cash; **zählen** vt, vi to count (*auf +akk* on); **~ zu** to be one of; **Zahlenschloss** nt combination lock; **Zähler** (-s, -) m (*Gerät*) counter; (*für Strom, Wasser*) meter; **zahlreich** adj numerous; **Zahlung** f payment; **Zahlungsanweisung** f money order; **Zahlungsbedingungen** pl terms pl of payment

zahm adj tame; **zähmen** vt to tame

Zahn (-(e)s, Zähne) m tooth; **Zahnarzt** m, **Zahnärztin** f dentist; **Zahnbürste** f toothbrush; **Zahncreme** f toothpaste; **Zahnersatz** m dentures pl; **Zahnfleisch** nt gums pl; **Zahnfleischbluten** nt bleeding gums pl; **Zahnfüllung** f filling; **Zahnklammer** f brace; **Zahnpasta** f, **Zahnpaste** f toothpaste; **Zahnradbahn** f rack railway (*Brit*) (*o* railroad (*US*));

Zahnschmerzen pl toothache sing; **Zahnseide** f dental floss; **Zahnspange** f brace; **Zahnstocher** (-s, -) m toothpick

Zange (-, -n) f pliers pl; (*Zuckerzange*) tongs pl; (*Beißzange, Zool*) pincers pl; (*Med*) forceps pl

zanken vi to quarrel ▷ vr **sich ~** to quarrel

Zäpfchen nt (*Anat*) uvula; (*Med*) suppository

zapfen vt (*Bier*) to pull; **Zapfsäule** f petrol (*Brit*) (*o* gas (*US*)) pump

zappeln vi to wriggle; (*unruhig sein*) to fidget

zappen vi to zap, to channel-hop

zart adj (*weich, leise*) soft; (*Braten etc*) tender; (*fein, schwächlich*) delicate; **zartbitter** adj (*Schokolade*) plain, dark

zärtlich adj tender, affectionate; **Zärtlichkeit** f tenderness; **~en** pl hugs and kisses pl

Zauber (-s, -) m magic; (*Bann*) spell; **Zauberei** f magic; **Zauberer** (-s, -) m magician; (*Künstler*) conjuror; **Zauberformel** f (magic) spell; **zauberhaft** adj enchanting; **Zauberin** f sorceress; **Zauberkünstler(in)** m(f) magician, conjuror; **Zaubermittel** nt magic cure; **zaubern** vi to do magic; (*Künstler*) to do conjuring tricks; **Zauberspruch** m (magic) spell

Zaun (-(e)s, Zäune) m fence

z. B. abk = **zum Beispiel** e.g., eg

Zebra (-s, -s) nt zebra; **Zebrastreifen** m zebra crossing (*Brit*), crosswalk (*US*)

Zechtour f pub crawl

Zecke (-, -n) f tick

Zehe (-, -n) f toe; (*Knoblauch*) clove; **Zehennagel** m toenail; **Zehenspitze** f tip of the toes

zehn num ten; **Zehnerkarte** f ticket valid for ten trips; **Zehnkampf** m decathlon; **Zehnkämpfer(in)** m(f) decathlete; **zehnmal** adv ten times; **zehntausend** num ten thousand; **zehnte(r, s)** adj tenth; siehe auch **dritte**; **Zehntel** (-s, -) nt (*Bruchteil*) tenth; **Zehntelsekunde** f tenth of a second

Zeichen (-s, -) nt sign; (*Schriftzeichen*) character; **Zeichenblock** m sketch pad; **Zeichenerklärung** f key; **Zeichensetzung** f punctuation; **Zeichensprache** f sign language; **Zeichentrickfilm** m cartoon

Z

zeichnen vt, vi to draw; **Zeichnung** f
drawing

Zeigefinger m index finger; **zeigen** vt
to show; **sie zeigte uns die Stadt** she
showed us around the town; **zeig mal!** let
me see ▷ vi to point (auf +akk to, at) ▷ vr
sich ~ to show oneself; **es wird sich
~ time** will tell; **Zeiger** (-s, -) m pointer;
(Uhr) hand

Zeile (-, -n) f line

Zeit (-, -en) f time; **ich habe keine ~** I
haven't got time; **lass dir ~** take your
time; **das hat ~** there's no rush; **von ~ zu
~** from time to time; **Zeitansage** f (Tel)
speaking clock (Brit), correct time (US);
Zeitarbeit f temporary work;
zeitgenössisch adj contemporary,
modern; **zeitgleich** adj simultaneous
▷ adv at exactly the same time; **zeitig**
adj early; **Zeitkarte** f season ticket;
zeitlich adj (Reihenfolge) chronological;
es passt ~ nicht it isn't a convenient
time; **ich schaff es ~ nicht** I'm not
going to make it; **Zeitlupe** f slow
motion; **Zeitplan** m schedule;
Zeitpunkt m point in time; **Zeitraum**
m period (of time); **Zeitschrift** f
magazine; (wissenschaftliche)
periodical

Zeitung f newspaper; **es steht in der
~** it's in the paper(s); **Zeitungsanzeige**
f newspaper advertisement;
Zeitungsartikel m newspaper article;
Zeitungskiosk m, **Zeitungsstand** m
newsstand

Zeitunterschied m time difference;
Zeitverschiebung f time lag;
Zeitvertreib (-(e)s, -e) m **zum ~** to pass
the time; **zeitweise** adv occasionally;
Zeitzone f time zone

Zelle (-, -n) f cell

Zellophan® (-s) nt cellophane®

Zelt (-(e)s, -e) nt tent; **zelten** vi to camp,
to go camping; **Zeltplatz** m campsite,
camping site

Zement (-(e)s, -e) m cement

Zentimeter m o nt centimetre

Zentner (-s, -) m (metric) hundredweight;
(in Deutschland) fifty kilos; (in Österreich und
der Schweiz) one hundred kilos

zentral adj central; **Zentrale** (-, -n) f
central office; (Tel) exchange;
Zentralheizung f central heating;

Zentralverriegelung f (Auto) central
locking; **Zentrum** (-s, Zentren) nt centre

zerbrechen irr vt, vi to break;
zerbrechlich adj fragile

Zeremonie (-, -n) f ceremony

zergehen irr vi to dissolve; (schmelzen) to
melt

zerkleinern vt to cut up; (zerhacken) to
chop (up); **zerkratzen** vt to scratch;
zerlegen vt to take to pieces; (Fleisch) to
carve; (Gerät, Maschine) to dismantle;
zerquetschen vt to squash; **zerreißen** irr
vt to tear to pieces ▷ vi to tear

zerren vt to drag; **sich** (dat) **einen Muskel
~** to pull a muscle ▷ vi to tug (an +dat at);
Zerrung f (Med) pulled muscle

zerschlagen irr vt to smash ▷ vr **sich
~** to come to nothing

zerschneiden irr vt to cut up

Zerstäuber (-s, -) m atomizer

zerstören vt to destroy; **Zerstörung** f
destruction

zerstreuen vt to scatter; (Menge) to
disperse; (Zweifel etc) to dispel ▷ vr **sich
~** (Menge) to disperse; **zerstreut** adj
scattered; (Mensch) absent-minded;
(kurzfristig) distracted

zerteilen vt to split up

Zertifikat (-(e)s, -e) nt certificate

Zettel (-s, -) m piece of paper; (Notizzettel)
note

Zeug (-(e)s, -e) nt (fam) stuff; (Ausrüstung)
gear; **dummes ~** nonsense

Zeuge (-n, -n) m, **Zeugin** f witness

Zeugnis nt certificate; (Schule) report;
(Referenz) reference

z. H(d). abk = **zu Händen von** attn

zickig adj (fam) touchy, bitchy

Zickzack (-(e)s, -e) m **im ~ fahren** to
zigzag (across the road)

Ziege (-, -n) f goat

Ziegel (-s, -) m brick; (Dach) tile

Ziegenkäse m goat's cheese;
Ziegenpeter m mumps

ziehen (zog, gezogen) vt to draw; (zerren) to
pull; (Spielfigur) to move; (züchten) to rear
▷ vi (zerren) to pull; (sich bewegen) to
move; (Rauch, Wolke etc) to drift; **den Tee
~ lassen** to let the tea stand ▷ vi impers **es
zieht** there's a draught ▷ vr **sich ~** (Treffen,
Rede) to drag on

Ziel (-(e)s, -e) nt (Reise) destination; (Sport)
finish; (Absicht) goal, aim; **zielen** vi to

aim (*auf +akk* at); **Zielgruppe** *f* target group; **zieilos** *adj* aimless; **Zielscheibe** *f* target

ziemlich *adj* considerable; **ein ~es Durcheinander** quite a mess; **mit ~er Sicherheit** with some certainty ▷ *adv* rather, quite; **~ viel** quite a lot

zierlich *adj* dainty; (*Frau*) petite

Ziffer (-, -*n*) *f* figure; **arabische/römische ~n** *pl* Arabic/Roman numerals *pl*; **Zifferblatt** *nt* dial, face

zig *adj* (*fam*) umpteen

Zigarette *f* cigarette; **Zigarettenautomat** *m* cigarette machine; **Zigarettenpapier** *nt* cigarette paper; **Zigarettenschachtel** *f* cigarette packet; **Zigarettenstummel** *m* cigarette end; **Zigarillo** (-s, -s) *m* cigarillo; **Zigarre** (-, -*n*) *f* cigar

Zigeuner(in) (-s, -) *m(f)* gipsy

Zimmer (-s, -) *nt* room; **haben Sie ein ~ für zwei Personen?** do you have a room for two?; **Zimmerlautstärke** *f* reasonable volume; **Zimmermädchen** *nt* chambermaid; **Zimmermann** *m* carpenter; **Zimmerpflanze** *f* house plant; **Zimmerschlüssel** *m* room key; **Zimmerservice** *m* room service; **Zimmervermittlung** *f* accommodation agency

Zimt (-(e)s, -e) *m* cinnamon; **Zimtstange** *f* cinnamon stick

Zink (-(e)s) *nt* zinc

Zinn (-(e)s) *nt* (*Element*) tin; (*legiertes*) pewter

Zinsen *pl* interest *sing*

Zipfel (-s, -) *m* corner; (*spitz*) tip; (*Hemd*) tail; (*Wurst*) end; (*fam: Penis*) willy; **Zipfelmütze** *f* pointed hat

zirka *adv* about, approximately

Zirkel (-s, -) *m* (*Math*) (pair of) compasses *pl*

Zirkus (-, -se) *m* circus

zischen *vi* to hiss

Zitat (-(e)s, -e) *nt* quotation (*aus* from); **zitieren** *vt* to quote

Zitronat *nt* candied lemon peel; **Zitrone** (-, -*n*) *f* lemon; **Zitronenlimonade** *f* lemonade; **Zitronensaft** *m* lemon juice

zittern *vi* to tremble (*vor +dat* with)

zivil *adj* civilian; (*Preis*) reasonable; **Zivil** (-s) *nt* plain clothes *pl*; (*Mil*) civilian

clothes *pl*; **Zivildienst** *m* community service (*for conscientious objectors*)

zocken *vi* (*fam*) to gamble

Zoff (-s) *m* (*fam*) trouble

zog *imperf von* **ziehen**

zögerlich *adj* hesitant; **zögern** *vi* to hesitate

Zoll (-(e)s, Zölle) *m* customs *pl*; (*Abgabe*) duty; **Zollabfertigung** *f* customs clearance; **Zollamt** *nt* customs office; **Zollbeamte(r)** *m*, **-beamtin** *f* customs official; **Zollerklärung** *f* customs declaration; **zollfrei** *adj* duty-free; **Zollgebühren** *pl* customs duties *pl*; **Zollkontrolle** *f* customs check; **Zöllner(in)** *m(f)* customs officer; **zollpflichtig** *adj* liable to duty

Zombie (-s, -s) *m* zombie

Zone (-, -*n*) *f* zone

Zoo (-s, -s) *m* zoo

Zoom (-s, -s) *nt* zoom (shot); (*Objektiv*) zoom (lens)

Zopf (-(e)s, Zöpfe) *m* plait (*Brit*), braid (*US*)

Zorn (-(e)s) *m* anger; **zornig** *adj* angry (*über etw akk* about sth, *auf jdn* with sb)

◯ SCHLÜSSELWORT

zu *präp +dat* **1** (*örtlich*) to; **zum Bahnhof/ Arzt gehen** to go to the station/doctor; **zur Schule/Kirche gehen** to go to school/church; **sollen wir zu euch gehen?** shall we go to your place?; **sie sah zu ihm hin** she looked towards him; **zum Fenster herein** through the window; **zu meiner Linken** to *od* on my left

2 (*zeitlich*) at; **zu Ostern** at Easter; **bis zum 1. Mai** until May 1st; (*nicht später als*) by May 1st; **zu meiner Zeit** in my time

3 (*Zusatz*) with; **Wein zum Essen trinken** to drink wine with one's meal; **sich zu jdm setzen** to sit down beside sb; **setz dich doch zu uns** (come and) sit with us; **Anmerkungen zu etw** notes on sth

4 (*Zweck*) for; **Wasser zum Waschen** water for washing; **Papier zum Schreiben** paper to write on; **etw zum Geburtstag bekommen** to get sth for one's birthday

5 (*Veränderung*) into; **zu etw werden** to turn into sth; **jdn zu etw machen** to make sb (into) sth; **zu Asche verbrennen** to burn to ashes

z

6 (*mit Zahlen*); **3 zu 2** (*Sport*) 3-2; **das Stück zu 5 Euro** at 5 euros each; **zum ersten Mal** for the first time
7: **zu meiner Freude** *etc* to my joy *etc*; **zum Glück** luckily; **zu Fuß** on foot; **es ist zum Weinen** it's enough to make you cry
▷ *konj* to; **etw zu essen** sth to eat; **um besser sehen zu können** in order to see better; **ohne es zu wissen** without knowing it; **noch zu bezahlende Rechnungen** bills that are still to be paid
▷ *adv* **1** (*allzu*) too; **zu sehr** too much; **zu viel** too much; **zu wenig** too little
2 (*örtlich*) toward(s); **er kam auf mich zu** he came up to me
3 (*geschlossen*) shut, closed; **die Geschäfte haben zu** the shops are closed; „**auf/zu**" (*Wasserhahn etc*) "on/off"
4 (*umg: los*): **nur zu!** just keep on!; **mach zu!** hurry up!

zuallererst *adv* first of all; **zuallerletzt** *adv* last of all
Zubehör (-(*e*)*s*, -*e*) *nt* accessories *pl*
zu|bereiten *vt* to prepare; **Zubereitung** *f* preparation
zu|binden *irr vt* to do (*o* tie) up
Zucchini *pl* courgettes *pl* (*Brit*), zucchini *pl* (*US*)
züchten *vt* (*Tiere*) to breed; (*Pflanzen*) to grow
zucken *vi* to jerk; (*krampfhaft*) to twitch; (*Strahl etc*) to flicker; **mit den Schultern ~** to shrug (one's shoulders)
Zucker (-*s*, -) *m* sugar; (*Med*) diabetes *sing*; **Zuckerdose** *f* sugar bowl; **zuckerkrank** *adj* diabetic; **Zuckerrohr** *nt* sugar cane; **Zuckerrübe** *f* sugar beet; **Zuckerwatte** *f* candy-floss (*Brit*), cotton candy (*US*)
zu|decken *vt* to cover up
zu|drehen *vt* to turn off
zueinander *adv* to one another; (*mit Verb*) together; **~ halten** to stick together
zuerst *adv* first; (*zu Anfang*) at first; **~ einmal** first of all
Zufahrt *f* access; (*Einfahrt*) drive(way); **Zufahrtsstraße** *f* access road; (*Autobahn*) slip road (*Brit*), ramp (*US*)
Zufall *m* chance; (*Ereignis*) coincidence; **durch ~** by accident; **so ein ~!** what a coincidence; **zufällig** *adj* chance ▷ *adv* by chance; **weißt du ~, ob ...?** do you happen to know whether ...?

zufrieden *adj* content(ed); (*befriedigt*) satisfied; **sich mit etw ~ geben** to settle for sth; **lass sie ~** leave her alone (*o* in peace); **sie ist schwer ~ zu stellen** she is hard to please; **Zufriedenheit** *f* contentment; (*Befriedigtsein*) satisfaction
zu|fügen *vt* to add (*dat* to); **jdm Schaden/Schmerzen ~** to cause sb harm/pain
Zug (-(*e*)*s*, Züge) *m* (*Eisenb*) train; (*Luft*) draught; (*Ziehen*) pull; (*Gesichtszug*) feature; (*Schach*) move; (*Charakterzug*) trait; (*an Zigarette*) puff, drag; (*Schluck*) gulp
Zugabe *f* extra; (*in Konzert etc*) encore
Zugabteil *nt* train compartment
Zugang *m* access; „**kein ~!**" 'no entry!'
Zugauskunft *f* (*Stelle*) train information office/desk; **Zugbegleiter(in)** *m(f)* guard (*Brit*), conductor (*US*)
zu|geben *irr vt* (*zugestehen*) admit; **zugegeben** *adv* admittedly
zu|gehen *irr vi* (*schließen*) to shut; **auf jdn/etw ~** to walk towards sb/sth; **dem Ende ~** to be coming to a close ▷ *vi impers* (*sich ereignen*) to happen; **es ging lustig zu** we/they had a lot of fun; **dort geht es streng zu** it's strict there
Zügel (-*s*, -) *m* rein
Zugführer(in) *m(f)* guard (*Brit*), conductor (*US*)
zugig *adj* draughty
zügig *adj* speedy
Zugluft *f* draught
Zugpersonal *nt* train staff
zu|greifen *irr vi* (*fig*) to seize the opportunity; (*beim Essen*) to help oneself; **~ auf** (+*akk*) (*Inform*) to access
Zugrestauraunt *nt* dining car, diner (*US*)
Zugriffsberechtigung *f* (*Inform*) access right
zugrunde *adv* **~ gehen** to perish; **~ gehen an** (+*dat*) (*sterben*) to die of
Zugschaffner(in) *m(f)* ticket inspector; **Zugunglück** *nt* train crash
zugunsten *prep* +*gen o dat* in favour of
Zugverbindung *f* train connection
zu|haben *irr vi* to be closed
zu|halten *irr vt* **sich** (*dat*) **die Nase ~** to hold one's nose; **sich** (*dat*) **die Ohren ~** to hold one's hands over one's ears; **die Tür ~** to hold the door shut
Zuhause (-*s*) *nt* home

zu|hören vi to listen (dat to); **Zuhörer(in)** m(f) listener

zu|kleben vt to seal

zu|kommen irr vi to come up (auf +akk to); **jdm etw ~ lassen** to give/send sb sth; **etw auf sich** (akk) **~ lassen** to take sth as it comes

zu|kriegen vt **ich krieg den Koffer nicht zu** I can't shut the case

Zukunft (-, Zukünfte) f future; **zukünftig** adj future ▷ adv in future

zu|lassen irr vt (hereinlassen) to admit; (erlauben) to permit; (Auto) to license; (fam: nicht öffnen) to keep shut; **zulässig** adj permissible, permitted

zuletzt adv finally, at last

zuliebe adv **jdm ~** for sb's sake

zum kontr von **zu dem; ~ dritten Mal** for the third time; **~ Scherz** as a joke; **~ Trinken** for drinking

zu|machen vt to shut; (Kleidung) to do up ▷ vi to shut

zumindest adv at least

zu|muten vt **jdm etw ~** to expect sth of sb ▷ vr **sich** (dat) **zu viel ~** to overdo things

zunächst adv first of all; **~ einmal** to start with

Zunahme (-, -n) f increase

Zuname m surname, last name

zünden vt, vi (Auto) to ignite, to fire; **Zündholz** nt match; **Zündkabel** f (Auto) ignition cable; **Zündkerze** f (Auto) spark plug; **Zündschloss** nt ignition lock; **Zündschlüssel** m ignition key; **Zündung** f ignition

zu|nehmen irr vi to increase; (Mensch) to put on weight ▷ vt **5 Kilo ~** to put on 5 kilos

Zunge (-, -n) f tongue

Zungenkuss m French kiss

zunichte adv **~ machen** to ruin

zunutze adv **sich** (dat) **etw ~ machen** to make use of sth

zu|parken vt to block

zur kontr von **zu der**

zurecht|finden irr vr **sich ~** to find one's way around; **zurecht|kommen** irr vi to cope (mit etw with sth); **zurecht|machen** vt to prepare ▷ vr **sich ~** to get ready

Zürich (-s) nt Zurich

zurück adv back

zurück|bekommen irr vt to get back;

zurück|blicken vi to look back (auf +akk at); **zurück|bringen** irr vt (hierhin) to bring back; (woandershin) to take back; **zurück|erstatten** vt to refund; **zurück|fahren** irr vi to go back; **zurück|geben** irr vt to give back; (antworten) to answer; **zurück|gehen** irr vi to go back; (zeitlich) to date back (auf +akk to)

zurück|halten irr vt to hold back; (hindern) to prevent ▷ vr **sich ~** to hold back; **zurückhaltend** adj reserved

zurück|holen vt to fetch back; **zurück|kommen** irr vi to come back; **auf etw** (akk) **~ to return** (o get back) to sth; **zurück|lassen** irr vt to leave behind; **zurück|legen** vt to put back; (Geld) to put by; (reservieren) to keep back; (Strecke) to cover; **zurück|nehmen** irr vt to take back; **zurück|rufen** irr vt to call back; **zurück|schicken** vt to send back; **zurück|stellen** vt to put back; **zurück|treten** irr vi to step back; (von Amt) to retire; **zurück|verlangen** vt **etw ~ to ask for sth back; zurück|zahlen** vt to pay back

zurzeit adv at present

Zusage f promise; (Annahme) acceptance; **zu|sagen** vt to promise ▷ vi to accept; **jdm ~** (gefallen) to appeal to sb

zusammen adv together

Zusammenarbeit f collaboration; **zusammen|arbeiten** vi to work together

zusammen|brechen irr vi to collapse; (psychisch) to break down; **Zusammenbruch** m collapse; (psychischer) breakdown

zusammen|fassen vt to summarize; (vereinigen) to unite; **zusammenfassend** adj summarizing ▷ adv to summarize; **Zusammenfassung** f summary

zusammen|gehören vi to belong together; **zusammen|halten** irr vi to stick together

Zusammenhang m connection; **im/aus dem ~** in/out of context; **zusammen|hängen** irr vi to be connected; **zusammenhängend** adj coherent; **zusammenhang(s)los** adj incoherent

zusammen|klappen vi, vt to fold up

zusammen|knüllen vt to screw up

zusammen|kommen irr vi to meet;

z

(*sich ereignen*) to happen together;
zusammen|legen vt to fold up ▷ vi (*Geld sammeln*) to club together;
zusammen|nehmen irr vt to summon up; **alles zusammengenommen** all in all ▷ vr **sich ~** to pull oneself together; (*fam*) to get a grip, to get one's act together;
zusammen|passen vi to go together; (*Personen*) to be suited;
zusammen|rechnen vt to add up
Zusammensein (-s) nt get-together
zusammen|setzen vt to put together ▷ vr **sich ~ aus** to be composed of;
Zusammensetzung f composition
Zusammenstoß m crash, collision;
zusammen|stoßen irr vi to crash (*mit* into)
zusammen|zählen vt to add up
zusammen|ziehen irr vi (*in Wohnung etc*) to move in together
Zusatz m addition; **Zusatzgerät** nt attachment; (*Inform*) add-on; **zusätzlich** adj additional ▷ adv in addition
zu|schauen vi to watch; **Zuschauer(in)** (-s, -) m(f) spectator; **die ~** (pl) (*Theat*) the audience sing; **Zuschauertribüne** f stand
zu|schicken vt to send
Zuschlag m extra charge; (*Fahrkarte*) supplement
zuschlagpflichtig adj subject to an extra charge; (*Eisenb*) subject to a supplement
zu|schließen irr vt to lock up
zu|sehen irr vi to watch (*jdm* sb); **~, dass** (*dafür sorgen*) to make sure that
zu|sichern vt **jdm etw ~** to assure sb of sth
Zustand m state, condition; **sie bekommt Zustände, wenn sie das sieht** (*fam*) she'll have a fit if she sees that
zustande adv **~ bringen** to bring about; **~ kommen** to come about
zuständig adj (*Behörde*) relevant; **~ für** responsible for
Zustellung f delivery
zu|stimmen vi to agree (*einer Sache* dat to sth, *jdm* with sb); **Zustimmung** f approval
zu|stoßen irr vi (*fig*) to happen (*jdm* to sb)
Zutaten pl ingredients pl
zu|trauen vt **jdm etw ~** to think sb is capable of sth; **das hätte ich ihm nie zugetraut** I'd never have thought he was capable of it; **ich würde es ihr ~** (*etw*

Negatives) I wouldn't put it past her;
Zutrauen (-s) nt confidence (*zu* in);
zutraulich adj trusting; (*Tier*) friendly
zu|treffen irr vi to be correct; **~ auf** (+akk) to apply to; **Zutreffendes bitte streichen** please delete as applicable
Zutritt m entry; (*Zugang*) access; **~ verboten!** no entry
zuverlässig adj reliable; **Zuverlässigkeit** f reliability
Zuversicht f confidence; **zuversichtlich** adj confident
zuvor adv before; (*zunächst*) first; **zuvor|kommen** irr vi **jdm ~** to beat sb to it; **zuvorkommend** adj obliging
Zuwachs (-es, Zuwächse) m increase, growth; (*fam: Baby*) addition to the family
zuwider adv **es ist mir ~** I hate (*o detest*) it
zuzüglich prep +gen plus
zwang imperf von **zwingen**
Zwang (-(e)s, Zwänge) m (*innerer*) compulsion; (*Gewalt*) force
zwängen vt to squeeze (*in* +akk into) ▷ vr **sich ~** to squeeze (*in* +akk into)
zwanglos adj informal
zwanzig num twenty; **zwanzigste(r, s)** adj twentieth; *siehe auch* **dritte**
zwar adv **und ~ ...** (*genauer*) ..., to be precise; **das ist ~ schön, aber ...** it is nice, but ...; **ich kenne ihn ~, aber ...** I know him all right, but ...
Zweck (-(e)s, -e) m purpose; **zwecklos** adj pointless
zwei num two; **Zwei** (-, -en) f two; (*Schulnote*) ≈ B; **Zweibettzimmer** nt twin room; **zweideutig** adj ambiguous; (*unanständig*) suggestive; **zweifach** adj, adv double
Zweifel (-s, -) m doubt; **zweifellos** adv undoubtedly; **zweifeln** vi to doubt (*an etw* dat sth); **Zweifelsfall** m **im ~** in case of doubt
Zweig (-(e)s, -e) m branch
Zweigstelle f branch
zweihundert num two hundred; **zweimal** adv twice; **zweisprachig** adj bilingual; **zweispurig** adj (*Auto*) two-lane; **zweit** adv **wir sind zu ~** there are two of us; **zweite(r, s)** adj second; *siehe auch* **dritte eine ~ Portion** a second helping; **zweitens** adv secondly; (*bei Aufzählungen*)

second; **zweitgrößte(r, s)** *adj* second
largest; **Zweitschlüssel** *m* spare key
Zwerchfell *nt* diaphragm
Zwerg(in) *(-(e)s, -e) m(f)* dwarf
Zwetschge *(-, -n) f* plum
zwicken *vt* to pinch
Zwieback *(-(e)s, -e) m* rusk
Zwiebel *(-, -n) f* onion; (*von Blume*) bulb;
Zwiebelsuppe *f* onion soup
Zwilling *(-s, -e) m* twin; **~e** (*pl*) (*Astr*)
Gemini *sing*
zwingen (*zwang, gezwungen*) *vt* to force
zwinkern *vi* to blink; (*absichtlich*) to wink
zwischen *prep +akk o dat* between
Zwischenablage *f* (*Inform*) clipboard
zwischendurch *adv* in between
Zwischenfall *m* incident
Zwischenlandung *f* stopover
zwischenmenschlich *adj* interpersonal
Zwischenraum *m* space
Zwischenstopp *(-s, -s) m* stopover
Zwischensumme *f* subtotal
Zwischenzeit *f* **in der ~** in the meantime
zwitschern *vt, vi* to twitter, to chirp
zwölf *num* twelve; **zwölfte(r, s)** *adj*
twelfth; *siehe auch* **dritte**
Zylinder *(-s, -) m* cylinder; (*Hut*) top hat;
Zylinderkopfdichtung *f* cylinder-head
gasket
zynisch *adj* cynical
Zypern *(-s) nt* Cyprus
Zyste *(-, -n) f* cyst

z

a

abdomen ['æbdəmən] n Unterleib m
ability [ə'bɪlɪtɪ] n Fähigkeit f; **able** ['eɪbl] adj fähig; **to be ~ to do sth** etw tun können
abnormal [æb'nɔːml] adj anormal
aboard [ə'bɔːd] adv, prep an Bord +gen
abolish [ə'bɒlɪʃ] vt abschaffen
aborigine [æbə'rɪdʒɪniː] n Ureinwohner(in) m(f) (Australiens)
abort [ə'bɔːt] vt (Med: foetus) abtreiben; (Space: mission) abbrechen; **abortion** [ə'bɔːʃən] n Abtreibung f

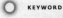 **KEYWORD**

about [ə'baʊt] adv **1** (approximately) etwa, ungefähr; **about a hundred/thousand** etc etwa hundert/tausend etc; **at about 2 o'clock** etwa um 2 Uhr; **I've just about finished** ich bin gerade fertig
2 (referring to place) herum, umher; **to leave things lying about** Sachen herumliegen lassen; **to run/walk** etc **about** herumrennen/gehen etc
3: **to be about to do sth** im Begriff sein, etw zu tun; **he was about to go to bed** er wollte gerade ins Bett gehen
▷ prep **1** (relating to) über +acc; **a book about London** ein Buch über London; **what is it about?** worum geht es?; (book etc) wovon handelt es?; **we talked about it** wir haben darüber geredet; **what** or **how about doing this?** wollen wir das machen?
2 (referring to place) um (... herum); **to walk about the town** in der Stadt herumgehen; **her clothes were scattered about the room** ihre Kleider waren über das ganze Zimmer verstreut

above [ə'bʌv] adv oben; **children aged 8 and ~** Kinder ab 8 Jahren; **on the floor ~** ein Stockwerk höher ▷ prep über; **~ 40 degrees** über 40 Grad; **~ all** vor allem ▷ adj obig
abroad [ə'brɔːd] adv im Ausland; **to go ~** ins Ausland gehen
abrupt [ə'brʌpt] adj (sudden) plötzlich, abrupt
abscess ['æbsɪs] n Geschwür nt
absence ['æbsəns] n Abwesenheit f; **absent** ['æbsənt] adj abwesend; **to be ~ fehlen**; **absent-minded** adj zerstreut

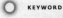 **KEYWORD**

a [eɪ, ə] (before vowel or silent h: an) indef art
1 ein; eine; **a woman** eine Frau; **a book** ein Buch; **an eagle** ein Adler; **she's a doctor** sie ist Ärztin
2 (instead of the number "one") ein, eine; **a year ago** vor einem Jahr; **a hundred/thousand** etc **pounds** (ein) hundert/(ein) tausend etc Pfund
3 (in expressing ratios, prices etc) pro; **3 a day/week** 3 pro Tag/Woche 3 am Tag/in der Woche; **10 km an hour** 10 km pro Stunde/in der Stunde

AA abbr = **Automobile Association** britischer Automobilklub, ≈ ADAC m
aback adv **taken ~** erstaunt
abandon [ə'bændən] vt (desert) verlassen; (give up) aufgeben
abbey ['æbɪ] n Abtei f
abbreviate [əbriː'vɪeɪt] vt abkürzen; **abbreviation** [əbriːvɪ'eɪʃən] n Abkürzung f
ABC ['eɪbiː'siː] n (a. fig) Abc nt
abdicate ['æbdɪkeɪt] vi (king) abdanken; **abdication** [æbdɪ'keɪʃən] n Abdankung f

absolute ['æbsəlu:t] *adj* absolut; *(power)* unumschränkt; *(rubbish)* vollkommen, total; **absolutely** *adv* absolut; *(true, stupid)* vollkommen; **~!** genau!; **you're ~ right** du hast/Sie haben völlig Recht

absorb [əb'zɔ:b] *vt* absorbieren; *(fig: information)* in sich aufnehmen; **absorbed** *adj* **~ in sth** in etw vertieft; **absorbent** *adj* absorbierend; **~ cotton** *(US)* Watte *f*; **absorbing** *adj (fig)* faszinierend, fesselnd

abstain [əb'steɪn] *vi* **to ~ (from voting)** sich (der Stimme) enthalten

abstract ['æbstrækt] *adj* abstrakt

absurd [əb'sɜ:d] *adj* absurd

abundance [ə'bʌndəns] *n* Reichtum *m (of* an +dat)

abuse [ə'bju:s] *n (rude language)* Beschimpfungen *pl*; *(mistreatment)* Missbrauch *m* ▷ [ə'bju:z] *vt (misuse)* missbrauchen; **abusive** [ə'bju:sɪv] *adj* beleidigend

AC *abbr* = **alternating current** Wechselstrom *m* ▷ *abbr* = **air conditioning** Klimaanlage

a/c *abbr* = **account** Kto.

academic [ækə'demɪk] *n* Wissenschaftler(in) *m(f)* ▷ *adj* akademisch, wissenschaftlich

accelerate [æk'seləreɪt] *vi (car etc)* beschleunigen; *(driver)* Gas geben; **acceleration** [æksələ'reɪʃən] *n* Beschleunigung *f*; **accelerator** [ək'seləreɪtə*] *n* Gas(pedal) *nt*

accent ['æksent] *n* Akzent *m*

accept [ək'sept] *vt* annehmen; *(agree to)* akzeptieren; *(responsibility)* übernehmen; **acceptable** [ək'septəbl] *adj* annehmbar

access ['ækses] *n* Zugang *m*; *(Inform)* Zugriff *m*; **accessible** [æk'sesəbl] *adj* (leicht) zugänglich/erreichbar; *(place)* (leicht) erreichbar

accessory [æk'sesərɪ] *n* Zubehörteil *nt*

access road *n* Zufahrtsstraße *f*

accident ['æksɪdənt] *n* Unfall *m*; **by ~** zufällig; **accidental** [æksɪ'dentl] *adj* unbeabsichtigt; *(meeting)* zufällig; *(death)* durch Unfall; **~ damage** Unfallschaden *m*; **accident-prone** *adj* vom Pech verfolgt

acclimatize [ə'klaɪmətaɪz] *vt* **to ~ oneself** sich gewöhnen (to an +akk)

accommodate [ə'kɒmədeɪt] *vt* unterbringen; **accommodation(s)** [əkɒmə'deɪʃən(z)] *n* Unterkunft *f*

accompany [ə'kʌmpənɪ] *vt* begleiten

accomplish [ə'kʌmplɪʃ] *vt* erreichen

accord [ə'kɔ:d] *n* **of one's own ~** freiwillig; **according to** *prep* nach, laut +dat

account [ə'kaʊnt] *n (in bank etc)* Konto *nt*; *(narrative)* Bericht *m*; **on ~ of** wegen; **on no ~** auf keinen Fall; **to take into ~** berücksichtigen, in Betracht ziehen; **accountant** [ə'kaʊntənt] *n* Buchhalter(in) *m(f)*; **account for** *vt (explain)* erklären; *(expenditure)* Rechenschaft ablegen für; **account number** *n* Kontonummer *f*

accumulate [ə'kju:mjʊleɪt] *vt* ansammeln ▷ *vi* sich ansammeln

accuracy ['ækjʊrəsɪ] *n* Genauigkeit *f*; **accurate** ['ækjʊrɪt] *adj* genau

accusation [ækjʊ'zeɪʃən] *n* Anklage *f*, Beschuldigung *f*

accusative [ə'kju:zətɪv] *n* Akkusativ *m*

accuse [ə'kju:z] *vt* beschuldigen; *(Jur)* anklagen *(of* wegen +gen*)*; **~ sb of doing sth** jdn beschuldigen, etw getan zu haben; **accused** *n (Jur)* Angeklagte(r) *mf*

accustom [ə'kʌstəm] *vt* gewöhnen (to an +akk); **accustomed** *adj* gewohnt; **to get ~ to sth** sich an etw akk gewöhnen

ace [eɪs] *n* Ass *nt* ▷ *adj* Star-

ache [eɪk] *n* Schmerz *m* ▷ *vi* wehtun

achieve [ə'tʃi:v] *vt* erreichen; **achievement** *n* Leistung *f*

acid ['æsɪd] *n* Säure *f* ▷ *adj* sauer; **~ rain** saurer Regen

acknowledge [ək'nɒlɪdʒ] *vt (recognize)* anerkennen; *(admit)* zugeben; *(receipt of letter etc)* bestätigen; **acknowledgement** *n* Anerkennung *f*; *(of letter)* Empfangsbestätigung *f*

acne ['æknɪ] *n* Akne *f*

acorn ['eɪkɔ:n] *n* Eichel *f*

acoustic [ə'ku:stɪk] *adj* akustisch; **acoustics** [ə'ku:stɪks] *npl* Akustik *f*

acquaintance [ə'kweɪntəns] *n (person)* Bekannte(r) *mf*

acquire [ə'kwaɪə*] *vt* erwerben, sich aneignen; **acquisition** [ækwɪ'zɪʃn] *n (of skills etc)* Erwerb *m*; *(object)* Anschaffung *f*

acrobat ['ækrəbæt] *n* Akrobat(in) *m(f)*

across [ə'krɒs] *prep* über +akk; **he lives ~ the street** er wohnt auf der anderen

Seite der Straße ▷ *adv* hinüber, herüber; **100m ~** 100m breit

act [ækt] *n* (*deed*) Tat *f*; (*Jur: law*) Gesetz *nt*; (*Theat*) Akt *m*; (*fig: pretence*) Schau *f*; **it's all an ~** es ist alles nur Theater; **to be in the ~ of doing sth** gerade dabei sein, etw zu tun ▷ *vi* (*take action*) handeln; (*behave*) sich verhalten; (*Theat*) spielen; **to ~ as** (*person*) fungieren als; (*thing*) dienen als ▷ *vt* (*a part*) spielen

action ['ækʃən] *n* (*of play, novel etc*) Handlung *f*; (*in film etc*) Action *f*; (*Mil*) Kampf *m*; **to take ~** etwas unternehmen; **out of ~** (*machine*) außer Betrieb; **to put a plan into ~** einen Plan in die Tat umsetzen; **action replay** *n* (*Sport, Tv*) Wiederholung *f*

active ['æktɪv] *adj* aktiv; (*child*) lebhaft; **activity** [æk'tɪvɪtɪ] *n* Aktivität *f*; (*occupation*) Beschäftigung *f*; (*organized event*) Veranstaltung *f*

actor ['æktə*] *n* Schauspieler(in) *m(f)*; **actress** ['æktrɪs] *n* Schauspielerin *f*

actual ['æktjʊəl] *adj* wirklich; **actually** *adv* eigentlich; (*said in surprise*) tatsächlich

acupuncture ['ækjʊpʌŋktʃə*] *n* Akupunktur *f*

acute [ə'kjuːt] *adj* (*pain*) akut; (*sense of smell*) fein; (*Math: angle*) spitz

ad [æd] *abbr* = **advertisement**

AD *abbr* = **Anno Domini** nach Christi, n. Chr.

adapt [ə'dæpt] *vi* sich anpassen (*to* +dat) ▷ *vt* anpassen (*to* +dat); (*rewrite*) bearbeiten (*for* für); **adaptable** *adj* anpassungsfähig; **adaptation** *n* (*of book etc*) Bearbeitung *f*; **adapter** *n* (*Elec*) Zwischenstecker *m*, Adapter *m*

add [æd] *vt* (*ingredient*) hinzufügen; (*numbers*) addieren; **add up** *vi* (*make sense*) stimmen ▷ *vt* (*numbers*) addieren

addict ['ædɪkt] *n* Süchtige(r) *mf*; **addicted** [ə'dɪktɪd] *adj* **~ to alcohol/drugs** alkohol-/drogensüchtig

addition [ə'dɪʃən] *n* Zusatz *m*; (*to bill*) Aufschlag *m*; (*Math*) Addition *f*; **in ~** außerdem, zusätzlich (*to* zu); **additional** *adj* zusätzlich, weiter; **additive** ['ædɪtɪv] *n* Zusatz *m*; **add-on** ['ædɒn] *n* Zusatzgerät *nt*

address [ə'dres] *n* Adresse *f* ▷ *vt* (*letter*) adressieren; (*person*) anreden

adequate ['ædɪkwɪt] *adj* (*appropriate*)

angemessen; (*sufficient*) ausreichend; (*time*) genügend

adhesive [əd'hiːsɪv] *n* Klebstoff *m*; **adhesive tape** *n* Klebstreifen *m*

adjacent [ə'dʒeɪsənt] *adj* benachbart

adjective ['ædʒəktɪv] *n* Adjektiv *nt*

adjoining [ə'dʒɔɪnɪŋ] *adj* benachbart, Neben-

adjust [ə'dʒʌst] *vt* einstellen; (*put right also*) richtig stellen; (*speed, flow*) regulieren; (*in position*) verstellen ▷ *vi* sich anpassen (*to* +dat); **adjustable** *adj* verstellbar

admin [əd'mɪn] *n* (*fam*) Verwaltung *f*; **administration** [ədmɪnɪs'treɪʃən] *n* Verwaltung *f*; (*Pol*) Regierung *f*

admirable ['ædmərəbl] *adj* bewundernswert; **admiration** [ædmɪ'reɪʃən] *n* Bewunderung *f*; **admire** [əd'maɪə*] *vt* bewundern

admission [əd'mɪʃən] *n* (*entrance*) Zutritt *m*; (*to university etc*) Zulassung *f*; (*fee*) Eintritt *m*; (*confession*) Eingeständnis *nt*; **admission charge**, **admission fee** *n* Eintrittspreis *m*; **admit** [əd'mɪt] *vt* (*let in*) hereinlassen (*to* in +akk); (*to university etc*) zulassen; (*confess*) zugeben, gestehen; **to be ~ted to hospital** ins Krankenhaus eingeliefert werden

adolescent [ædə'lesnt] *n* Jugendliche(r) *mf*

adopt [ə'dɒpt] *vt* (*child*) adoptieren; (*idea*) übernehmen; **adoption** [ə'dɒpʃn] *n* (*of child*) Adoption *f*; (*of idea*) Übernahme *f*

adorable [ə'dɔːrəbl] *adj* entzückend; **adore** [ə'dɔː*] *vt* anbeten; (*person*) über alles lieben, vergöttern

adult ['ædʌlt] *adj* (*person*) erwachsen; (*film etc*) für Erwachsene ▷ *n* Erwachsene(r) *mf*

adultery [ə'dʌltərɪ] *n* Ehebruch *m*

advance [əd'vɑːns] *n* (*money*) Vorschuss *m*; (*progress*) Fortschritt *m*; **in ~** im Voraus; **to book in ~** vorbestellen ▷ *vi* (*move forward*) vorrücken ▷ *vt* (*money*) vorschießen; **advance booking** *n* Reservierung *f*; (*Theat*) Vorverkauf *m*; **advanced** *adj* (*modern*) fortschrittlich; (*course, study*) für Fortgeschrittene; **advance payment** *n* Vorauszahlung *f*

advantage [əd'vɑːntɪdʒ] *n* Vorteil *m*; **to take ~ of** (*exploit*) ausnutzen; (*profit from*)

Nutzen ziehen aus; **it's to your ~** es ist in deinem/Ihrem Interesse
adventure [əd'ventʃə*] n Abenteuer nt; **adventure holiday** n Abenteuerurlaub m; **adventure playground** n Abenteuerspielplatz m; **adventurous** [əd'ventʃərəs] adj (person) abenteuerlustig
adverb ['ædvɜ:b] n Adverb nt
adverse ['ædvɜ:s] adj (conditions etc) ungünstig; (effect, comment etc) negativ
advert ['ædvɜ:t] n Anzeige f; **advertise** ['ædvətaɪz] vt werben für; (in newspaper) inserieren; (job) ausschreiben ▷ vi Reklame machen; (in newspaper) annoncieren (for für); **advertisement** [əd'vɜ:tɪsmənt] n Werbung f; (announcement) Anzeige f; **advertising** n Werbung f
advice [əd'vaɪs] n Rat(schlag) m; **word o piece of ~** Ratschlag m; **take my ~** hör auf mich; **advisable** [əd'vaɪzəbl] adj ratsam; **advise** [əd'vaɪz] vt raten (sb jdm); **to ~ sb to do sth/not to do sth** jdm zuraten/abraten, etw zu tun
Aegean [i:'dʒi:ən] n **the ~ (Sea)** die Ägäis
aerial ['eərɪəl] n Antenne f ▷ adj Luft-
aerobatics [ɛərəʊ'bætɪks] npl Kunstfliegen nt
aerobics [ɛə'rəʊbɪks] nsing Aerobic nt
aeroplane ['eərəpleɪn] n Flugzeug nt
afaik abbr = **as far as I know**; (SMS) ≈ soweit ich weiß
affair [ə'fɛə*] n (matter, business) Sache f, Angelegenheit f; (scandal) Affäre f; (love affair) Verhältnis nt
affect [ə'fekt] vt (influence) (ein)wirken auf +akk; (health, organ) angreifen; (move deeply) berühren; (concern) betreffen; **affection** [ə'fekʃən] n Zuneigung f; **affectionate** [ə'fekʃənɪt] adj liebevoll
affluent ['æfluənt] adj wohlhabend
afford [ə'fɔ:d] vt sich leisten; **I can't ~ it** ich kann es mir nicht leisten; **affordable** [ə'fɔ:dəbl] adj erschwinglich
Afghanistan [æf'gænɪstæn] n Afghanistan nt
aforementioned [əfɔ:'menʃənd] adj oben genannt
afraid [ə'freɪd] adj **to be ~** Angst haben (of vor +dat); **to be ~ that ...** fürchten, dass ...; **I'm ~ I don't know** das weiß ich leider nicht

Africa ['æfrɪkə] n Afrika nt; **African** adj afrikanisch ▷ n Afrikaner(in) m(f); **African American**, **Afro-American** n Afroamerikaner(in) m(f)
after ['ɑ:ftə*] prep nach; **ten ~ five** (US) zehn nach fünf; **to be ~ sb/sth** (following, seeking) hinter jdm/etw her sein; **~ all** schließlich; (in spite of everything) (schließlich) doch ▷ conj nachdem ▷ adv **soon ~** bald danach; **aftercare** n Nachbehandlung f; **after-effect** n Nachwirkung f
afternoon n Nachmittag m; **~, good ~** guten Tag!; **in the ~** nachmittags
afters npl Nachtisch m; **after-sales service** n Kundendienst m; **after-shave (lotion)** n Rasierwasser nt; **after-sun lotion** n After-Sun-Lotion f; **afterwards** adv nachher; (after that) danach
again [ə'gen] adv wieder; (one more time) noch einmal; **not ~!** (nicht) (nicht) schon wieder; **~ and ~** immer wieder; **the same ~ please** das Gleiche noch mal bitte
against [ə'genst] prep gegen; **~ my will** wider Willen; **~ the law** unrechtmäßig, illegal
age [eɪdʒ] n Alter nt; (period of history) Zeitalter nt; **at the ~ of four** im Alter von vier (Jahren); **what ~ is she?, what is her ~?** wie alt ist sie?; **to come of ~** volljährig werden; **under ~** minderjährig ▷ vi altern, alt werden; **aged** adj **~ thirty** dreißig Jahre alt; **a son ~ twenty** ein zwanzigjähriger Sohn ▷ adj ['eɪdʒɪd] (elderly) betagt; **age group** n Altersgruppe f; **ageism** n Diskriminierung f aufgrund des Alters; **age limit** n Altersgrenze f
agency ['eɪdʒənsɪ] n Agentur f
agenda [ə'dʒendə] n Tagesordnung f
agent ['eɪdʒənt] n (Comm) Vertreter(in) m(f); (for writer, actor etc) Agent(in) m(f)
aggression [ə'greʃn] n Aggression f; **aggressive** [ə'gresɪv] adj aggressiv
agitated adj aufgeregt; **to get ~** sich aufregen
AGM abbr = **Annual General Meeting** JHV f
ago [ə'gəʊ] adv **two days ~** heute vor zwei Tagen; **not long ~** (erst) vor kurzem
agonize ['ægənaɪz] vi sich den Kopf zerbrechen (over über dat); **agonizing** adj qualvoll; **agony** ['ægənɪ] n Qual f
agree [ə'gri:] vt (date, price etc)

vereinbaren; **to ~ to do sth** sich bereit erklären, etw zu tun; **to ~ that ...** sich *dat* einig sein, dass ...; (*decide*) beschließen, dass ...; (*admit*) zugeben, dass ... ▷ *vi* (*have same opinion, correspond*) übereinstimmen (*with* mit); (*consent*) zustimmen; (*come to an agreement*) sich einigen (*about, on* auf +*akk*); (*food*) **not to ~ with sb** jdm nicht bekommen; **agreement** *n* (*agreeing*) Übereinstimmung *f*; (*contract*) Abkommen *nt*, Vereinbarung *f*

agricultural [ægrɪˈkʌltʃərəl] *adj* landwirtschaftlich, Landwirtschafts-; **agriculture** [ˈægrɪkʌltʃə*] *n* Landwirtschaft *f*

ahead [əˈhed] *adv* **to be ~** führen, vorne liegen; **~ of** vor +*dat*; **to be ~ of sb** (*person*) jdm voraus sein; (*thing*) vor jdm liegen; **to be 3 metres ~** 3 Meter Vorsprung haben

aid [eɪd] *n* Hilfe *f*; **in ~ of** zugunsten +*gen*; **with the ~ of** mithilfe +*gen* ▷ *vt* helfen +*dat*; (*support*) unterstützen

Aids [eɪdz] *n acr* = **acquired immune deficiency syndrome** Aids *nt*

aim [eɪm] *vt* (*gun, camera*) richten (*at* auf +*akk*) ▷ *vi* **to ~ at** (*with gun etc*) zielen auf +*akk*; (*fig*) abzielen auf +*akk*; **to ~ to do sth** beabsichtigen, etw zu tun ▷ *n* Ziel *nt*

air [ɛə*] *n* Luft *f*; **in the open ~** im Freien; (*Radio, TV*) **to be on the ~** (*programme*) auf Sendung sein; (*station*) senden ▷ *vt* lüften; **airbag** *n* (*Auto*) Airbag *m*; **air-conditioned** *adj* mit Klimaanlage; **air-conditioning** *n* Klimaanlage *f*; **aircraft** *n* Flugzeug *nt*; **airfield** *n* Flugplatz *m*; **air force** *n* Luftwaffe *f*; **airgun** *n* Luftgewehr *nt*; **airline** *n* Fluggesellschaft *f*; **airmail** *n* Luftpost *f*; **by ~** mit Luftpost; **airplane** *n* (*US*) Flugzeug *nt*; **air pollution** *n* Luftverschmutzung *f*; **airport** *n* Flughafen *m*; **airsick** *adj* luftkrank; **airtight** *adj* luftdicht; **air-traffic controller** *n* Fluglotse *m*, Fluglotsin *f*; **airy** *adj* luftig; (*manner*) lässig

aisle [aɪl] *n* Gang *m*; (*in church*) Seitenschiff *nt*; **~ seat** Sitz *m* am Gang

ajar [əˈdʒɑ:*] *adj* (*door*) angelehnt

alarm [əˈlɑ:m] *n* (*warning*) Alarm *m*; (*bell etc*) Alarmanlage *f* ▷ *vt* beunruhigen; **alarm clock** *n* Wecker *m*; **alarmed** *adj* (*protected*) alarmgesichert; **alarming** *adj* beunruhigend

Albania [ælˈbeɪnɪə] *n* Albanien *nt*; **Albanian** *adj* albanisch ▷ *n* (*person*) Albaner(in) *m(f)*; (*language*) Albanisch *nt*

album [ˈælbəm] *n* Album *nt*

alcohol [ˈælkəhɒl] *n* Alkohol *m*; **alcohol-free** *adj* alkoholfrei; **alcoholic** [ælkəˈhɒlɪk] *adj* (*drink*) alkoholisch ▷ *n* Alkoholiker(in) *m(f)*; **alcoholism** *n* Alkoholismus *m*

ale [eɪl] *n* Ale *nt* (*helles englisches Bier*)

alert [əˈlɜ:t] *adj* wachsam ▷ *n* Alarm *m* ▷ *vt* warnen (*to* vor +*dat*)

algebra [ˈældʒɪbrə] *n* Algebra *f*

Algeria [ælˈdʒɪərɪə] *n* Algerien *nt*

alibi [ˈælɪbaɪ] *n* Alibi *nt*

alien [ˈeɪlɪən] *n* (*foreigner*) Ausländer(in) *m(f)*; (*from space*) Außerirdische(r) *mf*

align [əˈlaɪn] *vt* ausrichten (*with* auf +*akk*)

alike [əˈlaɪk] *adj, adv* gleich; (*similar*) ähnlich

alive [əˈlaɪv] *adj* lebendig; **to keep sth ~** etw am Leben erhalten; **he's still ~** er lebt noch

⊙ **KEYWORD**

all [ɔ:l] *adj* alle (r, s); **all day/night** den ganzen Tag/die ganze Nacht; **all men are equal** alle Menschen sind gleich; **all five came** alle fünf kamen; **all the books/food** die ganzen Bücher/das ganze Essen; **all the time** die ganze Zeit (über); **all his life** sein ganzes Leben (lang)
▷ *pron* **1** alles; **I ate it all, I ate all of it** ich habe alles gegessen; **all of us/the boys went** wir gingen alle/die Jungen gingen; **we all sat down** wir setzten uns alle
2 (*in phrases*): **above all** vor allem; **after all** schließlich; **at all**: **not at all** (*in answer to question*) überhaupt nicht; (*in answer to thanks*) gern geschehen; **I'm not at all tired** ich bin überhaupt nicht müde; **anything at all will do** es ist egal, welche(r, s); **all in all** alles in allem
▷ *adv* ganz; **all alone** ganz allein; **it's not as hard as all that** so schwer ist es nun auch wieder nicht; **all the more/the better** umso mehr/besser; **all but** fast; **the score is 2 all** es steht 2 zu 2

allegation [ælɪˈɡeɪʃən] *n* Behauptung *f*; **alleged** *adj* angeblich

allergic [ə'lɜːdʒɪk] *adj* allergisch (*to* gegen); **allergy** ['ælədʒɪ] *n* Allergie *f*

alleviate [ə'liːvɪeɪt] *vt* (*pain*) lindern

alley ['ælɪ] *n* (enge) Gasse; (*passage*) Durchgang *m*; (*bowling*) Bahn *f*

alliance [ə'laɪəns] *n* Bündnis *nt*

alligator ['ælɪgeɪtə*] *n* Alligator *m*

all-night *adj* (*café, cinema*) die ganze Nacht geöffnet

allocate ['æləkeɪt] *vt* zuweisen, zuteilen (*to dat*)

allotment *n* (*plot*) Schrebergarten *m*

allow [ə'laʊ] *vt* (*permit*) erlauben (*sb* jdm); (*grant*) bewilligen; (*time*) einplanen; **allow for** *vt* berücksichtigen; (*cost etc*) einkalkulieren; **allowance** *n* (*from state*) Beihilfe *f*; (*from parent*) Unterhaltsgeld *nt*

all right ['ɔːl'raɪt] *adj* okay, in Ordnung; **I'm ~** mir geht's gut ▷ *adv* (*satisfactorily*) ganz gut ▷ *interj* okay

all-time *adj* (*record, high*) aller Zeiten

allusion [ə'luːʒn] *n* Anspielung *f* (*to* auf +*akk*)

all-wheel drive ['ɔːlwiːl'draɪv] *n* (*Auto*) Allradantrieb *m*

ally ['ælaɪ] *n* Verbündete(r) *mf*; (*Hist*) Alliierte(r) *mf*

almond ['ɑːmənd] *n* Mandel *f*

almost ['ɔːlməʊst] *adv* fast

alone [ə'ləʊn] *adj, adv* allein

along [ə'lɒŋ] *prep* entlang +*akk*; **~ the river** den Fluss entlang; (*position*) am Fluss entlang ▷ *adv* (*onward*) weiter; **~ with** zusammen mit; **all ~** die ganze Zeit; **alongside** *prep* neben +*dat* ▷ *adv* (*walk*) nebenher

aloud [ə'laʊd] *adv* laut

alphabet ['ælfəbet] *n* Alphabet *nt*

alpine ['ælpaɪn] *adj* alpin; **Alps** [ælps] *npl* **the ~** die Alpen

already [ɔːl'redɪ] *adv* schon, bereits

Alsace ['ælsæs] *n* Elsass *nt*; **Alsatian** [æl'seɪʃən] *adj* elsässisch ▷ *n* Elsässer(in) *m(f)*; (*Brit: dog*) Schäferhund *m*

also ['ɔːlsəʊ] *adv* auch

altar ['ɔːltə*] *n* Altar *m*

alter ['ɔːltə*] *vt* ändern; **alteration** [ɔːltə'reɪʃən] *n* Änderung *f*; **~s** (*to building*) Umbau *m*

alternate [ɔːl'tɜːnət] *adj* abwechselnd ▷ ['ɔːltəneɪt] *vi* abwechseln (*with* mit); **alternating current** *n* Wechselstrom *m*

alternative [ɔːl'tɜːnətɪv] *adj* Alternativ- ▷ *n* Alternative *f*

although [ɔːl'ðəʊ] *conj* obwohl

altitude ['æltɪtjuːd] *n* Höhe *f*

altogether [ɔːltə'geðə*] *adv* (*in total*) insgesamt; (*entirely*) ganz und gar

aluminium, **aluminum** (*US*) [æljʊ'mɪnɪəm, ə'luːmɪnəm] *n* Aluminium *nt*

always ['ɔːlweɪz] *adv* immer

am [æm] *present of* **be**; bin

am, **a.m.** *abbr* = **ante meridiem** vormittags, vorm.

amateur ['æmətə*] *n* Amateur(in) *m(f)* ▷ *adj* Amateur-; (*theatre, choir*) Laien-

amaze [ə'meɪz] *vt* erstaunen; **amazed** *adj* erstaunt (*at* über +*akk*); **amazing** *adj* erstaunlich

Amazon ['æməzən] *n* **~** (*river*) Amazonas *m*

ambassador [æm'bæsədə*] *n* Botschafter *m*

amber ['æmbə*] *n* Bernstein *m*

ambiguity [æmbɪ'gjʊɪtɪ] *n* Zweideutigkeit *f*; **ambiguous** [æm'bɪgjʊəs] *adj* zweideutig

ambition [æm'bɪʃən] *n* Ambition *f*; (*ambitious nature*) Ehrgeiz *m*; **ambitious** [æm'bɪʃəs] *adj* ehrgeizig

ambulance ['æmbjʊləns] *n* Krankenwagen *m*

amend [ə'mend] *vt* (*law etc*) ändern

America [ə'merɪkə] *n* Amerika *nt*; **American** *adj* amerikanisch ▷ *n* Amerikaner(in) *m(f)*; **native ~** Indianer(in) *m(f)*

amiable ['eɪmɪəbl] *adj* liebenswürdig

amicable ['æmɪkəbl] *adj* freundlich; (*relations*) freundschaftlich; (*Jur: settlement*) gütlich

amnesia [æm'niːzɪə] *n* Gedächtnisverlust *m*

among(st) [ə'mʌŋ(st)] *prep* unter +*dat*

amount [ə'maʊnt] *n* (*quantity*) Menge *f*; (*of money*) Betrag *m*; **a large/small ~ of ...** ziemlich viel/wenig ... ▷ *vi* **to ~ to** (*total*) sich belaufen auf +*akk*

amp, **ampere** [æmp, 'æmpeə*] *n* Ampere *nt*

amplifier ['æmplɪfaɪə*] *n* Verstärker *m*

amputate ['æmpjʊteɪt] *vt* amputieren

Amtrak® ['æmtræk] *n* amerikanische Eisenbahngesellschaft

amuse [əˈmjuːz] vt amüsieren; (entertain) unterhalten; **amused** adj **I'm not ~** das finde ich gar nicht lustig; **amusement** n (enjoyment) Vergnügen nt; (recreation) Unterhaltung f; **amusement arcade** n Spielhalle f; **amusement park** n Vergnügungspark m; **amusing** adj amüsant

an [æn, ən] art ein(e)

anaemic [əˈniːmɪk] adj blutarm

anaesthetic [ænɪsˈθetɪk] n Narkose f; (substance) Narkosemittel nt

analyse, analyze [ˈænəlaɪz] vt analysieren; **analysis** [əˈnælɪsɪs] n Analyse f

anatomy [əˈnætəmɪ] n Anatomie f; (structure) Körperbau m

ancestor [ˈænsestə*] n Vorfahr m

anchor [ˈæŋkə*] n Anker m ▷ vt verankern; **anchorage** n Ankerplatz m

anchovy [ˈæntʃəvɪ] n Sardelle f

ancient [ˈeɪnʃənt] adj alt; (fam: person, clothes etc) uralt

and [ænd, ənd] conj und

Andorra [ænˈdɔːrə] n Andorra nt

anemic adj (US) see **anaemic**

anesthetic n (US) see **anaesthetic**

angel [ˈeɪndʒəl] n Engel m

anger [ˈæŋɡə*] n Zorn m ▷ vt ärgern

angina, angina pectoris [ænˈdʒaɪnə(ˈpektərɪs)] n Angina Pectoris f

angle [ˈæŋɡl] n Winkel m; (fig) Standpunkt m

angler [ˈæŋɡlə*] n Angler(in) m(f); **angling** [ˈæŋɡlɪŋ] n Angeln nt

angry [ˈæŋɡrɪ] adj verärgert; (stronger) zornig; **to be ~ with sb** auf jdn böse sein

angular [ˈæŋɡjʊlə*] adj eckig; (face) kantig

animal [ˈænɪməl] n Tier nt; **animal rights** npl Tierrechte pl

animated [ˈænɪmeɪtɪd] adj lebhaft; **~ film** Zeichentrickfilm m

aniseed [ˈænɪsiːd] n Anis m

ankle [ˈæŋkl] n (Fuß)knöchel m

annex [ˈæneks] n Anbau m

anniversary [ænɪˈvɜːsərɪ] n Jahrestag m

announce [əˈnaʊns] vt bekannt geben; (officially) bekannt machen; (on radio, TV etc) (Radio, TV) ansagen; **announcement** n Bekanntgabe f; (official) Bekanntmachung f; (Radio, TV) Ansage f;

announcer n (Radio, TV) Ansager(in) m(f)

annoy [əˈnɔɪ] vt ärgern; **annoyance** n Ärger m; **annoyed** adj ärgerlich; **to be ~ with sb (about sth)** sich über jdn (über etw) ärgern; **annoying** adj ärgerlich; (person) lästig, nervig

annual [ˈænjʊəl] adj jährlich ▷ n Jahrbuch nt

anonymous [əˈnɒnɪməs] adj anonym

anorak [ˈænəræk] n Anorak m; (Brit fam: pej) Freak m

anorexia [ænəˈreksɪə] n Magersucht f; **anorexic** adj magersüchtig

another [əˈnʌðə*] adj, pron (different) ein(e) andere(r, s); (additional) noch eine(r, s); **let me put it ~ way** lass es mich anders sagen

answer [ˈɑːnsə*] n Antwort f (to auf +akk); (solution) Lösung f (+gen ▷ vi antworten; (on phone) sich melden ▷ vt (person) antworten +dat; (letter, question) beantworten; (telephone) gehen an +akk, abnehmen; (door) öffnen; **answer back** vi widersprechen; **answering machine, answerphone** n Anrufbeantworter m

ant [ænt] n Ameise f

Antarctic [ænˈtɑːktɪk] n Antarktis f; **Antarctic Circle** n südlicher Polarkreis

antelope [ˈæntɪləʊp] n Antilope f

antenna [ænˈtenə] (pl **antennae**) n (Zool) Fühler m; (Radio) Antenne f

anti- [ˈæntɪ] pref Anti-, anti-; **antibiotic** [ˈæntɪbaɪˈɒtɪk] n Antibiotikum nt

anticipate [ænˈtɪsɪpeɪt] vt (expect: trouble, question) erwarten, rechnen mit; **anticipation** [æntɪsɪˈpeɪʃən] n Erwartung f

anticlimax [æntɪˈklaɪmæks] n Enttäuschung f; **anticlockwise** [æntɪˈklɒkwaɪz] adv entgegen dem Uhrzeigersinn

antidote [ˈæntɪdəʊt] n Gegenmittel nt; **antifreeze** n Frostschutzmittel nt

Antipodes [ænˈtɪpədiːz] npl Australien und Neuseeland

antiquarian [æntɪˈkwɛərɪən] adj **~ bookshop** Antiquariat nt

antique [ænˈtiːk] n Antiquität f ▷ adj antik; **antique shop** n Antiquitätengeschäft nt

anti-Semitism [æntɪ'semɪtɪzm] n
Antisemitismus m; **antiseptic**
[æntɪ'septɪk] n Antiseptikum nt ▷ adj
antiseptisch; **antisocial** adj (person)
ungesellig; (behaviour) unsozial,
asozial

antlers ['æntləz] npl Geweih nt

anxiety [æŋ'zaɪətɪ] n Sorge f (about um);
anxious ['æŋkʃəs] adj besorgt (about um);
(apprehensive) ängstlich

 KEYWORD

any ['enɪ] adj **1** (in questions etc): **have you
any butter?** haben Sie (etwas) Butter?;
have you any children? haben Sie
Kinder?; **if there are any tickets left** falls
noch Karten da sind
2 (with negative): **I haven't any
money/books** ich habe kein Geld/keine
Bücher
3 (no matter which) jede(r, s) (beliebige); **any
colour (at all)** jede beliebige Farbe;
choose any book you like nehmen Sie ein
beliebiges Buch
4 (in phrases): **in any case** in jedem Fall;
any day now jeden Tag; **at any
moment** jeden Moment; **at any rate**
auf jeden Fall
▷ pron **1** (in questions etc): **have you got
any?** haben Sie welche?; **can any of you
sing?** kann (irgend)einer von euch singen?
2 (with negative): **I haven't any (of them)**
ich habe keinen/keines (davon)
3 (no matter which one(s)): **take any of
those books (you like)** nehmen Sie
irgendeines dieser Bücher
▷ adv **1** (in questions etc): **do you want any
more soup/sandwiches?** möchten Sie
noch Suppe/Brote?; **are you feeling any
better?** fühlen Sie sich etwas besser?
2 (with negative): **I can't hear him any
more** ich kann ihn nicht mehr hören

 KEYWORD

anything ['enɪθɪŋ] pron **1** (in questions etc)
(irgend)etwas; **can you see anything?**
können Sie etwas sehen?
2 (with negative): **I can't see anything** ich
kann nichts sehen
3 (no matter what): **you can say anything**

you like Sie können sagen, was Sie
wollen; **anything will do**
irgendetwas(, wird genügen)
irgendeine(r, s) (wird genügen); **he'll eat
anything** er ißt alles

apart [ə'pɑːt] adv auseinander; **~ from**
außer; **live ~** getrennt leben
apartment [ə'pɑːtmənt] n (esp US)
Wohnung f; **apartment block** n (esp US)
Wohnblock m
ape [eɪp] n (Menschen)affe m
aperitif [ə'perɪtɪf] n Aperitif m
aperture ['æpətjuə*] n Öffnung f; (Foto)
Blende f
apologize [ə'pɒlədʒaɪz] vi sich
entschuldigen; **apology** n
Entschuldigung f
apostrophe [ə'pɒstrəfɪ] n Apostroph m
appalled [ə'pɔːld] adj entsetzt (at über
+akk); **appalling** adj entsetzlich
apparatus [æpə'reɪtəs] n Apparat m;
(piece of apparatus) Gerät nt
apparent [ə'pærənt] adj (obvious)
offensichtlich (to für); (seeming) scheinbar;
apparently adv anscheinend
appeal [ə'piːl] vi (dringend) bitten (for
um, to +akk); (Jur) Berufung einlegen; **to
~ to sb** (be attractive) jdm zusagen ▷ n
Aufruf m (to an +akk); (Jur) Berufung f;
(attraction) Reiz m; **appealing** adj
ansprechend, attraktiv
appear [ə'pɪə*] vi erscheinen; (Theat)
auftreten; (seem) scheinen; **appearance** n
Erscheinen nt; (Theat) Auftritt m; (look)
Aussehen nt
appendicitis [əpendɪ'saɪtɪs] n
Blinddarmentzündung f; **appendix**
[ə'pendɪks] n Blinddarm m; (to book)
Anhang m
appetite ['æpɪtaɪt] n Appetit m; (fig:
desire) Verlangen nt; (sexual) Lust f;
appetizing ['æpɪtaɪzɪŋ] adj appetitlich,
appetitanregend
applause [ə'plɔːz] n Beifall m, Applaus m
apple ['æpl] n Apfel m; **apple crumble** n
mit Streuseln bestreutes Apfeldessert; **apple
juice** n Apfelsaft m; **apple pie** n
gedeckter Apfelkuchen m; **apple puree**,
apple sauce n Apfelmus nt; **apple tart** n
Apfelkuchen m; **apple tree** n Apfelbaum m
appliance [ə'plaɪəns] n Gerät nt;
applicable [ə'plɪkəbl] adj anwendbar; (on

forms) zutreffend; **applicant** ['æplɪkənt] n
Bewerber(in) m(f); **application**
[æplɪ'keɪʃən] n (request) Antrag m (for auf
+akk); (for job) Bewerbung f (for um);
application form n Anmeldeformular nt;
apply [ə'plaɪ] vi (be relevant) zutreffen
(to auf +akk); (for job etc) sich bewerben
(for um) ▷ vt (cream, paint etc) auftragen;
(put into practice) anwenden; (brakes)
betätigen
appoint [ə'pɔɪnt] vt (to post) ernennen;
appointment n Verabredung f; (at doctor,
hairdresser etc, in business) Termin m; **by
~** nach Vereinbarung
appreciate [ə'priːʃɪeɪt] vt (value) zu
schätzen wissen; (understand) einsehen; **to
be much ~d** richtig gewürdigt werden ▷ vi
(increase in value) im Wert steigen;
appreciation [əpriːʃɪ'eɪʃən] n (esteem)
Anerkennung f, Würdigung f; (of person
also) Wertschätzung f
apprehensive [æprɪ'hensɪv] adj
ängstlich
apprentice [ə'prentɪs] n Lehrling m
approach [ə'prəʊtʃ] vi sich nähern ▷ vt
(place) sich nähern +dat; (person)
herantreten an +akk; (problem) angehen
appropriate [ə'prəʊprɪət] adj passend;
(to occasion) angemessen; (remark)
treffend; **appropriately** adv passend;
(expressed) treffend
approval [ə'pruːvəl] n (show of
satisfaction) Anerkennung f; (permission)
Zustimmung f (of zu); **approve** [ə'pruːv]
vt billigen ▷ vi **to ~ of sth/sb** etw
billigen/von jdm etwas halten; **I don't
~** ich missbillige das
approx [ə'prɒks] abbr = **approximately**
ca.; **approximate** [ə'prɒksɪmɪt] adj
ungefähr; **approximately** adv ungefähr,
circa
apricot ['eɪprɪkɒt] n Aprikose f
April ['eɪprəl] n April m; see also
September
apron ['eɪprən] n Schürze f
aptitude [æptɪtjuːd] n Begabung f
aquaplaning ['ækwəpleɪnɪŋ] n (Auto)
Aquaplaning nt
aquarium [ə'kweərɪəm] n Aquarium nt
Aquarius [ə'kweərɪəs] n (Astr)
Wassermann m
Arab ['ærəb] n Araber(in) m(f); (horse)
Araber m; **Arabian** [ə'reɪbɪən] adj

arabisch; **Arabic** ['ærəbɪk] n (language)
Arabisch nt ▷ adj arabisch
arbitrary ['ɑːbɪtrərɪ] adj willkürlich
arcade [ɑː'keɪd] n Arkade f; (shopping
arcade) Einkaufspassage f
arch [ɑːtʃ] n Bogen m
archaeologist, archeologist (US)
[ɑːkɪ'ɒlədʒɪst] n Archäologe m,
Archäologin f; **archaeology, archeology**
(US) [ɑːkɪ'ɒlədʒɪ] n Archäologie f
archaic [ɑː'keɪɪk] adj veraltet
archbishop [ɑːtʃ'bɪʃəp] n Erzbischof m
archery ['ɑːtʃərɪ] n Bogenschießen nt
architect ['ɑːkɪtekt] n Architekt(in)
m(f); **architecture** [ɑːkɪ'tektʃə] n
Architektur f
archive(s) ['ɑːkaɪv(z)] n(pl) Archiv nt
archway ['ɑːtʃweɪ] n Torbogen m
Arctic ['ɑːktɪk] n Arktis f; **Arctic Circle** n
nördlicher Polarkreis
are [ə], unstressed [ɑː*] present of **be**
area ['eərɪə] n (region, district) Gebiet nt,
Gegend f; (amount of space) Fläche f;
(part of building etc) Bereich m, Zone f; (fig:
field) Bereich m; **the London ~** der
Londoner Raum; **area code** n (US)
Vorwahl f
aren't [ɑːnt] contr of **are not**
Argentina [ɑːdʒən'tiːnə] n Argentinien
nt
argue ['ɑːgjuː] vi streiten (about, over über
+akk); **to ~ that ...** behaupten, dass ...; **to
~ for/against ...** sprechen für/gegen ...;
argument n (reasons) Argument nt;
(quarrel) Streit m; **to have an ~** sich
streiten
Aries ['eəriːz] nsing (Astr) Widder m
arise [ə'raɪz] (arose, arisen) vi sich
ergeben, entstehen; (problem, question,
wind) aufkommen
aristocracy [ærɪs'tɒkrəsɪ] n (class) Adel
m; **aristocrat** ['ærɪstəkræt] n Adlige(r)
mf; **aristocratic** [ærɪstə'krætɪk] adj
aristokratisch, adlig
arm [ɑːm] n Arm m; (sleeve) Ärmel m; (of
armchair) Armlehne f ▷ vt bewaffnen;
armchair ['ɑːmtʃeə*] n Lehnstuhl m
armed [ɑːmd] adj bewaffnet
armpit ['ɑːmpɪt] n Achselhöhle f
arms [ɑːmz] npl Waffen pl
army ['ɑːmɪ] n Armee f, Heer nt
A road ['eɪrəʊd] n (Brit) ≈ Bundesstraße f
aroma [ə'rəʊmə] n Duft m, Aroma nt;

aromatherapy [ərəʊmə'θerəpɪ] *n*
Aromatherapie *f*

arose [ə'rəʊz] *pt of* **arise**

around [ə'raʊnd] *adv* herum, umher;
(*present*) hier (irgendwo); (*approximately*)
ungefähr; (*with time*) gegen; **he's
~ somewhere** er ist hier irgendwo in der
Nähe ▷ *prep* (*surrounding*) um ... (herum);
(*about in*) in ... herum

arr. *abbr* = **arrival, arrives** Ank.

arrange [ə'reɪndʒ] *vt* (*put in order*)
(an)ordnen; (*alphabetically*) ordnen;
(*artistically*) arrangieren; (*agree to: meeting
etc*) vereinbaren, festsetzen; (*holidays*)
festlegen; (*organize*) planen; **to ~ that ...**
es so einrichten, dass ...; **we ~d to meet
at eight o'clock** wir haben uns für acht
Uhr verabredet; **it's all ~d** es ist alles
arrangiert; **arrangement** *n* (*layout*)
Anordnung *f*; (*agreement*) Vereinbarung
f, Plan *m*; **make ~s** Vorbereitungen
treffen

arrest [ə'rest] *vt* (*person*) verhaften ▷ *n*
Verhaftung *f*; **under ~** verhaftet

arrival [ə'raɪvəl] *n* Ankunft *f*; **new
~** (*person*) Neuankömmling *m*; **arrivals** *n*
(*airport*) Ankunftshalle *f*; **arrive** [ə'raɪv] *vi*
ankommen (*at* bei, *in* +*dat*); **to ~ at a
solution** eine Lösung finden

arrogant ['ærəgənt] *adj* arrogant

arrow ['ærəʊ] *n* (=*weapon, sign*) Pfeil *m*

art [ɑːt] *n* Kunst *f*, **~s** (*pl*)
Geisteswissenschaften *pl*

artery ['ɑːtərɪ] *n* (*Med*) Schlagader *f*,
Arterie *f*

art gallery *n* Kunstgalerie *f*,
Kunstmuseum *nt*

arthritis [ɑː'θraɪtɪs] *n* Arthritis *f*

artichoke ['ɑːtɪtʃəʊk] *n* Artischocke *f*

article ['ɑːtɪkl] *n* Artikel *m*; (*object*)
Gegenstand *m*

artificial [ɑːtɪ'fɪʃəl] *adj* künstlich, Kunst-;
(*smile etc*) gekünstelt

artist ['ɑːtɪst] *n* Künstler(in) *m(f)*; **artistic**
[ɑː'tɪstɪk] *adj* künstlerisch

🔵 **KEYWORD**

as [æz] *conj* **1** (*referring to time*) als; **as
the years went by** mit den Jahren; **he
came in as I was leaving** als er
hereinkam, ging ich gerade; **as from
tomorrow** ab morgen

2 (*in comparisons*): **as big as** so groß wie;
twice as big as zweimal so groß wie; **as
much/many as** so viel/so viele wie; **as
soon as** sobald

3 (*since, because*) da; **he left early as he
had to be home by 10** er ging früher, da er
um 10 zu Hause sein musste

4 (*referring to manner, way*) wie; **do as you
wish** mach was du willst; **as she said** wie
sie sagte

5 (*concerning*): **as for or to that** was das
betrifft *or* angeht

6: **as if** *or* **though** als ob
▷ *prep* als; *see also* **long**; **he works as a
driver** er arbeitet als Fahrer; *see also*
such; **he gave it to me as a present** er
hat es mir als Geschenk gegeben; *see also*
well

asap [eɪeseɪ'piː, 'eɪsæp] *acr* = **as soon as
possible** möglichst bald

ascertain [æsə'teɪn] *vt* feststellen

ash [æʃ] *n* (*dust*) Asche *f*; (*tree*)
Esche *f*

ashamed [ə'ʃeɪmd] *adj* beschämt; **to
be ~ (of sb/sth)** sich (für jdn/etw)
schämen

ashore [ə'ʃɔː*] *adv* an Land

ashtray ['æʃtreɪ] *n* Aschenbecher *m*

Asia ['eɪʃə] *n* Asien *nt*; **Asian** *adj* asiatisch
▷ *n* Asiat(in) *m(f)*

aside [ə'saɪd] *adv* beiseite, zur Seite;
~ from (*esp US*) außer

ask [ɑːsk] *vt, vi* fragen; (*question*) stellen;
(*request*) bitten um; (*invite*) einladen; **to
~ sb the way** jdn nach dem Weg fragen;
to ~ sb to do sth jdn darum bitten, etw zu
tun; **ask for** *vt* bitten um

asleep [ə'sliːp] *adj, adv* **to be ~** schlafen;
to fall ~ einschlafen

asparagus [əs'pærəgəs] *n* Spargel *m*

aspect ['æspekt] *n* Aspekt *m*

aspirin ['æsprɪn] *n* Aspirin® *nt*

ass [æs] *n* (*a. fig*) Esel *m*

assassinate [ə'sæsɪneɪt] *vt* ermorden;
assassination [ə'sæsɪneɪʃn] *n*
Ermordung *f*; **~ attempt** Attentat *nt*

assault [ə'sɔːlt] *n* Angriff *m*; (*Jur*)
Körperverletzung *f* ▷ *vt* überfallen,
herfallen über +*akk*

assemble [ə'sembl] *vt* (*parts*)
zusammensetzen; (*people*)
zusammenrufen ▷ *vi* sich versammeln;

assembly [ə'sɛmblɪ] n (of people)
Versammlung f; (putting together)
Zusammensetzen nt; **assembly hall** n
Aula f

assert [ə'sɜːt] vt behaupten; **assertion**
[ə'sɜːʃən] n Behauptung f

assess [ə'ses] vt einschätzen;
assessment n Einschätzung f

asset ['æset] n Vermögenswert m; (fig)
Vorteil m; **~s** pl Vermögen nt

assign [ə'saɪn] vt zuweisen; **assignment**
n Aufgabe f; (mission) Auftrag m

assist [ə'sɪst] vt helfen +dat; **assistance** n
Hilfe f; **assistant** n Assistent(in) m(f),
Mitarbeiter(in) m(f); (in shop) Verkäufer(in)
m(f)

associate [ə'səʊʃɪət] n (partner)
Partner(in) m(f), Teilhaber(in) m(f)
▷ [ə'səʊʃɪeɪt] vt verbinden (with mit);
association [əsəʊsɪ'eɪʃən] n (organization)
Verband m, Vereinigung f; **in ~ with ...** in
Zusammenarbeit mit ...

assorted [ə'sɔːtɪd] adj gemischt;
assortment n Auswahl f (of an +dat); (of
sweets) Mischung f

assume [ə'sjuːm] vt annehmen (that
... dass ...); (role, responsibility)
übernehmen; **assumption** [ə'sʌmpʃən] n
Annahme f

assurance [ə'ʃʊərəns] n Versicherung f;
(confidence) Zuversicht f; **assure** [ə'ʃʊə*] vt
(say confidently) versichern +dat; **to ~ sb of**
sth jdm etw zusichern; **to be ~d of sth**
einer Sache sicher sein

asterisk ['æstərɪsk] n Sternchen nt

asthma ['æsmə] n Asthma nt

astonish [əs'tɒnɪʃ] vt erstaunen;
astonished adj erstaunt (at über);
astonishing adj erstaunlich;
astonishment n Erstaunen nt

astound [ə'staʊnd] vt sehr erstaunen;
astounding adj erstaunlich

astray [ə'streɪ] adv **to go ~** (letter etc)
verloren gehen; (person) vom Weg
abkommen; **to lead ~** irreführen, verführen

astrology [əs'trɒlədʒɪ] n Astrologie f

astronaut ['æstrənɔːt] n Astronaut(in)
m(f)

astronomy [əs'trɒnəmɪ] n Astronomie
f

asylum [ə'saɪləm] n (home) Anstalt f;
(political asylum) Asyl nt; **asylum seeker** n
Asylbewerber(in) m(f)

○ **KEYWORD**

at [æt] prep **1** (referring to position, direction)
an +dat, bei +dat; (with place) in +dat; **at the**
top an der Spitze; **at home/school** zu
Hause, zuhause (österreichisch,
schweizerisch)/in der Schule; **at the**
baker's beim Bäcker; **to look at sth** auf
etw acc blicken; **to throw sth at sb** etw
nach jdm werfen
2 (referring to time): **at 4 o'clock** um 4 Uhr;
at night bei Nacht; **at Christmas** zu
Weihnachten; **at times** manchmal
3 (referring to rates, speed etc): **at £1 a kilo** zu £1
pro Kilo; **two at a time** zwei auf einmal;
at 50 km/h mit 50 km/h
4 (referring to manner): **at a stroke** mit
einem Schlag; **at peace** in Frieden
5 (referring to activity): **to be at work** bei
der Arbeit sein; **to play at cowboys**
Cowboy spielen; **to be good at sth** gut in
etw dat sein
6 (referring to cause): **shocked/surprised/**
annoyed at sth schockiert/überrascht/
verärgert über etw acc; **I went at his**
suggestion ich ging auf seinen Vorschlag
hin

ate [et, eɪt] pt of **eat**

athlete ['æθliːt] n Athlet(in) m(f); (track
and field) Leichtathlet(in) m(f); (sportsman)
Sportler(in) m(f); **~'s foot** Fußpilz m;
athletic [æθ'letɪk] adj sportlich; (build)
athletisch; **athletics** npl Leichtathletik f

Atlantic [ət'læntɪk] n **the ~ (Ocean)** der
Atlantik

atlas ['ætləs] n Atlas m

ATM abbr = **automated teller machine**
Geldautomat m

atmosphere ['ætməsfɪə*] n Atmosphäre
f; (fig) Stimmung f

atom ['ætəm] n Atom nt; **atom(ic) bomb**
n Atombombe f; **atomic** [ə'tɒmɪk] adj
Atom-; **~ energy** Atomenergie f; **~ power**
Atomkraft f

A to Z® ['eɪtə'zed] n Stadtplan m (in
Buchform)

atrocious [ə'trəʊʃəs] adj grauenhaft;
atrocity [ə'trɒsɪtɪ] n Grausamkeit f;
(deed) Gräueltat f

attach [ə'tætʃ] vt befestigen, anheften (to
an +dat); **to ~ importance to sth** Wert auf

etw *akk* legen; **to be ~ed to sb/sth** an
jdm/etw hängen; **attachment**
[ə'tætʃmənt] *n* (*affection*) Zuneigung *f*;
(*Inform*) Attachment *nt*, Anhang *m*,
Anlage *f*

attack [ə'tæk] *vt, vi* angreifen ▷ *n* Angriff
+*akk* (*on* auf *m*); (*Med*) Anfall *m*

attempt [ə'tempt] *n* Versuch *m*; **to make
an ~ to do sth** versuchen, etw zu tun ▷ *vt*
versuchen

attend [ə'tend] *vt* (*go to*) teilnehmen an
+*dat*; (*lectures, school*) besuchen ▷ *vi* (*be
present*) anwesend sein; **attend to** *vt* sich
kümmern um; (*customer*) bedienen;
attendance *n* (*presence*) Anwesenheit *f*;
(*people present*) Teilnehmerzahl *f*;
attendant *n* (*in car park etc*) Wächter(in)
m(f); (*in museum*) Aufseher(in) *m(f)*

attention [ə'tenʃən] *n* Aufmerksamkeit *f*;
(**your**) **~ please** Achtung!; **to pay ~ to sth**
etw beachten; **to pay ~ to sb** jdm
aufmerksam zuhören; (*listen*) jdm/etw
aufmerksam zuhören; **for the ~ of ...** zu
Händen von ...; **attentive** [ə'tentɪv] *adj*
aufmerksam

attic ['ætɪk] *n* Dachboden *m*; (*lived in*)
Mansarde *f*

attitude ['ætɪtjuːd] *n* (*mental*) Einstellung
f (*to, towards* zu); (*more general, physical*)
Haltung *f*

attorney [ə'tɜːnɪ] *n* (US: *lawyer*)
Rechtsanwalt *m*, Rechtsanwältin *f*

attract [ə'trækt] *vt* anziehen; (*attention*)
erregen; **to be ~ed to o by sb** sich zu jdm
hingezogen fühlen; **attraction**
[ə'trækʃən] *n* Anziehungskraft *f*; (*thing*)
Attraktion *f*; **attractive** *adj* attraktiv;
(*thing, idea*) reizvoll

aubergine ['əʊbəʒiːn] *n* Aubergine *f*

auction ['ɔːkʃən] *n* Versteigerung *f*,
Auktion *f* ▷ *vt* versteigern

audible ['ɔːdɪbl] *adj* hörbar

audience ['ɔːdɪəns] *n* Publikum *nt*;
(*Radio*) Zuhörer *pl*; (*Tv*) Zuschauer *pl*

audio ['ɔːdɪəʊ] *adj* Ton-

audition [ɔː'dɪʃən] *n* Probe *f* ▷ *vi* (*Theat*)
vorspielen, vorsingen

auditorium [ɔːdɪ'tɔːrɪəm] *n*
Zuschauerraum *m*

Aug *abbr* = **August**

August ['ɔːɡəst] *n* August *m*; *see also*
September

aunt [ɑːnt] *n* Tante *f*

au pair [əʊ'peə*] *n* Aupairmädchen *nt*,
Aupairjunge *m*

Australia [ɒ'streɪlɪə] *n* Australien *nt*;
Australian *adj* australisch ▷ *n*
Australier(in) *m(f)*

Austria ['ɒstrɪə] *n* Österreich *nt*;
Austrian *adj* österreichisch ▷ *n*
Österreicher(in) *m(f)*

authentic [ɔː'θentɪk] *adj* echt; (*signature*)
authentisch; **authenticity** [ɔː'θen'tɪsɪtɪ] *n*
Echtheit *f*

author ['ɔː'θə*] *n* Autor(in) *m(f)*; (*of report
etc*) Verfasser(in) *m(f)*

authority [ɔː'θɒrɪtɪ] *n* (*power, expert*)
Autorität *f*; **an ~ on sth** eine Autorität auf
dem Gebiet einer Sache; **the authorities**
(*pl*) die Behörden *pl*; **authorize** ['ɔː'θəraɪz]
vt (*permit*) genehmigen; **to be ~d to do
sth** offiziell berechtigt sein, etw zu tun

auto ['ɔːtəʊ] (*pl* **-s**) *n* (*US*) Auto *nt*

autobiography [ɔːtəʊbaɪ'ɒɡrəfɪ] *n*
Autobiographie *f*; **autograph** ['ɔːtəɡrɑːf]
n Autogramm *nt*

automatic [ɔːtə'mætɪk] *adj*
automatisch; **~ gear change** (*Brit*), **~ gear
shift** (*US*) Automatikschaltung *f* ▷ *n* (*car*)
Automatikwagen *m*

automobile ['ɔːtəməbiːl] *n* (*US*)
Auto(mobil) *nt*; **autotrain** ['ɔːtəʊtreɪn] *n*
(*US*) Autoreisezug *m*

autumn ['ɔːtəm] *n* (*Brit*) Herbst *m*

auxiliary [ɔːɡ'zɪlɪərɪ] *adj* Hilfs-; **~ verb**
Hilfsverb *nt* ▷ *n* Hilfskraft *f*

availability [əveɪlə'bɪlɪtɪ] *n* (*of product*)
Lieferbarkeit *f*; (*of resources*) Verfügbarkeit
f; **available** *adj* erhältlich; (*existing*)
vorhanden; (*product*) lieferbar; (*person*)
erreichbar; **to be/make ~ to sb** jdm zur
Verfügung stehen/stellen; **they're only
~ in black** es gibt sie nur in Schwarz, sie
sind nur in Schwarz erhältlich

avalanche ['ævəlɑːnʃ] *n* Lawine *f*

Ave *abbr* = **avenue**

avenue ['ævənjuː] *n* Allee *f*

average ['ævrɪdʒ] *n* Durchschnitt *m*; **on
~** im Durchschnitt ▷ *adj* durchschnittlich;
~ speed Durchschnittsgeschwindigkeit *f*;
of ~ height von mittlerer Größe

aviation [eɪvɪ'eɪʃən] *n* Luftfahrt *f*

avocado [ævə'kɑːdəʊ] (*pl* **-s**) *n* Avocado *f*

avoid [ə'vɔɪd] *vt* vermeiden; **to ~ sb** jdm
aus dem Weg gehen; **avoidable** *adj*
vermeidbar

awake [ə'weɪk] (**awoke, awoken**) vi
aufwachen ▷ adj wach

award [ə'wɔːd] n (prize) Preis m; (for
bravery etc) Auszeichnung f ▷ vt
zuerkennen (to sb jdm); (present) verleihen
(to sb jdm)

aware [ə'wɛə*] adj bewusst; **to be ~ of
sth** sich dat einer Sache gen bewusst sein; **I
was not ~ that ...** es war mir nicht klar,
dass ...

away [ə'weɪ] adv weg; **to look
~** wegsehen; **he's ~** er ist nicht da; (on a
trip) er ist verreist; (from school, work) er
fehlt; (Sport) **they are (playing) ~** sie
spielen auswärts; (with distance) **three
miles ~** drei Meilen (von hier) entfernt; **to
work ~** drauflos arbeiten

awful ['ɔːfʊl] adj schrecklich, furchtbar;
awfully adv furchtbar

awkward ['ɔːkwəd] adj (clumsy)
ungeschickt; (embarrassing) peinlich;
(difficult) schwierig

awning ['ɔːnɪŋ] n Markise f

awoke [ə'wəʊk] pt of **awake**; **awoken**
[ə'wəʊkən] pp of **awake**

ax (US), **axe** [æks] n Axt f

axle ['æksl] n (Tech) Achse f

BA *abbr* = **Bachelor of Arts**

BSc *abbr* = **Bachelor of Science**

babe [beɪb] *n* (*fam*) Baby *nt*; (*fam: affectionate*) Schatz *m*, Kleine(r) *mf*

baby ['beɪbɪ] *n* Baby *nt*; (*of animal*) Junge(s) *nt*; (*fam: affectionate*) Schatz *m*, Kleine(r) *mf*; **to have a ~** ein Kind bekommen; **it's your ~** (*fam: responsibility*) das ist dein Bier; **baby carriage** *n* (*US*) Kinderwagen *m*; **baby food** *n* Babynahrung *f*; **babyish** *adj* kindisch; **baby shower** *n* (*US*) Party für die werdende Mutter; **baby-sit** *irr vi* babysitten; **baby-sitter** *n* Babysitter(in) *m(f)*

bachelor ['bætʃələ*] *n* Junggeselle *m*; **Bachelor of Arts/Science** *erster akademischer Grad*, ≈ Magister/Diplom; **bachelorette** *n* Junggesellin *f*; **bachelorette party** *n* (*US*) Junggesellinnenabschied; **bachelor party** *n* (*US*) Junggesellenabschied

back [bæk] *n* (*of person, animal*) Rücken *m*; (*of house, coin etc*) Rückseite *f*; (*of chair*) Rückenlehne *f*; (*of car*) Rücksitz *m*; (*of train*) Ende *nt*; (*Sport: defender*) Verteidiger(in) *m(f)*; **at the ~ of ...,** (*US*) **in ~ of** (*inside*) hinten in ...; (*outside*) hinter ...; **~ to front** verkehrt herum ▷ *vt* (*support*) unterstützen; (*car*) rückwärts fahren ▷ *vi* (*go backwards*) rückwärts gehen o fahren ▷ *adj* Hinter-; **~ wheel** Hinterrad *nt* ▷ *adv* zurück; **they're ~** sie sind wieder da; **back away** *vi* sich zurückziehen; **back down** *vi* nachgeben; **back up** *vi* (*car etc*) zurücksetzen ▷ *vt* (*support*) unterstützen; (*Inform*) sichern; (*car*) zurückfahren

backache *n* Rückenschmerzen *pl*; **backbone** *n* Rückgrat *nt*; **backdate** *vt* zurückdatieren; **backdoor** *n* Hintertür *f*; **backfire** *vi* (*plan*) fehlschlagen; (*Auto*) fehlzünden; **background** *n* Hintergrund *m*; **backhand** *n* (*Sport*) Rückhand *f*; **backlog** *n* (*of work*) Rückstand *m*; **backpack** *n* (*US*) Rucksack *m*; **backpacker** *n* Rucksacktourist(in) *m(f)*; **backpacking** *n* Rucksacktourismus *m*; **back seat** *n* Rücksitz *m*; **backside** *n* (*fam*) Po *m*; **back street** *n* Seitensträßchen *nt*; **backstroke** *n* Rückenschwimmen *nt*; **back-up** *n* (*support*) Unterstützung *f*; **~** (*copy*) (*Inform*) Sicherungskopie *f*; **backward** *adj* (*child*) zurückgeblieben; (*region*) rückständig; **~ movement** Rückwärtsbewegung *f*; **backwards** *adv* rückwärts; **backyard** *n* Hinterhof *m*

bacon ['beɪkən] *n* Frühstücksspeck *m*

bacteria [bæk'tɪərɪə] *npl* Bakterien *pl*

bad [bæd] (**worse, worst**) *adj* schlecht, schlimm; (*smell*) übel; **I have a ~ back** mir tut der Rücken weh; **I'm ~ at maths/sport** ich bin schlecht in Mathe/Sport; **to go ~** schlecht werden, verderben

badge [bædʒ] *n* Abzeichen *nt*

badger ['bædʒə*] *n* Dachs *m*

badly ['bædlɪ] *adv* schlecht; **~ wounded** schwer verwundet; **to need sth ~** etw dringend brauchen; **bad-tempered** ['bæd'tempəd] *adj* schlecht gelaunt

bag [bæg] *n* (*small*) Tüte *f*; (*larger*) Beutel *m*; (*handbag*) Tasche *f*; **my ~s** (*luggage*) mein Gepäck; **it's not my ~** (*fam*) das ist nicht mein Ding

baggage ['bægɪdʒ] *n* Gepäck *nt*; **baggage allowance** *n* Freigepäck *nt*; **baggage (re)claim** *n* Gepäckrückgabe *f*

baggy ['bægɪ] *adj* (*zu*) weit; (*trousers, suit*) ausgebeult

bag lady ['bæɡleɪdɪ] *n* Stadtstreicherin *f*

bagpipes ['bæɡpaɪps] *npl* Dudelsack *m*

Bahamas [bə'hɑːməz] *npl* **the ~** die Bahamas *pl*

bail [beɪl] *n* (*money*) Kaution *f*

bait [beɪt] *n* Köder *m*

bake [beɪk] *vt, vi* backen; **baked beans** *npl* weiße Bohnen in Tomatensoße; **baked potato** (*pl* **-es**) *n* in der Schale gebackene Kartoffel, Ofenkartoffel *f*; **baker** *n* Bäcker(in) *m(f)*; **bakery** ['beɪkərɪ] *n* Bäckerei *f*; **baking powder** *n* Backpulver *nt*

balance ['bæləns] *n* (*equilibrium*) Gleichgewicht *nt* ▷ *vt* (*make up for*) ausgleichen; **balanced** *adj* ausgeglichen; **balance sheet** *n* Bilanz *f*

balcony ['bælkənɪ] *n* Balkon *m*

bald [bɔːld] *adj* kahl; **to be ~** eine Glatze haben

Balkans ['bɔːlkənz] *npl* **the ~** der Balkan, die Balkanländer *pl*

ball [bɔːl] *n* Ball *m*; **to have a ~** (*fam*) sich prima amüsieren

ballet ['bæleɪ] *n* Ballett *nt*; **ballet dancer** *n* Balletttänzer(in) *m(f)*

balloon [bə'luːn] *n* (Luft)ballon *m*

ballot ['bælət] *n* (geheime) Abstimmung; **ballot box** *n* Wahlurne *f*; **ballot paper** *n* Stimmzettel *m*

ballpoint (pen) ['bɔːlpɔɪnt] *n* Kugelschreiber *m*

ballroom ['bɔːlruːm] *n* Tanzsaal *m*

Baltic ['bɔːltɪk] *adj* **~ Sea** Ostsee *f*; **the ~ States** die baltischen Staaten

bamboo [bæm'buː] *n* Bambus *m*; **bamboo shoots** *npl* Bambussprossen *pl*

ban [bæn] *n* Verbot *nt* ▷ *vt* verbieten

banana [bə'nɑːnə] *n* Banane *f*; **he's ~s** ist völlig durchgeknallt; **banana split** *n* Bananensplit *nt*

band [bænd] *n* (*group*) Gruppe *f*; (*of criminals*) Bande *f*; (*Mus*) Kapelle *f*; (*pop, rock etc*) Band *f*; (*strip*) Band *nt*

bandage ['bændɪdʒ] *n* Verband *m*; (*elastic*) Bandage *f* ▷ *vt* verbinden

B & B *abbr* = **bed and breakfast**

bang [bæŋ] *n* (*noise*) Knall *m*; (*blow*) Schlag *m* ▷ *vt, vi* knallen; (*door*) zuschlagen, zuknallen; **banger** [bæŋə*] *n* (*Brit fam: firework*) Knallkörper *m*; (*sausage*) Würstchen *nt*; (*fam: old car*) Klapperkiste *f*

bangs [bæŋz] *npl* (*US: of hair*) Pony *m*

banish ['bænɪʃ] *vt* verbannen

banister(s) ['bænɪstə*] *n* (Treppen)geländer *nt*

bank [bæŋk] *n* (*Fin*) Bank *f*; (*of river etc*) Ufer *nt*; **bank account** *n* Bankkonto *nt*; **bank balance** *n* Kontostand *m*; **bank card** *n* Bankkarte *f*; **bank code** *n* Bankleitzahl *f*; **bank holiday** *n* gesetzlicher Feiertag

● **bank holiday**
●
● Als **bank holiday** wird in
● Großbritannien ein gesetzlicher
● Feiertag bezeichnet, an dem die
● Banken geschlossen sind. Die
● meisten dieser Feiertage, abgesehen
● von Weihnachten und Ostern, fallen
● auf Montage im Mai und August. An
● diesen langen Wochenenden (bank
● holiday weekends) fahren viele
● Briten in Urlaub, so dass dann auf
● den Straßen, Flughäfen und bei der
● Bahn sehr viel Betrieb ist.

bank manager *n* Filialleiter(in) *m(f)*; **banknote** *n* Banknote *f*

bankrupt *vt* ruinieren; **to go ~** Pleite gehen

bank statement *n* Kontoauszug *m*

baptism ['bæptɪzəm] *n* Taufe *f*; **baptize** ['bæptaɪz] *vt* taufen

bar [bɑː*] *n* (*for drinks*) Bar *f*; (*less smart*) Lokal *nt*; (*rod*) Stange *f*; (*of chocolate etc*) Riegel *m*, Tafel *f*; (*of soap*) Stück *nt*; (*counter*) Theke *f* ▷ *prep* außer; **~ none** ohne Ausnahme

barbecue ['bɑːbɪkjuː] *n* (*device*) Grill *m*; (*party*) Barbecue *nt*, Grillfete *f*; **to have a ~** grillen

barbed wire ['bɑːbd'waɪə*] *n* Stacheldraht *m*

barber ['bɑːbə*] *n* (Herren)friseur *m*

bar code ['bɑːkəʊd] *n* Strichkode *m*

bare [bɛə*] *adj* nackt; **~ patch** kahle Stelle; **barefoot** *adj, adv* barfuß; **bareheaded** *adj, adv* ohne Kopfbedeckung; **barely** *adv* kaum; (*with age*) knapp

bargain ['bɑːgɪn] *n* (*cheap offer*) günstiges Angebot, Schnäppchen *nt*; (*transaction*) Geschäft *nt*; **what a ~** das ist aber günstig! ▷ *vi* (ver)handeln

barge [bɑːdʒ] n (for freight) Lastkahn m; (unpowered) Schleppkahn m

bark [bɑːk] n (of tree) Rinde f; (of dog) Bellen nt ▷ vi (dog) bellen

barley ['bɑːlɪ] n Gerste f

barmaid ['bɑːmeɪd] n Bardame f; **barman** ['bɑːmən] (pl **-men**) n Barkeeper m

barn [bɑːn] n Scheune f

barometer [bə'rɒmɪtə*] n Barometer nt

baroque [bə'rɒk] adj barock, Barock-

barracks ['bærəks] npl Kaserne f

barrel ['bærəl] n Fass nt; **barrel organ** n Drehorgel f

barricade [bærɪ'keɪd] n Barrikade f

barrier ['bærɪə*] n (obstruction) Absperrung f, Barriere f; (across road etc) Schranke f

barrow ['bærəʊ] n (cart) Schubkarren m

bartender ['bɑːtendə*] n (US) Barkeeper m

base [beɪs] n Basis f; (of lamp, pillar etc) Fuß m; (Mil) Stützpunkt m ▷ vt gründen (on auf +akk); **to be ~d on sth** etw auf etw dat basieren; **baseball** n Baseball m; **baseball cap** n Baseballmütze f; **basement** n Kellergeschoss nt

bash [bæʃ] (fam) n Schlag m; (fam) Party f ▷ vt hauen

basic ['beɪsɪk] adj einfach; (fundamental) Grund-; (importance, difference) grundlegend; (in principle) grundsätzlich; **the accomodation is very ~** die Unterkunft ist sehr bescheiden; **basically** adv im Grunde; **basics** npl **the ~** das Wesentliche

basil ['bæzl] n Basilikum nt

basin ['beɪsn] n (for washing, valley) (Wasch)becken nt

basis ['beɪsɪs] n Basis f; **on the ~ of** aufgrund +gen; **on a monthly ~** monatlich

basket ['bɑːskɪt] n Korb m; **basketball** n Basketball m

Basque [bæsk] n (person) Baske m, Baskin f; (language) Baskisch nt ▷ adj baskisch

bass [beɪs] n (Mus) Bass m; (Zool) Barsch m ▷ adj (Mus) Bass-

bastard ['bɑːstəd] n (vulg: awful person) Arschloch nt

bat [bæt] n (Zool) Fledermaus f; (Sport: cricket, baseball) Schlagholz nt; (table tennis) Schläger m

batch [bætʃ] n Schwung m; (fam: of letters, books etc) Stoß m

bath [bɑːθ] n Bad nt; (tub) Badewanne f; **to have a ~** baden ▷ vt (child etc) baden

bathe [beɪð] vt, vi (wound etc) baden; **bathing cap** n Badekappe f; **bathing costume**, **bathing suit** (US) n Badeanzug m

bathmat ['bɑːθmæt] n Badevorleger m; **bathrobe** n Bademantel m; **bathroom** n Bad(ezimmer) nt; **baths** [bɑːðz] npl (Schwimm)bad nt; **bath towel** n Badetuch nt; **bathtub** n Badewanne f

baton ['bætən] n (Mus) Taktstock m; (police) Schlagstock m

batter ['bætə*] n Teig m ▷ vt heftig schlagen; **battered** adj übel zugerichtet; (hat, car) verbeult; (wife, baby) misshandelt

battery ['bætərɪ] n (Elec) Batterie f; **battery charger** n Ladegerät nt

battle ['bætl] n Schlacht f; (fig) Kampf m (for um +akk); **battlefield** n Schlachtfeld nt; **battlements** npl Zinnen pl

Bavaria [bə'veərɪə] n Bayern nt; **Bavarian** adj bay(e)risch ▷ n Bayer(in) m(f)

bay [beɪ] n (of sea) Bucht f; (on house) Erker m; (tree) Lorbeerbaum m; **bay leaf** n Lorbeerblatt nt; **bay window** n Erkerfenster nt

BBC abbr = **British Broadcasting Corporation** BBC f

BC abbr = **before Christ** vor Christi Geburt, v. Chr.

◯ **KEYWORD**

be [biː] (pt **was, were**, pp **been**) aux vb **1** (with present participle: forming continuous tenses); **what are you doing?** was machst du (gerade)?; **it is raining** es regnet; **I've been waiting for you for hours** ich warte schon seit Stunden auf dich

2 (with pp: forming passives): **to be killed** getötet werden; **the thief was nowhere to be seen** der Dieb war nirgendwo zu sehen

3 (in tag questions): **it was fun, wasn't it?** es hat Spaß gemacht, nicht wahr?

4 (+to +infin): **the house is to be sold** das Haus soll verkauft werden; **he's not to open it** er darf es nicht öffnen

▷ *vb* +complement **1** (*usu*) sein; **I'm tired** ich bin müde; **I'm hot/cold** mir ist heiß/kalt; **he's a doctor** er ist Arzt; **2 and 2 are 4** 2 und 2 ist *or* sind 4; **she's tall/pretty** sie ist groß/hübsch; **be careful/quiet** sei vorsichtig/ruhig **2** (*of health*): **how are you?** wie geht es dir?; **he's very ill** er ist sehr krank; **I'm fine now** jetzt geht es mir gut **3** (*of age*): **how old are you?** wie alt bist du?; **I'm sixteen (years old)** ich bin sechzehn (Jahre alt) **4** (*cost*): **how much was the meal?** was *or* wie viel hat das Essen gekostet?; **that'll be £5.75, please** das macht £5.75, bitte ▷ *vi* **1** (*exist, occur etc*): **is there a God?** gibt es einen Gott?; **be that as it may** wie dem auch sei; **so be it** also gut **2** (*referring to place*) sein; **I won't be here tomorrow** iche werde morgen nicht hier sein **3** (*referring to movement*); **where have you been?** wo bist du gewesen?; **I've been in the garden** ich war im Garten ▷ *impers vb* **1** (*referring to time, distance, weather*) sein; **it's 5 o'clock** es ist 5 Uhr; **it's 10 km to the village** es sind 10 km bis zum Dorf; **it's too hot/cold** es ist zu heiß/kalt **2** (*emphatic*): **it's me** ich bins; **it's the postman** es ist der Briefträger

beach [biːtʃ] *n* Strand *m*; **beachwear** *n* Strandkleidung *f*
bead [biːd] *n* (*of glass, wood etc*) Perle *f*; (*drop*) Tropfen *m*
beak [biːk] *n* Schnabel *m*
beam [biːm] *n* (*of wood etc*) Balken *m*; (*of light*) Strahl *m* ▷ *vi* (*smile etc*) strahlen
bean [biːn] *n* Bohne *f*; **bean curd** *n* Tofu *m*
bear [bɛə*] *n* (*carry*) (**bore, borne**) *vt* tragen; (*tolerate*) ertragen ▷ *n* Bär *m*; **bearable** *adj* erträglich
beard [bɪəd] *n* Bart *m*
beast [biːst] *n* Tier *nt*; (*brutal person*) Bestie *f*; (*disliked person*) Biest *nt*
beat [biːt] (**beat, beaten**) *vt* schlagen; (*as punishment*) prügeln; **to ~ sb at tennis** jdn im Tennis schlagen ▷ *n* (*of heart, drum etc*) Schlag *m*; (*Mus*) Takt *m*; (*type of music*) Beat *m*; **beat up** *vt* zusammenschlagen
beaten [ˈbiːtn] *pp of* **beat**; **of the ~ track** abgelegen
beautiful [ˈbjuːtɪful] *adj* schön; (*splendid*)

herrlich; **beauty** [ˈbjuːtɪ] *n* Schönheit *f*; **beauty spot** *n* (*place*) lohnendes Ausflugsziel
beaver [ˈbiːvə*] *n* Biber *m*
became [bɪˈkeɪm] *pt of* **become**
because [bɪˈkɒz] *adv, conj* weil ▷ *prep* **~ of** wegen +*gen o dat*
become [bɪˈkʌm] (**became, become**) *vt* werden; **what's ~ of him?** was ist aus ihm geworden?
bed [bed] *n* Bett *nt*; (*in garden*) Beet *nt*; **bed and breakfast** *n* Übernachtung *f* mit Frühstück; **bedclothes** *npl* Bettwäsche *f*; **bedding** *n* Bettzeug *nt*; **bed linen** *n* Bettwäsche *f*; **bedroom** *n* Schlafzimmer *nt*; **bed-sit(ter)** *n* (*fam*) möblierte Einzimmerwohnung; **bedspread** *n* Tagesdecke *f*; **bedtime** *n* Schlafenszeit *f*
bee [biː] *n* Biene *f*
beech [biːtʃ] *n* Buche *f*
beef [biːf] *n* Rindfleisch *nt*; **beefburger** *n* Hamburger *m*; **beef tomato** (*pl* **-es**) *n* Fleischtomate *f*
beehive [ˈbiːhaɪv] *n* Bienenstock *m*
been [biːn] *pp of* **be**
beer [bɪə*] *n* Bier *nt*; **beer garden** *n* Biergarten *m*
beetle [ˈbiːtl] *n* Käfer *m*
beetroot [ˈbiːtruːt] *n* Rote Bete *f*
before [bɪˈfɔː*] *prep* vor; **the year ~ last** vorletztes Jahr; **the day ~ yesterday** vorgestern ▷ *conj* bevor ▷ *adv* (*of time*) vorher; **have you been there ~?** waren Sie/warst du schon einmal dort?; **beforehand** *adv* vorher
beg [beg] *vt* **to ~ sb to do sth** jdn inständig bitten, etw zu tun ▷ *vi* (*beggar*) betteln (*for* um +*akk*)
began [bɪˈgæn] *pt of* **begin**
beggar [ˈbegə*] *n* Bettler(in) *m(f)*
begin [bɪˈgɪn] (**began, begun**), *vt, vi* anfangen, beginnen; **to ~ to do sth** anfangen, etw zu tun; **beginner** *n* Anfänger(in) *m(f)*; **beginning** *n* Anfang *m*
begun [bɪˈgʌn] *pp of* **begin**
behalf [bɪˈhɑːf] *n* **on ~ of, in ~ of** (*US*) im Namen/Auftrag von; **on my ~** für mich
behave [bɪˈheɪv] *vi* sich benehmen; **~ yourself!** benimm dich!; **behavior** (*US*), **behaviour** [bɪˈheɪvjə*] *n* Benehmen *nt*
behind [bɪˈhaɪnd] *prep* hinter; **to be ~ time** Verspätung haben ▷ *adv* hinten; **to be ~ with one's work** mit seiner Arbeit

im Rückstand sein ▷ n (fam) Hinterteil nt

beige [beɪʒ] adj beige

being ['biːɪŋ] n (existence) Dasein nt; (person) Wesen nt

Belarus [beləˈrʊs] n Weißrussland nt

belch [beltʃ] n Rülpser m ▷ vi rülpsen

belfry ['belfrɪ] n Glockenturm m

Belgian ['beldʒən] adj belgisch ▷ n Belgier(in) m(f); **Belgium** ['beldʒəm] n Belgien nt

belief [bɪˈliːf] n Glaube m (in an +akk); (conviction) Überzeugung f; **it's my ~ that ...** ich bin der Überzeugung, dass ...; **believe** [bɪˈliːv] vt glauben; **believe in** vi glauben an +akk; **believer** n (Rel) Gläubige(r) mf

bell [bel] n (church) Glocke f; (bicycle, door) Klingel f; **bellboy** ['belbɔɪ] n (esp US) Page m

bellows ['beləʊz] npl (for fire) Blasebalg m

belly ['belɪ] n Bauch m; **bellyache** n Bauchweh nt ▷ vi (fam) meckern; **belly button** n (fam) Bauchnabel m; **bellyflop** n (fam) Bauchklatscher m

belong [bɪˈlɒŋ] vi gehören (to sb jdm); (to club) angehören +dat; **belongings** npl Habe f

below [bɪˈləʊ] prep unter ▷ adv unten

belt [belt] n (round waist) Gürtel m; (safety belt) Gurt m; **below the ~** unter der Gürtellinie ▷ vi (fam: go fast) rasen, düsen; **beltway** n (US) Umgehungsstraße f

bench [bentʃ] n Bank f

bend [bend] n Biegung f; (in road) Kurve f ▷ vt (bent, bent) (curve) biegen; (head, arm) beugen ▷ vi sich biegen; (person) sich beugen; **bend down** vi sich bücken

beneath [bɪˈniːθ] prep unter ▷ adv darunter

beneficial [benɪˈfɪʃl] adj gut, nützlich (to für); **benefit** ['benɪfɪt] n (advantage) Vorteil m; (profit) Nutzen m; **for your/his ~** deinetwegen/seinetwegen; **unemployment ~** Arbeitslosengeld nt ▷ vt gut tun +dat ▷ vi Nutzen ziehen (from aus)

Benelux ['benɪlʌks] n Beneluxländer pl

benign [bɪˈnaɪn] adj (person) gütig; (climate) mild; (Med) gutartig

bent [bent] pt, pp of **bend** ▷ adj krumm; (fam) korrupt

beret ['bereɪ] n Baskenmütze f

Bermuda [bəˈmjuːdə] n **the ~s** pl die Bermudas pl ▷ adj **~ shorts** pl Bermudashorts pl; **the ~ triangle** das Bermudadreieck

berry ['berɪ] n Beere f

berth [bɜːθ] n (for ship) Ankerplatz m; (in ship) Koje f; (in train) Bett nt ▷ vt am Kai festmachen ▷ vi anlegen

beside [bɪˈsaɪd] prep neben; **~ the sea/lake** am Meer/See; **besides** [bɪˈsaɪdz] prep außer ▷ adv außerdem

besiege [bɪˈsiːdʒ] vt belagern

best [best] adj beste(r, s); **my ~ friend** mein bester o engster Freund; **the ~ thing (to do) would be to ...** das Beste wäre zu ...; (on food packaging) **~ before ...** mindestens haltbar bis ... ▷ n der/die/das Beste; **all the ~** alles Gute; **to make the ~ of it** das Beste daraus machen ▷ adv am besten; **I like this ~** das mag ich am liebsten; **best-before date** n Mindesthaltbarkeitsdatum nt; **best man** ['best'mæn] (pl men) n Trauzeuge m; **bestseller** ['bestselə*] n Bestseller m

bet [bet] n (bet, bet) vt, vi wetten (on auf +akk); **I ~ him £5 that ...** ich habe mit ihm um 5 Pfund gewettet, dass ...; **you ~** (fam) und ob!; **I ~ he'll be late** er kommt mit Sicherheit zu spät ▷ n Wette f

betray [bɪˈtreɪ] vt verraten; **betrayal** n Verrat m

better ['betə*] adj, adv besser; **to get ~** (healthwise) sich erholen, wieder gesund werden; (improve) sich verbessern; **I'm much ~ today** es geht mir heute viel besser; **you'd ~ go** du solltest lieber gehen; **a change for the ~** eine Wendung zum Guten

betting ['betɪŋ] n Wetten nt; **betting shop** n Wettbüro nt

between [bɪˈtwiːn] prep zwischen; (among) unter; **~ you and me, ...** unter uns gesagt, ... ▷ adv (in) **~** dazwischen

beverage ['bevərɪdʒ] n (formal) Getränk nt

beware [bɪˈwɛə*] vt **to ~ of sth** sich vor etw +dat hüten; **'~ of the dog'** „Vorsicht, bissiger Hund!'

bewildered [bɪˈwɪldəd] adj verwirrt

beyond [bɪˈjɒnd] prep (place) jenseits +gen; (time) über ... hinaus; (out of reach) außerhalb +gen; **it's ~ me** da habe ich keine Ahnung, da bin ich überfragt ▷ adv darüber hinaus

bias ['baɪəs] n (prejudice) Vorurteil nt, Voreingenommenheit f

bias(s)ed adj voreingenommen

bib [bɪb] n Latz m

Bible ['baɪbl] n Bibel f

bicycle ['baɪsɪkl] n Fahrrad nt

bid [bɪd] (**bid, bid**) vt (offer) bieten ▷ n (attempt) Versuch m; (offer) Gebot nt

big [bɪg] adj groß; **it's no ~ deal** (fam) es ist nichts Besonderes; **big dipper** n (Brit) Achterbahn f; **bigheaded** [bɪg'hedɪd] adj eingebildet

bike [baɪk] n (fam) Rad nt

bikini [bɪ'ki:nɪ] n Bikini m

bilberry ['bɪlbərɪ] n Heidelbeere f

bilingual [baɪ'lɪŋgwəl] adj zweisprachig

bill [bɪl] n (account) Rechnung f; (US: banknote) Banknote f; (Pol) Gesetzentwurf m; (Zool) Schnabel m; **billfold** ['bɪlfəʊld] n (US) Brieftasche f

billiards ['bɪlɪədz] nsing Billard nt; **billiard table** Billardtisch m

billion ['bɪlɪən] n Milliarde f

bin [bɪn] n Behälter m; (rubbish bin) (Müll)eimer m; (for paper) Papierkorb m

bind [baɪnd] (**bound, bound**) vt binden; (bind together) zusammenbinden; (wound) verbinden; **binding** n (ski) Bindung f; (book) Einband m

binge [bɪndʒ] n (fam: drinking) Sauferei f; **to go on a ~** auf Sauftour gehen

bingo ['bɪŋgəʊ] n Bingo nt

binoculars [bɪ'nɒkjʊləz] npl Fernglas nt

biodegradable ['baɪəʊdɪ'greɪdəbl] adj biologisch abbaubar

biography [baɪ'ɒgrəfɪ] n Biografie f

biological [baɪə'lɒdʒɪkəl] adj biologisch; **biology** [baɪ'ɒlədʒɪ] n Biologie f

birch [bɜːtʃ] n Birke f

bird [bɜːd] n Vogel m; (Brit fam: girl, girlfriend) Tussi f; **bird watcher** n Vogelbeobachter(in) m(f)

birth [bɜːθ] n Geburt f; **birth certificate** n Geburtsurkunde f; **birth control** n Geburtenkontrolle f; **birthday** n Geburtstag m; **happy ~** herzlichen Glückwunsch zum Geburtstag; **birthday card** n Geburtstagskarte f; **birthday party** n Geburtstagsfeier f; **birthplace** n Geburtsort m

biscuit ['bɪskɪt] n (Brit) Keks m

bisexual [baɪ'seksjʊəl] adj bisexuell

bishop ['bɪʃəp] n Bischof m; (in chess) Läufer m

bit [bɪt] pt of **bite** ▷ n (piece) Stück(chen) nt; (Inform) Bit nt; **a ~ (of ...)** (small amount) ein bisschen ...; **a ~ tired** etwas müde; **~ by ~** allmählich; (time) **for a ~** ein Weilchen; **quite a ~** (a lot) ganz schön viel

bitch [bɪtʃ] n (dog) Hündin f; **bitchy** adj gemein, zickig

bite [baɪt] (**bit, bitten**) vt, vi beißen ▷ n Biss m; (mouthful) Bissen m; (insect) Stich m; **to have a ~** eine Kleinigkeit essen; **bitten** pp of **bite**

bitter ['bɪtə*] adj bitter; (memory etc) schmerzlich ▷ n (Brit: beer) halbdunkles Bier; **bitter lemon** n Bitter Lemon nt

bizarre [bɪ'zɑː*] adj bizarr

black [blæk] adj schwarz; **blackberry** n Brombeere f; **blackbird** n Amsel f; **blackboard** n (Wand)tafel f; **black box** n (Aviat) Flugschreiber m; **blackcurrant** n Schwarze Johannisbeere; **black eye** n blaues Auge; **Black Forest** n Schwarzwald m; **Black Forest gateau** n Schwarzwälder Kirschtorte f; **blackmail** n Erpressung f ▷ vt erpressen; **black market** n Schwarzmarkt m; **blackout** n (Med) Ohnmacht f; **to have a ~** ohnmächtig werden; **black pudding** n ≈ Blutwurst f; **Black Sea** n **the ~** das Schwarze Meer; **blacksmith** n Schmied(in) m(f); **black tie** n Abendanzug m, Smoking m; **is it ~?** ist/besteht da Smokingzwang?

bladder ['blædə*] n Blase f

blade [bleɪd] n (of knife) Klinge f; (of propeller) Blatt nt; (of grass) Halm m

blame [bleɪm] n Schuld f ▷ vt **to ~ sth on sb** jdm die Schuld an etw dat geben; **he is to ~** er ist daran schuld

bland [blænd] adj (taste) fade; (comment) nichts sagend

blank [blæŋk] adj (page, space) leer, unbeschrieben; (look) ausdruckslos; **~ cheque** Blankoscheck m

blanket ['blæŋkɪt] n (Woll)decke f

blast [blɑːst] n (of wind) Windstoß m; (of explosion) Druckwelle f ▷ vt (blow up) sprengen; **~!** (fam) Mist!, verdammt!

blatant ['bleɪtənt] adj (undisguised) offen; (obvious) offensichtlich

blaze [bleɪz] vi lodern; (sun) brennen ▷ n

(building) Brand m; (other fire) Feuer nt; **a ~ of colour** eine Farbenpracht

blazer ['bleɪzə*] n Blazer m

bleach [bliːtʃ] n Bleichmittel nt ▷ vt bleichen

bleak [bliːk] adj öde, düster; (future) trostlos

bleary ['blɪərɪ] adj (eyes) trübe, verschlafen

bleed [bliːd] (**bled, bled**) vi bluten

bleep [bliːp] n Piepton m ▷ vi piepen; **bleeper** n (fam) Piepser m

blend [blend] n Mischung f ▷ vt mischen ▷ vi sich mischen; **blender** n Mixer m

bless [bles] vt segnen; **~ you!** Gesundheit!; **blessing** n Segen m

blew [bluː] pt of **blow**

blind [blaɪnd] adj blind; (corner) unübersichtlich; **to turn a ~ eye to sth** bei etw ein Auge zudrücken ▷ n (for window) Rollo nt ▷ vt blenden; **blind alley** n Sackgasse f; **blind spot** n (Auto) toter Winkel; (fig) schwacher Punkt

blink [blɪŋk] vi blinzeln; (light) blinken

bliss [blɪs] n (Glück)seligkeit f

blister ['blɪstə*] n Blase f

blizzard ['blɪzəd] n Schneesturm m

bloated ['bləʊtɪd] adj aufgedunsen

block [blɒk] n (of wood, stone, ice) Block m, Klotz m; (of buildings) Häuserblock m; **~ of flats** (Brit) Wohnblock m ▷ vt (road etc) blockieren; (pipe, nose) verstopfen; **blockage** n ['blɒkɪdʒ] n Verstopfung f; **blockbuster** ['blɒkbʌstə*] n Knüller m; **block letters** npl Blockschrift f

bloke [bləʊk] n (Brit fam) Kerl m, Typ m

blonde [blɒnd] adj blond ▷ n (person) Blondine f, blonder Typ

blood [blʌd] n Blut nt; **blood count** n Blutbild nt; **blood donor** n Blutspender(in) m(f); **blood group** n Blutgruppe f; **blood poisoning** n Blutvergiftung f; **blood pressure** n Blutdruck m; **blood sample** n Blutprobe f; **bloodsports** npl Sportarten, bei denen Tiere getötet werden; **bloodthirsty** adj blutrünstig; **bloody** adj (Brit fam) verdammt, Scheiß-; (literal sense) blutig

bloom [bluːm] n Blüte f ▷ vi blühen

blossom ['blɒsəm] n Blüte f ▷ vi blühen

blot ['blɒt] n (of ink) Klecks m; (fig) Fleck m

blouse [blaʊz] n Bluse f; **big girl's ~** (fam) Schwächling m, femininer Typ

blow [bləʊ] n Schlag m ▷ vi, vt (**blew, blown**) (wind) wehen, blasen; (person: trumpet etc) blasen; **to ~ one's nose** sich dat die Nase putzen; **blow out** vt (candle etc) ausblasen; **blow up** vi explodieren ▷ vt sprengen; (balloon, tyre) aufblasen; (Foto: enlarge) vergrößern; **blow-dry** vt föhnen; **blowjob** n (fam) **to give sb a ~** jdm einen blasen; **blown** [bləʊn] pp of **blow; blow-out** n (Auto) geplatzter Reifen

BLT n abbr = **bacon, lettuce and tomato sandwich** mit Frühstücksspeck, Kopfsalat und Tomaten belegtes Sandwich

blue [bluː] adj blau; (fam: unhappy) trübsinnig, niedergeschlagen; (film) pornografisch; (joke) anzüglich; (language) derb; **bluebell** n Glockenblume f; **blueberry** n Blaubeere f; **blue cheese** n Blauschimmelkäse m; **blues** npl **the ~** (Mus) der Blues; **to have the ~** (fam) niedergeschlagen sein

blunder ['blʌndə*] n Schnitzer m

blunt [blʌnt] adj (knife) stumpf; (fig) unverblümt; **bluntly** adv geradeheraus

blurred [blɜːd] adj verschwommen, unklar

blush [blʌʃ] vi erröten

board [bɔːd] n (of wood) Brett nt; (committee) Ausschuss m; (of firm) Vorstand m; **~ and lodging** Unterkunft und Verpflegung; **on ~** an Bord ▷ vt (train, bus) einsteigen in +akk; (ship) an Bord +gen gehen; **boarder** n Pensionsgast m; (school) Internatsschüler(in) m(f); **board game** n Brettspiel nt; **boarding card** n, **boarding pass** n Bordkarte f, Einsteigekarte f; **boarding school** n Internat nt; **board meeting** n Vorstandssitzung f; **boardroom** n Sitzungssaal m (des Vorstands)

boast [bəʊst] vi prahlen (about mit) ▷ n Prahlerei f

boat [bəʊt] n Boot nt; (ship) Schiff nt; **boatman** n (hirer) Bootsverleiher m; **boat race** n Regatta f; **boat train** n Zug m mit Schiffsanschluss

bob(sleigh) ['bɒbsleɪ] n Bob m

bodily ['bɒdɪlɪ] adj körperlich ▷ adv (forcibly) gewaltsam; **body** ['bɒdɪ] n Körper m; (dead) Leiche f; (of car) Karosserie f; **bodybuilding** n Bodybuilding nt; **bodyguard** n Leibwächter m; (group) Leibwache f; **body jewellery** n Intimschmuck m; **body odour** n Körpergeruch m; **body piercing** n Piercing nt; **bodywork** n Karosserie f

boil [bɔɪl] vt, vi kochen ▷ n (Med) Geschwür nt; **boiler** n Boiler m; **boiling** adj (water etc) kochend (heiß); **I was ~** (hot) mir war fürchterlich heiß; (with rage) ich kochte vor Wut; **boiling point** n Siedepunkt m

bold [bəʊld] adj kühn, mutig; (colours) kräftig; (type) fett

Bolivia [bə'lɪvɪə] n Bolivien nt

bolt [bəʊlt] n (lock) Riegel m; (screw) Bolzen m ▷ vt verriegeln

bomb [bɒm] n Bombe f ▷ vt bombardieren

bond [bɒnd] n (link) Bindung f; (Fin) Obligation f

bone [bəʊn] n Knochen m; (of fish) Gräte f; **boner** n (US fam) Schnitzer m; (erection) Ständer m

bonfire ['bɒnfaɪə*] n Feuer nt (im Freien)

bonnet ['bɒnɪt] n (Brit Auto) Haube f; (for baby) Häubchen nt

bonny ['bɒnɪ] adj (esp Scottish) hübsch

bonus ['bəʊnəs] n Bonus m, Prämie f

boo [buː] vt auspfeifen, ausbuhen ▷ vi buhen ▷ n Buhruf m

book [bʊk] n Buch nt; (of tickets, stamps) Heft nt ▷ vt (ticket etc) bestellen; (hotel, flight etc) buchen; (Sport) verwarnen; **fully ~ed (up)** ausgebucht; (performance) ausverkauft; **book in** vt eintragen; **to be ~ed in at a hotel** ein Zimmer in einem Hotel bestellt haben; **bookable** adj im Vorverkauf erhältlich; **bookcase** n Bücherregal nt; **booking** n Buchung f; **booking office** n (Rail) Fahrkartenschalter m; (Theat) Vorverkaufsstelle f; **book-keeping** n Buchhaltung f; **booklet** n Broschüre f; **bookmark** n (a. Inform) Lesezeichen nt; **bookshelf** n Bücherbord nt; **bookshelves** Bücherregal nt; **bookshop, bookstore** n (esp US) Buchhandlung f

boom [buːm] n (of business) Boom m; (noise) Dröhnen nt ▷ vi (business) boomen; (fam) florieren; (voice etc) dröhnen

boomerang ['buːməræŋ] n Bumerang m

boost [buːst] n Auftrieb m ▷ vt (production, sales) ankurbeln; (power, profits etc) steigern; **booster (injection)** n Wiederholungsimpfung f

boot [buːt] n Stiefel m; (Brit Auto) Kofferraum m ▷ vt (Inform) laden, booten

booth [buːð] n (at fair etc) Bude f; (at trade fair etc) Stand m

booze [buːz] n (fam) Alkohol m ▷ vi (fam) saufen

border ['bɔːdə*] n Grenze f; (edge) Rand m; **north/south of the Border** in Schottland/England; **borderline** n Grenze f

bore [bɔː*] pt of **bear** ▷ vt (hole etc) bohren; (person) langweilen ▷ n (person) Langweiler(in) m(f), langweiliger Mensch; (thing) langweilige Sache; **bored** adj **to be ~** sich langweilen; **boredom** n Langeweile f; **boring** adj langweilig

born [bɔːn] adj **he was ~ in London** er ist in London geboren

borne [bɔːn] pp of **bear**

borough ['bʌrə] n Stadtbezirk m

borrow ['bɒrəʊ] vt borgen

Bosnia-Herzegovina ['bɒznɪəhɜːtsəgəʊ'viːnə] n Bosnien-Herzegowina nt; **Bosnian** ['bɒznɪən] adj bosnisch ▷ n Bosnier(in) m(f)

boss [bɒs] n Chef(in) m(f), Boss m; **boss around** vt herumkommandieren; **bossy** adj herrisch

botanical [bə'tænɪkəl] adj botanisch; **~ garden(s)** botanischer Garten

both [bəʊθ] adj beide; **~ the books** beide Bücher ▷ pron (people) beide; (things) beides; **~ (of) the boys** beide Jungs; **I like ~ of them** ich mag sie (alle) beide ▷ adv **~ X and Y** sowohl X als auch Y

bother ['bɒðə*] vt ärgern, belästigen; **it doesn't ~ me** das stört mich nicht; **he can't be ~ed with details** mit Details gibt er sich nicht ab; **I'm not ~ed** das ist mir egal ▷ vi sich kümmern (about um); **don't ~** (das ist) nicht nötig, lass es! ▷ n (trouble) Mühe f; (annoyance) Ärger m

bottle ['bɒtl] n Flasche f ▷ vt (in Flaschen) abfüllen; **bottle out** vi (fam) den Mut verlieren, aufgeben; **bottle bank** n Altglascontainer m; **bottled** adj in Flaschen; **~ beer** Flaschenbier nt; **bottleneck** n (fig) Engpass m; **bottle opener** n Flaschenöffner m

bottom ['bɒtəm] n (of container) Boden m; (underside) Unterseite f; (fam: of person) Po m; **at the ~ of the sea/table/page** auf dem Meeresgrund/am Tabellenende/unten auf der Seite ▷ adj unterste(r, s); **to be ~ of the class/league** Klassenletzte(r)/Tabellenletzte(r) sein; **~ gear** (Auto) erster Gang

bought [bɔːt] pt, pp of **buy**

bounce [baʊns] vi (ball) springen, aufprallen; (cheque) platzen; **~ up and down** (person) herumhüpfen; **bouncy** adj (ball) gut springend; (person) munter; **bouncy castle®** n Hüpfburg f

bound [baʊnd] pt, pp of **bind** ▷ adj (tied up) gebunden; (obliged) verpflichtet; **to be ~ to do sth** (sure to) etw bestimmt tun (werden); (have to) etw tun müssen; **it's ~ to happen** es muss so kommen; **to be ~ for ...** auf dem Weg nach ... sein; **boundary** ['baʊndərɪ] n Grenze f

bouquet [bʊ'keɪ] n (flowers) Strauß m; (of wine) Blume f

boutique [buːˈtiːk] n Boutique f

bow [baʊ] n (ribbon) Schleife f; (instrument, weapon) Bogen m ▷ [baʊ] vi sich verbeugen ▷ [baʊ] n (with head) Verbeugung f; (of ship) Bug m

bowels ['baʊəlz] npl Darm m

bowl [bəʊl] n (basin) Schüssel f; (shallow) Schale f; (for animal) Napf m ▷ vt, vi (in cricket) werfen

bowler ['bəʊlə*] n (in cricket) Werfer(in) m(f); (hat) Melone f

bowling ['bəʊlɪŋ] n Kegeln nt; **bowling alley** n Kegelbahn f; **bowling green** n Rasen m zum Bowling-Spiel; **bowls** [bəʊlz] nsing (game) Bowling-Spiel nt

bow tie [bəʊ'taɪ] n Fliege f

box [bɒks] n Schachtel f; (cardboard) Karton m; (bigger) Kasten m; (space on form) Kästchen nt; (Theat) Loge f; **boxer** n Boxer(in) m(f); **boxers, boxer shorts** npl Boxershorts pl; **boxing** n (Sport) Boxen nt; **Boxing Day** n zweiter Weihnachtsfeiertag

boxing gloves npl Boxhandschuhe pl; **boxing ring** n Boxring m

box number n Chiffre f

box office n Kasse f

boy [bɔɪ] n Junge m

boycott ['bɔɪkɒt] n Boykott m ▷ vt boykottieren

boyfriend ['bɔɪfrend] n (fester) Freund m; **boy scout** n Pfadfinder m

bra [brɑː] n BH m

brace [breɪs] n (Tech) Strebe f; (on teeth) Spange f

bracelet ['breɪslɪt] n Armband nt

braces ['breɪsɪz] npl (Brit) Hosenträger pl

bracket ['brækɪt] n (in text) Klammer f; (Tech) Träger m ▷ vt einklammern

brag [bræg] vi angeben

Braille [breɪl] n Blindenschrift f

brain [breɪn] n (Anat) Gehirn nt; (mind) Verstand m; **~s** (pl) (intelligence) Grips m; **brainwave** n Geistesblitz m; **brainy** adj schlau, clever

braise [breɪz] vt schmoren

brake [breɪk] n Bremse f ▷ vi bremsen; **brake fluid** n Bremsflüssigkeit f; **brake light** n Bremslicht nt; **brake pedal** n Bremspedal nt

branch [brɑːntʃ] n (of tree) Ast m; (of family, subject) Zweig m; (of firm) Filiale f, Zweigstelle f; **branch off** vi (road) abzweigen

brand [brænd] n (Comm) Marke f

brand-new ['brænd'njuː] adj (funkel)nagelneu

brandy ['brændɪ] n Weinbrand m

brass [brɑːs] n Messing nt; (Brit fam: money) Knete f; **brass band** n Blaskapelle f

brat [bræt] n (pej, fam) Gör nt

brave [breɪv] adj tapfer, mutig; **bravery** ['breɪvərɪ] n Mut m

brawl [brɔːl] n Schlägerei f

brawn [brɔːn] n (strength) Muskelkraft f; (Gastr) Sülze f; **brawny** adj muskulös

Brazil [brə'zɪl] n Brasilien nt; **Brazilian** adj brasilianisch ▷ n Brasilianer(in) m(f); **brazil nut** n Paranuss f

bread [bred] n Brot nt; **breadbin** (Brit),

breadbox (US) n Brotkasten m;
breadcrumbs npl Brotkrumen pl; (Gastr)
Paniermehl nt; **breaded** adj paniert;
breadknife n Brotmesser nt
breadth [bredθ] n Breite f
break [breɪk] n (fracture) Bruch m; (rest)
Pause f; (short holiday) Kurzurlaub m; **give
me a ~** gib mir eine Chance, hör auf
damit! ▷ vt (**broke, broken**) (fracture)
brechen; (in pieces) zerbrechen; (toy, device)
kaputtmachen; (promise) nicht halten;
(silence) brechen; (law) verletzen; (journey)
unterbrechen; (news) mitteilen (to sb jdm);
I broke my leg ich habe mir das Bein
gebrochen; **he broke it to her gently** er
hat es ihr schonend beigebracht ▷ vi
(come apart) (auseinander) brechen; (in
pieces) zerbrechen; (toy, device)
kaputtgehen; (person) zusammenbrechen;
(day, dawn) anbrechen; (news) bekannt
werden; **break down** vi (car) eine Panne
haben; (machine) versagen; (person)
zusammenbrechen; **break in** vi (burglar)
einbrechen; **break into** vt einbrechen in
+akk; **break off** vi, vt abbrechen; **break
out** vi ausbrechen; **to ~ in a rash** einen
Ausschlag bekommen; **break up** vi
aufbrechen; (meeting, organisation) sich
auflösen; (marriage) in die Brüche gehen;
(couple) sich trennen; **school breaks up on
Friday** am Freitag beginnen die Ferien
▷ vt aufbrechen; (marriage) zerstören;
(meeting) auflösen; **breakable** adj
zerbrechlich; **breakage** n Bruch m;
breakdown n (of car) Panne f; (of machine)
Störung f; (of person, relations, system)
Zusammenbruch m; **breakdown service**
n Pannendienst m; **breakdown truck** n
Abschleppwagen m
breakfast ['brekfəst] n Frühstück nt; **to
have ~** frühstücken; **breakfast cereal** n
Cornflakes, Muesli etc; **breakfast television**
n Frühstücksfernsehen nt
break-in ['breɪkɪn] n Einbruch m;
breakup ['breɪkʌp] n (of meeting,
organization) Auflösung f; (of marriage)
Zerrüttung f
breast [brest] n Brust f; **breastfeed** vt
stillen; **breaststroke** n Brustschwimmen
nt
breath [breθ] n Atem m; **out of ~** außer
Atem; **breathalyse, breathalyze**
['breθəlaɪz] vt (ins Röhrchen) blasen

lassen; **breathalyser, breathalyzer** n
Promillemesser m; **breathe** [briːð] vt, vi
atmen; **breathe in** vt, vi einatmen;
breathe out vt, vi ausatmen;
breathless ['breθlɪs] adj atemlos;
breath-taking ['breθteɪkɪŋ] adj
atemberaubend
bred [bred] pt, pp of **breed**
breed [briːd] n (race) Rasse f ▷ vi (**bred,
bred**) sich vermehren ▷ vt züchten;
breeder n Züchter(in) m(f); (fam) Hetero
m; **breeding** n (of animals) Züchtung f; (of
person) (gute) Erziehung
breeze [briːz] n Brise f
brevity ['brevɪtɪ] n Kürze f
brew [bruː] vt (beer) brauen; (tea) kochen;
brewery n Brauerei f
bribe ['braɪb] n Bestechungsgeld nt ▷ vt
bestechen; **bribery** ['braɪbərɪ] n
Bestechung f
brick [brɪk] n Backstein m; **bricklayer** n
Maurer(in) m(f)
bride [braɪd] n Braut f; **bridegroom** n
Bräutigam m; **bridesmaid** n Brautjungfer
f
bridge [brɪdʒ] n Brücke f; (cards) Bridge nt
brief [briːf] adj kurz ▷ vt instruieren (on
über +akk); **briefcase** n Aktentasche f;
briefs npl Slip m
bright [braɪt] adj hell; (colour) leuchtend;
(cheerful) heiter; (intelligent) intelligent;
(idea) glänzend; **brighten up** vt aufhellen;
(person) aufheitern ▷ vi sich aufheitern;
(person) fröhlicher werden
brilliant ['brɪljənt] adj (sunshine, colour)
strahlend; (person) brillant; (idea)
glänzend; (Brit fam) **it was ~** es war
fantastisch
brim [brɪm] n Rand m
bring [brɪŋ] (**brought, brought**) vt
bringen; (with one) mitbringen; **bring
about** vt herbeiführen, bewirken; **bring
back** vt zurückbringen; (memories)
wecken; **bring down** vt (reduce) senken;
(government etc) zu Fall bringen; **bring in** vt
hereinbringen; (introduce) einführen; **bring
out** vt herausbringen; **bring round**,
bring to vt wieder zu sich bringen; **bring
up** vt (child) aufziehen; (question) zur
Sprache bringen
brisk [brɪsk] adj (trade) lebhaft; (wind)
frisch
bristle ['brɪsl] n Borste f

Brit [brɪt] n (fam) Brite m, Britin f; **Britain** ['brɪtn] n Großbritannien nt; **British** ['brɪtɪʃ] adj britisch; **the ~ Isles** (pl) die Britischen Inseln pl ▷ n **the ~** (pl) die Briten pl

Brittany ['brɪtənɪ] n die Bretagne

brittle ['brɪtl] adj spröde

broad [brɔːd] adj breit; (accent) stark; **in ~ daylight** am helllichten Tag ▷ (US fam) Frau f

B road [biːrəʊd] n (Brit) ≈ Landstraße f

broadcast ['brɔːdkɑːst] n Sendung f ▷ irr vt, vi senden; (event) übertragen

broaden ['brɔːdn] vt **to ~ the mind** den Horizont erweitern; **broad-minded** adj tolerant

broccoli ['brɒkəlɪ] n Brokkoli pl

brochure ['brəʊʃjʊə*] n Prospekt m, Broschüre f

broke [brəʊk] pt of **break** ▷ adj (Brit fam) pleite; **broken** ['brəʊkən] pp of **break**; **broken-hearted** adj untröstlich

broker ['brəʊkə*] n Makler(in) m(f)

brolly ['brɒlɪ] n (Brit fam) Schirm m

bronchitis [brɒŋ'kaɪtɪs] n Bronchitis f

bronze [brɒnz] n Bronze f

brooch [brəʊtʃ] n Brosche f

broom [bruːm] n Besen m

Bros [brɒs] abbr = **brothers** Gebr.

broth [brɒθ] n Fleischbrühe f

brothel ['brɒθl] n Bordell nt

brother ['brʌðə*] n Bruder m; **~s** (pl) (Comm) Gebrüder pl; **brother-in-law** (pl **brothers-in-law**) n Schwager m

brought [brɔːt] pt, pp of **bring**

brow [braʊ] n (eyebrow) (Augen)braue f; (forehead) Stirn f

brown [braʊn] adj braun; **brown bread** n Mischbrot nt; (wholemeal) Vollkornbrot nt; **brownie** ['braʊnɪ] n (Gastr) Brownie m; (Brit) junge Pfadfinderin; **brown paper** n Packpapier nt; **brown rice** n Naturreis m; **brown sugar** n brauner Zucker

browse [braʊz] vi (in book) blättern; (in shop) schmökern, herumschauen; **browser** n (Inform) Browser m

bruise [bruːz] n blauer Fleck ▷ vt **to ~ one's arm** sich dat einen blauen Fleck (am Arm) holen

brunette [bruː'net] n Brünette f

brush [brʌʃ] n Bürste f; (for sweeping) Handbesen m; (for painting) Pinsel m ▷ vt bürsten; (sweep) fegen; **to ~ one's teeth** sich dat die Zähne putzen; **brush up** vt (French etc) auffrischen

Brussels sprouts [brʌsl'spraʊts] npl Rosenkohl m, Kohlsprossen pl

brutal ['bruːtl] adj brutal; **brutality** [bruː'tælɪtɪ] n Brutalität f

BSE abbr = **bovine spongiform encephalopathy** BSE f

bubble ['bʌbl] n Blase f; **bubble bath** n Schaumbad nt; **bubbly** ['bʌblɪ] adj sprudelnd; (person) temperamentvoll ▷ n (fam) Schampus m

buck [bʌk] n (animal) Bock m; (US fam) Dollar m

bucket ['bʌkɪt] n Eimer m

● **Buckingham Palace**

● Der **Buckingham Palace** ist die offizielle
● Londoner Residenz der britischen
● Monarchen und liegt am St James's
● Park. Der Palast wurde 1703 für den
● Herzog von Buckingham erbaut, 1762
● von George III gekauft, zwischen 1821
● und 1836 von John Nash umgebaut,
● und Anfang des 20. Jahrhunderts
● teilweise neu gestaltet. Teile des
● Buckingham Palace sind heute der
● Öffentlichkeit zugänglich.

buckle ['bʌkl] n Schnalle f ▷ vi (Tech) sich verbiegen ▷ vt zuschnallen

bud [bʌd] n Knospe f

Buddhism ['bʊdɪzəm] n Buddhismus m; **Buddhist** adj buddhistisch ▷ n Buddhist(in) m(f)

buddy ['bʌdɪ] n (fam) Kumpel m

budget ['bʌdʒɪt] n Budget nt

budgie ['bʌdʒɪ] n (fam) Wellensittich m

buff [bʌf] adj (US) muskulös; **in the ~** nackt ▷ n (enthusiast) Fan m

buffalo ['bʌfələʊ] n (pl **-es**) n Büffel m

buffer ['bʌfə*] n (a. Inform) Puffer m

buffet ['bʊfeɪ] n (food) (kaltes) Büfett nt

bug [bʌg] n (Inform) Bug m, Programmfehler m; (listening device) Wanze f; (US: insect) Insekt nt; (fam: illness) Infektion f ▷ vt (fam) nerven

bugger ['bʌgə*] n (vulg) Scheißkerl m ▷ interj (vulg) Scheiße f; **bugger off** vi (vulg) abhauen, Leine ziehen

buggy® ['bʌgɪ] n (for baby) Buggy® m; (US: pram) Kinderwagen m

build [bɪld] (**built, built**) vt bauen; **build up** vt aufbauen; **builder** n Bauunternehmer(in) m(f); **building** n Gebäude nt; **building site** n Baustelle f; **building society** n Bausparkasse f

built pt, pp of **build**; **built-in** adj (cupboard) Einbau-, eingebaut

bulb [bʌlb] n (Bot) (Blumen)zwiebel f; (Elec) Glühbirne f

Bulgaria [bʌl'gɛərɪə] n Bulgarien nt; **Bulgarian** adj bulgarisch ▷ n (person) Bulgare m, Bulgarin f; (language) Bulgarisch nt

bulimia [bə'lɪmɪə] n Bulimie f

bulk [bʌlk] n (size) Größe f; (greater part) Großteil m (of +gen); **in ~** en gros; **bulky** adj (goods) sperrig; (person) stämmig

bull [bʊl] n Stier m; **bulldog** n Bulldogge f; **bulldoze** [ˈbʊldəʊz] vt planieren; **bulldozer** n Planierraupe f

bullet [ˈbʊlɪt] n Kugel f

bulletin [ˈbʊlɪtɪn] n Bulletin nt; (announcement) Bekanntmachung f; (Med) Krankenbericht m; **bulletin board** n (US: Inform) schwarzes Brett

bullfight [ˈbʊlfaɪt] n Stierkampf m; **bullshit** n (fam) Scheiß m

bully [ˈbʊlɪ] n Tyrann m

bum [bʌm] n (Brit fam: backside) Po m; (US: vagrant) Penner m; (worthless person) Rumtreiber m; **bum around** vi herumgammeln

bumblebee [ˈbʌmblbiː] n Hummel f

bump [bʌmp] n (fam: swelling) Beule f; (road) Unebenheit f; (blow) Stoß m ▷ vt stoßen; **to ~ one's head** sich dat den Kopf anschlagen (on an +dat); **bump into** vt stoßen gegen; (fam: meet) (zufällig) begegnen +dat; **bumper** n (Auto) Stoßstange f ▷ adj (edition etc) Riesen-; (crop etc) Rekord-; **bumpy** [ˈbʌmpɪ] adj holp(e)rig

bun [bʌn] n süßes Brötchen

bunch [bʌntʃ] n (of flowers) Strauß m; (fam: of people) Haufen m; **~ of keys** Schlüsselbund m; **~ of grapes** Weintraube f

bundle [ˈbʌndl] n Bündel nt

bungalow [ˈbʌŋgələʊ] n Bungalow m

bungee jumping [ˈbʌndʒɪdʒʌmpɪŋ] n Bungeejumping nt

bunk [bʌŋk] n Koje f; **bunk bed(s)** n(pl) Etagenbett nt

bunker [ˈbʌŋkə*] n (Mil) Bunker m

bunny [ˈbʌnɪ] n Häschen nt

buoy [bɔɪ] n Boje f; **buoyant** [ˈbɔɪənt] adj (floating) schwimmend

BUPA [ˈbuːpə] abbr (Brit) private Krankenkasse

burden [ˈbɜːdn] n Last f

bureau [ˈbjuːrəʊ] n Büro nt; (government department) Amt nt; **bureaucracy** [bjʊ'rɒkrəsɪ] n Bürokratie f; **bureaucratic** [bjuːrə'krætɪk] adj bürokratisch; **bureau de change** [ˈbjuːrəʊ də ˈʃɒnʒ] n Wechselstube f

burger [ˈbɜːgə*] n Hamburger m

burglar [ˈbɜːglə*] n Einbrecher(in) m(f); **burglar alarm** n Alarmanlage f; **burglarize** vt (US) einbrechen in +akk; **burglary** n Einbruch m; **burgle** [ˈbɜːgl] vt einbrechen in +akk

burial [ˈberɪəl] n Beerdigung f

burn [bɜːn] (**burnt** o **burned, burnt** o **burned**) vt verbrennen; (food, slightly) anbrennen; **to ~ one's hand** sich dat die Hand verbrennen ▷ vi brennen ▷ n (injury) Brandwunde f; (on material) verbrannte Stelle; **burn down** vt, vi abbrennen

burp [bɜːp] vi rülpsen ▷ vt (baby) aufstoßen lassen

bursary [ˈbɜːsərɪ] n Stipendium nt

burst [bɜːst] (**burst, burst**) vt platzen lassen ▷ vi platzen; **to ~ into tears** in Tränen ausbrechen

bury [ˈberɪ] vt begraben; (in grave) beerdigen; (hide) vergraben

bus [bʌs] n Bus m; **bus driver** n Busfahrer(in) m(f)

bush [bʊʃ] n Busch m

business [ˈbɪznɪs] n Geschäft nt; (enterprise) Unternehmen nt; (concern, affair) Sache f; **I'm here on ~** ich bin geschäftlich hier; **it's none of your ~** das geht dich nichts an; **business card** n Visitenkarte f; **business class** n (Aviat) Businessclass f; **business hours** npl Geschäftsstunden pl; **businessman** (pl **-men**) n Geschäftsmann m; **business studies** npl Betriebswirtschaftslehre f; **businesswoman** (pl **-women**) n Geschäftsfrau f

bus service n Busverbindung f; **bus shelter** n Wartehäuschen nt; **bus station** n Busbahnhof m; **bus stop** n Bushaltestelle f

bust [bʌst] n Büste f ▷ adj (broken) kaputt; **to go ~** Pleite gehen; **bust-up** n (fam) Krach m

busy ['bɪzɪ] adj beschäftigt; (street, place) belebt; (esp US: telephone) besetzt; **~ signal** (US) Besetztzeichen nt

○ KEYWORD

but [bʌt] conj **1** (yet) aber; **not X but Y** nicht X sondern Y

2 (however): **I'd love to come, but I'm busy** ich würde gern kommen, bin aber beschäftigt

3 (showing disagreement, surprise etc): **but that's fantastic!** (aber) das ist ja fantastisch!

▷ prep (apart from, except); **nothing but trouble** nichts als Ärger; **no-one but him can do it** niemand außer ihn kann es machen; **but for you/your help** ohne dich/deine Hilfe; **anything but that** alles, nur das nicht

▷ adv (just, only); **she's but a child** sie ist noch ein Kind; **had I but known** wenn ich es nur gewusst hätte; **I can but try** ich kann es immerhin versuchen; **all but finished** so gut wie fertig

butcher ['bʊtʃə*] n Fleischer(in) m(f), Metzger(in) m(f)

butler ['bʌtlə*] n Butler m

butter ['bʌtə*] n Butter f ▷ vt buttern; **buttercup** n Butterblume f; **butterfly** n Schmetterling m

buttocks ['bʌtəks] npl Gesäß nt

button ['bʌtn] n Knopf m; (badge) Button m ▷ vt zuknöpfen; **buttonhole** n Knopfloch nt

buy [baɪ] n Kauf m ▷ vt (bought, bought) kaufen (from von); **he bought me a ring** er hat mir einen Ring gekauft; **buyer** n Käufer(in) m(f)

buzz [bʌz] n Summen nt; **to give sb a ~** (fam) jdn anrufen ▷ vi summen; **buzzer** ['bʌzə*] n Summer m; **buzz word** n (fam) Modewort nt

○ KEYWORD

by [baɪ] prep **1** (referring to cause, agent) von durch; **killed by lightning** vom Blitz getötet; **a painting by Picasso** ein Gemälde von Picasso

2 (referring to method, manner): **by bus/car/train** mit dem Bus/Auto/Zug; **to pay by cheque** per Scheck bezahlen; **by moonlight** bei Mondschein; **by saving hard, he ...** indem er eisern sparte, ... er ...

3 (via, through) über +acc; **he came in by the back door** er kam durch die Hintertür herein

4 (close to, past) bei an +dat; **a holiday by the sea** ein Urlaub am Meer; **she rushed by me** sie eilte an mir vorbei

5 (not later than): **by 4 o'clock** bis 4 Uhr; **by this time tomorrow** morgen um diese Zeit; **by the time I got here it was too late** als ich hier ankam, war es zu spät

6 (during): **by day** bei Tag

7 (amount): **by the kilo/metre** kiloweise/meterweise; **paid by the hour** stundenweise bezahlt

8 (Math, measure): **to divide by 3** durch 3 teilen; **to multiply by 3** mit 3 malnehmen; **a room 3 metres by 4** ein Zimmer 3 mal 4 Meter; **it's broader by a metre** es ist (um) einem Meter breiter

9 (according to) nach; **it's all right by me** von mir aus gern

10: **(all) by oneself** etc ganz allein

11: **by the way** übrigens

▷ adv **1**: see **go**, **pass** etc

2: **by and by** irgendwann; (with past tenses) nach einiger Zeit; **by and large** (on the whole) im Großen und Ganzen

bye-bye ['baɪ'baɪ] interj (fam) Wiedersehen, tschüss

by-election n Nachwahl f; **bypass** n Umgehungsstraße f; (Med) Bypass m; **byproduct** n Nebenprodukt nt; **byroad** n Nebenstraße f; **bystander** n Zuschauer(in) m(f)

byte [baɪt] n Byte nt

C

C [siː] *abbr* = **Celsius** C

c *abbr* = **circa** ca

cab [kæb] *n* Taxi *nt*

cabbage ['kæbɪdʒ] *n* Kohl *m*

cabin ['kæbɪn] *n* (*Naut*) Kajüte *f*; (*Aviat*) Passagierraum *m*; (*wooden house*) Hütte *f*; **cabin crew** *n* Flugbegleitpersonal *nt*; **cabin cruiser** *n* Kajütboot *nt*

cabinet ['kæbɪnɪt] *n* Schrank *m*; (*for display*) Vitrine *f*; (*Pol*) Kabinett *nt*

cable ['keɪbl] *n* (*Elec*) Kabel *nt*; **cable-car** *n* Seilbahn *f*; **cable railway** *n* Drahtseilbahn *f*; **cable television**, **cablevision** (*US*) *n* Kabelfernsehen *nt*

cactus ['kæktəs] *n* Kaktus *m*

CAD *abbr* = **computer-aided design** CAD *nt*

Caesarean [siː'zɛərɪən] *adj* ~ (**section**) Kaiserschnitt *m*

café ['kæfeɪ] *n* Café *nt*; **cafeteria** [kæfɪ'tɪərɪə] *n* Cafeteria *f*; **cafetiere** [kæfə'tjɛə*] *n* Kaffeebereiter *m*

caffein(e) ['kæfiːn] *n* Koffein *nt*

cage [keɪdʒ] *n* Käfig *m*

Cairo ['kaɪərəʊ] *n* Kairo *nt*

cake [keɪk] *n* Kuchen *m*; **cake shop** *n* Konditorei *f*

calamity [kə'læmɪtɪ] *n* Katastrophe *f*

calculate ['kælkjʊleɪt] *vt* berechnen; (*estimate*) kalkulieren; **calculating** *adj* berechnend; **calculation** [kælkjʊ'leɪʃən] *n* Berechnung *f*; (*estimate*) Kalkulation *f*; **calculator** ['kælkjʊleɪtə*] *n* Taschenrechner *m*

calendar ['kælɪndə*] *n* Kalender *m*

calf [kɑːf] (*pl* **calves**) *n* Kalb *nt*; (*Anat*) Wade *f*

California [kælɪ'fɔːnɪə] *n* Kalifornien *nt*

call [kɔːl] *vt* rufen; (*name, describe as*) nennen; (*Tel*) anrufen; (*Inform, Aviat*) aufrufen; **what's this ~ed?** wie heißt das?; **that's what I ~ service** das nenne ich guten Service ▷ *vi* (*shout*) rufen (*for help* um Hilfe); (*visit*) vorbeikommen; **to ~ at the doctor's** beim Arzt vorbeigehen; (*of train*) **to ~ at ...** in ... halten ▷ *n* (*shout*) Ruf *m*; (*Tel*) Anruf; (*Inform, Aviat*) Aufruf *m*; **to make a ~** telefonieren; **to give sb a ~** jdn anrufen; **to be on ~** Bereitschaftsdienst haben; **call back** *vt, vi* zurückrufen; **call for** *vt* (*come to pick up*) abholen; (*demand, require*) verlangen; **call off** *vt* absagen

call centre *n* Callcenter *nt*; **caller** *n* Besucher(in) *m(f)*; (*Tel*) Anrufer(in) *m(f)*

calm [kɑːm] *n* Stille *f*; (*also of person*) Ruhe *f*; (*of sea*) Flaute *f* ▷ *vt* beruhigen ▷ *adj* ruhig; **calm down** *vi* sich beruhigen

calorie ['kælərɪ] *n* Kalorie *f*

calves [kɑːvz] *pl of* **calf**

Cambodia [kæm'bəʊdɪə] *n* Kambodscha *nt*

camcorder ['kæmkɔːdə*] *n* Camcorder *m*

came [keɪm] *pt of* **come**

camel ['kæməl] *n* Kamel *nt*

camera ['kæmərə] *n* Fotoapparat *m*, Kamera *f*

camomile ['kæməmaɪl] *n* Kamille *f*

camouflage ['kæməflɑːʒ] *n* Tarnung *f*

camp [kæmp] *n* Lager *nt*; (*camping place*) Zeltplatz *m* ▷ *vi* zelten, campen ▷ *adj* (*fam*) theatralisch, tuntig

campaign [kæm'peɪn] *n* Kampagne *f*; (*Pol*) Wahlkampf *m* ▷ *vi* sich einsetzen (*for/against* für/gegen)

campbed ['kæmpbed] *n* Campingliege *f*; **camper** ['kæmpə*] *n* (*person*) Camper(in) *m(f)*; (*van*) Wohnmobil *nt*; **camping** ['kæmpɪŋ] *n* Zelten *nt*, Camping *nt*; **campsite** ['kæmpsaɪt] *n* Zeltplatz *m*, Campingplatz *m*

campus ['kæmpəs] n (of university)
Universitätsgelände nt, Campus m
can¹ [kæn] (**could, been able**) vb aux (be
able) können; (permission) dürfen; **I ~not** o
~'t see ich kann nichts sehen; **~ I go now?**
darf ich jetzt gehen? ▷ n (for food, beer)
Dose f; (for water, milk) Kanne f

○ KEYWORD

can² [kæn] (negative **cannot, can't**,
conditional **could**) aux vb **1** (be able to, know
how to) können; **I can see you tomorrow,
if you like** ich könnte Sie morgen sehen,
wenn Sie wollen; **I can swim** ich kann
schwimmen; **can you speak German?**
sprechen Sie Deutsch?
2 (may) können dürfen; **could I have a
word with you?** könnte ich Sie kurz
sprechen?

Canada ['kænədə] n Kanada nt;
Canadian [kə'neɪdjən] adj kanadisch ▷ n
Kanadier(in) m(f)
canal [kə'næl] n Kanal m
canary [kə'nɛərɪ] n Kanarienvogel m
cancel ['kænsəl] vt (plans) aufgeben;
(meeting, event) absagen; (Comm: order etc)
stornieren; (contract) kündigen; (Inform)
löschen; (Aviat: flight) streichen; **to be ~led**
(event, train, bus) ausfallen; **cancellation**
[kænsə'leɪʃən] n Absage f; (Comm)
Stornierung f; (Aviat) gestrichener Flug
cancer ['kænsə*] n (Med) Krebs m; **Cancer**
n (Astr) Krebs m
candid ['kændɪd] adj (person, conversation)
offen
candidate ['kændɪdət] n (for post)
Bewerber(in) m(f); (Pol) Kandidat(in) m(f)
candle ['kændl] n Kerze f; **candlelight** n
Kerzenlicht nt; **candlestick** n
Kerzenhalter m
candy ['kændɪ] n (US) Bonbon nt;
(quantity) Süßigkeiten pl; **candy-floss** n
(Brit) Zuckerwatte f
cane [keɪn] n Rohr nt; (stick) Stock
m
cannabis ['kænəbɪs] n Cannabis m
canned [kænd] adj Dosen-
cannot ['kænɒt] contr of **can not**
canny ['kænɪ] adj (shrewd) schlau
canoe [kə'nuː] n Kanu nt; **canoeing** n
Kanufahren nt

canopener ['kænəʊpnə*] n Dosenöffner m
canopy ['kænəpɪ] n Baldachin m; (awning)
Markise f; (over entrance) Vordach nt
can't [kɑːnt] contr of **can not**
canteen [kæn'tiːn] n (in factory) Kantine
f; (in university) Mensa f
canvas ['kænvəs] n (for sails, shoes)
Segeltuch nt; (for tent) Zeltstoff m; (for
painting) Leinwand f
canvass ['kænvəs] vi um Stimmen
werben (for für)
canyon ['kænjən] n Felsenschlucht f;
canyoning ['kænjənɪŋ] n Canyoning nt
cap [kæp] n Mütze f; (lid) Verschluss m,
Deckel m
capability [keɪpə'bɪlɪtɪ] n Fähigkeit f;
capable ['keɪpəbl] adj fähig; **to be ~ of
sth** zu etw fähig (o imstande) sein; **to be
~ of doing sth** etw tun können
capacity [kə'pæsɪtɪ] n (of building,
container) Fassungsvermögen nt; (ability)
Fähigkeit f; (function) **in his ~ as ...** in
seiner Eigenschaft als ...
cape [keɪp] n (garment) Cape nt, Umhang
m; (Geo) Kap nt
caper ['keɪpə*] n (for cooking) Kaper f
capital ['kæpɪtl] n (Fin) Kapital nt; (letter)
Großbuchstabe m; **~ (city)** Hauptstadt f;
capitalism n Kapitalismus m; **capital
punishment** n die Todesstrafe
Capricorn ['kæprɪkɔːn] n (Astr) Steinbock
m
capsize [kæp'saɪz] vi kentern
capsule ['kæpsjuːl] n Kapsel f
captain ['kæptɪn] n Kapitän m; (army)
Hauptmann m
caption ['kæpʃən] n Bildunterschrift f
captive ['kæptɪv] n Gefangene(r) mf;
capture ['kæptʃə*] vt (person) fassen,
gefangen nehmen; (town etc) einnehmen;
(Inform: data) erfassen ▷ n
Gefangennahme f; (Inform) Erfassung f
car [kɑː*] n Auto nt; (US Rail) Wagen m
carafe [kə'ræf] n Karaffe f
carambola [kærəm'bəʊlə] n Sternfrucht f
caramel ['kærəmel] n Karamelle f
caravan ['kærəvæn] n Wohnwagen m;
caravan site n Campingplatz m für
Wohnwagen
caraway (seed) ['kærəweɪ] n Kümmel m
carbohydrate [kɑːbəʊ'haɪdreɪt] n
Kohle(n)hydrat nt
car bomb n Autobombe f

carbon ['kɑːbən] n Kohlenstoff m

car boot sale n auf einem Parkplatz stattfindender Flohmarkt

carburettor, carburetor (US) ['kɑːbjʊretə*] n Vergaser m

card [kɑːd] n Karte f; (material) Pappe f; **cardboard** n Pappe f; ~ (**box**) Karton m; (smaller) Pappschachtel f; **card game** n Kartenspiel nt

cardiac ['kɑːdɪæk] adj Herz-

cardigan ['kɑːdɪgən] n Strickjacke f

card index n Kartei f; **cardphone** ['kɑːdfəʊn] n Kartentelefon nt

care [kɛə*] n (worry) Sorge f; (carefulness) Sorgfalt f; (looking after things, people) Pflege f; **with** ~ sorgfältig; (cautiously) vorsichtig; **to take** ~ (watch out) vorsichtig sein; (in address) ~ **of** bei; **to take** ~ **of** sorgen für, sich kümmern um ▷ vi **I don't** ~ **es** ist mir egal; **to** ~ **about sth** Wert auf etw akk legen; **he ~s about her** sie liegt ihm am Herzen; **care for** vt (look after) sorgen für, sich kümmern um; (like) mögen

career [kə'rɪə*] n Karriere f, Laufbahn f; **career woman** (pl **women**) n Karrierefrau f; **careers adviser** n Berufsberater(in) m(f)

carefree ['kɛəfriː] adj sorgenfrei; **careful, carefully** adj, adv sorgfältig; (cautious, cautiously) vorsichtig; **careless, carelessly** adj, adv nachlässig; (driving etc) leichtsinnig; (remark) unvorsichtig; **carer** ['kɛərə*] n Betreuer(in) m(f), Pfleger(in) m(f); **caretaker** ['kɛəteɪkə*] n Hausmeister(in) m(f); **careworker** n Pfleger(in) m(f)

car-ferry ['kɑːferɪ] n Autofähre f

cargo ['kɑːgəʊ] (pl -(**e)s**) n Ladung f

car hire, car hire company n Autovermietung f

Caribbean [kærɪ'biːən] n Karibik f ▷ adj karibisch

caring ['kɛərɪŋ] adj mitfühlend; (parent, partner) liebevoll; (looking after sb) fürsorglich

car insurance n Kraftfahrzeugversicherung f

carnation [kɑː'neɪʃən] n Nelke f

carnival ['kɑːnɪvəl] n Volksfest nt; (before Lent) Karneval m

carol ['kærəl] n Weihnachtslied nt

carp [kɑːp] n (fish) Karpfen m

car park n (Brit) Parkplatz m; (multi-storey car park) Parkhaus nt

carpenter ['kɑːpəntə*] n Zimmermann m; **carpet** ['kɑːpɪt] n Teppich m

car phone n Autotelefon nt; **carpool** n Fahrgemeinschaft f; (vehicles) Fuhrpark m ▷ vi eine Fahrgemeinschaft bilden; **car rental** n Autovermietung f

carriage ['kærɪdʒ] n (Brit Rail: coach) Wagen m; (compartment) Abteil nt; (horse-drawn) Kutsche f; (transport) Beförderung f; **carriageway** n (Brit: on road) Fahrbahn f

carrier ['kærɪə*] n (Comm) Spediteur(in) m(f); **carrier bag** n Tragetasche f

carrot ['kærət] n Karotte f

carry ['kærɪ] vt tragen; (in vehicle) befördern; (have on one) bei sich haben; **carry on** vi (continue) weitermachen; (fam: make a scene) ein Theater machen ▷ vt (continue) fortführen; **to** ~ **on working** weiter arbeiten; **carry out** vt (orders, plan) ausführen, durchführen

carrycot n Babytragetasche f

carsick ['kɑːsɪk] adj **he gets** ~ ihm wird beim Autofahren übel

cart [kɑːt] n Wagen m, Karren m; (US: shopping trolley) Einkaufswagen m

carton ['kɑːtən] n (Papp)karton m; (of cigarettes) Stange f

cartoon [kɑː'tuːn] n Cartoon m o nt; (one drawing) Karikatur f; (film) (Zeichen)trickfilm m

cartridge ['kɑːtrɪdʒ] n (for film) Kassette f; (for gun, pen, printer) Patrone f; (for copier) Kartusche f

carve [kɑːv] vt, vi (wood) schnitzen; (stone) meißeln; (meat) schneiden, tranchieren; **carving** n (in wood) Schnitzerei f; (in stone) Skulptur f; (Ski) Carving nt

car wash n Autowaschanlage f

case [keɪs] n (crate) Kiste f; (box) Schachtel f; (for jewels) Schatulle f; (for spectacles) Etui nt; (Jur, matter) Fall m; **in** ~ falls; **in that** ~ in dem Fall; **in** ~ **of fire** bei Brand; **it's a** ~ **of ...** es handelt sich hier um ...

cash [kæʃ] n Bargeld nt; **in** ~ bar; ~ **on delivery** per Nachnahme ▷ vt (cheque) einlösen; **cash desk** n Kasse f; **cash dispenser** n Geldautomat m; **cashier** [kæ'ʃɪə*] n Kassierer(in) m(f); **cash machine** n (Brit) Geldautomat m

cashmere ['kæʃmɪə*] n Kaschmirwolle f
cash payment n Barzahlung f;
cashpoint n (Brit) Geldautomat m
casing ['keɪsɪŋ] n Gehäuse nt
casino [kə'siːnəʊ] (pl **-s**) n Kasino nt
cask [kɑːsk] n Fass nt
casserole ['kæsərəʊl] n Kasserole f; (food)
Schmortopf m
cassette [kæ'set] n Kassette f; **cassette
recorder** n Kassettenrekorder m
cast [kɑːst] (**cast, cast**) vt (throw) werfen;
(Theat, Cine) besetzen; (roles) verteilen ▷ n
(Theat, Cine) Besetzung f; (Med)
Gipsverband m; **cast off** vi (Naut)
losmachen
caster ['kɑːstə*] n ~ **sugar** Streuzucker
m
castle ['kɑːsl] n Burg f
castrate [kæs'treɪt] vt kastrieren
casual ['kæʒjʊəl] adj (arrangement, remark)
beiläufig; (attitude, manner) (nach)lässig,
zwanglos; (dress) leger; (work, earnings)
Gelegenheits-; (look, glance) flüchtig;
~ **wear** Freizeitkleidung f; ~ **sex**
Gelegenheitssex m; **casually** adv (remark,
say) beiläufig; (meet) zwanglos; (dressed)
leger
casualty ['kæʒjʊəltɪ] n Verletzte(r) mf;
(dead) Tote(r) mf; (department in hospital)
Notaufnahme f
cat [kæt] n Katze f; (male) Kater m
catalog (US), **catalogue** ['kætəlɒg] n
Katalog m ▷ vt katalogisieren
cataract ['kætərækt] n Wasserfall m;
(Med) grauer Star
catarrh [kə'tɑː*] n Katarr(h) m
catastrophe [kə'tæstrəfɪ] n Katastrophe
f
catch [kætʃ] n (fish etc) Fang m ▷ vt
(**caught, caught**) fangen; (thief) fassen;
(train, bus etc) nehmen; (not miss)
erreichen; **to ~ a cold** sich erkälten; **to
~ fire** Feuer fangen; **I didn't ~ that** das
habe ich nicht mitgekriegt; **catch on** vi
(become popular) Anklang finden; **catch up**
vt, vi **to ~ with sb** jdn einholen; **to ~ on
sth** etw nachholen; **catching** adj
ansteckend
category ['kætɪgərɪ] n Kategorie f
cater ['keɪtə*] vi die Speisen und Getränke
liefern (for für); **cater for** vt (have facilities
for) eingestellt sein auf +akk; **catering** n
Versorgung f mit Speisen und Getränken,

Gastronomie f; **catering service** n
Partyservice m
caterpillar ['kætəpɪlə*] n Raupe f
cathedral [kə'θiːdrəl] n Kathedrale f,
Dom m
Catholic ['kæθəlɪk] adj katholisch
▷ Katholik(in) m(f)
cat nap n (Brit) kurzer Schlaf; **cat's eyes**
['kætsaɪz] npl (in road) Katzenaugen pl,
Reflektoren pl
catsup ['kætsəp] n (US) Ketschup nt o m
cattle ['kætl] npl Vieh nt
caught [kɔːt] pt, pp of **catch**
cauliflower ['kɒlɪflaʊə*] n Blumenkohl m;
cauliflower cheese n Blumenkohl m in
Käsesoße
cause [kɔːz] n (origin) Ursache f (of für);
(reason) Grund m (for zu); (purpose) Sache f;
for a good ~ für wohltätige Zwecke; **no
~ for alarm/complaint** kein Grund zur
Aufregung/Klage ▷ vt verursachen
causeway ['kɔːzweɪ] n Damm m
caution ['kɔːʃən] n Vorsicht f; (Jur, Sport)
Verwarnung f ▷ vt (ver)warnen; **cautious**
['kɔːʃəs] adj vorsichtig
cave [keɪv] n Höhle f; **cave in** vi
einstürzen
cavity ['kævɪtɪ] n Hohlraum m; (in tooth)
Loch nt
cayenne (pepper) [keɪ'en] n
Cayennepfeffer m
CCTV abbr = **closed circuit television**
Videoüberwachungsanlage f
CD abbr = **Compact Disc** CD f; **CD player** n
CD-Spieler m; **CD-ROM** abbr = **Compact
Disc Read Only Memory** CD-ROM f;
CD-RW abbr = **Compact Disc Rewritable**
CD-RW f
cease [siːs] vi aufhören ▷ vt beenden; **to
~ doing sth** aufhören, etw zu tun; **cease
fire** n Waffenstillstand m
ceiling ['siːlɪŋ] n Decke f
celebrate ['selɪbreɪt] vt, vi feiern;
celebrated adj gefeiert; **celebration**
[selɪ'breɪʃən] n Feier f; **celebrity**
[sɪ'lebrɪtɪ] n Berühmtheit f, Star m
celeriac [sə'lerɪæk] n (Knollen)sellerie m
o f; **celery** ['selərɪ] n (Stangen)sellerie m
o f
cell [sel] n Zelle f; (US) see **cellphone**
cellar ['selə*] n Keller m
cello ['tʃeləʊ] (pl **-s**) n Cello nt
cellphone ['selfəʊn], **cellular phone**

['seljʊlə* 'fəʊn] n Mobiltelefon nt, Handy nt

Celt [kelt] n Kelte m, Keltin f; **Celtic** ['keltɪk] adj keltisch ▷ n (language) Keltisch nt

cement [sɪ'ment] n Zement m

cemetery ['semɪtrɪ] n Friedhof m

censorship ['sensəʃɪp] n Zensur f

cent [sent] n (of dollar, euro etc) Cent m

center n (US) see centre

centiliter (US), **centilitre** ['sentɪliːtə*] n Zentiliter m; **centimeter** (US), **centimetre** ['sentɪmiːtə*] n Zentimeter m

central ['sentrəl] adj zentral; **Central America** n Mittelamerika nt; **Central Europe** n Mitteleuropa nt; **central heating** n Zentralheizung f; **centralize** vt zentralisieren; **central locking** n (Auto) Zentralverriegelung f; **central reservation** n (Brit) Mittelstreifen m; **central station** n Hauptbahnhof m

centre ['sentə*] n Mitte f; (building, of city) Zentrum nt ▷ vt zentrieren; **centre forward** n (Sport) Mittelstürmer m

century ['sentjʊrɪ] n Jahrhundert nt

ceramic [sɪ'ræmɪk] adj keramisch

cereal ['sɪərɪəl] n (any grain) Getreide nt; (breakfast cereal) Frühstücksflocken pl

ceremony ['serɪmənɪ] n Feier f, Zeremonie f

certain ['sɜːtən] adj sicher (of +gen); (particular) bestimmt; **for ~** mit Sicherheit; **certainly** adv sicher; (without doubt) bestimmt; **~!** aber sicher!; **~ not** ganz bestimmt nicht!

certificate [sə'tɪfɪkɪt] n Bescheinigung f; (in school, of qualification) Zeugnis nt; **certify** ['sɜːtɪfaɪ] vt, vi bescheinigen

cervical smear ['sɜːvɪkəl smɪə*] n Abstrich m

CFC abbr = **chlorofluorocarbon** FCKW nt

chain [tʃeɪn] n Kette f ▷ vt **to ~ (up)** anketten; **chain reaction** n Kettenreaktion f; **chain store** n Kettenladen m

chair [tʃeə*] n Stuhl m; (university) Lehrstuhl m; (armchair) Sessel m; (chairperson) Vorsitzende(r) mf; **chairlift** n Sessellift m; **chairman** (pl -men) n Vorsitzende(r) m; (of firm) Präsident m; **chairperson** n Vorsitzende(r) mf; (of firm) Präsident(in) m(f); **chairwoman** (pl

-women) n Vorsitzende f; (of firm) Präsidentin f

chalet ['ʃæleɪ] n (in mountains) Berghütte f; (holiday dwelling) Ferienhäuschen nt

chalk ['tʃɔːk] n Kreide f

challenge ['tʃælɪndʒ] n Herausforderung f ▷ vt (person) herausfordern; (statement) bestreiten

chambermaid ['tʃeɪmbə*meɪd] n Zimmermädchen nt

chamois leather ['ʃæmwɑː'leðə*] n (for windows) Fensterleder nt

champagne [ʃæm'peɪn] n Champagner m

champion ['tʃæmpɪən] n (Sport) Meister(in) m(f); **championship** n Meisterschaft f; **Champions League** n Champions League f

chance [tʃɑːns] n (fate) Zufall m; (possibility) Möglichkeit f; (opportunity) Gelegenheit f; (risk) Risiko nt; **by ~** zufällig; **he doesn't stand a ~ (of winning)** er hat keinerlei Chance(, zu gewinnen)

chancellor ['tʃɑːnsələ*] n Kanzler(in) m(f)

chandelier [ʃændɪ'lɪə*] n Kronleuchter m

change [tʃeɪndʒ] vt verändern; (alter) ändern; (money, wheel, nappy) wechseln; (exchange) (um)tauschen; **to ~ one's clothes** sich umziehen; **to ~ trains** umsteigen; **to ~ gear** (Auto) schalten ▷ vi sich ändern; (esp outwardly) sich verändern; (get changed) sich umziehen ▷ n Veränderung f; (alteration) Änderung f; (money) Wechselgeld nt; (coins) Kleingeld nt; **for a ~** zur Abwechslung; **can you give me ~ for £10?** können Sie mir auf 10 Pfund herausgeben?; **change down** vi (Brit Auto) herunterschalten; **change over** vi sich umstellen (to auf +akk); **change up** vi (Brit Auto) hochschalten

changeable adj (weather) veränderlich, wechselhaft; **change machine** n Geldwechsler m; **changing room** n Umkleideraum m

channel ['tʃænl] n Kanal m; (Radio, Tv) Kanal m, Sender m; **the (English) Channel** der Ärmelkanal; **the Channel Islands** die Kanalinseln; **the Channel Tunnel** der Kanaltunnel; **channel-hopping** n Zappen nt

chaos ['keɪɒs] n Chaos nt; **chaotic** [keɪ'ɒtɪk] adj chaotisch

chap [tʃæp] n (Brit fam) Bursche m, Kerl m

chapel ['tʃæpəl] n Kapelle f

chapped ['tʃæpt] adj (lips) aufgesprungen

chapter ['tʃæptə*] n Kapitel nt

character ['kærəktə*] n Charakter m, Wesen nt; (in a play, novel etc) Figur f; (Typo) Zeichen nt; **he's a real ~** er ist ein echtes Original; **characteristic** [kærəktə'rıstık] n typisches Merkmal

charcoal ['tʃɑ:kəʊl] n Holzkohle f

charge [tʃɑ:dʒ] n (cost) Gebühr f; (Jur) Anklage f; **free of ~** gratis, kostenlos; **to be in ~ of** verantwortlich sein für ▷ vt (money) verlangen; (Jur) anklagen; (battery) laden; **charge card** n Kundenkreditkarte f

charity ['tʃærıtı] n (institution) wohltätige Organisation f; **a collection for ~** eine Sammlung für wohltätige Zwecke; **charity shop** n Geschäft einer 'charity', in dem freiwillige Helfer gebrauchte Kleidung, Bücher etc verkaufen

charm [tʃɑ:m] n Charme m ▷ vt bezaubern; **charming** adj reizend, charmant

chart [tʃɑ:t] n Diagramm nt; (map) Karte f; **the ~s** pl die Charts, die Hitliste

charter ['tʃɑ:tə*] n Urkunde f ▷ vt (Naut, Aviat) chartern; **charter flight** n Charterflug m

chase [tʃeıs] vt jagen, verfolgen ▷ n Verfolgungsjagd f; (hunt) Jagd f

chassis ['ʃæsı] n (Auto) Fahrgestell nt

chat [tʃæt] vi plaudern; (Inform) chatten ▷ n Plauderei f; **chat up** vt anmachen, anbaggern; **chatroom** n (Inform) Chatroom m; **chat show** n Talkshow f; **chatty** adj geschwätzig

chauffeur ['ʃəʊfə*] n Chauffeur(in) m(f), Fahrer(in) m(f)

cheap [tʃi:p] adj billig; (of poor quality) minderwertig

cheat [tʃi:t] vt, vi betrügen; (in school, game) mogeln

Chechen ['tʃetʃen] adj tschetschenisch ▷ n Tschetschene m, Tschetschenin f; **Chechnya** ['tʃetʃnıə] n Tschetschenien nt

check [tʃek] vt (examine) überprüfen (for auf +akk); (Tech: adjustment etc) kontrollieren; (US: tick) abhaken; (Aviat: luggage) einchecken; (US: coat) abgeben ▷ n (examination, restraint) Kontrolle f; (US: restaurant bill) Rechnung f; (pattern) Karo(muster) nt; (US) see **cheque**; **check in** vt, vi (Aviat) einchecken; (into hotel) sich

anmelden; **check out** vi sich abmelden, auschecken; **check up** vi nachprüfen; **to ~ on sb** Nachforschungen über jdn anstellen

checkers ['tʃekəz] nsing (US) Damespiel nt

check-in ['tʃekın] n (airport) Check-in m; (hotel) Anmeldung f; **check-in desk** n Abfertigungsschalter m; **checking account** n (US) Scheckkonto nt; **check list** n Kontrollliste f; **checkout** n (supermarket) Kasse f; **checkout time** n (hotel) Abreise(zeit) f; **checkpoint** n Kontrollpunkt m; **checkroom** n (US) Gepäckaufbewahrung f; **checkup** n (Med) (ärztliche) Untersuchung

cheddar ['tʃedə*] n Cheddarkäse m

cheek [tʃi:k] n Backe f, Wange f; (insolence) Frechheit f; **what a ~** so eine Frechheit!; **cheekbone** n Backenknochen m; **cheeky** adj frech

cheer [tʃıə*] n Beifallsruf m; **~s** (when drinking) prost!; (Brit fam: thanks) danke; (Brit: goodbye) tschüs ▷ vt zujubeln +dat ▷ vi jubeln; **cheer up** vt aufmuntern ▷ vi fröhlicher werden; **~!** Kopf hoch!; **cheerful** ['tʃıəfʊl] adj fröhlich

cheese [tʃi:z] n Käse m; **cheeseboard** n Käsebrett nt; (as course) (gemischte) Käseplatte; **cheesecake** n Käsekuchen m

chef [ʃef] n Koch m; (in charge of kitchen) Küchenchef(in) m(f)

chemical ['kemıkəl] adj chemisch ▷ n Chemikalie f; **chemist** ['kemıst] n (pharmacist) Apotheker(in) m(f); (industrial chemist) Chemiker(in) m(f); **~'s (shop)** Apotheke f; **chemistry** n Chemie f

cheque [tʃek] n (Brit) Scheck m; **cheque account** n (Brit) Girokonto nt; **cheque book** n (Brit) Scheckheft nt; **cheque card** n (Brit) Scheckkarte f

chequered ['tʃekəd] adj kariert

cherish ['tʃerıʃ] vt (look after) liebevoll sorgen für; (hope) hegen; (memory) bewahren

cherry ['tʃerı] n Kirsche f; **cherry tomato** (pl **-es**) n Kirschtomate f

chess [tʃes] n Schach nt; **chessboard** n Schachbrett nt

chest [tʃest] n Brust f; (box) Kiste f; **~ of drawers** Kommode f

chestnut ['tʃesnʌt] n Kastanie f

chew [tʃu:] vt, vi kauen; **chewing gum** n Kaugummi m

chick [tʃɪk] n Küken nt; **chicken** n Huhn nt; (food: roast) Hähnchen nt; (coward) Feigling m; **chicken breast** n Hühnerbrust f; **chicken Kiev** n paniertes Hähnchen, mit Knoblauchbutter gefüllt; **chickenpox** n Windpocken pl; **chickpea** n Kichererbse f

chicory ['tʃɪkərɪ] n Chicorée f

chief [tʃiːf] n (of department etc) Leiter(in) m(f); (boss) Chef(in) m(f); (of tribe) Häuptling m ▷ adj Haupt-; **chiefly** adv hauptsächlich

child [tʃaɪld] (pl children) n Kind nt; **child abuse** n Kindesmisshandlung f; **child allowance, child benefit** (Brit) n Kindergeld nt; **childbirth** n Geburt f, Entbindung f; **childhood** n Kindheit f; **childish** adj kindisch; **child lock** n Kindersicherung f; **childproof** adj kindersicher; **children** ['tʃɪldrən] pl of child; **child seat** n Kindersitz m

Chile ['tʃɪlɪ] n Chile nt

chill [tʃɪl] n Kühle f; (Med) Erkältung f ▷ vt (wine) kühlen; **chill out** vi (fam) relaxen; **chilled** adj gekühlt

chilli ['tʃɪlɪ] n Pepperoni pl; (spice) Chili m; **chilli con carne** ['tʃɪlɪkɒn'kɑːnɪ] n Chili con carne nt

chilly ['tʃɪlɪ] adj kühl, frostig

chimney ['tʃɪmnɪ] n Schornstein m; **chimneysweep** n Schornsteinfeger(in) m(f)

chimpanzee [tʃɪmpæn'ziː] n Schimpanse m

chin [tʃɪn] n Kinn nt

china ['tʃaɪnə] n Porzellan nt

China ['tʃaɪnə] n China nt; **Chinese** [tʃaɪ'niːz] adj chinesisch ▷ n (person) Chinese m, Chinesin f; (language) Chinesisch nt; **Chinese leaves** npl Chinakohl m

chip [tʃɪp] n (of wood etc) Splitter m; (damage) angeschlagene Stelle; (Inform) Chip m; **-s** (Brit: potatoes) Pommes frites pl; (US: crisps) Kartoffelchips pl ▷ vt anschlagen, beschädigen; **chippie** (fam), **chip shop** n Frittenbude f

chiropodist [kɪ'rɒpədɪst] n Fußpfleger(in) m(f)

chirp [tʃɜːp] vi zwitschern

chisel ['tʃɪzl] n Meißel m

chitchat ['tʃɪttʃæt] n Gerede nt

chives [tʃaɪvz] npl Schnittlauch m

chlorine ['klɔːriːn] n Chlor nt

chocaholic, chocoholic [tʃɒkə'hɒlɪk] n Schokoladenfreak m; **choc-ice** ['tʃɒkaɪs] n Eis nt mit Schokoladenüberzug; **chocolate** ['tʃɒklɪt] n Schokolade f; (chocolate-coated sweet) Praline f; **a bar of ~** eine Tafel Schokolade; **a box of ~s** eine Schachtel Pralinen; **chocolate cake** n Schokoladenkuchen m; **chocolate sauce** n Schokoladensoße f

choice [tʃɔɪs] n Wahl f, (selection) Auswahl f ▷ adj auserlesen; (product) Qualitäts-

choir ['kwaɪə*] n Chor m

choke [tʃəʊk] vi sich verschlucken; (Sport) die Nerven verlieren ▷ vt erdrosseln ▷ n (Auto) Choke m

cholera ['kɒlərə] n Cholera f

cholesterol [kə'lestərəl] n Cholesterin nt

choose [tʃuːz] (chose, chosen) vt wählen; (pick out) sich aussuchen; **there are three to ~ from** es stehen drei zur Auswahl

chop [tʃɒp] vt (zer)hacken; (meat etc) klein schneiden ▷ n (meat) Kotelett nt; **to get the ~** gefeuert werden; **chopper** n Hackbeil nt; (fam: helicopter) Hubschrauber m; **chopsticks** npl Essstäbchen pl

chorus ['kɔːrəs] n Chor m; (in song) Refrain m

chose, chosen [tʃəʊz, 'tʃəʊzn] pt, pp of choose

chowder ['tʃaʊdə*] n (US) dicke Suppe mit Meeresfrüchten

christen ['krɪsn] vt taufen; **christening** n Taufe f, **Christian** ['krɪstɪən] adj christlich ▷ n Christ(in) m(f); **Christian name** n (Brit) Vorname m

Christmas ['krɪsməs] n Weihnachten pl; **Christmas card** n Weihnachtskarte f; **Christmas carol** n Weihnachtslied nt; **Christmas Day** n der erste Weihnachtstag; **Christmas Eve** n Heiligabend m; **Christmas pudding** n Plumpudding m; **Christmas tree** n Weihnachtsbaum m

chronic ['krɒnɪk] adj (Med, fig) chronisch; (fam: very bad) miserabel

chrysanthemum [krɪ'sænθɪməm] n Chrysantheme f

chubby ['tʃʌbɪ] adj (child) pummelig; (adult) rundlich

chuck [tʃʌk] vt (fam) schmeißen; **chuck in**
vt (fam: job) hinschmeißen; **chuck out** vt
(fam) rausschmeißen; **chuck up** vi (fam)
kotzen

chunk [tʃʌŋk] n Klumpen m; (of bread)
Brocken m; (of meat) Batzen m; **chunky** adj
(person) stämmig

Chunnel ['tʃʌnəl] n (fam) Kanaltunnel m

church [tʃɜ:tʃ] n Kirche f; **churchyard** n
Kirchhof m

chute [ʃu:t] n Rutsche f

chutney ['ʃʌtnɪ] n Chutney m

CIA abbr = **Central Intelligence Agency**
(US) CIA f

CID abbr = **Criminal Investigation
Department** (Brit) ≈ Kripo f

cider ['saɪdə*] n ≈ Apfelmost m

cigar [sɪ'gɑ:*] n Zigarre f; **cigarette**
[sɪgə'ret] n Zigarette f

cinema ['sɪnəmə] n Kino nt

cinnamon ['sɪnəmən] n Zimt m

circa ['sɜ:kə] prep zirka

circle ['sɜ:kl] n Kreis m ▷ vi kreisen;
circuit ['sɜ:kɪt] n Rundfahrt f; (on foot)
Rundgang m; (for racing) Rennstrecke f;
(Elec) Stromkreis m; **circular** ['sɜ:kjʊlə*]
adj (kreis)rund, kreisförmig ▷ n
Rundschreiben nt; **circulation**
[sɜ:kjʊ'leɪʃən] n (of blood) Kreislauf m; (of
newspaper) Auflage f

circumstances ['sɜ:kəmstənsəz] npl
(facts) Umstände pl; (financial condition)
Verhältnisse pl; **in/under the ~** unter den
Umständen; **under no ~** auf keinen Fall

circus ['sɜ:kəs] n Zirkus m

cissy ['sɪsɪ] n (fam) Weichling m

cistern ['sɪstən] n Zisterne f; (of WC)
Spülkasten m

cite [saɪt] vt zitieren

citizen ['sɪtɪzn] n Bürger(in) m(f); (of
nation) Staatsangehörige(r) mf;
citizenship n Staatsangehörigkeit f

city ['sɪtɪ] n Stadt f; (large) Großstadt f;
the ~ (London's financial centre) die
(Londoner) City; **city centre** n Innenstadt
f, Zentrum nt

civil ['sɪvl] adj (of town) Bürger-; (of state)
staatsbürgerlich; (not military) zivil; **civil
ceremony** n standesamtliche Hochzeit;
civil engineering n Hoch- und Tiefbau m,
Bauingenieurwesen nt; **civilian** [sɪ'vɪljən]
n Zivilist(in) m(f); **civilization**
[sɪvɪlaɪ'zeɪʃən] n Zivilisation f, Kultur f;

civilized ['sɪvɪlaɪzd] adj zivilisiert,
kultiviert; **civil partnership** n
eingetragene Partnerschaft; **civil rights**
npl Bürgerrechte pl; **civil servant** n
(Staats)beamte(r) m, (Staats)beamtin f;
civil service n Staatsdienst m; **civil war**
n Bürgerkrieg m

CJD abbr = **Creutzfeld-Jakob disease**
Creutzfeld-Jakob-Krankheit f

cl abbr = **centilitre(s)** cl

claim [kleɪm] vt beanspruchen; (apply for)
beantragen; (demand) fordern; (assert)
behaupten (that dass) ▷ n (demand)
Forderung f (for für); (right) Anspruch m (to
auf +akk); **~ for damages**
Schadenersatzforderung f; **to make** o **put
in a ~** (insurance) Ansprüche geltend
machen; **claimant** n Antragsteller(in)
m(f)

clam [klæm] n Venusmuschel f; **clam
chowder** n (US) dicke Muschelsuppe (mit
Sellerie, Zwiebeln etc)

clap [klæp] vi (Beifall) klatschen

claret ['klærɪt] n roter Bordeaux(wein)

clarify ['klærɪfaɪ] vt klären

clarinet [klærɪ'net] n Klarinette f

clarity ['klærɪtɪ] n Klarheit f

clash [klæʃ] vi (physically)
zusammenstoßen (with mit); (argue) sich
auseinandersetzen (with mit); (fig: colours)
sich beißen ▷ n Zusammenstoß m;
(argument) Auseinandersetzung f

clasp [klɑ:sp] n (on belt) Schnalle f

class [klɑ:s] n Klasse f ▷ vt einordnen,
einstufen

classic ['klæsɪk] adj (mistake, example etc)
klassisch ▷ n Klassiker m; **classical**
['klæsɪkəl] adj (music, ballet etc) klassisch

classification [klæsɪfɪ'keɪʃn] n
Klassifizierung f; **classify** ['klæsɪfaɪ] vt
klassifizieren; **classified advertisement**
Kleinanzeige f

classroom ['klɑ:srʊm] n Klassenzimmer
nt

classy ['klɑ:sɪ] adj (fam) nobel, exklusiv

clatter ['klætə*] vi klappern

clause [klɔ:z] n (Ling) Satz m; (Jur) Klausel
f

claw [klɔ:] n Kralle f

clay [kleɪ] n Lehm m; (for pottery) Ton m

clean [kli:n] adj sauber; **~ driving licence**
Führerschein ohne Strafpunkte ▷ adv
(completely) glatt ▷ vt sauber machen;

(*carpet etc*) reinigen; (*window, shoes, vegetables*) putzen; (*wound*) säubern; **clean up** *vt* sauber machen ▷ *vi* aufräumen; **cleaner** *n* (*person*) Putzmann *m*, Putzfrau *f*; (*substance*) Putzmittel *nt*; **~'s** (*firm*) Reinigung *f*

cleanse [klɛnz] *vt* reinigen; (*wound*) säubern; **cleanser** *n* Reinigungsmittel *nt*

clear ['klɪə*] *adj* klar; (*distinct*) deutlich; (*conscience*) rein; (*free, road etc*) frei; **to be ~ about sth** sich über etw im Klaren sein ▷ *adv* **to stand ~** zurücktreten ▷ *vt* (*road, room etc*) räumen; (*table*) abräumen; (*Jur: find innocent*) freisprechen (*of* von) ▷ *vi* (*fog, mist*) sich verziehen; (*weather*) aufklaren; **clear away** *vt* wegräumen; (*dishes*) abräumen; **clear off** *vi* (*fam*) abhauen; **clear up** *vi* (*tidy up*) aufräumen; (*weather*) sich aufklären ▷ *vt* (*room*) aufräumen; (*litter*) wegräumen; (*matter*) klären

clearance sale *n* Räumungsverkauf *m*; **clearing** *n* Lichtung *f*; **clearly** *adv* klar; (*speak, remember*) deutlich; (*obviously*) eindeutig; **clearout** *n* Entrümpelungsaktion *f*; **clearway** *n* (*Brit*) Straße *f* mit Halteverbot *nt*

clench [klɛntʃ] *vt* (*fist*) ballen; (*teeth*) zusammenbeißen

clergyman ['klɜ:dʒɪmæn] (*pl* **-men**) *n* Geistliche(r) *m*

clerk [klɑ:k], (*US*) [klɜ:k] *n* (*in office*) Büroangestellte(r) *mf*; (*US: salesperson*) Verkäufer(in) *m(f)*

clever ['klɛvə*] *adj* schlau, klug; (*idea*) clever

cliché ['kli:ʃeɪ] *n* Klischee *nt*

click [klɪk] *n* Klicken *nt*; (*Inform*) Mausklick *m* ▷ *vi* klicken; **to ~ on sth** (*Inform*) etw anklicken; **it ~ed** (*fam*) ich hab's/er hat's etc geschnallt, es hat gefunkt, es hat Klick gemacht; **they ~ed** sie haben sich gleich verstanden; **click on** *vt* (*Inform*) anklicken

client ['klaɪənt] *n* Kunde *m*, Kundin *f*; (*Jur*) Mandant(in) *m(f)*

cliff [klɪf] *n* Klippe *f*

climate ['klaɪmɪt] *n* Klima *nt*

climax ['klaɪmæks] *n* Höhepunkt *m*

climb [klaɪm] *vi* (*person*) klettern; (*aircraft, sun*) steigen; (*road*) ansteigen ▷ *vt* (*mountain*) besteigen; (*tree etc*) klettern auf +*akk* ▷ *n* Aufstieg *m*; **climber** *n* (*mountaineer*) Bergsteiger(in) *m(f)*;

climbing *n* Klettern *nt*, Bergsteigen *nt*; **climbing frame** *n* Klettergerüst *nt*

cling [klɪŋ] (**clung, clung**) *vi* sich klammern (*to an* +*akk*); **cling film®** *n* Frischhaltefolie *f*

clinic ['klɪnɪk] *n* Klinik *f*; **clinical** *adj* klinisch

clip [klɪp] *n* Klammer *f* ▷ *vt* (*fix*) anklemmen (*to an* +*akk*); (*fingernails*) schneiden; **clipboard** *n* Klemmbrett *nt*; **clippers** *npl* Schere *f*; (*for nails*) Zwicker *m*

cloak [kləʊk] *n* Umhang *m*; **cloakroom** *n* (*for coats*) Garderobe *f*

clock [klɒk] *n* Uhr *f*; (*Auto: fam*) Tacho *m*; **round the ~** rund um die Uhr; **clockwise** *adv* im Uhrzeigersinn; **clockwork** *n* Uhrwerk *nt*

clog [klɒg] *n* Holzschuh *m* ▷ *vt* verstopfen

cloister ['klɔɪstə*] *n* Kreuzgang *m*

clone [kləʊn] *n* Klon *m* ▷ *vt* klonen

close [kləʊs] *adj* nahe (*to* +*dat*); (*friend, contact*) eng; (*resemblance*) groß; **~ to the beach** in der Nähe des Strandes; **~ win** knapper Sieg; **on ~r examination** bei näherer *o* genauerer Untersuchung ▷ *adv* [kləʊs] dicht; **he lives ~ by** er wohnt ganz in der Nähe ▷ *vt* [kləʊz] schließen; (*road*) sperren; (*discussion, matter*) abschließen ▷ *vi* [kləʊz] schließen ▷ *n* [kləʊz] Ende *nt*; **close down** *vi* schließen; (*factory*) stillgelegt werden ▷ *vt* (*shop*) schließen; (*factory*) stilllegen; **closed** *adj* (*road*) gesperrt; (*shop etc*) geschlossen; **closed circuit television** *n* Videoüberwachungsanlage *f*; **closely** *adv* (*related*) eng, nah; (*packed, follow*) dicht; (*attentively*) genau

closet ['klɒzɪt] *n* (*esp US*) Schrank *m*

close-up ['kləʊsʌp] *n* Nahaufnahme *f*

closing ['kləʊzɪŋ] *adj* **~ date** letzter Termin; (*for competition*) Einsendeschluss *m*; **~ time** (*of shop*) Ladenschluss *m*; (*Brit: of pub*) Polizeistunde *f*

clot [klɒt] (**blood**) **~** Blutgerinnsel *nt*; (*fam: idiot*) Trottel *m* ▷ *vi* (*blood*) gerinnen

cloth [klɒθ] *n* (*material*) Tuch *nt*; (*for cleaning*) Lappen *m*

clothe [kləʊð] *vt* kleiden; **clothes** *npl* Kleider *pl*, Kleidung *f*; **clothes line** *n* Wäscheleine *f*; **clothes peg, clothespin** (*US*) *n* Wäscheklammer *f*; **clothing** ['kləʊðɪŋ] *n* Kleidung *f*

clotted ['klɒtɪd] *adj* **~ cream** dicke Sahne (*aus erhitzter Milch*)

cloud [klaʊd] *n* Wolke *f*; **cloudy** *adj* (*sky*) bewölkt; (*liquid*) trüb

clove [kləʊv] *n* Gewürznelke *f*; **~ of garlic** Knoblauchzehe *f*

clover ['kləʊvə*] *n* Klee *m*; **cloverleaf** (*pl* **-leaves**) *n* Kleeblatt *nt*

clown [klaʊn] *n* Clown *m*

club [klʌb] *n* (*weapon*) Knüppel *m*; (*society*) Klub *m*, Verein *m*; (*nightclub*) Disko *f*; (*golf club*) Golfschläger *m*; **~s** (*Cards*) Kreuz *nt*; **clubbing** *n* **to go ~** in die Disko gehen; **club class** *n* (*Aviat*) Businessclass *f*

clue [klu:] *n* Anhaltspunkt *m*, Hinweis *m*; **he hasn't a ~** er hat keine Ahnung

clumsy ['klʌmzɪ] *adj* unbeholfen, ungeschickt

clung [klʌŋ] *pt, pp of* **cling**

clutch [klʌtʃ] *n* (*Auto*) Kupplung *f* ▷ *vt* umklammern; (*book etc*) an sich *akk* klammern

cm *abbr* = **centimetre(s)** cm

c/o *abbr* = **care of** bei

Co *abbr* = **company** Co

coach [kəʊtʃ] *n* (*Brit: bus*) Reisebus *m*; (*Rail*) (Personen)wagen *m*; (*Sport: trainer*) Trainer(in) *m(f)* ▷ *vt* Nachhilfeunterricht geben +*dat*; (*Sport*) trainieren; **coach (class)** *n* (*Aviat*) Economyclass *f*; **coach driver** *n* Busfahrer(in) *m(f)*; **coach station** *n* Busbahnhof *m*; **coach trip** *n* Busfahrt *f*; (*tour*) Busreise *f*

coal [kəʊl] *n* Kohle *f*

coalition [kəʊə'lɪʃən] *n* (*Pol*) Koalition *f*

coalmine ['kəʊlmaɪn] *n* Kohlenbergwerk *nt*; **coalminer** *n* Bergarbeiter *m*

coast [kəʊst] *n* Küste *f*; **coastguard** *n* Küstenwache *f*; **coastline** *n* Küste *f*

coat [kəʊt] *n* Mantel *m*; (*jacket*) Jacke *f*; (*on animals*) Fell *nt*, Pelz *m*; (*of paint*) Schicht *f*; **~ of arms** Wappen *nt*; **coathanger** *n* Kleiderbügel *m*; **coating** *n* Überzug *m*; (*layer*) Schicht *f*

cobble(stone)s ['kɒbl(stəʊn)z] *npl* Kopfsteine *pl*; (*surface*) Kopfsteinpflaster *nt*

cobweb ['kɒbweb] *n* Spinnennetz *nt*

cocaine [kə'keɪn] *n* Kokain *nt*

cock [kɒk] *n* Hahn *m*; (*vulg: penis*) Schwanz *m*; **cockerel** ['kɒkərəl] *n* junger Hahn

cockle ['kɒkl] *n* Herzmuschel *f*

cockpit ['kɒkpɪt] *n* (*in plane, racing car*) Cockpit *nt*; **cockroach** ['kɒkrəʊtʃ] *n* Kakerlake *f*; **cocksure** *adj* todsicher; **cocktail** ['kɒkteɪl] *n* Cocktail *m*; **cock-up** *n* (*Brit fam*) **to make a ~ of sth** bei etw Mist bauen; **cocky** ['kɒkɪ] *adj* großspurig, von sich selbst überzeugt

cocoa ['kəʊkəʊ] *n* Kakao *m*

coconut ['kəʊkənʌt] *n* Kokosnuss *f*

cod [kɒd] *n* Kabeljau *m*

COD *abbr* = **cash on delivery** per Nachnahme

code [kəʊd] *n* Kode *m*

coeducational [kəʊedjʊ'keɪʃənl] *adj* (*school*) gemischt

coffee ['kɒfɪ] *n* Kaffee *m*; **coffee bar** *n* Café *nt*; **coffee break** *n* Kaffeepause *f*; **coffee maker** *n* Kaffeemaschine *f*; **coffee pot** *n* Kaffeekanne *f*; **coffee shop** *n* Café *nt*; **coffee table** *n* Couchtisch *m*

coffin ['kɒfɪn] *n* Sarg *m*

coil [kɔɪl] *n* Rolle *f*; (*Elec*) Spule *f*; (*Med*) Spirale *f*

coin [kɔɪn] *n* Münze *f*

coincide [kəʊɪn'saɪd] *vi* (*happen together*) zusammenfallen (*with* mit); **coincidence** [kəʊ'ɪnsɪdəns] *n* Zufall *m*

coke [kəʊk] *n* Koks *m*; **Coke®** Cola *f*

cola ['kəʊlə] *n* Cola *f*

cold [kəʊld] *adj* kalt; **I'm ~** mir ist kalt, ich friere ▷ *n* Kälte *f*; (*illness*) Erkältung *f*, Schnupfen *m*; **to catch a ~** sich erkälten; **cold box** *n* Kühlbox *f*; **coldness** *n* Kälte *f*; **cold sore** *n* Herpes *m*; **cold turkey** *n* (*fam*) Totalentzug *m*; (*symptoms*) Entzugserscheinungen *pl*

coleslaw ['kəʊlslɔ:] *n* Krautsalat *m*

collaborate [kə'læbəreɪt] *vi* zusammenarbeiten (*with* mit); **collaboration** [kəlæbə'reɪʃən] *n* Zusammenarbeit *f*; (*of one party*) Mitarbeit *f*

collapse [kə'læps] *vi* zusammenbrechen; (*building etc*) einstürzen ▷ *n* Zusammenbruch *m*; (*of building*) Einsturz *m*; **collapsible** [kə'læpsəbl] *adj* zusammenklappbar, Klapp-

collar ['kɒlə*] *n* Kragen *m*; (*for dog, cat*) Halsband *nt*; **collarbone** *n* Schlüsselbein *nt*

colleague ['kɒli:g] *n* Kollege *m*, Kollegin *f*

collect [kə'lekt] *vt* sammeln; (*fetch*) abholen ▷ *vi* sich sammeln; **collect call** *n*

(US) R-Gespräch nt; **collected** adj (works) gesammelt; (person) gefasst; **collector** n Sammler(in) m(f); **collection** [kə'lekʃən] n Sammlung f; (Rel) Kollekte f; (from postbox) Leerung f

college ['kɒlɪdʒ] n (residential) College nt; (specialist) Fachhochschule f; (vocational) Berufsschule f; (US: university) Universität f; **to go to ~** (US) studieren

collide [kə'laɪd] vi zusammenstoßen; **collision** [kə'lɪʒən] n Zusammenstoß m

colloquial [kə'ləʊkwɪəl] adj umgangssprachlich

Cologne [kə'ləʊn] n Köln nt

colon ['kəʊlən] n (punctuation mark) Doppelpunkt m

colonial [kə'ləʊnɪəl] adj Kolonial-; **colonize** ['kɒlənaɪz] vt kolonisieren; **colony** ['kɒlənɪ] n Kolonie f

color n (US), **colour** ['kʌlə*] n Farbe f; (of skin) Hautfarbe f ▷ vt anmalen; (bias) färben; **colour-blind** adj farbenblind; **coloured** adj farbig; (biased) gefärbt; **colour film** n Farbfilm m; **colourful** adj (lit, fig) bunt; (life, past) bewegt; **colouring** n (in food etc) Farbstoff m; (complexion) Gesichtsfarbe f; **colourless** adj (lit, fig) farblos; **colour photo(graph)** n Farbfoto nt; **colour television** n Farbfernsehen nt

column ['kɒləm] n Säule f; (of print) Spalte f

comb [kəʊm] n Kamm m ▷ vt kämmen; **to ~ one's hair** sich kämmen

combination [kɒmbɪ'neɪʃən] n Kombination f; (mixture) Mischung f (of aus); **combine** [kəm'baɪn] vt verbinden (with mit); (two things) kombinieren

come [kʌm] (came, come) vi kommen; (arrive) ankommen; (on list, in order) stehen; (with adjective: become) werden; **~ and see us** besuchen Sie uns mal; **coming** ich komm ja schon!; **to ~ first/second** erster/zweiter werden; **to ~ true** wahr werden; **to ~ loose** sich lockern; **the years to ~** die kommenden Jahre; **there's one more to ~** es kommt noch eins/noch einer; **how ~ ...?** (fam) wie kommt es, dass ...?; **~ to think of it** (fam) wo es mir gerade einfällt; **come across** vt (find) stoßen auf +akk; **come back** vi zurückkommen; **I'll ~ to that** ich komme darauf zurück; **come down** vi herunterkommen; (rain, snow, price) fallen;

come from vt (result) kommen von; **where do you ~?** wo kommen Sie her?; **I ~ London** ich komme aus London; **come in** vi hereinkommen; (arrive) ankommen; (in race) **to ~ fourth** Vierter werden; **come off** vi (button, handle etc) abgehen; (succeed) gelingen; **to ~ well/badly** gut/schlecht wegkommen; **come on** vi (progress) vorankommen; **~!** komm!; (hurry) beeil dich!; (encouraging) los!; **come out** vi herauskommen; (photo) was werden; (homosexual) sich outen; **come round** vi (visit) vorbeikommen; (regain consciousness) wieder zu sich kommen; **come to** vi (regain consciousness) wieder zu sich kommen ▷ vt (sum) sich belaufen auf +akk; **when it comes to ...** wenn es um ... geht; **come up** vi hochkommen; (sun, moon) aufgehen; **to ~ (for discussion)** zur Sprache kommen; **come up to** vt (approach) zukommen auf +akk; (water) reichen bis zu; (expectations) entsprechen +dat; **come up with** vt (idea) haben; (solution, answer) kommen auf +akk; **to ~ a suggestion** einen Vorschlag machen

comedian [kə'miːdɪən] n Komiker(in) m(f)

comedown ['kʌmdaʊn] n Abstieg m

comedy ['kɒmədɪ] n Komödie f

come-on ['kʌmɒn] n **to give sb the ~** (fam) jdn anmachen

comfort ['kʌmfət] n Komfort m; (consolation) Trost m ▷ vt trösten; **comfortable** adj bequem; (income) ausreichend; (temperature, life) angenehm; **comfort station** n (US) Toilette f; **comforting** adj tröstlich

comic ['kɒmɪk] n (magazine) Comic(heft) nt; (comedian) Komiker(in) m(f) ▷ adj komisch

coming ['kʌmɪŋ] adj kommend; (event) bevorstehend

comma ['kɒmə] n Komma nt

command [kə'mɑːnd] n Befehl m; (control) Führung f; (Mil) Kommando nt ▷ vt befehlen +dat

commemorate [kə'meməreɪt] vt gedenken +gen; **commemoration** [kəmemə'reɪʃən] n **in ~ of** in Gedenken an +akk

comment ['kɒment] n (remark) Bemerkung f; (note) Anmerkung f; (official) Kommentar m (on zu); **no ~** kein

Kommentar ▷ *vi* sich äußern (*on* zu);
commentary ['kɒməntrɪ] *n* Kommentar
m (*on* zu); (*Tv, Sport*) Livereportage *f*;
commentator ['kɒmənteɪtə*] *n*
Kommentator(in) *m(f)*; (*Tv, Sport*)
Reporter(in) *m(f)*
commerce ['kɒmɜ:s] *n* Handel *m*;
commercial [kə'mɜ:ʃəl] *adj* kommerziell;
(*training*) kaufmännisch; **~ break**
Werbepause *f*; **~ vehicle** Lieferwagen *m*
▷ *n* (*Tv*) Werbespot *m*
commission [kə'mɪʃən] *n* Auftrag *m*; (*fee*)
Provision *f*; (*reporting body*) Kommission *f*
▷ *vt* beauftragen
commit [kə'mɪt] *vt* (*crime*) begehen ▷ *vr*
to ~ oneself (*undertake*) sich verpflichten
(*to* zu); **commitment** *n* Verpflichtung *f*;
(*Pol*) Engagement *nt*
committee [kə'mɪtɪ] *n* Ausschuss *m*,
Komitee *nt*
commodity [kə'mɒdɪtɪ] *n* Ware *f*
common ['kɒmən] *adj* (*experience*)
allgemein, alltäglich; (*shared*) gemeinsam;
(*widespread, frequent*) häufig; (*pej*)
gewöhnlich, ordinär; **to have sth in ~** etw
gemein haben ▷ *n* (*Brit: land*)
Gemeindewiese *f*; **commonly** *adv* häufig,
allgemein; **commonplace** *adj* alltäglich;
(*pej*) banal; **commonroom** *n*
Gemeinschaftsraum *m*; **Commons** *n* (*Brit
Pol*) **the** (**House of**) **~** das Unterhaus;
common sense *n* gesunder
Menschenverstand; **Commonwealth** *n*
Commonwealth *nt*; **~ of Independent
States** Gemeinschaft *f* Unabhängiger
Staaten
communal ['kɒmjʊnl] *adj* gemeinsam;
(*of a community*) Gemeinschafts-,
Gemeinde-
communicate [kə'mju:nɪkeɪt] *vi*
kommunizieren (*with* mit);
communication [kəmju:nɪ'keɪʃən] *n*
Kommunikation *f*, Verständigung *f*;
communications satellite *n*
Nachrichtensatellit *m*;
communications technology *n*
Nachrichtentechnik *f*; **communicative**
adj gesprächig
communion [kə'mju:nɪən] *n* (**Holy**)
Communion Heiliges Abendmahl;
(*Catholic*) Kommunion *f*
communism ['kɒmjʊnɪzəm] *n*
Kommunismus *m*; **communist**

['kɒmjʊnɪst] *adj* kommunistisch ▷ *n*
Kommunist(in) *m(f)*
community [kə'mju:nɪtɪ] *n*
Gemeinschaft *f*; **community centre** *n*
Gemeindezentrum *nt*; **community
service** *n* (*Jur*) Sozialdienst *m*
commutation ticket [kɒmjʊ'teɪʃəntɪkɪt]
n (*US*) Zeitkarte *f*; **commute** [kə'mju:t] *vi*
pendeln; **commuter** *n* Pendler(in) *m(f)*
compact [kəm'pækt] *adj* kompakt
▷ ['kɒmpækt] *n* (*for make-up*) Puderdose *f*;
(*US: car*) ≈ Mittelklassewagen *m*; **compact
camera** *n* Kompaktkamera *f*; **compact
disc** *n* Compact Disc *f*, CD *f*
companion [kəm'pænɪən] *n*
Begleiter(in) *m(f)*
company ['kʌmpənɪ] *n* Gesellschaft *f*;
(*Comm*) Firma *f*; **to keep sb ~** jdm
Gesellschaft leisten; **company car** *n*
Firmenauto *nt*
comparable ['kɒmpərəbl] *adj*
vergleichbar (*with, to* mit)
comparative [kəm'pærətɪv] *adj* relativ
▷ *n* (*Ling*) Komparativ *m*; **comparatively**
adv verhältnismäßig
compare [kəm'pɛə*] *vt* vergleichen (*with,
to* mit); **~d with** *o* **to** im Vergleich zu;
beyond ~ unvergleichlich; **comparison**
[kəm'pærɪsn] *n* Vergleich *m*; **in ~ with** im
Vergleich mit (*o* zu)
compartment [kəm'pɑ:tmənt] *n* (*Rail*)
Abteil *nt*; (*in desk etc*) Fach *nt*
compass ['kʌmpəs] *n* Kompass *m*; **~es** *pl*
Zirkel *m*
compassion [kəm'pæʃən] *n* Mitgefühl *nt*
compatible [kəm'pætɪbl] *adj* vereinbar
(*with* mit); (*Inform*) kompatibel; **we're not
~** wir passen nicht zueinander
compensate ['kɒmpenseɪt] *vt* (*person*)
entschädigen (*for* für) ▷ *vi* **to ~ for sth**
Ersatz für etw leisten; (*make up for*) etw
ausgleichen; **compensation**
[kɒmpen'seɪʃən] *n* Entschädigung *f*;
(*money*) Schadenersatz *m*; (*Jur*) Abfindung *f*
compete [kəm'pi:t] *vi* konkurrieren (*for*
um); (*Sport*) kämpfen (*for* um); (*take part*)
teilnehmen (*in* an +*dat*)
competence ['kɒmpɪtəns] *n* Fähigkeit *f*;
(*Jur*) Zuständigkeit *f*; **competent** *adj*
fähig; (*Jur*) zuständig
competition [kɒmpɪ'tɪʃən] *n* (*contest*)
Wettbewerb *m*; (*Comm*) Konkurrenz *f* (*for*
um); **competitive** [kəm'petɪtɪv] *adj* (*firm,*

price, product) konkurrenzfähig;
competitor [kəm'petɪtə*] n (Comm)
Konkurrent(in) m(f); (Sport) Teilnehmer(in)
m(f)
complain [kəm'pleɪn] vi klagen; (formally)
sich beschweren (about über +akk);
complaint n Klage f; (formal) Beschwerde
f; (Med) Leiden nt
complement vt ergänzen
complete [kəm'pliːt] adj vollständig;
(finished) fertig; (failure, disaster) total;
(happiness) vollkommen; **are we ~?** sind
wir vollzählig? ▷ vt vervollständigen;
(finish) beenden; (form) ausfüllen;
completely adv völlig; **not ~ ...** nicht
ganz ...
complex ['kɒmpleks] adj komplex; (task,
theory etc) kompliziert ▷ n Komplex m
complexion [kəm'plekʃən] n
Gesichtsfarbe f, Teint m
complicated ['kɒmplɪkeɪtɪd] adj
kompliziert; **complication**
['kɒmplɪkeɪʃən] n Komplikation f
compliment ['kɒmplɪmənt] n
Kompliment nt; **complimentary**
[kɒmplɪ'mentərɪ] adj lobend; (free of
charge) Gratis-; **~ ticket** Freikarte f
comply [kəm'plaɪ] vi **to ~ with the
regulations** den Vorschriften
entsprechen
component [kəm'pəʊnənt] n
Bestandteil m
compose [kəm'pəʊz] vt (music)
komponieren; **to ~ oneself** sich
zusammennehmen; **composed** adj
gefasst; **to be ~ of** bestehen aus;
composer n Komponist(in) m(f);
composition [kɒmpə'zɪʃən] n (of a group)
Zusammensetzung f; (Mus) Komposition f
comprehend [kɒmprɪ'hend] vt
verstehen; **comprehension**
[kɒmprɪ'henʃən] n Verständnis nt
comprehensive [kɒmprɪ'hensɪv] adj
umfassend; **~ school** Gesamtschule f
compress [kəm'pres] vt komprimieren
comprise [kəm'praɪz] vt umfassen,
bestehen aus
compromise ['kɒmprəmaɪz] n
Kompromiss m ▷ vi einen Kompromiss
schließen
compulsory [kəm'pʌlsərɪ] adj
obligatorisch; **~ subject** Pflichtfach nt
computer [kəm'pjuːtə*] n Computer m;

computer aided adj computergestützt;
computer-controlled adj
rechnergesteuert; **computer game** n
Computerspiel nt; **computer-literate** adj
to be ~ mit dem Computer umgehen
können; **computer scientist** n
Informatiker(in) m(f); **computing** n
(subject) Informatik f
con [kɒn] (fam) n Schwindel m ▷ vt
betrügen (out of um)
conceal [kən'siːl] vt verbergen (from vor
+dat)
conceivable [kən'siːvəbl] adj denkbar,
vorstellbar; **conceive** [kən'siːv] vt
(imagine) sich vorstellen; (child)
empfangen
concentrate ['kɒnsəntreɪt] vi sich
konzentrieren (on auf +akk);
concentration [kɒnsən'treɪʃən] n
Konzentration f
concept ['kɒnsept] n Begriff m
concern [kən'sɜːn] n (affair)
Angelegenheit f; (worry) Sorge f;
(Comm: firm) Unternehmen nt; **it's not my
~** das geht mich nichts an; **there's
no cause for ~** kein Grund zur
Beunruhigung ▷ vt (affect) angehen;
(have connection with) betreffen; (be
about) handeln von; **those ~ed** die
Betroffenen; **as far as I'm ~ed** was
mich betrifft; **concerned** adj (anxious)
besorgt; **concerning** prep bezüglich,
hinsichtlich +gen
concert ['kɒnsət] n Konzert nt; **~ hall**
Konzertsaal m
concession [kən'seʃən] n Zugeständnis
nt; (reduction) Ermäßigung f
concise [kən'saɪs] adj knapp gefasst,
prägnant
conclude [kən'kluːd] vt (end) beenden,
(ab)schließen; (infer) folgern (from aus); **to
~ that ...** zu dem Schluss kommen, dass
...; **conclusion** [kən'kluːʒən] n Schluss m,
Schlussfolgerung f
concrete ['kɒnkriːt] n Beton m ▷ adj
konkret
concussion [kən'kʌʃən] n
Gehirnerschütterung f
condemn [kən'dem] vt verdammen; (esp
Jur) verurteilen
condensed milk n Kondensmilch f,
Dosenmilch f
condition [kən'dɪʃən] n (state) Zustand m;

(requirement) Bedingung f; **on ~ that ...** unter der Bedingung, dass ...; **~s** pl *(circumstances, weather)* Verhältnisse pl; **conditional** adj bedingt; *(Ling)* Konditional-; **conditioner** n Weichspüler m; *(for hair)* Pflegespülung f

condo ['kɒndəʊ] *(pl -s)* n see **condominium**

condolences [kən'dəʊlənsɪz] npl Beileid nt

condom ['kɒndəm] n Kondom nt

condominium [kɒndə'mɪniəm] n *(US: apartment)* Eigentumswohnung f

conduct ['kɒndʌkt] n *(behaviour)* Verhalten nt ▷ [kən'dʌkt] vt führen, leiten; *(orchestra)* dirigieren; **conductor** [kən'dʌktə*] n *(of orchestra)* Dirigent(in) m(f); *(in bus)* Schaffner(in) m(f); *(US: on train)* Zugführer(in) m(f)

cone [kəʊn] n Kegel m; *(for ice cream)* Waffeltüte f; *(fir cone)* (Tannen)zapfen m

conference ['kɒnfərəns] n Konferenz f

confess [kən'fes] vt, vi **to ~ that ...** gestehen, dass ...; **confession** [kən'feʃən] n Geständnis nt; *(Rel)* Beichte f

confetti [kən'fetɪ] n Konfetti nt

confidence ['kɒnfɪdəns] n Vertrauen nt *(in zu)*; *(assurance)* Selbstvertrauen nt; **confident** adj *(sure)* zuversichtlich *(that ... dass ...)*, überzeugt *(of von)*; *(self-assured)* selbstsicher; **confidential** [kɒnfɪ'denʃəl] adj vertraulich

confine [kən'faɪn] vt beschränken *(to auf +akk)*

confirm [kən'fɜːm] vt bestätigen; **confirmation** [kɒnfə'meɪʃən] n Bestätigung f; *(Rel)* Konfirmation f; **confirmed** adj überzeugt; *(bachelor)* eingefleischt

confiscate ['kɒnfɪskeɪt] vt beschlagnahmen, konfiszieren

conflict ['kɒnflɪkt] n Konflikt m

confuse [kən'fjuːz] vt verwirren; *(sth with sth)* verwechseln *(with mit)*; *(several things)* durcheinanderbringen; **confused** adj *(person)* konfus, verwirrt; *(account)* verworren; **confusing** adj verwirrend; **confusion** [kən'fjuːʒən] n Verwirrung f; *(of two things)* Verwechslung f; *(muddle)* Chaos nt

congested [kən'dʒestɪd] adj verstopft; *(overcrowded)* überfüllt; **congestion** [kən'dʒestʃən] n Stau m

congratulate [kən'grætjʊleɪt] vt gratulieren *(on zu)*; **congratulations** [kəngrætjʊ'leɪʃənz] npl Glückwünsche pl; **~!** gratuliere!, herzlichen Glückwunsch!

congregation [kɒŋgrɪ'geɪʃən] n *(Rel)* Gemeinde f

congress ['kɒŋgres] n Kongress m; *(US)* **Congress** der Kongress; **congressman** *(pl -men)*, **congresswoman** *(pl -women)* n *(US)* Mitglied nt des Repräsentantenhauses

conifer ['kɒnɪfə*] n Nadelbaum m

conjunction [kən'dʒʌŋkʃən] n *(Ling)* Konjunktion f; **in ~ with** in Verbindung mit

conk out [kɒŋk 'aʊt] vi *(fam: appliance, car)* den Geist aufgeben, streiken; *(person: die)* ins Gras beißen

connect [kə'nekt] vt verbinden *(with, to mit)*; *(Elec, Tech: appliance etc)* anschließen *(to an +akk)* ▷ vi *(train, plane)* Anschluss haben *(with an +akk)*; **~ing flight** Anschlussflug m; **~ing train** Anschlusszug m; **connection** [kə'nekʃən] n Verbindung f; *(link)* Zusammenhang m; *(for train, plane, electrical appliance)* Anschluss m *(with, to an +akk)*; *(business etc)* Beziehung f; **in ~ with** in Zusammenhang mit; **bad ~** *(Tel)* schlechte Verbindung; *(Elec)* Wackelkontakt m; **connector** n *(Inform: computer)* Stecker m

conscience ['kɒnʃəns] n Gewissen nt; **conscientious** [kɒnʃɪ'enʃəs] adj gewissenhaft

conscious ['kɒnʃəs] adj *(act)* bewusst; *(Med)* bei Bewusstsein; **to be ~** bei Bewusstsein sein; **consciousness** n Bewusstsein nt

consecutive [kən'sekjʊtɪv] adj aufeinander folgend

consent [kən'sent] n Zustimmung f ▷ vi zustimmen *(to dat)*

consequence ['kɒnsɪkwəns] n Folge f, Konsequenz f; **consequently** ['kɒnsɪkwəntlɪ] adv folglich

conservation [kɒnsə'veɪʃən] n Erhaltung f; *(of buildings)* Denkmalschutz m; *(nature conservation)* Naturschutz m; **conservation area** n Naturschutzgebiet nt; *(in town)* unter Denkmalschutz stehendes Gebiet

Conservative [kən'sɜːvətɪv] adj *(Pol)* konservativ

conservatory [kən'sɜːvətrɪ] n
(greenhouse) Gewächshaus nt; (room)
Wintergarten m

consider [kən'sɪdə*] vt (reflect on)
nachdenken über, sich überlegen; (take
into account) in Betracht ziehen; (regard)
halten für; **he is ~ed (to be)** ... er gilt als
...; **considerable** [kən'sɪdərəbl] adj
beträchtlich; **considerate** [kən'sɪdərɪt]
adj aufmerksam, rücksichtsvoll;
consideration [kənsɪdə'reɪʃən] n
(thoughtfulness) Rücksicht f; (thought)
Überlegung f; **to take sth into** ~ etw in
Betracht ziehen; **considering**
[kən'sɪdərɪŋ] prep in Anbetracht +gen
▷ conj da

consist [kən'sɪst] vi **to ~ of ...** bestehen
aus ...

consistent [kən'sɪstənt] adj (behaviour,
process etc) konsequent; (statements)
übereinstimmend; (argument) folgerichtig;
(performance, results) beständig

consolation [kɒnsə'leɪʃən] n Trost m;
console [kən'səʊl] vt trösten

consolidate [kən'sɒlɪdeɪt] vt festigen

consonant [ˈkɒnsənənt] n Konsonant m

conspicuous [kən'spɪkjʊəs] adj auffällig,
auffallend

conspiracy [kən'spɪrəsɪ] n Komplott nt;
conspire [kən'spaɪə*] vi sich
verschwören (against gegen)

constable [ˈkʌnstəbl] n (Brit) Polizist(in)
m(f)

Constance [ˈkɒnstəns] n Konstanz nt;
Lake ~ der Bodensee

constant [ˈkɒnstənt] adj (continual)
ständig, dauernd; (unchanging: temperature
etc) gleich bleibend; **constantly** adv
dauernd

consternation [kɒnstə'neɪʃən] n
(dismay) Bestürzung f

constituency [kən'stɪtjʊənsɪ] n
Wahlkreis m

constitution [kɒnstɪ'tjuːʃən] n
Verfassung f; (of person) Konstitution f

construct [kən'strʌkt] vt bauen;
construction [kən'strʌkʃən] n (process,
result) Bau m; (method) Bauweise f; **under**
~ im Bau befindlich; **construction site** n
Baustelle f; **construction worker** n
Bauarbeiter(in) m(f)

consulate [ˈkɒnsjʊlət] n Konsulat nt

consult [kən'sʌlt] vt um Rat fragen;

(doctor) konsultieren; (book) nachschlagen
in +dat; **consultant** n (Med) Facharzt m,
Fachärztin f; **consultation** [kɒnsəl'teɪʃən]
n Beratung f; (Med) Konsultation f

consume [kən'sjuːm] vt verbrauchen;
(food) konsumieren; **consumer** n
Verbraucher(in) m(f); **consumer-friendly**
adj verbraucherfreundlich

contact [ˈkɒntækt] n (touch) Berührung f;
(communication) Kontakt m; (person)
Kontaktperson f; **to be/keep in ~** (with
sb) (mit jdm) in Kontakt sein/bleiben ▷ vt
sich in Verbindung setzen mit; **contact
lenses** npl Kontaktlinsen pl

contagious [kən'teɪdʒəs] adj ansteckend

contain [kən'teɪn] vt enthalten;
container n Behälter m; (for transport)
Container m

contaminate [kən'tæmɪneɪt] vt
verunreinigen; (chemically) verseuchen; **~d
by radiation** strahlenverseucht,
verstrahlt; **contamination**
[kəntæmɪ'neɪʃən] n Verunreinigung f; (by
radiation) Verseuchung f

contemporary [kən'tempərərɪ] adj
zeitgenössisch

contempt [kən'tempt] n Verachtung f;
contemptuous adj verächtlich; **to be
~** voller Verachtung sein (of für)

content [kən'tent] adj zufrieden

content(s) [ˈkɒntent(s)] n pl Inhalt m

contest [ˈkɒntest] n (Wett)kampf m (for
um); (competition) Wettbewerb m
▷ [kən'test] vt kämpfen um +akk; (dispute)
bestreiten; **contestant** [kən'testənt] n
Teilnehmer(in) m(f)

context [ˈkɒntekst] n Zusammenhang m;
out of ~ aus dem Zusammenhang
gerissen

continent [ˈkɒntɪnənt] n Kontinent m,
Festland nt; **the Continent** (Brit) das
europäische Festland, der Kontinent;
continental [kɒntɪ'nentl] adj
kontinental; **~ breakfast** kleines
Frühstück mit Brötchen und Marmelade, Kaffee
oder Tee

continual [kən'tɪnjʊəl] adj (endless)
ununterbrochen; (constant) dauernd,
ständig; **continually** adv dauernd; (again
and again) immer wieder; **continuation**
[kəntɪnjʊ'eɪʃən] n Fortsetzung f;
continue [kən'tɪnjuː] vi weitermachen
(with mit); (esp talking) fortfahren (with

mit); (*travelling*) weiterfahren; (*state, conditions*) fortdauern, anhalten ▷ *vt* fortsetzen; **to be ~d** Fortsetzung folgt; **continuous** [kən'tɪnjuəs] *adj* (*endless*) ununterbrochen; (*constant*) ständig

contraceptive [kɒntrə'septɪv] *n* Verhütungsmittel *nt*

contract ['kɒntrækt] *n* Vertrag *m*

contradict [kɒntrə'dɪkt] *vt* widersprechen +*dat*; **contradiction** [kɒntrə'dɪkʃən] *n* Widerspruch *m*

contrary ['kɒntrərɪ] *n* Gegenteil *nt*; **on the ~** im Gegenteil ▷ *adj* **~ to** entgegen +*dat*

contrast ['kɒntrɑːst] *n* Kontrast *m*, Gegensatz *m*; **in ~ to** im Gegensatz zu ▷ [kən'trɑːst] *vt* entgegensetzen

contribute [kən'trɪbjuːt] *vt*, *vi* beitragen (*to* zu); (*money*) spenden (*to* für); **contribution** [kɒntrɪ'bjuːʃən] *n* Beitrag *m*

control [kən'trəʊl] *vt* (*master*) beherrschen; (*temper etc*) im Griff haben; (*esp Tech*) steuern; **to ~ oneself** sich beherrschen ▷ *n* Kontrolle *f*; (*mastery*) Beherrschung *f*; (*of business*) Leitung *f*; (*esp Tech*) Steuerung *f*; **~s** *pl* (*knobs, switches etc*) Bedienungselemente *pl*; (*collectively*) Steuerung *f*; **to be out of ~** außer Kontrolle sein; **control knob** *n* Bedienungsknopf *m*; **control panel** *n* Schalttafel *f*

controversial [kɒntrə'vɜːʃəl] *adj* umstritten

convalesce [kɒnvə'les] *vi* gesund werden; **convalescence** *n* Genesung *f*

convenience [kən'viːnɪəns] *n* (*quality, thing*) Annehmlichkeit *f*; **at your ~** wann es Ihnen passt; **with all modern ~s** mit allem Komfort; **convenience food** *n* Fertiggericht *nt*; **convenient** *adj* günstig, passend

convent ['kɒnvənt] *n* Kloster *nt*

convention [kən'venʃən] *n* (*custom*) Konvention *f*; (*meeting*) Konferenz *f*; **the Geneva Convention** die Genfer Konvention; **conventional** *adj* herkömmlich, konventionell

conversation [kɒnvə'seɪʃən] *n* Gespräch *nt*, Unterhaltung *f*

conversion [kən'vɜːʃən] *n* Umwandlung *f* (*into* in +*akk*); (*of building*) Umbau *m* (*into* zu); (*calculation*) Umrechnung *f*;

conversion table *n* Umrechnungstabelle *f*; **convert** [kən'vɜːt] *vt* umwandeln; (*person*) bekehren; (*Inform*) konvertieren; **to ~ into Euros** in Euro umrechnen; **convertible** *n* (*Auto*) Kabrio *nt* ▷ *adj* umwandelbar

convey [kən'veɪ] *vt* (*carry*) befördern; (*feelings*) vermitteln; **conveyor belt** *n* Förderband *nt*, Fließband *nt*

convict [kən'vɪkt] *vt* verurteilen (*of* wegen) ▷ ['kɒnvɪkt] *n* Strafgefangene(r) *mf*; **conviction** *n* (*Jur*) Verurteilung *f*; (*strong belief*) Überzeugung *f*

convince [kən'vɪns] *vt* überzeugen (*of* von); **convincing** *adj* überzeugend

cook [kʊk] *vt*, *vi* kochen ▷ *n* Koch *m*, Köchin *f*; **cookbook** *n* Kochbuch *nt*; **cooker** *n* Herd *m*; **cookery** *n* Kochkunst *f*; **~ book** Kochbuch *nt*; **cookie** *n* (*US*) Keks *m*; **cooking** *n* Kochen *nt*; (*style of cooking*) Küche *f*

cool [kuːl] *adj* kühl, gelassen; (*fam: brilliant*) cool, stark ▷ *vt*, *vi* (ab)kühlen; **~ it** reg dich ab! ▷ *n* **to keep/lose one's ~** (*fam*) ruhig bleiben/durchdrehen; **cool down** *vi* abkühlen; (*calm down*) sich beruhigen

cooperate [kəʊ'ɒpəreɪt] *vi* zusammenarbeiten, kooperieren; **cooperation** [kəʊɒpə'reɪʃən] *n* Zusammenarbeit *f*, Kooperation *f*; **cooperative** [kəʊ'ɒpərətɪv] *adj* hilfsbereit ▷ *n* Genossenschaft *f*

coordinate [kəʊ'ɔːdɪneɪt] *vt* koordinieren

cop [kɒp] *n* (*fam: policeman*) Bulle *m*

cope [kəʊp] *vi* zurechtkommen, fertig werden (*with* mit)

Copenhagen [kəʊpən'heɪgən] *n* Kopenhagen *nt*

copier ['kɒpɪə*] *n* Kopierer *m*

copper ['kɒpə*] *n* Kupfer *nt*; (*Brit fam: policeman*) Bulle *m*; (*fam: coin*) Kupfermünze *f*; **~s** Kleingeld *nt*

copy ['kɒpɪ] *n* Kopie *f*; (*of book*) Exemplar *nt* ▷ *vt* kopieren; (*imitate*) nachahmen; **copyright** *n* Urheberrecht *nt*

coral ['kɒrəl] *n* Koralle *f*

cord [kɔːd] *n* Schnur *f*; (*material*) Kordsamt *m*

cordial ['kɔːdɪəl] *adj* freundlich

cordless ['kɔːdlɪs] *adj* (*phone*) schnurlos

core [kɔː*] *n* (*a. fig*) Kern *m*; (*of apple, pear*)

Kerngehäuse *nt*; **core business** *n*
Kerngeschäft *nt*
cork [kɔːk] *n* (*material*) Kork *m*; (*stopper*)
Korken *m*; **corkscrew** ['kɔːkskruː] *n*
Korkenzieher *m*
corn [kɔːn] *n* Getreide *nt*, Korn *nt*; (*US:*
maize) Mais *m*; (*on foot*) Hühnerauge *nt*;
~ on the cob (gekochter) Maiskolben;
corned beef *n* Cornedbeef *nt*
corner ['kɔːnə*] *n* Ecke *f*; (*on road*) Kurve *f*;
(*Sport*) Eckstoß *m* ▷ *vt* in die Enge treiben;
corner shop *n* Laden *m* an der Ecke
cornflakes ['kɔːfleɪks] *npl* Cornflakes *pl*;
cornflour ['kɔːnflaʊə*] (*Brit*), **cornstarch**
['kɔːnstɑːtʃ] (*US*) *n* Maismehl *nt*
Cornish ['kɔːnɪʃ] *adj* kornisch; **~ pasty** *mit*
Fleisch und Kartoffeln gefüllte Pastete;
Cornwall ['kɔːnwəl] *n* Cornwall *nt*
coronary ['kɒrənərɪ] *n* (*Med*) Herzinfarkt
m
coronation [kɒrə'neɪʃən] *n* Krönung *f*
corporation [kɔːpə'reɪʃən] *n* (*US Comm*)
Aktiengesellschaft *f*
corpse [kɔːps] *n* Leiche *f*
correct [kə'rekt] *adj* (*accurate*) richtig;
(*proper*) korrekt ▷ *vt* korrigieren,
verbessern; **correction** *n* (*esp written*)
Korrektur *f*
correspond [kɒrɪ'spɒnd] *vi* entsprechen
(*to dat*); (*two things*) übereinstimmen;
(*exchange letters*) korrespondieren;
corresponding *adj* entsprechend
corridor ['kɒrɪdɔː*] *n* (*in building*) Flur *m*;
(*in train*) Gang *m*
corrupt [kə'rʌpt] *adj* korrupt
cosmetic [kɒz'metɪk] *adj* kosmetisch;
cosmetics *npl* Kosmetika *pl*; **cosmetic**
surgeon *n* Schönheitschirurg(in) *m(f)*;
cosmetic surgery *n* Schönheitschirurgie *f*
cosmopolitan [kɒzmə'pɒlɪtən] *adj*
international; (*attitude*) weltoffen
cost [kɒst] *n* (*cost, cost*) *vt* kosten ▷ *n*
Kosten *pl*; **at all ~s, at any ~** um jeden
Preis; **~ of living** Lebenshaltungskosten
pl; **costly** *adj* kostspielig
costume ['kɒstjuːm] *n* (*Theat*) Kostüm *nt*
cosy ['kəʊzɪ] *adj* gemütlich
cot [kɒt] *n* (*Brit*) Kinderbett *nt*; (*US*)
Campingliege *f*
cottage ['kɒtɪdʒ] *n* kleines Haus; (*country*
cottage) Landhäuschen *nt*; **cottage cheese**
n Hüttenkäse *m*; **cottage pie** *n*
Hackfleisch mit Kartoffelbrei überbacken

cotton ['kɒtn] *n* Baumwolle *f*; **cotton**
candy *n* (*US*) Zuckerwatte *f*; **cotton wool**
n (*Brit*) Watte *f*
couch [kaʊtʃ] *n* Couch *f*; (*sofa*) Sofa *nt*;
couchette [kuː'ʃet] *n* Liegewagen(platz)
m
cough [kɒf] *vi* husten ▷ *n* Husten *m*;
cough mixture *n* Hustensaft *m*; **cough**
sweet *n* Hustenbonbon *nt*
could [kʊd] *pt of* **can** konnte; *conditional*
könnte; **~ you come earlier?** könntest du
früher kommen?
couldn't *contr of* **could not**
council ['kaʊnsl] *n* (*Pol*) Rat *m*; (*local ~*)
Gemeinderat *m*; (*town ~*) Stadtrat *m*;
council estate *n* Siedlung *f* des sozialen
Wohnungsbaus; **council house** *n*
Sozialwohnung *f*; **councillor** ['kaʊnsɪlə*]
n Gemeinderat *m*, Gemeinderätin *f*;
council tax *n* Gemeindesteuer *f*
count [kaʊnt] *vt, vi* zählen; (*include*)
mitrechnen ▷ *n* Zählung *f*; (*noble*) Graf *m*;
count on *vt* (*rely on*) sich verlassen auf
+akk; (*expect*) rechnen mit
counter ['kaʊntə*] *n* (*in shop*) Ladentisch *m*;
(*in café*) Theke *f*; (*in bank, post office*)
Schalter *m*; **counter attack** *n*
Gegenangriff *m* ▷ *vi* zurückschlagen;
counter-clockwise *adv* (*US*) entgegen
dem Uhrzeigersinn
counterfoil ['kaʊntəfɔɪl] *n*
(Kontroll)abschnitt *m*
counterpart ['kaʊntəpɑːt] *n* Gegenstück
nt (*of zu*)
countess *n* Gräfin *f*
countless ['kaʊntlɪs] *adj* zahllos,
unzählig
country ['kʌntrɪ] *n* Land *nt*; **in the ~** auf
dem Land(e); **in this ~** hierzulande;
country cousin *n* (*fam*) Landei *nt*;
country dancing *n* Volkstanz *m*;
country house *n* Landhaus *nt*;
countryman *n* (*compatriot*) Landsmann
m; **country music** *n* Countrymusic *f*;
country road *n* Landstraße *f*;
countryside *n* Landschaft *f*; (*rural area*)
Land *nt*
county ['kaʊntɪ] *n* (*Brit*) Grafschaft *f*; (*US*)
Verwaltungsbezirk *m*; **county town** *n*
(*Brit*) ≈ Kreisstadt *f*
couple ['kʌpl] *n* Paar *nt*; **a ~ of** ein paar
coupon ['kuːpɒn] *n* (*voucher*) Gutschein
m

courage ['kʌrɪdʒ] n Mut m; **courageous** [kə'reɪdʒəs] adj mutig

courgette [kʊə'ʒet] n (Brit) Zucchini f

courier ['kʊrɪə*] n (for tourists) Reiseleiter(in) m(f); (messenger) Kurier m

course [kɔːs] n (of study) Kurs m; (for race) Strecke f; (Naut, Aviat) Kurs m; (at university) Studiengang m; (in meal) Gang m; **of ~** natürlich; **in the ~ of** während

court [kɔːt] n (Sport) Platz m; (Jur) Gericht nt

courteous ['kɜːtɪəs] adj höflich; **courtesy** ['kɜːtəsɪ] n Höflichkeit f; **~ bus/coach** (gebührenfreier) Zubringerbus

courthouse ['kɔːthaʊs] n (US) Gerichtsgebäude nt; **court order** n Gerichtsbeschluss m; **courtroom** n Gerichtssaal m

courtyard ['kɔːtjɑːd] n Hof m

cousin ['kʌzn] n (male) Cousin m; (female) Cousine f

cover ['kʌvə*] vt bedecken (in, with mit); (distance) zurücklegen; (loan, costs) decken ▷ n (for bed etc) Decke f; (of cushion) Bezug m; (lid) Deckel m; (of book) Umschlag m; (**insurance**) **~** Versicherungsschutz m; **cover up** vt zudecken; (error etc) vertuschen; **coverage** n Berichterstattung f (of über +akk); **cover charge** n Kosten pl für ein Gedeck; **covering** n Decke f; **covering letter** n Begleitbrief m; **cover story** n (newspaper) Titelgeschichte f

cow [kaʊ] n Kuh f

coward ['kaʊəd] n Feigling m; **cowardly** adj feig(e)

cowboy ['kaʊbɔɪ] n Cowboy m

coy [kɔɪ] adj gespielt schüchtern, kokett

cozy ['kəʊzɪ] adj (US) gemütlich

CPU abbr = **central processing unit** Zentraleinheit f

crab [kræb] n Krabbe f

crabby ['kræbɪ] adj mürrisch, reizbar

crack [kræk] n Riss m; (in pottery, glass) Sprung m; (drug) Crack nt; **to have a ~ at sth** etw ausprobieren ▷ vi (pottery, glass) einen Sprung bekommen; (wood, ice etc) einen Riss bekommen; **to get ~ing** (fam) loslegen ▷ vt (bone) anbrechen; (nut, code) knacken

cracker ['krækə*] n (biscuit) Kräcker m;

(Christmas ~) Knallbonbon nt; **crackers** adj (fam) verrückt, bekloppt; **he's ~** er hat nicht alle Tassen im Schrank

crackle ['krækl] vi knistern; (telephone, radio) knacken; **crackling** n (Gastr) Kruste f (des Schweinebratens)

cradle ['kreɪdl] n Wiege f

craft [krɑːft] n Handwerk nt; (art) Kunsthandwerk nt; (Naut) Boot nt; **craftsman** (pl **-men**) n Handwerker m; **craftsmanship** n Handwerkskunst f; (ability) handwerkliches Können

crafty ['krɑːftɪ] adj schlau

cram [kræm] vt stopfen (into in +akk); **to be ~med with ...** mit ... voll gestopft sein ▷ vi (revise for exam) pauken (for für)

cramp [kræmp] n Krampf m

cranberry ['krænbərɪ] n Preiselbeere f

crane [kreɪn] n (machine) Kran m; (bird) Kranich m

crash [kræʃ] vi einen Unfall haben; (two vehicles) zusammenstoßen; (plane, computer) abstürzen; (economy) zusammenbrechen; **to ~ into sth** gegen etw knallen ▷ vt einen Unfall haben mit ▷ n (car) Unfall m; (train) Unglück nt; (collision) Zusammenstoß m; (Aviat, Inform) Absturz m; (noise) Krachen nt; **crash barrier** n Leitplanke f; **crash course** n Intensivkurs m; **crash helmet** n Sturzhelm m; **crash landing** n Bruchlandung f

crate [kreɪt] n Kiste f; (of beer) Kasten m

crater ['kreɪtə*] n Krater m

craving ['kreɪvɪŋ] n starkes Verlangen, Bedürfnis nt

crawl [krɔːl] vi kriechen; (baby) krabbeln ▷ n (swimming) Kraul nt; **crawler lane** n Kriechspur f

crayfish ['kreɪfɪʃ] n Languste f

crayon ['kreɪən] n Buntstift m

crazy ['kreɪzɪ] adj verrückt (about nach)

cream [kriːm] n (from milk) Sahne f, Rahm m; (polish, cosmetic) Creme f ▷ adj cremefarben; **cream cake** n (small) Sahnetörtchen nt; (big) Sahnetorte f; **cream cheese** n Frischkäse m; **creamer** n Kaffeeweißer m; **cream tea** n (Brit) Nachmittagstee mit Törtchen, Marmelade und Schlagsahne; **creamy** adj sahnig

crease [kriːs] n Falte f ▷ vt falten; (untidy) zerknittern

create [kri'eit] vt schaffen; (cause) verursachen; **creative** [kri:'eitiv] adj schöpferisch; (person) kreativ; **creature** ['kri:tʃə*] n Geschöpf nt

crèche [kreiʃ] n Kinderkrippe f

credible ['kredibl] adj (person) glaubwürdig; **credibility** n Glaubwürdigkeit f

credit ['kredit] n (Fin: amount allowed) Kredit m; (amount possessed) Guthaben nt; (recognition) Anerkennung f; **~s** (of film) Abspann m; **credit card** n Kreditkarte f

creep [kri:p] (crept, crept) vi kriechen; **creeps** n **he gives me the ~** er ist mir nicht ganz geheuer; **creepy** ['kri:pi] adj (frightening) gruselig, unheimlich

crept [krept] pt, pp of **creep**

cress [kres] n Kresse f

crest [krest] n Kamm m; (coat of arms) Wappen nt

crew [kru:] n Besatzung f, Mannschaft f

crib [krib] n (US) Kinderbett nt

cricket ['krikit] n (insect) Grille f; (game) Kricket nt

crime [kraim] n Verbrechen nt; **criminal** ['kriminl] n Verbrecher(in) m(f) ▷ adj kriminell, strafbar

cripple ['kripl] n Krüppel m ▷ vt verkrüppeln, lähmen

crisis ['kraisis] (pl crises) n Krise f

crisp [krisp] adj knusprig; **crisps** npl (Brit) Chips pl; **crispbread** n Knäckebrot nt

criterion [krai'tiəriən] n Kriterium nt; **critic** ['kritik] n Kritiker(in) m(f); **critical** adj kritisch; **critically** adv kritisch; **~ ill/injured** schwer krank/verletzt; **criticism** ['kritisizəm] n Kritik f; **criticize** ['kritisaiz] vt kritisieren

Croat ['krəuæt] n Kroate m, Kroatin f; **Croatia** [krəu'eiʃə] n Kroatien nt; **Croatian** [krəu'eiʃən] adj kroatisch

crockery ['krokəri] n Geschirr nt

crocodile ['krokədail] n Krokodil nt

crocus ['krəukəs] n Krokus m

crop [krop] n (harvest) Ernte f; **crops** npl Getreide nt; **crop up** vi auftauchen

croquette [krə'ket] n Krokette f

cross [kros] n Kreuz nt; **to mark sth with a ~** etw ankreuzen ▷ vt (road, river etc) überqueren; (legs) übereinander schlagen; **it ~ed my mind** es fiel mir ein; **to ~ one's fingers** die Daumen drücken ▷ adj ärgerlich, böse; **cross out** vt durchstreichen

crossbar n (of bicycle) Stange f; (Sport) Querlatte f; **cross-country** adj **~ running** Geländelauf m; **~ skiing** Langlauf m; **cross-examination** n Kreuzverhör nt; **cross-eyed** adj **to be ~** schielen; **crossing** n (crossroads) (Straßen)kreuzung f; (for pedestrians) Fußgängerüberweg m; (on ship) Überfahrt f; **crossroads** nsing o pl Straßenkreuzung f; **cross section** n Querschnitt m; **crosswalk** n (US) Fußgängerüberweg m; **crossword (puzzle)** n Kreuzworträtsel nt

crouch [krautʃ] vi hocken

crouton ['kru:ton] n Croûton m

crow [krəu] n Krähe f

crowbar [krəuba:*] n Brecheisen nt

crowd [kraud] n Menge f ▷ vi sich drängen (into in +akk; round um); **crowded** adj überfüllt

crown [kraun] n Krone f ▷ vt krönen; (fam) **and to ~ it all ...** und als Krönung ...; **crown jewels** npl Kronjuwelen pl

crucial ['kru:ʃəl] adj entscheidend

crude [kru:d] adj primitiv; (humour, behaviour) derb, ordinär ▷ n **~ (oil)** Rohöl nt

cruel ['kruəl] adj grausam (to zu, gegen); (unfeeling) gefühllos; **cruelty** n Grausamkeit f; **~ to animals** Tierquälerei f

cruise [kru:z] n Kreuzfahrt f ▷ vi (ship) kreuzen; (car) mit Reisegeschwindigkeit fahren; **cruise liner** n Kreuzfahrtschiff nt; **cruise missile** n Marschflugkörper m; **cruising speed** n Reisegeschwindigkeit f

crumb [krʌm] n Krume f

crumble ['krʌmbl] vt, vi zerbröckeln ▷ n mit Streuseln überbackenes Kompott

crumpet ['krʌmpit] n weiches Hefegebäck zum Toasten; (fam: attractive woman) Schnecke f

crumple ['krʌmpl] vt zerknittern; **crumple zone** n (Auto) Knautschzone f

crunchy ['krʌntʃi] adj (Brit) knusprig

crusade [kru:'seid] n Kreuzzug m

crush [krʌʃ] vt zerdrücken; (finger etc) quetschen; (spices, stone) zerstoßen ▷ n **to have a ~ on sb** in jdn verknallt sein; **crushing** adj (defeat, remark) vernichtend

crust [krʌst] n Kruste f; **crusty** adj knusprig

crutch [krʌtʃ] n Krücke f
cry [kraɪ] vi (call) rufen; (scream) schreien; (weep) weinen ▷ n (call) Ruf m; (louder) Schrei m
crypt [krɪpt] n Krypta f
crystal ['krɪstl] n Kristall m
cu abbr = **see you** (SMS, E-Mail) bis bald
cub [kʌb] n (animal) Junge(s) nt
Cuba ['kjuːbə] n Kuba nt
cube [kjuːb] n Würfel m
cubic ['kjuːbɪk] adj Kubik-
cubicle ['kjuːbɪkl] n Kabine f
cuckoo ['kʊkuː] n Kuckuck m
cucumber ['kjuːkʌmbə*] n Salatgurke f
cuddle ['kʌdl] vt in den Arm nehmen; (amorously) schmusen mit ▷ n Liebkosung f, Umarmung f; **to have a ~** schmusen; **cuddly** adj verschmust; **cuddly toy** n Plüschtier nt
cuff [kʌf] n Manschette f; (US: trouser ~) Aufschlag m; **off the ~** aus dem Stegreif; **cufflink** n Manschettenknopf m
cuisine [kwɪ'ziːn] n Kochkunst f, Küche f
cul-de-sac ['kʌldəsæk] n (Brit) Sackgasse f
culprit ['kʌlprɪt] n Schuldige(r) mf; (fig) Übeltäter(in) m(f)
cult [kʌlt] n Kult m
cultivate ['kʌltɪveɪt] vt (Agr: land) bebauen; (crop) anbauen; **cultivated** adj (person) kultiviert, gebildet
cultural ['kʌltʃərəl] adj kulturell, Kultur-; **culture** ['kʌltʃə*] n Kultur f; **cultured** adj gebildet, kultiviert; **culture vulture** (Brit fam) n Kulturfanatiker(in) m(f)
cumbersome ['kʌmbəsəm] adj (object) unhandlich
cumin ['kʌmɪn] n Kreuzkümmel m
cunning ['kʌnɪŋ] adj schlau; (person a.) gerissen
cup [kʌp] n Tasse f; (prize) Pokal m; **it's not his ~ of tea** das ist nicht sein Fall; **cupboard** ['kʌbəd] n Schrank m; **cup final** n Pokalendspiel nt; **cup tie** n Pokalspiel nt
cupola ['kjuːpələ] n Kuppel f
curable ['kjʊrəbəl] adj heilbar
curb [kɜːb] n (US) see **kerb**
curd [kɜːd] n **~ cheese**, **~s** ≈ Quark m
cure [kjʊə*] n Heilmittel nt (for gegen); (process) Heilung f ▷ vt heilen; (Gastr) pökeln; (smoke) räuchern
curious ['kjʊərɪəs] adj neugierig; (strange) seltsam

curl [kɜːl] n Locke f ▷ vi sich kräuseln; **curly** adj lockig
currant ['kʌrənt] n (dried) Korinthe f; (red, black) Johannisbeere f
currency ['kʌrənsɪ] n Währung f; **foreign ~** Devisen pl
current ['kʌrənt] n (in water) Strömung f; (electric ~) Strom m ▷ adj (issue, affairs) aktuell, gegenwärtig; (expression) gängig; **current account** n Girokonto nt; **currently** adv zur Zeit
curriculum [kə'rɪkjʊləm] n Lehrplan m; **curriculum vitae** [kə'rɪkjʊləm'viːtaɪ] n (Brit) Lebenslauf m
curry ['kʌrɪ] n Currygericht nt; **curry powder** n Curry(pulver) nt
curse [kɜːs] vi (swear) fluchen (at auf +akk) ▷ n Fluch m
cursor ['kɜːsə*] n (Inform) Cursor m
curt [kɜːt] adj schroff, kurz angebunden
curtain ['kɜːtn] n Vorhang m; **it was ~s for Benny** für Benny war alles vorbei
curve [kɜːv] n Kurve f ▷ vi einen Bogen machen; **curved** adj gebogen
cushion ['kʊʃn] n Kissen nt
custard ['kʌstəd] n dicke Vanillesoße, die warm oder kalt zu vielen englischen Nachspeisen gegessen wird
custom ['kʌstəm] n Brauch m; (habit) Gewohnheit f; **customary** ['kʌstəmrɪ] adj üblich; **custom-built** adj nach Kundenangaben gefertigt; **customer** ['kʌstəmə*] n Kunde m, Kundin f; **customer loyalty card** n Kundenkarte f; **customer service** n Kundendienst m
customs ['kʌstəmz] npl (organization, location) Zoll m; **to pass through ~** durch den Zoll gehen; **customs officer** n Zollbeamte(r) m, Zollbeamtin f
cut [kʌt] n (cut, cut) vt schneiden; (cake) anschneiden; (wages, benefits) kürzen; (prices) heruntersetzen; **I ~ my finger** ich habe mir in den Finger geschnitten ▷ n Schnitt m; (wound) Schnittwunde f; (reduction) Kürzung f (in gen); **price/tax ~** Preissenkung/Steuersenkung f; **to be a ~ above the rest** eine Klasse besser als die anderen sein; **cut back** vt (workforce etc) reduzieren; **cut down** vt (tree) fällen; **to ~ on sth** etwas einschränken; **cut in** vi (Auto) scharf einscheren; **to ~ on sb** jdn schneiden; **cut off** vt abschneiden; (gas,

electricity) abdrehen, abstellen; *(Tel)* **I was ~** ich wurde unterbrochen

cutback *n* Kürzung *f*

cute [kjuːt] *adj* putzig, niedlich; *(US: shrewd)* clever

cutlery ['kʌtləri] *n* Besteck *nt*

cutlet ['kʌtlɪt] *n* *(pork)* Kotelett *nt*; *(veal)* Schnitzel *nt*

cut-price *adj* verbilligt

cutting ['kʌtɪŋ] *n* *(from paper)* Ausschnitt *m*; *(of plant)* Ableger *m* ▷ *adj* *(comment)* verletzend

CV *abbr* = **curriculum vitae**

cwt *abbr* = **hundredweight** ≈ Zentner, Ztr.

cybercafé [saɪbə'kæfeɪ] *n* Internetcafé *nt*; **cyberspace** *n* Cyberspace *m*

cyclamen ['sɪkləmən] *n* Alpenveilchen *nt*

cycle ['saɪkl] *n* Fahrrad *nt* ▷ *vi* Rad fahren; **cycle lane**, **cycle path** *n* Radweg *m*; **cycling** *n* Radfahren *nt*; **cyclist** ['saɪklɪst] *n* Radfahrer(in) *m(f)*

cylinder ['sɪlɪndə*] *n* Zylinder *m*

cynical ['sɪnɪkəl] *adj* zynisch

cypress ['saɪprɪs] *n* Zypresse *f*

Cypriot ['sɪprɪət] *adj* zypriotisch ▷ *n* Zypriote *m*, Zypriotin *f*; **Cyprus** ['saɪprəs] *n* Zypern *nt*

czar [zɑː*] *n* Zar *m*; **czarina** [zɑˈriːnə] *n* Zarin *f*

Czech [tʃek] *adj* tschechisch ▷ *n* *(person)* Tscheche *m*, Tschechin *f*; *(language)* Tschechisch *nt*; **Czech Republic** *n* Tschechische Republik, Tschechien *nt*

dab [dæb] *vt* (*wound, nose etc*) betupfen (*with* mit)

dachshund ['dækshʊnd] *n* Dackel *m*

dad(dy) ['dæd(ɪ)] *n* Papa *m*, Vati *m*; **daddy-longlegs** *nsing* (*Brit*) Schnake; (*US*) Weberknecht *m*

daffodil ['dæfədɪl] *n* Osterglocke *f*

daft [dɑ:ft] *adj* (*fam*) blöd, doof

dahlia ['deɪlɪə] *n* Dahlie *f*

daily ['deɪlɪ] *adj, adv* täglich ▷ *n* (*paper*) Tageszeitung *f*

dairy ['dɛərɪ] *n* (*on farm*) Molkerei *f*; **dairy products** *npl* Milchprodukte *pl*

daisy ['deɪzɪ] *n* Gänseblümchen *nt*

dam [dæm] *n* Staudamm *m* ▷ *vt* stauen

damage ['dæmɪdʒ] *n* Schaden *m*; **~s** *pl* (*Jur*) Schadenersatz *m* ▷ *vt* beschädigen; (*reputation, health*) schädigen, schaden +*dat*

damn [dæm] *adj* (*fam*) verdammt ▷ *vt* (*condemn*) verurteilen; **~ (it)!** verflucht! ▷ *n* **he doesn't give a ~** es ist ihm völlig egal

damp [dæmp] *adj* feucht ▷ *n* Feuchtigkeit *f*; **dampen** ['dæmpən] *vt* befeuchten

dance [dɑ:ns] *n* Tanz *m*; (*event*) Tanzveranstaltung *f* ▷ *vi* tanzen; **dance floor** *n* Tanzfläche *f*; **dancer** *n* Tänzer(in) *m(f)*; **dancing** *n* Tanzen *nt*

dandelion ['dændɪlaɪən] *n* Löwenzahn *m*

dandruff ['dændrəf] *n* Schuppen *pl*

Dane [deɪn] *n* Däne *m*, Dänin *f*

danger ['deɪndʒə*] *n* Gefahr *f*; **~ (sign)** Achtung!; **to be in ~** in Gefahr sein; **dangerous** *adj* gefährlich

Danish ['deɪnɪʃ] *adj* dänisch ▷ *n* (*language*) Dänisch *nt*; **the ~** *pl* die Dänen; **Danish pastry** *n* Plundergebäck *nt*

Danube ['dænju:b] *n* Donau *f*

dare [dɛə*] *vi* **to ~ (to) do sth** es wagen, etw zu tun; **I didn't ~ ask** ich traute mich nicht, zu fragen; **how ~ you** was fällt dir ein! ; **daring** *adj* (*person*) mutig; (*film, clothes etc*) gewagt

dark [dɑ:k] *adj* dunkel; (*gloomy*) düster, trübe; (*sinister*) finster; **~ chocolate** Bitterschokolade *f*; **~ green/blue** dunkelgrün/dunkelblau ▷ *n* Dunkelheit *f*; **in the ~** im Dunkeln; **dark glasses** *npl* Sonnenbrille *f*; **darkness** *n* Dunkelheit *nt*

darling ['dɑ:lɪŋ] *n* Schatz *m*; (*also favourite*) Liebling *m*

dart [dɑ:t] *n* Wurfpfeil *m*; **darts** *nsing* (*game*) Darts *nt*

dash [dæʃ] *vi* stürzen, rennen ▷ *vt* **to ~ hopes** Hoffnungen zerstören ▷ *n* (*in text*) Gedankenstrich *m*; (*of liquid*) Schuss *m*; **dashboard** *n* Armaturenbrett *nt*

data ['deɪtə] *npl* Daten *pl*; **data bank, data base** *n* Datenbank *f*; **data capture** *n* Datenerfassung *f*; **data processing** *n* Datenverarbeitung *f*; **data protection** *n* Datenschutz *m*

date [deɪt] *n* Datum *nt*; (*for meeting, delivery etc*) Termin *m*; (*with person*) Verabredung *f*; (*with girlfriend etc*) Date *nt*; (*fruit*) Dattel *f*; **what's the ~ (today)?** der Wievielte ist heute?; **out of ~** *adj* veraltet; **up to ~** *adj* (*news*) aktuell; (*fashion*) zeitgemäß ▷ *vt* (*letter etc*) datieren; (*person*) gehen mit; **dated** *adj* altmodisch; **date of birth** *n* Geburtsdatum *nt*; **dating agency** *n* Partnervermittlung *f*

dative ['deɪtɪv] *n* Dativ *m*

daughter ['dɔ:tə*] *n* Tochter *f*; **daughter-in-law** (*pl* **daughters-in-law**) Schwiegertochter *f*

dawn [dɔ:n] *n* Morgendämmerung *f* ▷ *vi*

dämmern; **it ~ed on me** mir ging ein Licht auf

day [deɪ] n Tag m; **one ~** eines Tages; **by ~** bei Tage; **~ after ~, ~ by ~** Tag für Tag; **the ~ after/before** am Tag danach/zuvor; **the ~ before yesterday** vorgestern; **the ~ after tomorrow** übermorgen; **these ~s** heutzutage; **in those ~s** damals; **let's call it a ~** Schluss für heute!; **daybreak** n Tagesanbruch m; **daydream** n Tagtraum m ▷ vi (mit offenen Augen) träumen; **daylight** n Tageslicht nt; **in ~** bei Tage; **daylight saving time** n Sommerzeit f; **day nursery** n Kindertagesstätte f; **day return** n (Brit Rail) Tagesrückfahrkarte f; **daytime** n **in the ~** bei Tage, tagsüber; **daytrip** n Tagesausflug m

dazed [deɪzd] adj benommen

dazzle ['dæzl] vt blenden; **dazzling** adj blendend, glänzend

dead [dɛd] adj tot; (limb) abgestorben ▷ adv genau; (fam) total, völlig; **~ tired** adj todmüde; **~ slow** (sign) Schritt fahren; **dead end** n Sackgasse f; **deadline** n Termin m; (period) Frist f; **~ for applications** Anmeldeschluss m; **deadly** adj tödlich ▷ adv **~ dull** todlangweilig

deaf [dɛf] adj taub; **deafen** vt taub machen; **deafening** adj ohrenbetäubend

deal [di:l] (**dealt, dealt**) vt, vi (cards) geben, austeilen ▷ n (business ~) Geschäft nt; (agreement) Abmachung f; **it's a ~** abgemacht!; **a good/great ~ of** ziemlich/sehr viel; **deal in** vt handeln mit; **deal with** vt (matter) sich beschäftigen mit; (book, film) behandeln; (successfully: person, problem) fertig werden mit; (matter) erledigen; **dealer** n (Comm) Händler(in) m(f); (drugs) Dealer(in) m(f); **dealings** npl (Comm) Geschäfte pl

dealt [dɛlt] pt, pp of **deal**

dear [dɪə*] adj lieb, teuer; **Dear Sir or Madam** Sehr geehrte Damen und Herren; **Dear David** Lieber David ▷ n Schatz m; (as address) mein Schatz, Liebling; **dearly** adv (love) (heiß und) innig; (pay) teuer

death [dɛθ] n Tod m; (of project, hopes) Ende nt; **~s** pl Todesfälle; (in accident) Todesopfer; **death certificate** n Totenschein m; **death penalty** n Todesstrafe f; **death toll** n Zahl f der Todesopfer; **death trap** n Todesfalle f

debatable [dɪ'beɪtəbl] adj fraglich; (question) strittig; **debate** [dɪ'beɪt] n Debatte f ▷ vt debattieren

debauched [dɪ'bɔ:tʃt] adj ausschweifend

debit ['dɛbɪt] n Soll nt ▷ vt (account) belasten; **debit card** n Geldkarte f

debris ['dɛbri:] n Trümmer pl

debt [dɛt] n Schuld f; **to be in ~** verschuldet sein

decade ['dɛkeɪd] n Jahrzehnt nt

decadent ['dɛkədənt] adj dekadent

decaff ['di:kæf] n (fam) koffeinfreier Kaffee; **decaffeinated** [di:'kæfɪneɪtɪd] adj koffeinfrei

decanter [dɪ'kæntə*] n Dekanter m, Karaffe f

decay [dɪ'keɪ] n Verfall m; (rotting) Verwesung f; (of tooth) Fäule f ▷ vi verfallen; (rot) verwesen; (wood) vermodern; (teeth) faulen; (leaves) verrotten

deceased [dɪ'si:st] n **the ~** der/die Verstorbene

deceit [dɪ'si:t] n Betrug m; **deceive** [dɪ'si:v] vt täuschen

December [dɪ'sɛmbə*] n Dezember m; see also **September**

decent ['di:sənt] adj anständig

deception [dɪ'sɛpʃən] n Betrug m; **deceptive** [dɪ'sɛptɪv] adj täuschend, irreführend

decide [dɪ'saɪd] vt (question) entscheiden; (body of people) beschließen; **I can't ~ what to do** ich kann mich nicht entscheiden, was ich tun soll ▷ vi sich entscheiden; **to ~ on sth** (in favour of sth) sich für etw entscheiden, sich zu etw entschließen; **decided** adj entschieden; (clear) deutlich; **decidedly** adv entschieden

decimal ['dɛsɪməl] adj Dezimal-; **decimal system** n Dezimalsystem nt

decipher [dɪ'saɪfə*] vt entziffern

decision [dɪ'sɪʒən] n Entscheidung f (on über +akk); (of committee, jury etc) Beschluss m; **to make a ~** eine Entscheidung treffen; **decisive** [dɪ'saɪsɪv] adj entscheidend; (person) entscheidungsfreudig

deck [dɛk] n (Naut) Deck nt; (of cards) Blatt nt; **deckchair** n Liegestuhl m

declaration [dɛklə'reɪʃən] n Erklärung f; **declare** [dɪ'klɛə*] vt erklären; (state) behaupten (that dass); (at customs) **have**

d

you anything to ~? haben Sie etwas zu verzollen?

decline [dɪˈklaɪn] n Rückgang m ▷ vt (invitation, offer) ablehnen ▷ vi (become less) sinken, abnehmen; (health) sich verschlechtern

decode [diːˈkəʊd] vt entschlüsseln

decompose [diːkəmˈpəʊz] vi sich zersetzen

decontaminate [diːkənˈtæmɪneɪt] vt entgiften; (from radioactivity) entseuchen

decorate [ˈdekəreɪt] vt (aus)schmücken; (wallpaper) tapezieren; (paint) anstreichen; **decoration** [dekəˈreɪʃən] n Schmuck m; (process) Schmücken nt; (wallpapering) Tapezieren nt; (painting) Anstreichen nt; **Christmas ~s** Weihnachtsschmuck m; **decorator** n Maler(in) m(f)

decrease [ˈdiːkriːs] n Abnahme f ▷ [diːˈkriːs] vi abnehmen

dedicate [ˈdedɪkeɪt] vt widmen (to sb jdm); **dedicated** adj (person) engagiert; **dedication** [dedɪˈkeɪʃən] n Widmung f; (commitment) Hingabe f, Engagement nt

deduce [dɪˈdjuːs] vt folgern, schließen (from aus, that dass)

deduct [dɪˈdʌkt] vt abziehen (from von); **deduction** [dɪˈdʌkʃən] n (of money) Abzug m; (conclusion) (Schluss)folgerung f

deed [diːd] n Tat f

deep [diːp] adj tief; **deepen** vt vertiefen; **deep-freeze** n Tiefkühltruhe f; (upright) Gefrierschrank m; **deep-fry** vt frittieren

deer [dɪə*] n Reh nt; (with stag) Hirsch m

defeat [dɪˈfiːt] n Niederlage f; **to admit ~** sich geschlagen geben ▷ vt besiegen

defect [ˈdiːfekt] n Defekt m, Fehler m; **defective** [dɪˈfektɪv] adj fehlerhaft

defence [dɪˈfens] n Verteidigung f; **defend** [dɪˈfend] vt verteidigen; **defendant** [dɪˈfendənt] n (Jur) Angeklagte(r) mf; **defender** n (Sport) Verteidiger(in) m(f); **defensive** [dɪˈfensɪv] adj defensiv

deficiency [dɪˈfɪʃənsɪ] n Mangel m; **deficient** adj mangelhaft; **deficit** [ˈdefɪsɪt] n Defizit nt

define [dɪˈfaɪn] vt (word) definieren; (duties, powers) bestimmen; **definite** [ˈdefɪnɪt] adj (clear) klar, eindeutig; (certain) sicher; **it's ~** es steht fest; **definitely** adv bestimmt; **definition** [defɪˈnɪʃən] n Definition f; (Foto) Schärfe f

deflate [diːˈfleɪt] vt die Luft ablassen aus

defrost [diːˈfrɒst] vt (fridge) abtauen; (food) auftauen

degrading [dɪˈgreɪdɪŋ] adj erniedrigend

degree [dɪˈgriː] n Grad m; (at university) akademischer Grad; **a certain/high ~ of** ein gewisses/hohes Maß an +dat; **to a certain ~** einigermaßen; **I have a ~ in chemistry** ≈ ich habe Chemie studiert

dehydrated [diːhaɪˈdreɪtɪd] adj (food) getrocknet, Trocken-; (person) ausgetrocknet

de-ice [diːˈaɪs] vt enteisen

delay [dɪˈleɪ] vt (postpone) verschieben, aufschieben; **to be ~ed** (event) sich verzögern; **the train/flight was ~ed** der Zug/die Maschine hatte Verspätung ▷ vi warten; (hesitate) zögern ▷ n Verzögerung f; (of train etc) Verspätung f; **without ~** unverzüglich; **delayed** adj (train etc) verspätet

delegate n [ˈdelɪgət] Delegierte(r) mf ▷ [ˈdelɪgeɪt] vt delegieren; **delegation** [delɪˈgeɪʃən] n Abordnung f; (foreign) Delegation f

delete [dɪˈliːt] vt (aus)streichen; (Inform) löschen; **deletion** n Streichung f; (Inform) Löschung f

deli [ˈdelɪ] n (fam) Feinkostgeschäft nt

deliberate [dɪˈlɪbərət] adj (intentional) absichtlich; **deliberately** adv mit Absicht, extra

delicate [ˈdelɪkɪt] adj (fine) fein; (fragile) zart; (a. Med) empfindlich; (situation) heikel

delicatessen [delɪkəˈtesn] nsing Feinkostgeschäft nt

delicious [dɪˈlɪʃəs] adj köstlich, lecker

delight [dɪˈlaɪt] n Freude f ▷ vt entzücken; **delighted** adj sehr erfreut (with über +akk); **delightful** adj entzückend; (weather, meal etc) herrlich

deliver [dɪˈlɪvə*] vt (goods) liefern (to sb jdm); (letter, parcel) zustellen; (speech) halten; (baby) entbinden; **delivery** n Lieferung f; (of letter, parcel) Zustellung f; (of baby) Entbindung f; **delivery van** n Lieferwagen m

delude [dɪˈluːd] vt täuschen; **don't ~ yourself** mach dir nichts vor; **delusion** n Irrglaube m

de luxe [dɪˈlʌks] adj Luxus-

demand [dɪˈmɑːnd] vt verlangen (from

von); (*time, patience etc*) erfordern ▷ *n*
(*request*) Forderung *f*, Verlangen *nt* (*for
nach*); (*Comm: for goods*) Nachfrage *f*; **on
~** auf Wunsch; **very much in ~** sehr
gefragt; **demanding** *adj* anspruchsvoll
demented [dɪˈmentɪd] *adj* wahnsinnig
demerara [deməˈrɛərə] *n* **~ (sugar)**
brauner Zucker
demister *n* Defroster *m*
demo [ˈdeməʊ] (*pl* **-s**) *n* (*fam*) Demo *f*
democracy [dɪˈmɒkrəsɪ] *n* Demokratie *f*;
democrat, Democrat (*US Pol*)
[ˈdeməkræt] Demokrat(in) *m(f)*;
democratic *adj* demokratisch; **the
Democratic Party** (*US Pol*) die
Demokratische Partei
demolish [dɪˈmɒlɪʃ] *vt* abreißen; (*fig*)
zerstören; **demolition** [deməˈlɪʃən] *n*
Abbruch *m*
demonstrate [ˈdemənstreɪt] *vt*, *vi*
demonstrieren, beweisen;
demonstration *n* Demonstration *f*
demoralize [dɪˈmɒrəlaɪz] *vt*
demoralisieren
denationalization [ˈdiːnæʃnəlaɪˈzeɪʃən]
n Privatisierung *f*
denial [dɪˈnaɪəl] *n* Leugnung *f*; (*official ~*)
Dementi *nt*
denim [ˈdenɪm] *n* Jeansstoff *m*; **denim
jacket** *n* Jeansjacke *f*; **denims** *npl*
Bluejeans *pl*
Denmark [ˈdenmɑːk] *n* Dänemark *nt*
denomination [dɪnɒmɪˈneɪʃən] *n* (*Rel*)
Konfession *f*; (*Comm*) Nennwert *m*
dense [dens] *adj* dicht; (*fam: stupid*)
schwer von Begriff; **density** [ˈdensɪtɪ] *n*
Dichte *f*
dent [dent] *n* Beule *f*, Delle *f* ▷ *vt*
einbeulen
dental [ˈdentl] *adj* Zahn-; **~ care**
Zahnpflege *f*; **~ floss** Zahnseide *f*; **dentist**
[ˈdentɪst] *n* Zahnarzt *m*, Zahnärztin;
dentures [ˈdentʃəz] *npl* Zahnprothese *f*;
(*full*) Gebiss *nt*
deny [dɪˈnaɪ] *vt* leugnen, bestreiten;
(*refuse*) ablehnen
deodorant [diːˈəʊdərənt] *n* Deo(dorant)
nt; **~ spray** Deospray *nt* *o* *m*
depart [dɪˈpɑːt] *vi* abreisen; (*bus, train*)
abfahren (*for nach, from von*); (*plane*)
abfliegen (*for nach, from von*)
department [dɪˈpɑːtmənt] *n* Abteilung *f*;
(*at university*) Institut *nt*; (*Pol: ministry*)

Ministerium *nt*; **department store** *n*
Kaufhaus *nt*
departure [dɪˈpɑːtʃə*] *n* (*of person*)
Weggang *m*; (*on journey*) Abreise *f* (*for
nach*); (*of train etc*) Abfahrt *f* (*for nach*); (*of
plane*) Abflug *m* (*for nach*); **departure
lounge** *n* (*Aviat*) Abflughalle *f*;
departure time *n* Abfahrtzeit *f*; (*Aviat*)
Abflugzeit *f*
depend [dɪˈpend] *vi* **it ~s** es kommt
darauf an (*whether, if ob*); **depend on** *vt*
(*thing*) abhängen von; (*person: rely on*) sich
verlassen auf +*akk*; (*person, area etc*)
angewiesen sein auf +*akk*; **it ~s on the
weather** es kommt auf das Wetter an;
dependable *adj* zuverlässig;
dependence *n* Abhängigkeit *f* (*on von*);
dependent *adj* abhängig (*on von*)
deplorable [dɪˈplɔːrəbl] *adj* bedauerlich;
deplore *vt* bedauern
deport [dɪˈpɔːt] *vt* ausweisen,
abschieben; **deportation** [diːpɔːˈteɪʃən] *n*
Abschiebung *f*
deposit [dɪˈpɒzɪt] *n* (*down payment*)
Anzahlung *f*; (*security*) Kaution *f*; (*for bottle*)
Pfand *nt*; (*to bank account*) Einzahlung *f*; (*in
river etc*) Ablagerung *f* ▷ *vt* (*put down*)
abstellen, absetzen; (*to bank account*)
einzahlen; (*sth valuable*) deponieren;
deposit account *n* Sparkonto *nt*
depot [ˈdepəʊ] *n* Depot *nt*
depreciate [dɪˈpriːʃɪeɪt] *vi* an Wert
verlieren
depress [dɪˈpres] *vt* (*in mood*)
deprimieren; **depressed** *adj* (*person*)
niedergeschlagen, deprimiert; **~ area**
Notstandsgebiet *nt*; **depressing** *adj*
deprimierend; **depression** [dɪˈpreʃən] *n*
(*mood*) Depression *f*; (*Meteo*) Tief *nt*
deprive [dɪˈpraɪv] *vt* **to ~ sb of sth** jdn
einer Sache berauben; **deprived** *adj*
(*child*) (*sozial*) benachteiligt
dept *abbr* = **department** Abt.
depth [depθ] *n* Tiefe *f*
deputy [ˈdepjʊtɪ] *adj* stellvertretend,
Vize- ▷ *n* Stellvertreter(in) *m(f)*; (*US Pol*)
Abgeordnete(r) *mf*
derail [dɪˈreɪl] *vt* entgleisen lassen; **to be
~ed** entgleisen
deranged [dɪˈreɪndʒd] *adj* geistesgestört
derivation [derɪˈveɪʃən] *n* Ableitung *f*;
derive [dɪˈraɪv] *vt* ableiten (*from von*)
▷ abstammen (*from von*)

d

dermatitis [dɜ:məˈtaɪtɪs] n
Hautentzündung f
derogatory [dɪˈrɒɡətərɪ] adj abfällig
descend [dɪˈsend] vt, vi hinabsteigen,
hinuntergehen; (person) **to ~** o be ~ed
from abstammen von; **descendant** n
Nachkomme m; **descent** [dɪˈsent] n
(coming down) Abstieg m; (origin)
Abstammung f
describe [dɪsˈkraɪb] vt beschreiben;
description [dɪˈskrɪpʃən] n Beschreibung
f
desert [ˈdezət] n Wüste f ▷ [dɪˈzɜ:t] vt
verlassen; (abandon) im Stich lassen;
deserted adj verlassen; (empty)
menschenleer
deserve [dɪˈzɜ:v] vt verdienen
design [dɪˈzaɪn] n (plan) Entwurf m; (of
vehicle, machine) Konstruktion f; (of object)
Design nt; (planning) Gestaltung f ▷ vt
entwerfen; (machine etc) konstruieren; **~ed
for sb/sth** (intended) für jdn/etw
konzipiert
designate [ˈdezɪɡneɪt] vt bestimmen
designer [dɪˈzaɪnə*] n Designer(in) m(f);
(Tech) Konstrukteur(in) m(f); **designer
drug** n Designerdroge f
desirable [dɪˈzaɪərəbl] n wünschenswert;
(person) begehrenswert; **desire** [dɪˈzaɪə*]
n Wunsch m (for nach); (esp sexual)
Begierde f (for nach) ▷ vt wünschen; (ask
for) verlangen; **if ~d** auf Wunsch
desk [desk] n Schreibtisch m; (reception ~)
Empfang m; (at airport etc) Schalter m;
desktop publishing n Desktoppublishing
nt
desolate [ˈdesəlɪt] adj trostlos
despair [dɪsˈpeə*] n Verzweiflung f (at
über +akk) ▷ vi verzweifeln (of an +dat)
despatch [dɪˈspætʃ] see dispatch
desperate [ˈdespərɪt] adj verzweifelt;
(situation) hoffnungslos; **to be ~ for sth**
etw dringend brauchen, unbedingt
wollen; **desperation** [despəˈreɪʃən] n
Verzweiflung f
despicable [dɪˈspɪkəbl] adj
verachtenswert; **despise** [dɪˈspaɪz] vt
verachten
despite [dɪˈspaɪt] prep trotz +gen
dessert [dɪˈzɜ:t] n Nachtisch m;
dessertspoon n Dessertlöffel m
destination [destɪˈneɪʃən] n (of person)
(Reise)ziel nt; (of goods) Bestimmungsort

m; **destine** vt we're ~d for Hull wir sind
auf dem Weg nach Hull; **he was ~d to die
young** er sollte früh sterben; **destiny**
[ˈdestɪnɪ] n Schicksal nt
destroy [dɪˈstrɔɪ] vt zerstören;
(completely) vernichten; **destruction**
[dɪˈstrʌkʃən] n Zerstörung f; (complete)
Vernichtung f; **destructive** [dɪˈstrʌktɪv]
adj zerstörerisch; (esp fig) destruktiv
detach [dɪˈtætʃ] vt abnehmen; (from form
etc) abtrennen; (free) lösen (from von);
detachable adj abnehmbar; (from form
etc) abtrennbar; **detached** adj (attitude)
distanziert, objektiv; **~ house** Einzelhaus
nt
detail [ˈdi:teɪl,] (US) [di:ˈteɪl] n Einzelheit
f, Detail nt; (further) ~s from ... Näheres
erfahren Sie bei ...; **to go into ~** ins Detail
gehen; **in ~** ausführlich; **detailed** adj
detailliert, ausführlich
detain [dɪˈteɪn] vt aufhalten; (police) in
Haft nehmen
detect [dɪˈtekt] vt entdecken; (notice)
wahrnehmen; **detective** [dɪˈtektɪv] n
Detektiv(in) m(f); **detective story** n
Detektivroman, Krimi m
detention [dɪˈtenʃən] n Haft f; (Sch)
Nachsitzen nt
deter [dɪˈtɜ:*] vt abschrecken (from
von)
detergent [dɪˈtɜ:dʒənt] n
Reinigungsmittel nt; (soap powder)
Waschmittel nt
deteriorate [dɪˈtɪərɪəreɪt] vi sich
verschlechtern
determination [dɪtɜ:mɪˈneɪʃən] n
Entschlossenheit f; **determine** [dɪˈtɜ:mɪn]
vt bestimmen; **determined** adj (fest)
entschlossen
deterrent [dɪˈterənt] n
Abschreckungsmittel nt
detest [dɪˈtest] vt verabscheuen;
detestable adj abscheulich
detour [ˈdi:tʊə*] n Umweg m; (of traffic)
Umleitung f
deuce [dju:s] n (Tennis) Einstand m
devalue [di:ˈvælju:] vt abwerten
devastate [ˈdevəsteɪt] vt verwüsten;
devastating [ˈdevəsteɪtɪŋ] adj
verheerend
develop [dɪˈveləp] vt entwickeln; (illness)
bekommen ▷ vi sich entwickeln;
developing country n Entwicklungsland

nt; **development** n Entwicklung f; (of land) Erschließung f

device [dɪˈvaɪs] n Vorrichtung f, Gerät nt

devil [ˈdevl] n Teufel m; **devilish** adj teuflisch

devote [dɪˈvəʊt] vt widmen (to dat); **devoted** adj liebend; (servant etc) treu ergeben; **devotion** n Hingabe f

devour [dɪˈvaʊə*] vt verschlingen

dew [djuː] n Tau m

diabetes [daɪəˈbiːtiːz] n Diabetes m, Zuckerkrankheit f; **diabetic** [daɪəˈbetɪk] adj zuckerkrank, für Diabetiker ▷ n Diabetiker(in) m(f)

diagnosis (diagnoses) [daɪəgˈnəʊsɪs] (pl diagnoses) n Diagnose f

diagonal [daɪˈægənl] adj diagonal

diagram [ˈdaɪəgræm] n Diagramm nt

dial [ˈdaɪəl] n Skala f; (of clock) Zifferblatt nt ▷ vt (Tel) wählen; **dial code** n (US) Vorwahl f

dialect [ˈdaɪəlekt] n Dialekt m

dialling code n (Brit) Vorwahl f; **dialling tone** n (Brit) Amtszeichen nt

dialogue, dialog (US) [ˈdaɪəlɒg] n Dialog m

dial tone n (US) Amtszeichen nt

dialysis [daɪˈæləsɪs] n (Med) Dialyse f

diameter [daɪˈæmɪtə*] n Durchmesser m

diamond [ˈdaɪəmənd] n Diamant m; (Cards) Karo nt

diaper [ˈdaɪpə*] n (US) Windel f

diarrhoea [daɪəˈriːə] n Durchfall m

diary [ˈdaɪərɪ] n (Taschen)kalender m; (account) Tagebuch nt

dice [daɪs] npl Würfel pl; **diced** adj in Würfel geschnitten

dictate [dɪkˈteɪt] vt diktieren; **dictation** [dɪkˈteɪʃən] n Diktat nt

dictator [dɪkˈteɪtə*] n Diktator(in) m(f); **dictatorship** [dɪkˈteɪtəʃɪp] n Diktatur f

dictionary [ˈdɪkʃənrɪ] n Wörterbuch nt

did [dɪd] pt of **do**

didn't [ˈdɪdnt] contr of **did not**

die [daɪ] vi sterben (of an +dat); (plant, animal) eingehen; (engine) absterben; **to be dying to do sth** darauf brennen, etw zu tun; **I'm dying for a drink** ich brauche unbedingt was zu trinken; **die away** vi schwächer werden; (wind) sich legen; **die down** vi nachlassen; **die out** vi aussterben

diesel [ˈdiːzəl] n (fuel, car) Diesel m; **~ engine** Dieselmotor m

diet [ˈdaɪət] n Kost f; (special food) Diät f ▷ vi eine Diät machen

differ [ˈdɪfə*] vi (be different) sich unterscheiden; (disagree) anderer Meinung sein; **difference** [ˈdɪfrəns] n Unterschied m; **it makes no ~ (to me)** es ist (mir) egal; **it makes a big ~** es macht viel aus; **different** adj andere(r, s); (with pl) verschieden; **to be quite ~** ganz anders sein (from als); (two people, things) völlig verschieden sein; **a ~ person** ein anderer Mensch; **differentiate** [dɪfəˈrenʃɪeɪt] vt, vi unterscheiden; **differently** [ˈdɪfrəntlɪ] adv anders (from als); (from one another) unterschiedlich

difficult [ˈdɪfɪkəlt] adj schwierig; **I find it ~** es fällt mir schwer; **difficulty** n Schwierigkeit f; **with ~** nur schwer; **to have ~ in doing sth** etw nur mit Mühe machen können

dig [dɪg] (dug, dug) vt, vi (hole) graben; **dig in** vi (fam: to food) reinhauen; **~!** greif(t) zu!; **dig up** vt ausgraben

digest [daɪˈdʒest] vt (a. fig) verdauen; **digestible** [dɪˈdʒestəbl] adj verdaulich; **digestion** [dɪˈdʒestʃən] n Verdauung f; **digestive** [dɪˈdʒestɪv] adj **~ biscuit** (Brit) Vollkornkeks m

digit [ˈdɪdʒɪt] n Ziffer f; **digital** [ˈdɪdʒɪtəl] adj digital; **~ computer** Digitalrechner m; **~ watch/clock** Digitaluhr f; **digital camera** n Digitalkamera f

dignified [ˈdɪgnɪfaɪd] adj würdevoll; **dignity** [ˈdɪgnɪtɪ] n Würde f

dilapidated [dɪˈlæpɪdeɪtɪd] adj baufällig

dilemma [daɪˈlemə] n Dilemma nt

dill [dɪl] n Dill m

dilute [daɪˈluːt] vt verdünnen

dim [dɪm] adj (light) schwach; (outline) undeutlich; (stupid) schwer von Begriff ▷ vt verdunkeln; (US Auto) abblenden; **~med headlights** (US) Abblendlicht nt

dime [daɪm] n (US) Zehncentstück nt

dimension [daɪˈmenʃən] n Dimension f; **~s** pl Maße pl

diminish [dɪˈmɪnɪʃ] vt verringern ▷ vi sich verringern

dimple [ˈdɪmpl] n Grübchen nt

dine [daɪn] vi speisen; **dine out** vi außer Haus essen; **diner** n Gast m; (Rail) Speisewagen m; (US) Speiselokal nt

dinghy ['dɪŋɪ] n Ding(h)i nt; (inflatable) Schlauchboot nt

dingy ['dɪndʒɪ] adj düster; (dirty) schmuddelig

dining car ['daɪnɪŋkɑ:*] n Speisewagen m; **dining room** n Esszimmer nt; (in hotel) Speiseraum m; **dining table** n Esstisch m

dinner ['dɪnə*] n Abendessen nt; (lunch) Mittagessen nt; (public) Diner nt; **to be at ~** beim Essen sein; **to have ~** zu Abend/Mittag essen; **dinner jacket** n Smoking m; **dinner party** n Abendgesellschaft f (mit Essen); **dinnertime** n Essenszeit f

dinosaur ['daɪnəsɔ:*] n Dinosaurier m

dip [dɪp] vt tauchen (in in +akk); **to ~** (one's headlights) (Brit Auto) abblenden; **~ped headlights** Abblendlicht nt ▷ n (in ground) Bodensenke f; (sauce) Dip m

diploma [dɪ'pləʊmə] n Diplom nt

diplomat ['dɪpləmæt] n Diplomat(in) m(f); **diplomatic** [dɪplə'mætɪk] adj diplomatisch

dipstick ['dɪpstɪk] n Ölmessstab m

direct [daɪ'rɛkt] adj direkt; (cause, consequence) unmittelbar; **~ debit** (mandate) Einzugsermächtigung f; (transaction) Abbuchung f im Lastschriftverfahren; **~ train** durchgehender Zug ▷ vt (aim, send) richten (at, to an +akk); (film) die Regie führen bei; (traffic) regeln; **direct current** n (Elec) Gleichstrom m

direction [dɪ'rɛkʃən] n (course) Richtung f; (Cine) Regie f; **in the ~ of ...** in Richtung ...; **~s** pl **for use** Gebrauchsanweisung f; **~s** pl (to a place) Wegbeschreibung f

directly [dɪ'rɛktlɪ] adv direkt; (at once) sofort

director [dɪ'rɛktə*] n Direktor(in) m(f), Leiter(in) m(f); (of film) Regisseur(in) m(f)

directory [dɪ'rɛktərɪ] n Adressbuch nt; (Tel) Telefonbuch nt; **~ enquiries** o (US) **assistance** (Tel) Auskunft f

dirt [dɜ:t] n Schmutz m, Dreck m; **dirt cheap** adj spottbillig; **dirt road** n unbefestigte Straße; **dirty** adj schmutzig

disability [dɪsə'bɪlɪtɪ] n Behinderung f; **disabled** [dɪs'eɪbld] adj behindert, Behinderten- ▷ npl **the ~** die Behinderten

disadvantage [dɪsəd'vɑ:ntɪdʒ] n Nachteil m; **at a ~** benachteiligt;

disadvantageous [dɪsædvɑ:n'teɪdʒəs] adj nachteilig, ungünstig

disagree [dɪsə'griː] vi anderer Meinung sein; (two people) sich nicht einig sein; (two reports etc) nicht übereinstimmen; **to ~ with sb** mit jdm nicht übereinstimmen; (food) jdm nicht bekommen; **disagreeable** adj unangenehm; (person) unsympathisch; **disagreement** n Meinungsverschiedenheit f

disappear [dɪsə'pɪə*] vi verschwinden; **disappearance** n Verschwinden nt

disappoint [dɪsə'pɔɪnt] vt enttäuschen; **disappointing** adj enttäuschend; **disappointment** n Enttäuschung f

disapproval [dɪsə'pruːvl] n Missbilligung f; **disapprove** [dɪsə'pruːv] vi missbilligen (of akk)

disarm [dɪs'ɑːm] vt entwaffnen ▷ vi (Pol) abrüsten; **disarmament** n Abrüstung f; **disarming** adj (smile, look) gewinnend

disaster [dɪ'zɑːstə*] n Katastrophe f; **disastrous** [dɪ'zɑːstrəs] adj katastrophal

disbelief [dɪsbə'liːf] n Ungläubigkeit f

disc [dɪsk] n Scheibe f, CD f; see also **disk** (Anat) Bandscheibe f; **disc brake** n Scheibenbremse f

discharge [dɪstʃɑːdʒ] n (Med) Ausfluss m ▷ [dɪs'tʃɑːdʒ] vt (person) entlassen; (emit) ausstoßen; (Med) ausscheiden

discipline ['dɪsɪplɪn] n Disziplin f

disc jockey ['dɪskdʒɒkɪ] n Diskjockey m

disclose [dɪs'kləʊz] vt bekannt geben; (secret) enthüllen

disco ['dɪskəʊ] n (pl **-s**) n Disko f, Diskomusik f

discomfort [dɪs'kʌmfət] n (slight pain) leichte Schmerzen pl; (unease) Unbehagen nt

disconnect [dɪskə'nɛkt] vt (electricity, gas, phone) abstellen; (unplug) **to ~ the TV (from the mains)** den Stecker des Fernsehers herausziehen; (Tel) **I've been ~ed** das Gespräch ist unterbrochen worden

discontent [dɪskən'tɛnt] n Unzufriedenheit f; **discontented** adj unzufrieden

discontinue [dɪskən'tɪnjuː] vt einstellen; (product) auslaufen lassen

discotheque ['dɪskəʊtɛk] n Diskothek f

discount ['dɪskaʊnt] n Rabatt m

discover [dɪs'kʌvə*] vt entdecken;
  discovery n Entdeckung f
discredit [dɪs'kredɪt] vt in Verruf bringen
  ▷ n Misskredit m
discreet [dɪs'kriːt] adj diskret
discrepancy [dɪs'krepənsɪ] n
  Unstimmigkeit f, Diskrepanz f
discriminate [dɪs'krɪmɪneɪt] vi
  unterscheiden; **to ~ against sb** jdn
  diskriminieren; **discrimination**
  [dɪskrɪmɪ'neɪʃən] n (different treatment)
  Diskriminierung f
discus ['dɪskəs] n Diskus m
discuss [dɪs'kʌs] vt diskutieren,
  besprechen; **discussion** [dɪs'kʌʃən] n
  Diskussion f
disease [dɪ'ziːz] n Krankheit f
disembark [dɪsɪm'bɑːk] vi von Bord
  gehen
disentangle ['dɪsɪn'tæŋgl] vt entwirren
disgrace [dɪs'greɪs] n Schande f ▷ vt
  Schande machen +dat; (family etc) Schande
  bringen über +akk; (less strong) blamieren;
  disgraceful adj skandalös; **it's ~** es ist
  eine Schande
disguise [dɪs'gaɪz] vt verkleiden; (voice)
  verstellen ▷ n Verkleidung f; **in**
  ~ verkleidet
disgust [dɪs'gʌst] n Abscheu m; (physical)
  Ekel m ▷ vt anekeln, anwidern;
  disgusting adj widerlich; (physically)
  ekelhaft
dish [dɪʃ] n Schüssel f; (food) Gericht nt;
  ~es pl (crockery) Geschirr nt; **to do/wash**
  the ~es abwaschen; **dishcloth** n (for
  washing) Spültuch nt; (for drying)
  Geschirrtuch nt
dishearten [dɪs'hɑːtən] vt entmutigen;
  don't be ~ed lass den Kopf nicht
  hängen!
dishonest [dɪs'ɒnɪst] adj unehrlich
dishonour [dɪs'ɒnə*] n Schande f
dish towel n (US) Geschirrtuch nt; **dish**
  washer n Geschirrspülmaschine f
dishy ['dɪʃɪ] adj (Brit fam) klasse, attraktiv
disillusioned [dɪsɪ'luːʒənd] adj
  desillusioniert
disinfect [dɪsɪn'fekt] vt desinfizieren;
  disinfectant n Desinfektionsmittel nt
disintegrate [dɪs'ɪntɪgreɪt] vi zerfallen;
  (group) sich auflösen
disjointed [dɪs'dʒɔɪntɪd] adj
  unzusammenhängend

disk [dɪsk] n (Inform: floppy) Diskette f;
  disk drive n Diskettenlaufwerk nt;
  diskette [dɪ'sket] n Diskette f
dislike [dɪs'laɪk] n Abneigung f ▷ vt nicht
  mögen; **to ~ doing sth** etw ungern tun
dislocate ['dɪsləʊkeɪt] vt (Med)
  verrenken, ausrenken
dismal ['dɪzməl] adj trostlos
dismantle [dɪs'mæntl] vt auseinander
  nehmen; (machine) demontieren
dismay [dɪs'meɪ] n Bestürzung f;
  dismayed adj bestürzt
dismiss [dɪs'mɪs] vt (employee) entlassen;
  dismissal n Entlassung f
disobedience [dɪsə'biːdɪəns] n
  Ungehorsam m; **disobedient** adj
  ungehorsam; **disobey** [dɪsə'beɪ] vt nicht
  gehorchen +dat
disorder [dɪs'ɔːdə*] n (mess) Unordnung
  f; (riot) Aufruhr m; (Med) Störung f, Leiden
  nt
disorganized [dɪs'ɔːgənaɪzd] adj
  chaotisch
disparaging adj geringschätzig
dispatch [dɪ'spætʃ] vt abschicken,
  abfertigen
dispensable [dɪ'spensəbl] adj
  entbehrlich; **dispense** vt verteilen;
  dispense with vt verzichten auf +akk;
  dispenser n Automat m
disperse [dɪ'spɜːs] vi sich zerstreuen
display [dɪ'spleɪ] n (exhibition)
  Ausstellung f, Show f; (of goods) Auslage f;
  (Tech) Anzeige f, Display nt ▷ vt zeigen;
  (goods) ausstellen
disposable [dɪ'spəʊzəbl] adj (container,
  razor etc) Wegwerf-; **~ nappy**
  Wegwerfwindel f; **disposal** [dɪ'spəʊzəl] n
  Loswerden nt; (of waste) Beseitigung f; **to be**
  at sb's ~ jdm zur Verfügung stehen; **dispose**
  of vt loswerden; (waste etc) beseitigen
dispute [dɪ'spjuːt] n Streit m; (industrial)
  Auseinandersetzung f ▷ vt bestreiten
disqualification [dɪskwɒlɪfɪ'keɪʃən] n
  Disqualifikation f; **disqualify**
  [dɪs'kwɒlɪfaɪ] vt disqualifizieren
disregard [dɪsrɪ'gɑːd] vt nicht beachten
disreputable [dɪs'repjʊtəbl] adj verrufen
disrespect [dɪsrɪ'spekt] n
  Respektlosigkeit f
disrupt [dɪs'rʌpt] vt stören; (interrupt)
  unterbrechen; **disruption** [dɪs'rʌpʃən] n
  Störung f; (interruption) Unterbrechung f

dissatisfied [dɪs'sætɪsfaɪd] *adj*
unzufrieden

dissent [dɪ'sent] *n* Widerspruch *m*

dissolve [dɪ'zɒlv] *vt* auflösen ▷ *vi* sich
auflösen

dissuade [dɪ'sweɪd] *vt* (*davon abbringen*)
to ~ sb from doing sth jdn davon
abbringen, etw zu tun

distance ['dɪstəns] *n* Entfernung *f*; **in
the/from a ~** in/aus der Ferne; **distant**
adj (*a. in time*) fern; (*relative etc*) entfernt;
(*person*) distanziert

distaste [dɪs'teɪst] *n* Abneigung *f* (*for*
gegen)

distil [dɪ'stɪl] *vt* destillieren; **distillery** *n*
Brennerei *f*

distinct [dɪ'stɪŋkt] *adj* verschieden; (*clear*)
klar, deutlich; **distinction** [dɪ'stɪŋkʃən] *n*
(*difference*) Unterschied *m*; (*in exam etc*)
Auszeichnung *f*; **distinctive** *adj*
unverkennbar; **distinctly** *adv* deutlich

distinguish [dɪ'stɪŋgwɪʃ] *vt*
unterscheiden (*sth from sth* etw von
etw)

distort [dɪ'stɔːt] *vt* verzerren; (*truth*)
verdrehen

distract [dɪ'strækt] *vt* ablenken;
distraction [dɪ'strækʃən] *n* Ablenkung *f*;
(*diversion*) Zerstreuung *f*

distress [dɪ'stres] *n* (*need, danger*) Not *f*;
(*suffering*) Leiden *nt*; (*mental*) Qual *f*; (*worry*)
Kummer *m* ▷ *vt* mitnehmen, erschüttern;
distressed area *n* Notstandsgebiet *nt*;
distress signal *n* Notsignal *nt*

distribute [dɪ'strɪbjuːt] *vt* verteilen;
(*Comm: goods*) vertreiben; **distribution**
[dɪstrɪ'bjuːʃən] *n* Verteilung *f*; (*Comm: of
goods*) Vertrieb *m*; **distributor**
[dɪ'strɪbjʊtə*] *n* (*Auto*) Verteiler *m*; (*Comm*)
Händler(in) *m(f)*

district ['dɪstrɪkt] *n* Gegend *f*;
(*administrative*) Bezirk *m*; **district attorney**
n (*US*) Staatsanwalt *m*, Staatsanwältin *f*

distrust [dɪs'trʌst] *vt* misstrauen +*dat* ▷ *n*
Misstrauen *nt*

disturb [dɪ'stɜːb] *vt* stören; (*worry*)
beunruhigen; **disturbance** *n* Störung *f*;
disturbing *adj* beunruhigend

ditch [dɪtʃ] *n* Graben *m* ▷ *vt* (*fam: person*)
den Laufpass geben +*dat*; (*plan etc*)
verwerfen

ditto ['dɪtəʊ] *n* dito, ebenfalls

dive [daɪv] *n* (*into water*) Kopfsprung *m*;
(*Aviat*) Sturzflug *m*; (*fam*) zwielichtiges
Lokal ▷ *vi* (*under water*) tauchen; **diver** *n*
Taucher(in) *m(f)*

diverse [daɪ'vɜːs] *adj* verschieden;
diversion [daɪ'vɜːʃən] *n* (*of traffic*)
Umleitung *f*; (*distraction*) Ablenkung *f*;
divert [daɪ'vɜːt] *vt* ablenken; (*traffic*)
umleiten

divide [dɪ'vaɪd] *vt* teilen; (*in several parts,
between people*) aufteilen ▷ *vi* sich teilen;
dividend ['dɪvɪdend] *n* Dividende *f*

divine [dɪ'vaɪn] *adj* göttlich

diving ['daɪvɪŋ] *n* (*Sport*)tauchen *nt*;
(*jumping in*) Springen *nt*; (*Sport: from board*)
Kunstspringen *nt*; **diving board** *n*
Sprungbrett *nt*; **diving goggles** *npl*
Taucherbrille *f*; **diving mask** *n*
Tauchmaske *f*

division [dɪ'vɪʒən] *n* Teilung *f*; (*Math*)
Division *f*; (*department*) Abteilung *f*; (*Sport*)
Liga *f*

divorce [dɪ'vɔːs] *n* Scheidung *f* ▷ *vt* sich
scheiden lassen von; **divorced** *adj*
geschieden; **to get ~** sich scheiden lassen;
divorcee [dɪvɔː'siː] *n* Geschiedene(r) *mf*

DIY [diː'aɪwaɪ] *abbr* = **do-it-yourself**; **DIY
centre** *n* Baumarkt *m*

dizzy ['dɪzɪ] *adj* schwindlig

DJ [diː'dʒeɪ] *abbr* = **dinner jacket** Smoking
m ▷ *abbr* = **disc jockey** Diskjockey *m*, DJ *m*

DNA *abbr* = **desoxyribonucleic acid** DNS *f*

○ KEYWORD

do [duː] (*pt* **did**, *pp* **done**) *n* (*inf: party etc*)
Fete *f*

▷ *aux vb* **1** (*in negative constructions and
questions*): **I don't understand** ich
verstehe nicht; **didn't you know?**
wusstest du das nicht?; **what do you
think?** was meinen Sie?

2 (*for emphasis, in polite phrases*): **she does
seem rather tired** sie scheint wirklich
sehr müde zu sein; **do sit down/help
yourself** setzen Sie sich doch hin/greifen
Sie doch zu

3 (*used to avoid repeating vb*): **she swims
better than I do** sie schwimmt besser als
ich; **she lives in Glasgow — so do I** sie
wohnt in Glasgow — ich auch

4 (*in tag questions*): **you like him, don't
you?** du magst ihn doch, oder?

▷ *vt* **1** (*carry out, perform etc*) tun machen;

what are you doing tonight? was macht du heute Abend?; **I've got nothing to do** ich habe nichts zu tun; **to do one's hair/nails** sich die Haare/Nägel machen

2 (Aut etc) fahren

▷ vi **1** (act, behave): **do as I do** mach es wie ich

2 (get on, fare): **he's doing well/badly at school** er ist gut/schlecht in der Schule; **how do you do?** guten Tag

3 (be suitable) gehen (be sufficient) reichen; **to make do (with)** auskommen mit;
  do away with vt (kill) umbringen (abolish) (law etc) abschaffen;
  do up vt (laces, dress, buttons) zumachen (renovate) (room, house) renovieren;
  do with vt (need) brauchen (be connected) zu tun haben mit;
  do without vt, vi auskommen ohne

dock [dɒk] n Dock nt; (Jur) Anklagebank f; **docker** n Hafenarbeiter m; **dockyard** n Werft f

doctor ['dɒktə*] n Arzt m, Ärztin; (in title, also academic) Doktor m

document ['dɒkjʊmənt] n Dokument nt; **documentary** [dɒkjʊ'mentərɪ] n Dokumentarfilm m; **documentation** [dɒkjʊmən'teɪʃən] n Dokumentation f

docusoap ['dɒkjʊsəʊp] n Reality-Serie f, Dokusoap f

doddery ['dɒdərɪ] adj tatterig

dodgem ['dɒdʒəm] n Autoskooter m

dodgy [dɒdʒɪ] adj nicht ganz in Ordnung; (dishonest, unreliable) zwielichtig; **he has a ~ stomach** er hat sich den Magen verdorben

dog [dɒg] n Hund m; **dog food** n Hundefutter nt; **doggie bag** ['dɒgɪˈbæg] n Tüte oder Box, in der Essensreste aus dem Restaurant mit nach Hause genommen werden können

do-it-yourself ['duːɪtjə'self] n Heimwerken nt, Do-it-yourself nt ▷ adj Heimwerker-; **do-it-yourselfer** n Bastler(in) m(f), Heimwerker(in) m(f)

doll [dɒl] n Puppe f

dollar ['dɒlə*] n Dollar m

dolphin ['dɒlfɪn] n Delphin m

domain n Domäne f; (Inform) Domain f

dome [dəʊm] n Kuppel f

domestic [də'mestɪk] adj häuslich; (within country) Innen-, Binnen-; **domestic animal** n Haustier nt; **domesticated** [də'mestɪkeɪtɪd] adj (person) häuslich; (animal) zahm; **domestic flight** n Inlandsflug m

domicile ['dɒmɪsaɪl] n (ständiger) Wohnsitz

dominant ['dɒmɪnənt] adj dominierend, vorherrschend; **dominate** ['dɒmɪneɪt] vt beherrschen

dominoes ['dɒmɪnəʊz] npl Domino(spiel) nt

donate [dəʊ'neɪt] vt spenden; **donation** n Spende f

done [dʌn] pp of **do** ▷ adj (cooked) gar; **well ~** durchgebraten

doner (kebab) ['dɒnəkə'bæb] n Döner (Kebab) m

donkey ['dɒŋkɪ] n Esel m

donor ['dəʊnə] n Spender(in) m(f)

don't [dəʊnt] contr of **do not**

doom [duːm] n Schicksal nt; (downfall) Verderben nt

door [dɔː*] n Tür f; **doorbell** n Türklingel f; **door handle** n Türknauf m; **doorknob** n Türknauf m; **doormat** n Fußabtreter m; **doorstep** n Türstufe f; **right on our ~** direkt vor unserer Haustür

dope [dəʊp] n (for athlete) Aufputschmittel nt ▷ vt dopen; **dopey** adj (fam) bekloppt; (from drugs) benebelt; (sleepy) benommen

dormitory ['dɔːmɪtrɪ] n Schlafsaal m; (US) Studentenwohnheim nt

dosage ['dəʊsɪdʒ] n Dosierung f; **dose** [dəʊs] n Dosis f ▷ vt dosieren

dot [dɒt] n Punkt m; **on the ~** auf die Minute genau, pünktlich

dotcom ['dɒtkɒm] n **~ (company)** Internetfirma f, Dotcom-Unternehmen nt

dote on [dəʊt ɒn] vt abgöttisch lieben

dotted line n punktierte Linie

double ['dʌbl] adj, adv doppelt; **~ the quantity** die zweifache Menge, doppelt so viel ▷ vt verdoppeln ▷ n (person) Doppelgänger(in) m(f); (Cine) Double nt; **double bass** n Kontrabass m; **double bed** n Doppelbett nt; **double-click** vt (Inform) doppelklicken; **double cream** n Sahne mit hohem Fettgehalt; **doubledecker** n Doppeldecker m; **double glazing** n Doppelverglasung f; **double-park** vi in zweiter Reihe parken; **double room** n

Doppelzimmer nt; **doubles** npl (Sport: also match) Doppel nt

doubt [daʊt] n Zweifel m; **no ~** ohne Zweifel, zweifellos, wahrscheinlich; **to have one's ~s** Bedenken haben ▷ vt bezweifeln; (statement, word) anzweifeln; **I ~ it** das bezweifle ich; **doubtful** adj zweifelhaft, zweifelnd; **it is ~ whether ...** es ist fraglich, ob ...; **doubtless** adv ohne Zweifel, sicherlich

dough [daʊ] n Teig m; **doughnut** n Donut m (rundes Hefegebäck)

dove [dʌv] n Taube f

down [daʊn] n Daunen pl; (fluff) Flaum m ▷ adv unten; (motion) nach unten; (towards speaker) herunter; (away from speaker) hinunter; **~ here/there** hier/dort unten; (downstairs) **they came ~ for breakfast** sie kamen zum Frühstück herunter; (southwards) **he came ~ from Scotland** er kam von Schottland herunter ▷ prep (towards speaker) herunter; (away from speaker) hinunter; **to drive ~ the hill/road** den Berg/die Straße hinunter fahren; (along) **to walk ~ the street** die Straße entlang gehen; **he's ~ the pub** (fam) er ist in der Kneipe ▷ vt (fam: drink) runterkippen ▷ adj niedergeschlagen, deprimiert

down-and-out adj heruntergekommen ▷ n Obdachlose(r) mf, Penner(in) m(f); **downcast** adj niedergeschlagen; **downfall** n Sturz m; **down-hearted** adj entmutigt; **downhill** adv bergab; **he's going ~** (fig) mit ihm geht es bergab

● **Downing Street**
●
●
● **Downing Street** ist die Straße in
● London, die von Whitehall zum St
● James's Park führt, und in der sich
● der offizielle Wohnsitz des
● Premierministers (Nr. 10) und des
● Finanzministers (Nr. 11) befindet. Im
● weiteren Sinne bezieht sich der
● Begriff „Downing Street" auf die
● britische Regierung.

download ['daʊnləʊd] vt downloaden, herunterladen; **downmarket** adj für den Massenmarkt; **down payment** n Anzahlung f; **downpour** n Platzregen m; **downs** npl Hügelland nt; **downsize** vt

(business) verkleinern ▷ vi sich verkleinern

Down's syndrome ['daʊnz'sɪndrəʊm] n (Med) Downsyndrom nt

downstairs [daʊn'steəz] adv unten; (motion) nach unten; **downstream** adv flussabwärts; **downtime** n Ausfallzeit f; **downtown** adv (be, work etc) in der Innenstadt; (go) in die Innenstadt ▷ adj (US) in der Innenstadt; **~ Chicago** die Innenstadt von Chicago; **down under** adv (fam: in/to Australia) in/nach Australien; (in/to New Zealand) in/nach Neuseeland; **downwards** adv, adj nach unten; (movement, trend) Abwärts-

doze [dəʊz] vi dösen ▷ n Nickerchen nt

dozen ['dʌzn] n Dutzend nt; **two ~ eggs** zwei Dutzend Eier; **~s of times** x-mal

DP abbr = **data processing** DV f

drab [dræb] adj trist; (colour) düster

draft [drɑːft] n (outline) Entwurf m; (US Mil) Einberufung f

drag [dræg] vt schleppen ▷ n (fam) **to be a ~** (boring) stinklangweilig sein; (laborious) ein ziemlicher Schlauch sein; **drag on** vi sich in die Länge ziehen

dragon ['drægən] n Drache m; **dragonfly** n Libelle f

drain [dreɪn] n Abfluss m ▷ vt (water, oil) ablassen; (vegetables etc) abgießen; (land) entwässern, trockenlegen ▷ vi (of water) abfließen; **drainpipe** n Abflussrohr nt

drama ['drɑːmə] n (a. fig) Drama nt; **dramatic** [drə'mætɪk] adj dramatisch

drank [dræŋk] pt of **drink**

drapes [dreɪps] npl (US) Vorhänge pl

drastic ['dræstɪk] adj drastisch

draught [drɑːft] n (Luftzug) m; **there's a ~** es zieht; **on ~** (beer) vom Fass; **draughts** nsing Damespiel nt; **draughty** adj zugig

draw [drɔː] (drew, drawn) vt (pull) ziehen; (crowd) anlocken, anziehen; (picture) zeichnen ▷ vi (Sport) unentschieden spielen ▷ n (Sport) Unentschieden nt; (attraction) Attraktion f; (for lottery) Ziehung f; **draw out** vt herausziehen; (money) abheben; **draw up** vt (formulate) entwerfen; (list) erstellen ▷ vi (car) anhalten; **drawback** n Nachteil m; **drawbridge** n Zugbrücke f

drawer ['drɔː*] n Schublade f

drawing ['drɔːɪŋ] n Zeichnung f; **drawing pin** n Reißzwecke f

drawn [drɔːn] *pp of* **draw**

dread [dred] *n* Furcht *f* (*of* vor +*dat*) ▷ *vt* sich fürchten vor +*dat*; **dreadful** *adj* furchtbar; **dreadlocks** *npl* Rastalocken *pl*

dream [driːm] (**dreamed** *o* **dreamt**, **dreamed** *o* **dreamt**) *vt*, *vi* träumen (*about* von) ▷ *n* Traum *m*; **dreamt** [dremt] *pt*, *pp of* **dream**

dreary ['drɪərɪ] *adj* (*weather, place*) trostlos; (*book etc*) langweilig

drench [drentʃ] *vt* durchnässen

dress [dres] *n* Kleidung *f*; (*garment*) Kleid *nt* ▷ *vt* anziehen; (*Med: wound*) verbinden; **to get ~ed** sich anziehen; **dress up** *vi* sich fein machen; (*in costume*) sich verkleiden (*as* als); **dress circle** *n* (*Theat*) erster Rang; **dresser** *n* Anrichte *f*; (*US: dressing table*) (Frisier)kommode *f*; **dressing** *n* (*Gastr*) Dressing *nt*, Soße *f*; (*Med*) Verband *m*; **dressing gown** *n* Morgenmantel *m*; **dressing room** *n* (*Sport*) Umkleideraum *m*; (*Theat*) Künstlergarderobe *f*; **dressing table** *n* Frisierkommode *f*; **dress rehearsal** *n* (*Theat*) Generalprobe *f*

drew [druː] *pt of* **draw**

dried [draɪd] *adj* getrocknet; (*milk, flowers*) Trocken-; **~ fruit** Dörrobst *nt*; **drier** ['draɪə*] *n see* **dryer**

drift [drɪft] *vi* treiben ▷ *n* (*of snow*) Verwehung *f*; (*fig*) Tendenz *f*; **if you get my ~** wenn du mich richtig verstehst

drill [drɪl] *n* Bohrer *m* ▷ *vt*, *vi* bohren

drink [drɪŋk] (**drank, drunk**) *vt*, *vi* trinken ▷ *n* Getränk *nt*; (*alcoholic*) Drink *m*; **drink-driving** *n* (*Brit*) Trunkenheit *f* am Steuer; **drinking water** *n* Trinkwasser *nt*

drip [drɪp] *n* Tropfen *m* ▷ *vi* tropfen; **drip-dry** *adj* bügelfrei; **dripping** *n* Bratenfett *nt* ▷ *adj* **~ (wet)** tropfnass

drive [draɪv] (**drove, driven**) *vt* (*car, person in car*) fahren; (*force: person, animal*) treiben; (*Tech*) antreiben; **to ~ sb mad** jdn verrückt machen ▷ *vi* fahren ▷ *n* Fahrt *f*; (*entrance*) Einfahrt *f*, Auffahrt *f*; (*Inform*) Laufwerk *nt*; **to go for a ~** spazieren fahren; **drive away, drive off** *vi* wegfahren ▷ *vt* vertreiben

drive-in *adj* Drive-in-; **~ cinema** (*US*) Autokino *nt*

driven ['drɪvn] *pp of* **drive**

driver ['draɪvə*] *n* Fahrer(in) *m(f)*; (*Inform*) Treiber *m*; **~'s license** (*US*) Führerschein *m*;

~'s seat Fahrersitz *m*; **driving** ['draɪvɪŋ] *n* (Auto)fahren *nt*; **he likes ~** er fährt gern Auto; **driving lesson** *n* Fahrstunde *f*; **driving licence** *n* (*Brit*) Führerschein *m*; **driving school** *n* Fahrschule *f*; **driving seat** *n* (*Brit*) Fahrersitz *m*; **to be in the ~** alles im Griff haben; **driving test** *n* Fahrprüfung *f*

drizzle ['drɪzl] *n* Nieselregen *m* ▷ *vi* nieseln

drop [drɒp] *n* (*of liquid*) Tropfen *m*; (*fall in price etc*) Rückgang *m* ▷ *vt* (*a. fig: give up*) fallen lassen ▷ *vi* (*fall*) herunterfallen; (*figures, temperature*) sinken, zurückgehen; **drop by, drop in** *vi* vorbeikommen; **drop off** *vi* (*to sleep*) einnicken; **drop out** *vi* (*withdraw*) aussteigen; (*university*) das Studium abbrechen; **dropout** *n* Aussteiger(in) *m(f)*

drought [draʊt] *n* Dürre *f*

drove [drəʊv] *pt of* **drive**

drown [draʊn] *vi* ertrinken ▷ *vt* ertränken

drowsy ['draʊzɪ] *adj* schläfrig

drug [drʌg] *n* (*Med*) Medikament *nt*, Arznei *f*; (*addictive*) Droge *f*; (*narcotic*) Rauschgift *nt*; **to be on ~s** drogensüchtig sein ▷ *vt* (mit Medikamenten) betäuben; **drug addict** *n* Rauschgiftsüchtige(r) *mf*; **drug dealer** *n* Drogenhändler(in) *m(f)*; **druggist** *n* (*US*) Drogist(in) *m(f)*; **drugstore** *n* (*US*) Drogerie *f*

drum [drʌm] *n* Trommel *f*; **~s** *pl* Schlagzeug *nt*; **drummer** *n* Schlagzeuger(in) *m(f)*

drunk [drʌŋk] *pp of* **drink** ▷ *adj* betrunken; **to get ~** sich betrinken ▷ *n* Betrunkene(r) *mf*; (*alcoholic*) Trinker(in) *m(f)*; **drunk-driving** *n* (*US*) Trunkenheit *f* am Steuer; **drunken** *adj* betrunken, besoffen

dry [draɪ] *adj* trocken ▷ *vt* trocknen; (*dishes, oneself, one's hands etc*) abtrocknen ▷ *vi* trocknen, trocken werden; **dry out** *vi* trocknen; **dry up** *vi* austrocknen; **dry-clean** *vt* chemisch reinigen; **dry-cleaning** *n* chemische Reinigung; **dryer** *n* Trockner *m*; (*for hair*) Föhn *m*; (*overhead*) Trockenhaube *f*

DTP *abbr* = **desktop publishing** DTP *nt*

dual ['djʊəl] *adj* doppelt; **~ carriageway** (*Brit*) zweispurige Schnellstraße *f*; **~ nationality** doppelte

d

Staatsangehörigkeit; **dual-purpose** *adj* Mehrzweck-

dubbed [dʌbd] *adj* (*film*) synchronisiert

dubious ['djuːbɪəs] *adj* zweifelhaft

duchess ['dʌtʃəs] *n* Herzogin *f*

duck [dʌk] *n* Ente *f*

dude [duːd] *n* (*US fam*) Typ *m*; **a cool ~** ein cooler Typ

due [djuː] *adj* (*time*) fällig; (*fitting*) angemessen; **in ~ course** zu gegebener Zeit; **~ to** infolge +*gen*, wegen +*gen* ▷ *adv* **~ south/north etc** direkt nach Norden/Süden etc

dug [dʌg] *pt, pp of* **dig**

duke [djuːk] *n* Herzog *m*

dull [dʌl] *adj* (*colour, light, weather*) trübe; (*boring*) langweilig

duly ['djuːlɪ] *adv* ordnungsgemäß; (*as expected*) wie erwartet

dumb [dʌm] *adj* stumm; (*fam: stupid*) doof, blöde

dumb-bell ['dʌmbel] *n* Hantel *f*

dummy ['dʌmɪ] *n* (*sham*) Attrappe *f*; (*in shop*) Schaufensterpuppe *f*; (*Brit: teat*) Schnuller *m*; (*fam: person*) Dummkopf *m* ▷ *adj* unecht, Schein-; **~ run** Testlauf *m*

dump [dʌmp] *n* Abfallhaufen *m*; (*fam: place*) Kaff *nt* ▷ *vt* (*lit, fig*) abladen; (*fam*) **he ~ed her** er hat mir ihr Schluss gemacht

dumpling ['dʌmplɪŋ] *n* Kloß *m*, Knödel *m*

dune [djuːn] *n* Düne *f*

dung [dʌŋ] *n* Dung *m*; (*manure*) Mist *m*

dungarees [dʌŋgə'riːz] *npl* Latzhose *f*

dungeon ['dʌndʒən] *n* Kerker *m*

duplex ['djuːpleks] *n* zweistöckige Wohnung; (*US*) Doppelhaushälfte *f*

duplicate ['djuːplɪkɪt] *n* Duplikat *nt* ▷ ['djuːplɪkeɪt] *vt* (*make copies of*) kopieren; (*repeat*) wiederholen

durable ['djʊərəbl] *adj* haltbar; **duration** [djʊəˈreɪʃən] *n* Dauer *f*

during ['djʊərɪŋ] *prep* (*time*) während +*gen*

dusk [dʌsk] *n* Abenddämmerung *f*

dust [dʌst] *n* Staub *m* ▷ *vt* abstauben; **dustbin** *n* (*Brit*) Mülleimer *m*; **dustcart** *n* (*Brit*) Müllwagen *m*; **duster** *n* Staubtuch *nt*; **dust jacket** *n* Schutzumschlag *m*; **dustman** *n* (*Brit*) Müllmann *m*; **dustpan** *n* Kehrschaufel *f*; **dusty** *adj* staubig

Dutch [dʌtʃ] *adj* holländisch ▷ *n* (*language*) Holländisch *nt*; **to speak/talk double ~** (*fam*) Quatsch reden; **the ~** *pl* die Holländer; **Dutchman** (*pl* **-men**) *n*

Holländer *m*; **Dutchwoman** (*pl* **-women**) *n* Holländerin *f*

duty ['djuːtɪ] *n* Pflicht *f*; (*task*) Aufgabe *f*; (*tax*) Zoll *m*; **on/off ~** im Dienst/nicht im Dienst; **to be on ~** Dienst haben; **duty-free** *adj* zollfrei; **~ shop** Dutyfreeshop *m*

duvet ['duːveɪ] *n* Federbett *nt*

DVD *n abbr* = **digital versatile disk** DVD *f*

dwarf [dwɔːf] (*pl* **dwarves**) *n* Zwerg(in) *m(f)*

dwelling ['dwelɪŋ] *n* Wohnung *f*

dwindle ['dwɪndl] *vi* schwinden

dye [daɪ] *n* Farbstoff *m* ▷ *vt* färben

dynamic [daɪˈnæmɪk] *adj* dynamisch

dynamo ['daɪnəməʊ] *n* Dynamo *m*

dyslexia [dɪsˈleksɪə] *n* Legasthenie *f*; **dyslexic** *adj* legasthenisch; **to be ~** Legastheniker(in) sein

dyspepsia [dɪsˈpepsɪə] *n* Verdauungsstörung *f*

e

E [iː] *abbr* = **east** O

E111 form *n* ≈ Auslandskrankenschein *m*

each [iːtʃ] *adj* jeder/jede/jedes ▷ *pron* jeder/jede/jedes; **I'll have one of ~** ich nehme von jedem eins; **they ~ have a car** jeder von ihnen hat ein Auto; **~ other** einander, sich; **for/against ~ other** füreinander/gegeneinander ▷ *adv* je; **they cost 10 euros ~** sie kosten je 10 Euro, sie kosten 10 Euro das Stück

eager ['iːgə*] *adj* eifrig; **to be ~ to do sth** darauf brennen, etw zu tun

eagle ['iːgl] *n* Adler *m*

ear [ɪə*] *n* Ohr *nt*; **earache** *n* Ohrenschmerzen *pl*; **eardrum** *n* Trommelfell *nt*

earl [ɜːl] *n* Graf *m*

early ['ɜːlɪ] *adj, adv* früh; **to be 10 minutes ~** 10 Minuten zu früh kommen; **at the earliest** frühestens; **in ~ June/2008** Anfang Juni/2008; **~ retirement** vorzeitiger Ruhestand; **~ warning system** Frühwarnsystem *nt*

earn [ɜːn] *vt* verdienen

earnest ['ɜːnɪst] *adj* ernst; **in ~** im Ernst

earnings ['ɜːnɪŋz] *npl* Verdienst *m*, Einkommen *nt*

earphones ['ɪəfəʊnz] *npl* Kopfhörer *m*; **earplug** *n* Ohrenstöpsel *m*, Ohropax® *nt*; **earring** *n* Ohrring *m*

earth [ɜːθ] *n* Erde *f*; **what on ~ ...?** was in aller Welt ...? ▷ *vt* erden; **earthenware** *n* Tonwaren *pl*; **earthquake** *n* Erdbeben *nt*

earwig ['ɪəwɪg] *n* Ohrwurm *m*

ease [iːz] *vt* (*pain*) lindern; (*burden*) erleichtern ▷ *n* (*easiness*) Leichtigkeit *f*; **to feel at ~** sich wohl fühlen; **to feel ill at ~** sich nicht wohl fühlen; **easily** ['iːzɪlɪ] *adv* leicht; **he is ~ the best** er ist mit Abstand der Beste

east [iːst] *n* Osten *m*; **to the ~ of** östlich von ▷ *adv* (*go, face*) nach Osten ▷ *adj* Ost-; **~ wind** Ostwind *m*; **eastbound** *adj* (in) Richtung Osten

Easter ['iːstə*] *n* Ostern *nt*; **at ~** zu Ostern; **Easter egg** *n* Osterei *nt*; **Easter Sunday** *n* Ostersonntag *m*

eastern ['iːstən] *adj* Ost-, östlich; **Eastern Europe** Osteuropa *nt*; **East Germany** *n* Ostdeutschland *nt*; **former ~** die ehemalige DDR, die neuen Bundesländer; **eastwards** ['iːstwədz] *adv* nach Osten

easy ['iːzɪ] *adj* leicht; (*task, solution*) einfach; (*life*) bequem; (*manner*) ungezwungen; **easy-care** *adj* pflegeleicht; **easy-going** *adj* gelassen

eat [iːt] (**ate, eaten**) *vt* essen; (*animal*) fressen; **eat out** *vi* zum Essen ausgehen; **eat up** *vt* aufessen; (*animal*) auffressen

eaten ['iːtn] *pp of* **eat**

eavesdrop ['iːvzdrɒp] *vi* (heimlich) lauschen; **to ~ on sb** jdn belauschen

eccentric [ɪk'sentrɪk] *adj* exzentrisch

echo ['ekəʊ] (*pl* **-es**) *n* Echo *nt* ▷ *vi* widerhallen

ecological [iːkə'lɒdʒɪkl] *adj* ökologisch; **~ disaster** Umweltkatastrophe *f*; **ecology** [ɪ'kɒlədʒɪ] *n* Ökologie *f*

economic [iːkə'nɒmɪk] *adj* wirtschaftlich, Wirtschafts-; **~ aid** Wirtschaftshilfe *f*; **economical** *adj* wirtschaftlich; (*person*) sparsam; **economics** *nsing o pl* Wirtschaftswissenschaft *f*; **economist** [ɪ'kɒnəmɪst] *n* Wirtschaftswissenschaftler(in) *m(f)*; **economize** [ɪ'kɒnəmaɪz] *vi* sparen (*on an +dat*); **economy** [ɪ'kɒnəmɪ] *n* (*of state*)

Wirtschaft f; (thrift) Sparsamkeit f;
economy class n (Aviat) Economyclass f
ecstasy ['ekstəsɪ] n Ekstase f; (drug)
Ecstasy f
eczema ['eksɪmə] n Ekzem nt
edge [edʒ] n Rand m; (of knife) Schneide f;
on ~ nervös; **edgy** ['edʒɪ] adj nervös
edible ['edɪbl] adj essbar
Edinburgh ['edɪnbərə] n Edinburg nt
edit ['edɪt] vt (series, newspaper etc)
herausgeben; (text) redigieren; (film)
schneiden; (Inform) editieren; **edition**
[ɪ'dɪʃən] n Ausgabe f; **editor** n
Redakteur(in) m(f); (of series etc)
Herausgeber(in) m(f); **editorial**
[edɪ'tɔːrɪəl] adj Redaktions- ⊳ n
Leitartikel m
educate ['edjʊkeɪt] vt (child) erziehen; (at
school, university) ausbilden; (public)
aufklären; **educated** adj gebildet;
education [edjʊ'keɪʃən] n Erziehung f;
(studies, training) Ausbildung f; (subject of
study) Pädagogik f; (system) Schulwesen nt;
(knowledge) Bildung f; **educational** adj
pädagogisch; (instructive) lehrreich;
~ television Schulfernsehen nt
eel [iːl] n Aal m
eerie ['ɪərɪ] adj unheimlich
effect [ɪ'fekt] n Wirkung f (on auf +akk); **to
come into ~** in Kraft treten; **effective** adj
wirksam, effektiv
effeminate [ɪ'femɪnət] adj (of man)
tuntig
efficiency [ɪ'fɪʃənsɪ] n Leistungsfähigkeit
f; (of method) Wirksamkeit f; **efficient** adj
(Tech) leistungsfähig; (method) wirksam,
effizient
effort ['efət] n Anstrengung f; (attempt)
Versuch m; **to make an ~** sich anstrengen;
effortless adj mühelos
eg abbr = **exempli gratia (for example)** z.
B.
egg [eg] n Ei nt; **eggcup** n Eierbecher m;
eggplant n (US) Aubergine f; **eggshell** n
Eierschale f
ego ['iːgəʊ] (pl **-s**) n Ich nt; (self-esteem)
Selbstbewusstsein nt; **ego(t)ist**
['egəʊ(t)ɪst] n Egozentriker(in) m(f)
Egypt ['iːdʒɪpt] n Ägypten nt; **Egyptian**
[ɪ'dʒɪpʃən] adj ägyptisch ⊳ n Ägypter(in)
m(f)
eiderdown ['aɪdədaʊn] n Daunendecke f
eight [eɪt] num acht; **at the age of ~** im

Alter von acht Jahren; **it's ~ (o'clock)** es ist
acht Uhr ⊳ n (a. bus etc) Acht f; (boat)
Achter m; **eighteen** [eɪ'tiːn] num
achtzehn ⊳ n Achtzehn f; see also **eight**;
eighteenth adj achtzehnte(r, s); see also
eighth; **eighth** [eɪtθ] adj achte(r, s); **the
~ of June** der achte Juni ⊳ n (fraction)
Achtel nt; **an ~ of a litre** ein Achtelliter;
eightieth ['eɪtɪəθ] adj achtzigste(r, s); see
also **eighth**; **eighty** ['eɪtɪ] num achtzig
⊳ n Achtzig f; see also **eight**
Eire ['ɛərə] n die Republik Irland
either ['aɪðə*] conj **~ ... or** entweder ...
oder ⊳ pron **~ of the two** eine(r, s) von
beiden ⊳ adj **on ~ side** auf beiden Seiten
⊳ adv **I won't go ~** ich gehe auch nicht
eject [ɪ'dʒekt] vt ausstoßen; (person)
vertreiben
elaborate [ɪ'læbərət] adj (complex)
kompliziert; (plan) ausgeklügelt;
(decoration) kunstvoll ⊳ vi [ɪ'læbəreɪt]
could you ~ on that? könntest du mehr
darüber sagen?
elastic [ɪ'læstɪk] adj elastisch; **~ band**
Gummiband nt
elbow ['elbəʊ] n Ellbogen m
elder ['eldə*] adj (of two) älter ⊳ n
Ältere(r) mf; (Bot) Holunder m; **elderly** adj
ältere(r, s) ⊳ n **the ~** die älteren Leute;
eldest ['eldɪst] adj älteste(r, s)
elect [ɪ'lekt] vt wählen; **he was ~ed
chairman** er wurde zum Vorsitzenden
gewählt; **election** [ɪ'lekʃən] n Wahl f;
election campaign n Wahlkampf m;
electioneering [ɪlekʃə'nɪərɪŋ] n
Wahlpropaganda f; **electorate** [ɪ'lektərɪt]
n Wähler pl
electric [ɪ'lektrɪk] adj elektrisch; (car,
motor, razor etc) Elektro-; **~ blanket**
Heizdecke f; **~ cooker** Elektroherd m;
~ current elektrischer Strom; **~ shock**
Stromschlag m; **electrical** adj elektrisch;
~ goods/appliances Elektrogeräte;
electrician [ɪlek'trɪʃən] n Elektriker(in)
m(f); **electricity** [ɪlek'trɪsɪtɪ] n
Elektrizität f; **electrocute** [ɪ'lektrəʊkjuːt]
vt durch einen Stromschlag töten;
electronic [ɪlek'trɒnɪk] adj elektronisch
elegance ['elɪgəns] n Eleganz f; **elegant**
adj elegant
element ['elɪmənt] n Element nt; **an ~ of
truth** ein Körnchen Wahrheit;
elementary [elɪ'mentərɪ] adj einfach;

(*basic*) grundlegend; **~ stage** Anfangsstadium *nt*; **~ school** (*US*) Grundschule *f*; **~ maths/French** Grundkenntnisse in Mathematik/Französisch

elephant ['elɪfənt] *n* Elefant *m*

elevator ['elɪveɪtə*] *n* (*US*) Fahrstuhl *m*

eleven [ɪ'levn] *num* elf ▷ *n* (*team, bus etc*) Elf *f see* **eight**; **eleventh** [ɪ'levnθ] *adj* elfte(r, s) ▷ *n* (*fraction*) Elftel *nt see* **eighth**

eligible ['elɪdʒəbl] *adj* in Frage kommend; (*for grant etc*) berechtigt; **~ for a pension/competition** pensions-/teilnahmeberechtigt; **~ bachelor** begehrter Junggeselle

eliminate [ɪ'lɪmɪneɪt] *vt* ausschließen (*from aus*), ausschalten; (*problem etc*) beseitigen; **elimination** *n* Ausschluss *m* (*from aus*); (*of problem etc*) Beseitigung *f*

elm [elm] *n* Ulme *f*

elope [ɪ'ləʊp] *vi* durchbrennen (*with sb mit jdm*)

eloquent ['eləkwənt] *adj* redegewandt

else [els] *adv* **anybody/anything ~** (*in addition*) sonst (noch) jemand/etwas; (*other*) ein anderer/etwas anderes; **somebody ~** jemand anders; **everyone ~** alle anderen; **or ~** sonst; **elsewhere** *adv* anderswo, woanders; (*direction*) woandershin

ELT *abbr* = **English Language Teaching**

e-mail, E-mail ['i:meɪl] *vi, vt* mailen (*sth to sb jdm etw*) ▷ *n* E-Mail *f*; **e-mail address** *n* E-Mail-Adresse *f*

emancipated [ɪ'mænsɪpeɪtɪd] *adj* emanzipiert

embankment [ɪm'bæŋkmənt] *n* Böschung *f*; (*for railway*) Bahndamm *m*

embargo [ɪm'bɑːgəʊ] (*pl* **-es**) *n* Embargo *nt*

embark [ɪm'bɑːk] *vi* an Bord gehen

embarrass [ɪm'bærəs] *vt* in Verlegenheit bringen; **embarrassed** *adj* verlegen; **embarrassing** *adj* peinlich

embassy ['embəsɪ] *n* Botschaft *f*

embrace [ɪm'breɪs] *vt* umarmen ▷ *n* Umarmung *f*

embroider [ɪm'brɔɪdə*] *vt* besticken; **embroidery** *n* Stickerei *f*

embryo ['embrɪəʊ] (*pl* **-s**) *n* Embryo *m*

emerald ['emərəld] *n* Smaragd *m*

emerge [ɪ'mɜːdʒ] *vi* auftauchen; **it ~d that ...** es stellte sich heraus, dass ...

emergency [ɪ'mɜːdʒənsɪ] *n* Notfall *m* ▷ *adj* Not-; **~ exit** Notausgang *m*; **~ room** (*US*) Unfallstation *f*; **~ service** Notdienst *m*; **~ stop** Vollbremsung *f*

emigrate ['emɪgreɪt] *vi* auswandern

emit [ɪ'mɪt] *vt* ausstoßen; (*heat*) abgeben

emotion [ɪ'məʊʃən] *n* Emotion *f*, Gefühl *nt*; **emotional** *adj* (*person*) emotional; (*experience, moment, scene*) ergreifend

emperor ['empərə*] *n* Kaiser *m*

emphasis ['emfəsɪs] *n* Betonung *f*; **emphasize** ['emfəsaɪz] *vt* betonen; **emphatic, emphatically** [ɪm'fætɪk, -lɪ] *adj, adv* nachdrücklich

empire ['empaɪə*] *n* Reich *nt*

employ [ɪm'plɔɪ] *vt* beschäftigen; (*hire*) anstellen; (*use*) anwenden; **employee** [emplɔɪˈiː] *n* Angestellte(r) *mf*; **employer** *n* Arbeitgeber(in) *m(f)*; **employment** *n* Beschäftigung *f*; (*position*) Stellung *f*; **employment agency** *n* Stellenvermittlung *f*

empress ['emprɪs] *n* Kaiserin *f*

empty ['emptɪ] *adj* leer ▷ *vt* (*contents*) leeren; (*container*) ausleeren

enable [ɪ'neɪbl] *vt* **to ~ sb to do sth** es jdm ermöglichen, etw zu tun

enamel [ɪ'næməl] *n* Email *nt*; (*of teeth*) Zahnschmelz *m*

enchanting [ɪn'tʃɑːntɪŋ] *adj* bezaubernd

enclose [ɪn'kləʊz] *vt* einschließen; (*in letter*) beilegen (*in, with dat*); **enclosure** [ɪn'kləʊʒə*] *n* (*for animals*) Gehege *nt*; (*in letter*) Anlage *f*

encore ['ɒŋkɔː*] *n* Zugabe *f*

encounter [ɪn'kaʊntə*] *n* Begegnung *f* ▷ *vt* (*person*) begegnen +*dat*; (*difficulties*) stoßen auf +*akk*

encourage [ɪn'kʌrɪdʒ] *vt* ermutigen; **encouragement** *n* Ermutigung *f*

encyclopaedia [ensaɪkləʊ'piːdɪə] *n* Lexikon *nt*, Enzyklopädie *f*

end [end] *n* Ende *nt*; (*of film, play etc*) Schluss *m*; (*purpose*) Zweck *m*; **at the ~ of May** Ende Mai; **in the ~** schließlich; **to come to an ~** zu Ende gehen ▷ *vt* beenden ▷ *vi* enden; **end up** *vi* enden

endanger [ɪn'deɪndʒə*] *vt* gefährden; **~ed species** vom Aussterben bedrohte Art

endeavour [ɪn'devə*] *n* Bemühung *f* ▷ *vt* sich bemühen (*to do sth etw zu tun*)

ending ['endɪŋ] *n* (*of book*) Ausgang *m*; (*last part*) Schluss *m*; (*of word*) Endung *f*

e

endive [ˈendaɪv] n Endiviensalat m

endless [ˈendlɪs] adj endlos; (possibilities) unendlich

endurance [ɪnˈdjʊərəns] n Ausdauer f; **endure** [ɪnˈdjʊə*] vt ertragen

enemy [ˈenɪmɪ] n Feind(in) m(f) ▷ adj feindlich

energetic [enəˈdʒetɪk] adj energiegeladen; (active) aktiv; **energy** [ˈenədʒɪ] n Energie f

enforce [ɪnˈfɔːs] vt durchsetzen; (obedience) erzwingen

engage [ɪnˈgeɪdʒ] vt (employ) einstellen; (singer, performer) engagieren; **engaged** adj verlobt; (toilet, telephone line) besetzt; **to get ~** sich verloben (to mit); **engaged tone** n (Brit Tel) Belegzeichen nt; **engagement** n (to marry) Verlobung f; **~ ring** Verlobungsring m; **engaging** adj gewinnend

engine [ˈendʒɪn] n (Auto) Motor m; (Rail) Lokomotive f; **~ failure** (Auto) Motorschaden m; **~ trouble** (Auto) Defekt m am Motor; **engineer** [endʒɪˈnɪə*] n Ingenieur(in) m(f); (US Rail) Lokomotivführer(in) m(f); **engineering** [endʒɪˈnɪərɪŋ] n Technik f; (mechanical ~) Maschinenbau m; (subject) Ingenieurwesen nt; **engine immobilizer** n (Auto) Wegfahrsperre f

England [ˈɪŋglənd] n England nt; **English** adj englisch; **he's ~** er ist Engländer; **the ~ Channel** der Ärmelkanal ▷ n (language) Englisch nt; **in ~** auf Englisch; **to translate into ~** ins Englische übersetzen; (people) **the ~** pl die Engländer; **Englishman** (pl **-men**) n Engländer m; **Englishwoman** (pl **-women**) n Engländerin f

engrave [ɪnˈgreɪv] vt eingravieren; **engraving** n Stich m

engrossed [ɪnˈgrəʊst] adj vertieft (in sth in etw akk)

enigma [ɪˈnɪgmə] n Rätsel nt

enjoy [ɪnˈdʒɔɪ] vt genießen; **I ~ reading** ich lese gern; **he ~s teasing her** es macht ihm Spaß, sie aufzuziehen; **did you ~ the film?** hat dir der Film gefallen?; **enjoyable** adj angenehm; (entertaining) unterhaltsam; **enjoyment** n Vergnügen nt; (stronger) Freude f (of an +dat)

enlarge [ɪnˈlɑːdʒ] vt vergrößern; (expand) erweitern; **enlargement** n Vergrößerung f

enormous, enormously [ɪˈnɔːməs, -lɪ] adj, adv riesig, ungeheuer

enough [ɪˈnʌf] adj genug; **that's ~** das reicht!; (stop it) Schluss damit!; **I've had ~** das hat mir gereicht; (to eat) ich bin satt ▷ adv genug, genügend

enquire [ɪnˈkwaɪə*] vi sich erkundigen (about nach); **enquiry** [ɪnˈkwaɪərɪ] n (question) Anfrage f; (for information) Erkundigung f (about über +akk); (investigation) Untersuchung f; **'Enquiries'** „Auskunft"

enrol [ɪnˈrəʊl] vi sich einschreiben; (for course, school) sich anmelden; **enrolment** n Einschreibung f, Anmeldung f

en suite [ɒnˈswiːt] adj, n **room with ~** (bathroom) Zimmer nt mit eigenem Bad

ensure [ɪnˈʃʊə*] vt sicherstellen

enter [ˈentə*] vt eintreten in +akk, betreten; (drive into) einfahren in +akk; (country) einreisen in +akk; (in list) eintragen; (Inform) eingeben; (race, contest) teilnehmen an +dat ▷ vi (towards speaker) hereinkommen; (away from speaker) hineingehen

enterprise [ˈentəpraɪz] n (Comm) Unternehmen nt

entertain [entəˈteɪn] vt (guest) bewirten; (amuse) unterhalten; **entertaining** adj unterhaltsam; **entertainment** n (amusement) Unterhaltung f

enthusiasm [ɪnˈθjuːzɪæzəm] n Begeisterung f; **enthusiastic** [ɪnθjuːzɪˈæstɪk] adj begeistert (about von)

entice [ɪnˈtaɪs] vt locken; (lead astray) verleiten

entire, entirely [ɪnˈtaɪə*, -lɪ] adj, adv ganz

entitle [ɪnˈtaɪtl] vt (qualify) berechtigen (to zu); (name) betiteln

entrance [ˈentrəns] n Eingang m; (for vehicles) Einfahrt f; (entering) Eintritt m; (Theat) Auftritt m; **entrance exam** n Aufnahmeprüfung f; **entrance fee** n Eintrittsgeld nt

entrust [ɪnˈtrʌst] vt **to ~ sb with sth** jdm etw anvertrauen

entry [ˈentrɪ] n (way in) Eingang m; (entering) Eintritt m; (in vehicle) Einfahrt f; (into country) Einreise f; (admission) Zutritt m; (in diary, accounts) Eintrag m; **'no ~'** „Eintritt verboten"; (for vehicles) „Einfahrt verboten"; **entry phone** n Türsprechanlage f

E-number n (food additive) E-Nummer f
envelope ['envələʊp] n (Brief)umschlag
m
enviable ['enviəbl] adj beneidenswert;
envious ['enviəs] adj neidisch
environment [ɪn'vaɪərənmənt] n
Umgebung f; (ecology) Umwelt f;
environmental [ɪnvaɪərən'məntəl] adj
Umwelt-; ~ **pollution**
Umweltverschmutzung f;
environmentalist n Umweltschützer(in)
m(f)
envy ['envi] n Neid m (of auf +akk) ▷ vt
beneiden (sb sth jdn um etw)
epic ['epɪk] n Epos nt; (film)
Monumentalfilm m
epidemic [epɪ'demɪk] n Epidemie f
epilepsy [epɪ'lepsɪ] n Epilepsie f;
epileptic [epɪ'leptɪk] adj epileptisch
episode ['epɪsəʊd] n Episode f; (Tv)
Fortsetzung f, Folge f
epoch ['i:pɒk] n Zeitalter nt, Epoche f
equal ['i:kwl] adj gleich (to +dat) ▷ n
Gleichgestellte(r) mf ▷ vt gleichen;
(match) gleichkommen +dat; **two times
two ~s four** zwei mal zwei ist gleich vier;
equality [ɪ'kwɒlɪtɪ] n Gleichheit f; (equal
rights) Gleichberechtigung f; **equalize** vi
(Sport) ausgleichen; **equalizer** n (Sport)
Ausgleichstreffer m; **equally** adv gleich;
(on the other hand) andererseits; **equation**
[ɪ'kweɪʒən] n (Math) Gleichung f
equator [ɪ'kweɪtə*] n Äquator m
equilibrium [i:kwɪ'lɪbrɪəm] n
Gleichgewicht nt
equip [ɪ'kwɪp] vt ausrüsten; (kitchen)
ausstatten; **equipment** n Ausrüstung f;
(for kitchen) Ausstattung f; **electrical
~** Elektrogeräte pl
equivalent [ɪ'kwɪvələnt] adj
gleichwertig (to dat); (corresponding)
entsprechend (to dat) ▷ n Äquivalent nt;
(amount) gleiche Menge; (in money)
Gegenwert m
era ['ɪərə] n Ära f, Zeitalter nt
erase [ɪ'reɪz] vt ausradieren; (tape, disk)
löschen; **eraser** n Radiergummi m
erect [ɪ'rekt] adj aufrecht ▷ vt (building,
monument) errichten; (tent) aufstellen;
erection n Errichtung f; (Anat) Erektion f
erode [ɪ'rəʊd] vt zerfressen; (land)
auswaschen; (rights, power) aushöhlen;
erosion [ɪ'rəʊʒən] n Erosion f

erotic [ɪ'rɒtɪk] adj erotisch
err [ɜ:*] vi sich irren
errand ['erənd] n Besorgung f
erratic [ɪ'rætɪk] adj (behaviour)
unberechenbar; (bus link etc)
unregelmäßig; (performance) unbeständig
error ['erə*] n Fehler m; **in**
~ irrtümlicherweise; **error message** n
(Inform) Fehlermeldung f
erupt [ɪ'rʌpt] vi ausbrechen
escalator ['eskəleɪtə*] n Rolltreppe f
escalope ['eskələp] n Schnitzel nt
escape [ɪ'skeɪp] n Flucht f; (from prison etc)
Ausbruch m; **to have a narrow ~** gerade
noch davonkommen; **there's no ~** (fig) es
gibt keinen Ausweg ▷ vt (pursuers)
entkommen +dat; (punishment etc)
entgehen +dat ▷ vi (from pursuers)
entkommen (from dat); (from prison etc)
ausbrechen (from dat); (leak: gas)
ausströmen; (water) auslaufen
escort ['eskɔ:t] n (companion)
Begleiter(in) m(f); (guard) Eskorte f ▷ vt
[ɪ'skɔ:t] (lady) begleiten
especially [ɪ'speʃəlɪ] adv besonders
espionage ['espɪəna:ʒ] n Spionage f
Esquire [ɪ'skwaɪə*] n (Brit: in address) **J.
Brown, Esq** Herrn J. Brown
essay ['eseɪ] n Aufsatz m; (literary) Essay
m
essential [ɪ'senʃəl] adj (necessary)
unentbehrlich, unverzichtbar; (basic)
wesentlich ▷ n **the ~s** pl das Wesentliche;
essentially adv im Wesentlichen
establish [ɪ'stæblɪʃ] vt (set up) gründen;
(introduce) einführen; (relations)
aufnehmen; (prove) nachweisen; **to
~ that ...** feststellen, dass ...;
establishment n Institution f; (business)
Unternehmen nt
estate [ɪ'steɪt] n Gut nt; (of deceased)
Nachlass m; (housing ~) Siedlung f; (country
house) Landsitz m; **estate agent** n (Brit)
Grundstücksmakler(in) m(f),
Immobilienmakler(in) m(f); **estate car** n
(Brit) Kombiwagen m
estimate ['estɪmət] n Schätzung f;
(Comm: of price) Kostenvoranschlag m
▷ ['estɪmeɪt] vt schätzen
estuary ['estjʊərɪ] n Mündung f
etching ['etʃɪŋ] n Radierung f
eternal, eternally [ɪ'tɜ:nl, -nəlɪ] adj, adv
ewig; **eternity** n Ewigkeit f

ethical ['eθɪkəl] *adj* ethisch; **ethics** ['eθɪks] *npl* Ethik *f*

Ethiopia [i:θɪ'əʊpɪə] *n* Äthiopien *nt*

ethnic ['eθnɪk] *adj* ethnisch; *(clothes etc)* landesüblich; **~ minority** ethnische Minderheit

EU *abbr* = **European Union** EU *f*

euphemism ['ju:fɪmɪzəm] *n* Euphemismus *m*

euro ['jʊərəʊ] *(pl* **-s)** *n (Fin)* Euro *m*; **~ symbol** Eurozeichen *nt*; **Eurocheque** ['jʊərəʊtʃek] *n* Euroscheck *m*; **Europe** ['jʊərəp] *n* Europa *nt*; **European** [jʊərə'pi:ən] *adj* europäisch; **~ Parliament** Europäisches Parlament; **~ Union** Europäische Union ▷ *n* Europäer(in) *m(f)*; **Eurosceptic** ['jʊərəʊskeptɪk] *n* Euroskeptiker(in) *m(f)*; **Eurotunnel** *n* Eurotunnel *m*

evacuate [ɪ'vækjʊeɪt] *vt (place)* räumen; *(people)* evakuieren

evade [ɪ'veɪd] *vt* ausweichen +*dat*; *(pursuers)* sich entziehen +*dat*

evaluate [ɪ'væljʊeɪt] *vt* auswerten

evaporate [ɪ'væpəreɪt] *vi* verdampfen; *(fig)* verschwinden; **~d milk** Kondensmilch *f*

even ['i:vən] *adj (flat)* eben; *(regular)* gleichmäßig; *(equal)* gleich; *(number)* gerade; **the score is ~** es steht unentschieden ▷ *adv* sogar; **~ you** selbst *(o* sogar*)* du; **~ if** selbst wenn, wenn auch; **~ though** obwohl; **not ~** nicht einmal; **~ better** noch besser; **even out** *vi (prices)* sich einpendeln

evening ['i:vnɪŋ] *n* Abend *m*; **in the ~** abends, am Abend; **this ~** heute Abend; **evening class** *n* Abendkurs *m*; **evening dress** *n (generally)* Abendkleidung *f*; *(woman's)* Abendkleid *nt*

evenly ['i:vənlɪ] *adv* gleichmäßig

event [ɪ'vent] *n* Ereignis *nt*; *(organized)* Veranstaltung *f*; *(Sport: discipline)* Disziplin *f*; **in the ~ of** im Falle +*gen*; **eventful** *adj* ereignisreich

eventual [ɪ'ventʃʊəl] *adj (final)* letztendlich; **eventually** [ɪ'ventʃʊəlɪ] *adv (at last)* am Ende; *(given time)* schließlich

ever ['evə*] *adv (at any time)* je(mals); **don't ~ do that again** tu das ja nie wieder; **he's the best ~** er ist der Beste, den es je gegeben hat; **have you ~ been to the States?** bist du schon einmal in den Staaten gewesen?; **for ~** (für) immer; **for ~ and ~** auf immer und ewig; **~ so ...** *(fam)* äußerst ...; **~ so drunk** ganz schön betrunken

every ['evrɪ] *adj* jeder/jede/jedes; **~ day** jeden Tag; **~ other day** jeden zweiten Tag; **~ five days** alle fünf Tage; **I have ~ reason to believe that ...** ich habe allen Grund anzunehmen, dass ...; **everybody** *pron* jeder, alle *pl*; **everyday** *adj (commonplace)* alltäglich; *(clothes, language etc)* Alltags-; **everyone** *pron* jeder, alle *pl*; **everything** *pron* alles; **everywhere** *adv* überall; *(with direction)* überallhin

evidence ['evɪdəns] *n* Beweise *pl*; *(single piece)* Beweis *m*; *(testimony)* Aussage *f*; *(signs)* Spuren *pl*; **evident, evidently** *adj, adv* offensichtlich

evil ['i:vl] *adj* böse ▷ *n* Böse(s) *nt*; **an ~** ein Übel

evolution [i:və'lu:ʃən] *n* Entwicklung *f*; *(of life)* Evolution *f*; **evolve** [ɪ'vɒlv] *vi* sich entwickeln

ex- [eks] *pref* Ex-, ehemalig; **~wife** frühere Frau, Exfrau *f*; **ex** *n (fam)* Verflossene(r) *mf*, Ex *mf*

exact [ɪg'zækt] *adj* genau; **exactly** *adv* genau; **not ~ fast** nicht gerade schnell

exaggerate [ɪg'zædʒəreɪt] *vt, vi* übertreiben; **exaggerated** *adj* übertrieben; **exaggeration** *n* Übertreibung *f*

exam [ɪg'zæm] *n* Prüfung *f*; **examination** [ɪgzæmɪ'neɪʃən] *n (Med etc)* Untersuchung *f*, Prüfung *f*; *(at university)* Examen *nt*; *(at customs etc)* Kontrolle *f*; **examine** [ɪg'zæmɪn] *vt* untersuchen *(for* auf +*akk)*; *(check)* kontrollieren, prüfen; **examiner** *n* Prüfer(in) *m(f)*

example [ɪg'zɑ:mpl] *n* Beispiel *nt*; **for ~** zum Beispiel

excavation [ekskə'veɪʃən] *n* Ausgrabung *f*

exceed [ɪk'si:d] *vt* überschreiten, übertreffen; **exceedingly** *adv* äußerst

excel [ɪk'sel] *vt* übertreffen; **he ~led himself** er hat sich selbst übertroffen ▷ *vi* sich auszeichnen *(in* in +*dat*, *at* bei); **excellent, excellently** ['eksələnt, -lɪ] *adj, adv* ausgezeichnet

except [ɪk'sept] *prep* **~** außer +*dat*; **~ for** abgesehen von ▷ *vt* ausnehmen; **exception** [ɪk'sepʃən] *n* Ausnahme *f*;

exceptional, exceptionally [ɪk'sepʃənl, -nəlɪ] adj, adv außergewöhnlich

excess [ek'ses] n Übermaß nt (of an +dat); **excess baggage** n Übergepäck nt; **excesses** npl Exzesse pl; (drink, sex) Ausschweifungen pl; **excess fare** n Nachlösegebühr f; **excessive, excessively** adj, adv übermäßig; **excess weight** n Übergewicht nt

exchange [ɪks'tʃeɪndʒ] n Austausch m (for gegen); (of bought items) Umtausch m (for gegen); (Fin) Wechsel m; (Tel) Vermittlung f, Zentrale f ▷ vt austauschen; (goods) tauschen; (bought items) umtauschen (for gegen); (money, blows) wechseln; **exchange rate** n Wechselkurs m

excite [ɪk'saɪt] vt erregen; **excited** adj aufgeregt; **to get ~** sich aufregen; **exciting** adj aufregend; (book, film) spannend

exclamation [ekskləˈmeɪʃən] n Ausruf m; **exclamation mark, exclamation point** (US) n Ausrufezeichen nt

exclude [ɪks'kluːd] vt ausschließen; **exclusion** [ɪks'kluːʒən] n Ausschluss m; **exclusive** [ɪks'kluːsɪv] adj (select) exklusiv; (sole) ausschließlich; **exclusively** adv ausschließlich

excrement ['ekskrɪmənt] n Kot m, Exkremente pl

excruciating [ɪks'kruːʃɪeɪtɪŋ] adj fürchterlich, entsetzlich

excursion [ɪks'kɜːʃən] n Ausflug m

excusable [ɪks'kjuːzəbl] adj entschuldbar; **excuse** [ɪks'kjuːz] vt entschuldigen; **~ me** Entschuldigung!; **to ~ sb for sth** jdm etw verzeihen; **to ~ sb from sth** jdn von etw befreien ▷ [ɪks'kjuːs] n Entschuldigung f, Ausrede f

ex-directory [eksdaɪ'rektərɪ] adj **to be ~** (Brit Tel) nicht im Telefonbuch stehen

execute ['eksɪkjuːt] vt (carry out) ausführen; (kill) hinrichten; **execution** (killing) Hinrichtung f; (carrying out) Ausführung f; **executive** [ɪg'zekjʊtɪv] n (Comm) leitender Angestellter, leitende Angestellte

exemplary [ɪg'zemplərɪ] adj beispielhaft

exempt [ɪg'zempt] adj befreit (from von) ▷ vt befreien

exercise ['eksəsaɪz] n (in school, sports) Übung f; (movement) Bewegung f; **to get more ~** mehr Sport treiben; **exercise bike**

n Heimtrainer m; **exercise book** n Heft nt

exert [ɪg'zɜːt] vt (influence) ausüben

exhaust [ɪg'zɔːst] n (fumes) Abgase pl; (Auto) Auspuff m; **exhausted** adj erschöpft; **exhausting** adj anstrengend

exhibit [ɪg'zɪbɪt] n (in exhibition) Ausstellungsstück nt; **exhibition** [eksɪ'bɪʃən] n Ausstellung f; **exhibitor** n Aussteller(in) m(f)

exhilarating [ɪg'zɪləreɪtɪŋ] adj belebend, erregend

exile ['eksaɪl] n Exil nt; (person) Verbannte(r) mf ▷ vt verbannen

exist [ɪg'zɪst] vi existieren; (live) leben (on von); **existence** n Existenz f; **to come into ~** entstehen; **existing** adj bestehend

exit ['eksɪt] n Ausgang m; (for vehicles) Ausfahrt f; **exit poll** n Umfrage direkt nach dem Wahlgang

exorbitant [ɪg'zɔːbɪtənt] adj astronomisch

exotic [ɪg'zɒtɪk] adj exotisch

expand [ɪks'pænd] vt ausdehnen, erweitern ▷ vi sich ausdehnen; **expansion** [ɪks'pænʃən] n Expansion f, Erweiterung f

expect [ɪk'spekt] vt erwarten; (suppose) annehmen; **he ~s me to do it** er erwartet, dass ich es mache; **I ~ it'll rain** es wird wohl regnen; **I ~ so** ich denke schon ▷ vi **to be ~ing** ein Kind erwarten

expedition [ekspɪ'dɪʃən] n Expedition f

expenditure [ɪk'spendɪtʃə*] n Ausgaben pl

expense [ɪk'spens] n Kosten pl; (single cost) Ausgabe f; (business) **~s** pl Spesen pl; **at sb's ~** auf jds Kosten; **expensive** [ɪk'spensɪv] adj teuer

experience [ɪk'spɪərɪəns] n Erfahrung f; (particular incident) Erlebnis nt; **by/from ~** aus Erfahrung ▷ vt erfahren, erleben; (hardship) durchmachen; **experienced** adj erfahren

experiment [ɪk'sperɪmənt] n Versuch m, Experiment nt ▷ vi experimentieren

expert ['ekspɜːt] n Experte m, Expertin f; (professional) Fachmann m, Fachfrau f; (Jur) Sachverständige(r) mf ▷ adj fachmännisch; **expertise** [ekspəˈtiːz] n Sachkenntnis f

expire [ɪk'spaɪə*] vi (end) ablaufen; **expiry date** [ɪk'spaɪərɪdeɪt] n Verfallsdatum nt

explain [ɪk'spleɪn] vt erklären (sth to sb jdm etw); **explanation** [eksplə'neɪʃən] n Erklärung f

explicit [ɪk'splɪsɪt] adj ausdrücklich, deutlich

explode [ɪk'spləʊd] vi explodieren

exploit [ɪk'splɔɪt] vt ausbeuten

explore [ɪk'splɔː*] vt erforschen

explosion [ɪk'spləʊʒən] n Explosion f; **explosive** [ɪk'spləʊsɪv] adj explosiv ▷ n Sprengstoff m

export [ek'spɔːt] vt, vi exportieren ▷ ['ekspɔːt] n Export m ▷ adj (trade) Export-

expose [ɪk'spəʊz] vt (to danger etc) aussetzen (to dat); (uncover) freilegen; (imposter) entlarven; **exposed** adj (position) ungeschützt; **exposure** [ɪk'spəʊʒə*] n (Med) Unterkühlung f; (Foto: time) Belichtung(szeit) f; **24 ~s** 24 Aufnahmen

express [ɪk'spres] adj (speedy) Express-, Schnell-; **~ delivery** Eilzustellung f ▷ n (Rail) Schnellzug m ▷ vt ausdrücken ▷ vr **to ~ oneself** sich ausdrücken; **expression** [ɪk'spreʃən] n (phrase) Ausdruck m; (look) Gesichtsausdruck m; **expressive** adj ausdrucksvoll; **expressway** n (US) Schnellstraße f

extend [ɪk'stend] vt (arms) ausstrecken; (lengthen) verlängern; (building) vergrößern, ausbauen; (business, limits) erweitern; **extension** [ɪk'stenʃən] n (lengthening) Verlängerung f; (of building) Anbau m; (Tel) Anschluss m; (of business, limits) Erweiterung f; **extensive** [ɪk'stensɪv] adj (knowledge) umfangreich; (use) häufig; **extent** [ɪk'stent] n (length) Länge f; (size) Ausdehnung f; (scope) Umfang m, Ausmaß nt; **to a certain/large ~** in gewissem/hohem Maße

exterior [ek'stɪərɪə*] n Äußere(s) nt

external [ek'stɜːnl] adj äußere(r, s), Außen-; **externally** adv äußerlich

extinct [ɪk'stɪŋkt] adj (species) ausgestorben

extinguish [ɪk'stɪŋgwɪʃ] vt löschen; **extinguisher** n Löschgerät nt

extra ['ekstrə] adj zusätzlich; **~ charge** Zuschlag m; **~ time** (Sport) Verlängerung f ▷ adv besonders; **~ large** (clothing) übergroß ▷ npl **~s** zusätzliche Kosten pl;

(food) Beilagen pl; (accessories) Zubehör nt; (for car etc) Extras pl

extract [ɪk'strækt] vt herausziehen (from aus); (tooth) ziehen ▷ ['ekstrækt] n (from book etc) Auszug m

extraordinary [ɪk'strɔːdnrɪ] adj außerordentlich; (unusual) ungewöhnlich; (amazing) erstaunlich

extreme [ɪk'striːm] adj äußerste(r, s); (drastic) extrem ▷ n Extrem nt; **extremely** adv äußerst, höchst; **extreme sports** npl Extremsportarten pl; **extremist** [ɪk'striːmɪst] adj extremistisch ▷ n Extremist m

extricate ['ekstrɪkeɪt] vt befreien (from aus)

extrovert ['ekstrəʊvɜːt] adj extrovertiert

exuberance [ɪg'zuːbərəns] n Überschwang m; **exuberant** adj überschwänglich

exultation [egzʌl'teɪʃən] n Jubel m

eye [aɪ] n Auge nt; **to keep an ~ on sb/sth** auf jdn/etw aufpassen ▷ vt mustern; **eyebrow** n Augenbraue f; **eyelash** n Wimper f; **eyelid** n Augenlid nt; **eyeliner** n Eyeliner m; **eyeopener** n **that was an ~** das hat mir die Augen geöffnet; **eyeshadow** n Lidschatten m; **eyesight** n Sehkraft f; **eyesore** n Schandfleck m; **eye witness** n Augenzeuge m, Augenzeugin f

f

fabric ['fæbrɪk] n Stoff m
fabulous ['fæbjʊləs] adj sagenhaft
façade [fə'sɑːd] n (a. fig) Fassade f
face [feɪs] n Gesicht nt; (of clock)
Zifferblatt nt; (of mountain) Wand f; **in the
~ of** trotz +gen; **to be ~ to ~** (people)
einander gegenüberstehen ▷ vt, vi
(person) gegenüberstehen +dat; (at table)
gegenübersitzen +dat; **to ~ north** (room)
nach Norden gehen; **to ~ (up to) the
facts** den Tatsachen ins Auge sehen; **to
be ~d with sth** mit etw konfrontiert
sein; **face cream** n Gesichtscreme f;
face lift n Gesichtsstraffung f; (fig)
Verschönerung f; **face powder** n
Gesichtspuder m
facet ['fæsɪt] n (fig) Aspekt m
face value n Nennwert m
facial ['feɪʃəl] adj Gesichts- ▷ n (fam)
(kosmetische) Gesichtsbehandlung
facilitate [fə'sɪlɪteɪt] vt erleichtern
facility [fə'sɪlɪtɪ] n (building etc to be used)
Einrichtung f, Möglichkeit f; (installation)
Anlage f; (skill) Gewandtheit f
fact [fækt] n Tatsache f; **as a matter of ~,
in ~** eigentlich, tatsächlich
factor ['fæktə*] n Faktor m

factory ['fæktərɪ] n Fabrik f; **factory
outlet** n Fabrikverkauf m
factual ['fæktjʊəl] adj sachlich
faculty ['fækəltɪ] n Fähigkeit f; (at
university) Fakultät f; (US: teaching staff)
Lehrkörper m
fade [feɪd] vi (a. fig) verblassen; **faded** adj
verblasst, verblichen
faff about ['fæfəbaʊt] vi (Brit fam)
herumwursteln
fag [fæg] n (Brit fam: cigarette) Kippe f; (US
fam pej) Schwule(r) m
Fahrenheit ['færənhaɪt] n Fahrenheit
fail [feɪl] vt (exam) nicht bestehen ▷ vi
versagen; (plan, marriage) scheitern;
(student) durchfallen; (eyesight)
nachlassen; **words ~ me** ich bin sprachlos;
failing n Schwäche f; **failure** ['feɪljə*] n
(person) Versager(in) m(f); (act) (a. Tech)
Versagen nt; (of engine etc) Ausfall m; (of
plan, marriage) Scheitern nt
faint [feɪnt] adj schwach; (sound) leise;
(fam) **I haven't the ~est (idea)** ich habe
keine Ahnung ▷ vi ohnmächtig werden
(with vor +dat); **faintness** n (Med)
Schwächegefühl nt
fair [feə*] adj (hair) blond; (skin) hell; (just)
gerecht, fair; (reasonable) ganz ordentlich;
(in school) befriedigend; (weather) schön;
(wind) günstig; **a ~ number/amount of**
ziemlich viele/viel ▷ adv **to play ~** fair
spielen; (fig) fair sein; **~ enough** in
Ordnung! ▷ n (fun~) Jahrmarkt m; (Comm)
Messe f; **fair-haired** adj blond; **fairly** adv
(honestly) fair; (rather) ziemlich
fairy ['feərɪ] n Fee f; **fairy tale** n Märchen
nt
faith [feɪθ] n (trust) Vertrauen nt (in sb zu
jdm); (Rel) Glaube m; **faithful, faithfully**
adj, adv treu; **Yours ~ly** Hochachtungsvoll
fake [feɪk] n (thing) Fälschung f ▷ adj
vorgetäuscht ▷ vt fälschen
falcon ['fɔːlkən] n Falke m
fall [fɔːl] (**fell, fallen**) vi fallen; (from a
height, badly) stürzen; **to ~ ill** krank
werden; **to ~ asleep** einschlafen; **to ~ in
love** sich verlieben ▷ n Fall m; (accident,
fig: of regime) Sturz m; (decrease) Sinken nt
(in +gen); (US: autumn) Herbst m; **fall apart**
vi auseinanderfallen; **fall behind** vi
zurückbleiben; (with work, rent) in
Rückstand geraten; **fall down** vi (person)
hinfallen; **fall off** vi herunterfallen;

(*decrease*) zurückgehen; **fall out** vi herausfallen; (*quarrel*) sich streiten; **fall over** vi hinfallen; **fall through** vi (*plan etc*) ins Wasser fallen

fallen ['fɔːlən] pp of **fall**

fallout ['fɔːlaʊt] n radioaktiver Niederschlag, Fall-out m

false [fɔːls] adj falsch; (*artificial*) künstlich; **false alarm** n blinder Alarm; **false start** n (*Sport*) Fehlstart m; **false teeth** npl (künstliches) Gebiss

fame [feɪm] n Ruhm m

familiar [fə'mɪlɪə*] adj vertraut, bekannt; **to be ~ with** vertraut sein mit, gut kennen; **familiarity** [fəmɪlɪ'ærɪtɪ] n Vertrautheit f

family ['fæmɪlɪ] n Familie f; (*including relations*) Verwandtschaft f; **family man** n Familienvater m; **family name** n Familienname m, Nachname m

famine ['fæmɪn] n Hungersnot f; **famished** ['fæmɪʃt] adj (*fam*) ausgehungert

famous ['feɪməs] adj berühmt

fan [fæn] n (*hand-held*) Fächer m; (*Elec*) Ventilator m; (*admirer*) Fan m

fanatic [fə'nætɪk] n Fanatiker(in) m(f)

fancy ['fænsɪ] adj (*elaborate*) kunstvoll; (*unusual*) ausgefallen ▷ vt (*like*) gern haben; **he fancies her** er steht auf sie; **~ that** stell dir vor!, so was!; **fancy dress** n Kostüm nt, Verkleidung f

fan heater ['fænhiːtə*] n Heizlüfter m; **fanlight** n Oberlicht nt

fan mail n Fanpost f

fantasise ['fæntəsaɪz] vi träumen (*about* von); **fantastic** [fæn'tæstɪk] adj (*a. fam*) fantastisch; **that's ~** (*fam*) das ist ja toll!; **fantasy** ['fæntəzɪ] n Fantasie f

far [fɑː*] (*further o* **farther, furthest** *o* **farthest**) adj weit; **the ~ end of the room** das andere Ende des Zimmers; **the Far East** der Ferne Osten ▷ adv weit; **~ better** viel besser; **by ~ the best** bei weitem der/die/das Beste; **as ~ as ...** bis zum *o* zur ...; (*with place name*) bis nach ...; **as ~ as I'm concerned** was mich betrifft, von mir aus; **so ~** soweit, bisher; **faraway** adj weit entfernt; (*look*) verträumt

fare [fɛə*] n Fahrpreis m; (*money*) Fahrgeld nt

farm [fɑːm] n Bauernhof m, Farm f; **farmer** n Bauer m, Bäuerin f,

Landwirt(in) m(f); **farmhouse** n Bauernhaus nt; **farming** n Landwirtschaft f; **farmland** n Ackerland nt; **farmyard** n Hof m

far-reaching ['fɑːriːtʃɪŋ] adj weit reichend; **far-sighted** adj weitsichtig; (*fig*) weitblickend

farther ['fɑːðə*] adj, adv comparative of **far**; see **further**

farthest ['fɑːðɪst] adj, adv superlative of **far**; see **furthest**

fascinating ['fæsɪneɪtɪŋ] adj faszinierend; **fascination** n Faszination f

fascism ['fæʃɪzəm] n Faschismus m; **fascist** ['fæʃɪst] adj faschistisch ▷ n Faschist(in) m(f)

fashion ['fæʃən] n (*clothes*) Mode f; (*manner*) Art (und Weise) f; **to be in ~** (in) Mode sein; **out of ~** unmodisch; **fashionable, fashionably** adj, adv (*clothes, person*) modisch; (*author, pub etc*) in Mode

fast [fɑːst] adj schnell; (*dye*) waschecht; **to be ~** (*clock*) vorgehen ▷ adv schnell; (*firmly*) fest; **to be ~ asleep** fest schlafen ▷ n Fasten nt ▷ vi fasten; **fastback** n (*Auto*) Fließheck nt

fasten ['fɑːsn] vt (*attach*) befestigen (*to* an +dat); (*do up*) zumachen; **~ your seatbelts** bitte anschnallen; **fastener**, **fastening** n Verschluss m

fast food n Fast Food nt; **fast forward** n (*for tape*) Schnellvorlauf m; **fast lane** n Überholspur f

fat [fæt] adj dick; (*meat*) fett ▷ n (*Anat, Gastr, Chem*) Fett nt

fatal ['feɪtl] adj tödlich

fate [feɪt] n Schicksal nt

fat-free adj (*food*) fettfrei

father ['fɑːðə*] n Vater m; (*priest*) Pfarrer m ▷ vt (*child*) zeugen; **Father Christmas** n der Weihnachtsmann; **father-in-law** (*pl* **fathers-in-law**) n Schwiegervater m

fatigue [fə'tiːg] n Ermüdung f

fattening ['fætnɪŋ] adj **to be ~** dick machen; **fatty** ['fætɪ] adj (*food*) fettig

faucet ['fɔːsɪt] n (*US*) Wasserhahn m

fault [fɔːlt] n Fehler m; (*Tech*) Defekt m; (*Elec*) Störung f; (*blame*) Schuld f; **it's your ~** du bist daran schuld; **faulty** adj fehlerhaft; (*Tech*) defekt

favor (*US*), **favour** ['feɪvə*] n (*approval*) Gunst f; (*kindness*) Gefallen m; **in ~ of** für;

I'm in ~ (of going) ich bin dafür(, dass wir gehen); **to do sb a ~** jdm einen Gefallen tun ▷ vt (prefer) vorziehen; **favourable** adj günstig (to, for für); **favourite** ['feɪvərɪt] n Liebling m, Favorit(in) m(f) ▷ adj Lieblings-

fax [fæks] vt faxen ▷ n Fax nt; **fax number** n Faxnummer f

faze [feɪz] vt (fam) aus der Fassung bringen

FBI abbr = **Federal Bureau of Investigation** FBI nt

fear [fɪə*] n Angst f (of vor +dat) ▷ vt befürchten; **I ~ that most** davor habe ich am meisten Angst; **fearful** adj (timid) ängstlich, furchtsam; (terrible) fürchterlich; **fearless** adj furchtlos

feasible ['fi:zəbl] adj machbar

feast [fi:st] n Festessen nt

feather ['feðə*] n Feder f

feature ['fi:tʃə*] n (facial) (Gesichts)zug m; (characteristic) Merkmal nt; (of car etc) Ausstattungsmerkmal nt; (in the press) (Cine) Feature nt ▷ vt bringen, (als Besonderheit) zeigen; **feature film** n Spielfilm m

February ['februərɪ] n Februar m; see also **September**

fed [fed] pt, pp of **feed**

federal ['fedərəl] adj Bundes-; **the Federal Republic of Germany** die Bundesrepublik Deutschland

fed-up [fed'ʌp] adj **to be ~ with sth** etw satt haben; **I'm ~** ich habe die Nase voll

fee [fi:] n Gebühr f; (of doctor, lawyer) Honorar nt

feeble ['fi:bl] adj schwach

feed [fi:d] (**fed, fed**) vt (baby, animal) füttern; (support) ernähren ▷ n (for baby) Mahlzeit f; (for animals) Futter nt; (Inform: paper ~) Zufuhr f; **feed in** vt (information) eingeben; **feedback** n (information) Feed-back nt

feel [fi:l] (**felt, felt**) vt (sense) fühlen; (pain) empfinden; (touch) anfassen; (think) meinen ▷ vi (person) sich fühlen; **I ~ cold** mir ist kalt; **do you ~ like a walk?** hast du Lust, spazieren zu gehen?; **feeling** n Gefühl nt

feet [fi:t] pl of **foot**

fell [fel] pt of **fall** ▷ vt (tree) fällen

fellow ['feləʊ] n Kerl m, Typ m; **~ citizen** Mitbürger(in) m(f); **~ countryman**

Landsmann m; **~ worker** Mitarbeiter(in) m(f)

felt [felt] pt, pp of **feel** ▷ n Filz m; **felt tip, felt-tip pen** n Filzstift m

female ['fi:meɪl] n (of animals) Weibchen nt ▷ adj weiblich; **~ doctor** Ärztin f; **~ dog** Hündin f; **feminine** ['femɪnɪn] adj weiblich; **feminist** ['femɪnɪst] n Feminist(in) m(f) ▷ adj feministisch

fence [fens] n Zaun m

fencing n (Sport) Fechten nt

fender ['fendə*] n (US Auto) Kotflügel m

fennel ['fenl] n Fenchel m

fern [fɜ:n] n Farn m

ferocious [fə'rəʊʃəs] adj wild

ferry ['ferɪ] n Fähre f ▷ vt übersetzen

fertile ['fɜ:taɪl] adj fruchtbar; **fertility** [fə'tɪlɪtɪ] n Fruchtbarkeit f; **fertilize** ['fɜ:tɪlaɪz] vt (Bio) befruchten; (Agr: land) düngen; **fertilizer** n Dünger m

festival ['festɪvəl] n (Rel) Fest nt; (Art, Mus) Festspiele pl; (pop music) Festival nt; **festive** ['festɪv] adj festlich; **festivities** [fe'stɪvɪtɪz] n Feierlichkeiten pl

fetch [fetʃ] vt holen; (collect) abholen; (in sale, money) einbringen; **fetching** adj reizend

fetish ['fetɪʃ] n Fetisch m

fetus ['fi:təs] n (US) Fötus m

fever ['fi:və*] n Fieber nt; **feverish** adj (Med) fiebrig; (fig) fieberhaft

few [fju:] adj, pron pl wenige pl; **a ~** ein paar; **fewer** adj weniger; **fewest** adj wenigste(r, s)

fiancé [fɪ'ɑ̃:nseɪ] n Verlobte(r) m; **fiancée** n Verlobte f

fiasco [fɪ'æskəʊ] (pl -s o US -es) n Fiasko nt

fiber (US), **fibre** ['faɪbə*] n Faser f; (material) Faserstoff m

fickle ['fɪkl] adj unbeständig

fiction ['fɪkʃən] n (novels) Prosaliteratur f; **fictional, fictitious** [fɪk'tɪʃəs] adj erfunden

fiddle ['fɪdl] n Geige f; (trick) Betrug m ▷ vt (accounts, results) frisieren; **fiddle with** vt herumfummeln an +dat; **fiddly** adj knifflig

fidelity [fɪ'delɪtɪ] n Treue f

fidget ['fɪdʒɪt] vi zappeln; **fidgety** adj zappelig

field [fi:ld] n Feld nt; (grass-covered) Wiese f; (fig: of work) (Arbeits)gebiet nt

fierce [fɪəs] adj heftig; (animal, appearance) wild; (criticism, competition) scharf

fifteen [fɪfˈtiːn] num fünfzehn ▷ n Fünfzehn f; see also **eight**; **fifteenth** adj fünfzehnte(r, s); see also **eighth**; **fifth** [fɪfθ] adj fünfte(r, s) ▷ n (fraction) Fünftel nt; see also **eighth**; **fifty** [ˈfɪftɪ] num fünfzig ▷ n Fünfzig f; see also **eight**; **fiftieth** adj fünfzigste(r, s); see also **eighth**

fig [fɪg] n Feige f

fight [faɪt] (**fought, fought**) vi kämpfen (with, against gegen, for, over um) ▷ vt (person) kämpfen mit; (fig: disease, fire etc) bekämpfen ▷ n Kampf m; (brawl) Schlägerei f; (argument) Streit m; **fight back** vi zurückschlagen; **fight off** vt abwehren; **fighter** n Kämpfer(in) m(f)

figurative [ˈfɪɡərətɪv] adj übertragen

figure [ˈfɪɡə*] n (person) Gestalt f; (of person) Figur f; (number) Zahl f, Ziffer f; (amount) Betrag m; **a four-figure sum** eine vierstellige Summe ▷ vt (US: think) glauben ▷ vi (appear) erscheinen; **figure out** vt (work out) herausbekommen; **I can't figure him out** ich werde aus ihm nicht schlau; **figure skating** n Eiskunstlauf m

file [faɪl] n (tool) Feile f; (dossier) Akte f; (Inform) Datei f; (folder) Aktenordner m; **on ~** in den Akten ▷ vt (metal, nails) feilen; (papers) ablegen (under unter) ▷ vi **to ~ in/out** hintereinander hereinkommen/hinausgehen; **filing cabinet** n Aktenschrank m

fill [fɪl] vt füllen; (tooth) plombieren; (post) besetzen; **fill in** vt (hole) auffüllen; (form) ausfüllen; (tell) informieren (on über); **fill out** vt (form) ausfüllen; **fill up** vi (Auto) voll tanken

fillet [ˈfɪlɪt] n Filet nt

filling [ˈfɪlɪŋ] n (Gastr) Füllung f; (for tooth) Plombe f; **filling station** n Tankstelle f

film [fɪlm] n Film m ▷ vt (scene) filmen; **film star** n Filmstar m; **film studio** n Filmstudio nt

filter [ˈfɪltə*] n Filter m; (traffic lane) Abbiegespur f ▷ vt filtern

filth [fɪlθ] n Dreck m; **filthy** adj dreckig

fin [fɪn] n Flosse f

final [ˈfaɪnl] adj letzte(r, s); (stage, round) End-; (decision, version) endgültig; **~ score**

Schlussstand m ▷ n (Sport) Endspiel nt; (competition) Finale nt; **~s** pl Abschlussexamen nt; **finalize** vt die endgültige Form geben +dat; **finally** adv (lastly) zuletzt; (eventually) schließlich, endlich

finance [faɪˈnæns] n Finanzwesen nt; **~s** pl Finanzen pl ▷ vt finanzieren; **financial** [faɪˈnænʃəl] adj finanziell; (adviser, crisis, policy etc) Finanz-

find [faɪnd] (**found, found**) vt finden; **he was found dead** er wurde tot aufgefunden; **I ~ myself in difficulties** ich befinde mich in Schwierigkeiten; **she ~s it difficult/easy** es fällt ihr schwer/leicht; **find out** vt herausfinden; **findings** npl (Jur) Ermittlungsergebnis nt; (of report, Med) Befund m

fine [faɪn] adj (thin) dünn, fein; (good) gut; (splendid) herrlich; (clothes) elegant; (weather) schön; **I'm ~** es geht mir gut; **that's ~** das ist OK ▷ adv (well) gut ▷ n (Jur) Geldstrafe f ▷ vt (Jur) mit einer Geldstrafe belegen; **fine arts** npl **the ~** die schönen Künste pl; **finely** adv (cut) dünn; (ground) fein

finger [ˈfɪŋɡə*] n Finger m ▷ vt herumfingern an +dat; **fingernail** n Fingernagel m; **fingerprint** n Fingerabdruck m; **fingertip** n Fingerspitze f

finicky [ˈfɪnɪkɪ] adj (person) pingelig; (work) knifflig

finish [ˈfɪnɪʃ] n Ende nt; (Sport) Finish nt; (line) Ziel nt; (of product) Verarbeitung f ▷ vt beenden; (book etc) zu Ende lesen; (food) aufessen; (drink) austrinken ▷ vi zu Ende gehen; (song, story) enden; (person) fertig sein; (stop) aufhören; **have you ~ed?** bist du fertig?; **to ~ first/second** (Sport) als erster/zweiter durchs Ziel gehen; **finishing line** n Ziellinie f

Finland [ˈfɪnlənd] n Finnland nt; **Finn** n Finne m, Finnin f; **Finnish** adj finnisch ▷ n (language) Finnisch nt

fir [fɜ:*] n Tanne f

fire [faɪə*] n Feuer nt; (house etc) Brand m; **to set ~ to sth** etw in Brand stecken; **to be on ~** brennen ▷ vt (bullets, rockets) abfeuern; (fam: dismiss) feuern ▷ vi (Auto: engine) zünden; **to ~ at sb** auf jdn schießen; **fire alarm** n Feuermelder m; **fire brigade** n Feuerwehr f; **fire engine**

n Feuerwehrauto *nt*; **fire escape** *n* Feuerleiter *f*; **fire extinguisher** *n* Feuerlöscher *m*; **firefighter** *n* Feuerwehrmann *m*, Feuerwehrfrau *f*; **fireman** *n* Feuerwehrmann *m*; **fireplace** *n* (offener) Kamin; **fireproof** *adj* feuerfest; **fire station** *n* Feuerwache *f*; **firewood** *n* Brennholz *nt*; **fireworks** *npl* Feuerwerk *nt*

firm [fɜːm] *adj* fest; (*person*) **to be ~** entschlossen auftreten ▷ *n* Firma *f*

first [fɜːst] *adj* erste(r, s) ▷ *adv* (*at first*) zuerst; (*firstly*) erstens; (*arrive, finish*) als erste(r); (*happen*) zum ersten Mal; **~ of all** zuallererst ▷ *n* (*person*) Erste(r) *mf*; (*Auto: gear*) erster Gang; **at ~** zuerst, anfangs; **first aid** *n* erste Hilfe; **first-class** *adj* erstklassig; (*compartment, ticket*) erster Klasse; **~ mail** (*Brit*) bevorzugt beförderte Post ▷ *adv* (*travel*) erster Klasse; **first floor** *n* (*Brit*) erster Stock; (*US*) Erdgeschoss *nt*; **first lady** *n* (*US*) Frau *f* des Präsidenten; **firstly** *adv* erstens; **first name** *n* Vorname *m*; **first night** *n* (*Theat*) Premiere *f*; **first-rate** *adj* erstklassig

fir tree *n* Tannenbaum *m*

fish [fɪʃ] *n* Fisch *m*; **~ and chips** (*Brit*) frittierter Fisch mit Pommes frites ▷ *vi* fischen; (*with rod*) angeln; **to go ~ing** fischen/angeln gehen; **fishbone** *n* Gräte *f*; **fishcake** *n* Fischfrikadelle *f*; **fish farm** *n* Fischzucht *f*; **fish finger** *n* (*Brit*) Fischstäbchen *nt*; **fishing** ['fɪʃɪŋ] *n* Fischen *nt*; (*with rod*) Angeln *nt*; (*as industry*) Fischerei *f*; **fishing boat** *n* Fischerboot *nt*; **fishing line** *n* Angelschnur *f*; **fishing rod** *n* Angelrute *f*; **fishing village** *n* Fischerdorf *nt*; **fishmonger** ['fɪʃmʌŋgə*] *n* Fischhändler(in) *m(f)*; **fish stick** *n* (*US*) Fischstäbchen *nt*; **fish tank** *n* Aquarium *nt*

fishy ['fɪʃɪ] *adj* (*fam: suspicious*) faul

fist [fɪst] *n* Faust *f*

fit [fɪt] *adj* (*Med*) gesund; (*Sport*) in Form, fit; (*suitable*) geeignet; **to keep ~** sich in Form halten ▷ *vt* passen +*dat*; (*attach*) anbringen (*to* an +*dat*); (*install*) einbauen (*in* in +*akk*) ▷ *vi* passen; (*in space, gap*) hineinpassen ▷ *n* (*of clothes*) Sitz *m*; (*Med*) Anfall *m*; **it's a good ~** es passt gut; **fit in** *vt* (*accommodate*) unterbringen; (*find time for*) einschieben ▷ *vi* (*in space*)

hineinpassen; (*plans, ideas*) passen; **he doesn't ~ (here)** er passt nicht hierher; **to ~ with sb's plans** sich mit jds Plänen vereinbaren lassen; **fitness** *n* (*Med*) Gesundheit *f*; (*Sport*) Fitness *f*; **fitted carpet** *n* Teppichboden *m*; **fitted kitchen** *n* Einbauküche *f*; **fitting** *adj* passend ▷ *n* (*of dress*) Anprobe *f*; **~s** *pl* Ausstattung *f*

five [faɪv] *num* fünf ▷ *n* Fünf *f*; *see also* **eight**; **fiver** *n* (*Brit fam*) Fünfpfundschein *m*

fix [fɪks] *vt* befestigen (*to* an +*dat*); (*settle*) festsetzen; (*place, time*) ausmachen; (*repair*) reparieren; **fixer** *n* (*drug addict*) Fixer(in) *m(f)*; **fixture** ['fɪkstʃə*] *n* (*Sport*) Veranstaltung *f*; (*match*) Spiel *nt*; (*in building*) Installationsteil *nt*; **~s (and fittings)** *pl* Ausstattung *f*

fizzy ['fɪzɪ] *adj* sprudelnd; **~ drink** Limo *f*

flabbergasted ['flæbəgɑːstɪd] *adj* (*fam*) platt

flabby ['flæbɪ] *adj* (*fat*) wabbelig

flag [flæg] *n* Fahne *f*; **flagstone** *n* Steinplatte *f*

flake [fleɪk] *n* Flocke *f* ▷ *vi* **to ~ (off)** abblättern

flamboyant [flæm'bɔɪənt] *adj* extravagant

flame [fleɪm] *n* Flamme *f*; (*person*) **an old ~** eine alte Liebe

flan [flæn] *n* (*fruit ~*) Obstkuchen *m*

flannel ['flænl] *n* Flanell *m*; (*Brit: face ~*) Waschlappen *m*; (*fam: waffle*) Geschwafel *nt* ▷ *vi* herumlabern

flap [flæp] *n* Klappe *f*; (*fam*) **to be in a ~** rotieren ▷ *vt* (*wings*) schlagen mit ▷ *vi* flattern

flared [fleəd] *adj* (*trousers*) mit Schlag; **flares** *npl* Schlaghose *f*

flash [flæʃ] *n* Blitz *m*; (*news ~*) Kurzmeldung *f*; (*Foto*) Blitzlicht *nt*; **in a ~** im Nu ▷ *vt* **to ~ one's (head)lights** die Lichthupe betätigen ▷ *vi* aufblinken; (*brightly*) aufblitzen; **flashback** *n* Rückblende *f*, Flashback *m*; **flashlight** ['flæʃlaɪt] *n* (*Photo*) Blitzlicht *nt*; (*US: torch*) Taschenlampe *f*; **flashy** *adj* grell, schrill; (*pej*) protzig

flat [flæt] *adj* flach; (*surface*) eben; (*drink*) abgestanden; (*tyre*) platt; (*battery*) leer; (*refusal*) glatt ▷ *n* (*Brit: rooms*) Wohnung *f*; (*Auto*) Reifenpanne *f*; **flat screen** *n*

(*Inform*) Flachbildschirm *m*; **flatten** *vt*
platt machen, einebnen

flatter ['flætə*] *vt* schmeicheln +*dat*;
flattering *adj* schmeichelhaft

flatware ['flætwɛə] *n* (*US*) Besteck *nt*

flavor (*US*), **flavour** ['fleɪvə*] *n* Geschmack
m ▷ *vt* Geschmack geben +*dat*; (*with
spices*) würzen; **flavouring** *n* Aroma *nt*

flaw [flɔ:] *n* Fehler *m*; **flawless** *adj*
fehlerlos; (*complexion*) makellos

flea [fli:] *n* Floh *m*

fled [fled] *pt, pp of* **flee**

flee [fli:] (**fled, fled**) *vi* fliehen

fleece [fli:s] *n* (*of sheep*) Vlies *nt*; (*soft
material*) Fleece *m*; (*jacket*) Fleecejacke *f*

fleet [fli:t] *n* Flotte *f*

Flemish ['flemɪʃ] *adj* flämisch ▷ *n*
(*language*) Flämisch *nt*

flesh [fleʃ] *n* Fleisch *nt*

flew [flu:] *pt of* **fly**

flex [fleks] *n* (*Brit Elec*) Schnur *f*

flexibility [fleksɪ'bɪlɪtɪ] *n* Biegsamkeit *f*;
(*fig*) Flexibilität *f*; **flexible** ['fleksɪbl] *adj*
biegsam; (*plans, person*) flexibel; **flexitime**
n gleitende Arbeitszeit, Gleitzeit *f*

flicker ['flɪkə*] *vi* flackern; (*Tv*) flimmern

flies [flaɪz] *pl of* **fly** ▷ *n*

flight [flaɪt] *n* Flug *m*; (*escape*) Flucht *f*; **~ of
stairs** Treppe *f*; **flight attendant** *n*
Flugbegleiter(in) *m(f)*; **flight recorder** *n*
Flugschreiber *m*

flimsy ['flɪmzɪ] *adj* leicht gebaut, nicht
stabil; (*thin*) hauchdünn; (*excuse*)
fadenscheinig

fling [flɪŋ] (**flung, flung**) *vt* schleudern
▷ *n* **to have a ~** eine (kurze) Affäre
haben

flint [flɪnt] *n* Feuerstein *m*

flip [flɪp] *vt* schnippen; **to ~ a coin** eine
Münze werfen; **flip through** *vt* (*book*)
durchblättern; **flipchart** *n* Flipchart *f*

flipper ['flɪpə*] *n* Flosse *f*

flirt [flɜ:t] *vi* flirten

float [fləʊt] *n* (*for fishing*) Schwimmer *m*;
(*in procession*) Festwagen *m*; (*money*)
Wechselgeld *nt* ▷ *vi* schwimmen; (*in air*)
schweben

flock [flɒk] *n* (*of sheep*) (*Rel*) Herde *f*; (*of
birds*) Schwarm *m*; (*of people*) Schar *f*

flog [flɒg] *vt* auspeitschen; (*Brit fam*)
verscheuern

flood [flʌd] *n* Hochwasser *nt*,
Überschwemmung *f*; (*fig*) Flut *f* ▷ *vt*

überschwemmen; **floodlight** *n* Flutlicht
nt; **floodlit** *adj* (*building*) angestrahlt

floor [flɔ:*] *n* Fußboden *m*; (*storey*) Stock
m; **ground ~** (*Brit*), **first ~** (*US*)
Erdgeschoss *nt*; **first ~** (*Brit*), **second
~** (*US*) erster Stock; **floorboard** *n* Diele *f*

flop [flɒp] *n* (*fam: failure*) Reinfall *m*, Flop *m*
▷ *vi* misslingen, floppen

floppy disk ['flɒpɪ'dɪsk] *n* Diskette *f*

Florence ['flɒrəns] *n* Florenz *nt*

florist ['flɒrɪst] *n* Blumenhändler(in) *m(f)*

flounder ['flaʊndə*] *n* (*fish*) Flunder *f*

flour ['flaʊə*] *n* Mehl *nt*

flourish ['flʌrɪʃ] *vi* gedeihen; (*business*) gut
laufen; (*boom*) florieren ▷ *vt* (*wave about*)
schwenken; **flourishing** *adj* blühend

flow [fləʊ] *n* Fluss *m*; **to go with the ~** mit
dem Strom schwimmen ▷ *vi* fließen

flower ['flaʊə*] *n* Blume *f* ▷ *vi* blühen;
flower bed *n* Blumenbeet *nt*; **flowerpot** *n*
Blumentopf *m*

flown [fləʊn] *pp of* **fly**

flu [flu:] *n* (*fam*) Grippe *f*

fluent *adj* (*Italian etc*) fließend; **to be ~ in
German** fließend Deutsch sprechen

fluid ['flu:ɪd] *n* Flüssigkeit *f* ▷ *adj* flüssig

flung [flʌŋ] *pt, pp of* **fling**

fluorescent [flʊə'resnt] *adj*
fluoreszierend, Leucht-

flush [flʌʃ] *n* (*lavatory*) Wasserspülung *f*;
(*blush*) Röte *f* ▷ *vi* (*lavatory*) spülen

flute [flu:t] *n* Flöte *f*

fly [flaɪ] (**flew, flown**) *vt, vi* fliegen; **how
time flies** wie die Zeit vergeht! ▷ *n* (*insect*)
Fliege *f*; **~/flies** (*pl*) (*on trousers*)
Hosenschlitz *m*; **fly-drive** *n* Urlaub *m* mit
Flug und Mietwagen; **flyover** *n* (*Brit*)
Straßenüberführung *f*,
Eisenbahnüberführung *f*; **flysheet** *n*
Überzelt *nt*

FM *abbr* = **frequency modulation** ≈ UKW

FO *abbr* = **Foreign Office** ≈ AA *nt*

foal [fəʊl] *n* Fohlen *nt*

foam [fəʊm] *n* Schaum *m* ▷ *vi* schäumen

fob off [fɒb ɒf] *vt* **to fob sb off with sth**
jdm etw abspeisen

focus ['fəʊkəs] *n* Brennpunkt *m*; **in/out of
~** (*photo*) scharf/unscharf; (*camera*)
scharf/unscharf eingestellt ▷ *vt* (*camera*)
scharf stellen ▷ *vi* sich konzentrieren (*on*
auf +*akk*)

foetus ['fi:təs] *n* Fötus *m*

fog [fɒg] *n* Nebel *m*; **foggy** *adj* neblig; **fog**

light n (Auto: at rear) Nebelschlussleuchte f

foil [fɔɪl] vt vereiteln ▷ n Folie f

fold [fəʊld] vt falten ▷ vi (fam: business) eingehen ▷ n Falte f; **fold up** vt (map etc) zusammenfalten; (chair etc) zusammenklappen ▷ vi (fam: business) eingehen; **folder** n (portfolio) Aktenmappe f; (pamphlet) Broschüre f; (Inform) Ordner m; **folding** adj zusammenklappbar; (bicycle, chair) Klapp-

folk [fəʊk] n Leute pl; (Mus) Folk m; **my ~s** pl (fam) meine Leute ▷ adj Volks-

follow ['fɒləʊ] vt folgen +dat; (pursue) verfolgen; (understand) folgen können +dat; (career, news etc) verfolgen; **as ~s** wie folgt ▷ vi folgen; (result) sich ergeben (from aus); **follow up** vt (request, rumour) nachgehen +dat, weiter verfolgen; **follower** n Anhänger(in) m(f); **following** adj folgend; **the ~ day** am (darauf)folgenden Tag ▷ prep nach; **follow up** n (event, book etc) Fortsetzung f

fond [fɒnd] adj **to be ~ of** gern haben; **fondly** adv (with love) liebevoll; **fondness** n Vorliebe f; (for people) Zuneigung f

fondue ['fɒndu:] n Fondue nt

font [fɒnt] n Taufbecken nt; (Typo) Schriftart f

food [fu:d] n Essen nt, Lebensmittel pl; (for animals) Futter n; (groceries) Lebensmittel pl; **food poisoning** n Lebensmittelvergiftung f; **food processor** n Küchenmaschine f; **foodstuff** n Lebensmittel nt

fool [fu:l] n Idiot m, Narr m; **to make a ~ of oneself** sich blamieren ▷ vt (deceive) hereinlegen ▷ vi **to ~ around** herumalbern; (waste time) herumtrödeln; **foolish** adj dumm; **foolproof** adj idiotensicher

foot [fʊt] (pl **feet**) n [fi:t] Fuß m; (measure) Fuß m (30,48 cm); **on ~** zu Fuß ▷ vt (bill) bezahlen; **foot-and-mouth disease** n Maul- und Klauenseuche f; **football** n Fußball m; (US: American ~) Football m; **footballer** n Fußballspieler(in) m(f); **footbridge** n Fußgängerbrücke f; **footing** n (hold) Halt m; **footlights** npl Rampenlicht nt; **footnote** n Fußnote f; **footpath** n Fußweg m;

footprint n Fußabdruck m; **footwear** n Schuhwerk nt

KEYWORD

for [fɔ:*] prep **1** für; **is this for me?** ist das für mich?; **the train for London** der Zug nach London; **he went for the paper** er ging die Zeitung holen; **give it to me — what for?** gib es mir — warum?

2 (because of) wegen; **for this reason** aus diesem Grunde

3 (referring to distance); **there are roadworks for 5 km** die Baustelle ist 5 km lang; **we walked for miles** wir sind meilenweit gegangen

4 (referring to time) seit; (: with future sense) für; **he was away for 2 years** er war zwei Jahre lang weg

5 (+infin clauses): **it is not for me to decide** das kann ich nicht entscheiden; **for this to be possible ...** damit dies möglich wird/wurde ...

6 (in spite of) trotz +gen or (inf) dat; **for all his complaints** obwohl er sich ständig beschwert
▷ conj denn

forbade [fə'bæd] pt of **forbid**

forbid [fə'bɪd] (**forbade**, **forbidden**) vt verbieten

force [fɔ:s] n Kraft f; (compulsion) Zwang m, Gewalt f; **to come into ~** in Kraft treten; **the Forces** pl die Streitkräfte ▷ vt zwingen; **forced** adj (smile) gezwungen; **~ landing** Notlandung f; **forceful** adj kraftvoll

forceps ['fɔ:seps] npl Zange f

forearm ['fɔ:rɑ:m] n Unterarm m

forecast ['fɔ:kɑ:st] vt voraussagen; (weather) vorhersagen ▷ n Vorhersage f

forefinger ['fɔ:fɪŋgə*] n Zeigefinger m

foreground ['fɔ:graʊnd] n Vordergrund m

forehand ['fɔ:hænd] n (Sport) Vorhand f

forehead ['fɔ:hed, 'fɒrɪd] n Stirn f

foreign ['fɒrən] adj ausländisch; **foreigner** n Ausländer(in) m(f); **foreign exchange** n Devisen pl; **foreign language** n Fremdsprache f; **foreign minister**, **foreign secretary** n Außenminister(in) m(f); **foreign policy** n Außenpolitik f

foremost ['fɔːməʊst] adj erste(r, s); (leading) führend

forerunner ['fɔːrʌnə*] n Vorläufer(in) m(f)

foresee [fɔːˈsiː] irr vt vorhersehen; **foreseeable** adj absehbar

forest ['fɒrɪst] n Wald m; **forestry** ['fɒrɪstrɪ] n Forstwirtschaft f

forever [fəˈrevə*] adv für immer

forgave [fəˈgeɪv] pt of **forgive**

forge [fɔːdʒ] n Schmiede f ▷ vt schmieden; (fake) fälschen; **forger** n Fälscher(in) m(f); **forgery** n Fälschung f

forget [fəˈget] (**forgot, forgotten**) vt, vi vergessen; **to ~ about sth** etw vergessen; **forgetful** adj vergesslich; **forgetfulness** n Vergesslichkeit f; **forget-me-not** n Vergissmeinnicht nt

forgive [fəˈgɪv] (**forgave, forgiven**) irr vt verzeihen; **to ~ sb for sth** jdm etw verzeihen

forgot [fəˈgɒt] pt of **forget**

forgotten [fəˈgɒtn] pp of **forget**

fork [fɔːk] n Gabel f; (in road) Gabelung f ▷ vi (road) sich gabeln

form [fɔːm] n (shape) Form f, Klasse f; (document) Formular nt; (person) **to be in (good) ~** in Form sein ▷ vt bilden

formal ['fɔːməl] adj förmlich, formell; **formality** [fɔːˈmælɪtɪ] n Formalität f

format ['fɔːmæt] n Format nt ▷ vt (Inform) formatieren

former ['fɔːmə*] adj frühere(r, s); (opposite of latter) erstere(r, s); **formerly** adv früher

formidable ['fɔːmɪdəbl] adj gewaltig; (opponent) stark

formula ['fɔːmjʊlə] n Formel f

formulate ['fɔːmjʊleɪt] vt formulieren

forth [fɔːθ] adv **and so ~** und so weiter; **forthcoming** [fɔːθˈkʌmɪŋ] adj kommend, bevorstehend

fortify ['fɔːtɪfaɪ] vt verstärken; (for protection) befestigen

fortieth ['fɔːtɪəθ] adj vierzigste(r, s); see also **eighth**

fortnight ['fɔːtnaɪt] n vierzehn Tage pl

fortress ['fɔːtrɪs] n Festung f

fortunate ['fɔːtʃənɪt] adj glücklich; **I was ~** ich hatte Glück; **fortunately** adv zum Glück; **fortune** ['fɔːtʃən] n (money) Vermögen nt; **good ~** Glück nt; **fortune-teller** n Wahrsager(in) m(f)

forty ['fɔːtɪ] num vierzig ▷ n Vierzig f; see also **eight**

forward ['fɔːwəd] adv vorwärts ▷ n (Sport) Stürmer(in) m(f) ▷ vt (send on) nachsenden; (Inform) weiterleiten; **forwards** adv vorwärts

foster child ['fɒstətʃaɪld] n Pflegekind nt; **foster parents** npl Pflegeeltern pl

fought [fɔːt] pt, pp of **fight**

foul [faʊl] adj (weather) schlecht; (smell) übel ▷ n (Sport) Foul nt

found [faʊnd] pt, pp of **find** (establish) gründen; **foundations** [faʊnˈdeɪʃənz] npl Fundament nt

fountain ['faʊntɪn] n Springbrunnen m; **fountain pen** n Füller m

four [fɔː*] num vier ▷ n Vier f; see also **eight**; **fourteen** ['fɔːˈtiːn] num vierzehn ▷ n Vierzehn f; see also **eight**; **fourteenth** adj vierzehnte(r, s); see also **eighth**; **fourth** [fɔːθ] adj vierte(r, s); see also **eighth**

four-wheel drive n Allradantrieb m; (car) Geländewagen m

fowl [faʊl] n Geflügel nt

fox [fɒks] n (a. fig) Fuchs m

fraction ['frækʃən] n (Math) Bruch m; (part) Bruchteil m; **fracture** ['fræktʃə*] n (Med) Bruch m ▷ vt brechen

fragile ['frædʒaɪl] adj zerbrechlich

fragment ['frægmənt] n Bruchstück nt

fragrance ['freɪgrəns] n Duft m; **fragrant** adj duftend

frail [freɪl] adj gebrechlich

frame [freɪm] n Rahmen m; (of spectacles) Gestell nt; **~ of mind** Verfassung f ▷ vt einrahmen; **to ~ sb** (fam: incriminate) jdm etwas anhängen; **framework** n Rahmen m, Struktur f

France [frɑːns] n Frankreich nt

frank [fræŋk] adj offen

frankfurter ['fræŋkfɜːtə*] n (Frankfurter) Würstchen nt

frankly ['fræŋklɪ] adv offen gesagt; **quite ~** ganz ehrlich; **frankness** n Offenheit f

frantic ['fræntɪk] adj (activity) hektisch; (effort) verzweifelt; **~ with worry** außer sich vor Sorge

fraud [frɔːd] n (trickery) Betrug m; (person) Schwindler(in) m(f)

freak [friːk] n Anomalie f; (animal, person) Missgeburt f; (fam: fan) Fan m, Freak m ▷ adj (conditions)

außergewöhnlich, seltsam; **freak out** vi
(fam) ausflippen

freckle ['frekl] n Sommersprosse f

free [fri:] adj, adv frei; (without payment)
gratis, kostenlos; **for ~** umsonst ▷ vt
befreien; **freebie** ['fri:bɪ] n (fam)
Werbegeschenk nt; **it was a ~** es war
gratis; **freedom** ['fri:dəm] n Freiheit f;
freefone ['fri:fəʊn] adj **a ~ number** eine
gebührenfreie Nummer; **free kick** n
(Sport) Freistoß m

freelance ['fri:lɑːns] adj freiberuflich
tätig; (artist) freischaffend ▷ n
Freiberufler(in) m(f)

free-range ['fri:reɪndʒ] adj (hen) frei
laufend; **~ eggs** pl Freilandeier pl

freeway ['fri:weɪ] n (US) (gebührenfreie)
Autobahn

freeze [fri:z] (froze, frozen) vi (feel cold)
frieren; (of lake etc) zufrieren; (water etc)
gefrieren ▷ vt einfrieren; **freezer** n
Tiefkühltruhe f; (in fridge) Gefrierfach
nt; **freezing** adj eiskalt; **I'm ~** mir ist
eiskalt; **freezing point** n Gefrierpunkt m

freight [freɪt] n (goods) Fracht f; (money
charged) Frachtgebühr f; **freight car** n
(US) Güterwagen m; **freight train** n (US)
Güterzug m

French [frentʃ] adj französisch ▷ n
(language) Französisch nt; **the ~** pl die
Franzosen; **French bean** n grüne Bohne;
French bread n Baguette f; **French
dressing** n Vinaigrette f; **French fries**
(US) npl Pommes frites pl; **French kiss** n
Zungenkuss m; **Frenchman** (pl -men) n
Franzose m; **French toast** n (US) in Ei und
Milch getunktes gebratenes Brot; **French
window(s)** n(pl) Balkontür f,
Terrassentür f; **Frenchwoman** (pl
-women) n Französin f

frequency ['fri:kwənsɪ] n Häufigkeit
f; (Phys) Frequenz f; **frequent**
['fri:kwənt] adj häufig; **frequently** adv
häufig

fresco ['freskəʊ] n (pl -es) n Fresko nt

fresh [freʃ] adj frisch; (new) neu; **freshen**
vi **to ~ (up)** (person) sich frisch machen;
freshman (pl -men) n Erstsemester nt;
freshwater fish n Süßwasserfisch m

Fri abbr = **Friday** Fr

friction ['frɪkʃən] n (a. fig) Reibung f

Friday ['fraɪdeɪ] n Freitag m; see also
Tuesday

fridge [frɪdʒ] n Kühlschrank m

fried [fraɪd] adj gebraten; **~ potatoes**
Bratkartoffeln pl; **~ egg** Spiegelei nt; **~ rice**
gebratener Reis

friend [frend] n Freund(in) m(f); (less
close) Bekannte(r) mf; **to make ~s with sb**
sich mit jdm anfreunden; **we're good ~s**
wir sind gut befreundet; **friendly** adj
freundlich; **to be ~ with sb** mit jdm
befreundet sein ▷ n (Sport)
Freundschaftsspiel nt; **friendship**
['frendʃɪp] n Freundschaft f

fright [fraɪt] n Schrecken m; **frighten** vt
erschrecken; **to be ~ed** Angst haben;
frightening adj beängstigend

frill [frɪl] n Rüsche f; **~s** (fam)
Schnickschnack

fringe [frɪndʒ] n (edge) Rand m; (on shawl
etc) Fransen pl; (hair) Pony m

frivolous ['frɪvələs] adj leichtsinnig;
(remark) frivol

frizzy ['frɪzɪ] adj kraus

frog [frɒg] n Frosch m

 KEYWORD

from [frɒm] prep **1** (indicating starting
place) von; (indicating origin etc) aus +dat; **a
letter/telephone call from my sister** ein
Brief/Anruf von meiner Schwester; **where
do you come from?** woher kommen Sie?;
to drink from the bottle aus der Flasche
trinken

2 (indicating time) von ... an; (:past)
seit; **from one o'clock to or until or till
two** von ein Uhr bis zwei; **from January
(on)** ab Januar

3 (indicating distance) von ... (entfernt)

4 (indicating price, number etc) ab +dat; **from
£10** ab £10; **there were from 20 to 30
people there** es waren zwischen 20 und
30 Leute da

5 (indicating difference): **he can't tell red
from green** er kann nicht zwischen Rot
und Grün unterscheiden; **to be
different from sb/sth** anders sein als
jd/etw

6 (because of, based on): **from what he says**
aus dem, was er sagt; **weak from hunger**
schwach vor Hunger

front [frʌnt] n Vorderseite f; (of house)
Fassade f; (in war, of weather) Front f; (at

seaside) Promenade *f*; **in ~**, **at the ~** vorne; **in ~ of** vor; **up ~** (*in advance*) vorher, im Voraus ▷ *adj* vordere(r, s), Vorder-; (*first*) vorderste(r, s); **~ door** Haustür *f*; **~ page** Titelseite *f*; **~ seat** Vordersitz *m*; **~ wheel** Vorderrad *nt*

frontier ['frʌntɪə*] *n* Grenze *f*

front-wheel drive *n* (*Auto*) Frontantrieb *m*

frost [frɒst] *n* Frost *m*; (*white ~*) Reif *m*; **frosting** *n* (*US*) Zuckerguss *m*; **frosty** *adj* frostig

froth [frɒθ] *n* Schaum *m*; **frothy** *adj* schaumig

frown [fraʊn] *vi* die Stirn runzeln

froze [frəʊz] *pt of* **freeze**

frozen [frəʊzn] *pp of* **freeze** ▷ *adj* (*food*) tiefgekühlt, Tiefkühl-

fruit [fruːt] *n* (*as collective, a. type*) Obst *nt*; (*single ~, a. fig*) Frucht *f*; **fruit machine** *n* Spielautomat *m*; **fruit salad** *n* Obstsalat *m*

frustrated [frʌˈstreɪtɪd] *adj* frustriert; **frustratration** *n* Frustration *f*, Frust *m*

fry [fraɪ] *vt* braten; **frying pan** *n* Bratpfanne *f*

fuchsia ['fjuːʃə] *n* Fuchsie *f*

fuck [fʌk] *vt* (*vulg*) ficken; **~ off** verpiss dich!; **fucking** *adj* (*vulg*) Scheiß-

fudge [fʌdʒ] *n* weiche Karamellsüßigkeit

fuel [fjʊəl] *n* Kraftstoff *m*; (*for heating*) Brennstoff *m*; **fuel consumption** *n* Kraftstoffverbrauch *m*; **fuel gauge** *n* Benzinuhr *f*; **fuel oil** *n* Gasöl *nt*; **fuel rod** *n* Brennstab *m*; **fuel tank** *n* Tank *m*; (*for oil*) Öltank *m*

fugitive ['fjuːdʒɪtɪv] *n* Flüchtling *m*

fulfil [fʊlˈfɪl] *vt* erfüllen

full [fʊl] *adj* voll; (*person: satisfied*) satt; (*member, employment*) Voll(zeit)-; (*complete*) vollständig; **~ of ...** voller ... *gen*; **full beam** *n* (*Auto*) Fernlicht *nt*; **full moon** *n* Vollmond *m*; **full stop** *n* Punkt *m*; **full-time** *adj* **~ job** Ganztagsarbeit *f*; **fully** *adv* völlig; (*recover*) voll und ganz; (*discuss*) ausführlich

fumble ['fʌmbl] *vi* herumfummeln (*with, at* an +*dat*)

fumes [fjuːmz] *npl* Dämpfe *pl*; (*of car*) Abgase *pl*

fun [fʌn] *n* Spaß *m*; **for ~** zum Spaß; **it's ~** es macht Spaß; **to make ~ of** sich lustig machen über +*akk*

function ['fʌŋkʃən] *n* Funktion *f*; (*event*)

Feier *f*; (*reception*) Empfang *m* ▷ *vi* funktionieren; **function key** *n* (*Inform*) Funktionstaste *f*

fund [fʌnd] *n* Fonds *m*; **~s** *pl* Geldmittel *pl*

fundamental [fʌndəˈmentl] *adj* grundlegend; **fundamentally** *adv* im Grunde

funding ['fʌndɪŋ] *n* finanzielle Unterstützung

funeral ['fjuːnərəl] *n* Beerdigung *f*

funfair ['fʌnfɛə*] *n* Jahrmarkt *m*

fungus ['fʌŋɡəs] (*pl* **fungi** *o* **funguses**) *n* Pilz *m*

funicular [fjuːˈnɪkjʊlə*] *n* Seilbahn *f*

funnel ['fʌnl] *n* Trichter *m*; (*of steamer*) Schornstein *m*

funny ['fʌnɪ] *adj* (*amusing*) komisch, lustig; (*strange*) seltsam

fur [fɜː*] *n* Pelz *m*; (*of animal*) Fell *nt*

furious ['fjʊərɪəs] *adj* wütend (*with sb* auf jdn)

furnished ['fɜːnɪʃd] *adj* möbliert; **furniture** ['fɜːnɪtʃə*] *n* Möbel *pl*; **piece of ~** Möbelstück *nt*

further ['fɜːðə*] *comparative of* **far** ▷ *adj* weitere(r, s); **~ education** Weiterbildung *f*; **until ~ notice** bis auf weiteres ▷ *adv* weiter; **furthest** ['fɜːðɪst] *superlative of* **far** ▷ *adj* am weitesten entfernt ▷ *adv* am weitesten

fury ['fjʊərɪ] *n* Wut *f*

fuse [fjuːz] *n* (*Elec*) Sicherung *f* ▷ *vi* (*Elec*) durchbrennen; **fuse box** *n* Sicherungskasten *m*

fuss [fʌs] *n* Theater *nt*; **to make a ~** ein Theater machen; **fussy** *adj* (*difficult*) schwierig, kompliziert; (*attentive to detail*) pingelig

future ['fjuːtʃə*] *adj* künftig ▷ *n* Zukunft *f*

fuze (*US*) *see* **fuse**

fuzzy ['fʌzɪ] *adj* (*indistinct*) verschwommen; (*hair*) kraus

g

gable ['geɪbl] *n* Giebel *m*

gadget ['gædʒɪt] *n* Vorrichtung *f*, Gerät *nt*

Gaelic ['geɪlɪk] *adj* gälisch ▷ *n* (*language*) Gälisch *nt*

gain [geɪn] *vt* (*obtain, win*) gewinnen; (*advantage, respect*) sich verschaffen; (*wealth*) erwerben; (*weight*) zunehmen ▷ *vi* (*improve*) gewinnen (*in an +dat*); (*clock*) vorgehen ▷ *n* Gewinn *m* (*in an +dat*)

gale [geɪl] *n* Sturm *m*

gall bladder ['gɔ:lblædə*] *n* Gallenblase *f*

gallery ['gælərɪ] *n* Galerie *f*, Museum *nt*

gallon ['gælən] *n* Gallone *f*; ((*Brit*) 4,546 l, (*US*) 3,79 l)

gallop ['gæləp] *n* Galopp *m* ▷ *vi* galoppieren

gallstone ['gɔ:lstəʊn] *n* Gallenstein *m*

Gambia ['gæmbɪə] *n* Gambia *nt*

gamble ['gæmbl] *vi* um Geld spielen, wetten ▷ *n* **it's a ~** es ist riskant; **gambling** *n* Glücksspiel *nt*

game [geɪm] *n* Spiel *nt*; (*animals*) Wild *nt*; **a ~ of chess** eine Partie Schach; **~s** (*in school*) Sport *m*; **game show** *n* (*TV*) Gameshow *f*

gammon ['gæmən] *n* geräucherter Schinken

gang [gæŋ] *n* (*of criminals, youths*) Bande *f*, Gang *f*, Clique *f* ▷ *vt* **to ~ up on** sich verschwören gegen

gangster ['gæŋstə*] *n* Gangster *m*

gangway ['gæŋweɪ] *n* (*for ship*) Gangway *f*; (*Brit: aisle*) Gang *m*, Gangway *f*

gap [gæp] *n* (*hole*) Lücke *f*; (*in time*) Pause *f*; (*in age*) Unterschied *m*

gape [geɪp] *vi* (mit offenem Mund) starren

gap year *n* Jahr zwischen Schulabschluss und Studium, das oft zu Auslandsaufenthalten genutzt wird

garage ['gærɑːʒ] *n* Garage *f*; (*for repair*) (Auto)werkstatt *f*; (*for fuel*) Tankstelle *f*

garbage ['gɑːbɪdʒ] *n* (*US*) Müll *m*; (*fam: nonsense*) Quatsch *m*; **garbage can** *n* (*US*) Mülleimer *m*; (*outside*) Mülltonne *f*; **garbage truck** *n* (*US*) Müllwagen *m*

garbled ['gɑːbld] *adj* (*story*) verdreht

garden ['gɑːdn] *n* Garten *m*; (**public**) **~s** Park *m*; **garden centre** *n* Gartencenter *nt*; **gardener** *n* Gärtner(in) *m(f)*; **gardening** *n* Gartenarbeit *f*

gargle ['gɑːgl] *vi* gurgeln

gargoyle ['gɑːgɔɪl] *n* Wasserspeier *m*

garlic ['gɑːlɪk] *n* Knoblauch *m*; **garlic bread** *n* Knoblauchbrot *nt*; **garlic butter** *n* Knoblauchbutter *f*

gas [gæs] *n* Gas *nt*; (*US: petrol*) Benzin *nt*; **to step on the ~** Gas geben; **gas cooker** *n* Gasherd *m*; **gas cylinder** *n* Gasflasche *f*; **gas fire** *n* Gasofen *m*

gasket ['gæskɪt] *n* Dichtung *f*

gas lighter *n* (*for cigarettes*) Gasfeuerzeug *nt*; **gas mask** *n* Gasmaske *f*; **gas meter** *n* Gaszähler *m*

gasoline ['gæsəliːn] *n* (*US*) Benzin *nt*

gasp [gɑːsp] *vi* keuchen; (*in surprise*) nach Luft schnappen

gas pedal *n* (*US*) Gaspedal *nt*; **gas pump** *n* (*US*) Zapfsäule *f*; **gas station** *n* (*US*) Tankstelle *f*; **gas tank** *n* (*US*) Benzintank *m*

gastric ['gæstrɪk] *adj* Magen-; **~ flu** Magen-Darm-Grippe *f*; **~ ulcer** Magengeschwür *nt*

gasworks ['gæswɜːks] *n* Gaswerk *nt*

gate [geɪt] *n* Tor *nt*; (*barrier*) Schranke *f*; (*Aviat*) Gate *nt*, Flugsteig *m*

gateau ['gætəʊ] *n* Torte *f*

gateway *n* Tor *nt*

gather ['gæðə*] vt (collect) sammeln; **to ~ speed** beschleunigen ▷ vi (assemble) sich versammeln; (understand) schließen (from aus); **gathering** n Versammlung f

gauge [geɪdʒ] n Meßgerät nt

gauze [gɔːz] n Gaze f; (for bandages) Mull m

gave [geɪv] pt of **give**

gay [geɪ] adj (homosexual) schwul

gaze [geɪz] n Blick m ▷ vi starren

GCSE abbr = **general certificate of secondary education** (school) Abschlussprüfung f der Sekundarstufe, ≈ mittlere Reife

gear [gɪə*] n (Auto) Gang m; (equipment) Ausrüstung f; (clothes) Klamotten pl; **to change ~** schalten; **gearbox** n Getriebe nt; **gear change**, **gear shift** (US) n Gangschaltung f; **gear lever**, **gear stick** (US) n Schalthebel m

geese [giːs] pl of **goose**

gel [dʒel] n Gel nt ▷ vi gelieren; **they really ~led** sie verstanden sich auf Anhieb

gelatine ['dʒelətiːn] n Gelatine f

gem [dʒem] n Edelstein m; (fig) Juwel nt

Gemini ['dʒemɪniː] nsing (Astr) Zwillinge pl

gender ['dʒendə*] n Geschlecht nt

gene [dʒiːn] n Gen nt

general ['dʒenərəl] adj allgemein; **~ knowledge** Allgemeinbildung f; **~ election** Parlamentswahlen pl; **generalize** ['dʒenrəlaɪz] vi verallgemeinern; **generally** ['dʒenrəlɪ] adv im Allgemeinen

generation [dʒenə'reɪʃən] n Generation f; **generation gap** n Generationsunterschied m

generator ['dʒenəreɪtə*] n Generator m

generosity [dʒenə'rɒsɪtɪ] n Großzügigkeit f; **generous** ['dʒenərəs] adj großzügig; (portion) reichlich

genetic [dʒɪ'netɪk] adj genetisch; **genetically modified** adj gentechnisch verändert, genmanipuliert; see also **GM**

Geneva [dʒɪ'niːvə] n Genf nt; **Lake ~** der Genfer See

genitals ['dʒenɪtlz] npl Geschlechtsteile pl

genitive ['dʒenɪtɪv] n Genitiv m

genius ['dʒiːnɪəs] n Genie nt

gentle ['dʒentl] adj sanft; (touch) zart;

gentleman (pl **-men**) n Herr m; (polite man) Gentleman m

gents [dʒents] n '**~**' (lavatory) „Herren"; **the ~** pl die Herrentoilette

genuine ['dʒenjʊɪn] adj echt

geographical [dʒɪə'græfɪkəl] adj geografisch; **geography** [dʒɪ'ɒgrəfɪ] n Geografie f; (at school) Erdkunde f

geological [dʒɪəʊ'lɒdʒɪkəl] adj geologisch; **geology** [dʒɪ'ɒlədʒɪ] n Geologie f

geometry [dʒɪ'ɒmɪtrɪ] n Geometrie f

geranium [dʒɪ'reɪnɪəm] n Geranie f

germ [dʒɜːm] n Keim m; (Med) Bazillus m

German ['dʒɜːmən] adj deutsch; **she's ~** sie ist Deutsche; **~ shepherd** Deutscher Schäferhund ▷ n (person) Deutsche(r) mf; (language) Deutsch nt; **in ~** auf Deutsch; **German measles** n sing Röteln pl; **Germany** ['dʒɜːmənɪ] n Deutschland nt

gesture ['dʒestʃə*] n Geste f

KEYWORD

get [gɛt] (pt, pp **got**, pp **gotten** (US)) vi
1 (become, be) werden; **to get old/tired** alt/müde werden; **to get married** heiraten
2 (go) (an)kommen gehen
3 (begin): **to get to know sb** jdn kennen lernen; **let's get going or started!** fangen wir an!
4 (modal aux vb): **you've got to do it** du musst es tun
▷ vt 1: **to get sth done** (do) etw machen: (have done) etw machen lassen; **to get sth going or to go** etw in Gang bringen or bekommen; **to get sb to do sth** jdn dazu bringen, etw zu tun
2 (obtain: money, permission, results) erhalten; (find: job, flat) finden; (fetch: person, object) holen; **to get sth for sb** jdm etw besorgen; **get me Mr Jones, please** (Tel) verbinden Sie mich bitte mit Mr Jones
3 (receive: present, letter) bekommen kriegen (acquire: reputation etc) erwerben
4 (catch) bekommen kriegen; (hit: target etc) treffen erwischen; **get him!** (to dog) fass!
5 (take, move) bringen; **to get sth to sb** jdm etw bringen

6 (*understand*) verstehen; (*hear*)
mitbekommen; **I've got it!** ich habs!
7 (*have, possess*): **to have got sth** etw
haben

get about *vi* herumkommen; (*news*) sich
verbreiten

get along *vi* (*people*) (gut)
zurechtkommen; (*depart*) sich *acc* auf den
Weg machen

get at *vt* (*facts*) herausbekommen; **to
get at sb** (*nag*) an jdm herumnörgeln

get away *vi* (*leave*) sich *acc* davonmachen
(*escape*); **to get away from sth** von etw
dat entkommen; **to get away with sth**
mit etw davonkommen

get back *vi* (*return*) zurückkommen ⊳ *vt*
zurückbekommen

get by *vi* (*pass*) vorbeikommen; (*manage*)
zurechtkommen

get down *vi* (her)untergehen ⊳ *vt*
(*depress*) fertig machen; **to get down to**
in Angriff nehmen; (*find time to do*)
kommen zu

get in *vi* (*train*) ankommen; (*arrive home*)
heimkommen

get into *vt* (*enter*) hinein-/hereinkommen
in +*acc*; (: *car, train etc*) einsteigen in +*acc*;
(*clothes*) anziehen

get off *vi* (*from train etc*) aussteigen; (*from
horse*) absteigen ⊳ *vt* aussteigen aus;
absteigen von

get on *vi* (*progress*) vorankommen; (*be
friends*) auskommen; (*age*) alt werden;
(*onto train etc*) einsteigen; (*onto horse*)
aufsteigen ⊳ *vt* einsteigen in +*acc*; auf
etw *acc* aufsteigen

get out *vi* (*of house*) herauskommen; (*of
vehicle*) aussteigen ⊳ *vt* (*take out*)
herausholen

get out of *vt* (*duty etc*) herumkommen
um

get over *vt* (*illness*) sich *acc* erholen von
(*surprise*) verkraften; (*news*) fassen; (*loss*)
sich abfinden mit

get round *vt* herumkommen; (*fig:
person*) herumkriegen

get through to *vt* (*Tel*) durchkommen zu

get together *vi* zusammenkommen

get up *vi* aufstehen ⊳ *vt* hinaufbringen;
(*go up*) hinaufgehen; (*organize*) auf die
Beine stellen

get up to *vt* (*reach*) erreichen; (*prank etc*)
anstellen

Ghana ['gɑ:nə] *n* Ghana *nt*

gherkin ['gɜ:kɪn] *n* Gewürzgurke *f*

ghetto ['getəu] (*pl* **-es**) *n* Ghetto *nt*

ghost [gəust] *n* Gespenst *nt*; (*of sb*) Geist
m

giant ['dʒaɪənt] *n* Riese *m* ⊳ *adj* riesig

giblets ['dʒɪblɪts] *npl* Geflügelinnereien *pl*

Gibraltar [dʒɪ'brɔ:ltə*] *n* Gibraltar *nt*

giddy ['gɪdɪ] *adj* schwindlig

gift [gɪft] *n* Geschenk *nt*; (*talent*)
Begabung *f*; **gifted** *adj* begabt; **giftwrap**
vt als Geschenk verpacken

gigantic [dʒaɪ'gæntɪk] *adj* riesig

giggle ['gɪgl] *vi* kichern ⊳ *n* Gekicher *nt*

gill [gɪl] *n* (*of fish*) Kieme *f*

gimmick ['gɪmɪk] *n* (*for sales, publicity*)
Gag *m*

gin [dʒɪn] *n* Gin *m*

ginger ['dʒɪndʒə*] *n* Ingwer *m* ⊳ *adj*
(*colour*) kupferrot; (*cat*) rötlichgelb; **ginger
ale** *n* Gingerale *nt*; **ginger beer** *n*
Ingwerlimonade *f*; **gingerbread** *n*
Lebkuchen *m* (*mit Ingwergeschmack*);
ginger(-haired) *adj* rotblond; **gingerly**
adv (*move*) vorsichtig

gipsy ['dʒɪpsɪ] *n* Zigeuner(in) *m(f)*

giraffe [dʒɪ'rɑ:f] *n* Giraffe *f*

girl [gɜ:l] *n* Mädchen *nt*; **girlfriend** *n*
(*feste*) Freundin *f*; **girl guide** *n* (*Brit*), **girl
scout** (*US*) Pfadfinderin *f*

gist [dʒɪst] *n* **to get the ~** (*of it*) das
Wesentliche verstehen

give [gɪv] (**gave, given**) *vt* geben; (*as
present*) schenken (*to sb jdm*); (*state: name
etc*) angeben; (*speech*) halten; (*blood*)
spenden; **to ~ sb sth** jdm etw
geben/schenken ⊳ *vi* (*yield*) nachgeben;
give away *vt* (*give free*) verschenken;
(*secret*) verraten; **give back** *vt*
zurückgeben; **give in** *vi* aufgeben; **give
up** *vt, vi* aufgeben; **give way** *vi* (*collapse,
yield*) nachgeben; (*traffic*) die Vorfahrt
beachten

given ['gɪvn] *pp of* **give** ⊳ *adj* (*fixed*)
festgesetzt; (*certain*) bestimmt; **~ name**
(*US*) Vorname *m* ⊳ *conj* **~ that ...**
angesichts der Tatsache, dass ...

glacier ['glæsɪə*] *n* Gletscher *m*

glad [glæd] *adj* froh (*about über*); **I was
~** (*to hear*) **that ...** es hat mich gefreut,
dass ...; **gladly** ['glædlɪ] *adv* gerne

glance [glɑ:ns] *n* Blick *m* ⊳ *vi* einen Blick
werfen (*at auf* +*akk*)

g

gland [glænd] n Drüse f; **glandular fever**
n Drüsenfieber nt

glare [gleə*] n grelles Licht; (stare)
stechender Blick ▷ vi (angrily) **to ~ at sb**
jdn böse anstarren; **glaring** adj (mistake)
krass

glass [glɑːs] n Glas nt; **~es** pl Brille f

glen [glen] n (SCOT) (enges) Bergtal nt

glide [glaɪd] vi gleiten; (hover) schweben;
glider n Segelflugzeug nt; **gliding** n
Segelfliegen nt

glimmer ['glɪmə*] n (of hope) Schimmer m

glimpse [glɪmps] n flüchtiger Blick

glitter ['glɪtə*] vi glitzern; (eyes) funkeln

glitzy [glɪtsɪ] adj (fam) glanzvoll,
Schickimicki-

global ['gləʊbəl] adj global, Welt-;
~ warming die Erwärmung der
Erdatmosphäre; **globe** [gləʊb] n (sphere)
Kugel f; (world) Erdball m; (map) Globus m

gloomily ['gluːmɪlɪ], **gloomy** adv, adj
düster

glorious ['glɔːrɪəs] adj (victory, past)
ruhmreich; (weather, day) herrlich; **glory**
['glɔːrɪ] n Herrlichkeit f

gloss [glɒs] n (shine) Glanz m

glossary ['glɒsərɪ] n Glossar nt

glossy ['glɒsɪ] adj (surface) glänzend ▷ n
(magazine) Hochglanzmagazin nt

glove [glʌv] n Handschuh m; **glove
compartment** n Handschuhfach nt

glow [gləʊ] vi glühen

glucose ['gluːkəʊs] n Traubenzucker m

glue [gluː] n Klebstoff m ▷ vt kleben

glutton ['glʌtn] n Vielfraß m; **a ~ for
punishment** (fam) Masochist m

GM abbr = **genetically modified** Gen-;
~ foods gentechnisch veränderte
Lebensmittel

GMT abbr = **Greenwich Mean Time** WEZ f

go [gəʊ] (**went, gone**) vi gehen; (in vehicle,
travel) fahren; (plane) fliegen; (road) führen
(to nach); (depart: train, bus) (ab)fahren;
(person) (fort)gehen; (disappear)
verschwinden; (time) vergehen; (function)
gehen, funktionieren; (machine, engine)
laufen; (fit, suit) passen (with zu); (fail)
nachlassen; **I have to ~ to the doctor/to
London** ich muss zum Arzt/nach London;
to ~ shopping einkaufen gehen; **to ~ for a
walk/swim** spazieren/schwimmen
gehen; **has he gone yet?** ist er schon
weg?; **the wine ~es in the cupboard** der

Wein kommt in den Schrank; **to get sth
~ing** etw in Gang setzen; **to keep ~ing**
weitermachen; (machine etc) weiterlaufen;
how's the job ~ing? was macht der Job?;
his memory/eyesight is going sein
Gedächtnis lässt nach/seine Augen
werden schwach; **to ~ deaf/mad/grey**
taub/verrückt/grau werden ▷ vb aux **to
be ~ing to do sth** etw tun werden; **I was
~ing to do it** ich wollte es tun ▷ n (pl **-es**)
(attempt) Versuch m; **can I have another
~?** darf ich noch mal (probieren)?; **it's my
~** ich bin dran; **in one ~** auf einen Schlag;
(drink) in einem Zug; **go after** vt
nachlaufen +dat; (in vehicle) nachfahren
+dat; **go ahead** vi (in front) vorausgehen;
(start) anfangen; **go away** vi weggehen;
(on holiday, business) verreisen; **go back** vi
(return) zurückgehen; **we ~ a long way**
(fam) wir kennen uns schon ewig; **go by** vi
vorbeigehen; (vehicle) vorbeifahren; (years,
time) vergehen ▷ vt (judge by) gehen nach;
go down vi (sun, ship) untergehen; (flood,
temperature) zurückgehen; (price) sinken;
to ~ well/badly gut/schlecht ankommen;
go in vi hineingehen; **go into** vt (enter)
hineingehen in +akk; (crash) fahren gegen,
hineinfahren in +akk; **to
~ teaching/politics/the army** Lehrer
werden/in die Politik gehen/zum Militär
gehen; **go off** vi (depart) weggehen; (in
vehicle) wegfahren; (lights) ausgehen; (milk
etc) sauer werden; (gun, bomb, alarm)
losgehen ▷ vt (dislike) nicht mehr mögen;
go on vi (continue) weitergehen; (lights)
angehen; **to ~ with** o doing sth etw
weitermachen; **go out** vi (leave house)
hinausgehen; (fire, light, person socially)
ausgehen; **to ~ for a meal** essen gehen;
go up vi (temperature, price) steigen; (lift)
hochfahren; **go without** vt verzichten
auf +akk; (food, sleep) auskommen ohne

go-ahead ['gəʊəhed] adj (progressive)
fortschrittlich ▷ n grünes Licht

goal [gəʊl] n (aim) Ziel nt; (Sport) Tor nt;
goalie, **goalkeeper** n Torwart m, Torfrau
f; **goalpost** n Torpfosten m

goat [gəʊt] n Ziege f

gob [gɒb] n (Brit fam) Maul nt; **shut your
~** halt's Maul! ▷ vi spucken; **gobsmacked**
(fam: surprised) platt

god [gɒd] n Gott m; **thank God** Gott sei
Dank; **godchild** (pl **-children**) n

Patenkind nt; **goddaughter** n
Patentochter f; **goddess** ['gɒdes] n
Göttin f; **godfather** n Pate m;
godmother n Patin f; **godson** n
Patensohn m
goggles npl Schutzbrille f; (for skiing)
Skibrille f; (for diving) Taucherbrille f
going ['gəʊɪŋ] adj (rate) üblich; **goings-on**
npl Vorgänge pl
go-kart ['gəʊkɑ:t] n Gokart m
gold [gəʊld] n Gold nt ▷ adj golden;
goldfish n Goldfisch m; **gold-plated** adj
vergoldet
golf [gɒlf] n Golf nt; **golf ball** n Golfball
m; **golf club** n Golfschläger m;
(association) Golfklub m; **golf course** n
Golfplatz m; **golfer** n Golfspieler(in) m(f)
gone [gɒn] pp of go; **he's ~** er ist weg
▷ prep **just ~ three** gerade drei Uhr vorbei
good [gʊd] n (benefit) Wohl nt; (morally
good things) Gute(s) nt; **for the ~ of** zum
Wohle +gen; **it's for your own ~** es ist zu
deinem Besten o Vorteil; **it's no ~** (doing
sth) es hat keinen Sinn o Zweck; (thing) es
taugt nichts; **for ~** für immer ▷ adj
(better, best) gut; (suitable) passend;
(thorough) gründlich; (well-behaved) brav;
(kind) nett, lieb; **to be ~ at sport/maths**
gut in Sport/Mathe sein; **to be no ~ at**
sport/maths schlecht in Sport/Mathe
sein; **it's ~ for you** es tut dir gut; **this is**
~ for colds das ist gut gegen Erkältungen;
too ~ to be true zu schön, um wahr zu
sein; **this is just not ~ enough** so geht das
nicht; **a ~ three hours** gute drei Stunden;
~ morning/evening guten
Morgen/Abend; **~ night** gute Nacht; **to**
have a ~ time sich gut amüsieren
goodbye [gʊd'baɪ] interj auf Wiedersehen
Good Friday n Karfreitag m
good-looking adj gut aussehend
goods [gʊdz] npl Waren pl, Güter pl;
goods train n (Brit) Güterzug m
goodwill [gʊd'wɪl] n Wohlwollen nt
goose [gu:s] n (pl geese) n Gans f ▷ vt
(fam) **to ~ s.o.** jdn in den Arsch kneifen;
gooseberry ['gʊzbərɪ] n Stachelbeere f;
goose bumps n, **goose pimples** npl
Gänsehaut f
gorge [gɔ:dʒ] n Schlucht f
gorgeous ['gɔ:dʒəs] adj wunderschön;
he's ~ er sieht toll aus
gorilla [gə'rɪlə] n Gorilla m

gossip ['gɒsɪp] n (talk) Klatsch m; (person)
Klatschtante f ▷ vi klatschen, tratschen
got [gɒt] pt, pp of **get**
gotten ['gɒtn] (US) pp of **get**
govern ['gʌvən] vt regieren; (province etc)
verwalten; **government** n Regierung f;
governor n Gouverneur(in) m(f); **govt**
abbr = **government** Regierung f
gown [gaʊn] n Abendkleid nt; (academic)
Robe f
GP abbr = **General Practitioner**
praktischer Arzt
GPS n abbr = **global positioning system**
GPS nt
grab [græb] vt packen; (person)
schnappen
grace [greɪs] n Anmut f; (prayer)
Tischgebet nt; **5 days' ~** 5 Tage Aufschub;
graceful adj anmutig
grade [greɪd] n Niveau nt; (of goods)
Güteklasse f; (mark) Note f; (US: year)
Klasse f; **to make the ~** es schaffen; **grade**
crossing n (US) Bahnübergang m; **grade**
school n (US) Grundschule f
gradient ['greɪdɪənt] n (upward) Steigung
f; (downward) Gefälle nt
gradual, gradually ['grædjʊəl, -lɪ] adj, adv
allmählich
graduate ['grædjʊɪt] n Uniabsolvent(in)
m(f), Akademiker(in) m(f),
Hochschulabsolvent(in) m(f)
▷ ['grædjʊeɪt] vi einen akademischen
Grad erwerben
grain [greɪn] n (cereals) Getreide nt;
(of corn, sand) Korn nt; (in wood) Maserung
f
gram [græm] n Gramm nt
grammar ['græmə*] n Grammatik f;
grammar school n (Brit) ≈ Gymnasium nt
gran [græn] n (fam) Oma f
grand [grænd] adj (pej) hochnäsig; (posh)
vornehm ▷ n (fam) 1000 Pfund bzw. 1000
Dollar
grand(d)ad n (fam) Opa m;
granddaughter n Enkelin f; **grandfather**
n Großvater m; **grandma** n (fam) Oma f;
grandmother n Großmutter f; **grandpa**
n (fam) Opa m; **grandparents** npl
Großeltern pl; **grandson** n Enkel m
grandstand n (Sport) Tribüne f
granny ['grænɪ] n (fam) Oma f
grant [grɑ:nt] vt gewähren (sb sth jdm
etw); **to take sb/sth for ~ed** jdn/etw als

selbstverständlich hinnehmen ▷ n Subvention f, finanzielle Unterstützung f; (for university) Stipendium nt

grape [greip] n Weintraube f; **grapefruit** n Grapefruit f; **grape juice** n Traubensaft m

graph [grɑːf] n Diagramm nt; **graphic** ['græfik] adj grafisch; (description) anschaulich

grasp [grɑːsp] vt ergreifen; (understand) begreifen

grass [grɑːs] n Gras nt; (lawn) Rasen m; **grasshopper** n Heuschrecke f

grate [greit] n Feuerrost m ▷ vi kratzen ▷ vt (cheese) reiben

grateful, gratefully ['greitful, -fəli] adj, adv dankbar

grater ['greitə*] n Reibe f

gratifying ['grætifaiiŋ] adj erfreulich

gratitude ['grætitjuːd] n Dankbarkeit f

grave [greiv] n Grab nt ▷ adj ernst; (mistake) schwer

gravel ['grævəl] n Kies m

graveyard ['greivjɑːd] n Friedhof m

gravity ['græviti] n Schwerkraft f; (seriousness) Ernst m

gravy ['greivi] n Bratensoße f

gray [grei] adj (US) grau

graze [greiz] vi (of animals) grasen ▷ vt (touch) streifen; (Med) abschürfen ▷ n (Med) Abschürfung f

grease [griːs] n (fat) Fett nt; (lubricant) Schmiere f ▷ vt einfetten; (Tech) schmieren; **greasy** ['griːsi] adj fettig; (hands, tools) schmierig; (fam: person) schleimig

great [greit] adj groß; (fam: good) großartig, super; **a ~ deal of** viel; **Great Britain** ['greit'britn] n Großbritannien nt; **great-grandfather** n Urgroßvater m; **great-grandmother** n Urgroßmutter f; **greatly** adv sehr; **~ disappointed** zutiefst enttäuscht

Greece [griːs] n Griechenland nt

greed [griːd] n Gier f (for nach); (for food) Gefräßigkeit f; **greedy** adj gierig; (for food) gefräßig

Greek [griːk] adj griechisch ▷ n (person) Grieche m, Griechin f; (language) Griechisch nt

green [griːn] adj grün ▷ n (colour, for golf) Grün nt; (village ~) Dorfwiese f; **~s** (vegetables) grünes Gemüse; **the Greens,**

the **Green Party** (Pol) die Grünen; **green card** n (US: work permit) Arbeitserlaubnis f; (Brit: for car) grüne Versicherungskarte; **greengage** n Reneklode f; **greengrocer** n Obst- und Gemüsehändler(in) m(f); **greenhouse** n Gewächshaus nt; **~ effect** Treibhauseffekt m; **Greenland** n Grönland nt; **green pepper** n grüner Paprika; **green salad** n grüner Salat

Greenwich Mean Time ['grenidʒ'miːntaim] n westeuropäische Zeit

greet [griːt] vt grüßen; **greeting** n Gruß m

grew [gruː] pt of **grow**

grey [grei] adj grau; **grey-haired** adj grauhaarig; **greyhound** n Windhund m

grid [grid] n Gitter nt; **gridlock** n Verkehrsinfarkt m; **gridlocked** adj (roads) völlig verstopft; (talks) festgefahren

grief [griːf] n Kummer m; (over loss) Trauer f

grievance ['griːvəns] n Beschwerde f

grieve [griːv] vi trauern (for um)

grill [gril] n (on cooker) Grill m ▷ vt grillen

grim [grim] adj (face, humour) grimmig; (situation, prospects) trostlos

grin [grin] n Grinsen nt ▷ vi grinsen

grind [graind] (ground, ground) vt mahlen; (sharpen) schleifen; (US: meat) durchdrehen, hacken

grip [grip] n Griff m; **get a ~** nimm dich zusammen; **to get to ~s with sth** etw in den Griff bekommen ▷ vt packen; **gripping** adj (exciting) spannend

gristle ['grisl] n Knorpel m

groan [grəun] vi stöhnen (with vor +dat)

grocer ['grəusə*] n Lebensmittelhändler(in) m(f); **groceries** npl Lebensmittel pl

groin [grɔin] n (Anat) Leiste f; **groin strain** n (Med) Leistenbruch m

groom [gruːm] n Bräutigam m ▷ vt well **~ed** gepflegt

groovy ['gruːvi] adj (fam) cool

grope [grəup] vi tasten ▷ vt (sexually harrass) befummeln

gross [grəus] adj (coarse) derb; (extreme: negligence, error) grob; (disgusting) ekelhaft; (Comm) brutto; **~ national product** Bruttosozialprodukt nt; **~ salary** Bruttogehalt nt

grotty ['grɔti] adj (fam) mies, vergammelt

ground [graʊnd] pt, pp of **grind** ▷ n
Boden m, Erde f; (Sport) Platz m; **~s** pl
(around house) (Garten)anlagen pl; (reasons)
Gründe pl; (of coffee) Satz m; **on (the) ~s of**
aufgrund von; **ground floor** n (Brit)
Erdgeschoss nt; **ground meat** n (US)
Hackfleisch nt

group [gru:p] n Gruppe f ▷ vt
gruppieren

grouse [graʊs] (pl **-**) n (bird) Schottisches
Moorhuhn; (complaint) Nörgelei f

grow [grəʊ] (**grew, grown**) vi wachsen;
(increase) zunehmen (in an); (become)
werden; **to ~ old** alt werden; **to ~ into ...**
sich entwickeln zu ... ▷ vt (crop, plant)
ziehen; (commercially) anbauen; **I'm ~ing a
beard** ich lasse mir einen Bart wachsen;
grow up vi aufwachsen; (mature)
erwachsen werden; **growing** adj
wachsend; **a ~ number of people** immer
mehr Leute

growl [graʊl] vi knurren

grown [grəʊn] pp of **grow**

grown-up [grəʊnʌp] adj erwachsen ▷ n
Erwachsene(r) mf; **growth** [grəʊθ] n
Wachstum nt; (increase) Zunahme f; (Med)
Wucherung f

grubby [ˈgrʌbɪ] adj schmuddelig

grudge [grʌdʒ] n Abneigung f (against
gegen) ▷ vt **to ~ sb sth** jdm etw nicht
gönnen

gruelling [ˈgrʊəlɪŋ] adj aufreibend; (pace)
mörderisch

gruesome [ˈgruːsəm] adj grausig

grumble [ˈgrʌmbl] vi murren (about über
+akk)

grumpy [ˈgrʌmpɪ] adj (fam) mürrisch,
grantig

grunt [grʌnt] vi grunzen

G-string [ˈdʒiːstrɪŋ] n ≈ Tanga m

guarantee [gærənˈtiː] n Garantie f (of
für); **it's still under ~** es ist noch Garantie
darauf ▷ vt garantieren

guard [gɑːd] n (sentry) Wache f; (in prison)
Wärter(in) m(f); (Brit Rail) Schaffner(in)
m(f) ▷ vt bewachen; **a closely ~ed secret**
ein streng gehütetes Geheimnis

guardian [ˈgɑːdɪən] n Vormund m;
~ angel Schutzengel m

guess [ges] n Vermutung f; (estimate)
Schätzung f; **have a ~** rate mal! ▷ vt, vi
raten; (estimate) schätzen; **I ~ you're right**
du hast wohl recht; **I ~ so** ich glaube

schon; **guesstimate** [ˈgestɪmɪt] n (fam)
grobe Schätzung

guest [gest] n Gast m; **be my ~** nur zu!;
guest-house n Pension f; **guest room** n
Gästezimmer nt

guidance [ˈgaɪdəns] n (direction) Leitung
f; (advice) Rat m; (counselling) Beratung f;
for your ~ zu Ihrer Orientierung; **guide**
[gaɪd] n (person) Führer(in) m(f); (tour)
Reiseleiter(in) m(f); (book) Führer m; (girl ~)
Pfadfinderin f ▷ vt führen; **guidebook** n
Reiseführer m; **guide dog** n Blindenhund
m; **guided tour** n Führung f (of durch);
guidelines npl Richtlinien pl

guilt [gɪlt] n Schuld f; **guilty** adj schuldig
(of gen); (look) schuldbewusst; **to have a
~ conscience** ein schlechtes Gewissen
haben

guinea pig [ˈgɪnɪ pɪg] n
Meerschweinchen nt; (person)
Versuchskaninchen nt

guitar [gɪˈtɑː*] n Gitarre f

gulf [gʌlf] n Golf m; (gap) Kluft f; **Gulf
States** npl Golfstaaten pl

gull [gʌl] n Möwe f

gullible [ˈgʌlɪbl] adj leichtgläubig

gulp [gʌlp] n (kräftiger) Schluck ▷ vi
schlucken

gum [gʌm] n (around teeth, usu pl)
Zahnfleisch nt; (chewing ~) Kaugummi m

gun [gʌn] n Schusswaffe f; (rifle) Gewehr
nt; (pistol) Pistole f; **gunfire** n Schüsse pl,
Geschützfeuer nt; **gunpowder** n
Schießpulver nt; **gunshot** n Schuss m

gush [gʌʃ] vi (heraus)strömen (from aus)

gut [gʌt] n Darm m; **~s** pl (intestines)
Eingeweide; (courage) Mumm m

gutter [ˈgʌtə*] n (for roof) Dachrinne f; (in
street) Rinnstein m, Gosse f; **gutter press**
n Skandalpresse f

guy [gaɪ] n (man) Typ m, Kerl m; **~s** pl (US)
Leute pl

gym [dʒɪm] n Turnhalle f; (for working out)
Fitnesscenter nt; **gymnasium**
[dʒɪmˈneɪzɪəm] n Turnhalle f; **gymnastics**
[dʒɪmˈnæstɪks] nsing Turnen nt;
gym-toned adj durchtrainiert

gynaecologist [gaɪnɪˈkɒlədʒɪst] n
Frauenarzt m, Frauenärztin f, Gynäkologe
m, Gynäkologin f; **gynaecology** n
Gynäkologie f, Frauenheilkunde f

gypsy [ˈdʒɪpsɪ] n Zigeuner(in) m(f)

h

habit ['hæbɪt] *n* Gewohnheit *f;* **habitual** [hə'bɪtjʊəl] *adj* gewohnt; *(drinker, liar)* gewohnheitsmäßig

hack [hæk] *vt* hacken; **hacker** *n* (*Inform*) Hacker(in) *m(f)*

had [hæd] *pt, pp of* **have**

haddock ['hædək] *n* Schellfisch *m*

hadn't ['hædnt] *contr of* **had not**

haemophiliac, hemophiliac (US) [hi:məʊ'fɪlɪæk] *n* Bluter(in) *m(f);* **haemorrhage, hemorrhage** (US) ['hemərɪdʒ] *n* Blutung *f* ▷ *vi* bluten; **haemorrhoids, hemorrhoids** (US) ['hemərɔɪdz] *npl* Hämorrhoiden *pl*

haggis ['hægɪs] *n* (*Scot*) mit gehackten Schafsinnereien und Haferschrot gefüllter Schafsmagen

Hague [heɪɡ] *n* **the ~** Den Haag

hail [heɪl] *n* Hagel *m* ▷ *vi* hageln ▷ *vt* **to ~ sb as sth** jdn als etw feiern; **hailstone** *n* Hagelkorn *nt;* **hailstorm** *n* Hagelschauer *m*

hair [hɛə*] *n* Haar *nt,* Haare *pl;* **to do one's ~** sich frisieren; **to get one's ~ cut** sich *dat* die Haare schneiden lassen; **hairbrush** *n* Haarbürste *f;* **hair conditioner** *n* Haarspülung *f;* **haircut** *n*

Haarschnitt *m;* **to have a ~** sich *dat* die Haare schneiden lassen; **hairdo** (*pl* **-s**) *n* Frisur *f;* **hairdresser** *n* Friseur *m,* Friseuse *f;* **hairdryer** *n* Haartrockner *m;* (*hand-held*) Fön® *m;* (*over head*) Trockenhaube *f;* **hair gel** *n* Haargel *nt;* **hairpin** *n* Haarnadel *f;* **hair remover** *n* Enthaarungsmittel *nt;* **hair spray** *n* Haarspray *nt;* **hair style** *n* Frisur *f;* **hairy** *adj* haarig, behaart; (*fam: dangerous*) brenzlig

hake [heɪk] *n* Seehecht *m*

half [hɑːf] (*pl* **halves**) *n* Hälfte *f;* (*Sport: of game*) Halbzeit *f;* **to cut in ~** halbieren ▷ *adj* halb; **three and a ~ pounds** dreieinhalb Pfund; **~ an hour, a ~ hour** eine halbe Stunde; **one and a ~** eineinhalb, anderthalb ▷ *adv* halb, zur Hälfte; **~ past three, ~ three** halb vier; **at ~ past** um halb; **~ asleep** fast eingeschlafen; **she's ~ German** sie ist zur Hälfte Deutsche; **~ as big (as)** halb so groß (wie); **half board** *n* Halbpension *f;* **half fare** *n* halber Fahrpreis; **half-hearted** *adj* halbherzig; **half-hour** *n* halbe Stunde; **half moon** *n* Halbmond *m;* **half pint** *n* ≈ Viertelliter *m o nt;* **half price** *n* (**at**) **~** zum halben Preis; **half-term** *n* (*at school*) Ferien *pl* in der Mitte des Trimesters; **half-time** *n* Halbzeit *f;* **halfway** *adv* auf halbem Wege; **halfwit** *n* (*fam*) Trottel *m*

halibut ['hælɪbət] *n* Heilbutt *m*

hall [hɔːl] *n* (*building*) Halle *f;* (*for audience*) Saal *m;* (*entrance ~*) Flur *m;* (*large*) Diele *f;* **~ of residence** (*Brit*) Studentenwohnheim *nt*

hallmark ['hɔːlmɑːk] *n* Stempel *m;* (*fig*) Kennzeichen *nt*

hallo [hʌ'ləʊ] *interj* hallo

Hallowe'en [hæləʊ'iːn] *n* Halloween *nt* (*Tag vor Allerheiligen, an dem sich Kinder verkleiden und von Tür zu Tür gehen*)

• Hallowe'en

Hallowe'en ist der 31. Oktober, der Vorabend von Allerheiligen und nach altem Glauben der Abend, an dem man Geister und Hexen sehen kann. In Großbritannien und vor allem in den USA feiern die Kinder Hallowe'en, indem sie sich verkleiden und mit selbst gemachten

Laternen aus Kürbissen von Tür zu Tür ziehen.

halo ['heɪləʊ] (pl -es) n (of saint) Heiligenschein m

halt [hɔːlt] n Pause f, Halt m; **to come to a ~** zum Stillstand kommen ▷ vt, vi anhalten

halve [hɑːv] vt halbieren

ham [hæm] n Schinken m; **~ and eggs** Schinken mit Spiegelei

hamburger ['hæmbɜːgə*] n (Gastr) Hamburger m

hammer ['hæmə*] n Hammer m ▷ vt, vi hämmern

hammock ['hæmək] n Hängematte f

hamper ['hæmpə*] vt behindern ▷ n (as gift) Geschenkkorb m; (for picnic) Picknickkorb m

hamster ['hæmstə*] n Hamster m

hand [hænd] n Hand f; (of clock, instrument) Zeiger m; (in card game) Blatt nt; **to be made by ~** Handarbeit sein; **~s up!** Hände hoch!; (at school) meldet euch!; **~s off!** Finger weg!; **on the one ~ ..., on the other ~...** einerseits ..., andererseits ...; **to give sb a ~** jdm helfen (with bei); **it's in his ~s** er hat es in der Hand; **to be in good ~s** gut aufgehoben sein; **to get out of ~** außer Kontrolle geraten ▷ vt (pass) reichen (to sb jdm); **hand down** vt (tradition) überliefern; (heirloom) vererben; **hand in** vt einreichen; (at school, university etc) abgeben; **hand out** vt verteilen; **hand over** vt übergeben

handbag n Handtasche f; **handbook** n Handbuch nt; **handbrake** n (Brit) Handbremse f; **hand cream** n Handcreme f; **handcuffs** npl Handschellen pl; **handful** n Handvoll f; **handheld PC** n Handheld m

handicap ['hændɪkæp] n Behinderung f, Handikap nt ▷ vt benachteiligen; **handicapped** adj behindert; **the ~** die Behinderten

handicraft ['hændɪkrɑːft] n Kunsthandwerk nt

handkerchief ['hæŋkətʃɪf] n Taschentuch nt

handle ['hændl] n Griff m; (of door) Klinke f; (of cup etc) Henkel m; (for winding) Kurbel f ▷ vt (touch) anfassen; (deal with: matter) sich befassen mit; (people, machine etc)

umgehen mit; (situation, problem) fertig werden mit; **handlebars** npl Lenkstange f

hand luggage ['hændlʌgɪdʒ] n Handgepäck nt; **handmade** adj handgefertigt; **to be ~** Handarbeit sein; **handout** n (sheet) Handout nt, Thesenpapier nt; **handset** n Hörer m; **please replace the ~** bitte legen Sie auf; **hands-free phone** n Freisprechanlage f; **handshake** n Händedruck m

handsome ['hænsəm] adj (man) gut aussehend

hands-on [hændz'ɒn] adj praxisorientiert; **~ experience** praktische Erfahrung

handwriting ['hændraɪtɪŋ] n Handschrift f

handy ['hændɪ] adj (useful) praktisch

hang [hæŋ] (hung, hung) vt (auf)hängen; (execute: hanged, hanged) hängen; **to ~ sth on sth** etw an etw akk hängen ▷ vi hängen ▷ n **he's got the ~ of it** er hat den Dreh raus; **hang about** vi sich herumtreiben, rumhängen; **hang on** vi sich festhalten (to an +dat); (fam: wait) warten; **to ~ to sth** etw behalten; **hang up** vi (Tel) auflegen ▷ vt aufhängen

hangar ['hæŋə*] n Flugzeughalle f

hanger ['hæŋə*] n Kleiderbügel m

hang glider ['hæŋglaɪdə*] n (Flug)drachen m; (person) Drachenflieger(in) m(f); **hang-gliding** n Drachenfliegen nt

hangover ['hæŋəʊvə*] n (bad head) Kater m; (relic) Überbleibsel nt

hankie ['hæŋkɪ] n (fam) Taschentuch nt

happen ['hæpən] vi geschehen; (sth strange, unpleasant) passieren; **if anything should ~ to me** wenn mir etwas passieren sollte; **it won't ~ again** es wird nicht wieder vorkommen; **I ~ed to be passing** ich kam zufällig vorbei; **happening** n Ereignis nt, Happening nt

happily ['hæpɪlɪ] adv fröhlich, glücklich; (luckily) glücklicherweise; **happiness** ['hæpɪnɪs] n Glück nt; **happy** ['hæpɪ] adj glücklich; (satisfied) **~ with sth** mit etw zufrieden; (willing) **to be ~ to do sth** etw gerne tun; **Happy Christmas** fröhliche Weihnachten!; **Happy New Year** ein glückliches Neues Jahr!; **Happy Birthday** herzlichen Glückwunsch zum Geburtstag!; **happy hour** n Happy Hour f

(Zeit, in der man in Bars Getränke zu günstigeren Preisen bekommt)

harass ['hærəs] vt (ständig) belästigen; **harassment** n Belästigung f; (at work) Mobbing nt; **sexual ~** sexuelle Belästigung

harbor (US), **harbour** ['hɑːbə*] n Hafen m

hard [hɑːd] adj hart; (difficult) schwer, schwierig; (harsh) hart(herzig); **don't be ~ on him** sei nicht zu streng zu ihm; **it's ~ to believe** es ist kaum zu glauben ▷ adv (work) schwer; (run) schnell; (rain, snow) stark; **to try ~/~er** sich dat große/mehr Mühe geben; **hardback** n gebundene Ausgabe; **hard-boiled** adj (egg) hart gekocht; **hard copy** n (Inform) Ausdruck m; **hard disk** n (Inform) Festplatte f; **harden** vt härten ▷ vi hart werden; **hardened** adj (person) abgehärtet (to gegen); **hard-hearted** adj hartherzig; **hardliner** n Hardliner(in) m(f); **hardly** ['hɑːdlɪ] adv kaum; **~ ever** fast nie; **hardship** ['hɑːdʃɪp] n Not f; **hard shoulder** n (Brit) Standspur f; **hardware** n (Inform) Hardware f, Haushalts- und Eisenwaren pl; **hard-working** adj fleißig, tüchtig

hare [hɛə*] n Hase m

harm [hɑːm] n Schaden m; (bodily) Verletzung f; **it wouldn't do any ~** es würde nicht schaden ▷ vt schaden +dat; (person) verletzen; **harmful** adj schädlich; **harmless** adj harmlos

harp [hɑːp] n Harfe f

harsh [hɑːʃ] adj (climate, voice) rau; (light, sound) grell; (severe) hart, streng

harvest ['hɑːvɪst] n Ernte f; (time) Erntezeit f ▷ vt ernten

has [hæz] pres of **have**

hash [hæʃ] n (Gastr) Haschee nt; (fam: hashish) Haschisch nt; **to make a ~ of sth** etw vermasseln; **hash browns** npl (US) ≈ Kartoffelpuffer pl

hassle ['hæsl] n Ärger m; (fuss) Theater nt; **no ~** kein Problem ▷ vt bedrängen

hasn't ['hæznt] contr of **has not**

haste [heɪst] n Eile f; **hastily, hasty** adv, adj hastig; (rash) vorschnell

hat [hæt] n Hut m

hatch [hætʃ] n (Naut) Luke f; (in house) Durchreiche f; **hatchback** ['hætʃbæk] n (car) Wagen m mit Hecktür

hate [heɪt] vt hassen; **I ~ doing this** ich mache das sehr ungern ▷ n Hass m (of auf +akk)

haul [hɔːl] vt ziehen, schleppen ▷ n (booty) Beute f; **haulage** ['hɔːlɪdʒ] n Transport m; (trade) Spedition f; **haunted** adj **a ~ house** ein Haus, in dem es spukt

Ⓞ **KEYWORD**

have [hæv] (pt, pp **had**) aux vb **1** haben (esp with vbs of motion) sein; **to have arrived/slept** angekommen sein/geschlafen haben; **to have been gewesen** sein; **having eaten** or **when he had eaten, he left** nachdem er gegessen hatte, ging er

2 (in tag questions): **you've done it, haven't you?** du hast es doch gemacht, oder nicht?

3 (in short answers and questions): **you've made a mistake — so I have/no I haven't** du hast einen Fehler gemacht — ja, stimmt/nein; **we haven't paid — yes we have!** wir haben nicht bezahlt — doch; **I've been there before, have you?** ich war schon einmal da, du auch?

▷ modal aux vb (be obliged); **to have (got) to do sth** etw tun müssen; **you haven't to tell her** du darfst es ihr nicht erzählen

▷ vt **1** (possess) haben; **he has (got) blue eyes** er hat blaue Augen; **I have (got) an idea** ich habe eine Idee

2 (referring to meals etc): **to have breakfast/a cigarette** frühstücken/eine Zigarette rauchen

3 (receive, obtain etc) haben; **may I have your address?** kann ich Ihre Adresse haben?; **to have a baby** ein Kind bekommen

4 (maintain, allow): **he will have it that he is right** er besteht darauf, dass er Recht hat; **I won't have it** das lasse ich mir nicht bieten

5: **to have sth done** etw machen lassen; **to have sb do sth** jdn etw machen lassen; **he soon had them all laughing** er brachte sie alle zum Lachen

6 (experience, suffer): **she had her bag stolen** man hat ihr die Tasche gestohlen; **he had his arm broken** er hat sich den Arm gebrochen

7 (+noun: take, hold etc); **to have a walk/rest** spazieren gehen/sich ausruhen; **to have a meeting/party** eine Besprechung/Party haben
have out vt: **to have it out with sb** (settle problem) etw mit jdm bereden

Hawaii [həˈwaiː] n Hawaii nt
hawk [hɔːk] n Habicht m
hay [heɪ] n Heu nt; **hay fever** n Heuschnupfen m
hazard [ˈhæzəd] n Gefahr f; (risk) Risiko nt; **hazardous** adj gefährlich; **~ waste** Sondermüll m; **hazard warning lights** npl Warnblinkanlage f
haze [heɪz] n Dunst m
hazelnut [ˈheɪzlnʌt] n Haselnuss f
hazy [ˈheɪzɪ] adj (misty) dunstig; (vague) verschwommen
he [hiː] pron er
head [hed] n Kopf m; (leader) Leiter(in) m(f); (at school) Schulleiter(in) m(f); **~ of state** Staatsoberhaupt nt; **at the ~ of** an der Spitze von; (tossing coin) **~s or tails?** Kopf oder Zahl? ⊳ adj (leading) Ober-; **~ boy** Schulsprecher m; **~ girl** Schulsprecherin f ⊳ vt anführen; (organization) leiten; **head for** vt zusteuern auf +akk; **he's heading for trouble** er wird Ärger bekommen
headache [ˈhedeɪk] n Kopfschmerzen pl, Kopfweh nt; **header** n (football) Kopfball m; (dive) Kopfsprung m; **headfirst** adj kopfüber; **headhunt** vt (Comm) abwerben; **heading** n Überschrift f; **headlamp, headlight** n Scheinwerfer m; **headline** n Schlagzeile f; **headmaster** n Schulleiter m; **headmistress** n Schulleiterin f; **head-on collision** adj Frontalzusammenstoß m; **headphones** npl Kopfhörer m; **headquarters** npl (of firm) Zentrale f; **headrest, head restraint** n Kopfstütze f; **headscarf** (pl **-scarves**) n Kopftuch nt; **head teacher** n Schulleiter(in) m(f)
heal [hiːl] vt, vi heilen
health [helθ] n Gesundheit f; **good/bad for one's ~** gesund/ungesund; **your ~!** zum Wohl!; **health centre** n Ärztezentrum nt; **health club** n Fitnesscenter nt; **health food** n Reformkost f; **~ store** Bioladen m; **health insurance** n Krankenversicherung f;

health service n Gesundheitswesen nt; **healthy** adj gesund
heap [hiːp] n Haufen m; **~s of** (fam) jede Menge ⊳ vt, vi häufen
hear [hɪə*] (**heard, heard**) vt, vi hören; **to ~ about sth** von etw erfahren; **I've ~d of it/him** ich habe schon davon/von ihm gehört; **hearing** n Gehör nt; (Jur) Verhandlung f; **hearing aid** n Hörgerät nt; **hearsay** n **from ~** vom Hörensagen
heart [hɑːt] n Herz nt; **to loose/take ~** den Mut verlieren/Mut fassen; **to learn by ~** auswendig lernen; (cards) **~s** Herz nt; **queen of ~s** Herzdame f; **heart attack** n Herzanfall m; **heartbeat** n Herzschlag m; **heartbreaking** adj herzzerreißend; **heartbroken** adj todunglücklich, untröstlich; **heartburn** n Sodbrennen nt; **heart failure** n Herzversagen nt; **heartfelt** adj tief empfunden; **heartless** adj herzlos; **heart-throb** n (fam) Schwarm m; **heart-to-heart** n offene Aussprache; **hearty** [ˈhɑːtɪ] adj (meal, appetite) herzhaft; (welcome) herzlich
heat [hiːt] n Hitze f (pleasant) Wärme f; (temperature) Temperatur f; (Sport) Vorlauf m ⊳ vt (house, room) heizen; **heat up** vi warm werden ⊳ vt aufwärmen; **heated** adj beheizt; (fig) hitzig; **heater** n Heizofen m; (Auto) Heizung f
heath [hiːθ] n (Brit) Heide f; **heather** [ˈheðə*] n Heidekraut nt
heating [ˈhiːtɪŋ] n Heizung f; **heat resistant** adj hitzebeständig; **heatstroke** n Hitzschlag m; **heatwave** n Hitzewelle f
heaven [ˈhevn] n Himmel m; **heavenly** adj himmlisch
heavily [ˈhevɪlɪ] adv (rain, drink etc) stark; **heavy** [ˈhevɪ] adj schwer; (rain, traffic, smoker etc) stark; **heavy goods vehicle** n Lastkraftwagen m
Hebrew [ˈhiːbruː] adj hebräisch ⊳ n (language) Hebräisch nt
hectic [ˈhektɪk] adj hektisch
he'd [hiːd] contr of **he had**; **he would**
hedge [hedʒ] n Hecke f
hedgehog [ˈhedʒhɒg] n Igel m
heel [hiːl] n (Anat) Ferse f; (of shoe) Absatz m
hefty [ˈheftɪ] adj schwer; (person) stämmig; (fine, amount) saftig
height [haɪt] n Höhe f; (of person) Größe f

h

heir [ɛə*] n Erbe m; **heiress** ['ɛərɪs] n
Erbin f

held [held] pt, pp of **hold**

helicopter ['helɪkɒptə*] n Hubschrauber
m; **heliport** ['helɪpɔːt] n
Hubschrauberlandeplatz m

hell [hel] n Hölle f; **go to ~** scher dich zum
Teufel ▷ interj verdammt; **that's a ~ of a
lot of money** das ist verdammt viel Geld

he'll [hiːl] contr of **he will; he shall**

hello [hʌ'ləʊ] interj hallo

helmet ['helmɪt] n Helm m

help [help] n Hilfe f ▷ vt, vi helfen +dat
(with bei); **to ~ sb (to) do sth** jdm helfen,
etw zu tun; **can I ~?** kann ich (Ihnen)
behilflich sein?; **I couldn't ~ laughing** ich
musste einfach lachen; **I can't ~ it** ich
kann nichts dafür; **~ yourself** bedienen Sie
sich; **helpful** adj (person) hilfsbereit;
(useful) nützlich; **helping** n Portion f;
helpless adj hilflos

hem [hem] n Saum m

hemophiliac [hiːməʊ'fɪlɪæk] n (US)
Bluter m; **hemorrhage** ['hemərɪdʒ] n (US)
Blutung f; **hemorrhoids** ['hemərɔɪdz] npl
(US) Hämorrhoiden pl

hen [hen] n Henne f

hen night n (Brit)
Junggesellinnenabschied m

hence [hens] adv (reason) daher

henpecked ['henpekt] adj **to be ~** unter
dem Pantoffel stehen

hepatitis [hepə'taɪtɪs] n Hepatitis f

her [hɜː*] adj ihr; **she's hurt ~ leg** sie hat
sich dat das Bein verletzt ▷ pron (direct
object) sie; (indirect object) ihr; **do you
know ~?** kennst du sie?; **can you help ~?**
kannst du ihr helfen?; **it's ~** sie ist's

herb [hɜːb] n Kraut nt

herbal medicine ['hɜːbəl-] n
Pflanzenheilkunde f; **herbal tea** n
Kräutertee m

herd [hɜːd] n Herde f; **herd instinct** n
Herdentrieb m

here [hɪə*] adv hier; (to this place) hierher;
come ~ komm her; **I won't be ~ for lunch**
ich bin zum Mittagessen nicht da; **~ and
there** hier und da, da und dort

hereditary [hɪ'redɪtərɪ] adj erblich;
hereditary disease n Erbkrankheit f;
heritage ['herɪtɪdʒ] n Erbe nt

hernia ['hɜːnɪə] n Leistenbruch m,
Eingeweidebruch m

hero ['hɪərəʊ] (pl **-es**) n Held m

heroin ['herəʊɪn] n Heroin nt

heroine ['herəʊɪn] n Heldin f; **heroism**
['herəʊɪzəm] n Heldentum nt

herring ['herɪŋ] n Hering m

hers [hɜːz] pron ihre(r, s); **this is ~** das
gehört ihr; **a friend of ~** ein Freund von ihr

herself [hɜː'self] pron (reflexive); **she's
bought ~ a flat** sie hat sich eine Wohnung
gekauft; **she needs it for ~** sie braucht es
für sich (selbst); (emphatic) **she did it ~**
hat es selbst gemacht; (all) **by ~** allein

he's [hiːz] contr of **he is; he has**

hesitant ['hezɪtənt] adj zögernd;
hesitate ['hezɪteɪt] vi zögern; **don't ~ to
ask** fragen Sie ruhig; **hesitation** n Zögern
nt; **without ~** ohne zu zögern

heterosexual [hetərəʊ'sekʃʊəl] adj
heterosexuell ▷ n Heterosexuelle(r) mf

HGV abbr = **heavy goods vehicle** LKW m

hi [haɪ] interj hi, hallo

hiccup ['hɪkʌp] n Schluckauf m; (minor
problem) Problemchen nt; **to have (the) ~s**
Schluckauf haben

hid [hɪd] pt of **hide**

hidden ['hɪdn] pp of **hide**

hide [haɪd] (**hid, hidden**) vt verstecken
(from vor +dat); (feelings, truth) verbergen;
(cover) verdecken ▷ vi sich verstecken
(from vor +dat)

hideous ['hɪdɪəs] adj scheußlich

hiding ['haɪdɪŋ] n (beating) Tracht f
Prügel; (concealment) **to be in ~** sich
versteckt halten; **hiding place** n Versteck
nt

hi-fi ['haɪfaɪ] n Hi-Fi nt; (system)
Hi-Fi-Anlage f

high [haɪ] adj hoch; (wind) stark; (living)
im großen Stil; (on drugs) high ▷ adv hoch
▷ n (Meteo) Hoch nt; **highchair** n
Hochstuhl m; **higher** adj höher; **higher
education** n Hochschulbildung f; **high
flier** n Hochbegabte(r) (m)f; **high heels**
npl Stöckelschuhe pl; **high jump** n
Hochsprung m; **Highlands** npl
(schottisches) Hochland nt; **highlight** n
(in hair) Strähnchen nt; (fig) Höhepunkt m
▷ vt (with pen) hervorheben; **highlighter**
n Textmarker m; **highly** adv hoch, sehr;
~ paid hoch bezahlt; **I think ~ of him** ich
habe eine hohe Meinung von ihm;
high-performance adj Hochleistungs-;
high pressure n Hochdruck m; **high**

school n (US) Highschool f, ≈ Gymnasium nt; **high-speed** adj Schnell-; **~ train** Hochgeschwindigkeitszug m; **high street** n Hauptstraße f; **high tech** adj Hightech- ▷ n Hightech nt; **high tide** n Flut f; **highway** n (US) ≈ Autobahn f; (Brit) Landstraße f

hijack ['haɪdʒæk] vt entführen, hijacken; **hijacker** n Entführer(in) m(f), Hijacker m

hike [haɪk] vi wandern ▷ n Wanderung f; **hiker** n Wanderer m, Wanderin f; **hiking** n Wandern nt

hilarious [hɪ'leərɪəs] adj zum Schreien komisch

hill [hɪl] n Hügel m; (higher) Berg m; **hilly** adj hügelig

him [hɪm] pron (direct object) ihn; (indirect object) ihm; **do you know ~?** kennst du ihn?; **can you help ~?** kannst du ihm helfen?; **it's ~** er ist's; **~ too** er auch

himself [hɪm'self] pron (reflexive) sich; **he's bought ~ a flat** er hat sich eine Wohnung gekauft; **he needs it for ~** er braucht es für sich (selbst); (emphatic) **he did it ~** er hat es selbst gemacht; (all) **by ~** allein

hinder ['hɪndə*] vt behindern; **hindrance** ['hɪndrəns] n Behinderung f

Hindu ['hɪnduː] adj hinduistisch ▷ n Hindu m; **Hinduism** ['hɪnduːɪzəm] n Hinduismus m

hinge [hɪndʒ] n Scharnier nt; (on door) Angel f

hint [hɪnt] n Wink m, Andeutung f; (trace) Spur f ▷ vi andeuten (at akk)

hip [hɪp] n Hüfte f ▷ adj (trend) hip, trendy

hippopotamus [hɪpə'pɒtəməs] n Nilpferd nt

hire ['haɪə*] vt (worker) anstellen; (car, bike etc) mieten ▷ n Miete f; **for ~** (taxi) frei; **hire(d) car** n Mietwagen m; **hire purchase** n Ratenkauf m

his [hɪz] adj sein; **he's hurt ~ leg** er hat sich dat das Bein verletzt ▷ pron seine(r, s); **it's ~** es gehört ihm; **a friend of ~** ein Freund von ihm

historic [hɪ'stɒrɪk] adj (significant) historisch; **historical** adj (monument etc) historisch; (studies etc) geschichtlich; **history** ['hɪstərɪ] n Geschichte f

hit [hɪt] n (blow) Schlag m; (on target) Treffer m; (success) Erfolg m; (Mus) Hit m ▷ vt (hit, hit) schlagen; (bullet, stone etc)

treffen; **the car ~ the tree** das Auto fuhr gegen einen Baum; **to ~ one's head on sth** sich dat den Kopf an etw dat stoßen; **hit (up)on** vt stoßen auf +akk; **hit-and-run** adj **~ accident** Unfall m mit Fahrerflucht

hitch [hɪtʃ] vt (pull up) hochziehen ▷ n Schwierigkeit f; **without a ~** reibungslos

hitch-hike ['hɪtʃhaɪk] vi trampen; **hitch-hiker** n Tramper(in) m(f); **hitchhiking** n Trampen nt

HIV abbr = **human immunodeficiency virus** HIV nt; **~ positive/negative** HIV-positiv/negativ

hive [haɪv] n Bienenstock m

HM abbr = **His/Her Majesty**

HMS abbr = **His/Her Majesty's Ship**

hoarse [hɔːs] adj heiser

hoax [həʊks] n Streich m, Jux m; (false alarm) blinder Alarm

hob [hɒb] n (of cooker) Kochfeld nt

hobble ['hɒbl] vi humpeln

hobby ['hɒbɪ] n Hobby nt

hobo ['həʊbəʊ] (pl **-es**) n (US) Penner(in) m(f)

hockey ['hɒkɪ] n Hockey nt

hold [həʊld] (**held, held**) vt halten; (contain) enthalten; (be able to contain) fassen; (post, office) innehaben; (value) behalten; (meeting) abhalten; (person as prisoner) gefangen halten; **to ~ one's breath** den Atem anhalten; **to ~ hands** Händchen halten; **~ the line** (Tel) bleiben Sie am Apparat ▷ vi halten; (weather) sich halten ▷ n (grasp) Halt m; (of ship, aircraft) Laderaum m; **hold back** vt zurückhalten; (keep secret) verheimlichen; **hold on** vi sich festhalten; (wait) warten; (Tel) dranbleiben; **to ~ to sth** etw festhalten; **hold out** vt ausstrecken; (offer) hinhalten; (offer) bieten ▷ vi durchhalten; **hold up** vt hochhalten; (support) stützen; (delay) aufhalten; **holdall** n Reisetasche f; **holder** n (person) Inhaber(in) m(f); **holdup** n (in traffic) Stau m; (robbery) Überfall m

hole [həʊl] n Loch nt; (of fox, rabbit) Bau m; **~ in the wall** (cash dispenser) Geldautomat m

holiday ['hɒlɪdeɪ] n (day off) freier Tag; (public ~) Feiertag m; (vacation) Urlaub m; (at school) Ferien pl; **on ~** im Urlaub; **to go on ~** Urlaub machen; **holiday camp** n Ferienlager nt; **holiday home** n

Ferienhaus nt; (flat) Ferienwohnung f;
holidaymaker n Urlauber(in) m(f);
holiday resort n Ferienort m

Holland ['hɒlənd] n Holland nt

hollow ['hɒləʊ] adj hohl; (words) leer ▷ n
Vertiefung f

holly ['hɒlɪ] n Stechpalme f

holy ['həʊlɪ] adj heilig; **Holy Week** n
Karwoche f

home [həʊm] n Zuhause nt; (area, country)
Heimat f; (institution) Heim nt; **at ~** zu
Hause; **to make oneself at ~** es sich dat
bequem machen; **away from ~** verreist
▷ adv **to go ~** nach Hause gehen/fahren;
home address n Heimatadresse f; **home
country** n Heimatland nt; **home game** n
(Sport) Heimspiel nt; **homeless** adj
obdachlos; **homely** adj häuslich; (US:
ugly) unscheinbar; **home-made** adj selbst
gemacht; **home movie** n Amateurfilm
m; **Home Office** n (Brit)
Innenministerium nt

homeopathic adj (US) see
homoeopathic

home page ['həʊmpeɪdʒ] n (Inform)
Homepage f; **Home Secretary** n (Brit)
Innenminister(in) m(f); **homesick** adj **to
be ~** Heimweh haben; **home town** n
Heimatstadt f; **homework** n
Hausaufgaben pl

homicide ['hɒmɪsaɪd] n (US) Totschlag m

homoeopathic [həʊmɪəʊ'pæθɪk] adj
homöopathisch

homosexual [hɒməʊ'sekʃʊəl] adj
homosexuell ▷ n Homosexuelle(r) mf

Honduras [hɒn'djʊərəs] n Honduras nt

honest ['ɒnɪst] adj ehrlich; **honesty** n
Ehrlichkeit f

honey ['hʌnɪ] n Honig m; **honeycomb** n
Honigwabe f; **honeydew melon** n
Honigmelone f; **honeymoon** n
Flitterwochen pl

Hong Kong [hɒŋ 'kɒŋ] n Hongkong nt

honor (US) see **honour**; **honorary**
['ɒnərərɪ] adj (member, title etc) Ehren-,
ehrenamtlich; **honour** ['ɒnə*] vt ehren;
(cheque) einlösen; (contract) einhalten ▷ n
Ehre f; **in ~ of** zu Ehren von; **honourable**
adj ehrenhaft; **honours degree** n
akademischer Grad mit Prüfung im
Spezialfach

hood [hʊd] n Kapuze f; (Auto) Verdeck nt;
(US Auto) Kühlerhaube f

hoof [huːf] (pl hooves) n Huf m

hook [hʊk] n Haken m; **hooked** adj (keen)
besessen (on von); (drugs) abhängig sein
(on von)

hooligan ['huːlɪgən] n Hooligan m

hoot [huːt] vi (Auto) hupen

Hoover® ['huːvə] n Staubsauger m;
hoover vi, vt staubsaugen

hop [hɒp] vi hüpfen ▷ n (Bot) Hopfen m

hope [həʊp] vi, vt hoffen (for auf +akk); **I
~ so/~ not** hoffentlich/hoffentlich nicht; **I
~ (that) we'll meet** ich hoffe, dass wir uns
sehen werden ▷ n Hoffnung f; **there's no
~** es ist aussichtslos; **hopeful** adj
hoffnungsvoll; **hopefully** adv (full of hope)
hoffnungsvoll; (I hope so) hoffentlich;
hopeless adj hoffnungslos; (incompetent)
miserabel

horizon [hə'raɪzn] n Horizont m;
horizontal [hɒrɪ'zɒntl] adj horizontal

hormone ['hɔːməʊn] n Hormon nt

horn [hɔːn] n Horn nt; (Auto) Hupe f

hornet ['hɔːnɪt] n Hornisse f

horny ['hɔːnɪ] adj (fam) geil

horoscope ['hɒrəskəʊp] n Horoskop nt

horrible, horribly ['hɒrɪbl, -blɪ] adj, adv
schrecklich; **horrid, horridly** ['hɒrɪd, -lɪ]
adj, adv abscheulich; **horrify** ['hɒrɪfaɪ] vt
entsetzen; **horror** ['hɒrə*] n Entsetzen
nt; **~s** (things) Schrecken pl

hors d'œuvre [ɔː'dɜːvr] n Vorspeise f

horse [hɔːs] n Pferd nt; **horse chestnut** n
Rosskastanie f; **horsepower** n
Pferdestärke f, PS nt; **horse racing** n
Pferderennen nt; **horseradish** n
Meerrettich m; **horse riding** n Reiten nt;
horseshoe n Hufeisen nt

horticulture ['hɔːtɪkʌltʃə*] n Gartenbau
m

hose, hosepipe [həʊz, 'həʊzpaɪp] n
Schlauch m

hospitable [hɒ'spɪtəbl] adj
gastfreundlich

hospital ['hɒspɪtl] n Krankenhaus nt

hospitality [hɒspɪ'tælɪtɪ] n
Gastfreundschaft f

host [həʊst] n Gastgeber m; (Tv: of show)
Moderator(in) m(f), Talkmaster(in) m(f)
▷ vt (party) geben; (TV show)
moderieren

hostage ['hɒstɪdʒ] n Geisel f

hostel ['hɒstəl] n Wohnheim nt; (youth ~)
Jugendherberge f

hostess ['həʊstɪs] n (of a party)
Gastgeberin f

hostile ['hɒstaɪl] adj feindlich; **hostility**
[hɒs'tɪlɪtɪ] n Feindseligkeit f

hot [hɒt] adj heiß; (drink, food, water)
warm; (spiced) scharf; **I'm (feeling)** ~ mir
ist heiß; **hot cross bun** n Rosinenbrötchen
mit einem Kreuz darauf, hauptsächlich zu
Ostern gegessen; **hot dog** n Hotdog nt

hotel [həʊ'tel] n Hotel nt; **hotel room** n
Hotelzimmer nt

hothouse n Treibhaus nt; **hotline** n
Hotline f; **hotplate** n Kochplatte f;
hotpot n Fleischeintopf mit Kartoffeleinlage;
hot-water bottle n Wärmflasche f

hour ['aʊə*] n Stunde f; **to wait for ~s**
stundenlang warten; **~s** pl (of shops etc)
Geschäftszeiten pl; **hourly** adj stündlich

house [haʊs] (pl **houses**) n Haus nt; **at
my ~** bei mir (zu Hause); **to my ~** zu mir
(nach Hause); **on the ~** auf Kosten des
Hauses; **the House of Commons/Lords**
das britische Unterhaus/Oberhaus; **the
Houses of Parliament** das britische
Parlamentsgebäude ▷ [haʊz] vt
unterbringen; **houseboat** n Hausboot nt;
household n Haushalt m; **~ appliance**
Haushaltsgerät nt; **house-husband** n
Hausmann m; **housekeeping** n
Haushaltung f; (money) Haushaltsgeld nt;
house-trained adj stubenrein;
house-warming (party) n Einzugsparty
f; **housewife** (pl **-wives**) n Hausfrau f;
house wine n Hauswein m; **housework**
n Hausarbeit f

housing ['haʊzɪŋ] n (houses) Wohnungen
pl; (house building) Wohnungsbau m;
housing benefit n Wohngeld nt;
housing development, **housing estate**
(Brit) n Wohnsiedlung f

hover ['hɒvə*] vi schweben; **hovercraft** n
Luftkissenboot nt

how [haʊ] adv wie; **~ many** wie viele;
~ much wie viel; **~ are you?** wie geht es
Ihnen?; **~ are things?** wie geht's?; **~'s
work?** was macht die Arbeit?; **~ about ...?**
wie wäre es mit ...?; **however** [haʊ'evə*]
conj (but) jedoch, aber ▷ adv (no matter
how) wie ... auch; **~ much it costs** wie viel
es auch kostet; **~ you do it** wie man es
auch macht

howl [haʊl] vi heulen; **howler** ['haʊlə*] n
(fam) grober Schnitzer

HP, **hp** n (Brit) abbr = **hire purchase**
Ratenkauf m ▷ abbr = **horsepower** PS

HQ abbr = **headquarters**

hubcap ['hʌbkæp] n Radkappe f

hug [hʌg] vt umarmen ▷ n Umarmung f

huge [hjuːdʒ] adj riesig

hum [hʌm] vi, vt summen

human ['hjuːmən] adj menschlich;
~ rights Menschenrechte pl ▷ n **~ (being)**
Mensch m; **humanitarian**
[hjuːmænɪ'teərɪən] adj humanitär;
humanity [hjuː'mænɪtɪ] n Menschheit f;
(kindliness) Menschlichkeit f; **humanities**
Geisteswissenschaften pl

humble ['hʌmbl] adj demütig; (modest)
bescheiden

humid ['hjuːmɪd] adj feucht; **humidity**
[hjuː'mɪdɪtɪ] n (Luft)feuchtigkeit f

humiliate [hjuː'mɪlɪeɪt] vt demütigen;
humiliation [hjuːmɪlɪ'eɪʃn] n
Erniedrigung f, Demütigung f

humor (US) see **humour**; **humorous**
['hjuːmərəs] adj humorvoll; (story) lustig,
witzig; **humour** ['hjuːmə*] n Humor m;
sense of ~ Sinn m für Humor

hump [hʌmp] n Buckel m

hunch [hʌntʃ] n Gefühl nt, Ahnung f ▷ vt
(back) krümmen; **hunchback** n
Bucklige(r) mf

hundred ['hʌndrəd] num **one ~, a
~** (ein)hundert; **a ~ and one**
hundert(und)eins; **two ~** zweihundert;
hundredth adj hundertste(r, s) ▷ n
(fraction) Hundertstel nt; **hundredweight**
n Zentner m (50,8 kg)

hung [hʌŋ] pt, pp of **hang**

Hungarian [hʌŋ'geərɪən] adj ungarisch
▷ n (person) Ungar(in) m(f); (language)
Ungarisch nt; **Hungary** ['hʌŋgərɪ] n
Ungarn nt

hunger ['hʌŋgə*] n Hunger m; **hungry**
['hʌŋgrɪ] adj hungrig; **to be ~** Hunger
haben

hunk [hʌŋk] n (fam) gut aussehender
Mann

hunt [hʌnt] n Jagd f; (search) Suche f (for
nach) ▷ vt, vi jagen; (search) suchen (for
nach); **hunting** n Jagen nt, Jagd f

hurdle ['hɜːdl] n (a. fig) Hürde f; **the
400m ~s** die 400m-Hürdenlauf

hurl [hɜːl] vt schleudern

hurray [hʊ'reɪ] interj hurra

hurricane ['hʌrɪkən] n Orkan m

hurried ['hʌrɪd] *adj* eilig; **hurry** ['hʌrɪ] *n*
Eile *f*; **to be in a ~** es eilig haben; **there's
no ~** es eilt nicht ▷ *vi* sich beeilen; **~ (up)**
mach schnell! ▷ *vt* antreiben

hurt [hɜːt] **(hurt, hurt)** *vt* wehtun +*dat*;
(*wound: person, feelings*) verletzen; **I've
~ my arm** ich habe mir am Arm wehgetan
▷ *vi* wehtun; **my arm ~s** mir tut der Arm
weh

husband ['hʌzbənd] *n* Ehemann *m*

husky ['hʌskɪ] *adj* rau ▷ *n* Schlittenhund
m

hut [hʌt] *n* Hütte *f*

hyacinth ['haɪəsɪnθ] *n* Hyazinthe *f*

hybrid ['haɪbrɪd] *n* Kreuzung *f*

hydroelectric ['haɪdrəʊɪ'lektrɪk] *adj*
~ power station Wasserkraftwerk *nt*

hydrofoil ['haɪdrəʊfɔɪl] *n*
Tragflächenboot *nt*

hydrogen ['haɪdrədʒən] *n* Wasserstoff *m*

hygiene ['haɪdʒiːn] *n* Hygiene *f*; **hygienic**
[haɪ'dʒiːnɪk] *adj* hygienisch

hymn [hɪm] *n* Kirchenlied *nt*

hypermarket ['haɪpəmɑːkɪt] *n*
Großmarkt *m*; **hypersensitive** *adj*
überempfindlich

hyphen ['haɪfən] *n* Bindestrich *m*

hypnosis [hɪp'nəʊsɪs] *n* Hypnose *f*;
hypnotize ['hɪpnətaɪz] *vt* hypnotisieren

hypochondriac [haɪpəʊ'kɒndriæk] *n*
eingebildete(r) Kranke(r), eingebildete
Kranke

hypocrisy [hɪ'pəkrəsɪ] *n* Heuchelei *f*;
hypocrite ['hɪpəkrɪt] *n* Heuchler(in) *m(f)*

hypodermic [haɪpə'dɜmɪk] *adj, n*
~ (needle) Spritze *f*

hypothetical [haɪpəʊ'θetɪkəl] *adj*
hypothetisch

hysteria [hɪ'stɪərɪə] *n* Hysterie *f*;
hysterical [hɪ'sterɪkəl] *adj* hysterisch;
(*amusing*) zum Totlachen

identical [aɪˈdentɪkəl] adj identisch;
~ twins eineiige Zwillinge
identify [aɪˈdentɪfaɪ] vt identifizieren;
identity [aɪˈdentɪtɪ] n Identität f;
identity card n Personalausweis m
idiom [ˈɪdɪəm] n Redewendung f;
idiomatic adj idiomatisch
idiot [ˈɪdɪət] n Idiot(in) m(f)
idle [ˈaɪdl] adj (doing nothing) untätig;
(worker) unbeschäftigt; (machines) außer
Betrieb; (lazy) faul; (promise, threat) leer
idol [ˈaɪdl] n Idol nt; **idolize** [ˈaɪdəlaɪz] vt
vergöttern
idyllic [ɪˈdɪlɪk] adj idyllisch
i.e. abbr = **id est** d.h.

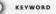

KEYWORD

if [ɪf] conj **1** wenn (in case also) falls; **if I**
were you wenn ich Sie wäre
2 (although): **(even) if** (selbst or auch)
wenn
3 (whether) ob
4: **if so/not** wenn ja/nicht; **if only ...**
wenn ... doch nur ...; **if only I could** wenn
ich doch nur könnte; see also **as**

I [aɪ] pron ich
ice [aɪs] n Eis nt ▷ vt (cake) glasieren;
iceberg n Eisberg m; **iceberg lettuce** n
Eisbergsalat m; **icebox** n (US)
Kühlschrank m; **icecold** adj eiskalt;
ice cream n Eis nt; **ice cube** n
Eiswürfel m; **iced** adj eisgekühlt; (coffee,
tea) Eis-; (cake) glasiert; **ice hockey** n
Eishockey nt
Iceland [ˈaɪslənd] n Island nt; **Icelander** n
Isländer(in) m(f); **Icelandic** [aɪsˈlændɪk]
adj isländisch ▷ n (language) Isländisch nt
ice lolly [ˈaɪslɒlɪ] n (Brit) Eis nt am Stiel;
ice rink n Kunsteisbahn f; **ice skating** n
Schlittschuhlaufen nt
icing [ˈaɪsɪŋ] n (on cake) Zuckerguss m
icon [ˈaɪkɒn] n Ikone f; (Inform) Icon nt,
Programmsymbol nt
icy [ˈaɪsɪ] adj (slippery) vereist; (cold) eisig
I'd [aɪd] contr of **I would**; **I had**
ID abbr = **identification** Ausweis m
idea [aɪˈdɪə] n Idee f; **(I've) no ~** (ich habe)
keine Ahnung; **that's my ~ of ...** so stelle
ich mir ... vor
ideal [aɪˈdɪəl] n Ideal nt ▷ adj ideal;
ideally adv ideal; (before statement)
idealerweise

ignition [ɪgˈnɪʃən] n Zündung f; **ignition**
key n (Auto) Zündschlüssel m
ignorance [ˈɪgnərəns] n Unwissenheit f;
ignorant adj unwissend; **ignore** [ɪgˈnɔː*]
vt ignorieren, nicht beachten
I'll [aɪl] contr of **I will**; **I shall**
ill [ɪl] adj krank; **~ at ease** unbehaglich
illegal [ɪˈliːgəl] adj illegal
illegitimate [ɪlɪˈdʒɪtɪmət] adj unzulässig;
(child) unehelich
illiterate [ɪˈlɪtərət] adj **to be**
~ Analphabet(in) sein
illness [ˈɪlnəs] n Krankheit f
illuminate [ɪˈluːmɪneɪt] vt beleuchten;
illuminating adj (remark)
aufschlussreich
illusion [ɪˈluːʒən] n Illusion f; **to be under**
the ~ that ... sich einbilden, dass ...
illustrate [ˈɪləstreɪt] vt illustrieren;
illustration n Abbildung f, Bild nt
I'm [aɪm] contr of **I am**
image [ˈɪmɪdʒ] n Bild nt; (public ~) Image
nt; **imaginable** [ɪˈmædʒɪnəbl] adj
denkbar; **imaginary** [ɪˈmædʒɪnərɪ] adj
eingebildet; **~ world** Fantasiewelt f;
imagination [ɪmædʒɪˈneɪʃən] n Fantasie

f; (*mistaken*) Einbildung f; **imaginative**
[ɪ'mædʒɪnətɪv] *adj* fantasievoll; **imagine**
[ɪ'mædʒɪn] *vt* sich vorstellen; (*wrongly*)
sich einbilden; **~!** stell dir vor!

imbecile ['ɪmbəsiːl] *n* Trottel *m*

imitate ['ɪmɪteɪt] *vt* nachahmen,
nachmachen; **imitation** *n* Nachahmung f
▷ *adj* imitiert; **~ leather** Kunstleder *nt*

immaculate [ɪ'mækjʊlɪt] *adj* tadellos;
(*spotless*) makellos

immature [ɪmə'tjʊə*] *adj* unreif

immediate [ɪ'miːdɪət] *adj* unmittelbar;
(*instant*) sofortig; (*reply*) umgehend;
immediately *adv* sofort

immense, immensely [ɪ'mens, -lɪ] *adj*,
adv riesig, enorm

immersion heater [ɪ'mɜːʃn hiːtə] *n*
Boiler *m*

immigrant ['ɪmɪgrənt] *n* Einwanderer *m*,
Einwanderin f; **immigration** [ɪmɪ'greɪʃən]
n Einwanderung f; (*facility*)
Einwanderungskontrolle f

immobilize [ɪ'məʊbɪlaɪz] *vt* lähmen;
immobilizer *n* (*Auto*) Wegfahrsperre f

immoral [ɪ'mɒrəl] *adj* unmoralisch

immortal [ɪ'mɔːtl] *adj* unsterblich

immune [ɪ'mjuːn] *adj* (*Med*) immun (*from*,
to gegen); **immune system** *n*
Immunsystem *nt*

impact ['ɪmpækt] *n* Aufprall *m*; (*effect*)
Auswirkung f (*on* auf +*akk*)

impatience [ɪm'peɪʃəns] *n* Ungeduld f;
impatient, impatiently *adj*, *adv*
ungeduldig

impeccable [ɪm'pekəbl] *adj* tadellos

impede [ɪm'piːd] *vt* behindern

imperative [ɪm'perətɪv] *adj* unbedingt
erforderlich ▷ *n* (*Ling*) Imperativ *m*

imperfect [ɪm'pɜːfɪkt] *adj*
unvollkommen; (*goods*) fehlerhaft ▷ *n*
(*Ling*) Imperfekt *nt*; **imperfection**
[ɪmpə'fekʃən] *n* Unvollkommenheit f;
(*fault*) Fehler *m*

imperial [ɪm'pɪərɪəl] *adj* kaiserlich,
Reichs-; **imperialism** *n* Imperialismus *m*

impertinence [ɪm'pɜːtɪnəns] *n*
Unverschämtheit f, Zumutung f;
impertinent *adj* unverschämt

implant ['ɪmplɑːnt] *n* (*Med*) Implantat *nt*

implausible [ɪm'plɔːzəbl] *adj*
unglaubwürdig

implement ['ɪmplɪmənt] *n* Werkzeug *nt*,
Gerät *nt* ▷ [ɪmplɪ'ment] *vt* durchführen

implication [ɪmplɪ'keɪʃən] *n* Folge f,
Auswirkung f; (*logical*) Schlussfolgerung f;
implicit [ɪm'plɪsɪt] *adj* implizit,
unausgesprochen; **imply** [ɪm'plaɪ] *vt*
(*indicate*) andeuten; (*mean*) bedeuten; **are
you ~ing that ...** wollen Sie damit sagen,
dass ...

impolite [ɪmpə'laɪt] *adj* unhöflich

import [ɪm'pɔːt] *vt* einführen,
importieren ▷ *n* ['ɪmpɔːt] Einfuhr f,
Import *m*

importance [ɪm'pɔːtəns] *n* Bedeutung f;
of no ~ unwichtig; **important** *adj* wichtig
(*to sb* für jdn); (*significant*) bedeutend;
(*influential*) einflussreich

import duty ['ɪmpɔːtdjuːtɪ] *n*
Einfuhrzoll *m*; **import licence** *n*
Einfuhrgenehmigung f

impose [ɪm'pəʊz] *vt* (*conditions*)
auferlegen (*on dat*); (*penalty, sanctions*)
verhängen (*on* gegen); **imposing**
[ɪm'pəʊzɪŋ] *adj* eindrucksvoll, imposant

impossible [ɪm'pɒsəbl] *adj* unmöglich

impotence ['ɪmpətəns] *n* Machtlosigkeit
f; (*sexual*) Impotenz f; **impotent** *adj*
machtlos; (*sexually*) impotent

impractical [ɪm'præktɪkəl] *adj*
unpraktisch; (*plan*) undurchführbar

impress [ɪm'pres] *vt* beeindrucken;
impression [ɪm'preʃən] *n* Eindruck *m*;
impressive *adj* eindrucksvoll

imprison [ɪm'prɪzn] *vt* inhaftieren;
imprisonment *n* Inhaftierung f

improbability [ɪmprəbə'bɪlɪtɪ] *n*
Unwahrscheinlichkeit f; **improbable**
[ɪm'prɒbəbl] *adj* unwahrscheinlich

improper [ɪm'prɒpə*] *adj* (*indecent*)
unanständig; (*use*) unsachgemäß

improve [ɪm'pruːv] *vt* verbessern ▷ *vi*
sich verbessern, besser werden; (*patient*)
Fortschritte machen; **improvement** *n*
Verbesserung f (*in* +*gen*; *on* gegenüber); (*in
appearance*) Verschönerung f

improvise ['ɪmprəvaɪz] *vt*, *vi*
improvisieren

impulse ['ɪmpʌls] *n* Impuls *m*; **impulsive**
[ɪm'pʌlsɪv] *adj* impulsiv

🔵 **KEYWORD**

in [ɪn] *prep* **1** (*indicating place, position*) in
+*dat*; (*with motion*) in +*acc*; **in here/there**
hier/dort; **in London** in London; **in the**

United States in den Vereinigten Staaten

2 (*indicating time: during*) in +*dat*; **in summer** im Sommer; **in 1988** (im Jahre) 1988; **in the afternoon** nachmittags, am Nachmittag

3 (*indicating time: in the space of*) innerhalb von; **I'll see you in 2 weeks** *or* **in 2 weeks' time** ich sehe Sie in zwei Wochen

4 (*indicating manner, circumstances, state etc*) in +*dat*; **in the sun/rain** in der Sonne/im Regen; **in English/French** auf Englisch/Französisch; **in a loud/soft voice** mit lauter/leiser Stimme

5 (*with ratios, numbers*): **1 in 10** jeder Zehnte; **20 pence in the pound** 20 Pence pro Pfund; **they lined up in twos** sie stellten sich in Zweierreihe auf

6 (*referring to people, works*): **the disease is common in children** die Krankheit ist bei Kindern häufig; **in Dickens** bei Dickens; **we have a loyal friend in him** er ist uns ein treuer Freund

7 (*indicating profession etc*): **to be in teaching/the army** Lehrer in/beim Militär sein; **to be in publishing** im Verlagswesen arbeiten

8 (*with present participle*): **in saying this, I** ... wenn ich das sage, ... ich; **in accepting this view, he** ... weil er diese Meinung akzeptierte, ... er

▷ *adv*; **to be in** (*person: at home, work*) da sein (*train, ship, plane*) angekommen sein (*in fashion*) in sein: **to ask sb in** jdn hereinbitten; **to run/limp** *etc* **in** hereingerannt/gehumpelt *etc* kommen

▷ *n*; **the ins and outs** (*of proposal, situation etc*) die Feinheiten

inability [ɪnəˈbɪlɪtɪ] *n* Unfähigkeit *f*
inaccessible [ɪnækˈsesəbl] *adj* (*a. fig*) unzugänglich
inaccurate [ɪnˈækjʊrɪt] *adj* ungenau
inadequate [ɪnˈædɪkwət] *adj* unzulänglich
inapplicable [ɪnəˈplɪkəbl] *adj* unzutreffend
inappropriate [ɪnəˈprəʊprɪət] *adj* unpassend; (*clothing*) ungeeignet; (*remark*) unangebracht
inborn [ˈɪnˈbɔːn] *adj* angeboren
incapable [ɪnˈkeɪpəbl] *adj* unfähig (*of* zu);

to be ~ of doing sth nicht imstande sein, etw zu tun

incense [ˈɪnsens] *n* Weihrauch *m*
incentive [ɪnˈsentɪv] *n* Anreiz *m*
incessant, incessantly [ɪnˈsesnt, -lɪ] *adj, adv* unaufhörlich
incest [ˈɪnsest] *n* Inzest *m*
inch [ɪntʃ] *n* Zoll *m* (2,54 cm)
incident [ˈɪnsɪdənt] *n* Vorfall *m*; (*disturbance*) Zwischenfall *m*; **incidentally** [ɪnsɪˈdentlɪ] *adv* nebenbei bemerkt, übrigens
inclination [ɪnklɪˈneɪʃən] *n* Neigung *f*; **inclined** [ˈɪnklaɪnd] *adj* **to be ~ to do sth** dazu neigen, etw zu tun
include [ɪnˈkluːd] *vt* einschließen; (*on list, in group*) aufnehmen; **including** *prep* einschließlich (+*gen*); **not ~ service** Bedienung nicht inbegriffen; **inclusive** [ɪnˈkluːsɪv] *adj* einschließlich (*of* +*gen*); (*price*) Pauschal-
incoherent [ɪnkəʊˈhɪərənt] *adj* zusammenhanglos
income [ˈɪnkʌm] *n* Einkommen *nt*; (*from business*) Einkünfte *pl*; **income tax** *n* Einkommensteuer *f*; (*on wages, salary*) Lohnsteuer *f*; **incoming** [ˈɪnkʌmɪŋ] *adj* ankommend; (*mail*) eingehend
incompatible [ɪnkəmˈpætəbl] *adj* unvereinbar; (*people*) unverträglich; (*Inform*) nicht kompatibel
incompetent [ɪnˈkɒmpɪtənt] *adj* unfähig
incomplete [ɪnkəmˈpliːt] *adj* unvollständig
incomprehensible [ɪnkɒmprɪˈhensəbl] *adj* unverständlich
inconceivable [ɪnkənˈsiːvəbl] *adj* unvorstellbar
inconsiderate [ɪnkənˈsɪdərət] *adj* rücksichtslos
inconsistency [ɪnkənˈsɪstənsɪ] *n* Inkonsequenz *f*; (*contradictory*) Widersprüchlichkeit *f*; **inconsistent** *adj* inkonsequent; (*contradictory*) widersprüchlich; (*work*) unbeständig
inconvenience [ɪnkənˈviːnɪəns] *n* Unannehmlichkeit *f*; (*trouble*) Umstände *pl*; **inconvenient** *adj* ungünstig, unbequem; (*time*) **it's ~ for me** es kommt mir ungelegen; **if it's not too ~ for you** wenn es dir passt
incorporate [ɪnˈkɔːpəreɪt] *vt* aufnehmen (*into* in +*akk*); (*include*) enthalten

incorrect ['ɪnkərekt] adj falsch; (improper) inkorrekt

increase ['ɪnkriːs] n Zunahme f (in an +dat); (in amount, speed) Erhöhung f (in +gen); **~ in size** Vergrößerung f ▷ [ɪn'kriːs] vt (price, taxes, salary, speed etc) erhöhen; (wealth) vermehren; (number) vergrößern; (business) erweitern ▷ vi (Auto) zunehmen (in an +dat); (prices) steigen; (in size) größer werden; (in number) sich vermehren; **increasingly** [ɪn'kriːsɪŋlɪ] adv zunehmend

incredible, incredibly [ɪn'kredəbl, -blɪ] adj, adv unglaublich; (very good) fantastisch

incredulous [ɪn'kredjʊləs] adj ungläubig, skeptisch

incriminate [ɪn'krɪmɪneɪt] vt belasten

incubator ['ɪnkjʊbeɪtə*] n Brutkasten m

incurable [ɪn'kjʊərəbl] adj unheilbar

indecent [ɪn'diːsnt] adj unanständig

indecisive [ɪndɪ'saɪsɪv] adj (person) unentschlossen; (result) nicht entscheidend

indeed [ɪn'diːd] adv tatsächlich; (as answer) allerdings; **very hot ~** wirklich sehr heiß

indefinite [ɪn'defɪnɪt] adj unbestimmt; **indefinitely** adv endlos; (postpone) auf unbestimmte Zeit

independence [ɪndɪ'pendəns] n Unabhängigkeit f

● **Independence Day**
●
● Der **Independence Day**, der 4. Juli, ist in
● den USA ein gesetzlicher Feiertag
● zum Gedenken an die
● Unabhängigkeitserklärung am 4. Juli
● 1776, mit der die 13 amerikanischen
● Kolonien ihre Freiheit und
● Unabhängigkeit von Großbritannien
● erklärten.

independent [ɪndɪ'pendənt] adj unabhängig (of von); (person) selbstständig

indescribable [ɪndɪ'skraɪbəbl] adj unbeschreiblich

index ['ɪndeks] n Index m, Verzeichnis nt; **index finger** n Zeigefinger m

India ['ɪndɪə] n Indien nt; **Indian** ['ɪndɪən] adj indisch; (Native American) indianisch

▷ n Inder(in) m(f); (Native American) Indianer(in) m(f); **Indian Ocean** n Indischer Ozean; **Indian summer** n Spätsommer m, Altweibersommer m

indicate ['ɪndɪkeɪt] vt (show) zeigen; (instrument) anzeigen; (suggest) hinweisen auf +akk ▷ vi (Auto) blinken; **indication** [ɪndɪ'keɪʃn] n (sign) Anzeichen nt (of für); **indicator** ['ɪndɪkeɪtə*] n (Auto) Blinker m

indifferent [ɪn'dɪfrənt] adj (not caring) gleichgültig (to, towards gegenüber); (mediocre) mittelmäßig

indigestible [ɪndɪ'dʒestəbl] adj unverdaulich; **indigestion** [ɪndɪ'dʒestʃən] n Verdauungsstörung f

indignity [ɪn'dɪgnɪtɪ] n Demütigung f

indirect, indirectly [ɪndɪ'rekt, -lɪ] adj, adv indirekt

indiscreet [ɪndɪ'skriːt] adj indiskret

indispensable [ɪndɪ'spensəbl] adj unentbehrlich

indisposed [ɪndɪ'spəʊzd] adj unwohl

indisputable [ɪndɪ'spjuːtəbl] adj unbestreitbar; (evidence) unanfechtbar

individual [ɪndɪ'vɪdjʊəl] n Einzelne(r) mf ▷ adj einzeln; (distinctive) eigen, individuell; **~ case** Einzelfall m; **individually** adv (separately) einzeln

Indonesia [ɪndəʊ'niːzjə] n Indonesien nt

indoor ['ɪndɔː*] adj (shoes) Haus-; (plant, games) Zimmer-; (Sport: football, championship, record etc) Hallen-; **indoors** adv drinnen, im Haus

indulge [ɪn'dʌldʒ] vi **to ~ in sth** sich dat etw gönnen; **indulgence** n Nachsicht f; (enjoyment) (übermäßiger) Genuss; (luxury) Luxus m; **indulgent** adj nachsichtig (with gegenüber)

industrial [ɪn'dʌstrɪəl] adj Industrie-, industriell; **~ estate** Industriegebiet nt; **industry** ['ɪndəstrɪ] n Industrie f

inedible [ɪn'edɪbl] adj nicht essbar, ungenießbar

ineffective [ɪnɪ'fektɪv] adj unwirksam, wirkungslos; **inefficient** adj unwirksam; (use, machine) unwirtschaftlich; (method etc) unrationell

ineligible [ɪn'elɪdʒəbl] adj nicht berechtigt (for zu)

inequality [ɪnɪ'kwɒlɪtɪ] n Ungleichheit f

inevitable [ɪn'evɪtəbl] adj unvermeidlich; **inevitably** adv zwangsläufig

inexcusable [ɪnɪksˈkjuːzəbl] adj
unverzeihlich; **that's ~** das kann man
nicht verzeihen

inexpensive [ɪnɪksˈpensɪv] adj
preisgünstig

inexperience [ɪnɪksˈpɪərɪəns] n
Unerfahrenheit f; **inexperienced** adj
unerfahren

inexplicable [ɪnɪksˈplɪkəbl] adj
unerklärlich

infallible [ɪnˈfæləbl] adj unfehlbar

infamous [ˈɪnfəməs] adj (person)
berüchtigt (for wegen); (deed)
niederträchtig

infancy [ˈɪnfənsɪ] n frühe Kindheit;
infant [ˈɪnfənt] n Säugling m; (small child)
Kleinkind nt; **infant school** n Vorschule f

infatuated [ɪnˈfætjʊeɪtɪd] adj vernarrt
(with in +akk), verknallt (with in +akk)

infect [ɪnˈfekt] vt (person) anstecken;
(wound) infizieren; **infection** [ɪnˈfekʃən] n
Infektion f; **infectious** [ɪnˈfekʃəs] adj
ansteckend

inferior [ɪnˈfɪərɪə*] adj (in quality)
minderwertig; (in rank) untergeordnet;
inferiority [ɪnfɪərɪˈɒrɪtɪ] n
Minderwertigkeit f; **~ complex**
Minderwertigkeitskomplex m

infertile [ɪnˈfɜːtaɪl] adj unfruchtbar

infidelity [ɪnfɪˈdelɪtɪ] n Untreue f

infinite [ˈɪnfɪnɪt] adj unendlich

infinitive [ɪnˈfɪnɪtɪv] n (Ling) Infinitiv m

infinity [ɪnˈfɪnɪtɪ] n Unendlichkeit f

infirmary [ɪnˈfɜːmərɪ] n Krankenhaus nt

inflame [ɪnˈfleɪm] vt (Med) entzünden;
inflammation [ɪnfləˈmeɪʃən] n (Med)
Entzündung f

inflatable [ɪnˈfleɪtəbl] adj aufblasbar;
~ dinghy Schlauchboot nt; **inflate** [ɪnˈfleɪt]
vt aufpumpen; (by blowing) aufblasen;
(prices) hochtreiben

inflation [ɪnˈfleɪʃən] n Inflation f

inflexible [ɪnˈfleksəbl] adj unflexibel

inflict [ɪnˈflɪkt] vt **to ~ sth on sb** jdm etw
zufügen; (punishment) jdm etw auferlegen;
(wound) jdm etw beibringen

in-flight [ɪnˈflaɪt] adj (catering, magazine)
Bord-; **~ entertainment** Bordprogramm
nt

influence [ˈɪnfluəns] n Einfluss m (on auf
+akk) ▷ vt beeinflussen; **influential**
[ɪnfluˈenʃəl] adj einflussreich

influenza [ɪnfluˈenzə] n Grippe f

inform [ɪnˈfɔːm] vt informieren (of, about
über +akk); **to keep sb ~ed** jdn auf dem
Laufenden halten

informal [ɪnˈfɔːməl] adj zwanglos,
ungezwungen

information [ɪnfəˈmeɪʃən] n Auskunft f,
Informationen pl; **for your ~** zu Ihrer
Information; **further ~** weitere
Informationen, weiteres; **information
desk** n Auskunftsschalter m;
information technology n
Informationstechnik f; **informative**
[ɪnˈfɔːmətɪv] adj aufschlussreich

infra-red [ˈɪnfrəˈred] adj infrarot

infrastructure n Infrastruktur f

infuriate [ɪnˈfjʊərɪeɪt] vt wütend
machen; **infuriating** adj äußerst
ärgerlich

infusion [ɪnˈfjuːʒən] n (herbal tea)
Aufguss m; (Med) Infusion f

ingenious [ɪnˈdʒiːnɪəs] adj (person)
erfinderisch; (device) raffiniert; (idea)
genial

ingredient [ɪnˈgriːdɪənt] n (Gastr) Zutat f

inhabit [ɪnˈhæbɪt] vt bewohnen;
inhabitant n Einwohner(in) m(f)

inhale [ɪnˈheɪl] vt einatmen; (cigarettes,
Med) inhalieren; **inhaler** n
Inhalationsgerät nt

inherit [ɪnˈherɪt] vt erben; **inheritance** n
Erbe nt

inhibited [ɪnˈhɪbɪtɪd] adj gehemmt;
inhibition [ɪnhɪˈbɪʃən] n Hemmung f

in-house [ˈɪnhaʊs] adj intern

inhuman [ɪnˈhjuːmən] adj unmenschlich

initial [ɪˈnɪʃəl] adj anfänglich; **~ stage**
Anfangsstadium nt ▷ vt mit Initialen
unterschreiben; **initially** adv anfangs;
initials npl Initialen pl

initiative [ɪˈnɪʃɪətɪv] n Initiative f

inject [ɪnˈdʒekt] vt (drug etc) einspritzen;
to ~ sb with sth jdm etw (ein)spritzen;
injection n Spritze f, Injektion f

in-joke [ˈɪndʒəʊk] n Insiderwitz m

injure [ˈɪndʒə*] vt verletzen; **to ~ one's
leg** sich dat das Bein verletzen; **injury**
[ˈɪndʒərɪ] n Verletzung f

injustice [ɪnˈdʒʌstɪs] n Ungerechtigkeit f

ink [ɪŋk] n Tinte f; **ink-jet printer** n
Tintenstrahldrucker m

inland [ˈɪnlənd] adj Binnen- ▷ adv
landeinwärts; **inland revenue** n (Brit)
Finanzamt nt

in-laws ['ɪnlɔːz] npl (fam)
Schwiegereltern pl

inline skates ['ɪnlaɪnskeɪts] npl
Inlineskates pl, Inliner pl

inmate ['ɪnmeɪt] n Insasse m

inn [ɪn] n Gasthaus nt

innate [ɪ'neɪt] adj angeboren

inner ['ɪnə*] adj innere(r, s); **~ city**
Innenstadt f

innocence ['ɪnəsns] n Unschuld f;
innocent adj unschuldig

innovation [ɪnəʊ'veɪʃən] n Neuerung f

innumerable [ɪ'njuː'mərəbl] adj
unzählig

inoculate [ɪ'nɒkjʊleɪt] vt impfen (against
gegen); **inoculation** [ɪnɒkjʊ'leɪʃən] n
Impfung f

in-patient ['ɪnpeɪʃənt] n stationärer
Patient, stationäre Patientin

input ['ɪnpʊt] n (contribution) Beitrag m;
(Inform) Eingabe f

inquest ['ɪnkwest] n gerichtliche
Untersuchung (einer Todesursache)

inquire [ɪn'kwaɪə*] see **enquire**; **inquiry**
[ɪn'kwaɪərɪ] see **enquiry**

insane [ɪn'seɪn] adj wahnsinnig; (Med)
geisteskrank; **insanity** [ɪn'sænɪtɪ] n
Wahnsinn m

insatiable [ɪn'seɪʃəbl] adj unersättlich

inscription [ɪn'skrɪpʃən] n (on stone etc)
Inschrift f

insect ['ɪnsekt] n Insekt nt; **insecticide**
[ɪn'sektɪsaɪd] n
Insektenbekämpfungsmittel nt; **insect
repellent** n Insektenschutzmittel nt

insecure [ɪnsɪ'kjʊə*] adj (person)
unsicher; (shelves) instabil

insensitive [ɪn'sensɪtɪv] adj
unempfindlich (to gegen); (unfeeling)
gefühllos; **insensitivity** [ɪnsensɪ'tɪvɪtɪ] n
Unempfindlichkeit f (to gegen); (unfeeling
nature) Gefühllosigkeit f

inseparable [ɪn'sepərəbl] adj
unzertrennlich

insert [ɪn'sɜːt] vt einfügen; (coin)
einwerfen; (key etc) hineinstecken ▷ n (in
magazine) Beilage f; **insertion** n (in text)
Einfügen nt

inside ['ɪn'saɪd] n **the ~** das Innere;
(surface) die Innenseite; **from the ~** von
innen ▷ adj innere(r, s), Innen-; **~ lane**
(Auto) Innenspur f; (Sport) Innenbahn f
▷ adv (place) innen; (direction) hinein; **to**

go ~ hineingehen ▷ prep (place) in +dat;
(into) in +akk ... hinein; (time, within)
innerhalb +gen; **inside out** adv verkehrt
herum; (know) in- und auswendig; **insider**
n Eingeweihte(r) mf, Insider(in) m(f)

insight ['ɪnsaɪt] n Einblick m (into in
+akk)

insignificant [ɪnsɪg'nɪfɪkənt] adj
unbedeutend

insincere [ɪnsɪn'sɪə*] adj unaufrichtig,
falsch

insinuate [ɪn'sɪnjʊeɪt] vt andeuten;
insinuation [ɪnsɪnjʊ'eɪʃən] n Andeutung
f

insist [ɪn'sɪst] vi darauf bestehen; **to ~ on
sth** auf etw dat bestehen; **insistent** adj
hartnäckig

insoluble [ɪn'sɒljʊbl] adj unlösbar

insomnia [ɪn'sɒmnɪə] n Schlaflosigkeit f

inspect [ɪn'spekt] vt prüfen,
kontrollieren; **inspection** n Prüfung f;
(check) Kontrolle f; **inspector** n (police ~)
Inspektor(in) m(f); (senior) Kommissar(in)
m(f); (on bus etc) Kontrolleur(in) m(f)

inspiration [ɪnspɪ'reɪʃən] n Inspiration f;
inspire [ɪn'spaɪə*] vt (respect) einflößen
(in dat); (person) inspirieren

install [ɪn'stɔːl] vt (software) installieren;
(furnishings) einbauen

installment, instalment [ɪn'stɔːlmənt] n
Rate f; (of story) Folge f; **to pay in ~s** auf
Raten zahlen; **installment plan** n (US)
Ratenkauf m

instance ['ɪnstəns] n (of discrimination)
Fall m; (example) Beispiel nt; **for ~** zum
Beispiel

instant ['ɪnstənt] n Augenblick m ▷ adj
sofortig; **instant coffee** n Instantkaffee
m; **instantly** adv sofort

instead [ɪn'sted] adv stattdessen;
instead of prep (an)statt +gen; **~ of me** an
meiner Stelle; **~ of going** (an)statt zu
gehen

instinct ['ɪnstɪŋkt] n Instinkt m;
instinctive, instinctively [ɪn'stɪŋktɪv, -lɪ]
adj, adv instinktiv

institute ['ɪnstɪtjuːt] n Institut nt;
institution [ɪnstɪ'tjuːʃən] n (organisation)
Institution f, Einrichtung f; (home) Anstalt f

instruct [ɪn'strʌkt] vt anweisen;
instruction [ɪn'strʌkʃən] n (teaching)
Unterricht m; (command) Anweisung f; **~s
for use** Gebrauchsanweisung f;

instructor n Lehrer(in) m(f); (US) Dozent(in) m(f)

instrument ['ɪnstrʊmənt] n Instrument nt; **instrument panel** n Armaturenbrett nt

insufficient [ɪnsə'fɪʃənt] adj ungenügend

insulate ['ɪnsjʊleɪt] vt (Elec) isolieren; **insulating tape** n Isolierband nt; **insulation** [ɪnsjʊ'leɪʃən] n Isolierung f

insulin ['ɪnsjʊlɪn] n Insulin nt

insult ['ɪnsʌlt] n Beleidigung f ▷ [ɪn'sʌlt] vt beleidigen; **insulting** [ɪn'sʌltɪŋ] adj beleidigend

insurance [ɪn'ʃʊərəns] n Versicherung f; **~ company** Versicherungsgesellschaft f; **~ policy** Versicherungspolice f; **insure** [ɪn'ʃʊə*] vt versichern (against gegen)

intact [ɪn'tækt] adj intakt

intake ['ɪnteɪk] n Aufnahme f

integrate [ɪntɪ'greɪt] vt integrieren (into in +akk); **integration** n Integration f

integrity [ɪn'tegrətɪ] n Integrität f, Ehrlichkeit f

intellect ['ɪntɪlekt] n Intellekt m; **intellectual** [ɪntɪ'lektjʊəl] adj intellektuell; (interests etc) geistig

intelligence [ɪn'telɪdʒəns] n (understanding) Intelligenz f; **intelligent** adj intelligent

intend [ɪn'tend] vt beabsichtigen; **to ~ to do sth** vorhaben, etw zu tun

intense [ɪn'tens] adj intensiv; (pressure) enorm; (competition) heftig; **intensity** n Intensität f; **intensive** adj intensiv; **intensive care unit** n Intensivstation f; **intensive course** n Intensivkurs m

intent [ɪn'tent] adj **to be ~ on doing sth** fest entschlossen sein, etw zu tun; **intention** [ɪn'tenʃən] n Absicht f; **intentional, intentionally** adj, adv absichtlich

interact [ɪntər'ækt] vi aufeinander einwirken; **interaction** n Interaktion f, Wechselwirkung f; **interactive** adj interaktiv

interchange ['ɪntətʃeɪndʒ] n (of motorways) Autobahnkreuz nt; **interchangeable** [ɪntə'tʃeɪndʒəbl] adj austauschbar

intercity [ɪntə'sɪtɪ] n Intercityzug m, IC m

intercom ['ɪntəkɒm] n (Gegen)sprechanlage f

intercourse ['ɪntəkɔːs] n (sexual) Geschlechtsverkehr m

interest ['ɪntrest] n Interesse nt; (Fin: on money) Zinsen pl; (Comm: share) Anteil m; **to be of ~** von Interesse sein (to für) ▷ vt interessieren; **interested** adj interessiert (in an +dat); **to be ~ed in** sich interessieren für; **are you ~ in coming?** hast du Lust, mitzukommen?; **interest-free** adj zinsfrei; **interesting** adj interessant; **interest rate** n Zinssatz m

interface ['ɪntəfeɪs] n (Inform) Schnittstelle f

interfere [ɪntə'fɪə*] vi (meddle) sich einmischen (with, in in +akk); **interference** n Einmischung f; (Tv, Radio) Störung f

interior [ɪn'tɪərɪə*] adj Innen- ▷ n Innere(s) nt; (of car) Innenraum m; (of house) Innenausstattung f

intermediate [ɪntə'miːdɪət] adj Zwischen-; **~ stage** Zwischenstadium nt

intermission [ɪntə'mɪʃən] n Pause f

intern [ɪn'tɜːn] n Assistent(in) m(f)

internal [ɪn'tɜːnl] adj innere(r, s); (flight) Inlands-; **~ revenue** (US) Finanzamt nt; **internally** adv innen; (in body) innerlich

international [ɪntə'næʃnəl] adj international; **~ match** Länderspiel nt; **~ flight** Auslandsflug m ▷ n (Sport: player) Nationalspieler(in) m(f)

Internet ['ɪntənet] n (Inform) Internet nt; **Internet banking** n Onlinebanking nt; **Internet café** n Internetcafé nt; **Internet provider** n Internetprovider m

interpret [ɪn'tɜːprɪt] vi, vt (translate) dolmetschen; (explain) interpretieren; **interpretation** [ɪntɜːprɪ'teɪʃən] n Interpretation f; **interpreter** [ɪn'tɜːprɪtə*] n Dolmetscher(in) m(f)

interrogate [ɪn'terəgeɪt] vt verhören; **interrogation** n Verhör nt

interrupt [ɪntə'rʌpt] vt unterbrechen; **interruption** [ɪntə'rʌpʃən] n Unterbrechung f

intersection [ɪntə'sekʃən] n (of roads) Kreuzung f

interstate [ɪntə'steɪt] n (US) zwischenstaatlich; **~ highway =** Bundesautobahn f

interval ['ɪntəvəl] n (space, time) Abstand m; (theatre etc) Pause f

intervene [ɪntə'viːn] vi eingreifen (in in);

intervention [ɪntə'venʃən] n Eingreifen nt; (Pol) Intervention f

interview ['ɪntəvjuː] n Interview nt; (for job) Vorstellungsgespräch nt ▷ vt interviewen; (job applicant) ein Vorstellungsgespräch führen mit; **interviewer** n Interviewer(in) m(f)

intestine [ɪn'testɪn] n Darm m; **~s** pl Eingeweide pl

intimate ['ɪntɪmət] adj (friends) vertraut, eng; (atmosphere) gemütlich; (sexually) intim

intimidate [ɪn'tɪmɪdeɪt] vt einschüchtern; **intimidation** n Einschüchterung f

into ['ɪntʊ] prep in +akk; (crash) gegen; **to change ~ sth** (turn ~) zu etw werden; (put on) sich dat etw anziehen; **to translate ~ French** ins Französische übersetzen; **to be ~ sth** (fam) auf etw akk stehen

intolerable [ɪn'tɒlərəbl] adj unerträglich

intolerant [ɪn'tɒlərənt] adj intolerant

intoxicated [ɪn'tɒksɪkeɪtɪd] adj betrunken; (fig) berauscht

intricate ['ɪntrɪkət] adj kompliziert

intrigue [ɪn'triːg] vt faszinieren; **intriguing** adj faszinierend, fesselnd

introduce [ɪntrə'djuːs] vt (person) vorstellen (to sb jdm); (sth new) einführen (to in +akk); **introduction** [ɪntrə'dʌkʃən] n Einführung f (to in +akk); (to book) Einleitung f (to zu); (to person) Vorstellung f

introvert ['ɪntrəʊvɜːt] n Introvertierte(r) mf

intuition [ɪntjuː'ɪʃn] n Intuition f

invade [ɪn'veɪd] vt einfallen in +akk

invalid ['ɪnvəlɪd] n Kranke(r) mf; (disabled) Invalide m ▷ adj [ɪn'vælɪd] (not valid) ungültig

invaluable [ɪn'væljʊəbl] adj äußerst wertvoll, unschätzbar

invariably [ɪn'vɛərɪəblɪ] adv ständig; (every time) jedes Mal, ohne Ausnahme

invasion [ɪn'veɪʒən] n Invasion f (of in +akk)

invent [ɪn'vent] vt erfinden; **invention** [ɪn'venʃən] n Erfindung f; **inventor** n Erfinder(in) m(f)

inverted commas [ɪn'vɜːtɪd 'kɒməz] npl Anführungszeichen pl

invest [ɪn'vest] vt, vi investieren (in in +akk)

investigate [ɪn'vestɪgeɪt] vt untersuchen; **investigation** [ɪnvestɪ'geɪʃən] n Untersuchung f (into +gen)

investment [ɪn'vestmənt] n Investition f; **it's a good ~** es ist eine gute Anlage; (it'll be useful) es macht sich bezahlt

invigorating [ɪn'vɪgəreɪtɪŋ] adj erfrischend, belebend; (tonic) stärkend

invisible [ɪn'vɪzəbl] adj unsichtbar

invitation [ɪnvɪ'teɪʃən] n Einladung f; **invite** [ɪn'vaɪt] vt einladen

invoice ['ɪnvɔɪs] n (bill) Rechnung f

involuntary [ɪn'vɒləntərɪ] adj unbeabsichtigt

involve [ɪn'vɒlv] vt verwickeln (in sth in etw akk); (entail) zur Folge haben; **to be ~d in sth** (participate in) an etw dat beteiligt sein; **I'm not ~d** (affected) ich bin nicht betroffen

inward ['ɪnwəd] adj innere(r, s); **inwardly** adv innerlich; **inwards** adv nach innen

iodine ['aɪədiːn] n Jod nt

IOU [aɪəʊ'juː] abbr = **I owe you** Schuldschein m

IQ abbr = **intelligence quotient** IQ m

Iran [ɪ'rɑːn] n der Iran

Iraq [ɪ'rɑːk] n der Irak

Ireland ['aɪələnd] n Irland nt

iris ['aɪrɪs] n (flower) Schwertlilie f; (of eye) Iris f

Irish ['aɪrɪʃ] adj irisch; **~ coffee** Irishcoffee m; **~ Sea** die Irische See ▷ n (language) Irisch nt; **the ~** pl die Iren pl; **Irishman** (pl **-men**) n Ire m; **Irishwoman** (pl **-women**) n Irin f

iron ['aɪən] n Eisen nt; (for ironing) Bügeleisen nt ▷ adj eisern ▷ vt bügeln

ironic(al) [aɪ'rɒnɪk(əl)] adj ironisch

ironing board n Bügelbrett nt

irony ['aɪrənɪ] n Ironie f

irrational [ɪ'ræʃənl] adj irrational

irregular [ɪ'regjʊlə*] adj unregelmäßig; (shape) ungleichmäßig

irrelevant [ɪ'relɪvənt] adj belanglos, irrelevant

irreplaceable [ɪrɪ'pleɪsəbl] adj unersetzlich

irresistible [ɪrɪ'zɪstəbl] adj unwiderstehlich

irrespective of [ɪrɪ'spektɪv ɒv] prep ungeachtet +gen

irresponsible [ɪrɪ'spɒnsəbl] *adj* verantwortungslos
irretrievable [ɪrɪ'triːvəbl] *adv* unwiederbringlich; (*loss*) unersetzlich
irritable ['ɪrɪtəbl] *adj* reizbar; **irritate** ['ɪrɪteɪt] *vt* (*annoy*) ärgern; (*deliberately*) reizen; **irritation** [ɪrɪ'teɪʃən] *n* (*anger*) Ärger *m*; (*Med*) Reizung *f*
IRS *abbr* = **Internal Revenue Service** (*US*) Finanzamt *nt*
is [ɪz] *present of* **be** ist
Islam ['ɪzlɑːm] *n* Islam *m*; **Islamic** [ɪz'læmɪk] *adj* islamisch
island ['aɪlənd] *n* Insel *f*; **Isle** [aɪl] *n* (*in names*) **the ~ of Man** die Insel Man; **the ~ of Wight** die Insel Wight; **the British ~s** die Britischen Inseln
isn't ['ɪznt] *contr of* **is not**
isolate ['aɪsəleɪt] *vt* isolieren; **isolated** *adj* (*remote*) abgelegen; (*cut off*) abgeschnitten (*from von*); **an ~ case** ein Einzelfall; **isolation** [aɪsə'leɪʃən] *n* Isolierung *f*
Israel ['ɪzreɪl] *n* Israel *nt*; **Israeli** [ɪz'reɪlɪ] *adj* israelisch ▷ *n* Israeli *m o f*
issue ['ɪʃuː] *n* (*matter*) Frage *f*; (*problem*) Problem *nt*; (*subject*) Thema *nt*; (*of newspaper etc*) Ausgabe *f*; **that's not the ~** darum geht es nicht ▷ *vt* ausgeben; (*document*) ausstellen; (*orders*) erteilen; (*book*) herausgeben

🔘 KEYWORD

it [ɪt] *pron* **1** (*specific: subject*) er/sie/es; (: *direct object*) ihn/sie/es; (: *indirect object*) ihm/ihr/ihm; **about/from/in/of it** darüber/davon/darin/davon
2 (*impers*) es; **it's raining** es regnet; **it's Friday tomorrow** morgen ist Freitag; **who is it? — it's me** wer ist da? — ich (bins)

IT *abbr* = **information technology** IT *f*
Italian [ɪ'tæljən] *adj* italienisch ▷ *n* Italiener(in) *m(f)*; (*language*) Italienisch *nt*
italic [ɪ'tælɪk] *adj* kursiv ▷ *npl* **in ~s** kursiv
Italy ['ɪtəlɪ] *n* Italien *nt*
itch [ɪtʃ] *n* Juckreiz *m*; **I have an ~** mich juckt es ▷ *vi* jucken; **he is ~ing to ...** es juckt ihn, zu ...; **itchy** *adj* juckend
it'd ['ɪtd] *contr of* **it would; it had**
item ['aɪtəm] *n* (*article*) Gegenstand *m*; (*in catalogue*) Artikel *m*; (*on list, in accounts*) Posten *m*; (*on agenda*) Punkt *m*; (*in show programme*) Nummer *f*; (*in news*) Bericht *m*; (*Tv: radio*) Meldung *f*
itinerary [aɪ'tɪnərərɪ] *n* Reiseroute *f*
it'll ['ɪtl] *contr of* **it will; it shall**
its [ɪts] *pron* sein; (*feminine form*) ihr
it's [ɪts] *contr of* **it is; it has**
itself [ɪt'self] *pron* (*reflexive*) sich; (*emphatic*) **the house ~ is OK** das Haus selbst *o* an sich ist in Ordnung; **by ~** allein; **the door closes (by) ~** die Tür schließt sich von selbst
I've [aɪv] *contr of* **I have**
ivory ['aɪvərɪ] *n* Elfenbein *nt*
ivy ['aɪvɪ] *n* Efeu *m*

i

j

jab [dʒæb] n (needle, knife) stechen (into in +akk) ▷ n (fam) Spritze f

jack [dʒæk] n (Auto) Wagenheber m; (Cards) Bube m; **jack in** vt (fam) aufgeben, hinschmeißen; **jack up** vt (car etc) aufbocken

jacket ['dʒækɪt] n Jacke f; (of man's suit) Jackett nt; (of book) Schutzumschlag m; **jacket potato** (pl **-es**) n (in der Schale) gebackene Kartoffel

jack-knife ['dʒæknaɪf] (pl **jack-knives**) n Klappmesser nt ▷ vi (truck) sich quer stellen

jackpot ['dʒækpɒt] n Jackpot m

jacuzzi® [dʒə'kuːzɪ] n (bath) Whirlpool® m

jail [dʒeɪl] n Gefängnis nt ▷ vt einsperren

jam [dʒæm] n Konfitüre f, Marmelade f; (traffic ~) Stau m ▷ vt (street) verstopfen; (machine) blockieren; **to be ~med** (stuck) klemmen; **to ~ on the brakes** eine Vollbremsung machen

Jamaica [dʒə'meɪkə] n Jamaika nt

jam-packed adj proppenvoll

janitor ['dʒænɪtə*] n (US) Hausmeister(in) m(f)

Jan abbr = **January** Jan

January ['dʒænjʊərɪ] n Januar m

Japan [dʒə'pæn] n Japan nt; **Japanese** [dʒæpə'niːz] adj japanisch ▷ n (person) Japaner(in) m(f); (language) Japanisch nt

jar [dʒɑː*] n Glas nt

jaundice ['dʒɔːndɪs] n Gelbsucht f

javelin ['dʒævlɪn] n Speer m; (Sport) Speerwerfen nt

jaw [dʒɔː] n Kiefer m

jazz [dʒæz] n Jazz m

jealous ['dʒeləs] adj eifersüchtig (of auf +akk); **don't make me ~** mach mich nicht neidisch; **jealousy** n Eifersucht f

jeans [dʒiːnz] npl Jeans pl

jeep® [dʒiːp] n Jeep® m

jelly ['dʒelɪ] n Gelee nt; (on meat) Gallert nt; (dessert) Götterspeise f; (US: jam) Marmelade f; **jelly baby** n (sweet) Gummibärchen nt; **jellyfish** n Qualle f

jeopardize ['dʒepədaɪz] vt gefährden

jerk [dʒɜːk] n Ruck m; (fam: idiot) Trottel m ▷ vt ruckartig bewegen ▷ vi (rope) rucken; (muscles) zucken

Jerusalem [dʒə'ruːsələm] n Jerusalem nt

jet [dʒet] n (of water etc) Strahl m; (nozzle) Düse f; (aircraft) Düsenflugzeug nt; **jet foil** n Tragflächenboot nt; **jetlag** n Jetlag m (Müdigkeit nach langem Flug)

jetty ['dʒetɪ] n Landesteg m; (larger) Landungsbrücke f

Jew [dʒuː] n Jude m, Jüdin f

jewel ['dʒuːəl] n Edelstein m; (esp fig) Juwel nt; **jeweller, jeweler** (US) n Juwelier(in) m(f); **jewellery, jewelery** (US) n Schmuck m

Jewish ['dʒuːɪʃ] adj jüdisch; **she's ~** sie ist Jüdin

jigsaw (puzzle) ['dʒɪgsɔː(ˌpʌzl)] n Puzzle nt

jilt [dʒɪlt] vt den Laufpass geben +dat

jingle ['dʒɪŋgl] n (advert) Jingle m; (verse) Reim m

jitters ['dʒɪtərz] npl (fam) **to have the ~** Bammel haben; **jittery** adj (fam) ganz nervös

job [dʒɒb] n (piece of work) Arbeit f; (task) Aufgabe f; (occupation) Stellung f, Job m; **what's your ~?** was machen Sie beruflich?; **it's a good ~ you did that** gut, dass du das gemacht hast; **jobcentre** n Arbeitsvermittlungsstelle f, Arbeitsamt nt; **job-hunting** n **to go ~** auf Arbeitssuche gehen; **jobless** adj

arbeitslos; **job seeker** n
Arbeitssuchende(r) mf; **jobseeker's
allowance** n Arbeitslosengeld nt;
job-sharing n Arbeitsplatzteilung f
jockey ['dʒɒkɪ] n Jockey m
jog [dʒɒg] vt (person) anstoßen ▷ vi (run)
joggen; **jogging** n Jogging nt; **to go
~** joggen gehen
john [dʒɒn] n (US fam) Klo nt
join [dʒɔɪn] vt (put together) verbinden (to
mit); (club etc) beitreten +dat; **to ~ sb** sich
jdm anschließen; (sit with) sich zu jdm
setzen ▷ vi (unite) sich vereinigen; (rivers)
zusammenfließen ▷ n Verbindungsstelle
f; (seam) Naht f; **join in** vi, vt mitmachen
(sth bei etw)
joinery ['dʒɔɪnərɪ] n Schreinerei f
joint [dʒɔɪnt] n (of bones) Gelenk nt; (in pipe
etc) Verbindungsstelle f; (of meat) Braten
m; (of marijuana) Joint m ▷ adj gemeinsam;
joint account n Gemeinschaftskonto nt;
jointly adv gemeinsam
joke [dʒəʊk] n Witz m; (prank) Streich m;
for a ~ zum Spaß; **it's no ~** das ist nicht
zum Lachen ▷ vi Witze machen; **you
must be joking** das ist ja wohl nicht dein
Ernst!
jolly ['dʒɒlɪ] adj lustig, vergnügt
Jordan ['dʒɔːdən] n (country) Jordanien nt;
(river) Jordan m
jot down [dʒɒt daʊn] vt sich notieren;
jotter n Notizbuch nt
journal ['dʒɜːnl] n (diary) Tagebuch nt;
(magazine) Zeitschrift f; **journalism** n
Journalismus m; **journalist** n
Journalist(in) m(f)
journey ['dʒɜːnɪ] n Reise f; (esp on stage,
by car, train) Fahrt f
joy [dʒɔɪ] n Freude f (at über +akk);
joystick n (Inform) Joystick m; (Aviat)
Steuerknüppel m
judge [dʒʌdʒ] n Richter(in) m(f); (Sport)
Punktrichter(in) m(f) ▷ vt beurteilen (by
nach); **as far as I can ~** meinem Urteil
nach ▷ vi urteilen (by nach); **judg(e)ment**
n (Jur) Urteil nt; (opinion) Ansicht f; **an
error of ~** Fehleinschätzung f
judo ['dʒuːdəʊ] n Judo nt
jug [dʒʌg] n Krug m
juggle ['dʒʌgl] vi (lit, fig) jonglieren (with
mit)
juice [dʒuːs] n Saft m; **juicy** adj saftig;
(story, scandal) pikant

July [dʒuːˈlaɪ] n Juli m; see also **September**
jumble ['dʒʌmbl] n Durcheinander nt ▷ vt
to ~ (up) durcheinander werfen; (facts)
durcheinander bringen; **jumble sale** n
(for charity) Wohltätigkeitsbasar m
jumbo ['dʒʌmbəʊ] adj (sausage etc)
Riesen-; **jumbo jet** n Jumbojet m
jump [dʒʌmp] vi springen; (nervously)
zusammenzucken; **to ~ to conclusions**
voreilige Schlüsse ziehen; **to ~ from one
thing to another** dauernd das Thema
wechseln ▷ vt (a. fig: omit) überspringen;
to ~ the lights bei Rot über die Kreuzung
fahren; **to ~ the queue** sich vordrängen
▷ n Sprung m; (for horses) Hindernis nt;
jumper n Pullover m; (US: dress)
Trägerkleid nt; (person, horse) Springer(in)
m(f); **jumper cables** npl (US), **jump leads**
npl (Brit Auto) Starthilfekabel nt
junction ['dʒʌŋkʃən] n (of roads) Kreuzung
f; (Rail) Knotenpunkt m
June [dʒuːn] n Juni m; see also **September**
jungle ['dʒʌŋgl] n Dschungel m
junior ['dʒuːnɪə*] adj (younger) jünger;
(lower position) untergeordnet (to sb jdm)
▷ n **she's two years my ~** sie ist zwei
Jahre jünger als ich; **junior high (school)**
n (US) ≈ Mittelschule f; **junior school** n
(Brit) Grundschule f
junk [dʒʌŋk] n (trash) Plunder m;
junkfood n Nahrungsmittel pl mit
geringem Nährwert, Junkfood nt; **junkie**
n (fam) Junkie m, Fixer(in) m(f); (fig: fan)
Freak m; **junk mail** n Reklame f; (Inform)
Junkmail f; **junk shop** n Trödelladen m
jury ['dʒʊərɪ] n Geschworene pl; (in
competition) Jury f
just [dʒʌst] adj gerecht ▷ adv (recently)
gerade; (exactly) genau; **~ as expected**
genau wie erwartet; **~ as nice** genauso
nett; (barely) **~ in time** gerade noch
rechtzeitig; (immediately) **~ before/after
...** gleich vor/nach ...; (small distance)
~ round the corner gleich um die Ecke; (a
little) **~ over an hour** etwas mehr als eine
Stunde; (only) **~ the two of us** nur wir
beide; **~ a moment** Moment mal;
(absolutely, simply) **it was ~ fantastic** es
war einfach klasse; **~ about** so etwa;
(more or less) mehr oder weniger; **~ about
ready** fast fertig
justice ['dʒʌstɪs] n Gerechtigkeit f;
justifiable [dʒʌstɪˈfaɪəbl] adj

berechtigt; **justifiably** *adv* zu
Recht; **justify** ['dʒʌstɪfaɪ] *vt*
rechtfertigen
jut [dʒʌt] *vi* **to ~ (out)** herausragen
juvenile ['dʒuːvənaɪl] *n adj* Jugend-,
jugendlich ▷ *n* Jugendliche(r) *mf*

k

k *abbr* = **thousand**; **15k** 15 000

K *abbr* = **kilobyte** KB

kangaroo [kæŋɡə'ruː] *n* Känguru *nt*

karaoke [kærɪ'əʊkɪ] *n* Karaoke *nt*

karate [kə'rɑːtɪ] *n* Karate *nt*

kart [kɑːt] *n* Gokart *m*

kayak ['kaɪæk] *n* Kajak *m o nt*

Kazakhstan [kæzæk'stɑːn] *n* Kasachstan *nt*

kebab [kə'bæb] *n* (*shish ~*) Schaschlik *nt o m*; (*doner ~*) Kebab *m*

keel [kiːl] *n* (*Naut*) Kiel *m*; **keel over** *vi* (*boat*) kentern; (*person*) umkippen

keen [kiːn] *adj* begeistert (*on* von); (*hardworking*) eifrig; (*mind, wind*) scharf; (*interest, feeling*) stark; **to be ~ on sb** von jdm angetan sein; **she's ~ on riding** sie reitet gern; **to be ~ to do sth** darauf erpicht sein, etw zu tun

keep [kiːp] (**kept, kept**) *vt* (*retain*) behalten; (*secret*) für sich behalten; (*observe*) einhalten; (*promise*) halten; (*run: shop, diary, accounts*) führen; (*animals*) halten; (*support, family etc*) unterhalten, versorgen; (*store*) aufbewahren; **to ~ sb waiting** jdn warten lassen; **to ~ sb from doing sth** jdn davon abhalten, etw zu tun; **to ~ sth clean/secret** etw sauber/geheim halten; **'~ clear'** „(bitte) freihalten"; **~ this to yourself** behalten Sie das für sich ▷ *vi* (*food*) sich halten; (*remain, with adj*) bleiben; **~ quiet** sei ruhig!; **~ left** links fahren; **to ~ doing sth** (*repeatedly*) etw immer wieder tun; **~ at it** mach weiter so!; **it ~s happening** es passiert immer wieder ▷ *n* (*livelihood*) Unterhalt *m*; **keep back** *vi* zurückbleiben ▷ *vt* zurückhalten; (*information*) verschweigen (*from sb* jdm); **keep off** *vt* (*person, animal*) fernhalten; **'~ off the grass'** „Betreten des Rasens verboten"; **keep on** *vi* weitermachen; (*walking*) weitergehen; (*in car*) weiterfahren; **to ~ doing sth** (*persistently*) etw immer wieder tun ▷ *vt* (*coat etc*) anbehalten; **keep out** *vt* nicht hereinlassen ▷ *vi* draußen bleiben; **~** (*on sign*) Eintritt verboten; **keep to** *vt* (*road, path*) bleiben auf +*dat*; (*plan etc*) sich halten an +*akk*; **to ~ the point** bei der Sache bleiben; **keep up** *vi* Schritt halten (*with* mit) ▷ *vt* (*maintain*) aufrechterhalten; (*speed*) halten; **to ~ appearances** den Schein wahren; **keep it up!** (*fam*) weiter so!

keeper *n* (*museum etc*) Aufseher(in) *m(f)*; (*goal~*) Torwart *m*; (*zoo ~*) Tierpfleger(in) *m(f)*; **keep-fit** *n* Fitnesstraining *nt*; **~ exercises** Gymnastik *f*

kennel ['kenl] *n* Hundehütte *f*; **kennels** *n* Hundepension *f*

Kenya ['kenjə] *n* Kenia *nt*

kept [kept] *pt, pp of* **keep**

kerb [kɜːb] *n* Randstein *m*

kerosene ['kerəsiːn] *n* (*US*) Petroleum *nt*

ketchup ['ketʃʌp] *n* Ket(s)chup *nt o m*

kettle ['ketl] *n* Kessel *m*

key [kiː] *n* Schlüssel *m*; (*of piano, computer*) Taste *f*; (*Mus*) Tonart *f*; (*for map etc*) Zeichenerklärung *f* ▷ *vt* **to ~ (in)** (*Inform*) eingeben ▷ *adj* entscheidend; **keyboard** *n* (*piano, computer*) Tastatur *f*; **keyhole** *n* Schlüsselloch *nt*; **keypad** *n* (*Inform*) Nummernblock *m*; **keyring** *n* Schlüsselring *m*

kick [kɪk] *n* Tritt *m*; (*Sport*) Stoß *m*; **I get a ~ out of it** (*fam*) es turnt mich an ▷ *vt, vi* treten; **kick out** *vt* (*fam*) rausschmeißen (*of* aus); **kick-off** *n* (*Sport*) Anstoß *m*

kid [kɪd] *n* (*child*) Kind *nt* ▷ *vt* (*tease*) auf den Arm nehmen ▷ *vi* Witze machen;

you're ~ding das ist doch nicht dein Ernst!; no ~ding aber echt!

kidnap ['kɪdnæp] vt entführen; **kidnapper** n Entführer(in) m(f); **kidnapping** n Entführung f

kidney ['kɪdnɪ] n Niere f; **kidney machine** n künstliche Niere

kill [kɪl] vt töten; (esp intentionally) umbringen; (weeds) vernichten; **killer** n Mörder(in) m(f)

kilo ['ki:ləʊ] (pl -s) n Kilo nt; **kilobyte** n Kilobyte nt; **kilogramme** n Kilogramm nt; **kilometer** (US), **kilometre** n Kilometer m; **~s per hour** Stundenkilometer pl; **kilowatt** n Kilowatt nt

kilt [kɪlt] n Schottenrock m

kind [kaɪnd] adj nett, freundlich (to zu) ▷ n Art f; (of coffee, cheese etc) Sorte f; **what ~ of ...?** was für ein(e) ...?; **this ~ of ...** so ein(e) ...; **~ of** (+ adj) irgendwie

kindergarten ['kɪndəgaːtn] n Kindergarten m

kindly ['kaɪndlɪ] adj nett, freundlich ▷ adv liebenswürdigerweise; **kindness** ['kaɪndnəs] n Freundlichkeit f

king [kɪŋ] n König m; **kingdom** n Königreich nt; **kingfisher** n Eisvogel m; **king-size** adj im Großformat; (bed) extra groß

kipper ['kɪpə*] n Räucherhering m

kiss [kɪs] n Kuss m; **~ of life** Mund-zu-Mund-Beatmung f ▷ vt küssen

kit [kɪt] n (equipment) Ausrüstung f; (fam) Sachen pl; (sports ~) Sportsachen pl; (belongings, clothes) Sachen pl; (for building sth) Bausatz m

kitchen ['kɪtʃɪn] n Küche f; **kitchen foil** n Alufolie f; **kitchen scales** n Küchenwaage f; **kitchen unit** n Küchenschrank m; **kitchenware** n Küchengeschirr nt

kite [kaɪt] n Drachen m

kitten ['kɪtn] n Kätzchen nt

kiwi ['ki:wi:] n (fruit) Kiwi f

km abbr = **kilometres** km

knack [næk] n Dreh m, Trick m; **to get/have got the ~** den Dreh herauskriegen/heraushaben; **knackered** ['nækəd] adj (Brit fam) fix und fertig, kaputt

knee [ni:] n Knie nt; **kneecap** n Kniescheibe f; **knee-jerk** adj (reaction) reflexartig; **kneel** [ni:l] (**knelt** o **kneeled,** **knelt** o **kneeled**) vi knien; (action, ~ down) sich hinknien

knelt [nelt] pt, pp of **kneel**

knew [nju:] pt of **know**

knickers ['nɪkəz] npl (Brit) Schlüpfer m

knife [naɪf] (pl **knives**) n Messer nt

knight [naɪt] n Ritter m; (in chess) Pferd nt, Springer m

knit [nɪt] vt, vi stricken; **knitting** n (piece of work) Strickarbeit f; (activity) Stricken nt; **knitting needle** n Stricknadel f; **knitwear** n Strickwaren pl

knob [nɒb] n (on door) Knauf m; (on radio etc) Knopf m

knock [nɒk] vt (with hammer etc) schlagen; (accidentally) stoßen; **to ~ one's head** sich dat den Kopf anschlagen ▷ vi klopfen (on, at an +akk) ▷ n (blow) Schlag m; (on door) Klopfen nt; **there was a ~ (at the door)** es hat geklopft; **knock down** vt (object) umstoßen; (person) niederschlagen; (with car) anfahren; (building) abreißen; **knock out** vt (stun) bewusstlos schlagen; (boxer) k.o. schlagen; **knock over** vt umstoßen; (with car) anfahren; **knocker** n Türklopfer m; **knockout** n Knockout m, K.o. m

knot [nɒt] n Knoten m

know [nəʊ] (**knew, known**) vt, vi wissen; (be acquainted with: people, places) kennen; (recognize) erkennen; (language) können; **I'll let you ~** ich sage dir Bescheid; **I ~ some French** ich kann etwas Französisch; **to get to ~ sb** jdn kennen lernen; **to be ~n as** bekannt sein als; **know about** vt Bescheid wissen über +akk; (subject) sich auskennen in +dat; (cars, horses etc) sich auskennen mit; **know of** vt kennen; **not that I ~** nicht dass ich wüsste; **know-all** n (fam) Klugscheißer m; **know-how** n Kenntnis f, Know-how nt; **knowing** adj wissend; (look, smile) vielsagend; **knowledge** ['nɒlɪdʒ] n Wissen nt; (of a subject) Kenntnisse pl; **to (the best of) my ~** meines Wissens

known [nəʊn] pp of **know**

knuckle ['nʌkl] n (Finger)knöchel m; (Gastr) Hachse f; **knuckle down** vi sich an die Arbeit machen

Koran [kɒ'raːn] n Koran m

Korea [kə'rɪə] n Korea nt

Kosovo ['kɒsəvəʊ] n der Kosovo

kph abbr = **kilometres per hour** km/h

Kremlin ['kremlɪn] *n* **the ~** der
Kreml
Kurd [kɛːd] *n* Kurde *m*, Kurdin *f*; **Kurdish**
adj kurdisch
Kuwait [kʊ'weɪt] *n* Kuwait *nt*

L abbr (Brit Auto) = **learner**

LA abbr = **Los Angeles**

lab [læb] n (fam) Labor nt

label ['leɪbl] n Etikett nt; (tied) Anhänger m; (adhesive) Aufkleber m; (record ~) Label nt ▷ vt etikettieren; (pej) abstempeln

laboratory [ləˈbɒrətərɪ] n Labor nt

● **Labor Day**
●
● Der **Labor Day** ist in den USA und
● Kanada der Name für den Tag der
● Arbeit. Er wird dort als gesetzlicher
● Feiertag am ersten Montag im
● September begangen.

laborious [ləˈbɔːrɪəs] adj mühsam; **labor** (US), **labour** ['leɪbə*] n Arbeit f; (Med) Wehen pl; **to be in ~** Wehen haben ▷ adj (Pol) Labour-; **~ Party** Labour Party f; **labor union** n (US) Gewerkschaft f; **labourer** n Arbeiter(in) m(f)

lace [leɪs] n (fabric) Spitze f; (of shoe) Schnürsenkel m ▷ vt **to ~ (up)** zuschnüren; **lace-up** n Schnürschuh m

lack [læk] vt, vi **to be ~ing** fehlen; **sb ~s o is ~ing in sth** es fehlt jdm an etw dat; **we**

~ the time uns fehlt die Zeit ▷ n Mangel m; **for ~ of** aus Mangel an +dat

lacquer ['lækə*] n Lack m; (Brit: hair ~) Haarspray nt

lad [læd] n Junge m

ladder ['lædə*] n Leiter f; (in tight) Laufmasche f

laddish ['lædɪʃ] adj (Brit) machohaft

laden ['leɪdn] adj beladen (with mit)

ladies ['leɪdɪz], **ladies' room** n Damentoilette f; **lady** ['leɪdɪ] n Dame f; (as title) Lady f; **ladybird**, **ladybug** (US) n Marienkäfer m

lag [læg] vi **to ~ (behind)** zurückliegen ▷ vt (pipes) isolieren

lager ['lɑːɡə*] n helles Bier; **~ lout** betrunkener Rowdy

lagging ['lægɪŋ] n Isolierung f

laid [leɪd] pt, pp of **lay**; **laid-back** adj (fam) cool, gelassen

lain [leɪn] pp of **lie**

lake [leɪk] n See m; **the Lake District** Seengebiet im Nordwesten Englands

lamb [læm] n Lamm nt; (meat) Lammfleisch nt; **lamb chop** n Lammkotelett nt

lame [leɪm] adj lahm; (excuse) faul; (argument) schwach

lament [ləˈment] n Klage f ▷ vt beklagen

laminated ['læmɪneɪtɪd] adj beschichtet

lamp [læmp] n Lampe f; (in street) Laterne f; (in car) Licht nt, Scheinwerfer m; **lamppost** n Laternenpfahl m; **lampshade** n Lampenschirm m

land [lænd] n Land nt ▷ vi (from ship) an Land gehen; (Aviat) landen ▷ vt (passengers) absetzen; (goods) abladen; (plane) landen; **landing** n Landung f; (on stairs) Treppenabsatz m; **landing stage** n Landesteg m; **landing strip** n Landebahn f

landlady n Hauswirtin f, Vermieterin f; **landlord** n (of house) Hauswirt m, Vermieter m; (of pub) Gastwirt m; **landmark** n Wahrzeichen nt; (event) Meilenstein m; **landowner** n Grundbesitzer(in) m(f); **landscape** n Landschaft f; (format) Querformat nt; **landslide** n (Geo) Erdrutsch m

lane [leɪn] n (in country) enge Landstraße, Weg m; (in town) Gasse f; (of motorway) Spur f; (Sport) Bahn f; **to get in ~** (in car) sich einordnen

language ['læŋgwɪdʒ] n Sprache f; (style) Ausdrucksweise f

lantern ['læntən] n Laterne f

lap [læp] n Schoß m; (in race) Runde f ▷ vt (in race) überholen

lapse [læps] n (mistake) Irrtum m; (moral) Fehltritt m ▷ vi ablaufen

laptop ['læptɒp] n Laptop m

large [lɑːdʒ] adj groß; **by and ~** im Großen und Ganzen; **largely** adv zum größten Teil; **large-scale** adj groß angelegt, Groß-

lark [lɑːk] n (bird) Lerche f

laryngitis [lærɪn'dʒaɪtɪs] n Kehlkopfentzündung f; **larynx** ['lærɪŋks] n Kehlkopf m

laser ['leɪzə*] n Laser m; **laser printer** n Laserdrucker m

lash [læʃ] vt peitschen; **lash out** vi (with fists) um sich schlagen; (spend money) sich in Unkosten stürzen (on mit)

lass [læs] n Mädchen nt

last [lɑːst] adj letzte(r, s); **the ~ but one** der/die/das vorletzte; **~ night** gestern Abend; **~ but not least** nicht zuletzt ▷ adv zuletzt; (last time) das letzte Mal; **at ~** endlich ▷ n (person) Letzte(r) mf; (thing) Letzte(s) nt; **he was the ~ to leave** er ging als Letzter ▷ vi (continue) dauern; (remain in good condition) durchhalten; (remain good) sich halten; (money) ausreichen; **lasting** adj dauerhaft; (impression) nachhaltig; **lastly** adv schließlich; **last-minute** adj in letzter Minute; **last name** n Nachname m

late [leɪt] adj spät; (after proper time) zu spät; (train etc) verspätet; (dead) verstorben; **to be ~** zu spät kommen; (train etc) Verspätung haben ▷ adv spät; (after proper time) zu spät; **late availibility flight** n Last-Minute-Flug m; **lately** adv in letzter Zeit; **late opening** n verlängerte Öffnungszeiten pl; **later** ['leɪtə*] adj, adv später; **see you ~** bis später; **latest** ['leɪtɪst] adj späteste(r, s); (most recent) neueste(r, s) ▷ n **the ~** (news) das Neueste; **at the ~** spätestens

Latin ['lætɪn] n Latein nt ▷ adj lateinisch; **Latin America** n Lateinamerika nt; **Latin-American** adj lateinamerikanisch ▷ n Lateinamerikaner(in) m(f)

latitude ['lætɪtjuːd] n (Geo) Breite f

latter ['lætə*] adj (second of two) letztere(r, s); (last: part, years) letzte(r, s), später

Latvia ['lætvɪə] n Lettland nt

laugh [lɑːf] n Lachen nt; **for a ~** aus Spaß ▷ vi lachen (at, about über +akk); **to ~ at sb** sich über jdn lustig machen; **it's no ~ing matter** es ist nicht zum Lachen; **laughter** ['lɑːftə*] n Gelächter nt

launch [lɔːntʃ] n (launching, of ship) Stapellauf m; (of rocket) Abschuss m; (of product) Markteinführung f; (with hype) Lancierung f; (event) Eröffnungsfeier f ▷ vt (ship) vom Stapel lassen; (rocket) abschießen; (product) einführen; (with hype) lancieren; (project) in Gang setzen

launder ['lɔːndə*] vt waschen und bügeln; (fig: money) waschen; **laundrette** [lɔːn'dret] n (Brit), **laundromat** ['lɔːndrəmæt] n (US) Waschsalon m; **laundry** ['lɔːndrɪ] n (place) Wäscherei f; (clothes) Wäsche f

lavatory ['lævətrɪ] n Toilette f

lavender ['lævɪndə*] n Lavendel m

lavish ['lævɪʃ] adj verschwenderisch; (furnishings etc) üppig; (gift) großzügig

law [lɔː] n Gesetz nt; (system) Recht nt; (for study) Jura; (of sport) Regel f; **against the ~** gesetzwidrig; **law-abiding** adj gesetzestreu; **law court** n Gerichtshof m; **lawful** adj rechtmäßig

lawn [lɔːn] n Rasen m; **lawnmower** n Rasenmäher m

lawsuit ['lɔːsuːt] n Prozess m; **lawyer** ['lɔːjə*] n Rechtsanwalt m, Rechtsanwältin f

laxative ['læksətɪv] n Abführmittel nt

lay [leɪ] pt of **lie** ▷ vt (laid, laid) legen; (table) decken; (vulg) poppen, bumsen; (egg) legen ▷ adj Laien-; **lay down** vt hinlegen; **lay off** vt (workers) (vorübergehend) entlassen; (stop attacking) in Ruhe lassen; **lay on** vt (provide) anbieten; (organize) veranstalten, bereitstellen; **layabout** n Faulenzer(in) m(f); **lay-by** n Parkbucht f; (bigger) Parkplatz m

layer ['leɪə*] n Schicht f

layman ['leɪmən] n Laie m

layout ['leɪaut] n Gestaltung f; (of book etc) Lay-out nt

laze [leɪz] vi faulenzen; **laziness** ['leɪzɪnɪs] n Faulheit f; **lazy** ['leɪzɪ] adj faul; (day, time) gemütlich

lb *abbr* = **pound** Pfd.

lead [led] *n* Blei *nt* ▷ *vt, vi* [li:d] (**led, led**) führen; (*group etc*) leiten; **to ~ the way** vorangehen; **this is ~ing us nowhere** das bringt uns nicht weiter ▷ [li:d] *n* (*race*) Führung *f*; (*distance, time ahead*) Vorsprung *m* (*over* vor +*dat*); (*of police*) Spur *f*; (*Theat*) Hauptrolle *f*; (*dog's*) Leine *f*; (*Elec: flex*) Leitung *f*; **lead astray** *vt* irreführen; **lead away** *vt* wegführen; **lead back** *vi* zurückführen; **lead on** *vt* anführen; **lead to** *vt* (*street*) hinführen nach; (*result in*) führen zu; **lead up to** *vt* (*drive*) führen zu

leaded ['lɛdɪd] *adj* (*petrol*) verbleit

leader ['li:dəʳ] *n* Führer(in) *m(f)*; (*of party*) Vorsitzende(r) *mf*; (*of project, expedition*) Leiter(in) *m(f)*; (*Sport: in race*) der/die Erste; (*in league*) Tabellenführer *m*; **leadership** ['li:dəʃɪp] *n* Führung *f*

lead-free ['lɛd'fri:] *adj* (*petrol*) bleifrei

leading ['li:dɪŋ] *adj* führend, wichtig

leaf [li:f] (*pl* **leaves**) *n* Blatt *nt*; **leaflet** ['li:flɪt] *n* Prospekt *m*; (*pamphlet*) Flugblatt *nt*; (*with instructions*) Merkblatt *nt*

league [li:g] *n* Bund *m*; (*Sport*) Liga *f*

leak [li:k] *n* (*gap*) undichte Stelle; (*escape*) Leck *nt*; **to take a ~** (*fam*) pinkeln gehen ▷ *vi* (*pipe etc*) undicht sein; (*liquid etc*) auslaufen; **leaky** *adj* undicht

lean [li:n] *adj* (*meat*) mager; (*face*) schmal; (*person*) drahtig ▷ *vi* (**leant** *o* **leaned, leant** *o* **leaned**) (*not vertical*) sich neigen; (*rest*) **to ~ against sth** sich an etw *akk* lehnen; (*support oneself*) **to ~ on sth** sich auf etw *akk* stützen ▷ *vt* lehnen (*on, against* an +*akk*); **lean back** *vi* sich zurücklehnen; **lean forward** *vi* sich vorbeugen; **lean over** *vi* sich hinüberbeugen; **lean towards** *vt* tendieren zu

leant [lɛnt] *pt, pp of* **lean**

leap [li:p] *n* Sprung *m* ▷ *vi* (**lept** *o* **leaped, lept** *o* **leaped**) springen; **leap year** *n* Schaltjahr *nt*

learn [lɜ:n] (**learnt** *o* **learned, learnt** *o* **learned**) *vt, vi* lernen; (*find out*) erfahren; **to ~ (how) to swim** schwimmen lernen; **learned** ['lɜ:nɪd] *adj* gelehrt; **learner** *n* Anfänger(in) *m(f)*; (*Brit: driver*) Fahrschüler(in) *m(f)*

learnt [lɜ:nt] *pt, pp of* **learn**

lease [li:s] *n* (*of land, premises etc*) Pacht *f*; (*contract*) Pachtvertrag *m*; (*of house, car etc*)

Miete *f*; (*contract*) Mietvertrag *m* ▷ *vt* pachten; (*house, car etc*) mieten; **lease out** *vt* vermieten; **leasing** ['li:sɪŋ] *n* Leasing *nt*

least [li:st] *adj* wenigste(r, s); (*slightest*) geringste(r, s) ▷ *adv* am wenigsten; **~ expensive** billigste(r, s) ▷ *n* **the ~** das Mindeste; **not in the ~** nicht im geringsten; **at ~** wenigstens; (*with number*) mindestens

leather ['lɛðəʳ] *n* Leder *nt* ▷ *adj* ledern, Leder-

leave [li:v] *n* (*time off*) Urlaub *m*; **on ~** auf Urlaub; **to take one's ~** Abschied nehmen (*of* von) ▷ *vt* (**left, left**) (*place, person*) verlassen; (*not remove, not change*) lassen; (*~ behind: message, scar etc*) hinterlassen; (*forget*) hinter sich lassen; (*after death*) hinterlassen (*to sb* jdm); (*entrust*) überlassen (*to sb* jdm); **to be left** (*remain*) übrig bleiben; **~ me alone** lass mich in Ruhe!; **don't ~ it to the last minute** warte nicht bis zur letzten Minute ▷ *vi* (*weg*)gehen, (*weg*)fahren; (*on journey*) abreisen; (*bus, train*) abfahren (*for* nach); **leave behind** *vt* zurücklassen; (*scar etc*) hinterlassen; (*forget*) hinter sich lassen; **leave out** *vt* auslassen; (*person*) ausschließen (*of* von)

leaves [li:vz] *pl of* **leaf**

leaving do [li:vɪŋdu:] *n* Abschiedsfeier *f*

Lebanon ['lɛbənən] *n* **the ~** der Libanon

lecture ['lɛktʃəʳ] *n* Vortrag *m*; (*at university*) Vorlesung *f*; **to give a ~** einen Vortrag/eine Vorlesung halten; **lecturer** *n* Dozent(in) *m(f)*; **lecture theatre** *n* Hörsaal *m*

led [lɛd] *pt, pp of* **lead**

LED *abbr* = **light-emitting diode** Leuchtdiode *f*

ledge [lɛdʒ] *n* Leiste *f*; (*window ~*) Sims *m* *o* *nt*

leek [li:k] *n* Lauch *m*

left [lɛft] *pt, pp of* **leave** ▷ *adj* linke(r, s) ▷ *adv* (*position*) links; (*movement*) nach links ▷ *n* (*side*) linke Seite; **the Left** (*Pol*) die Linke; **to the ~** links (*of* von); **move/fall to the ~** nach links rücken/fallen; **left-hand** *adj* linke(r, s); **~ bend** Linkskurve *f*; **~ drive** Linkssteuerung *f*; **left-handed** *adj* linkshändig; **left-hand side** *n* linke Seite

left-luggage locker n
Gepäckschließfach nt; **left-luggage office**
n Gepäckaufbewahrung f
left-overs npl Reste pl
left wing n linker Flügel; **left-wing** adj
(Pol) linksgerichtet
leg [leg] n Bein nt; (of meat) Keule f
legacy ['legəsɪ] n Erbe nt, Erbschaft f
legal ['liːgəl] adj Rechts-, rechtlich;
(allowed) legal; (limit, age) gesetzlich; **~ aid**
Rechtshilfe f; **legalize** vt legalisieren;
legally adv legal
legend ['ledʒənd] n Legende f
legible, legibly ['ledʒəbl, -blɪ] adj, adv
leserlich
legislation [ledʒɪs'leɪʃn] n Gesetze pl
legitimate [lɪ'dʒɪtɪmət] adj rechtmäßig,
legitim
legroom ['legrʊm] n Platz m für die Beine
leisure ['leʒə*] n (time) Freizeit f ▷ adj
Freizeit-; **~ centre** Freizeitzentrum nt;
leisurely ['leʒəlɪ] adj gemächlich
lemon ['lemən] n Zitrone f; **lemonade**
[lemə'neɪd] n Limonade f; **lemon curd** n
Brotaufstrich aus Zitronen, Butter, Eiern und
Zucker; **lemon juice** n Zitronensaft m;
lemon sole n Seezunge f
lend [lend] (lent, lent) vt leihen; **to ~ sb**
sth jdm etw leihen; **to (sb) ~ a hand** (jdm)
behilflich sein; **lending library** n
Leihbücherei f
length [lenθ] n Länge f; **4 metres in ~** 4
Meter lang; **what ~ is it?** wie lange ist es?;
for any ~ of time für längere Zeit; **at**
~ (lengthily) ausführlich; **lengthen**
['lenθən] vt verlängern; **lengthy** adj sehr
lange; (dragging) langwierig
lenient ['liːnɪənt] adj nachsichtig
lens [lenz] n Linse f; (Foto) Objektiv nt
lent [lent] pt, pp of **lend**
Lent [lent] n Fastenzeit f
lentil ['lentl] n (Bot) Linse f
Leo ['liːəʊ] (pl **-s**) (Astr) Löwe m
leopard ['lepəd] n Leopard m
lept [lept] pt, pp of **leap**
lesbian ['lezbɪən] adj lesbisch ▷ n Lesbe f
less [les] adj, adv, n weniger; **~ and**
~ immer weniger; (~ often) immer
seltener; **lessen** ['lesn] vi abnehmen,
nachlassen ▷ vt verringern; (pain) lindern;
lesser ['lesə*] adj geringer; (amount)
kleiner
lesson ['lesn] n (at school) Stunde f; (unit

of study) Lektion f; (fig) Lehre f; (Rel) Lesung
f; **~s start at 9** der Unterricht beginnt
um 9
let [let] (let, let) vt lassen; (lease)
vermieten; **to ~ sb have sth** jdm etw
geben; **~'s go** gehen wir; **to ~ go** (of sth)
(etw) loslassen; **let down** vt
herunterlassen; (fail to help) im Stich
lassen; (disappoint) enttäuschen; **let in** vt
hereinlassen; **let off** vt (bomb) hochgehen
lassen; (person) laufen lassen; **let out** vt
hinauslassen; (secret) verraten; (scream etc)
ausstoßen; **let up** vi nachlassen; (stop)
aufhören
lethal ['liːθəl] adj tödlich
let's contr = **let us**
letter ['letə*] n (of alphabet) Buchstabe m;
(message) Brief m; (official ~) Schreiben nt;
letter bomb n Briefbombe f; **letterbox** n
Briefkasten m
lettuce ['letɪs] n Kopfsalat m
leukaemia, leukemia (US) [luː'kiːmɪə] n
Leukämie f
level ['levl] adj (horizontal) waagerecht;
(ground) eben; (two things, two runners) auf
selber Höhe; **to be ~ with sb/sth** mit
jdm/etw auf gleicher Höhe sein; **~ on**
points punktgleich ▷ adv (run etc) auf
gleicher Höhe, gleich auf; **to draw ~** (in
race) gleichziehen (with mit); (in game)
ausgleichen ▷ n (altitude) Höhe f;
(standard) Niveau nt; (amount, degree) Grad
m; **to be on a ~ with** auf gleicher Höhe
sein mit ▷ vt (ground) einebnen; **level**
crossing n (Brit) (schienengleicher)
Bahnübergang m; **level-headed** adj
vernünftig
lever ['liːvə*], (US) ['levə*] n Hebel m;
(fig) Druckmittel nt; **lever up** vt
hochstemmen
liability [laɪə'bɪlɪtɪ] n Haftung f; (burden)
Belastung f; (obligation) Verpflichtung f;
liable ['laɪəbl] adj **to be ~ for sth**
(responsible) für etw haften; **~ for tax**
steuerpflichtig
liar ['laɪə*] n Lügner(in) m(f)
Lib Dem [lɪb'dem] abbr = **Liberal**
Democrat
liberal ['lɪbərəl] adj (generous) großzügig;
(broad-minded) liberal; **Liberal Democrat** n
(Brit Pol) Liberaldemokrat(in) m(f) ▷ adj
liberaldemokratisch; **the ~ Party** die
Liberaldemokratische Partei

liberate ['lɪbəreɪt] vt befreien; **liberation** [lɪbə'reɪʃn] n Befreiung f

Liberia [laɪ'bɪərɪə] n Liberia nt

liberty ['lɪbətɪ] n Freiheit f

Libra ['li:brə] n (Astr) Waage f

library ['laɪbrərɪ] n Bibliothek f; (lending ~) Bücherei f

Libya ['lɪbɪə] n Libyen nt

lice [laɪs] pl of **louse**

licence ['laɪsəns] n (permit) Genehmigung f; (Comm) Lizenz f; (driving ~) Führerschein m; **license** ['laɪsəns] n (US) see **licence** ▷ vt genehmigen; **licensed** adj (restaurant etc) mit Schankerlaubnis; **license plate** n (US Auto) Nummernschild nt; **licensing hours** npl Ausschankzeiten pl

lick [lɪk] vt lecken ▷ n Lecken nt

licorice ['lɪkərɪs] n Lakritze f

lid [lɪd] n Deckel m; (eye~) Lid nt

lie [laɪ] n Lüge f; **~ detector** Lügendetektor m ▷ vi lügen; **to ~ to sb** jdn belügen ▷ vi **(lay, lain)** (rest, be situated) liegen; (~ down) sich legen; (snow) liegen bleiben; **to be lying third** an dritter Stelle liegen; **lie about** vi herumliegen; **lie down** vi sich hinlegen

Liechtenstein ['lɪktənstaɪn] n Liechtenstein nt

lie in [laɪ'ɪn] n **to have a ~** ausschlafen

life [laɪf] (pl **lives**) n Leben nt; **to get ~** lebenslänglich bekommen; **there isn't much ~ here** hier ist nicht viel los; **how many lives were lost?** wie viele sind ums Leben gekommen?; **life assurance** n Lebensversicherung f; **lifebelt** n Rettungsring m; **lifeboat** n Rettungsboot nt; **lifeguard** n Bademeister(in) m(f), Rettungsschwimmer(in) m(f); **life insurance** n Lebensversicherung f; **life jacket** n Schwimmweste f; **lifeless** adj (dead) leblos; **lifelong** adj lebenslang; **life preserver** n (US) Rettungsring m; **life-saving** adj lebensrettend; **life-size(d)** adj in Lebensgröße; **life span** n Lebensspanne f; **life style** n Lebensstil m; **lifetime** n Lebenszeit f

lift [lɪft] vt (hoch)heben; (ban) aufheben ▷ n (Brit: elevator) Aufzug m, Lift m; **to give sb a ~** jdn im Auto mitnehmen; **lift up** vt hochheben; **lift-off** n Start m

ligament ['lɪgəmənt] n Band nt

light [laɪt] (**lit** o **lighted**, **lit** o **lighted**) vt beleuchten; (fire, cigarette) anzünden ▷ n Licht nt; (lamp) Lampe f; **~s** pl (Auto) Beleuchtung f; (traffic ~s) Ampel f; **in the ~ of** angesichts +gen ▷ adj (bright) hell; (not heavy, easy) leicht; (punishment) milde; (taxes) niedrig; **~ blue/green** hellblau/hellgrün; **light up** vt (illuminate) beleuchten ▷ vi (a. eyes) aufleuchten

light bulb n Glühbirne f

lighten ['laɪtn] vi hell werden ▷ vt (give light to) erhellen; (make less heavy) leichter machen; (fig) erleichtern

lighter ['laɪtə*] n (cigarette ~) Feuerzeug nt

light-hearted adj unbeschwert; **lighthouse** n Leuchtturm m; **lighting** n Beleuchtung f; **lightly** adv leicht; **light meter** n (Foto) Belichtungsmesser m

lightning ['laɪtnɪŋ] n Blitz m

lightweight adj leicht

like [laɪk] vt mögen, gern haben; **he ~s swimming** er schwimmt gern; **would you ~ ...?** hätten Sie gern ...?; **I'd ~ to go home** ich möchte nach Hause (gehen); **I don't ~ the film** der Film gefällt mir nicht ▷ prep wie; **what's it/he ~?** wie ist es/er?; **he looks ~ you** er sieht dir ähnlich; **~ that/this** so; **likeable** ['laɪkəbl] adj sympathisch

likelihood ['laɪklɪhʊd] n Wahrscheinlichkeit f; **likely** ['laɪklɪ] adj wahrscheinlich; **the bus is ~ to be late** der Bus wird wahrscheinlich Verspätung haben; **he's not (at all) ~ to come** (höchst)wahrscheinlich kommt er nicht

like-minded [laɪk'maɪndɪd] adj gleich gesinnt

likewise ['laɪkwaɪz] adv ebenfalls; **to do ~** das Gleiche tun

liking ['laɪkɪŋ] n (for person) Zuneigung f; (for type, things) Vorliebe f (for für)

lilac ['laɪlək] n Flieder m ▷ adj fliederfarben

lily ['lɪlɪ] n Lilie f; **~ of the valley** Maiglöckchen nt

limb [lɪm] n Glied nt

limbo ['lɪmbəʊ] n **in ~** (plans) auf Eis gelegt

lime [laɪm] n (tree) Linde f; (fruit) Limone f; (substance) Kalk m; **lime juice** n Limonensaft m; **limelight** n (fig) Rampenlicht nt

limerick ['lɪmərɪk] n Limerick m (fünfzeiliges komisches Gedicht)

limestone ['laɪmstəʊn] n Kalkstein m

limit ['lɪmɪt] n Grenze f; (for pollution etc) Grenzwert m; **there's a ~ to that** dem sind Grenzen gesetzt; **to drive over the ~** das Tempolimit überschreiten; **that's the ~** jetzt reicht's!, das ist die Höhe! ▷ vt beschränken (to auf +akk); (freedom, spending) einschränken; **limitation** [lɪmɪ'teɪʃən] n Beschränkung f; (of freedom, spending) Einschränkung f; **limited** adj begrenzt; **~ liability company** Gesellschaft f mit beschränkter Haftung, GmbH f; **public ~ company** Aktiengesellschaft f

limousine ['lɪməzi:n] n Limousine f

limp [lɪmp] vi hinken ▷ adj schlaff

line [laɪn] n Linie f; (written) Zeile f; (rope) Leine f; (on face) Falte f; (row) Reihe f; (US: queue) Schlange f; (Rail) Bahnlinie f; (between A and B) Strecke f; (Tel) Leitung f; (range of items) Kollektion f; **hold the ~** bleiben Sie am Apparat; **to stand in ~** Schlange stehen; **in ~ with** in Übereinstimmung mit; **something along those ~s** etwas in dieser Art; **drop me a ~** schreib mir ein paar Zeilen; **~s** (Theat) Text m ▷ vt (clothes) füttern; (streets) säumen; **lined** adj (paper) liniert; (face) faltig; **line up** vi sich aufstellen; (US: form queue) sich anstellen

linen ['lɪnɪn] n Leinen nt; (sheets etc) Wäsche f

liner ['laɪnə*] n Überseedampfer m, Passagierschiff nt

linesman ['laɪnzmən] n (pl -men) n (Sport) Linienrichter m

linger ['lɪŋɡə*] vi verweilen; (smell) nicht weggehen

lingerie ['lænʒəri:] n Damenunterwäsche f

lining ['laɪnɪŋ] n (of clothes) Futter nt; (brake ~) Bremsbelag m

link [lɪŋk] n (connection) Verbindung f; (of chain) Glied nt; (relationship) Beziehung f (with zu); (between events) Zusammenhang m; (Internet) Link m ▷ vt verbinden

lion ['laɪən] n Löwe m; **lioness** n Löwin f

lip [lɪp] n Lippe f; **lipstick** n Lippenstift m

liqueur [lɪ'kjʊə*] n Likör m

liquid ['lɪkwɪd] n Flüssigkeit f ▷ adj flüssig

liquidate ['lɪkwɪdeɪt] vt liquidieren

liquidizer ['lɪkwɪdaɪzə*] n Mixer m

liquor ['lɪkə*] n Spirituosen pl

liquorice ['lɪkərɪs] n Lakritze f

Lisbon ['lɪzbən] n Lissabon nt

lisp [lɪsp] vt, vi lispeln

list [lɪst] n Liste f ▷ vi (ship) Schlagseite haben ▷ vt auflisten, aufzählen; **~ed building** unter Denkmalschutz stehendes Gebäude

listen ['lɪsn] vi zuhören, horchen (for sth auf etw akk); **listen to** vt (person) zuhören +dat; (radio) hören; (advice) hören auf; **listener** n Zuhörer(in) m(f); (to radio) Hörer(in) m(f)

lit [lɪt] pt, pp of **light**

liter ['li:tə*] n (US) Liter m

literacy ['lɪtərəsɪ] n Fähigkeit f zu lesen und zu schreiben; **literal** ['lɪtərəl] adj (translation, meaning) wörtlich; (actual) buchstäblich; **literally** adv (translate, take sth) wörtlich; (really) buchstäblich, wirklich; **literary** ['lɪtərərɪ] adj literarisch; (critic, journal etc) Literatur-; (language) gehoben; **literature** ['lɪtrətʃə*] n Literatur f; (brochures etc) Informationsmaterial nt

Lithuania [lɪθju:'eɪnjə] n Litauen nt

litre ['li:tə*] n Liter m

litter ['lɪtə*] n Abfälle pl; (of animals) Wurf m ▷ vt **to be ~ed with** übersät sein mit; **litter bin** n Abfalleimer m

little ['lɪtl] adj (**smaller, smallest**) klein; (in quantity) wenig; **a ~ while ago** vor kurzer Zeit ▷ adv, n (**fewer, fewest**) wenig; **a ~** ein bisschen, ein wenig; **as ~ as possible** so wenig wie möglich; **for as ~ as £5** ab nur 5 Pfund; **I see very ~ of them** ich sehe sie sehr selten; **~ by ~** nach und nach; **little finger** n kleiner Finger

live [laɪv] adj lebendig; (Elec) geladen, unter Strom; (Tv, Radio: event) live; **~ broadcast** Direktübertragung f ▷ [lɪv] vi leben; (not die) überleben; (dwell) wohnen; **you ~ and learn** man lernt nie aus ▷ vt (life) führen; **to ~ a life of luxury** im Luxus leben; **live on** vi weiterleben ▷ vt **to ~ sth** von etw leben; (feed) sich von etw ernähren; **to earn enough to ~** genug verdienen, um davon zu leben; **live together** vi zusammenleben; **live up to** vt (reputation) gerecht werden +dat; (expectations) entsprechen +dat; **live with** vt (parents etc) wohnen bei; (partner) zusammenleben mit; (difficulty) **you'll just have to ~ it** du musst dich eben damit abfinden

liveliness ['laɪvlɪnɪs] n Lebhaftigkeit f; **lively** ['laɪvlɪ] adj lebhaft

liver ['lɪvə*] n Leber f

lives [laɪvz] pl of **life**

livestock ['laɪvstɒk] n Vieh nt

living ['lɪvɪŋ] n Lebensunterhalt m; **what do you do for a ~?** was machen Sie beruflich? ▷ adj lebend; **living room** n Wohnzimmer nt

lizard ['lɪzəd] n Eidechse f

load [ləʊd] n Last f; (cargo) Ladung f; (Tech, fig) Belastung f; **~s of** (fam) massenhaft; **it was a ~ of rubbish** (fam) es war grottenschlecht ▷ vt (vehicle) beladen; (Inform) laden; (film) einlegen

loaf [ləʊf] (pl **loaves**) n ~ **(of bread)** Brot nt; **loaf about** vi faulenzen

loan [ləʊn] n (item leant) Leihgabe f; (Fin) Darlehen nt; **on ~** geliehen ▷ vt leihen (to sb jdm)

loathe [ləʊð] vt verabscheuen

loaves [ləʊvz] pl of **loaf**

lobby ['lɒbɪ] n Vorhalle f; (Pol) Lobby f

lobster ['lɒbstə*] n Hummer m

local ['ləʊkəl] adj (traffic, time etc) Orts-; (radio, news, paper) Lokal-; (government, authority) Kommunal-; (anaesthetic) örtlich; **~ call** (Tel) Ortsgespräch nt; **~ elections** Kommunalwahlen pl; **~ time** Ortszeit f; **~ train** Nahverkehrszug m; **the ~ shops** die Geschäfte am Ort ▷ n (pub) Stammlokal nt; **the ~s** pl die Ortsansässigen pl; **locally** adv örtlich, am Ort

locate [ləʊ'keɪt] vt (find) ausfindig machen; (position) legen; (establish) errichten; **to be ~d** sich befinden (in, at in +dat); **location** [ləʊ'keɪʃən] n (position) Lage f; (Cine) Drehort m

loch [lɒx] n (Scot) See m

lock [lɒk] n Schloss nt; (Naut) Schleuse f; (of hair) Locke f ▷ vt (door etc) abschließen ▷ vi (door etc) sich abschließen lassen; (wheels) blockieren; **lock in** vt einschließen, einsperren; **lock out** vt aussperren; **lock up** vt (house, abschließen; (person) einsperren

locker ['lɒkə*] n Schließfach nt; **locker room** n (US) Umkleideraum m

locksmith ['lɒksmɪθ] n Schlosser(in) m(f)

locust ['ləʊkəst] n Heuschrecke f

lodge [lɒdʒ] n (small house) Pförtnerhaus nt; (porter's ~) Pförtnerloge f ▷ vi in Untermiete wohnen (with bei); (get stuck) stecken bleiben; **lodger** n Untermieter(in) m(f); **lodging** n Unterkunft f

loft [lɒft] n Dachboden m

log [lɒg] n Klotz m; (Naut) Log nt; **to keep a ~ of sth** über etw Buch führen; **log in** vi (Inform) sich einloggen; **log off** vi (Inform) sich ausloggen; **log on** vi (Inform) sich einloggen; **log out** vi (Inform) sich ausloggen

logic ['lɒdʒɪk] n Logik f; **logical** adj logisch

logo ['lɒgəʊ] (pl **-s**) n Logo nt

loin [lɔɪn] n Lende f

loiter ['lɔɪtə*] vi sich herumtreiben

lollipop ['lɒlɪpɒp] n Lutscher m; **~ man/lady** (Brit) Schülerlotse m, Schülerlotsin f

lolly ['lɒlɪ] n Lutscher m; (fam: money) Knete f

London ['lʌndən] n London nt; **Londoner** n Londoner(in) m(f)

loneliness ['ləʊnlɪnɪs] n Einsamkeit f; **lonely** ['ləʊnlɪ], (esp US) **lonesome** ['ləʊnsəm] adj einsam

long [lɒŋ] adj lang; (distance) weit; **it's a ~ way** es ist weit (to nach); **for a ~ time** lange; **how ~ is the film?** wie lange dauert der Film?; **in the ~ run** auf die Dauer ▷ adv lange; **not for ~** nicht lange; **~ ago** vor langer Zeit; **before ~** bald; **all day ~** den ganzen Tag; **no ~er** nicht mehr; **as ~ as** solange ▷ vi sich sehnen (for nach); (be waiting) sehnsüchtig warten (for auf); **long-distance call** n Ferngespräch nt; **long drink** n Longdrink m; **long-haul flight** n Langstreckenflug m; **longing** n Sehnsucht f (for nach); **longingly** adv sehnsüchtig; **longitude** ['lɒŋgɪtjuːd] n Länge f; **long jump** n Weitsprung m; **long-life milk** n H-Milch f; **long-range** adj Langstrecken-, Fern-; **~ missile** Langstreckenrakete f; **long-sighted** adj weitsichtig; **long-standing** adj alt, langjährig; **long-term** adj langfristig; (car park, effect etc) Langzeit-; **~ unemployment** Langzeitarbeitslosigkeit f; **long wave** n Langwelle f

loo [luː] n (Brit fam) Klo nt

look [lʊk] n Blick m; (appearance) ~(s) pl Aussehen nt; **I'll have a** ~ ich schau mal nach; **to have a** ~ **at sth** sich dat etw ansehen; **can I have a** ~? darf ich mal sehen? ▷ vi schauen, gucken; (with prep) sehen; (search) nachsehen; (appear) aussehen; **(I'm) just** ~**ing** ich schaue nur; **it** ~**s like rain** es sieht nach Regen aus ▷ vt ~ **what you've done** sieh dir mal an, was du da angestellt hast; (appear) **he** ~**s his age** man sieht ihm sein Alter an; **to** ~ **one's best** sehr vorteilhaft aussehen; **look after** vt (care for) sorgen für; (keep an eye on) aufpassen auf +akk; **look at** vt ansehen, anschauen; **look back** vi sich umsehen; (fig) zurückblicken; **look down on** vt (fig) herabsehen auf +akk; **look for** vt suchen; **look forward to** vt sich freuen auf +akk; **look into** vt (investigate) untersuchen; **look out** vi hinaussehen (of the window zum Fenster); (watch out) Ausschau halten (for nach); (be careful) aufpassen, Acht geben (for auf +akk); ~! Vorsicht!; **look up** vi aufsehen ▷ vt (word etc) nachschlagen; **look up to** vt aufsehen zu

loony ['luːnɪ] adj (fam) bekloppt

loop [luːp] n Schleife f

loose [luːs] adj locker; (knot, button) lose; **loosen** vt lockern; (knot) lösen

loot [luːt] n Beute f

lop-sided ['lɒp'saɪdɪd] adj schief

lord [lɔːd] n (ruler) Herr m; (Brit: title) Lord m; **the Lord** (God) Gott der Herr; **the (House of) Lords** (Brit) das Oberhaus

lorry ['lɒrɪ] n (Brit) Lastwagen m

lose [luːz] (**lost, lost**) vt verlieren; (chance) verpassen; **to** ~ **weight** abnehmen; **to** ~ **one's life** umkommen ▷ vi verlieren; (clock, watch) nachgehen; **loser** n Verlierer(in) m(f); **loss** [lɒs] n Verlust m; **lost** [lɒst] pt, pp of **lose**; **we're** ~ wir haben uns verlaufen ▷ adj verloren; **lost-and-found** (US), **lost property (office)** n Fundbüro nt

lot [lɒt] n (fam: batch) Menge f, Haufen m, Stoß m; **this is the first** ~ das ist die erste Ladung; **a** ~ viel(e); **a** ~ **of money** viel Geld; ~**s of people** viele Leute; **the (whole)** ~ alles; (people) alle; **(parking)** ~ (US) Parkplatz m

lotion ['ləʊʃən] n Lotion f

lottery ['lɒtərɪ] n Lotterie f

loud [laʊd] adj laut; (colour) schreiend; **loudspeaker** n Lautsprecher m; (of stereo) Box f

lounge [laʊndʒ] n Wohnzimmer nt; (in hotel) Aufenthaltsraum m; (at airport) Warteraum m ▷ vi sich herumlümmeln

louse [laʊs] (pl **lice**) n Laus f; **lousy** ['laʊzɪ] adj (fam) lausig

lout [laʊt] n Rüpel m

lovable ['lʌvəbl] adj liebenswert

love [lʌv] n Liebe f (of zu); (person, address) Liebling m, Schatz m; (Sport) null; **to be in** ~ verliebt sein (with sb in jdn); **to fall in** ~ sich verlieben (with sb in jdn); **to make** ~ (sexually) sich lieben; **to make** ~ **to** (o **with**) **sb** mit jdm schlafen; (in letter) **he sends his** ~ er lässt grüßen; **give her my** ~ grüße sie von mir; ~, **Tom** liebe Grüße, Tom ▷ vt (person) lieben; (activity) sehr gerne mögen; **to** ~ **to do sth** etw für sein Leben gerne tun; **I'd** ~ **a cup of tea** ich hätte liebend gern eine Tasse Tee; **love affair** n (Liebes)verhältnis nt; **love letter** n Liebesbrief m; **love life** n Liebesleben nt; **lovely** ['lʌvlɪ] adj schön, wunderschön; (charming) reizend; **we had a** ~ **time** es war sehr schön; **lover** ['lʌvə] n Liebhaber(in) m(f); **loving** adj liebevoll

low [ləʊ] adj niedrig; (rank) niedere(r, s); (level, note, neckline) tief; (intelligence, density) gering; (quality, standard) schlecht; (not loud) leise; (depressed) niedergeschlagen; **we're** ~ **on petrol** wir haben kaum noch Benzin ▷ n (Meteo) Tief nt; **low-calorie** adj kalorienarm; **lowcut** adj (dress) tief ausgeschnitten; **low-emission** adj schadstoffarm; **lower** ['ləʊə*] adj niedriger; (storey, class etc) untere(r, s) ▷ vt herunterlassen; (eyes, price) senken; (pressure) verringern; **low-fat** adj fettarm; **low tide** [ləʊ'taɪd] n Ebbe f

loyal ['lɔɪəl] adj treu; **loyalty** n Treue f

lozenge ['lɒzɪndʒ] n Pastille f

● **L-Plates**
●
● Als **L-Plates** werden in
● Großbritannien die weißen Schilder
● mit einem roten „L" bezeichnet, die
● vorn und hinten an jedem von einem
● Fahrschüler gesteuerten Fahrzeug

● befestigt werden müssen.
● Fahrschüler müssen einen
● vorläufigen Führerschein
● beantragen und dürfen damit unter
● der Aufsicht eines erfahrenen
● Autofahrers auf allen Straßen außer
● Autobahnen fahren.

Ltd *abbr* = **limited** ≈ GmbH *f*
lubricant ['lu:brɪkənt] *n* Schmiermittel
nt, Gleitmittel *nt*
luck [lʌk] *n* Glück *nt*; **bad ~** Pech *nt*;
luckily *adv* glücklicherweise, zum Glück;
lucky *adj* (*number, day etc*) Glücks-; **to be
~** Glück haben; **~ coincidence** glücklicher
Zufall
ludicrous ['lu:dɪkrəs] *adj* grotesk
luggage ['lʌgɪdʒ] *n* Gepäck *nt*; **luggage
compartment** *n* Gepäckraum *m*;
luggage rack *n* Gepäcknetz *nt*
lukewarm ['lu:kwɔ:m] *adj* lauwarm
lullaby ['lʌləbaɪ] *n* Schlaflied *nt*
lumbago [lʌm'beɪgəʊ] *n* Hexenschuss
m
luminous ['lu:mɪnəs] *adj* leuchtend
lump [lʌmp] *n* Klumpen *m*; (*Med*)
Schwellung *f*; (*in breast*) Knoten *m*; (*of
sugar*) Stück *nt*; **lump sum** *n*
Pauschalsumme *f*; **lumpy** *adj* klumpig
lunacy ['lu:nəsɪ] *n* Wahnsinn *m*; **lunatic**
['lu:nətɪk] *adj* wahnsinnig ▷ *n*
Wahnsinnige(r) *mf*
lunch, luncheon [lʌntʃ, -ən] *n*
Mittagessen *nt*; **to have ~** zu Mittag
essen; **lunch break, lunch hour** *n*
Mittagspause *f*; **lunch packet** *n*
Lunchpaket *nt*; **lunchtime** *n* Mittagszeit *f*
lung [lʌŋ] *n* Lunge *f*
lurid ['ljʊərɪd] *adj* (*colour*) grell; (*details*)
widerlich
lurk [lɜ:k] *vi* lauern
lust [lʌst] *n* (sinnliche) Begierde (*for* nach)
luster (*US*), **lustre** ['lʌstə*] *n* Glanz *m*
Luxembourg ['lʌksəmbɜ:g] *n*
Luxemburg *nt*; **Luxembourger**
[lʌksəm'bɜ:gə*] *n* Luxemburger(in) *m(f)*
luxurious [lʌg'ʒʊərɪəs] *adj* luxuriös,
Luxus-; **luxury** ['lʌkʃərɪ] *n* (*a. luxuries pl*)
Luxus *m*; **~ goods** Luxusgüter *pl*
lynx [lɪŋks] *n* Luchs *m*
lyrics *npl* (*words for song*) Liedtext *m*

m

m *abbr* = **metre** m

M *abbr* (*street*) = **Motorway** A; (*size*) =
medium M

MA *abbr* = **Master of Arts** Magister Artium
m

ma [ma:] *n* (*fam*) Mutti *f*

mac [mæk] *n* (*Brit fam*) Regenmantel *m*

Macedonia [mæʃə'dəʊnɪə] *n*
Mazedonien *nt*

machine [mə'ʃi:n] *n* Maschine *f*;
machine gun *n* Maschinengewehr *nt*;
machinery [mə'ʃi:nərɪ] *n* Maschinen *pl*;
(*fig*) Apparat *m*; **machine washable** *adj*
waschmaschinenfest

mackerel ['mækrəl] *n* Makrele *f*

macro ['mækrəʊ] (*pl* **-s**) *n* (*Inform*) Makro
nt

mad [mæd] *adj* wahnsinnig, verrückt;
(*dog*) tollwütig; (*angry*) wütend, sauer (*at*
auf +*akk*); (*fam*) **~ about** (*fond of*) verrückt
nach; **to work like ~** wie verrückt
arbeiten; **are you ~?** spinnst du?

madam ['mædəm] *n* gnädige Frau

mad cow disease [mæd'kaʊdɪzi:z] *n*
Rinderwahnsinn *m*; **maddening** *adj* zum
Verrücktwerden

made [meɪd] *pt, pp of* **make**

made-to-measure ['meɪdtə'meʒə*] *adj*
nach Maß; **~ suit** Maßanzug *m*

madly ['mædlɪ] *adv* wie verrückt; (*with
adj*) wahnsinnig; **madman** ['mædmən] (*pl*
-men) *n* Verrückte(r) *m*; **madwoman**
['mædwʊmən] (*pl* **-women**) *n* Verrückte *f*;
madness ['mædnɪs] *n* Wahnsinn *m*

magazine [mægə'zi:n] *n* Zeitschrift *f*

maggot ['mægət] *n* Made *f*

magic ['mædʒɪk] *n* Magie *f*; (*activity*)
Zauberei *f*; (*fig: effect*) Zauber *m*; **as if by
~** wie durch Zauberei ▷ *adj* Zauber-;
(*powers*) magisch; **magician** [mə'dʒɪʃən] *n*
Zauberer *m*, Zaub(r)erin *f*

magnet ['mægnɪt] *n* Magnet *m*;
magnetic [mæg'netɪk] *adj* magnetisch;
magnetism ['mægnɪtɪzəm] *n* (*fig*)
Anziehungskraft *f*

magnificent, magnificently
[mæg'nɪfɪsənt, -lɪ] *adj, adv* herrlich,
großartig

magnify ['mægnɪfaɪ] *vt* vergrößern;
magnifying glass *n* Vergrößerungsglas
nt, Lupe *f*

magpie ['mægpaɪ] *n* Elster *f*

maid [meɪd] *n* Dienstmädchen *nt*;
maiden name *n* Mädchenname *m*;
maiden voyage *n* Jungfernfahrt *f*

mail [meɪl] *n* Post *f*; (*e-mail*) Mail *f* ▷ *vt*
(*post*) aufgeben; (*send*) mit der Post
schicken (*to* an +*akk*); **mailbox** *n* (*US*)
Briefkasten *m*; (*Inform*) Mailbox *f*; **mailing
list** *n* Adressenliste *f*; **mailman** *n* (*pl*
-men) (*US*) Briefträger *m*; **mail order** *n*
Bestellung *f* per Post; **mail order firm** *n*
Versandhaus *nt*; **mailshot** *n* Mailing *nt*

main [meɪn] *adj* Haupt-; **~ course**
Hauptgericht *nt*; **the ~ thing** die
Hauptsache ▷ *n* (*pipe*) Hauptleitung *f*;
mainframe *n* Großrechner *m*; **mainland**
n Festland *nt*; **mainly** *adv* hauptsächlich;
main road *n* Hauptverkehrsstraße *f*;
main street *n* (*US*) Hauptstraße *f*

maintain [meɪn'teɪn] *vt* (*keep up*)
aufrechterhalten; (*machine, roads*) instand
halten; (*service*) warten; (*claim*)
behaupten; **maintenance** ['meɪntənəns]
n Instandhaltung *f*; (*Tech*) Wartung *f*

maize [meɪz] *n* Mais *m*

majestic [mə'dʒestɪk] *adj* majestätisch;
majesty ['mædʒɪstɪ] *n* Majestät *f*;
his/her Majesty seine/ihre Majestät

major ['meɪdʒə*] *adj* (*bigger*) größer; (*important*) bedeutend; **~ part** Großteil *m*; (*role*) wichtige Rolle; **~ road** Hauptverkehrsstraße *f*; (*Mus*) **A ~** A-Dur *nt* ▷ *vi* (*US*) **to ~ in sth** etw als Hauptfach studieren

Majorca [mə'jɔːkə] *n* Mallorca *nt*

majority [mə'dʒɒrɪtɪ] *n* Mehrheit *f*; **to be in the ~** in der Mehrzahl sein

make [meɪk] *n* Marke *f* ▷ *vt* (**made, made**) machen; (*manufacture*) herstellen; (*clothes*) anfertigen; (*dress*) nähen; (*soup*) zubereiten; (*bread, cake*) backen; (*tea, coffee*) kochen; (*speech*) halten; (*earn*) verdienen; (*decision*) treffen; **it's made of gold** es ist aus Gold; **to ~ sb do sth** jdn dazu bringen, etw zu tun; (*force*) jdn zwingen, etw zu tun; **she made us wait** sie ließ uns warten; **what ~s you think that?** wie kommen Sie darauf?; **it ~s the room look smaller** es lässt den Raum kleiner wirken; **to ~** (**it to**) **the airport** (*reach*) den Flughafen erreichen; (*in time*) es zum Flughafen schaffen; **he never really made it** er hat es nie zu etwas gebracht; **she didn't ~ it through the night** sie hat die Nacht nicht überlebt; (*calculate*) **I ~ it £5/a quarter to six** nach meiner Rechnung sind es auf 5 Pfund/nach meiner Uhr ist es dreiviertel sechs; **he's just made for this job** er ist für diese Arbeit wie geschaffen; **make for** *vt* zusteuern auf +*akk*; **make of** *vt* (*think of*) halten von; **I couldn't ~ anything of it** ich wurde daraus nicht schlau; **make off** *vi* sich davonmachen (*with* mit); **make out** *vi* zurechtkommen ▷ *vt* (*cheque*) ausstellen; (*list*) aufstellen; (*understand*) verstehen; (*discern*) ausmachen; **to ~** (**that**) **…** es so hinstellen, als ob …; **make up** *vt* (*team etc*) bilden; (*face*) schminken; (*invent: story etc*) erfinden; **to ~ one's mind** sich entscheiden; **to make it up with sb** sich mit jdm aussöhnen ▷ *vi* sich versöhnen; **make up for** *vt* ausgleichen; (*time*) aufholen

make-believe *adj* Fantasie-; **makeover** *n* gründliche Veränderung, Verschönerung *f*; **maker** *n* (*Comm*) Hersteller(in) *m(f)*; **makeshift** *adj* behelfsmäßig; **make-up** *n* Make-up *nt*, Schminke *f*; **making** ['meɪkɪŋ] *n* Herstellung *f*

maladjusted [mælə'dʒʌstɪd] *adj* verhaltensgestört

malaria [mə'lɛərɪə] *n* Malaria *f*

Malaysia [mə'leɪʒɪə] *n* Malaysia *nt*

male [meɪl] *n* Mann *m*; (*animal*) Männchen *nt* ▷ *adj* männlich; **~ chauvinist** Chauvi *m*, Macho *m*; **~ nurse** Krankenpfleger *m*

malfunction [mæl'fʌŋkʃən] *vi* nicht richtig funktionieren ▷ *n* Defekt *m*

malice ['mælɪs] *n* Bosheit *f*; **malicious** [mə'lɪʃəs] *adj* boshaft; (*behaviour, action*) böswillig; (*damage*) mutwillig

malignant [mə'lɪgnənt] *adj* bösartig

mall [mɔːl] *n* (*US*) Einkaufszentrum *nt*

malnutrition [mælnjuː'trɪʃən] *n* Unterernährung *f*

malt [mɔːlt] *n* Malz *nt*

Malta ['mɔːltə] *n* Malta *nt*; **Maltese** [mɔːl'tiːz] *adj* maltesisch ▷ *n* (*person*) Malteser(in) *m(f)*; (*language*) Maltesisch *nt*

maltreat [mæl'triːt] *vt* schlecht behandeln; (*violently*) misshandeln

mammal ['mæməl] *n* Säugetier *nt*

mammoth ['mæməθ] *adj* Mammut-, Riesen-

man [mæn] (*pl* **men**) *n* (*male*) Mann *m*; (*human race*) der Mensch, die Menschen *pl*; (*in chess*) Figur *f* ▷ *vt* besetzen

manage ['mænɪdʒ] *vi* zurechtkommen; **can you ~?** schaffst du es?; **to ~ without sth** ohne etw auskommen, auf etw verzichten können ▷ *vt* (*control*) leiten; (*musician, sportsman*) managen; (*cope with*) fertig werden mit; (*task, portion, climb etc*) schaffen; **to ~ to do sth** es schaffen, etw zu tun; **manageable** *adj* (*object*) handlich; (*task*) zu bewältigen; **management** *n* Leitung *f*; (*directors*) Direktion *f*; (*subject*) Management *nt*, Betriebswirtschaft *f*; **management consultant** *n* Unternehmensberater(in) *m(f)*; **manager** *n* Geschäftsführer(in) *m(f)*; (*departmental ~*) Abteilungsleiter(in) *m(f)*; (*of branch, bank*) Filialleiter(in) *m(f)*; (*of musician, sportsman*) Manager(in) *m(f)*; **managing director** *n* Geschäftsführer(in) *m(f)*

mane [meɪn] *n* Mähne *f*

maneuver (*US*) *see* **manoeuvre**

mango ['mæŋgəʊ] (*pl* **-es**) *n* Mango *f*

man-hour *n* Arbeitsstunde *f*

manhunt *n* Fahndung *f*

mania ['meɪnɪə] *n* Manie *f*; **maniac**

['meɪnɪæk] n Wahnsinnige(r) mf; (fan) Fanatiker(in) m(f)

manicure ['mænɪkjʊə*] n Maniküre f

manipulate [mə'nɪpjʊleɪt] vt manipulieren

mankind [mæn'kaɪnd] n Menschheit f

manly ['mænlɪ] adj männlich

man-made ['mænmeɪd] adj (product) künstlich

manner ['mænə*] n Art f; **in this ~** auf diese Art und Weise; **~s** pl Manieren pl

manoeuvre [mə'nu:və*] n Manöver nt ▷ vt, vi manövrieren

manor ['mænə*] n **~ (house)** Herrenhaus nt

manpower ['mænpaʊə*] n Arbeitskräfte pl

mansion ['mænʃən] n Villa f; (of old family) Herrenhaus nt

manslaughter ['mænslɔ:tə*] n Totschlag m

mantelpiece ['mæntlpi:s] n Kaminsims m

manual ['mænjʊəl] adj manuell, Hand- ▷ n Handbuch nt

manufacture [mænjʊ'fæktʃə*] vt herstellen ▷ n Herstellung f; **manufacturer** n Hersteller m

manure [mə'njʊə*] n Dung m; (esp artificial) Dünger m

many ['menɪ] (**more, most**) adj, pron viele; **~ times** oft; **not ~ people** nicht viele Leute; **too ~ problems** zu viele Probleme

map [mæp] n Landkarte f; (of town) Stadtplan m

maple ['meɪpl] n Ahorn m

marathon ['mærəθən] n Marathon m

marble ['mɑ:bl] n Marmor m; (for playing) Murmel f

march [mɑ:tʃ] vi marschieren ▷ n Marsch m; (protest) Demonstration f

March [mɑ:tʃ] n März m; see also **September**

mare [meə] n Stute f

margarine [mɑ:dʒə'ri:n] n Margarine f

margin ['mɑ:dʒɪn] n Rand m; (extra amount) Spielraum m; (Comm) Gewinnspanne f; **marginal** adj (difference etc) geringfügig

marijuana [mærjuː'ɑ:nə] n Marihuana nt

marinade ['mærɪneɪd] n (Gastr)

Marinade f; **marinated** ['mærɪneɪtd] adj mariniert

marine [mə'ri:n] adj Meeres-

marital ['mærɪtl] adj ehelich; **~ status** Familienstand m

maritime ['mærɪtaɪm] adj See-

marjoram ['mɑ:dʒərəm] n Majoran m

mark [mɑ:k] n (spot) Fleck m; (at school) Note f; (sign) Zeichen nt ▷ vt (make ~) Flecken machen auf +akk; (indicate) markieren; (schoolwork) benoten, korrigieren, Flecken machen auf +akk; **markedly** ['mɑ:kɪdlɪ] adv merklich; (with comp adj) wesentlich; **marker** n (in book) Lesezeichen nt; (pen) Marker m

market ['mɑ:kɪt] n Markt m; (stock ~) Börse f ▷ vt (Comm: new product) auf den Markt bringen; (goods) vertreiben; **marketing** n Marketing nt; **market leader** n Marktführer m; **market place** n Marktplatz m; **market research** n Marktforschung f

marmalade ['mɑ:məleɪd] n Orangenmarmelade f

maroon [mə'ru:n] adj rötlich braun

marquee [mɑ:'ki:] n großes Zelt

marriage ['mærɪdʒ] n Ehe f; (wedding) Heirat f (to mit); **married** ['mærɪd] adj (person) verheiratet

marrow ['mærəʊ] n (bone ~) Knochenmark nt; (vegetable) Kürbis m

marry ['mærɪ] vt heiraten; (join) trauen; (take as husband, wife) heiraten ▷ vi **to ~ / to get married** heiraten

marsh [mɑ:ʃ] n Marsch f, Sumpf m

marshal ['mɑ:ʃəl] n (at rally etc) Ordner m; (US: police) Bezirkspolizeichef m

martial arts ['mɑ:ʃəl'ɑ:ts] npl Kampfsportarten pl

martyr ['mɑ:tə*] n Märtyrer(in) m(f)

marvel ['mɑ:vəl] n Wunder nt ▷ vi staunen (at über +akk); **marvellous, marvelous** (US) adj wunderbar

marzipan [mɑ:zɪ'pæn] n Marzipan nt o m

mascara [mæ'skɑ:rə] n Wimperntusche f

mascot ['mæskɒt] n Maskottchen nt

masculine ['mæskjʊlɪn] adj männlich

mashed [mæʃt] adj **~ potatoes** pl Kartoffelbrei m, Kartoffelpüree nt

mask [mɑ:sk] n (a. Inform) Maske f ▷ vt (feelings) verbergen

masochist ['mæsəʊkɪst] n Masochist(in) m(f)

mason ['meɪsn] n (stone~) Steinmetz(in) m(f); **masonry** n Mauerwerk nt
mass [mæs] n Masse f; (of people) Menge f; (Rel) Messe f; **~es of** massenhaft
massacre ['mæsəkə*] n Blutbad nt
massage ['mæsɑːʒ] n Massage f ▷ vt massieren
massive ['mæsɪv] adj (powerful) gewaltig; (very large) riesig
mass media ['mæs'miːdɪə] npl Massenmedien pl; **mass-produce** vt in Massenproduktion herstellen; **mass production** n Massenproduktion f
master ['mɑːstə*] n Herr m; (of dog) Besitzer m, Herrchen nt; (teacher) Lehrer m; (artist) Meister m ▷ vt meistern; (language etc) beherrschen; **masterly** adj meisterhaft; **masterpiece** n Meisterwerk nt
masturbate ['mæstəbeɪt] vi masturbieren
mat [mæt] n Matte f; (for table) Untersetzer m
match [mætʃ] n Streichholz nt; (Sport) Wettkampf m; (ball games) Spiel nt; (tennis) Match nt ▷ vt (be like, suit) passen zu; (equal) gleichkommen +dat ▷ vi zusammenpassen; **matchbox** n Streichholzschachtel f; **matching** adj (one item) passend; (two items) zusammenpassend
mate [meɪt] n (companion) Kumpel m; (of animal) Weibchen nt/Männchen nt ▷ vi sich paaren
material [mə'tɪərɪəl] n Material nt; (for book etc, cloth) Stoff m; **materialistic** [mətɪərɪə'lɪstɪk] adj materialistisch; **materialize** [mə'tɪərɪəlaɪz] vi zustande kommen; (hope) wahr werden
maternal [mə'tɜːnl] adj mütterlich; **maternity** [mə'tɜːnɪtɪ] adj **~ dress** Umstandskleid nt; **~ leave** Elternzeit f (der Mutter); **~ ward** Entbindungsstation f
math [mæθ] n (US fam) Mathe f; **mathematical** [mæθə'mætɪkəl] adj mathematisch; **mathematics** [mæθə'mætɪks] nsing Mathematik f; **maths** [mæθs] nsing (Brit fam) Mathe f
matinée ['mætɪneɪ] n Nachmittagsvorstellung f
matter ['mætə*] n (substance) Materie f; (affair) Sache f; **a personal ~** eine

persönliche Angelegenheit; **a ~ of taste** eine Frage des Geschmacks; **no ~ how/what** egal wie/was; **what is the ~?** was ist los?; **as a ~ of fact** eigentlich; **a ~ of time** eine Frage der Zeit ▷ vi darauf ankommen, wichtig sein; **it doesn't ~** es macht nichts; **matter-of-fact** adj sachlich, nüchtern
mattress ['mætrəs] n Matratze f
mature [mə'tjʊə*] adj reif ▷ vi reif werden; **maturity** [mə'tjʊərɪtɪ] n Reife f
maximum ['mæksɪməm] adj Höchst-, höchste(r, s); **~ speed** Höchstgeschwindigkeit f ▷ n Maximum nt
may [meɪ] (might) vb aux (be possible) können; (have permission) dürfen; **it ~ rain** es könnte regnen; **~ I smoke?** darf ich rauchen?; **it ~ not happen** es passiert vielleicht gar nicht; **we ~ as well go** wir können ruhig gehen
May [meɪ] n Mai m; see also **September**
maybe ['meɪbiː] adv vielleicht
May Day ['meɪdeɪ] n der erste Mai
mayo ['meɪəʊ] (US fam), **mayonnaise** [meɪə'neɪz] n Mayo f, Mayonnaise f, Majonäse f
mayor [mɛə*] n Bürgermeister m
maze [meɪz] n Irrgarten m; (fig) Wirrwarr nt
MB abbr = **megabyte** MB nt

○ KEYWORD

me [miː] pron **1** (direct) mich; **it's me** ich bins
2 (indirect) mir; **give them to me** gib sie mir
3 (after prep: +acc) mich; (+dat) mir; **with/without me** mit mir/ohne mich

meadow ['medəʊ] n Wiese f
meal [miːl] n Essen nt, Mahlzeit f; **to go out for a ~** essen gehen; **meal pack** n (US) tiefgekühltes Fertiggericht; **meal time** n Essenszeit f
mean [miːn] (meant, meant) vt (signify) bedeuten; (have in mind) meinen; (intend) vorhaben; **I ~ it** ich meine das ernst; **what do you ~ (by that)?** was willst du damit sagen?; **to ~ to do sth** etw tun wollen; **it was ~t for you** es war für dich bestimmt (o gedacht); **it was ~t to be a joke** es

sollte ein Witz sein ▷ vi **he ~s well** er
meint es gut ▷ adj (stingy) geizig; (spiteful)
gemein (to zu); **meaning** ['miːnɪŋ] n
Bedeutung f; (of life, poem) Sinn m;
meaningful adj sinnvoll; **meaningless**
adj (text) ohne Sinn
means [miːnz] (pl **means**) n Mittel nt; (pl:
funds) Mittel pl; **by ~ of** durch, mittels; **by
all ~** selbstverständlich; **by no
~** keineswegs; **~ of transport**
Beförderungsmittel
meant [ment] pt, pp of **mean**
meantime [miːn'taɪm] adv **in the
~** inzwischen; **meanwhile** [miːn'waɪl]
adv inzwischen
measles ['miːzlz] nsing Masern pl;
German ~ Röteln pl
measure ['meʒə*] vt, vi messen ▷ n (unit,
device for measuring) Maß nt; (step)
Maßnahme f; **to take ~s** Maßnahmen
ergreifen; **measurement** n (amount
measured) Maß nt
meat [miːt] n Fleisch nt; **meatball** n
Fleischbällchen nt
mechanic [mɪ'kænɪk] n Mechaniker(in)
m(f); **mechanical** adj mechanisch;
mechanics nsing Mechanik f;
mechanism ['mekənɪzəm] n
Mechanismus m
medal ['medl] n Medaille f; (decoration)
Orden m; **medalist** (US), **medallist**
['medəlɪst] n Medaillengewinner(in) m(f)
media ['miːdɪə] npl Medien pl
median strip ['miːdɪən strɪp] n (US)
Mittelstreifen m
mediate ['miːdɪeɪt] vi vermitteln
medical ['medɪkəl] adj medizinisch;
(treatment etc) ärztlich; **~ student** n
Medizinstudent(in) m(f) ▷ n
Untersuchung f; **Medicare** ['medɪkɛə*] n
(US) Krankenkasse f für ältere Leute;
medication [medɪ'keɪʃən] n
Medikamente pl; **to be on ~** Medikamente
nehmen; **medicinal** [me'dɪsɪnl] adj Heil-;
~ herbs Heilkräuter pl; **medicine**
['medsɪn] n Arznei f; (science) Medizin f
medieval [medɪ'iːvəl] adj mittelalterlich
mediocre [miːdɪ'əʊkə*] adj mittelmäßig
meditate ['medɪteɪt] vi meditieren; (fig)
nachdenken (on über +akk)
Mediterranean [medɪtə'reɪnɪən] n (sea)
Mittelmeer nt; (region) Mittelmeerraum m
medium ['miːdɪəm] adj (quality, size)

mittlere(r, s); (steak) halbdurch; **~ (dry)**
(wine) halbtrocken; **~ sized** mittelgroß;
~ wave Mittelwelle f ▷ n (pl **media**)
Medium nt; (means) Mittel nt
meet [miːt] (**met, met**) vt treffen; (by
arrangement) sich treffen mit; (difficulties)
stoßen auf +akk; (get to know) kennen
lernen; (requirement, demand) gerecht
werden +dat; (deadline) einhalten; **pleased
to ~ you** sehr angenehm!; **to ~ sb at the
station** jdn vom Bahnhof abholen ▷ vi
sich treffen; (become acquainted) sich
kennen lernen; **we've met** (before) wir
kennen uns schon; **meet up** vt sich
treffen (with mit); **meet with** vt (group)
zusammenkommen mit; (difficulties,
resistance etc) stoßen auf +akk; **meeting** n
Treffen nt; (business ~) Besprechung f; (of
committee) Sitzung f; (assembly)
Versammlung f; **meeting place**, **meeting
point** n Treffpunkt m
megabyte ['megəbaɪt] n Megabyte nt
melody ['melədɪ] n Melodie f
melon ['melən] n Melone f
melt [melt] vt, vi schmelzen
member ['membə*] n Mitglied nt;
(of tribe, species) Angehörige(r) mf;
Member of Parliament
Parlamentsabgeordnete(r) mf;
membership n Mitgliedschaft f;
membership card n Mitgliedskarte f
memento [mə'mentəʊ] (pl **-es**) n
Andenken nt (of an +akk)
memo ['meməʊ] (pl **-s**) n Mitteilung f,
Memo nt; **memo pad** n Notizblock m
memorable ['memərəbl] adj
unvergesslich; **memorial** [mɪ'mɔːrɪəl] n
Denkmal nt (to für); **memorize**
['meməraɪz] vt sich einprägen,
auswendig lernen; **memory** ['memərɪ] n
Gedächtnis nt; (Inform: of computer)
Speicher m; (sth recalled) Erinnerung f; **in
~ of** zur Erinnerung an +akk
men [men] pl of **man**
menace ['menɪs] n Bedrohung f; (danger)
Gefahr f
mend [mend] vt reparieren; (clothes)
flicken ▷ n **to be on the ~** auf dem Wege
der Besserung sein
meningitis [menɪn'dʒaɪtɪs] n
Hirnhautentzündung f
menopause ['menəʊpɔːz] n
Wechseljahre pl

m

mental ['mentl] adj geistig; **~ hospital** psychiatrische Klinik; **mentality** [men'tælıtı] n Mentalität f; **mentally** ['mentəlı] adv geistig; **~ handicapped** geistig behindert; **~ ill** geisteskrank

mention ['menʃən] n Erwähnung f ▷ vt erwähnen (to sb jdm gegenüber); **don't ~ it** bitte sehr, gern geschehen

menu ['menju:] n Speisekarte f; (Inform) Menü nt

merchandise ['mɜ:tʃəndaız] n Handelsware f; **merchant** ['mɜ:tʃənt] adj Handels-

merciful ['mɜ:sıfʊl] adj gnädig; **mercifully** adv glücklicherweise

mercury ['mɜ:kjʊrı] n Quecksilber nt

mercy ['mɜ:sı] n Gnade f

mere [mıə*] adj bloß; **merely** ['mıəlı] adv bloß, lediglich

merge [mɜ:dʒ] vi verschmelzen; (Auto) sich einfädeln; (Comm) fusionieren; **merger** n (Comm) Fusion f

meringue [mə'ræŋ] n Baiser nt

merit ['merıt] n Verdienst nt; (advantage) Vorzug m

merry ['merı] adj fröhlich; (fam: tipsy) angeheitert; **Merry Christmas** Fröhliche Weihnachten!; **merry-go-round** n Karussell nt

mess [mes] n Unordnung f; (muddle) Durcheinander nt; (dirty) Schweinerei f; (trouble) Schwierigkeiten pl; **in a ~** (muddled) durcheinander; (untidy) unordentlich; (fig: person) in der Klemme; **to make a ~ of sth** etw verpfuschen; **to look a ~** unmöglich aussehen; **mess about** vi (tinker with) herummurksen (with an +dat); (play the fool) herumalbern; (do nothing in particular) herumgammeln; **mess up** vt verpfuschen; (make untidy) in Unordnung bringen; (dirty) schmutzig machen

message ['mesıdʒ] n Mitteilung f, Nachricht f; (meaning) Botschaft f; **can I give him a ~?** kann ich ihm etwas ausrichten?; **please leave a ~** (on answerphones) bitte hinterlassen Sie eine Nachricht; **I get the ~** ich hab's verstanden

messenger ['mesındʒə*] n Bote m

messy ['mesı] adj (untidy) unordentlich; (situation etc) verfahren

met [met] pt, pp of **meet**

metal ['metl] n Metall nt; **metallic** [mı'tælık] adj metallisch

meteorology [mi:tıə'rɒlədʒı] n Meteorologie f

meter ['mi:tə*] n Zähler m; (parking meter) Parkuhr f; (US) see **metre**

method ['meθəd] n Methode f; **methodical** [mı'θɒdıkəl] adj methodisch

meticulous [mı'tıkjʊləs] adj (peinlich) genau

metre ['mi:tə*] n Meter m o nt; **metric** ['metrık] adj metrisch; **~ system** Dezimalsystem nt

Mexico ['meksıkəʊ] n Mexiko nt

mice [maıs] pl of **mouse**

mickey ['mıkı] n **to take the ~ (out of sb)** (fam) (jdn) auf den Arm nehmen

microchip ['maıkrəʊtʃıp] n (Inform) Mikrochip m; **microphone** n Mikrofon nt; **microscope** n Mikroskop nt; **microwave (oven)** n Mikrowelle(nherd) f(m)

mid [mıd] adj **in ~ January** Mitte Januar; **he's in his ~ forties** er ist Mitte vierzig

midday ['mıd'deı] n Mittag m; **at ~** mittags

middle ['mıdl] n Mitte f; (waist) Taille f; **in the ~ of** mitten in +dat; **to be in the ~ of doing sth** gerade dabei sein, etw zu tun ▷ adj mittlere(r, s), Mittel-; **the ~ one** der/die/das Mittlere; **middle-aged** adj mittleren Alters; **Middle Ages** npl **the ~** das Mittelalter; **middle-class** adj mittelständisch; (bourgeois) bürgerlich; **middle classes** npl **the ~** der Mittelstand; **Middle East** n **the ~** der Nahe Osten; **middle name** n zweiter Vorname

Midlands ['mıdləndz] npl **the ~** Mittelengland nt

midnight ['mıdnaıt] n Mitternacht f

midst [mıdst] n **in the ~ of** mitten in +dat

midsummer ['mıdsʌmə*] n Hochsommer m; **Midsummer's Day** Sommersonnenwende f

midway [mıd'weı] adv auf halbem Wege; **~ through the film** nach der Hälfte des Films; **midweek** [mıd'wi:k] adj, adv in der Mitte der Woche

midwife ['mıdwaıf] (pl **-wives**) n Hebamme f

midwinter [mıd'wıntə*] n tiefster Winter

might [maıt] pt of **may**; (possibility) könnte; (permission) dürfte; (would) würde;

they ~ still come sie könnten noch
kommen; **he ~ have let me know** er hätte
mir doch Bescheid sagen können; **I
thought she ~ change her mind** ich
dachte schon, sie würde sich anders
entscheiden ⊳ n Macht f, Kraft f

mighty ['maɪtɪ] adj gewaltig; (powerful)
mächtig

migraine ['miːgreɪn] n Migräne f

migrant ['maɪgrənt] n (bird) Zugvogel m;
~ worker Gastarbeiter(in) m(f); **migrate**
[maɪˈgreɪt] vi abwandern; (birds) nach
Süden ziehen

mike [maɪk] n (fam) Mikro nt

Milan [mɪˈlæn] n Mailand nt

mild [maɪld] adj mild; (person) sanft;
mildly adv **to put it ~** gelinde gesagt;
mildness n Milde f

mile [maɪl] n Meile f (= 1,609 km); **for ~s
(and ~s)** = kilometerweit; **~s per hour**
Meilen pro Stunde; **~s better than**
hundertmal besser als; **mileage** n Meilen
pl, Meilenzahl f; **mileometer**
[maɪˈlɒmɪtə*] n = Kilometerzähler m;
milestone n (a. fig) Meilenstein m

militant ['mɪlɪtənt] adj militant; **military**
['mɪlɪtərɪ] adj Militär-, militärisch

milk [mɪlk] n Milch f ⊳ vt melken; **milk
chocolate** n Vollmilchschokolade f;
milkman (pl **-men**) n Milchmann m; **milk
shake** n Milkshake m, Milchmixgetränk
nt

mill [mɪl] n Mühle f; (factory) Fabrik f

millennium [mɪˈlenɪəm] n Jahrtausend nt

millet ['mɪlɪt] n Hirse f

milligramme ['mɪlɪgræm] n Milligramm
nt; **milliliter** (US), **millilitre** n Milliliter m;
millimeter (US), **millimetre** n Millimeter
m

million ['mɪljən] n Million f; **five ~** fünf
Millionen; **~s of people** Millionen von
Menschen; **millionaire** [mɪljəˈnɛə*] n
Millionär(in) m(f)

mime [maɪm] n Pantomime f ⊳ vt, vi
mimen; **mimic** ['mɪmɪk] n Imitator(in)
m(f) ⊳ vt, vi nachahmen; **mimicry**
['mɪmɪkrɪ] n Nachahmung f

mince [mɪns] vt (zer)hacken ⊳ n (meat)
Hackfleisch nt; **mincemeat** n süße
Gebäckfüllung aus Rosinen, Äpfeln, Zucker,
Gewürzen und Talg, **mince pie** n mit
'mincemeat' gefülltes süßes Weihnachtsgebäck

mind [maɪnd] n (intellect) Verstand m;
(also person) Geist m; **out of sight, out of
~** aus den Augen, aus dem Sinn; **he is out
of his ~** er ist nicht bei Verstand; **to keep
sth in ~** etw im Auge behalten; **do you
have sth in ~?** denken Sie an etwas
Besonderes?; **I've a lot on my ~** mich
beschäftigt so vieles im Moment; **to
change one's ~** es sich dat anders
überlegen ⊳ vt (look after) aufpassen auf
+akk; (object to) etwas haben gegen;
~ you, ... allerdings ...; **I wouldn't ~ ...** ich
hätte nichts gegen ...; **'~ the step'**
„Vorsicht Stufe!" ⊳ vi etwas dagegen
haben; **do you ~ if I ...** macht es Ihnen
etwas aus, wenn ich ...; **I don't ~** es ist mir
egal, meinetwegen; **never ~** macht nichts

mine [maɪn] pron meine(r, s); **this is ~** das
gehört mir; **a friend of ~** ein Freund von
mir ⊳ n (coalmine) Bergwerk nt; (Mil) Mine
f; **miner** n Bergarbeiter m

mineral ['mɪnərəl] n Mineral nt; **mineral
water** n Mineralwasser nt

mingle ['mɪŋgl] vi sich mischen (with
unter +akk)

miniature ['mɪnɪtʃə*] adj Miniatur-

minibar ['mɪnɪbɑː] n Minibar f; **minibus**
n Kleinbus m; **minicab** n Kleintaxi nt

minimal ['mɪnɪml] adj minimal;
minimize ['mɪnɪmaɪz] vt auf ein
Minimum reduzieren; **minimum**
['mɪnɪməm] n Minimum nt ⊳ adj
Mindest-

mining ['maɪnɪŋ] n Bergbau m

miniskirt n Minirock m

minister ['mɪnɪstə*] n (Pol) Minister(in)
m(f); (Rel) Pastor(in) m(f), Pfarrer(in) m(f);
ministry ['mɪnɪstrɪ] n (Pol) Ministerium
nt

minor ['maɪnə*] adj kleiner; (insignificant)
unbedeutend; (operation, offence) harmlos;
~ road Nebenstraße f; (Mus) **A ~** a-Moll nt
⊳ n (Brit: under 18) Minderjährige(r) mf;
minority [maɪˈnɒrɪtɪ] n Minderheit f

mint [mɪnt] n Minze f; (sweet)
Pfefferminz(bonbon) nt; **mint sauce** n
Minzsoße f

minus ['maɪnəs] prep minus; (without)
ohne

minute [maɪˈnjuːt] adj winzig; **in ~ detail**
genauestens ⊳ ['mɪnɪt] n Minute f; **just a
~** Moment mal; **any ~** jeden Augenblick;
~s pl (of meeting) Protokoll nt

miracle ['mɪrəkl] n Wunder nt;

miraculous [mɪˈrækjʊləs] *adj*
unglaublich

mirage [ˈmɪrɑːʒ] *n* Fata Morgana *f*,
Luftspiegelung *f*

mirror [ˈmɪrə*] *n* Spiegel *m*

misbehave [mɪsbɪˈheɪv] *vi* sich schlecht
benehmen

miscalculation [ˈmɪskælkjʊˈleɪʃən] *n*
Fehlkalkulation *f*; (*misjudgement*)
Fehleinschätzung *f*

miscarriage [mɪsˈkærɪdʒ] *n* (*Med*)
Fehlgeburt *f*

miscellaneous [mɪsɪˈleɪnɪəs] *adj*
verschieden

mischief [ˈmɪstʃɪf] *n* Unfug *m*;
mischievous [ˈmɪstʃɪvəs] *adj* (*person*)
durchtrieben; (*glance*) verschmitzt

misconception [mɪskənˈsepʃən] *n*
falsche Vorstellung

misconduct [mɪsˈkɒndʌkt] *n* Vergehen
nt

miser [ˈmaɪzə*] *n* Geizhals *m*

miserable [ˈmɪzərəbl] *adj* (*person*)
todunglücklich; (*conditions, life*) elend; (*pay,
weather*) miserabel

miserly [ˈmaɪzəlɪ] *adj* geizig

misery [ˈmɪzərɪ] *n* Elend *nt*; (*suffering*)
Qualen *pl*

misfit [ˈmɪsfɪt] *n* Außenseiter(in) *m(f)*

misfortune [mɪsˈfɔːtʃən] *n* Pech *nt*

misguided [mɪsˈgaɪdɪd] *adj* irrig;
(*optimism*) unangebracht

misinform [mɪsɪnˈfɔːm] *vt* falsch
informieren

misinterpret [mɪsɪnˈtɜːprɪt] *vt* falsch
auslegen

misjudge [mɪsˈdʒʌdʒ] *vt* falsch
beurteilen

mislay [mɪsˈleɪ] *irr vt* verlegen

mislead [mɪsˈliːd] *irr vt* irreführen;
misleading *adj* irreführend

misprint [ˈmɪsprɪnt] *n* Druckfehler *m*

mispronounce [mɪsprəˈnaʊns] *vt* falsch
aussprechen

miss [mɪs] *vt* (*fail to hit, catch*) verfehlen;
(*not notice, hear*) nicht mitbekommen; (*be
too late for*) verpassen; (*chance*) versäumen;
(*regret the absence of*) vermissen; **I ~ you** du
fehlst mir ▷ *vi* nicht treffen; (*shooting*)
danebenschießen; (*ball, shot etc*)
danebengehen; **miss out** *vt* auslassen
▷ *vi* **to ~ on sth** etw verpassen

Miss [mɪs] *n* (*unmarried woman*) Fräulein *nt*

missile [ˈmɪsaɪl] *n* Geschoss *nt*; (*rocket*)
Rakete *f*

missing [ˈmɪsɪŋ] *adj* (*person*) vermisst;
(*thing*) fehlend; **to be/go ~** vermisst
werden, fehlen

mission [ˈmɪʃən] *n* (*Pol, Mil, Rel*) Auftrag
m, Mission *f*; **missionary** [ˈmɪʃənrɪ] *n*
Missionar(in) *m(f)*

mist [mɪst] *n* (*feiner*) Nebel *m*; (*haze*)
Dunst *m*; **mist over**, **mist up** *vi* sich
beschlagen

mistake [mɪsˈteɪk] *n* Fehler *m*; **by ~** aus
Versehen ▷ *irr vt* (**mistook, mistaken**)
(*misunderstand*) falsch verstehen; (*mix up*)
verwechseln (*for* mit); **there's no
mistaking ...** ... ist unverkennbar;
(*meaning*) ... ist unmissverständlich;
mistaken *adj* (*idea, identity*) falsch; **to be
~** sich irren, falsch liegen

mistletoe [ˈmɪsltəʊ] *n* Mistel *f*

mistreat [mɪsˈtriːt] *vt* schlecht
behandeln

mistress [ˈmɪstrɪs] *n* (*lover*) Geliebte *f*

mistrust [mɪsˈtrʌst] *n* Misstrauen *nt* (*of
gegen*) ▷ *vt* misstrauen +*dat*

misty [ˈmɪstɪ] *adj* neblig; (*hazy*) dunstig

misunderstand [mɪsʌndəˈstænd] *irr vt, vi*
falsch verstehen; **misunderstanding** *n*
Missverständnis *nt*; (*disagreement*)
Differenz *f*

mitten [ˈmɪtn] *n* Fausthandschuh *m*

mix [mɪks] *n* (*mixture*) Mischung *f* ▷ *vt*
mischen; (*blend*) vermischen (*with* mit);
(*drinks, music*) mixen; **to ~ business with
pleasure** das Angenehme mit dem
Nützlichen verbinden ▷ *vi* (*liquids*) sich
vermischen lassen; **mix up** *vt* (*mix*)
zusammenmischen; (*confuse*) verwechseln
(*with* mit); **mixed** *adj* gemischt; **a
~ bunch** eine bunt gemischte Truppe;
~ grill Mixedgrill *m*; **~ vegetables**
Mischgemüse *nt*; **mixer** *n* (*for food*) Mixer
m; **mixture** [ˈmɪkstʃə*] *n* Mischung *f*;
(*Med*) Saft *m*; **mix-up** *n* Durcheinander *nt*

ml *abbr* = **millilitre** ml

mm *abbr* = **millimetre** mm

moan [məʊn] *n* Stöhnen *nt*; (*complaint*)
Gejammer *nt* ▷ *vi* stöhnen; (*complain*)
jammern, meckern (*about* über +*akk*)

mobile [ˈməʊbaɪl] *adj* beweglich; (*on
wheels*) fahrbar ▷ *n* (*phone*) Handy *nt*;
mobile phone *n* Mobiltelefon *nt*, Handy
nt

mobility [məʊ'bɪlɪtɪ] n Beweglichkeit f

mock [mɒk] vt verspotten ▷ adj Schein-;
mockery n Spott m

mod cons ['mɒd'kɒnz] abbr = **modern
conveniences** (moderner) Komfort

mode [məʊd] n Art f; (Inform) Modus m

model ['mɒdl] n Modell nt; (example)
Vorbild nt; (fashion ~) Model m ▷ adj
(miniature) Modell-; (perfect) Muster- ▷ vt
(make) formen ▷ vi **she ~s for Versace** sie
arbeitet als Model bei Versace

modem ['məʊdem] n Modem nt

moderate ['mɒdərət] adj mäßig; (views,
politics) gemäßigt; (income, success)
mittelmäßig ▷ n (Pol) Gemäßigte(r) mf
▷ ['mɒdəreɪt] vt mäßigen; **moderation**
[mɒdə'reɪʃən] n Mäßigung f; **in ~** mit
Maßen

modern ['mɒdən] adj modern; **~ history**
neuere Geschichte; **~ Greek**
Neugriechisch nt; **modernize** ['mɒdənaɪz]
vt modernisieren

modest ['mɒdɪst] adj bescheiden;
modesty n Bescheidenheit f

modification [mɒdɪfɪ'keɪʃən] n
Abänderung f; **modify** ['mɒdɪfaɪ] vt
abändern

moist [mɔɪst] adj feucht; **moisten**
['mɔɪsn] vt befeuchten; **moisture**
['mɔɪstʃə*] n Feuchtigkeit f; **moisturizer**
n Feuchtigkeitscreme f

molar ['məʊlə*] n Backenzahn m

mold (US) see **mould**

mole [məʊl] n (spot) Leberfleck m; (animal)
Maulwurf m

molecule ['mɒlɪkjuːl] n Molekül nt

molest [məʊ'lest] vt belästigen

molt (US) see **moult**

molten ['məʊltən] adj geschmolzen

mom [mɒm] n (US) Mutti f

moment ['məʊmənt] n Moment m,
Augenblick m; **just a ~** Moment mal; **at** (o
for) **the ~** im Augenblick; **in a ~** gleich

momentous [məʊ'mentəs] adj
bedeutsam

Monaco ['mɒnəkəʊ] n Monaco nt

monarchy ['mɒnəkɪ] n Monarchie f

monastery ['mɒnəstrɪ] n (for monks)
Kloster nt

Monday ['mʌndeɪ] n Montag m; see also
Tuesday

monetary ['mʌnɪtərɪ] adj (reform, policy,
union) Währungs-; **~ unit** Geldeinheit f

money ['mʌnɪ] n Geld nt; **to get one's ~'s
worth** auf seine Kosten kommen; **money
order** n Postanweisung f

mongrel ['mʌŋgrəl] n
Promenadenmischung f

monitor ['mɒnɪtə*] n (screen) Monitor m
▷ vt (progress etc) überwachen;
(broadcasts) abhören

monk [mʌŋk] n Mönch m

monkey ['mʌŋkɪ] n Affe m; **~ business**
Unfug m

monopolize [mə'nɒpəlaɪz] vt
monopolisieren; (fig: person, thing) in
Beschlag nehmen; **monopoly** [mə'nɒpəlɪ]
n Monopol nt

monotonous [mə'nɒtənəs] adj eintönig,
monoton

monsoon [mɒn'suːn] n Monsun m

monster ['mɒnstə*] n (animal, thing)
Monstrum nt ▷ adj Riesen-; **monstrosity**
[mɒn'strɒsɪtɪ] n Monstrosität f; (thing)
Ungetüm nt

month [mʌnθ] n Monat m; **monthly** adj
monatlich; (ticket, salary) Monats- ▷ adv
monatlich ▷ n (magazine)
Monats(zeit)schrift f

monty ['mɒntɪ] n **to go the full ~** (fam:
strip) alle Hüllen fallen lassen; (go the whole
hog) aufs Ganze gehen

monument ['mɒnjʊmənt] n Denkmal nt
(to für); **monumental** [mɒnjʊ'mentl] adj
(huge) gewaltig

mood [muːd] n (of person) Laune f; (a.
general) Stimmung f; **to be in a good/bad
~** gute/schlechte Laune haben,
gut/schlecht drauf sein; **to be in the ~ for
sth** zu etw aufgelegt sein; **I'm not in the
~** ich fühle mich nicht danach; **moody** adj
launisch

moon [muːn] n Mond m; **to be over the
~** (fam) überglücklich sein; **moonlight** n
Mondlicht m ▷ vi schwarzarbeiten;
moonlit adj (night, landscape) mondhell

moor [mɔː*] n Moor nt ▷ vt, vi
festmachen; **moorings** npl Liegeplatz m;
moorland nt Moorland nt, Heideland nt

moose [muːs] n (pl -) n Elch m

mop [mɒp] n Mopp m; **mop up** vt
aufwischen

mope [məʊp] vi Trübsal blasen

moped ['məʊped] n (Brit) Moped nt

moral ['mɒrəl] adj moralisch; (values)
sittlich ▷ n Moral f; **~s** pl Moral f; **morale**

[mɒˈrɑːl] n Stimmung f, Moral f; **morality**
[məˈrælɪtɪ] n Moral f, Ethik f
morbid [ˈmɔːbɪd] adj krankhaft

 KEYWORD

more [mɔː*] adj (greater in number etc)
mehr; (additional) noch mehr; **do you
want (some) more tea?** möchten Sie
noch etwas Tee?; **I have no** or **I don't have
any more money** ich habe kein Geld mehr
▷ pron (greater amount) mehr; (further or
additional amount) noch mehr; **is there any
more?** gibt es noch mehr?; (left over) ist
noch etwas da?; **there's no more** es ist
nichts mehr da ▷ adv mehr; **more
dangerous/easily** etc **(than)**
gefährlicher/einfacher etc (als); **more and
more** immer mehr; **more and more
excited** immer aufgeregter; **more or less**
mehr oder weniger; **more than ever** mehr
denn je; **more beautiful than ever**
schöner denn je

morgue [mɔːg] n Leichenschauhaus nt
morning [ˈmɔːnɪŋ] n Morgen m; **in the
~** am Morgen, morgens; (tomorrow)
morgen früh; **this ~** heute morgen ▷ adj
Morgen-; (early) Früh-; (walk etc)
morgendlich; **morning after pill** n die
Pille danach; **morning sickness** n
Schwangerschaftsübelkeit f
Morocco [məˈrɒkəʊ] n Marokko nt
moron [ˈmɔːrɒn] n Idiot(in) m(f)
morphine [ˈmɔːfiːn] n Morphium nt
morsel [ˈmɔːsl] n Bissen m
mortal [ˈmɔːtl] adj sterblich; (wound)
tödlich ▷ n Sterbliche(r) mf; **mortality**
[mɔːˈtælɪtɪ] n (death rate)
Sterblichkeitsziffer f; **mortally** adv
tödlich
mortgage [ˈmɔːgɪdʒ] n Hypothek f ▷ vt
mit einer Hypothek belasten
mortified [ˈmɔːtɪfaɪd] adj **I was ~** es war
mir schrecklich peinlich
mortuary [ˈmɔːtjʊərɪ] n Leichenhalle f
mosaic [məʊˈzeɪɪk] n Mosaik nt
Moscow [ˈmɒskəʊ] n Moskau nt
Moslem [ˈmɒzlem] adj, n see **Muslim**
mosque [mɒsk] n Moschee f
mosquito [mɒsˈkiːtəʊ] (pl **-es**) n
(Stech)mücke f; (tropical) Moskito m; **~ net**
Moskitonetz nt

moss [mɒs] n Moos nt
most [məʊst] adj meiste pl, die meisten;
in ~ cases in den meisten Fällen ▷ adv
(with verbs) am meisten; (with adj) ...ste;
(with adv) am ...sten; (very) äußerst,
höchst; **he ate (the) ~** er hat am meisten
gegessen; **the ~ beautiful/interesting**
der/die/das schönste/interessanteste;
~ interesting hochinteressant! ▷ n das
meiste, der größte Teil; (people) die
meisten; **~ of the money/players** das
meiste Geld/die meisten Spieler; **for the
~ part** zum größten Teil; **five at the
~** höchstens fünf; **to make the ~ of sth**
etw voll ausnützen; **mostly** adv (most of
the time) meistens; (mainly) hauptsächlich;
(for the most part) größtenteils
MOT abbr = Ministry of Transport;
~ (test) ≈ TÜV m
motel [məʊˈtel] n Motel nt
moth [mɒθ] n Nachtfalter m; (wool-eating)
Motte f; **mothball** n Mottenkugel f
mother [ˈmʌðə*] n Mutter f ▷ vt
bemuttern; **mother-in-law** (pl
mothers-in-law) n Schwiegermutter f;
mother-to-be (pl **mothers-to-be**) n
werdende Mutter
motif [məʊˈtiːf] n Motiv nt
motion [ˈməʊʃən] n Bewegung f; (in
meeting) Antrag m; **motionless** adj
bewegungslos
motivate [ˈməʊtɪveɪt] vt motivieren;
motive [ˈməʊtɪv] n Motiv nt
motor [ˈməʊtə*] n Motor m; (fam: car)
Auto nt ▷ adj Motor-; **Motorail train®** n
(Brit) Autoreisezug m; **motorbike** n
Motorrad nt; **motorboat** n Motorboot nt;
motorcycle n Motorrad nt; **motor
industry** n Automobilindustrie f;
motoring [ˈməʊtərɪŋ] n Autofahren nt;
~ organization Automobilklub m;
motorist [ˈməʊtərɪst] n Autofahrer(in)
m(f); **motor oil** n Motorenöl nt; **motor
racing** n Autorennsport m; **motor
scooter** n Motorroller m; **motor show** n
Automobilausstellung f; **motor vehicle** n
Kraftfahrzeug nt; **motorway** n (Brit)
Autobahn f
motto [ˈmɒtəʊ] n (pl **-es**) n Motto nt
mould [məʊld] n Form f; (mildew)
Schimmel m ▷ vt (a. fig) formen; **mouldy**
[ˈməʊldɪ] adj schimmelig
moult [məʊlt] vi sich mausern, haaren

mount [maʊnt] vt (horse) steigen auf +akk; (exhibition etc) organisieren; (painting) mit einem Passepartout versehen ▷ vi **to ~** (**up**) (an)steigen ▷ n Passepartout nt

mountain ['maʊntɪn] n Berg m; **mountain bike** n Mountainbike nt; **mountaineer** [maʊntɪ'nɪə*] n Bergsteiger(in) m(f); **mountaineering** [maʊntɪ'nɪərɪŋ] n Bergsteigen nt; **mountainous** adj bergig; **mountainside** n Berghang m

mourn [mɔ:n] vt betrauern ▷ vi trauern (for um); **mourner** n Trauernde(r) mf; **mournful** adj trauervoll; **mourning** n Trauer f; **to be in ~** trauern (for um)

mouse [maʊs] (pl **mice**) n (a. Inform) Maus f; **mouse mat**, **mouse pad** (US) n Mauspad nt; **mouse trap** n Mausefalle f

mousse [mu:s] n (Gastr) Creme f; (styling ~) Schaumfestiger m

moustache [mə'stɑ:ʃ] n Schnurrbart m

mouth [maʊθ] n Mund m; (of animal) Maul nt; (of cave) Eingang m; (of bottle etc) Öffnung f; (of river) Mündung f; **to keep one's ~ shut** (fam) den Mund halten; **mouthful** n (of drink) Schluck m; (of food) Bissen m; **mouth organ** n Mundharmonika f; **mouthwash** n Mundwasser nt; **mouthwatering** adj appetitlich, lecker

move [mu:v] n (movement) Bewegung f; (in game) Zug m; (step) Schritt m; (moving house) Umzug m; **to make a ~** (in game) ziehen; (leave) sich auf den Weg machen; **to get a ~ on** (**with sth**) sich (mit etw) beeilen ▷ vt bewegen; (object) rücken; (car) wegfahren; (transport: goods) befördern; (people) transportieren; (in job) versetzen; (emotionally) bewegen, rühren; **I can't ~ it** (stuck, too heavy) ich bringe es nicht von der Stelle; **to ~ house** umziehen ▷ vi sich bewegen; (change place) gehen; (vehicle, ship) fahren; (move house, town etc) umziehen; (in game) ziehen; **move about** vi sich bewegen; (travel) unterwegs sein; **move away** vi weggehen; (move town) wegziehen; **move in** vi (to house) einziehen; **move off** vi losfahren; **move on** vi weitergehen; (vehicle) weiterfahren; **move out** vi ausziehen; **move up** vi (in queue etc) aufrücken; **movement** n Bewegung f

movie ['mu:vɪ] n Film m; **the ~s** (the cinema) das Kino

moving ['mu:vɪŋ] adj (emotionally) ergreifend, berührend

mow [məʊ] (**mowed**, **mown** o **mowed**) vt mähen; **mower** n (lawn~) Rasenmäher m

mown [məʊn] pp of **mow**

Mozambique [məʊzæm'bi:k] n Mosambik nt

MP abbr = **Member of Parliament** Parlamentsabgeordnete(r) mf

mph abbr = **miles per hour** Meilen pro Stunde

MPV abbr = **multi-purpose vehicle** Mehrzweckfahrzeug nt

MP3 n MP3 nt

Mr [mɪstə*] n (form of address) Herr

Mrs ['mɪsɪz] n (form of address) Frau

Ms [məz] n (form of address for any woman, married or unmarried) Frau

MS n abbr = **multiple sclerosis** MS f

Mt abbr = **Mount** Berg m

much [mʌtʃ] (**more, most**) adj viel; **we haven't got ~ time** wir haben nicht viel Zeit; **how ~ money?** wie viel Geld? ▷ adv viel; (with verb) sehr; **~ better** viel besser; **I like it very ~** es gefällt mir sehr gut; **I don't like it ~** ich mag es nicht besonders; **thank you very ~** danke sehr; **I thought as ~** das habe ich mir gedacht; **~ as I like him** so sehr ich ihn mag; **we don't see them ~** wir sehen sie nicht sehr oft; **~ the same** fast gleich ▷ n viel; **as ~ as you want** so viel du willst; **he's not ~ of a cook** er ist kein großer Koch

muck [mʌk] n (fam) Dreck m; **muck about** vi (fam) herumalbern; **muck up** vt (fam) dreckig machen; (spoil) vermasseln; **mucky** adj dreckig

mucus ['mju:kəs] n Schleim m

mud [mʌd] n Schlamm m

muddle ['mʌdl] n Durcheinander nt; **to be in a ~** ganz durcheinander sein ▷ vt **to ~** (**up**) durcheinander bringen; **muddled** adj konfus

muddy ['mʌdɪ] adj schlammig; (shoes) schmutzig; **mudguard** ['mʌdgɑ:d] n Schutzblech nt

muesli ['mju:zlɪ] n Müsli nt

muffin ['mʌfɪn] n Muffin m; (Brit) weiches, flaches Milchbrötchen aus Hefeteig, das meist getoastet und mit Butter gegessen wird

muffle ['mʌfl] vt (sound) dämpfen; **muffler** n (US) Schalldämpfer m

mug [mʌg] n (cup) Becher m; (fam: fool) Trottel m ▷ vt (attack and rob) überfallen; **mugging** n Raubüberfall m

muggy ['mʌgɪ] adj (weather) schwül

mule [mju:l] n Maulesel m

mull over [mʌl 'əʊvə*] vt nachdenken über +akk

mulled [mʌld] adj ~ **wine** Glühwein m

multicolored (US), **multicoloured** ['mʌltɪ'kʌləd] adj bunt; **multicultural** adj multikulturell; **multi-grade** adj ~ **oil** Mehrbereichsöl nt; **multilingual** adj mehrsprachig; **multinational** n (company) Multi m

multiple ['mʌltɪpl] n Vielfache(s) nt ▷ adj mehrfach; (several) mehrere; **multiple-choice (method)** n Multiple-Choice-Verfahren nt; **multiple sclerosis** ['mʌltɪplskle'rəʊsɪs] n Multiple Sklerose f

multiplex ['mʌltɪpleks] adj, n ~ **(cinema)** Multiplexkino nt

multiplication [mʌltɪplɪ'keɪʃən] n Multiplikation f; **multiply** ['mʌltɪplaɪ] vt multiplizieren (by mit) ▷ vi sich vermehren

multi-purpose ['mʌltɪ'pɜːpəs] adj Mehrzweck-; **multistorey (car park)** n Parkhaus nt; **multitasking** n (Inform) Multitasking nt

mum [mʌm] n (fam: mother) Mutti f, Mami f

mumble ['mʌmbl] vt, vi murmeln

mummy ['mʌmɪ] n (dead body) Mumie f; (fam: mother) Mutti f, Mami f

mumps [mʌmps] nsing Mumps m

munch [mʌntʃ] vt, vi mampfen

Munich ['mju:nɪk] n München nt

municipal [mju:'nɪsɪpəl] adj städtisch

mural ['mjʊərəl] n Wandgemälde nt

murder ['mɜːdə*] n Mord m; **the traffic was ~** der Verkehr war die Hölle ▷ vt ermorden; **murderer** n Mörder(in) m(f)

murky ['mɜːkɪ] adj düster; (water) trüb

murmur ['mɜːmə*] vt, vi murmeln

muscle ['mʌsl] n Muskel m; **muscular** ['mʌskjʊlə*] adj (strong) muskulös; (cramp, pain etc) Muskel-

museum [mju:'zɪəm] n Museum nt

mushroom ['mʌʃru:m] n (essbarer) Pilz; (button ~) Champignon m ▷ vi (fig) emporschießen

mushy ['mʌʃɪ] adj breiig; ~ **peas** Erbsenmus nt

music ['mju:zɪk] n Musik f; (printed) Noten pl; **musical** adj (sound) melodisch; (person) musikalisch; ~ **instrument** Musikinstrument nt ▷ n (show) Musical nt; **musically** adv musikalisch; **musician** [mju:'zɪʃən] n Musiker(in) m(f)

Muslim ['mʊzlɪm] adj moslemisch ▷ n Moslem m, Muslime f

mussel ['mʌsl] n Miesmuschel f

must [mʌst] (had to, had to) vb aux (need to) müssen; (in negation) dürfen; **I ~n't forget that** ich darf das nicht vergessen; (certainty) **he ~ be there by now** er ist inzwischen bestimmt schon da; (assumption) **I ~ have lost it** ich habe es wohl verloren; **~ you?** muss das sein? ▷ n Muss nt

mustache ['mʌstæʃ] n (US) Schnurrbart m

mustard ['mʌstəd] n Senf m; **to cut the ~** es bringen

mustn't ['mʌsnt] contr of **must not**

mute [mju:t] adj stumm

mutter ['mʌtə*] vt, vi murmeln

mutton ['mʌtn] n Hammelfleisch nt

mutual ['mju:tjʊəl] adj gegenseitig; **by ~ consent** in gegenseitigem Einvernehmen

my [maɪ] adj mein; **I've hurt ~ leg** ich habe mir das Bein verletzt

Myanmar ['maɪænmɑ:] n Myanmar nt

myself [maɪ'self] pron (reflexive) mich akk, mir dat; **I've hurt ~** ich habe mich verletzt; **I've bought ~ a flat** ich habe mir eine Wohnung gekauft; **I need it for ~** ich brauche es für mich (selbst); (emphatic) **I did it ~** ich habe es selbst gemacht; (all) **by ~** allein

mysterious [mɪ'stɪərɪəs] adj geheimnisvoll, mysteriös; (inexplicable) rätselhaft; **mystery** ['mɪstərɪ] n Geheimnis nt; (puzzle) Rätsel nt; **it's a ~ to me** es ist mir schleierhaft; **mystify** ['mɪstɪfaɪ] vt verblüffen

myth [mɪθ] n Mythos m; (fig: untrue story) Märchen nt; **mythical** adj mythisch; (fig: untrue) erfunden; **mythology** [mɪ'θɒlədʒɪ] n Mythologie f

N *abbr* = **north** N

nag [næg] *vt, vi* herumnörgeln (*sb* an jdm); **nagging** *n* Nörgelei *f*

nail [neɪl] *n* Nagel *m* ▷ *vt* nageln (*to* an); **nail down** *vt* festnageln; **nailbrush** *n* Nagelbürste *f*; **nail clippers** *npl* Nagelknipser *m*; **nailfile** *n* Nagelfeile *f*; **nail polish** *n* Nagellack *m*; **nail polish remover** *n* Nagellackentferner *m*; **nail scissors** *npl* Nagelschere *f*; **nail varnish** *n* Nagellack *m*

naive [naɪˈiːv] *adj* naiv

naked [ˈneɪkɪd] *adj* nackt

name [neɪm] *n* Name *m*; **his ~ is ...** er heißt ...; **what's your ~?** wie heißen Sie?; (*reputation*) **to have a good/bad ~** einen guten/schlechten Ruf haben ▷ *vt* nennen (*after* nach); (*sth new*) benennen; (*nominate*) ernennen (*as* als/zu); **a boy ~d ...** ein Junge namens ...; **namely** *adv* nämlich; **name plate** *n* Namensschild *nt*

nan bread [ˈnɑːnˈbred] *n* (*warm serviertes*) *indisches Fladenbrot*

nanny [ˈnænɪ] *n* Kindermädchen *nt*

nap [næp] *n* **to have a ~** ein Nickerchen machen

napkin [ˈnæpkɪn] *n* (*at table*) Serviette *f*

Naples [ˈneɪplz] *n* Neapel *nt*

nappy [ˈnæpɪ] *n* (*Brit*) Windel *f*

narcotic [nɑːˈkɒtɪk] *n* Rauschgift *nt*

narrate [nəˈreɪt] *vt* erzählen; **narration** [nəˈreɪʃən], **narrative** [ˈnærətɪv] *n* Erzählung *f*; **narrator** [nəˈreɪtə*] *n* Erzähler(in) *m(f)*

narrow [ˈnærəʊ] *adj* eng, schmal; (*victory, majority*) knapp; **to have a ~ escape** mit knapper Not davonkommen ▷ *vi* sich verengen; **narrow down** *vt* einschränken (*to sth* auf etw *akk*); **narrow-minded** *adj* engstirnig

nasty [ˈnɑːstɪ] *adj* ekelhaft; (*person*) fies; (*remark*) gehässig; (*accident, wound etc*) schlimm

nation [ˈneɪʃən] *n* Nation *f*; **national** [ˈnæʃənl] *adj* national; **~ anthem** Nationalhymne *f*; **National Health Service** (*Brit*) staatlicher Gesundheitsdienst; **~ insurance** (*Brit*) Sozialversicherung *f*; **~ park** Nationalpark *m*; **~ service** Wehrdienst *m*; **~ socialism** (*Hist*) Nationalsozialismus *m* ▷ *n* Staatsbürger(in) *m(f)*

nationality [næʃˈnælɪtɪ] *n* Staatsangehörigkeit *f*, Nationalität *f*; **nationalize** [ˈnæʃnəlaɪz] *vt* verstaatlichen; **nationwide** *adj, adv* landesweit

● **National Trust**
●
● Der **National Trust** ist ein 1895
● gegründeter Natur- und
● Denkmalschutzverband in
● Großbritannien, der Gebäude und
● Gelände von besonderem
● historischem oder ästhetischem
● Interesse erhält und der
● Öffentlichkeit zugänglich macht.

native [ˈneɪtɪv] *adj* einheimisch; (*inborn*) angeboren, natürlich; **Native American** Indianer(in) *m(f)*; **~ country** Heimatland *nt*; **a ~ German** ein gebürtiger Deutscher, eine gebürtige Deutsche; **~ language** Muttersprache *f*; **~ speaker** Muttersprachler(in) *m(f)* ▷ *n* Einheimische(r) *mf*; (*in colonial context*) Eingeborene(r) *mf*

nativity play [nəˈtɪvətɪpleɪ] *n* Krippenspiel *nt*

NATO ['neɪtəʊ] *acr* = **North Atlantic Treaty Organization** Nato *f*

natural ['nætʃrəl] *adj* natürlich; (*law, science, forces etc*) Natur-; (*inborn*) angeboren; **~ gas** Erdgas *nt*; **~ resources** Bodenschätze *pl*; **naturally** *adv* natürlich; (*by nature*) von Natur aus; **it comes ~ to her** es fällt ihr leicht

nature ['neɪtʃə*] *n* Natur *f*; (*type*) Art *f*; **it is not in my ~** es entspricht nicht meiner Art; **by ~** von Natur aus; **nature reserve** *n* Naturschutzgebiet *nt*

naughty ['nɔ:tɪ] *adj* (*child*) ungezogen; (*cheeky*) frech

nausea ['nɔ:sɪə] *n* Übelkeit *f*

nautical ['nɔ:tɪkəl] *adj* nautisch; **~ mile** Seemeile *f*

nave [neɪv] *n* Hauptschiff *nt*

navel ['neɪvəl] *n* Nabel *m*

navigate ['nævɪgeɪt] *vi* navigieren; (*in car*) lotsen, dirigieren; **navigation** [nævɪ'geɪʃən] *n* Navigation *f*; (*in car*) Lotsen *nt*

navy ['neɪvɪ] *n* Marine *f*; **~ blue** Marineblau *nt*

Nazi ['nɑːtsɪ] *n* Nazi *m*

NB *abbr* = **nota bene** NB

NE *abbr* = **northeast** NO

near [nɪə*] *adj* nahe; **my ~est relations** meine nächsten Verwandten; **in the ~ future** in nächster Zukunft; **that was a ~ miss** (*o thing*) das war knapp; (*with price*) **... or ~est offer** Verhandlungsbasis ... ▷ *adv* in der Nähe; **so ~** so nahe; **come ~er** näher kommen; (*event*) näher rücken ▷ *prep* **~ (to)** (*space*) nahe an +*dat*; (*vicinity*) in der Nähe +*gen*; **~ the sea** nahe am Meer; **~ the station** in der Nähe des Bahnhofs, in Bahnhofsnähe; **nearby** *adj* nahe gelegen ▷ *adv* in der Nähe; **nearly** *adv* fast; **nearside** *n* (*Auto*) Beifahrerseite *f*; **near-sighted** *adj* kurzsichtig

neat ['ni:t] *adj* ordentlich; (*work, writing*) sauber; (*undiluted*) pur

necessarily [nesə'serəlɪ] *adv* notwendigerweise; **not ~** nicht unbedingt; **necessary** ['nesəsərɪ] *adj* notwendig, nötig; **it's ~ to ...** man muss ...; **it's not ~ for him to come** er braucht nicht mitzukommen; **necessity** [nɪ'sesɪtɪ] *n* Notwendigkeit *f*; **the bare necessities** das absolut Notwendigste; **there is no**

~ to ... man braucht nicht (zu) ..., man muss nicht ...

neck [nek] *n* Hals *m*; (*size*) Halsweite *f*; **back of the ~** Nacken *m*; **necklace** ['neklɪs] *n* Halskette *f*; **necktie** *n* (*US*) Krawatte *f*

nectarine ['nektərɪn] *n* Nektarine *f*

née [neɪ] *adj* geborene

need [ni:d] *n* (*requirement*) Bedürfnis *nt* (*for* für); (*necessity*) Notwendigkeit *f*; (*poverty*) Not *f*; **to be in ~ of sth** etw brauchen; **if ~(s) be** wenn nötig; **there is no ~ to ...** man braucht nicht (zu) ..., man muss nicht ... ▷ *vt* brauchen; **I ~ to speak to you** ich muss mit dir reden; **you ~n't go** du brauchst nicht (zu) gehen, du musst nicht gehen

needle ['ni:dl] *n* Nadel *f*

needless, needlessly ['ni:dlɪs, -lɪ] *adj, adv* unnötig; **~ to say** selbstverständlich

needy ['ni:dɪ] *adj* bedürftig

negative ['negətɪv] *n* (*Ling*) Verneinung *f*; (*Foto*) Negativ *nt* ▷ *adj* negativ; (*answer*) verneinend

neglect [nɪ'glekt] *n* Vernachlässigung *f* ▷ *vt* vernachlässigen; **to ~ to do sth** es versäumen, etw zu tun; **negligence** ['neglɪdʒəns] *n* Nachlässigkeit *f*; **negligent** *adj* nachlässig

negligible ['neglɪdʒəbl] *adj* unbedeutend; (*amount*) geringfügig

negotiate [nɪ'gəʊʃɪeɪt] *vi* verhandeln; **negotiation** [nɪgəʊʃɪ'eɪʃən] *n* Verhandlung *f*

neigh [neɪ] *vi* (*horse*) wiehern

neighbor (*US*), **neighbour** ['neɪbə*] *n* Nachbar(in) *m(f)*; **neighbo(u)rhood** *n* Nachbarschaft *f*; **neighbo(u)ring** *adj* benachbart

neither ['naɪðə*] *adj, pron* keine(r, s) von beiden; **~ of you/us** keiner von euch/uns beiden ▷ *adv* **~ ... nor ...** weder ... noch ... ▷ *conj* **I'm not going - ~ am I** ich gehe nicht - ich auch nicht

neon ['ni:ɒn] *n* Neon *nt*; **~ sign** (*advertisement*) Leuchtreklame *f*

nephew ['nefju:] *n* Neffe *m*

nerd [nɜ:v] *n* (*fam*) Schwachkopf *m*; **he's a real computer ~** er ist ein totaler Computerfreak

nerve [nɜ:v] *n* Nerv *m*; **he gets on my ~s** er geht mir auf die Nerven; (*courage*) **to keep/lose one's ~** die Nerven

behalten/verlieren; (cheek) **to have the
~ to do sth** die Frechheit besitzen, etw zu
tun; **nerve-racking** adj
nervenaufreibend; **nervous** ['nɜːvəs] adj
(apprehensive) ängstlich; (on edge) nervös;
nervous breakdown n
Nervenzusammenbruch m
nest [nest] n Nest nt ▷ vi nisten
net [net] n Netz nt; **the Net** (Internet) das
Internet; **on the ~** im Netz ▷ adj (price,
weight) Netto-; **~ profit** Reingewinn m;
netball n Netzball m
Netherlands ['neðələndz] npl **the ~** die
Niederlande pl
nettle ['netl] n Nessel f
network ['netwɜːk] n Netz nt; (Tv, Radio)
Sendenetz nt; (Inform) Netzwerk nt
neurosis [njʊəˈrəʊsɪs] n Neurose f;
neurotic [njʊəˈrɒtɪk] adj neurotisch
neuter ['njuːtə*] adj (Bio) geschlechtslos;
(Ling) sächlich
neutral ['njuːtrəl] adj neutral ▷ n (gear in
car) Leerlauf m
never ['nevə*] adv nie(mals); **~ before**
noch nie; **~ mind** macht nichts!;
never-ending adj endlos; **nevertheless**
[nevəðə'les] adv trotzdem
new [njuː] adj neu; **this is all ~ to me** das
ist für mich noch ungewohnt; **newcomer**
n Neuankömmling m; (in job, subject)
Neuling m
New England [njuːˈɪŋglənd] n
Neuengland nt
Newfoundland ['njuːfəndlənd] n
Neufundland nt
newly ['njuːlɪ] adv neu; **~ made** (cake)
frisch gebacken; **newly-weds** npl
Frischvermählte pl; **new moon** n
Neumond m
news [njuːz] nsing (item of ~) Nachricht f;
(Radio, Tv) Nachrichten pl; **good ~** ein
erfreuliche Nachricht; **what's the ~?** was
gibt's Neues?; **have you heard the ~?** hast
du das Neueste gehört?; **that's ~ to me**
das ist mir neu; **newsagent, news dealer**
(US) n Zeitungshändler(in) m(f); **news
bulletin** n Nachrichtensendung f; **news
flash** n Kurzmeldung f; **newsgroup** n
(Inform) Diskussionsforum nt, Newsgroup
f; **newsletter** n Mitteilungsblatt nt;
newspaper ['njuːspeɪpə*] n Zeitung f
New Year ['njuːˈjɪə*] n das neue Jahr;
Happy ~ (ein) frohes Neues Jahr!; (toast)

Prosit Neujahr!; **~'s Day** Neujahr nt,
Neujahrstag m; **~'s Eve** Silvesterabend m;
~'s resolution guter Vorsatz fürs neue Jahr
New York [njuːˈjɔːk] n New York nt
New Zealand [njuːˈziːlənd] n
Neuseeland nt ▷ adj neuseeländisch; **New
Zealander** n Neuseeländer(in) m(f)
next [nekst] adj nächste(r, s); **the week
after ~** übernächste Woche; **~ time I see
him** wenn ich ihn das nächste Mal sehe;
you're ~ du bist jetzt dran ▷ adv als
Nächstes; (then) dann, darauf; **~ to** neben
+dat; **~ to last** vorletzte(r, s); **~ to
impossible** nahezu unmöglich; **the ~ best
thing** das Nächstbeste; **~ door** nebenan
NHS abbr = **National Health Service**
Niagara Falls [naɪˈægrəˈfɔːlz] npl
Niagarafälle pl
nibble ['nɪbl] vt knabbern an +dat;
nibbles npl Knabberzeug nt
Nicaragua [nɪkəˈrægjʊə] n Nicaragua nt
nice [naɪs] adj nett, sympathisch; (taste,
food, drink) gut; (weather) schön; **~ and ...**
schön ...; **be ~ to him** sei nett zu ihm;
have a ~ day (US) schönen Tag noch!;
nicely adv nett; (well) gut; **that'll do
~** das genügt vollauf
nick [nɪk] vt (fam: steal) klauen; (capture)
schnappen
nickel ['nɪkl] n (Chem) Nickel nt; (US: coin)
Nickel m
nickname ['nɪkneɪm] n Spitzname m
nicotine ['nɪkətiːn] n Nikotin nt;
nicotine patch n Nikotinpflaster nt
niece [niːs] n Nichte f
Nigeria [naɪˈdʒɪərɪə] n Nigeria nt
night [naɪt] n Nacht f; (before bed) Abend
m; **good ~** gute Nacht!; **at** (o by) **~** nachts;
to have an early ~ früh schlafen gehen;
nightcap n Schlummertrunk m;
nightclub n Nachtklub m; **nightdress** n
Nachthemd nt; **nightie** ['naɪtɪ] n (fam)
Nachthemd nt
nightingale ['naɪtɪŋgeɪl] n Nachtigall f
night life ['naɪtlaɪf] n Nachtleben nt;
nightly adv (every evening) jeden Abend;
(every night) jede Nacht; **nightmare**
['naɪtmeə*] n Albtraum m; **nighttime** n
Nacht f; **at ~** nachts
nil [nɪl] n (Sport) null
Nile [naɪl] n Nil m
nine [naɪn] num neun; **~ times out of ten**
so gut wie immer ▷ n (a. bus etc) Neun f;

n

see also **eight**; **nineteen** [naɪn'tiːn] *num*
neunzehn ▷ *n* (*a. bus etc*) Neunzehn *f*; *see*
also **eight**; **nineteenth** *adj* neunzehnte(r,
s); *see also* **eighth**; **ninetieth** ['naɪntɪəθ]
adj neunzigste(r, s); *see also* **eighth**;
ninety ['naɪntɪ] *num* neunzig ▷ *n*
Neunzig *f*; *see also* **eight**; **ninth** [naɪnθ]
adj neunte(r, s) ▷ *n* (*fraction*) Neuntel *nt*;
see also **eighth**

nipple ['nɪpl] *n* Brustwarze *f*

nitrogen ['naɪtrədʒən] *n* Stickstoff *m*

○ KEYWORD

no [nəʊ] (*pl* **noes** *adv* (*opposite of yes*) nein;
to answer no (*to question*) mit Nein
antworten; (*to request*) Nein *or* nein sagen;
no thank you nein, danke
▷ *adj* (*not any*) kein(e); **I have no**
money/time ich habe kein Geld/keine
Zeit; **"no smoking"** "Rauchen
verboten"
▷ *n* Nein *nt* (*no vote*) Neinstimme *f*

nobility [nəʊ'bɪlɪtɪ] *n* Adel *m*; **noble**
['nəʊbl] *adj* (*rank*) adlig; (*quality*) edel ▷ *n*
Adlige(r) *mf*

nobody ['nəʊbədɪ] *pron* niemand;
(*emphatic*) keiner; **~ knows** keiner weiß es;
~ else sonst niemand, kein anderer ▷ *n*
Niemand *m*

no-claims bonus [nəʊ'kleɪmzbəʊnəs] *n*
Schadenfreiheitsrabatt *m*

nod [nɒd] *vi, vt* nicken; **nod off** *vi*
einnicken

noise [nɔɪz] *n* (*loud*) Lärm *m*; (*sound*)
Geräusch *nt*; **noisy** *adj* laut; (*crowd*)
lärmend

nominate ['nɒmɪneɪt] *vt* (*in election*)
aufstellen; (*appoint*) ernennen

nominative ['nɒmɪnətɪv] *n* (*Ling*)
Nominativ *m*

nominee [nɒmɪ'niː] *n* Kandidat(in) *m(f)*

non- [nɒn] *pref* Nicht-; (*with adj*) nicht-,
un-; **non-alcoholic** *adj* alkoholfrei

none [nʌn] *pron* keine(r, s); **~ of them**
keiner von ihnen; **~ of it is any use** nichts
davon ist brauchbar; **there are ~ left** es
sind keine mehr da; (*with comparative*) **to**
be ~ the wiser auch nicht schlauer sein; **I**
was ~ the worse for it es hat mir nichts
geschadet

nonentity [nɒ'nentɪtɪ] *n* Null *f*

nonetheless [nʌnðə'les] *adv*
nichtsdestoweniger, dennoch

non-event *n* Reinfall *m*; **non-existent**
adj nicht vorhanden; **non-fiction** *n*
Sachbücher *pl*; **non-iron** *adj* bügelfrei;
non-polluting *adj* schadstofffrei;
non-resident *n* **'open to ~s'** „auch für
Nichthotelgäste" **non-returnable** *adj*
~ bottle Einwegflasche *f*

nonsense ['nɒnsəns] *n* Unsinn *m*; **don't**
talk ~ red keinen Unsinn

non-smoker [nɒn'sməʊkə*] *n*
Nichtraucher(in) *m(f)*; **non-smoking** *adj*
Nichtraucher-; **~ area**
Nichtraucherbereich *m*; **non-standard** *adj*
nicht serienmäßig; **nonstop** *adj* (*train*)
durchgehend; (*flight*) Nonstop- ▷ *adv*
(*talk*) ununterbrochen; (*travel*) ohne
Unterbrechung; (*fly*) ohne
Zwischenlandung; **non-violent** *adj*
gewaltfrei

noodles ['nuːdlz] *npl* Nudeln *pl*

noon [nuːn] *n* Mittag *m*; **at ~** um 12 Uhr
mittags

no one ['nəʊwʌn] *pron* niemand;
(*emphatic*) keiner; **~ else** sonst niemand,
kein anderer

nor [nɔː] *conj* **neither ... ~ ...** weder ...
noch ...; **I don't smoke, ~ does he** ich
rauche nicht, er auch nicht

norm [nɔːm] *n* Norm *f*

normal ['nɔːməl] *adj* normal; **to get back**
to ~ sich wieder normalisieren; **normally**
adv (*usually*) normalerweise

north [nɔːθ] *n* Norden *m*; **to the ~ of**
nördlich von ▷ *adv* (*go, face*) nach Norden
▷ *adj* Nord-; **~ wind** Nordwind *m*; **North**
America *n* Nordamerika *nt*; **northbound**
adj (in) Richtung Norden; **northeast** *n*
Nordosten *m*; **to the ~ of** nordöstlich von
▷ *adv* (*go, face*) nach Nordosten ▷ *adj*
Nordost-; **northern** ['nɔːðən] *adj*
nördlich; **~ France** Nordfrankreich *nt*;
Northern Ireland *n* Nordirland *nt*; **North**
Pole *n* Nordpol *m*; **North Sea** *n* Nordsee
f; **northwards** *adv* nach Norden;
northwest *n* Nordwesten *m*; **to the ~ of**
nordwestlich von ▷ *adv* (*go, face*) nach
Nordwesten ▷ *adj* Nordwest-

Norway ['nɔːweɪ] *n* Norwegen *nt*;
Norwegian [nɔː'wiːdʒən] *adj*
norwegisch ▷ *n* (*person*) Norweger(in)
m(f); (*language*) Norwegisch *nt*

nos. *abbr* = **numbers** Nr.

nose [nəʊz] *n* Nase *f*; **nose around** *vi* herumschnüffeln; **nosebleed** *n* Nasenbluten *nt*; **nose-dive** *n* Sturzflug *m*; **to take a ~** abstürzen

nosey ['nəʊzɪ] *see* **nosy**

nostalgia [nɒ'stældʒɪə] *n* Nostalgie *f* (*for* nach); **nostalgic** *adj* nostalgisch

nostril ['nɒstrɪl] *n* Nasenloch *nt*

nosy ['nəʊzɪ] *adj* neugierig

not [nɒt] *adv* nicht; **~ a** kein; **~ one of them** kein einziger von ihnen; **he is ~ an expert** er ist kein Experte; **I told him ~ to** (**do it**) ich sagte ihm, er solle es nicht tun; **~ at all** überhaupt nicht, keineswegs; (*don't mention it*) gern geschehen; **~ yet** noch nicht

notable ['nəʊtəbl] *adj* bemerkenswert; **note** [nəʊt] *n* (*written*) Notiz *f*; (*short letter*) paar Zeilen *pl*; (*on scrap of paper*) Zettel *m*; (*comment in book etc*) Anmerkung *f*; (*bank~*) Schein *m*; (*Mus: sign*) Note *f*; (*sound*) Ton *m*; **to make a ~ of sth** sich *dat* etw notieren; **~s** (*of lecture etc*) Aufzeichnungen *pl*; **to take ~s** sich *dat* Notizen machen (*of* über +*akk*) ▷ *vt* (*notice*) bemerken (*that* dass); (*write down*) notieren; **notebook** *n* Notizbuch *nt*; (*Inform*) Notebook *nt*; **notepad** *n* Notizblock *m*; **notepaper** *n* Briefpapier *nt*

nothing ['nʌθɪŋ] *n* nichts; **~ but ...** lauter ...; **for ~** umsonst; **he thinks ~ of it** er macht sich nichts daraus

notice ['nəʊtɪs] *n* (*announcement*) Bekanntmachung *f*; (*on ~ board*) Anschlag *m*; (*attention*) Beachtung *f*; (*advance warning*) Ankündigung *f*; (*to leave job, flat etc*) Kündigung *f*; **at short ~** kurzfristig; **until further ~** bis auf weiteres; **to give sb ~** jdm kündigen; **to hand in one's ~** kündigen; **to take (no) ~ of (sth)** etw (nicht) beachten; **take no ~** kümmere dich nicht darum! ▷ *vt* bemerken; **noticeable** *adj* erkennbar; (*visible*) sichtbar; **to be ~** auffallen; **notice board** *n* Anschlagtafel *f*

notification [nəʊtɪfɪ'keɪʃən] *n* Benachrichtigung *f* (*of* von); **notify** ['nəʊtɪfaɪ] *vt* benachrichtigen (*of* von)

notion ['nəʊʃən] *n* Idee *f*

notorious [nəʊ'tɔːrɪəs] *adj* berüchtigt

nought [nɔːt] *n* Null *f*

noun [naʊn] *n* Substantiv *nt*

nourish ['nʌrɪʃ] *vt* nähren; **nourishing** *adj* nahrhaft; **nourishment** *n* Nahrung *f*

novel ['nɒvəl] *n* Roman *m* ▷ *adj* neuartig; **novelist** *n* Schriftsteller(in) *m(f)*; **novelty** *n* Neuheit *f*

November [nəʊ'vembə*] *n* November *m*; *see also* **September**

novice ['nɒvɪs] *n* Neuling *m*

now [naʊ] *adv* (*at the moment*) jetzt; (*introductory phrase*) also; **right ~** jetzt gleich; **just ~** gerade; **by ~** inzwischen; **from ~ on** ab jetzt; **~ and again** (*o then*) ab und zu; **nowadays** *adv* heutzutage

nowhere ['nəʊwɛə*] *adv* nirgends; **we're getting ~** wir kommen nicht weiter; **~ near** noch lange nicht

nozzle ['nɒzl] *n* Düse *f*

nuclear ['njuːklɪə*] *adj* (*energy etc*) Kern-; **~ power station** Kernkraftwerk *nt*; **nuclear waste** *n* Atommüll *m*

nude [njuːd] *adj* nackt ▷ *n* (*person*) Nackte(r) *mf*; (*painting etc*) Akt *m*

nudge [nʌdʒ] *vt* stupsen; **nudist** ['njuːdɪst] *n* Nudist(in) *m(f)*, FKK-Anhänger(in) *m(f)*; **nudist beach** *n* FKK-Strand *m*

nuisance ['njuːsns] *n* Ärgernis *nt*; (*person*) Plage *f*; **what a ~** wie ärgerlich!

nuke [njuːk] (*US fam*) *n* (*bomb*) Atombombe *f* ▷ *vt* eine Atombombe werfen auf +*akk*

numb [nʌm] *adj* taub, gefühllos ▷ *vt* betäuben

number ['nʌmbə*] *n* Nummer *f*; (*Math*) Zahl *f*; (*quantity*) (An)zahl *f*; **in small/large ~s** in kleinen/großen Mengen; **a ~ of times** mehrmals ▷ *vt* (*give a number to*) nummerieren; (*count*) zählen (*among* zu); **his days are ~ed** seine Tage sind gezählt; **number plate** *n* (*Brit Auto*) Nummernschild *nt*

numeral ['njuːmərəl] *n* Ziffer *f*; **numerical** [njuː'merɪkəl] *adj* numerisch; (*superiority*) zahlenmäßig; **numerous** ['njuːmərəs] *adj* zahlreich

nun [nʌn] *n* Nonne *f*

Nuremberg ['njʊərəmbɜːg] *n* Nürnberg *nt*

nurse [nɜːs] *n* Krankenschwester *f*; (*male ~*) Krankenpfleger *m* ▷ *vt* (*patient*) pflegen; (*baby*) stillen; **nursery** *n* Kinderzimmer *nt*; (*for plants*) Gärtnerei *f*; (*tree*) Baumschule *f*; **nursery rhyme** *n* Kinderreim *m*; **nursery school** *n* Kindergarten *m*; **~ teacher**

Kindergärtner(in) *m(f)*, Erzieher(in) *m(f)*;
nursing *n* (*profession*) Krankenpflege *f*;
~ home Privatklinik *f*
nut [nʌt] *n* Nuss *f*; (*Tech: for bolt*) Mutter *f*;
nutcase *n* (*fam*) Spinner(in) *m(f)*;
nutcracker *n*, **nutcrackers** *npl*
Nussknacker *m*
nutmeg ['nʌtmeg] *n* Muskat *m*,
Muskatnuss *f*
nutrient ['njuːtrɪənt] *n* Nährstoff *m*
nutrition [njuːˈtrɪʃən] *n* Ernährung *f*;
nutritious [njuːˈtrɪʃəs] *adj* nahrhaft
nuts [nʌts] (*fam*) *adj* verrückt; **to be
~ about sth** nach etw verrückt sein ▷ *npl*
(*testicles*) Eier *pl*
nutshell ['nʌtʃel] *n* Nussschale *f*; **in a
~** kurz gesagt
nutter ['nʌtə*] *n* (*fam*) Spinner(in) *m(f)*;
nutty ['nʌtɪ] *adj* (*fam*) verrückt
NW *abbr* = **northwest** NW
nylon® ['naɪlɒn] *n* Nylon® *nt* ▷ *adj*
Nylon-

O [əʊ] *n (Tel)* Null *f*

oak [əʊk] *n* Eiche *f* ▷ *adj* Eichen-

OAP *abbr = old-age pensioner* Rentner(in) *m(f)*

oar [ɔː*] *n* Ruder *nt*

oasis [əʊˈeɪsɪs] *(pl* **oases***) n* Oase *f*

oatcake [ˈəʊtkeɪk] *n* Haferkeks *m*

oath [əʊθ] *n (statement)* Eid *m*

oats [əʊts] *npl* Hafer *m; (Gastr)* Haferflocken *pl*

obedience [əˈbiːdɪəns] *n* Gehorsam *m;* **obedient** *adj* gehorsam; **obey** [əˈbeɪ] *vt, vi* gehorchen +*dat*

object [ˈɒbdʒekt] *n* Gegenstand *m; (abstract)* Objekt *nt; (purpose)* Ziel *nt* ▷ [əbˈdʒekt] *(raise objection)* Einwände erheben *(to* gegen); *(morally)* Anstoß nehmen *(to* an +*dat*); **do you ~ to my smoking?** haben Sie etwas dagegen, wenn ich rauche?; **objection** [əbˈdʒekʃən] *n* Einwand *m*

objective [əbˈdʒektɪv] *n* Ziel *nt* ▷ *adj* objektiv; **objectivity** [ɒbdʒekˈtɪvɪti] *n* Objektivität *f*

obligation [ɒblɪˈɡeɪʃən] *n (duty)* Pflicht *f; (commitment)* Verpflichtung *f;* **no ~** unverbindlich; **obligatory** [əˈblɪɡətərɪ]

adj obligatorisch; **oblige** [əˈblaɪdʒ] *vt* **to ~ sb to do sth** jdn (dazu) zwingen, etw zu tun; **he felt ~d to accept the offer** er fühlte sich verpflichtet, das Angebot anzunehmen

oblique [əˈbliːk] *adj* schräg; *(angle)* schief

oblong [ˈɒblɒŋ] *n* Rechteck *nt* ▷ *adj* rechteckig

oboe [ˈəʊbəʊ] *n* Oboe *f*

obscene [əbˈsiːn] *adj* obszön

obscure [əbˈskjʊə*] *adj* unklar; *(unknown)* unbekannt

observant [əbˈzɜːvənt] *adj* aufmerksam; **observation** [ɒbzəˈveɪʃən] *n (watching)* Beobachtung *f; (remark)* Bemerkung *f;* **observe** [əbˈzɜːv] *vt (notice)* bemerken; *(watch)* beobachten; *(customs)* einhalten

obsessed [əbˈsest] *adj* besessen *(with an idea etc* von einem Gedanken etc); **obsession** [əbˈseʃən] *n* Manie *f*

obsolete [ˈɒbsəliːt] *adj* veraltet

obstacle [ˈɒbstəkl] *n* Hindernis *nt (to* für); **to be an ~ to sth** einer Sache im Weg stehen

obstinate [ˈɒbstɪnət] *adj* hartnäckig

obstruct [əbˈstrʌkt] *vt* versperren; *(pipe)* verstopfen; *(hinder)* behindern, aufhalten; **obstruction** [əbˈstrʌkʃən] *n* Blockierung *f; (of pipe)* Verstopfung *f; (obstacle)* Hindernis *nt*

obtain [əbˈteɪn] *vt* erhalten; **obtainable** *adj* erhältlich

obvious [ˈɒbvɪəs] *adj* offensichtlich; **it was ~ to me that ...** es war mir klar, dass ...; **obviously** *adj* offensichtlich

occasion [əˈkeɪʒən] *n* Gelegenheit *f; (special event)* (großes) Ereignis; **on the ~ of** anlässlich +*gen;* **special ~** besonderer Anlass; **occasional, occasionally** *adj, adv* gelegentlich

occupant [ˈɒkjʊpənt] *n (of house)* Bewohner(in) *m(f); (of vehicle)* Insasse *m,* Insassin *f;* **occupation** [ɒkjʊˈpeɪʃən] *n* Beruf *m; (pastime)* Beschäftigung *f; (of country etc)* Besetzung *f;* **occupied** *adj (country, seat, toilet)* besetzt; *(person)* beschäftigt; **to keep sb/oneself ~** jdn/sich beschäftigen; **occupy** [ˈɒkjʊpaɪ] *vt (country)* besetzen; *(time)* beanspruchen; *(mind, person)* beschäftigen

occur [əˈkɜː*] *vi* vorkommen; **~ to sb** jdm

einfallen; **occurrence** [əˈkʌrəns] n (event) Ereignis nt; (presence) Vorkommen nt

ocean [ˈəʊʃən] n Ozean m; (US: sea) das Meer nt

o'clock [əˈklɒk] adv **5** ~ 5 Uhr; **at 10** ~ um 10 Uhr

octagon [ˈɒktəgən] n Achteck nt

October [ɒkˈtəʊbə*] n Oktober m; see also **September**

octopus [ˈɒktəpəs] n Tintenfisch m

odd [ɒd] adj (strange) sonderbar; (not even) ungerade; (one missing) einzeln; **to be the ~ one out** nicht dazugehören; **~ jobs** Gelegenheitsarbeiten pl; **odds** npl Chancen pl; **against all ~** entgegen allen Erwartungen; **~ and ends** (fam) Kleinkram pl

odometer [əʊˈdɒmətə*] n (US Auto) Meilenzähler m

odor (US), **odour** [ˈəʊdə*] n Geruch m

🔵 **KEYWORD**

of [ɒv, əv] prep **1** von +dat ≈ use of gen; **the history of Germany** die Geschichte Deutschlands; **a friend of ours** ein Freund von uns; **a boy of 10** ein 10-jähriger Junge; **that was kind of you** das war sehr freundlich von Ihnen

2 (expressing quantity, amount, dates etc): **a kilo of flour** ein Kilo Mehl; **how much of this do you need?** wie viel brauchen Sie (davon)?; **there were 3 of them** (people) sie waren zu dritt; (objects) es gab 3 (davon); **a cup of tea/vase of flowers** eine Tasse Tee/Vase mit Blumen; **the 5th of July** der 5 Juli

3 (from, out of) aus; **a bridge made of wood** eine Holzbrücke eine Brücke aus Holz

---

off [ɒf] adv (away) weg, fort; (free) frei; (switch) ausgeschaltet; (milk) sauer; **a mile ~** eine Meile entfernt; **I'll be ~ now** ich gehe jetzt; **to have the day/Monday ~** heute/Montag freihaben; **the lights are ~** die Lichter sind aus; **the concert is ~** das Konzert fällt aus; **I got 10% ~** ich habe 10% Nachlass bekommen ▷ prep (away from) von; **to jump/fall ~ the roof** vom Dach springen/fallen; **to get ~ the bus** aus dem Bus aussteigen; **he's ~ work/school** er hat frei/schulfrei; **to take £20 ~ the**

price den Preis um 20 Pfund herabsetzen

offence [əˈfens] n (crime) Straftat f; (minor) Vergehen nt; (to feelings) Kränkung f; **to cause/take ~** Anstoß erregen/nehmen; **offend** [əˈfend] vt kränken; (eye, ear) beleidigen; **offender** n Straffällige(r) mf; **offense** (US) see **offence**; **offensive** [əˈfensɪv] adj anstößig; (insulting) beleidigend; (smell) übel, abstoßend ▷ n (Mil) Offensive f

offer [ˈɒfə*] n Angebot nt; **on ~** (Comm) im Angebot ▷ vt anbieten (to sb jdm); (money, a chance etc) bieten

offhand [ɒfˈhænd] adj lässig ▷ adv (say) auf Anhieb

office [ˈɒfɪs] n Büro nt; (position) Amt nt; **doctor's ~** (US) Arztpraxis f; **office block** n Bürogebäude nt; **office hours** npl Dienstzeit f; (notice) Geschäftszeiten pl; **officer** [ˈɒfɪsə*] n (Mil) Offizier(in) m(f); (official) Polizeibeamte(r) m, Polizeibeamtin f; **office worker** [ˈɒfɪswɜːkə*] n Büroangestellte(r) mf; **official** [əˈfɪʃəl] adj offiziell; (report etc) amtlich; **~ language** Amtssprache f ▷ n Beamte(r) m, Beamtin f, Repräsentant(in) m(f)

off-licence [ˈɒflaɪsəns] n (Brit) Wein- und Spirituosenhandlung f; **off-line** adj (Inform) offline; **off-peak** adj außerhalb der Stoßzeiten; (rate, ticket) verbilligt; **off-putting** adj abstoßend, entmutigend, irritierend; **off-season** adj außerhalb der Saison

offshore [ˈɒfʃɔː*] adj küstennah, Küsten-; (oil rig) im Meer; **offside** [ˈɒfsaɪd] n (Auto) Fahrerseite f; (Sport) Abseits nt

often [ˈɒfən] adv oft; **every so ~** von Zeit zu Zeit

oil [ɔɪl] n Öl nt ▷ vt ölen; **oil level** n Ölstand m; **oil painting** n Ölgemälde nt; **oil-rig** n (Öl)bohrinsel f; **oil slick** n Ölteppich m; **oil tanker** n Öltanker m; (truck) Tankwagen m; **oily** adj ölig; (skin, hair) fettig

ointment [ˈɔɪntmənt] n Salbe f

OK, **okay** [əʊˈkeɪ] adj (fam) okay, in Ordnung; **that's ~ by** (o **with**) **me** das ist mir recht

old [əʊld] adj alt; **old age** n Alter nt; **~ pension** Rente f; **~ pensioner** Rentner(in) m(f); **old-fashioned** adj

altmodisch; **old people's home** n
Altersheim nt

olive ['ɒlɪv] n Olive f; **olive oil** n Olivenöl
nt

Olympic [əʊ'lɪmpɪk] adj olympisch; **the
~ Games, the ~s** pl die Olympischen Spiele
pl, die Olympiade

omelette ['ɒmlət] n Omelett nt

omission [əʊ'mɪʃən] n Auslassung f; **omit**
[əʊ'mɪt] vt auslassen

KEYWORD

on [ɒn] prep **1** (indicating position) auf +dat;
(with vb of motion) auf +acc; (on vertical
surface, part of body) an +dat/acc; **it's on the
table** es ist auf dem Tisch; **she put the
book on the table** sie legte das Buch auf
den Tisch; **on the left** links

2 (indicating means, method, condition etc):
on foot (go, be) zu Fuß; **on the
train/plane** (go) mit dem Zug/Flugzeug;
(be) im Zug/Flugzeug; **on the
telephone/television** am Telefon/im
Fernsehen; **to be on drugs** Drogen
nehmen; **to be on holiday/business** im
Urlaub/auf Geschäftsreise sein

3 (referring to time): **on Friday** (am)
Freitag; **on Fridays** freitags; **on June 20th**
am 20. Juni; **a week on Friday** Freitag in
einer Woche; **on arrival he ...** als er
ankam, ... er ...

4 (about, concerning) über +acc
▷ adv **1** (referring to dress) an; **she put her
boots/hat on** sie zog ihre Stiefel
an/setzte ihren Hut auf

2 (further, continuously) weiter; **to walk on**
weitergehen
▷ adj **1** (functioning, in operation: machine,
TV, light) an; (: tap) aufgedreht; (: brakes)
angezogen; **is the meeting still on?**
findet die Versammlung noch statt?;
there's a good film on es läuft ein guter
Film

2: **that's not on!** (inf: of behaviour) das
liegt nicht drin!

once [wʌns] adv (one time, in the past)
einmal; **at ~** sofort; (at the same time)
gleichzeitig; **~ more** noch einmal; **for
~** ausnahmsweise (einmal); **~ in a while**
ab und zu mal ▷ conj wenn ... einmal;

~ you've got used to it sobald Sie sich
daran gewöhnt haben

oncoming ['ɒnkʌmɪŋ] adj
entgegenkommend; **~ traffic**
Gegenverkehr m

KEYWORD

one [wʌn] num eins (with noun, referring
back to noun) ein/eine/ein; **it is one
(o'clock)** es ist eins es ist ein Uhr; **one
hundred and fifty** einhundertfünfzig
▷ adj **1** (sole) einzige(r, s); **the one book
which** das einzige Buch, welches
2 (same) derselbe/dieselbe/dasselbe;
they came in the one car sie kamen alle
in dem einen Auto
3 (indef): **one day I discovered ...** eines
Tages bemerkte ich ...
▷ pron **1** eine(r, s); **do you have a red
one?** haben Sie einen roten/eine rote/ein
rotes?; **this one** diese(r, s); **that one**
der/die/das; **which one?** welche(r, s)?;
one by one einzeln
2: **one another** einander; **do you two
ever see one another?** seht ihr beide
euch manchmal?
3 (impers) man; **one never knows** man
kann nie wissen; **to cut one's finger** sich
in den Finger schneiden

onion ['ʌnjən] n Zwiebel f

on-line ['ɒnlaɪn] adj (Inform) online;
~ banking Homebanking nt

only ['əʊnlɪ] adv nur; (with time) erst;
~ yesterday erst gestern; **he's ~ four** er
ist erst vier; **~ just arrived** gerade erst
angekommen ▷ adj einzige(r, s); **~ child**
Einzelkind nt

o.n.o. abbr = **or nearest offer** VB

onside [ɒn'saɪd] adv (Sport) nicht im
Abseits

onto ['ɒntʊ] prep auf +akk; (vertical surface)
an +akk; **to be ~ sb** jdm auf die Schliche
gekommen sein

onwards ['ɒnwədz] adv voran, vorwärts;
from today ~ von heute an, ab heute

opaque [əʊ'peɪk] adj undurchsichtig

open ['əʊpən] adj offen; **in the ~ air** im
Freien; **~ to the public** für die
Öffentlichkeit zugänglich; **the shop is
~ all day** das Geschäft hat den ganzen Tag

offen ▷ *vt* öffnen, aufmachen; (*meeting, account, new building*) eröffnen; (*road*) dem Verkehr übergeben ▷ *vi* (*door, window etc*) aufgehen, sich öffnen; (*shop, bank*) öffnen, aufmachen; (*begin*) anfangen (*with* mit); **open-air** *adj* Freiluft-; **open day** *n* Tag *m* der offenen Tür; **opening** *n* Öffnung *f*; (*beginning*) Anfang *m*; (*official, of exhibition etc*) Eröffnung *f*; (*opportunity*) Möglichkeit *f*; **~ hours** (*o times*) Öffnungszeiten *pl*; **openly** *adv* offen; **open-minded** *adj* aufgeschlossen; **open-plan** *adj* **~ office** Großraumbüro *nt*

opera ['ɒpərə] *n* Oper *f*; **opera glasses** *npl* Opernglas *nt*; **opera house** *n* Oper *f*, Opernhaus *nt*; **opera singer** *n* Opernsänger(in) *m(f)*

operate ['ɒpəreɪt] *vt* (*machine*) bedienen; (*brakes, lights*) betätigen ▷ *vi* (*machine*) laufen; (*bus etc*) verkehren (*between* zwischen); **to ~ (on sb)** (*Med*) (jdn) operieren; **operating theatre** *n* Operationssaal *m*; **operation** [ɒpə'reɪʃən] *n* (*of machine*) Bedienung *f*; (*functioning*) Funktionieren *nt*; (*Med*) Operation *f* (*on* an +*dat*); (*undertaking*) Unternehmen *nt*; **in ~** (*machine*) in Betrieb; **to have an ~** operiert werden (*for* wegen); **operator** ['ɒpəreɪtə*] *n* **to phone the ~** die Vermittlung anrufen

opinion [ə'pɪnjən] *n* Meinung *f* (*on* zu); **in my ~** meiner Meinung nach

opponent [ə'pəʊnənt] *n* Gegner(in) *m(f)*

opportunity [ɒpə'tju:nɪtɪ] *n* Gelegenheit *f*

oppose [ə'pəʊz] *vt* sich widersetzen +*dat*; (*idea*) ablehnen; **opposed** *adj* **to be ~ to sth** gegen etw sein; **as ~ to** im Gegensatz zu; **opposing** *adj* (*team*) gegnerisch; (*points of view*) entgegengesetzt

opposite ['ɒpəzɪt] *adj* (*house*) gegenüberliegend; (*direction*) entgegengesetzt; **the ~ sex** das andere Geschlecht ▷ *adv* gegenüber ▷ *prep* gegenüber; **~ me** mir gegenüber ▷ *n* Gegenteil *nt*

opposition [ɒpə'zɪʃən] *n* Widerstand *m* (*to* gegen); (*Pol*) Opposition *f*

oppress [ə'pres] *vt* unterdrücken; **oppressive** *adj* (*heat*) drückend

opt [ɒpt] *vi* **to ~ for sth** sich für etw

entscheiden; **to ~ to do sth** sich entscheiden, etw zu tun

optician [ɒp'tɪʃən] *n* Optiker(in) *m(f)*

optimist ['ɒptɪmɪst] *n* Optimist(in) *m(f)*; **optimistic** [ɒptɪ'mɪstɪk] *adj* optimistisch

optimum ['ɒptɪməm] *adj* optimal

option ['ɒpʃən] *n* Möglichkeit *f*; (*Comm*) Option *f*; **to have no ~** keine Wahl haben; **optional** *adj* freiwillig; **~ extras** (*Auto*) Extras *pl*

or [ɔ:*] *conj* oder; (*otherwise*) sonst; (*after neg*) noch; **hurry up, ~** (*else*) **we'll be late** beeil dich, sonst kommen wir zu spät

oral ['ɔ:rəl] *adj* mündlich; **~ sex** Oralverkehr *m* ▷ *n* (*exam*) Mündliche(s) *nt*

orange ['ɒrɪndʒ] *n* Orange *f* ▷ *adj* orangefarben; **orange juice** *n* Orangensaft *m*

orbit ['ɔ:bɪt] *n* Umlaufbahn *f*; **to be out of ~** (*fam*) nicht zu erreichen sein ▷ *vt* umkreisen

orchard ['ɔ:tʃəd] *n* Obstgarten *m*

orchestra ['ɔ:kɪstrə] *n* Orchester *nt*; (*US Theat*) Parkett *nt*

orchid ['ɔ:kɪd] *n* Orchidee *f*

ordeal [ɔ:'di:l] *n* Tortur *f*; (*emotional*) Qual *f*

order ['ɔ:də*] *n* (*sequence*) Reihenfolge *f*; (*good arrangement*) Ordnung *f*; (*command*) Befehl *m*; (*Jur*) Anordnung *f*; (*condition*) Zustand *m*; (*Comm*) Bestellung *f*; **out of ~** (*not functioning*) außer Betrieb; (*unsuitable*) nicht angebracht; **in ~** (*items*) richtig geordnet; (*all right*) in Ordnung; **in ~ to do sth** um etw zu tun ▷ *vt* (*arrange*) ordnen; (*command*) befehlen; **to ~ sb to do sth** jdm befehlen, etw zu tun; (*food, product*) bestellen; **order form** *n* Bestellschein *m*

ordinary ['ɔ:dnrɪ] *adj* gewöhnlich, normal; (*average*) durchschnittlich

ore [ɔ:*] *n* Erz *nt*

organ ['ɔ:gən] *n* (*Mus*) Orgel *f*; (*Anat*) Organ *nt*

organic [ɔ:'gænɪk] *adj* organisch; (*farming, vegetables*) Bio-, Öko-; **~ farmer** Biobauer *m*, Biobäuerin *f*; **~ food** Biokost *f*

organization [ɔ:gənaɪ'zeɪʃən] *n* Organisation *f*; (*arrangement*) Ordnung *f*; **organize** ['ɔ:gənaɪz] *vt* organisieren; **organizer** *n* (elektronisches) Notizbuch

orgasm ['ɔ:gæzəm] *n* Orgasmus *m*

orgy ['ɔːdʒɪ] n Orgie f
oriental [ɔːrɪ'entəl] adj orientalisch
orientation ['ɔːrɪenteɪʃən] n
Orientierung f
origin ['ɒrɪdʒɪn] n Ursprung m; (of person)
Herkunft f; **original** [ə'rɪdʒɪnl] adj (first)
ursprünglich; (painting) original; (idea)
originell ▷ n Original nt; **originality**
[ərɪdʒɪ'nælɪtɪ] n Originalität f; **originally**
adv ursprünglich
Orkneys ['ɔːknɪz] npl, **Orkney Islands**
npl Orkneyinseln pl
ornament ['ɔːnəmənt] n
Schmuckgegenstand m; **ornamental**
[ɔːnə'mentl] adj dekorativ
orphan ['ɔːfən] n Waise f, Waisenkind nt;
orphanage ['ɔːfənɪdʒ] n Waisenhaus nt
orthodox ['ɔːθədɒks] adj orthodox
orthopaedic, **orthopedic** (US)
[ɔːθəʊ'piːdɪk] adj orthopädisch
ostentatious [ɒsten'teɪʃəs] adj protzig
ostrich ['ɒstrɪtʃ] n (Zool) Strauß m
other ['ʌðə*] adj, pron andere(r, s); **any**
~ questions? sonst noch Fragen?; **the**
~ day neulich; **every ~ day** jeden zweiten
Tag; **any person ~ than him** alle außer
ihm; **someone/something or ~** irgend
jemand/irgend etwas; **otherwise** adv
sonst; (differently) anders
OTT adj abbr = **over the top** übertrieben
otter ['ɒtə*] n Otter m
ought [ɔːt] vb aux (obligation) sollte;
(probability) dürfte; (stronger) müsste; **you**
~ to do that Sie sollten das tun; **he ~ to**
win er müsste gewinnen; **that ~ to do** das
müsste (o dürfte) reichen
ounce [aʊns] n Unze f (28,35 g)
our [aʊə*] adj unser; **ours** pron unsere(r,
s); **this is ~** das gehört uns; **a friend of**
~ ein Freund von uns; **ourselves** pron
(reflexive) uns; **we enjoyed ~** wir haben uns
amüsiert; **we've got the house to ~** wir
haben das Haus für uns; (emphatic) **we did**
it ~ wir haben es selbst gemacht; **(all) by**
~ allein
out [aʊt] adv hinaus/heraus; (not indoors)
draußen; (not at home) nicht zu Hause; (not
alight) aus; (unconscious) bewusstlos;
(published) herausgekommen; (results)
bekannt gegeben; **have you been ~ yet?**
waren Sie schon draußen?; **I was ~ when**
they called ich war nicht da, als sie
vorbeikamen; **to be ~ and about**

unterwegs sein; **the sun is ~** die Sonne
scheint; **the fire is ~** das Feuer ist
ausgegangen; (wrong) **the calculation is**
(way) ~ die Kalkulation stimmt (ganz und
gar) nicht; **they're ~ to get him** sie sind
hinter ihm her
outback ['aʊtbæk] n (in Australia) **the**
~ das Hinterland
outboard ['aʊtbɔːd] adj **~ motor**
Außenbordmotor m
outbreak ['aʊtbreɪk] n Ausbruch m
outburst ['aʊtbɜːst] n Ausbruch m
outcome ['aʊtkʌm] n Ergebnis nt
outcry ['aʊtkraɪ] n (public protest)
Protestwelle f (against gegen)
outdo [aʊt'duː] irr vt übertreffen
outdoor ['aʊtdɔː*] adj Außen-; (Sport) im
Freien; **~ swimming pool** Freibad nt;
outdoors [aʊt'dɔːz] adv draußen, im
Freien
outer ['aʊtə*] adj äußere(r, s); **outer**
space n Weltraum m
outfit ['aʊtfɪt] n Ausrüstung f; (clothes)
Kleidung f
outgoing ['aʊtgəʊɪŋ] adj kontaktfreudig
outgrow [aʊt'grəʊ] irr vt (clothes)
herauswachsen aus
outing ['aʊtɪŋ] n Ausflug m
outlet ['aʊtlet] n Auslass m, Abfluss m;
(US) Steckdose f; (shop) Verkaufsstelle f
outline ['aʊtlaɪn] n Umriss m; (summary)
Abriss m
outlive [aʊt'lɪv] vt überleben
outlook ['aʊtlʊk] n Aussicht(en) f(pl);
(prospects) Aussichten pl; (attitude)
Einstellung f (on zu)
outnumber [aʊt'nʌmbə*] vt
zahlenmäßig überlegen sein +dat; **~ed**
zahlenmäßig unterlegen
out of ['aʊtɒv] prep (motion, motive, origin)
aus; (position, away from) außerhalb +gen;
~ danger/sight/breath außer
Gefahr/Sicht/Atem; **made ~ wood** aus
Holz gemacht; **we are ~ bread** wir haben
kein Brot mehr; **out-of-date** adj veraltet;
out-of-the-way adj abgelegen
outpatient ['aʊtpeɪʃənt] n ambulanter
Patient, ambulante Patientin
output ['aʊtpʊt] n Produktion f; (of
engine) Leistung f; (Inform) Ausgabe f
outrage ['aʊtreɪdʒ] n (great anger)
Empörung f (at über); (wicked deed)
Schandtat f; (crime) Verbrechen nt;

(*indecency*) Skandal *m*; **outrageous** [aʊt'reɪdʒəs] *adj* unerhört; (*clothes, behaviour etc*) unmöglich, schrill

outright ['aʊtraɪt] *adv* (*killed*) sofort ▷ *adj* total; (*denial*) völlig; (*winner*) unbestritten

outside [aʊt'saɪd] *n* Außenseite *f*; **on the ~** außen ▷ *adj* äußere(r, s), Außen-; (*chance*) sehr gering ▷ *adv* außen; **to go ~** nach draußen gehen ▷ *prep* außerhalb +*gen*; **outsider** *n* Außenseiter(in) *m(f)*

outsize ['aʊtsaɪz] *adj* übergroß; (*clothes*) in Übergröße

outskirts ['aʊtskɜːts] *npl* (*of town*) Stadtrand *m*

outstanding [aʊt'stændɪŋ] *adj* hervorragend; (*debts etc*) ausstehend

outward ['aʊtwəd] *adj* äußere(r, s); **~ journey** Hinfahrt *f*; **outwardly** *adv* nach außen hin; **outwards** *adv* nach außen

oval ['əʊvəl] *adj* oval

ovary ['əʊvərɪ] *n* Eierstock *m*

ovation [əʊ'veɪʃən] *n* Ovation *f*, Applaus *m*

oven ['ʌvn] *n* Backofen *m*; **oven glove** *n* Topfhandschuh *m*; **ovenproof** *adj* feuerfest; **oven-ready** *adj* bratfertig

over ['əʊvə*] *prep* (*position*) über +*dat*; (*motion*) über +*akk*; **they spent a long time ~ it** sie haben lange dazu gebraucht; **from all ~ England** aus ganz England; **~ £20** mehr als 20 Pfund; **~ the phone/radio** am Telefon/im Radio; **to talk ~ a glass of wine** sich bei einem Glas Wein unterhalten; **~ and above this** darüber hinaus; **~ the summer** während des Sommers ▷ *adv* (*across*) hinüber/herüber; (*finished*) vorbei; (*match, play etc*) zu Ende; (*left*) übrig; (*more*) mehr; **~ there/in America** da drüben/drüben in Amerika; **~ to you** Sie sind dran; **it's (all) ~ between us** es ist aus zwischen uns; **~ and ~ again** immer wieder; **to start (all) ~ again** noch einmal von vorn anfangen; **children of 8 and ~** Kinder von 8 Jahren und darüber

over- ['əʊvə*] *pref* über-

overall ['əʊvərɔːl] *n* (*Brit*) Kittel *m* ▷ *adj* (*situation*) allgemein; (*length*) Gesamt-; **~ majority** absolute Mehrheit ▷ *adv* insgesamt; **overalls** *npl* Overall *m*

overboard ['əʊvəbɔːd] *adv* über Bord

overbooked [əʊvə'bʊkt] *adj* überbucht; **overbooking** *n* Überbuchung *f*

overcharge [əʊvə'tʃɑːdʒ] *vt* zu viel verlangen von

overcoat ['əʊvəkəʊt] *n* Wintermantel *m*

overcome [əʊvə'kʌm] *irr vt* überwinden; **~ by sleep/emotion** von Schlaf/Rührung übermannt; **we shall ~** wir werden siegen

overcooked [əʊvə'kʊkt] *adj* zu lange gekocht; (*meat*) zu lange gebraten

overcrowded [əʊvə'kraʊdɪd] *adj* überfüllt

overdo [əʊvə'duː] *irr vt* übertreiben; **you're ~ing it** du übertreibst es; (*doing too much*) Sie übernehmen sich; **overdone** *adj* übertrieben; (*food*) zu lange gekocht; (*meat*) zu lange gebraten

overdose ['əʊvədəʊs] *n* Überdosis *f*

overdraft ['əʊvədrɑːft] *n* Kontoüberziehung *f*; **overdrawn** [əʊvə'drɔːn] *adj* überzogen

overdue [əʊvə'djuː] *adj* überfällig

overestimate [əʊvər'estɪmeɪt] *vt* überschätzen

overexpose [əʊvərɪks'pəʊz] *vt* (*Foto*) überbelichten

overflow [əʊvə'fləʊ] *vi* überlaufen

overhead ['əʊvəhed] *adj* (*Aviat*) **~ locker** Gepäckfach *nt*; **~ projector** Overheadprojektor *m*; **~ railway** Hochbahn *f* ▷ [əʊvə'hed] *adv* oben

overhear [əʊvə'hɪə*] *irr vt* zufällig mit anhören

overheat [əʊvə'hiːt] *vi* (*engine*) heiß laufen

overjoyed [əʊvə'dʒɔɪd] *adj* überglücklich (*at* über)

overland ['əʊvəlænd] *adj* Überland- ▷ [əʊvə'lænd] *adv* (*travel*) über Land

overlap [əʊvə'læp] *vi* (*dates etc*) sich überschneiden; (*objects*) sich teilweise decken

overload [əʊvə'ləʊd] *vt* überladen

overlook [əʊvə'lʊk] *vt* (*view from above*) überblicken; (*not notice*) übersehen; (*pardon*) hinwegsehen über +*akk*

overnight [əʊvə'naɪt] *adj* (*journey, train*) Nacht-; **~ bag** Reisetasche *f*; **~ stay** Übernachtung *f* ▷ *adv* über Nacht

overpass ['əʊvəpɑːs] *n* Überführung *f*

overpay [əʊvə'peɪ] *vt* überbezahlen

overrule [əʊvə'ruːl] *vt* verwerfen; (*decision*) aufheben

overseas [əʊvəˈsiːz] *adj* Übersee-; *(fam)* Auslands-; **~ students** Studenten aus Übersee ▷ *adv* *(go)* nach Übersee; *(live, work)* in Übersee

oversee [əʊvəˈsiː] *irr vt* beaufsichtigen

overshadow [əʊvəˈʃædəʊ] *vt* überschatten

overshoot [əʊvəˈʃuːt] *irr vt* *(runway)* hinausschießen über +*akk*; *(turning)* vorbeifahren +*dat*

oversight [ˈəʊvəsaɪt] *n* Versehen *nt*

oversimplify [əʊvəˈsɪmplɪfaɪ] *vt* zu sehr vereinfachen

oversleep [əʊvəˈsliːp] *irr vi* verschlafen

overtake [əʊvəˈteɪk] *irr vt, vi* überholen

overtime [ˈəʊvətaɪm] *n* Überstunden *pl*

overturn [əʊvəˈtɜːn] *vt, vi* umkippen

overweight [əʊvəˈweɪt] *adj* **to be ~** Übergewicht haben

overwhelm [əʊvəˈwelm] *vt* überwältigen; **overwhelming** *adj* überwältigend

overwork [əʊvəˈwɜːk] *n* Überarbeitung *f* ▷ *vi* sich überarbeiten; **overworked** *adj* überarbeitet

owe [əʊ] *vt* schulden; **to ~ sth to sb** *(money)* jdm etw schulden; *(favour etc)* jdm etw verdanken; **how much do I ~ you?** was bin ich Ihnen schuldig?; **owing to** *prep* wegen +*gen*

owl [aʊl] *n* Eule *f*

own [əʊn] *vt* besitzen ▷ *adj* eigen; **on one's ~** allein; **he has a flat of his ~** er hat eine eigene Wohung; **own up** *vi* **to ~ to sth** etw zugeben; **owner** *n* Besitzer(in) *m(f)*; *(of business)* Inhaber(in) *m(f)*; **ownership** *n* Besitz *m*; **under new ~** unter neuer Leitung

ox [ɒks] *(pl oxen) n* Ochse *m*; **oxtail** [ˈɒksteɪl] *n* Ochsenschwanz *m*; **~ soup** Ochsenschwanzsuppe *f*; **oxygen** [ˈɒksɪdʒən] *n* Sauerstoff *m*

oyster [ˈɔɪstə*] *n* Auster *f*

oz *abbr* = **ounces** Unzen *pl*

Oz [ˈɒz] *n (fam)* Australien *nt*

ozone [ˈəʊzəʊn] *n* Ozon *nt*; **~ layer** Ozonschicht *f*

o

p *abbr* = **page** S.; *abbr* = **penny, pence**
p.a. *abbr* = **per annum**
pace [peɪs] *n* (*speed*) Tempo *nt*; (*step*)
Schritt *m*; **pacemaker** *n* (*Med*)
Schrittmacher *m*
Pacific [pə'sɪfɪk] *n* **the ~ (Ocean)** der
Pazifik; **Pacific Standard Time** *n*
pazifische Zeit
pacifier ['pæsɪfaɪə] *n* (*US: for baby*)
Schnuller *m*
pack [pæk] *n* (*of cards*) Spiel *nt*; (*esp US: of
cigarettes*) Schachtel *f*; (*gang*) Bande *f*; (*US:
backpack*) Rucksack *m* ▷ *vt* (*case*) packen;
(*clothes*) einpacken ▷ *vi* (*for holiday*)
packen; **pack in** *vt* (*Brit fam: job*)
hinschmeißen; **package** ['pækɪdʒ] *n* (*a.
Inform, fig*) Paket *nt*; **package deal** *n*
Pauschalangebot *nt*; **package holiday**,
package tour *n* Pauschalreise *f*;
packaging *n* (*material*) Verpackung *f*;
packed lunch *n* (*Brit*) Lunchpaket *nt*;
packet *n* Päckchen *nt*; (*of cigarettes*)
Schachtel *f*
pad [pæd] *n* (*of paper*) Schreibblock *m*;
(*padding*) Polster *nt*; **padded envelope** *n*
wattierter Umschlag; **padding** *n*
(*material*) Polsterung *f*

paddle ['pædl] *n* (*for boat*) Paddel *nt* ▷ *vi*
(*in boat*) paddeln; **paddling pool** *n* (*Brit*)
Planschbecken *nt*
padlock ['pædlɒk] *n* Vorhängeschloss *nt*
page [peɪdʒ] *n* (*of book etc*) Seite *f*
pager ['peɪdʒə*] *n* Piepser *m*
paid [peɪd] *pt, pp of* **pay** ▷ *adj* bezahlt
pain [peɪn] *n* Schmerz *m*; **to be in**
~ Schmerzen haben; **she's a (real) ~** sie
nervt; **painful** *adj* (*physically*)
schmerzhaft; (*embarrassing*) peinlich;
painkiller *n* schmerzstillendes Mittel
painstaking *adj* sorgfältig
paint [peɪnt] *n* Farbe *f* ▷ *vt* anstreichen;
(*picture*) malen; **paintbrush** *n* Pinsel *m*;
painter *n* Maler(in) *m(f)*; **painting** *n*
(*picture*) Bild *nt*, Gemälde *nt*
pair [peə*] *n* Paar *nt*; **a ~ of shoes** ein Paar
Schuhe; **a ~ of scissors** eine Schere; **a ~ of**
trousers eine Hose
pajamas [pə'dʒɑːməz] *npl* (*US*)
Schlafanzug *m*
Pakistan [pɑːkɪ'stɑːn] *n* Pakistan *nt*
pal [pæl] *n* (*fam*) Kumpel *m*
palace ['pæləs] *n* Palast *m*
pale [peɪl] *adj* (*face*) blass, bleich; (*colour*)
hell
palm [pɑːm] *n* (*of hand*) Handfläche *f*;
~ (tree) Palme *f*; **palmtop (computer)** *n*
Palmtop(computer) *m*
pamper ['pæmpə*] *vt* verhätscheln
pan [pæn] *n* (*saucepan*) Topf *m*; (*frying pan*)
Pfanne *f*; **pancake** ['pænkeɪk] *n*
Pfannkuchen *m*; **Pancake Day** *n* (*Brit*)
Fastnachtsdienstag *m*
panda ['pændə] *n* Panda *m*
pane [peɪn] *n* Scheibe *f*
panel ['pænl] *n* (*of wood*) Tafel *f*; (*in*
discussion) Diskussionsteilnehmer *pl*
panic ['pænɪk] *n* Panik *f* ▷ *vi* in Panik
geraten; **panicky** ['pænɪkɪ] *adj* panisch
pansy ['pænzɪ] *n* (*flower*) Stiefmütterchen
nt
panties ['pæntɪz] *npl* (Damen)slip *m*
pantomime ['pæntəmaɪm] *n* (*Brit*) *um die*
Weihnachtszeit aufgeführte Märchenkomödie
pants [pænts] *npl* Unterhose *f*; (*esp US:*
trousers) Hose *f*
pantyhose ['pæntɪhəʊz] *npl* (*US*)
Strumpfhose *f*; **panty-liner** *n* Slipeinlage
f
paper ['peɪpə*] *n* Papier *nt*; (*newspaper*)
Zeitung *f*; (*exam*) Klausur *f*; (*for reading at*

conference) Referat nt; **~s** pl (identity papers)
Papiere pl; **~ bag** Papiertüte f; **~ cup**
Pappbecher m ▷ vt (wall) tapezieren;
paperback n Taschenbuch nt; **paper clip**
n Büroklammer f; **paper feed** n (of printer)
Papiereinzug m; **paper round** n **to do a**
~ Zeitungen austragen; **paperwork** n
Schreibarbeit f

parachute ['pærəʃuːt] n Fallschirm m
▷ vi abspringen

paracetamol [pærə'siːtəmɒl] n (tablet)
Paracetamoltablette f

parade [pə'reɪd] n (procession) Umzug m;
(Mil) Parade f ▷ vi vorbeimarschieren

paradise ['pærədaɪs] n Paradies nt

paragliding ['pærəɡlaɪdɪŋ] n
Gleitschirmfliegen nt

paragraph ['pærəɡrɑːf] n Absatz m

parallel ['pærəlel] adj parallel ▷ n (Math,
fig) Parallele f

paralyze ['pærəlaɪz] vt lähmen; (fig)
lahm legen

paranoid ['pærənɔɪd] adj paranoid

paraphrase ['pærəfreɪz] vt umschreiben;
(sth spoken) anders ausdrücken

parasailing ['pærəseɪlɪŋ] n Parasailing nt

parasol ['pærəsɒl] n Sonnenschirm m

parcel ['pɑːsl] n Paket nt

pardon ['pɑːdn] n (Jur) Begnadigung f;
~ me/I beg your ~ verzeihen Sie bitte;
(objection) aber ich bitte Sie; **I beg your ~?/**
~ me? wie bitte?

parent ['peərənt] n Elternteil m; **~s** pl
Eltern pl; **~s-in-law** pl Schwiegereltern pl;
parental [pə'rentl] adj elterlich, Eltern-

parish ['pærɪʃ] n Gemeinde f

park [pɑːk] n Park m ▷ vt, vi parken;
parking n Parken nt; **'no ~'** „Parken
verboten"; **parking brake** n (US)
Handbremse f; **parking disc** n
Parkscheibe f; **parking fine** n Geldbuße f
für falsches Parken; **parking lights** npl
(US) Standlicht nt; **parking lot** n (US)
Parkplatz m; **parking meter** n Parkuhr f;
parking place, parking space n
Parkplatz m; **parking ticket** n
Strafzettel m

parliament ['pɑːləmənt] n Parlament nt

parrot ['pærət] n Papagei m

parsley ['pɑːslɪ] n Petersilie f

parsnip ['pɑːsnɪp] n Pastinake f
(längliches, weißes Wurzelgemüse)

part [pɑːt] n Teil m; (of machine) Teil nt;

(Theat) Rolle f; (US: in hair) Scheitel m; **to**
take ~ teilnehmen (in an +dat); **for the**
most ~ zum größten Teil ▷ adj Teil- ▷ vt
(separate) trennen; (hair) scheiteln ▷ vi
(people) sich trennen

partial ['pɑːʃəl] adj (incomplete) teilweise,
Teil-; (biased) parteiisch

participant [pɑː'tɪsɪpənt] n
Teilnehmer(in) m(f); **participate**
[pɑː'tɪsɪpeɪt] vi teilnehmen (in an +dat)

particular [pə'tɪkjʊlə*] adj (specific)
bestimmt; (exact) genau; (fussy) eigen; **in**
~ insbesondere ▷ n **~s** pl (details)
Einzelheiten pl; (about person) Personalien
pl; **particularly** adv besonders

parting ['pɑːtɪŋ] n (farewell) Abschied m;
(Brit: in hair) Scheitel m

partly ['pɑːtlɪ] adv teilweise

partner ['pɑːtnə*] n Partner(in) m(f);
partnership n Partnerschaft f

partridge ['pɑːtrɪdʒ] n Rebhuhn nt

part-time ['pɑːt'taɪm] adj Teilzeit- ▷ adv
to work ~ Teilzeit arbeiten

party ['pɑːtɪ] n (celebration) Party f;
(Pol, Jur) Partei f; (group) Gruppe f ▷ vi
feiern

pass [pɑːs] vt (on foot) vorbeigehen an
+dat; (in car etc) vorbeifahren an +dat;
(time) verbringen; (exam) bestehen; (law)
verabschieden; **to ~ sth to sb, to ~ sb sth**
jdm etw reichen; **to ~ the ball to sb** jdm
den Ball zuspielen ▷ vi (on foot)
vorbeigehen; (in car etc) vorbeifahren;
(years) vergehen; (in exam) bestehen ▷ n
(document) Ausweis m; (Sport) Pass m; **pass**
away vi (die) verscheiden; **pass by** vi (on
foot) vorbeigehen; (in car etc) vorbeifahren
▷ vt (on foot) vorbeigehen an +dat; (in car
etc) vorbeifahren an +dat; **pass on** vt
weitergeben (to an +akk); (disease)
übertragen (to auf +akk); **pass out** vi
(faint) ohnmächtig werden; **pass round** vt
herumreichen

passage ['pæsɪdʒ] n (corridor) Gang m; (in
book, music) Passage f; **passageway** n
Durchgang m

passenger ['pæsɪndʒə*] n Passagier(in)
m(f); (on bus) Fahrgast m; (on train)
Reisende(r) mf; (in car) Mitfahrer(in) m(f)

passer-by ['pɑːsə'baɪ] (pl passers-by) n
Passant(in) m(f)

passion ['pæʃən] n Leidenschaft f;
passionate ['pæʃənɪt] adj

leidenschaftlich; **passion fruit** n
Passionsfrucht

passive ['pæsɪv] adj passiv ▷ n ~ (**voice**)
(Ling) Passiv nt

passport ['pɑːspɔːt] n (Reise)pass m;
passport control n Passkontrolle f

password ['pɑːswɜːd] n (Inform)
Passwort nt

past [pɑːst] n Vergangenheit f ▷ adv (by)
vorbei; **it's five ~** es ist fünf nach ▷ adj
(years) vergangen; (president etc) ehemalig;
in the ~ two months in den letzten zwei
Monaten ▷ prep (telling time) nach; **it's
half ~ 10** es ist halb 11; **to go ~ sth** an etw
dat vorbeigehen/-fahren

pasta ['pæstə] n Nudeln pl

paste [peɪst] vt (stick) kleben; (Inform)
einfügen ▷ n (glue) Kleister m

pastime ['pɑːstaɪm] n Zeitvertreib m

pastry ['peɪstrɪ] n Teig m; (cake)
Stückchen

pasty ['pæstɪ] n (Brit) Pastete f

patch [pætʃ] n (area) Fleck m; (for mending)
Flicken ▷ vt flicken; **patchy** adj (uneven)
ungleichmäßig

pâté ['pæteɪ] n Pastete f

paternal [pə'tɜːnl] adj väterlich;
~ grandmother Großmutter f
väterlicherseits; **paternity leave**
[pə'tɜːnɪtɪliːv] n Elternzeit f (des Vaters)

path [pɑːθ] n (a. Inform) Pfad m; (a. fig)
Weg m

pathetic [pə'θetɪk] adj (bad) kläglich,
erbärmlich; **it's ~** es ist zum Heulen

patience ['peɪʃəns] n Geduld f; (Brit Cards)
Patience f; **patient** adj geduldig ▷ n
Patient(in) m(f)

patio ['pætɪəʊ] n Terrasse f

patriotic [pætrɪ'ɒtɪk] adj patriotisch

patrol car [pə'trəʊlkɑː*] n Streifenwagen
m; **patrolman** (pl -men) n (US)
Streifenpolizist m

patron ['peɪtrən] n (sponsor) Förderer m,
Förderin f; (in shop) Kunde m, Kundin f

patronize ['pætrənaɪz] vt (treat
condescendingly) von oben herab
behandeln; **patronizing** adj (attitude)
herablassend

pattern ['pætən] n Muster nt

pause [pɔːz] n Pause f ▷ vi (speaker)
innehalten

pavement n (Brit) Bürgersteig m; (US)
Pflaster nt

pay [peɪ] (**paid, paid**) vt bezahlen; **he
paid (me) £20 for it** er hat (mir) 20 Pfund
dafür gezahlt; **to ~ attention** Acht geben
(to auf +akk); **to ~ sb a visit** jdn besuchen
▷ vi zahlen; (be profitable) sich bezahlt
machen; **to ~ for sth** etw bezahlen ▷ n
Bezahlung f, Lohn m; **pay back** vt (money)
zurückzahlen; **pay in** vt (into account)
einzahlen; **payable** adj zahlbar; (due)
fällig; **payday** n Zahltag m; **payee** [peɪ'iː]
n Zahlungsempfänger(in) m(f); **payment**
n Bezahlung f; (money) Zahlung f;
pay-per-view n (TV) Pay-per-View-; **pay
phone** n Münzfernsprecher m; **pay TV** n
Pay-TV nt

PC abbr = **personal computer** PC
m; abbr = **politically correct** politisch
korrekt

PDA abbr = **personal digital assistant**
PDA m

PE abbr = **physical education** (school)
Sport m

pea [piː] n Erbse f

peace [piːs] n Frieden m; **peaceful** adj
friedlich

peach [piːtʃ] n Pfirsich m

peacock ['piːkɒk] n Pfau m

peak [piːk] n (of mountain) Gipfel m; (fig)
Höhepunkt m; **peak period** n Stoßzeit f;
(season) Hochsaison

peanut ['piːnʌt] n Erdnuss f; **peanut
butter** n Erdnussbutter f

pear [peə*] n Birne f

pearl [pɜːl] n Perle f

pebble ['pebl] n Kiesel m

pecan [prɪ'kæn] n Pekannuss

peck [pek] vt, vi picken; **peckish** adj (Brit
fam) ein bisschen hungrig

peculiar [prɪ'kjuːlɪə*] adj (odd) seltsam;
~ to charakteristisch für; **peculiarity**
[pɪkjʊlɪ'ærɪtɪ] n (singular quality)
Besonderheit f; (strangeness)
Eigenartigkeit f

pedal ['pedl] n Pedal nt

pedestrian [prɪ'destrɪən] n Fußgänger(in)
m(f); **pedestrian crossing** n
Fußgängerüberweg m

pee [piː] vi (fam) pinkeln

peel [piːl] n Schale f ▷ vt schälen ▷ vi
(paint etc) abblättern; (skin etc) sich
schälen

peer [pɪə*] n Gleichaltrige(r) mf ▷ vi
starren

peg [peg] *n* (*for coat etc*) Haken *m*; (*for tent*) Hering *m*; (**clothes**) ~ (Wäsche)klammer *f*

pelvis ['pelvɪs] *n* Becken *nt*

pen [pen] *n* (*ball-point*) Kuli *m*, Kugelschreiber; (*fountain* ~) Füller *m*

penalize ['piːnəlaɪz] *vt* (*punish*) bestrafen; **penalty** ['penltɪ] *n* (*punishment*) Strafe *f*; (*in football*) Elfmeter *m*

pence [pens] *pl of* **penny**

pencil ['pensl] *n* Bleistift *m*; **pencil sharpener** *n* (Bleistift)spitzer *m*

penetrate ['penɪtreɪt] *vt* durchdringen; (*enter into*) eindringen in +*akk*

penfriend ['penfrend] *n* Brieffreund(in) *m(f)*

penguin ['peŋgwɪn] *n* Pinguin *m*

penicillin [penɪ'sɪlɪn] *n* Penizillin *nt*

peninsula [pɪ'nɪnsjʊlə] *n* Halbinsel *f*

penis ['piːnɪs] *n* Penis *m*

penknife ['pennaɪf] (*pl* **penknives**) *n* Taschenmesser *nt*

penny ['penɪ] (*pl* **pence** *o* **pennies**) *n* (*Brit*) Penny *m*; (*US*) Centstück *nt*

pension ['penʃən] *n* Rente *f*; (*for civil servants, executives etc*) Pension *f*; **pensioner** *n* Rentner(in) *m(f)*; **pension plan, pension scheme** *n* Rentenversicherung *f*

penultimate [pɪ'nʌltɪmət] *adj* vorletzte(r, s)

people ['piːpl] *npl* (*persons*) Leute *pl*; (*von Staat*) Volk *nt*; (*inhabitants*) Bevölkerung *f*; **people carrier** *n* Minivan *m*

pepper ['pepə*] *n* Pfeffer *m*; (*vegetable*) Paprika *m*; **peppermint** *n* (*sweet*) Pfefferminz *m*

per [pɜː*] *prep* pro; ~ **annum** pro Jahr; ~ **cent** Prozent *nt*

percentage [pə'sentɪdʒ] *n* Prozentsatz *m*

perceptible [pə'septəbl] *adj* wahrnehmbar

percolator ['pɜːkəleɪtə*] *n* Kaffeemaschine *f*

percussion [pɜː'kʌʃən] *n* (*Mus*) Schlagzeug *nt*

perfect ['pɜːfɪkt] *adj* perfekt; (*utter*) völlig ▷ [pə'fekt] *vt* vervollkommnen; **perfectly** *adv* perfekt; (*utterly*) völlig

perform [pə'fɔːm] *vt* (*task*) ausführen; (*play*) aufführen; (*Med: operation*) durchführen ▷ *vi* (*Theat*) auftreten;

performance *n* (*show*) Vorstellung *f*; (*efficiency*) Leistung *f*

perfume ['pɜːfjuːm] *n* Duft *m*; (*substance*) Parfüm *nt*

perhaps [pə'hæps] *adv* vielleicht

peril ['perɪl] *n* Gefahr *f*

period ['pɪərɪəd] *n* (*length of time*) Zeit *f*; (*in history*) Zeitalter *nt*; (*school*) Stunde *f*; (*Med*) Periode *f*; (*US: full stop*) Punkt *m*; **for a ~ of three years** für einen Zeitraum von drei Jahren; **periodical** [pɪərɪ'ɒdɪkəl] *n* Zeitschrift *f*

peripheral [pə'rɪfərəl] *n* (*Inform*) Peripheriegerät *nt*

perish ['perɪʃ] *vi* (*die*) umkommen; (*material*) verderben

perjury ['pɜːdʒərɪ] *n* Meineid *m*

perm [pɜːm] *n* Dauerwelle *f*

permanent, permanently ['pɜːmənənt, -lɪ] *adj, adv* ständig

permission [pə'mɪʃən] *n* Erlaubnis *f*; **permit** ['pɜːmɪt] *n* Genehmigung *f* ▷ [pə'mɪt] *vt* erlauben, zulassen; **to ~ sb to do sth** jdm erlauben, etw zu tun

persecute ['pɜːsɪkjuːt] *vt* verfolgen

perseverance [pɜːsɪ'vɪərəns] *n* Ausdauer *f*

Persian ['pɜːʃən] *adj* persisch

persist [pə'sɪst] *vi* (*in belief etc*) bleiben (*in* bei); (*rain, smell*) andauern; **persistent** *adj* beharrlich

person ['pɜːsn] *n* Mensch *m*; (*in official context*) Person *f*; **in ~** persönlich; **personal** *adj* persönlich; (*private*) privat; **personality** [pɜːsə'nælɪtɪ] *n* Persönlichkeit *f*; **personal organizer** *n* Organizer *m*; **personal stereo** (*pl* **-s**) *n* Walkman® *m*; **personnel** [pɜːsə'nel] *n* Personal *nt*

perspective [pə'spektɪv] *n* Perspektive *f*

perspire [pə'spaɪə*] *vi* schwitzen

persuade [pə'sweɪd] *vt* überreden; (*convince*) überzeugen; **persuasive** [pə'sweɪsɪv] *adj* überzeugend

perverse [pə'vɜːs] *adj* pervers; (*obstinate*) eigensinnig; **pervert** [pə'vɜːt] *n* Perverse(r) *mf* ▷ [pə'vɜːt] *vt* (*morally*) verderben

pessimist ['pesɪmɪst] *n* Pessimist(in) *m(f)*; **pessimistic** [pesɪ'mɪstɪk] *adj* pessimistisch

pest [pest] *n* (*insect*) Schädling *m*; (*fig: person*) Nervensäge *f*; (*thing*) Plage *f*;

pester ['pestə*] vt plagen; **pesticide** ['pestɪsaɪd] n Schädlingsbekämpfungsmittel nt

pet [pet] n (animal) Haustier nt; (person) Liebling m

petal ['petl] n Blütenblatt nt

petition [pə'tɪʃən] n Petition f

petrol ['petrəl] n (Brit) Benzin nt; **petrol pump** n (at garage) Zapfsäule f; **petrol station** n Tankstelle f; **petrol tank** n Benzintank m

pharmacy ['fɑːməsɪ] n (shop) Apotheke f

phase [feɪz] n Phase f

PhD abbr = **Doctor of Philosophy** Dr. phil; (dissertation) Doktorarbeit f; **to do one's ~** promovieren

pheasant ['feznt] n Fasan m

phenomenon [fɪ'nɒmɪnən] (pl **phenomena**) n Phänomen nt

Philippines ['fɪlɪpiːnz] npl Philippinen pl

philosophical [fɪlə'sɒfɪkəl] adj philosophisch; (fig) gelassen; **philosophy** [fɪ'lɒsəfɪ] n Philosophie f

phone [fəʊn] n Telefon nt ▷ vt, vi anrufen; **phone book** n Telefonbuch nt; **phone bill** n Telefonrechnung f; **phone booth**, **phone box** (Brit) n Telefonzelle f; **phonecall** n Telefonanruf m; **phonecard** n Telefonkarte f; **phone-in** n Rundfunkprogramm, bei dem Hörer anrufen können; **phone number** n Telefonnummer f

photo ['fəʊtəʊ] (pl -s) n Foto nt; **photo booth** n Fotoautomat m; **photocopier** ['fəʊtəʊ'kɒpɪə*] n Kopiergerät nt; **photocopy** ['fəʊtəʊkɒpɪ] n Fotokopie f ▷ vt fotokopieren; **photograph** ['fəʊtəgrɑːf] n Fotografie f, Aufnahme f ▷ vt fotografieren; **photographer** [fə'tɒgrəfə*] n Fotograf(in) m(f); **photography** [fə'tɒgrəfɪ] n Fotografie f

phrase [freɪz] n (expression) Redewendung f, Ausdruck m; **phrase book** n Sprachführer m

physical ['fɪzɪkəl] adj (bodily) körperlich, physisch ▷ n ärztliche Untersuchung; **physically** adv (bodily) körperlich, physisch; **~ handicapped** körperbehindert

physician [fɪ'zɪʃən] n Arzt m, Ärztin f

physics ['fɪzɪks] nsing (=subject) Physik f

physiotherapy [fɪzɪə'θerəpɪ] n Physiotherapie f

physique [fɪ'ziːk] n Körperbau m

piano ['pjɑːnəʊ] (pl -s) n Klavier nt

pick [pɪk] vt (flowers, fruit) pflücken; (choose) auswählen; (team) aufstellen; **pick out** vt auswählen; **pick up** vt (lift up) aufheben; (collect) abholen; (learn) lernen

pickle ['pɪkl] n (food) (Mixed) Pickles pl ▷ vt einlegen

pickpocket ['pɪkpɒkɪt] n Taschendieb(in) m(f)

picnic ['pɪknɪk] n Picknick nt

picture ['pɪktʃə*] n Bild nt; **to go to the ~s** (Brit) ins Kino gehen ▷ vt (visualize) sich vorstellen; **picture book** n Bilderbuch nt; **picturesque** [pɪktʃə'resk] adj malerisch

pie [paɪ] n (meat) Pastete f; (fruit) Kuchen m

piece [piːs] n Stück nt; (part) Teil nt; (in chess) Figur f; (in draughts) Stein m; **a ~ of cake** ein Stück Kuchen; **to fall to ~s** auseinanderfallen

pier [pɪə*] n Pier m

pierce [pɪəs] vt durchstechen, durchbohren; (cold, sound) durchdringen; **pierced** adj (part of body) gepierct; **piercing** adj durchdringend

pig [pɪg] n Schwein nt

pigeon ['pɪdʒən] n Taube f; **pigeonhole** n (compartment) Ablegefach nt

piggy ['pɪgɪ] adj (fam) verfressen; **pigheaded** ['pɪg'hedɪd] adj dickköpfig; **piglet** ['pɪglət] n Ferkel nt; **pigsty** ['pɪgstaɪ] n Schweinestall m; **pigtail** ['pɪgteɪl] n Zopf m

pile [paɪl] n (heap) Haufen m; (one on top of another) Stapel m; **pile up** vi (accumulate) sich anhäufen

piles [paɪlz] npl Hämorr(ho)iden pl

pile-up ['paɪlʌp] n (Auto) Massenkarambolage f

pilgrim ['pɪlgrɪm] n Pilger(in) m(f)

pill [pɪl] n Tablette f; **the ~** die (Antibaby)pille; **to be on the ~** die Pille nehmen

pillar ['pɪlə*] n Pfeiler m

pillow ['pɪləʊ] n (Kopf)kissen nt; **pillowcase** n (Kopf)kissenbezug m

pilot ['paɪlət] n (Aviat) Pilot(in) m(f)

pimple ['pɪmpl] n Pickel m

pin [pɪn] n (for fixing) Nadel f; (in sewing) Stecknadel f; (Tech) Stift m; **I've got ~s and needles in my leg** mein Bein ist mir eingeschlafen ▷ vt (fix with ~) heften (to an +akk)

PIN [pɪn] acr = **personal identification number**, **PIN** (number) PIN f, Geheimzahl f

pincers ['pɪnsəz] npl (tool) Kneifzange f

pinch [pɪntʃ] n (of salt) Prise f ▷ vt zwicken; (fam: steal) klauen ▷ vi (shoe) drücken

pine [paɪn] n Kiefer f

pineapple ['paɪnæpl] n Ananas f

pink [pɪŋk] adj rosa

pinstripe(d) ['pɪnstraɪp(t)] adj Nadelstreifen-

pint [paɪnt] n Pint nt (Brit: 0,57 l, US: 0,473l); (Brit: glass of beer) Bier nt

pious ['paɪəs] adj fromm

pip [pɪp] n (of fruit) Kern m

pipe [paɪp] n (for smoking) Pfeife f; (for water, gas) Rohrleitung f

pirate ['paɪərɪt] n Pirat(in) m(f); **pirated copy** n Raubkopie f

Pisces ['paɪsiːz] nsing (Astr) Fische pl; **she's a ~** sie ist Fisch

pistachio [pɪˈstɑːʃɪəʊ] (pl -s) n Pistazie f

piste [piːst] n (Ski) Piste f

pistol ['pɪstl] n Pistole f

pit [pɪt] n (hole) Grube f; (coalmine) Zeche f; **the ~s** (in motor racing) die Box; **to be the ~s** (fam) grottenschlecht sein

pitch [pɪtʃ] n (Sport) Spielfeld nt; (Mus: of instrument) Tonlage f; (of voice) Stimmlage f ▷ vt (tent) aufschlagen; (throw) werfen; **pitch-black** adj pechschwarz

pitcher ['pɪtʃə*] n (US: jug) Krug m

pitiful ['pɪtɪfʊl] adj (contemptible) jämmerlich

pitta bread ['pɪtəbred] n Pittabrot nt

pity ['pɪtɪ] n Mitleid nt; **what a ~** wie schade; **it's a ~** es ist schade ▷ vt Mitleid haben mit

pizza ['piːtsə] n Pizza f

place [pleɪs] n m (spot, in text) Stelle f; (town etc) Ort; (house) Haus nt; (position, seat, on course) Platz m; **~ of birth** Geburtsort m; **at my ~** bei mir; **in third ~** in dritter Platz; **to three decimal ~s** bis auf drei Stellen nach dem Komma; **out of ~** nicht an der richtigen Stelle; (fig: remark) unangebracht; **in ~ of** anstelle

von; **in the first ~** (firstly) erstens; (immediately) gleich; (in any case) überhaupt ▷ vt (put) stellen, setzen; (lay flat) legen; (advertisement) setzen (in in +akk); (Comm: order) aufgeben; **place mat** n Set nt

plague [pleɪg] n Pest f

plaice [pleɪs] n Scholle f

plain [pleɪn] adj (clear) klar, deutlich; (simple) einfach; (not beautiful) unattraktiv; (yoghurt) Natur-; (Brit: chocolate) (Zart)bitter- ▷ n Ebene f; **plainly** adv (frankly) offen; (simply) einfach; (obviously) eindeutig

plait [plæt] n Zopf m ▷ vt flechten

plan [plæn] n Plan m; (for essay etc) Konzept nt ▷ vt planen; **to ~ to do sth, to ~ on doing sth** vorhaben, etw zu tun ▷ vi planen

plane [pleɪn] n (aircraft) Flugzeug nt; (tool) Hobel m; (Math) Ebene f

planet ['plænɪt] n Planet m

plank [plæŋk] n Brett nt

plant [plɑːnt] n Pflanze f; (equipment) Maschinen pl; (factory) Werk nt ▷ vt (tree etc) pflanzen; **plantation** [plæn'teɪʃən] n Plantage f

plaque [plæk] n Gedenktafel f; (on teeth) Zahnbelag m

plaster ['plɑːstə*] n (Brit Med: sticking plaster) Pflaster m; (on wall) Verputz m; **to have one's arm in ~** den Arm in Gips haben

plastered ['plɑːstəd] adj (fam) besoffen; **to get (absolutely) ~** sich besaufen

plastic ['plæstɪk] n Kunststoff m; **to pay with ~** mit Kreditkarte bezahlen ▷ adj Plastik-; **plastic bag** n Plastiktüte f; **plastic surgery** n plastische Chirurgie f

plate [pleɪt] n (for food) Teller m; (flat sheet) Platte f; (plaque) Schild nt

platform ['plætfɔːm] n (Rail) Bahnsteig m; (at meeting) Podium nt

platinum ['plætɪnəm] n Platin nt

play [pleɪ] n Spiel nt; (Theat) (Theater)stück nt ▷ vt spielen; (another player or team) spielen gegen; **to ~ the piano** Klavier spielen; **to ~ a part in** (fig) eine Rolle spielen ▷ vi spielen; **play at** vt **what are you ~ing at?** was soll das?; **play back** vt abspielen; **play down** vt herunterspielen

playacting n Schauspielerei f; **playback**
n Wiedergabe f; **player** n Spieler(in) m(f);
playful adj (person) verspielt; (remark)
scherzhaft; **playground** n Spielplatz m;
(in school) Schulhof m; **playgroup** n
Spielgruppe f; **playing card** n Spielkarte
f; **playing field** n Sportplatz m;
playmate n Spielkamerad(in) m(f);
playwright n Dramatiker(in) m(f)

plc abbr = **public limited company** AG f

plea [pliː] n Bitte f (for um)

plead [pliːd] vi dringend bitten (with sb
jdn); (Jur) **to ~ guilty** sich schuldig
bekennen

pleasant, **pleasantly** ['pleznt, -lɪ] adj, adv
angenehm

please [pliːz] adv bitte; **more tea? - yes,
~** noch Tee? - ja, bitte ▷ vt (be agreeable to)
gefallen +dat; **~ yourself** wie du willst;
pleased adj zufrieden; (glad) erfreut; **~ to
meet you** freut mich, angenehm;
pleasing adj erfreulich; **pleasure**
['pleʒə*] n Vergnügen nt, Freude f; **it's a
~** gern geschehen

pledge [pledʒ] n (promise) Versprechen nt
▷ vt (promise) versprechen

plenty ['plentɪ] n **~ of** eine Menge, viel(e);
to be ~ genug sein, reichen; **I've got ~** ich
habe mehr als genug ▷ adv (US fam) ganz
schön

pliable ['plaɪəbl] adj biegsam

pliers ['plaɪəz] npl (Kombi)zange f

plimsolls ['plɪmsəlz] npl (Brit)
Turnschuhe pl

plonk [plɒŋk] n (Brit fam: wine) billiger
Wein ▷ vt **to ~ sth** (**down**) etw
hinknallen

plot [plɒt] n (of story) Handlung f;
(conspiracy) Komplott nt; (of land) Stück nt
Land, Grundstück nt ▷ vi ein Komplott
schmieden

plough, **plow** (US) [plaʊ] n Pflug m ▷ vt, vi
(Agr) pflügen; **ploughman's lunch** n (Brit)
in einer Kneipe serviertes Gericht aus Käse,
Brot, Mixed Pickles etc

pluck [plʌk] vt (eyebrows, guitar) zupfen;
(chicken) rupfen; **pluck up** vt **to ~ (one's)
courage** Mut aufbringen

plug [plʌg] n (for sink, bath) Stöpsel m;
(Elec) Stecker m; (Auto) (Zünd)kerze f; (fam:
publicity) Schleichwerbung f ▷ vt (fam:
advertise) Reklame machen für; **plug in** vt
anschließen

plum [plʌm] n Pflaume f ▷ adj (fam: job
etc) Super-

plumber ['plʌmə*] n Klempner(in) m(f);
plumbing ['plʌmɪŋ] n (fittings)
Leitungen pl; (craft) Installieren nt

plump [plʌmp] adj rundlich

plunge [plʌndʒ] vt (knife) stoßen; (into
water) tauchen ▷ vi stürzen; (into water)
tauchen

plural ['plʊərəl] n Plural m

plus [plʌs] prep plus; (as well as) und ▷ adj
Plus-; **20 ~** mehr als 20 ▷ n (fig) Plus nt

plywood ['plaɪwʊd] n Sperrholz nt

pm abbr = **post meridiem at 3 ~** um 3 Uhr
nachmittags; **at 8 ~** um 8 Uhr abends

pneumonia [njuːˈməʊnɪə] n
Lungenentzündung f

poached [pəʊtʃt] adj (egg) pochiert,
verloren

PO Box abbr = **post office box** Postfach nt

pocket ['pɒkɪt] n Tasche f ▷ vt (put in ~)
einstecken; **pocketbook** n (US: wallet)
Brieftasche f; **pocket calculator** n
Taschenrechner m; **pocket money** n
Taschengeld nt

poem ['pəʊəm] n Gedicht nt; **poet** ['pəʊɪt]
n Dichter(in) m(f); **poetic** [pəʊˈetɪk] adj
poetisch; **poetry** ['pəʊɪtrɪ] n (art)
Dichtung f; (poems) Gedichte pl

point [pɔɪnt] n Punkt m; (spot) Stelle f;
(sharp tip) Spitze f; (moment) Zeitpunkt m;
(purpose) Zweck m; (idea) Argument nt;
(decimal) Dezimalstelle f; **~s** pl (Rail)
Weiche f; **~ of view** Standpunkt m; **three
~ two** drei Komma zwei; **at some
~** irgendwann (mal); **to get to the ~** zur
Sache kommen; **there's no ~** es hat
keinen Sinn; **I was on the ~ of leaving** ich
wollte gerade gehen ▷ vt (gun etc) richten
(at auf +akk); **to ~ one's finger at** mit dem
Finger zeigen auf +akk ▷ vi (with finger etc)
zeigen (at, to auf +akk); **point out** vt
(indicate) aufzeigen; (mention) hinweisen
auf +akk; **pointed** adj spitz; (question)
gezielt; **pointer** n (on dial) Zeiger m; (tip)
Hinweis m; **pointless** adj sinnlos

poison ['pɔɪzn] n Gift nt ▷ vt vergiften;
poisonous adj giftig

poke [pəʊk] vt (with stick, finger) stoßen,
stupsen; (put) stecken

Poland ['pəʊlənd] n Polen nt

polar ['pəʊlə*] adj Polar-, polar; **~ bear**
Eisbär m

pole [pəʊl] n Stange f; (Geo, Elec) Pol m
Pole [pəʊl] n Pole m, Polin f
pole vault n Stabhochsprung m
police [pə'liːs] n Polizei f; **police car** n
Polizeiwagen m; **policeman** (pl -men) n
Polizist m; **police station** n
(Polizei)wache f; **policewoman** (pl
-women) n Polizistin f
policy ['pɒlɪsɪ] n (plan) Politik f; (principle)
Grundsatz m; (insurance ~)
(Versicherungs)police f
polio ['pəʊlɪəʊ] n Kinderlähmung f
polish ['pɒlɪʃ] n (for furniture) Politur f; (for
floor) Wachs nt; (for shoes) Creme f; (shine)
Glanz m; (fig) Schliff m ▷ vt polieren;
(shoes) putzen; (fig) den letzten Schliff
geben +dat
Polish ['pəʊlɪʃ] adj polnisch ▷ n Polnisch
nt
polite [pə'laɪt] adj höflich; **politeness** n
Höflichkeit f
political, politically [pə'lɪtɪkəl, -ɪ] adj, adv
politisch; **~ly correct** politisch korrekt;
politician [pɒlɪ'tɪʃən] n Politiker(in) m(f);
politics ['pɒlɪtɪks] nsing o pl Politik f
poll [pəʊl] n (election) Wahl f; (opinion ~)
Umfrage f
pollen ['pɒlən] n Pollen m, Blütenstaub m;
pollen count n Pollenflug m
polling station ['pəʊlɪŋsteɪʃən] n
Wahllokal nt
pollute [pə'luːt] vt verschmutzen;
pollution [pə'luːʃən] n Verschmutzung f
pompous ['pɒmpəs] adj aufgeblasen;
(language) geschwollen
pond [pɒnd] n Teich m
ponder ['pɒndə*] vt nachdenken über
+akk
pony ['pəʊnɪ] n Pony nt; **ponytail** n
Pferdeschwanz m
poodle ['puːdl] n Pudel m
pool [puːl] n (swimming ~) Schwimmbad
nt; (private) Swimmingpool m; (of spilt
liquid, blood) Lache f; (game) Poolbillard nt
▷ vt (money etc) zusammenlegen
poor [pɔː*] adj arm; (not good) schlecht
▷ npl **the ~** die Armen pl; **poorly** adv
(badly) schlecht ▷ adj (Brit) krank
pop [pɒp] n (music) Pop m; (noise) Knall m
▷ vt (put) stecken; (balloon) platzen lassen
▷ vi (balloon) platzen; (cork) knallen; **to**
~ in (person) vorbeischauen; **pop concert**
n Popkonzert nt; **popcorn** n Popcorn nt

Pope [pəʊp] n Papst m
pop group ['pɒpgruːp] n Popgruppe f;
pop music n Popmusik f
poppy ['pɒpɪ] n Mohn m
Popsicle® ['pɒpsɪkl] n (US) Eis nt am
Stiel
pop star ['pɒpstɑː*] n Popstar m
popular ['pɒpjʊlə*] adj (well-liked) beliebt
(with bei); (widespread) weit verbreitet
population [pɒpjʊ'leɪʃən] n Bevölkerung
f; (of town) Einwohner pl
porcelain ['pɔːslɪn] n Porzellan nt
porch [pɔːtʃ] n Vorbau m; (US: verandah)
Veranda f
porcupine ['pɔːkjʊpaɪn] n
Stachelschwein nt
pork [pɔːk] n Schweinefleisch nt; **pork**
chop n Schweinekotelett; **pork pie** n
Schweinefleischpastete f
porn [pɔːn] n Porno m; **pornographic**
[pɔːnə'græfɪk] adj pornografisch;
pornography [pɔː'nɒgrəfɪ] n
Pornografie f
porridge ['pɒrɪdʒ] n Haferbrei m
port [pɔːt] n (harbour) Hafen m; (town)
Hafenstadt f; (Naut: left side) Backbord nt;
(wine) Portwein m; (Inform) Anschluss m
portable ['pɔːtəbl] adj tragbar; (radio)
Koffer-
portal ['pɔːtl] n (Inform) Portal nt
porter ['pɔːtə*] n Pförtner(in) m(f); (for
luggage) Gepäckträger m
porthole ['pɔːthəʊl] n Bullauge nt
portion ['pɔːʃən] n Teil m; (of food) Portion
f
portrait ['pɔːtrɪt] n Porträt nt
portray [pɔː'treɪ] vt darstellen
Portugal ['pɔːtjʊgl] n Portugal nt;
Portuguese [pɔːtjʊ'giːz] adj
portugiesisch ▷ n Portugiese m,
Portugiesin f; (language) Portugiesisch nt
pose [pəʊz] n Haltung f ▷ vi posieren ▷ vt
(threat, problem) darstellen
posh [pɒʃ] adj (fam) piekfein
position [pə'zɪʃən] n Stellung f; (place)
Position f, Lage f; (job) Stelle f; (opinion)
Standpunkt m; **to be in a ~ to do sth** in
der Lage sein, etw zu tun; **in third ~** auf
dem dritten Platz ▷ vt aufstellen; (Inform:
cursor) positionieren
positive ['pɒzɪtɪv] adj positiv; (convinced)
sicher; (definite) eindeutig
possess [pə'zes] vt besitzen; **possession**

P

[pə'zeʃən] n ~(s pl) Besitz m; **possessive**
adj (person) Besitz ergreifend
possibility [pɒsə'bɪlɪtɪ] n Möglichkeit f;
possible ['pɒsəbl] adj möglich; **if ~** wenn
möglich; **as big/soon as ~** so groß/bald
wie möglich; **possibly** adv (perhaps)
vielleicht; **I've done all I ~ can** ich habe
mein Möglichstes getan
post [pəust] n (mail) Post f; (pole) Pfosten
m; (job) Stelle f ▷ vt (letters) aufgeben; **to
keep sb ~ed** jdn auf dem Laufenden
halten; **postage** ['pəustɪdʒ] n Porto nt;
~ and packing Porto und Verpackung;
postal adj Post-; (Brit) **~ order**
Postanweisung f; **postbox** n Briefkasten
m; **postcard** n Postkarte f; **postcode** n
(Brit) Postleitzahl f
poster ['pəustə*] n Plakat nt, Poster nt
postgraduate [pəust'grædjuıt] n jmd, der
seine Studien nach dem ersten akademischen
Grad weiterführt
postman ['pəustmən] (pl **-men**) n
Briefträger m; **postmark** n Poststempel
m
postmortem [pəust'mɔ:təm] n Autopsie
f
post office ['pəustɒfɪs] n Post® f; **post
office box** n Postfach nt
postpone [pə'spəun] vt verschieben (till
auf +akk)
posture ['pɒstʃə*] n Haltung f
pot [pɒt] n Topf m; (tea~, coffee ~) Kanne f;
(fam: marijuana) Pot n ▷ vt (plant)
eintopfen
potato [pə'teɪtəu] (pl **-es**) n Kartoffel f;
potato chips (US) npl Kartoffelchips pl;
potato peeler n Kartoffelschäler m
potent ['pəutənt] adj stark
potential [pəu'tenʃəl] adj potenziell ▷ n
Potenzial nt; **potentially** adv potenziell
pothole ['pɒthəul] n Höhle f; (in road)
Schlagloch nt
potter about ['pɒtərəbaut] vi
herumhantieren
pottery ['pɒtərɪ] n (objects) Töpferwaren
pl
potty ['pɒtɪ] adj (Brit fam) verrückt ▷ n
Töpfchen nt
poultry ['pəultrɪ] n Geflügel nt
pounce [pauns] vi **to ~ on** sich stürzen
auf +akk
pound [paund] n (money) Pfund nt;
(weight) Pfund nt (0,454 kg); **a ~ of cherries**

ein Pfund Kirschen; **ten-~ note**
Zehnpfundschein m
pour [pɔ:*] vt (liquid) gießen; (rice, sugar
etc) schütten; **to ~ sb sth** (drink) jdm etw
eingießen; **pouring** adj (rain) strömend
poverty ['pɒvətɪ] n Armut f
powder ['paudə*] n Pulver nt; (cosmetic)
Puder m; **powdered milk** n Milchpulver
nt; **powder room** n Damentoilette f
power ['pauə*] n Macht f; (ability)
Fähigkeit f; (strength) Stärke f; (Elec) Strom
m; **to be in ~** an der Macht sein ▷ vt
betreiben, antreiben; **power-assisted
steering** n Servolenkung f; **power cut** n
Stromausfall m; **powerful** adj (politician
etc) mächtig; (engine, government) stark;
(argument) durchschlagend; **powerless**
adj machtlos; **power station** n
Kraftwerk nt
p&p abbr = **postage and packing**
PR abbr = **public relations** ▷ abbr =
proportional representation
practical, practically ['præktɪkəl, -ɪ] adj,
adv praktisch; **practice** ['præktɪs] n
(training) Übung f; (custom) Gewohnheit f;
(doctor's, lawyer's) Praxis f; **in ~** (in reality) in
der Praxis; **out of ~** außer Übung; **to put
sth into ~** etw in die Praxis umsetzen ▷ vt,
vi (US) see **practise**; **practise** ['præktɪs] vt
(instrument, movement) üben; (profession)
ausüben ▷ vi üben; (doctor, lawyer)
praktizieren
Prague [prɑ:g] n Prag nt
praise [preɪz] n Lob nt ▷ vt loben
pram [præm] n (Brit) Kinderwagen m
prawn [prɔ:n] n Garnele f, Krabbe f;
prawn crackers npl Krabbenchips pl
pray [preɪ] vi beten; **to ~ for sth** (fig)
stark auf etw akk hoffen; **prayer** ['preə*] n
Gebet nt
pre- [pri:] pref vor-, prä-
preach [pri:tʃ] vi predigen
prearrange [pri:ə'reɪndʒ] vt im Voraus
vereinbaren
precaution [prɪ'kɔ:ʃən] n
Vorsichtsmaßnahme f
precede [prɪ'si:d] vt vorausgehen +dat;
preceding adj vorhergehend
precinct ['pri:sɪŋkt] n (Brit: pedestrian ~)
Fußgängerzone f; (Brit: shopping ~)
Einkaufsviertel nt; (US: district) Bezirk m
precious ['preʃəs] adj kostbar; **~ stone**
Edelstein m

précis ['preɪsiː] n Zusammenfassung f
precise, **precisely** [prɪ'saɪs, -lɪ] adj, adv
genau
precondition [priːkən'dɪʃən] n
Vorbedingung f
predecessor ['priːdɪsesə*] n
Vorgänger(in) m(f)
predicament [prɪ'dɪkəmənt] n missliche
Lage
predict [prɪ'dɪkt] vt voraussagen;
predictable adj vorhersehbar; (person)
berechenbar
predominant [prɪ'dɒmɪnənt] adj
vorherrschend; **predominantly** adv
überwiegend
preface ['prefɪs] n Vorwort nt
prefer [prɪ'fɜː*] vt vorziehen (to dat),
lieber mögen (to als); **to ~ to do sth** etw
lieber tun; **preferably** ['prefrəblɪ] adv
vorzugsweise, am liebsten; **preference**
['prefərəns] n (liking) Vorliebe f;
preferential [prefə'renʃəl] adj **to get
~ treatment** bevorzugt behandelt
werden
prefix ['priːfɪks] n (US Tel) Vorwahl f
pregnancy ['pregnənsɪ] n
Schwangerschaft f; **pregnant** ['pregnənt]
adj schwanger; **two months ~** im zweiten
Monat schwanger
prejudice ['predʒʊdɪs] n Vorurteil nt;
prejudiced adj (person)
voreingenommen
preliminary [prɪ'lɪmɪnərɪ] adj (measures)
vorbereitend; (results) vorläufig; (remarks)
einleitend
premature ['premətʃʊə*] adj vorzeitig;
(hasty) voreilig
premiere ['premɪeə*] n Premiere f
premises ['premɪsɪz] npl (offices)
Räumlichkeiten pl; (of factory, school)
Gelände nt
premium-rate ['priːmɪəmreɪt] adj (Tel)
zum Höchsttarif
preoccupied [priː'ɒkjʊpaɪd] adj **to be
~ with sth** mit etw sehr beschäftigt sein
prepaid [priː'peɪd] adj vorausbezahlt;
(envelope) frankiert
preparation [prepə'reɪʃən] n
Vorbereitung f; **prepare** [prɪ'peə*] vt
vorbereiten (for auf +akk); (food)
zubereiten; **to be ~d to do sth** bereit sein,
etw zu tun ▷ vi sich vorbereiten (for auf
+akk)

prerequisite [priː'rekwɪzɪt] n
Voraussetzung f
prescribe [prɪ'skraɪb] vt vorschreiben;
(Med) verschreiben; **prescription**
[prɪ'skrɪpʃən] n Rezept nt
presence ['prezns] n Gegenwart f;
present ['preznt] adj (in attendance)
anwesend (at bei); (current) gegenwärtig;
~ tense Gegenwart f, Präsens nt ▷ n
Gegenwart f; (gift) Geschenk nt; **at
~** zurzeit ▷ [prɪ'zent] vt (Tv, Radio)
präsentieren; (problem) darstellen; (report
etc) vorlegen; **to ~ sb with sth** jdm etw
überreichen; **present-day** adj heutig;
presently adv bald; (at present) zurzeit
preservative [prɪ'zɜːvətɪv] n
Konservierungsmittel nt; **preserve**
[prɪ'zɜːv] vt erhalten; (food) einmachen,
konservieren
president ['prezɪdənt] n Präsident(in)
m(f); **presidential** [prezɪ'denʃəl] adj
Präsidenten-; (election) Präsidentschafts-
press [pres] n (newspapers, machine) Presse
f ▷ vt (push) drücken; **to ~ a button** auf
einen Knopf drücken ▷ vi (push) drücken;
pressing adj dringend; **press-stud** n
Druckknopf m; **press-up** n (Brit)
Liegestütz m; **pressure** ['preʃə*] n Druck
m; **to be under ~** unter Druck stehen; **to
put ~ on sb** jdn unter Druck setzen;
pressure cooker n Schnellkochtopf m;
pressurize ['preʃəraɪz] vt (person) unter
Druck setzen
presumably [prɪ'zjuːməblɪ] adv
vermutlich; **presume** [prɪ'zjuːm] vt, vi
annehmen
presumptuous [prɪ'zʌmptʊəs] adj
anmaßend
presuppose [priːsə'pəʊz] vt
voraussetzen
pretend [prɪ'tend] vt **to ~ that** so tun als
ob; **to ~ to do sth** vorgeben, etw zu tun
▷ vi **she's ~ing** sie tut nur so
pretentious [prɪ'tenʃəs] adj anmaßend;
(person) wichtigtuerisch
pretty ['prɪtɪ] adj hübsch ▷ adv ziemlich
prevent [prɪ'vent] vt verhindern; **to ~ sb
from doing sth** jdn daran hindern, etw zu
tun
preview ['priːvjuː] n (Cine)
Voraufführung f; (trailer) Vorschau f
previous, **previously** ['priːvɪəs, -lɪ] adj,
adv früher

P

prey [preɪ] n Beute f
price [praɪs] n Preis m ▷ vt **it's ~d at £10**
es ist mit 10 Pfund ausgezeichnet;
priceless adj unbezahlbar; **price list** n
Preisliste f; **price tag** n Preisschild nt
prick [prɪk] n Stich m; (vulg: penis)
Schwanz m; (vulg: person) Arsch m ▷ vt
stechen in +akk; **to ~ one's finger** sich dat
in den Finger stechen; **prickly** ['prɪklɪ] adj
stachelig
pride [praɪd] n Stolz m; (arrogance)
Hochmut m ▷ vt **to ~ oneself on sth** auf
etw akk stolz sein
priest [priːst] n Priester m
primarily ['praɪmərɪlɪ] adv vorwiegend;
primary ['praɪmərɪ] adj Haupt-;
~ education Grundschulausbildung f;
~ school Grundschule f
prime [praɪm] adj Haupt-; (excellent)
erstklassig ▷ n **in one's ~** in den besten
Jahren; **prime minister** n
Premierminister(in) m(f); **prime time** n
(TV) Hauptsendezeit f
primitive ['prɪmɪtɪv] adj primitiv
primrose ['prɪmrəʊz] n Schlüsselblume f
prince [prɪns] n Prinz m; (ruler) Fürst m;
princess [prɪn'ses] n Prinzessin f; (wife of
ruler) Fürstin f
principal ['prɪnsɪpəl] adj
Haupt-, wichtigste(r, s) ▷ n (school)
Rektor(in) m(f)
principle ['prɪnsəpl] n Prinzip nt; **in ~** im
Prinzip; **on ~** aus Prinzip
print [prɪnt] n (picture) Druck m; (Foto)
Abzug m; (made by feet, fingers) Abdruck m;
out of ~ vergriffen ▷ vt drucken; (photo)
abziehen; (write in block letters) in
Druckschrift schreiben; **print out** vt
(Inform) ausdrucken; **printed matter** n
Drucksache f; **printer** n Drucker m;
printout n (Inform) Ausdruck m
prior ['praɪə*] adj früher; **a
~ engagement** eine vorher getroffene
Verabredung; **~ to sth** vor etw dat; **~ to
going abroad, she had ...** bevor sie ins
Ausland ging, hatte sie ...
priority [praɪ'ɒrɪtɪ] n (thing having
precedence) Priorität f
prison ['prɪzn] n Gefängnis nt; **prisoner** n
Gefangene(r) mf; **~ of war**
Kriegsgefangene(r) mf
privacy ['prɪvəsɪ] n Privatleben nt;
private ['praɪvɪt] adj privat; (confidential)

vertraulich ▷ n einfacher Soldat; **in
~** privat; **privately** adv privat;
(confidentially) vertraulich; **privatize**
['praɪvətaɪz] vt privatisieren
privilege ['prɪvɪlɪdʒ] n Privileg nt;
privileged adj privilegiert
prize [praɪz] n Preis m; **prize money** n
Preisgeld m; **prizewinner** n Gewinner(in)
m(f); **prizewinning** adj preisgekrönt
pro [prəʊ] (pl -s) n (professional) Profi m;
the ~s and cons pl das Für und Wider
pro- [prəʊ] pref pro-
probability [prɒbə'bɪlɪtɪ] n
Wahrscheinlichkeit f; **probable, probably**
['prɒbəbl, -blɪ] adj, adv wahrscheinlich
probation [prə'beɪʃən] n Probezeit f; (Jur)
Bewährung f
probe [prəʊb] n (investigation)
Untersuchung f ▷ vt untersuchen
problem ['prɒbləm] n Problem nt; **no
~** kein Problem!
procedure [prə'siːdʒə*] n Verfahren nt
proceed [prə'siːd] vi (continue)
fortfahren; (set about sth) vorgehen ▷ vt
to ~ to do sth anfangen, etw zu tun;
proceedings npl (Jur) Verfahren nt;
proceeds ['prəʊsiːds] npl Erlös m
process ['prəʊses] n Prozess m, Vorgang
m; (method) Verfahren nt ▷ vt (application
etc) bearbeiten; (food, data) verarbeiten;
(film) entwickeln
procession [prə'seʃən] n Umzug m
processor ['prəʊsesə*] n (Inform)
Prozessor m; (Gastr) Küchenmaschine f
produce ['prɒdjuːs] n (Agr) Produkte pl,
Erzeugnisse pl ▷ [prə'djuːs] vt
(manufacture) herstellen, produzieren; (on
farm) erzeugen; (film, play, record)
produzieren; (cause) hervorrufen; (evidence,
results) liefern; **producer** n (manufacturer)
Hersteller(in) m(f); (of film, play, record)
Produzent(in) m(f); **product** ['prɒdʌkt] n
Produkt nt, Erzeugnis nt; **production**
[prə'dʌkʃən] n Produktion f; (Theat)
Inszenierung f; **productive** [prə'dʌktɪv]
adj produktiv; (land) ertragreich
prof [prɒf] n (fam) Professor(in) m(f)
profession [prə'feʃən] n Beruf m;
professional [prə'feʃnl] n Profi m ▷ adj
beruflich; (expert) fachlich; (sportsman,
actor etc) Berufs-
professor [prə'fesə*] n Professor(in) m(f);
(US: lecturer) Dozent(in) m(f)

proficient [prə'fɪʃənt] *adj* kompetent (*in* in +*dat*)

profile ['prəʊfaɪl] *n* Profil *nt*; **to keep a low ~** sich rar machen

profit ['prɒfɪt] *n* Gewinn *m* ▷ *vi* profitieren (*by, from* von); **profitable** *adj* rentabel

profound [prə'faʊnd] *adj* tief; (*idea, thinker*) tiefgründig; (*knowledge*) profund

program ['prəʊgræm] *n* (*Inform*) Programm *nt*; (*US*) *see* **programme** ▷ *vt* (*Inform*) programmieren; (*US*) *see* **programme**

programme ['prəʊgræm] *n* Programm *nt*; (*Tv, Radio*) Sendung *f* ▷ *vt* programmieren; **programmer** *n* Programmierer(in) *m(f)*; **programming** *n* (*Inform*) Programmierung *nt*; **~ language** Programmiersprache *f*

progress ['prəʊgres] *n* Fortschritt *m*; **to make ~** Fortschritte machen ▷ [prə'gres] *vi* (*work, illness etc*) fortschreiten; (*improve*) Fortschritte machen; **progressive** [prə'gresɪv] *adj* (*person, policy*) fortschrittlich; **progressively** [prə'gresɪvlɪ] *adv* zunehmend

prohibit [prə'hɪbɪt] *vt* verbieten

project ['prɒdʒekt] *n* Projekt *nt*

projector [prə'dʒektə*] *n* Projektor *m*

prolong [prə'lɒŋ] *vt* verlängern

prom [prɒm] *n* (*at seaside*) Promenade *f*; (*Brit: concert*) Konzert *nt* (*bei dem ein Großteil des Publikums im Parkett Stehplätze hat*); (*US: dance*) Ball für die Schüler und Studenten von Highschools oder Colleges

prominent ['prɒmɪnənt] *adj* (*politician, actor etc*) prominent; (*easily seen*) auffallend

promiscuous [prə'mɪskjʊəs] *adj* promisk

promise ['prɒmɪs] *n* Versprechen *nt* ▷ *vt* versprechen; **to ~ sb sth** jdm etw versprechen; **to ~ to do sth** versprechen, etw zu tun ▷ *vi* versprechen; **promising** *adj* viel versprechend

promote [prə'məʊt] *vt* (*in rank*) befördern; (*help on*) fördern; (*Comm*) werben für; **promotion** [prə'məʊʃən] *n* (*in rank*) Beförderung *f*; (*Comm*) Werbung *f* (*of* für)

prompt [prɒmpt] *adj* prompt; (*punctual*) pünktlich ▷ *adv* **at two o'clock ~** Punkt zwei Uhr ▷ *vt* (*Theat: actor*) soufflieren +*dat*

prone [prəʊn] *adj* **to be ~ to sth** zu etw neigen

pronounce [prə'naʊns] *vt* (*word*) aussprechen; **pronounced** *adj* ausgeprägt; **pronunciation** [prənʌnsɪ'eɪʃən] *n* Aussprache *f*

proof [pruːf] *n* Beweis *m*; (*of alcohol*) Alkoholgehalt *m*

prop [prɒp] *n* Stütze *f*; (*Theat*) Requisit *nt* ▷ *vt* **to ~ sth against sth** etw gegen etw lehnen; **prop up** *vt* stützen; (*fig*) unterstützen

proper ['prɒpə*] *adj* richtig; (*morally correct*) anständig

property ['prɒpətɪ] *n* (*possession*) Eigentum *nt*; (*house*) Haus *nt*; (*land*) Grundbesitz *m*; (*characteristic*) Eigenschaft *f*

proportion [prə'pɔːʃən] *n* Verhältnis *nt*; (*share*) Teil *m*; **~s** *pl* (*size*) Proportionen *pl*; **in ~ to** im Verhältnis zu; **proportional** *adj* proportional; **~ representation** Verhältniswahlrecht *nt*

proposal [prə'pəʊzl] *n* Vorschlag *m*; **~ (of marriage)** (Heirats)antrag *m*; **propose** [prə'pəʊz] *vt* vorschlagen ▷ *vi* (*offer marriage*) einen Heiratsantrag machen (*to sb* jdm)

proprietor [prə'praɪətə*] *n* Besitzer(in) *m(f)*; (*of pub, hotel*) Inhaber(in) *m(f)*

prose [prəʊz] *n* Prosa *f*

prosecute ['prɒsɪkjuːt] *vt* verfolgen (*for* wegen)

prospect ['prɒspekt] *n* Aussicht *f*

prosperity [prɒ'sperɪtɪ] *n* Wohlstand *m*; **prosperous** *adj* wohlhabend; (*business*) gut gehend

prostitute ['prɒstɪtjuːt] *n* Prostituierte(r) *mf*

protect [prə'tekt] *vt* schützen (*from, against* vor +*dat*, gegen); **protection** [prə'tekʃən] *n* Schutz *m* (*from, against* vor +*dat*, gegen); **protective** *adj* beschützend; (*clothing etc*) Schutz-

protein ['prəʊtiːn] *n* Protein *nt*, Eiweiß *nt*

protest ['prəʊtest] *n* Protest *m*; (*demonstration*) Protestkundgebung *f* ▷ [prə'test] *vi* protestieren (*against* gegen); (*demonstrate*) demonstrieren

Protestant ['prɒtəstənt] *adj* protestantisch ▷ *n* Protestant(in) *m(f)*

proud, proudly [praʊd, -lɪ] *adj, adv* stolz (*of* auf +*akk*)

prove [pru:v] *vt* beweisen; *(turn out to be)* sich erweisen als

proverb ['prɒvɜ:b] *n* Sprichwort *nt*

provide [prə'vaɪd] *vt* zur Verfügung stellen; *(drinks, music etc)* sorgen für; *(person)* versorgen (*with* mit); **provide for** *vt (family etc)* sorgen für; **provided** *conj* ~ **(that)** vorausgesetzt, dass; **provider** *n* (*Inform*) Provider *m*

provision [prə'vɪʒən] *n (condition)* Bestimmung *f*; **~s** *pl (food)* Proviant *m*

provisional, provisionally [prə'vɪʒnl, -ɪ] *adj, adv* provisorisch

provoke [prə'vəʊk] *vt* provozieren; *(cause)* hervorrufen

proximity [prɒk'sɪmɪtɪ] *n* Nähe *f*

prudent ['pru:dənt] *adj* klug; *(person)* umsichtig

prudish ['pru:dɪʃ] *adj* prüde

prune [pru:n] *n* Backpflaume *f* ▷ *vt (tree etc)* zurechtstutzen

PS *abbr* = **postscript** PS *nt*

psalm [sɑ:m] *n* Psalm *m*

pseudo ['sju:dəʊ] *adj* pseudo-, Pseudo-; **pseudonym** ['sju:dənɪm] *n* Pseudonym *nt*

PST *abbr* = **Pacific Standard Time**

psychiatric [saɪkɪ'ætrɪk] *adj* psychiatrisch; *(illness)* psychisch; **psychiatrist** [saɪ'kaɪətrɪst] *n* Psychiater(in) *m(f)*; **psychiatry** [saɪ'kaɪətrɪ] *n* Psychiatrie *f*; **psychic** ['saɪkɪk] *adj* übersinnlich; **I'm not ~** ich kann keine Gedanken lesen; **psychoanalysis** [saɪkəʊə'næləsɪs] *n* Psychoanalyse *f*; **psychoanalyst** [saɪkəʊ'ænəlɪst] *n* Psychoanalytiker(in) *m(f)*; **psychological** [saɪkə'lɒdʒɪkəl] *adj* psychologisch; **psychology** [saɪ'kɒlədʒɪ] *n* Psychologie *f*; **psychopath** ['saɪkəʊpæθ] *n* Psychopath(in) *m(f)*

pt *abbr* = **pint**

pto *abbr* = **please turn over** b.w.

pub [pʌb] *n (Brit)* Kneipe *f*

● **pub**

● Ein **pub** ist ein Gasthaus mit einer
● Lizenz zum Ausschank von
● alkoholischen Getränken. Ein „Pub"
● besteht meist aus verschiedenen
● gemütlichen (**lounge, snug**) oder
● einfacheren (**public bar**) Räumen, in

● denen oft auch Spiele wie Darts,
● Domino und Poolbillard zur
● Verfügung stehen. In „Pubs" werden
● vor allem mittags auch Mahlzeiten
● angeboten (**pub lunch**). „Pubs" sind
● normalerweise von 11 bis 23 Uhr
● geöffnet, aber manchmal
● nachmittags geschlossen.

puberty ['pju:bətɪ] *n* Pubertät *f*

public ['pʌblɪk] *n* **the (general) ~** die (breite) Öffentlichkeit; **in ~** in der Öffentlichkeit ▷ *adj* öffentlich; *(relating to the State)* Staats-; **~ convenience** *(Brit)* öffentliche Toilette; **~ holiday** gesetzlicher Feiertag; **~ opinion** die öffentliche Meinung; **~ relations** *pl* Öffentlichkeitsarbeit *f*, Public Relations *pl*; **~ school** *(Brit)* Privatschule *f*; **publication** [pʌblɪ'keɪʃən] *n* Veröffentlichung *f*; **publicity** [pʌb'lɪsɪtɪ] *n* Publicity *f*; *(advertisements)* Werbung *f*; **publish** ['pʌblɪʃ] *vt* veröffentlichen; **publisher** *n* Verleger(in) *m(f)*; *(company)* Verlag *m*; **publishing** *n* Verlagswesen *nt*

pub lunch ['pʌb'lʌntʃ] *n (oft einfacheres) Mittagessen in einer Kneipe*

pudding ['pʊdɪŋ] *n (course)* Nachtisch *m*

puddle ['pʌdl] *n* Pfütze *f*

puff [pʌf] *vi (pant)* schnaufen

puffin ['pʌfɪn] *n* Papageientaucher *m*

puff paste *(US)*, **puff pastry** ['pʌf'peɪstrɪ] *n* Blätterteig *m*

pull [pʊl] *n* Ziehen *nt*; **to give sth a ~** an etw *dat* ziehen ▷ *vt (cart, tooth)* ziehen; *(rope, handle)* ziehen an +*dat*; *(fam: date)* abschleppen; **to ~ a muscle** sich *dat* einen Muskel zerren; **to ~ sb's leg** jdn auf den Arm nehmen ▷ *vi* ziehen; **pull apart** *vt (separate)* auseinander ziehen; **pull down** *vt (blind)* herunterziehen; *(house)* abreißen; **pull in** *vi* hineinfahren; *(stop)* anhalten; **pull off** *vt (clothes)* ausziehen; *(deal etc)* zuwege bringen; **pull on** *vt (clothes)* anziehen; **pull out** *vi (car from lane)* ausscheren; *(train)* abfahren; *(withdraw)* aussteigen (*of* aus) ▷ *vt* herausziehen; *(tooth)* ziehen; *(troops)* abziehen; **pull round, pull through** *vi* durchkommen; **pull up** *vt (raise)* hochziehen; *(chair)* heranziehen ▷ *vi* anhalten

pullover ['pʊləʊvə*] *n* Pullover *m*

pulp [pʌlp] n Brei m; (of fruit) Fruchtfleisch nt

pulpit ['pʊlpɪt] n Kanzel f

pulse [pʌls] n Puls m

pump [pʌmp] n Pumpe f; (in petrol station) Zapfsäule f; **pump up** vt (tyre etc) aufpumpen

pumpkin ['pʌmpkɪn] n Kürbis m

pun [pʌn] n Wortspiel nt

punch [pʌntʃ] n (blow) (Faust)schlag m; (tool) Locher m; (hot drink) Punsch m; (cold drink) Bowle f ▷ vt (strike) schlagen; (ticket, paper) lochen

punctual, punctually ['pʌŋktjʊəl, -ɪ] adj, adv pünktlich

punctuation [pʌŋktjʊ'eɪʃən] n Interpunktion f; **punctuation mark** n Satzzeichen nt

puncture ['pʌŋktʃə*] n (flat tyre) Reifenpanne f

punish ['pʌnɪʃ] vt bestrafen; **punishment** n Strafe f; (action) Bestrafung f

pupil ['pjuːpl] n (school) Schüler(in) m(f)

puppet ['pʌpɪt] n Puppe f; (string ~) Marionette f

puppy ['pʌpɪ] n junger Hund

purchase ['pɜːtʃɪs] n Kauf m ▷ vt kaufen

pure [pjʊə*] adj rein; (clean) sauber; (utter) pur; **purely** ['pjʊəlɪ] adv rein; **purify** ['pjʊərɪfaɪ] vt reinigen; **purity** ['pjʊərɪtɪ] n Reinheit f

purple ['pɜːpl] adj violett

purpose ['pɜːpəs] n Zweck m; (of person) Absicht f; **on ~** absichtlich

purr [pɜː*] vi (cat) schnurren

purse [pɜːs] n Geldbeutel m; (US: handbag) Handtasche f

pursue [pə'sjuː] vt (person, car) verfolgen; (hobby, studies) nachgehen +dat; **pursuit** [pə'sjuːt] n (chase) Verfolgung f; (occupation) Beschäftigung f; (hobby) Hobby nt

pus [pʌs] n Eiter m

push [pʊʃ] n Stoß m ▷ vt (person) stoßen; (car, chair etc) schieben; (button) drücken; (drugs) dealen ▷ vi (in crowd) drängeln; **push in** vi (in queue) sich vordrängeln; **push off** vi (fam: leave) abhauen; **push on** vi (with job) weitermachen; **push up** vt (prices) hochtreiben; **pushchair** n (Brit) Sportwagen m; **pusher** n (of drugs) Dealer(in) m(f); **push-up** n (US)

Liegestütz m; **pushy** adj (fam) aufdringlich, penetrant

put [pʊt] (put, put) vt tun; (upright) stellen; (flat) legen; (express) ausdrücken; (write) schreiben; **he ~ his hand in his pocket** er steckte die Hand in die Tasche; **he ~ his hand on her shoulder** er legte ihr die Hand auf die Schulter; **to ~ money into one's account** Geld auf sein Konto einzahlen; **put aside** vt (money) zurücklegen; **put away** vt (tidy away) wegräumen; **put back** vt zurücklegen; (clock) zurückstellen; **put down** vt (in writing) aufschreiben; (Brit: animal) einschläfern; (rebellion) niederschlagen; **to put the phone down** (den Hörer) auflegen; **to put one's name down for sth** sich für etw eintragen; **put forward** vt (idea) vorbringen; (name) vorschlagen; (clock) vorstellen; **put in** vt (install) einbauen; (submit) einreichen; **put off** vt (switch off) ausschalten; (postpone) verschieben; **to put sb off doing sth** jdn davon abbringen, etw zu tun; **put on** vt (switch on) anmachen; (clothes) anziehen; (hat, glasses) aufsetzen; (make-up, CD) auflegen; (play) aufführen; **to put the kettle on** Wasser aufsetzen; **to put weight on** zunehmen; **put out** vt (hand, foot) ausstrecken; (light, cigarette) ausmachen; **put up** vt (hand) hochheben; (picture) aufhängen; (tent) aufstellen; (building) errichten; (price) erhöhen; (person) unterbringen; **to ~ with** sich abfinden mit; **I won't ~ with it** das lasse ich mir nicht gefallen

putt [pʌt] vt, vi (Sport) putten

puzzle ['pʌzl] n Rätsel nt; (toy) Geduldsspiel nt; (jigsaw) ~ Puzzle nt ▷ vt vor ein Rätsel stellen; **it ~s me** es ist mir ein Rätsel; **puzzling** adj rätselhaft

pyjamas [pɪ'dʒɑːməz] npl Schlafanzug m

pylon ['paɪlən] n Mast m

pyramid ['pɪrəmɪd] n Pyramide f

P

quack [kwæk] *vi* quaken

quaint [kweɪnt] *adj* (*idea, tradition*) kurios; (*picturesque*) malerisch

qualification [kwɒlɪfɪ'keɪʃən] *n* (*for job*) Qualifikation *f*; (*from school, university*) Abschluss *m*; **qualified** ['kwɒlɪfaɪd] *adj* (*for job*) qualifiziert; **qualify** *vt* (*limit*) einschränken; **to be qualified to do sth** berechtigt sein, etw zu tun ▷ *vi* (*finish training*) seine Ausbildung abschließen; (*Sport*) sich qualifizieren

quality ['kwɒlɪtɪ] *n* Qualität *f*; (*characteristic*) Eigenschaft *f*

quantity ['kwɒntɪtɪ] *n* Menge *f*, Quantität *f*

quarantine ['kwɒrəntiːn] *n* Quarantäne *f*

quarrel ['kwɒrəl] *n* Streit *m* ▷ *vi* sich streiten; **quarrelsome** *adj* streitsüchtig

quarter ['kwɔːtə*] *n* Viertel *nt*; (*of year*) Vierteljahr *nt*; (*US: coin*) Vierteldollar *m*; **a ~ of an hour** eine Viertelstunde; **~ to/past** (*Brit*) (*o* **~ of/after** (*US*)) **three** Viertel vor/nach drei ▷ *vt* vierteln; **quarter final** *n* Viertelfinale *nt*; **quarters** *npl* (*Mil*) Quartier *nt*

quartet [kwɔː'tet] *n* Quartett *nt*

quay [kiː] *n* Kai *m*

queasy ['kwiːzɪ] *adj* **I feel ~** mir ist übel

queen [kwiːn] *n* Königin *f*; (*in cards, chess*) Dame *f*

queer [kwɪə*] *adj* (*strange*) seltsam, sonderbar; (*pej: homosexual*) schwul ▷ *n* (*pej*) Schwule(r) *m*

quench [kwentʃ] *vt* (*thirst*) löschen

query ['kwɪərɪ] *n* Frage *f* ▷ *vt* in Frage stellen; (*bill*) reklamieren

question ['kwestʃən] *n* Frage *f*; **that's out of the ~** das kommt nicht in Frage ▷ *vt* (*person*) befragen; (*suspect*) verhören; (*express doubt about*) bezweifeln; **questionable** *adj* zweifelhaft; (*improper*) fragwürdig; **question mark** *n* Fragezeichen *nt*; **questionnaire** [kwestʃə'nɛə*] *n* Fragebogen *m*

queue [kjuː] *n* (*Brit*) Schlange *f*; **to jump the ~** sich vordrängeln ▷ *vi* **to ~ (up)** Schlange stehen

quibble ['kwɪbl] *vi* kleinlich sein; (*argue*) streiten

quiche [kiːʃ] *n* Quiche *f*

quick [kwɪk] *adj* schnell; (*short*) kurz; **be ~** mach schnell!; **quickly** *adv* schnell

quid [kwɪd] (*pl* **quid**) *n* (*Brit fam*) Pfund *nt*; **20 ~** 20 Pfund

quiet ['kwaɪət] *adj* (*not noisy*) leise; (*peaceful, calm*) still, ruhig; **be ~** sei still!; **to keep ~ about sth** über etw *akk* nichts sagen ▷ *n* Stille *f*, Ruhe *f*; **quiet down** (*US*), **quieten down** ['kwaɪətən'daʊn] *vi* sich beruhigen ▷ *vt* beruhigen; **quietly** *adv* leise; (*calmly*) ruhig

quilt [kwɪlt] *n* (Stepp)decke *f*

quit [kwɪt] (**quit** *o* **quitted**, **quit** *o* **quitted**) *vt* (*leave*) verlassen; (*job*) aufgeben; **to ~ doing sth** aufhören, etw zu tun ▷ *vi* aufhören; (*resign*) kündigen

quite [kwaɪt] *adv* (*fairly*) ziemlich; (*completely*) ganz, völlig; **I don't ~ understand** ich verstehe das nicht ganz; **~ a few** ziemlich viele; **~ so** richtig!

quits [kwɪts] *adj* **to be ~ with sb** mit jdm quitt sein

quiver ['kwɪvə*] *vi* zittern

quiz [kwɪz] *n* (*competition*) Quiz *nt*

quota ['kwəʊtə] *n* Anteil *m*; (*Comm, Pol*) Quote *f*

quotation [kwəʊ'teɪʃən] *n* Zitat *nt*; (*price*)
Kostenvoranschlag *m*; **quotation marks**
npl Anführungszeichen *pl*; **quote** [kwəʊt]
vt (*text, author*) zitieren; (*price*) nennen ▷ *n*
Zitat *nt*; (*price*) Kostenvoranschlag *m*; **in ~s**
in Anführungszeichen

r

rabbi ['ræbaɪ] n Rabbiner m

rabbit ['ræbɪt] n Kaninchen nt

rabies ['reɪbiːz] nsing Tollwut f

raccoon [rə'kuːn] n Waschbär m

race [reɪs] n (competition) Rennen nt; (people) Rasse f ▷ vt um die Wette laufen/fahren ▷ vi (rush) rennen; **racecourse** n Rennbahn f; **racehorse** n Rennpferd nt; **racetrack** n Rennbahn f

racial ['reɪʃəl] adj Rassen-; **~ discrimination** Rassendiskriminierung f

racing ['reɪsɪŋ] n (horse) **~** Pferderennen nt; (motor) **~** Autorennen nt; **racing car** n Rennwagen m

racism ['reɪsɪzəm] n Rassismus m; **racist** n Rassist(in) m(f) ▷ adj rassistisch

rack [ræk] n Ständer m, Gestell nt ▷ vt **to ~ one's brains** sich dat den Kopf zerbrechen

racket ['rækɪt] n (Sport) Schläger m; (noise) Krach m

radar ['reɪdɑ:*] n Radar nt o m; **radar trap** n Radarfalle f

radiation [reɪdɪ'eɪʃən] n (radioactive) Strahlung f

radiator ['reɪdɪeɪtə*] n Heizkörper m; (Auto) Kühler m

radical ['rædɪkəl] adj radikal

radio ['reɪdɪəʊ] (pl **-s**) n Rundfunk m, Radio nt

radioactivity [reɪdɪəʊæk'tɪvɪtɪ] n Radioaktivität f

radio alarm ['reɪdɪəʊə'lɑːm] n Radiowecker m; **radio station** n Rundfunkstation f

radiotherapy [reɪdɪəʊ'θerəpɪ] n Strahlenbehandlung f

radish ['rædɪʃ] n Radieschen nt

radius ['reɪdɪəs] n Radius m; **within a five-mile ~** im Umkreis von fünf Meilen (of um)

raffle ['ræfl] n Tombola f; **raffle ticket** n Los nt

raft [rɑːft] n Floß nt

rag [ræg] n Lumpen m; (for cleaning) Lappen m

rage [reɪdʒ] n Wut f; **to be all the ~** der letzte Schrei sein ▷ vi toben; (disease) wüten

raid [reɪd] n Überfall m (on auf +akk); (by police) Razzia f (on gegen) ▷ vt (bank etc) überfallen; (by police) eine Razzia machen in +dat

rail [reɪl] n (on stairs, balcony etc) Geländer nt; (of ship) Reling f; (Rail) Schiene f; **railcard** n (Brit) ≈ Bahncard® f; **railing** n Geländer nt; **~s** pl (fence) Zaun m; **railroad** n (US) Eisenbahn f; **railroad station** n (US) Bahnhof m; **railway** n (Brit) Eisenbahn f; **railway line** n Bahnlinie f; (track) Gleis m; **railway station** n Bahnhof m

rain [reɪn] n Regen m ▷ vi regnen; **it's ~ing** es regnet; **rainbow** n Regenbogen m; **raincoat** n Regenmantel m; **rainfall** n Niederschlag m; **rainforest** n Regenwald m; **rainy** adj regnerisch

raise [reɪz] n (US: of wages/salary) Gehalts-/Lohnerhöhung f ▷ vt (lift) hochheben; (increase) erhöhen; (family) großziehen; (livestock) züchten; (money) aufbringen; (objection) erheben; **to ~ one's voice** (in anger) laut werden

raisin ['reɪzən] n Rosine f

rally ['rælɪ] n (Pol) Kundgebung f; (Auto) Rallye f; (Tennis) Ballwechsel m

RAM [ræm] acr = **random access memory** RAM m

ramble ['ræmbl] n Wanderung f ▷ vi (walk) wandern; (talk) schwafeln

ramp [ræmp] n Rampe f

ran [ræn] pt of **run**

ranch [rɑːntʃ] n Ranch f

rancid ['rænsɪd] adj ranzig

random ['rændəm] adj willkürlich ▷ n **at ~** (choose) willkürlich; (fire) ziellos

randy ['rændɪ] adj (Brit fam) geil, scharf

rang [ræŋ] pt of **ring**

range [reɪndʒ] n (selection) Auswahl f (of an +dat); (Comm) Sortiment nt (of an +dat); (of missile, telescope) Reichweite f; (of mountains) Kette f; **in this price ~** in dieser Preisklasse ▷ vi **to ~ from ... to ...** gehen von ... bis ...; (temperature, sizes, prices) liegen zwischen ... und ...

rank [ræŋk] n (Mil) Rang m; (social position) Stand m ▷ vt einstufen ▷ vi **to ~ among** zählen zu

ransom ['rænsəm] n Lösegeld nt

rap [ræp] n (Mus) Rap m

rape [reɪp] n Vergewaltigung f ▷ vt vergewaltigen

rapid, rapidly ['ræpɪd, -lɪ] adj, adv schnell

rapist ['reɪpɪst] n Vergewaltiger m

rare [reə*] adj selten, rar; (especially good) vortrefflich; (steak) blutig; **rarely** adv selten; **rarity** ['reərɪtɪ] n Seltenheit f

rash [ræʃ] adj unbesonnen ▷ n (Med) (Haut)ausschlag m

rasher ['ræʃə*] n **~ (of bacon)** (Speck)scheibe f

raspberry ['rɑːzbərɪ] n Himbeere f

rat [ræt] n Ratte f; (pej: person) Schwein nt

rate [reɪt] n (proportion, frequency) Rate f; (speed) Tempo nt; **~ (of exchange)** (Wechsel)kurs m; **~ of inflation** Inflationsrate f; **~ of interest** Zinssatz m; **at any ~** auf jeden Fall ▷ vt (evaluate) einschätzen (as als)

rather ['rɑːðə*] adv (in preference) lieber; (fairly) ziemlich; **I'd ~ stay here** ich würde lieber hier bleiben; **I'd ~ not** lieber nicht; **or ~** (more accurately) vielmehr

ratio ['reɪʃɪəʊ] (pl **-s**) n Verhältnis nt

rational ['ræʃənl] adj rational; **rationalize** ['ræʃnəlaɪz] vt rationalisieren

rattle ['rætl] n (toy) Rassel f ▷ vt (keys, coins) klimpern mit; (person) durcheinander bringen ▷ vi (window) klappern; (bottles) klirren; **rattle off** vt herunterrasseln; **rattlesnake** n Klapperschlange f

rave [reɪv] vi (talk wildly) fantasieren; (rage) toben; (enthuse) schwärmen (about von) ▷ n (Brit: event) Raveparty f

raven ['reɪvn] n Rabe m

raving ['reɪvɪŋ] adv **~ mad** total verrückt

ravishing ['rævɪʃɪŋ] adj hinreißend

raw [rɔː] adj (food) roh; (skin) wund; (climate) rau

ray [reɪ] n (of light) Strahl m; **~ of hope** Hoffnungsschimmer m

razor ['reɪzə*] n Rasierapparat m; **razor blade** n Rasierklinge f

Rd n abbr = **road** Str.

re [riː] prep (Comm) betreffs +gen

RE abbr = **religious education**

reach [riːtʃ] n **within/out of (sb's) ~** in/außer (jds) Reichweite; **within easy ~ of the shops** nicht weit von den Geschäften ▷ vt (arrive at, contact) erreichen; (come down/up as far as) reichen bis zu; (contact) **can you ~ it?** kommen Sie dran?; **reach for** vt greifen nach; **reach out** vi die Hand ausstrecken; **to ~ for** greifen nach

react [riːˈækt] vi reagieren (to auf +akk); **reaction** [riːˈækʃən] n Reaktion f (to auf +akk); **reactor** [rɪˈæktə*] n Reaktor m

read [riːd] (**read, read**) vt lesen; (meter) ablesen; **to ~ sth to sb** jdm etw vorlesen ▷ vi lesen; **to ~ to sb** jdm vorlesen; **it ~s well** es liest sich gut; **it ~s as follows** es lautet folgendermaßen; **read out** vt vorlesen; **read through** vt durchlesen; **read up on** vt nachlesen über +akk; **readable** adj (book) lesenswert; (handwriting) lesbar; **reader** n Leser(in) m(f)

readily ['redɪlɪ] adv (willingly) bereitwillig; **~ available** leicht erhältlich

reading ['riːdɪŋ] n (action) Lesen nt; (from meter) Zählerstand m; **reading glasses** npl Lesebrille f; **reading lamp** n Leselampe f; **reading list** n Leseliste f; **reading matter** n Lektüre f

readjust [riːəˈdʒʌst] vt (mechanism etc) neu einstellen ▷ vi sich wieder anpassen (to an +akk)

ready ['redɪ] adj fertig, bereit; **to be ~ to do sth** (willing) bereit sein, etw zu tun; **are you ~ to go?** bist du so weit?; **to get sth ~** etw fertig machen; **to get (oneself) ~** sich fertig machen; **ready cash** n

Bargeld nt; **ready-made** adj (product)
Fertig-; (clothes) Konfektions-; **~ meal**
Fertiggericht nt

real [rɪəl] adj wirklich; (actual) eigentlich;
(genuine) echt; (idiot etc) richtig; **for ~** echt;
this time it's for ~ diesmal ist es ernst;
get ~ sei realistisch! ▷ adv (fam, esp US)
echt ▷ n **for ~** echt; **this time it's for
~** diesmal ist es ernst; **get ~** sei
realistisch!; **real ale** n Ale nt; **real estate**
n Immobilien pl

realistic, realistically [rɪə'lɪstɪk, -əlɪ] adj,
adv realistisch; **reality** [rɪ'ælɪtɪ] n
Wirklichkeit f; **in ~** in Wirklichkeit; **reality
TV** n Reality-TV nt; **realization**
[rɪəlaɪ'zeɪʃən] n (awareness) Erkenntnis f;
realize ['rɪəlaɪz] vt (understand) begreifen;
(plan, idea) realisieren; **I ~d (that) ...** mir
wurde klar, dass ...

really ['rɪəlɪ] adv wirklich

real time [rɪəl'taɪm] n (Inform) **in ~** in
Echtzeit

realtor ['rɪəltɔ*] n (US)
Grundstücksmakler(in) m(f)

reappear [riːə'pɪə*] vi wieder erscheinen

rear [rɪə*] adj hintere(r, s), Hinter- ▷ n (of
building, vehicle) hinterer Teil; **at the ~ of**
hinter +dat; (inside) hinten in +dat; **rear
light** n (Auto) Rücklicht nt

rearm [riː'ɑːm] vt, vi wieder aufrüsten

rearrange [riːə'reɪndʒ] vt (furniture,
system) umstellen; (meeting) verlegen (for
auf +akk)

rear-view mirror ['rɪəvjuː'mɪrə*] n
Rückspiegel m; **rear window** n (Auto)
Heckscheibe f

reason ['riːzn] n (cause) Grund m (for für);
(ability to think) Verstand m; (common sense)
Vernunft f; **for some ~** aus irgendeinem
Grund ▷ vi **to ~ with sb** mit jdm
vernünftig reden; **reasonable** adj (person,
price) vernünftig; (offer) akzeptabel;
(chance) reell; (food, weather) ganz gut;
reasonably adv vernünftig; (fairly)
ziemlich

reassure [riːə'ʃʊə*] vt beruhigen; **she ~d
me that ...** sie versicherte mir, dass ...

rebel ['rebl] n Rebell(in) m(f) ▷ [rɪ'bel] vi
rebellieren; **rebellion** [rɪ'beliən] n
Aufstand m

reboot [riː'buːt] vt, vi (Inform) rebooten

rebound [rɪ'baʊnd] vi (ball etc)
zurückprallen

rebuild [riː'bɪld] irr vt wieder aufbauen

recall [rɪ'kɔːl] vt (remember) sich erinnern
an +akk; (call back) zurückrufen

recap ['riːkæp] vt, vi rekapitulieren

receipt [rɪ'siːt] n (document) Quittung f;
(receiving) Empfang m; **~s** pl (money)
Einnahmen pl

receive [rɪ'siːv] vt (news etc) erhalten,
bekommen; (visitor) empfangen; **receiver**
n (Tel) Hörer m; (Radio) Empfänger m

recent ['riːsnt] adj (event) vor kurzem
stattgefunden; (photo) neueste(r,s);
(invention) neu; **in ~ years** in den letzten
Jahren; **recently** adv vor kurzem; (in the
last few days or weeks) in letzter Zeit

reception [rɪ'sepʃən] n Empfang m;
receptionist n (in hotel) Empfangschef m,
Empfangsdame f; (woman in firm)
Empfangsdame f; (Med)
Sprechstundenhilfe f

recess [rɪ'ses] n (in wall) Nische f; (US: in
school) Pause f

recession [rɪ'seʃən] n Rezession f

recharge [riː'tʃɑːdʒ] vt (battery) aufladen;
rechargeable [riː'tʃɑːdʒəbl] adj wieder
aufladbar

recipe ['resɪpɪ] n Rezept nt (for für)

recipient [rɪ'sɪpɪənt] n Empfänger(in)
m(f)

reciprocal [rɪ'sɪprəkəl] adj gegenseitig

recite [rɪ'saɪt] vt vortragen; (details)
aufzählen

reckless ['rekləs] adj leichtsinnig; (driving)
gefährlich

reckon ['rekən] vt (calculate) schätzen;
(think) glauben ▷ vi **to ~ with** rechnen mit

reclaim [rɪ'kleɪm] vt (baggage) abholen;
(expenses, tax) zurückverlangen

recline [rɪ'klaɪn] vi (person) sich
zurücklehnen; **reclining seat** n Liegesitz
m

recognition [rekəg'nɪʃən] n
(acknowledgement) Anerkennung f; **in ~ of**
in Anerkennung +gen; **recognize**
['rekəgnaɪz] vt erkennen; (approve
officially) anerkennen

recommend [rekə'mend] vt empfehlen;
recommendation [rekəmen'deɪʃən] n
Empfehlung f

reconcile ['rekənsaɪl] vt (people)
versöhnen; (facts) (miteinander)
vereinbaren

reconsider [riːkən'sɪdə*] vt noch einmal

überdenken ▷ vi es sich *dat* noch einmal überlegen

reconstruct [ri:kən'strʌkt] vt wieder aufbauen; (*crime*) rekonstruieren

record ['rekɔːd] n (*Mus*) (Schall)platte f; (*best performance*) Rekord m; **~s** pl (*files*) Akten pl; **to keep a ~ of** Buch führen über +akk ▷ adj (*time etc*) Rekord- ▷ [ri'kɔːd] vt (*write down*) aufzeichnen; (*on tape etc*) aufnehmen; **~ed message** Ansage f; **recorded delivery** n (*Brit*) **by ~** per Einschreiben

recorder [ri'kɔːdə*] n (*Mus*) Blockflöte f; (**cassette**) **~** (Kassetten)rekorder m; **recording** [ri'kɔːdɪŋ] n (*on tape etc*) Aufnahme f; **record player** ['rekɔːdpleɪə*] n Plattenspieler m

recover [ri'kʌvə*] vt (*money, item*) zurückbekommen; (*appetite, strength*) wiedergewinnen ▷ vi sich erholen

recreation [rekri'eɪʃən] n Erholung f; **recreational** adj Freizeit-; **~ vehicle** (*US*) Wohnmobil nt

recruit [ri'kruːt] n (*Mil*) Rekrut(in) m(f); (*in firm, organization*) neues Mitglied ▷ vt (*Mil*) rekrutieren; (*members*) anwerben; (*staff*) einstellen; **recruitment agency** n Personalagentur f

rectangle ['rektæŋgl] n Rechteck nt; **rectangular** [rek'tæŋgʊlə*] adj rechteckig

rectify ['rektɪfaɪ] vt berichtigen

recuperate [ri'kuːpəreɪt] vi sich erholen

recyclable [riː'saɪkləbl] adj recycelbar, wieder verwertbar; **recycle** [riː'saɪkl] vt recyceln, wieder verwerten; **~d paper** Recyclingpapier nt; **recycling** n Recycling nt, Wiederverwertung f

red [red] adj rot ▷ n **in the ~** in den roten Zahlen; **Red Cross** n Rotes Kreuz; **red cabbage** n Rotkohl m; **redcurrant** n (rote) Johannisbeere

redeem [ri'diːm] vt (*Comm*) einlösen

red-handed [red'hændɪd] adj **to catch sb ~** jdn auf frischer Tat ertappen; **redhead** n Rothaarige(r) mf

redial [riː'daɪəl] vt, vi nochmals wählen

redirect [riːdaɪ'rekt] vt (*traffic*) umleiten; (*forward*) nachsenden

red light [red'laɪt] n (*traffic signal*) rotes Licht; **to go through the ~** bei Rot über die Ampel fahren; **red meat** n Rind-, Lamm-, Rehfleisch

redo [riː'duː] irr vt nochmals machen

reduce [ri'djuːs] vt reduzieren (**to** auf +akk, **by** um); **reduction** [ri'dʌkʃən] n Reduzierung f; (*in price*) Ermäßigung f

redundant [ri'dʌndənt] adj überflüssig; **to be made ~** entlassen werden

red wine [red'waɪn] n Rotwein m

reef [riːf] n Riff nt

reel [riːl] n Spule f; (*on fishing rod*) Rolle f; **reel off** vt herunterrasseln

ref [ref] n (*fam: referee*) Schiri m

refectory [ri'fektərɪ] n (*at college*) Mensa f

refer [ri'fɜː*] vt **to ~ sb to sb/sth** jdn an jdn/etw verweisen; **to ~ sth to sb** (*query, problem*) etw an jdn weiterleiten ▷ vi **to ~ to** (*mention, allude to*) sich beziehen auf +akk; (*book*) nachschlagen in +dat

referee [refə'riː] n Schiedsrichter(in) m(f); (*in boxing*) Ringrichter m; (*Brit: for job*) Referenz f

reference ['refrəns] n (*allusion*) Anspielung f (**to** auf +akk); (*for job*) Referenz f; (*in book*) Verweis m; **~ (number)** (*in document*) Aktenzeichen nt; **with ~ to** mit Bezug auf +akk; **reference book** n Nachschlagewerk nt

referendum [refə'rendəm] (pl **referenda**) n Referendum nt

refill ['riːfɪl] vt [riː'fɪl] nachfüllen ▷ n (*for ballpoint pen*) Ersatzmine f

refine [ri'faɪn] vt (*purify*) raffinieren; (*improve*) verfeinern; **refined** adj (*genteel*) fein

reflect [ri'flekt] vt reflektieren; (*fig*) widerspiegeln ▷ vi nachdenken (**on** über +akk); **reflection** [ri'flekʃən] n (*image*) Spiegelbild nt; (*thought*) Überlegung f

reflex ['riːfleks] n Reflex m

reform [ri'fɔːm] n Reform f ▷ vt reformieren; (*person*) bessern

refrain [ri'freɪn] vi **to ~ from doing sth** es unterlassen, etw zu tun

refresh [ri'freʃ] vt erfrischen; **refresher course** n Auffrischungskurs m; **refreshing** adj erfrischend; **refreshments** npl Erfrischungen pl

refrigerator [ri'frɪdʒəreɪtə*] n Kühlschrank m

refuel [riː'fjʊəl] vt, vi auftanken

refuge ['refjuːdʒ] n Zuflucht f (*from* vor +dat); **to take ~** sich flüchten (*from* vor +dat, *in* in +akk); **refugee** [refjʊ'dʒiː] n Flüchtling m

refund ['riːfʌnd] *n* (*of money*) Rückerstattung *f*; **to get a ~ (on sth)** sein Geld (für etw) zurückbekommen ▷ [rɪ'fʌnd] *vt* zurückerstatten

refusal [rɪ'fjuːzəl] *n* (*to do sth*) Weigerung *f*; **refuse** ['refjuːs] *n* Müll *m*, Abfall *m* ▷ [rɪ'fjuːz] *vt* ablehnen; **to ~ sb sth** jdm etw verweigern; **to ~ to do sth** sich weigern, etw zu tun ▷ *vi* sich weigern

regain [rɪ'geɪn] *vt* wiedergewinnen, wiedererlangen; **to ~ consciousness** wieder zu Bewusstsein kommen

regard [rɪ'gɑːd] *n* **with ~ to** in Bezug auf +*akk*; **in this ~** in dieser Hinsicht; **~s** (*at end of letter*) mit freundlichen Grüßen; **give my ~s to ...** viele Grüße an ...+*akk* ▷ *vt* **to ~ sb/sth as sth** jdn/etw als etw betrachten; **as ~s ...** was ... betrifft; **regarding** *prep* bezüglich +*gen*; **regardless** *adj* **~ of** ohne Rücksicht auf +*akk* ▷ *adv* trotzdem; **to carry on ~** einfach weitermachen

regime [reɪ'ʒiːm] *n* (*Pol*) Regime *nt*

region ['riːdʒən] *n* (*of country*) Region *f*, Gebiet *nt*; **in the ~ of** (*about*) ungefähr; **regional** *adj* regional

register ['redʒɪstə*] *n* Register *nt*; (*school*) Namensliste *f* ▷ *vt* (*with an authority*) registrieren lassen; (*birth, death, vehicle*) anmelden ▷ *vi* (*at hotel, for course*) sich anmelden; (*at university*) sich einschreiben; **registered** *adj* eingetragen; (*letter*) eingeschrieben; **by ~ post** per Einschreiben; **registration** [redʒɪ'streɪʃən] *n* (*for course*) Anmeldung *f*; (*at university*) Einschreibung *f*; (*Auto: number*) (polizeiliches) Kennzeichen; **registration form** *n* Anmeldeformular *nt*; **registration number** (*Auto*) (polizeiliches) Kennzeichen; **registry office** ['redʒɪstrɪfɪs] *n* Standesamt *nt*

regret [rɪ'gret] *n* Bedauern *nt* ▷ *vt* bedauern; **regrettable** *adj* bedauerlich

regular ['regjʊlə*] *adj* regelmäßig; (*size*) normal ▷ *n* (*client*) Stammkunde *m*, Stammkundin *f*; (*in bar*) Stammgast *m*; (*petrol*) Normalbenzin *nt*; **regularly** *adv* regelmäßig

regulate ['regjʊleɪt] *vt* regulieren; (*using rules*) regeln; **regulation** [regjʊ'leɪʃən] *n* (*rule*) Vorschrift *f*

rehabilitation [riːəbɪlɪ'teɪʃən] *n* Rehabilitation *f*

rehearsal [rɪ'hɜːsəl] *n* Probe *f*; **rehearse** *vt, vi* proben

reign [reɪn] *n* Herrschaft *f* ▷ *vi* herrschen (*over über* +*akk*)

reimburse [riːɪm'bɜːs] *vt* (*person*) entschädigen; (*expenses*) zurückerstatten

reindeer ['reɪndɪə*] *n* Rentier *nt*

reinforce [riːɪn'fɔːs] *vt* verstärken

reinstate [riːɪn'steɪt] *vt* (*employee*) wieder einstellen; (*passage in text*) wieder aufnehmen

reject ['riːdʒekt] *n* (*Comm*) Ausschussartikel *m* ▷ [rɪ'dʒekt] *vt* ablehnen; **rejection** [rɪ'dʒekʃən] *n* Ablehnung *f*

relapse [rɪ'læps] *n* Rückfall *m*

relate [rɪ'leɪt] *vt* (*story*) erzählen; (*connect*) in Verbindung bringen (*to mit*) ▷ *vi* **to ~ to** (*refer*) sich beziehen auf +*akk*; **related** *adj* verwandt (*to mit*); **relation** [rɪ'leɪʃən] *n* (*relative*) Verwandte(r) *mf*; (*connection*) Beziehung *f*; **~s** *pl* (*dealings*) Beziehungen *pl*; **relationship** *n* (*connection*) Beziehung *f*; (*between people*) Verhältnis *nt*

relative ['relətɪv] *n* Verwandte(r) *mf* ▷ *adj* relativ; **relatively** *adv* relativ, verhältnismäßig

relax [rɪ'læks] *vi* sich entspannen; **~!** reg dich nicht auf! ▷ *vt* (*grip, conditions*) lockern; **relaxation** [riːlæk'seɪʃən] *n* (*rest*) Entspannung *f*; **relaxed** *adj* entspannt; **relaxing** *adj* entspannend

release [rɪ'liːs] *n* (*from prison*) Entlassung *f*; **new/recent ~** (*film, CD*) Neuerscheinung *f* ▷ *vt* (*animal, hostage*) freilassen; (*prisoner*) entlassen; (*handbrake*) lösen; (*news*) veröffentlichen; (*film, CD*) herausbringen

relent [rɪ'lent] *vi* nachgeben; **relentless, relentlessly** *adj, adv* (*merciless*) erbarmungslos; (*neverending*) unaufhörlich

relevance ['reləvəns] *n* Relevanz *f* (*to für*); **relevant** *adj* relevant (*to für*)

reliable, reliably [rɪ'laɪəbl, -blɪ] *adj, adv* zuverlässig; **reliant** [rɪ'laɪənt] *adj* **~ on** abhängig von

relic ['relɪk] *n* (*from past*) Relikt *nt*

relief [rɪ'liːf] *n* (*from anxiety, pain*) Erleichterung *f*; (*assistance*) Hilfe *f*; **relieve** [rɪ'liːv] *vt* (*pain*) lindern; (*boredom*) überwinden; (*take over from*) ablösen; **I'm ~d** ich bin erleichtert

religion [rɪ'lɪdʒən] n Religion f; **religious** [rɪ'lɪdʒəs] adj religiös

relish ['relɪʃ] n (for food) würzige Soße ▷ vt (enjoy) genießen; **I don't ~ the thought of getting up early** der Gedanke, früh aufzustehen, behagt mir gar nicht

reluctant [rɪ'lʌktənt] adj widerwillig; **to be ~ to do sth** etw nur ungern tun; **reluctantly** adv widerwillig

rely on [rɪ'laɪ ɒn] vt sich verlassen auf +akk; (depend on) abhängig sein von

remain [rɪ'meɪn] vi bleiben; (be left over) übrig bleiben; **remainder** n (a. Math) Rest m; **remaining** adj übrig; **remains** npl Überreste pl

remark [rɪ'mɑːk] n Bemerkung f ▷ vt **to ~ that** bemerken, dass ▷ vi **to ~ on sth** über etw akk eine Bemerkung machen; **remarkable, remarkably** adj, adv bemerkenswert

remarry [riː'mærɪ] vi wieder heiraten

remedy ['remɪdɪ] n Mittel nt (for gegen) ▷ vt abhelfen +dat

remember [rɪ'membə*] vt sich erinnern an +akk; **to ~ to do sth** daran denken, etw zu tun; **I ~ seeing her** ich erinnere mich daran, sie gesehen zu haben; **I must ~ that** das muss ich mir merken ▷ vi sich erinnern

Remembrance Day [rɪ'membrəns'deɪ] n (Brit) ≈ Volkstrauertag m

● **Remembrance Day**
●
● **Remembrance Sunday/Day** ist der
● britische Gedenktag für die
● Gefallenen der beiden Weltkriege
● und anderer Kriege. Er fällt auf einen
● Sonntag vor oder nach dem 11.
● November (am 11.11.1918 endete der
● Erste Weltkrieg) und wird mit einer
● Schweigeminute,
● Kranzniederlegungen an
● Kriegerdenkmälern und dem Tragen
● von Ansteckhnadeln in Form einer
● Mohnblume begangen.

remind [rɪ'maɪnd] vt **to ~ sb of/about sb/sth** jdn an jdn/etw erinnern; **to ~ sb to do sth** jdn daran erinnern, etw zu tun; **that ~s me** dabei fällt mir ein ...; **reminder** n (to pay) Mahnung f

reminisce [remɪ'nɪs] vi in Erinnerungen schwelgen (about an +akk); **reminiscent** [remɪ'nɪsənt] adj **to be ~ of** erinnern an +akk

remittance n Überweisung f (to an +akk)

remnant ['remnənt] n Rest m

remote [rɪ'məʊt] adj (place) abgelegen; (slight) gering ▷ n (Tv) Fernbedienung f; **remote control** n Fernsteuerung f; (device) Fernbedienung f

removal [rɪ'muːvəl] n Entfernung f; (Brit: move from house) Umzug m; **removal firm** n (Brit) Spedition f; **remove** [rɪ'muːv] vt entfernen; (lid) abnehmen; (clothes) ausziehen; (doubt, suspicion) zerstreuen

rename [riː'neɪm] vt umbenennen

renew [rɪ'njuː] vt erneuern; (licence, passport, library book) verlängern lassen

renounce [rɪ'naʊns] vt verzichten auf +akk; (faith, opinion) abschwören +dat

renovate ['renəveɪt] vt renovieren

renowned [rɪ'naʊnd] adj berühmt (for für)

rent [rent] n Miete f; **for ~** (US) zu vermieten ▷ vt (as hirer, tenant) mieten; (as owner) vermieten; **~ed car** Mietwagen m; **rent out** vt vermieten; **rental** n Miete f; (for car, TV etc) Leihgebühr f ▷ adj Miet-

reorganize [riː'ɔːgənaɪz] vt umorganisieren

rep [rep] n (Comm) Vertreter(in) m(f)

repair [rɪ'peə*] n Reparatur f ▷ vt reparieren; (damage) wieder gutmachen; **repair kit** n Flickzeug nt

repay [riː'peɪ] irr vt (money) zurückzahlen; **to ~ sb for sth** (fig) sich bei jdm für etw revanchieren

repeat [rɪ'piːt] n (Radio, Tv) Wiederholung f ▷ vt wiederholen; **repetition** [repə'tɪʃən] n Wiederholung f; **repetitive** [rɪ'petɪtɪv] adj sich wiederholend

rephrase [riː'freɪz] vt anders formulieren

replace [rɪ'pleɪs] vt ersetzen (with durch); (put back) zurückstellen, zurücklegen; **replacement** n (thing, person) Ersatz m; (temporarily in job) Vertretung f; **replacement part** n Ersatzteil nt

replay ['riːpleɪ] n (action) ~ Wiederholung f ▷ [riː'pleɪ] vt (game) wiederholen

replica ['replɪkə] n Kopie f

reply [rɪ'plaɪ] n Antwort f ▷ vi antworten; **to ~ to sb/sth** jdm/auf etw

r

akk antworten ▷ *vt* **to ~ that** antworten, dass

report [rɪ'pɔːt] *n* Bericht *m*; (*school*) Zeugnis *nt* ▷ *vt* (*tell*) berichten; (*give information against*) melden; (*to police*) anzeigen ▷ *vi* (*present oneself*) sich melden; **to ~ sick** sich krankmelden; **report card** *n* (*US: school*), Zeugnis *nt*; **reporter** *n* Reporter(in) *m(f)*

represent [reprɪ'zent] *vt* darstellen; (*speak for*) vertreten; **representation** [reprɪzen'teɪʃən] *n* (*picture etc*) Darstellung *f*; **representative** [reprɪ'zentətɪv] *n* Vertreter(in) *m(f)*; (*US Pol*) Abgeordnete(r) *mf* ▷ *adj* repräsentativ (*of* für)

reprimand ['reprɪmɑːnd] *n* Tadel *m* ▷ *vt* tadeln

reprint ['riːprɪnt] *n* Nachdruck *m*

reproduce [riːprə'djuːs] *vt* (*copy*) reproduzieren ▷ *vi* (*Bio*) sich fortpflanzen; **reproduction** [riːprə'dʌkʃən] *n* (*copy*) Reproduktion *f*; (*Bio*) Fortpflanzung *f*

reptile ['reptaɪl] *n* Reptil *nt*

republic [rɪ'pʌblɪk] *n* Republik *f*; **republican** *adj* republikanisch ▷ *n* Republikaner(in) *m(f)*

repulsive [rɪ'pʌlsɪv] *adj* abstoßend

reputable ['repjʊtəbl] *adj* seriös

reputation [repjʊ'teɪʃən] *n* Ruf *m*; **he has a ~ for being difficult** er hat den Ruf, schwierig zu sein

request [rɪ'kwest] *n* Bitte *f* (*for* um); **on ~** auf Wunsch ▷ *vt* bitten um; **to ~ sb to do sth** jdn bitten, etw zu tun

require [rɪ'kwaɪə*] *vt* (*need*) brauchen; (*desire*) verlangen; **what qualifications are ~d?** welche Qualifikationen sind erforderlich?; **required** *adj* erforderlich; **requirement** *n* (*condition*) Anforderung *f*; (*need*) Bedingung *f*

rerun ['riːrʌn] *n* Wiederholung *f*

rescue ['reskjuː] *n* Rettung *f*; **to come to sb's ~** jdm zu Hilfe kommen ▷ *vt* retten; **rescue party** *n* Rettungsmannschaft *f*

research [rɪ'sɜːtʃ] *n* Forschung *f* ▷ *vi* forschen (*into* über +*akk*) ▷ *vt* erforschen; **researcher** *n* Forscher(in) *m(f)*

resemblance [rɪ'zembləns] *n* Ähnlichkeit *f* (*to* mit); **resemble** [rɪ'zembl] *vt* ähneln +*dat*

resent [rɪ'zent] *vt* übel nehmen

reservation [rezə'veɪʃən] *n* (*booking*) Reservierung *f*; (*doubt*) Vorbehalt *m*; **I**

have a ~ (*in hotel, restaurant*) ich habe reserviert; **reserve** [rɪ'zɜːv] *n* (*store*) Vorrat *m* (*of* an +*dat*); (*manner*) Zurückhaltung *f*; (*Sport*) Reservespieler(in) *m(f)*; (*game ~*) Naturschutzgebiet *nt* ▷ *vt* (*book in advance*) reservieren; **reserved** *adj* reserviert

reservoir ['rezəvwɑː*] *n* (*for water*) Reservoir *nt*

reside [rɪ'zaɪd] *vi* wohnen; **residence** ['rezɪdəns] *n* Wohnsitz *m*; (*living*) Aufenthalt *m*; **~ permit** Aufenthaltsgenehmigung *f*; **~ hall** Studentenwohnheim *nt*; **resident** ['rezɪdənt] *n* (*in house*) Bewohner(in) *m(f)*; (*in town, area*) Einwohner(in) *m(f)*

resign [rɪ'zaɪn] *vt* (*post*) zurücktreten von; (*job*) kündigen ▷ *vi* (*from post*) zurücktreten; (*from job*) kündigen; **resignation** [rezɪg'neɪʃən] *n* (*from post*) Rücktritt *m*; (*from job*) Kündigung *f*; **resigned** *adj* resigniert; **he is ~ to it** er hat sich damit abgefunden

resist [rɪ'zɪst] *vt* widerstehen +*dat*; **resistance** *n* Widerstand *m* (*to* gegen)

resit [riː'sɪt] (*Brit*) *irr vt* wiederholen ▷ ['riːsɪt] *n* Wiederholungsprüfung *f*

resolution [rezə'luːʃən] *n* (*intention*) Vorsatz *m*; (*decision*) Beschluss *m*

resolve [rɪ'zɒlv] *vt* (*problem*) lösen

resort [rɪ'zɔːt] *n* (*holiday ~*) Urlaubsort *m*; (*health ~*) Kurort *m*; **as a last ~** als letzter Ausweg ▷ *vi* **to ~ to** greifen zu; (*violence*) anwenden

resources [rɪ'sɔːsɪz] *npl* (*money*) (Geld)mittel *pl*; (*mineral ~*) Bodenschätze *pl*

respect [rɪ'spekt] *n* Respekt *m* (*for* vor +*dat*); (*consideration*) Rücksicht *f* (*for* auf +*akk*); **with ~ to** in Bezug auf +*akk*; **in this ~** in dieser Hinsicht; **in all due ~** bei allem Respekt ▷ *vt* respektieren; **respectable** [rɪ'spektəbl] *adj* (*person, family*) angesehen; (*district*) anständig; (*achievement, result*) beachtlich; **respected** [rɪ'spektɪd] *adj* angesehen

respective [rɪ'spektɪv] *adj* jeweilig; **respectively** *adv* **5% and 10% ~** 5% beziehungsweise 10%

respiratory [rɪ'spɪrətərɪ] *adj* **~ problems** (*o trouble*) Atembeschwerden *pl*

respond [rɪ'spɒnd] *vi* antworten (*to* auf +*akk*); (*react*) reagieren (*to* auf +*akk*); (*to*

treatment) ansprechen (to auf +akk);
response [rɪ'spɒns] n Antwort f;
(reaction) Reaktion f; **in ~ to** als Antwort
auf +akk

responsibility [rɪspɒnsə'bɪlɪtɪ] n
Verantwortung f; **that's her ~** dafür ist sie
verantwortlich; **responsible** [rɪ'spɒnsəbl]
adj verantwortlich (for für); (trustworthy)
verantwortungsbewusst; (job)
verantwortungsvoll

rest [rest] n (relaxation) Ruhe f; (break)
Pause f; (remainder) Rest m; **to have** (o
take) **a ~** sich ausruhen; (break) Pause
machen; **the ~ of the wine/the people**
der Rest des Weins/der Leute ▷ vi (relax)
sich ausruhen; (lean) lehnen (on, against an
+dat, gegen)

restaurant ['restərɒnt] n Restaurant nt;
restaurant car n (Brit) Speisewagen m

restful ['restful] adj (holiday etc)
erholsam, ruhig; **restless** ['restləs] adj
unruhig

restore [rɪ'stɔː*] vt (painting, building)
restaurieren; (order) wiederherstellen;
(give back) zurückgeben

restrain [rɪ'streɪn] vt (person, feelings)
zurückhalten; **to ~ oneself** sich
beherrschen

restrict [rɪ'strɪkt] vt beschränken (to auf
+akk); **restricted** adj beschränkt;
restriction [rɪ'strɪkʃən] n Einschränkung
f (on +gen)

rest room ['restruːm] n (US) Toilette f

result [rɪ'zʌlt] n Ergebnis nt; (consequence)
Folge f; **as a ~ of** infolge +gen ▷ vi **to ~ in**
führen zu; **to ~ from** sich ergeben aus

resume [rɪ'zjuːm] vt (work, negotiations)
wieder aufnehmen; (journey) fortsetzen

résumé ['rezjumeɪ] n Zusammenfassung
f; (US: curriculum vitae) Lebenslauf m

resuscitate [rɪ'sʌsɪteɪt] vt wieder
beleben

retail ['riːteɪl] adv im Einzelhandel;
retailer n Einzelhändler(in) m(f)

retain [rɪ'teɪn] vt behalten; (heat) halten

rethink [riː'θɪŋk] irr vt noch einmal
überdenken

retire [rɪ'taɪə*] vi (from work) in den
Ruhestand treten; (withdraw) sich
zurückziehen; **retired** adj (person)
pensioniert; **retirement** n (time of life)
Ruhestand m; **retirement age** n
Rentenalter nt

retrace [rɪ'treɪs] vt zurückverfolgen

retrain [riː'treɪn] vi sich umschulen
lassen

retreat [rɪ'triːt] n (Mil) Rückzug m (from
aus); (refuge) Zufluchtsort m ▷ vi (Mil) sich
zurückziehen; (step back) zurückweichen

retrieve [rɪ'triːv] vt (recover)
wiederbekommen; (rescue) retten; (data)
abrufen

retrospect ['retrəuspekt] n **in
~** rückblickend; **retrospective**
[retrəu'spektɪv] adj rückblickend; (pay rise)
rückwirkend

return [rɪ'tɜːn] n (going back) Rückkehr f;
(giving back) Rückgabe f; (profit) Gewinn m;
(Brit: ~ ticket) Rückfahrkarte f; (plane ticket)
Rückflugticket nt; (Tennis), Return m; **in
~** als Gegenleistung (for für); **many happy
~s (of the day)** herzlichen Glückwunsch
zum Geburtstag! ▷ vi (person)
zurückkehren; (doubts, symptoms) wieder
auftreten; **to ~ to school/work** wieder in
die Schule/die Arbeit gehen ▷ vt (give
back) zurückgeben; **I ~ed his call** ich habe
ihn zurückgerufen; **returnable** adj (bottle)
Pfand-; **return flight** n (Brit) Rückflug m;
(both ways) Hin- und Rückflug m; **return
key** n (Inform) Eingabetaste f; **return
ticket** n (Brit) Rückfahrkarte f; (for plane)
Rückflugticket nt

reunification [riːjuːnɪfɪ'keɪʃən] n
Wiedervereinigung f

reunion [riː'juːnjən] n (party) Treffen nt;
reunite [riːju'naɪt] vt wieder vereinigen

reusable [riː'juːzəbl] adj wieder
verwendbar

reveal [rɪ'viːl] vt (make known) enthüllen;
(secret) verraten; (show) zeigen; **revealing**
adj aufschlussreich; (dress) freizügig

revenge [rɪ'vendʒ] n Rache f; (in game)
Revanche f; **to take ~ on sb (for sth)** sich
an jdm (für etw) rächen

revenue ['revənjuː] n Einnahmen pl

reverse [rɪ'vɜːs] n (back) Rückseite f;
(opposite) Gegenteil nt; (Auto) **~ (gear)**
Rückwärtsgang m ▷ adj **in ~ order** in
umgekehrter Reihenfolge ▷ vt (order)
umkehren; (decision) umstoßen; (car)
zurücksetzen; **to ~ the charges** (Brit) ein
R-Gespräch führen ▷ vi (Auto) rückwärts
fahren

review [rɪ'vjuː] n (of book, film etc)
Rezension f; **to be under ~** überprüft

r

werden ▷ vt (book, film etc) rezensieren; (re-examine) überprüfen

revise [rɪ'vaɪz] vt revidieren; (text) überarbeiten; (Brit: in school) wiederholen ▷ vi (Brit: in school) den Stoff wiederholen; **revision** [rɪ'vɪʒən] n (of text) Überarbeitung f; (Brit: in school) Wiederholung f

revitalize [ri:'vaɪtəlaɪz] vt neu beleben

revive [rɪ'vaɪv] vt (person) wieder beleben; (tradition, interest) wieder aufleben lassen ▷ vi (regain consciousness) wieder zu sich kommen

revolt [rɪ'vəʊlt] n Aufstand m; **revolting** adj widerlich

revolution [revə'lu:ʃən] n (Pol, fig) Revolution f; (turn) Umdrehung f; **revolutionary** adj revolutionär ▷ n Revolutionär(in) m(f)

revolve [rɪ'vɒlv] vi sich drehen (around um); **revolver** n Revolver m; **revolving door** n Drehtür f

reward [rɪ'wɔ:d] n Belohnung f ▷ vt belohnen; **rewarding** adj lohnend

rewind [ri:'waɪnd] irr vt (tape) zurückspulen

rewrite [ri:'raɪt] irr vt (write again; recast) umschreiben

rheumatism ['ru:mətɪzəm] n Rheuma nt

Rhine [raɪn] n Rhein m

rhinoceros [raɪ'nɒsərəs] n Nashorn nt

Rhodes [rəʊdz] n Rhodos nt

rhubarb ['ru:bɑ:b] n Rhabarber m

rhyme [raɪm] n Reim m ▷ vi sich reimen (with auf +akk)

rhythm ['rɪðəm] n Rhythmus m

rib [rɪb] n Rippe f

ribbon ['rɪbən] n Band nt

rice [raɪs] n Reis m; **rice pudding** n Milchreis m

rich [rɪtʃ] adj reich; (food) schwer ▷ npl **the ~** die Reichen pl

rickety ['rɪkɪtɪ] adj wackelig

rid [rɪd] (**rid, rid**) vt **to get ~ of sb/sth** jdn/etw loswerden

ridden ['rɪdn] pp of **ride**

riddle ['rɪdl] n Rätsel nt

ride [raɪd] (**rode, ridden**) vt (horse) reiten; (bicycle) fahren ▷ vi (on horse) reiten; (on bike) fahren ▷ n (in vehicle, on bike) Fahrt f; (on horse) (Aus)ritt m; **to go for a ~** (in car, on bike) spazieren fahren; (on horse) reiten gehen; **to take sb for a ~** (fam) jdn

verarschen; **rider** n (on horse) Reiter(in) m(f); (on bike) Fahrer(in) m(f)

ridiculous [rɪ'dɪkjʊləs] adj lächerlich; **don't be ~** red keinen Unsinn!

riding ['raɪdɪŋ] n Reiten nt; **to go ~** reiten gehen ▷ adj Reit-

rifle ['raɪfl] n Gewehr nt

rig [rɪg] n **oil ~** Bohrinsel f ▷ vt (election etc) manipulieren

right [raɪt] adj (correct, just) richtig; (opposite of left) rechte(r, s); (clothes, job etc) passend; **to be ~** (person) Recht haben; (clock) richtig gehen; **that's ~** das stimmt! ▷ n Recht nt (to auf +akk); (side) rechte Seite; **the Right** (Pol) die Rechte; **to take a ~** (Auto) rechts abbiegen; **on the ~** rechts (of von); **to the ~** nach rechts; (on the ~) rechts (of von) ▷ adv (towards the ~) nach rechts; (directly) direkt; (exactly) genau; **to turn ~** (Auto) rechts abbiegen; **~ away** sofort; **~ now** im Moment; (immediately) sofort; **right angle** n rechter Winkel; **right-hand drive** n Rechtssteuerung f ▷ adj rechtsgesteuert; **right-handed** adj **he is ~** er ist Rechtshänder; **right-hand side** n rechte Seite; **on the ~** auf der rechten Seite; **rightly** adv zu Recht; **right of way** n **to have ~** (Auto) Vorfahrt haben; **right wing** n (Pol, Sport) rechter Flügel; **right-wing** adj Rechts-; **~ extremist** Rechtsradikale(r) mf

rigid ['rɪdʒɪd] adj (stiff) starr; (strict) streng

rigorous, rigorously ['rɪgərəs, -lɪ] adj, adv streng

rim [rɪm] n (of cup etc) Rand m; (of wheel) Felge f

rind [raɪnd] n (of cheese) Rinde f; (of bacon) Schwarte f; (of fruit) Schale f

ring [rɪŋ] (**rang, rung**) vt, vi (bell) läuten; (Tel) anrufen ▷ n (on finger, in boxing) Ring m; (circle) Kreis m; (at circus) Manege f; **to give sb a ~** (Tel) jdn anrufen; **ring back** vt, vi zurückrufen; **ring up** vt, vi anrufen

ring binder n Ringbuch nt

ringing tone n (Tel) Rufzeichen nt

ringleader n Anführer(in) m(f)

ring road n (Brit) Umgehungsstraße f

ringtone n Klingelton m

rink [rɪŋk] n (ice ~) Eisbahn f; (for roller-skating) Rollschuhbahn f

rinse [rɪns] vt spülen

riot ['raɪət] n Aufruhr m

rip [rɪp] n Riss m ▷ vt zerreißen; **to ~ sth**

open etw aufreißen ▷ vi reißen; **rip off** vt (fam: person) übers Ohr hauen; **rip up** vt zerreißen

ripe [raɪp] adj (fruit) reif; **ripen** vi reifen

rip-off ['rɪpɒf] n **that's a ~** (fam: too expensive) das ist Wucher

rise [raɪz] (**rose, risen**) vi (from sitting, lying) aufstehen; (sun) aufgehen; (prices, temperature) steigen; (ground) ansteigen; (in revolt) sich erheben ▷ n (increase) Anstieg m (in +gen); (pay ~) Gehaltserhöhung f; (to power, fame) Aufstieg m (to u); (slope) Steigung f; **risen** ['rɪzn] pp of **rise**

risk [rɪsk] n Risiko nt ▷ vt riskieren; **to ~ doing sth** es riskieren, etw zu tun; **risky** adj riskant

risotto [rɪ'zɒtəʊ] (pl **-s**) n Risotto nt

ritual ['rɪtjʊəl] n Ritual nt ▷ adj rituell

rival ['raɪvəl] n Rivale m, Rivalin f (for um); (Comm) Konkurrent(in) m(f); **rivalry** n Rivalität f; (Comm, Sport) Konkurrenz f

river ['rɪvə*] n Fluss m; **the River Thames** (Brit), **the Thames River** (US) die Themse; **riverside** n Flussufer nt ▷ adj am Flussufer

road [rəʊd] n Straße f; (fig) Weg m; **on the ~** (travelling) unterwegs, mit dem Auto/Bus etc fahren; **roadblock** n Straßensperre f; **roadmap** n Straßenkarte f; **road rage** n aggressives Verhalten im Straßenverkehr; **roadside** n **at** (o **by**) **the ~** am Straßenrand; **roadsign** n Verkehrsschild nt; **road tax** n Kraftfahrzeugsteuer f; **roadworks** npl Straßenarbeiten pl; **roadworthy** adj fahrtüchtig

roar [rɔ:*] n (of person, lion) Brüllen nt; (von Verkehr) Donnern nt ▷ vi (person, lion) brüllen (with vor +dat)

roast [rəʊst] n Braten m ▷ adj **~ beef** Rinderbraten m; **~ chicken** Brathähnchen nt; **~ pork** Schweinebraten m; **~ potatoes** pl im Backofen gebratene Kartoffeln ▷ vt (meat) braten

rob [rɒb] vt bestehlen; (bank, shop) ausrauben; **robber** n Räuber(in) m(f); **robbery** n Raub m

robe [rəʊb] n (US: dressing gown) Morgenrock m; (of judge, priest etc) Robe f, Talar m

robin ['rɒbɪn] n Rotkehlchen nt

robot ['rəʊbɒt] n Roboter m

robust [rəʊ'bʌst] adj robust; (defence) stark

rock [rɒk] n (substance) Stein m; (boulder) Felsbrocken m; (Mus) Rock m; **stick of ~** (Brit) Zuckerstange f; **on the ~s** (drink) mit Eis; (marriage) gescheitert ▷ vt, vi (swing) schaukeln; (dance) rocken; **rock climbing** n Klettern nt; **to go ~** klettern gehen

rocket ['rɒkɪt] n Rakete f; (in salad) Rucola f

rocking chair ['rɒkɪŋtʃeə*] n Schaukelstuhl m

rocky ['rɒkɪ] adj (landscape) felsig; (path) steinig

rod [rɒd] n (bar) Stange f; (fishing ~) Rute f

rode [rəʊd] pt of **ride**

rogue [rəʊg] n Schurke m, Gauner m

role [rəʊl] n Rolle f; **role model** n Vorbild nt

roll [rəʊl] n (of film, paper etc) Rolle f; (bread ~) Brötchen nt ▷ vt (move by ~ing) rollen; (cigarette) drehen ▷ vi (move by ~ing) rollen; (ship) schlingern; (camera) laufen; **roll out** vt (pastry) ausrollen; **roll over** vi (person) sich umdrehen; **roll up** vi (fam: arrive) antanzen ▷ vt (carpet) aufrollen; **to roll one's sleeves up** die Ärmel hochkrempeln

roller n (hair ~) (Locken)wickler m; **Rollerblades®** npl Inlineskates pl; **rollerblading** n Inlineskaten nt; **roller coaster** n Achterbahn f; **roller skates** npl Rollschuhe pl; **roller-skating** n Rollschuhlaufen nt; **rolling pin** n Nudelholz nt; **roll-on (deodorant)** n Deoroller m

ROM [rɒm] acr = **read only memory** ROM m

Roman ['rəʊmən] adj römisch ▷ n Römer(in) m(f); **Roman Catholic** adj römisch-katholisch ▷ n Katholik(in) m(f)

romance [rəʊ'mæns] n Romantik f; (love affair) Romanze f

Romania [rəʊ'meɪnɪə] n Rumänien nt; **Romanian** adj rumänisch ▷ n Rumäne m, Rumänin f; (language) Rumänisch nt

romantic [rəʊ'mæntɪk] adj romantisch

roof [ru:f] n Dach nt; **roof rack** n Dachgepäckträger m

rook [rʊk] n (in chess) Turm m

room [ru:m] n Zimmer nt, Raum m; (large, for gatherings etc) Saal m; (space) Platz m; (fig) Spielraum m; **to make ~ for** Platz

machen für; **roommate** n
Zimmergenosse m, Zimmergenossin f; (US:
sharing apartment) Mitbewohner(in) m(f);
room service n Zimmerservice m; **roomy**
adj geräumig; (garment) weit

root [ruːt] n Wurzel f; **root out** vt
(eradicate) ausrotten; **root vegetable** n
Wurzelgemüse nt

rope [rəʊp] n Seil nt; **to know the ~s** (fam)
sich auskennen

rose [rəʊz] pt of **rise** ▷ n Rose f

rosé ['rəʊzeɪ] n Rosé(wein) m

rot [rɒt] vi verfaulen

rota ['rəʊtə] n (Brit) Dienstplan m

rotate [rəʊ'teɪt] vt (turn) rotieren lassen
▷ vi rotieren; **rotation** [rəʊ'teɪʃən] n
(turning) Rotation f; **in ~** abwechselnd

rotten ['rɒtn] adj (decayed) faul; (mean)
gemein; (unpleasant) scheußlich; (ill) elend

rough [rʌf] adj (not smooth) rau; (path)
uneben; (coarse, violent) grob; (crossing)
stürmisch; (without comforts) hart;
(unfinished, makeshift) grob; (approximate)
ungefähr; **~ draft** Rohentwurf m; **I have a
~ idea** ich habe eine ungefähre
Vorstellung ▷ adv **to sleep ~** im Freien
schlafen ▷ vt **to ~ it** primitiv leben ▷ n **to
write sth in ~** etw ins Unreine schreiben;
roughly adv grob; (approximately)
ungefähr

round [raʊnd] adj rund ▷ adv **all ~** (on all
sides) rundherum; **the long way ~** der
längere Weg; **I'll be ~ at 8** ich werde um
acht Uhr da sein; **the other way
~** umgekehrt ▷ prep (surrounding) um (…
herum); **~** (about) (approximately)
ungefähr; **~ the corner** um die Ecke; **to go
~ the world** um die Welt reisen; **she lives
~ here** sie wohnt hier in der Gegend ▷ n
Runde f; (of bread, toast) Scheibe f; **it's my
~** (of drinks) die Runde geht auf mich ▷ vt
(corner) biegen um; **round off** vt
abrunden; **round up** vt (number, price)
aufrunden

roundabout n (Brit Auto) Kreisverkehr m;
(Brit: merry-go-round) Karussell nt ▷ adj
umständlich; **round-the-clock** adj rund
um die Uhr; **round trip** n Rundreise f;
round-trip ticket n (US) Rückfahrkarte f;
(for plane) Rückflugticket nt

rouse [raʊz] vt (from sleep) wecken

route [ruːt] n Route f; (bus, plane etc
service) Linie f; (fig) Weg m

routine [ruː'tiːn] n Routine f ▷ adj
Routine-

row [rəʊ] n (line) Reihe f; **three times in a
~** dreimal hintereinander ▷ vt, vi (boat)
rudern ▷ [raʊ] n (noise) Krach m; (dispute)
Streit m

rowboat ['rəʊbəʊt] n (US) Ruderboot nt

row house ['rəʊhaʊs] n (US) Reihenhaus
nt

rowing ['rəʊɪŋ] n Rudern nt; **rowing boat**
n (Brit) Ruderboot nt; **rowing machine** n
Rudergerät nt

royal ['rɔɪəl] adj königlich; **royalty** n
(family) Mitglieder pl der königlichen
Familie; **royalties** pl (from book, music)
Tantiemen pl

RSPCA abbr = **Royal Society for the
Prevention of Cruelty to Animals**
britischer Tierschutzverein

RSPCC abbr = **Royal Society for the
Prevention of Cruelty to Children**
britischer Kinderschutzverein

RSVP abbr = **répondez s'il vous plaît** u. A.
w. g.

rub [rʌb] vt reiben; **rub in** vt
einmassieren; **rub out** vt (with eraser)
ausradieren

rubber ['rʌbə*] n Gummi m; (Brit: eraser)
Radiergummi m; (US fam: contraceptive)
Gummi m; **rubber band** n Gummiband
nt; **rubber stamp** n Stempel m

rubbish ['rʌbɪʃ] n Abfall m; (nonsense)
Quatsch m; (poor-quality thing) Mist m;
don't talk ~ red keinen Unsinn!; **rubbish
bin** n Mülleimer m; **rubbish dump** n
Müllabladeplatz m

rubble ['rʌbl] n Schutt m

ruby ['ruːbɪ] n (stone) Rubin m

rucksack ['rʌksæk] n Rucksack m

rude [ruːd] adj (impolite) unhöflich;
(indecent) unanständig

rug [rʌg] n Teppich m; (next to bed)
Bettvorleger m; (for knees) Wolldecke f

rugby ['rʌgbɪ] n Rugby nt

rugged ['rʌgɪd] adj (coastline) zerklüftet;
(features) markant

ruin ['ruːɪn] n Ruine f; (financial, social)
Ruin m ▷ vt ruinieren

rule [ruːl] n Regel f; (governing) Herrschaft
f; **as a ~** in der Regel ▷ vt, vi (govern)
regieren; (decide) entscheiden; **ruler** n
Lineal nt; (person) Herrscher(in) m(f)

rum [rʌm] n Rum m

rumble ['rʌmbl] vi (stomach) knurren; (train, truck) rumpeln

rummage ['rʌmɪdʒ] vi ~ (**around**) herumstöbern

rumor (US), **rumour** ['ru:mə*] n Gerücht nt

run [rʌn] (**ran**, **run**) vt (race, distance) laufen; (machine, engine, computer program, water) laufen lassen; (manage) leiten, führen; (car) unterhalten; **I ran her home** ich habe sie nach Hause gefahren ▷ vi laufen; (move quickly) rennen; (bus, train) fahren; (path etc) verlaufen; (machine, engine, computer program) laufen; (flow) fließen; (colours, make-up) verlaufen; **to ~ for President** für die Präsidentschaft kandidieren; **to be ~ning low** knapp werden; **my nose is ~ning** mir läuft die Nase; **it ~s in the family** es liegt in der Familie ▷ n (on foot) Lauf m; (in car) Spazierfahrt f; (series) Reihe f; (sudden demand) Ansturm m (on auf +akk); (in tights) Laufmasche f; (in cricket, baseball) Lauf m; **to go for a ~** laufen gehen; (in car) eine Spazierfahrt machen; **in the long ~** auf die Dauer; **on the ~** auf der Flucht (from vor +dat); **run about** vi herumlaufen; **run away** vi weglaufen; **run down** vt (with car) umfahren; (criticize) heruntermachen; **to be ~** (tired) abgespannt sein; **run into** vt (meet) zufällig treffen; (problem) stoßen auf +akk; **run off** vi weglaufen; **run out** vi (person) hinausrennen; (liquid) auslaufen; (lease, time) ablaufen; (money, supplies) ausgehen; **he ran ~ of money** ihm ging das Geld aus; **run over** vt (with car) überfahren; **run up** vt (debt, bill) machen

rung [rʌŋ] pp of **ring**

runner ['rʌnə*] n (athlete) Läufer(in) m(f); **to do a ~** (fam) wegrennen; **runner beans** npl (Brit) Stangenbohnen pl

running ['rʌnɪŋ] n (Sport) Laufen nt; (management) Leitung f, Führung f ▷ adj (water) fließend; **~ costs** Betriebskosten pl; (for car) Unterhaltskosten pl; **3 days ~** 3 Tage hintereinander

runny ['rʌnɪ] adj (food) flüssig; (nose) laufend

runway ['rʌnweɪ] n Start- und Landebahn f

rural ['rʊərəl] adj ländlich

rush [rʌʃ] n Eile f; (for tickets etc) Ansturm m (for auf +akk); **to be in a ~** es eilig haben; **there's no ~** es eilt nicht ▷ vt (do too quickly) hastig machen; (meal) hastig essen; **to ~ sb to hospital** jdn auf dem schnellsten Weg ins Krankenhaus bringen; **don't ~ me** dräng mich nicht ▷ vi (hurry) eilen; **don't ~** lass dir Zeit; **rush hour** n Hauptverkehrszeit f

rusk [rʌsk] n Zwieback m

Russia ['rʌʃə] n Russland nt; **Russian** adj russisch ▷ n Russe m, Russin f; (language) Russisch nt

rust [rʌst] n Rost m ▷ vi rosten; **rustproof** ['rʌstpru:f] adj rostfrei; **rusty** ['rʌstɪ] adj rostig

ruthless ['ru:θləs] adj rücksichtslos; (treatment, criticism) schonungslos

rye [raɪ] n Roggen m; **rye bread** n Roggenbrot nt

r

S *abbr* = **south** S

sabotage ['sæbətɑːʒ] *vt* sabotieren

sachet ['sæʃeɪ] *n* Päckchen *nt*

sack [sæk] *n* (*bag*) Sack *m*; **to get the ~** (*fam*) rausgeschmissen werden ▷ *vt* (*fam*) rausschmeißen

sacred ['seɪkrɪd] *adj* heilig

sacrifice ['sækrɪfaɪs] *n* Opfer *nt* ▷ *vt* opfern

sad [sæd] *adj* traurig

saddle ['sædl] *n* Sattel *m*

sadistic [sə'dɪstɪk] *adj* sadistisch

sadly ['sædlɪ] *adv* (*unfortunately*) leider

safari [sə'fɑːrɪ] *n* Safari

safe [seɪf] *adj* (*free from danger*) sicher; (*out of danger*) in Sicherheit; (*careful*) vorsichtig; **have a ~ journey** gute Fahrt! ▷ *n* Safe *m*; **safeguard** *n* Schutz *m* ▷ *vt* schützen (*against* vor +*dat*); **safely** *adv* sicher; (*arrive*) wohlbehalten; (*drive*) vorsichtig; **safety** *n* Sicherheit *f*; **safety belt** *n* Sicherheitsgurt *m*; **safety pin** *n* Sicherheitsnadel *f*

Sagittarius [sædʒɪ'tɛərɪəs] *n* (*Astr*) Schütze *m*

Sahara [sə'hɑːrə] *n* **the ~** (**Desert**) die (Wüste) Sahara

said [sed] *pt, pp of* **say**

sail [seɪl] *n* Segel *nt*; **to set ~** losfahren (*for* nach) ▷ *vi* (*in yacht*) segeln; (*on ship*) mit dem Schiff fahren; (*ship*) auslaufen (*for* nach) ▷ *vt* (*yacht*) segeln mit; (*ship*) steuern; **sailboat** *n* (*US*) Segelboot *nt*; **sailing** *n* **to go ~** segeln gehen; **sailing boat** *n* (*Brit*) Segelboot *nt*; **sailor** *n* Seemann *m*; (*in navy*) Matrose *m*

saint [seɪnt] *n* Heilige(r) *mf*

sake [seɪk] *n* **for the ~ of** um +*gen* ... willen; **for your ~** deinetwegen, dir zuliebe

salad ['sæləd] *n* Salat *m*; **salad cream** *n* (*Brit*) majonäseartige Salatsoße; **salad dressing** *n* Salatsoße *f*

salary ['sælərɪ] *n* Gehalt *nt*

sale [seɪl] *n* Verkauf *m*; (*at reduced prices*) Ausverkauf *m*; **the ~s** *pl* (*in summer, winter*) der Schlussverkauf; **for ~** zu verkaufen; **sales clerk** *n* (*US*) Verkäufer(in) *m(f)*; **salesman** (*pl* -**men**) *n* Verkäufer *m*; (*rep*) Vertreter *m*; **sales rep** *n* Vertreter(in) *m(f)*; **sales tax** *n* (*US*) Verkaufssteuer *f*; **saleswoman** (*pl* -**women**) *n* Verkäuferin *f*; (*rep*) Vertreterin *f*

saliva [sə'laɪvə] *n* Speichel *m*

salmon ['sæmən] *n* Lachs *m*

saloon [sə'luːn] *n* (*ship's lounge*) Salon *m*; (*US: bar*) Kneipe *f*

salt [sɔːlt] *n* Salz *nt* ▷ *vt* (*flavour*) salzen; (*roads*) mit Salz streuen; **salt cellar**, **salt shaker** (*US*) *n* Salzstreuer *m*; **salty** *adj* salzig

salvage ['sælvɪdʒ] *vt* bergen (*from* aus); (*fig*) retten

same [seɪm] *adj* **the ~** (*similar*) der/die/das gleiche, die gleichen *pl*; (*identical*) der-/die-/dasselbe, dieselben *pl*; **they live in the ~ house** sie wohnen im selben Haus ▷ *pron* **the ~** (*similar*) der/die/das Gleiche, die Gleichen *pl*; (*identical*) der-/die-/dasselbe, dieselben *pl*; **I'll have the ~ again** ich möchte noch mal das Gleiche; **all the ~** trotzdem; **the ~ to you** gleichfalls; **it's all the ~ to me** es ist mir egal ▷ *adv* **the ~** gleich; **they look the ~** sie sehen gleich aus

sample ['sɑːmpl] *n* Probe *f*; (*of fabric*) Muster *nt* ▷ *vt* probieren

sanctions ['sæŋkʃənz] *npl* (*Pol*) Sanktionen *pl*

sanctuary ['sæŋktjʊərɪ] n (refuge) Zuflucht f; (for animals) Schutzgebiet nt

sand [sænd] n Sand m

sandal ['sændl] n Sandale f

sandpaper n Sandpapier nt ▷ vt schmirgeln

sandwich ['sænwɪdʒ] n Sandwich nt

sandy ['sændɪ] adj (full of sand) sandig; **~ beach** Sandstrand m

sane [seɪn] adj geistig gesund, normal; (sensible) vernünftig

sang [sæŋ] pt of **sing**

sanitary ['sænɪtərɪ] adj hygienisch; **sanitary napkin** (US), **sanitary towel** n Damenbinde f

sank [sæŋk] pt of **sink**

Santa (Claus) ['sæntə('klɔːz)] n der Weihnachtsmann

sarcastic [sɑːˈkæstɪk] adj sarkastisch

sardine [sɑːˈdiːn] n Sardine f

Sardinia [sɑːˈdɪnɪə] n Sardinien nt

sari [sɑːrɪ] n Sari m (von indischen Frauen getragenes Gewand)

sat [sæt] pt, pp of **sit**

Sat abbr = **Saturday** Sa.

satellite ['sætəlaɪt] n Satellit m; **satellite dish** n Satellitenschüssel f; **satellite TV** n Satellitenfernsehen nt

satin ['sætɪn] n Satin m

satisfaction [sætɪsˈfækʃən] n (contentment) Zufriedenheit f; **is that to your ~?** sind Sie damit zufrieden?; **satisfactory** [sætɪsˈfæktərɪ] adj zufrieden stellend; **satisfied** ['sætɪsfaɪd] adj zufrieden (with mit); **satisfy** ['sætɪsfaɪ] vt zufrieden stellen; (convince) überzeugen; (conditions) erfüllen; (need, demand) befriedigen; **satisfying** adj befriedigend

Saturday ['sætədeɪ] n Samstag m, Sonnabend m; see also **Tuesday**

sauce [sɔːs] n Soße f; **saucepan** n Kochtopf m; **saucer** n Untertasse f

saucy ['sɔːsɪ] adj frech

Saudi Arabia ['saʊdɪəˈreɪbɪə] n Saudi-Arabien nt

sauna ['sɔːnə] n Sauna f

sausage ['sɒsɪdʒ] n Wurst f; **sausage roll** n mit Wurst gefülltes Blätterteigröllchen

savage ['sævɪdʒ] adj (person, attack) brutal; (animal) wild

save [seɪv] vt (rescue) retten (from vor +dat); (money, time, electricity etc) sparen; (strength) schonen; (Inform) speichern; **to ~ sb's life** jdm das Leben retten ▷ vi sparen ▷ n (in football) Parade f; **save up** vi sparen (for auf +akk); **saving** n (of money) Sparen nt; **~s** pl Ersparnisse pl; **~s account** Sparkonto nt

savory (US), **savoury** ['seɪvərɪ] adj (not sweet) pikant

saw [sɔː] (**sawed**, **sawn**) vt, vi sägen ▷ n (tool) Säge f ▷ pt of **see**; **sawdust** n Sägemehl nt

saxophone ['sæksəfəʊn] n Saxophon nt

say [seɪ] (**said**, **said**) vt sagen (to sb jdm); (prayer) sprechen; **what does the letter ~?** was steht im Brief?; **the rules ~ that ...** in den Regeln heißt es, dass ...; **he's said to be rich** er soll reich sein ▷ n **to have a ~ in sth** bei etw ein Mitspracherecht haben ▷ adv zum Beispiel; **saying** n Sprichwort nt

scab [skæb] n (on cut) Schorf m

scaffolding ['skæfəʊldɪŋ] n (Bau)gerüst nt

scale [skeɪl] n (of map etc) Maßstab m; (on thermometer etc) Skala f; (of pay) Tarifsystem nt; (Mus) Tonleiter f; (of fish, snake) Schuppe f; **to ~** maßstabsgerecht; **on a large/small ~** in großem/kleinem Umfang; **scales** npl (for weighing) Waage f

scalp [skælp] n Kopfhaut f

scan [skæn] vt (examine) genau prüfen; (read quickly) überfliegen; (Inform) scannen ▷ n (Med) Ultraschall m; **scan in** vt (Inform) einscannen

scandal ['skændl] n Skandal m; **scandalous** adj skandalös

Scandinavia [skændɪˈneɪvɪə] n Skandinavien nt; **Scandinavian** adj skandinavisch ▷ n Skandinavier(in) m(f)

scanner ['skænə*] n Scanner m

scapegoat ['skeɪpgəʊt] n Sündenbock m

scar [skɑː*] n Narbe f

scarce ['skeəs] adj selten; (in short supply) knapp; **scarcely** adv kaum

scare ['skeə*] n (general alarm) Panik f ▷ vt erschrecken; **to be ~d** Angst haben (of vor +dat)

scarf [skɑːf] (pl **-scarves**) n Schal m; (on head) Kopftuch nt

scarlet ['skɑːlət] adj scharlachrot; **scarlet fever** n Scharlach m

scary ['skeərɪ] adj (film, story) gruselig

scatter ['skætə*] vt verstreuen; (seed,

gravel) streuen; (*disperse*) auseinander treiben

scene [si:n] n (*location*) Ort m; (*division of play*) (*Theat*) Szene f; (*view*) Anblick m; **to make a ~** eine Szene machen; **scenery** ['si:nərɪ] n (*landscape*) Landschaft f; (*Theat*) Kulissen pl; **scenic** ['si:nɪk] adj (*landscape*) malerisch; **~ route** landschaftlich schöne Strecke

scent [sɛnt] n (*perfume*) Parfüm nt; (*smell*) Duft m

sceptical ['skɛptɪkəl] adj (*Brit*) skeptisch

schedule ['ʃɛdjuːl, 'skɛdʒʊəl] n (*plan*) Programm nt; (*of work*) Zeitplan m; (*list*) Liste f; (*US: of trains, buses, air traffic*) Fahr-, Flugplan m; **on ~** planmäßig; **to be behind ~ with sth** mit etw in Verzug sein ▷ vt **the meeting is ~d for next Monday** die Besprechung ist für nächsten Montag angesetzt; **scheduled** adj (*departure, arrival*) planmäßig; **~ flight** Linienflug m

scheme [ski:m] n (*plan*) Plan m; (*project*) Projekt nt; (*dishonest*) Intrige f ▷ vi intrigieren

schizophrenic [skɪtsəˈfrɛnɪk] adj schizophren

scholar ['skɒlə*] n Gelehrte(r) mf; **scholarship** n (*grant*) Stipendium nt

school [skuːl] n Schule f; (*university department*) Fachbereich m; (*US: university*) Universität f; **school bag** n Schultasche f; **schoolbook** n Schulbuch nt; **schoolboy** n Schüler m; **school bus** n Schulbus m; **schoolgirl** n Schülerin f; **schoolteacher** n Lehrer(in) m(f); **schoolwork** n Schularbeiten pl

sciatica [saɪˈætɪkə] n Ischias m

science ['saɪəns] n Wissenschaft f; (*natural ~*) Naturwissenschaft f; **science fiction** n Sciencefiction f; **scientific** [saɪənˈtɪfɪk] adj wissenschaftlich; **scientist** ['saɪəntɪst] n Wissenschaftler(in) m(f); (*in natural sciences*) Naturwissenschaftler(in) m(f)

scissors ['sɪzəz] npl Schere f

scone [skɒn] n kleines süßes Hefebrötchen mit oder ohne Rosinen, das mit Butter oder Dickrahm und Marmelade gegessen wird

scoop [skuːp] n (*exclusive story*) Exklusivbericht m; **a ~ of ice-cream** eine Kugel Eis ▷ vt **to ~ (up)** schaufeln

scooter ['skuːtə*] n (*Motor*)roller m; (*toy*) (*Tret*)roller m

scope [skəʊp] n Umfang m; (*opportunity*) Möglichkeit f

score [skɔː*] n (*Sport*) Spielstand m; (*final result*) Spielergebnis nt; (*in quiz etc*) Punktestand m; (*Mus*) Partitur f; **to keep (the) ~** mitzählen ▷ vt (*goal*) schießen; (*points*) machen ▷ vi (*keep ~*) mitzählen; **scoreboard** n Anzeigetafel f

scorn [skɔːn] n Verachtung f; **scornful** adj verächtlich

Scorpio ['skɔːpɪəʊ] (*pl* **-s**) n (*Astr*) Skorpion m

scorpion ['skɔːpɪən] n Skorpion m

Scot [skɒt] n Schotte m, Schottin f; **Scotch** [skɒtʃ] adj schottisch ▷ n (*whisky*) schottischer Whisky, Scotch m

Scotch tape® n (*US*) Tesafilm® m

Scotland ['skɒtlənd] n Schottland nt; **Scotsman** (*pl* **-men**) n Schotte m; **Scotswoman** (*pl* **-women**) n Schottin f; **Scottish** adj schottisch

scout [skaʊt] n (*boy ~*) Pfadfinder m

scowl [skaʊl] vi finster blicken

scrambled eggs npl Rührei nt

scrap [skræp] n (*bit*) Stückchen nt, Fetzen m; (*metal*) Schrott m ▷ vt (*car*) verschrotten; (*plan*) verwerfen; **scrapbook** n Sammelalbum nt

scrape [skreɪp] n (*scratch*) Kratzer m ▷ vt (*car*) schrammen; (*wall*) streifen; **to ~ one's knee** sich das Knie schürfen; **scrape through** vi (*exam*) mit knapper Not bestehen

scrap heap ['skræphiːp] n Schrotthaufen m; **scrap metal** n Schrott m; **scrap paper** n Schmierpapier nt

scratch ['skrætʃ] n (*mark*) Kratzer m; **to start from ~** von vorne anfangen ▷ vt kratzen; (*car*) zerkratzen; **to ~ one's arm** sich am Arm kratzen ▷ vi kratzen; (*~ oneself*) sich kratzen

scream [skriːm] n Schrei m ▷ vi schreien (*with* vor +dat); **to ~ at sb** jdn anschreien

screen [skriːn] n (*Tv, Inform*) Bildschirm m; (*Cine*) Leinwand f ▷ vt (*protect*) abschirmen; (*hide*) verdecken; (*film*) zeigen; (*applicants, luggage*) überprüfen; **screenplay** n Drehbuch nt; **screen saver** n (*Inform*) Bildschirmschoner m

screw [skruː] n Schraube f ▷ vt (*vulg: have sex with*) poppen; **to ~ sth to sth** etw an etw akk schrauben; **to ~ off/on** (*lid*) ab-/aufschrauben; **screw up** vt (*paper*) zusammenknüllen; (*make a mess of*) vermasseln; **screwdriver** *n* Schraubenzieher *m*; **screw top** *n* Schraubverschluss *m*

scribble ['skrɪbl] *vt, vi* kritzeln

script [skrɪpt] *n* (*of play*) Text *m*; (*of film*) Drehbuch *nt*; (*style of writing*) Schrift *f*

scroll down ['skrəʊl'daʊn] *vi* (*Inform*) runterscrollen; **scroll up** *vi* (*Inform*) raufscrollen; **scroll bar** *n* (*Inform*) Scrollbar *f*

scrub [skrʌb] *vt* schrubben; **scrubbing brush**, **scrub brush** (*US*) *n* Scheuerbürste *f*

scruffy ['skrʌfɪ] *adj* vergammelt

scrupulous, scrupulously ['skru:pjʊləs, -lɪ] *adj, adv* gewissenhaft; (*painstaking*) peinlich genau

scuba-diving ['sku:bədaɪvɪŋ] *n* Sporttauchen *nt*

sculptor ['skʌlptə*] *n* Bildhauer(in) *m(f)*; **sculpture** ['skʌlptʃə*] *n* (*Art*) Bildhauerei *f*; (*statue*) Skulptur *f*

sea [si:] *n* Meer *nt*, See *f*; **seafood** *n* Meeresfrüchte *pl*; **sea front** *n* Strandpromenade *f*; **seagull** *n* Möwe *f*

seal [si:l] *n* (*animal*) Robbe *f*; (*stamp, impression*) Siegel *nt*; (*Tech*) Verschluss *m*; (*ring etc*) Dichtung *f* ▷ *vt* versiegeln; (*envelope*) zukleben

seam [si:m] *n* Naht *f*

seaport ['si:pɔ:t] *n* Seehafen *m*

search [sɜ:tʃ] *n* Suche *f* (*for* nach); **to do a ~** *for* (*Inform*) suchen nach; **in ~ of** auf der Suche nach ▷ *vi* suchen (*for* nach) ▷ *vt* durchsuchen; **search engine** *n* (*Inform*) Suchmaschine *f*

seashell ['si:ʃel] *n* Muschel *f*; **seashore** *n* Strand *m*; **seasick** *adj* seekrank; **seaside** *n* **at the ~** am Meer; **to go to the ~** ans Meer fahren; **seaside resort** *n* Seebad *nt*

season ['si:zn] *n* Jahreszeit *f*; (*Comm*) Saison *f*; **high/low ~** Hoch-/Nebensaison *f* ▷ *vt* (*flavour*) würzen

seasoning *n* Gewürz *nt*

season ticket *n* (*Rail*) Zeitkarte *f*; (*Theat*) Abonnement *nt*; (*Sport*) Dauerkarte *f*

seat [si:t] *n* (*place*) Platz *m*; (*chair*) Sitz *m*; **take a ~** setzen Sie sich ▷ *vt* **the hall ~s 300** der Saal hat 300 Sitzplätze; **please be ~ed** bitte setzen Sie sich; **to remain ~ed** sitzen bleiben; **seat belt** *n* Sicherheitsgurt *m*

sea view ['si:vju:] *n* Seeblick *m*; **seaweed** *n* Seetang *m*

secluded [sɪ'klu:dɪd] *adj* abgelegen

second ['sekənd] *adj* zweite(r, s); **the ~ of June** der zweite Juni ▷ *adv* (*in ~ position*) an zweiter Stelle; (*secondly*) zweitens; **he came ~** er ist Zweiter geworden ▷ *n* (*of time*) Sekunde *f*; (*moment*) Augenblick *m*; **~ (gear)** der zweite Gang; (*~ helping*) zweite Portion; **just a ~!** (einen) Augenblick!; **secondary** *adj* (*less important*) zweitrangig; **~ education** höhere Schulbildung *f*; **~ school** weiterführende Schule; **second-class** *adj* (*ticket*) zweiter Klasse; **~ stamp** *Briefmarke für nicht bevorzugt beförderte Sendungen* ▷ *adv* (*travel*) zweiter Klasse; **secondhand** *adj, adv* gebraucht; (*information*) aus zweiter Hand; **secondly** *adv* zweitens; **second-rate** *adj* (*pej*) zweitklassig

secret ['si:krət] *n* Geheimnis *nt* ▷ *adj* geheim; (*admirer*) heimlich

secretary ['sekrətrɪ] *n* Sekretär(in) *m(f)*; (*minister*) Minister(in) *m(f)*; **Secretary of State** *n* (*US*) Außenminister(in) *m(f)*

secretive ['si:krətɪv] *adj* (*person*) geheimnistuerisch; **secretly** ['si:krətlɪ] *adv* heimlich

sect [sekt] *n* Sekte *f*

section ['sekʃən] *n* (*part*) Teil *m*; (*of document*) Abschnitt *m*; (*department*) Abteilung *f*

secure [sɪ'kjʊə*] *adj* (*safe*) sicher (*from* vor +dat); (*firmly fixed*) fest ▷ *vt* (*make firm*) befestigen; (*window, door*) fest verschließen; (*obtain*) sich sichern; **securely** *adv* fest; (*safely*) sicher; **security** [sɪ'kjʊərɪtɪ] *n* Sicherheit *f*

sedative ['sedətɪv] *n* Beruhigungsmittel *nt*

seduce [sɪ'dju:s] *vt* verführen; **seductive** [sɪ'dʌktɪv] *adj* verführerisch; (*offer*) verlockend

see [si:] (*saw, seen*) *vt* sehen; (*understand*) verstehen; (*check*) nachsehen; (*accompany*) bringen; (*visit*) besuchen; (*talk to*) sprechen; **to ~ the doctor** zum Arzt gehen; **to ~ sb home** jdn nach Hause begleiten; **I saw him swimming** ich habe ihn schwimmen sehen; **~ you** tschüs!; **~ you on Friday** bis Freitag! ▷ *vi* sehen; (*understand*) verstehen; (*check*) nachsehen;

(you) ~ siehst du!; **we'll** ~ mal sehen; **see about** vt (attend to) sich kümmern um; **see off** vt (say goodbye to) verabschieden; **see out** vt (show out) zur Tür bringen; **see through** vt **to see sth through** etw zu Ende bringen; **to** ~ **sb/sth** jdn/etw durchschauen; **see to** vt sich kümmern um; ~ **it that ...** sieh zu, dass ...

seed [siːd] n (of plant) Samen m; (in fruit) Kern m; **seedless** adj kernlos

seek [siːk] (**sought, sought**) vt suchen; (fame) streben nach; **to** ~ **sb's advice** jdn um Rat fragen

seem [siːm] vi scheinen; **he ~s (to be) honest** er scheint ehrlich zu sein; **it ~s to me that ...** es scheint mir, dass ...

seen [siːn] pp of **see**

seesaw ['siːsɔː] n Wippe f

segment ['segmənt] n Teil m

seize [siːz] vt packen; (confiscate) beschlagnahmen; (opportunity, power) ergreifen

seldom ['seldəm] adv selten

select [sɪ'lekt] adj (exclusive) exklusiv ▷ vt auswählen; **selection** [sɪ'lekʃən] n Auswahl f (of an +dat); **selective** adj (choosy) wählerisch

self [self] (pl **selves**) n Selbst nt, Ich nt; **he's his old** ~ **again** er ist wieder ganz der Alte; **self-adhesive** adj selbstklebend; **self-assured** n selbstsicher; **self-catering** adj für Selbstversorger; **self-centred** adj egozentrisch; **self-confidence** n Selbstbewusstsein nt; **self-confident** adj selbstbewusst; **self-conscious** adj befangen, verklemmt; **self-contained** adj (flat) separat; **self-control** n Selbstbeherrschung f; **self-defence** n Selbstverteidigung f; **self-employed** adj selbstständig; **self-evident** adj offensichtlich

selfish, selfishly ['selfɪʃ, -lɪ] adj, adv egoistisch, selbstsüchtig; **selfless, selflessly** adj, adv selbstlos

self-pity [self'pɪtɪ] n Selbstmitleid nt; **self-portrait** n Selbstporträt nt; **self-respect** n Selbstachtung f; **self-service** n Selbstbedienung f ▷ adj Selbstbedienungs-

sell [sel] (**sold, sold**) vt verkaufen; **to** ~ **sb sth, to** ~ **sth to sb** jdm etw verkaufen; **do you** ~ **postcards?** haben Sie Postkarten?

▷ vi (product) sich verkaufen; **sell out** vt **to be sold** ~ ausverkauft sein; **sell-by date** n Haltbarkeitsdatum nt

Sellotape® ['seləteɪp] n (Brit) Tesafilm® m

semester [sɪ'mestə*] n Semester nt

semi ['semɪ] n (Brit: house) Doppelhaushälfte f; **semicircle** n Halbkreis m; **semicolon** n Semikolon nt; **semidetached (house)** n (Brit) Doppelhaushälfte f; **semifinal** n Halbfinale nt

seminar ['semɪnɑː*] n Seminar nt

semiskimmed milk ['semɪskɪmd'mɪlk] n Halbfettmilch f

senate ['senət] n Senat m; **senator** n Senator(in) m(f)

send [send] (**sent, sent**) vt schicken; **to** ~ **sb sth, to** ~ **sth to sb** jdm etw schicken; ~ **her my best wishes** grüße sie von mir; **send away** vt wegschicken ▷ vi **to** ~ **for** anfordern; **send back** vt zurückschicken; **send for** vt (person) holen lassen; (by post) anfordern; **send off** vt (by post) abschicken; **send out** vt (invitations etc) verschicken ▷ vi **to** ~ **for sth** etw holen lassen

sender ['sendə*] n Absender(in) m(f)

senior ['siːnɪə*] adj (older) älter; (high-ranking) höher; (pupils) älter; **he is** ~ **to me** er ist mir übergeordnet ▷ n **he's eight years my** ~ er ist acht Jahre älter als ich; **senior citizen** n Senior(in) m(f)

sensation [sen'seɪʃən] n Gefühl nt; (excitement, person, thing) Sensation f; **sensational** adj sensationell

sense [sens] n (faculty, meaning) Sinn m; (feeling) Gefühl nt; (understanding) Verstand m; ~ **of smell/taste** Geruchs-/Geschmackssinn m; **to have a** ~ **of humour** Humor haben; **to make** ~ (sentence etc) einen Sinn ergeben; (be sensible) Sinn machen; **in a** ~ gewissermaßen ▷ vt spüren; **senseless** adj (stupid) sinnlos

sensible, sensibly ['sensəbl, -blɪ] adj, adv vernünftig

sensitive ['sensɪtɪv] adj empfindlich (to gegen); (easily hurt) sensibel; (subject) heikel

sensual ['sensjʊəl] adj sinnlich

sensuous ['sensjʊəs] adj sinnlich

sent [sent] pt, pp of **send**

sentence ['sentəns] n (Ling) Satz m; (Jur) Strafe f ▷ vt verurteilen (to zu)

sentiment ['sentɪmənt] n (sentimentality) Sentimentalität f; (opinion) Ansicht f; **sentimental** [sentɪ'mentl] adj sentimental

separate ['seprət] adj getrennt, separat; (individual) einzeln ▷ ['sepəreɪt] vt trennen (from von); **they are ~d** (couple) sie leben getrennt ▷ vi sich trennen; **separately** adv getrennt; (singly) einzeln

September [sep'tembə*] n September m; **in ~** im September; **on the 2nd of ~** am 2. September; **at the beginning/in the middle/at the end of ~** Anfang/Mitte/Ende September; **last/next ~** letzten/nächsten September

septic ['septɪk] adj vereitert

sequel ['siːkwəl] n (to film, book) Fortsetzung f (to von)

sequence ['siːkwəns] n (order) Reihenfolge f

Serb ['sɜːb] n Serbe m, Serbin f; **Serbia** ['sɜːbjə] n Serbien nt

sergeant ['sɑːdʒənt] n Polizeimeister(in) m(f); (Mil) Feldwebel(in) m(f)

serial ['sɪərɪəl] n (Tv) Serie f; (in newspaper etc) Fortsetzungsroman m ▷ adj (Inform) seriell; **~ number** Seriennummer f

series ['sɪəriːz] nsing Reihe f; (Tv, Radio) Serie f

serious ['sɪərɪəs] adj ernst; (injury, illness, mistake) schwer; (discussion) ernsthaft; **are you ~?** ist das dein Ernst?; **seriously** adv ernsthaft; (hurt) schwer; **~?** im Ernst?; **to take sb ~** jdn ernst nehmen

sermon ['sɜːmən] n (Rel) Predigt f

servant ['sɜːvənt] n Diener(in) m(f);

serve [sɜːv] vt (customer) bedienen; (food) servieren; (one's country etc) dienen +dat; (sentence) verbüßen; **I'm being ~d** ich werde schon bedient; **it ~s him right** es geschieht ihm recht ▷ vi dienen (as als), aufschlagen ▷ n Aufschlag m

server n (Inform) Server m

service ['sɜːvɪs] n (in shop, hotel) Bedienung f; (activity, amenity) Dienstleistung f; (set of dishes) Service nt; (Auto) Inspektion f; (Tech) Wartung f; (Rel) Gottesdienst m, Aufschlag m; **train/bus ~** Zug-/Busverbindung f; **'~ not included'** „Bedienung nicht inbegriffen" ▷ vt (Auto, Tech) warten;

service area n (on motorway) Raststätte f (mit Tankstelle); **service charge** n Bedienung f; **service provider** n (Inform) Provider m; **service station** n Tankstelle f

serving ['sɜːvɪŋ] n (portion) Portion f

session ['seʃən] n (of court, assembly) Sitzung f

set [set] (**set**, **set**) vt (place) stellen; (lay flat) legen; (arrange) anordnen; (table) decken; (trap, record) aufstellen; (time, price) festsetzen; (watch, alarm) stellen (for auf +akk); **to ~ sb a task** jdm eine Aufgabe stellen; **to ~ free** freilassen; **to ~ a good example** ein gutes Beispiel geben; **the novel is ~ in London** der Roman spielt in London ▷ vi (sun) untergehen; (become hard) fest werden; (bone) zusammenwachsen ▷ n (collection of things) Satz m; (of cutlery, furniture) Garnitur f; (group of people) Kreis m; (Radio, Tv) Apparat m, Satz m; (Theat) Bühnenbild nt; (Cine) (Film)kulisse f ▷ adj (agreed, prescribed) festgelegt; (ready) bereit; **~ meal** Menü nt; **set aside** vt (money) beiseite legen; (time) einplanen; **set off** vi aufbrechen (for nach) ▷ vt (alarm) auslösen; (enhance) hervorheben; **set out** vi aufbrechen (for nach) ▷ vt (chairs, chesspieces etc) aufstellen; (state) darlegen; **to ~ to do sth** (intend) beabsichtigen, etw zu tun; **set up** vt (firm, organization) gründen; (stall, tent, camera) aufbauen; (meeting) vereinbaren ▷ vi **to ~ as a doctor** sich als Arzt niederlassen

setback n Rückschlag m

settee [se'tiː] n Sofa nt, Couch f

setting ['setɪŋ] n (of novel, film) Schauplatz m; (surroundings) Umgebung f

settle ['setl] vt (bill, debt) begleichen; (dispute) beilegen; (question) klären; (stomach) beruhigen ▷ vi **to ~ (down)** (feel at home) sich einleben; (calm down) sich beruhigen; **settle in** vi (in place) sich einleben; (in job) sich eingewöhnen; **settle up** vi (be)zahlen; **to ~ with sb** mit jdm abrechnen; **settlement** n (of bill, debt) Begleichung f; (colony) Siedlung f; **to reach a ~** sich einigen

setup ['setʌp] n (organization) Organisation f; (situation) Situation f

seven ['sevn] num sieben ▷ n Sieben f; see also **eight**; **seventeen** ['sevn'tiːn] num

siebzehn ▷ n Siebzehn f; see also **eight**;
seventeenth adj siebzehnte(r, s); see also
eighth; **seventh** ['sevnθ] adj siebte(r, s)
▷ n (fraction) Siebtel nt; see also **eighth**;
seventieth ['sevntɪɪθ] adj siebzigste(r, s);
see also **eighth**; **seventy** ['sevntɪ] num
siebzig; **~-one** einundsiebzig ▷ n Siebzig f;
to be in one's seventies in den Siebzigern
sein; see also **eight**

several ['sevrəl] adj, pron mehrere

severe [sɪ'vɪə*] adj (strict) streng; (serious)
schwer; (pain) stark; (winter) hart;
severely adv (harshly) hart; (seriously)
schwer

sew [səu] (**sewed, sewn**) vt, vi nähen

sewage ['su:ɪdʒ] n Abwasser nt; **sewer**
['suə*] n Abwasserkanal m

sewing ['səuɪŋ] n Nähen nt; **sewing
machine** n Nähmaschine f

sewn [səun] pp of **sew**

sex [seks] n Sex m; (gender) Geschlecht nt;
to have ~ Sex haben (with mit); **sexism**
['seksɪzəm] n Sexismus m; **sexist**
['seksɪst] adj sexistisch ▷ n Sexist(in)
m(f); **sex life** n Sex(ual)leben nt

sexual ['seksjuəl] adj sexuell;
~ discrimination/harassment sexuelle
Diskriminierung/Belästigung;
~ intercourse Geschlechtsverkehr m;
sexuality [seksju'ælɪtɪ] n Sexualität f;
sexually adv sexuell

sexy ['seksɪ] adj sexy

Seychelles ['seɪʃelz] npl Seychellen pl

shabby ['ʃæbɪ] adj schäbig

shack [ʃæk] n Hütte f

shade [ʃeɪd] n (shadow) Schatten m; (for
lamp) (Lampen)schirm m; (colour) Farbton
m; **~s** (US: sunglasses) Sonnenbrille f ▷ vt
(from sun) abschirmen; (in drawing)
schattieren

shadow ['ʃædəu] n Schatten m

shady ['ʃeɪdɪ] adj schattig; (fig)
zwielichtig

shake [ʃeɪk] (**shook, shaken**) vt
schütteln; (shock) erschüttern; **to ~ hands
with sb** jdm die Hand geben; **to ~ one's
head** den Kopf schütteln ▷ vi (tremble)
zittern; (building, ground) schwanken;
shake off vt abschütteln; **shaken** ['ʃeɪkn]
pp of **shake**; **shaky** ['ʃeɪkɪ] adj (trembling)
zittrig; (table, chair, position) wackelig;
(weak) unsicher

shall [ʃæl] (**should**) vb aux werden; (in

questions) sollen; **I ~ do my best** ich werde
mein Bestes tun; **~ I come too?** soll ich
mitkommen?; **where ~ we go?** wo gehen
wir hin?

shallow ['ʃæləu] adj (a. fig) seicht; (person)
oberflächlich

shame [ʃeɪm] n (feeling of ~) Scham f;
(disgrace) Schande f; **what a ~** wie schade!;
~ on you schäm dich!; **it's a ~ that ...**
schade, dass ...

shampoo [ʃæm'pu:] n Shampoo nt; **to
have a ~ and set** sich die Haare waschen
und legen lassen ▷ vt (hair) waschen;
(carpet) schamponieren

shandy ['ʃændɪ] n Radler m, Alsterwasser
nt

shan't [ʃɑ:nt] contr of **shall not**

shape [ʃeɪp] n Form f; (unidentified figure)
Gestalt f; **in the ~ of** in Form +gen; **to be in
good ~** (healthwise) in guter Verfassung
sein; **to take ~** (plan, idea) Gestalt
annehmen ▷ vt (clay, person) formen;
-shaped [ʃeɪpt] suf -förmig;
heart~ herzförmig; **shapeless** adj
formlos

share [ʃɛə*] n Anteil +dat (in, of an m); (Fin)
Aktie f ▷ vt, vi teilen; **shareholder** n
Aktionär(in) m(f)

shark [ʃɑ:k] n (Zool) Haifisch m

sharp [ʃɑ:p] adj scharf; (pin) spitz; (person)
scharfsinnig; (pain) heftig; (increase, fall)
abrupt; **C/F ~** (Mus) Cis/Dis nt ▷ adv **at 2
o'clock ~** Punkt 2 Uhr; **sharpen** vt (knife)
schärfen; (pencil) spitzen; **sharpener** n
(pencil ~) Spitzer m

shatter ['ʃætə*] vt zerschmettern; (fig)
zerstören ▷ vi zerspringen; **shattered** adj
(exhausted) kaputt

shave [ʃeɪv] (**shaved, shaved** o **shaven**) vt
rasieren ▷ vi sich rasieren ▷ n Rasur f;
that was a close ~ (fig) das war knapp;
shave off vt **to shave one's beard off**
sich den Bart abrasieren; **shaven** ['ʃeɪvn]
pp of **shave** ▷ adj (head) kahl geschoren;
shaver n (Elec) Rasierapparat m; **shaving
brush** n Rasierpinsel m; **shaving foam** n
Rasierschaum m

shawl [ʃɔ:l] n Tuch nt

she [ʃi:] pron sie

shed [ʃed] (**shed, shed**) n Schuppen m
▷ vt (tears, blood) vergießen; (hair, leaves)
verlieren

she'd [ʃi:d] contr of **she had; she would**

sheep [ʃiːp] (pl -) n Schaf nt; **sheepdog** n Schäferhund m; **sheepskin** n Schaffell nt

sheer [ʃɪə*] adj (madness) rein; (steep) steil; (transparent) hauchdünn; **by ~ chance** rein zufällig

sheet [ʃiːt] n (on bed) Betttuch nt; (of paper) Blatt nt; (of metal) Platte f; (of glass) Scheibe f; **a ~ of paper** ein Blatt Papier

shelf [ʃelf] (pl shelves) n Bücherbord nt, Regal nt; **shelves** pl (item of furniture) Regal nt

she'll [ʃiːl] contr of **she will; she shall**

shell [ʃel] n (of egg, nut) Schale f; (sea~) Muschel f ▷ vt (peas, nuts) schälen; **shellfish** n (as food) Meeresfrüchte pl

shelter ['ʃeltə*] n (protection) Schutz m; (accommodation) Unterkunft f; (bus ~) Wartehäuschen nt ▷ vt schützen (from vor +dat) ▷ vi sich unterstellen; **sheltered** adj (spot) geschützt; (life) behütet

shelve [ʃelv] vt (fig) aufschieben; **shelves** pl of **shelf**

shepherd ['ʃepəd] n Schäfer m; **shepherd's pie** n Hackfleischauflauf mit Decke aus Kartoffelpüree

sherry ['ʃerɪ] n Sherry m

she's [ʃiːz] contr of **she is; she has**

shield [ʃiːld] n Schild m; (fig) Schutz m ▷ vt schützen (from vor +dat)

shift [ʃɪft] n (change) Veränderung f; (period at work, workers) Schicht f; (on keyboard) Umschalttaste f ▷ vt (furniture etc) verrücken; (stain) entfernen; **to ~ gear(s)** (US Auto) schalten ▷ vi (move) sich bewegen; (move up) rutschen; **shift key** n Umschalttaste f

shin [ʃɪn] n Schienbein nt

shine [ʃaɪn] (shone, shone) vi (be shiny) glänzen; (sun) scheinen; (lamp) leuchten ▷ vt (polish) polieren ▷ n Glanz m

shingles ['ʃɪŋglz] nsing (Med) Gürtelrose f

shiny ['ʃaɪnɪ] adj glänzend

ship [ʃɪp] n Schiff nt ▷ vt (send) versenden; (by ship) verschiffen; **shipment** n (goods) Sendung f; (sent by ship) Ladung f; **shipwreck** n Schiffbruch m; **shipyard** n Werft f

shirt [ʃɜːt] n Hemd nt

shiver ['ʃɪvə*] vi zittern (with vor +dat)

shock [ʃɒk] n (mental, emotional) Schock m; **to be in ~** unter Schock stehen; **to get a ~** (Elec) einen Schlag bekommen ▷ vt schockieren; **shock absorber** n Stoßdämpfer m; **shocked** adj schockiert (by über +akk); **shocking** adj schockierend; (awful) furchtbar

shoe [ʃuː] n Schuh m; **shoehorn** n Schuhlöffel m; **shoelace** n Schnürsenkel m; **shoe polish** n Schuhcreme f

shone [ʃɒn] pt, pp of **shine**

shook [ʃʊk] pt of **shake**

shoot [ʃuːt] (shot, shot) vt (wound) anschießen; (kill) erschießen; (Cine) drehen; (fam: heroin) drücken ▷ vi (with gun, move quickly) schießen; **to ~ at sb** auf jdn schießen ▷ n (of plant) Trieb m; **shooting** n (exchange of gunfire) Schießerei f; (killing) Erschießung f

shop [ʃɒp] n Geschäft nt, Laden m ▷ vi einkaufen; **shop assistant** n Verkäufer(in) m(f); **shopkeeper** n Geschäftsinhaber(in) m(f); **shoplifting** n Ladendiebstahl m; **shopper** n Käufer(in) m(f); **shopping** n (activity) Einkaufen nt; (goods) Einkäufe pl; **to do the ~** einkaufen; **to go ~** einkaufen gehen; **shopping bag** n Einkaufstasche f; **shopping cart** n (US) Einkaufswagen m; **shopping center** (US), **shopping centre** n Einkaufszentrum nt; **shopping list** n Einkaufszettel m; **shopping trolley** n (Brit) Einkaufswagen m; **shop window** n Schaufenster nt

shore [ʃɔː*] n Ufer nt; **on ~** an Land

short [ʃɔːt] adj kurz; (person) klein; **to be ~ of money** knapp bei Kasse sein; **to be ~ of time** wenig Zeit haben; **~ of breath** kurzatmig; **to cut ~** (holiday) abbrechen; **we are two ~** wir haben zwei zu wenig; **it's ~ for ...** das ist die Kurzform von ... ▷ n (drink, Elec) Kurze(r) m; **shortage** n Knappheit f (of an +dat); **shortbread** n Buttergebäck nt; **short circuit** n Kurzschluss m; **shortcoming** n Unzulänglichkeit f; (of person) Fehler m; **shortcut** n (quicker route) Abkürzung f; (Inform) Shortcut m; **shorten** vt kürzen; (in time) verkürzen; **shorthand** n Stenografie f; **shortlist** n **to be on the ~** in der engeren Wahl sein; **short-lived** adj kurzlebig; **shortly** adv bald; **shorts** npl Shorts pl; **short-sighted** adj (a. fig) kurzsichtig; **short-sleeved** adj kurzärmelig; **short-stay car park** n

S

Kurzzeitparkplatz m; **short story** n
Kurzgeschichte f; **short-term** adj
kurzfristig; **short wave** n Kurzwelle f

shot [ʃɒt] pt, pp of **shoot** ▷ n (from gun, in
football) Schuss m; (Foto, Cine) Aufnahme f;
(injection) Spritze f; (of alcohol) Schuss m

should [ʃʊd] pt of **shall** ▷ vb aux **I ~ go
now** ich sollte jetzt gehen; **what ~ I do?**
was soll ich tun?; **you ~n't have said that**
das hättest du nicht sagen sollen; **that
~ be enough** das müsste reichen

shoulder [ˈʃəʊldə*] n Schulter f

shouldn't [ˈʃʊdnt] contr of **should not**

should've [ˈʃʊdəv] contr of **should have**

shout [ʃaʊt] n Schrei m; (call) Ruf m ▷ vt
rufen; (order) brüllen ▷ vi schreien; **to ~ at**
anschreien; **to ~ for help** um Hilfe rufen

shove [ʃʌv] vt (person) schubsen; (car, table
etc) schieben ▷ vi (in crowd) drängeln

shovel [ˈʃʌvl] n Schaufel f ▷ vt
schaufeln

show [ʃəʊ] (showed, shown) vt zeigen;
to ~ sb sth, to ~ sth to sb jdm etw zeigen;
to ~ sb in jdn hereinführen; **to ~ sb out**
jdn zur Tür bringen ▷ n (Cine, Theat)
Vorstellung f; (TV) Show f; (exhibition)
Ausstellung f; **show off** vi (pej) angeben;
show round vt herumführen; **to show sb
round the house/the town** jdm das
Haus/die Stadt zeigen; **show up** vi
(arrive) auftauchen

shower [ˈʃaʊə*] n Dusche f; (rain) Schauer
m; **to have** (o **take) a ~** duschen ▷ vi
(wash) duschen

showing [ˈʃəʊɪŋ] n (Cine) Vorstellung f

shown [ʃəʊn] pp of **show**

showroom [ˈʃəʊruːm] n
Ausstellungsraum m

shrank [ʃræŋk] pt of **shrink**

shred [ʃred] n (of paper, fabric) Fetzen m
▷ vt (in shredder) (im Reißwolf)
zerkleinern; **shredder** n (for paper)
Reißwolf m

shrimp [ʃrɪmp] n Garnele f

shrink [ʃrɪŋk] (shrank, shrunk) vi
schrumpfen; (clothes) eingehen

shrivel [ˈʃrɪvl] vi **to ~ (up)** schrumpfen;
(skin) runzlig werden; (plant) welken

Shrove Tuesday [ˈʃrəʊvˈtjuːzdeɪ] n
Fastnachtsdienstag m

shrub [ʃrʌb] n Busch m, Strauch m

shrug [ʃrʌg] vt, vi **to ~ (one's shoulders)**
mit den Achseln zucken

shrunk [ʃrʌŋk] pp of **shrink**

shudder [ˈʃʌdə*] vi schaudern; (ground,
building) beben

shuffle [ˈʃʌfl] vt, vi mischen

shut [ʃʌt] (shut, shut) vt zumachen,
schließen; **~ your mouth** (fam) halt den
Mund! ▷ vi schließen ▷ adj geschlossen;
we're ~ wir haben geschlossen; **shut
down** vt schließen; (computer)
ausschalten ▷ vi schließen; (computer)
sich ausschalten; **shut in** vt einschließen;
shut out vt (lock out) aussperren; **to shut
oneself out** sich aussperren; **shut up** vt
(lock up) abschließen; (silence) zum
Schweigen bringen ▷ vi (keep quiet) den
Mund halten; **~!** halt den Mund!; **shutter**
n (on window) (Fenster)laden m; **shutter
release** n Auslöser m; **shutter speed** n
Belichtungszeit f

shuttle bus [ˈʃʌtlbʌs] n Shuttlebus m

shuttlecock [ˈʃʌtlkɒk] n Federball m

shuttle service [ˈʃʌtlsɜːvɪs] n
Pendelverkehr m

shy [ʃaɪ] adj schüchtern; (animal) scheu

Siberia [saɪˈbɪərɪə] n Sibirien nt

Sicily [ˈsɪsɪlɪ] n Sizilien nt

sick [sɪk] adj krank; (joke) makaber; **to be
~** (Brit: vomit) sich übergeben; **to be off
~** wegen Krankheit fehlen; **I feel ~** mir ist
schlecht; **to be ~ of sb/sth** jdn/etw satt
haben; **it makes me ~** (fig) es ekelt mich
an; **sickbag** n Spucktüte f; **sick leave** n
to be on ~ krankgeschrieben sein;
sickness n Krankheit f; (Brit: nausea)
Übelkeit f; **sickness benefit** n (Brit)
Krankengeld nt

side [saɪd] n Seite f; (of road) Rand m; (of
mountain) Hang m; (Sport) Mannschaft f;
by my ~ neben mir; **~ by ~** nebeneinander
▷ adj (door, entrance) Seiten-; **sideboard** n
Anrichte f; **sideboards, sideburns** (US) npl
Koteletten pl; **side dish** n Beilage f; **side
effect** n Nebenwirkung f; **sidelight** n
(Brit Auto) Parklicht nt; **side order** n
Beilage f; **side road** n Nebenstraße f; **side
street** n Seitenstraße f; **sidewalk** n (US)
Bürgersteig m; **sideways** adv seitwärts

sieve [sɪv] n Sieb nt

sift [sɪft] vt (flour etc) sieben

sigh [saɪ] vi seufzen

sight [saɪt] n (power of seeing)
Sehvermögen nt; (view, thing seen) Anblick
m; **~s** pl (of city etc) Sehenswürdigkeiten pl;

to have bad ~ schlecht sehen; **to lose ~ of** aus den Augen verlieren; **out of ~** außer Sicht; **sightseeing** *n* **to go ~** Sehenswürdigkeiten besichtigen; **~ tour** Rundfahrt *f*

sign [saın] *n* Zeichen *nt*; (*notice, road ~*) Schild *nt* ▷ *vt* unterschreiben ▷ *vi* unterschreiben; **to ~ for sth** den Empfang einer Sache *gen* bestätigen; **to ~ in/out** sich ein-/austragen; **sign on** *vi* (*Brit: register as unemployed*) sich arbeitslos melden; **sign up** *vi* (*for course*) sich einschreiben; (*Mil*) sich verpflichten

signal ['sıgnl] *n* Signal *nt* ▷ *vi* (*car driver*) blinken

signature ['sıgnətʃə*] *n* Unterschrift *f*

significant [sıg'nıfıkənt] *adj* (*important*) bedeutend, wichtig; (*meaning sth*) bedeutsam; **significantly** *adv* (*considerably*) bedeutend

sign language ['saınlæŋgwıdʒ] *n* Zeichensprache *f*; **signpost** *n* Wegweiser *m*

silence ['saıləns] *n* Stille *f*; (*of person*) Schweigen *nt*; **~!** Ruhe! ▷ *vt* zum Schweigen bringen; **silent** *adj* still; (*taciturn*) schweigsam; **she remained ~** sie schwieg

silk [sılk] *n* Seide *f* ▷ *adj* Seiden-

silly ['sılı] *adj* dumm, albern; **don't do anything ~** mach keine Dummheiten

silver ['sılvə*] *n* Silber *nt*; (*coins*) Silbermünzen *pl* ▷ *adj* Silber-, silbern; **silver-plated** *adj* versilbert; **silver wedding** *n* silberne Hochzeit

similar ['sımılə*] *adj* ähnlich (*to dat*); **similarity** [sımı'lærıtı] *n* Ähnlichkeit *f* (*to* mit); **similarly** *adv* (*equally*) ebenso

simple ['sımpl] *adj* einfach; (*unsophisticated*) schlicht; **simplify** ['sımplıfaı] *vt* vereinfachen; **simply** *adv* einfach; (*merely*) bloß; (*dress*) schlicht

simulate ['sımjʊleıt] *vt* simulieren

simultaneous, **simultaneously** [sıməl'teınıəs, -lı] *adj, adv* gleichzeitig

sin [sın] *n* Sünde *f* ▷ *vi* sündigen

since [sıns] *adv* seitdem; (*in the meantime*) inzwischen ▷ *prep* seit +*dat*; **ever ~ 1995** schon seit 1995 ▷ *conj* (*time*) seit, seitdem; (*because*) da, weil; **ever ~ I've known her** seit ich sie kenne; **it's ages ~ I've seen him** ich habe ihn seit langem nicht mehr gesehen

sincere [sın'sıə*] *adj* aufrichtig; **sincerely** *adv* aufrichtig; **Yours ~** mit freundlichen Grüßen

sing [sıŋ] (**sang, sung**) *vt, vi* singen

Singapore [sıŋgə'pɔː*] *n* Singapur *nt*

singer ['sıŋə*] *n* Sänger(in) *m(f)*

single ['sıŋgl] *adj* (*one only*) einzig; (*not double*) einfach; (*bed, room*) Einzel-; (*unmarried*) ledig; (*Brit: ticket*) einfach ▷ *n* (*Brit: ticket*) einfache Fahrkarte; (*Mus*) Single *f*; **a ~ to London, please** (*Brit Rail*) einfach nach London, bitte; **single out** *vt* (*choose*) auswählen; **single-handed**, **single-handedly** *adv* im Alleingang; **single parent** *n* Alleinerziehende(r) *mf*; **single supplement** *n* (*for hotel room*) Einzelzimmerzuschlag *m*

singular ['sıŋgjʊlə*] *n* Singular *m*

sinister ['sınıstə*] *adj* unheimlich

sink [sıŋk] (**sank, sunk**) *vt* (*ship*) versenken ▷ *vi* sinken ▷ *n* Spülbecken *nt*; (*in bathroom*) Waschbecken *nt*

sip [sıp] *vt* nippen an +*dat*

sir [sɜː*] *n* **yes, ~** ja(, mein Herr); **can I help you, ~?** kann ich Ihnen helfen?; **Sir James** (*title*) Sir James

sister ['sıstə*] *n* Schwester *f*; (*Brit: nurse*) Oberschwester *f*; **sister-in-law** (*pl* **sisters-in-law**) *n* Schwägerin *f*

sit [sıt] (**sat, sat**) *vi* (*be sitting*) sitzen; (*~ down*) sich setzen; (*committee, court*) tagen ▷ *vt* (*Brit: exam*) machen; **sit down** *vi* sich hinsetzen; **sit up** *vi* (*from lying position*) sich aufsetzen

sitcom ['sıtkɒm] *n* Situationskomödie *f*

site [saıt] *n* Platz *m*; (*building ~*) Baustelle *f*; (*web~*) Site *f*

sitting ['sıtıŋ] *n* (*meeting, for portrait*) Sitzung *f*; **sitting room** *n* Wohnzimmer *nt*

situated ['sıtjʊeıtıd] *adj* **to be ~** liegen

situation [sıtjʊ'eıʃən] *n* (*circumstances*) Situation *f*, Lage *f*; (*job*) Stelle *f*; **'~s vacant/wanted'** (*Brit*) „Stellenangebote/Stellengesuche"

six [sıks] *num* sechs ▷ *n* Sechs *f*; *see also* **eight**; **sixpack** *n* (*of beer etc*) Sechserpack *nt*; **sixteen** ['sıks'tiːn] *num* sechzehn ▷ *n* Sechzehn *f*; *see also* **eight**; **sixteenth** *adj* sechzehnte(r, s); *see also* **eighth**; **sixth** [sıksθ] *adj* sechste(r, s); **~ form** (*Brit*) ≈ Oberstufe *f* ▷ *n* (*fraction*) Sechstel *nt*; *see also* **eighth**; **sixtieth** ['sıkstııθ] *adj*

sechzigste(r, s); *see also* **eighth**; **sixty**
['sɪkstɪ] *num* sechzig; **~~one**
einundsechzig ▷ *n* Sechzig *f*; **to be in
one's sixties** in den Sechzigern sein; *see
also* **eight**

size [saɪz] *n* Größe *f*; **what ~ are you?**
welche Größe haben Sie?; **a ~ too big** eine
Nummer zu groß

sizzle ['sɪzl] *vi* (*Gastr*) brutzeln

skate [skeɪt] *n* Schlittschuh *m*; (*roller-~*)
Rollschuh *m* ▷ *vi* Schlittschuh laufen;
(*roller-~*) Rollschuh laufen; **skateboard** *n*
Skateboard *nt*; **skating** *n* Eislauf *m*;
(*roller-~*) Rollschuhlauf *m*; **skating rink** *n*
Eisbahn *f*; (*for roller-skating*) Rollschuhbahn
f

skeleton ['skelɪtn] *n* (*a. fig*) Skelett *nt*

skeptical *n* (*US*) *see* **sceptical**

sketch [sketʃ] *n* Skizze *f*; (*Theat*) Sketch *m*
▷ *vt* skizzieren; **sketchbook** *n*
Skizzenbuch *nt*

ski [skiː] *n* Ski *m* ▷ *vi* Ski laufen; **ski boot**
n Skistiefel *m*

skid [skɪd] *vi* (*Auto*) schleudern

skier ['skiːə*] *n* Skiläufer(in) *m(f)*; **skiing** *n*
Skilaufen *nt*; **to go ~** Ski laufen gehen;
~ holiday Skiurlaub *m*; **skiing instructor**
n Skilehrer(in) *m(f)*

skilful, skilfully ['skɪlfʊl, -fəlɪ] *adj, adv*
geschickt

ski-lift ['skiːlɪft] *n* Skilift *m*

skill [skɪl] *n* Geschick *nt*; (*acquired
technique*) Fertigkeit *f*; **skilled** *adj*
geschickt (*at, in* in +*dat*); (*worker*) Fach-;
(*work*) fachmännisch

skim [skɪm] *vt* **to ~ (off)** (*fat etc*)
abschöpfen; **to ~ (through)** (*read*)
überfliegen; **skimmed milk** *n*
Magermilch *f*

skin [skɪn] *n* Haut *f*; (*fur*) Fell *nt*; (*peel*)
Schale *f*; **skin diving** *n* Sporttauchen *nt*;
skinny *adj* dünn

skip [skɪp] *vi* hüpfen; (*with rope*) Seil
springen ▷ *vt* (*miss out*) überspringen;
(*meal*) ausfallen lassen; (*school, lesson*)
schwänzen

ski pants ['skiːpænts] *npl* Skihose *f*; **ski
pass** *n* Skipass *m*; **ski pole** *n* Skistock *m*;
ski resort *n* Skiort *m*

skirt [skɜːt] *n* Rock *m*

ski run ['skiːrʌn] *n* (Ski)abfahrt *f*; **ski
stick** *n* Skistock *m*; **ski tow** *n* Schlepplift
m

skittle ['skɪtl] *n* Kegel *m*; **~s** (*game*) Kegeln
nt

skive [skaɪv] *vi* **to ~ (off)** (*Brit fam*) sich
drücken; (*from school*) schwänzen; (*from
work*) blaumachen

skull [skʌl] *n* Schädel *m*

sky [skaɪ] *n* Himmel *m*; **skydiving** *n*
Fallschirmspringen *nt*; **skylight** *n*
Dachfenster *nt*; **skyscraper** *n*
Wolkenkratzer *m*

slam [slæm] *vt* (*door*) zuschlagen; **slam
on** *vt* **to slam the brakes on** voll auf die
Bremse treten

slander ['slɑːndə*] *n* Verleumdung *f* ▷ *vt*
verleumden

slang [slæŋ] *n* Slang *m*

slap [slæp] *n* Klaps *m*; (*across face*)
Ohrfeige *f* ▷ *vt* schlagen; **to ~ sb's face**
jdn ohrfeigen

slash [slæʃ] *n* (*punctuation mark*)
Schrägstrich *m* ▷ *vt* (*face, tyre*)
aufschlitzen; (*prices*) stark herabsetzen

slate [sleɪt] *n* (*rock*) Schiefer *m*; (*roof ~*)
Schieferplatte *f*

slaughter ['slɔːtə*] *vt* (*animals*)
schlachten; (*people*) abschlachten

Slav [slɑːv] *adj* slawisch ▷ *n* Slawe *m*,
Slawin *f*

slave [sleɪv] *n* Sklave *m*, Sklavin *f*; **slave
away** *vi* schuften; **slave-driver** *n* (*fam*)
Sklaventreiber(in) *m(f)*; **slavery** ['sleɪvərɪ]
n Sklaverei *f*

sleaze [sliːz] *n* (*corruption*) Korruption *f*;
sleazy *adj* (*bar, district*) zwielichtig

sledge ['sledʒ] *n* Schlitten *m*

sleep [sliːp] (**slept, slept**) *vi* schlafen; **to
~ with sb** mit jdm schlafen ▷ *n* Schlaf *m*;
to put to ~ (*animal*) einschläfern; **sleep in**
vi (*lie in*) ausschlafen; **sleeper** *n* (*Rail:
train*) Schlafwagenzug *m*; (*carriage*)
Schlafwagen *m*; **sleeping bag** *n*
Schlafsack *m*; **sleeping car** *n*
Schlafwagen *m*; **sleeping pill** *n*
Schlaftablette *f*; **sleepless** *adj* schlaflos;
sleepy *adj* schläfrig; (*place*) verschlafen

sleet [sliːt] *n* Schneeregen *m*

sleeve [sliːv] *n* Ärmel *m*; **sleeveless** *adj*
ärmellos

sleigh [sleɪ] *n* (Pferde)schlitten *m*

slender ['slendə*] *adj* schlank; (*fig*)
gering

slept [slept] *pt, pp of* **sleep**

slice [slaɪs] *n* Scheibe *f*; (*of cake, tart, pizza*)

Stück nt ▷ vt **to ~ (up)** in Scheiben schneiden; **sliced bread** n geschnittenes Brot

slid [slɪd] pt, pp of **slide**

slide [slaɪd] (**slid, slid**) vt gleiten lassen; (push) schieben ▷ vi gleiten; (slip) rutschen ▷ n (Foto) Dia nt; (in playground) Rutschbahn f; (Brit: for hair) Spange f

slight [slaɪt] adj leicht; (problem, difference) klein; **not in the ~est** nicht im Geringsten; **slightly** adv etwas; (injured) leicht

slim [slɪm] adj (person) schlank; (book) dünn; (chance, hope) gering ▷ vi abnehmen

slime [slaɪm] n Schleim m; **slimy** adj schleimig

sling [slɪŋ] (**slung, slung**) vt werfen ▷ n (for arm) Schlinge f

slip [slɪp] n (mistake) Flüchtigkeitsfehler m; **~ of paper** Zettel m ▷ vt (put) stecken; **to ~ on/off** (garment) an-/ausziehen; **it ~ped my mind** ich habe es vergessen ▷ vi (lose balance) (aus)rutschen; **slip away** vi (leave) sich wegstehlen; **slipper** n Hausschuh m; **slippery** adj (path, road) glatt; (soap, fish) glitschig; **slip-road** n (Brit: onto motorway) Auffahrt f; (off motorway) Ausfahrt f

slit [slɪt] (**slit, slit**) vt aufschlitzen ▷ n Schlitz m

slope [sləʊp] n Neigung f; (side of hill) Hang m ▷ vi (be sloping) schräg sein; **slope down** vi (land, road) abfallen; **sloping** adj (floor, roof) schräg

sloppy ['slɒpɪ] adj (careless) schlampig; (sentimental) rührselig

slot [slɒt] n (opening) Schlitz m; (Inform) Steckplatz m; **we have a ~ free at 2** (free time) um 2 ist noch ein Termin frei; **slot machine** n Automat m; (for gambling) Spielautomat m

Slovak ['sləʊvæk] adj slowakisch ▷ n (person) Slowake m, Slowakin f; (language) Slowakisch nt; **Slovakia** [sləʊ'vækɪə] n Slowakei f

Slovene ['sləʊviːn], **Slovenian** [sləʊ'viːnɪən] adj slowenisch ▷ n (person) Slowene m, Slowenin f; (language) Slowenisch nt; **Slovenia** [sləʊ'viːnɪə] n Slowenien nt

slow [sləʊ] adj langsam; (business) flau; **to be ~** (clock) nachgehen; (stupid)

begriffsstutzig sein; **slow down** vi langsamer werden; (when driving/walking) langsamer fahren/gehen; **slowly** adv langsam; **slow motion** n **in ~** in Zeitlupe

slug [slʌg] n (Zool) Nacktschnecke f

slum [slʌm] n Slum m

slump [slʌmp] n Rückgang m (in an +dat) ▷ vi (onto chair etc) sich fallen lassen; (prices) stürzen

slung [slʌŋ] pt, pp of **sling**

slur [slɜː*] n (insult) Verleumdung f; **slurred** [slɜːd] adj undeutlich

slush [slʌʃ] n (snow) Schneematsch m; **slushy** adj matschig; (fig) schmalzig

slut [slʌt] n (pej) Schlampe f

smack [smæk] n Klaps m ▷ vt **to ~ sb** jdm einen Klaps geben ▷ vi **to ~ of** riechen nach

small [smɔːl] adj klein; **small ads** npl (Brit) Kleinanzeigen pl; **small change** n Kleingeld nt; **small letters** npl **in ~** in Kleinbuchstaben; **smallpox** n Pocken pl; **small print** n **the ~** das Kleingedruckte; **small-scale** adj (map) in kleinem Maßstab; **small talk** n Konversation f, Smalltalk m

smart [smɑːt] adj (elegant) schick; (clever) clever; **smart card** n Chipkarte f; **smartly** adv (dressed) schick

smash [smæʃ] n (car crash) Zusammenstoß m, Schmetterball m ▷ vt (break) zerschlagen; (fig: record) brechen, deutlich übertreffen ▷ vi (break) zerbrechen; **to ~ into** (car) krachen gegen; **smashing** adj (fam) toll

smear [smɪə*] n (mark) Fleck m; (Med) Abstrich m; (fig) Verleumdung f ▷ vt (spread) schmieren; (make dirty) beschmieren; (fig) verleumden

smell [smel] (**smelt** o **smelled, smelt** o **smelled**) vt riechen ▷ vi riechen (of nach); (unpleasantly) stinken ▷ n Geruch m; (unpleasant) Gestank m; **smelly** adj übel riechend; **smelt** [smelt] pt, pp of **smell**

smile [smaɪl] n Lächeln nt ▷ vi lächeln; **to ~ at sb** jdn anlächeln

smock [smɒk] n Kittel m

smog [smɒg] n Smog m

smoke [sməʊk] n Rauch m ▷ vt rauchen; (food) räuchern ▷ vi rauchen; **smoke alarm** n Rauchmelder m; **smoked** adj (food) geräuchert; **smoke-free** adj (zone, building) rauchfrei; **smoker** n Raucher(in)

S

m(f); **smoking** *n* Rauchen *nt*; **'no ~'**
„Rauchen verboten"

smooth [smu:ð] *adj* glatt; *(flight,*
crossing) ruhig; *(movement)* geschmeidig;
(without problems) reibungslos; *(pej:*
person) aalglatt ▷ *vt* *(hair, dress)* glatt
streichen; *(surface)* glätten; **smoothly**
adv reibungslos; **to run ~** *(engine)* ruhig
laufen

smudge [smʌdʒ] *vt* *(writing, lipstick)*
verschmieren

smug [smʌg] *adj* selbstgefällig

smuggle ['smʌgl] *vt* schmuggeln; **to**
~ in/out herein-/herausschmuggeln

smutty ['smʌtɪ] *adj* *(obscene)* schmutzig

snack [snæk] *n* Imbiss *m*; **to have a ~** eine
Kleinigkeit essen; **snack bar** *n*
Imbissstube *f*

snail [sneɪl] *n* Schnecke *f*; **snail mail** *n*
(fam) Schneckenpost *f*

snake [sneɪk] *n* Schlange *f*

snap [snæp] *n* *(photo)* Schnappschuss *m*
▷ *adj* *(decision)* spontan ▷ *vt* *(break)*
zerbrechen; *(rope)* zerreißen ▷ *vi* *(break)*
brechen; *(rope)* reißen; *(bite)* schnappen *(at*
nach); **snap off** *vt* *(break)* abbrechen;
snap fastener *n* *(US)* Druckknopf *m*;
snapshot *n* Schnappschuss *m*

snatch [snætʃ] *vt* *(grab)* schnappen

sneak [sni:k] *vi* *(move)* schleichen;
sneakers *npl* *(US)* Turnschuhe *pl*

sneeze [sni:z] *vi* niesen

sniff [snɪf] *vi* schniefen; *(smell)* schnüffeln
(at an +*dat*) ▷ *vt* schnuppern an +*dat*;
(glue) schnüffeln

snob [snɒb] *n* Snob *m*; **snobbish** *adj*
versnobt

snog [snɒg] *vi, vt* knutschen

snooker ['snu:kə*] *n* Snooker *nt*

snoop [snu:p] *vi* **to ~ (around)**
(herum)schnüffeln

snooze [snu:z] *n, vi* **to (have a) ~** ein
Nickerchen machen

snore [snɔ:*] *vi* schnarchen

snorkel ['snɔ:kl] *n* Schnorchel *m*;
snorkelling *n* Schnorcheln *nt*; **to go**
~ schnorcheln gehen

snout [snaʊt] *n* Schnauze *f*

snow [snəʊ] *n* Schnee *m* ▷ *vi* schneien;
snowball *n* Schneeball *m*; **snowboard** *n*
Snowboard *nt*; **snowboarding** *n*
Snowboarding *nt*; **snowdrift** *n*
Schneewehe *f*; **snowdrop** *n*

Schneeglöckchen *nt*; **snowflake** *n*
Schneeflocke *f*; **snowman** *(pl* **-men)** *n*
Schneemann *m*; **snowplough**, **snowplow**
(US) n Schneepflug *m*; **snowstorm** *n*
Schneesturm *m*; **snowy** *adj* *(region)*
schneereich; *(landscape)* verschneit

snug [snʌg] *adj* *(person, place)* gemütlich

snuggle up ['snʌglʌp] *vi* **to ~ to sb** sich
an jdn ankuscheln

◯ **KEYWORD**

so [səʊ] *adv* **1** *(thus)* so; *(likewise)* auch; **so**
saying he walked away indem er das
sagte, ging er; **if so** wenn ja; **I didn't do it**
— you did so! ich hab das nicht gemacht
— hast du wohl!; **so do I, so am I** *etc* ich
auch; **so it is!** tatsächlich!; **I hope/think**
so hoffentlich/ich glaube schon; **so far** bis
jetzt

2 *(in comparisons etc: to such a degree)* so;
so quickly/big (that) so schnell/groß,
dass; **I'm so glad to see you** ich freue
mich so, dich zu sehen

3: **so many so** viele; **so much work** so viel
Arbeit; **I love you so much** ich liebe dich
so sehr

4 *(phrases)*: **10 or so** etwa 10; **so long!** *(inf:*
goodbye) tschüss!

▷ *conj* **1** *(expressing purpose)*: **so as to** um …
zu; **so (that)** damit

2 *(expressing result)* also; **so I was right**
after all ich hatte also doch Recht; **so you**
see … wie du siehst …

soak [səʊk] *vt* durchnässen; *(leave in*
liquid) einweichen; **I'm ~ed** ich bin
durchnässt; **soaking** *adj* **~ (wet)**
durchnässt

soap [səʊp] *n* Seife *f*; **soap (opera)** *n*
Seifenoper *f*; **soap powder** *n*
Waschpulver *nt*

sob [sɒb] *vi* schluchzen

sober ['səʊbə*] *adj* nüchtern; **sober up** *vi*
nüchtern werden

so-called ['səʊ'kɔ:ld] *adj* so genannt

soccer ['sɒkə*] *n* Fußball *m*

sociable ['səʊʃəbl] *adj* gesellig

social ['səʊʃəl] *adj* sozial; *(sociable)*
gesellig; **socialist** *adj* sozialistisch ▷ *n*
Sozialist(in) *m(f)*; **socialize** *vi* unter die
Leute gehen; **social security** *n* *(Brit)*
Sozialhilfe *f*; *(US)* Sozialversicherung *f*

society [sə'saɪətɪ] n Gesellschaft f; (club) Verein m

sock [sɒk] n Socke f

socket ['sɒkɪt] n (Elec) Steckdose f

soda ['səʊdə] n (~ water) Soda f; (US: pop) Limo f; **soda water** n Sodawasser nt

sofa ['səʊfə] n Sofa nt; **sofa bed** n Schlafcouch f

soft [sɒft] adj weich; (quiet) leise; (lighting) gedämpft; (kind) gutmütig; (weak) nachgiebig; **~ drink** alkoholfreies Getränk; **softly** adv sanft; (quietly) leise; **software** n (Inform) Software f

soil [sɔɪl] n Erde f; (ground) Boden m

solar ['səʊlə*] adj Sonnen-, Solar-

solarium [sə'lɛərɪəm] n Solarium nt

sold [səʊld] pt, pp of **sell**

soldier ['səʊldʒə*] n Soldat(in) m(f)

sole [səʊl] n Sohle f; (fish) Seezunge f ▷ vt besohlen ▷ adj einzig; (owner, responsibility) alleinig; **solely** adv nur

solemn ['sɒləm] adj feierlich; (person) ernst

solicitor [sə'lɪsɪtə*] n (Brit) Rechtsanwalt m, Rechtsanwältin f

solid ['sɒlɪd] adj (hard) fest; (gold, oak etc) massiv; (~ly built) solide; (meal) kräftig; **three hours ~** drei volle Stunden

solitary ['sɒlɪtərɪ] adj einsam; (single) einzeln; **solitude** ['sɒlɪtjuːd] n Einsamkeit f

solo ['səʊləʊ] n (Mus) Solo nt

soluble ['sɒljʊbl] adj löslich; (problem) lösbar; **solution** [sə'luːʃən] n Lösung f (to +gen); **solve** [sɒlv] vt lösen

somber (US), **sombre** ['sɒmbə*] adj düster

KEYWORD

some [sʌm] adj **1** (a certain amount or number of) einige; (a few) ein paar; (with singular nouns) etwas; **some tea/biscuits** etwas Tee/ein paar Plätzchen; **I've got some money, but not much** ich habe ein bisschen Geld, aber nicht viel

2 (certain: in contrasts) manche(r, s); **some people say that ...** manche Leute sagen, dass ...

3 (unspecified) irgendein(e); **some woman was asking for you** da hat eine Frau nach Ihnen gefragt; **some day** eines Tages;

some day next week irgendwann nächste Woche

▷ pron **1** (a certain number) einige; **have you got some?** haben Sie welche?

2 (a certain amount) etwas; **I've read some of the book** ich habe das Buch teilweise gelesen

▷ adv : **some 10 people** etwa 10 Leute

somebody pron jemand; **~ (or other)** irgendjemand; **~ else** jemand anders; **someday** adv irgendwann; **somehow** adv irgendwie; **someone** pron see **somebody**; **someplace** adv (US) see **somewhere**; **something** ['sʌmθɪŋ] pron etwas; **~ (or other)** irgendetwas; **~ else** etwas anderes; **~ nice** etwas Nettes; **would you like ~ to drink?** möchten Sie etwas trinken? ▷ adv **~ like 20** ungefähr 20; **sometime** adv irgendwann; **sometimes** adv manchmal; **somewhat** adv ein wenig; **somewhere** adv irgendwo; (to a place) irgendwohin; **~ else** irgendwo anders; (to another place) irgendwo anders hin; **~ around 6** ungefähr 6

son [sʌn] n Sohn m

song [sɒŋ] n Lied nt

son-in-law ['sʌnɪnlɔː] (pl sons-in-law) n Schwiegersohn m

soon [suːn] adv bald; (early) früh; **too ~** zu früh; **as ~ as I ...** sobald ich ...; **as ~ as possible** so bald wie möglich; **sooner** adv (time) früher; (for preference) lieber

soot [sʊt] n Ruß m

soothe [suːð] vt beruhigen; (pain) lindern

sophisticated [sə'fɪstɪkeɪtɪd] adj (person) kultiviert; (machine) hoch entwickelt; (plan) ausgeklügelt

sophomore ['sɒfəmɔː*] n (US) College-Student(in) m(f) im zweiten Jahr

soppy ['sɒpɪ] adj (fam) rührselig

soprano [sə'prɑːnəʊ] n Sopran m

sore [sɔː*] adj **to be ~** weh tun; **to have a ~ throat** Halsschmerzen haben ▷ n wunde Stelle

sorrow ['sɒrəʊ] n Kummer m

sorry ['sɒrɪ] adj (sad) traurig; (I'm) **~ (excusing)** Entschuldigung!; **I'm ~ (regretful)** es tut mir leid; **~?** wie bitte?; **I feel ~ for him** er tut mir leid

S

sort [sɔːt] *n* Art *f*; **what ~ of film is it?**
was für ein Film ist das?; **a ~ of** eine Art
+*gen*; **all ~s of things** alles Mögliche ▷ *adv*
~ of (*fam*) irgendwie ▷ *vt* sortieren;
everything's ~ed (*dealt with*) alles ist
geregelt; **sort out** *vt* (*classify etc*)
sortieren; (*problems*) lösen

sought [sɔːt] *pt, pp of* **seek**

soul [səʊl] *n* Seele *f*; (*music*) Soul *m*

sound [saʊnd] *adj* (*healthy*) gesund; (*safe*)
sicher; (*sensible*) vernünftig; (*theory*)
stichhaltig; (*thrashing*) tüchtig ▷ *adv* **to be
~ asleep** fest schlafen ▷ *n* (*noise*)
Geräusch *nt*; (*Mus*) Klang *m*; (*Tv*) Ton *m* ▷ *vt*
to ~ the alarm Alarm schlagen; **to ~ one's
horn** hupen ▷ *vi* (*seem*) klingen (*like* wie);
soundcard *n* (*Inform*) Soundkarte *f*;
sound effects *npl* Klangeffekte *pl*;
soundproof *adj* schalldicht; **soundtrack**
n (*of film*) Filmmusik *f*, Soundtrack *m*

soup [suːp] *n* Suppe *f*

sour [saʊə*] *adj* sauer; (*fig*) mürrisch

source [sɔːs] *n* Quelle *f*; (*fig*) Ursprung
m

sour cream [saʊə'kriːm] *n* saure Sahne

south [saʊθ] *n* Süden *m*; **to the ~ of**
südlich von ▷ *adv* (*go, face*) nach Süden
▷ *adj* Süd-; **South Africa** *n* Südafrika *nt*;
South African *adj* südafrikanisch ▷ *n*
Südafrikaner(in) *m(f)*; **South America** *n*
Südamerika *nt*; **South American** *adj*
südamerikanisch ▷ *n* Südamerikaner(in)
m(f); **southbound** *adj* (in) Richtung
Süden; **southern** ['sʌðən] *adj*
Süd-, südlich; **~ Europe** Südeuropa *nt*;
southwards ['saʊθwədz] *adv* nach Süden

souvenir [suːvə'nɪə*] *n* Andenken *nt* (*of*
an +*akk*)

sow [saʊ] (**sowed, sown** *o* **sowed**) *vt* (*a.
fig*) säen; (*field*) besäen ▷ [saʊ] *n* (*pig*)
Sau *f*

soya bean ['sɔɪə'biːn] *n* Sojabohne *f*

soy sauce ['sɔɪ'sɔːs] *n* Sojasoße *f*

spa [spɑː] *n* (*place*) Kurort *m*

space [speɪs] *n* (*room*) Platz *m*, Raum *m*;
(*outer ~*) Weltraum *m*; (*gap*) Zwischenraum
m; (*for parking*) Lücke *f*; **space bar** *n*
Leertaste *f*; **spacecraft** (*pl* -) *n*
Raumschiff *nt*; **space ship** *n* Raumschiff
nt; **space shuttle** *n* Raumfähre *f*

spacing ['speɪsɪŋ] *n* (*in text*)
Zeilenabstand *m*; **double ~** zweizeiliger
Abstand

spacious ['speɪʃəs] *adj* geräumig

spade [speɪd] *n* Spaten *m*; **~s** Pik *nt*

spaghetti [spə'getɪ] *nsing* Spaghetti *pl*

Spain [speɪn] *n* Spanien *nt*

spam [spæm] *n* (*Inform*) Spam *m*

Spaniard ['spænɪəd] *n* Spanier(in) *m(f)*;
Spanish ['spænɪʃ] *adj* spanisch ▷ *n*
(*language*) Spanisch *nt*

spanner ['spænə*] *n* (*Brit*)
Schraubenschlüssel *m*

spare [speə*] *adj* (*as replacement*) Ersatz-;
~ part Ersatzteil *nt*; **~ room** Gästezimmer
nt; **~ time** Freizeit *f*; **~ tyre** Ersatzreifen *m*
▷ *n* (*~ part*) Ersatzteil *nt* ▷ *vt* (*lives,
feelings*) verschonen; **can you ~ (me) a
moment?** hätten Sie einen Moment Zeit?

spark [spɑːk] *n* Funke *m*; **sparkle**
['spɑːkl] *vi* funkeln; **sparkling wine** *n*
Schaumwein *m*, Sekt *m*; **spark plug**
['spɑːkplʌg] *n* Zündkerze *f*

sparrow ['spærəʊ] *n* Spatz *m*

sparse [spɑːs] *adj* spärlich; **sparsely** *adv*
~ populated dünn besiedelt

spasm ['spæzəm] *n* (*Med*) Krampf *m*

spat [spæt] *pt, pp of* **spit**

speak [spiːk] (**spoke, spoken**) *vt*
sprechen; **can you ~ French?** sprechen Sie
Französisch?; **to ~ one's mind** seine
Meinung sagen ▷ *vi* sprechen (*to* mit, zu);
(*make speech*) reden; **~ing** (*Tel*) am Apparat;
so to ~ sozusagen; **~ for yourself** das
meinst auch nur du!; **speak up** *vi* (*louder*)
lauter sprechen; **speaker** *n* Sprecher(in)
m(f); (*public ~*) Redner(in) *m(f)*; (*loud~*)
Lautsprecher *m*

spear [spɪə*] *n* Speer *m*

special ['speʃəl] *adj* besondere(r, s),
speziell ▷ *n* (*on menu*) Tagesgericht *nt*; (*Tv,
Radio*) Sondersendung *f*; **special delivery**
n Eilzustellung *f*; **special effects** *npl*
Spezialeffekte *pl*; **specialist** *n*
Spezialist(in) *m(f)*; (*Tech*) Fachmann *m*,
Fachfrau *f*; (*Med*) Facharzt *m*, Fachärztin *f*;
speciality [speʃɪ'ælɪtɪ] *n* Spezialität *f*;
specialize *vi* sich spezialisieren (*in* auf
+*akk*); **specially** *adv* besonders;
(*specifically*) extra; **special offer** *n*
Sonderangebot *nt*; **specialty** *n* (*US*) *see*
speciality

species ['spiːʃiːz] *nsing* Art *f*

specific [spə'sɪfɪk] *adj* spezifisch; (*precise*)
genau; **specify** ['spesɪfaɪ] *vt* genau
angeben

specimen ['spesɪmən] n (sample) Probe f;
(example) Exemplar nt

specs [speks] npl (fam) Brille f

spectacle ['spektəkl] n Schauspiel nt

spectacles npl Brille f

spectacular [spek'tækjʊlə*] adj
spektakulär

spectator [spek'teɪtə*] n Zuschauer(in)
m(f)

sped [sped] pt, pp of **speed**

speech [spiːtʃ] n (address) Rede f; (faculty)
Sprache f; **to make a ~** eine Rede halten;
speechless adj sprachlos (with vor +dat)

speed [spiːd] (**sped** o **speeded, sped** o
speeded) vi rasen; (exceed ~ limit) zu
schnell fahren ▷ n Geschwindigkeit f; (of
film) Lichtempfindlichkeit f; **speed up** vt
beschleunigen ▷ vi schneller
werden/fahren; (drive faster) schneller
fahren; **speedboat** n Rennboot nt; **speed
bump** n Bodenschwelle f; **speed camera**
n Blitzgerät nt; **speed limit** n
Geschwindigkeitsbegrenzung f;
speedometer [spɪ'dɒmɪtə*] n
Tachometer m; **speed trap** n Radarfalle f;
speedy adj schnell

spell [spel] (**spelt** o **spelled, spelt** o
spelled) vt buchstabieren; **how do you
~ ...?** wie schreibt man ...? ▷ n (period)
Weile f; (enchantment) Zauber m; **a
cold/hot ~** (weather) ein
Kälteeinbruch/eine Hitzewelle;
spellchecker n (Inform)
Rechtschreibprüfung f; **spelling** n
Rechtschreibung f; (of a word)
Schreibweise f; **~ mistake** Schreibfehler m

spelt [spelt] pt, pp of **spell**

spend [spend] (**spent, spent**) vt (money)
ausgeben (on für); (time) verbringen;
spending money n Taschengeld nt

spent [spent] pt, pp of **spend**

sperm [spɜːm] n Sperma nt

sphere [sfɪə*] n (globe) Kugel f; (fig)
Sphäre f

spice [spaɪs] n Gewürz nt; (fig) Würze f
▷ vt würzen; **spicy** ['spaɪsɪ] adj würzig;
(fig) pikant

spider ['spaɪdə*] n Spinne f

spike [spaɪk] n (on railing etc) Spitze f; (on
shoe, tyre) Spike m

spill [spɪl] (**spilt** o **spilled, spilt** o **spilled**)
vt verschütten

spin [spɪn] (**spun, spun**) vi (turn) sich

drehen; (washing) schleudern; **my head is
~ning** mir dreht sich alles ▷ vt (turn)
drehen; (coin) hochwerfen ▷ n (turn)
Drehung f

spinach ['spɪnɪtʃ] n Spinat m

spin-drier ['spɪndraɪə*] n
Wäscheschleuder f; **spin-dry** vt
schleudern

spine [spaɪn] n Rückgrat nt; (of animal,
plant) Stachel m; (of book) Rücken m

spiral ['spaɪrəl] n Spirale f ▷ adj
spiralförmig; **spiral staircase** n
Wendeltreppe f

spire ['spaɪə*] n Turmspitze f

spirit ['spɪrɪt] n (essence, soul) Geist m;
(humour, mood) Stimmung f; (courage) Mut
m; (verve) Elan m; **~s** pl (drinks) Spirituosen
pl

spiritual ['spɪrɪtjʊəl] adj geistig; (Rel)
geistlich

spit [spɪt] (**spat, spat**) vi spucken ▷ n (for
roasting) (Brat)spieß m; (saliva) Spucke f;
spit out vt ausspucken

spite [spaɪt] n Boshaftigkeit f; **in ~ of**
trotz +gen; **spiteful** adj boshaft

spitting image ['spɪtɪŋ'ɪmɪdʒ] n **he's the
~ of you** er ist dir wie aus dem Gesicht
geschnitten

splash [splæʃ] vt (person, object)
bespritzen ▷ vi (liquid) spritzen; (play in
water) planschen

splendid ['splendɪd] adj herrlich

splinter ['splɪntə*] n Splitter m

split [splɪt] (**split, split**) vt (stone, wood)
spalten; (share) teilen ▷ vi (stone, wood)
sich spalten; (seam) platzen ▷ n (in stone,
wood) Spalt m; (in clothing) Riss m; (fig)
Spaltung f; **split up** vi (couple) sich
trennen ▷ vt (divide up) aufteilen; **split
ends** npl (Haar)spliss m; **splitting** adj
(headache) rasend

spoil [spɔɪl] (**spoiled** o **spoilt, spoiled** o
spoilt) vt verderben; (child) verwöhnen
▷ vi (food) verderben

spoilt [spɔɪlt] pt, pp of **spoil**

spoke [spəʊk] pt of **speak** ▷ n Speiche f

spoken ['spəʊkən] pp of **speak**

spokesperson ['spəʊkspɜːsən] (pl
-people) n Sprecher(in) m(f)

sponge [spʌndʒ] n
Schwamm m; **sponge bag** n Kulturbeutel
m; **sponge cake** n Biskuitkuchen m

sponsor ['spɒnsə*] n (of event, programme)

Sponsor(in) *m(f)* ▷ *vt* unterstützen; (*event, programme*) sponsern

spontaneous, spontaneously [spɒn'teɪnɪəs, -lɪ] *adj, adv* spontan

spool [spuːl] *n* Spule *f*

spoon [spuːn] *n* Löffel *m*

sport [spɔːt] *n* Sport *m*; **sports car** *n* Sportwagen *m*; **sports centre** *n* Sportzentrum *nt*; **sports club** *n* Sportverein *m*; **sportsman** (*pl* -**men**) *n* Sportler *m*; **sportswear** *n* Sportkleidung *f*; **sportswoman** (*pl* -**women**) *n* Sportlerin *f*; **sporty** *adj* sportlich

spot [spɒt] *n* (*dot*) Punkt *m*; (*of paint, blood etc*) Fleck *m*; (*place*) Stelle *f*; (*pimple*) Pickel *m*; **on the ~** vor Ort; (*at once*) auf der Stelle ▷ *vt* (*notice*) entdecken; (*difference*) erkennen; **spotless** *adj* (*clean*) blitzsauber; **spotlight** *n* (*lamp*) Scheinwerfer *m*; **spotty** *adj* (*pimply*) pickelig

spouse [spaʊs] *n* Gatte *m*, Gattin *f*

spout [spaʊt] *n* Schnabel *m*

sprain [spreɪn] *n* Verstauchung *f* ▷ *vt* **to ~ one's ankle** sich den Knöchel verstauchen

sprang [spræŋ] *pt of* **spring**

spray [spreɪ] *n* (*liquid in can*) Spray *nt o m*; (~ (*can*)) Spraydose *f* ▷ *vt* (*plant, insects*) besprühen; (*car*) spritzen

spread [spred] (**spread, spread**) *vt* (*open out*) ausbreiten; (*news, disease*) verbreiten; (*butter, jam*) streichen; (*bread, surface*) bestreichen ▷ *vi* (*news, disease, fire*) sich verbreiten ▷ *n* (*of disease, religion etc*) Verbreitung *f*; (*for bread*) Aufstrich *m*; **spreadsheet** *n* (*Inform*) Tabellenkalkulation *f*

spring [sprɪŋ] (**sprang, sprung**) *vi* (*leap*) springen ▷ *n* (*season*) Frühling *m*; (*coil*) Feder *f*; (*water*) Quelle *f*; **springboard** *n* Sprungbrett *nt*; **spring onion** *n* (*Brit*) Frühlingszwiebel *f*; **spring roll** *n* (*Brit*) Frühlingsrolle *f*; **springy** *adj* (*mattress*) federnd

sprinkle ['sprɪŋkl] *vt* streuen; (*liquid*) (be)träufeln; **to ~ sth with sth** etw mit etw bestreuen; (*with liquid*) etw mit etw besprengen; **sprinkler** *n* (*for lawn*) Rasensprenger *m*; (*for fire*) Sprinkler *m*

sprint [sprɪnt] *vi* rennen; (*Sport*) sprinten

sprout [spraʊt] *n* (*of plant*) Trieb *m*; (*from* seed) Keim *m*; (**Brussels**) **~s** *pl* Rosenkohl *m* ▷ *vi* sprießen

sprung [sprʌŋ] *pp of* **spring**

spun [spʌn] *pt, pp of* **spin**

spy [spaɪ] *n* Spion(in) *m(f)* ▷ *vi* spionieren; **to ~ on sb** jdm nachspionieren ▷ *vt* erspähen

squad [skwɒd] *n* (*Sport*) Mannschaft *f*; (*police* ~) Kommando *nt*

square [skwɛə*] *n* (*shape*) Quadrat *nt*; (*open space*) Platz *m*; (*on chessboard etc*) Feld *nt* ▷ *adj* (*in shape*) quadratisch; **2 ~ metres** 2 Quadratmeter; **2 metres ~** 2 Meter im Quadrat ▷ *vt* **3 ~d** 3 hoch 2; **square root** *n* Quadratwurzel *f*

squash [skwɒʃ] *n* (*drink*) Fruchtsaftgetränk *nt*; (*Sport*) Squash *nt*; (*US: vegetable*) Kürbis *m* ▷ *vt* zerquetschen

squat [skwɒt] *vi* (*be crouching*) hocken; **to ~ (down)** sich (hin)hocken

squeak [skwiːk] *vi* (*door, shoes etc*) quietschen; (*animal*) quieken

squeal [skwiːl] *vi* (*person*) kreischen (*with* vor +*dat*)

squeeze [skwiːz] *vt* drücken; (*orange*) auspressen ▷ *vi* **to ~ into the car** sich in den Wagen hineinzwängen; **squeeze up** *vi* (*on bench etc*) zusammenrücken

squid [skwɪd] *n* Tintenfisch *m*

squint [skwɪnt] *vi* schielen; (*in bright light*) blinzeln

squirrel ['skwɪrəl] *n* Eichhörnchen *nt*

squirt [skwɜːt] *vt, vi* (*liquid*) spritzen

Sri Lanka [srɪ'læŋkə] *n* Sri Lanka *nt*

st *abbr* = **stone** Gewichtseinheit (6,35 *kg*)

St *abbr* = **saint** St.; *abbr* = **street** Str.

stab [stæb] *vt* (*person*) einstechen auf +*akk*; (*to death*) erstechen; **stabbing** *adj* (*pain*) stechend

stabilize ['steɪbəlaɪz] *vt* stabilisieren ▷ *vi* sich stabilisieren

stable ['steɪbl] *n* Stall *m* ▷ *adj* stabil

stack [stæk] *n* (*pile*) Stapel *m* ▷ *vt* **to ~ (up)** (auf)stapeln

stadium ['steɪdɪəm] *n* Stadion *nt*

staff [stɑːf] *n* (*personnel*) Personal *nt*, Lehrkräfte *pl*

stag [stæg] *n* Hirsch *m*

stag night *n* (*Brit*) Junggesellenabschied *m*

stage [steɪdʒ] *n* (*Theat*) Bühne *f*; (*of project, life etc*) Stadium *nt*; (*of journey*) Etappe *f*; **at this ~** zu diesem Zeitpunkt ▷ *vt* (*Theat*)

aufführen, inszenieren; (*demonstration*) veranstalten

stagger ['stægə*] vi wanken ▷ vt (*amaze*) verblüffen; **staggering** adj (*amazing*) umwerfend; (*amount, price*) Schwindel erregend

stagnant ['stægnənt] adj (*water*) stehend; **stagnate** [stæg'neɪt] vi (*fig*) stagnieren

stain [steɪn] n Fleck m; **stained-glass window** n Buntglasfenster nt; **stainless steel** n rostfreier Stahl; **stain remover** n Fleck(en)entferner m

stair [steə*] n (Treppen)stufe f; **~s** pl Treppe f; **staircase** n Treppe f

stake [steɪk] n (*post*) Pfahl m; (*in betting*) Einsatz m; (*Fin*) Anteil m (*in* an +*dat*); **to be at ~** auf dem Spiel stehen

stale [steɪl] adj (*bread*) alt; (*beer*) schal

stalk [stɔːk] n Stiel m ▷ vt (*wild animal*) sich anpirschen an +*akk*; (*person*) nachstellen +*dat*

stall [stɔːl] n (*in market*) (Verkaufs)stand m; (*in stable*) Box f; **~s** pl (*Theat*) Parkett nt ▷ vt (*engine*) abwürgen ▷ vi (*driver*) den Motor abwürgen; (*car*) stehen bleiben; (*delay*) Zeit schinden

stamina ['stæmɪnə] n Durchhaltevermögen nt

stammer ['stæmə*] vi, vt stottern

stamp [stæmp] n (*postage ~*) Briefmarke f; (*for document*) Stempel m ▷ vt (*passport etc*) stempeln; (*mail*) frankieren; **stamped addressed envelope** n frankierter Rückumschlag

stand [stænd] (**stood, stood**) vi stehen; (*as candidate*) kandidieren ▷ vt (*place*) stellen; (*endure*) aushalten; **I can't ~ her** ich kann sie nicht ausstehen ▷ n (*stall*) Stand m; (*seats in stadium*) Tribüne f; (*for coats, bicycles*) Ständer m; (*for small objects*) Gestell nt; **stand around** vi herumstehen; **stand by** vi (*be ready*) sich bereithalten; (*be inactive*) danebenstehen ▷ vt (*fig: person*) halten zu; (*decision, promise*) stehen zu; **stand for** vt (*represent*) stehen für; (*tolerate*) hinnehmen; **stand in for** vt einspringen für; **stand out** vi (*be noticeable*) auffallen; **stand up** vi (*get up*) aufstehen ▷ vt (*girlfriend, boyfriend*) versetzen; **stand up for** vt sich einsetzen für; **stand up to** vt **to ~ sb** jdm die Stirn bieten

standard ['stændəd] n (*norm*) Norm f; **~ of living** Lebensstandard m ▷ adj Standard-

standardize ['stændədaɪz] vt vereinheitlichen

stand-by ['stændbaɪ] n (*thing in reserve*) Reserve f; **on ~** in Bereitschaft ▷ adj (*flight, ticket*) Standby-; **standing order** n (*at bank*) Dauerauftrag m; **standpoint** ['stændpɔɪnt] n Standpunkt m; **standstill** ['stændstɪl] n Stillstand m; **to come to a ~** stehen bleiben; (*fig*) zum Erliegen kommen

stank [stæŋk] pt of **stink**

staple ['steɪpl] n (*for paper*) Heftklammer f ▷ vt heften (*to* an +*akk*); **stapler** n Hefter m

star [stɑː*] n Stern m; (*person*) Star m ▷ vt **the film ~s Hugh Grant** der Film zeigt Hugh Grant in der Hauptrolle ▷ vi die Hauptrolle spielen

starch [stɑːtʃ] n Stärke f

stare [steə*] vi starren; **to ~ at** anstarren

starfish ['stɑːfɪʃ] n Seestern m

star sign ['stɑːsaɪn] n Sternzeichen nt

start [stɑːt] n (*beginning*) Anfang m, Beginn m; (*Sport*) Start m; (*lead*) Vorsprung m; **from the ~** von Anfang an ▷ vt anfangen; (*car, engine*) starten; (*business, family*) gründen; **to ~ to do sth, to ~ doing sth** anfangen, etw zu tun ▷ vi (*begin*) anfangen; (*car*) anspringen; (*on journey*) aufbrechen; (*Sport*) starten; (*jump*) zusammenfahren; **~ing from Monday** ab Montag; **start off** vt (*discussion, process etc*) anfangen, beginnen ▷ vi (*begin*) anfangen, beginnen; (*on journey*) aufbrechen; **start over** vi (*US*) wieder anfangen; **start up** vi (*in business*) anfangen ▷ vt (*car, engine*) starten; (*business*) gründen; **starter** n (*Brit: first course*) Vorspeise f; (*Auto*) Anlasser m; **starting point** n (*a. fig*) Ausgangspunkt m

startle ['stɑːtl] vt erschrecken; **startling** adj überraschend

starve [stɑːv] vi hungern; (*to death*) verhungern; **I'm ~ing** ich habe einen Riesenhunger

state [steɪt] n (*condition*) Zustand m; (*Pol*) Staat m; **~ of health/mind** Gesundheits-/Geisteszustand m; **the (United) States** die (Vereinigten) Staaten

▷ *adj* Staats-; *(control, education)* staatlich
▷ *vt* erklären; *(facts, name etc)* angeben;
stated *adj (fixed)* festgesetzt
statement ['steɪtmənt] *n (official
declaration)* Erklärung *f*; *(to police)* Aussage
f; *(from bank)* Kontoauszug *m*
state-of-the-art [steɪtəvðiː'ɑːt] *adj*
hochmodern, auf dem neuesten Stand der
Technik
static ['stætɪk] *adj (unchanging)*
konstant
station ['steɪʃən] *n (for trains, buses)*
Bahnhof *m*; *(underground ~)* Station *f*; *(police
~, fire ~)* Wache *f*; *(Tv, Radio)* Sender *m* ▷ *vt*
(Mil) stationieren
stationer's ['steɪʃənəz] *n ~ (shop)*
Schreibwarengeschäft *nt*; **stationery** *n*
Schreibwaren *pl*
station wagon ['steɪʃənwægən] *n (US)*
Kombiwagen *m*
statistics [stə'tɪstɪks] *nsing (science)*
Statistik *f*; *(figures)* Statistiken *pl*
statue ['stætjuː] *n* Statue *f*
status ['steɪtəs] *n* Status *m*; *(prestige)*
Ansehen *nt*; **status bar** *n (Inform)*
Statuszeile *f*
stay [steɪ] *n* Aufenthalt *m* ▷ *vi* bleiben;
(with friends, in hotel) wohnen *(with bei)*; **to
~ the night** übernachten; **stay away** *vi*
wegbleiben; **to ~ from sb** sich von jdm
fern halten; **stay behind** *vi*
zurückbleiben; *(at work)* länger bleiben;
stay in *vi (at home)* zu Hause bleiben;
stay out *vi (not come home)* wegbleiben;
stay up *vi (at night)* aufbleiben
steady ['stedɪ] *adj (speed)* gleichmäßig;
(progress, increase) stetig; *(job, income,
girlfriend)* fest; *(worker)* zuverlässig; *(hand)*
ruhig; **they've been going ~ for two
years** sie sind seit zwei Jahren fest
zusammen ▷ *vt (nerves)* beruhigen; **to
~ oneself** Halt finden
steak [steɪk] *n* Steak *nt*; *(of fish)* Filet *nt*
steal [stiːl] **(stole, stolen)** *vt* stehlen; **to
~ sth from sb** jdm etw stehlen
steam [stiːm] *n* Dampf *m* ▷ *vt (Gastr)*
dämpfen; **steam up** *vi (window)*
beschlagen; **steamer** *n (Gastr)*
Dampfkochtopf *m*; *(ship)* Dampfer *m*;
steam iron *n* Dampfbügeleisen *nt*
steel [stiːl] *n* Stahl *m* ▷ *adj* Stahl-
steep [stiːp] *adj* steil
steeple ['stiːpl] *n* Kirchturm *m*

steer [stɪə*] *vt, vi* steuern; *(car, bike etc)*
lenken; **steering** *n (Auto)* Lenkung *f*;
steering wheel *n* Steuer *nt*, Lenkrad *nt*
stem [stem] *n (of plant, glass)* Stiel *m*
step [step] *n* Schritt *m*; *(stair)* Stufe *f*;
(measure) Maßnahme *f*; **~ by ~** Schritt für
Schritt ▷ *vi* treten; **~ this way, please**
hier entlang, bitte; **step down** *vi (resign)*
zurücktreten
stepbrother *n* Stiefbruder *m*; **stepchild**
(pl **-children)** *n* Stiefkind *nt*; **stepfather** *n*
Stiefvater *m*
stepladder *n* Trittleiter *f*
stepmother *n* Stiefmutter *f*; **stepsister**
n Stiefschwester *f*
stereo ['sterɪəʊ] *(pl* **-s)** *n ~ (system)*
Stereoanlage *f*
sterile ['steraɪl] *adj* steril; **sterilize**
['sterɪlaɪz] *vt* sterilisieren
sterling ['stɜːlɪŋ] *n (Fin)* das Pfund
Sterling
stern [stɜːn] *adj* streng ▷ *n* Heck *nt*
stew [stjuː] *n* Eintopf *m*
steward ['stjuːəd] *n (on plane, ship)*
Steward *m*; **stewardess** *n* Stewardess *f*
stick [stɪk] **(stuck, stuck)** *vt (with glue etc)*
kleben; *(pin etc)* stecken; *(fam: put)* tun ▷ *vi*
(get jammed) klemmen; *(hold fast)* haften
▷ *n* Stock *m*; *(hockey ~)* Schläger *m*; *(of
chalk)* Stück *nt*; *(of celery, rhubarb)* Stange *f*;
stick out *vt* **to stick one's tongue out
(at sb)** *(jdm)* die Zunge herausstrecken
▷ *vi (protrude)* vorstehen; *(ears)* abstehen;
(be noticeable) auffallen; **stick to** *vi (rules,
plan etc)* sich halten an +*akk*; **sticker**
['stɪkə*] *n* Aufkleber *m*; **sticky** ['stɪkɪ] *adj*
klebrig; *(weather)* schwül; **~ label**
Aufkleber *m*; **~ tape** Klebeband *nt*
stiff [stɪf] *adj* steif
stifle ['staɪfl] *vt (yawn etc, opposition)*
unterdrücken; **stifling** *adj* drückend
still [stɪl] *adj* still; *(drink)* ohne
Kohlensäure ▷ *adv (yet, even now)* (immer)
noch; *(all the same)* immerhin; *(sit, stand)*
still; **he ~ doesn't believe me** er glaubt
mir immer noch nicht; **keep ~** halt still!;
bigger/better ~ noch größer/besser
still life *(pl* **still lives)** *n* Stillleben *nt*
stimulate ['stɪmjʊleɪt] *vt* anregen,
stimulieren; **stimulating** *adj* anregend;
stimulus ['stɪmjʊləs] *n (incentive)* Anreiz
m
sting [stɪŋ] **(stung, stung)** *vt (wound with*

~) stechen ▷ vi (eyes, ointment etc) brennen ▷ n (insect wound) Stich m

stingy ['stɪndʒɪ] adj (fam) geizig

stink [stɪŋk] (**stank, stunk**) vi stinken (of nach) ▷ n Gestank m

stir [stɜ:*] vt (mix) (um)rühren; **stir up** vt (mob) aufhetzen; (memories) wachrufen; **to ~ trouble** Unruhe stiften; **stir-fry** vt (unter Rühren) kurz anbraten

stitch [stɪtʃ] n (in sewing) Stich m; (in knitting) Masche f; **to have a ~** (pain) Seitenstechen haben; **he had to have ~es** er musste genäht werden; **she had her ~es out** ihr wurden die Fäden gezogen; **to be in ~es** (fam) sich kaputtlachen ▷ vt nähen; **stitch up** vt (hole, wound) nähen

stock [stɒk] n (supply) Vorrat m (of an +dat); (of shop) Bestand m; (for soup etc) Brühe f; **~s and shares** pl Aktien und Wertpapiere pl; **to be in/out of ~** vorrätig/nicht vorrätig sein; **to take ~** Inventur machen; (fig) Bilanz ziehen ▷ vt (keep in shop) führen; **stock up** vi sich eindecken (on, with mit)

stockbroker n Börsenmakler(in) m(f)

stock cube n Brühwurfel m

stock exchange n Börse f

stocking ['stɒkɪŋ] n Strumpf m

stock market ['stɒkmɑ:kɪt] n Börse f

stole [stəʊl] pt of **steal**; **stolen** ['stəʊlən] pp of **steal**

stomach ['stʌmək] n Magen m; (belly) Bauch m; **on an empty ~** auf leeren Magen; **stomach-ache** n Magenschmerzen pl; **stomach upset** n Magenverstimmung f

stone [stəʊn] n Stein m; (seed) Kern m, Stein m; (weight) britische Gewichtseinheit (6,35 kg) ▷ adj Stein-, aus Stein; **stony** adj (ground) steinig

stood [stʊd] pt, pp of **stand**

stool [stu:l] n Hocker m

stop [stɒp] n Halt m; (for bus, tram, train) Haltestelle f; **to come to a ~** anhalten ▷ vt (vehicle, passer-by) anhalten; (put an end to) ein Ende machen +dat; (cease) aufhören mit; (prevent from happening) verhindern; (bleeding) stillen; (engine, machine) abstellen; (payments) einstellen; (cheque) sperren; **to ~ doing sth** aufhören, etw zu tun; **to ~ sb (from) doing sth** jdn daran hindern, etw zu tun; **~ it** hör auf (damit)! ▷ vi (vehicle) anhalten; (during journey) Halt machen; (pedestrian, clock, heart) stehen bleiben; (rain, noise) aufhören; (stay) bleiben; **stop by** vi vorbeischauen; **stop over** vi Halt machen; (overnight) übernachten; **stopover** n (on journey) Zwischenstation f; **stopper** n Stöpsel m; **stop sign** n Stoppschild nt; **stopwatch** n Stoppuhr f

storage ['stɔ:rɪdʒ] n Lagerung f; **store** [stɔ:*] n (supply) Vorrat m (of an +dat); (place for storage) Lager nt; (large shop) Kaufhaus nt; (US: shop) Geschäft nt ▷ vt lagern; (Inform) speichern; **storecard** n Kundenkreditkarte f; **storeroom** n Lagerraum m

storey ['stɔ:rɪ] n (Brit) Stock m, Stockwerk nt

storm [stɔ:m] n Sturm m; (thunder~) Gewitter nt ▷ vt, vi (with movement) stürmen; **stormy** adj stürmisch

story ['stɔ:rɪ] n Geschichte f; (plot) Handlung f; (US: of building) Stock m, Stockwerk nt

stout [staʊt] adj (fat) korpulent; (shoes) fest

stove [stəʊv] n Herd m; (for heating) Ofen m

stow [stəʊ] vt verstauen; **stowaway** n blinder Passagier

straight [streɪt] adj (not curved) gerade; (hair) glatt; (honest) ehrlich (with zu); (fam: heterosexual) hetero ▷ adv (directly) direkt; (immediately) sofort; (drink) pur; (think) klar; **~ ahead** geradeaus; **to go ~ on** geradeaus weitergehen/weiterfahren; **straightaway** adv sofort; **straightforward** adj einfach; (person) aufrichtig

strain [streɪn] n Belastung f ▷ vt (eyes) überanstrengen; (rope, relationship) belasten; (vegetables) abgießen; **to ~ a muscle** sich einen Muskel zerren; **strained** adj (laugh, smile) gezwungen; (relations) gespannt; **~ muscle** Muskelzerrung f; **strainer** n Sieb nt

strand [strænd] n (of wool) Faden m; (of hair) Strähne f ▷ vt **to be (left) ~ed** (person) festsitzen

strange [streɪndʒ] adj seltsam; (unfamiliar) fremd; **strangely** adv seltsam; **~ enough** seltsamerweise; **stranger** n Fremde(r) mf; **I'm a ~ here** ich bin hier fremd

S

strangle ['stræŋgl] vt (kill) erdrosseln
strap [stræp] n Riemen m; (on dress etc)
Träger m; (on watch) Band nt ▷ vt (fasten)
festschnallen (to an +dat); **strapless** adj
trägerlos
strategy ['strætɪdʒɪ] n Strategie f
straw [strɔ:] n Stroh nt; (drinking ~)
Strohhalm m
strawberry n Erdbeere f
stray [streɪ] n streunendes Tier ▷ adj (cat,
dog) streunend ▷ vi streunen
streak ['stri:k] n (of colour, dirt) Streifen m;
(in hair) Strähne f; (in character) Zug m
stream [stri:m] n (flow of liquid) Strom m;
(brook) Bach m ▷ vi strömen; **streamer** n
(of paper) Luftschlange f
street [stri:t] n Straße f; **streetcar** n (US)
Straßenbahn f; **street lamp**, **street light**
n Straßenlaterne f; **street map** n
Stadtplan m
strength [streŋθ] n Kraft f, Stärke f;
strengthen vt verstärken; (fig) stärken
strenuous ['strenjʊəs] adj anstrengend
stress [stres] n Stress m; (on word)
Betonung f; **to be under ~** im Stress sein
▷ vt betonen; (on word) stressen;
stressed adj ~ (out) gestresst
stretch [stretʃ] n (of land) Stück nt; (of
road) Strecke f ▷ vt (material, shoes)
dehnen; (rope, canvas) spannen; (person in
job etc) fordern; **to ~ one's legs** (walk) sich
die Beine vertreten ▷ vi (person) sich
strecken; (area) sich erstrecken (to bis zu);
stretch out vt **to stretch one's
hand/legs out** die Hand/die Beine
ausstrecken, ausstrecken ▷ vi (reach) sich
strecken; (lie down) sich ausstrecken;
stretcher n Tragbahre f
strict, strictly [strɪkt, -lɪ] adj, adv
(severe(ly)) streng; (exact(ly)) genau
strike [straɪk] (**struck, struck**) vt (match)
anzünden; (hit) schlagen; (find) finden; **it
struck me as strange** es kam mir seltsam
vor ▷ vi (stop work) streiken; (attack)
zuschlagen; (clock) schlagen ▷ n (by
workers) Streik m; **to be on ~** streiken;
strike up vt (conversation) anfangen;
(friendship) schließen; **striking** adj
auffallend; (resemblance) verblüffend
string [strɪŋ] n (for tying) Schnur f; (Mus,
Tennis) Saite f; **the ~s** pl (section of orchestra)
die Streicher pl
strip [strɪp] n Streifen m; (Brit: of footballer

etc) Trikot nt ▷ vt (undress) ausziehen ▷ vi
(undress) sich ausziehen, strippen
stripe [straɪp] n Streifen m; **striped** adj
gestreift
stripper ['strɪpə*] n Stripper(in) m(f);
(paint ~) Farbentferner m
strip-search ['strɪpsɜ:tʃ] n
Leibesvisitation f (bei der man sich ausziehen
muss)
striptease ['strɪpti:z] n Striptease m
strive [straɪv] (**strove, striven**) vi **to ~ to
do sth** bemüht sein, etw zu tun; **to ~ for
sth** nach etw streben
stroke [strəʊk] n (Med, Tennis etc)
Schlag m; (of pen, brush) Strich m ▷ vt
streicheln
stroll [strəʊl] n Spaziergang m ▷ vi
spazieren; **stroller** n (US: for baby) Buggy
m
strong [strɒŋ] adj stark; (healthy) robust;
(wall, table) stabil; (shoes) fest; (influence,
chance) groß; **strongly** adv stark; (believe)
fest; (constructed) stabil
strove [strəʊv] pt of **strive**
struck [strʌk] pt, pp of **strike**
structural, structurally ['strʌktʃərəl, -lɪ]
adj strukturell; **structure** ['strʌktʃə*] n
Struktur f; (building, bridge) Konstruktion f,
Bau m
struggle ['strʌgl] n Kampf m (for um) ▷ vi
(fight) kämpfen (for um); (do sth with
difficulty) sich abmühen; **to ~ to do sth**
sich abmühen, etw zu tun
stub [stʌb] n (of cigarette) Kippe f; (of ticket,
cheque) Abschnitt m ▷ vt **to ~ one's toe**
sich dat den Zeh stoßen (on an +dat)
stubble ['stʌbl] n Stoppeln pl
stubborn ['stʌbən] adj (person) stur
stuck [stʌk] pt, pp of **stick** ▷ adj **to be
~** (jammed) klemmen; (at a loss) nicht mehr
weiterwissen; **to get ~** (car in snow etc)
stecken bleiben
student ['stju:dənt] n Student(in) m(f),
Schüler(in) m(f)
studio ['stju:dɪəʊ] (pl **-s**) n Studio nt
studious ['stju:dɪəs] adj fleißig
study ['stʌdɪ] n (investigation)
Untersuchung f; (studying) Studium nt;
(room) Arbeitszimmer nt ▷ vt, vi studieren;
to ~ for an exam sich auf eine Prüfung
vorbereiten
stuff [stʌf] n Zeug nt, Sachen pl ▷ vt
(push) stopfen; (Gastr) füllen; **to ~ oneself**

(*fam*) sich voll stopfen; **stuffing** n (*Gastr*) Füllung f

stuffy ['stʌfɪ] adj (*room*) stickig; (*person*) spießig

stumble ['stʌmbl] vi stolpern; (*when speaking*) stocken

stun [stʌn] vt (*shock*) fassungslos machen; **I was ~ned** ich war fassungslos (*o völlig überrascht*)

stung [stʌŋ] pt, pp of **sting**

stunk [stʌŋk] pp of **stink**

stunning ['stʌnɪŋ] adj (*marvellous*) fantastisch; (*beautiful*) atemberaubend; (*very surprising, shocking*) überwältigend; unfassbar

stunt [stʌnt] n (*Cine*) Stunt m

stupid ['stjuːpɪd] adj dumm; **stupidity** [stjuːˈpɪdɪtɪ] n Dummheit f

sturdy ['stɜːdɪ] adj robust; (*building, car*) stabil

stutter ['stʌtə*] vi, vt stottern

stye [staɪ] n (*Med*) Gerstenkorn nt

style [staɪl] n Stil m ▷ vt (*hair*) stylen; **styling mousse** n Schaumfestiger m; **stylish** ['staɪlɪʃ] adj elegant

subconscious [sʌbˈkɒnʃəs] adj unterbewusst ▷ n **the ~** das Unterbewusstsein

subdivide [sʌbdɪˈvaɪd] vt unterteilen

subject ['sʌbdʒɪkt] n (*topic*) Thema nt; (*in school*) Fach nt; (*citizen*) Staatsangehörige(r) mf; (*of kingdom*) Untertan(in) m(f); (*Ling*) Subjekt nt; **to change the ~** das Thema wechseln ▷ adj [səbˈdʒɛkt] **to be ~ to** (*dependent on*) abhängen von; (*under control of*) unterworfen sein +dat

subjective [səbˈdʒɛktɪv] adj subjektiv

sublet [sʌbˈlet] irr vt untervermieten (*to* an +akk)

submarine [sʌbməˈriːn] n U-Boot nt

submerge [səbˈmɜːdʒ] vt (*put in water*) eintauchen ▷ vi tauchen

submit [səbˈmɪt] vt (*application, claim*) einreichen ▷ vi (*surrender*) sich ergeben

subordinate [səˈbɔːdɪnət] adj untergeordnet (*to* +dat) ▷ n Untergebene(r) mf

subscribe [səbˈskraɪb] vi **to ~ to** (*magazine etc*) abonnieren; **subscription** [səbˈskrɪpʃən] n (*to magazine etc*) Abonnement nt; (*to club etc*) (Mitglieds)beitrag m

subsequent ['sʌbsɪkwənt] adj nach(folgend); **subsequently** adv später, anschließend

subside [səbˈsaɪd] vi (*floods*) zurückgehen; (*storm*) sich legen; (*building*) sich senken

substance ['sʌbstəns] n Substanz f

substantial [səbˈstænʃəl] adj beträchtlich; (*improvement*) wesentlich; (*meal*) reichhaltig; (*furniture*) solide

substitute ['sʌbstɪtjuːt] n Ersatz m; (*Sport*) Ersatzspieler(in) m(f) ▷ vt **to ~ A for B** B durch A ersetzen

subtitle ['sʌbtaɪtl] n Untertitel m

subtle ['sʌtl] adj (*difference, taste*) fein; (*plan*) raffiniert

subtotal ['sʌbtəutl] n Zwischensumme f

subtract [səbˈtrækt] vt abziehen (*from* von)

suburb ['sʌbɜːb] n Vorort m; **in the ~s** am Stadtrand; **suburban** [səˈbɜːbən] adj vorstädtisch, Vorstadt-

subway ['sʌbweɪ] n (*Brit*) Unterführung f; (*US Rail*) U-Bahn f

succeed [səkˈsiːd] vi erfolgreich sein; **he ~ed (in doing it)** es gelang ihm(, es zu tun) ▷ vt nachfolgen +dat; **succeeding** adj nachfolgend; **success** [səkˈses] n Erfolg m; **successful**, **successfully** adj, adv erfolgreich

successive [səkˈsesɪv] adj aufeinander folgend; **successor** n Nachfolger(in) m(f)

succulent ['sʌkjʊlənt] adj saftig

succumb [səˈkʌm] vi erliegen (*to* +dat)

such [sʌtʃ] adj solche(r, s); **~ a book** so ein Buch, ein solches Buch; **it was ~ a success that ...** es war solch ein Erfolg, dass ...; **~ as** wie so; **~ a hot day** so ein heißer Tag ▷ pron **as ~** als solche(r, s); **suchlike** adj derartig ▷ pron dergleichen

suck [sʌk] vt (*toffee etc*) lutschen; (*liquid*) saugen; **it ~s** (*fam*) das ist beschissen

Sudan [suˈdɑːn] n (**the**) **~** der Sudan

sudden ['sʌdn] adj plötzlich; **all of a ~** ganz plötzlich; **suddenly** adv plötzlich

sue [suː] vt verklagen

suede [sweɪd] n Wildleder nt

suffer ['sʌfə*] vt erleiden ▷ vi leiden; **to ~ from** (*Med*) leiden an +dat

sufficient, **sufficiently** [səˈfɪʃənt, -lɪ] adj, adv ausreichend

suffocate ['sʌfəkeɪt] vt, vi ersticken

sugar ['ʃʊgə*] n Zucker m ▷ vt zuckern;
sugar bowl n Zuckerdose f; **sugary** adj
(sweet) süß

suggest [sə'dʒest] vt vorschlagen; (imply)
andeuten; **I ~ saying nothing** ich schlage
vor, nichts zu sagen; **suggestion**
[sə'dʒestʃən] n (proposal) Vorschlag m;
suggestive adj vielsagend; (sexually)
anzüglich

suicide ['sʊɪsaɪd] n (act) Selbstmord m

suit [suːt] n (man's clothes) Anzug m; (lady's
clothes) Kostüm nt; (Cards) Farbe f ▷ vt (be
convenient for) passen +dat; (clothes, colour)
stehen +dat; (climate, food) bekommen
+dat; **suitable** adj geeignet (for für);
suitcase n Koffer m

suite [swiːt] n (of rooms) Suite f; (sofa and
chairs) Sitzgarnitur f

sulk [sʌlk] vi schmollen; **sulky** adj
eingeschnappt

sultana [sʌl'taːnə] n (raisin) Sultanine f

sum [sʌm] n Summe f; (money a.) Betrag
m; (calculation) Rechenaufgabe f; **sum up**
vt, vi (summarize) zusammenfassen

summarize ['sʌməraɪz] vt, vi
zusammenfassen; **summary** n
Zusammenfassung f

summer ['sʌmə*] n Sommer m; **summer
camp** n (US) Ferienlager nt; **summer
holidays** n Sommerferien pl;
summertime n in (the) **~** im Sommer

summit ['sʌmɪt] n (a. Pol) Gipfel m

summon ['sʌmən] vt (doctor, fire brigade
etc) rufen; (to one's office) zitieren;
summon up vt (courage, strength)
zusammennehmen

summons ['sʌmənz] nsing (Jur)
Vorladung f

sumptuous ['sʌmptjʊəs] adj luxuriös;
(meal) üppig

sun [sʌn] n Sonne f ▷ vt **to ~ oneself** sich
sonnen

Sun abbr = **Sunday** So.

sunbathe vi sich sonnen; **sunbathing**
n Sonnenbaden nt; **sunbed** n
Sonnenbank f; **sunblock** n Sonnenblocker m;
sunburn n Sonnenbrand m; **sunburnt** adj
to be/get ~ einen Sonnenbrand
haben/bekommen

sundae ['sʌndeɪ] n Eisbecher m

Sunday ['sʌndɪ] n Sonntag m; see also
Tuesday

sung [sʌŋ] pp of **sing**

sunglasses ['sʌnglaːsɪz] npl Sonnenbrille
f; **sunhat** n Sonnenhut m

sunk [sʌŋk] pp of **sink**

sunlamp ['sʌnlæmp] n Höhensonne f;
sunlight n Sonnenlicht nt; **sunny** ['sʌnɪ]
adj sonnig; **sun protection factor** n
Lichtschutzfaktor m; **sunrise** n
Sonnenaufgang m; **sunroof** n (Auto)
Schiebedach nt; **sunscreen** n
Sonnenschutzmittel nt; **sunset** n
Sonnenuntergang m; **sunshade** n
Sonnenschirm m; **sunshine** n
Sonnenschein m; **sunstroke** n
Sonnenstich m; **suntan** n
(Sonnen)bräune f; **to get/have a
~** braun werden/sein; **~ lotion** (o oil)
Sonnenöl nt

super ['suːpə*] adj (fam) toll

superb, superbly [suː'pɜːb, -lɪ] adj, adv
ausgezeichnet

superficial, superficially [suːpə'fɪʃəl, -ɪ]
adj, adv oberflächlich

superfluous [sʊ'pɜːflʊəs] adj überflüssig

superglue ['suːpəgluː] n Sekundenkleber
m

superior [sʊ'pɪərɪə*] adj (better) besser (to
als); (higher in rank) höher gestellt (to als),
höher ▷ n (in rank) Vorgesetzte(r) mf

supermarket ['suːpəmaːkɪt] n
Supermarkt m

supersede [suːpə'siːd] vt ablösen

supersonic [suːpə'sɒnɪk] adj Überschall-

superstitious [suːpə'stɪʃəs] adj
abergläubisch

superstore ['suːpəstɔː*] n
Verbrauchermarkt m

supervise ['suːpəvaɪz] vt beaufsichtigen;
supervisor ['suːpəvaɪzə] n Aufsicht f; (at
university) Doktorvater m

supper ['sʌpə*] n Abendessen nt;
(late-night snack) Imbiss

supplement ['sʌplɪmənt] n (extra
payment) Zuschlag m; (of newspaper)
Beilage f ▷ vt ergänzen; **supplementary**
[sʌplɪ'mentərɪ] adj zusätzlich

supplier [sə'plaɪə*] n Lieferant(in) m(f);
supply [sə'plaɪ] vt (deliver) liefern; (drinks,
music etc) sorgen für; **to ~ sb with sth**
(provide) jdn mit etw versorgen ▷ n (stock)
Vorrat m (of an +dat)

support [sə'pɔːt] n Unterstützung f;
(Tech) Stütze f ▷ vt (hold up) tragen,
stützen; (provide for) ernähren,

unterhalten; (*speak in favour of*)
unterstützen; **he ~s Manchester United**
er ist Manchester-United-Fan
suppose [sə'pəʊz] *vt* (*assume*) annehmen;
I ~ so ich denke schon; **I ~ not**
wahrscheinlich nicht; **you're not ~d to
smoke here** du darfst hier nicht rauchen;
supposedly [sə'pəʊzıdlı] *adv* angeblich;
supposing *conj* angenommen
suppress [sə'pres] *vt* unterdrücken
surcharge ['sɜːtʃɑːdʒ] *n* Zuschlag *m*
sure [ʃʊə*] *adj* sicher; **I'm (not) ~** ich bin
mir (nicht) sicher; **make ~ you lock up**
vergiss nicht abzuschließen ▷ *adv* **~!** klar!;
~ enough tatsächlich; **surely** *adv* **~ you
don't mean it?** das ist nicht dein Ernst,
oder?
surf [sɜːf] *n* Brandung *f* ▷ *vi* (*Sport*) surfen
▷ *vt* **to ~ the net** im Internet surfen
surface ['sɜːfıs] *n* Oberfläche *f* ▷ *vi*
auftauchen; **surface mail** *n* **by ~** auf dem
Land-/Seeweg
surfboard ['sɜːfbɔːd] *n* Surfbrett *nt*;
surfer *n* Surfer(in) *m(f)*; **surfing** *n* Surfen
nt; **to go ~** surfen gehen
surgeon ['sɜːdʒən] *n* Chirurg(in) *m(f)*;
surgery ['sɜːdʒərı] *n* (*operation*)
Operation *f*; (*room*) Praxis *f*, Sprechzimmer
nt; (*consulting time*) Sprechstunde *f*; **to
have ~** operiert werden
surname ['sɜːneım] *n* Nachname *m*
surpass [sɜː'pɑːs] *vt* übertreffen
surplus ['sɜːpləs] *n* Überschuss *m* (*of an
+dat*)
surprise [sə'praız] *n* Überraschung *f* ▷ *vt*
überraschen; **surprising** *adj*
überraschend; **surprisingly** *adv*
überraschenderweise, erstaunlicherweise
surrender [sə'rendə*] *vi* sich ergeben (*to
+dat*) ▷ *vt* (*weapon, passport*) abgeben
surround [sə'raʊnd] *vt* umgeben; (*stand
all round*) umringen; **surrounding** *adj*
(*countryside*) umliegend ▷ *n* **~s** *pl*
Umgebung *f*
survey ['sɜːveı] *n* (*opinion poll*) Umfrage
f; (*of literature etc*) Überblick *m* (*of über
+akk*); (*of land*) Vermessung *f* ▷ [sɜː'veı] *vt*
(*look out over*) überblicken; (*land*)
vermessen
survive [sə'vaıv] *vt*, *vi* überleben
susceptible [sə'septəbl] *adj* empfänglich
(*to für*); (*Med*) anfällig (*to für*)
suspect ['sʌspekt] *n* Verdächtige(r) *mf*

▷ *adj* verdächtig ▷ [sə'spekt] *vt*
verdächtigen (*of +gen*); (*think likely*)
vermuten
suspend [sə'spend] *vt* (*from work*)
suspendieren; (*payment*) vorübergehend
einstellen; (*player*) sperren; (*hang up*)
aufhängen; **suspender** *n* (*Brit*)
Strumpfhalter *m*; **~s** *pl* (US: *for trousers*)
Hosenträger *pl*
suspense [sə'spens] *n* Spannung *f*
suspicious [sə'spıʃəs] *adj* misstrauisch (*of
sb/sth* jdm/etw gegenüber); (*causing
suspicion*) verdächtig
swallow ['swɒləʊ] *n* (*bird*) Schwalbe *f*
▷ *vt*, *vi* schlucken
swam [swæm] *pt of* **swim**
swamp [swɒmp] *n* Sumpf *m*
swan [swɒn] *n* Schwan *m*
swap [swɒp] *vt*, *vi* tauschen; **to ~ sth for
sth** etw gegen etw eintauschen
sway [sweı] *vi* schwanken
swear [sweə*] (**swore, sworn**) *vi* (*promise*)
schwören; (*curse*) fluchen; **to ~ at sb** jdn
beschimpfen; **swear by** *vt* (*have faith in*)
schwören auf *+akk*; **swearword** *n* Fluch *m*
sweat [swet] *n* Schweiß *m* ▷ *vi*
schwitzen; **sweatband** *n* Schweißband
nt; **sweater** *n* Pullover *m*; **sweatshirt** *n*
Sweatshirt *nt*; **sweaty** *adj* verschwitzt
swede [swiːd] *n* Steckrübe *f*
Swede [swiːd] *n* Schwede *m*, Schwedin *f*;
Sweden *n* Schweden *nt*; **Swedish** *adj*
schwedisch ▷ *n* (*language*) Schwedisch *nt*
sweep [swiːp] (**swept, swept**) *vt*, *vi* (*with
brush*) kehren, fegen; **sweep up** *vt* (*dirt
etc*) zusammenkehren, zusammenfegen
sweet [swiːt] *n* (*Brit*: *candy*) Bonbon *nt*;
(*dessert*) Nachtisch *m* ▷ *adj* süß; (*kind*) lieb;
sweet-and-sour *adj* süßsauer;
sweetcorn *n* Mais *m*; **sweeten** *vt* (*tea
etc*) süßen; **sweetener** *n* (*substance*)
Süßstoff *m*
swell [swel] (**swelled, swollen** *o* **swelled**)
vi **to ~ (up)** (an)schwellen ▷ *adj* (US *fam*)
toll; **swelling** *n* (*Med*) Schwellung *f*
sweltering ['sweltərıŋ] *adj* (*heat*)
drückend
swept [swept] *pt*, *pp of* **sweep**
swift, swiftly [swıft] *adj*, *adv* schnell
swig [swıg] *n* (*fam*) Schluck *m*
swim [swım] (**swam, swum**) *vi*
schwimmen ▷ *n* **to go for a
~** schwimmen gehen; **swimmer** *n*

Schwimmer(in) *m(f)*; **swimming** *n*
Schwimmen *nt*; **to go ~** schwimmen
gehen; **swimming cap** *n* (*Brit*)
Badekappe *f*; **swimming costume** *n* (*Brit*)
Badeanzug *m*; **swimming pool** *n*
Schwimmbad *nt*; (*private, in hotel*)
Swimmingpool *m*; **swimming trunks** *npl*
(*Brit*) Badehose *f*; **swimsuit** *n* Badeanzug
m

swindle ['swɪndl] *vt* betrügen (*out of* um)

swine [swaɪn] *n* (*person*) Schwein *nt*

swing [swɪŋ] (**swung, swung**) *vt, vi*
(*object*) schwingen ▷ *n* (*for child*) Schaukel *f*

swipe [swaɪp] *vt* (*credit card etc*)
durchziehen; (*fam: steal*) klauen; **swipe
card** *n* Magnetkarte *f*

Swiss [swɪs] *adj* schweizerisch ▷ *n*
Schweizer(in) *m(f)*

switch [swɪtʃ] *n* (*Elec*) Schalter *m* ▷ *vt*
(*change*) wechseln; **to ~ sth for sth** etw
gegen etw eintauschen ▷ *vi* (*change*)
wechseln (*to* zu); **switch off** *vt*
abschalten, ausschalten; **switch on** *vt*
anschalten, einschalten; **switchboard** *n*
(*Tel*) Vermittlung *f*

Switzerland ['swɪtsələnd] *n* die Schweiz

swivel ['swɪvl] *vi* sich drehen ▷ *vt*
drehen; **swivel chair** *n* Drehstuhl *m*

swollen ['swəʊlən] *pp of* **swell** ▷ *adj* (*Med*)
geschwollen; (*stomach*) aufgebläht

swop [swɒp] *see* **swap**

sword [sɔːd] *n* Schwert *nt*

swore [swɔː*] *pt of* **swear**

sworn [swɔːn] *pp of* **swear**

swot [swɒt] *vi* (*Brit fam*) büffeln (*for* für)

swum [swʌm] *pp of* **swim**

swung [swʌŋ] *pt, pp of* **swing**

syllable ['sɪləbl] *n* Silbe *f*

syllabus ['sɪləbəs] *n* Lehrplan *m*

symbol ['sɪmbəl] *n* Symbol *nt*; **symbolic**
[sɪm'bɒlɪk] *adj* symbolisch; **symbolize** *vt*
symbolisieren

symmetrical [sɪ'metrɪkəl] *adj*
symmetrisch

sympathetic [sɪmpə'θetɪk] *adj*
mitfühlend; (*understanding*)
verständnisvoll; **sympathize** ['sɪmpəθaɪz]
vi mitfühlen (*with sb* mit jdm); **sympathy**
['sɪmpəθɪ] *n* Mitleid *nt*; (*after death*) Beileid
nt; (*understanding*) Verständnis *nt*

symphony ['sɪmfənɪ] *n* Sinfonie *f*

symptom ['sɪmptəm] *n* (*a. fig*) Symptom
nt

synagogue ['sɪnəgɒg] *n* Synagoge *f*

synonym ['sɪnənɪm] *n* Synonym *nt*;
synonymous [sɪ'nɒnɪməs] *adj* synonym
(*with* mit)

synthetic [sɪn'θetɪk] *adj* (*material*)
synthetisch

syphilis ['sɪfɪlɪs] *n* Syphilis *f*

Syria ['sɪrɪə] *n* Syrien *nt*

syringe [sɪ'rɪndʒ] *n* Spritze *f*

system ['sɪstəm] *n* System *nt*;
systematic [sɪstə'mætɪk] *adj*
systematisch; **system disk** *n* (*Inform*)
Systemdiskette *f*; **system(s) software** *n*
(*Inform*) Systemsoftware *f*

t

tab [tæb] n (for hanging up coat etc) Aufhänger m; (Inform) Tabulator m; **to pick up the ~** (fam) die Rechnung übernehmen

table ['teɪbl] n Tisch m; (list) Tabelle f; **~ of contents** Inhaltsverzeichnis nt; **tablecloth** n Tischdecke f; **tablelamp** n Tischlampe f; **tablemat** n Set nt; **tablespoon** n Servierlöffel m; (in recipes) Esslöffel m

tablet ['tæblət] n (Med) Tablette f

table tennis ['teɪbltənɪs] n Tischtennis nt; **table wine** n Tafelwein m

tabloid ['tæblɔɪd] n Boulevardzeitung f

taboo [tə'buː] n Tabu nt ▷ adj tabu

tacit, tacitly ['tæsɪt, -lɪ] adj, adv stillschweigend

tack [tæk] n (small nail) Stift m; (US: thumb~) Reißwecke f

tackle ['tækl] n (Sport) Angriff m; (equipment) Ausrüstung f ▷ vt (deal with) in Angriff nehmen; (Sport) angreifen; (verbally) zur Rede stellen (about wegen)

tact [tækt] n Takt m; **tactful, tactfully** adj, adv taktvoll; **tactic(s)** ['tæktɪk(s)] n(pl) Taktik f; **tactless, tactlessly** ['tæktləs, -lɪ] adj, adv taktlos

tag [tæg] n (label) Schild nt; (with maker's name) Etikett nt

Tahiti [tɑːˈhiːtɪ] n Tahiti nt

tail [teɪl] n Schwanz m; **heads or ~s?** Kopf oder Zahl?; **tailback** n (Brit) Rückstau m; **taillight** n (Auto) Rücklicht nt

tailor ['teɪlə*] n Schneider(in) m(f)

tailpipe ['teɪlpaɪp] n (US Auto) Auspuffrohr nt

tainted ['teɪntɪd] adj (US: food) verdorben

Taiwan [taɪˈwæn] n Taiwan nt

take [teɪk] (**took, taken**) vt nehmen; (~ along with one) mitnehmen; (~ to a place) bringen; (subtract) abziehen (from von); (capture: person) fassen; (gain, obtain) bekommen; (Fin, Comm) einnehmen; (train, taxi) nehmen, fahren mit; (trip, walk, holiday, exam, course, photo) machen; (bath) nehmen; (phone call) entgegennehmen; (decision, precautions) treffen; (risk) eingehen; (advice, job) annehmen; (consume) zu sich nehmen; (tablets) nehmen; (heat, pain) ertragen; (react to) aufnehmen; (have room for) Platz haben für; **I'll ~ it** (item in shop) ich nehme es; **how long does it ~?** wie lange dauert es?; **it ~s 4 hours** man braucht 4 Stunden; **do you ~ sugar?** nehmen Sie Zucker?; **I ~ it that ...** ich nehme an, dass ...; **to ~ place** stattfinden; **take after** vt nachschlagen +dat; **take along** vt mitnehmen; **take apart** vt auseinander nehmen; **take away** vt (remove) wegnehmen (from sb jdm); (subtract) abziehen (from von); **take back** vt (return) zurückbringen; (retract) zurücknehmen; (remind) zurückversetzen (to in +akk); **take down** vt (picture, curtains) abnehmen; (write down) aufschreiben; **take in** vt (understand) begreifen; (give accommodation to) aufnehmen; (deceive) hereinlegen; (include) einschließen; (show, film etc) mitnehmen; **take off** vi (plane) starten ▷ vt (clothing) ausziehen; (hat, lid) abnehmen; (deduct) abziehen; (Brit: imitate) nachmachen; **to take a day off** sich einen Tag freinehmen; **take on** vt (undertake) übernehmen; (employ) einstellen; (Sport) antreten gegen; **take out** vt (wallet etc) herausnehmen; (person, dog) ausführen; (insurance) abschließen; (money from bank) abheben; (book from library) ausleihen; **take over** vt übernehmen ▷ vi **he took over (from me)**

er hat mich abgelöst; **take to** vt **I've taken to her/it** ich mag sie/es; **to ~ doing sth** (begin) anfangen, etw zu tun; **take up** vt (carpet) hochnehmen; (space) einnehmen; (time) in Anspruch nehmen; (hobby) anfangen mit; (new job) antreten; (offer) annehmen

takeaway n (Brit: meal) Essen nt zum Mitnehmen

taken ['teɪkn] pp of **take** ▷ adj (seat) besetzt; **to be ~ with** angetan sein von

takeoff ['teɪkɒf] n (Aviat) Start m; (imitation) Nachahmung f; **takeout** (US) see **takeaway**; **takeover** n (Comm) Übernahme f

takings ['teɪkɪŋz] npl Einnahmen pl

tale [teɪl] n Geschichte f

talent ['tælənt] n Talent nt; **talented** adj begabt

talk [tɔ:k] n (conversation) Gespräch nt; (rumour) Gerede nt; (to audience) Vortrag m ▷ vi sprechen, reden; (have conversation) sich unterhalten; **to ~ to** (o with) sb (about sth) mit jdm (über etw akk) sprechen ▷ vt (language) sprechen; (nonsense) reden; (politics, business) reden über +akk; **to ~ sb into doing/out of doing sth** jdn überreden/jdm ausreden, etw zu tun; **talk over** vt besprechen

talkative adj gesprächig; **talk show** n Talkshow f

tall [tɔ:l] adj groß; (building, tree) hoch; **he is 6ft ~** er ist 1,80m groß

tame [teɪm] adj zahm; (joke, story) fade ▷ vt (animal) zähmen

tampon ['tæmpɒn] n Tampon m

tan [tæn] n (on skin) (Sonnen)bräune f; **to get/have a ~** braun werden/sein ▷ vi braun werden

tangerine [tændʒə'ri:n] n Mandarine f

tango ['tæŋgəʊ] n Tango m

tank [tæŋk] n Tank m; (for fish) Aquarium nt; (Mil) Panzer m

tanker ['tæŋkə*] n (ship) Tanker m; (vehicle) Tankwagen m

tanned [tænd] adj (by sun) braun

tantalizing ['tæntəlaɪzɪŋ] adj verlockend

Tanzania [tænzə'nɪə] n Tansania nt

tap [tæp] n (for water) Hahn m ▷ vt, vi (strike) klopfen; **to ~ sb on the shoulder** jdm auf die Schulter klopfen; **tap-dance** vi steppen

tape [teɪp] n (adhesive ~) Klebeband nt; (for

tape recorder) Tonband nt; (cassette) Kassette f; (video) Video nt ▷ vt (record) aufnehmen; **tape up** vt (parcel) zukleben; **tape measure** n Maßband nt; **tape recorder** n Tonbandgerät nt

tapestry ['tæpɪstrɪ] n Wandteppich m

tap water ['tæpwɔ:tə*] n Leitungswasser nt

tar [tɑ:*] n Teer m

target ['tɑ:gɪt] n Ziel nt; (board) Zielscheibe f

tariff ['tærɪf] n (price list) Preisliste f; (tax) Zoll m

tarmac ['tɑ:mæk] n (Aviat) Rollfeld nt

tart [tɑ:t] n (fruit ~) (Obst)kuchen m; (small) (Obst)törtchen nt; (fam, pej: prostitute) Nutte f; (fam: promiscuous person) Schlampe f

tartan ['tɑ:tən] n Schottenkaro nt; (material) Schottenstoff m

tartar(e) sauce ['tɑ:tə'sɔ:s] n Remouladensoße f

task [tɑ:sk] n Aufgabe f; (duty) Pflicht f; **taskbar** n (Inform) Taskbar f

Tasmania [tæz'meɪnɪə] n Tasmanien nt

taste [teɪst] n Geschmack m; (sense of ~) Geschmackssinn m; (small quantity) Kostprobe f; **it has a strange ~** es schmeckt komisch ▷ vt schmecken; (try) probieren ▷ vi (food) schmecken (of nach); **to ~ good/strange** gut/komisch schmecken; **tasteful, tastefully** adj, adv geschmackvoll; **tasteless, tastelessly** adj, adv geschmacklos; **tasty** adj schmackhaft

tattered ['tætəd] adj (clothes) zerlumpt; (fam: person) angespannt; **I'm absolutely ~** ich bin mit den Nerven am Ende

tattoo [tə'tu:] n (on skin) Tätowierung f

taught [tɔ:t] pt, pp of **teach**

Taurus ['tɔ:rəs] n (Astr) Stier m

tax [tæks] n Steuer f (on auf +akk) ▷ vt besteuern; **taxable** adj steuerpflichtig; **taxation** [tæk'seɪʃən] n Besteuerung f; **tax bracket** n Steuerklasse f; **tax disc** n (Brit Auto) Steuermarke f; **tax-free** adj steuerfrei

taxi ['tæksɪ] n Taxi nt ▷ vi (plane) rollen; **taxi driver** n Taxifahrer(in) m(f); **taxi rank** (Brit), **taxi stand** n Taxistand m

tax return ['tæksrɪ'tɜ:n] n Steuererklärung f

tea [ti:] n Tee m; (afternoon ~) ≈ Kaffee und Kuchen; (meal) frühes Abendessen; **teabag** n Teebeutel m; **tea break** n (Tee)pause f

teach [ti:tʃ] (**taught, taught**) vt (person, subject) unterrichten; **to ~ sb (how) to dance** jdm das Tanzen beibringen ▷ vi unterrichten; **teacher** n Lehrer(in) m(f); **teaching** n (activity) Unterrichten nt; (profession) Lehrberuf m

teacup ['ti:kʌp] n Teetasse f

team [ti:m] n (Sport) Mannschaft f, Team nt; **teamwork** n Teamarbeit f

teapot ['ti:pɒt] n Teekanne f

tear [tɪə*] n (in eye) Träne f

tear [tɛə*] (**tore, torn**) vt zerreißen; **to ~ a muscle** sich einen Muskel zerren ▷ n (in material etc) Riss m; **tear down** vt (building) abreißen; **tear up** vt (paper) zerreißen

tearoom ['ti:rʊm] n Teestube f, Café, in dem in erster Linie Tee serviert wird

tease [ti:z] vt (person) necken (about wegen)

tea set ['ti:set] n Teeservice nt; **teashop** n Teestube f; **teaspoon** n Teelöffel m; **tea towel** n Geschirrtuch nt

technical ['teknɪkəl] adj technisch; (knowledge, term, dictionary) Fach-; **technically** adv technisch; **technique** [tek'ni:k] n Technik f

techno ['teknəʊ] n Techno f

technological [teknə'lɒdʒɪkəl] adj technologisch; **technology** [tek'nɒlədʒɪ] n Technologie f

tedious ['ti:dɪəs] adj langweilig

teen(age) ['ti:n(eɪdʒ)] adj (fashions etc) Teenager-; **teenager** n Teenager m; **teens** [ti:nz] npl **in one's ~** im Teenageralter

teeth [ti:θ] pl of tooth

teetotal ['ti:'təʊtl] adj abstinent

telegraph pole ['telɪɡrɑ:fpəʊl] n (Brit) Telegrafenmast m

telephone ['telɪfəʊn] n Telefon nt ▷ vi telefonieren ▷ vt anrufen; **telephone banking** n Telefonbanking nt; **telephone book** n Telefonbuch nt; **telephone booth**, **telephone box** (Brit) n Telefonzelle f; **telephone call** n Telefonanruf m; **telephone directory** n Telefonbuch nt; **telephone number** n Telefonnummer f

telephoto lens ['telɪfəʊtəʊ'lenz] n Teleobjektiv nt

telescope ['telɪskəʊp] n Teleskop nt

televise ['telɪvaɪz] vt im Fernsehen übertragen; **television** ['telɪvɪʒən] n Fernsehen nt; **television programme** n Fernsehsendung f; **television set** n Fernsehapparat m

teleworking ['telɪwɜ:kɪŋ] n Telearbeit f

tell [tel] (**told, told**) vt (say, inform) sagen (sb sth jdm etw); (story) erzählen; (truth) sagen; (difference) erkennen; (reveal secret) verraten; **to ~ sb about sth** jdm von etw erzählen; **to ~ sth from sth** etw von etw unterscheiden ▷ vi (be sure) wissen; **tell apart** vt unterscheiden; **tell off** vt schimpfen

telling adj aufschlussreich

telly ['telɪ] n (Brit fam) Glotze f; **on (the) ~** in der Glotze

temp [temp] n Aushilfskraft f ▷ vi als Aushilfskraft arbeiten

temper ['tempə*] n (anger) Wut f; (mood) Laune f; **to lose one's ~** die Beherrschung verlieren; **to have a bad ~** jähzornig sein; **temperamental** [tempərə'mentl] adj (moody) launisch

temperature ['temprɪtʃə*] n Temperatur f; (Med: high ~) Fieber nt; **to have a ~** Fieber haben

temple ['templ] n Tempel m; (Anat) Schläfe f

tempo ['tempəʊ] (pl -s) n Tempo nt

temporarily ['tempərərɪlɪ] adv vorübergehend; **temporary** ['tempərərɪ] adj vorübergehend; (road, building) provisorisch

tempt [tempt] vt in Versuchung führen; **I'm ~ed to accept** ich bin versucht anzunehmen; **temptation** [temp'teɪʃən] n Versuchung f; **tempting** adj verlockend

ten [ten] num zehn ▷ n Zehn f; see also **eight**

tenant ['tenənt] n Mieter(in) m(f); (of land) Pächter(in) m(f)

tend [tend] vi **to ~ to do sth** (person) dazu neigen, etw zu tun; **to ~ towards** neigen zu; **tendency** ['tendənsɪ] n Tendenz f; **to have a ~ to do sth** (person) dazu neigen, etw zu tun

tender ['tendə*] adj (loving) zärtlich; (sore) empfindlich; (meat) zart

t

tendon ['tendən] n Sehne f
Tenerife [tenə'riːf] n Teneriffa nt
tenner ['tenə*] n (Brit fam: note)
Zehnpfundschein m; (amount) zehn Pfund
tennis ['tenɪs] n Tennis nt; **tennis ball** n
Tennisball m; **tennis court** n Tennisplatz
m; **tennis racket** n Tennisschläger m
tenor ['tenə*] n Tenor m
tenpin bowling, tenpins (US)
['tenpɪn'bəʊlɪŋ, 'tenpɪnz] n Bowling nt
tense [tens] adj angespannt; (stretched
tight) gespannt; **tension** ['tenʃən] n
Spannung f; (strain) Anspannung f
tent [tent] n Zelt nt
tenth [tenθ] adj zehnte(r, s) ▷ n (fraction)
Zehntel nt; see also **eighth**
tent peg ['tentpeg] n Hering m; **tent pole**
n Zeltstange f
term [tɜːm] n (in school, at university)
Trimester nt; (expression) Ausdruck m; ~s pl
(conditions) Bedingungen pl; **to be on good
~s with sb** mit jdm gut auskommen; **to
come to ~s with sth** sich mit etw
abfinden; **in the long/short
~** langfristig/kurzfristig; **in ~s of ...** was ...
betrifft
terminal ['tɜːmɪnl] n (bus ~ etc)
Endstation f; (Aviat) Terminal m; (Inform)
Terminal nt; (Elec) Pol m ▷ adj (Med)
unheilbar; **terminally** adv (ill) unheilbar
terminate ['tɜːmɪneɪt] vt (contract)
lösen; (pregnancy) abbrechen ▷ vi (train,
bus) enden
terminology [tɜːmɪ'nɒlədʒɪ] n
Terminologie f
terrace ['terəs] n (of houses) Häuserreihe f;
(in garden etc) Terrasse f; **terraced** adj
(garden) terrassenförmig angelegt;
terraced house n (Brit) Reihenhaus nt
terrible ['terəbl] adj schrecklich
terrific [tə'rɪfɪk] adj (very good)
fantastisch
terrify ['terɪfaɪ] vt erschrecken; **to be
terrified** schreckliche Angst haben (of vor
+dat)
territory ['terɪtərɪ] n Gebiet nt
terror ['terə*] n Schrecken m; (Pol) Terror
m; **terrorism** n Terrorismus m; **terrorist**
n Terrorist(in) m(f)
test [test] n Test m, Klassenarbeit f;
(driving ~) Prüfung f; **to put to the ~** auf die
Probe stellen ▷ vt testen, prüfen;
(patience, courage etc) auf die Probe stellen

Testament ['testəmənt] n **the Old/New
~** das Alte/Neue Testament
test-drive ['testdraɪv] vt Probe fahren
testicle ['testɪkl] n Hoden m
testify ['testɪfaɪ] vi (Jur) aussagen
test tube ['testjuːb] n Reagenzglas nt
tetanus ['tetənəs] n Tetanus m
text [tekst] n Text m; (of document)
Wortlaut m; (sent by mobile phone) SMS f
▷ vt (message) simsen, SMSen; **to ~ sb**
jdm simsen, jdm eine SMS schicken; **I'll ~ it to
you** ich schicke es dir per SMS
textbook n Lehrbuch nt
texting ['tekstɪŋ] n SMS-Messaging nt;
text message n SMS f; **text messaging**
n SMS-Messaging nt
texture ['tekstʃə*] n Beschaffenheit f
Thailand ['taɪlænd] n Thailand nt
Thames [temz] n Themse f
than [ðæn] prep, conj als; **bigger/faster
~ me** größer/schneller als ich; **I'd rather
walk ~ drive** ich gehe lieber zu Fuß als mit
dem Auto
thank [θæŋk] vt danken +dat; **~ you**
danke; **~ you very much** vielen Dank;
thankful adj dankbar; **thankfully** adv
(luckily) zum Glück; **thankless** adj
undankbar; **thanks** npl Dank m; **~!**
danke!; **~ to** dank +gen

● **Thanksgiving Day**
●
● **Thanksgiving (Day)** ist ein Feiertag in
● den USA, der auf den vierten
● Donnerstag im November fällt. Er
● soll daran erinnern, wie die
● Pilgerväter die gute Ernte im Jahre
● 1621 feierten. In Kanada gibt es einen
● ähnlichen Erntedanktag (, der aber
● nichts mit den Pilgervätern zu tun
● hat) am zweiten Montag im Oktober.

○ **KEYWORD**

that [ðæt, ðət] adj (demonstrative) (pl
those) der/die/das; jene(r, s); **that one** das
da ▷ pron
1 (demonstrative) (pl those) das;
who's/what's that? wer ist da/was ist
das?; **is that you?** bist du das?; **that's
what he said** genau das hat er gesagt;
what happened after that? was
passierte danach?; **that is** das heißt

2 (relative: subj) der/die/das die; (: direct obj) den/die/das die; (: indirect obj) dem/der/dem denen; **all (that) I have** alles, was ich habe
3 (relative: of time); **the day (that)** an dem Tag, als; **the winter (that) he came** in dem Winter, in dem er kam
▷ conj dass; **he thought that I was ill** er dachte, dass ich krank sei or er dachte, ich sei krank
▷ adv (demonstrative) so; **I can't work that much** ich kann nicht so viel arbeiten

that's [ðæts] contr of **that is; that has**
thaw [θɔː] vi tauen; (frozen food) auftauen
▷ vt auftauen lassen

○ KEYWORD

the [ðiː, ðə] def art **1** der/die/das; **to play the piano/violin** Klavier/Geige spielen; **I'm going to the butcher's/ the cinema** ich gehe zum Fleischer/ins Kino; **Elizabeth the First** Elisabeth die Erste
2 (+adj to form noun) das die; **the rich and the poor** die Reichen und die Armen
3 (in comparisons): **the more he works the more he earns** je mehr er arbeitet, desto mehr verdient er

theater (US), **theatre** ['θɪətə*] n Theater nt; (for lectures etc) Saal m
theft [θeft] n Diebstahl m
their [ðeə*] adj ihr; (unidentified person) sein; **they cleaned ~ teeth** sie putzten sich die Zähne; **someone has left ~ umbrella here** jemand hat seinen Schirm hier vergessen; **theirs** pron ihre(r, s); (unidentified person) seine(r, s); **it's ~** es gehört ihnen; **a friend of ~** ein Freund von ihnen; **someone has left ~ here** jemand hat seins hier liegen lassen
them [ðem, ðəm] pron (direct object) sie; (indirect object) ihnen; (unidentified person) ihn/ihm, sie/ihr; **do you know ~?** kennst du sie?; **can you help ~?** kannst du ihnen helfen?; **it's ~** sie sind's; **if anyone has a problem you should help ~** wenn jemand ein Problem hat, solltest du ihm helfen
theme [θiːm] n Thema nt; (Mus) Motiv nt; **~ park** Themenpark m; **~ song** Titelmusik f

themselves [ðəm'selvz] pron sich; **they hurt ~** sie haben sich verletzt; **they ~ were not there** sie selbst waren nicht da; **they did it ~** sie haben es selbst gemacht; **they are not dangerous in ~** an sich sind sie nicht gefährlich; **(all) by ~** allein
then [ðen] adv (at that time) damals; (next) dann; (therefore) also; (furthermore) ferner; **from ~ on** von da an; **by ~** bis dahin ▷ adj damalig; **our ~ boss** unser damaliger Chef
theoretical, theoretically [θɪə'retɪkəl, -ɪ] adj, adv theoretisch
theory ['θɪərɪ] n Theorie f; **in ~** theoretisch
therapy ['θerəpɪ] n Therapie f

○ KEYWORD

there [ðeə*] adv **1**: **there is, there are** es or da ist/sind; (there exists/exist also) es gibt; **there are 3 of them** (people, things) es gibt 3 davon; **there has been an accident** da war ein Unfall
2 (place) da dort; (direction) dahin, dorthin; **put it in/on there** leg es dahinein/dorthinauf
3: **there, there** (esp to child) na, na

thermometer [θə'mɒmɪtə*] n Thermometer nt
Thermos® ['θɜːməs] n **~ (flask)** Thermosflasche® f
these [ðiːz] pron, adj diese; **I don't like ~ apples** ich mag diese Äpfel nicht; **~ are not my books** das sind nicht meine Bücher
thesis ['θiːsɪs] (pl **theses**) n (for PhD) Doktorarbeit f
they [ðeɪ] pron pl sie; (people in general) man; (unidentified person) er/sie; **~ are rich** sie sind reich; **~ say that ...** man sagt, dass ...; **if anyone looks at this, ~ will see that ...** wenn sich jemand dies ansieht, wird er erkennen, dass ...
they'd [ðeɪd] contr of **they had; they would**
they'll [ðeɪl] contr of **they will; they shall**
they've [ðeɪv] contr of **they have**
thick [θɪk] adj dick; (liquid) dickflüssig; (fam: stupid) dumm; **thicken** vi (fog) dichter werden; (sauce) dick werden ▷ vt (sauce) eindicken

t

thief [θiːf] (*pl* **thieves**) *n* Dieb(in) *m(f)*
thigh [θaɪ] *n* Oberschenkel *m*
thimble ['θɪmbl] *n* Fingerhut *m*
thin [θɪn] *adj* dünn
thing [θɪŋ] *n* Ding *nt*; (*affair*) Sache *f*; **my ~s** *pl* meine Sachen *pl*; **how are ~s?** wie geht's?; **I can't see a ~** ich kann nichts sehen; **he knows a ~ or two about cars** er kennt sich mit Autos aus
think [θɪŋk] (**thought, thought**) *vt, vi* denken; (*believe*) meinen; **I ~ so** ich denke schon; **I don't ~ so** ich glaube nicht; **think about** *vt* denken an +*akk*; (*reflect on*) nachdenken über +*akk*; (*have opinion of*) halten von; **think of** *vt* denken an +*akk*; (*devise*) sich ausdenken; (*have opinion of*) halten von; (*remember*) sich erinnern an +*akk*; **think over** *vt* überdenken; **think up** *vt* sich ausdenken
third [θɜːd] *adj* dritte(r, s); **the Third World** die Dritte Welt ▷ *n* (*fraction*) Drittel *nt*; **in ~** (*gear*) im dritten Gang; *see also* **eighth**; **thirdly** *adv* drittens; **third-party insurance** *n* Haftpflichtversicherung *f*
thirst [θɜːst] *n* Durst *m* (**for** nach); **thirsty** *adj* **to be ~** Durst haben
thirteen ['θɜːˈtiːn] *num* dreizehn ▷ *n* Dreizehn *f; see also* **eight**; **thirteenth** *adj* dreizehnte(r, s); *see also* **eighth**; **thirtieth** ['θɜːtɪɪθ] *adj* dreißigste(r, s); *see also* **eighth**; **thirty** ['θɜːtɪ] *num* dreißig; **~-one** einunddreißig ▷ *n* Dreißig *f*; **to be in one's thirties** in den Dreißigern sein; *see also* **eight**

○ KEYWORD

this [ðɪs] *adj* (*demonstrative: pl these*) diese(r, s); **this evening** heute Abend; **this one** diese(r, s) (da)
▷ *pron* (*demonstrative: pl these*) dies das; **who/what is this?** wer/was ist das?; **this is where I live** hier wohne ich; **this is what he said** das hat er gesagt; **this is Mr Brown** dies ist Mr Brown; (*on telephone*) hier ist Mr Brown
▷ *adv* (*demonstrative*); **this high/long** *etc* so groß/lang *etc*

thistle ['θɪsl] *n* Distel *f*
thorn [θɔːn] *n* Dorn *m*, Stachel *m*
thorough ['θʌrə] *adj* gründlich;

thoroughly *adv* gründlich; (*agree etc*) völlig
those [ðəʊz] *pron* die da, jene; **~ who** diejenigen, die ▷ *adj* die, jene
though [ðəʊ] *conj* obwohl; **as ~** als ob ▷ *adv* aber
thought [θɔːt] *pt, pp of* **think** ▷ *n* Gedanke *m*; (*thinking*) Überlegung *f*; **thoughtful** *adj* (*kind*) rücksichtsvoll; (*attentive*) aufmerksam; (*in Gedanken versunken*) nachdenklich; **thoughtless** *adj* (*unkind*) rücksichtslos, gedankenlos
thousand ['θaʊzənd] *num* (**one**) ~, **a ~** tausend; **five ~** fünftausend; **~s of** Tausende von
thrash [θræʃ] *vt* (*hit*) verprügeln; (*defeat*) vernichtend schlagen
thread [θred] *n* Faden *m* ▷ *vt* (*needle*) einfädeln; (*beads*) auffädeln
threat [θret] *n* Drohung *f*; (*danger*) Bedrohung *f* (**to** für); **threaten** *vt* bedrohen; **threatening** *adj* bedrohlich
three [θriː] *num* drei ▷ *n* Drei *f; see also* **eight**; **three-dimensional** *adj* dreidimensional; **three-piece suit** *n* Anzug *m* mit Weste; **three-quarters** *npl* drei Viertel *pl*
threshold ['θreʃhəʊld] *n* Schwelle *f*
threw [θruː] *pt of* **throw**
thrifty ['θrɪftɪ] *adj* sparsam
thrilled [θrɪld] *adj* **to be ~** (**with sth**) sich (über etw *akk*) riesig freuen; **thriller** *n* Thriller *m*; **thrilling** *adj* aufregend
thrive [θraɪv] *vi* gedeihen (**on** bei); (*fig, business*) florieren
throat [θrəʊt] *n* Hals *m*, Kehle *f*
throbbing ['θrɒbɪŋ] *adj* (*pain, headache*) pochend
thrombosis [θrɒmˈbəʊsɪs] *n* Thrombose *f*; **deep vein ~** tiefe Venenthrombose *f*
throne [θrəʊn] *n* Thron *m*
through [θruː] *prep* durch; (*time*) während +*gen*; (*because of*) aus, durch; (*US: up to and including*) bis; **arranged ~ him** durch ihn arrangiert ▷ *adv* durch; **to put sb ~** (*Tel*) jdn verbinden (**to** mit) ▷ *adj* (*ticket, train*) durchgehend; **~ flight** Direktflug *m*; **to be ~ with sb/sth** mit jdm/etw fertig sein; **throughout** [θruːˈaʊt] *prep* (*place*) überall in +*dat*; (*time*) während +*gen*; **~ the night** die ganze Nacht hindurch ▷ *adv* überall; (*time*) die ganze Zeit

throw [θrəʊ] **(threw, thrown)** vt werfen; (rider) abwerfen; (party) geben; **to ~ sth to sb, to ~ sb sth** jdm etw zuwerfen; **I was ~n by his question** seine Frage hat mich aus dem Konzept gebracht ▷ n Wurf m; **throw away** vt wegwerfen; **throw in** vt (include) dazugeben; **throw out** vt (unwanted object) wegwerfen; (person) hinauswerfen (of aus); **throw up** vt, vi (fam: vomit) sich übergeben; **throw-in** n Einwurf m

thrown [θrəʊn] pp of **throw**

thru (US) see **through**

thrush [θrʌʃ] n Drossel f

thrust [θrʌst] **(thrust, thrust)** vt, vi (push) stoßen

thruway ['θru:weɪ] n (US) Schnellstraße f

thumb [θʌm] n Daumen m ▷ vt **to ~ a lift** per Anhalter fahren; **thumbtack** n (US) Reißzwecke f

thunder ['θʌndə*] n Donner m ▷ vi donnern; **thunderstorm** n Gewitter nt

Thur(s) abbr = **Thursday** Do.

Thursday ['θɜ:zdɪ] n Donnerstag m; see also **Tuesday**

thus [ðʌs] adv (in this way) so; (therefore) somit, also

thyme [taɪm] n Thymian m

Tibet [tɪ'bet] n Tibet nt

tick [tɪk] n (Brit: mark) Häkchen nt ▷ vt (name) abhaken; (box, answer) ankreuzen ▷ vi (clock) ticken

ticket ['tɪkɪt] n (for train, bus) (Fahr)karte f; (plane ~) Flugschein m, Ticket nt; (for theatre, match, museum etc) (Eintritts)karte f; (price ~) (Preis)schild nt; (raffle ~) Los nt; (for car park) Parkschein m; (for traffic offence) Strafzettel m; **ticket collector**, **ticket inspector** (Brit) n Fahrkartenkontrolleur(in) m(f); **ticket machine** n (for public transport) Fahrscheinautomat m; (in car park) Parkscheinautomat m; **ticket office** n (Rail) Fahrkartenschalter m; (Theat) Kasse f

tickle ['tɪkl] vt kitzeln; **ticklish** ['tɪklɪʃ] adj kitzlig

tide [taɪd] n Gezeiten pl; **the ~ is in/out** es ist Flut/Ebbe

tidy ['taɪdɪ] adj ordentlich ▷ vt aufräumen; **tidy up** vt, vi aufräumen

tie [taɪ] n (neck~) Krawatte f; (Sport) Unentschieden nt; (bond) Bindung f ▷ vt (attach, do up) binden (to an +akk); (~ together) zusammenbinden; (knot) machen ▷ vi (Sport) unentschieden spielen; **tie down** vt festbinden (to an +dat); (fig) binden; **tie up** vt (dog) anbinden; (parcel) verschnüren; (shoelace) binden; (boat) festmachen; **I'm tied up** (fig) ich bin beschäftigt

tiger ['taɪgə*] n Tiger m

tight [taɪt] adj (clothes) eng; (knot) fest; (screw, lid) fest sitzend; (control, security measures) streng; (timewise) knapp; (schedule) eng ▷ adv (shut) fest; (pull) stramm; **hold ~** festhalten!; **sleep ~** schlaf gut!; **tighten** vt (knot, rope, screw) anziehen; (belt) enger machen; (restrictions, control) verschärfen; **tights** npl (Brit) Strumpfhose f

tile [taɪl] n (on roof) Dachziegel m; (on wall, floor) Fliese f; **tiled** adj (roof) Ziegel-; (floor, wall) gefliest

till [tɪl] n Kasse f ▷ prep, conj see **until**

tilt [tɪlt] vt kippen; (head) neigen ▷ vi sich neigen

time [taɪm] n Zeit f; (occasion) Mal nt; (Mus) Takt m; **local ~** Ortszeit; **what ~ is it?, what's the ~?** wie spät ist es?, wie viel Uhr ist es?; **to take one's ~ (over sth)** sich (bei etw) Zeit lassen; **to have a good ~** Spaß haben; **in two weeks' ~** in zwei Wochen; **at ~s** manchmal; **at the same ~** gleichzeitig; **all the ~** die ganze Zeit; **by the ~ he ...** bis er ...; (in past) als er ...; **for the ~ being** vorläufig; **in ~** (not late) rechtzeitig; **on ~** pünktlich; **the first ~** das erste Mal; **this ~** diesmal; **five ~s** fünfmal; **five ~s six** fünf mal sechs; **four ~s a year** viermal im Jahr; **three at a ~** drei auf einmal ▷ vt (with stopwatch) stoppen; **you ~d that well** das hast du gut getimt; **time difference** n Zeitunterschied m; **time limit** n Frist f; **timer** n Timer m; (switch) Schaltuhr f; **time-saving** adj Zeit sparend; **time switch** n Schaltuhr f; **timetable** n (for public transport) Fahrplan m; (school) Stundenplan m; **time zone** n Zeitzone f

timid ['tɪmɪd] adj ängstlich

timing ['taɪmɪŋ] n (coordination) Timing nt, zeitliche Abstimmung

tin [tɪn] n (metal) Blech nt; (Brit: can) Dose f; **tinfoil** n Alufolie f; **tinned** [tɪnd] adj (Brit) aus der Dose; **tin opener** n (Brit) Dosenöffner m

t

tinsel ['tɪnsəl] n ≈ Lametta nt

tint [tɪnt] n (Farb)ton m; (in hair) Tönung f; **tinted** adj getönt

tiny ['taɪnɪ] adj winzig

tip [tɪp] n (money) Trinkgeld nt; (hint) Tipp m; (end) Spitze f; (of cigarette) Filter m; (Brit: rubbish ~) Müllkippe f ▷ vt (waiter) Trinkgeld geben +dat; **tip over** vt, vi (overturn) umkippen

tipsy ['tɪpsɪ] adj beschwipst

tiptoe ['tɪptəʊ] n **on ~** auf Zehenspitzen

tire ['taɪə*] n (US) see **tyre** ▷ vt müde machen ▷ vi müde werden; **tired** adj müde; **to be ~ of sb/sth** jdn/etw satt haben; **to be ~ of doing sth** es satt haben, etw zu tun; **tireless, tirelessly** adv unermüdlich; **tiresome** adj lästig; **tiring** adj ermüdend

Tirol [tɪ'rəʊl] see **Tyrol**

tissue ['tɪʃuː] n (Anat) Gewebe nt; (paper handkerchief) Tempotaschentuch® nt, Papier(taschen)tuch nt; **tissue paper** n Seidenpapier nt

tit [tɪt] n (bird) Meise f; (fam: breast) Titte f

title ['taɪtl] n Titel m

○ **KEYWORD**

to [tuː, tə] prep **1** (direction) zu nach; **I go to France/school** ich gehe nach Frankreich/zur Schule; **to the left** nach links
2 (as far as) bis
3 (with expressions of time) vor; **a quarter to 5** Viertel vor 5
4 (for, of) für; **secretary to the director** Sekretärin des Direktors
5 (expressing indirect object): **to give sth to sb** jdm etw geben; **to talk to sb** mit jdm sprechen; **I sold it to a friend** ich habe es einem Freund verkauft
6 (in relation to) zu; **30 miles to the gallon** 30 Meilen pro Gallone
7 (purpose, result) zu; **to my surprise** zu meiner Überraschung
▷ with vb **1** (infin): **to go/eat** gehen/essen; **to want to do sth** etw tun wollen; **to try/start to do sth** versuchen/anfangen, etw zu tun; **he has a lot to lose** er hat viel zu verlieren
2 (with vb omitted): **I don't want to** ich will (es) nicht

3 (purpose, result) um; **I did it to help you** ich tat es, um dir zu helfen
4 (after adj etc): **ready to use** gebrauchsfertig; **too old/young to ... zu** alt/jung, um ... zu ...
▷ adv ; **push/pull the door to** die Tür zuschieben/zuziehen

toad [təʊd] n Kröte f; **toadstool** n Giftpilz m

toast [təʊst] n (bread, drink) Toast m; **a piece** (o **slice**) **of ~** eine Scheibe Toast; **to propose a ~ to sb** einen Toast auf jdn ausbringen ▷ vt (bread) toasten; (person) trinken auf +akk; **toaster** n Toaster m

tobacco [tə'bækəʊ] (pl **-es**) n Tabak m; **tobacconist's** [tə'bækənɪsts] n **~ (shop)** Tabakladen m

toboggan [tə'bɒgən] n Schlitten m

today [tə'deɪ] adv heute; **a week ~** heute in einer Woche; **~'s newspaper** die Zeitung von heute

toddler ['tɒdlə*] n Kleinkind nt

toe [təʊ] n Zehe f, Zeh m; **toenail** n Zehennagel m

toffee ['tɒfɪ] n (sweet) Karamellbonbon nt; **toffee apple** n kandierter Apfel

tofu ['təʊfuː] n Tofu m

together [tə'geðə*] adv zusammen; **I tied them ~** ich habe sie zusammengebunden

toilet ['tɔɪlət] n Toilette f; **to go to the ~** auf die Toilette gehen; **toilet bag** n Kulturbeutel m; **toilet paper** n Toilettenpapier nt; **toiletries** ['tɔɪlətrɪz] npl Toilettenartikel pl; **toilet roll** n Rolle f Toilettenpapier

token ['təʊkən] n Marke f; (in casino) Spielmarke f; (voucher, gift ~) Gutschein m; (sign) Zeichen nt

Tokyo ['təʊkɪəʊ] n Tokio nt

told [təʊld] pt, pp of **tell**

tolerant ['tɒlərənt] adj tolerant (of gegenüber); **tolerate** ['tɒləreɪt] vt tolerieren; (noise, pain, heat) ertragen

toll [təʊl] n (charge) Gebühr f; **the death ~** die Zahl der Toten; **toll-free** adj, adv (US Tel) gebührenfrei; **toll road** n gebührenpflichtige Straße

tomato [tə'mɑːtəʊ] (pl **-es**) n Tomate f; **tomato juice** n Tomatensaft m; **tomato ketchup** n Tomatenket(s)chup m o nt;

tomato sauce n Tomatensoße f; (Brit: ketchup) Tomatenket(s)chup m o nt

tomb [tuːm] n Grabmal nt; **tombstone** n Grabstein m

tomorrow [təˈmɒrəʊ] adv morgen; **~ morning** morgen früh; **~ evening** morgen Abend; **the day after ~** übermorgen; **a week (from) ~/~ week** morgen in einer Woche

ton [tʌn] n (Brit) Tonne f (1016 kg); (US) Tonne f (907 kg); **~s of books** (fam) eine Menge Bücher

tone [təʊn] n Ton m; **tone down** vt mäßigen; **toner** [ˈtəʊnə*] n (for printer) Toner m; **toner cartridge** n Tonerpatrone f

tongs [tɒŋz] npl Zange f; (curling ~) Lockenstab m

tongue [tʌŋ] n Zunge f

tonic [ˈtɒnɪk] n (Med) Stärkungsmittel nt; **~ (water)** n Tonic nt; **gin and ~** Gin m Tonic

tonight [təˈnaɪt] adv heute Abend; (during night) heute Nacht

tonsils [ˈtɒnsɪz] n Mandeln pl; **tonsillitis** [tɒnsɪˈlaɪtɪs] n Mandelentzündung f

too [tuː] adv zu; (also) auch; **~ fast** zu schnell; **~ much/many** zu viel/viele; **me ~** ich auch; **she liked it ~** ihr gefiel es auch

took [tʊk] pt of **take**

tool [tuːl] n Werkzeug nt; **toolbar** n (Inform) Symbolleiste f; **toolbox** n Werkzeugkasten m

tooth [tuːθ] n (pl teeth) n Zahn m; **toothache** n Zahnschmerzen pl; **toothbrush** n Zahnbürste f; **toothpaste** n Zahnpasta f; **toothpick** n Zahnstocher m

top [tɒp] n (of tower, class, company etc) Spitze f; (of mountain) Gipfel m; (of tree) Krone f; (of street) oberes Ende; (of tube, pen) Kappe f; (of box) Deckel m; (of bikini) Oberteil nt; (sleeveless) Top nt; **at the ~ of the page** oben auf der Seite; **at the ~ of the league** an der Spitze der Liga; **on ~** oben; **on ~ of** auf +dat; (in addition to) zusätzlich zu; **in ~ (gear)** im höchsten Gang; **over the ~** übertrieben ▷ adj (floor, shelf) oberste(r, s); (price, note) höchste(r, s); (best) Spitzen-; (pupil, school) beste(r, s) ▷ vt (exceed) übersteigen; (be better than) übertreffen; (league) an erster Stelle liegen in +dat; **~ped with cream** mit Sahne obendrauf; **top up** vt auffüllen; **can I top you up?** darf ich dir nachschenken?

topic [ˈtɒpɪk] n Thema nt; **topical** adj aktuell

topless [ˈtɒpləs] adj, adv oben ohne

topping [ˈtɒpɪŋ] n (on top of pizza, ice-cream etc) Belag m, Garnierung f

top-secret [ˈtɒpˈsiːkrət] adj streng geheim

torch [tɔːtʃ] n (Brit) Taschenlampe f

tore [tɔː*] pt of **tear**

torment [ˈtɔːment] vt quälen

torn [tɔːn] pp of **tear**

tornado [tɔːˈneɪdəʊ] (pl -es) n Tornado m

torrential [təˈrenʃəl] adj (rain) sintflutartig

tortoise [ˈtɔːtəs] n Schildkröte f

torture [ˈtɔːtʃə*] n Folter f; (fig) Qual f ▷ vt foltern

Tory [ˈtɔːrɪ] (Brit) n Tory m, Konservative(r) mf ▷ adj Tory-

toss [tɒs] vt (throw) werfen; (salad) anmachen; **to ~ a coin** eine Münze werfen ▷ n **I don't give a ~** (fam) es ist mir scheißegal

total [ˈtəʊtl] n (of figures, money) Gesamtsumme f; **a ~ of 30** insgesamt 30; **in ~** insgesamt ▷ adj total; (sum etc) Gesamt- ▷ vt (amount to) sich belaufen auf +akk; **totally** adv total

touch [tʌtʃ] n (act of ~ing) Berührung f; (sense of ~) Tastsinn m; (trace) Spur f; **to be/keep in ~ with sb** mit jdm in Verbindung stehen/bleiben; **to get in ~ with sb** sich mit jdm in Verbindung setzen; **to lose ~ with sb** den Kontakt zu jdm verlieren ▷ vt (feel) berühren; (emotionally) bewegen; **touch on** vt (topic) berühren; **touchdown** n (Aviat) Landung f; (Sport) Touchdown m; **touching** adj (moving) rührend; **touch screen** n Touchscreen m, Berührungsbildschirm m; **touchy** adj empfindlich, zickig

tough [tʌf] adj hart; (meat) zäh; (material) robust; (meat) zäh

tour [ˈtʊə*] n Tour f (of durch); (of town, building) Rundgang m (of durch); (of pop group etc) Tournee f ▷ vt eine Tour/einen Rundgang/eine Tournee machen durch ▷ vi (on holiday) umherreisen; **tour guide** n Reiseleiter(in) m(f)

tourism [ˈtʊərɪzəm] n Tourismus m, Fremdenverkehr m; **tourist** n Tourist(in) m(f); **tourist class** n Touristenklasse f; **tourist guide** n (book) Reiseführer m;

(*person*) Fremdenführer(in) *m(f)*; **tourist office** *n* Fremdenverkehrsamt *nt*

tournament ['tʊənəmənt] *n* Tournier *nt*

tour operator ['tʊərɒpəreɪtə*] *n* Reiseveranstalter *m*

tow [təʊ] *vt* abschleppen; (*caravan, trailer*) ziehen; **tow away** *vt* abschleppen

towards [tə'wɔːdz] *prep* ~ **me** mir entgegen, auf mich zu; **we walked ~ the station** wir gingen in Richtung Bahnhof; **my feelings ~ him** meine Gefühle ihm gegenüber; **she was kind ~ me** sie war nett zu mir

towel ['taʊəl] *n* Handtuch *nt*

tower ['taʊə*] *n* Turm *m*; **tower block** *n* (*Brit*) Hochhaus *nt*

town [taʊn] *n* Stadt *f*; **town center** (*US*), **town centre** *n* Stadtmitte *f*, Stadtzentrum *nt*; **town hall** *n* Rathaus *nt*

towrope ['təʊrəʊp] *n* Abschleppseil *nt*; **tow truck** *n* (*US*) Abschleppwagen *m*

toxic ['tɒksɪk] *adj* giftig, Gift-

toy [tɔɪ] *n* Spielzeug *nt*; **toy with** *vt* spielen mit; **toyshop** *n* Spielwarengeschäft *nt*

trace [treɪs] *n* Spur *f*; **without ~** spurlos ▷ *vt* (*find*) ausfindig machen; **tracing paper** *n* Pauspapier *nt*

track [træk] *n* (*mark*) Spur *f*; (*path*) Weg *m*; (*Rail*) Gleis *nt*; (*on CD, record*) Stück *nt*; **to keep/lose ~ of sb/sth** jdn/etw im Auge behalten/aus den Augen verlieren; **track down** *vt* ausfindig machen; **trackball** *n* (*Inform*) Trackball *m*; **tracksuit** *n* Trainingsanzug *m*

tractor ['træktə*] *n* Traktor *m*

trade [treɪd] *n* (*commerce*) Handel *m*; (*business*) Geschäft *nt*; (*skilled job*) Handwerk *nt* ▷ *vi* handeln (*in* mit) ▷ *vt* (*exchange*) tauschen (*for* gegen); **trademark** *n* Warenzeichen *nt*; **tradesman** (*pl* **-men**) *n* (*shopkeeper*) Geschäftsmann *m*; (*workman*) Handwerker *m*; **trade(s) union** *n* (*Brit*) Gewerkschaft *f*

tradition [trə'dɪʃən] *n* Tradition *f*; **traditional, traditionally** *adj, adv* traditionell

traffic ['træfɪk] *n* Verkehr *m*; (*pej: trading*) Handel *m* (*in* mit); **traffic circle** *n* (*US*) Kreisverkehr *m*; **traffic island** *n* Verkehrsinsel *f*; **traffic jam** *n* Stau *m*;

traffic lights *npl* Verkehrsampel *f*; **traffic warden** *n* (*Brit*) ≈ Politesse *f*

tragedy ['trædʒədɪ] *n* Tragödie *f*; **tragic** ['trædʒɪk] *adj* tragisch

trail [treɪl] *n* Spur *f*; (*path*) Weg *m* ▷ *vt* (*follow*) verfolgen; (*drag*) schleppen; (*drag behind*) hinter sich herziehen; (*Sport*) zurückliegen hinter +*dat* ▷ *vi* (*hang loosely*) schleifen; (*Sport*) weit zurückliegen; **trailer** *n* Anhänger *m*; (*US: caravan*) Wohnwagen *m*; (*Cine*) Trailer *m*

train [treɪn] *n* (*Rail*) Zug *m* ▷ *vt* (*teach*) ausbilden; (*Sport*) trainieren ▷ *vi* (*Sport*) trainieren; **to ~ as** (*o* **to be**) **a teacher** eine Ausbildung als Lehrer machen; **trained** *adj* (*person, voice*) ausgebildet; **trainee** *n* Auszubildende(r) *mf*; (*academic, practical*) Praktikant(in) *m(f)*; **trainer** *n* (*Sport*) Trainer(in) *m(f)*; **~s** (*Brit: shoes*) Turnschuhe *pl*; **training** *n* Ausbildung *f*; (*Sport*) Training *nt*; **train station** *n* Bahnhof *m*

tram ['træm] *n* (*Brit*) Straßenbahn *f*

tramp [træmp] *n* Landstreicher(in) *m(f)* ▷ *vi* trotten

tranquillizer ['træŋkwɪlaɪzə*] *n* Beruhigungsmittel *nt*

transaction *n* (*piece of business*) Geschäft *nt*

transatlantic ['trænzət'læntɪk] *adj* transatlantisch; **~ flight** Transatlantikflug *m*

transfer ['trænsfə*] *n* (*of money*) Überweisung *f*; (*US: ticket*) Umsteigekarte *f* ▷ [træns'fɜː*] *vt* (*money*) überweisen (*to sb* an jdn); (*patient*) verlegen; (*employee*) versetzen; (*Sport*) transferieren ▷ *vi* (*on journey*) umsteigen; **transferable** [træns'fɜːrəbl] *adj* übertragbar

transform [træns'fɔːm] *vt* umwandeln; **transformation** [trænsfə'meɪʃən] *n* Umwandlung *f*

transfusion [træns'fjuːʒən] *n* Transfusion *f*

transistor [træn'zɪstə*] *n* Transistor *m*; **~ (radio)** Transistorradio *nt*

transition [træn'zɪʃən] *n* Übergang *m* (*from ... to* von ... zu)

transit lounge ['trænzɪtlaʊndʒ] *n* Transitraum *m*; **transit passenger** *n* Transitreisende(r) *mf*

translate [trænz'leɪt] *vt, vi* übersetzen; **translation** [trænz'leɪʃən] *n* Übersetzung f; **translator** [trænz'leɪtə*] n Übersetzer(in) m(f)

transmission [trænz'mɪʃən] n (Tv, Radio) Übertragung f; (Auto) Getriebe nt

transparent [træns'pærənt] adj durchsichtig; (fig) offenkundig

transplant [træns'plɑ:nt] (Med) vt transplantieren ▷ ['trænsplɑ:nt] n (operation) Transplantation f

transport ['trænspɔ:t] n (of goods, people) Beförderung f; **public ~** öffentliche Verkehrsmittel pl ▷ [træns'pɔ:t] vt befördern, transportieren; **transportation** [trænspɔ:'teɪʃən] n see **transport**

trap [træp] n Falle f ▷ vt **to be ~ped** (in snow, job etc) festsitzen

trash [træʃ] n (book, film etc) Schund m; (US: refuse) Abfall m; **trash can** n (US) Abfalleimer m; **trashy** adj niveaulos; (novel) Schund-

traumatic [trɔ:'mætɪk] adj traumatisch

travel ['trævl] n Reisen nt ▷ vi (journey) reisen ▷ vt (distance) zurücklegen; (country) bereisen; **travel agency, travel agent** n (company) Reisebüro nt; **traveler** (US) see **traveller; traveler's check** (US) see **traveller's cheque; travel insurance** n Reiseversicherung f; **traveller** n Reisende(r) mf; **traveller's cheque** n (Brit) Reisescheck m; **travelsick** n reisekrank

tray [treɪ] n Tablett nt; (for mail etc) Ablage f; (of printer, photocopier) Fach nt

tread [tred] n (on tyre) Profil nt; **tread on** [tred] (**trod, trodden**) vt treten auf +akk

treasure ['treʒə*] n Schatz m ▷ vt schätzen

treat [tri:t] n besondere Freude; **it's my ~** das geht auf meine Kosten ▷ vt behandeln; **to ~ sb (to sth)** jdn (zu etw) einladen; **to ~ oneself to sth** sich etw leisten; **treatment** ['tri:tmənt] n Behandlung f

treaty ['tri:tɪ] n Vertrag m

tree [tri:] n Baum m

tremble ['trembl] vi zittern

tremendous [trə'mendəs] adj gewaltig; (fam: very good) toll

trench [trentʃ] n Graben m

trend [trend] n Tendenz f; (fashion) Mode f, Trend m; **trendy** adj trendy

trespass ['trespəs] vi **'no ~ing'** „Betreten verboten"

trial ['traɪəl] n (Jur) Prozess m; (test) Versuch m; **by ~ and error** durch Ausprobieren; **trial period** n (for employee) Probezeit f

triangle ['traɪæŋgl] n Dreieck nt; (Mus) Triangel m; **triangular** [traɪ'æŋjʊlə*] adj dreieckig

tribe [traɪb] n Stamm m

trick [trɪk] n Trick m; (mischief) Streich m ▷ vt hereinlegen

tricky ['trɪkɪ] adj (difficult) schwierig; (situation) verzwickt

trifle ['traɪfl] n Kleinigkeit f; (Brit Gastr) Trifle nt (Nachspeise aus Biskuit, Wackelpudding, Obst, Vanillesoße und Sahne)

trigger ['trɪgə*] n (of gun) Abzug m ▷ vt **to ~ (off)** auslösen

trim [trɪm] vt (hair, beard) nachschneiden; (nails) schneiden; (hedge) stutzen ▷ n **just a ~, please** nur etwas nachschneiden, bitte; **trimmings** npl (decorations) Verzierungen pl; (extras) Zubehör nt; (Gastr) Beilagen pl

trip [trɪp] n Reise f; (outing) Ausflug m ▷ vi stolpern (over über +akk)

triple ['trɪpl] adj dreifach ▷ adv **~ the price** dreimal so teuer ▷ vi sich verdreifachen; **triplets** ['trɪplɪts] npl Drillinge pl

tripod ['traɪpɒd] n (Foto) Stativ nt

trite [traɪt] adj banal

triumph ['traɪʌmf] n Triumph m

trivial ['trɪvɪəl] adj trivial

trod [trɒd] pt of **tread**

trodden pp of **tread**

trolley ['trɒlɪ] n (Brit: in shop) Einkaufswagen m; (for luggage) Kofferkuli m; (serving ~) Teewagen m

trombone [trɒm'bəʊn] n Posaune f

troops [tru:ps] npl (Mil) Truppen pl

trophy ['trəʊfɪ] n Trophäe f

tropical ['trɒpɪkl] adj tropisch

trouble ['trʌbl] n (problems) Schwierigkeiten pl; (worry) Sorgen pl; (effort) Mühe f; (unrest) Unruhen pl; (Med) Beschwerden pl; **to be in ~** in Schwierigkeiten sein; **to get into ~ (with authority)** Ärger bekommen; **to make ~** Schwierigkeiten machen ▷ vt (worry) beunruhigen; (disturb) stören; **my back's troubling me** mein Rücken macht mir zu schaffen; **sorry to ~ you** ich muss dich leider kurz stören; **troubled** adj (worried) beunruhigt; **trouble-free** adj problemlos; **troublemaker** n Unruhestifter(in) m(f); **troublesome** adj lästig

trousers ['traʊzəz] npl Hose f; **trouser suit** n (Brit) Hosenanzug m

trout [traʊt] n Forelle f

truck [trʌk] n Lastwagen m; (Brit Rail) Güterwagen m; **trucker** n (US: driver) Lastwagenfahrer(in) m(f)

true [truː] adj (factually correct) wahr; (genuine) echt; **to come ~** wahr werden

truly ['truːlɪ] adv wirklich; **Yours ~** (in letter) mit freundlichen Grüßen

trump [trʌmp] n (Cards) Trumpf m

trumpet ['trʌmpɪt] n Trompete f

trunk [trʌŋk] n (of tree) Stamm m; (Anat) Rumpf m; (of elephant) Rüssel m; (piece of luggage) Überseekoffer m; (US Auto) Kofferraum m; **trunks** npl (swimming) ~ Badehose f

trust [trʌst] n (confidence) Vertrauen nt (in zu) ▷ vt vertrauen +dat; **trusting** adj vertrauensvoll; **trustworthy** adj vertrauenswürdig

truth [truːθ] n Wahrheit f; **truthful** adj ehrlich; (statement) wahrheitsgemäß

try [traɪ] n Versuch m ▷ vt (attempt) versuchen; (~ out) ausprobieren; (sample) probieren; (Jur: person) vor Gericht stellen; (courage, patience) auf die Probe stellen ▷ vi versuchen; (make effort) sich bemühen; **~ and come** versuch zu kommen; **try on** vt (clothes) anprobieren; **try out** vt ausprobieren

T-shirt ['tiːʃɜːt] n T-Shirt nt

tub [tʌb] n (for ice-cream, margarine) Becher m

tube [tjuːb] n (pipe) Rohr nt; (of rubber, plastic) Schlauch m; (for toothpaste, glue etc) Tube f; **the Tube** (in London) die U-Bahn

tube station ['tjuːbsteɪʃən] n U-Bahn-Station f

tuck [tʌk] vt (put) stecken; **tuck in** vt (shirt) in die Hose stecken; (blanket) feststecken; (person) zudecken ▷ vi (eat) zulangen

Tue(s) abbr = **Tuesday** Di.

Tuesday ['tjuːzdɪ] n Dienstag m; **on ~** (am) Dienstag; **on ~s** dienstags;

this/last/next ~ diesen/letzten/nächsten Dienstag; **(on) ~ morning/afternoon/evening** (am) Dienstag Morgen/Nachmittag/Abend; **every ~** jeden Dienstag; **a week on ~/ ~ week** Dienstag in einer Woche

tug [tʌg] vt ziehen; **she ~ged his sleeve** sie zog an seinem Ärmel ▷ vi ziehen (at an +dat)

tuition [tjuː'ɪʃən] n Unterricht m; (US: fees) Studiengebühren pl; **~ fees** pl Studiengebühren pl

tulip ['tjuːlɪp] n Tulpe f

tumble ['tʌmbl] vi (person, prices) fallen; **tumble dryer** n Wäschetrockner m; **tumbler** n (glass) (Becher)glas nt

tummy ['tʌmɪ] n (fam) Bauch m; **tummyache** n (fam) Bauchweh m

tumor (US), **tumour** ['tjuːmə*] n Tumor m

tuna ['tjuːnə] n Thunfisch m

tune [tjuːn] n Melodie f; **to be in/out of ~** (instrument) gestimmt/verstimmt sein; (singer) richtig/falsch singen ▷ vt (instrument) stimmen; (radio) einstellen (to auf +akk); **tuner** n (in stereo system) Tuner m

Tunisia [tjuː'nɪzɪə] n Tunesien nt

tunnel ['tʌnl] n Tunnel m; (under road, railway) Unterführung f

turban ['tɜːbən] n Turban m

turbulence ['tɜːbjʊləns] n (Aviat) Turbulenzen pl; **turbulent** adj stürmisch

Turk [tɜːk] n Türke m, Türkin f

turkey ['tɜːkɪ] n Truthahn m

Turkey ['tɜːkɪ] n die Türkei; **Turkish** adj türkisch ▷ n (language) Türkisch nt

turmoil ['tɜːmɔɪl] n Aufruhr m

turn [tɜːn] n (rotation) Drehung f; (performance) Nummer f; **to make a left ~** nach links abbiegen; **at the ~ of the century** um die Jahrhundertwende; **it's your ~** du bist dran; **in ~, by ~s** abwechselnd; **to take ~s** sich abwechseln ▷ vt (wheel, key, screw) drehen; (to face other way) umdrehen; (corner) biegen um; (page) umblättern; (transform) verwandeln (into in +akk) ▷ vi (rotate) sich drehen; (to face other way) sich umdrehen; (change direction: driver, car) abbiegen; (become) werden; (weather) umschlagen; **to ~ into sth** (become) sich in etw akk verwandeln; **to ~ cold/green** kalt/grün werden; **to ~ left/right** links/rechts abbiegen; **turn**

away vt (person) abweisen; **turn back** vt (person) zurückweisen ▷ vi (go back) umkehren; **turn down** vt (refuse) ablehnen; (radio, TV) leiser stellen; (heating) kleiner stellen; **turn off** vi abbiegen ▷ vt (switch off) ausschalten; (tap) zudrehen; (engine, electricity) abstellen; **turn on** vt (switch on) einschalten; (tap) aufdrehen; (engine, electricity) anstellen; (fam: person) anmachen, antörnen; **turn out** vt (light) ausmachen; (pockets) leeren ▷ vi (develop) sich entwickeln; **as it turned out** wie sich herausstellte; **turn over** vt onto other side, umdrehen; (page) umblättern ▷ vi (person) sich umdrehen; (car) sich überschlagen; (Tv) umschalten (to auf +akk); **turn round** vt (to face other way) umdrehen ▷ vi (person) sich umdrehen; (go back) umkehren; **turn to** vt sich zuwenden +dat; **turn up** vi (person, lost object) auftauchen ▷ vt (radio, TV) lauter stellen; (heating) höher stellen; **turning** n (in road) Abzweigung f; **turning point** n Wendepunkt m

turnip ['tɜ:nɪp] n Rübe f

turnover ['tɜ:nəʊvə*] n (Fin) Umsatz m

turnpike ['tɜ:npaɪk] n (US) gebührenpflichtige Autobahn

turntable ['tɜ:nteɪbl] n (on record player) Plattenteller m

turn-up ['tɜ:nʌp] n (Brit: on trousers) Aufschlag m

turquoise ['tɜ:kwɔɪz] adj türkis

turtle ['tɜ:tl] n (Brit) Wasserschildkröte f; (US) Schildkröte f

tutor ['tju:tə*] n (private) Privatlehrer(in) m(f); (Brit: at university) Tutor(in) m(f)

tuxedo [tʌk'si:dəʊ] (pl **-s**) n (US) Smoking m

TV ['ti:'vi:] n Fernsehen nt; (~ set) Fernseher m; **to watch ~** fernsehen; **on ~** im Fernsehen ▷ adj Fernseh-; **~ programme** Fernsehsendung f

tweed [twi:d] n Tweed m

tweezers ['twi:zəz] npl Pinzette f

twelfth [twelfθ] adj zwölfte(r, s); see also **eighth**; **twelve** [twelv] num zwölf ▷ n Zwölf f; see also **eight**

twentieth ['twentɪɪθ] adj zwanzigste(r, s); see also **eighth**; **twenty** ['twentɪ] num zwanzig; **~-one** einundzwanzig ▷ n

Zwanzig f; **to be in one's twenties** in den Zwanzigern sein; see also **eight**

twice [twaɪs] adv zweimal; **~ as much/many** doppelt so viel/viele

twig [twɪg] n Zweig m

twilight ['twaɪlaɪt] n (in evening) Dämmerung f

twin [twɪn] n Zwilling m ▷ adj (brother etc) Zwillings-; **~ beds** zwei Einzelbetten

twinge [twɪndʒ] n (pain) stechender Schmerz

twinkle ['twɪŋkl] vi funkeln

twin room ['twɪn'ru:m] n Zweibettzimmer nt; **twin town** n Partnerstadt f

twist [twɪst] vt (turn) drehen, winden; (distort) verdrehen; **I've ~ed my ankle** ich bin mit dem Fuß umgeknickt

two [tu:] num zwei; **to break sth in ~** etw in zwei Teile brechen ▷ n Zwei f; **the ~ of them** die beiden; see also **eight**; **two-dimensional** adj zweidimensional; (fig) oberflächlich; **two-faced** adj falsch, heuchlerisch; **two-piece** adj zweiteilig; **two-way** adj **~ traffic** Gegenverkehr

type [taɪp] n (sort) Art f; (typeface) Schrift(art) f; **what ~ of car is it?** was für ein Auto ist das?; **he's not my ~** er ist nicht mein Typ; **typeface** n Schrift(art) f; **typewriter** n Schreibmaschine f

typhoid ['taɪfɔɪd] n Typhus m

typhoon [taɪ'fu:n] n Taifun m

typical ['tɪpɪkəl] adj typisch (of für)

typing error ['taɪpɪŋerə*] n Tippfehler m

tyre [taɪə*] n (Brit) Reifen m; **tyre pressure** n Reifendruck m

Tyrol [tɪ'rəʊl] n **the ~** Tirol nt

t

UFO ['juːfəʊ] *acr* = **unidentified flying object** Ufo *nt*

Uganda [juːˈgændə] *n* Uganda *nt*

ugly ['ʌglɪ] *adj* hässlich; (*bad*) schlimm

UHT *adj abbr* = **ultra-heat treated ~ milk** H-Milch *f*

UK *abbr* = **United Kingdom**

Ukraine [juːˈkreɪn] *n* **the ~** die Ukraine

ulcer ['ʌlsə*] *n* Geschwür *nt*

ulterior [ʌlˈtɪərɪə*] *adj* **~ motive** Hintergedanke *m*

ultimate ['ʌltɪmət] *adj* (*final*) letzte(r, s); (*authority*) höchste(r, s); **ultimately** *adv* letzten Endes; (*eventually*) schließlich; **ultimatum** [ʌltɪˈmeɪtəm] *n* Ultimatum *nt*

ultra- ['ʌltrə] *pref* ultra-

ultrasound ['ʌltrəsaʊnd] *n* (*Med*) Ultraschall *m*

umbrella [ʌmˈbrelə] *n* Schirm *m*

umpire ['ʌmpaɪə*] *n* Schiedsrichter(in) *m(f)*

umpteen ['ʌmptiːn] *num* (*fam*) zig; **~ times** zigmal

un- [ʌn] *pref* un-

UN *nsing abbr* = **United Nations** UNO *f*

unable [ʌnˈeɪbl] *adj* **to be ~ to do sth** etw nicht tun können

unacceptable [ʌnəˈkseptəbl] *adj* unannehmbar

unaccountably [ʌnəˈkaʊntəblɪ] *adv* unerklärlicherweise

unaccustomed [ʌnəˈkʌstəmd] *adj* **to be ~ to sth** etw nicht gewohnt sein

unanimous, unanimously [juːˈnænɪməs, -lɪ] *adj, adv* einmütig

unattached [ʌnəˈtætʃt] *adj* (*without partner*) ungebunden

unattended [ʌnəˈtendɪd] *adj* (*luggage, car*) unbeaufsichtigt

unauthorized [ʌnˈɔːθəraɪzd] *adj* unbefugt

unavailable [ʌnəˈveɪləbl] *adj* nicht erhältlich; (*person*) nicht erreichbar

unavoidable [ʌnəˈvɔɪdəbl] *adj* unvermeidlich

unaware [ʌnəˈwɛə*] *adj* **to be ~ of sth** sich einer Sache *dat* nicht bewusst sein; **I was ~ that ...** ich wusste nicht, dass ...

unbalanced [ʌnˈbælənst] *adj* unausgewogen; (*mentally*) gestört

unbearable [ʌnˈbɛərəbl] *adj* unerträglich

unbeatable [ʌnˈbiːtəbl] *adj* unschlagbar

unbelievable [ʌnbɪˈliːvəbl] *adj* unglaublich

unblock [ʌnˈblɒk] *vt* (*pipe*) frei machen

unbutton [ʌnˈbʌtn] *vt* aufknöpfen

uncertain [ʌnˈsɜːtən] *adj* unsicher

uncle ['ʌŋkl] *n* Onkel *m*

uncomfortable [ʌnˈkʌmfətəbl] *adj* unbequem

unconditional [ʌnkənˈdɪʃənl] *adj* bedingungslos

unconscious [ʌnˈkɒnʃəs] *adj* (*Med*) bewusstlos; **to be ~ of sth** sich einer Sache *dat* nicht bewusst sein; **unconsciously** *adv* unbewusst

uncork [ʌnˈkɔːk] *vt* entkorken

uncover [ʌnˈkʌvə*] *vt* aufdecken

undecided [ʌndɪˈsaɪdɪd] *adj* unschlüssig

undeniable [ʌndɪˈnaɪəbl] *adj* unbestreitbar

under ['ʌndə*] *prep* (*beneath*) unter +*dat*; (*with motion*) unter +*akk*; **children ~ eight** Kinder unter acht; **~ an hour** weniger als eine Stunde ▷ *adv* (*beneath*) unten; (*with motion*) darunter; **children aged eight and ~** Kinder bis zu acht Jahren; **under-age** *adj* minderjährig

undercarriage ['ʌndəkærɪdʒ] *n* Fahrgestell *nt*

underdog ['ʌndədɒg] n Unterlegene(r) mf; (outsider) Außenseiter(in) m(f)

underdone [ʌndə'dʌn] adj (Gastr) nicht gar, durch; (deliberately) nicht durchgebraten

underestimate [ʌndər'estimeɪt] vt unterschätzen

underexposed [ʌndərɪks'pəʊzd] adj (Foto) unterbelichtet

undergo [ʌndə'gəʊ] irr vt (experience) durchmachen; (operation, test) sich unterziehen +dat

undergraduate [ʌndə'grædjʊət] n Student(in) m(f)

underground ['ʌndəgraʊnd] adj unterirdisch ▷ n (Brit Rail) U-Bahn f; **underground station** n U-Bahn-Station f

underlie [ʌndə'laɪ] irr vt zugrunde liegen +dat

underline [ʌndə'laɪn] vt unterstreichen

underlying [ʌndə'laɪɪŋ] adj zugrunde liegend

underneath [ʌndə'niːθ] prep unter; (with motion) unter +akk ▷ adv darunter

underpants ['ʌndəpænts] npl Unterhose f; **undershirt** ['ʌndəʃɜːt] n (US) Unterhemd nt; **undershorts** ['ʌndəʃɔːts] npl (US) Unterhose f

understand [ʌndə'stænd] irr vt, vi verstehen; **I ~ that ...** (been told) ich habe gehört, dass ...; (sympathize) ich habe Verständnis dafür, dass ...; **to make oneself understood** sich verständlich machen; **understandable** adj verständlich; **understanding** adj verständnisvoll

undertake [ʌndə'teɪk] irr vt (task) übernehmen; **to ~ to do sth** (been told) sich verpflichten, etw zu tun; **undertaker** n Leichenbestatter(in) m(f); **~'s** (firm) Bestattungsinstitut nt

underwater [ʌndə'wɔːtə*] adv unter Wasser ▷ adj Unterwasser-

underwear ['ʌndəweə*] n Unterwäsche f

undesirable [ʌndɪ'zaɪərəbl] adj unerwünscht

undo [ʌn'duː] irr vt (unfasten) aufmachen; (work) zunichte machen; (Inform) rückgängig machen

undoubtedly [ʌn'daʊtɪdlɪ] adv zweifellos

undress [ʌn'dres] vt ausziehen; **to get ~ed** sich ausziehen ▷ vi sich ausziehen

undue [ʌn'djuː] adj übermäßig

unduly [ʌn'djuːlɪ] adv übermäßig

unearth [ʌn'ɜːθ] vt (dig up) ausgraben; (find) aufstöbern

unease [ʌn'iːz] n Unbehagen nt; **uneasy** adj (person) unbehaglich; **I'm ~ about it** mir ist nicht wohl dabei

unemployed [ʌnɪm'plɔɪd] adj arbeitslos ▷ ▷ npl **the ~** die Arbeitslosen pl; **unemployment** [ʌnɪm'plɔɪmənt] n Arbeitslosigkeit f; **unemployment benefit** n Arbeitslosengeld nt

unequal [ʌn'iːkwəl] adj ungleich

uneven [ʌn'iːvən] adj (surface, road) uneben; (contest) ungleich

unexpected [ʌnɪk'spektɪd] adj unerwartet

unfair [ʌn'fɛə*] adj unfair

unfamiliar [ʌnfə'mɪljə*] adj **to be ~ with sb/sth** jdn/etw nicht kennen

unfasten [ʌn'fɑːsn] vt aufmachen

unfit [ʌn'fɪt] adj ungeeignet (for für); (in bad health) nicht fit

unforeseen [ʌnfɔː'siːn] adj unvorhergesehen

unforgettable [ʌnfə'getəbl] adj unvergesslich

unforgivable [ʌnfə'gɪvəbl] adj unverzeihlich

unfortunate [ʌn'fɔːtʃnət] adj (unlucky) unglücklich; **it is ~ that ...** es ist bedauerlich, dass ...; **unfortunately** adv leider

unfounded [ʌn'faʊndɪd] adj unbegründet

unhappy [ʌn'hæpɪ] adj (sad) unglücklich, unzufrieden; **to be ~ with sth** mit etw unzufrieden sein

unhealthy [ʌn'helθɪ] adj ungesund

unheard-of [ʌn'hɜːdɒv] adj (unknown) gänzlich unbekannt; (outrageous) unerhört

unhelpful [ʌn'helpfʊl] adj nicht hilfreich

unhitch [ʌn'hɪtʃ] vt (caravan, trailer) abkoppeln

unhurt [ʌn'hɜːt] adj unverletzt

uniform ['juːnɪfɔːm] n Uniform f ▷ adj einheitlich

unify ['juːnɪfaɪ] vt vereinigen

unimportant [ʌnɪm'pɔːtənt] adj unwichtig

uninhabited [ʌnɪn'hæbɪtɪd] adj unbewohnt

uninstall [ˌʌnɪnˈstɔːl] *vt* (*Inform*)
deinstallieren

unintentional [ˌʌnɪnˈtenʃənl] *adj*
unabsichtlich

union ['juːnjən] *n* (*uniting*) Vereinigung *f*;
(*alliance*) Union *f*; **Union Jack** *n* Union Jack
m (*britische Nationalflagge*)

unique [juːˈniːk] *adj* einzigartig

unit ['juːnɪt] *n* Einheit *f*; (*of system,
machine*) Teil *nt*; (*in school*) Lektion *f*

unite [juːˈnaɪt] *vt* vereinigen; **the United
Kingdom** das Vereinigte Königreich; **the
United Nations** *pl* die Vereinten Nationen
pl; **the United States (of America)** *pl* die
Vereinigten Staaten (von Amerika) *pl* ▷ *vi*
sich vereinigen

universe ['juːnɪvɜːs] *n* Universum *nt*

university [juːnɪˈvɜːsɪtɪ] *n* Universität *f*

unkind [ʌnˈkaɪnd] *adj* unfreundlich (*to* zu)

unknown [ʌnˈnəʊn] *adj* unbekannt (*to
+dat*)

unleaded [ʌnˈledɪd] *adj* bleifrei

unless [ənˈles] *conj* es sei denn, wenn ...
nicht; **don't do it ~ I tell you to** mach das
nicht, es sei denn, ich sage es dir; **~ I'm
mistaken ...** wenn ich mich nicht irre ...

unlicensed [ʌnˈlaɪsənst] *adj* (*to sell
alcohol*) ohne Lizenz

unlike [ʌnˈlaɪk] *prep* (*in contrast to*) im
Gegensatz zu; **it's ~ her to be late** es sieht
ihr gar nicht ähnlich, zu spät zu kommen;
unlikely [ʌnˈlaɪklɪ] *adj* unwahrscheinlich

unload [ʌnˈləʊd] *vt* ausladen

unlock [ʌnˈlɒk] *vt* aufschließen

unlucky [ʌnˈlʌkɪ] *adj* unglücklich; **to be
~** Pech haben

unmistakable [ʌnmɪˈsteɪkəbl] *adj*
unverkennbar

unnecessary [ʌnˈnesəsərɪ] *adj* unnötig

unobtainable [ʌnəbˈteɪnəbl] *adj* nicht
erhältlich

unoccupied [ʌnˈɒkjʊpaɪd] *adj* (*seat*) frei;
(*building, room*) leer stehend

unpack [ʌnˈpæk] *vt, vi* auspacken

unpleasant [ʌnˈpleznt] *adj* unangenehm

unplug [ʌnˈplʌg] *vt* **to ~ sth** den Stecker
von etw herausziehen

unprecedented [ʌnˈpresɪdəntɪd] *adj*
beispiellos

unpredictable [ʌnprɪˈdɪktəbl] *adj*
(*person, weather*) unberechenbar

unreasonable [ʌnˈriːznəbl] *adj*
unvernünftig; (*demand*) übertrieben

unreliable [ʌnrɪˈlaɪəbl] *adj* unzuverlässig

unsafe [ʌnˈseɪf] *adj* nicht sicher;
(*dangerous*) gefährlich

unscrew [ʌnˈskruː] *vt* abschrauben

unsightly [ʌnˈsaɪtlɪ] *adj* unansehnlich

unskilled [ʌnˈskɪld] *adj* (*worker*) ungelernt

unsuccessful [ʌnsəkˈsesfʊl] *adj* erfolglos

unsuitable [ʌnˈsuːtəbl] *adj* ungeeignet
(*for* für)

until [ənˈtɪl] *prep* bis; **not ~** erst; **from
Monday ~ Friday** von Montag bis Freitag; **he
didn't come home ~ midnight** er kam
erst um Mitternacht nach Hause; **~ then**
bis dahin ▷ *conj* bis; **she won't come
~ you invite her** sie kommt erst, wenn du
sie einlädst

unusual, unusually [ʌnˈjuːʒʊəl, -ɪ] *adj,
adv* ungewöhnlich

unwanted [ʌnˈwɒntɪd] *adj* unerwünscht,
ungewollt

unwell [ʌnˈwel] *adj* krank; **to feel ~** sich
nicht wohl fühlen

unwilling [ʌnˈwɪlɪŋ] *adj* **to be ~ to do sth**
nicht bereit sein, etw zu tun

unwind [ʌnˈwaɪnd] *irr vt* abwickeln ▷ *vi*
(*relax*) sich entspannen

unwrap [ʌnˈræp] *vt* auspacken

unzip [ʌnˈzɪp] *vt* den Reißverschluss
aufmachen an +*dat*; (*Inform*) entzippen

🔵 **KEYWORD**

up [ʌp] *prep*: **to be up sth** oben auf etw *dat*
sein; **to go up sth** (auf) etw *acc*
hinaufgehen; **go up that road** gehen Sie
die Straße hinauf

▷ *adv* **1** (*upwards, higher*) oben; **put it up a
bit higher** stell es etwas weiter nach
oben; **up there** da oben dort oben; **up
above** hoch oben

2: **to be up** (*out of bed*) auf sein (*prices,
level*) gestiegen sein (*building, tent*) stehen

3: **up to** (*as far as*) bis; **up to now** bis jetzt

4: **to be up to** (*depending on*): **it's up to
you** das hängt von dir ab; (*equal to*); **he's
not up to it** (*job, task etc*) er ist dem nicht
gewachsen (*inf: be doing: showing
disapproval, suspicion*): **what is he up to?**
was führt er im Schilde?; **it's not up to me
to decide** die Entscheidung liegt nicht bei
mir; **his work is not up to the required
standard** seine Arbeit entspricht nicht
dem geforderten Niveau

▷ n ; **ups and downs** (in life, career) Höhen und Tiefen pl

upbringing ['ʌpbrɪŋɪŋ] n Erziehung f

update [ʌp'deɪt] n (list etc) Aktualisierung f; (software) Update nt ▷ vt (list etc, person) auf den neuesten Stand bringen, aktualisieren

upgrade [ʌp'greɪd] vt (computer) aufrüsten; **we were ~d** das Hotel hat uns ein besseres Zimmer gegeben

upheaval [ʌp'hi:vəl] n Aufruhr m; (Pol) Umbruch m

uphill [ʌp'hɪl] adv bergauf

upon [ə'pɒn] prep see **on**

upper ['ʌpə*] adj obere(r, s); (arm, deck) Ober-

upright ['ʌpraɪt] adj, adv aufrecht

uprising ['ʌpraɪzɪŋ] n Aufstand m

uproar ['ʌprɔ:*] n Aufruhr m

upset [ʌp'set] irr vt (overturn) umkippen; (disturb) aufregen; (sadden) bestürzen; (offend) kränken; (plans) durcheinander bringen ▷ adj (disturbed) aufgeregt; (sad) bestürzt; (offended) gekränkt; **~ stomach** ['ʌpset] Magenverstimmung f

upside down [ʌpsaɪd'daʊn] adv verkehrt herum; (fig) drunter und drüber; **to turn sth ~** (box etc) etw umdrehen/durchwühlen

upstairs [ʌp'stɛəz] adv oben; (go, take) nach oben

up-to-date ['ʌptə'deɪt] adj modern; (fashion, information) aktuell; **to keep sb ~** jdn auf dem Laufenden halten

upwards ['ʌpwədz] adv nach oben

urban ['ɜ:bən] adj städtisch, Stadt-

urge [ɜ:dʒ] n Drang m ▷ vt **to ~ sb to do sth** jdn drängen, etw zu tun; **urgent, urgently** ['ɜ:dʒənt, -lɪ] adj, adv dringend

urine ['jʊərɪn] n Urin m

us [ʌs] pron uns; **do they know ~?** kennen sie uns?; **can he help ~?** kann er uns helfen?; **it's ~** wir sind's; **both of ~** wir beide

US, USA nsing abbr = **United States (of America)** USA pl

use [ju:s] n (using) Gebrauch m; (for specific purpose) Verwendung f; **to make ~ of** Gebrauch machen von; **in/out of ~** in/außer Gebrauch; **it's no ~ (doing that)** es hat keinen Zweck(, das zu tun); **it's (of) no ~ to me** das kann ich nicht

brauchen ▷ [ju:z] vt benutzen, gebrauchen; (for specific purpose) verwenden; (method) anwenden; **use up** vt aufbrauchen

used [ju:zd] adj (secondhand) gebraucht ▷ vb aux **to be ~d to sb/sth** an jdn/etw gewöhnt sein; **to get ~d to sb/sth** sich an jdn/etw gewöhnen; **she ~d to live here** sie hat früher mal hier gewohnt; **useful** adj nützlich; **useless** adj nutzlos; (unusable) unbrauchbar; (pointless) zwecklos; **user** ['ju:zə*] n Benutzer(in) m(f); **user-friendly** adj benutzerfreundlich

usual ['ju:ʒəl] adj üblich, gewöhnlich; **as ~** wie üblich; **usually** adv normalerweise

utensil [ju:'tensl] n Gerät nt

uterus ['ju:tərəs] n Gebärmutter f

utilize ['ju:tɪlaɪz] vt verwenden

utmost ['ʌtməʊst] adj äußerst; **to do one's ~** sein Möglichstes tun

utter ['ʌtə*] adj völlig ▷ vt von sich geben; **utterly** adv völlig

U-turn ['ju:tɜ:n] n (Auto) Wende f; **to do a ~** wenden; (fig) eine Kehrtwendung machen

V

vacancy ['veɪkənsɪ] n (job) offene
Stelle; (room) freies Zimmer; **vacant**
['veɪkənt] adj (room, seat) frei; (post)
offen; (building) leer stehend; **vacate**
[və'keɪt] vt (room, building) räumen;
(seat) frei machen

vacation [və'keɪʃən] n (US) Ferien pl,
Urlaub m; (at university) (Semester)ferien
pl; **to go on ~** in Urlaub fahren; **~ course**
Ferienkurs m

vaccinate ['væksɪneɪt] vt impfen;
vaccination [væksɪ'neɪʃən] n Impfung f;
~ card Impfpass m

vacuum ['vækjʊm] n Vakuum nt ▷ vt, vi
(staub)saugen; **vacuum cleaner** n
Staubsauger m

vagina [və'dʒaɪnə] n Scheide f

vague [veɪg] adj (imprecise) vage;
(resemblance) entfernt; **vaguely** adv in
etwa, irgendwie

vain [veɪn] adj (attempt) vergeblich;
(conceited) eitel; **vainly** adv (in vain)
vergeblich

valentine (card) ['væləntaɪn(kɑːd)] n
Valentinskarte f; **Valentine's Day** n
Valentinstag m

valid ['vælɪd] adj (ticket, passport etc)
gültig; (argument) stichhaltig; (claim)
berechtigt

valley ['vælɪ] n Tal nt

valuable ['væljʊəbl] adj wertvoll; (time)
kostbar; **valuables** npl Wertsachen pl

value ['væljuː] n Wert m ▷ vt (appreciate)
schätzen; **value added tax** n
Mehrwertsteuer f

valve [vælv] n Ventil nt

van [væn] n (Auto) Lieferwagen m

vanilla [və'nɪlə] n Vanille f

vanish ['vænɪʃ] vi verschwinden

vanity ['vænɪtɪ] n Eitelkeit f; **vanity case**
n Schminkkoffer m

vapor (US), **vapour** ['veɪpə*] n (mist)
Dunst m; (steam) Dampf m

variable ['veərɪəbl] adj (weather, mood)
unbeständig; (quality) unterschiedlich;
(speed, height) regulierbar; **varied** ['veərɪd]
adj (interests, selection) vielseitig; (career)
bewegt; (work, diet) abwechslungsreich;
variety [və'raɪətɪ] n (diversity)
Abwechslung f; (assortment) Vielfalt f (of an
+dat); (type) Art f; **various** ['veərɪəs] adj
verschieden

varnish ['vɑːnɪʃ] n Lack m ▷ vt
lackieren

vary ['veərɪ] vt (alter) verändern ▷ vi (be
different) unterschiedlich sein; (fluctuate)
sich verändern; (prices) schwanken

vase [vɑːz, ç veɪz] (US) n Vase f

vast [vɑːst] adj riesig; (area) weit

VAT abbr = value added tax
Mehrwertsteuer f, MwSt.

Vatican ['vætɪkən] n **the ~** der Vatikan

VCR abbr = video cassette recorder
Videorekorder m

VD abbr = venereal disease

VDU abbr = visual display unit

veal [viːl] n Kalbfleisch nt

vegan ['viːgən] n Veganer(in) m(f)

vegetable ['vedʒətəbl] n Gemüse nt

vegetarian [vedʒɪ'teərɪən] n
Vegetarier(in) m(f) ▷ adj vegetarisch

vehicle ['viːɪkl] n Fahrzeug nt

veil [veɪl] n Schleier m

vein [veɪn] n Ader f

Velcro® ['velkrəʊ] n Klettband nt

velvet ['velvɪt] n Samt m

vending machine ['vendɪŋməʃiːn] n
Automat m

venereal disease [vɪ'nɪərɪəldɪziːz] n
Geschlechtskrankheit f

venetian blind [vɪˈniːʃənˈblaɪnd] n
Jalousie f
Venezuela [veneˈzweɪlə] n Venezuela nt
vengeance [ˈvendʒəns] n Rache f
Venice [ˈvenɪs] n Venedig nt
venison [ˈvenɪsn] n Rehfleisch nt
vent [vent] n Öffnung f
ventilate [ˈventɪleɪt] vt lüften;
ventilation [ventɪˈleɪʃən] n Belüftung f;
ventilator [ˈventɪleɪtə*] n (in room)
Ventilator m; **to be on a ~** (Med) künstlich
beatmet werden
venture [ˈventʃə*] n (project)
Unternehmung f; (Comm) Unternehmen nt
▷ vi (go) (sich) wagen
venue [ˈvenjuː] n (for concert etc)
Veranstaltungsort m; (Sport)
Austragungsort m
verb [vɜːb] n Verb nt; **verbal** adj
(agreement) mündlich; (skills) sprachlich;
verbally adv mündlich
verdict [ˈvɜːdɪkt] n Urteil nt
verge [vɜːdʒ] n (of road) (Straßen)rand m;
to be on the ~ of doing sth im Begriff
sein, etw zu tun ▷ vi **to ~ on** grenzen an
+akk
verification [verɪfɪˈkeɪʃən] n
(confirmation) Bestätigung f; (check)
Überprüfung f; **verify** [ˈverɪfaɪ] vt
(confirm) bestätigen; (check) überprüfen
vermin [ˈvɜːmɪn] npl Schädlinge pl;
(insects) Ungeziefer nt
verruca [veˈruːkə] n Warze f
versatile [ˈvɜːsətaɪl] adj vielseitig
verse [vɜːs] n (poetry) Poesie f; (stanza)
Strophe f
version [ˈvɜːʃən] n Version f
versus [ˈvɜːsəs] prep gegen; (in contrast
to) im Gegensatz zu
vertical [ˈvɜːtɪkəl] adj senkrecht,
vertikal
very [ˈverɪ] adv sehr; **~ much** sehr ▷ adj
the ~ book I need genau das Buch, das ich
brauche; **at that ~ moment** gerade in
dem Augenblick; **at the ~ top** ganz oben;
the ~ best der/die/das Allerbeste
vest [vest] n (Brit) Unterhemd nt; (US:
waistcoat) Weste f
vet [vet] n Tierarzt m, Tierärztin f
veto [ˈviːtəʊ] (pl **-es**) n Veto nt ▷ vt sein
Veto einlegen gegen
VHF abbr = **very high frequency** UKW
via [ˈvaɪə] prep über +akk

viable [ˈvaɪəbl] adj (plan) realisierbar;
(company) rentabel
vibrate [vaɪˈbreɪt] vi vibrieren; **vibration**
[vaɪˈbreɪʃən] n Vibration f
vicar [ˈvɪkə*] n Pfarrer(in) m(f)
vice [vaɪs] n (evil) Laster nt; (Tech)
Schraubstock m ▷ pref Vize-;
~-chairman stellvertretender
Vorsitzender; **~-president**
Vizepräsident(in) m(f)
vice versa [ˈvaɪsˈvɜːsə] adv umgekehrt
vicinity [vɪˈsɪnɪtɪ] n **in the ~** in der Nähe
(of +gen)
vicious [ˈvɪʃəs] adj (violent) brutal;
(malicious) gemein; **vicious circle** n
Teufelskreis m
victim [ˈvɪktɪm] n Opfer nt
Victorian [vɪkˈtɔːrɪən] adj viktorianisch
victory [ˈvɪktərɪ] n Sieg m
video [ˈvɪdɪəʊ] (pl **-s**) adj Video- ▷ n Video
nt; (recorder) Videorekorder m ▷ vt (auf
Video) aufnehmen; **video camera** n
Videokamera f; **video cassette** n
Videokassette f; **video clip** n Videoclip m;
video game n Videospiel nt; **video
recorder** n Videorekorder m; **video shop**
n Videothek f; **videotape** n Videoband nt
▷ vt (auf Video) aufnehmen
Vienna [vɪˈenə] n Wien nt
Vietnam [vjetˈnæm] n Vietnam nt
view [vjuː] n (sight) Blick m (of auf +akk);
(vista) Aussicht f; (opinion) Ansicht f,
Meinung f; **in ~ of** angesichts +gen ▷ vt
(situation, event) betrachten; (house)
besichtigen; **viewer** n (for slides)
Diabetrachter m; (TV) Zuschauer(in) m(f);
viewpoint n (fig) Standpunkt m
vigilant [ˈvɪdʒɪlənt] adj wachsam
vile [vaɪl] adj abscheulich; (weather, food)
scheußlich
village [ˈvɪlɪdʒ] n Dorf nt; **villager** n
Dorfbewohner(in) m(f)
villain [ˈvɪlən] n Schurke m; (in film, story)
Bösewicht m
vine [vaɪn] n (Wein)rebe f
vinegar [ˈvɪnɪgə*] n Essig m
vineyard [ˈvɪnjəd] n Weinberg m
vintage [ˈvɪntɪdʒ] n (of wine) Jahrgang m;
vintage wine n edler Wein
vinyl [ˈvaɪnɪl] n Vinyl nt
viola [vɪˈəʊlə] n Bratsche f
violate [ˈvaɪəleɪt] vt (treaty) brechen;
(rights, rule) verletzen

violence ['vaɪələns] n (brutality) Gewalt f; (of person) Gewalttätigkeit f; **violent** adj (brutal) brutal; (death) gewaltsam

violet ['vaɪələt] n Veilchen nt

violin [vaɪə'lɪn] n Geige f, Violine f

VIP abbr = **very important person** VIP mf

virgin ['vɜ:dʒɪn] n Jungfrau f

Virgo ['vɜ:gəʊ] n (Astr) Jungfrau f

virile ['vɪraɪl] adj (man) männlich

virtual ['vɜ:tjʊəl] adj (Inform) virtuell; **virtually** adv praktisch; **virtual reality** n virtuelle Realität

virtue ['vɜ:tju:] n Tugend f; **by ~ of** aufgrund +gen; **virtuous** ['vɜ:tjʊəs] adj tugendhaft

virus ['vaɪrəs] n (Med, Inform) Virus nt

visa ['vi:zə] n Visum nt

visibility [vɪzɪ'bɪlɪtɪ] n (Meteo) Sichtweite f; **good/poor ~** gute/schlechte Sicht; **visible** ['vɪzəbl] adj sichtbar; (evident) sichtlich; **visibly** adv sichtlich

vision ['vɪʒən] n (power of sight) Sehvermögen nt; (foresight) Weitblick m; (dream, image) Vision f

visit ['vɪzɪt] n Besuch m; (stay) Aufenthalt m ▷ vt besuchen; **visiting hours** npl Besuchszeiten pl; **visitor** n Besucher(in) m(f); **~'s book** Gästebuch nt; **visitor centre** n Informationszentrum nt

visor ['vaɪzə*] n (on helmet) Visier nt; (Auto) Blende f

visual ['vɪzjʊəl] adj Seh-; (image, joke) visuell; **~ aid** Anschauungsmaterial nt; **~ display unit** Monitor m; **visualize** vt sich vorstellen; **visually** adv visuell; **~ impaired** sehbehindert

vital ['vaɪtl] adj (essential) unerlässlich, wesentlich; (argument, moment) entscheidend; **vitality** [vaɪ'tælɪtɪ] n Vitalität f; **vitally** adv äußerst

vitamin ['vɪtəmɪn] n Vitamin nt

vivacious [vɪ'veɪʃəs] adj lebhaft

vivid ['vɪvɪd] adj (description) anschaulich; (memory) lebhaft; (colour) leuchtend

V-neck ['vi:nek] n V-Ausschnitt m

vocabulary [vəʊ'kæbjʊlərɪ] n Wortschatz m, Vokabular nt

vocal ['vəʊkəl] adj (of the voice) Stimm-; (group) Gesangs-; (protest, person) lautstark

vocation [vəʊ'keɪʃən] n Berufung f; **vocational** adj Berufs-

vodka ['vɒdkə] n Wodka m

voice [vɔɪs] n Stimme f ▷ vt äußern; **voice mail** n Voicemail f

void [vɔɪd] n Leere f ▷ adj (Jur) ungültig; **~ of** (ganz) ohne

volcano [vɒl'keɪnəʊ] (pl **-es**) n Vulkan m

volley ['vɒlɪ] n (Tennis) Volley m; **volleyball** n Volleyball m

volt [vəʊlt] n Volt nt; **voltage** n Spannung f

volume ['vɒlju:m] n (of sound) Lautstärke f; (space occupied by sth) Volumen nt; (size, amount) Umfang m; (book) Band m; **volume control** n Lautstärkeregler m

voluntary, voluntarily ['vɒləntərɪ, -lɪ] adj, adv freiwillig; (unpaid) ehrenamtlich; **volunteer** [vɒlən'tɪə*] n Freiwillige(r) mf ▷ vi sich freiwillig melden ▷ vt **to ~ to do sth** sich anbieten, etw zu tun

voluptuous [və'lʌptjʊəs] adj sinnlich

vomit ['vɒmɪt] vi sich übergeben

vote [vəʊt] n Stimme f; (ballot) Wahl f; (result) Abstimmungsergebnis nt; (right to vote) Wahlrecht nt ▷ vt (elect) wählen; **they ~d him chairman** sie wählten ihn zum Vorsitzenden ▷ vi wählen; **to ~ for/against sth** für/gegen etw stimmen; **voter** n Wähler(in) m(f)

voucher ['vaʊtʃə*] n Gutschein m

vow [vaʊ] n Gelöbnis nt ▷ vt **to ~ to do sth** geloben, etw zu tun

vowel ['vaʊəl] n Vokal m

voyage ['vɔɪdʒ] n Reise f

vulgar ['vʌlgə*] adj vulgär, ordinär

vulnerable ['vʌlnərəbl] adj verwundbar; (sensitive) verletzlich

vulture ['vʌltʃə*] n Geier m

W

W abbr = **west** W

wade [weɪd] vi (in water) waten

wafer ['weɪfə*] n Waffel f; (Rel) Hostie f; **wafer-thin** adj hauchdünn

waffle ['wɒfl] n Waffel f; (Brit fam: empty talk) Geschwafel nt ▷ vi (Brit fam) schwafeln

wag [wæg] vt (tail) wedeln mit

wage [weɪdʒ] n Lohn m

waggon (Brit), **wagon** ['wægən] n (horse-drawn) Fuhrwerk nt; (Brit Rail) Waggon m; (US Auto) Wagen m

waist [weɪst] n Taille f; **waistcoat** n (Brit) Weste f; **waistline** n Taille f

wait [weɪt] n Wartezeit f ▷ vi warten (for auf +akk); **to ~ and see** abwarten; **~ a minute** Moment mal!; **wait up** vi aufbleiben

waiter n Kellner m; **~!** Herr Ober!

waiting n **'no ~'** „Halteverbot"; **waiting list** n Warteliste f; **waiting room** n (Med) Wartezimmer nt; (Rail) Wartesaal m

waitress n Kellnerin f

wake [weɪk] (**woke** o **waked**, **woken** o **waked**) vt wecken ▷ vi aufwachen; **wake up** vt aufwecken ▷ vi aufwachen; **wake-up call** n (Tel) Weckruf m

Wales ['weɪlz] n Wales nt

walk [wɔːk] n Spaziergang m; (ramble) Wanderung f; (route) Weg m; **to go for a ~** spazieren gehen; **it's only a five-minute ~** es sind nur fünf Minuten zu Fuß ▷ vi gehen; (stroll) spazieren gehen; (ramble) wandern ▷ vt (dog) ausführen; **walking** n **to go ~** wandern; **walking shoes** npl Wanderschuhe pl; **walking stick** n Spazierstock m

Walkman®(pl **-s**) n Walkman® m

wall [wɔːl] n (inside) Wand f; (outside) Mauer f

wallet ['wɒlɪt] n Brieftasche f

wallpaper ['wɔːlpeɪpə*] n Tapete f; (Inform) Bildschirmhintergrund m ▷ vt tapezieren

walnut ['wɔːlnʌt] n (nut) Walnuss f

waltz [wɔːlts] n Walzer m

wander ['wɒndə*] vi (person) herumwandern

want [wɒnt] n (lack) Mangel m (of an +dat); (need) Bedürfnis nt; **for ~ of** aus Mangel an +dat ▷ vt (desire) wollen; (need) brauchen; **I ~ to stay here** ich will hier bleiben; **he doesn't ~ to** er will nicht

WAP phone ['wæpfəʊn] n WAP-Handy nt

war [wɔː*] n Krieg m

ward [wɔːd] n (in hospital) Station f; (child) Mündel nt

warden ['wɔːdən] n Aufseher(in) m(f); (in youth hostel) Herbergsvater m, Herbergsmutter f

wardrobe ['wɔːdrəʊb] n Kleiderschrank m

warehouse ['weəhaʊs] n Lagerhaus nt

warfare ['wɔːfeə*] n Krieg m; (techniques) Kriegsführung f

warm [wɔːm] adj warm; (welcome) herzlich; **I'm ~** mir ist warm ▷ vt wärmen; (food) aufwärmen; **warm over** vt (US: food) aufwärmen; **warm up** vt (food) aufwärmen; (room) erwärmen ▷ vi (food, room) warm werden; (Sport) sich aufwärmen; **warmly** adv warm; (welcome) herzlich; **warmth** n Wärme f; (of welcome) Herzlichkeit f

warn [wɔːn] vt warnen (of, against vor +dat); **to ~ sb not to do sth** jdn davor warnen, etw zu tun; **warning** n Warnung f; **warning light** n Warnlicht nt; **warning triangle** n (Auto) Warndreieck nt

warranty ['wɒrəntɪ] n Garantie f

wart [wɔːt] n Warze f

W

wary ['wεərɪ] *adj* vorsichtig; (*suspicious*) misstrauisch

was [wɒz, wəz] *pt of* **be**

wash [wɒʃ] *n* **to have a ~** sich waschen; **it's in the ~** es ist in der Wäsche ▷ *vt* waschen; (*plates, glasses etc*) abwaschen; **to ~ one's hands** sich *dat* die Hände waschen; **to ~ the dishes** (das Geschirr) abwaschen ▷ *vi* (*clean oneself*) sich waschen; **wash off** *vt* abwaschen; **wash up** *vi* (*Brit: wash dishes*) abwaschen; (*US: clean oneself*) sich waschen; **washable** *adj* waschbar; **washbag** *n* (*US*) Kulturbeutel *m*; **washbasin** *n* Waschbecken *nt*; **washcloth** *n* (*US*) Waschlappen *m*; **washer** *n* (*Tech*) Dichtungsring *m*; (*washing machine*) Waschmaschine *f*; **washing** *n* (*laundry*) Wäsche *f*; **washing machine** *n* Waschmaschine *f*; **washing powder** *n* (*Brit*) Waschpulver *nt*; **washing-up** *n* (*Brit*) Abwasch *m*; **to do the ~** abwaschen; **washing-up liquid** *n* (*Brit*) Spülmittel *nt*; **washroom** *n* (*US*) Toilette *f*

wasn't ['wɒznt] *contr of* **was not**

wasp [wɒsp] *n* Wespe *f*

waste [weɪst] *n* (*materials*) Abfall *m*; (*wasting*) Verschwendung *f*; **it's a ~ of time** das ist Zeitverschwendung ▷ *adj* (*superfluous*) überschüssig ▷ *vt* verschwenden (*on an* +*akk*); (*opportunity*) vertun; **waste bin** *n* Abfalleimer *m*; **wastepaper basket** *n* Papierkorb *m*

watch [wɒtʃ] *n* (*timepiece*) (Armband)uhr *f* ▷ *vt* (*observe*) beobachten; (*guard*) aufpassen auf +*akk*; (*film, play, programme*) sich *dat* ansehen; **to ~ TV** fernsehen ▷ *vi* zusehen; (*guard*) Wache halten; **to ~ for sb/sth** nach jdm/etw Ausschau halten; **~ out** pass auf!; **watchdog** *n* Wachhund *m*; (*fig*) Aufsichtsbehörde *f*; **watchful** *adj* wachsam

water ['wɔːtə*] *n* Wasser *nt*; **~s** *pl* (*territory*) Gewässer *pl* ▷ *vt* (*plant*) gießen ▷ *vi* (*eye*) tränen; **my mouth is ~ing** mir läuft das Wasser im Mund zusammen; **water down** *vt* verdünnen; **watercolor** (*US*), **watercolour** *n* (*painting*) Aquarell *nt*; (*paint*) Wasserfarbe *f*; **watercress** *n* (Brunnen)kresse *f*; **waterfall** *n* Wasserfall *m*; **watering can** *n* Gießkanne *f*; **water level** *n* Wasserstand *m*; **watermelon** *n* Wassermelone *f*; **waterproof** *adj*

wasserdicht; **water-skiing** *n* Wasserskilaufen *nt*; **water sports** *npl* Wassersport *m*; **watertight** *adj* wasserdicht; **water wings** *npl* Schwimmflügel *pl*; **watery** *adj* wässerig

wave [weɪv] *n* Welle *f* ▷ *vt* (*move to and fro*) schwenken; (*hand, flag*) winken mit ▷ *vi* (*person*) winken; (*flag*) wehen; **wavelength** *n* Wellenlänge *f*; **to be on the same ~** (*fig*) die gleiche Wellenlänge haben; **wavy** ['weɪvɪ] *adj* wellig

wax [wæks] *n* Wachs *nt*; (*in ear*) Ohrenschmalz *nt*

way [weɪ] *n* Weg *m*; (*direction*) Richtung *f*; (*manner*) Art *f*; **can you tell me the ~ to ... ?** wie komme ich (am besten) zu ... ?; **we went the wrong ~** wir sind in die falsche Richtung gefahren/gegangen; **to lose one's ~** sich verirren; **to make ~ for sb/sth** jdm/etw Platz machen; **to get one's own ~** seinen Willen durchsetzen; **'give ~'** (*Auto*) "Vorfahrt achten"; **the other ~ round** andersherum; **one ~ or another** irgendwie; **in a ~** in gewisser Weise; **in the ~** im Weg; **by the ~** übrigens; **'~ in'** "Eingang"; **'~ out'** "Ausgang"; **no ~** (*fam*) kommt nicht infrage!

we [wiː] *pron* wir

weak [wiːk] *adj* schwach; **weaken** *vt* schwächen ▷ *vi* schwächer werden

wealth [welθ] *n* Reichtum *m*; **wealthy** *adj* reich

weapon ['wepən] *n* Waffe *f*

wear [wεə*] (**wore, worn**) *vt* (*have on*) tragen; **what shall I ~?** was soll ich anziehen? ▷ *vi* (*become worn*) sich abnutzen ▷ *n* **~ (and tear)** Abnutzung *f*; **wear off** *vi* (*diminish*) nachlassen; **wear out** *vt* abnutzen; (*person*) erschöpfen ▷ *vi* sich abnutzen

weary ['wɪərɪ] *adj* müde

weather ['weðə*] *n* Wetter *nt*; **I'm feeling under the ~** ich fühle mich nicht ganz wohl; **weather forecast** *n* Wettervorhersage *f*

weave [wiːv] (**wove** *o* **weaved, woven** *o* **weaved**) *vt* (*cloth*) weben; (*basket etc*) flechten

web [web] *n* (*a. fig*) Netz *nt*; **the Web** das Web, das Internet; **webcam** ['webkæm] *n* Webcam *f*; **web page** *n* Webseite *f*; **website** *n* Website *f*

we'd [wi:d] contr of **we had; we would**

Wed abbr = **Wednesday** Mi.

wedding ['wedɪŋ] n Hochzeit f; **wedding anniversary** n Hochzeitstag m; **wedding dress** n Hochzeitskleid nt; **wedding ring** n Ehering m

wedding shower n (US) Party für die zukünftige Braut

wedge [wedʒ] n (under door etc) Keil m; (of cheese etc) Stück nt, Ecke f

Wednesday ['wenzdeɪ] n Mittwoch m; see also **Tuesday**

wee [wi:] adj klein ▷ vi (fam) Pipi machen

weed [wi:d] n Unkraut nt ▷ vt jäten

week [wi:k] n Woche f; **twice a ~** zweimal in der Woche; **a ~ on Friday/Friday ~** Freitag in einer Woche; **a ~ last Friday** letzten Freitag vor einer Woche; **in two ~s' time, in two ~s** in zwei Wochen; **for ~s** wochenlang; **weekday** n Wochentag m; **weekend** n Wochenende nt; **weekly** adj, adv wöchentlich; (magazine) Wochen-

weep [wi:p] (**wept, wept**) vi weinen

weigh [weɪ] vt, vi wiegen; **it ~s 20 kilos** es wiegt 20 Kilo; **weigh up** vt abwägen; (person) einschätzen; **weight** [weɪt] n Gewicht nt; **to lose/put on ~** abnehmen/zunehmen; **weightlifting** n Gewichtheben nt; **weight training** n Krafttraining nt; **weighty** adj (important) schwer wiegend

weird [wɪəd] adj seltsam; **weirdo** ['wɪədəʊ] n Spinner(in) m(f)

welcome ['welkəm] n Empfang m ▷ adj willkommen; (news) angenehm; **~ to London** willkommen in London! ▷ vt begrüßen; **welcoming** adj freundlich

welfare ['welfeə*] n Wohl nt; (US: social security) Sozialhilfe f; **welfare state** n Wohlfahrtsstaat m

well [wel] n Brunnen m ▷ adj (in good health) gesund; **are you ~?** geht es dir gut?; **to feel ~** sich wohl fühlen; **get ~ soon** gute Besserung! ▷ interj nun; **~, I don't know** nun, ich weiß nicht ▷ adv gut; **~ done** gut gemacht!; **it may ~ be** das kann wohl sein; **as ~** (in addition) auch; **~ over 60** weit über 60

we'll [wi:l] contr of **we will; we shall**

well-behaved [welbɪ'heɪvd] adj brav; **well-being** n Wohl nt; **well-built** adj (person) gut gebaut; **well-done** adj (steak) durchgebraten; **well-earned** adj wohlverdient

wellingtons ['welɪŋtənz] npl Gummistiefel pl

well-known [wel'nəʊn] adj bekannt; **well-off** adj (wealthy) wohlhabend; **well-paid** adj gut bezahlt

Welsh [welʃ] adj walisisch ▷ n (language) Walisisch nt; **the ~** pl die Waliser pl; **Welshman** (pl **-men**) n Waliser m; **Welshwoman** (pl **-women**) n Waliserin f

went [went] pt of **go**

wept [wept] pt, pp of **weep**

were [wɜ:] pt of **be**

we're [wɪə*] contr of **we are**

weren't [wɜ:nt] contr of **were not**

west [west] n Westen m; **the West** (Pol) der Westen ▷ adv (go, face) nach Westen ▷ adj West-; **westbound** adj (in) Richtung Westen; **western** adj West-, westlich; **Western Europe** Westeuropa nt ▷ n (Cine) Western m; **West Germany** n (**the former**) ~ (das ehemalige) Westdeutschland, Westdeutschland n; **westwards** ['westwədz] adv nach Westen

wet [wet] (**wet, wet**) vt **to ~ oneself** in die Hose machen ▷ adj nass, feucht; **'~ paint'** „frisch gestrichen"; **wet suit** n Tauscheranzug m

we've [wi:v] contr of **we have**

whale [weɪl] n Wal m

wharf [wɔ:f] (pl **-s** o **wharves**) n Kai m

🅾 **KEYWORD**

what [wɒt] adj **1** (in questions) welche(r, s) was für ein(e); **what size is it?** welche Größe ist das?

2 (in exclamations) was für ein(e); **what a mess!** was für ein Durcheinander!

▷ pron (interrogative/relative) was; **what are you doing?** was machst du gerade?; **what are you talking about?** wovon reden Sie?; **what is it called?** wie heißt das?; **what about ...?** wie wärs mit ...?; **I saw what you did** ich habe gesehen, was du gemacht hast

▷ excl (disbelieving) wie was; **what, no coffee!** wie, kein Kaffee?; **I've crashed the car — what!** ich hatte einen Autounfall — was!

W

what's [wɒts] contr of **what is; what has**

wheat [wiːt] n Weizen m

wheel [wiːl] n Rad nt; (steering wheel) Lenkrad nt ▷ vt (bicycle, trolley) schieben; **wheelbarrow** n Schubkarren m; **wheelchair** n Rollstuhl m; **wheel clamp** n Parkkralle f

O KEYWORD

when [wɛn] adv wann ▷ conj **1** (at, during, after the time that) wenn; (in past) als; **she was reading when I came in** sie las, als ich hereinkam; **be careful when you cross the road** seien Sie vorsichtig, wenn Sie über die Straße gehen
2 (on, at which) als; **on the day when I met him** an dem Tag, an dem ich ihn traf
3 (whereas) wo ... doch

where [wɛə*] adv wo; **~ are you going?** wohin gehst du?; **~ are you from?** woher kommst du? ▷ conj wo; **that's ~ I used to live** da habe ich früher gewohnt; **whereabouts** [wɛərə'baʊts] adv wo ▷ npl ['wɛərəbaʊts] Aufenthaltsort m; **whereas** [wɛər'æz] conj während, wohingegen; **whereby** adv wodurch; **wherever** [wɛər'evə*] conj wo immer; **~ that may be** wo immer das sein mag; **~ I go** überall, wohin ich gehe

whether ['wɛðə*] conj ob

O KEYWORD

which [wɪtʃ] adj **1** (interrogative: direct, indirect) welche(r, s); **which one?** welche(r, s)?
2: **in which case** in diesem Fall; **by which time** zu dieser Zeit
▷ pron **1** (interrogative) welche(r, s); (of people also) wer
2 (relative) der/die/das (referring to people) was; **the apple which you ate/which is on the table** der Apfel, den du gegessen hast/der auf dem Tisch liegt; **he said he saw her, which is true** er sagte, er habe sie gesehen, was auch stimmt

while [waɪl] n **a ~** eine Weile; **for a ~** eine Zeit lang; **a short ~ ago** vor kurzem ▷ conj während; (although) obwohl

whine [waɪn] vi (person) jammern

whip [wɪp] n Peitsche f ▷ vt (beat) peitschen; **~ped cream** Schlagsahne f

whirl [wɜːl] vt, vi herumwirbeln; **whirlpool** n (in river, sea) Strudel m; (pool) Whirlpool m

whisk [wɪsk] n Schneebesen m ▷ vt (cream etc) schlagen

whisker ['wɪskə*] n (of animal) Schnurrhaar nt; **~s** pl (of man) Backenbart m

whisk(e)y ['wɪskɪ] n Whisky m

whisper ['wɪspə*] vi, vt flüstern; **to ~ sth to sb** jdm etw zuflüstern

whistle ['wɪsl] n Pfiff m; (instrument) Pfeife f ▷ vt, vi pfeifen

white [waɪt] n (of egg) Eiweiß nt; (of eye) Weiße nt ▷ adj weiß; (with fear) blass; (coffee) mit Milch; **White House** n the **~** das Weiße Haus; **white lie** n Notlüge f; **white meat** n helles Fleisch; **white sauce** n weiße Soße; **white water rafting** n Rafting nt; **white wine** n Weißwein m

Whitsun ['wɪtsn] n Pfingsten nt

O KEYWORD

who [huː] pron **1** (interrogative) wer; (acc) wen; (dat) wem; **who is it?, who's there?** wer ist da?
2 (relative) der/die/das; **the woman/man who spoke to me** die Frau/der Mann, die/der mit mir sprach

whole [həʊl] adj ganz ▷ n Ganze(s) nt; **the ~ of my family** meine ganze Familie; **on the ~** im Großen und Ganzen; **wholefood** n (Brit) Vollwertkost f; **wholeheartedly** adv voll und ganz; **wholemeal** adj (Brit) Vollkorn-; **wholesale** adv (buy, sell) im Großhandel; **wholesome** adj gesund; **wholewheat** adj Vollkorn-; **wholly** ['həʊlɪ] adv völlig

O KEYWORD

whom [huːm] pron **1** (interrogative: acc) wen; (: dat) wem; **whom did you see?** wen haben Sie gesehen?; **to whom did you give it?** wem haben Sie es gegeben?
2 (relative: acc) den/die/das; (: dat) dem/der/dem; **the man whom I saw/to**

whom I spoke der Mann, den ich sah/mit dem ich sprach

whooping cough ['hu:piŋkɒf] n Keuchhusten m

whose [hu:z] adj (in questions) wessen; (in relative clauses) dessen/deren/dessen, deren pl; **~ bike is that?** wessen Fahrrad ist das? ▷ pron (in questions) wessen; **~ is this?** wem gehört das?

 KEYWORD

why [waɪ] adv warum weshalb ▷ conj warum weshalb; **that's not why I'm here** ich bin nicht deswegen hier; **that's the reason why** deshalb ▷ excl (expressing surprise, shock) na so was (explaining) also dann; **why, it's you!** na so was, du bist es!

wicked ['wɪkɪd] adj böse; (fam: great) geil

wide [waɪd] adj breit; (skirt, trousers) weit; (selection) groß ▷ adv weit; **wide-angle lens** n Weitwinkelobjektiv nt; **wide-awake** adj hellwach; **widely** adv weit; **~ known** allgemein bekannt; **widen** vt verbreitern; (fig) erweitern; **wide-open** adj weit offen; **widescreen TV** n Breitbildfernseher m; **widespread** adj weit verbreitet

widow ['wɪdəʊ] n Witwe f; **widowed** adj verwitwet; **widower** n Witwer m

width [wɪdθ] n Breite f

wife [waɪf] (pl **wives**) n (Ehe)frau f

wig [wɪg] n Perücke f

wiggle ['wɪgl] vt wackeln mit

wild [waɪld] adj wild; (violent) heftig; (plan, idea) verrückt ▷ n **in the ~** in freier Wildbahn; **wildlife** n Tier- und Pflanzenwelt f; **wildly** adv wild; (enthusiastic, exaggerated) maßlos

 KEYWORD

will [wɪl] aux vb **1** (forms future tense) werden; **I will finish it tomorrow** ich mache es morgen zu Ende
2 (in conjectures, predictions): **he will or he'll be there by now** er dürfte jetzt da sein; **that will be the postman** das wird der Postbote sein
3 (in commands, requests, offers): **will you be**

quiet! sei endlich still!; **will you help me?** hilfst du mir?; **will you have a cup of tea?** trinken Sie eine Tasse Tee?; **I won't put up with it!** das lasse ich mir nicht gefallen!
▷ vt wollen
▷ n Wille m (Jur) Testament nt

willow ['wɪləʊ] n Weide f

willpower ['wɪlpaʊə*] n Willenskraft f

wimp [wɪmp] n Weichei nt

win [wɪn] (**won, won**) vt, vi gewinnen ▷ n Sieg m; **win over, win round** vt für sich gewinnen

wind [waɪnd] (**wound, wound**) vt (rope, bandage) wickeln; **wind down** vt (car window) herunterkurbeln; **wind up** vt (clock) aufziehen; (car window) hochkurbeln; (meeting, speech) abschließen; (person) aufziehen, ärgern

wind [wɪnd] n Wind m; (Med) Blähungen pl

wind instrument ['wɪndɪnstrʊmənt] n Blasinstrument nt; **windmill** n Windmühle f

window ['wɪndəʊ] n Fenster nt; (counter) Schalter m; **window box** n Blumenkasten m; **windowpane** n Fensterscheibe f; **window-shopping** n **to go ~** einen Schaufensterbummel machen; **windowsill** n Fensterbrett nt

windpipe ['wɪndpaɪp] n Luftröhre f; **windscreen** n (Brit) Windschutzscheibe f; **windscreen wiper** n (Brit) Scheibenwischer m; **windshield** n (US) Windschutzscheibe f; **windshield wiper** n (US) Scheibenwischer m; **windsurfer** n Windsurfer(in) m(f); (board) Surfbrett nt; **windsurfing** n Windsurfen nt

windy ['wɪndɪ] adj windig

wine [waɪn] n Wein m; **wine bar** n Weinlokal nt; **wineglass** n Weinglas nt; **wine list** n Weinkarte f; **wine tasting** n (event) Weinprobe f

wing [wɪŋ] n Flügel m; (Brit Auto) Kotflügel m; **~s** pl (Theat) Kulissen pl

wink [wɪŋk] vi zwinkern; **to ~ at sb** jdm zuzwinkern

winner ['wɪnə*] n Gewinner(in) m(f); (Sport) Sieger(in) m(f); **winning** adj (team, horse etc) siegreich; **~ number** Gewinnzahl f ▷ n **~s** pl Gewinn m

winter ['wɪntə*] n Winter m; **winter sports** npl Wintersport m; **wint(e)ry** ['wɪntrɪ] adj winterlich

W

wipe [waɪp] vt abwischen; **to ~ one's nose** sich dat die Nase putzen; **to ~ one's feet** (on mat) sich dat die Schuhe abtreten; **wipe off** vt abwischen; **wipe out** vt (destroy) vernichten; (data, debt) löschen; (epidemic etc) ausrotten

wire ['waɪə*] n Draht m; (Elec) Leitung f; (US: telegram) Telegramm nt ▷ vt (plug in) anschließen; (US Tel) telegrafieren (sb sth jdm etw); **wireless** ['waɪələs] adj drahtlos

wisdom ['wɪzdəm] n Weisheit f; **wisdom tooth** n Weisheitszahn m

wise, wisely [waɪz, -lɪ] adj, adv weise

wish [wɪʃ] n Wunsch m (for nach); **with best ~es** (in letter) herzliche Grüße ▷ vt wünschen, wollen; **to ~ sb good luck/Merry Christmas** jdm viel Glück/frohe Weihnachten wünschen; **I ~ I'd never seen him** ich wünschte, ich hätte ihn nie gesehen

witch [wɪtʃ] n Hexe f

◯ **KEYWORD**

with [wɪð, wɪθ] prep **1** (accompanying, in the company of) mit; **we stayed with friends** wir übernachteten bei Freunden; **I'll be with you in a minute** einen Augenblick ich bin sofort da; **I'm not with you** (I don't understand) das verstehe ich nicht; **to be with it** (inf) (up-to-date) auf dem Laufenden sein (ooo) (alert) (voll) da sein if

2 (descriptive, indicating manner etc) mit; **the man with the grey hat** der Mann mit dem grauen Hut; **red with anger** rot vor Wut

withdraw [wɪð'drɔː] irr vt zurückziehen; (money) abheben; (comment) zurücknehmen ▷ vi sich zurückziehen

wither ['wɪðə*] vi (plant) verwelken

withhold [wɪð'həʊld] irr vt vorenthalten (from sb jdm)

within [wɪð'ɪn] prep innerhalb +gen; **~ walking distance** zu Fuß erreichbar

without [wɪð'aʊt] prep ohne; **~ asking** ohne zu fragen

withstand [wɪð'stænd] irr vt standhalten +dat

witness ['wɪtnəs] n Zeuge m, Zeugin f ▷ vt Zeuge sein; **witness box, witness stand** (US) n Zeugenstand m

witty ['wɪtɪ] adj geistreich

wives [waɪvz] pl of **wife**

wobble ['wɒbl] vi wackeln; **wobbly** adj wackelig

wok [wɒk] n Wok m

woke [wəʊk] pt of **wake**

woken ['wəʊkn] pp of **wake**

wolf [wʊlf] (pl **wolves**) n Wolf m

woman ['wʊmən] (pl **women**) n Frau f

womb [wuːm] n Gebärmutter f

women ['wɪmɪn] pl of **woman**

won [wʌn] pt, pp of **win**

wonder ['wʌndə*] n (marvel) Wunder nt; (surprise) Staunen nt ▷ vt, vi (speculate) sich fragen; **I ~ what/if ...** ich frage mich, was/ob ...; **wonderful, wonderfully** adj, adv wunderbar

won't [wəʊnt] contr of **will not**

wood [wʊd] n Holz nt; **~s** Wald m; **wooden** adj Holz-; (fig) hölzern; **woodpecker** n Specht m; **woodwork** n (wooden parts) Holzteile pl; (in school) Werken nt

wool [wʊl] n Wolle f; **woollen, woolen** (US) adj Woll-

word [wɜːd] n Wort nt; (promise) Ehrenwort nt; **~s** pl (of song) Text m; **to have a ~ with sb** mit jdm sprechen; **in other ~s** mit anderen Worten ▷ vt formulieren; **wording** n Wortlaut m, Formulierung f; **word processing** n Textverarbeitung f; **word processor** n (program) Textverarbeitungsprogramm nt

wore [wɔː*] pt of **wear**

work [wɜːk] n Arbeit f; (of art, literature) Werk nt; **~ of art** Kunstwerk nt; **he's at ~** er ist in/auf der Arbeit; **out of ~** arbeitslos ▷ vi arbeiten (at, on an +dat); (machine, plan) funktionieren; (medicine) wirken; (succeed) klappen ▷ vt (machine) bedienen; **work out** vi (plan) klappen; (sum) aufgehen; (person) trainieren ▷ vt (price, speed etc) ausrechnen; (plan) ausarbeiten; **work up** vt **to get worked up** sich aufregen; **workaholic** [wɜːkə'hɒlɪk] n Arbeitstier nt; **worker** n Arbeiter(in) m(f); **working class** n Arbeiterklasse f; **workman** (pl **-men**) n Handwerker m; **workout** n (Sport) Fitnesstraining nt, Konditionstraining nt; **work permit** n Arbeitserlaubnis f; **workplace** n Arbeitsplatz m; **workshop** n Werkstatt f; (meeting) Workshop m;

work station n (Inform) Workstation f
world [wɜːld] n Welt f; **world
championship** n Weltmeisterschaft f;
World War n ~ I/II, the First/Second
~ der Erste/Zweite Weltkrieg; **world-wide**
adj, adv weltweit; **World Wide Web** n
World Wide Web nt
worm [wɜːm] n Wurm m
worn [wɔːn] pp of **wear** ▷ adj (clothes)
abgetragen; (tyre) abgefahren; **worn-out**
adj abgenutzt; (person) erschöpft
worried ['wʌrɪd] adj besorgt; **be ~ about**
sich dat Sorgen machen um; **worry** ['wʌrɪ]
n Sorge f ▷ vt Sorgen machen +dat ▷ vi
sich Sorgen machen (about um); **don't
~** keine Sorge!; **worrying** adj
beunruhigend
worse [wɜːs] adj comparative of **bad**;
schlechter; (pain, mistake etc) schlimmer
▷ adv comparative of **badly**; schlechter;
worsen vt verschlechtern ▷ vi sich
verschlechtern
worship ['wɜːʃɪp] vt anbeten,
anhimmeln
worst [wɜːst] adj superlative of **bad**;
schlechteste(r, s); (pain, mistake etc)
schlimmste(r, s) ▷ adv superlative of **badly**;
am schlechtesten ▷ n **the ~ is over** das
Schlimmste ist vorbei; **at (the)** ~
schlimmstenfalls
worth [wɜːθ] n Wert m; **£10 ~ of food**
Essen für 10 Pfund ▷ adj **it is ~ £50** es ist
50 Pfund wert; **~ seeing** sehenswert; **it's
~ it** (rewarding) es lohnt sich; **worthless**
adj wertlos; **worthwhile** adj lohnend,
lohnenswert; **worthy** ['wɜːðɪ] adj
(deserving respect) würdig; **to be ~ of sth**
etw verdienen

○ KEYWORD

would [wʊd] aux vb **1** (conditional tense): **if
you asked him he would do it** wenn du
ihn fragtest, würde er es tun; **if you had
asked him he would have done it** wenn
du ihn gefragt hättest, hätte er es getan
2 (in offers, invitations, requests): **would you
like a biscuit?** möchten Sie ein Plätzchen?;
would you ask him to come in? würden
Sie ihn bitte hereinbitten?
3 (in indirect speech): **I said I would do it** ich
sagte, ich würde es tun
4 (emphatic): **it WOULD have to snow**

today! es musste ja ausgerechnet heute
schneien!
5 (insistence): **she wouldn't behave** sie
wollte sich partout nicht anständig
benehmen
6 (conjecture): **it would have been
midnight** es mag ungefähr Mitternacht
gewesen sein; **it would seem so** es sieht
wohl so aus
7 (indicating habit): **he would go there on
Mondays** er ging jeden Montag dorthin

wouldn't ['wʊdnt] contr of **would not**
would've ['wʊdəv] contr of **would have**
wound [wuːnd] n Wunde f ▷ vt
verwunden; (fig) verletzen ▷ [waʊnd] pt,
pp of **wind**
wove [wəʊv] pt of **weave**
woven ['wəʊvn] pp of **weave**
wrap [ræp] vt (parcel, present) einwickeln;
to ~ sth round sth etw um etw wickeln;
wrap up vt (parcel, present) einwickeln
▷ vi (dress warmly) sich warm anziehen;
wrapper n (of sweet) Papier nt; **wrapping
paper** n Packpapier nt; (giftwrap)
Geschenkpapier nt
wreath [riːθ] n Kranz m
wreck [rek] n (ship, plane, car) Wrack nt; **a
nervous ~** ein Nervenbündel nt ▷ vt (car)
zu Schrott fahren; (fig) zerstören;
wreckage ['rekɪdʒ] n Trümmer pl
wrench [rentʃ] n (tool)
Schraubenschlüssel m
wrestling ['reslɪŋ] n Ringen nt
wring out ['rɪŋ'aʊt] (**wrung, wrung**) vt
auswringen
wrinkle ['rɪŋkl] n Falte f
wrist [rɪst] n Handgelenk nt; **wristwatch**
n Armbanduhr f
write [raɪt] (**wrote, written**) vt
schreiben; (cheque) ausstellen ▷ vi
schreiben; **to ~ to sb** jdm schreiben; **write
down** vt aufschreiben; **write off** vt (debt,
person) abschreiben; (car) zu Schrott
fahren ▷ vi **to ~ off for sth** etw anfordern;
write out vt (name etc) ausschreiben;
(cheque) ausstellen; **write-protected** adj
(Inform) schreibgeschützt; **writer** n
Verfasser(in) m(f); (author)
Schriftsteller(in) m(f); **writing** n Schrift f;
(profession) Schreiben nt; **writing paper** n
Schreibpapier nt
written ['rɪtən] pp of **write**

w

wrong [rɒŋ] *adj* (*incorrect*) falsch; (*morally*)
unrecht; **you're ~** du hast Unrecht;
what's ~ with your leg? was ist mit
deinem Bein los?; **you've got the
~ number** Sie sind falsch verbunden; **I
dialled the ~ number** ich habe mich
verwählt; **don't get me ~** versteh mich
nicht falsch; **to go ~** (*plan*) schief gehen;
wrongly *adv* falsch; (*unjustly*) zu Unrecht
wrote [rəʊt] *pt of* **write**
WWW *abbr* = **World Wide Web** WWW

xenophobia [zenə'fəʊbɪə] *n*
  Ausländerfeindlichkeit *f*
XL *abbr* = **extra large** XL, übergroß
Xmas ['eksməs] *n* Weihnachten *nt*
X-ray ['eksreɪ] *n* (*picture*)
  Röntgenaufnahme *f* ⊳ *vt* röntgen
xylophone ['zaɪləfəʊn] *n* Xylophon *nt*

Abend; **the day before ~** vorgestern; **~'s newspaper** die Zeitung von gestern

yet [jet] *adv* (*still*) noch; (*up to now*) bis jetzt; (*in a question: already*) schon; **he hasn't arrived ~** er ist noch nicht gekommen; **have you finished ~?** bist du schon fertig?; **~ again** schon wieder; **as ~** bis jetzt ▷ *conj* doch

yield [jiːld] *n* Ertrag *m* ▷ *vt* (*result, crop*) hervorbringen; (*profit, interest*) bringen ▷ *vi* nachgeben (*to* +*dat*); (*Mil*) sich ergeben (*to* +*dat*); **'~'** (*US Auto*) „Vorfahrt beachten"

yoga ['jəʊgə] *n* Joga *nt*

yog(h)urt ['jɒgət] *n* Jog(h)urt *m*

yolk [jəʊk] *n* Eigelb *nt*

Yorkshire pudding ['jɔː'kʃə'pʊdɪŋ] *n* gebackener Eierteig, der meist zum Roastbeef gegessen wird

 KEYWORD

you [juː] *pron* **1** (*subj, in comparisons: familiar form: sg*) du; (*: pl*) ihr; (*in letters also*) du ihr; (*: polite form*) Sie; **you Germans** ihr Deutschen; **she's younger than you** sie ist jünger als du/Sie
2 (*direct object, after prep* +*acc: familiar form: sg*) dich; (*: pl*) euch; (*in letters also*) dich euch; (*: polite form*) Sie; **I know you** ich kenne dich/euch/Sie
3 (*indirect object, after prep* +*dat: familiar form*) (*sg*) dir; (*: pl*) euch; (*in letters also*) dir euch; (*: polite form*) Ihnen; **I gave it to you** ich gab es dir/euch/Ihnen
4 (*impers: one: subj*) man; (*: direct object*) einen; (*indirect object*) einem; **fresh air does you good** frische Luft tut gut

you'd [juːd] *contr of* **you had**; **you would**; **~ better leave** du solltest gehen

you'll [juːl] *contr of* **you will**; **you shall**

young [jʌŋ] *adj* jung ▷ *n* **the ~** *pl* (*~ people*) die jungen Leute *pl*; (*animals*) die Jungen *pl*; **youngster** ['jʌŋstə*] *n* Jugendliche(r) *mf*

your ['jɔː*] *adj sing* dein; *polite form* Ihr; *pl* euer; *polite form* Ihr; **have you hurt ~ leg?** hast du dir das Bein verletzt?

you're ['jʊə*] *contr of* **you are**

yours ['jɔːz] *pron sing* deine(r, s); *polite form* Ihre(r, s); *pl* eure(r, s); *polite form* Ihre(r, s); **is this ~?** gehört das dir/Ihnen?; **a**

yacht [jɒt] *n* Jacht *f*; **yachting** *n* Segeln *nt*; **to go ~** segeln gehen

yard [jɑːd] *n* Hof *m*; (*US: garden*) Garten *m*; (*measure*) Yard *nt* (0,91 *m*)

yawn [jɔːn] *vi* gähnen

yd *abbr* = **yard(s)**

year ['jɪə*] *n* Jahr *nt*; **this/last/next ~** dieses/letztes/nächstes Jahr; **he is 28 ~s old** er ist 28 Jahre alt; **~s ago** vor Jahren; **a five-year-old** ein(e) Fünfjährige(r); **yearly** *adj, adv* jährlich

yearn [jɜːn] *vi* sich sehnen (*for* nach +*dat*); **to ~ to do sth** sich danach sehnen, etw zu tun

yeast [jiːst] *n* Hefe *f*

yell [jel] *vi, vt* schreien; **to ~ at sb** jdn anschreien

yellow ['jeləʊ] *adj* gelb; **~ card** (*Sport*) gelbe Karte; **~ fever** Gelbfieber *nt*; **~ line** (*Brit*) = Halteverbot *nt*; **double ~ line** (*Brit*) ≈ absolutes Halteverbot; **the Yellow Pages®** *pl* die Gelben Seiten *pl*

yes [jes] *adv* ja; (*answering negative question*) doch; **to say ~ to sth** ja zu etw sagen ▷ *n* Ja *nt*

yesterday ['jestədeɪ] *adv* gestern; **~ morning/evening** gestern Morgen/

friend of ~ ein Freund von dir/Ihnen; **~ ...**, dein/deine ..., Ihr/Ihre ...

yourself [jɔːˈself] *pron sing* dich; *polite form* sich; **have you hurt ~?** hast du dich/haben Sie sich verletzt?; **did you do it ~?** hast du es selbst gemacht?; **(all) by ~** allein; **yourselves** *pron pl* euch; *polite form* sich; **have you hurt ~?** habt ihr euch/haben Sie sich verletzt?; **did you do it ~?** habt ihr es selbst gemacht?; **(all) by ~** allein

youth [juːθ] *n* (*period*) Jugend *f*; (*young man*) junger Mann; (*young people*) Jugend *f*; **youth hostel** *n* Jugendherberge *f*

you've [juːv] *contr of* **you have**

yucky [ˈjʌkɪ] *adj* (*fam*) eklig

Yugoslav [juːɡəˈslɑːv] *adj* jugoslawisch ▷ *n* Jugoslawe *m*, Jugoslawin *f*; **Yugoslavia** *n* (*hist*) Jugoslawien *nt*; **the former ~** das ehemalige Jugoslawien; **Yugoslavian** *see* **Yugoslav**

yummy [ˈjʌmɪ] *adj* (*fam*) lecker

yuppie, **yuppy** [ˈjʌpɪ] *n* Yuppie *m*

Z

zoo [zuː] *n* Zoo *m*
zoom [zuːm] *vi* (*move fast*) brausen, sausen ▷ *n* **~ (lens)** Zoomobjektiv *nt*; **zoom in** *vi* (*Foto*) heranzoomen (*on an* +*akk*)
zucchini [zuːˈkiːnɪ] (*pl* **-(s)**) *n* (*US*) Zucchini *f*

zap [zæp] *vt* (*Inform*) löschen; (*in computer game*) abknallen ▷ *vi* (*Tv*) zappen; **zapper** *n* (*Tv*) Fernbedienung *f*; **zapping** *n* (*Tv*) ständiges Umschalten, Zapping *nt*
zebra [ˈzebrə, ç ˈziːbrə] (*US*) *n* Zebra *nt*; **zebra crossing** *n* (*Brit*) Zebrastreifen *m*
zero [ˈzɪərəʊ] (*pl* **-es**) *n* Null *f*; **10 degrees below ~** 10 Grad unter null
zest [zest] *n* (*enthusiasm*) Begeisterung *f*
zigzag [ˈzɪgzæg] *n* Zickzack *m* ▷ *vi* (*person, vehicle*) im Zickzack gehen/fahren; (*path*) im Zickzack verlaufen
zinc [zɪŋk] *n* Zink *nt*
zip [zɪp] *n* (*Brit*) Reißverschluss *m* ▷ *vt* **to ~ (up)** den Reißverschluss zumachen; (*Inform*) zippen; **zip code** *n* (*US*) Postleitzahl *f*; **Zip disk®** *n* (*Inform*) ZIP-Diskette® *f*; **Zip drive®** *n* (*Inform*) ZIP-Laufwerk® *nt*; **Zip file®** *n* (*Inform*) ZIP-Datei® *f*; **zipper** *n* (*US*) Reißverschluss *m*
zit [zɪt] *n* (*fam*) Pickel *m*
zodiac [ˈzəʊdɪæk] *n* Tierkreis *m*; **sign of the ~** Tierkreiszeichen *nt*
zone [zəʊn] *n* Zone *f*; (*area*) Gebiet *nt*; (*in town*) Bezirk *m*